Microsoft® SQL Server® 2008 Bible

Paul Nielsen
with Mike White
and Uttam Parui

Wiley Publishing, Inc.

Soli Deo Gloria
— Paul Nielsen

For my wife, Katy, who has been so patient during the lon
and weekends of research and writing.
— Mike White

To my wife, Shyama, and my daughters, Noyonika and Niharika
— Uttam Parui

Microsoft® SQL Server® 2008 Bible

Published by
Wiley Publishing, Inc.
10475 Crosspoint Boulevard
Indianapolis, IN 46256
www.wiley.com

Published simultaneously in Canada

ISBN: 978-0-470-25704-3

Manufactured in the United States of America

10 9 8 7 6 5 4 3

Library of Congress Control Number: 2009928744

About Paul Nielsen

Paul Nielsen, SQL Server MVP since 2004, focuses on database performance through excellent design — always normalized, generalized, and data driven. Continuing to push the envelope of database design, Paul experiments with Object/Relational designs, the open-source T-SQL solution for transforming SQL Server into an object database.

As an entrepreneur, Paul has developed an application that helps nonprofit organizations that give hope to children in developing counties.

As a consultant, he has developed small to very large SQL Server databases, and has helped several third-party software vendors improve the quality and performance of their databases.

As a presenter, Paul has given talks at Microsoft TechEd, PASS Summits, DevLink (Nashville), SQL Teach (Canada), Rocky Mountain Tech Tri-Fecta, ICCM, and numerous user groups. Paul recorded SQL Server 2005 Development with Total Training. He has presented his Smart Database Design Seminar in the U.S., Canada, U.K., and Denmark. Paul also provides private and public SQL Server developer and data architecture courses.

As a family guy, Paul lives in Colorado Springs with his very sweet wife, Edie, and Dasha, their five-year-old daughter. He has two adult children: Lauren, who will soon graduate from the University of Colorado at Boulder, to collect scores of apples as an elementary school teacher, and David, who has a genius within him. Paul's hobbies include photography, a little jazz guitar, great movies, and stunt kites.

Paul answers reader e-mails at pauln@SQLServerBile.com.

For links to blogs, Twitter, eNewsletter, seminars and courses, free SQL utilities, links, screencasts, and updates to this book, visit `www.SQLServerBible.com`.

About the Contributing Authors

Mary Chipman has been writing about databases and database development since SQL Server version 6.0. She is best known for the *Microsoft Access Developer's Guide to SQL Server,* which has maintained a five-star ranking on Amazon.com since it was published in 2000. Mary is currently part of the Business Platform Division at Microsoft, where she is dedicated to providing customers with the information they need to get the most out of Microsoft's data access technologies. Prior to joining Microsoft, Mary was a founding partner of MCW Technologies, spoke at industry conferences, authored several books, and created award-winning courseware and videos for Application Developers Training Company (`www.appdev.com/info.asp?page=experts_mchipman`). She was awarded MVP status every year from 1995 until she joined Microsoft in 2004. Mary contributed Chapter 38.

Scott Klein is a .Net and SQL Server developer in South Florida and the author of *Professional SQL Server 2005 XML (Programmer to Programmer)*. Scott contributed chapters 32, 33, and 34.

Uttam Parui is currently a Senior Premier Field Engineer at Microsoft. He has worked with SQL Server for over 11 years and joined Microsoft nine years ago with the SQL Server Developer Support team. Additionally, Uttam has assisted with training and mentoring the SQL Customer Support Services (CSS) and SQL Premier Field Engineering (PFE) teams, and was one of the first to train and assist in the development of Microsoft's SQL Server support teams in Canada and India. Uttam led the development of and successfully completed Microsoft's globally coordinated intellectual property for the "SQL Server 2005/2008: Failover Clustering" workshop. He received his master's degree in computer science from University of Florida at Gainesville and is a Microsoft Certified Trainer (MCT) and Microsoft Certified IT Professional (MCITP): Database Administrator 2008. He can be reached at uttam_parui@hotmail.com. Uttam wrote all but one of the chapters in Part VI, "Enterprise Data Management," Chapter 39, and Chapters 41 through 48.

Jacob Sebastian, SQL Server MVP, is a SQL Server Consultant specializing in XML based on Ahmedabad, India, and has been using SQL Server since version 6.5. Jacob compressed his vast knowledge of SQL Server and XML into Chapter 18.

Allen White, SQL Server MVP (with a minor in PowerShell), is a SQL Server Trainer with Scalability Experts. He has worked as a database administrator, architect and developer for over 30 years and blogs on `www.SQLBlog.com`. Allen expressed his passion for PowerShell in Chapter 7.

Michael White has focused on database development and administration since 1992. Concentrating on Microsoft's Business Intelligence (BI) tools and applications since 2000, he has architected and implemented large warehousing and Analysis Services applications, as well as nontraditional applications of BI tools. After many years in corporate IT and consulting, Mike currently works as a data architect for IntrinsiQ, LLC. He is a strong advocate for the underused BI toolset and a frequent speaker at SQL Server user groups and events. Mike wrote Chapter 37 and all the chapters (70 through 76) in Part X, "Business Intelligence."

About the Technical Reviewers

John Paul Cook is a database consultant based in Houston. His primary focus is on the development and tuning of custom SQL Server–based solutions for large enterprise customers. As a three-time Microsoft MVP for Virtual Machines, his secondary focus is using virtualization to facilitate application testing. You can read his blog at `http://sqlblog.com/blogs/john_paul_cook`.

Hilary Cotter has been a SQL Server MVP for eight years and specializes in replication, high availability, and full-text search. He lives in New Jersey and loves to play the piano and spend time with his wife and four kids. He has answered over 17,000 newsgroup questions, some of them correctly.

Louis Davidson has over 15 years of experience as a corporate database developer and architect. He has been the principal author on four editions of a book on database design, including *Professional SQL Server 2008 Relational Database Design and Implementation*. You can get more information about his books, blogs, and more at his web page, drsql.org.

Rob Farley lives in Adelaide, Australia, where the sun always shines and it hasn't rained (hardly at all) for a very long time. He runs the Adelaide SQL Server User Group, operates a SQL Server consultancy called LobsterPot Solutions, acts as a mentor for SQLskills Australia, and somehow finds time to be married with three amazing children. He is originally from the U.K., and his passions include serving at his church and supporting Arsenal Football Club. He blogs at `http://msmvps.com/blogs/robfarley` and can be reached via e-mail to rob@lobsterpot.com.au.

Hongfei Guo is a senior program manager in the SQL Server Manageability Team. Prior to Microsoft, she spent six years in database research and earned her PhD from University of Wisconsin at Madison. Hongfei's dissertation was "Data Quality Aware Caching" and she implemented it in the SQL Server Engine code base while interning at Microsoft Research. For the SQL Server 2008 release, Hongfei was a critical contributor to the Policy-Based Management feature (PBM) and witnessed its journey from birth to product. For SQL Server 11, Hongfei will continue her role as feature owner of PBM, and is dedicated to producing the next version that customers desire.

Allan Hirt has been using SQL Server in various guises since 1992. For the past 10 years, he has been consulting, training, developing content, speaking at events, as well as authoring books, white papers, and articles related to SQL Server architecture, high availability, administration, and more. His latest book is *Pro SQL Server 2008 Failover Clustering* (Apress, 2009). Before forming Megahirtz in 2007, he most recently worked for both Microsoft and Avanade, and still continues to work closely with Microsoft on various projects, including contributing to the recently published *SQL Server 2008 Upgrade Technical Reference Guide*. He can be contacted at allan@sqlha.com or via his website at www.sqlha.com.

Brian Kelley is a SQL Server author, blogger, columnist, and Microsoft MVP focusing primarily on SQL Server security. He is a contributing author for *How to Cheat at Securing SQL Server 2005* (Syngress, 2007) and *Professional SQL Server 2008 Administration* (Wrox, 2008). Brian currently serves as a database administrator/architect in order to concentrate on his passion: SQL Server. He can be reached at kbriankelley@acm.org.

Jonathan Kehayias is a SQL Server MVP and MCITP Database Administrator and Developer, who got started in SQL Server in 2004 as a database developer and report writer in the natural gas industry. He has experience in upgrading and consolidating SQL environments, and experience in running SQL Server in large virtual environments. His primary passion is performance tuning, and he frequently rewrites queries for better performance and performs in-depth analysis of index implementation and usage. He can be reached through his blog at http://sqlblog.com/blogs/jonathan_kehayias.

Hugo Kornelius, lead technical editor, is co-founder and R&D lead of perFact BV, a Dutch company that improves analysis methods and develops computer-aided tools to generate completely functional applications from the analysis deliverable on the SQL Server platform. In his spare time, Hugo likes to share and enhance his knowledge of SQL Server by frequenting newsgroups and forums, reading and writing books and blogs, and attending and speaking at conferences. As a result of these activities, he has been awarded MVP status since January 2006. Hugo blogs at http://sqlblog.com/blogs/hugo_kornelis. He can be reached by e-mail at hugo@perFact.info.

Marco Shaw, ITIL, RHCE, LCP, MCP, has been working in the IT industry for over 10 years. Marco runs a Virtual PowerShell User Group, and is one of the community directors of the PowerShell Community site www.powershellcommunity.org. Marco recently received the Microsoft MVP Award for the second year in a row (2008/2009) for contributions to the Windows PowerShell Community. Included in his recent authoring activities is writing PowerShell content for various books published in 2008 and 2009. Marco's blog is at http://marcoshaw.blogspot.com.

Simon Sabine is Database Architect for SQL Know How, a SQL Server Consultancy and Training provider in the U.K. He has particular expertise in the world of search, distributed architectures, business intelligence, and application development. He has worked with SQL Server since 1998, always focused on high-performance, reliable systems. Simon received the MVP award in 2006. He founded the first free SQL Server conference in the U.K., SQLBits, in 2007, along with other MVPs in the U.K. He is a regular speaker at SQL Server events and maintains a blog at www.sqlblogcasts.com/blogs/simons. He is married with children and lives in the U.K. You can contact him at Simon@sqlknowhow.com.

Peter Ward is the Chief Technical Architect for WARDY IT Solutions (www.wardyit.com). Peter is an active member in the Australian SQL Server community, and president of the Queensland SQL Server User Group. Peter is a highly regarded speaker at SQL Server events throughout Australia and is a sought-after SQL Server consultant and trainer, providing solutions for some of the largest SQL Server sites in Australia. He has been awarded Microsoft Most Valuable Professional status for his technical excellence and commitment to the SQL Server community.

Credits

Executive Editor
Bob Elliott

Senior Project Editor
Ami Frank Sullivan

Development Editor
Lori Cerreto

Lead Technical Editor
Hugo Kornelius

Technical Editors
John Paul Cook
Hilary Cotter
Louis Davidson
Rob Farley
Hongfei Guo
Allan Hirt
Jonathan Kehayias
Brian Kelley
Hugo Kornelius
Simon Sabine
Marco Shaw
Peter Ward

Production Editor
Dassi Zeidel

Copy Editor
Luann Rouff

Editorial Director
Robyn B. Siesky

Editorial Manager
Mary Beth Wakefield

Production Manager
Tim Tate

Vice President and Executive Group Publisher
Richard Swadley

Vice President and Executive Publisher
Barry Pruett

Associate Publisher
Jim Minatel

Project Coordinator, Cover
Lynsey Stanford

Proofreader
Publication Services, Inc.

Indexer
Jack Lewis

Cover Design
Michael E. Trent

Cover Image
Joyce Haughey

From Paul Nielsen: Of course, any book this size requires the efforts of several people.

Perhaps the greatest effort was made by my family as I spent long days, pulled all-nighters, and worked straight through weekends in the SQL Dungeon to finish the book. My first thank-you must go to my beautiful wife, Edie, and my kids, Lauren, David, and Dasha for their patience and love.

I also want to thank the folks at European Adoption Consultants who helped us with our adoption of Dasha from Russia in 2007. Every tiny detail was professional and we couldn't be more pleased. I encourage every healthy family to adopt an orphan. I know it's a stretch, but it's well worth it.

This was the second book that I did with the same team at Wiley: Bob Elliot, Ami Frank Sullivan, Mary Beth Wakefield, and Luann Rouff. What an amazing team, and I'm sure there are others with whom I didn't have direct contact. Ami is a pleasure to work with and one of the best editors in the business. I'm a lucky author to work with her.

I'm also lucky enough to be an MVP. By far the best benefit of being an MVP is the private newsgroup — reading the questions and dialogue between the MVPs more brilliant than me and the Microsoft development team. When Louis, Erland, Aaron, Hugo, Linchi, Alex, Simon, Greg, Denis, Adam, and, of course, Kalen, and the many others ask a question or dig into an issue, I pay attention. Whenever the MVPs meet I always feel like a fortunate guest to be among such a smart and insightful group.

Kalen Delaney deserves a special acknowledgment. Kalen is a gracious lady with the highest integrity, a deep knowledge of SQL Server, and always a kind word. Thank you, Kalen.

Louis Davidson has become a good friend. We co-present at many conferences and I hope that he's grown from our respectful and friendly debates as much as I have. And if you ever get a chance to see us on stage, be sure to ask Louis about denormalization. He'll like that.

To the other authors who contributed to this book, I thank you: Mike White, Uttam Parui, Allen White, Scott Klein, and Jacob Sebastian. Without you the book might not have come out before SQL 11 ships.

For any errors and omissions I take full credit; for what's right in the book you should credit the tech editors. I think it would be interesting to publish a book with all the tech editor comments and suggestions. Some authors don't like it when a tech editor disagrees or nitpicks. Personally, I think that's what makes a great tech editor, which is why I picked my friend Hugo Kornelius as the lead tech editor for this book. Hugo's a great tech editor, and this book had an incredible team of technical editors — all experts, and all went above and beyond in their quest for perfection: Louis Davidson (who tech edited the chapter on relational database design about five times!), Jonathan Kehayias, Simon Sabin, Hilary Cotter, Hongfei Guo, Peter Ward, Allan Hirt, John Paul Cook, Brian Kelley, Rob Farley, and Marco Shaw. I'm also honored to acknowledge the many comments, recommendations, and encouragement I've received from loyal readers. A few readers volunteered to help me polish this edition by serving as a pre-editorial board, adding significant comments and feedback to early versions of various chapters for this book: JJ Bienn, Viktor Gurevich, Steve Miller, Greg Low, Aaron Bertrand, Adam Greifer, Alan Horsman, Andrew Novick, Degmar Barbosa, Mesut Demir, Denis Gobo, Dominique Verrière, Erin Welker, Henry S. Hayden, James Beidleman, Joe Webb, Ken Scott, Kevin Cox, Kevin Lambert, Michael Shaya, Michael Wiles, Scott Stonehouse, and Scott Whigham. Thank you, all.

I really enjoy teaching and sharing SQL Server in the classroom, in seminars, at conferences, and on the street corner. To everyone who's joined me in these settings, thanks for your participation and enthusiasm.

To the many who contributed efforts to the two previous editions, thank you. This work builds on your foundation.

This was the second book that I did with the same team at Wiley: Bob Elliott, Ami Frank Sullivan, Mary Beth Wakefield, Dassi Zeidel, and Luann Rouff.

Finally, a warm thank you goes out to the Microsoft SQL Server team in Redmond. Thanks for building such a great database engine. Thanks for your close relationships with the MVPs. And thanks to those team members who spent time with me individually: Buck Woody, Hongfei Guo, Ed Lehman.

For those of you who follow me on Twitter and read my daily tweets about writing, this book was powered by Dr. Pepper. And now, I have a stunt kite that has been in its case far too long — there's a fair wind outside somewhere and I'm going to find it.

From Uttam Parui: I would like to thank my parents for their endless love and support and for giving me the best education they could provide, which has made me successful in life. I'd like to thank my loving wife, Shyama, and my two doting daughters, Noyonika and Niharika, for all their encouragement and understanding while I spent many nights and weekends working on the book. I would also like to thank Paul Nielsen, the lead author, for giving me this great opportunity to co-author this book, and for his support throughout the writing of it. Last but not least, I would like to thank everyone at Wiley for their help with this book.

Contents
at a Glance

Contents

Part III Beyond Relational

Part VII Security

Part VIII Monitoring and Auditing

Foreword

Can one book really cover everything you need to know about SQL Server 2008? As more and more books are covering fewer and fewer features of this huge product, before taking a close look at Paul's *SQL Server 2008 Bible*, I would have said no. And of course, the answer depends on how much you actually need to know about my favorite database system. For some, "information needed" could cover a lot of ground, but Paul's book comes closer to covering everything than any book I have ever seen.

Paul Nielsen brings his passion for SQL Server and his many years of experience with this product into every page of the *SQL Server 2008 Bible*. Every detail and every example is tested out by Paul personally, and I know for a fact that he had fun doing all this amazing writing and testing.

Of course, no book can go into great depth on every single area, but Paul takes you deeply enough into each topic that you, the reader, can decide whether that feature will be valuable to you. How can you know whether PowerShell or Spatial Data is something you want to dive deeply into unless you know something about its value? How can you know if you should look more deeply into Analysis Services or partitioning if you don't even know what those features are? How do you know which Transact-SQL language features will help you solve your data access problems if you don't know what features are available, and what features are new in SQL Server 2008? How can you know which high-availability technology or monitoring tool will work best in your environment if you don't know how they differ?

You can decide whether you want to use what Paul has presented as either a great breadth of SQL Server knowledge or a starting point for acquiring greater depth in areas of your own choosing.

As someone who writes about a very advanced, but limited, area within SQL Server, I am frequently asked by my readers what they can read to prepare them for reading my books. Now I have an answer not just for my readers, but for myself as well. Just as no one book can cover every aspect of SQL Server in great depth, no one person can know everything about this product. When I want to know how to get started with LINQ, Service Broker, or MDX, or any of dozens of other topics that my books don't cover, Paul's book is the place I'll start my education.

Kalen Delaney, SQL Server MVP and author of *SQL Server 2008 Internals*

Introduction

Welcome to the *SQL Server 2008 Bible*. SQL Server is an incredible database product. It offers an excellent mix of performance, reliability, ease of administration, and new architectural options, yet enables the developer or DBA to control minute details when desired. SQL Server is a dream system for a database developer.

If there's a theme to SQL Server 2008, it's this: enterprise-level excellence. SQL Server 2008 opens several new possibilities for designing more scalable and powerful systems. The first goal of this book is to share with you the pleasure of working with SQL Server.

Like all books in the Bible series, you can expect to find both hands-on tutorials and real-world practical applications, as well as reference and background information that provides a context for what you are learning. However, to cover every minute detail of every command of this very complex product would consume thousands of pages, so it is the second goal of this book to provide a concise yet comprehensive guide to SQL Server 2008 based on the information I have found most useful in my experience as a database developer, consultant, and instructor. By the time you have completed the *SQL Server 2008 Bible*, you will be well prepared to develop and manage your SQL Server 2008 database.

Some of you are repeat readers of mine (thanks!) and are familiar with my approach from the previous SQL Server Bibles. Even though you might be familiar with this approach and my tone, you will find several new features in this edition, including the following:

- A "what's new" sidebar in most chapters presents a timeline of the features so you can envision the progression.
- Several chapters are completely rewritten, especially my favorite topics.
- I've added much of the material from my Smart Database Design into this book.

A wise database developer once showed a box to an apprentice and asked, "How many sides do you see?" The apprentice replied, "There are six sides to the box." The experienced database developer then said, "Users may see six sides, but database developers see only two sides: the inside and the outside. To the database developer, the cool code goes inside the box." This book is about thinking inside the box.

Who Should Read This Book

I believe there are five distinct roles in the SQL Server space:

- Data architect/data modeler
- Database developer

- Database administrator
- BI (Business Intelligence) developer
- PTO performance tuning and optimization expert

This book has been carefully planned to address each of these roles.

Whether you are a database developer or a database administrator, whether you are just starting out or have one year of experience or five, this book contains material that will be useful to you.

While the book is targeted at intermediate-level database professionals, each chapter begins with the assumption that you've never seen the topic before, and then progresses through the subject, presenting the information that makes a difference.

At the higher end of the spectrum, the book pushes the intermediate professional into certain advanced areas where it makes the most sense. For example, there's very advanced material on T-SQL queries, index strategies, and data architecture.

How This Book Is Organized

SQL Server is a huge product with dozens of technologies and interrelated features. Seventy-six chapters! Just organizing a book of this scope is a daunting task.

A book of this size and scope must also be approachable as both a cover-to-cover read and a reference book. The ten parts of this book are organized by job role, project flow, and skills progression:

Part I: Laying the Foundation

Part II: Manipulating Data with Select

Part III: Beyond Relational

Part IV: Developing with SQL Server

Part V: Data Connectivity

Part VI: Enterprise Data Management

Part VII: Security

Part VIII: Monitoring and Auditing

Part IX: Performance Tuning and Optimization

Part X: Business Intelligence

SQL Server Books Online

This book is not a rehash of Books Online, and it doesn't pretend to replace Books Online. I avoid listing the complete syntax of every command — there's little value in reprinting Books Online.

Instead, I've designed this book to show you what you need to know in order to get the most out of SQL Server, so that you can learn from my experience and the experience of the co-authors.

In here you'll find each feature explained as if we are friends — you got a new job that requires a specific feature you're unfamiliar with, and you asked me to get you up to speed with what matters most.

The 76 chapters contain critical concepts, real-world examples, and best practices.

Conventions and Features

This book contains several different organizational and typographical features designed to help you get the most from the information.

Tips, Notes, Cautions, and Cross-References

Whenever the authors want to bring something important to your attention, the information will appear in a Tip, Note, or Caution.

CAUTION **This information is important and is set off in a separate paragraph with a special icon. Cautions provide information about things to watch out for, whether simply inconvenient or potentially hazardous to your data or systems.**

TIP **Tips generally are used to provide information that can make your work simpler — special shortcuts or methods for doing something easier than the norm. You will often find the relevant .sys files listed in a tip.**

NOTE **Notes provide additional, ancillary information that is helpful, but somewhat outside of the current presentation of information.**

CROSS-REF **Cross-references provide a roadmap to related content, be it on the Web, another chapter in this book, or another book.**

What's New and Best Practice Sidebars

Two sidebar features are specific to this book: the What's New sidebars and the Best Practice sidebars.

What's New with SQL Server Feature

Whenever possible and practical, a sidebar will be included that highlights the relevant new features covered in the chapter. Often, these sidebars also alert you to which features have been eliminated and which are deprecated. Usually, these sidebars are placed near the beginning of the chapter.

Best Practice

This book is based on the real-life experiences of SQL Server developers and administrators. To enable you to benefit from all that experience, the best practices have been pulled out in sidebar form wherever and whenever they apply.

www.SQLServerBible.com

This book has an active companion website where you'll find the following:

- Sample code: Most chapters have their own SQL script or two. All the chapter code samples are in a single zip file on the book's page.
- Sample databases: The sample database specific to this book, OBXKites, CHA2, and others are in the Sampledb.zip file also on the book's page.
- Watch free screencasts based on the examples and content of this book.
- Links to new downloads, and the best of the SQL Server community online.
- Get a free Euro-style SQL Sticker for your notebook.
- Get the latest versions of Paul's SQL Server queries and utilities.
- Paul's presentation schedule and a schedule of SQL Server community events.
- Link to BrainBench.com's SQL Server 2008 Programming Certification, the test that Paul designed.
- Sign up for the *SQL Server 2008 Bible* eNewsletter to stay current with new links, new queries, articles, updates, and announcements.

Where to Go from Here

There's a whole world of SQL Server. Dig in. Explore. Play with SQL Server. Try out new ideas, and e-mail me if you have questions or discover something cool.

I designed the BrainBench.com SQL Server 2008 Programming Certification, so read the book and then take the test.

Do sign up for the SQL Server Bible eNewsletter to keep up with updates and news.

Come to a conference or user group where I'm speaking. I'd love to meet you in person and sign your book. You can learn where and when I'll be speaking at SQLServerBible.com.

With a topic as large as SQL Server and a community this strong, a lot of resources are available. But there's a lot of hubris around SQL Server too, for recommended additional resources and SQL Server books, check the book's website.

Most important of all, e-mail me: pauln@SQLServerBible.com. I'd love to hear what you're doing with SQL Server.

Part I

Laying the Foundation

SQL Server is a vast product. If you're new to SQL Server it can be difficult to know where to start. You need at least an idea of the scope of the components, the theory behind databases, and how to use the UI to even begin playing with SQL Server.

That's where this part fits and why it's called "Laying the Foundation."

Chapter 1 presents an introduction to SQL Server's many components and how they work together. Even if you're an experienced DBA, this chapter is a quick way to catch up on what's new.

Database design and technology have both evolved faster since the millennium than at any other time since Dr. Edgar Codd introduced his revolutionary RDBMS concepts three decades earlier. Every year, the IT profession is getting closer to the vision of ubiquitous information. This is truly a time of change. Chapters 2 and 3 discuss database architecture and relational database design.

Installing and connecting to SQL Server is of course required before you can have any fun with joins, and two chapters cover those details.

Management Studio, one of my favorite features of SQL Server, and PowerShell, the new scripting tool, each deserve a chapter and round out the first part.

If SQL Server is the box, and developing is thinking inside the box, the first part of this book is an introduction to the box.

IN THIS PART

Chapter 1

The World of SQL Server

Welcome to SQL Server 2008.

At the Rocky Mountain Tech Tri-Fecta 2009 SQL keynote, I walked through the major SQL Server 2008 new features and asked the question, "Cool or Kool-Aid?"

I've worked with SQL Server since version 6.5 and I'm excited about this newest iteration because it reflects a natural evolution and maturing of the product. I believe it's the best release of SQL Server so far. There's no Kool-Aid here — it's all way cool.

SQL Server is a vast product and I don't know any sane person who claims to know all of it in depth. In fact, SQL Server is used by so many different types of professions to accomplish so many different types of tasks, it can be difficult to concisely define it, but here goes:

SQL Server 2008: Microsoft's enterprise client-server relational database product, with T-SQL as its primary programming language.

However, SQL Server is more than just a relational database engine:

- Connecting to SQL Server is made easy with a host of data connectivity options and a variety of technologies to import and export data, such as Tabular Data Stream (TDS), XML, Integration Services, bulk copy, SQL Native Connectivity, OLE DB, ODBC, and distributed query with Distributed Transaction Coordinator, to name a few.
- The engine works well with data (XML, spatial, words within text, and blob data).
- SQL Server has a full suite of OLAP/BI components and tools to work with multidimensional data, analyze data, build cubes, and mine data.

IN THIS CHAPTER

- SQL Server includes a complete reporting solution that serves up great-looking reports, enables users to create reports, and tracks who saw what when.
- SQL Server exposes an impressive level of diagnostic detail with Performance Studio, SQL Trace/Profiler, and Database Management Views and Functions.
- SQL Server includes several options for high availability with varying degrees of latency, performance, number of nines, physical distance, and synchronization.
- SQL Server can be managed declaratively using Policy-Based Management.
- SQL Server's Management Studio is a mature UI for both the database developer and the DBA.
- SQL Server is available in several different scalable editions in 32-bit and 64-bit for scaling up and out.

All of these components are included with SQL Server (at no additional cost or per-component cost), and together in concert, you can use them to build a data solution within a data architecture environment that was difficult or impossible a few years ago. SQL Server 2008 truly is an enterprise database for today.

A Great Choice

There are other good database engines, but SQL Server is a great choice for several reasons. I'll leave the marketing hype for Microsoft; here are my personal ten reasons for choosing SQL Server for my career:

- **Set-based SQL purity:** As a set-based data architect type of guy, I find SQL Server fun to work with. It's designed to function in a set-based manner. Great SQL Server code has little reason to include iterative cursors. SQL Server is pure set-based SQL.
- **Scalable performance:** SQL Server performance scales well — I've developed code on my notebook that runs great on a server with 32- and 64-bit dual-core CPUs and 48GB of RAM. I've yet to find a database application that doesn't run well with SQL Server given a good design and the right hardware.

  People sometimes write to the newsgroups that their database is huge — *"over a gig!"* — but SQL Server regularly runs databases in the terabyte size. I'd say that over a petabyte is huge, over a terabyte is large, 100 GB is normal, under 10 GB is small, and under 1 GB is tiny.
- **Scalable experience:** The SQL Server experience scales from nearly automated self-managed databases administered by the accidental DBA to finite control that enables expert DBAs to tune to their heart's content.
- **Industry acceptance:** SQL Server is a standard. I can find consulting work from small shops to the largest enterprises running SQL Server.
- **Diverse technologies:** SQL Server is broad enough to handle many types of problems and applications. From BI to spatial, to heavy transactional OLTP, to XML, SQL Server has a technology to address the problem.
- **SQL in the Cloud:** There are a number of options to host a SQL database in the cloud with great stability, availability, and performance.
- **Financial stability:** It's going to be here for a nice long time. When you choose SQL Server, you're not risking that your database vendor will be gone next year.

- **Ongoing development:** I know that Microsoft is investing heavily in the future of SQL Server, and new versions will keep up the pace of new cool features. I can promise you that SQL 11 will rock!
- **Fun community:** There's an active culture around SQL Server, including a lot of user groups, books, blogs, websites, code camps, conferences, and so on. Last year I presented 22 sessions at nine conferences, so it's easy to find answers and get plugged in. In fact, I recently read a blog comparing SQL Server and Oracle and the key differentiator is enthusiasm of the community and the copious amount of information it publishes. It's true: the SQL community is a fun place to be.
- **Affordable:** SQL Server is more affordable than the other enterprise database options, and the Developer Edition costs less than $50 on Amazon.

The Client/Server Database Model

Technically, the term *client/server* refers to any two cooperating processes. The client process requests a service from the server process, which in turn handles the request for the client. The client process and the server process may be on different computers or on the same computer: It's the cooperation between the processes that is significant, not the physical location.

For a client/server database, the client application (be it a front end, an ETL process, a middle tier, or a report) prepares a SQL request — just a small text message or remote procedure call (RPC) — and sends it to the database server, which in turn reads and processes the request. Inside the server, the security is checked, the indexes are searched, the data is retrieved or manipulated, any server-side code is executed, and the final results are sent back to the client. All the database work is performed within the database server. The actual data and indexes never leave the server.

In contrast, desktop file-based databases (such as Microsoft Access), may share a common file, but the desktop application does all the work as the data file is shared across the network.

The client/server–database model offers several benefits over the desktop database model:

- Reliability is improved because the data is not spread across the network and several applications. Only one process handles the data.
- Data integrity constraints and business rules can be enforced at the server level, resulting in a more thorough implementation of the rules.
- Security is improved because the database keeps the data within a single server. Hacking into a data file that's protected within the database server is much more difficult than hacking into a data file on a workstation. It's also harder to steal a physical storage device connected to a server, as most server rooms are adequately protected against intruders.
- Performance is improved and better balanced among workstations because the majority of the workload, the database processing, is being handled by the server; the workstations handle only the user-interface portion.

continued

continued

- Because the database server process has direct access to the data files, and much of the data is already cached in memory, database operations are much faster at the server than in a multi-user desktop-database environment. A database server is serving every user operating a database application; therefore, it's easier to justify the cost of a beefier server. For applications that require database access and heavy computational work, the computational work can be handled by the application, further balancing the load.
- Network traffic is greatly reduced. Compared to a desktop database's rush-hour traffic, client/server traffic is like a single motorcyclist carrying a slip of paper with all 10 lanes to himself. This is no exaggeration! Upgrading a heavily used desktop database to a well-designed client/server database will reduce database-related network traffic by more than 95 percent.
- A by-product of reducing network traffic is that well-designed client/server applications perform well in a distributed environment — even when using slower communications. So little traffic is required that even a 56KB dial-up line should be indistinguishable from a 100baseT Ethernet connection for a .NET-rich client application connected to a SQL Server database.

Client/server SQL Server: a Boeing 777. Desktop databases: a toy red wagon.

SQL Server Database Engine

SQL Server components can be divided into two broad categories: those within the engine, and external tools (e.g., user interfaces and components), as illustrated in Figure 1-1. Because the relational Database Engine is the core of SQL Server, I'll start there.

Database Engine

The SQL Server *Database Engine*, sometimes called the *Relational Engine*, is the core of SQL Server. It is the component that handles all the relational database work. SQL is a descriptive language, meaning it describes only the question to the engine; the engine takes over from there.

Within the Relational Engine are several key processes and components, including the following:

- **Algebrizer:** Checks the syntax and transforms a query to an internal representation that is used by the following components.
- **Query Optimizer:** SQL Server's Query Optimizer determines how to best process the query based on the costs of different types of query-execution operations. The estimated and actual query-execution plans may be viewed graphically, or in XML, using Management Studio or SQL Profiler.
- **Query Engine, or Query Processor:** Executes the queries according to the plan generated by the Query Optimizer.

- **Storage Engine:** Works for the Query Engine and handles the actual reading from and writing to the disk.
- **The Buffer Manager:** Analyzes the data pages being used and pre-fetches data from the data file(s) into memory, thus reducing the dependency on disk I/O performance.
- **Checkpoint:** Process that writes dirty data pages (modified pages) from memory to the data file.
- **Resource Monitor:** Optimizes the query plan cache by responding to memory pressure and intelligently removing older query plans from the cache.
- **Lock Manager:** Dynamically manages the scope of locks to balance the number of required locks with the size of the lock.
- **SQLOS:** SQL Server eats resources for lunch, and for this reason it needs direct control of the available resources (memory, threads, I/O request, etc.). Simply leaving the resource management to Windows isn't sophisticated enough for SQL Server. SQL Server includes its own OS layer, *SQLOS*, which manages all of its internal resources.

SQL Server 2008 supports installation of up to 16 (Workgroup Edition) or 50 (Standard or Enterprise Edition) instances of the Relational Engine on a physical server. Although they share some components, each instance functions as a complete separate installation of SQL Server.

FIGURE 1-1

SQL Server is a collection of components within the relational Database Engine and client components.

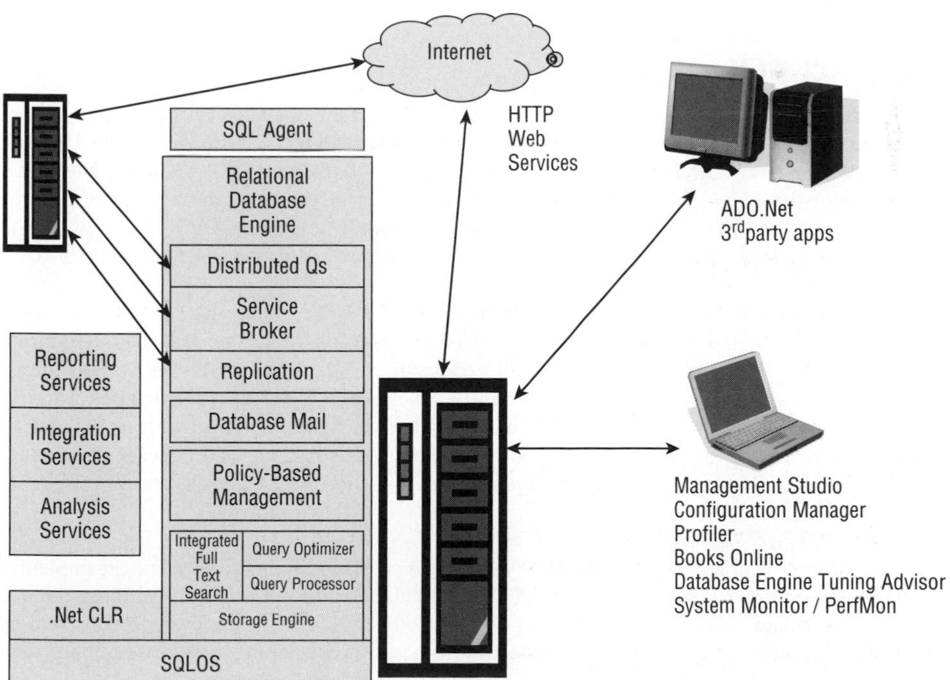

ACID and SQL Server's Transaction Log

SQL Server's Transaction Log is more than an optional appendix to the engine. It's integral to SQL Server's reputation for data integrity and robustness. Here's why:

Data integrity is defined by the acronym ACID, meaning transactions must be Atomic (one action — all or nothing), Consistent (the database must begin and end the transaction in a consistent state), Isolated (no transaction should affect another transaction), and Durable (once committed, always committed).

The transaction log is vital to the ACID capabilities of SQL Server. SQL Server writes to the transaction log as the first step of writing any change to the data pages (in memory), which is why it is sometimes called the *write-ahead transaction log*.

Every DML statement (Select, Insert, Update, Delete) is a complete transaction, and the transaction log ensures that the entire set-based operation takes place, thereby ensuring the atomicity of the transaction.

SQL Server can use the transaction log to roll back, or complete a transaction regardless of hardware failure, which is key to both the consistency and durability of the transaction.

CROSS-REF Chapter 40, "Policy-Based Management," goes into more detail about transactions.

Transact-SQL

SQL Server is based on the SQL standard, with some Microsoft-specific extensions. SQL was invented by E. F. Codd while he was working at the IBM research labs in San Jose in 1971. SQL Server is entry-level (Level 1) compliant with the ANSI SQL 92 standard. (The complete specifications for the ANSI SQL standard are found in five documents that can be purchased from `www.techstreet.com/ncits.html`. I doubt if anyone who doesn't know exactly what to look for will find these documents.) But it also includes many features defined in later versions of the standard (SQL-1999, SQL-2003).

While the ANSI SQL definition is excellent for the common data-selection and data-definition commands, it does not include commands for controlling SQL Server properties, or provide the level of logical control within batches required to develop a SQL Server–specific application. Therefore, the Microsoft SQL Server team has extended the ANSI definition with several enhancements and new commands, and has left out a few commands because SQL Server implemented them differently. The result is Transact-SQL, or T-SQL — the dialect of SQL understood by SQL Server.

Missing from T-SQL are very few ANSI SQL commands, primarily because Microsoft implemented the functionality in other ways. T-SQL, by default, also handles nulls, quotes, and padding differently than the ANSI standard, although that behavior can be modified. Based on my own development experience, I can say that none of these differences affect the process of developing a database application using SQL Server. T-SQL adds significantly more to ANSI SQL than it lacks.

Understanding SQL Server requires understanding T-SQL. The native language of the SQL Server engine is Transact-SQL. Every command sent to SQL Server must be a valid T-SQL command. Batches of stored T-SQL commands may be executed within the server as stored procedures. Other tools, such as Management Studio, which provide graphical user interfaces with which to control SQL Server, are at some level converting most of those mouse clicks to T-SQL for processing by the engine.

SQL and T-SQL commands are divided into the following three categories:

- **Data Manipulation Language (DML):** Includes the common SQL `SELECT`, `INSERT`, `UPDATE`, and `DELETE` commands. DML is sometimes mistakenly referred to as *Data Modification Language*; this is misleading, because the `SELECT` statement does not modify data. It does, however, manipulate the data returned.
- **Data Definition Language (DDL):** Commands that `CREATE`, `ALTER`, or `DROP` data tables, constraints, indexes, and other database objects.
- **Data Control Language (DCL):** Security commands such as `GRANT`, `REVOKE`, and `DENY` that control how a principal (user or role) can access a securable (object or data.)

In Honor of Dr. Jim Gray

Jim Gray, a Technical Fellow at Microsoft Research (MSR) in San Francisco, earned the ACM Turing Award in 1998 "for seminal contributions to database and transaction processing research and technical leadership in system implementation."

A friend of the SQL Server community, he often spoke at PASS Summits. His keynote address on the future of databases at the PASS 2005 Community Summit in Grapevine, Texas, was one of the most thrilling database presentations I've ever seen. He predicted that the exponential growth of cheap storage space will create a crisis for the public as they attempt to organize several terabytes of data in drives that will fit in their pockets. For the database community, Dr. Gray believed that the growth of storage space would eliminate the need for updating or deleting data; future databases will only have insert and select commands.

The following image of Microsoft's TerraServer appeared in the SQL Server 2000 Bible. TerraServer was Microsoft's SQL Server 2000 scalability project, designed by Jim Gray. His research in spatial data is behind the new spatial data types in SQL Server 2008.

Dr. Gray's research led to a project that rocked the SQL world: 48 SATA drives were configured to build a 24-TB data warehouse, achieving throughputs equal to a SAN at one-fortieth the cost.

On January 28, 2007, Jim Gray disappeared while sailing alone near the Farallon Islands just outside San Francisco Bay. An extensive sea search by the U.S. Coast Guard, a private search, and an Internet satellite image search all failed to reveal any clues.

continued

continued

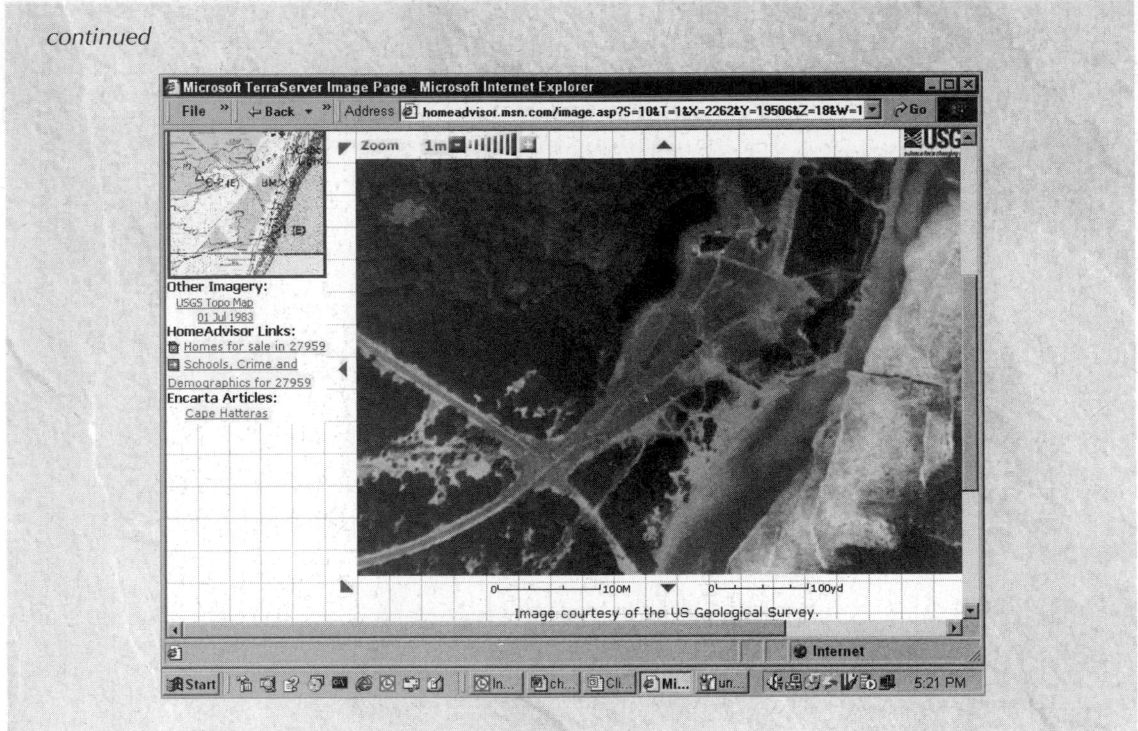

Policy-Based Management

Policy-based management, affectionately known as PBM, and new for SQL Server 2008, is the system within the engine that handles declarative management of the server, database, and any database object.

As declarative management, PBM replaces the chaos of scripts, manual operations, three-ring binders with daily run sheets and policies, and Post-it notes in the DBA's cubicle.

CROSS-REF **Chapter 40, "Policy-Based Management," discusses managing your server declaratively.**

.NET Common Language Runtime

Since SQL Server 2005, SQL Server has hosted an internal .Net Common Language Runtime, or CLR. Assemblies developed in Visual Studio can be deployed and executed inside SQL Server as stored procedures, triggers, user-defined functions, or user-defined aggregate functions. In addition, data types developed with Visual Studio can be used to define tables and store custom data.

SQL Server's internal operating system, SQLOS, actually hosts the .NET CLR inside SQL Server. There's value in SQLOS hosting the CLR, as it means that SQL Server is in control of the CLR resources. It can prevent a CLR problem, shut down and restart a CLR routine that's causing trouble, and ensure that the battle for memory is won by the right player.

While the CLR may sound appealing, Transact-SQL is the native language of SQL Server and it performs better and scales better than the CLR for nearly every task. The CLR is useful for coding tasks that require resources external to the database that cannot be completed using T-SQL. In this sense, the CLR is the replacement for the older extended stored procedures. In my opinion, the primary benefit of the CLR is that Microsoft can use it to extend and develop SQL Server.

By default, the common language runtime is disabled in SQL Server and must be specifically enabled using a T-SQL SET command. When enabled, each assembly's scope, or ability to access code outside SQL Server, can be carefully controlled.

CROSS-REF **.NET integration is discussed in Chapter 32, "Programming .NET CLR within SQL Server."**

Service Broker

Introduced in SQL Server 2005, Service Broker is a managed data queue, providing a key performance and scalability feature by leveling the load over time:

- Service Broker can buffer high volumes of calls to an HTTP Web Service or a stored procedure. Rather than a thousand Web Service calls launching a thousand stored procedure threads, the calls can be placed on a queue and the stored procedures can be executed by a few instances to handle the load more efficiently.
- Server-side processes that include significant logic or periods of heavy traffic can place the required data in the queue and return to the calling process without completing the logic. Service Broker will move through the queue calling another stored procedure to do the heavy lifting.

While it's possible to design your own queue within SQL Server, there are benefits to using Microsoft's work queue. SQL Server includes DDL commands to manage Service Broker, and there are T-SQL commands to place data on the queue or fetch data from the queue. Information about Service Broker queues are exposed in metadata views, Management Studio, and System Monitor. Most important, Service Broker is well tested and designed for heavy payloads under stress.

CROSS-REF **Service Broker is a key service in building a service-oriented architecture data store. For more information, see Chapter 35, "Building Asynchronous Applications with Service Broker."**

Replication services

SQL Server data is often required throughout national or global organizations, and SQL Server replication is often employed to move that data. Replication Services can move transactions one-way or merge updates from multiple locations using a publisher-distributor-subscriber topology.

CROSS-REF **Chapter 36, "Replicating Data," explains the various replication models and how to set up replication.**

Integrated Full-Text Search

Full-Text Search has been in SQL Server since version 7, but with each version this excellent service has been enhanced, and the name has evolved to Integrated Full-Text Search, or iFTS.

SQL queries use indexes to locate rows quickly. SQL Server b-tree indexes index the entire column. Searching for words within the column requires a scan and is a very slow process. Full-Text Search solves this problem by indexing every word within a column.

Once the full-text search has been created for the column, SQL Server queries can search the Full-Text Search indexes and return high-performance in-string word searches.

CROSS-REF **Chapter 19, "Using Integrated Full-Text Search," explains how to set up and use full-text searches within SQL queries.**

Server management objects

Server Management Objects (SMO) is the set of objects that exposes SQL Server's configuration and management features for two primary purposes: scripting and programming.

For administration scripting, PowerShell cmdlets use SMO to access SQL Server objects.

For programming, SMO isn't intended for development of database applications; rather, it's used by vendors when developing SQL Server tools such as Management Studio or a third-party management GUI or backup utility. SMO uses the namespace `Microsoft.SQLServer.SMO`.

Filestream

New for SQL Server 2008, Filestream technology adds the ability to write or read large BLOB data to Windows files through the database, complete with transactional control.

CROSS-REF **Chapter 15, "Modifying Data," covers how to use FileStream with `INSERT`, `UPDATE`, and `DELETE` commands.**

SQL Server Services

The following components are client processes for SQL Server used to control, or communicate with, SQL Server.

SQL Server Agent

The Server Agent is an optional process that, when running, executes SQL jobs and handles other automated tasks. It can be configured to automatically run when the system boots, or it can be started from SQL Server Configuration Manager or Management Studio's Object Explorer.

Database Mail

The Database Mail component enables SQL Server to send mail to an external mailbox through SMTP. Mail may be generated from multiple sources within SQL Server, including T-SQL code, jobs, alerts, Integration Services, and maintenance plans.

CROSS-REF **Chapter 43, "Automating Database Maintenance with SQL Server Agent," details SQL agents and jobs, as well as the SQL Server Agent. It also explains how to set up a mail profile for SQL Server and how to send mail.**

Distributed Transaction Coordinator (DTC)

The Distributed Transaction Coordinator is a process that handles dual-phase commits for transactions that span multiple SQL Servers. DTC can be started from within Windows' Computer Administration/Services. If the application regularly uses distributed transactions, you should start DTC when the operating system starts.

CROSS-REF **Chapter 31, "Executing Distributed Queries," explains dual-phase commitments and distributed transactions.**

A Brief History of SQL Server

SQL Server has grown considerably over the past two decades from its early roots with Sybase:

SQL Server 1.0 was jointly released in 1989 by Microsoft, Sybase, and Ashton-Tate. The product was based on Sybase SQL Server 3.0 for Unix and VMS.

SQL Server 4.2.1 for Windows NT was released in 1993. Microsoft began making changes to the code.

SQL Server 6.0 (code-named SQL 95) was released in 1995. In 1996, the 6.5 upgrade (Hydra) was released. It included the first version of Enterprise Manager (StarFighter I) and SQL Server Agent (StarFighter II).

SQL Server 7.0 (Sphinx) was released in 1999, and was a full rewrite of the Database Engine by Microsoft. From a code perspective, this was the first Microsoft SQL Server. SQL Server 7 also included English Query (Argo), OLAP Services (Plato), replication, Database Design and Query tools (DaVinci) and Full-Text Search (aptly code-named Babylon.) Data Transformation Services (DTS) is also introduced.

My favorite new feature? DTS.

SQL Server 2000 (Shiloh) 32-bit, version 8, introduced SQL Server to the enterprise with clustering, much better performance, and real OLAP. It supported XML though three different XML add-on packs. It added user-defined functions, indexed views, clustering support, Distributed Partition Views, and improved replication. SQL Server 2000 64-bit version for Intel Itanium (Liberty) was released in 2003, along with the first version of Reporting Services (Rosetta) and Data Mining tools (Aurum). DTS became more powerful and gained in popularity. Northwind joined Pubs as the sample database.

My favorite new feature? User-defined functions.

SQL Server 2005 (Yukon), version 9, was another rewrite of the Database Engine and pushed SQL Server further into the enterprise space. 2005 added a ton of new features and technologies, including Service Broker, Notification Services, CLR, XQuery and XML data types, and SQLOS. T-SQL gained try-catch and the system tables were replaced with Dynamic Management Views (DMVs). Management Studio replaced Enterprise Manager and Query Analyzer. DTS is replaced by Integration Services. English Query was removed, and stored procedure debugging was moved from the DBA interface to Visual Studio. AdventureWorks and AdventureWorksDW replaced Northwind and Pubs as the sample databases. SQL Server 2005 supported 32-bit, 64x, and Itanium CPUs. Steve Ballmer publically vowed to never again make customers wait five years between releases, and to return to a 2–3 year release cycle.

My favorite new features? T-SQL Try-Catch, Index Include columns, VarChar(max), windowing/ranking functions, and DMVs.

SQL Server 2008 (Katmai), version 10, is a natural evolution of SQL Server, adding Policy-Based Management, data compression, Resource Governor, and new beyond relational data types. Notification Services go the way of English Query. T-SQL finally gets date and time data types and table-valued parameters, the debugger returns, and Management Studio gets IntelliSense.

My favorite new features? Table-valued parameters and policy-based management.

continued

continued

What's next?

SQL Data Services is Microsoft's database in the cloud.

Kilimanjaro, estimated availability in mid-2010 extends SQL Server's BI suite with tighter integration with Office 14.

SQL11 continues the strategic direction of SQL Server 2008.

Business Intelligence

Business intelligence (BI) is the name given to the discipline and tools that enables the management of data for the purpose of analysis, exploration, reporting, mining, and visualization. While aspects of BI appear in many applications, the BI approach and toolset provides a rich and robust environment to understand data and trends.

SQL Server provides a great toolset to build BI applications, which explains Microsoft's continued gains in the growing BI market. SQL Server includes three services designed for business intelligence: Integration Services (IS, or sometimes called SSIS for SQL Server Integration Services), Reporting Services (RS), and Analysis Services (AS). Development for all three services can be done using the BI Development Studio.

Business Intelligence Development Studio

The BI Development Studio (BIDS) is a version of Visual Studio that hosts development of Analysis Services databases and mining models, Integration Services packages, and Reporting Services reports. When installed on a system that already has Visual Studio installed, these additional project types are added to the existing Visual Studio environment.

Integration Services

Integration Services (IS) moves data among nearly any type of data source and is SQL Server's extract-transform-load (ETL) tool. As shown in Figure 1-2, IS uses a graphical tool to define how data can be moved from one connection to another connection. Integration Services packages have the flexibility to either copy data column for column or perform complex transformations, lookups, and exception handling during the data move. Integration Services is extremely useful during data conversions, collecting data from many dissimilar data sources, or gathering for data warehousing data that can be analyzed using Analysis Services.

Integration Services has many advantages over using custom programming or T-SQL to move and transform data; chief among these are speed and traceability. If you have experience with other databases but are new to SQL Server, this is one of the tools that will most impress you. If any other company were marketing SSIS it would be their flagship product, but instead it's bundled inside SQL Server without much fanfare and at no extra charge. Be sure to find the time to explore Integration Services.

CROSS-REF **Chapter 37, "Performing ETL with Integration Services," describes how to create and execute an SSIS package.**

FIGURE 1-2

Integration Services graphically illustrates the data transformations within a planned data migration or conversion.

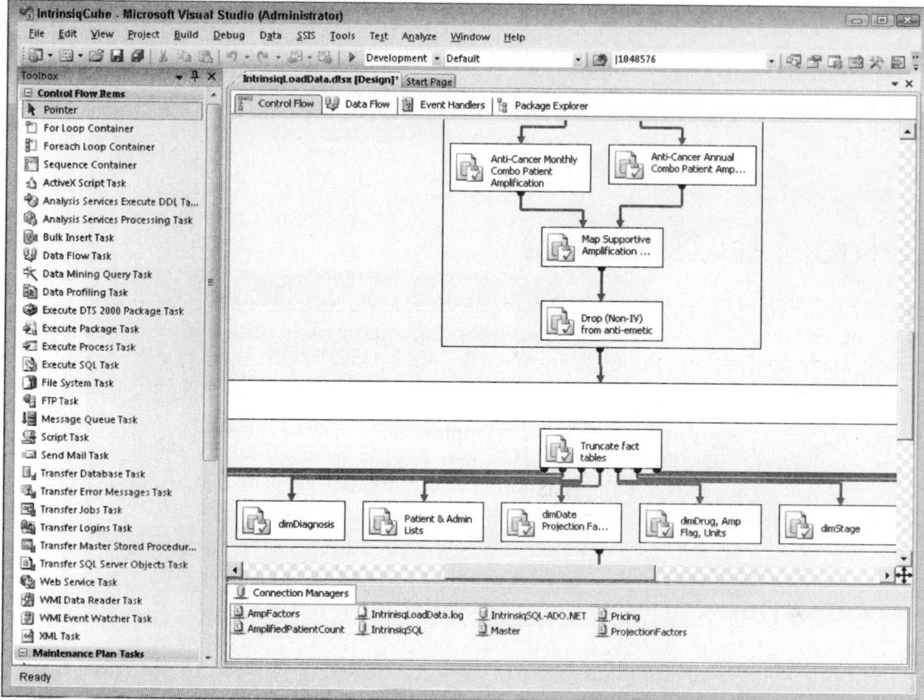

Analysis Services

The Analysis Services service hosts two key components of the BI toolset: *Online Analytical Processing (OLAP)* hosts multidimensional databases, whereby data is stored in cubes, while *Data Mining* provides methods to analyze data sets for non-obvious patterns in the data.

OLAP

Building cubes in a multidimensional database provides a fast, pre-interpreted, flexible analysis environment. Robust calculations can be included in a cube for later querying and reporting, going a long way toward the "one version of the truth" that is so elusive in many organizations. Results can be used as the basis for reports, but the most powerful uses involve interactive data exploration using tools such as Excel pivot tables or similar query and analysis applications. Tables and charts that summarize billions of rows can be generated in seconds, enabling users to understand the data in ways they never thought possible.

Whereas relational databases in SQL Server are queried using T-SQL, cubes are queried using Multidimensional Expressions (MDX), a set-based query language tailored to retrieving multidimensional data (see Figure 1-3). This enables relatively easy custom application development in addition to standard analysis and reporting tools.

FIGURE 1-3

Browsing a multidimensional cube within Analysis Services is a fluid way to compare various aspects of the data.

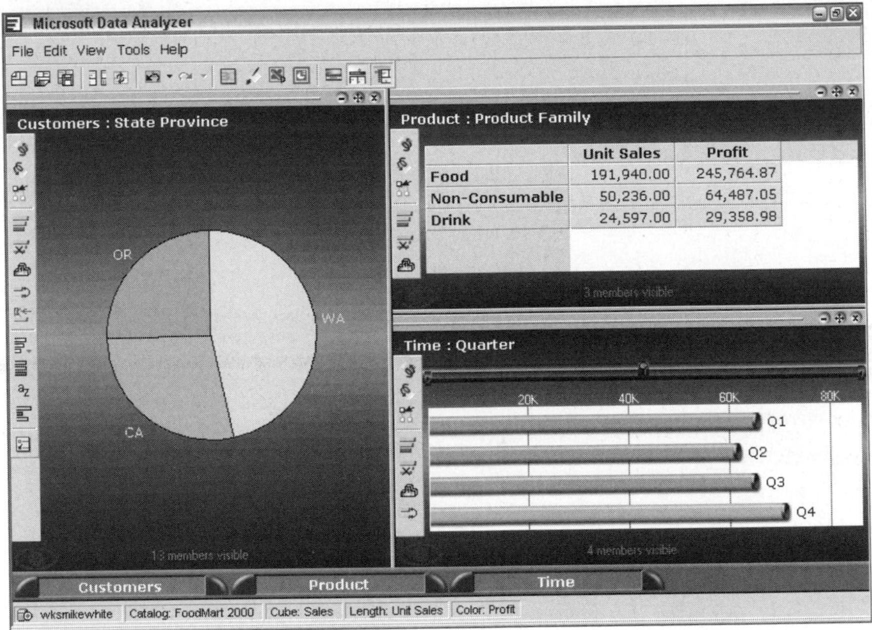

Data Mining

Viewing data from cubes or even relational queries can reveal the obvious trends and correlations in a data set, but data mining can expose the non-obvious ones. The robust set of mining algorithms enables tasks like finding associations, forecasting, and classifying cases into groups. Once a model is trained on an existing set of data, it can predict new cases that are likely to occur — for example, predicting the most profitable customers to spend scarce advertising dollars on or estimating expected component failure rates based on its characteristics.

CROSS-REF **Chapters 71, 72, and 76 cover designing cubes, data mining, and programming MDX queries with Analysis Services. Chapter 75 describes data analysis in Excel, including accessing cube data and using Excel's related data-mining functions.**

The BI Stack

The buzz today is around the BI stack; in other words, the suite of products that support an organization's BI efforts both inside and outside of SQL Server.

continued

continued

The SQL Server products described here are the BI platform of the stack, providing the data acquisition, storage, summarization, and reporting — the basis for analysis. Excel is a key analysis tool in the stack, exposing query results, pivot tables, basic data-mining functions, and a host of charting and formatting features. The 2007 version of Excel puts it on a par with many of the third-party data analysis tools available.

The PerformancePoint product enables the construction of dashboards and scorecards, exposing company performance metrics throughout the organization. Combined with a variety of reporting and charting options, key performance indicators, and data-mining trends, this product has the potential to change the way companies work day to day.

SharePoint has long been an excellent tool for collaboration, organizing and tracking documents, and searching all the associated content. Microsoft Office SharePoint Server 2007 (MOSS) adds several BI features to the SharePoint product, including Excel Services, which enables the sharing of Excel workbooks, tables, and charts via a web interface, rather than a download. MOSS also provides a great way to organize and share Reporting Services reports with related content (e.g., department reports from a department's website). In addition, BI Web Parts, SharePoint-hosted key performance indicators and Dashboards, and data connection libraries are all available within MOSS.

These additions to the BI platform provide important pieces to deliver BI solutions, presenting some very persuasive enhancements to how organizations work.

Reporting Services

Reporting Services (RS) for SQL Server 2005 is a full-featured, web-based, managed reporting solution. RS reports can be exported to PDF, Excel, or other formats with a single click, and are easy to build and customize.

Reports are defined graphically or programmatically and stored as `.rdl` files in the Reporting Services databases in SQL Server. They can be scheduled to be pre-created and cached for users, e-mailed to users, or generated by users on-the-fly with parameters. Reporting Services is bundled with SQL Server so there are no end-user licensing issues. It's essentially free, although most DBAs place it on its own dedicated server for better performance.

With SQL Server 2008, Reporting Services gets a facelift: slick new Dundas controls, a new Tablix control, a re-written memory management system, and a direct HTTP.sys access, so IIS is no longer needed. If you're still using Crystal Reports, why?

CROSS-REF **Chapters 73 and 74 deal with authoring and deploying reports using Reporting Services.**

UI and Tools

SQL Server 2008 retains most of the UI feel of SQL Server 2005, with a few significant enhancements.

SQL Server Management Studio

Management Studio is a Visual Studio-esque integrated environment that's used by database administrators and database developers. At its core is the visual Object Explorer, complete with filters and the capability to browse all the SQL Server servers (Database Engine, Analysis Services, Reporting Services, etc.). Management Studio's Query Editor is an excellent way to work with raw T-SQL code and it's integrated with the Solution Explorer to manage projects. Although the interface, shown in Figure 1-4, can look crowded, the windows are easily configurable and can auto-hide.

Chapter 6, "Using Management Studio," discusses the many tools within Management Studio and how to use this flexible development and management interface.

FIGURE 1-4

Management Studio's full array of windows and tools can seem overwhelming but it's flexible enough for you to configure it for your own purposes.

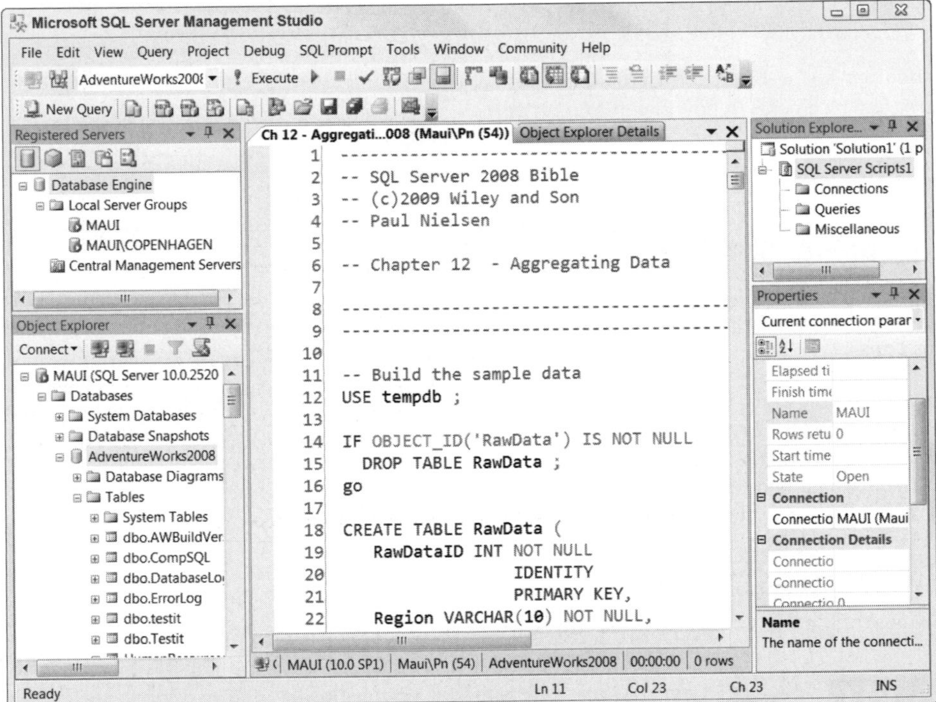

SQL Server Configuration Manager

This tool, shown in Figure 1-5, is used to start and stop any server, set the start-up options, and configure connectivity. It may be launched from the Start menu or from Management Studio.

FIGURE 1-5

Use the Configuration Manager to launch and control SQL Server's many servers.

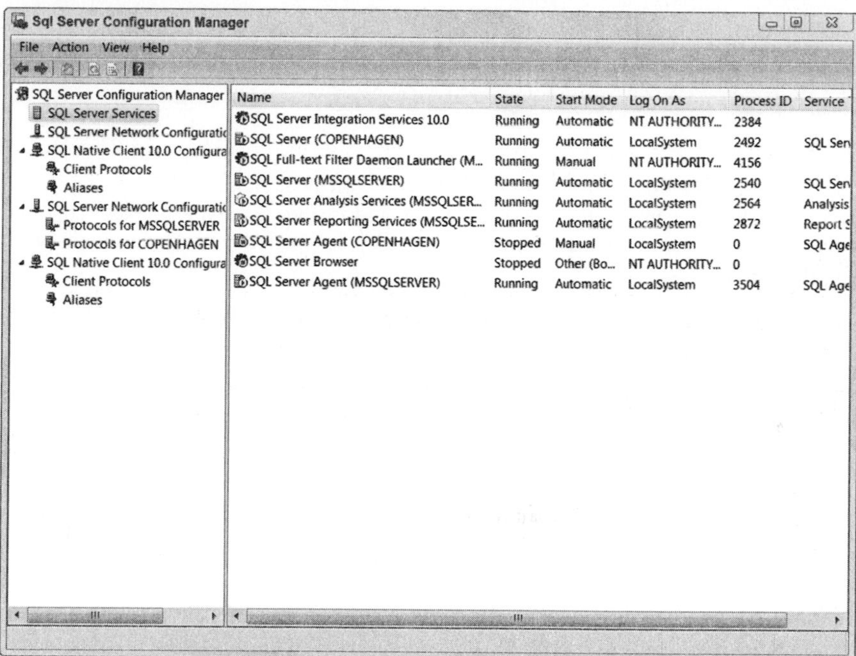

SQL Profiler/Trace

SQL Server is capable of exposing a trace of selected events and data points. The server-side trace has nearly no load on the server. SQL Profiler is the UI for viewing traces in real time (with some performance cost) or viewing saved trace files. Profiler is great for debugging an application or tuning the database. Using a two-monitor system, I often run Profiler on one monitor while I'm tuning and developing on the other monitor.

CROSS-REF **Chapter 56, "Tracing and Profiling," covers Performance Monitor.**

Performance Monitor

While Profiler records large sets of details concerning SQL traffic and SQL Server events, Performance Monitor is a visual window into the current status of the selected performance counters. Performance Monitor is found within Windows' administrative tools. When SQL Server is installed, it adds a ton of useful performance counters to Performance Monitor. It's enough to make a network administrator jealous.

Command-line utilities

Various command-line utilities may be used to execute SQL code (sqlcmd) or perform bulk-copy operations (bcp) from the DOS prompt or a command-line scheduler. Integration Services and SQL Server

Agent have rendered these tools somewhat obsolete, but in the spirit of extreme flexibility, Microsoft still includes them.

Management Studio has a mode that enables you to use the Query Editor as if it were the command-line utility sqlcmd.

CROSS-REF **Chapter 6, "Using Management Studio," has a sidebar discussing SQLCMD and Query Editor's SQLCMD mode.**

Books Online

The SQL Server documentation team did an excellent job with Books Online (BOL) — SQL Server's mega help on steroids. The articles tend to be complete and include several examples. The indexing method provides a short list of applicable articles. BOL may be opened from Management Studio or directly from the Start menu.

BOL is well integrated with the primary interfaces. Selecting a keyword within Management Studio's Query Editor and pressing F1 will launch BOL to the selected keyword. The Enterprise Manager help buttons also launch the correct BOL topic.

Management Studio also includes a dynamic help window that automatically tracks the cursor and presents help for the current keyword.

Searching returns both online and local MSDN articles. In addition, BOL searches the Codezone community for relevant articles. Both the Community Menu and Developer Center launch web pages that enable users to ask a question or learn more about SQL Server.

CROSS-REF **Microsoft regularly updates BOL. The new versions can be downloaded from `www.Microsoft.com/sql`, and I post a link to it on `www.SQLServerBible.com`.**

NOTE **If you haven't discovered CodePlex.com, allow me to introduce it to you. CodePlex.com is Microsoft's site for open-source code. That's where you'll find AdventureWorks2008, the official sample database for SQL Server 2008, along with AdventureWorksLT (a smaller version of AdventureWorks) and AdventureWorksDW (the BI companion to AdventureWorks). You'll also find copies of the older sample databases, Pubs and Northwind. I also have a few projects on CodePlex.com myself.**

SQL Server Editions

SQL Server is available in several editions (not to be confused with versions), which differ in terms of features, hardware, and cost. This section details the various editions and their respective features. Because Microsoft licensing and costs change, check with `www.microsoft.com/sql` or your Microsoft representative for license and cost specifics.

- **Enterprise (Developer) Edition:** This is the high-end edition, with the advanced performance and availability features (e.g., table partitioning, data compression) required to support thousands of connections and databases measured by terabytes.

  The Developer Edition is the same as the Enterprise Edition, but it's licensed only for development and testing and it can run on workstation versions of Windows.

- **Standard Edition:** The majority of medium to large production database needs will be well served by the SQL Server 2008 Standard Edition, the workhorse edition of SQL Server. This edition includes all the right features, including Integration Services, Analysis Services, Web

Services, database mirroring, and failover clustering. Don't blow your budget on Enterprise Edition unless you've proven that Standard Edition won't do the job.

NOTE With multi-core CPUs becoming commonplace in servers, the question is, how does this affect licensing? The good news is that Microsoft is licensing SQL Server by the CPU socket, not the number of CPU cores. This means that a dual CPU server running quad-core CPUs will function almost as if the server had eight CPUs, but you're only paying for two CPUs' worth of SQL Server licensing.

Although it's limited to four CPUs with multi-core CPUs, it is a lesser limitation than in the past and there's no limit to memory. With a well-designed four-way server running multi-core CPUs and plenty of RAM, Standard Edition can easily handle 500 concurrent users and a database pushing a terabyte of data.

- **Workgroup Edition:** Intended as a departmental database server, Workgroup Edition includes the right mix of features for a small transactional database that's connected to a Standard or Enterprise Edition.

  The key feature missing from Workgroup Edition is Integration Services, the rationale being that a workgroup database is likely the source of data that is integrated by other larger database servers but does not pull data from other sources itself. This may be the single factor that drives you to move up to Standard Edition. In my experience, a database of this size does occasionally require moving data even if for an upgrade of an Access database.

  I recommend Workgroup Edition for small businesses or departments that don't require extremely high availability or Analysis Services. A server with two dual-core CPUs, 3GB of RAM, and a well-designed disk subsystem could easily serve 100 busy users with Workgroup Edition.

- **Web Edition:** As the name implies, the Web Edition, new for SQL Server 2008 is licensed for hosting websites.**SQL Server Express Edition:** This free (no upfront cost, no royalties, no redistributable fees) version of SQL S**erver is not simply a plug-**in replacement for the Access Jet database engine. It's a full version of the SQL Server Database Engine intended to serve as an embedded database within an application. Express does have some limitations: a maximum database size limit of 4GB, only one CPU socket, and 1GB of RAM.

  I'd recommend SQL Server Express Edition for any small .NET application that needs a real database. It's more than suitable for applications with up to 25 users and less than 4GB of data.

- **SQL Server Compact Edition:** CE is technically a different Database Engine with a different feature set and a different set of commands. Its small footprint of only 1MB of RAM means that it can actually run well on a mobile smart device. Even though it runs on a handheld computer, it's a true ACID-compliant Database Engine. This book does not cover SQL Server CE.

Best Practice

I've spoken out and blogged about my pro-64-bit view. Any new server will sport shiny, new 64-bit multi-core CPUs, and considering the smoother memory addressing and performance gains, I see no reason why SQL Server is not a 64-bit only product — except for, perhaps, Developer and Express Editions. Do your shop a favor and don't even consider 32-bit SQL Server for production.

- **SQL Data Services (SDS):** The database side of Microsoft Azure is a full-featured relational SQL Server in the cloud that provides an incredible level of high availability and scalable performance without any capital expenses or software licenses at a very reasonable cost. I'm a huge fan of SDS and I host my ISV software business on SDS.

  Version 1 does have a few limitations: 10GB per database, no heaps (I can live with that), no access to the file system or other SQL Servers (distributed queries, etc.), and you're limited to SQL Server logins.

CROSS-REF **Besides the general descriptions here, Appendix A includes a chart detailing the differences between the multiple editions.**

Exploring the Metadata

When SQL Server is initially installed, it already contains several system objects. In addition, every new user database contains several system objects, including tables, views, stored procedures, and functions.

Within Management Studio's Object Explorer, the system databases appear under the Databases ➪ System Databases node.

System databases

SQL Server uses five system databases to store system information, track operations, and provide a temporary work area. In addition, the `model` database is a template for new user databases. These five system databases are as follows:

- **master:** Contains information about the server's databases. In addition, objects in `master` are available to other databases. For example, stored procedures in `master` may be called from a user database.
- **msdb:** Maintains lists of activities, such as backups and jobs, and tracks which database backup goes with which user database
- **model:** The template database from which new databases are created. Any object placed in the `model` database will be copied into any new database.
- **tempdb:** Used for ad hoc tables by all users, batches, stored procedures (including Microsoft stored procedures), and the SQL Server engine itself. If SQL Server needs to create temporary heaps or lists during query execution, it creates them in `tempdb`. `tempdb` is dropped and recreated when SQL Server is restarted.
- **resource:** This hidden database, added in SQL Server 2005, contains information that was previously in the master database and was split out from the master database to make service pack upgrades easier to install.

Metadata views

Metadata is data about data. One of Codd's original rules for relational databases is that information about the database schema must be stored in the database using tables, rows, and columns, just like user data. It is this data about the data that makes it easy to write code to navigate and explore the database schema and configuration. SQL Server has several types of metadata:

- **Catalog views:** Provide information about static metadata — such as tables, security, and server configuration

- **Dynamic management views (DMVs) and functions:** Yield powerful insight into the current state of the server and provide data about things such as memory, threads, stored procedures in cache, and connections
- **System functions and global variables:** Provide data about the current state of the server, the database, and connections for use in scalar expressions
- **Compatibility views:** Serve as backward compatibility views to simulate the system tables from previous versions of SQL Server 2000 and earlier. Note that compatibility views are deprecated, meaning they'll disappear in SQL Server 11, the next version of SQL Server.
- **Information schema views:** The ANSI SQL-92 standard nonproprietary views used to examine the schema of any database product. Portability as a database design goal is a lost cause, and these views are of little practical use for any DBA or database developer who exploits the features of SQL Server. Note that they have been updated for SQL Server 2008, so if you used these in the past they may need to be tweaked.

These metadata views are all listed in Management Studio's Object Explorer under the Database ➪ Views ➪ System Views node, or under the Database ➪ Programmability ➪ Functions ➪ Metadata Function node.

What's New?

There are about 50 new features in SQL Server 2008, as you'll discover in the What's New in 2008 sidebars in many chapters. Everyone loves lists (and so do I), so here's my list highlighting the best of what's new in SQL Server 2008.

Paul's top-ten new features in SQL Server 2008:

10. **PowerShell** — The new Windows scripting language has been integrated into SQL Server. If you are a DBA willing to learn PowerShell, this technology has the potential to radically change how you do your daily jobs.
9. **New data types** — Specifically, I'm more excited about Date, Time, and DateTime2 than Spatial and HierarchyID.
8. **Tablix** — Reporting Services gains the Tablix and Dundas controls, and loses that IIS requirement.
7. **Query processing optimizations** — The new star joins provide incredible out-of-the-box performance gains for some types of queries. Also, although partitioned tables were introduced in SQL Server 2005, the query execution plan performance improvements and new UI for partitioned tables in SQL Server 2008 will increase their adoption rate.
6. **Filtered indexes** — The ability to create a small targeted nonclustered index over a very large table is the perfect logical extension of indexing, and I predict it will be one of the most popular new features.
5. **Management Data Warehouse** — A new consistent method of gathering performance data for further analysis by Performance Studio or custom reports and third parties lays the foundation for more good stuff in the future.
4. **Data compression** — The ability to trade CPU cycles for reduced IO can significantly improve the scalability of some enterprise databases. I believe this is the sleeper feature that will be the compelling reason for many shops to upgrade to SQL Server 2008 Enterprise Edition.

The third top new feature is Management Studio's many enhancements. Even though it's just a tool and doesn't affect the performance of the engine, it will help database developers and DBAs be more productive and it lends a more enjoyable experience to every job role working with SQL Server:

3. **Management Studio** — The primary UI is supercharged with multi-server queries and configuration servers, IntelliSense, T-SQL debugger, customizable Query Editor tabs, Error list in Query Editor, easily exported data from Query Results, launch profiler from Query Editor, Object Search, a vastly improved Object Explorer Details page, a new Activity Monitor, improved ways to work with query plans, and it's faster.

And for the final top two new features, one for developers and one for DBAs:

2. `Merge` and **Table-valued parameters** — Wow! It's great to see new T-SQL features on the list. Table-valued parameters alone is the compelling reason I upgraded my Nordic software to SQL Server 2008. Table-valued parameters revolutionize the way application transactions communicate with the database, which earns it the top SQL Server 2008 database developer feature and number two in this list.

   The new `merge` command combines insert, update, and delete into a single transaction and is a slick way to code an upsert operation. I've recoded many of my upsert stored procedures to use `merge` with excellent results.

1. **Policy-based management (PBM)** — PBM means that servers and databases can be declaratively managed by applying and enforcing consistent policies, instead of running ad hoc scripts. This feature has the potential to radically change how enterprise DBAs do their daily jobs, which is why it earns the number one spot on my list of top ten SQL Server 2008 features.

Going, Going, Gone?

With every new version of SQL Server, some features change or are removed because they no longer make sense with the newer feature set. *Discontinued* means a feature used to work in a previous SQL Server version but no longer appears in SQL Server 2008.

Deprecated means the feature still works in SQL Server 2008, but it's going to be removed in a future version. There are two levels of deprecation; Microsoft releases both a list of the features that will be gone in the next version, and a list of the features that will be gone in some future version but will still work in the next version.

Books Online has details about all three lists (just search for deprecated), but here are the highlights:

Going Eventually (Deprecated)

These features are deprecated from a future version of SQL Server. You should try to remove these from your code:

- SQLOLEDB
- `Timestamp` (although the synonym `rowversion` continues to be supported)

continued

continued

- Text, ntext, and image data types
- Older full-text catalog commands
- Sp_configure 'user instances enabled'
- Sp_lock
- SQL-DMO
- Sp stored procedures for security, e.g., sp_adduser
- Setuser (use Execute as instead)
- System tables
- Group by all

Going Soon (Deprecated)

The following features are deprecated from the next version of SQL Server. You should definitely remove these commands from your code:

- Older backup and restore options
- SQL Server 2000 compatibility level
- DATABASEPROPERTY command
- sp_dboption
- FastFirstRow query hint (use Option(Fast n))
- ANSI-89 (legacy) outer join syntax (*=, =*); use ANSI-92 syntax instead
- Raiserror integer string format
- Client connectivity using DB-Lib and Embedded SQL for C

Gone (Discontinued)

The following features are discontinued in SQL Server 2008:

- SQL Server 6, 6.5, and 7 compatibility levels
- Surface Area Configuration Tool (unfortunately)
- Notification Services
- Dump and Load commands (use Backup and Restore)
- Backup log with No-Log

continued

continued

- `Backup log with truncate_only`
- `Backup transaction`
- `DBCC` Concurrencyviolation
- `sp_addgroup`, `sp_changegroup`, `sp_dropgroup`, and `sp_helpgroup` (use security roles instead)

The very useful Profiler trace feature can report the use of any deprecated features.

Summary

If SQL Server 2005 was the "kitchen sink" version of SQL Server, then SQL Server 2008 is the version that focuses squarely on managing the enterprise database.

Some have written that SQL Server 2008 is the second step of a two-step release. In the same way that SQL Server 2000 was part two to SQL Server 7, the theory is that SQL Server 2008 is part two to SQL Server 2005.

At first glance this makes sense, because SQL Server 2008 is an evolution of the SQL Server 2005 engine, in the same way that SQL Server 2000 was built on the SQL Server 7 engine. However, as I became intimate with SQL Server 2008, I changed my mind.

Consider the significant new technologies in SQL Server 2008: policy-based management, Performance Data Warehouse, PowerShell, data compression, and Resource Governor. None of these technologies existed in SQL Server 2005.

In addition, think of the killer technologies introduced in SQL Server 2005 that are being extended in SQL Server 2008. The most talked about new technology in SQL Server 2005 was CLR. Hear much about CLR in SQL Server 2008? Nope. Service Broker has some minor enhancements. Two SQL Server 2005 new technologies, HTTP endpoints and Notification Services, are actually discontinued in SQL Server 2008. Hmmm, I guess they should have been on the SQL Server 2005 deprecation list.

No, SQL Server 2008 is more than a SQL Server 2005 sequel. SQL Server 2008 is a fresh new vision for SQL Server. SQL Server 2008 is the first punch of a two-punch setup focused squarely at managing the enterprise-level database. SQL Server 2008 is a down payment on the big gains coming in SQL Server 11.

I'm convinced that the SQL Server Product Managers nailed it and that SQL Server 2008 is the best direction possible for SQL Server. There's no Kool-Aid here — it's all way cool.

Chapter 2

Data Architecture

You can tell by looking at a building whether there's an elegance to the architecture, but architecture is more than just good looks. Architecture brings together materials, foundations, and standards. In the same way, data architecture is the study of defining what a good database is and how one builds a good database. That's why data architecture is more than just data modeling, more than just server configuration, and more than just a collection of tips and tricks.

Data architecture is the overarching design of the database, how the database should be developed and implemented, and how it interacts with other software. In this sense, data architecture can be related to the architecture of a home, a factory, or a skyscraper. Data architecture is defined by the *Information Architecture Principle* and the six attributes by which every database can be measured.

Enterprise data architecture extends the basic ideas of designing a single database to include designing which types of databases serve which needs within the organization, how those databases share resources, and how they communicate with one another and other software. In this sense, enterprise data architecture is community planning or zoning, and is concerned with applying the best database meta-patterns (e.g., relational OTLP database, object-oriented database, multidimensional) to an organization's various needs.

IN THIS CHAPTER

Author's Note

Data architecture is a passion of mine, and without question the subject belongs in any comprehensive database book. Because it's the foundation for the rest of the book — the "why" behind the "how" of designing, developing, and operating a database — it makes sense to position it toward the beginning of the book. Even if you're not in the role of database architect yet, I hope you enjoy the chapter and that it presents a useful viewpoint for your database career. Keep in mind that you can return to read this chapter later, at any time when the information might be more useful to you.

Information Architecture Principle

For any complex endeavor, there is value in beginning with a common principle to drive designs, procedures, and decisions. A credible principle is understandable, robust, complete, consistent, and stable. When an overarching principle is agreed upon, conflicting opinions can be objectively measured, and standards can be decided upon that support the principle.

The Information Architecture Principle encompasses the three main areas of information management: database design and development, enterprise data center management, and business intelligence analysis.

> ***Information Architecture Principle****: Information is an organizational asset, and, according to its value and scope, must be organized, inventoried, secured, and made readily available in a usable format for daily operations and analysis by individuals, groups, and processes, both today and in the future.*

Unpacking this principle reveals several practical implications. There should be a known inventory of information, including its location, source, sensitivity, present and future value, and current owner. While most organizational information is stored in IT databases, un-inventoried critical data is often found scattered throughout the organization in desktop databases, spreadsheets, scraps of papers, Post-it notes, and (the most dangerous of all) inside the head of key employees.

Just as the value of physical assets varies from asset to asset and over time, the value of information is also variable and so must be assessed. Information value may be high for an individual or department, but less valuable to the organization as a whole; information that is critical today might be meaningless in a month; or information that may seem insignificant individually might become critical for organizational planning once aggregated.

If the data is to be made easily available in the future, then current designs must be loosely connected, or coupled, to avoid locking the data in a rigid, but brittle, database.

Database Objectives

Based on the Information Architecture Principle, every database can be architected or evaluated by six interdependent database objectives. Four of these objectives are primarily a function of design, development, and implementation: *usability, extensibility, data integrity*, and *performance*. *Availability* and *security* are more a function of implementation than design.

With sufficient design effort and a clear goal of meeting all six objectives, it is fully possible to design and develop an elegant database that does just that. The idea that one attribute is gained only at the expense of the other attributes is a myth.

Each objective can be measured on a continuum. The data architect is responsible for informing the organization about these six objectives, including the cost associated with meeting each objective, the risk of failing to meet the objective, and the recommended level for each objective.

It's the organization's privilege to then prioritize the objectives compared with the relative cost.

Usability

The usability of a data store (the architectural term for a database) involves the completeness of meeting the organization's requirements, the suitability of the design for its intended purpose, the effectiveness of the format of data available to applications, the robustness of the database, and the ease of extracting information (by programmers and power users). The most common reason why a database is less than usable is an overly complex or inappropriate design.

Usability is enabled in the design by ensuring the following:

- A thorough and well-documented understanding of the organizational requirements
- Life-cycle planning of software features
- Selecting the correct meta-pattern (e.g., relational OTLP database, object-oriented database, multidimensional) for the data store.
- Normalization and correct handling of optional data
- Simplicity of design
- A well-defined abstraction layer with stored procedures and views

Extensibility

The Information Architecture Principle states that the information must be readily available today and in the future, which requires the database to be *extensible*, able to be easily adapted to meet new requirements. Data integrity, performance, and availability are all mature and well understood by the computer science and IT professions. While there may be many badly designed, poorly performing, and often down databases, plenty of professionals in the field know exactly how to solve those problems. I believe the least understood database objective is extensibility.

Extensibility is incorporated into the design as follows:

- Normalization and correct handling of optional data
- Generalization of entities when designing the schema
- Data-driven designs that not only model the obvious data (e.g., orders, customers), but also enable the organization to store the behavioral patterns, or process flow.
- A well-defined abstraction layer with stored procedures and views that decouple the database from all client access, including client apps, middle tiers, ETL, and reports.
- Extensibility is also closely related to simplicity. Complexity breeds complexity, and inhibits adaptation.

Data integrity

The ability to ensure that persisted data can be retrieved without error is central to the Information Architecture Principle, and it was the first major problem tackled by the database world. Without data integrity, a query's answer cannot be guaranteed to be correct; consequently, there's not much point in availability or performance. Data integrity can be defined in multiple ways:

- **Entity integrity** involves the structure (primary key and its attributes) of the entity. If the primary key is unique and all attributes are scalar and fully dependent on the primary key, then the integrity of the entity is good. In the physical schema, the table's primary key enforces entity integrity.
- **Domain integrity** ensures that only valid data is permitted in the attribute. A domain is a set of possible values for an attribute, such as integers, bit values, or characters. Nullability (whether a null value is valid for an attribute) is also a part of domain integrity. In the physical schema, the data type and nullability of the row enforce domain integrity.
- **Referential integrity** refers to the domain integrity of foreign keys. Domain integrity means that if an attribute has a value, then that value must be in the domain. In the case of the foreign key, the domain is the list of values in the related primary key. Referential integrity, therefore, is not an issue of the integrity of the primary key but of the foreign key.
- **Transactional integrity** ensures that every logical unit of work, such as inserting 100 rows or updating 1,000 rows, is executed as a single transaction. The quality of a database product is measured by its transactions' adherence to the *ACID* properties: *atomic* — all or nothing, *consistent* — the database begins and ends the transaction in a consistent state, *isolated* — one transaction does not affect another transaction, and *durable* — once committed always committed.

In addition to these four generally accepted definitions of data integrity, I add user-defined data integrity:

- **User-defined integrity** means that the data meets the organization's requirements. Simple business rules, such as a restriction to a domain, limit the list of valid data entries. Check constraints are commonly used to enforce these rules in the physical schema.
- Complex business rules limit the list of valid data based on some condition. For example, certain tours may require a medical waiver. Implementing these rules in the physical schema generally requires stored procedures or triggers.
- Some data-integrity concerns can't be checked by constraints or triggers. Invalid, incomplete, or questionable data may pass all the standard data-integrity checks. For example, an order without any order detail rows is not a valid order, but no SQL constraint or trigger traps such an order. The abstraction layer can assist with this problem, and SQL queries can locate incomplete orders and help in identifying other less measurable data-integrity issues, including wrong data, incomplete data, questionable data, and inconsistent data.

Integrity is established in the design by ensuring the following:

- A thorough and well-documented understanding of the organizational requirements
- Normalization and correct handling of optional data
- A well-defined abstraction layer with stored procedures and views
- Data quality unit testing using a well-defined and understood set of test data
- Metadata and data audit trails documenting the source and veracity of the data, including updates

Performance/scalability

Presenting readily usable information is a key aspect of the Information Architecture Principle. Although the database industry has achieved a high degree of performance, the ability to scale that performance to very large databases with more connections is still an area of competition between database engine vendors.

Performance is enabled in the database design and development by ensuring the following:

- A well-designed schema with normalization and generalization, and correct handling of optional data
- Set-based queries implemented within a well-defined abstraction layer with stored procedures and views
- A sound indexing strategy that determines which queries should use bookmark lookups and which queries would benefit most from clustered and non-clustered covering indexes to eliminate bookmark lookups
- Tight, fast transactions that reduce locking and blocking
- Partitioning, which is useful for advanced scalability

Availability

The availability of information refers to the information's accessibility when required regarding uptime, locations, and the availability of the data for future analysis. Disaster recovery, redundancy, archiving, and network delivery all affect availability.

Availability is strengthened by the following:

- Quality, redundant hardware
- SQL Server's high-availability features
- Proper DBA procedures regarding data backup and backup storage
- Disaster recovery planning

Security

The sixth database objective based of the Information Architecture Principle is security. For any organizational asset, the level of security must be secured depending on its value and sensitivity.

Security is enforced by the following:

- Physical security and restricted access of the data center
- Defensively coding against SQL injection
- Appropriate operating system security
- Reducing the surface area of SQL Server to only those services and features required
- Identifying and documenting ownership of the data
- Granting access according to the principle of least privilege
- Cryptography — data encryption of live databases, backups, and data warehouses
- Meta-data and data audit trails documenting the source and veracity of the data, including updates

Planning Data Stores

The enterprise data architect helps an organization plan the most effective use of information throughout the organization. An organization's data store configuration includes multiple types of data stores, as illustrated in the following figure, each with a specific purpose:

- *Operational databases*, or *OLTP* (online transaction processing) *databases* collect first-generation transactional data that is essential to the day-to-day operation of the organization and unique to the organization. An organization might have an operational data store to serve each unit or function within it. Regardless of the organization's size, an organization with a singly focused purpose may very well have only one operational database.
- For performance, operational stores are tuned for a balance of data retrieval and updates, so indexes and locking are key concerns. Because these databases receive first-generation data, they are subject to data update anomalies, and benefit from normalization. A typical organizational data store configuration includes several operational data stores feeding multiple data marts and a single master data store (see graphic).

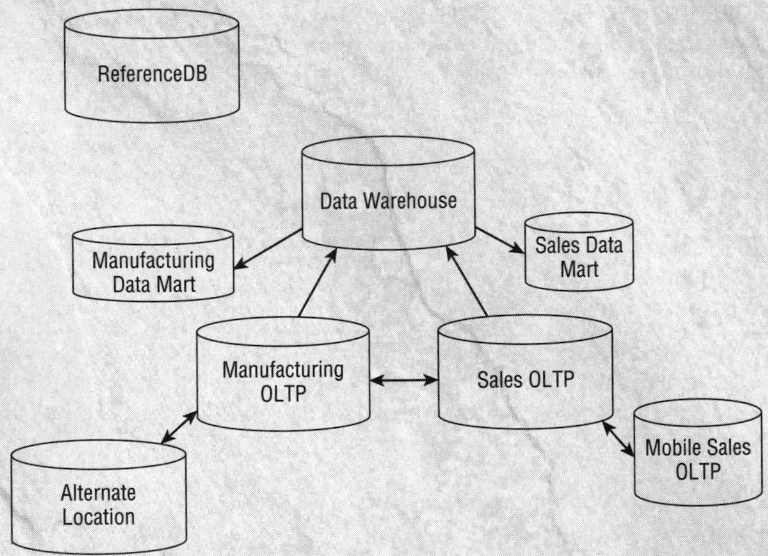

- *Caching data stores*, sometime called *reporting databases*, are optional read-only copies of all or part of an operational database. An organization might have multiple caching data stores to deliver data throughout the organization. Caching data stores

continued

continued

might use SQL Server replication or log shipping to populate the database and are tuned for high-performance data retrieval.

- *Reference data stores* are primarily read-only, and store generic data required by the organization but which seldom changes — similar to the reference section of the library. Examples of reference data might be unit of measure conversion factors or ISO country codes. A reference data store is tuned for high-performance data retrieval.
- *Data warehouses* collect large amounts of data from multiple data stores across the entire enterprise using an *extract-transform-load (ETL)* process to convert the data from the various formats and schema into a common format, designed for ease of data retrieval. Data warehouses also serve as the archival location, storing historical data and releasing some of the data load from the operational data stores. The data is also pre-aggregated, making research and reporting easier, thereby improving the accessibility of information and reducing errors.
- Because the primary task of a data warehouse is data retrieval and analysis, the data-integrity concerns present with an operational data store don't apply. Data warehouses are designed for fast retrieval and are not normalized like master data stores. They are generally designed using a basic star schema or snowflake design. Locks generally aren't an issue, and the indexing is applied without adversely affecting inserts or updates.

CROSS-REF **Chapter 70, "BI Design," discusses star schemas and snowflake designs used in data warehousing.**

- **The analysis process usually involves more than just SQL queries, and uses data cubes that consolidate gigabytes of data into dynamic pivot tables. Business intelligence (BI) is the combination of the ETL process, the data warehouse data store, and the acts of creating and browsing cubes.**
- **A common data warehouse is essential for ensuring that the entire organization researches the same data set and achieves the same result for the same query — a critical aspect of the Sarbanes-Oxley Act and other regulatory requirements.**
- ***Data marts* are subsets of the data warehouse with pre-aggregated data organized specifically to serve the needs of one organizational group or one data domain.**
- ***Master data store*, or *master data management* (MDM), refers to the data warehouse that combines the data from throughout the organization. The primary purpose of the master data store is to provide a single version of the truth for organizations with a complex set of data stores and multiple data warehouses.**

Smart Database Design

My career has focused on turning around database projects that were previously considered failures and recommending solutions for ISV databases that are performing poorly. In nearly every case, the root cause of the failure was the database design. It was too complex, too clumsy, or just plain inadequate.

Without exception, where I found poor database performance, I also found data modelers who insisted on modeling alone or who couldn't write SQL queries to save their lives.

Throughout my career, what began as an observation was reinforced into a firm conviction. The database schema is the foundation of the database project; and an elegant, simple database design outperforms a complex database both in terms of the development process and the final performance of the database application. This is the basic idea behind the Smart Database Design.

While I believe in a balanced set of goals for any database, including performance, usability, data integrity, availability, extensibility, and security, all things being equal, the crown goes to the database that always provides the right answer with lightning speed.

Database system

A database system is a complex system. By complex, I mean that the system consists of multiple components that interact with one another, as shown in Figure 2-1. The performance of one component affects the performance of other components and thus the entire system. Stated another way, the design of one component will set up other components, and the whole system, to either work well together or to frustrate those trying to make the system work.

FIGURE 2-1

The database system is the collective effort of the server environment, maintenance jobs, the client application, and the database.

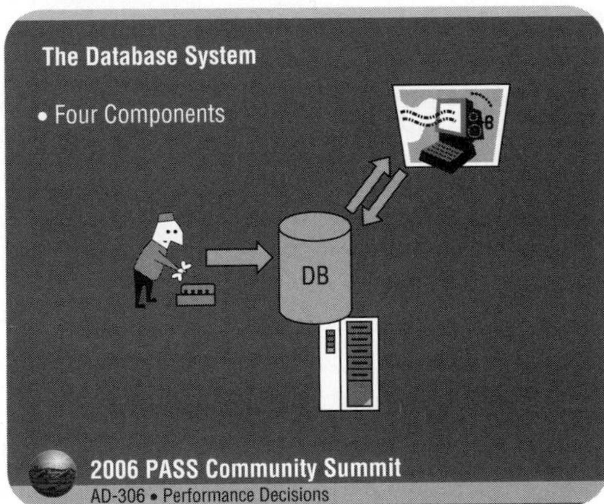

Instead of randomly trying performance tips (and the Internet has an overwhelming number of SQL Server performance and optimization tips), it makes more sense to think about the database as a system and then figure out how the components of the database system affect one another. You can then use this knowledge to apply the performance techniques in a way that provides the most benefit.

Every database system contains four broad technologies or components: the database itself, the server platform, the maintenance jobs, and the client's data access code, as illustrated in Figure 2-2. Each component affects the overall performance of the database system:

- The *server environment* is the physical hardware configuration (CPUs, memory, disk spindles, I/O bus), the operating system, and the SQL Server instance configuration, which together provide the working environment for the database. The server environment is typically optimized by balancing the CPUs, memory and I/O, and identifying and eliminating bottlenecks.
- The database *maintenance jobs* are the steps that keep the database running optimally (index defragmentation, DBCC integrity checks, and maintaining index statistics).
- The *client application* is the collection of data access layers, middle tiers, front-end applications, ETL (extract, transform, and load) scripts, report queries, or SSIS (SQL Server Integration Services) packages that access the database. These can not only affect the user's perception of database performance, but can also reduce the overall performance of the database system.
- Finally, the *database* component includes everything within the data file: the physical schema, T-SQL code (queries, stored procedures, user-defined functions (UDFs), and views), indexes, and data.

FIGURE 2-2

Smart Database Design is the premise that an elegant *physical schema* makes the data intuitively obvious and enables writing great set-based *queries* that respond well to *indexing*. This in turn creates short, tight transactions, which improves *concurrency* and *scalability*, while reducing the aggregate workload of the database. This flow from layer to layer becomes a methodology for designing and optimizing databases.

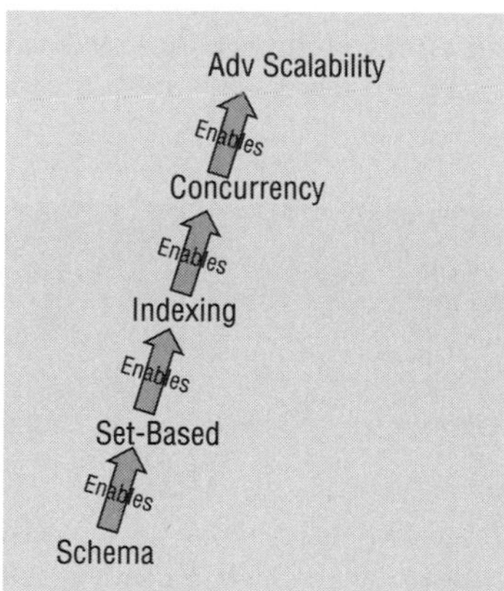

All four database components must function well together to produce a high-performance database system; if one of the components is weak, then the database system will fail or perform poorly.

However, of these four components, the database itself is the most difficult component to design and the one that drives the design of the other three components. For example, the database workload determines the hardware requirements. Maintenance jobs and data access code are both designed around the database; and an overly complex database will complicate both the maintenance jobs and the data access code.

Physical schema

The base layer of Smart Database Design is the database's physical schema. The physical schema includes the database's tables, columns, primary and foreign keys, and constraints. Basically, the "physical" schema is what the server creates when you run data definition language (DDL) commands. Designing an elegant, high-performance physical schema typically involves a team effort and requires numerous design iterations and reviews.

Well-designed physical schemas avoid overcomplexity by generalizing similar types of objects, thereby creating a schema with fewer entities. While designing the physical schema, make the data obvious to the developer and easy to query. The prime consideration when converting the logical database design into a physical schema is how much work is required in order for a query to navigate the data structures while maintaining a correctly normalized design. Not only is the schema then a joy to use, but it also makes it easier to code correct queries, reducing the chance of data integrity errors caused by faulty queries.

Other hallmarks of a well-designed schema include the following:

- The primary and foreign keys are designed for raw physical performance.
- Optional data (e.g., second address lines, name suffixes) is designed using patterns (nullable columns, surrogate nulls, or missing rows) that protect the integrity of the data both within the database and through the query.

Conversely, a poorly designed (either non-normalized or overly complex) physical schema encourages developers to write iterative code, code that uses temporary buckets to manipulate data, or code that will be difficult to debug or maintain.

Agile Modeling

Agile development is popular for good reasons. It gets the job done more quickly and often produces a better result than traditional methods. Agile development also fits well with database design and development.

The traditional waterfall process steps through four project phases: requirements gathering, design, development, and implementation. While this method may work well for some endeavors, when creating software, the users often don't know what they want until they see it, which pushes discovery beyond the requirements gathering phase and into the development phase.

Agile development addresses this problem by replacing the single long waterfall with numerous short cycles or iterations. Each iteration builds out a working model that can be tested, and enables users to play with the

continued

continued
software and further discover their needs. When users see rapid progress and trust that new features can be added, they become more willing to allow features to be planned into the life cycle of the software, instead of insisting that every feature be implemented in the next version.

When I'm developing a database, each iteration is usually 2–5 days long and is a mini cycle of discovery, coding, unit testing, and more discoveries with the client. A project might consist of a dozen of these tight iterations; and with each iteration, more features are fleshed out in the database and code.

Set-based queries

SQL Server is designed to handle data in sets. SQL is a declarative language, meaning that the SQL query describes the problem, and the Query Optimizer generates an execution plan to resolve the problem as a set.

Application programmers typically develop while-loops that handle data one row at a time. Iterative code is fine for application tasks such as populating a grid or combo box, but it is inappropriate for server-side code. Iterative T-SQL code, typically implemented via cursors, forces the database engine to perform thousands of wasteful single-row operations, instead of handling the problem in one larger, more efficient set. The performance cost of these single-row operations is huge. Depending on the task, SQL cursors perform about half as well as set-based code, and the performance differential grows with the size of the data. This is why set-based queries, based on an obvious physical schema, are so critical to database performance.

A good physical schema and set-based queries set up the database for excellent indexing, further improving the performance of the query (see Figure 2-2).

However, queries cannot overcome the errors of a poor physical schema and won't solve the performance issues of poorly written code. It's simply impossible to fix a clumsy database design by throwing code at it. Poor database designs tend to require extra code, which performs poorly and is difficult to maintain. Unfortunately, poorly designed databases also tend to have code that is tightly coupled (refers directly to tables), instead of code that accesses the database's abstraction layer (stored procedures and views). This makes it all that much harder to refactor the database.

Indexing

An index is an organized pointer used to locate information in a larger collection. An index is only useful when it matches the needs of a question. In this case, it becomes the shortcut between a question and the right answer. The key is to design the fewest number of shortcuts between the right questions and the right answers.

A sound indexing strategy identifies a handful of queries that represent 90% of the workload and, with judicious use of clustered indexes and covering indexes, solves the queries without expensive bookmark lookup operations.

An elegant physical schema, well-written set-based queries, and excellent indexing reduce transaction duration, which implicitly improves concurrency and sets up the database for scalability.

Nevertheless, indexes cannot overcome the performance difficulties of iterative code. Poorly written SQL code that returns unnecessary columns is much more difficult to index and will likely not take advantage of covering indexes. Moreover, it's extremely difficult to properly index an overly complex or non-normalized physical schema.

Concurrency

SQL Server, as an ACID-compliant database engine, supports transactions that are atomic, consistent, isolated, and durable. Whether the transaction is a single statement or an explicit transaction within `BEGIN TRAN...COMMIT TRAN` statements, locks are typically used to prevent one transaction from seeing another transaction's uncommitted data. Transaction isolation is great for data integrity, but locking and blocking hurt performance.

Multi-user concurrency can be tuned by limiting the extraneous code within logical transactions, setting the transaction isolation level no higher than required, keeping trigger code to a minimum, and perhaps using snapshot isolation.

A database with an excellent physical schema, well-written set-based queries, and the right set of indexes will have tight transactions and perform well with multiple users.

When a poorly designed database displays symptoms of locking and blocking issues, no amount of transaction isolation level tuning will solve the problem. The sources of the concurrency issue are the long transactions and additional workload caused by the poor database schema, lack of set-based queries, or missing indexes. Concurrency tuning cannot overcome the deficiencies of a poor database design.

Advanced scalability

With each release, Microsoft has consistently enhanced SQL Server for the enterprise. These technologies can enhance the scalability of heavy transaction databases.

The Resource Governor, new in SQL Server 2008, can restrict the resources available for different sets of queries, enabling the server to maintain the SLA agreement for some queries at the expense of other less critical queries.

Indexed views were introduced in SQL Server 2000. They actually materialize the view as a clustered index and can enable queries to select from joined data without hitting the joined tables, or to pre-aggregate data. In effect, an indexed view is a custom covering index that can cover across multiple tables.

Partitioned tables can automatically segment data across multiple filegroups, which can serve as an auto-archive device. By reducing the size of the active data partition, the requirements for maintaining the data, such as defragging the indexes, are also reduced.

Service Broker can collect transactional data and process it after the fact, thereby providing an "over-time" load leveling as it spreads a five-second peak load over a one-minute execution without delaying the calling transaction.

While these high-scalability features can extend the scalability of a well-designed database, they are limited in their ability to add performance to a poorly designed database, and they cannot overcome long transactions caused by a lack of indexes, iterative code, or all the multiple other problems caused by an overly complex database design.

The database component is the principle factor determining the overall monetary cost of the database. A well-designed database minimizes hardware costs, simplifies data access code and maintenance jobs, and significantly lowers both the initial and the total cost of the database system.

A performance framework

By describing the dependencies between the schema, queries, indexing, transactions, and scalability, Smart Database Design is a framework for performance.

The key to mastering Smart Database Design is understanding the interaction, or cause-and-effect relationship, between these hierarchical layers (schema, queries, indexing, concurrency). Each layer enables the next layer; conversely, no layer can overcome deficiencies in lower layers. The practical application of Smart Database Design takes advantage of these dependencies when developing or optimizing a database by employing the right best practices within each layer to support the next layer.

Reducing the aggregate workload of the database component has a positive effect on the rest of the database system. An efficient database component reduces the performance requirements of the server platform, increasing capacity. Maintenance jobs are easier to plan and also execute faster when the database component is designed well. There is less client access code to write and the code that needs to be written is easier to write and maintain. The result is an overall database system that's simpler to maintain, cheaper to run, easier to connect to from the data access layer, and that scales beautifully.

Although it's not a perfect analogy, picturing a water fountain on a hot summer day can help demonstrate how shorter transactions improve overall database performance. If everyone takes a small, quick sip from the fountain, then no queue forms; but as soon as someone fills up a liter-sized Big Gulp cup, others begin to wait. Regardless of the amount of hardware resources available to a database, time is finite, and the greatest performance gain is obtained by eliminating the excess work of wastefully long transactions, or throwing away the Big Gulp cup.

The quick sips of a well-designed query hitting an elegant, properly indexed database will outperform and be significantly easier on the budget than the Bug Gulp cup, with its poorly written query or cursor, on a poorly designed database missing an index.

Striving for database design excellence is a smart business move with an excellent estimated return on investment. From my experience, every day spent on database design saves two to three months of development and maintenance time. In the long term, it's far cheaper to design the database correctly than to throw money or labor at project overruns or hardware upgrades.

The cause-and-effect relationship between the layers helps diagnose performance problems as well. When a system is experiencing locking and blocking problems, the cause is likely found in the indexing or query layers. I've seen databases that were drowning under the weight of poorly written code. However, the root cause wasn't the code; it was the overly complex, anti-normalized database design that was driving the developers to write horrid code.

The bottom line? Designing an elegant database schema is the first step in maximizing the performance of the overall database system, while reducing costs.

Issues and objections

I've heard objections to the Smart Database Design framework and I like to address them here. Some say that buying more hardware is the best way to improve performance. I disagree. More hardware only masks the problem until it explodes later. Performance problems tend to grow exponentially as DB size grows, whereas hardware performance grows more or less linearly over time. One can almost predict when even the "best" hardware available no longer suffices to get acceptable performance. In several cases, I've seen companies spend incredible amounts to upgrade their hardware and they saw little or no improvement because the bottleneck was the transaction locking and blocking and poor code. Sometimes, a faster CPU only waits faster. Strategically, reducing the workload is cheaper than increasing the capacity of the hardware.

Some claim that fixing one layer can overcome deficiencies in lower layers. It's true that a poor schema will perform better when properly indexed than without indexes. However, adding the indexes doesn't really solve the deficiencies, it only masks the deficiencies. The code is still doing extra work to compensate for the poor schema. The cost of developing code and designing correct indexes is still higher for the poor schema. Any data integrity or extensibility risks are still there.

Some argue that they would like to apply Smart Database Design but they can't because the database is a third-party database and they can't modify the schema or the code. True, for most third-party products, the database schema and queries are not open for optimization, and this can be very frustrating if the database needs optimization. However, most vendors are interested in improving their product and keeping their clients happy. Both clients and vendors have contracted with me to help identify areas of opportunity and suggest solutions for the next revision.

Some say they'd like to apply Smart Database Design but they can't because any change to the schema would break hundreds of other objects. It's true — databases without abstraction layers are expensive to alter. An abstraction layer decouples the database from the client applications, making it possible to change the database component without affecting the client applications. In the absence of a well-designed abstraction layer, the first step toward gaining system performance is to create one. As expensive as it may seem to refactor the database and every application so that all communications go through an abstraction layer, the cost of not doing so could very well be that IT can't respond to the organization's needs, forcing the company to outsource or develop wasteful extra databases. At the worst, the failure of the database to be extensible could force the end of the organization.

In both the case of the third-party database and the lack of abstraction, it's still a good idea to optimize at the lowest level possible, and then move up the layers; but the best performance gains are made when you can start optimizing at the lowest level of the database component, the physical schema.

Some say that a poorly designed database can be solved by adding more layers of code and converting the database to an SOA-style application. I disagree. The database should be refactored with a clean normalized design and a proper abstraction layer. This will reduce the overall workload and solve a host of usability and performance issues much better than simply wrapping a poorly designed database with more code.

Summary

When introducing the optimization chapter in her book *Inside SQL Server 2000*, Kalen Delaney correctly writes that optimization can't be added to a database after it has been developed; it has to be designed into the database from the beginning.

This chapter presented the concept of the Information Architecture Principle, unpacked the six database objectives, and then discussed the Smart Database Design, showing the dependencies between the layers and how each layer enables the next layer.

In a chapter packed with ideas, I'd like to highlight the following:

- The database architect position should be equally involved in the enterprise-level design and the project-level designs.
- Any database design or implementation can be measured by six database objectives: usability, extensibility, data integrity, performance, availability, and security. These objectives don't have to compete — it's possible to design an elegant database that meets all six objectives.
- Each day spent on the database design will save three months later.
- Extensibility is the most expensive database objective to correct after the fact. A brittle database — one that has ad hoc SQL directly accessing the table from the client — is the worst design possible. It's simply impossible to fix a clumsy database design by throwing code at it.
- Smart Database Design is the premise that an elegant *physical schema* makes the data intuitively obvious and enables writing great set-based *queries* that respond well to *indexing*. This in turn creates short, tight transactions, which improves *concurrency* and *scalability* while reducing the aggregate workload of the database. This flow from layer to layer becomes a methodology for designing and optimizing databases.
- Reducing the aggregate workload of the database has a greater positive effect than buying more hardware.

From this overview of data architecture, the next chapter digs deeper into the concepts and patterns of relational database design, which are critical for usability, extensibility, data integrity, and performance.

Chapter 3

Relational Database Design

I play jazz guitar — well, I used to play before life became so busy. (You can listen to some of my MP3s on my "about" page on `www.sqlserverbible.com`.) There are some musicians who can hear a song and then play it; I'm not one of those. I can feel the rhythm, but I have to work through the chords and figure them out almost mathematically before I can play anything but a simple piece. To me, building chords and chord progressions is like drawing geometric patterns on the guitar neck using the frets and strings.

Music theory encompasses the scales, chords, and progressions used to make music. Every melody, harmony, rhythm, and song draws from music theory. For some musicians there's just a feeling that the song sounds right. For those who make music their profession, they understand the theory behind why a song feels right. Great musicians have both the feel and the theory in their music.

Designing databases is similar to playing music. Databases are designed by combining the right patterns to correctly model a specific solution to a problem. Normalization is the theory that shapes the design. There's both the mathematic theory of relational algebra and the intuitive feel of an elegant database.

Designing databases is both science and art.

IN THIS CHAPTER

Database Basics

The purpose of a database is to store the information required by an organization. Any means of collecting and organizing data is a database. Prior to the Information Age, information was primarily stored on cards, in file folders, or in ledger books. Before the adding machine, offices employed dozens of workers who spent all day adding columns of numbers and double-checking the math of others. The job title of those who had that exciting career was *computer*.

Author's Note

Welcome to the second of five chapters that deal with database design. Although they're spread out in the table of contents, they weave a consistent theme that good design yields great performance:

- Chapter 2, "Data Architecture," provides an overview of data architecture.
- This chapter details relational database theory.
- Chapter 20, "Creating the Physical Database Schema," discusses the DDL layer of database design and development.
- Partitioning the physical layer is covered in Chapter 68, "Partitioning."
- Designing data warehouses for business intelligence is covered in Chapter 70, "BI Design."

There's more to this chapter than the standard "Intro to Normalization." This chapter draws on the lessons I've learned over the years and has a few original ideas.

This chapter covers a book's worth of material (which is why I rewrote it three times), but I tried to concisely summarize the main ideas. The chapter opens with an introduction to database design term and concepts. Then I present the same concept from three perspectives: first with the common patterns, then with my custom Layered Design concept, and lastly with the normal forms. I've tried to make the chapter flow, but each of these ideas is easier to comprehend after you understand the other two, so if you have the time, read the chapter twice to get the most out of it.

As the number crunching began to be handled by digital machines, human labor, rather than being eliminated, shifted to other tasks. Analysts, programmers, managers, and IT staff have replaced the human "computers" of days gone by.

NOTE **Speaking of old computers, I collect abacuses, and I know how to use them too — it keeps me in touch with the roots of computing. On my office wall is a very cool nineteenth-century Russian abacus.**

Benefits of a digital database

The Information Age and the relational database brought several measurable benefits to organizations:

- Increased data consistency and better enforcement of business rules
- Improved sharing of data, especially across distances
- Improved ability to search for and retrieve information
- Improved generation of comprehensive reports
- Improved ability to analyze data trends

The general theme is that a computer database originally didn't save time in the entry of data, but rather in the retrieval of data and in the quality of the data retrieved. However, with automated data collection in manufacturing, bar codes in retailing, databases sharing more data, and consumers placing their own orders on the Internet, the effort required to enter the data has also decreased.

NOTE The previous chapter's sidebar titled "Planning Data Stores" discusses different types or styles of databases. This chapter presents the relational database design principles and patterns used to develop operational, or OLTP (online transaction processing), databases.

Some of the relational principles and patterns may apply to other types of databases, but databases that are not used for first-generation data (such as most BI, reporting databases, data warehouses, or reference data stores) do not necessarily benefit from normalization.

In this chapter, when I use the term "database," I'm referring exclusively to a relational, OLTP-style database.

Tables, rows, columns

A relational database collects related, or common, data in a single list. For example, all the product information may be listed in one table and all the customers in another table.

A table appears similar to a spreadsheet and is constructed of columns and rows. The appeal (and the curse) of the spreadsheet is its informal development style, which makes it easy to modify and add to as the design matures. In fact, managers tend to store critical information in spreadsheets, and many databases started as informal spreadsheets.

In both a spreadsheet and a database table, each row is an item in the list and each column is a specific piece of data concerning that item, so each cell should contain a single piece of data about a single item.

Whereas a spreadsheet tends to be free-flowing and loose in its design, database tables should be very consistent in terms of the meaning of the data in a column. Because row and column consistency is so important to a database table, the design of the table is critical.

Over the years, different development styles have referred to these concepts with various different terms, listed in Table 3-1.

TABLE 3-1

Comparing Database Terms

Development Style	The List of Common Items	An Item in the List	A Piece of Information in the List
Legacy software	File	Record	Field
Spreadsheet	Spreadsheet/worksheet/ named range	Row	Column/cell
Relational algebra/ logical design	Entity, or relation	Tuple (rhymes with couple)	Attribute
SQL DDL design	Table	Row	Column
Object-oriented design	Class	Object instance	Property

SQL Server developers generally refer to database elements as tables, rows, and columns when discussing the SQL DDL layer or physical schema, and sometimes use the terms entity, tuple, and attribute when discussing the logical design. The rest of this book uses the SQL terms (table, row, column), but this chapter is devoted to the theory behind the design, so I also use the relational algebra terms (entity, tuple, and attribute).

Database design phases

Traditionally, data modeling has been split into two phases, the logical design and the physical design; but Louis Davidson and I have been co-presenting at conferences on the topic of database design and I've become convinced that Louis is right when he defines three phases to database design. To avoid confusion with the traditional terms, I'm defining them as follows:

- **Conceptual Model:** The first phase digests the organizational requirements and identifies the entities, their attributes, and their relationships.

  The conceptual diagram model is great for understanding, communicating, and verifying the organization's requirements. The diagramming method should be easily understood by all the stakeholders — the subject-matter experts, the development team, and management.

  At this layer, the design is implementation independent: It could end up on Oracle, SQL Server, or even Access. Some designers refer to this as the "logical model."

- **SQL DDL Layer:** This phase concentrates on performance without losing the fidelity of the logical model as it applies the design to a specific version of a database engine — SQL Server 2008, for example, generating the DDL for the actual tables, keys, and attributes. Typically, the SQL DDL layer generalizes some entities, and replaces some natural keys with surrogate computer-generated keys.

  The SQL DDL layer might look very different than the conceptual model.

- **Physical Layer:** The implementation phase considers how the data will be physically stored on the disk subsystems using indexes, partitioning, and materialized views. Changes made to this layer won't affect how the data is accessed, only how it's stored on the disk.

  The physical layer ranges from simple, for small databases (under 20Gb), to complex, with multiple filegroups, indexed views, and data routing partitions.

This chapter focuses on designing the conceptual model, with a brief look at normalization followed by a repertoire of database patterns.

CAUTION **Implementing a database without working through the SQL DLL Layer design phase is a certain path to a poorly performing database. I've seen far too many database purists who didn't care to learn SQL Server implement conceptual designs only to blame SQL Server for the horrible performance.**

CROSS-REF **The SQL DLL Layer is covered in Chapter 20, "Creating the Physical Database Schema." Tuning the physical layer is discussed in Chapters 64, "Indexing Strategies," and 68, "Partitioning."**

Normalization

In 1970, Dr. Edgar F. Codd published "A Relational Model of Data for Large Shared Data Bank" and became the father of relational database. During the 1970s Codd wrote a series of papers that defined the concept of database normalization. He wrote his famous "Codd's 12 Rules" in 1985 to define what constitutes a relational database and to defend the relational database from software vendors who were falsely claiming to be relational. Since that time, others have amended and refined the concept of normalization.

The primary purpose of *normalization* is to improve the data integrity of the database by reducing or eliminating modification anomalies that can occur when the same fact is stored in multiple locations within the database.

Duplicate data raises all sorts of interesting problems for inserts, updates, and deletes. For example, if the product name is stored in the order detail table, and the product name is edited, should every order details row be updated? If so, is there a mechanism to ensure that the edit to the product name propagates down to every duplicate entry of the product name? If data is stored in multiple locations, is it safe to read just one of those locations without double-checking other locations? Normalization prevents these kinds of modification anomalies.

Besides the primary goal of consistency and data integrity, there are several other very good reasons to normalize an OLTP relational database:

- **Performance:** Duplicate data requires extra code to perform extra writes, maintain consistency, and manipulate data into a set when reading data. On my last large production contract (several terabytes, OLTP, 35K transactions per second), I tested a normalized version of the database vs. a denormalized version. The normalized version was 15% faster. I've found similar results in other databases over the years.

  Normalization also reduces locking contention and improves multiple-user concurrency
- **Development costs:** While it may take longer to design a normalized database, it's easier to work with a normalized database and it reduces development costs.
- **Usability:** By placing columns in the correct table, it's easier to understand the database and easier to write correct queries.
- **Extensibility:** A non-normalized database is often more complex and therefore more difficult to modify.

The three "Rules of One"

Normalization is well defined as normalized forms — specific issues that address specific potential errors in the design (there's a whole section on normal forms later in this chapter). But I don't design a database with errors and then normalize the errors away; I follow normalization from the beginning to the conclusion of the design process. That's why I prefer to think of normalization as positively stated principles.

When I teach normalization I open with the three "Rules of One," which summarize normalization from a positive point of view. One type of item is represented by one entity (table). The key to designing a schema that avoids update anomalies is to ensure that each single fact in real life is modeled by a single data point in the database. Three principles define a single data point:

- One group of similar things is represented by one entity (table).
- One thing is represented by one tuple (row).
- One descriptive fact about the thing is represented by one attribute (column).

Grok these three simple rules and you'll be a long way toward designing a properly normalized database.

Normalization As Story

The Time Traveler's Wife, by Audrey Niffenegger, is one of my favorite books. Without giving away the plot or any spoilers, it's an amazing sci-fi romance story. She moves through time conventionally, while he bounces uncontrollably through time and space. Even though the plot is more complex than the average novel, I love how Ms. Niffenegger weaves every detail together into an intricate flow. Every detail fits and builds the characters and the story.

In some ways, a database is like a good story. The plot of the story is in the data model, and the data represents the characters and the details. *Normalization* is the grammar of the database.

When two writers tell the same story, each crafts the story differently. There's no single correct way to tell a story. Likewise, there may be multiple ways to model the database. There's no single correct way to model a database — as long as the database contains all the information needed to extract the story and it follows the normalized grammar rules, the database will work. (Don't take this to mean that any design might be a correct design. While there may be multiple correct designs, there are many more incorrect designs.) A corollary is that just as some books read better than others, so do some database schemas flow well, while other database designs are difficult to query.

As with writing a novel, the foundation of data modeling is careful observation, an understanding of reality, and clear thinking. Based on those insights, the data modeler constructs a logical system — a new virtual world — that models a slice of reality. Therefore, how the designer views reality and identifies entities and their interactions will influence the design of the virtual world. Like postmodernism, there's no single perfect correct representation, only the viewpoint of the author/designer.

Identifying entities

The first step to designing a database conceptual diagram is to identify the entities (tables). Because any entity represents only one type of thing, it takes several entities together to represent an entire process or organization.

Entities are usually discovered from several sources:

- Examining existing documents (order forms, registration forms, patient files, reports)
- Interviews with subject-matter experts
- Diagramming the process flow

At this early stage the goal is to simply collect a list of possible entities and their facts. Some of the entities will be obvious nouns, such as customers, products, flights, materials, and machines.

Other entities will be verbs: shipping, processing, assembling parts to build a product. Verbs may be entities, or they may indicate a relationship between two entities.

The goal is to simply collect all the possible entities and their attributes. At this early stage, it's also useful to document as many known relationships as possible, even if those relationships will be edited several times.

Generalization

Normalization has a reputation of creating databases that are complex and unwieldy. It's true that some database schemas are far too complex, but I don't believe normalization, by itself, is the root cause.

I've found that the difference between elegant databases that are a joy to query and overly complex designs that make you want to polish your resume is the data modeler's view of entities.

When identifying entities, there's a continuum, illustrated in Figure 3-1, ranging from a broad all-inclusive view to a very specific narrow definition of the entity.

FIGURE 3-1

Entities can be identified along a continuum, from overly generalized with a single table, to overly specific with too many tables.

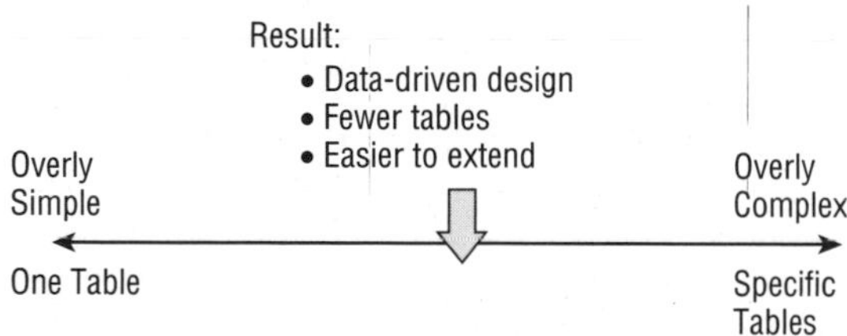

The overly simple view groups together entities that are in fact different types of things, e.g., storing machines, products, and processes in the single entity. This approach might risk data integrity for two reasons. First, it's difficult to enforce referential integrity (foreign key constraints) because the primary key attempts to represent multiple types of items. Second, these designs tend to merge entities with different attributes, which means that many of the attributes (columns) won't apply to various rows and will simply be left null. Many nullable columns means the data will probably be sparsely filled and inconsistent.

At the other extreme, the overly specific view segments entities that could be represented by a single entity into multiple entities, e.g., splitting different types of subassemblies and finished products into multiple different entities. This type of design risks flexibility and usability:

- The additional tables create additional work at every layer of the software.
- Database relationships become more complex because what could have been a single relationship is now multiple relationships. For example, instead of relating an assembly process between any part, the assembly relationship must now relate with multiple types of parts.

- The database has now hard-coded the specific types of similar entities, making it very difficult to add another similar type of entity. Using the manufacturing example again, if there's an entity for every type of subassembly, then adding another type of subassembly means changes at every level of the software.

The sweet spot in the middle generalizes, or combines, similar entities into single entities. This approach creates a more flexible and elegant database design that is easier to query and extend:

- Look for entities with similar attributes, or entities that share some attributes.
- Look for types of entities that might have an additional similar entity added in the future.
- Look for entities that might be summarized together in reports.

When designing a generalized entity, two techniques are essential:

- Use a lookup entity to organize the types of entities. For the manufacturing example, a `subassemblytype` attribute would serve the purpose of organizing the parts by subassembly type. Typically, this would be a foreign key to a `subassemblytype` entity.
- Typically, the different entity types that could be generalized together do have some differences (which is why a purist view would want to segment them). Employing the supertype/subtype (discussed in the "Data Design Patterns" section) solves this dilemma perfectly.

I've heard from some that generalization sounds like denormalization — it's not. When generalizing, it's critical that the entities comply with all the rules of normalization.

Generalized databases tend to be data-driven, have fewer tables, and are easier to extend. I was once asked to optimize a database design that was modeled by a very specific-style data modeler. His design had 78 entities, mine had 18 and covered more features. For which would you rather write stored procedures?

On the other hand, be careful to merge entities because they actually do share a root meaning in the data. Don't merge unlike entities just to save programming. The result will be more complex programming.

Best Practice

Granted, knowing when to generalize and when to segment can be an art form and requires a repertoire of database experience, but generalization is the buffer against database over-complexity; and consciously working at understanding generalization is the key to becoming an excellent data modeler.

In my seminars I use an extreme example of specific vs. generalized design, asking groups of three to four attendees to model the database in two ways: first using an overly specific data modeling technique, and then modeling the database trying to hit the generalization sweet spot.

Assume your team has been contracted to develop a database for a cruise ship's activity director — think Julie McCoy, the cruise director on the Love Boat.

The cruise offers a lot of activities: tango dance lessons, tweetups, theater, scuba lessons, hang-gliding, off-boat excursions, authentic Hawaiian luau, hula-dancing lessons, swimming lessons, Captain's dinners, aerobics, and the ever-popular shark-feeding scuba trips. These various activities have differing requirements, are offered multiple times throughout the cruise, and some are held at different locations. A passenger entity already exists; you're expected to extend the database with new entities to handle activities but still use the existing passenger entity.

In the seminars, the specialized designs often have an entity for every activity, every time an activity is offered, activities at different locations, and even activity requirements. I believe the maximum number of entities by a seminar group is 36. Admittedly, it's an extreme example for illustration purposes, but I've seen database designs in production using this style.

Each group's generalized design tends to be similar to the one shown in Figure 3-2. A generalized activity entity stores all activities and descriptions of their requirements organized by activity type. The `ActivityTime` entity has one tuple (row) for every instance or offering of an activity, so if hula-dance lessons are offered three times, there will be three tuples in this entity.

FIGURE 3-2

A generalized cruise activity design can easily accommodate new activities and locations.

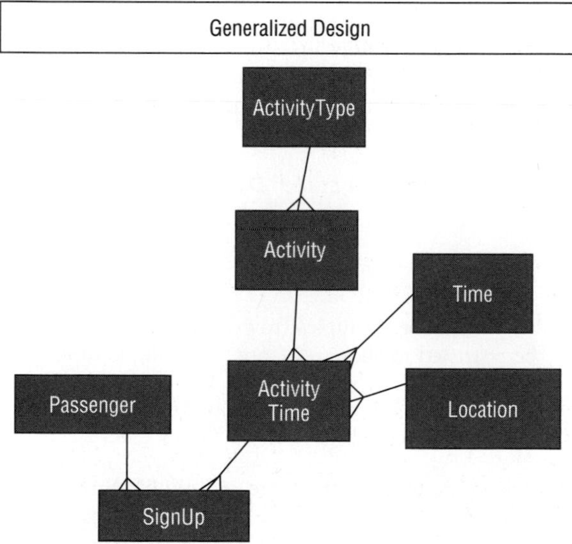

Primary keys

Perhaps the most important concept of an entity (table) is that it has a primary key — an attribute or set of attributes that can be used to uniquely identify the tuple (row). Every entity must have a primary key; without a primary key, it's not a valid entity.

By definition, a primary key must be unique and must have a value (not null).

For some entities, there might be multiple possible primary keys to choose from: employee number, driver's license number, national ID number (ssn). In this case, all the potential primary keys are known as *candidate keys*. Candidate keys that are not selected as the primary key are then known as *alternate keys*. It's important to document all the candidate keys because later, at the SQL DLL layer, they will need unique constraints.

At the conceptual diagramming phase, a primary key might be obvious — an employee number, an automobile VIN number, a state or region name — but often there is no clearly recognizable uniquely identifying value for each item in reality. That's OK, as that problem can be solved later during the SQL DLL layer.

Foreign keys

When two entities (tables) relate to one another, one entity is typically the primary entity and the other entity is the secondary entity.

The connection between the two entities is made by replicating the primary key from the primary entity in the secondary entity. The duplicated attributes in the secondary entity are known as a *foreign key*. Informally this type of relationship is sometimes called a parent-child relationship.

Enforcing the foreign key is referred to as *referential integrity*.

The classic example of a primary key and foreign key relationship is the *order* and *order details* relationship. Each order item (primary entity) can have multiple order detail rows (secondary entity). The order's primary key is duplicated in the order detail entity, providing the link between the two entities, as shown in Figure 3-3.

You'll see several examples of primary keys and foreign keys in the "Data Design Patterns" section later in this chapter.

Cardinality

The cardinality of the relationship describes the number of tuples (rows) on each side of the relationship. Either side of the relationship may be restricted to allow zero, one, or multiple tuples.

The type of key enforces the restriction of multiple tuples. Primary keys are by definition unique and enforce the single-tuple restriction, whereas foreign keys permit multiple tuples.

There are several possible cardinality combinations, as shown in Table 3-2. Within this section, each of the cardinality possibilities is examined in detail.

Optionality

The second property of the relationship is its *optionality*. The difference between an optional relationship and a mandatory relationship is critical to the data integrity of the database.

FIGURE 3-3

A one-to-many relationship consists of a primary entity and a secondary entity. The secondary entity's foreign key points to the primary entity's primary key. In this case, the Sales.SalesOrderDetail's SalesOrderID is the foreign key that relates to Sales.SalesOrderheader's primary key.

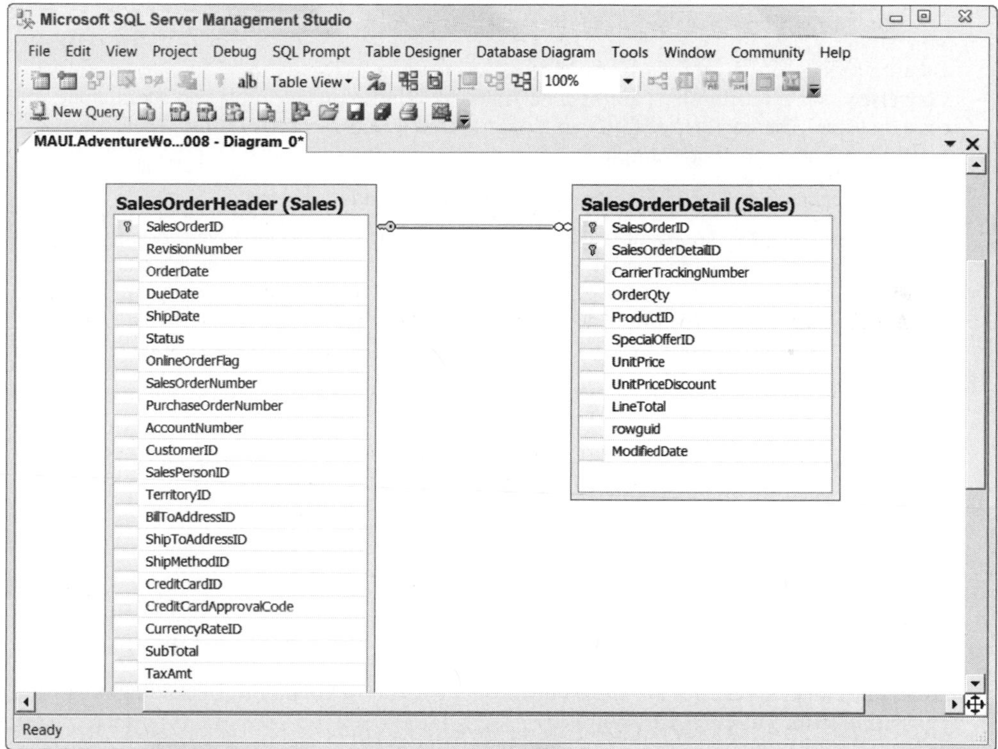

TABLE 3-2

Common Relationship Cardinalities

Relationship Type	First Entity's Key	Second Entity's Key
One-to-one	Primary entity–primary key–single tuple	Primary entity–primary key–single tuple
One-to-many	Primary entity–primary key–single tuple	Secondary entity–foreign key–multiple tuples
Many-to-many	Multiple tuples	Multiple tuples

Some relationships are mandatory, or strong. These secondary tuples (rows) require that the foreign key point to a primary key. The secondary tuple would be incomplete or meaningless without the primary entity. For the following examples, it's critical that the relationship be enforced:

- An order-line item without an order is meaningless.
- An order without a customer is invalid.
- In the `Cape Hatteras Adventures` database, an event without an associated tour tuple is a useless event tuple.

Conversely, some relationships are optional, or weak. The secondary tuple can stand alone without the primary tuple. The object in reality that is represented by the secondary tuple would exist with or without the primary tuple. For example:

- A customer is valid with or without a discount code.
- In the `OBXKites` sample database, an order may or may not have a priority code. Whether the order points to a valid tuple in the order priority entity or not, it's still a valid order.

Some database developers prefer to avoid optional relationships and so they design all relationships as mandatory and point tuples that wouldn't need a foreign key value to a surrogate tuple in the primary table. For example, rather than allow nulls in the discount attribute for customers without discounts, a "no discount" tuple is inserted into the `discount` entity and every customer without a discount points to that tuple.

There are two reasons to avoid surrogate null tuples (pointing to a "no discount" tuple): The design adds work when work isn't required (additional inserts and foreign key checks), and it's easier to locate a tuple without the relationship by selecting `where column is not null`. The null value is a standard and useful design element. Ignoring the benefits of nullability only creates additional work for both the developer and the database.

From a purist's point of view, a benefit of using the surrogate null tuple is that the "no discount" is explicit and a null value can then actually mean unknown or missing, rather than "no discount."

Some rare situations call for a complex optionality based on a condition. Depending on a rule, the relationship must be enforced, for example:

- If an organization sometimes sells ad hoc items that are not in the item entity, then the relationship may, depending on the item, be considered optional. The `orderdetail` entity can use two attributes for the item. If the `ItemID` attribute is used, then it must point to a valid `item` entity primary key.
- However, if the `NonStandardItemDescription` attribute is used instead, the `ItemID` attribute is left null.
- A check constraint ensures that for each row, either the `ItemID` or `NonStandardItemDescription` is null.

How the optionality is implemented is up to the SQL DDL layer. The only purpose of the conceptual design layer is to model the organization's objects, their relationships, and their business rules.

CROSS-REF **Data schema diagrams for the sample databases are in Appendix B. The code to create the sample database may be downloaded from `www.sqlserverbible.com`.**

Data-Model Diagramming

Data modelers use several methods to graphically work out their data models. The Chen ER diagramming method is popular, and Visio Professional includes it and five others. The method I prefer, Information Engineering — E/R Diagramming, is rather simple and works well on a whiteboard, as shown in Figure 3-4. The cardinality of the relationship is indicated by a single line or by three lines (crow's feet). If the relationship is optional, a circle is placed near the foreign key.

FIGURE 3-4

A simple method for diagramming logical schemas

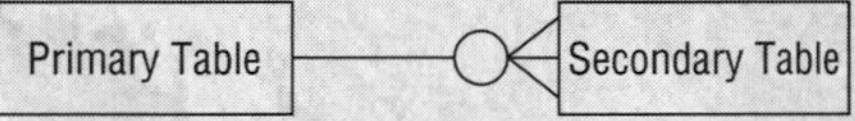

Another benefit of this simple diagramming method is that it doesn't require an advanced version of Visio. Visio is OK as a starting point, but it doesn't give you a nice life cycle like a dedicated modeling tool. There are several more powerful tools, but it's really a personal preference.

Data Design Patterns

Design is all about building something new by combining existing concepts or items using patterns. The same is true for database design. The building blocks are tables, rows, and columns, and the patterns are one-to-many, many-to-many, and others. This section explains these patterns.

Once the entities — nouns and verbs — are organized, the next step is to determine the relationships among the objects. Each relationship connects two entities using their primary and foreign keys.

Clients or business analysts should be able to describe the common relationships between the objects using terms such as *includes*, *has*, or *contains*. For example, a customer may place (has) many orders. An order may include (contains) many items. An item may be on many orders.

Based on these relationship descriptions, the best data design pattern may be chosen.

One-to-many pattern

By far the most common relationship is a one-to-many relationship; this is the classic parent-child relationship. Several tuples (rows) in the secondary entity relate to a single tuple in the primary entity. The relationship is between the primary entity's primary key and the secondary entity's foreign key, as illustrated in the following examples:

- In the `Cape Hatteras Adventures` database, each base camp may have several tours that originate from it. Each tour may originate from only one base camp, so the relationship is modeled as one base camp relating to multiple tours. The relationship is made between the BaseCamp's primary key and the Tour entity's BaseCampID foreign key, as diagrammed in Figure 3-5. Each Tour's foreign key attribute contains a copy of its BaseCamp's primary key.

FIGURE 3-5

The one-to-many relationship relates zero to many tuples (rows) in the secondary entity to a single tuple in the primary entity.

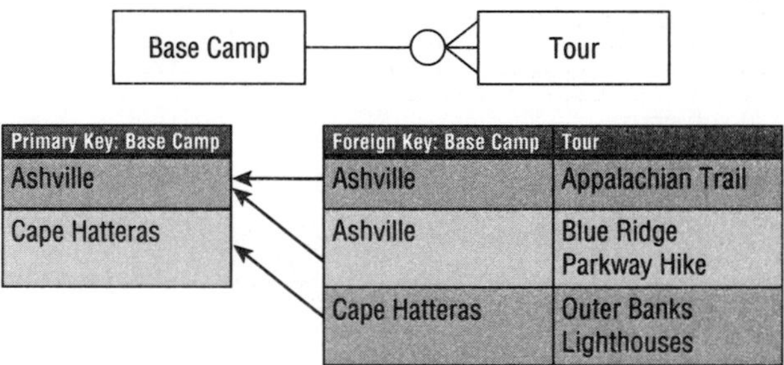

- Each customer may place multiple orders. While each order has its own unique OrderID primary key, the Order entity also has a foreign key attribute that contains the CustomerID of the customer who placed the order. The Order entity may have several tuples with the same CustomerID that defines the relationship as one-to-many.
- A non-profit organization has an annual pledge drive. As each donor makes an annual pledge, the pledges go into a secondary entity that can store an infinite number of years' worth of pledges — one tuple per year.

One-to-one pattern

At the conceptual diagram layer, one-to-one relationships are quite rare. Typically, one-to-one relationships are used in the SQL ODD or the physical layer to partition the data for some performance or security reason.

One-to-one relationships connect two entities with primary keys at both entities. Because a primary key must be unique, each side of the relationship is restricted to one tuple.

For example, an Employee entity can store general information about the employee. However, more sensitive classified information is stored in a separate entity as shown in Figure 3-6. While security can be applied on a per-attribute basis, or a view can project selected attributes, many organizations choose to model sensitive information as two one-to-one entities.

Many-to-many pattern

In a many-to-many relationship, both sides may relate to multiple tuples (rows) on the other side of the relationship. The many-to-many relationship is common in reality, as shown in the following examples:

FIGURE 3-6

This one-to-one relationship partitions employee data, segmenting classified information into a separate entity.

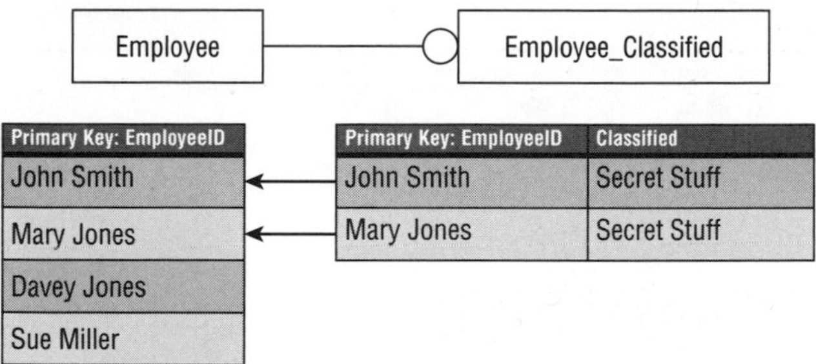

- The classic example is members and groups. A member may belong to multiple groups, and a group may have multiple members.
- In the `OBXKites` sample database, an order may have multiple items, and each item may be sold on multiple orders.
- In the `Cape Hatteras Adventures` sample database, a guide may qualify for several tours, and each tour may have several qualified guides.

In a conceptual diagram, the many-to-many relationship can be diagramed by signifying multiple cardinality at each side of the relationship, as shown in Figure 3-7.

FIGURE 3-7

The many-to-many logical model shows multiple tuples on both ends of the relationship.

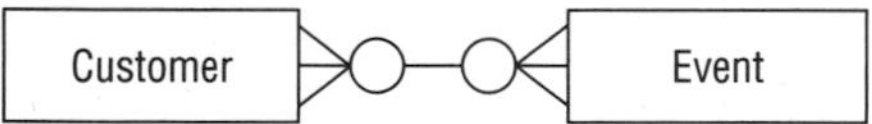

Many-to-many relationships are nearly always optional. For example, the many customers-to-many events relationship is optional because the customer and the tour/event are each valid without the other.

The one-to-one and the one-to-many relationship can typically be constructed from items within an organization that users can describe and understand. That's not always the case with many-to-many relationships.

To implement a many-to-many relationship in SQL DDL, a third table, called an *associative table* (sometimes called a *junction table*) is used, which artificially creates two one-to-many relationships between the two entities (see Figure 3-8).

Figure 3-9 shows the associative entity with data to illustrate how it has a foreign key to each of the two many-to-many primary entities. This enables each primary entity to assume a one-to-many relationship with the other entity.

FIGURE 3-8

The many-to-many implementation adds an associative table to create artificial one-to-many relationships for both tables.

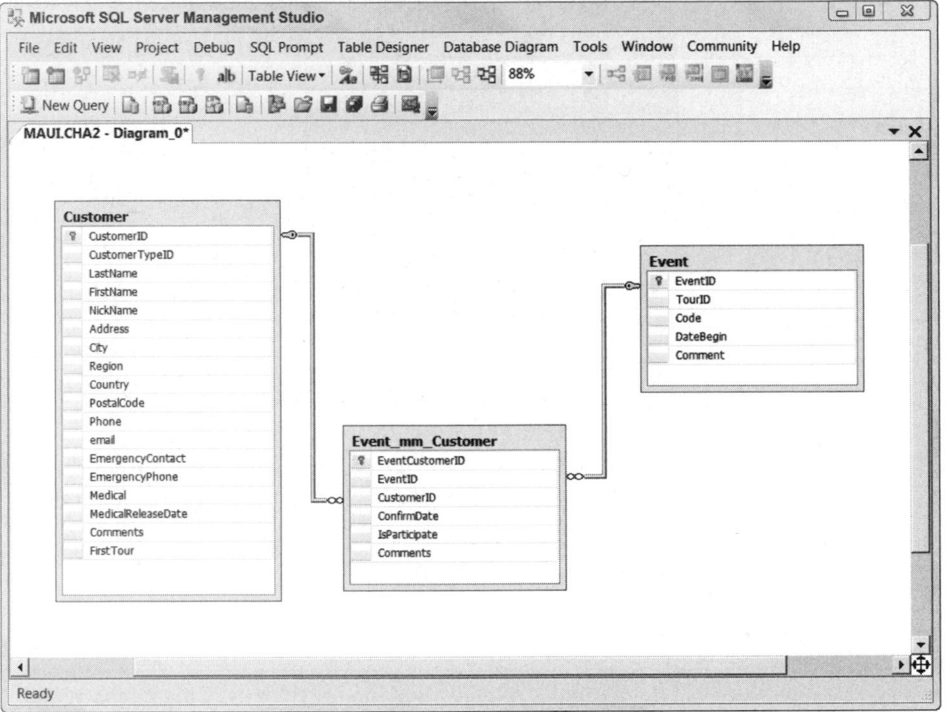

FIGURE 3-9

In the associative entity (Customer_mm_Event), each customer can be represented multiple times, which creates an artificial one-event-to-many-customers relationship. Likewise, each event can be listed multiple times in the associative entity, creating a one-customer-to-many-events relationship.

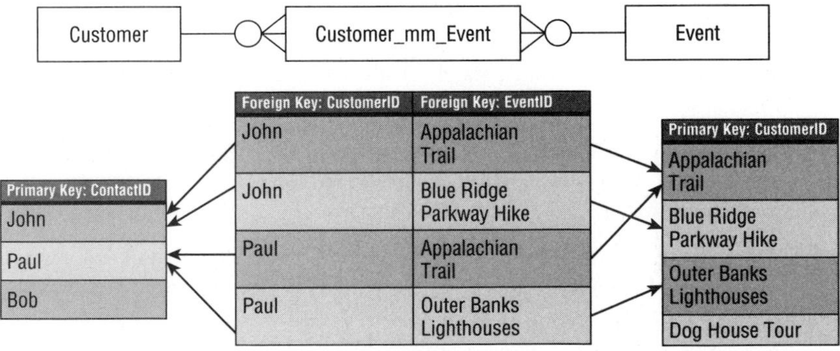

In some cases the subject-matter experts will readily recognize the associated table:

- In the case of the many orders to many products example, the associative entity is the `order details` entity.
- A class may have many students and each student may attend many classes. The associative entity would be recognized as the `registration` entity.

In other cases an organization might understand that the relationship is a many-to-many relationship, but there's no term to describe the relationship. In this case, the associative entity is still required to resolve the many-to-many relationship — just don't discuss it with the subject-matter experts.

Typically, additional facts and attributes describe the many-to-many relationship. These attributes belong in the associative entity. For example:

- In the case of the many orders to many products example, the associative entity (`order details` entity) would include the `quantity` and `sales price` attributes.
- In the members and groups example, the `member_groups` associative entity might include the `datejoined` and `status` attributes.

When designing attributes for associative entities, it's extremely critical that every attribute actually describe only the many-to-many relationship and not one of the primary entities. For example, including a product name describes the product entity and not the many orders to many products relationship.

Supertype/subtype pattern

One of my favorite design patterns, that I don't see used often enough, is the supertype/subtype pattern. It supports generalization, and I use it extensively in my designs. The supertype/subtype pattern is also perfectly suited to modeling an object-oriented design in a relational database.

The supertype/subtype relationship leverages the one-to-one relationship to connect one supertype entity with one or more subtype entities. This extends the supertype entity with what appears to be flexible attributes.

The textbook example is a database that needs to store multiple types of contacts. All contacts have basic contact data such as name, location, phone number, and so on. Some contacts are customers with customer attributes (credit limits, loyalty programs, etc.). Some contacts are vendors with vendor-specific data.

While it's possible to use separate entities for customers and vendors, an alternative design is to use a single `Contact` entity (the supertype) to hold every contact, regardless of their type, and the attributes common to every type (probably just the name and contact attributes). Separate entities (the subtypes) hold the attributes unique to customers and vendors. A customer would have a tuple (row) in the contact and the customer entities. A vendor would have tuples in both the contact and vendor entities. All three entities share the same primary key, as shown in Figure 3-10.

Sometime data modelers who use the supertype/subtype pattern add a `type` attribute in the supertype entity so it's easy to quickly determine the type by searching the subtypes. This works well but it restricts the tuples to a single subtype.

FIGURE 3-10

The supertype/subtype pattern uses an optional one-to-one relationship that relates a primary key to a primary key.

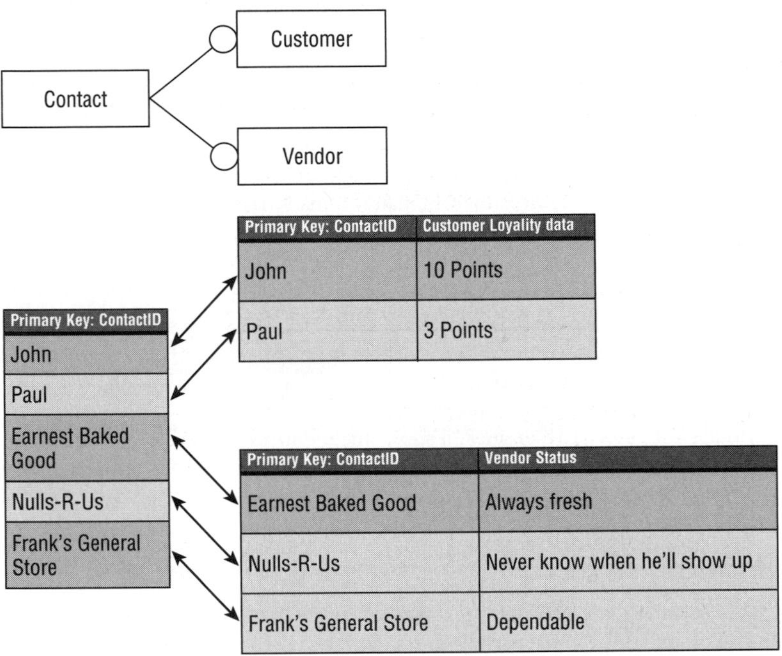

Without the `type` attribute, it's possible to allow tuples to belong to multiple subtypes. Sometimes this is referred to as allowing the supertype to have multiple roles. In the contact example, multiple roles (e.g. a contact who is both an employee and customer) could mean the tuple has data in the supertype entity (e.g. contact entity) and each role subtype entity (e.g. employee and customer entities.)

Nordic O/R DBMS

Nordic (New Object/Relational Design) is my open-source experiment to transform SQL Server into an object-oriented database.

Nordic builds on the supertype/subtype pattern and uses T-SQL code generation to create a T-SQL API façade that supports classes with multiple inheritance, attribute inheritance, polymorphism, inheritable class roles, object morphing, and inheritable class-defined workflow state. If you want to play with Nordic, go to `www.CodePlex.com/nordic`.

Domain integrity lookup pattern

The domain integrity lookup pattern, informally called the lookup table pattern, is very common in production databases. This pattern only serves to limit the valid options for an attribute, as illustrated in Figure 3-11.

FIGURE 3-11

The domain integrity lookup pattern uses a foreign key to ensure that only valid data is entered into the attribute.

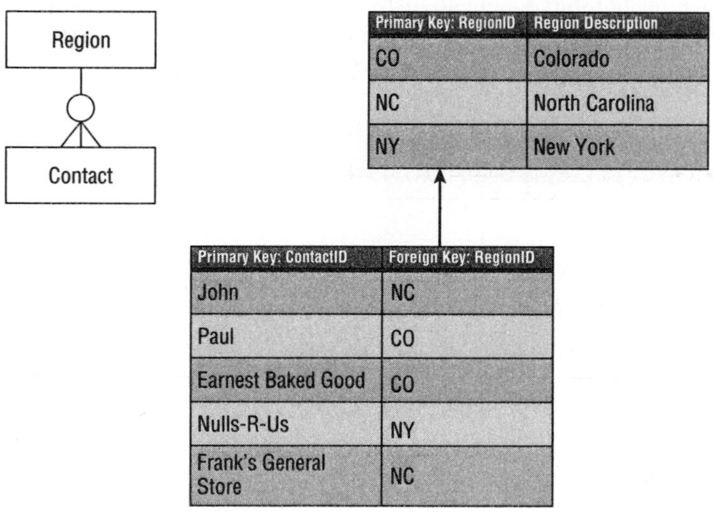

The classic example is the state, or region, lookup entity. Unless the organization regularly deals with several states as clients, the state lookup entity only serves to ensure that the state attributes in other entities are entered correctly. Its only purpose is data consistency.

Recursive pattern

A recursive relationship pattern (sometimes called a *self-referencing*, *unary*, or *self-join* relationship) is one that relates back to itself. In reality, these relationships are quite common:

- An organizational chart represents a person reporting to another person.
- A bill of materials details how a material is constructed from other materials.
- Within the `Family` sample database, a person relates to his or her mother and father.

CROSS-REF **Chapter 17, "Traversing Hierarchies," deals specifically with modeling and querying recursive relationships within SQL Server 2008.**

To use the standard organization chart as an example, each tuple in the `employee` entity represents one employee. Each employee reports to a supervisor who is also listed in the `employee` entity. The `ReportsToID` foreign key points to the supervisor's primary key.

Because `EmployeeID` is a primary key and `ReportsToID` is a foreign key, the relationship cardinality is one-to-many, as shown in Figure 3-12. One manager may have several direct reports, but each employee may have only one manager.

FIGURE 3-12

The reflexive, or recursive, relationship is a one-to-many relationship between two tuples of the same entity. This shows the organization chart for members of the Adventure Works IT department.

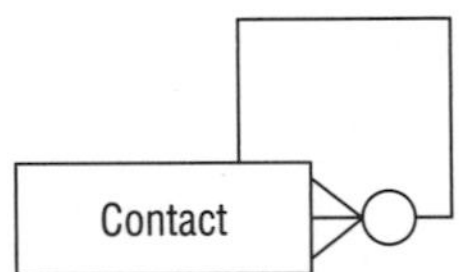

Primary Key: ContactID	Foreign Key: ReportsToID
Ken Sánchez	<NULL>
Jean Trenary	Ken Sánchez
Stephanie Conroy	Jean Trenary
François Ajenstat	Jean Trenary
Dan Wilson	Jean Trenary

A bill of materials is a more complex form of the recursive pattern because a part may be built from several source parts, and the part may be used to build several parts in the next step of the manufacturing process, as illustrated in Figure 3-13.

FIGURE 3-13

The conceptual diagram of a many-to-many recursive relationship shows multiple cardinality at each end of the relationship.

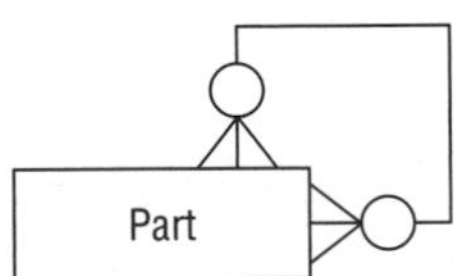

An associative entity is required to resolve the many-to-many relationship between the component parts being used and the part being assembled. In the `MaterialSpecification` sample database, the `BoM`

(bill of materials) associative entity has two foreign keys that both point to the `Part` entity, as shown in Figure 3-14. The first foreign key points to the part being built. The second foreign key points to the source parts.

FIGURE 3-14

The physical implementation of the many-to-many reflexive relationship must include a associative entity to resolve the many-to-many relationship, just like the many-to-many two-entity relationship.

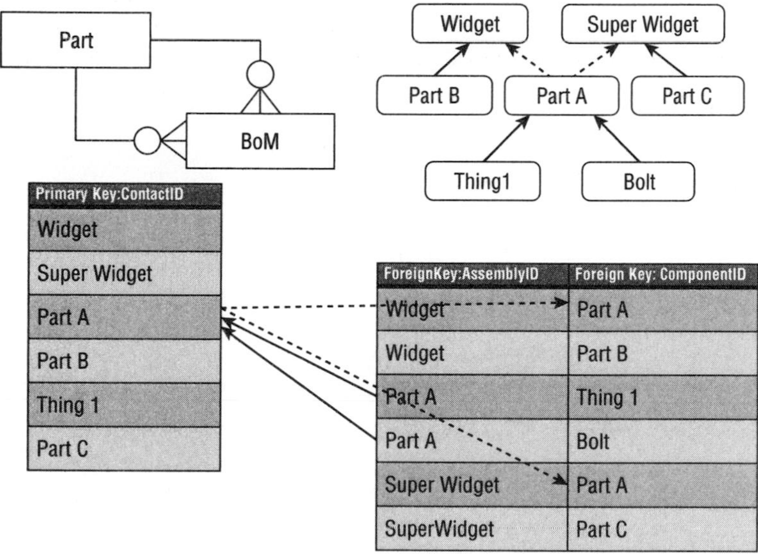

In the sample data, Part A is constructed from two parts (a Thing1 and a bolt) and is used in the assembly of two parts (Widget and SuperWidget).

The first foreign key points to the material being built. The second foreign key points to the source material.

Entity-Value Pairs Pattern

Every couple of months, I hear about data modelers working with the *entity-value pairs pattern,* also known as the *entity-attribute-value (EAV) pattern,* sometimes called the *generic pattern* or *property bag/property table pattern,* illustrated in Figure 3-15. In the *SQL Server 2000 Bible,* I called it the "dynamic/relational pattern."

continued

continued

FIGURE 3-15

The entity-values pairs pattern is a simple design with only four tables: class/type, attribute/column, object/item, and value. The value table stores every value for every attribute for every item — one long list.

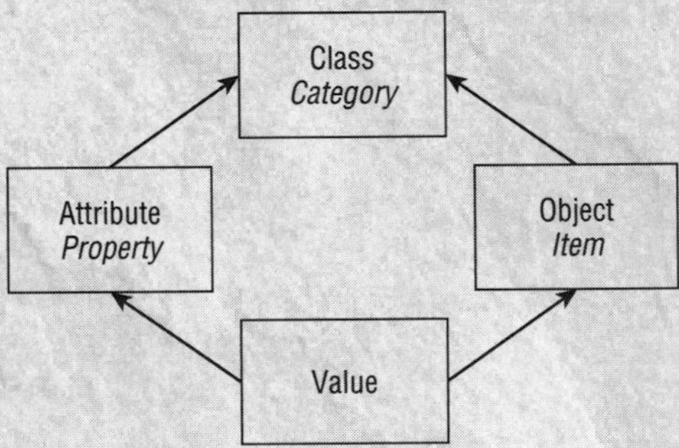

This design can be popular when applications require dynamic attributes. Sometimes it's used as an OO DBMS physical design within a RDBMS product. It's also gaining popularity with cloud databases.

At first blush, the entity-value pairs pattern is attractive, novel, and appealing. It offers unlimited logical design alterations without any physical schema changes — the ultimate flexible extensible design.

But there are problems. Many problems . . .

- The entity-value pairs pattern lacks data integrity — specifically, data typing. The data type is the most basic data constraint. The basic entity-value pairs pattern stores every value in a single `nvarchar` or `sql_variant` column and ignores data typing. One option that I wouldn't recommend is to create a value table for each data type. While this adds data typing, it certainly complicates the code.
- It's difficult to query the entity-value pairs pattern. I've seen two solutions. The most common method is hard-coding .NET code to extract and normalize the data. Another option is to code-gen a table-valued UDF or crosstab view for each class/type to extract the data and return a normalized data set. This has the advantage of being usable in normal SQL queries, but performance and inserts/updates remain difficult. Either solution defeats the dynamic goal of the pattern.
- Perhaps the greatest complaint against the entity-value pairs pattern is that it's nearly impossible to enforce referential integrity.

Can the value-pairs pattern be an efficient, practical solution? I doubt it. I continue to hear of projects using this pattern that initially look promising and then fail under the weight of querying once it's fully populated. Nulltheless, someday I'd like to build out a complete EAV code-gen tool and test it under a heavy load — just for the fun of it.

Database design layers

I've observed that every database can be visualized as three layers: domain integrity (lookup) layer, business visible layer, and supporting layer, as drawn in Figure 3-16.

FIGURE 3-16

Visualizing the database as three layers can be useful when designing the conceptual diagram and coding the SQL DLL implementation.

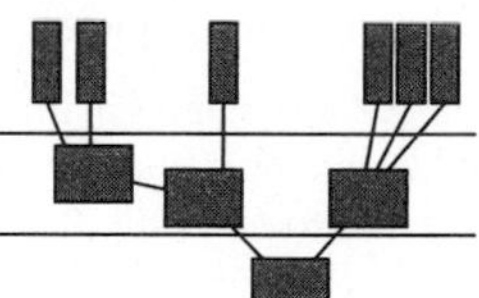

While you are designing the conceptual diagram, visualizing the database as three layers can help organize the entities and clarify the design. When the database design moves into the SQL DDL implementation phase, the database design layers become critical in optimizing the primary keys for performance.

The center layer contains those entities that the client or subject-matter expert would readily recognize and understand. These are the main work tables that contain working data such as transaction, account, or contact information. When a user enters data on a daily basis, these are the tables hit by the insert and update. I refer to this layer as the *visible layer* or the *business entity layer*.

Above the business entity layer is the domain integrity layer. This top layer has the entities used for validating foreign key values. These tables may or may not be recognizable by the subject-matter expert or a typical end-user. The key point is that they are used only to maintain the list of what's legal for a foreign key, and they are rarely updated once initially populated.

Below the visible layer live the tables that are a mystery to the end-user — associative tables used to materialize a many-to-many logical relationship are a perfect example of a supporting table. Like the visible layer, these tables are often heavily updated.

Normal Forms

Taking a detailed look at the normal forms moves this chapter into a more formal study of relational database design.

Contrary to popular opinion, the forms are not a progressive methodology, but they do represent a progressive level of compliance. Technically, you can't be in 2NF until 1NF has been met. Don't plan on designing an entity and moving it through first normal form to second normal form, and so on. Each normal form is simply a different type of data integrity fault to be avoided.

First normal form (1NF)

The first normalized form means the data is in an entity format, such that the following three conditions are met:

- *Every unit of data is represented within scalar attributes.* A scalar value is a value "capable of being represented by a point on a scale," according to Merriam-Webster.

  Every attribute must contain one unit of data, and each unit of data must fill one attribute. Designs that embed multiple pieces of information within an attribute violate the first normal form. Likewise, if multiple attributes must be combined in some way to determine a single unit of data, then the attribute design is incomplete.

- *All data must be represented in unique attributes.* Each attribute must have a unique name and a unique purpose. An entity should have no repeating attributes. If the attributes repeat, or the entity is very wide, then the object is too broadly designed.

  A design that repeats attributes, such as an order entity that includes `item1`, `item2`, and `item3` attributes to hold multiple line items, violates the first normal form.

- *All data must be represented within unique tuples.* If the entity design requires or permits duplicate tuples, that design violates the first normal form.

  If the design requires multiple tuples to represent a single item, or multiple items are represented by a single tuple, then the table violates first normal form.

For an example of the first normal form in action, consider the listing of base camps and tours from the `Cape Hatteras Adventures` database. Table 3-3 shows base camp data in a model that violates the first normal form. The repeating tour attribute is not unique.

TABLE 3-3

Violating the First Normal Form

BaseCamp	Tour1	Tour2	Tour3
Ashville	Appalachian Trail	Blue Ridge Parkway Hike	
Cape Hatteras	Outer Banks Lighthouses		
Freeport	Bahamas Dive		
Ft. Lauderdale	Amazon Trek		
West Virginia	Gauley River Rafting		

To redesign the data model so that it complies with the first normal form, resolve the repeating group of tour attributes into a single unique attribute, as shown in Table 3-4, and then move any multiple values to a unique tuple. The `BaseCamp` entity contains a unique tuple for each base camp, and the `Tour` entity's `BaseCampID` refers to the primary key in the `BaseCamp` entity.

TABLE 3-4

Conforming to the First Normal Form

Tour Entity		BaseCamp Entity	
BaseCampID(FK)	**Tour**	**BaseCampID (PK)**	**Name**
1	Appalachian Trail	1	Ashville
1	Blue Ridge Parkway Hike	2	Cape Hatteras
2	Outer Banks Lighthouses	3	Freeport
3	Bahamas Dive	4	Ft. Lauderdale
4	Amazon Trek	5	West Virginia
	Gauley River Rafting		

Another example of a data structure that desperately needs to adhere to the first normal form is a corporate product code that embeds the department, model, color, size, and so forth within the code. I've even seen product codes that were so complex they included digits to signify the syntax for the following digits.

In a theoretical sense, this type of design is wrong because the attribute isn't a scalar value. In practical terms, it has the following problems:

- Using a digit or two for each data element means that the database will soon run out of possible data values.
- Databases don't index based on the internal values of a string, so searches require scanning the entire table and parsing each value.
- Business rules are difficult to code and enforce.

Entities with non-scalar attributes need to be completely redesigned so that each individual data attribute has its own attribute. Smart keys may be useful for humans, but it is best if it is generated by combining data from the tables.

Second normal form (2NF)

The second normal form ensures that each attribute does in fact describe the entity. It's a dependency issue. Does the attribute depend on, or describe, the item identified by the primary key?

If the entity's primary key is a single value, this isn't too difficult. Composite primary keys can sometimes get into trouble with the second normal form if the attributes aren't dependent on every attribute in the primary key. If an attribute depends on one of the primary key attributes but not the other, that is a partial dependency, which violates the second normal form.

An example of a data model that violates the second normal form is one in which the base camp phone number is added to the `BaseCampTour` entity, as shown in Table 3-5. Assume that the primary key

(PK) is a composite of both the `BaseCamp` and the `Tour`, and that the phone number is a permanent phone number for the base camp, not a phone number assigned for each tour.

TABLE 3-5

Violating the Second Normal Form

PK-BaseCamp	PK-Tour	Base Camp PhoneNumber
Ashville	Appalachian Trail	828-555-1212
Ashville	Blue Ridge Parkway Hike	828-555-1212
Cape Hatteras	Outer Banks Lighthouses	828-555-1213
Freeport	Bahamas Dive	828-555-1214
Ft. Lauderdale	Amazon Trek	828-555-1215
West Virginia	Gauley River Rafting	828-555-1216

The problem with this design is that the phone number is an attribute of the base camp but not the tour, so the `PhoneNumber` attribute is only partially dependent on the entity's primary key.

An obvious practical problem with this design is that updating the phone number requires either updating multiple tuples or risking having two phone numbers for the same phone.

The solution is to remove the partially dependent attribute from the entity with the composite keys, and create an entity with a unique primary key for the base camp, as shown in Table 3-6. This new entity is then an appropriate location for the dependent attribute.

TABLE 3-6

Conforming to the Second Normal Form

Tour Entity		Base Camp Entity	
PK-Base Camp	**PK-Tour**	**PK-Base Camp**	**PhoneNumber**
Ashville	Appalachian Trail	Ashville	828-555-1212
Ashville	Blue Ridge Parkway Hike	Cape Hatteras	828-555-1213
Cape Hatteras	Outer Banks Lighthouses	Freeport	828-555-1214
Freeport	Bahamas Dive	Ft. Lauderdale	828-555-1215
Ft. Lauderdale	Amazon Trek	West Virginia	828-555-1216
West Virginia	Gauley River Rafting		

The PhoneNumber attribute is now fully dependent on the entity's primary key. Each phone number is stored in only one location, and no partial dependencies exist.

Third normal form (3NF)

The third normal form checks for transitive dependencies. A *transitive dependency* is similar to a partial dependency in that they both refer to attributes that are not fully dependent on a primary key. A dependency is transient when attribute1 is dependent on attribute2, which is dependent on the primary key.

The second normal form is violated when an attribute depends on part of the key. The third normal form is violated when the attribute does depend on the key but also depends on another non-key attribute.

The key phrase when describing third normal form is that every attribute "*must provide a fact about the key, the whole key, and nothing but the key.*"

Just as with the second normal form, the third normal form is resolved by moving the non-dependent attribute to a new entity.

Continuing with the Cape Hatteras Adventures example, a guide is assigned as the lead guide responsible for each base camp. The BaseCampGuide attribute belongs in the BaseCamp entity; but it is a violation of the third normal form if other information describing the guide is stored in the base camp, as shown in Table 3-7.

TABLE 3-7

Violating the Third Normal Form

Base Camp Entity			
BaseCampPK	**BaseCampPhoneNumber**	**LeadGuide**	**DateofHire**
Ashville	1-828-555-1212	Jeff Davis	5/1/99
Cape Hatteras	1-828-555-1213	Ken Frank	4/15/97
Freeport	1-828-555-1214	Dab Smith	7/7/2001
Ft. Lauderdale	1-828-555-1215	Sam Wilson	1/1/2002
West Virginia	1-828-555-1216	Lauren Jones	6/1/2000

The DateofHire describes the guide not the base, so the hire-date attribute is not directly dependent on the BaseCamp entity's primary key. The DateOfHire's dependency is transitive — it describes the key and a non-key attribute — in that it goes through the LeadGuide attribute.

Creating a Guide entity and moving its attributes to the new entity resolves the violation of the third normal form and cleans up the logical design, as demonstrated in Table 3-8.

TABLE 3-8

Conforming to the Third Normal Form

Tour Entity		LeadGuide Entity	
BaseCampPK	**LeadGuide**	**LeadGuidePK**	**DateofHire**
Ashville, NC	Jeff Davis	Jeff Davis	5/1/99
Cape Hatteras	Ken Frank	Ken Frank	4/15/97
Freeport	Dab Smith	Dab Smith	7/7/2001
Ft. Lauderdale	Sam Wilson	Sam Wilson	1/1/2002
West Virginia	Lauren Jones	Lauren Jones	6/1/2000

Best Practice

If the entity has a good primary key and every attribute is scalar and fully dependent on the primary key, then the logical design is in the third normal form. Most database designs stop at the third normal form.

The additional forms prevent problems with more complex logical designs. If you tend to work with mind-bending modeling problems and develop creative solutions, then understanding the advanced forms will prove useful.

The Boyce-Codd normal form (BCNF)

The Boyce-Codd normal form occurs between the third and fourth normal forms, and it handles a problem with an entity that has multiple candidate keys. One of the candidate keys is chosen as the primary key and the others become alternate keys. For example, a person might be uniquely identified by his or her social security number (ssn), employee number, and driver's license number. If the ssn is the primary key, then the employee number and driver's license number are the alternate keys.

The Boyce-Codd normal form simply stipulates that in such a case every attribute must describe every candidate key. If an attribute describes one of the candidate keys but not another candidate key, then the entity violates BCNF.

Fourth normal form (4NF)

The fourth normal form deals with problems created by complex composite primary keys. If two independent attributes are brought together to form a primary key along with a third attribute but the two attributes don't really uniquely identify the entity without the third attribute, then the design violates the fourth normal form.

For example, assume the following conditions:

1. The `BaseCamp` and the base camp's `LeadGuide` were used as a composite primary key.
2. An `Event` and the `Guide` were brought together as a primary key.
3. Because both used a guide all three were combined into a single entity.

The preceding example violates the fourth normal form.

The fourth normal form is used to help identify entities that should be split into separate entities. Usually this is only an issue if large composite primary keys have brought too many disparate objects into a single entity.

Fifth normal form (5NF)

The fifth normal form provides the method for designing complex relationships that involve multiple (three or more) entities. A *three-way* or *ternary* relationship, if properly designed, is in the fifth normal form. The cardinality of any of the relationships could be one or many. What makes it a ternary relationship is the number of related entities.

As an example of a ternary relationship, consider a manufacturing process that involves an operator, a machine, and a bill of materials. From one point of view, this could be an operation entity with three foreign keys. Alternately, it could be thought of as a ternary relationship with additional attributes.

Just like a two-entity many-to-many relationship, a ternary relationship requires a resolution entity in the physical schema design to resolve the many-to-many relationship into multiple artificial one-to-many relationships; but in this case the resolution entity has three or more foreign keys.

In such a complex relationship, the fifth normal form requires that each entity, if separated from the ternary relationship, remains a proper entity without any loss of data.

It's commonly stated that third normal form is enough. Boyce-Codd, fourth, and fifth normal forms may be complex, but violating them can cause severe problems. It's not a matter of more entities vs. fewer entities; it's a matter of properly aligned attributes and keys.

NOTE **As I mentioned earlier in this chapter, Louis Davidson (aka Dr. SQL) and I co-present a session at conferences on database design. I recommend his book *Pro SQL Server 2008 Relational Database Design and Implementation* (Apress, 2008).**

Summary

Relational database design, covered in Chapter 2, showed why the database physical schema is critical to the database's performance. This chapter looked at the theory behind the logical correctness of the database design and the many patterns used to assemble a database schema.

- There are three phases in database design: the conceptual (diagramming) phase, the SQL DDL (create table) phase, and the physical layer (partition and file location) phase. Databases designed with only the conceptual phase perform poorly.

- Normalization can be summed up as the three "Rules of One": one group of items = one table, one item = one row, one fact = one column.
- Generalization is the buffer against normalization over-complexity.

With smart database design and normalization as a foundation, the next few chapters move into installing SQL Server, connecting clients, and using the tools.

Chapter 4

Installing SQL Server 2008

The actual process of installing SQL Server is relatively easy; the trick is planning and configuring the server to meet the current and future needs of a production environment — planning the hardware, selecting the operating system, choosing the collation, and several other decisions should be settled prior to the SQL Server installation.

Not every SQL Server 2008 server will be a fresh installation. SQL Server 2000 and SQL Server 2005 servers can be upgraded to SQL Server 2008. Additionally, the data might reside in a foreign database, such as Microsoft Access, MySQL, or Oracle, and the project might involve porting the database to SQL Server.

Not every SQL Server 2008 server will run production databases — there are developer sandbox servers, quality test servers, integration test servers, performance test servers, and the list goes on. This chapter discusses all these situations to help you avoid surprises.

IN THIS CHAPTER

- **Server-hardware recommendations**
- **Planning an installation**
- **Installing multiple instances of SQL Server**
- **Upgrading from previous versions of SQL Server**
- **Migrating to SQL Server**

Selecting Server Hardware

The value per dollar for hardware has improved significantly and continues to do so. Nevertheless, large datacenters can still cost hundreds of thousands of dollars. This section provides some design guidelines for planning a server.

CPU planning

SQL Server needs plenty of raw CPU horsepower. Fortunately, the newer crop of CPUs perform very well and today's servers use multi-core CPUs. Microsoft licenses SQL Server by the CPU socket, not the number of cores. Comparing the dropping price of multi-core CPUs with the license cost of SQL Server, it makes sense to buy the most cores possible per socket. When planning your server, note the following:

- As a beginning point for planning, I recommend one CPU core per 500 transactions per second. Of course, you should test your application to determine the number of transactions a core can provide.
- A well-planned server will have CPUs running at 30%–50% utilization, as reflected by Performance Monitor.
- I also strongly recommend using 64-bit CPUs for their large memory addressing. If the server will see high transactions (>10K per second), then choose Itanium 64-bit CPUs because they have better throughput than x64 CPUs.

What's New with SQL Server Setup?

If you've been installing SQL Server servers for a while, the first thing you'll see is that the setup is brand-new. It's been completely rewritten from the ground up.

If running the Surface Area Configuration tool was part of your SQL Server 2005 installation process, you'll notice that it's gone, replaced with Policy-Based Management policies.

Copious memory

Memory is a magic elixir for SQL Server. Any time the data is already in cache it's a big win for performance. Balance the performance of the CPUs, memory, and disk subsystems, but focus on memory. More memory will reduce the I/O requirement and thus also reduce the CPU requirement.

When planning server memory, I recommend the following:

- The easy answer is to buy as much memory as you can afford. SQL Server consumes memory for cached query execution plans and cached data pages, so the amount of memory needed isn't based on the size of the database but on the number of queries. I recommend using this formula as a baseline for required memory: 2 Gb for the OS and SQL Server, plus 1 Gb per 1,000 queries per second. Of course, this greatly depends on the complexity of the query and the type of index access. An efficiently designed database (great schema, queries, and indexing) can support more queries per gigabyte than a poorly designed database.
- If the amount of memory will eventually exceed 4 Gb, I also strongly recommend using 64-bit versions of the operating system and SQL Server because the memory addressing is so much smoother than the 32-bit AWE solution.

NOTE **To enable AWE, SQL Server 2008 must run under an account that has the Lock Pages in Memory option turned on and the AWE Enabled option set to 1 using** `sp_configure`**.**

Disk-drive subsystems

The disk subsystem is critical for both performance and availability. Here are some guidelines for planning the disk subsystem:

- The scalability bottleneck is typically the disk subsystem throughput. If you can use a storage area network (SAN) for your disk subsystem, do so. A properly configured SAN will scale further than local disk subsystems. SANs offer four significant benefits: They spread the files across several disk spindles; they use a high-speed fiber optic connection; they typically include a very large RAM buffer to absorb bursts of traffic; and SANs can usually perform a hardware level snapshot backup and restore.

The cons are that SANs cost 40–50 times as much as local disk space and they are very difficult to configure and tune, so encourage the SAN administrator to focus on the database requirements and carefully configure the database LUNs (Logical Unit Number — similar to a virtual drive) so the database isn't lost in the organization's common file traffic. This can be very difficult to do, especially when file server and database traffic are combined on the same SAN.

- Never, never, ever try to use iSCSI devices that connect the server and the disk subsystem using Ethernet. The Ethernet simply won't keep up and the TCP/IP stack possessing will consume CPU cycles. It's a sure way to waste a lot of time (trust me).
- Watch the prices for the new solid-state drives (SSD) and move to them as soon as it's affordable. SSD drives will dramatically improve both database performance and availability. Even if you have a SAN, I'd use a local SSD drive for the database transaction log, `tempdb` and its transaction log.

If you aren't using a SAN, here are my recommendations for configuring local direct attached storage (DAS). Each DAS disk subsystem has its own disk controller:

- Using one large RAID 5 disk array and placing all the files on the array may be easy to configure, but it will cost performance. The goal of the disk subsystem is more than redundancy. You want to separate different files onto dedicated disks for specific purposes.
- SATA drives don't wait for a write to complete before telling Windows they're finished with the task. While this might be great for a PC, it shortcuts the SQL Server write-ahead transaction log verification and compromises data durability. Don't use SATA drives for production, use SCSI drives.
- The goal for database disk subsystems is not to use the largest disk available, but to use more spindles. Using four 36GB drives is far better than a single 146GB drive. More spindles is always better than fewer spindles. If a byte is striped across 8 drives, then the controller can read the entire byte in one-eighth of the time it would take if the byte were on a single drive. Use RAID striping, multiple filegroups, or a SAN to spread the load across multiple spindles.
- When choosing drives, choose the highest spindle speed and throughput you can afford.
- SQL Server is optimized to read and write sequentially from the disk subsystem for both data files and transaction logs, so use RAID 1 (mirrored) or RAID 10 (mirrored and striped), which is also optimized for sequential operations, rather than RAID 5, which is better for random access.
- While software options are available to provide behavior similar to RAID, they are not as efficient as RAID-specific hardware solutions. The software solutions tie up CPU cycles to perform the RAID activities that could be used for server processing. Don't use software RAID for a production SQL Server.
- The transaction log for any database that sees a significant value of writes should be on a dedicated DAS so that the heads can stay near the end of the transaction log without moving to other files. In addition, be sure to put enough memory into the disk controller to buffer a burst of transactions, but ensure that the disk controller buffer has an on-board battery.

- SQL Server adds additional threads to handle additional data files, so it's far better to use three data files on three DAS subsystems than a single larger file. Using multiple files to spread the load across multiple drives is better than manually using multiple filegroups to separate tables.
- SQL Server's Query Processor makes heavy use of `tempdb`. The best disk optimization you can do is to dedicate a DAS to `tempdb` and, of course, another disk to `tempdb`'s transaction log. Placing `tempdb` on multiple files across multiple DAS disk subsystems is another good idea.
- Windows wants to have a quick swap file. Regardless of how much physical memory is in the server, configure a large swap file and place it on a dedicated disk subsystem.
- To recap scaling out a non-SAN disk subsystem, Table 4-1 lists one possible configuration of disk subsystems. Each drive letter might actually be configured for multiple striped drives. They're listed by priority — for example, if you only have four drive subsystems, then break out the transaction log, first data file, and `tempdb` transaction log.

TABLE 4-1

Scaling Non-SAN Disk Subsystems

Logical Drive	Purpose
C:	Windows system and SQL Server executables
D:	Transaction log
E:	First data file
F:	tempdb transaction log
G:	tempdb data file
H:	Windows swap file
I: ...	Additional data files

RAID Illustrated

RAID stands for Redundant Array of Independent/Inexpensive Disks. It is a category of disk drives that utilizes two or more drives in combination for increased performance and fault tolerance. RAID applications are typically found in high-performance disk systems utilized by servers to improve the persistence and availability of data. Table 4-2 describes the various levels of RAID.

Network performance

Typical motherboards today include built-in network interface cards (NICs) capable of auto-switching between 10/100/1,000Mbps. As with most built-in devices, these tend to utilize the CPU for required processing, which affects performance. A variety of manufacturers today offer NIC cards that include onboard TCP/IP stack possessing, freeing up those tasks from the CPU. This improves overall network performance while reducing the CPU load, and I highly recommended them.

TABLE 4-2

RAID Levels

RAID Level	Diagram	Redundancy Percentage (percent of disks dedicated to redundancy)	Description
JBOD	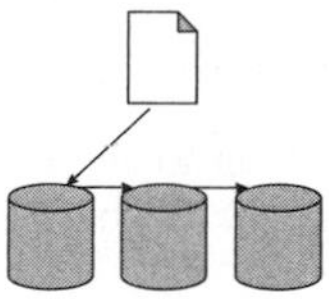	0%	*Just a Bunch of Disks* — Each extra disk extends the storage as if the disk were replaced with a larger one.
0	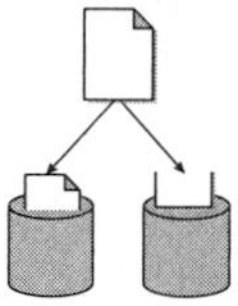	0%	*Data striping* — Data is spread out across multiple drives, speeding up data writes and reads. No parity, redundancy, or fault tolerance is available.
1	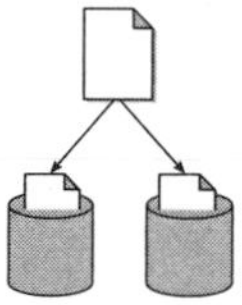	50%	*Data mirroring* — Data is written to two drives and read from either drive, providing better fault tolerance.
5	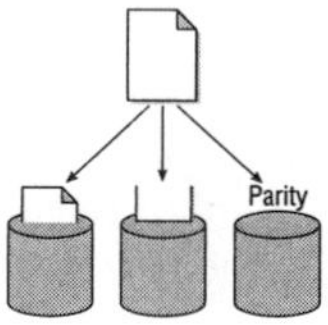 Parity	1/(n-1) For example, if the RAID array has five drives, then $\frac{1}{4}$, or 25% of the array is used for redundancy.	Data striping with a parity bit written to one of the drives. Because of the parity bit, any single drive can fail and the disk subsystem can still function. When the failed disk drive is replaced, the disk subsystem can recreate the data on the failed drive it contained.
6	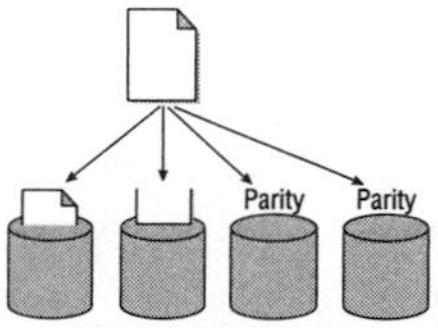 Parity Parity	Depends on the number of drives (e.g., if ten drives and the last two are used for parity, then 25%) Or use a formula: 2/(n-2)	RAID 6 is similar to RAID 5, except the parity bit is mirrored to two drives, so any data drive and one of the parity drives could fail simultaneously and the drive subsystem could continue to function.
10	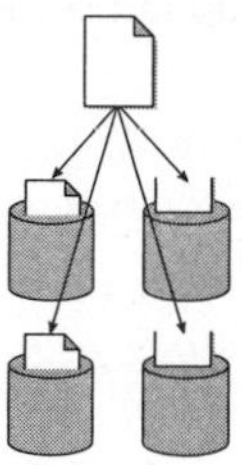	50%	*Mirrored striped drives* — These offer the speed of data striping and the protection of data Mirroring.

Preparing the Server

With the server in place, it's time to configure the operating system and set up the service accounts.

Dedicated server

I strongly recommend running any production SQL Server on a dedicated server — don't use the server for file or printer services, and no exchange, and no IIS — for two reasons:

- **Availability:** Multiple services running on the same server increases how often the server requires service pack installations, adjustments, and possibly rebooting. A dedicated SQL Server installation increases database availability.
- **Economics:** SQL Server is both resource intensive and expensive. SQL Server eats memory for lunch. It doesn't make economic sense to share the server resources between the expensive SQL Server license and other less expensive software.

When to Consolidate and Virtualize?

Server consolidation and virtual servers is a hot topic in the IT world. Running several logical servers on one large box can be cost effective and attractive in a spreadsheet. The question is, when is it a good idea for SQL Server?

- **CTP testing:** Personally, I'm a big fan of Microsoft Virtual PC and I often build up a SQL Server instance using VPC. Until the SQL Server 2008 RTM version is available, I only run Katmai CTP builds in a VPC. (I wrote this entire book with Katmai CTPs running on a VPC full-screen on one monitor and Word running on the host operating system on a second monitor.) Virtual PC is so easy to set up, and so safe, it doesn't make any sense to run a pre-RTM version of any software on the host operating system.
- **Developer sandboxes:** Developer Edition is so inexpensive that I recommend all developers have a license for Developer Edition on their own machine, rather than use a virtualized server.
- **QA, test, integration testing, and pre-prod servers:** Every organization has its own way of pushing code from the developer to production, or from the vendor to production. Because these applications demand strict application compatibility, but not performance compatibility, VPCs are perfect for this type of testing.
- **Service pack testing:** A virtual server is a great way to build up test servers for these configurations, or for testing Microsoft service packs.
- **Performance testing:** Depending on the scope of performance testing, a virtual server may be able to show performance gains for a new rev of the database code; but if the

continued

continued

performance test is to prove the database can handle *n* tps, then the performance test environment needs to be identical to production and that counts out virtualization.

- **Production:** With Windows Server 2008 and HyperV, running multiple SQL Server servers in a virtualized environment for production is a very reasonable alternative.

The other obvious option of SQL Server consolidation is running multiple SQL Server instances on the same physical server. This still enables each instance to have its own server settings and service pack level. My primary concern with multiple instances is that I want to avoid any resource contention.

Operating system

SQL Server 2008 installs and runs on various operating systems — from Windows XP to Windows Server 2003 Enterprise Edition, with the more feature-rich versions running on the higher-end operating systems. Appendix A, "SQL Server 2008 Specs," includes a table listing the supported operating systems by edition.

Service accounts

The SQL Server services require Windows login accounts to run and access the file system. It's possible to allow SQL Server to run using the local service account, but creating a specific Windows user account for SQL Server services provides better security and reliability. You can configure these accounts with the required minimum set of permissions (user, not administrator) and access to the data files.

The accounts can be specified independently during installation by selecting the "Customize for each service account" option. By default, SQL Server, SQL Server Agent, Analysis Server, and SQL Browser share the same login account. Ensure that the assigned Windows login account for each service has the appropriate file and resource permissions. Each login account and service relationship is listed in Table 4-3.

If the installation will include servers that will communicate and perform distributed queries or replication, then the login account must be a domain-level account.

Server instances

SQL Server 2008 Enterprise Edition supports up to 50 instances of SQL Server running on the same physical server, including instances of different editions (Enterprise, Standard, or Developer). The advantage of multiple instances is that each instance can have its own server-level configuration and service pack level.

CAUTION **Using multiple instances of SQL Server to provide multiple databases on the same server negatively affects performance. Each instance requires its own resources as well as CPU cycles to handle requests. While using a multi-core processor could mitigate the performance issues to an extent, using a large virtualized server or a single SQL Server to handle multiple databases is the best solution.**

TABLE 4-3

Startup Accounts for SQL Server Services

SQL Server Service Name	Default Account	Optional Accounts
SQL Server	SQL Express on Windows 2000–local system SQL Express on all other operating systems–network service All other editions on all operating systems–domain user	SQL Express–domain user, local system, network service All other editions–domain user, local system, network service
SQL Server Agent	Domain user	Domain user, local system, network service
Analysis Services	Domain user	Domain user, local system, network service, local service
Reporting Services	Domain user	Domain user, local system, network service, local service
Integration Services	Windows 2000–local system All other operating systems–network service	Domain user, local system, network service, local service
Full-Text Search	Same as SQL Server	Domain user, local system, network service, local service
SQL Server Browser	SQL Express on Windows 2000–local system SQL Express on all other operating systems–local service All other editions on all operating systems–domain user	Domain user, local system, network service, local service
SQL Server Active Directory Helper	Network service	Local system, network service
SQL Writer	Local system	Local system

The default location for SQL Server and associated files will be similar to the following:

```
C:\Program Files\Microsoft SQL Server\MSSQL.#
```

An instance can be installed as the default instance (with the same name as the server) or a named instance (with the name as *servername\instancename*). I recommend installing only named instances on a production server as a security measure. Depending on the hack, the hacker needs to know the instance name as well as the server name.

Not all installed services are shared among the multiple instances. Table 4-4 shows a list of shared versus instance services. Instance-specific services will have their own installed components.

TABLE 4-4

Shared SQL Server Services

Service	Shared	Instance Specific?
SQL Browser	Yes	
SQL Server Active Directory Helper	Yes	
SQL Writer	Yes	
SQL Server		Yes
SQL Server Agent		Yes
Analysis Services		Yes
Report Services		Yes
Full-Text Search		Yes

Performing the Installation

Once the installation plan has been created and the server is set up to meet the SQL Server requirements, it is time to install the software.

`Setup.exe` opens the SQL Server Installation Center, shown in Figure 4-1, which brings together into one UI a broad collection of installation utilities and resources — from the planning stage to advanced options.

In the Planning page there's an option to install the Upgrade Advisor. If you're upgrading an existing database to SQL Server, I recommend running this utility on the existing database to check for any potential issues.

By default, the Installation Center will choose the highest CPU level available on the server (x86, x64, IA-64). If you want to install a different CPU version of SQL Server, the Installation Center's Options page is the only location for this option.

Attended installations

A new installation is initiated from the Installation page ➪ "New SQL Server stand-alone installation or add features to an existing installation." The installation process moves through several pages according to the type of installation and components selected.

Errors, or missing items, appear at the bottom of the page with red Xs. You cannot progress past any page with an error.

FIGURE 4-1

The SQL Server Installation Center is the launch point for numerous planning, set-up, and advanced options.

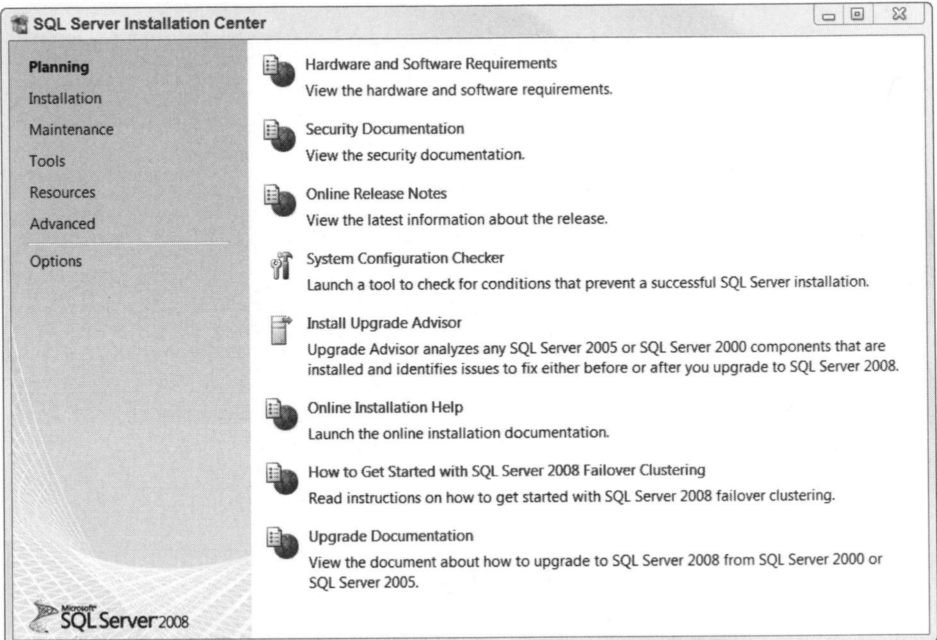

Setup Support Rules and Support Files pages

The first step of the installation, shown in Figure 4-2, checks the current configuration and status of the server to ensure that it's capable of a SQL Server installation.

Pressing OK, assuming the server passed all the tests, launches the Setup Support Files installation. This page simply installs all the support files needed for the SQL Server installation. When the setup support files are installed, SQL Server Setup will rerun the Setup Support Rules. This time it performs additional checks to ensure that the support files and components installed into the OS properly.

Installation Type page

The Installation Type page simply allows you to choose to install a new installation or modify the feature set of an existing SQL Server instance.

Product Key and License Terms pages

As the name implies, the Product Key page is used to authenticate your license of SQL Server or choose to install a free edition — Evaluation Enterprise Edition, Express Edition, or Express Edition with Advanced Services. Copies downloaded from MSDN often have the product key supplied automatically.

The License Terms page has the obligatory and ubiquitous "I accept the license terms" check box.

FIGURE 4-2

The Setup Support Rules page ensures that the server complies with the rules, or requirements, for setup. In this case, which is very common, my server has a pending reboot from a previous installation or Windows upgrade.

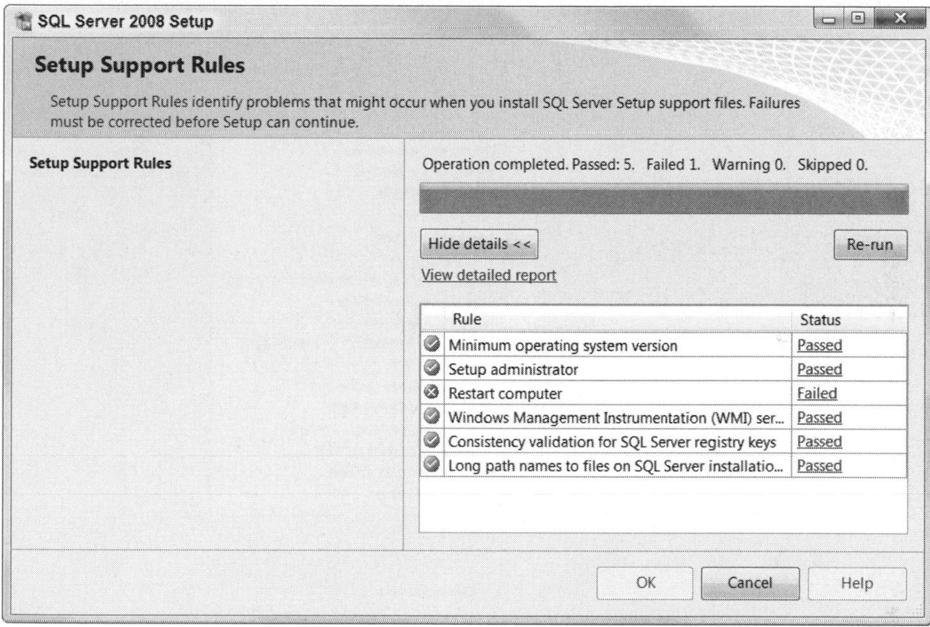

Feature Selection page

The Feature Selection page, shown in Figure 4-3, presents a tree view of the possible components and services. Selected by default are the shared components, Books Online, and the client tools. The real choice here is whether to install the relational Database Engine Services and its options, Replication and Integrated Full-Text Search; or Analysis Services; or Reporting Services.

A common error on this page is to forget to select Full-Text Search. Depending on the services selected, additional pages may be added to the rest of the setup process.

Instance Configuration page

This page is used to select a default or named instance and provide a name for the named instance (up to 16 characters), as well as to configure the instance ID, and specify the file path of the instance root directory.

Disk Space Requirements page

The Disk Space Requirements page simply informs you of the disk requirements for the selected components and ensures that the server has enough space to continue setup.

FIGURE 4-3

Use the Feature Selection page to select the major services and components to install.

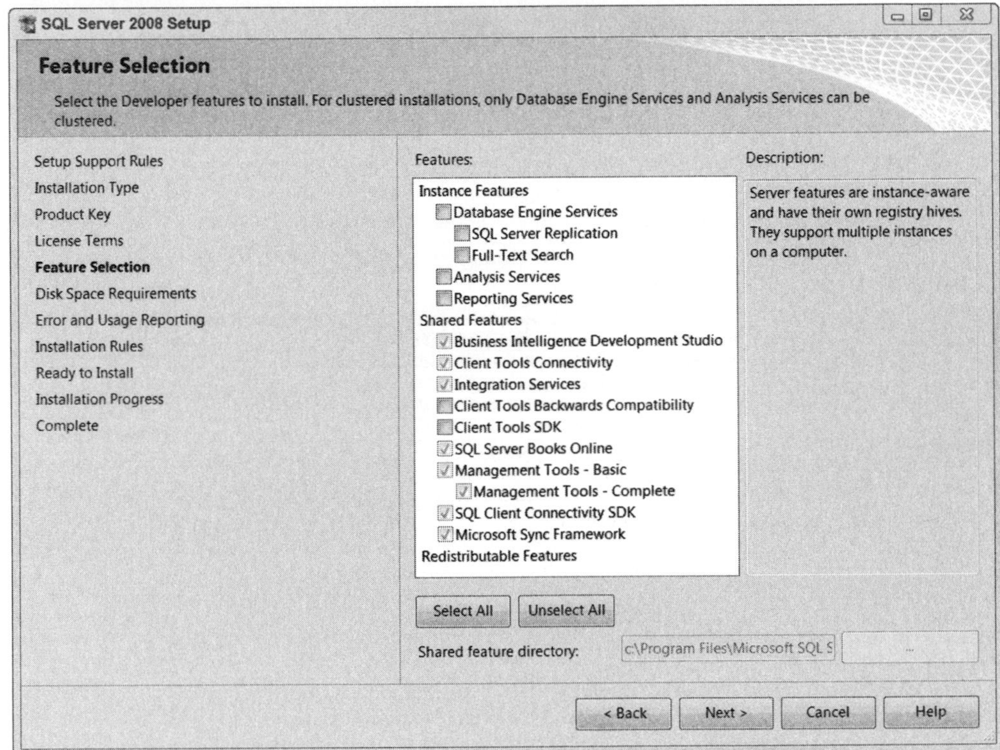

Server Configuration page

This page supplies server options for the Database Engine component. Here is where the Windows service account is configured so that SQL Server will have permission to execute and access to files.

Also configured on this page is the initial startup type, which determines whether the services start automatically when Windows starts or whether they require manual starting.

A common error on this page is to miss the Collation tab on this page. The default is probably OK for most installations, but be careful that you don't miss this important step.

Database Engine Configuration page

There are three tabs on the Database Engine Configuration page: Account Provisioning, Data Directories, and Filestream.

Account Provisioning configures SQL Server to only accept users based on their Windows account or mixed mode, which also allows SQL Server-defined users. If mixed mode is selected, then the SA account must be created with a strong P@s$w0rD. Windows authenticated accounts may also be added on this page and automatically added to the server sysadmin role.

CROSS-REF **Securing databases is discussed in more detail in Part VII: "Security."**

The Directories tab is used to configure the default directories for user database and transaction log files, the tempdb database and transaction log file, and the default backup directory.

The Filestream tab is where Filestream is enabled for the server. If there's any chance you might want to try any sample code that runs in AdventureWorks2008 (like nearly all of Books Online and much of the code in this book), then enable Filestream. AdventureWorks2008 can't be installed without Filestream enabled for the server.

Analysis Services Configuration page

This optional page, which appears only if Analysis Services was selected in the Feature Selection page, is used to add initial users with administrative permission and configure the default directories for Analysis Services.

Reporting Services Configuration page

If Reporting Services was selected in the Feature Selection page, this page is used to select the native configuration or SharePoint configuration.

Error and Usage Reporting page

The Microsoft SQL Server team really does use this information to collect usage statistics on SQL Server features and error reports. This information is key to determining where the team's efforts should be invested. Please enable these options.

Installation Rules and Ready to Install pages

This rendition of the Rules page verifies the installation configuration. The Ready to Install page reports the complete configuration in a tree view, and the location of the created .ini file with these configuration options. Clicking the Install button will launch the actual installation.

Unattended installations

SQL Server 2008 continues its tradition of offering the capability to perform an unattended installation based on an .ini configuration file. A well-commented sample .ini file, template.ini, can be found at the root of the SQL Server installation CD. This file contains the [Options] section, which must be customized for the type of installation to perform.

CAUTION **The clear-text installation .ini file does not provide any security for logins and passwords that are embedded. Take appropriate measures to restrict access to this file if it contains logins and passwords.**

The following example command shows the syntax for starting an unattended installation:

```
setup.exe  /settings  <full path to .ini file>
```

For example, to install SQL Server with the settings specified in an `.ini` file named `mySQLSettings.ini` located in a SQLTemp folder in the root of the system drive, the following command would be executed:

```
setup.exe /settings  c:\SQLTemp\mySQLSettings.ini
```

The following command-line switches affect installation behavior:

- `/qn` performs a silent installation with no dialogs.
- `/qb` displays only progress dialogs.

Once an installation configuration file has been created, it can be used for either an unattended installation or even a remote installation.

Remote installations

SQL Server 2008 may be installed on a remote network computer. A remote installation begins with the same configuration `.ini` file that an unattended install uses, but adds three additional values in the remote configuration `.ini` file, as described in Table 4-5.

NOTE **Remote installation can be performed only in a domain environment, not on a workgroup computer.**

TABLE 4-5

Remote Install Required .ini Options

Option	Description
`TargetComputer`	The network computer name on which SQL Server will be installed
`AdminAccount`	The admin user account of the target server where SQL Server will be installed
`AdminPassword`	The password for the admin user account of the target server

Upgrading from Previous Versions

SQL Server 2008 includes upgrade support for SQL Server 2000 and 2005. Prior to any upgrade, run the Upgrade Advisor to determine any effects the upgrade may have.

Microsoft supports installing SQL Server 2008 over an installation of SQL Server 2000 or 2005, but I strongly recommend that you use a side-by-side upgrade process. This method begins with a fresh installation of SQL Server 2008 on a newly set up Windows Server box and then moves any user databases to the new server using either backup/restore, or detach/attach. This method is also excellent for testing the new configuration prior to the actual production go-live date.

Upgrading from SQL Server 2005

The Database Engine, Migration Analysis Services, Reporting Services, and Integration Services may all be upgraded to SQL Server 2008. While some of these components may co-reside, others may not. Table 4-6 illustrates how the components may be installed.

TABLE 4-6

Component Upgrade Types

Server Component	Side-by-Side	Upgraded	Migration Required
Database Engine	Yes	Yes	No
Migration Analysis Services	Yes	Yes	Yes
Reporting Services	No	Yes[1]	Yes[2]
Notification Services	No	No	Yes[3]
Data Transformation Services	Yes	Yes	Yes

[1]The upgrade is transparent when on a default installation with no modifications.
[2]When installing to a modified/non-default installation. Otherwise, migration is not required.
[3]Migration occurs after the 2005 Database Engine and Notification Services have been installed.

If access to SQL Server 2000 components and data is required, then installing SQL Server 2005 side-by-side with the 2000 installation is the way to go.

When upgrading SQL 2000 servers, upgrade the client and target database servers first to ensure minimal data failures of the primary servers.

Migrating to SQL Server

During the data life cycle there are distinct points when the conversion to a new database proves beneficial and provides value. During these nexuses, a determination of the new database's features, requirements, value, and business needs must be made. Should enough evidence support the migration, then time-consuming projects begin to translate the data, schemas, and business logic to the new database. Aware of the time and cost inherent in these activities, Microsoft has provided the SQL Server Migration Assistant (SSMA), coinciding with the release of SQL Server 2005, to aid in migrations from alternative databases.

Migrating from Access

Microsoft and other third-party vendors provide upsizing wizards that are intended to port a database from MS Access to SQL Server. Avoid these at all costs. I've never seen a smooth automatic migration from Access to SQL Server. The best practices and common design patterns for Access translate into worst practices for SQL Server.

The only route is to analyze the Access schema, create a new fresh schema in SQL Server, build out appropriate stored procedures, and then port the data to SQL Server.

Migration Assistant

The initial release of SSMA includes support for migrating from Oracle to SQL Server 2000. SSMA provides a significant step forward in determining the complexity of a database project at a fraction of the cost and time associated with traditional determination means. Schema, data, constraint, migration, and validation can be accomplished through the new IDE.

All migrations go through the following phases: assessment, schema conversion, data migration, business logic conversion, validation, integration, and performance analysis.

Assessment

SSMA provides an assessment that includes an estimate of the labor required and provides information on what can be migrated automatically versus manually. Approximately 100 statistics are provided to characterize the database and offer insight into the complexity. SSMA also provides an estimate regarding the hours required to manually accomplish the conversion tasks.

While SSMA provides faster insight into the complexity of the database, it will still take time to identify the complexity of client software at the application and middle-tier levels.

Schema conversion

After it is connected to a source Oracle and target SQL database, the IDE displays the various attributes and objects of the databases. The source PL/SQL can be viewed along with the converted T-SQL for comparison. The IDE supports direct editing of the displayed SQL.

Oracle system functions that do not have a counterpart in SQL will be supported through the use of additional UDFs and stored procedures. Constraints, views, and indexes will all convert to their corresponding entities on SQL Server.

Data migration

The Oracle schema can be automatically converted to the SQL Server schema, and all specified data migrated to the SQL Server database. During migration, the administrator must be aware of possible constraints, triggers, and other dependencies that could prevent the record insertions, on a per-table basis, from completing.

Business logic conversion

Table 4-7 illustrates the conversions that take place from PL/SQL to SQL Server.

Transactions in SQL Server can be implicit by using `SET IMPLICIT_TRANSACTIONS ON`, or explicit by using `BEGIN TRAN` and `COMMIT TRAN`.

If exceptions are disabled on the target SQL Server, then no exception handling will occur. If exception handling is enabled, then exceptions are converted using `IF/GOTO` statements and UDFs.

TABLE 4-7

PL/SQL to T-SQL Conversions

PL/SQL	T-SQL
Outer (+) joins	ANSI-standard outer joins
Hints	Supported hints include First_Rows, Index, Append, Merge_Aj, Merge_Sj, Merge Unsupported hints will be ignored.
Boolean	Smallint
String parameters with unspecified length	Varchar(8000)
Numeric parameters with unspecified length and precision	Numeric (38,10)
Functions	User-defined functions (UDFs)
Triggers Before After Row-level Multiple	Triggers Instead Of After Emulated using cursors Combined into one
Package functions	UDFs using *PackageName_FunctionName* convention
Package procedures	Stored procedures using *PackageName_ProcedureName* convention
Package variables	Emulated with a table and support functions
System functions	System functions or UDFs
If-Elsif. . .Elsif-Else-End	Nested IF statements
NULL	SYSDB.SYS.DB_NULL_STATEMENT
Case	Case
Goto	Goto
Loop with Exit or Exit When	While (1=1) with a Break
While	While
For	While
Cursors With parameters FOR loop Close cursor_name	Cursors Multiple cursors Cursor with local variables Close cursor_name and Deallocate cursor_name

TABLE 4-7 *(continued)*

PL/SQL	T-SQL
Return	Return
Comments	Comments
Variables Static with %Type with %Rowtype Records	Variables Resolved at conversion time Group of local variables Group of local variables
Procedure calls	Procedure calls
Function calls	Function calls
Begin Tran Commit Rollback	Begin Tran Commit Rollback
SavePoint	Save Transaction
Exceptions	Emulated in T-SQL

Validation and Integration

The IDE provides a view of the SQL, similar to a code tool that displays differences between the source and newer versions of code, and supports the capability to modify, accept, and/or discard the proposed changes. Additional synchronization options include being able to overwrite the database objects with the current workspace objects, overwrite the workspace objects from the database, and merge objects.

Removing SQL Server

To remove SQL Server, use the Add/Remove Programs option in the Windows Control Panel. If there are multiple instances, removing a single instance will leave the other instances intact and able to function.

User databases will not be deleted by the uninstall and their directory structure remains intact.

Detaching and copying a database to another server prior to removing an instance of SQL Server enables continued access to the data. If that is not possible, back up and restore the database to another server or attach the orphaned database to another server.

Summary

SQL Server 2008 is easy to install with proper planning, With the 2008 release, Microsoft has introduced additional tools to aid in migration and configuration, and refined existing tools to assist with the install and upgrade paths. Default installations continue to be straightforward, and a little planning and forethought will help for installations that deviate from the fresh install. Following the "secure by default" philosophy, SQL Server 2008 disables the bulk of its features, especially for fresh installs. Enabled features prior to an upgrade remain enabled once 2008 has been installed.

If you've had painful upgrade experiences in the past, be hopeful — I've heard nothing but good stories about SQL Server 2008 upgrades.

With SQL Server installed, the next chapter moves on to connecting clients to SQL Server.

Chapter 5

Client Connectivity

SQL Server 2008 follows Microsoft's philosophy of "secure by default" and reduces the surface area of the application. The initial installation allows local access only — no network connections for the Express and Developer editions (i.e., remote client applications will not be able to connect).

IN THIS CHAPTER

Enabling server connectivity

SQL Native Client development features

Client software connectivity

CROSS-REF **Chapter 4, "Installing SQL Server 2008" discusses SQL Server surface area configuration as part of the installation process.**

The Server Configuration Manager tool installed with SQL Server can nearly always communicate with SQL Server so you can configure the server connectivity options and open the server up for network access. The connectivity relies on open paths between the client and server machines. At times, there will be firewall issues to deal with.

With network access allowed on the SQL Server, SQL Server provides clients with a new means of accessing functionality and features through the new SQL Server Native Client (SNAC). Before getting into the SNAC, network access for the new server must be enabled.

Enabling Server Connectivity

When initially installed, SQL Server enables the Shared Memory protocol and disables the remaining protocols. This provides the greatest default security because only applications running locally to the SQL Server can connect.

To broaden SQL Server availability, additional network protocols must be enabled on the server.

What's New in 2008 Connectivity

SNAC supports table value parameters. Table-valued parameters are a new parameter type in SQL Server 2008.

There is a new SNAC OLE DB provider. You'll need to get version 10 of SNAC.

Also of note for developers, Microsoft Data Access Components (MDAC) is compatible with SQL 2008 but will not be enhanced to support the new 2008 SQL Server features.

CROSS-REF **Chapter 39, "Configuring SQL Server," discusses SQL Server configuration in detail.**

Server Configuration Manager

When managing SQL Server services, configuring network protocols used by SQL server, or managing the network connectivity configuration from client computers, SQL Server Configuration Manager is the tool you need.

Network protocols define the common set of rules and formats that computers and applications use when communicating with one another. Table 5-1 lists the protocols available in SQL Server.

TABLE 5-1

SQL Server Protocols

Protocol	Description
Shared Memory	This is an in-memory protocol and thus is only suitable for applications that are running on the same machine as the SQL Server.
Named Pipes	This is an interprocess communications protocol (IPC) that enables a process to communicate with another process, possibly running on a different computer, through the use of shared memory. This protocol typically works well in small and fast local area networks, as it generates additional network traffic during use. In larger and slower networks, TCP/IP works better.
TCP/IP	TCP/IP, or Transmission Control Protocol/Internet Protocol, is widely used today. TCP guarantees the delivery and order of the information sent between computers, while IP defines the format or structure of the data sent. TCP/IP also contains advanced security features that make it attractive to security-sensitive organizations and users. This protocol works well in larger networks and slower networks.

With the Configuration Manager, you can enable, disable, and configure these various protocols as appropriate for the operational environment. The utility may be launched from the Start menu by selecting Start ➪ All Programs ➪ Microsoft SQL Server 2008 ➪ Configuration Tools ➪ SQL Server Configuration Manager. The Server Configuration Manager presents a list of all the available protocols and communication options, as shown in Figure 5-1.

FIGURE 5-1

The SQL Server Configuration Manager establishes the connectivity protocols used by SQL Server to communicate with clients.

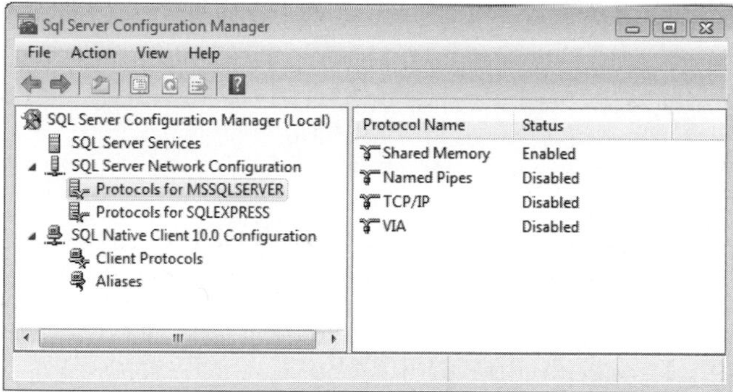

All TCP/IP communications is done over a specified port. Well-known ports include HTTP (port 80), FTP (port 21), and SSL (port 443). In most cases, SQL Server communicates over port 1433 when using TCP/IP. If communications are sent through a firewall, this can cause the communication to block. Port 1433 must be opened in a firewall in order for communications to be possible.

You can change the port number for instances of SQL Server. In this way, you can map instances to specific TCP/IP ports. When you do this, make sure that there is an opening in the firewall for any ports that you need.

Having trouble connecting with your SQL Server? Check these items:

- Does the server allow remote connections?
- Do both the server and the client speak the same protocol?
- Can the client ping the server?
- Is port 1433 (the SQL Server default port) open on the server's firewall?
- Is SQL Browser service running?

SQL Native Client Connectivity (SNAC)

The SQL Native Client connectivity is managed through the same Server Configuration Manager. SNAC installations will initially default the network protocols to enabling Shared Memory, TCP/IP, and Named Pipes, as shown in Figure 5-2.

FIGURE 5-2

The SQL Server Configuration Manager view for SQL Native Client Configuration Client Protocols.

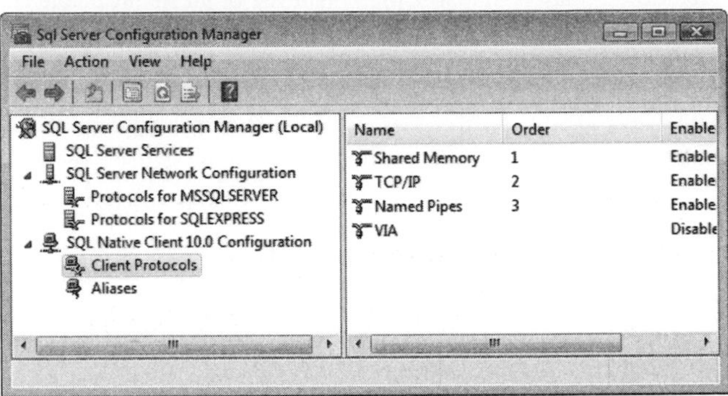

SNAC also adds support for large User Defined Types (UDT). This enables developers to create custom types of any arbitrary size. In addition, SNAC supports table value parameters. New to 2008 are table-valued parameters, which are used to send multiple rows of data to a T-SQL statement or routine without creating multiple other parameters or a temporary table. You declare a table-valued parameter with user-defined table types.

There is also a new SNAC OLE DB provider, which offers much better performance. It also makes parameterized queries much more efficient.

If SNAC access is not needed or supported by your organization, disabling the appropriate network protocols will reduce your security risks (surface area).

SQL Server Native Client Features

The development community gains access to the new features of SQL Server 2008 through the SQL Server Native Client (SNAC). If the new features are not needed and managed code is a requirement for data access, then ADO.NET will suffice. While a detailed examination of the features is beyond the scope of this chapter, a summary of each is provided.

NOTE **ADO.NET is an umbrella label applied to the .NET functionality that supports connections to a variety of data sources. Classes within this library supply the programmatic capability to create, maintain, dispose of, and execute actions against a database.**

For developers, Microsoft Data Access Components (MDAC) is compatible with SQL 2008 but will not be enhanced to support the new 2008 Server features.

NOTE **Because SQL Server Native Client is a component of SQL Server 2008, it must be installed separately on the development machine and must be included with the application setup. Microsoft has included the `sqlncli.msi` file on the SQL Server installation DVD. This file installs SQL Server Native Client without requiring the full SQL Server installation DVDs.**

Requirements

The software requirements for installing and running SQL Server Native Client are listed in Table 5-2. The operating system dictates the hardware requirements, including memory, hard disk capacities, CPU, and so on.

Chapter 4, "Installing SQL Server 2008," provides details about SQL Server installation requirements.

TABLE 5-2

SNAC Installation Requirements

Installer	Operating Systems	Compatible SQL Server
Windows Installer 3.0	Windows XP SP1 or later Windows 2000 Professional Windows 2000 Server Windows 2000 Advanced Server Windows 2000 Datacenter Windows 2003 Server Windows 2003 Enterprise Server Windows 2003 Datacenter Server Windows Vista Windows 2008 Server Windows 2008 Enterprise Server	SQL Server 7.0 or later supports connectivity.

Asynchronous operations

There are times when not waiting on a return from the database call is desirable. It is now possible to open and close a database connection without waiting by setting the appropriate property.

Additionally, asynchronous calls returning result sets can be made. In these cases, a valid result set will exist but may still be populating. Therefore, it is necessary to test the asynchronous status of the result set and process it when it is complete.

There are some caveats to performing asynchronous operations such as connection pooled objects and use of the cursor's engine. The asynchronous status is not exposed.

Multiple Active Result Sets (MARS)

SQL Server 2008 provides support for multiple active SQL statements on the same connection. This capability includes being able to interleave reading from multiple results sets and being able to execute additional commands while a result set is open.

Microsoft guidelines for applications using MARS include the following:

- Result sets should be short-lived per SQL statement.

- If a result set is long-lived or large, then server cursors should be used.
- Always read to the end of the results and use API/property calls to change connection properties.

By default, MARS functionality is not enabled. Turn it on by using a connection string value — `MarsConn` for the OLE DB provider and `Mars_Connection` for the ODBC provider.

XML data types

Much like the current `VarChar` data type that persists variable character values, a new XML data type persists XML documents and fragments. This type is available for variable declarations within stored procedures, parameter declarations, and return types and conversions.

User-defined types

These types are defined using .NET common language runtime (CLR) code. This would include the popular C# and VB.NET languages. The data itself is exposed as fields and properties, with the behavior exposed through the class methods.

Large value types

Three new data types have been introduced to handle values up to 2 ^ 31-1 bytes long. This includes variables, thus allowing for text values in excess of the old 8K limit. The new types and their corresponding old types are listed in Table 5-3.

TABLE 5-3

New SQL Server 2008 Large Values Types

New Large Data Types	Prior Data Types
varchar(max)	Text
nvarchar(max)	ntext
varbinary(max)	image

Handling expired passwords

This new feature of SQL Server 2008 enables users to change their expired password at the client without the intervention of an administrator.

A user's password may be changed in any of the following ways:

- Programmatically changing the password such that both the old and new passwords are provided in the connection string
- A prompt via the user interface to change the password prior to expiration
- A prompt via the user interface to change the password after expiration

Best Practice

If the old and new passwords are supplied on the connection string, then ensure that this information has not been persisted in some external file. Instead, build it dynamically to mitigate any security concerns.

Snapshot isolation

The new snapshot isolation feature enhances concurrency and improves performance by avoiding reader-writer blocking.

Snapshot isolation relies on the row versioning feature. A transaction begins when the `BeginTransaction` call is made but is not assigned a sequence transaction number until the first T-SQL statement is executed. The temporary logical copies used to support row versioning are stored in `tempdb`.

NOTE **If `tempdb` does not have enough space for the version store, then various features and operations such as triggers, MARS, indexing, client executed T-SQL, and row versioning will fail, so ensure that `tempdb` has more than enough space for anticipated uses.**

Summary

SQL Server Configuration Manager now provides the server and SQL Native Client protocol management. SQL Server 2008 supports new features that enrich the client and programmatic data experience. By accessing these new features through the SQL Server Native Client (SNAC), developers are now able to enhance the user experience by providing integrated password changes, improved blocking, and better user interface response with asynchronous calls. In addition, stability increases significantly with the use of mirrored servers and other useful features.

Chapter 6

Using Management Studio

IN THIS CHAPTER

A UI worthy of SQL Server 2008

Navigating SQL Server's objects

Organizing projects

Maximizing productivity with Query Editor

SQL Server's primary user interface is SQL Server Management Studio (SSMS), a powerful set of tools within a Visual Studio shell that enables the developer or DBA to create database projects and manage SQL Server with either a GUI interface or T-SQL code. For business intelligence (BI) work with Integration Services, Reporting Services, and Analysis Services, there's a companion tool called SQL Server Business Intelligence Development Studio (BIDS).

Like many things in life, Management Studio's greatest strength is also its greatest weakness. Its numerous tasks, tree nodes, and tools can overwhelm the new user. The windows can dock, float, or become tabbed, so the interface can appear cluttered, without any sense of order.

However, once the individual pages are understood, and the interface options mastered, the studios are very flexible, and interfaces can be configured to meet the specific needs of any database task. Personally, I love Management Studio — it's one of my favorite features of SQL Server 2008.

Much of using Management Studio is obvious to experienced IT professionals, and subsequent chapters in this book explain how to accomplish tasks using Management Studio, so I'm not going to explain every feature or menu item in this chapter. Instead, this chapter is a navigational guide to the landscape, pointing out the more interesting features along the way.

TIP **Management Studio is backwardly compatible, so you can use it to manage SQL Server 2008 and SQL Server 2005 servers. It's SMO-based, so some features may work with SQL Server 2000, but it's not guaranteed to be compatible.**

A common misconception among new SQL Server DBAs is that Management Studio *is* SQL Server. It's not. Management Studio is a front-end client tool used to manage SQL Server and develop databases. Typically, Management Studio is run on a workstation, and connects to the actual server. Management Studio sends T-SQL commands to SQL Server, or uses SQL Management Objects (SMOs), just like any other client application. It also inspects SQL Server and presents the data and configuration for viewing.

CROSS-REF **It's interesting to watch the commands sent by Management Studio to SQL Server. While Management Studio can generate a script for nearly every action, the actual traffic between SQL Server and its clients may be viewed using SQL Profiler, which is discussed in Chapter 56, "Tracing and Profiling."**

What's New in Management Studio?

SQL Server 2008's Management Studio is an evolution of SQL Server 2005's Management Studio, which was a merger of the old Enterprise Manager and Query Analyzer. Besides a few new nodes in Object Explorer and small tweaks to the UI, Management Studio has two new very cool powerful features worth mentioning:

- Using Registered Servers and Server Groups, the Query Editor can now send T-SQL statements to multiple servers with a single execute.
- The Query Editor now includes a very nice IntelliSense that completes table and column names, and a code outlining feature that collapses multi-line statements and procedures.

For SQL Server 2008, Buck Woody (SSMS 2008 Product Manager) and his team went all out with enhancements, tweaks, and new features. The new supercharged Management Studio is one of my personal favorite new features of SQL Server 2008, with at least 28 (count 'em) features:

- Using Registered Servers and Server Groups, the Query Editor can now send T-SQL statements to multiple servers with a single execute.
- Registered servers can now point to a configuration server, a central server that holds the configuration settings for several instances of SSMS so DBAs can share server configurations.
- Partitioning is easier to configure using a new wizard.
- Performance Studio presents drill-through reports of information gathered by the Performance Data Warehouse.
- The Activity Monitor can be launched for the SPID currently being viewed.
- Table Designer and Database Designer have new safety features to prevent accidental data loss.
- Setting security permissions has been redesigned for fewer required clicks and better display of a principal's effective permissions.
- Many SSMSs offer an Info-bar that provides user guidance.
- Info-bar color can be set on a per-server basis. For example, the development server could be green while the production server is red.

continued

continued

- A new Activity Monitor designed for the DBA provides better information, including active sessions, wait states, file I/O, and long-running queries.

Object Explorer has several enhancements:

- A new Object Explorer Details page displays a ton of information about the object, including configuration columns and a Vista-like properties panel at the bottom of the page.
- Object Search makes it easier to locate the right object.
- Data can be copied from the Object Explorer Details grid as tab-delimited data with headers.
- The number of rows returned by selecting Object Explorer ⇨ Select Top n Rows and Object Explorer ⇨ Edit Top n Rows can be set in Options.
- PowerShell can be launched from most nodes in Object Explorer.
- Service Broker can now be configured and controlled from Object Explorer.

The Query Editor alone has several enhancements:

- IntelliSense completes table and column names.
- IntelliSense tooltips provide detailed information about objects and parameters.
- Code outlining features collapse multi-line statements and procedures.
- Customizable tabs
- Launch profiler from the Query Editor
- The Error List recalls the last T-SQL errors.
- The T-SQL debugger is back!
- The results grid context menu is now capable of copying, copying with headers, and saving the results to CSV or tab-delimited files.

Working with query execution plans, also called showplans, is improved with new options:

- An XML query plan (from `sys.dm_exec_query_plan`) can be opened as a graphical query plan.
- XML showplans are now formatted for easier viewing.
- Graphic execution plans can be converted to XML showplans.
- Saved graphic execution plans can be converted back into the original query.

In addition, the framework on which SSMS is based received an overhaul focused on improving load time and overall performance. In addition, one of Ken Henderson's final tasks with Microsoft before his untimely passing was performance-tuning the queries that SSMS sends to SQL Server. (Ken was the author of the famous *SQL Server Guru* series of books, a popular conference speaker, a friend of the SQL community, and a brilliant SQL programmer. He is missed by the SQL community.)

Organizing the Interface

Management Studio includes a wide variety of functionality organized into 13 tools, which may be opened from either the View menu, the standard toolbar, or the associated hotkey:

- **Object Explorer** (F8): Used for administering and developing SQL Server database objects. The Object Explorer Details page presents a list of objects under the selected node.

TIP **In SQL Server 2005 Management Studio, F8 opened Object Explorer. That was removed in SQL Server 2008. To get that functionality back, revert to SQL Server 2000 keyboard layout (Tool ➪ Options ➪ Environment ➪ Keyboard). Object Explorer will now open with F8, even after resetting the keyboard layout to Standard.**

- **Registered Servers** (Ctrl+Alt+G): Used to manage the connections to multiple SQL Server 2005 engines. You can register database engines, Analysis Services, Report Servers, SQL Server Mobile, and Integration Services servers.
- **Template Explorer** (Ctrl+Alt+T): Used to create and manage T-SQL code templates
- **Solution Explorer** (Ctrl+Alt+L): Organizes projects and manages source code control
- **Properties window** (F4): Displays properties for the selected object
- **Bookmarks window** (Ctrl+K, Ctrl+W): Lists current bookmarks from within the Query Editor
- **Web Browser** (Ctrl+Alt+R): Used by the Query Editor to display XML or HTML results
- **Output window** (Ctrl+Alt+O): Displays messages from Management Studio's integrated development tools.
- **Query Editor:** The descendant of SQL Server 2000's Query Analyzer, the Query Editor is used to create, edit, and execute T-SQL batches. Query Editor may be opened from the File ➪ New menu by opening an existing query file (assuming you have the `.sql` file extension associated with Management Studio); by clicking the New Query toolbar button; or by launching a query script from an object in Object Explorer.
- **Toolbox** (Ctrl+Alt+X): Used to hold tools for some tasks
- **Error List** (Ctrl+\, Ctrl+E): Lists multiple errors
- **Task List** (Ctrl+Alt+K): Tracks tasks for solutions

The most commonly used tools — Query Editor, Object Explorer, Template Explorer, and Properties windows — are available on the standard toolbar.

NOTE **This chapter primarily discusses Management Studio because it is used with the Relational Engine, but Management Studio is used with the Business Intelligence (BI) tools as well. Part 10 covers the BI tools.**

Window placement

Using the Visual Studio look and feel, most windows may float, be docked, be part of a tabbed window, or be hidden off to one side. The exception is the Query Editor, which shares the center window — the document window. Here, multiple documents are presented, with tabs enabling selection of a document.

Any window's mode may be changed by right-clicking on the window's title bar, selecting the down arrow on the right side of a docked window, or from the Window menu. In addition, grabbing a window and moving it to the desired location also changes the window's mode. Following are the available options by either dragging the tool's window or using the tool's context menu:

- Setting the mode to *floating* instantly removes the window from Management Studio's window. A floating window behaves like a non-modal dialog box.
- Setting the mode to *tabbed* immediately moves the window to a tabbed document location in the center of Management Studio, adding it as a tab to any existing documents already there. In effect, this makes the tool appear to become a tab in the Query Editor. Dragging a tab to a side location creates a new tabbed document. Any location (center, right, left, top, bottom) can hold several tabbed tools or documents. The center document location displays the tabs on the top of the documents, the other locations display the tabs at the bottom.

  A tabbed document area can hold more documents than the space allows to display the tabs. There are two ways to view the hidden tabs. Ctrl+Tab opens the active tool's window and scrolls through the open files, or the Active File arrow in the upper right-hand corner of the tabbed document area opens a drop-down list of the tabs.
- While a *dockable* window is being moved, Management Studio displays several blue docking indicators (see Figure 6-1). Dropping a window on the arrow will dock it in the selected location. Dropping the window on the center blue spot adds the window to the center location as a tabbed document.

CROSS-REF **The free screencast *Using SQL Server Management Studio*, demonstrates the various ways to move, dock, and hide Management Studio's windows. See `www.SQLServerBible.com`.**

- Opening several windows will keep the tools right at hand, but unless you have a mega monitor (a 24″ widescreen works well!), the windows will likely use too much real estate. One solution is *auto-hiding* any docked window that you want out of the way until the window's tab is clicked. To auto-hide a window, use the View ➪ Auto-Hide menu command or toggle the pin icon in the window's title bar. When the pin is vertical, the window stays open. When the window is unpinned, the window auto-hides. An auto-hidden window must be pinned back to normal before its mode can be changed to floating or tabbed. Unfortunately, I find that I accidentally open the hidden tab so much that I avoid auto-hiding windows, but you might be more coordinated and find the feature useful.

TIP **Ctrl+Tab displays all windows and documents. You can click on a window or document with the Ctrl key still pressed to select it. You can also use the arrow keys with the Ctrl key still pressed and release Ctrl when the window you need is selected. One press of Ctrl+Tab will select the most recently selected document. Repeatedly pressing Ctrl+Tab will cycle though all the documents in the center location. I use Ctrl+Tab regularly.**

To reset Management Studio to its default configuration (Object Explorer ➪ Tabbed Documents ➪ Property Window) use the Window ➪ Reset Window Layout menu command. Fortunately, this command does not reset any custom toolbar modifications.

To hide all the docked windows and keep only the tabbed documents in the center visible, use the Window ➪ Auto Hide All menu command.

This flexible positioning of the windows means you can configure the interface to give you access to the tools in whatever way makes you the most comfortable and productive. Personally, I tend to close every window but the Query Editor and work with multiple scripts using the vertical split panes, as shown in Figure 6-2.

FIGURE 6-1

Moving a floating window in Management Studio presents several drop points. The shaded area indicates where the dropped window will be placed.

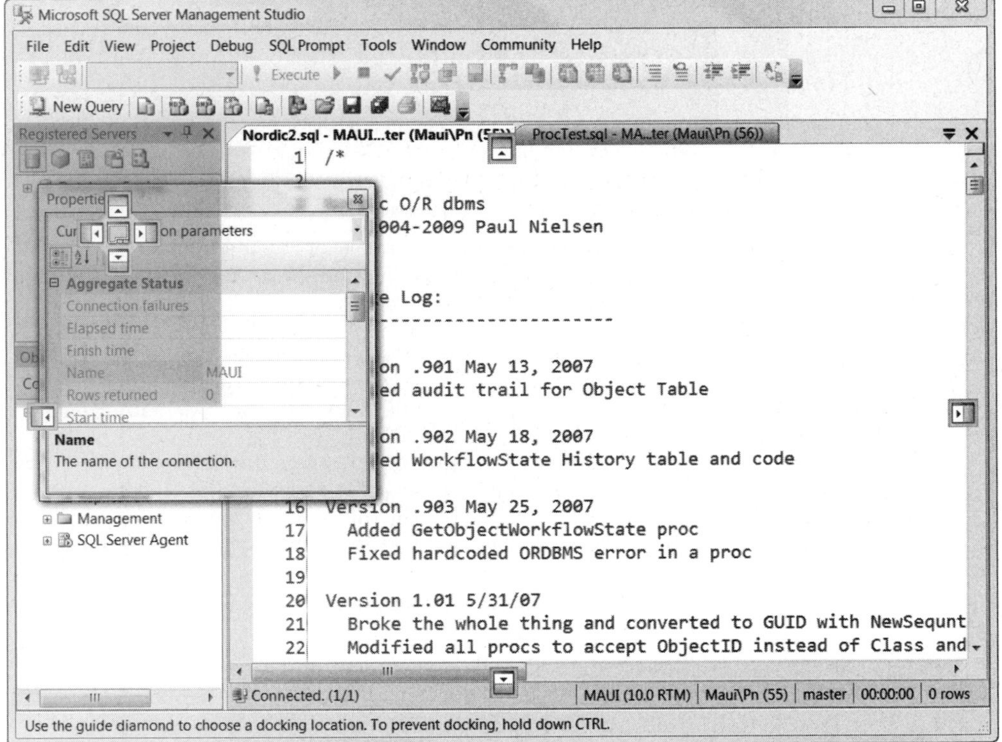

The Context Menu

In keeping with the Microsoft Windows interface standards, the context menu (accessed via right-click) is the primary means of selecting actions or viewing properties throughout Management Studio. The context menu for most object types includes submenus for new objects, and tasks. These are the workhorse menus within Management Studio.

Add `/nosplash` to your SQL Server Management Studio shortcut(s) to improve startup time.

FIGURE 6-2

Although Management Studio can be configured with multiple windows, this is my most common configuration for doing development work: Object Explorer Details for searches and Query Editor for script-style coding in the tabbed view, with a little Object Explorer on the side.

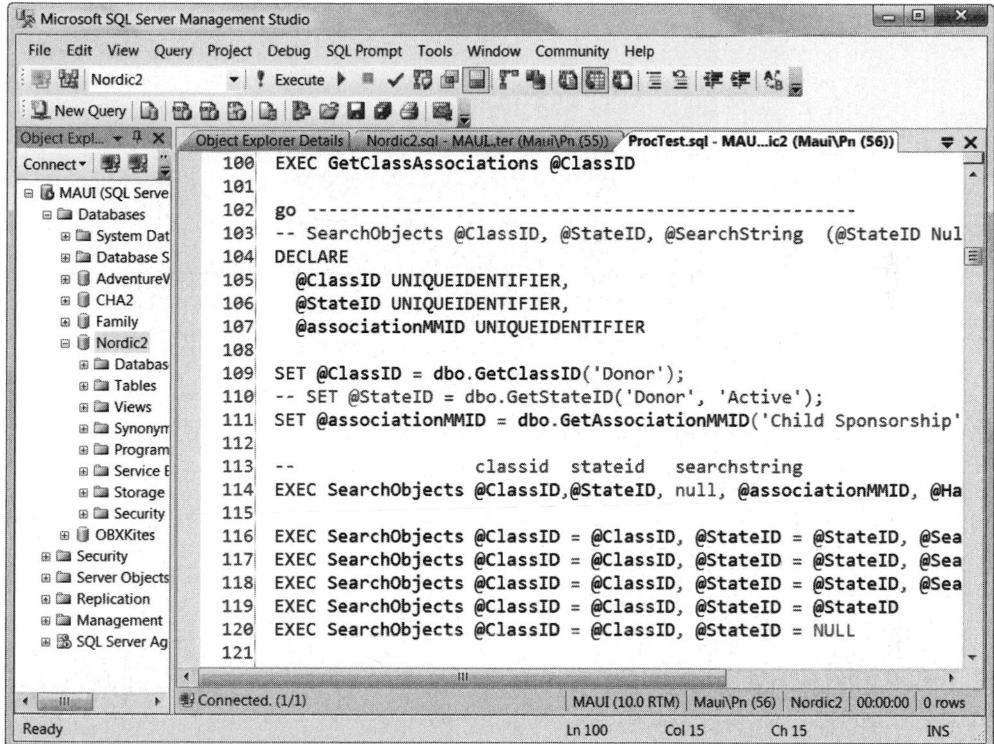

Registered Servers

Registered Servers is an optional feature. If you manage only one or a few SQL Servers, then Registered Servers offers little benefit. If, however, you are responsible for many SQL Servers, then this is the right place to take control.

Using Registered Servers, connection information can be maintained for connections to the Database Engine, Analysis Services, Reporting Services, SQL Server Mobile Edition Databases, and Integration Services. The toolbar at the top of Registered Servers enables selection among the types of services.

Managing Servers

Servers are easily registered using the context menu and supplying the Properties page with the server name, authentication, and maybe the connection information. One key benefit of registering a server is that it can be given an alias, or Registered Server Name, in the Properties page, which is great if you're a DBA managing dozens of servers with the serial number as the server name.

Once a server is registered, you can easily select it, and using the context menu, connect to it with Object Explorer or the Query Editor. While this is a good thing, the server aliases don't propagate to Object Explorer, which can lead to confusion. The workaround is to keep Object Explorer free from all other connections except those currently in use.

The Server context menu, shown in Figure 6-3, can also be used to connect to the server with Object Explorer or the Query Editor, or to apply Policies. Other tasks include starting and stopping the service, and opening the server's Registration Properties page.

To share your registered server list, or move from one SSMS installation to another, import and export the server configurations by selecting the context menu ➪ Tasks ➪ Import/Export, respectively.

FIGURE 6-3

Registered Servers is the tool used to manage multiple servers. Here, a new query was opened from the Local Server Groups node in Registered Servers. The new query is connected to both the Maui and Maui/Copenhagen servers. The Query Editor Results pane adds the Server Name column as it combines the results from both servers.

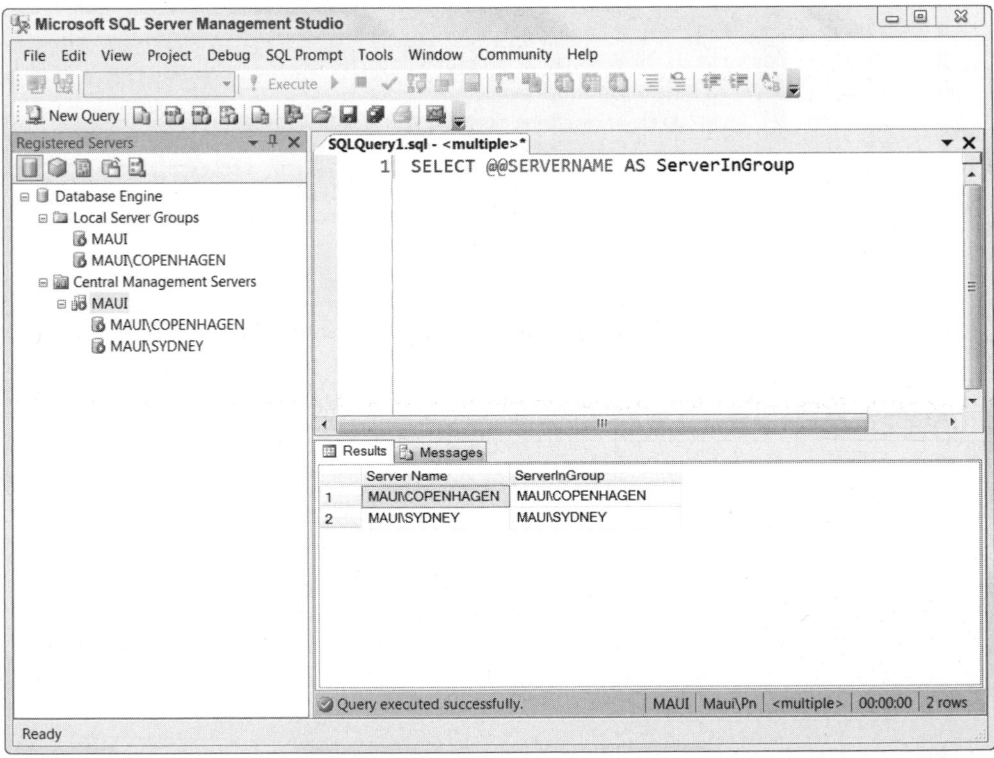

Server Groups

Within the Registered Servers tree, servers may be organized by server groups. This not only organizes the servers, but enables new group actions as well.

- **Local Server Groups:** Stores the connection information in the local file system. Think of these as Management Studio groups.
- **Configuration Server Groups:** New in SQL Server 2008, these store the connection information in a specified server. Groups are then created under the configuration server, so the tree in Registered Servers flows from Database Engine to Configuration Servers to the server selected as the configuration server, to a configuration group, to all the servers in the configuration group, as shown in Figure 6-3.

The server group (local or configuration servers) context menu includes the same Object Explorer, Query Editor, and Policy commands as registered servers, but when these commands are executed from the group, they apply to all servers in the group or group.

- **Object Explorer:** Opens Object Explorer and connects every server in the server group.
- **Query Editor:** Opens with a connection to the group instead of a connection to the server. T-SQL commands are then submitted to every server simultaneously.

  The Query Editor merges (unions) the results from every server and adds two columns, server name and login, to indicate which server returned each row. The columns, and whether results are merged or returned in separate result sets, can be configured in Tools ➪ Options – Query Results ➪ SQL Server ➪ MultiServer Results, or Query Editor ➪ Query Options ➪ Results ➪ MultiServer. Messages will now include the server name and login.
- Declarative Management Framework **Policies** may be applied to every server in the group.

CROSS-REF ***SSMS: Registered Server Groups and MultiServer Queries*** **is an online screencast that demonstrates setting up server groups and sending T-SQL to multiple servers. See** `www.SQLServerBible.com`**.**

The Great Graphical vs. Scripts Debate

Sorry for the hype — there isn't really any debate because the SQL Server development team's goal for Management Studio is to enable you to perform any task using your choice of graphical or script. In addition, you should be able to script any graphical action to a script. This is part of what I was referring to in Chapter 1 when I said that I like SQL Server because the experience is scalable. You choose how you want to work with SQL Server.

Personally, I write scripts by hand, but it's a common practice to prepare changes in the graphical tool, and then script them but not actually execute them.

There are several advantages to working with scripts. Scripts (especially alter scripts) can be developed on the dev server, checked into SourceSafe, deployed to test, and then production. I think of DDL as source code. Scripts can be checked into source control. Graphical clicks cannot.

CROSS-REF **Management Studio is not the only way to submit T-SQL scripts to SQL Server. For details on running the command-line interface, SQLCmd, refer to Chapter 42, "Maintaining the Database."**

Object Explorer

Object Explorer offers a well-organized view of the world of SQL Server. The top level of the tree lists the connected servers. Object Explorer can connect to a server regardless of whether the server is known by Registered Servers. The server icon color indicates whether or not the server is running.

Navigating the tree

In keeping with the Explorer metaphor, Object Explorer (see Figure 6-4) is a hierarchical, expandable view of the objects available within the connected servers.

Each Database Engine server node includes Databases, Security, Server Objects, Replication, Management, and SQL Server Agent. Most of the tree structure is fixed, but additional nodes are added as objects are created within the server.

The Databases node contains all the server's databases. When you right-click on a database, the context menu includes a host of options and commands. Under each database are standard nodes (refer to Figure 6-4), which manage the following database objects:

- **Database Diagrams:** Illustrates several tables and their relationships. A database may contain multiple diagrams, and each diagram does not need to display all the tables. This makes it easy to organize large databases into modular diagrams.
- **Tables:** Used to create and modify the design of tables, view and edit the contents of tables, and work with the tables' indexes, permissions, and publications. Triggers, stored procedures that respond to data-modification operations (insert, update, and delete), may be created and edited here. The only way to launch the Query Designer is from the table listing.
- **Views:** Stored SQL statements are listed, created, and edited, and the results viewed, from this node.
- **Synonyms:** These are alternative names for SQL Server database objects.
- **Programmability:** A large section that includes most of the development objects, stored procedures, functions, database triggers, assemblies, types, rules, and defaults
- **Service Broker:** Used to view Server Broker objects, such as queues and contracts
- **Storage:** Used to manage non-standard storage such as full-text search, and table partitions
- **Security:** Used to manage security at the database level

FIGURE 6-4

Object Explorer's tree structure invites you to explore the various components of SQL Server management and development.

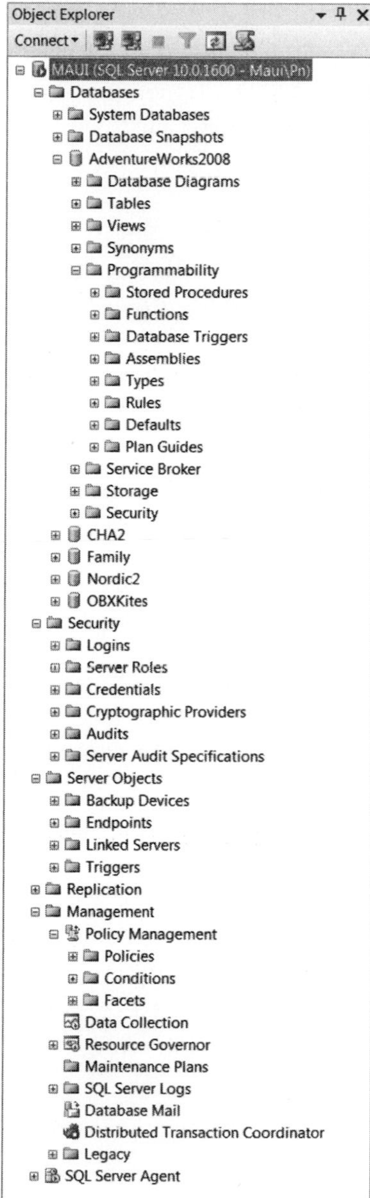

The Security node is used to manage server-wide security:

- **Logins:** Server-level authentication of logins
- **Server Roles:** Predefined security roles
- **Credentials:** Lists credentials
- **Cryptographic Providers:** Used for advanced data encryption
- **Audits:** Part of SQL Audit, collects data from Extended Events
- **Server Audit Specifications:** Defines a SQL Audit for a server-level audit

The Server Objects node holds server-wide items:

- **Backup Devices:** Organizes tapes and files
- **Endpoints:** HTTP endpoints used by database mirroring, Service Broker, SOAP, and T-SQL
- **Linked Servers:** Lists predefined server credentials for distributed queries
- **Triggers:** Contains server-level DDL triggers

The Replication node is used to set up and monitor replication:

- **Local Publications:** Lists publications available from this server
- **Local Subscriptions:** Lists subscriptions this server subscribes to from other servers

The Management node contains several server-wide administration tools:

- **Policy Management:** SQL Server's new policy-based management
- **Data Collection:** Define data collection points for SQL Server's Management Data Warehouse
- **Resource Governor:** Control Enterprise Edition's CPU and Memory Resource Governor
- **Maintenance Plans:** Create and manage maintenance plans
- **SQL Server Logs:** SQL Server creates a new log with every restart. View them all here.
- **Database Mail:** Configure and monitor Database Mail
- **Distributed Transaction Coordinator:** Manage DTC for transactions involving multiple servers
- **Legacy:** Contains deprecated objects such as DTS packages and older database maintenance plans

The final node links to SQL Server Agent tools (if SQL Server Agent is running):

- **Jobs:** Control SQL Server Agent jobs
- **Job Activity Monitor:** View job activity
- **Alerts:** Configure SQL Server Agent alerts
- **Operators:** Set up SQL Server Agent operators
- **Proxies:** Manage SQL Server Agent externally
- **Error Logs:** View SQL Server Error Logs

CAUTION **Because Management Studio and SQL Server are communicating as client and server, the two processes are not always in sync. Changes on the server are often not immediately reflected in Management Studio unless Management Studio is refreshed, which is why nearly every tool has a refresh icon, and refresh is in nearly every context menu.**

Filtering Object Explorer

Some databases are huge. To ease navigating these objects, Microsoft has included a filter for portions of the tree that include user-defined objects, such as tables or views. The filter icon is in the toolbar at the top of the Object Explorer. The icon is only enabled when the top node for a type of user-defined object is selected. For example, to filter the tables, select the tree node and then click on the filter icon or right-click to open the tree's context menu, and select Filter ➪ Filter Settings.

The Filter Settings dialog box enables you to filter the object by name, schema, or creation date. To remove the filter, use the same context menu, or open the Filter Settings dialog box and choose Clear Filter. Note that the filter accepts only single values for each parameter; Boolean operators are not permitted.

TIP **System objects are organized in their own folder, but if you prefer to hide them altogether, you can do so by selecting Tools ➪ Options – Environment ➪ General tab.**

Object Explorer Details

The Object Explorer Details page is completely redesigned and now sports several way cool features. If you upgrade to SQL Server 2008 and just keep using it the way you used Management Studio 2005, you're missing out:

- Object Explorer Details has dozens of additional columns that may be added to the grid. Right-click on the grid headers to select additional columns.
- The columns can be rearranged and the rows sorted by any column.
- Data can be selected (highlighted) and copied to the clipboard (Ctrl+C) in a tabbed format with header columns — perfect for pasting into Excel and graphing.
- The pane below the grid displays several properties depending on the size of the pane. The sort order of those properties was hand-picked by Buck Woody (real DBA and SSMS 2008 Product Manager).

The Object Explorer Details Search is one of the best-kept secrets of SQL Server:

- If Object Explorer is at the server-node level, then the Object Explorer Details Search searches every object in the server.
- If Object Explorer is at any node at or under the database node level, then it searches the current database.
- The Object Explorer Details page is rather object-type generic and so is its context menu. The best solution is to use the synchronize toolbar button or context menu command to quickly jump to the object in Object Explorer.
- If the back button in Object Explorer Details returns to search results, it will automatically re-execute the search to ensure that the list is as up-to-date as possible.

The Table Designer

Creating a new table, or modifying the design of an existing table, is easy with the Table Designer. The Table Designer, shown in Figure 6-5, is very similar to MS Access and other database design tool interfaces.

Create a new table by selecting the Tables node in the tree and then selecting New Table from the context menu. The design of existing tables may be altered by selecting the table, right-clicking, and selecting Design from the context menu.

FIGURE 6-5

Tables may be created or their designs edited using the Table Designer tool.

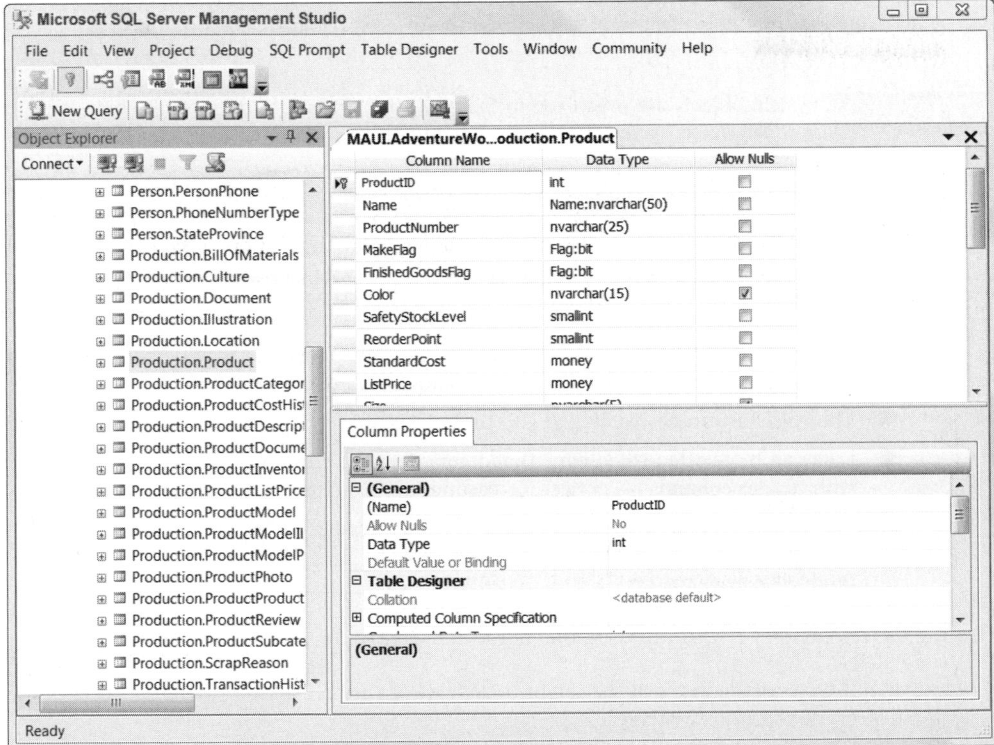

Columns may be individually selected and edited in the top pane. The column properties for the selected column are listed in the bottom pane. Dialog boxes for modifying foreign keys and indexes can be opened using the Table Designer menu or toolbar.

Although I'm a code guy myself and prefer Query Editor to the GUI tools, I must admit that the Table Designer page is a clean, straightforward UI, and it generates scripts for every modification. I recommend opening the Properties window as well, because some table properties are only visible there.

CROSS-REF **The logical design of tables and columns is covered in Chapter 3, "Relational Database Design." The realities of implementing the logical design, and how to script tables using DDL, are discussed in Chapter 20, "Creating the Physical Database Schema."**

Building database diagrams

The Database Diagram tool takes the Table Designer up a notch by adding custom table design views (see Figure 6-6) and a multi-table view of the foreign-key relationships. The Database Diagram tool has its own node under each database, and each database may contain multiple diagrams, which makes working with very large databases easier because each module, or schema, of the database may be represented by a diagram.

FIGURE 6-6

The OBXKites database relationships viewed with the Database Diagram tool. The Location table has been changed to Standard view.

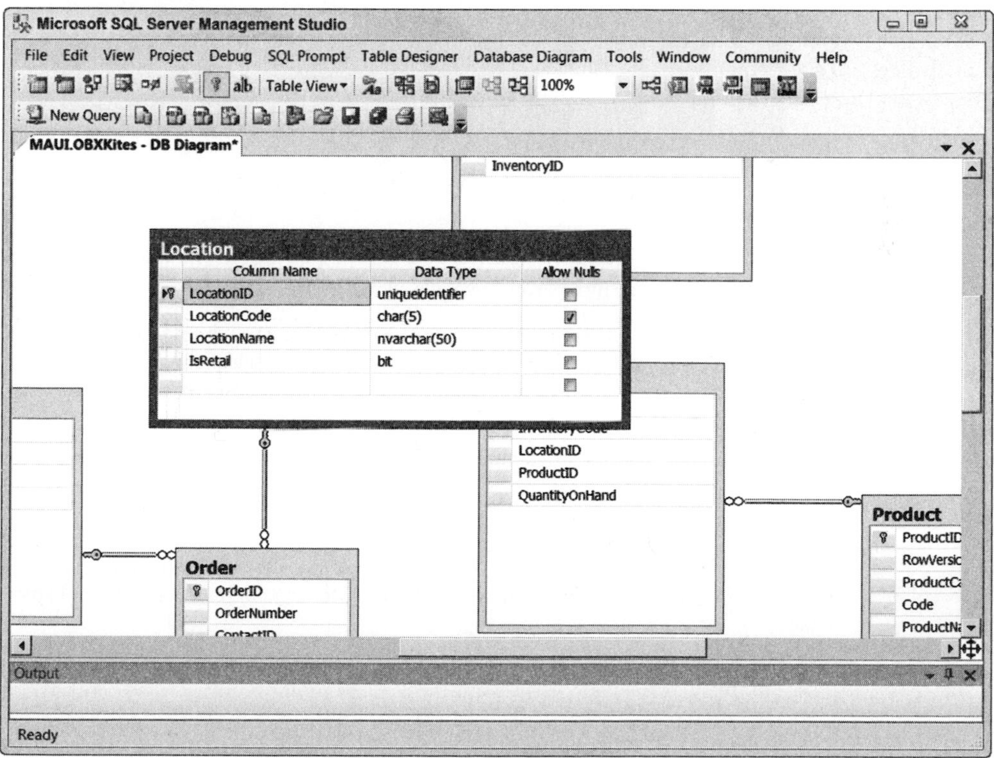

Personally, I like the Database Diagram tool (as far as GUI tools go). Although I don't develop using the tool, sometimes it's useful to visually explore the schemas of very large databases. Unfortunately, the Database Diagram tool suffers from a few clumsy issues:

- It makes sense to create a separate diagram for each section of a large database, and databases can be organized by schemas (as AdventureWorks is); unfortunately, the Database Diagram tool is schema unaware.
- It does not display the table schema in the diagram. To view the schema, open the Property window and select the table in the diagram.
- There's no way to select all of the tables of a schema and add them to the diagram as a set. Object Explorer will not permit selecting multiple tables. The Object Explorer Details page allows multiple table selection, but it does not permit dragging the tables to the design. Even worse, the Add Table dialog box in the Database Diagram tool does not sort by the table's schema. The Add Related Tables option on the table's context menu helps solve this problem.
- Relationship lines have the frustrating tendency to become pretzels when tables or lines are moved.

Best Practice

If your goal is to print the database diagram, be sure to check the page breaks and arrange the tables first, or chances are good you'll end up wasting a lot of paper. To view the page breaks, use the tool's context menu or the Database Diagram menu.

The Query Designer

The Query Designer is a popular tool for data retrieval and modification, although it's not the easiest tool to find within Management Studio. You can open it two ways:

- Using Object Explorer, select a table. Using the context menu, choose Edit Top 200 Rows. This will open the Query Designer, showing the return from a "select top(200)" query in the results pane. The other panes may now be opened using the Query Designer menu or the toolbar.
- When using the Query Editor, use the Query Designer button on the toolbar, use the Query ⇨ Design Query in Editor menu command, or use the Query Editor's own context menu.

  Note that when the Query Designer is opened from the Query Editor, it's a modal dialog box and the results pane is disabled.

TIP **If editing 200 rows, or viewing 1000 rows, seems like too many (or not enough) for your application, you can edit those values in the Options ⇨ SQL Server Object Explorer ⇨ Command tab.**

Unlike other query tools that alternate between a graphic view, a SQL text view, and the query results, Management Studio's Query Designer simultaneously displays multiple panes (see Figure 6-7), as selected with the view buttons in the toolbar:

- **Diagram pane:** Multiple tables or views may be added to the query and joined together in this graphic representation of the `SELECT` statement's `FROM` clause.

- **Grid pane:** Lists the columns being displayed, filtered, or sorted
- **SQL pane:** The raw SQL `SELECT` statement may be entered or edited in this pane.
- **Results pane:** When the query is executed with the Run button (!), the results are captured in the results pane. If the results are left untouched for too long, Management Studio requests permission to close the connection.

One of my favorite features in Management Studio is the capability to create and graphically join derived tables within Query Designer's Diagram pane. Way cool!

FIGURE 6-7

Object Explorer's Query Designer

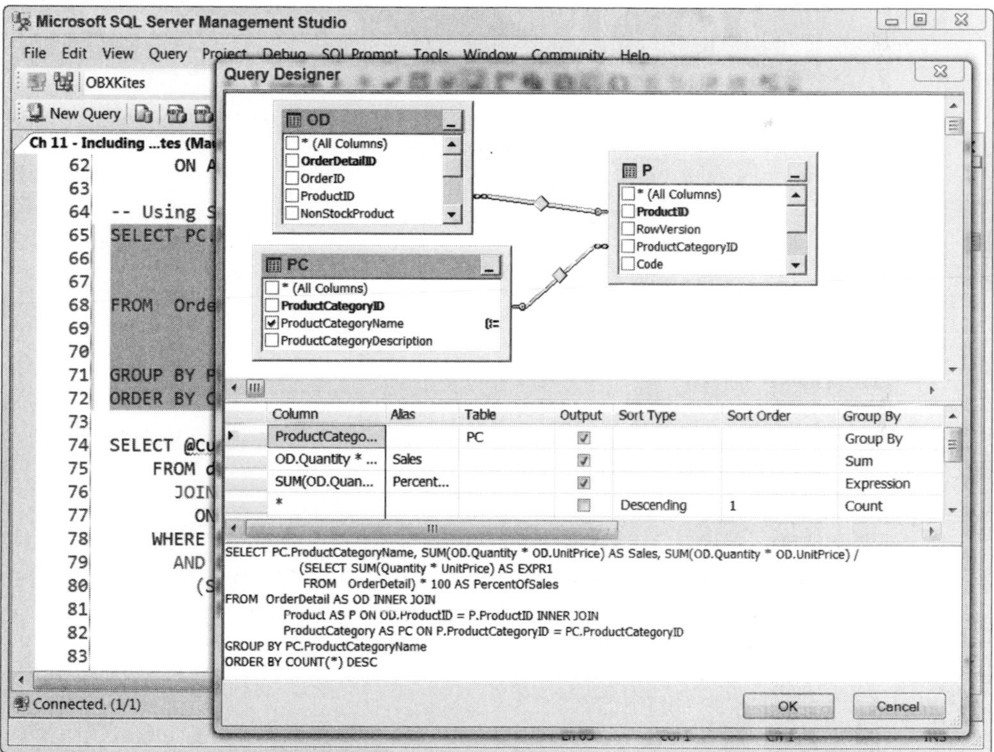

The Query Designer can perform *Data Manipulation Language (DML)* queries other than `SELECT`. The Change Type drop-down list in the Query Designer toolbar can change the query from a default `SELECT` query to the following queries: Insert Results, Insert Values, Update, Delete, or Make Table.

However, the Query Designer is no substitute for the Query Editor. Unlike the Query Editor, it cannot perform batches or non-DML commands. Nor can it execute SQL statements using F5. Table and column names can't be dragged from the Object Explorer to the SQL pane.

The Query Designer may be used to edit data directly in the results pane — a quick-and-dirty way to correct or mock up data.

Navigating the Query Designer should feel familiar to experienced Windows users. While Books Online lists several pages of keyboard shortcuts, most are standard Windows navigation commands. The one worth mentioning here is Ctrl+0, which enters a `null` into the result pane.

Object Explorer reports

No section on Object Explorer would be complete without mentioning the dozens of great reports hidden within it, one of which is shown in Figure 6-8. These reports can be found in the context menus of the Server, Database, and Security ⇨ login nodes. While I won't list every report here, they're an excellent resource and one of the most underused features of Management Studio.

FIGURE 6-8

The server or database standard reports are a great way to quickly investigate your SQL Server.

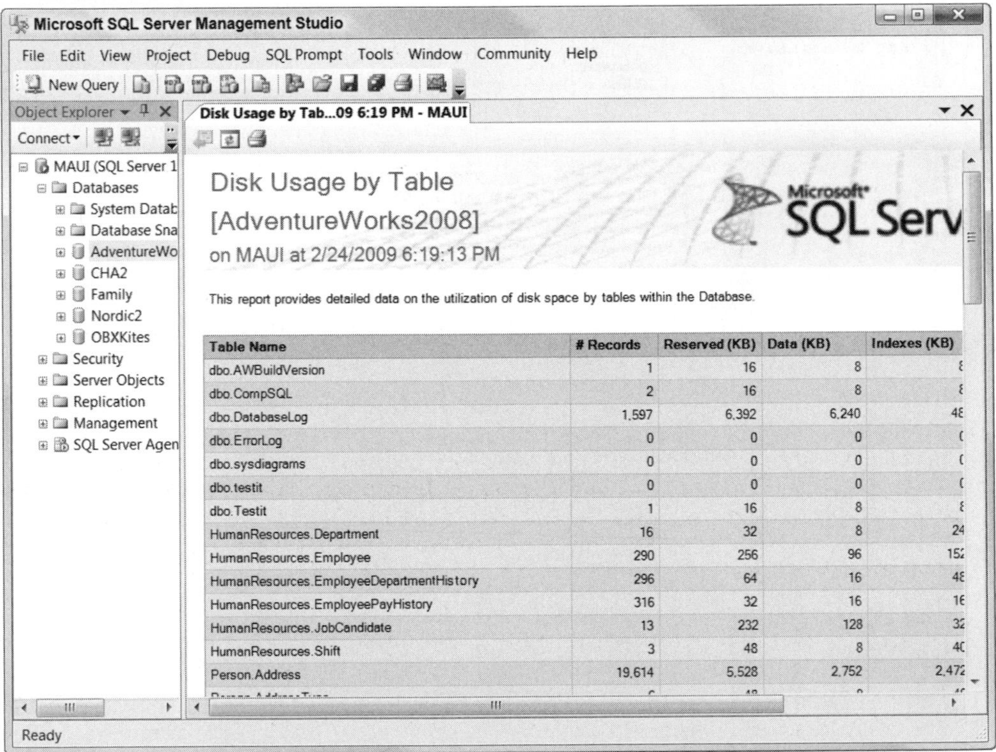

Custom reports can be installed in any Object Explorer node by placing the report definition file in the following directory: ...\Documents and Settings\{user}\Documents\SQL Server Management Studio\Custom Reports.

For more details, see `http://msdn2.microsoft.com/en-us/library/bb153684.aspx`.

Using the Query Editor

The Query Editor carries on the legacy of SQL Server's historic Query Analyzer as the primary UI for database developers. While SQL Server 2005 introduced Management Studio and the Query Editor, with SQL Server 2008, it rocks!

Opening a query connecting to a server

The Query Editor can maintain multiple open query documents and connections within the tabbed document area. In fact, different queries may be connected as different users, which is very useful for testing security. In addition, the Query Editor can open and work with a `.sql` file even when not connected to a server.

When Query Editor first opens, it prompts for an initial login. To make further connections, use the File ➪ New Connection menu command.

The New Query toolbar button opens a new Query Editor document. There's some intelligence in how it selects the current database for the new query. If Object Explorer had focus before the New Query button is pressed, then the new query is connected to Object Explorer's currently selected database. If the Query Editor had focus, then the new query opens to the same database as the Query Editor's current query.

You can also switch a query's connection to another server using the Query ➪ Connection menu, the Change Connection toolbar button, or the Query Editor's context menu.

By default, the Query tab displays the current SQL Server and database name merged with the filename; but it's too long to fit, so it's cut off in the middle.

Don't forget that with SQL Server 2008, you can now open a new query connected to multiple servers using the Registered Server's server group context menu.

TIP **In some extreme cases, if SQL Server cannot seem to accept new connections, it listens on a dedicated port for a special diagnostic connection and tries to make a connection. A Dedicated Administrator Connection (DAC) is only possible if you are a member of the server's sysadmin role. To attempt a DAC connection using Query Editor, connect to the server with a prefix of `admin:` before the server name. For example, my notebook's name is Maui, so connecting to it as `admin:maui` opens a DAC connection. DAC connections are also possible using the SQLCMD utility. For more details about the DAC connection, see Chapter 42, "Maintaining the Database."**

TIP **You can set the display color of the Query Editor's connection bar (at the bottom of the Query Editor) per connected server. This is a great visual cue. I recommend setting the development server to green and the production server to red. When connecting to a server, open the connection dialog's options and select Use Custom Color to set the color for that server.**

Opening a .sql file

There are multiple ways to open a saved query batch file, and one huge trap you want to avoid:

- If Management Studio is not open, then double-clicking a `.sql` file in Windows File Explorer will launch Management Studio, prompt you for a connection, and open the file. Here's the gotcha: If you select multiple `.sql` files in Windows File Explorer and open them as a group, Windows will launch a separate instance of Management Studio for each file — not a good thing. You'll end up running several copies of Management Studio.

- If Management Studio is already open, then double-clicking will open the file or selected files in a Query Editor document. Each file will prompt you for a connection.
- Multiple `.sql` files may be dragged from Windows File Explorer and dropped on Management Studio. Each file will open a Query Editor after prompting for a connection.
- The most recently viewed files are listed in the Files ➪ Recent Files menu. Selecting a file will open it in the Query Editor.
- The File ➪ File Open menu or toolbar command will open a dialog box to select one or more files.

Real-World Developing with the Query Editor

I admit it, I dream in T-SQL — so here are my favorite tips for using the Query Editor as a developer:

- View multiple scripts at the same time in Query Editor by right-clicking on one of the documents and selecting New Vertical Tab Group. The selected document is the one that becomes the new tab to the right.
- I usually develop using three scripts. The first script contains schema, triggers, indexes, and stored procedures. The second script is the inserts for the unit test sample data, and the third script — called ProcTest — executes every stored procedure. I like dragging the documents so that the tabs are in the correct order to run the three scripts in sequence.
- I use bookmarks liberally to save points in the script to which I'll need to refer back. For example, I'll bookmark a table's DDL code and the CRUD stored procedures for that table while I'm working on the stored procedures.
- I begin every script with `use database` and `set nocount on` (these commands are covered in Chapter 21, "Programming with T-SQL.") Every script ends with `use tempdb`. That way, if I run all the scripts, no script stays in the user database and the initial create script can easily `drop` and recreate the database.
- Line numbers can be a good thing when navigating a long script. They can be turned on by using Options – Text Editor ➪ All Languages ➪ General.
- Maybe it's just my eyes, but the default text is way too small. I find Consolas 14-point to be far more readable than the default.
- When there are more documents than can be displayed as tabs, the easy way to select the correct tab is to use the Active Documents drop-down list, at the far right of the

continued

continued

Query Editor by the close document "x" button. This is also the best way to determine whether a script is still executing, but it does sometimes reorder the tabs.

- If there's an error in the script, double-clicking on the error message jumps to a spot near the error.
- I'm compulsive about indenting, and I like indents of two spaces. I uppercase all reserved words in the outer query, and then use PascalCase (sometimes called CamelCase) for user-defined objects and reserved words in subqueries.
- IntelliSense rocks! Finally.
- I sometimes use code outlining to collapse large sections of code. The Code Outliner can collapse multi-line statements.
- IntelliSense and Code Outlining can be turned off in Options – Text Editor ➪ Transact-SQL ➪ Advanced.
- The Query Editor provides a quick visual indicator of lines that have been edited. The Track Changes Indicator displays a thin, yellow bar to the left of the line if the text is modified, and a green bar if that change has been saved.
- Use the SQLCMD toolbar button or the Query ➪ SQLCMD Mode menu command to switch the editor to work with SQLCMD utility scripts.
- While working with T-SQL code in the Query Editor, you can get Books Online (BOL) keyword help by pressing F1. Alternately, the dynamic help window in Management Studio will follow your work and display appropriate help topics as you move though the code (which is actually a bit spooky).

TIP **Out of the box, Management Studio's Query Editor does not provide automatic formatting of T-SQL. There are some free websites that enable you to submit a SQL statement and will then format the code, but I've been using SQL Prompt from Red Gate and I've come to depend on it for consistent formatting. Highly recommended.**

Shortcuts and bookmarks

Bookmarks are a great way to navigate large scripts. Bookmarks can be set manually, or automatically set using the Find command. Bookmarks work with double Control key combinations. For example, holding down the Ctrl key and pressing K and then N moves to the next bookmark. The Ctrl+K keys also control some of the other editing commands, such as commenting code. Bookmarks are also controlled using the Edit ➪ Bookmarks menu or the bookmark next and previous toolbar buttons. Table 6-1 lists the shortcuts I find especially useful.

The Bookmark window displays a list of all bookmarks and offers tools to control bookmarks, navigate bookmarks, and even change the name of a bookmark.

Bookmarks are lost if the file is simply saved as a `.sql` file, but if the query is saved within a solution in the Solution Explorer, then bookmarks are saved from session to session.

TABLE 6-1

Useful Query Editor Shortcuts

Shortcut	Description
Ctrl+Shift+R	Refresh IntelliSense
Ctrl+K+K	Add or remove a bookmark
Ctrl+K+A	Enable all bookmarks
Ctrl+K+N	Move to the next bookmark
Ctrl+K+P	Move to the previous bookmark
Ctrl+K+L	Clear all bookmarks
Ctrl+K+C	Comment the selection
Ctrl+K+U	Uncomment the selection
Ctrl+K+W	Open the Bookmark window

Query options

When a batch is sent from the Query Editor to SQL Server, several query option settings are included with the batch. The defaults for these settings can be set in Tools ➪ Options ➪ Query Execution ➪ SQL Server. The current query options can be viewed or changed in Query ➪ Query Options, as shown in Figure 6-9.

FIGURE 6-9

Advanced and ANSI query options can be viewed and set using the Query Options dialog. This view shows the Advanced Query Options.

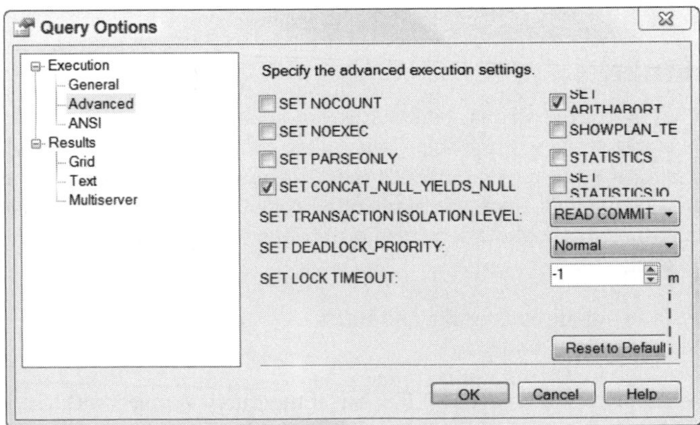

Executing SQL batches

As a developer's tool, the Query Editor is designed to execute T-SQL batches, which are collections of multiple T-SQL statements. To submit a batch to SQL Server for processing, use Query ➪ Execute Query, click the Run Query toolbar button, use the F5 key, or press Ctrl+E. (Personally, I've always wanted a large button like the Staples® Easy button plugged into USB and programmed to F5 that I can slam to execute the query.)

Because batches tend to be long, and it's often desirable to execute a single T-SQL command or a portion of the batch for testing or stepping through the code, the SQL Server team provides you with a convenient feature. If no text is highlighted, then the entire batch is executed. If text is highlighted, only that text is executed.

You'll learn more about this in Chapter 21, "Programming with T-SQL," but technically, when the Query Editor sends the script to SQL Server, it breaks it up into smaller batches separated by the batch separator – `go`.

It's worth pointing out that the Parse Query menu command and toolbar button checks only the SQL code. It does not check object names (tables, columns, stored procedures, and so on). This actually is a feature, not a bug. By not including object name–checking in the syntax check, SQL Server permits batches that create objects, and then references them.

The T-SQL batch will execute within the context of a current database. The current database is displayed, and may be changed, within the database combo box in the toolbar.

Results!

The results of the query are displayed in the bottom pane, along with the Messages tab, and optionally the Client Statistics or Query Execution Plan tabs. The Results tab format may be either text or grid; you can switch using Ctrl+T or Ctrl+D, respectively. The new format will be applied to the next batch execution.

Alternately, the results can be displayed in another tab, instead of at the bottom of the query document. In Options, use the Query Results ➪ SQL Server ➪ Results to Grid tab, or the Query context menu Results tab and choose the "Display results in a separate tab" option.

Another useful result option is to play the Windows default beep sound file when a query completes. This can only be set in the Query ➪ Option, Query Results ➪ SQL Server tab.

SQL Server 2000's Query Editor had a toolbar button to open or close the results pane. It disappeared with SQL Server 2005, but Ctrl+R still toggles the Query Editor results pane. The command is still in the Customize Toolbar dialog, so you can fix the toolbar if you'd like. It's called Show Results Pane, and it's not in the Query category where you'd expect to find it, but hiding in the Window category.

Viewing query execution plans

One of Query Editor's most significant features is its ability to graphically view query execution plans (see Figure 6-10).

FIGURE 6-10

Query Editor's ability to graphically display the execution plan of a query is perhaps its most useful feature.

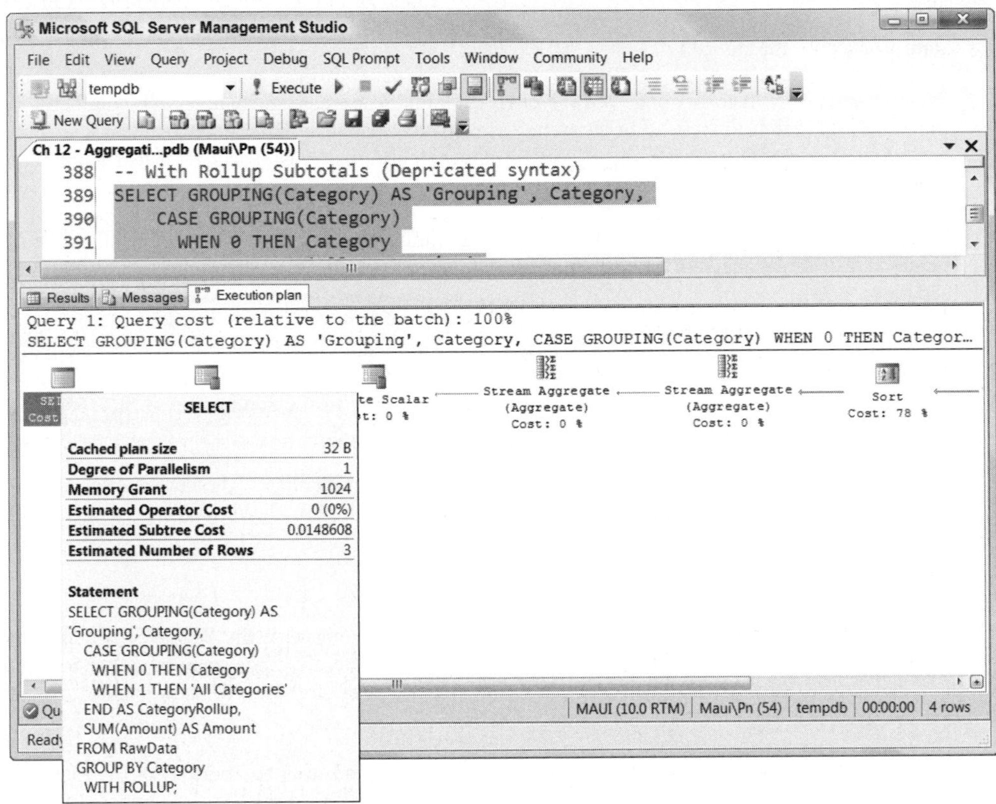

What makes the query execution plans even more important is that SQL is a descriptive language, so it doesn't tell the Query Optimizer exactly how to get the data, but only which data to retrieve. While some performance tuning can be applied to the way the query is stated, most of the tuning is accomplished by adjusting the indexes, which greatly affects how the Query Optimizer can compile the query. The query execution plan reveals how SQL Server will optimize the query, take advantage of indexes, pull data from other data sources, and perform joins. Reading the query execution plans and understanding their interaction with the database schema and indexes is both a science and an art.

CROSS-REF **Chapter 63, "Interpreting Query Execution Plans," includes a full discussion on reading the query execution plan.**

Query Editor can display either an estimated query execution plan prior to executing the query or the actual plan after the query is run. Both display the exact same plan, the only difference (besides the wait) is that the actual plan can display both the estimated and actual row counts for each operation, whereas the estimated query execution plan provides only the estimated row count.

In addition to the query execution plan, the Query Editor can display the client statistics, which is a quick way to see the server execution times for the batch (although Profiler is a much better tool for detail work.) Enable Include Client Statistics using the Query menu or toolbar to add this tab to the results.

Using the Solution Explorer

The optional Solution Explorer enables you to organize files and connections within *solutions*, which contain *projects*, similar to the Solution Explorer in Visual Studio. You don't need to use it; File ➪ Open and Save work well without Solution Explorer, but if you work on several database projects, you may find that Solution Explorer helps keep your life organized — or at least your code organized. You can find Solution Explorer in the View menu, and the Solution Explorer icon may be added to the Standard toolbar using the Customize toolbar.

To use Solution Explorer for managing query scripts, use the Solution Explorer context menu to create a new project. This will create the nodes and directories for the files. Once the project exists, use it to create new queries.

Other than simply organizing your project, Solution Explorer offers two practical benefits. One, if queries are saved within a solution, bookmarks are retained. Two, Solution Explorer can be used with source control.

Visual SourceSafe Integration

It's possible to integrate Solution Explorer with Visual Studio SourceSafe or a third-party version control utility to provide solid document management and version control.

When source control is installed and enabled, scripts under the control of Solution Explorer will automatically use the source control. The following commands are added to Solution Explorer's object context menu:

- Check Out for Edit
- Get Latest Version
- Compare
- Get
- View History
- Undo Checkout

Whether you use SourceSafe or integrate Management Studio with source control, I strongly suggest that you use some method of checking your scripts into source control.

Jump-Starting Code with Templates

Management Studio templates are useful because they provide a starting point when programming new types of code and they help make the code consistent.

Using templates

To use a template, open the Template Explorer, select a template, and double-click. This will open a new query in the Query Editor using code from the template.

You can also drag a template from the Template Explorer to an open Query and deposit the template code into the query.

The new query will likely include several template parameters. Rather than edit these in text, you can use a dialog box by selecting Query ➪ Specify Values for Template Parameters (Crtl+Shift+M). Sorry, but I didn't find any way to automatically open this dialog, which has an entry for every parameter and automatically fills in the parameters within the query. If you make an error, the only way to go back is to undo each parameter change (Ctrl+Z).

Managing templates

The templates are simply stored SQL scripts within a directory structure, which means it's easy to create your own templates or modify the existing ones. Simply save the `.SQL` scripts in the following directory:

```
...\Documents and Settings\{user}\Application Data\Microsoft\
Microsoft SQL Server\100\Tools\Shell\Templates\
```

There's more to saving templates than meets the eye. A common copy is stored here:

```
%ProgramFiles%\Microsoft
SQLServer\100\Tools\Binn\
VSShell\Common7\IDE\sqlworkbenchprojectitems
```

When Management Studio launches, it checks the two folders and any template in the common folder that's not in the local folder is copied to the local user folder.

To add parameters to your custom templates, add the parameter name, the type, and the default value inside angle brackets, like this:

```
<parameter name, data type, default value>
```

The data type is optional.

For developers or organizations desiring consistency in their own development styles or standards, I highly recommend taking advantage of Management Studio's templates.

Summary

Management Studio's Object Explorer and Query Editor are the two primary DBA and developer interfaces for SQL Server. Mastering the navigation of both these tools is vital to your success with SQL Server.

Here are the few chapter takeaways:

- Management Studio can be visually intimidating — so many windows. I recommend closing any window not needed for the task at hand. Remove the distractions and get the job done.
- If you upgraded from SQL Server 2005 and haven't taken the time to explore the new Management Studio, you're missing some of the best parts of SQL Server 2008.
- You may not need Registered Servers. It's only useful if you have a lot of servers.
- Management Studio offers a scalable experience. The accidental DBA can use the wizards and GUI, while the master DBA can work with raw T-SQL, DMV, and wait states.
- The T-SQL Debugger is back!
- As the Query Editor is really the place where T-SQL happens, take the time to master its little features, such as bookmarks, in order to get the most out of SQL Server.
- IntelliSense takes some getting used to, but when mastered, it's great.
- Query Editor can now connect to multiple servers from a single tab — very useful for server farm management.

The next chapter rounds out Part I, "Laying the Foundation," with a new interface for SQL Server that holds a lot of promise for the power DBA: PowerShell.

Chapter 7

Scripting with PowerShell

PowerShell is the new scripting environment for the Microsoft Windows platform. For administrators who don't have access to the Visual Studio environment, or for the IT professional who prefers scripting to compiled code, PowerShell provides access to most of the .NET Framework and the objects available within it. PowerShell is available as a free download from Microsoft at `www.microsoft.com/powershell/`. It's also automatically installed when SQL Server 2008 is installed, unless it's already present. PowerShell is included with the Windows Server 2008 and later operating systems, but must be installed on Windows 2003, Windows XP (SP2 or later), and Windows Vista. It will not run on operating systems earlier than those mentioned here.

PowerShell was introduced in late 2006 to enable administrators to develop scripts for automating processes they did regularly. Prior to the introduction of PowerShell, most administrators used command-line batch files, VBScript, or some third-party proprietary application designed for this function.

Batch files had somewhat limited functionality, and significant security problems. It was easy using batch files to "hijack" actual operating system commands by creating a batch file with the same name and placing it in a directory in the PATH environment variable, or in the current directory. Batch files also suffer significant limitations with regard to iterative processes.

VBScript was a better solution to the problem of iterative processes and provided interfaces to many of the server products offered, but it lacked consistency and was reliant on the COM object model. The introduction of the .NET Framework rendered the COM object model obsolete (or nearly so).

PowerShell addresses these limitations through a strong security foundation that prevents command-line hijacking by only allowing the user (by default) to run digitally signed scripts, and by forcing the user to specify the directory for each command run from the script environment. It also supports the .NET Framework (2.0 and later), so the functionality built in the framework is available in this scripting environment.

IN THIS CHAPTER

Introduction to PowerShell and PowerShell Scripting

Using PowerShell with SMO to automate SQL Server administration

Using PowerShell to extract SQL Server data

New SQL Server 2008 PowerShell features

Why Use PowerShell?

In today's business world it's important to get as much done in as little time as possible. The most successful people are finding ways to automate every repetitive task for which they're responsible. Consistency is important when automating tasks so that every administrator on the team is equally capable of stepping in to help other team members when necessary.

Microsoft has designated PowerShell as part of its *common engineering criteria (CEC)* for all server products. This means that an administrator who's responsible for Exchange or Active Directory will probably have spent time learning PowerShell, and scripts written to manage SQL Server using PowerShell can be understood by administrators without specific SQL Server knowledge. Companies will be able to run more efficiently with this common scripting language and administrators with skills in PowerShell will be more valuable to their companies.

Basic PowerShell

PowerShell, like any language, consists of commands, variables, functions, flow control methods, and other features necessary to enable work to be done. Because it is an interpreted language, the scripts don't have to be compiled into an executable form to be run.

Language features

A *cmdlet* (command-let) is a command-line utility built into PowerShell to provide some functionality. These cmdlets use a verb-noun naming convention, so it's fairly easy to understand what they're doing. Microsoft has provided about 130 built-in cmdlets with the default installation of PowerShell (1.0), and additional cmdlets are installed depending on various server products that may be running. PowerShell 2.0 is expected in mid-2009, but because it wasn't ready for release when SQL Server 2008 was shipped, the focus of this chapter is on PowerShell 1.0. (Version 2.0 expands the PowerShell language and introduces an integrated development environment, similar to Visual Studio.)

Cmdlets are frequently aliased. In other words, a different command can be entered to run the cmdlet, rather than using its own name. For example, when browsing a directory, the PowerShell cmdlet to view the contents of the current directory is `Get-ChildItem`. Users of the DOS operating system (or `cmd.exe` on current windows systems) are familiar with the `dir` command, and Unix users are familiar with the `ls` command. All three of these commands do the same thing, and both `dir` and `ls` are included with PowerShell as aliases of the `Get-ChildItem` cmdlet.

A feature of Unix shell scripting environments is the capability to "pipe" the results of one command into another command's input buffer. This is a feature of shell scripting that makes it so powerful — the ability to string multiple commands together to provide information quickly. PowerShell provides this ability, but differs from Unix shell scripting in that the Unix pipe sends text from one command to another, whereas PowerShell pipes objects from one cmdlet to another. Unix scripts must parse the text from one command using commands such as `grep`, `awk`, and `sed` to format the text in a form the next command expects. PowerShell's objects are understood by the receiving cmdlet and no such parsing is required.

The PowerShell environment can be started in a number of different ways:

- Select the Start button ➪ Programs ➪ Windows PowerShell 1.0, and then select Windows PowerShell.
- From the `cmd.exe` command line, the "powershell" command will launch the environment as well.
- There's also the new SQL Server wrapper called `sqlps.exe`, which is discussed later in the chapter.

The examples here are based on the standard `powershell.exe` environment. Normally, in the PowerShell environment, the user is informed of this by the prompt "`PS>`" at the beginning of the line where the next command is to be entered.

Here's an example of using a series of cmdlets, piping the results of one to the next, and then filtering the results to get useful information. In this set of commands, the `get-process` command is used to return a set of all processes on the system, pipe the results into a sort on the size of the workingset, or the amount of memory each process is using, in descending order, and then select just the first 10, returning the biggest memory hogs on the system:

```
get-process | sort-object workingset -descending |
select-object -first 10
```

Notice that PowerShell is not case sensitive. In addition, the alias `sort` could have been used instead of the proper name of `sort-object`, and `select` could have been used instead of `select-object`. This set of commands produces results like this:

```
Handles  NPM(K)    PM(K)      WS(K) VM(M)   CPU(s)     Id ProcessName
-------  ------    -----      ----- -----   ------     -- -----------
    637      82   163668     157312  1228   232.92   2132 sqlservr
    535      80   120208     117256  1225   261.53   1344 sqlservr
    562      18    99972      77364   357   457.14   3580 Ssms
    598      11    52048      50352   179    57.86   4012 powershell
    308      73    61612      45740  1155   156.54    728 sqlservr
    602      17    57452      37956   255   298.60   1400 Reporting
                                                          ServicesService
    494      10    26636      33144   155     5.93   3308 SQLPS
    713      46    36704      27984   210   241.31   1264 msmdsrv
   1011      42    12872      19556    80   144.29    808 svchost
    158       4    12248      13272   104     2.22   1204 MsDtsSrvr
```

PowerShell variables are declared by preceding the variable name with the dollar sign ($) character. Variables are really objects of a particular type, and that data type can be created by preceding the variable name with the data type in brackets ([]). For example, a variable called `$counter` that's an integer object can be created and set to a value of 7 as follows:

```
PS> $counter = 7
```

However, a string object variable with the value of `'7'` can be created as follows:

```
PS> [string] $counter = '7'
```

Variables can also contain objects or collections. Collections are just a group of objects, such as an array. It's easy to create a collection just by assigning a list of values to a variable, like this:

```
PS> $stuff = 1,2,4,6,8
```

The list of numbers is grouped into a collection of integer objects and placed in the variable `$stuff`. Individual elements within the collection can be accessed by using their ordinal number:

```
PS> $stuff[2]
4
PS>
```

Addressing individual elements of an array is nice, but the power of collections is realized by being able to iterate through the members of the collection. PowerShell offers two versions of `foreach` logic, the first being a cmdlet to which a collection is piped, like this:

```
PS> $stuff | foreach-object {write-output $_}
1
2
4
6
8
```

Notice the variable $_, which is defined as the current object in the set of objects the cmdlet is iterating through. The other version is the `foreach` language element, which enables naming of the member:

```
PS> foreach ($thing in $stuff) {write-output $thing}
1
2
4
6
8
```

Now, within the script block operating on the members of the collection, conditions can be checked. For example, if the script should only operate on elements with a value not greater than 4, the script would read as follows:

```
PS> $stuff | foreach-object { if ($_ -gt 4) {break}
else {write-output $_}}
1
2
4
```

Table 7-1 shows most of the comparison operators within PowerShell.

TABLE 7-1

Comparison Operators

Operator	Description
-lt	less than
-le	less than or equal to
-gt	greater than
-ge	greater than or equal to
-eq	equal to
-ne	not equal to
-like	like wildcard pattern matching

Suppose you have a text file called `servers.txt` that contains a list of servers, one server name per line. The file might resemble something like this:

```
SQLTBWS
SQLTBXP
SQLTBW7
SQLPROD1
SQLPROD2
```

By using the `Get-Content` cmdlet, this list of servers can easily be brought into a PowerShell variable as a collection by issuing the following command:

```
$servers = Get-Content 'servers.txt'
```

Each element in the collection can be addressed by its ordinal number, so the first item is referenced by `$servers[0]`, the second item by `$servers[1]`, and so on. This ability to create collections will come in handy later in this discussion.

Comments, always good in any language, are specified in PowerShell 1.0 by using the pound (#) character, with the comments following that character on the line. (PowerShell 2.0 will support an additional comment operator, enabling multi-line comments, e.g., `<# Multi-Line Comment #>`.)

Referencing the `$servers` collection, each element in the collection is a string object, and string objects have a `Length` property, so the element can be tested to determine whether it has a value using the following commands:

```
if ($servers[0].Length -gt 0) {
  #work
  }
```

Control flow is handled by the commands shown in Table 7-2.

To help with logic flow, PowerShell provides a group of "object" cmdlets, as shown in Table 7-3.

For example, in the earlier example of the `$servers` collection, the collection can be iterated through using the following commands:

```
$servers | Foreach-Object {
    Write-Output $_
    }
```

TABLE 7-2

Control Flow Commands

If	`if ($val -eq "target") {`
	`  #work`
	`  }`

For	`For ($i=0; $i -lt 10; $i++) {`
	`  #work`
	`  }`

Switch	`Switch ($val) {`
	`  "Val1" {`
	`          #work`
	`          }`
	`  "Val2" {`
	`          #work`
	`          }`
	`  }`

Do Until	`Do {`
	`  #work`
	`  }`
	`  Until ($val -eq "target")`

Do While	`Do {`
	`  #work`
	`  }`
	`  While ($val -eq "target")`

While	`While ($val -eq "target") {`
	`  #work`
	`  }`

TABLE 7-3

Object cmdlets in PowerShell

Cmdlet	Alias	Description
ForEach-Object	%	Executes once for each member in the collection
Where-Object	?	Filters objects based on conditions
Select-Object	select	Pipes only the specified properties
Sort-Object	sort	Sorts the objects
Tee-Object	tee	Sends the objects in two directions

These cmdlets will be very useful when scripting. For example, they enable iteration through a collection of properties in objects, as shown here:

```
get-service | where-object {$_.Status -eq "Running"}
```

The preceding produced the following results:

```
Status   Name                DisplayName
------   ----                -----------
Running  1-vmsrvc            Virtual Machine Additions Services ...
Running  AeLookupSvc         Application Experience Lookup Service
Running  Browser             Computer Browser
Running  CryptSvc            Cryptographic Services
Running  DcomLaunch          DCOM Server Process Launcher
Running  Dhcp                DHCP Client
Running  dmserver            Logical Disk Manager
Running  Dnscache            DNS Client
Running  ERSvc               Error Reporting Service
Running  Eventlog            Event Log
Running  EventSystem         COM+ Event System
Running  helpsvc             Help and Support
Running  HTTPFilter          HTTP SSL
Running  lanmanserver        Server
Running  lanmanworkstation   Workstation
Running  LmHosts             TCP/IP NetBIOS Helper
Running  MSDTC               Distributed Transaction Coordinator
Running  MsDtsServer100      SQL Server Integration Services 10.0
Running  MSOLAP$INST01       SQL Server Analysis Services (INST01)
Running  MSSQL$INST01        SQL Server (INST01)
Running  MSSQL$INST02        SQL Server (INST02)
```

In this example, PowerShell sifts through the current services on the system and returns only those services that are currently running. Note the braces ({}) delimiting the operation of the `where-object` cmdlet. These braces allow embedded operations within loop-type structures; and together with the script content between them, are referred to as a *script block*.

NOTE **Most important, help is always available using the `Get-Help` cmdlet. It can also be called using the `help` or `man` aliases. Either way, help can be obtained for any cmdlet; and it will return syntax, description, and related links. `Get-Help` has options to return normal, full, detailed, or examples.**

To get help on any cmdlet, type **Get-Help** followed by the cmdlet. To get help on `Get-Help`, type the following:

```
PS> Get-Help Get-Help
NAME
    Get-Help

SYNOPSIS
    Displays information about Windows PowerShell cmdlets and concepts.


SYNTAX
    Get-Help [[-name] <string>] [-component <string[]>]
[-functionality <string[]>] [-role <string[]>] [-category <stri
    ng[]>] [-full] [<CommonParameters>]

    Get-Help [[-name] <string>] [-component <string[]>]
[-functionality <string[]>] [-role <string[]>] [-category <stri
    ng[]>] [-detailed] [<CommonParameters>]

    Get-Help [[-name] <string>] [-component <string[]>]
[-functionality <string[]>] [-role <string[]>] [-category <stri
    ng[]>] [-examples] [<CommonParameters>]

    Get-Help [[-name] <string>] [-component <string[]>]
[-functionality <string[]>] [-role <string[]>] [-category <stri
    ng[]>] [-parameter <string>] [<CommonParameters>]


DETAILED DESCRIPTION
    The Get-Help cmdlet displays information about Windows PowerShell
cmdlets and concepts. You can also use "Help {<cm
    dlet name> | <topic-name>" or "<cmdlet-name> /?".
"Help" displays the help topics one page at a time. The "/?" disp
    lays help for cmdlets on a single page.


RELATED LINKS
    Get-Command
    Get-PSDrive
    Get-Member
```

```
REMARKS
    For more information, type: "get-help Get-Help -detailed".
    For technical information, type: "get-help Get-Help -full".
```

Creating scripts

While it's sometimes useful to enter ad hoc commands into PowerShell to evaluate system state or other information, the real power of PowerShell comes with writing scripts. A good collection of scripts to perform normal administrative functions is a sign of an effective administrator.

For example it's a good idea to have information about the physical servers on which SQL Server is running. Windows Management Instrumentation (WMI) provides this information through simple queries, available to PowerShell through the `Get-WMIObject` cmdlet (aliased as `gwmi`). A simple script to gather this information is shown in Listing 7-1. In this script, four different WMI classes are polled, and their results are piped into the `select-object` cmdlet (aliased as `select`), where the specific properties needed are retrieved. Those results are then piped into the `format-list` cmdlet for presentation.

LISTING 7-1

Get System Info

```
#getsysinfo.ps1
# Use WMI queries to retrieve information about the computer, operating
# system and disk devices

gwmi -query "select * from Win32_ComputerSystem" | select Name, Model,
  Manufacturer, Description, DNSHostName, Domain, DomainRole,
  PartOfDomain, NumberOfProcessors, SystemType, TotalPhysicalMemory,
  UserName, Workgroup | format-list


gwmi -query "select * from Win32_OperatingSystem" | select Name,
  Version, FreePhysicalMemory, OSLanguage, OSProductSuite, OSType,
  ServicePackMajorVersion, ServicePackMinorVersion | format-list

gwmi -query "select * from Win32_PhysicalMemory" | select Name,
  Capacity, DeviceLocator, Tag | format-table -Autosize

gwmi -query "select * from Win32_LogicalDisk where
  DriveType=3" | select Name, FreeSpace, Size | format-table -Autosize
```

When this script is run on a server it will return results like this:

```
Name                 : SQLTBWS
Model                : Virtual Machine
Manufacturer         : Microsoft Corporation
Description          : AT/AT COMPATIBLE
DNSHostName          : sqltbws
```

```
Domain              : WORKGROUP
DomainRole          : 2
PartOfDomain        : False
NumberOfProcessors  : 1
SystemType          : X86-based PC
TotalPhysicalMemory : 1073192960
UserName            : SQLTBWS\Administrator
Workgroup           :

Name                    : Microsoft Windows Server 2003 R2
Enterprise Edition|C:\WINDOWS|
Version                 : 5.2.3790
FreePhysicalMemory      : 340816
OSLanguage              : 1033
OSProductSuite          : 274
OSType                  : 18
ServicePackMajorVersion : 2
ServicePackMinorVersion : 0

Name            Capacity DeviceLocator Tag
----            -------- ------------- ---
Physical Memory 16777216 DIMM1         Physical Memory 0
Physical Memory 16777216 DIMM2         Physical Memory 1
Physical Memory 16777216 DIMM2         Physical Memory 2
Physical Memory 16777216 DIMM2         Physical Memory 3

Name   FreeSpace         Size
----   ---------         ----
C:   60792463360 68705730560
E:   16124747776 17173573632
F:   17087807488 17173573632
```

Anytime a set of commands will be used repeatedly, it's useful to encapsulate those commands in a function. Functions must be defined before they can be used, because PowerShell is an interpretive language and doesn't "read ahead" to see what functions might be defined later.

Best Practice

Begin all PowerShell scripts with the set of functions that will be used in the script, with the main part of the script listed at the very end. PowerShell cannot forward-reference function code, so the function must have been read before it's called in the main part of the script.

The basic format of a function is as follows:

```
Function MyFunction {
    #work
    }
```

This, of course, doesn't do anything. Between the braces the real work needs to be coded, but most often functions need parameters. You can add functions in a number of ways, but two ways are most commonly used. The first, most obvious, format is like this:

```
Function MyFunction ($param) {
    #work
    }
```

This works fine, but the recommended method is to use a `param` block within the function, which enables the specification of multiple parameters, the specification of the data type for each parameter, and even default values for each parameter:

```
Function MyFunction {
    param (
           [int]$x = 7,
           [int]$y = 9
           )
    #work
    }
```

The `GetSysInfo.ps1` script shown in Listing 7-1 is useful when run on an individual server, but would be even more so if it could be run against all servers in the data center. By putting the working code from `GetSysInfo.ps1` into a function (and adding the `-computername` parameter to each `Get-WMIObject` command within the function to specify which server to run the command against) it's possible to iterate through the set of servers in the `$servers` collection discussed earlier.

Listing 7-2 shows exactly how to do this. The function with the calls to the four WMI classes is defined first, followed by the main part of the script. Note that before attempting to get the server information, the main part of the script uses the WMI class `Win32_PingStatus` to determine whether the computer is reachable through the network. This saves time because the script doesn't attempt to run the four main queries against a server that doesn't respond.

LISTING 7-2

ServerStatus.ps1

```
function getwmiinfo ($svr) {
    gwmi -query "select * from
        Win32_ComputerSystem" -computername $svr | select Name,
        Model, Manufacturer, Description, DNSHostName,
        Domain, DomainRole, PartOfDomain, NumberOfProcessors,
```

```
            SystemType, TotalPhysicalMemory, UserName,
            Workgroup | format-list

        gwmi -query "select * from
            Win32_OperatingSystem" -computername $svr | select Name,
            Version, FreePhysicalMemory, OSLanguage, OSProductSuite,
            OSType, ServicePackMajorVersion,
            ServicePackMinorVersion | format-list

        gwmi -query "select * from
            Win32_PhysicalMemory" -computername $svr | select
            Name, Capacity, DeviceLocator, Tag | format-table -Autosize

        gwmi -query "select * from Win32_LogicalDisk
            where DriveType=3" -computername $svr | select Name, FreeSpace,
            Size | format-table -Autosize

}

$servers = get-content 'servers.txt'

foreach ($server in $servers) {
    $results = gwmi -query "select StatusCode from Win32_PingStatus
        where Address = '$server'"
    $responds = $false
    foreach ($result in $results) {
        if ($result.statuscode -eq 0) {
            $responds = $true
            break
        }
    }

    if ($responds) {
        getwmiinfo $server
    } else {
        Write-Output "$server does not respond"
    }
}
```

The results of this script look like this:

```
Name                  : SQLTBWS
Model                 : Virtual Machine
Manufacturer          : Microsoft Corporation
Description           : AT/AT COMPATIBLE
DNSHostName           : sqltbws
Domain                : WORKGROUP
DomainRole            : 2
```

```
PartOfDomain        : False
NumberOfProcessors  : 1
SystemType          : X86-based PC
TotalPhysicalMemory : 1073192960
UserName            : SQLTBWS\Administrator
Workgroup           :

Name                    : Microsoft Windows Server 2003 R2
Enterprise Edition|C:\WINDOWS|
Version                 : 5.2.3790
FreePhysicalMemory      : 341320
OSLanguage              : 1033
OSProductSuite          : 274
OSType                  : 18
ServicePackMajorVersion : 2
ServicePackMinorVersion : 0

Name            Capacity DeviceLocator Tag
----            -------- ------------- ---
Physical Memory 16777216 DIMM1         Physical Memory 0
Physical Memory 16777216 DIMM2         Physical Memory 1
Physical Memory 16777216 DIMM2         Physical Memory 2
Physical Memory 16777216 DIMM2         Physical Memory 3

Name   FreeSpace        Size
----   ---------        ----
C:   60792463360 68705730560
E:   16124743680 17173573632
F:   17088528384 17173573632

SQLTBXP does not respond
SQLTBW7 does not respond
SQLPROD1 does not respond
SQLPROD2 does not respond
```

NOTE **The day after I wrote this script for this book, I was on a consulting engagement that called for collecting server data for more than 70 SQL Server instances, and I was able to use this script as a starting point for my data collection. After I completed the script I wrote an article about it for the *Simple-Talk* newsletter. The article is available at** `www.simple-talk.com/sql/database-administration/let-powershell-do-an-inventory-of-your-servers/`.

Errors are handled using a `Trap` function. The Try-Catch mechanism for error handling will be added to PowerShell in version 2.0, but for the time being the best method is to create a `Trap` function at the beginning of the script, like this:

```
Function Error_Handler {
  $errmsg = "Error Category: " + $error[0].CategoryInfo.Category
  $errmsg = $errmsg + ". Error Object: " + $error[0].TargetObject
```

```
  $errmsg = $errmsg + " Error Message: " + $error[0].Exception.Message
  $errmsg = $errmsg + " Error Message: " +
$error[0].FullyQualifiedErrorId

  $log = New-Object System.Diagnostics.EventLog('Application')
  $log.set_source("MyPowerShellScript")
  $log.WriteEntry($errmsg)
  }

Trap {
  # Handle the error
  Error_Handler
  # End the program.
  break;
  }
# Your code here
```

Then, the event log can be queried using the following cmdlet:

```
get-Eventlog application | where-Object {$_.Message -like
"Error*"} | format-Table
```

This enables consistent notification of errors in PowerShell scripts.

Communicating with SQL Server

The two main reasons for communicating with SQL Server are to manage the server and to use the data contained on the server in some way. Not only are administrators expected to manage the server efficiently, they're also frequently asked to extract some corporate data to send to another application, to make quick updates to correct a problem, or other such requests. SQL Server management can be done from PowerShell or any other .NET language using the Server Management Objects library, and the data can be accessed using ADO.NET.

SQL Server Management Objects

SQL Server Management Objects (SMO) and its related sisters (RMO for Replication Management Objects and AMO for Analysis Services Management Objects) are object libraries that provide a programmatic way to manage Microsoft SQL. SMO can be used to manage SQL Server 2000, 2005, and 2008. It was introduced with SQL Server 2005, but supports the management of SQL Server 2000 instances as well. SMO was built using the .NET Framework, so the objects it exposes are available in PowerShell.

SMO has been designed to be easier to use and more efficient than its predecessor DMO (Distributed Management Objects). For example, when returning the collection of databases for a server, SMO will only return the name and the schema for the databases on the server. DMO would return the fully instantiated collections of every database on that server, taking time to both populate that entire collection and increase the network bandwidth required to pass it over the wire.

Before using SMO within PowerShell, the SMO assembly must be loaded into the environment. If PowerShell is started from within SQL Server Management Studio or from SQL Server Agent, the `sqlps.exe` program is run, not basic PowerShell. `Sqlps.exe` is discussed later in this chapter. When running the native PowerShell environment interactively, the following commands are required:

```
  [System.Reflection.Assembly]::LoadWithPartialName('Microsoft
.SqlServer.SMO')  | out-null
[System.Reflection.Assembly]::LoadWithPartialName('Microsoft
.SqlServer.SMOExtended')  | out-null
```

If SMO objects are going to be loaded on a regular basis, these commands can be loaded into a profile file. User profiles are generally loaded into `%UserProfile%\My Documents\WindowsPowerShell\Microsoft.PowerShell_profile.ps1`, where `%UserProfile%` is usually in `c:\Users\username`.

The results of the command are piped to the `out-null` device because the version number of the library is generally not needed.

After loading the SMO libraries, it's easy to connect to a server (using Windows Authentication) by issuing the following command:

```
$sqlsvr = new-object ('Microsoft.SqlServer.Management
.Smo.Server') 'MyServer'
```

The `$sqlsvr` variable now contains a `Server` object for the `MyServer` instance of SQL Server. The properties and methods of the `Server` object can be seen by piping the variable into the `Get-Member` cmdlet:

```
$sqlsvr | Get-Member
```

The SMO object library is best represented in a chart for ease in understanding. The basic object is the `Server` object, and managing the server starts with connecting to that object. For example, the SMO objects used in managing user databases is shown in Figure 7-1.

Creating databases and database objects using SMO may seem counterintuitive, as usually these objects are created using Transact-SQL scripts, but automating the processes that create the objects can provide consistency in an area that is usually quite inconsistent.

FIGURE 7-1

Database objects

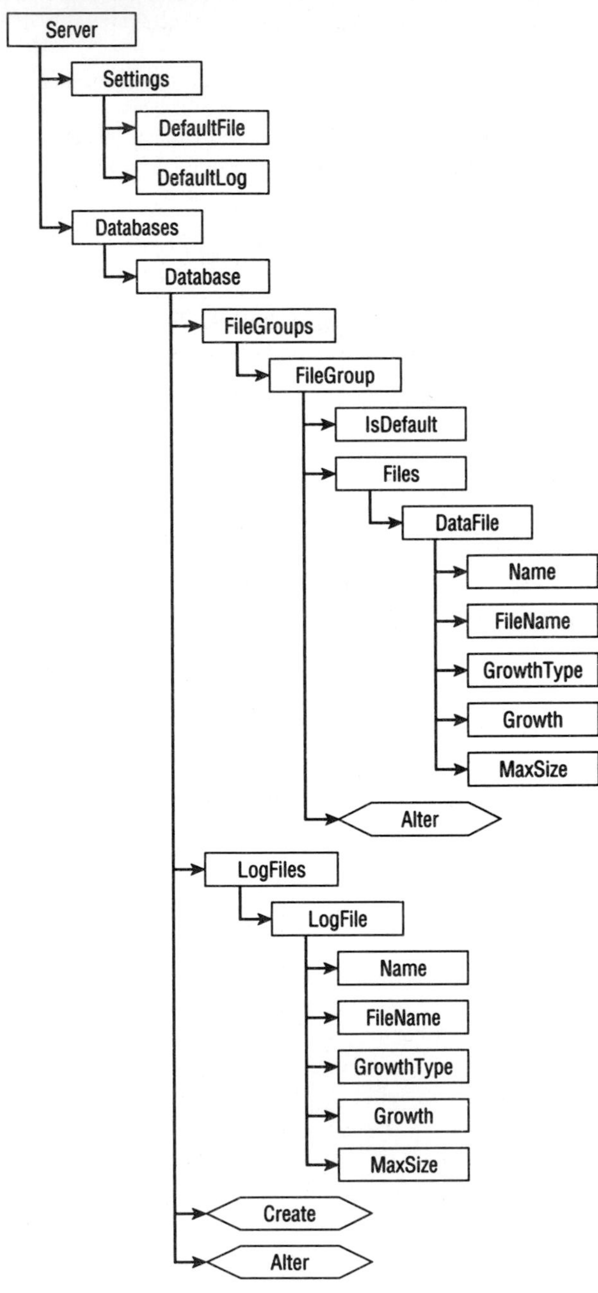

SQL Server requires that a database have a PRIMARY filegroup and that the system tables (the database meta-data) reside in that filegroup. It is recommended that you keep your application data out of the PRIMARY filegroup, both from a manageability perspective and a performance perspective. When creating a database using SQL Server Management Studio (SSMS), it can be tedious to create a database with the desired size and file location and with a separate, default filegroup to hold the application data. This is a relatively simple process using SMO.

Best Practice

Don't place application data in the primary filegroup, because the size and location of application file groups are easier to control and manage, especially as the size of the database grows. The database metadata must exist in the primary filegroup, and once the primary filegroup is online, the database is considered available. As each additional filegroup becomes available, the data within it is usable by applications, but smaller, discrete filegroups can improve the overall uptime for the application data.

Listing 7-3 shows the script to create a database. The example database is a database called `MyAppDB`, which will have a 5MB file in the primary filegroup to hold the database metadata. This file will be allowed to grow by 25% when required, but it shouldn't be required. The percentage or fixed growth size chosen depends on the actual usage history for the application, but a growth size too small can cause excessive fragmentation, and a growth size too large can take too much time when the autogrow event occurs. The logical name `MyAppDB_SysData` will be used for this file and it will be placed in the default data path for the server.

The application data will be located in a second filegroup called `AppFG`, which will then be set to be the default filegroup for the database. The filegroup will contain one file with a logical name of `MyAppDB_AppData` and will also be housed in the default data path for the server. The initial size will be set to 25MB and it will be allowed to grow by 25% each time it is required, but set a maximum size of 100MB.

Log files in SQL Server do not use filegroups, so a log file named `MyAppDB_Log` will be added to the `LogFiles` collection of the database, and it will be housed in the default log file path for the server. Its initial size will be set to 10MB and it will be allowed to grow by 25% each time it is required, but you won't set a maximum size for the log file.

Once the structural objects have been created for the database, the `Create()` method is executed, but SQL Server automatically sets the default filegroup to primary when a database is created. Once it has been created, the script sets the default filegroup to `AppFG` using the `Alter()` method at both the FileGroup and Database levels. Because of a bug in SMO, the `DefaultFile` and `DefaultLog` properties in the Server object's `Settings` collection don't properly initialize. Therefore, the script places the files in the same location as the master database data and log files, as defined in the `MasterDBPath` and `MasterDBLogPath` properties in the `Server` object's `Information` collection.

LISTING 7-3

CreateDB.ps1

```
#createdb.ps1
#Creates a new database using our specifications
[System.Reflection.Assembly]::LoadWithPartialName('Microsoft.SqlServer.SMO')
| out-null

# Instantiate a new SMO Server object and connect to server SQLTBWS\INST01
$s =
  new-object ('Microsoft.SqlServer.Management.Smo.Server') 'SQLTBWS\INST01'
$dbname = 'SMO_DB'

# Set the database logical and physical names
$syslogname = $dbname + '_SysData'
$applogname = $dbname + '_AppData'
$loglogname = $dbname + '_Log'

# An SMO bug in SQL 2005 and SQL 2008 cause the default locations to possibly
be null
$fileloc = $s.Settings.DefaultFile
$logloc = $s.Settings.DefaultLog
if ($fileloc.Length = 0) {
    $fileloc = $s.Information.MasterDBPath
    }
if ($logloc.Length = 0) {
    $logloc = $s.Information.MasterDBLogPath
    }

# Place the files in the same location as the master database
$dbsysfile = $fileloc + '\' + $syslogname + '.mdf'
$dbappfile = $fileloc + '\' + $applogname + '.ndf'
$dblogfile = $logloc + '\' + $loglogname + '.ldf'


# Instantiate the database object and add the filegroups
$db =
 new-object ('Microsoft.SqlServer.Management.Smo.Database') ($s, $dbname)
$sysfg =
 new-object ('Microsoft.SqlServer.Management.Smo.FileGroup') ($db, 'PRIMARY')
$db.FileGroups.Add($sysfg)
$appfg = new-object ('Microsoft.SqlServer.Management.Smo.FileGroup') ($db,
'AppFG')
$db.FileGroups.Add($appfg)

# Create the file for the system tables
$dbdsysfile = new-object ('Microsoft.SqlServer.Management.Smo.DataFile')
($sysfg, $syslogname)
$sysfg.Files.Add($dbdsysfile)
$dbdsysfile.FileName = $dbsysfile
$dbdsysfile.Size = [double](5.0 * 1024.0)
```

```
$dbdsysfile.GrowthType = 'None'
$dbdsysfile.IsPrimaryFile = 'True'

# Create the file for the Application tables
$dbdappfile = new-object ('Microsoft.SqlServer.Management.Smo.DataFile')
($appfg, $applogname)
$appfg.Files.Add($dbdappfile)
$dbdappfile.FileName = $dbappfile
$dbdappfile.Size = [double](25.0 * 1024.0)
$dbdappfile.GrowthType = 'Percent'
$dbdappfile.Growth = 25.0
$dbdappfile.MaxSize = [double](100.0 * 1024.0)

# Create the file for the log
$dblfile = new-object ('Microsoft.SqlServer.Management.Smo.LogFile') ($db,
$loglogname)
$db.LogFiles.Add($dblfile)
$dblfile.FileName = $dblogfile
$dblfile.Size = [double](10.0 * 1024.0)
$dblfile.GrowthType = 'Percent'
$dblfile.Growth = 25.0

# Create the database
$db.Create()

# Set the default filegroup to AppFG
$appfg = $db.FileGroups['AppFG']
$appfg.IsDefault = $true
$appfg.Alter()
$db.Alter()
```

ADO.NET

ADO.NET consists of a set of object libraries that enable communication between client programs and the source of the data, in this case SQL Server. Two groups of objects are defined within ADO.NET: a set of *connected objects*, which enable the client to communicate with the server using an active connection, and a set of *disconnected objects*, which act as an offline data cache, enabling the client application to work with the data independently of the server. These two groups of objects are listed in Table 7-4 and Table 7-5, respectively.

The first thing needed for a session using ADO.NET is a connection to the database. The `SqlConnection` object is initialized using the following commands:

```
$connstring = "Data Source=myServerAddress;Initial
Catalog=myDataBase;Integrated Security=SSPI;"
# or its equivalent
$connstring = "Server=myServerAddress;
Database=myDataBase;Trusted_Connection=True;"
$cn = new-object system.data.SqlClient.SqlConnection($connstring)
```

TABLE 7-4

Connected Objects

Object	Description
Connection object	A connection to the data source
Command object	Can represent a query against a database, a call to a stored procedure, or a direct request to return the contents of a specific table
DataReader object	Designed to return query results as quickly as possible
Transaction object	Groups a number of changes to a database and treats them as a single unit of work
	The Connection object has a BeginTransaction method that can be used to create Transaction objects
Parameter object	Allows the specification of parameters for stored procedures or parameterized queries
DataAdapter object	Acts as a bridge between the database and the disconnected objects in the ADO.NET object model

TABLE 7-5

Disconnected Objects

Object	Description
DataTable object	Allows the examination of data through collections of rows and columns
DataColumn object	Corresponds to a column in a table
Constraint object	Defines and enforces column constraints
DataRow object	Provides access to the DataTable's Rows collection
DataSet object	The container for a number of DataTable objects
DataRelation object	Defines the relations between DataTables in the DataSet object
DataView object	Allows the examination of DataTable data in different ways

Many options are available for configuring connection strings, most of which are available at `www.connectionstrings.com/sql-server-2008`.

Once the connection object is initialized, the connection can be used to send queries to SQL Server. Listing 7-4 shows an example using the `AdventureWorks` sample database, returning query results to a `DataSet` object, and then presenting it to the user.

LISTING 7-4

EmployeeExtract.ps1

```
#employeeextract.ps1
#This script pulls info from the Person.Contact table in AdventureWorks
and presents it to the user

$cn = new-object system.data.SqlClient.SqlConnection("Data Source=SQLTBWS\INST01;
Integrated Security=SSPI;Initial Catalog=AdventureWorks");
$ds = new-object "System.Data.DataSet" "dsPersonData"
$q = "SELECT TOP 25 [ContactID]"
$q = $q + "      ,[FirstName]"
$q = $q + "      ,[LastName]"
$q = $q + "      ,[EmailAddress]"
$q = $q + "      ,[Phone]"
$q = $q + "  FROM [AdventureWorks].[Person].[Contact]"
$da = new-object "System.Data.SqlClient.SqlDataAdapter" ($q, $cn)
$da.Fill($ds)

$dtPerson = new-object "System.Data.DataTable" "dtPersonData"
$dtPerson = $ds.Tables[0]
$dtPerson | FOREACH-OBJECT { [string]$_.ContactID + ": " + $_.FirstName + ", " +
$_.LastName + ", " + $_.EmailAddress + ", " + $_.Phone }
```

The script first connects with the database server, and then builds a string containing the query to be run. That query and the connection object are then supplied as parameters to a `SqlDataAdapter` object. Using the `DataAdapter`'s `Fill` method, a `DataSet` is populated with the query results. One table results from the query, so the `DataTable` object is populated using the first table in the `DataSet`. This `DataTable` is then iterated through to return results to the user. Running this script produces these results:

```
25
1: Gustavo, Achong, gustavo0@adventure-works.com, 398-555-0132
2: Catherine, Abel, catherine0@adventure-works.com, 747-555-0171
3: Kim, Abercrombie, kim2@adventure-works.com, 334-555-0137
4: Humberto, Acevedo, humberto0@adventure-works.com, 599-555-0127
5: Pilar, Ackerman, pilar1@adventure-works.com, 1 (11) 500 555-0132
6: Frances, Adams, frances0@adventure-works.com, 991-555-0183
7: Margaret, Smith, margaret0@adventure-works.com, 959-555-0151
8: Carla, Adams, carla0@adventure-works.com, 107-555-0138
9: Jay, Adams, jay1@adventure-works.com, 158-555-0142
10: Ronald, Adina, ronald0@adventure-works.com, 453-555-0165
11: Samuel, Agcaoili, samuel0@adventure-works.com, 554-555-0110
12: James, Aguilar, james2@adventure-works.com, 1 (11) 500 555-0198
13: Robert, Ahlering, robert1@adventure-works.com, 678-555-0175
14: François, Ferrier, françois1@adventure-works.com, 571-555-0128
15: Kim, Akers, kim3@adventure-works.com, 440-555-0166
16: Lili, Alameda, lili0@adventure-works.com, 1 (11) 500 555-0150
```

```
17: Amy, Alberts, amy1@adventure-works.com, 727-555-0115
18: Anna, Albright, anna0@adventure-works.com, 197-555-0143
19: Milton, Albury, milton0@adventure-works.com, 492-555-0189
20: Paul, Alcorn, paul2@adventure-works.com, 331-555-0162
21: Gregory, Alderson, gregory0@adventure-works.com, 968-555-0153
22: J. Phillip, Alexander, jphillip0@adventure-works.com, 845-555-0187
23: Michelle, Alexander, michelle0@adventure-works.com, 115-555-0175
24: Sean, Jacobson, sean2@adventure-works.com, 555-555-0162
25: Phyllis, Allen, phyllis0@adventure-works.com, 695-555-0111
```

Scripting SQL Server Tasks

While using PowerShell interactively to perform maintenance tasks may be fun and interesting, it doesn't save much time. Scripting enables administrators to perform the same function the same way every time, saving the time it might take to remember how to solve a problem and enabling the administrator to focus on new problems as they occur. Typically, administrators create scripts for two basic categories of tasks: *administrative tasks*, those that perform normal administrative functions, and *data-based tasks*.

Administrative tasks

A script showing how to create a database was shown in Listing 7-3, but nearly every administrative activity required of a SQL Server DBA can be scripted using PowerShell and SMO.

The most important task a DBA must perform is backing up databases. First, the backup directory is needed so SQL Server knows where to put the backup files. Getting this information using Transact-SQL isn't possible (without using extended stored procedures to poll the system registry values, that is), but it's quite easy by using the objects shown in Figure 7-2 to get the `BackupDirectory` property from the server's `Settings` collection.

FIGURE 7-2

The SMO objects used to access the location of the backup directory

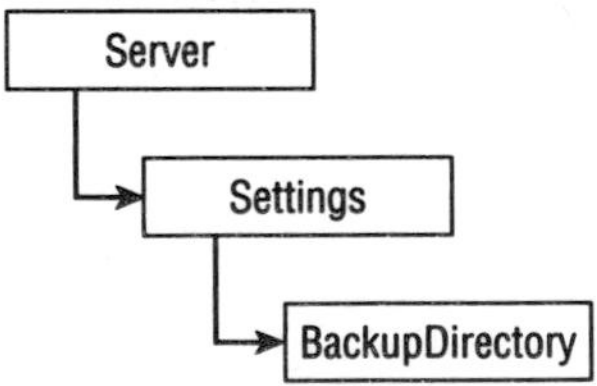

Once the backup directory is known, it's easy to set the properties necessary to perform the backup. Figure 7-3 shows the SMO objects needed to back up the database.

The `Action` object determines whether the backup is a Database, Differential, or Log backup. The `BackupSetDescription` and `BackupSetName` are descriptive information for the backup. The

Database property tells SQL Server which database to back up, and the MediaDescription defines whether the backup is sent to disk or tape (disk is much more efficient, in general). Each file or tape device used as a destination for the backup is defined and added to the backup's Devices collection. Once these properties have been set, the SqlBackup method is called to perform the backup.

FIGURE 7-3

The SMO backup properties and methods

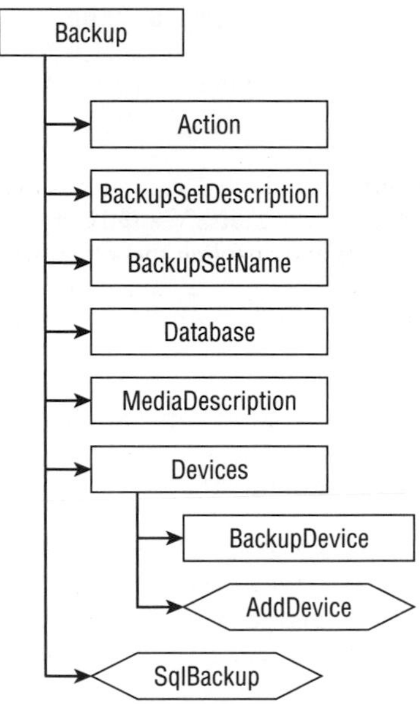

The example script in Listing 7-5 loops through the databases for which the IsSystemObject property is set to False and the IsMirroringEnabled property is also set to False. It uses the Get-Date cmdlet to get the current system date and time and puts that into the filename for the backup file. If the database that has been backed up is not in SIMPLE recovery mode, the script also performs a transaction log backup.

LISTING 7-5

Backup.ps1

```
#backup.ps1
#Performs a Full backup followed by a transaction log backup on all user
databases

[System.Reflection.Assembly]::LoadWithPartialName('Microsoft.SqlServer.SMO')
| out-null
[System.Reflection.Assembly]::LoadWithPartialName('Microsoft.SqlServer
.SmoExtended') | out-null
```

```
$s = new-object ('Microsoft.SqlServer.Management.Smo.Server') 'SQLTBWS\INST01'
$bkdir = $s.Settings.BackupDirectory
$dbs = $s.Databases
$dbs | foreach-object {
    $db = $_

    if ($db.IsSystemObject -eq $False -and $db.IsMirroringEnabled -eq $False) {
        $dbname = $db.Name
        $dt = get-date -format yyyyMMddHHmmss
        $dbbk = new-object ('Microsoft.SqlServer.Management.Smo.Backup')
        $dbbk.Action = 'Database'
        $dbbk.BackupSetDescription = "Full backup of " + $dbname
        $dbbk.BackupSetName = $dbname + " Backup"
        $dbbk.Database = $dbname
        $dbbk.MediaDescription = "Disk"
        $dbbk.Devices.AddDevice($bkdir + "\" + $dbname + "_db_" + $dt +
".bak", 'File')
        $dbbk.SqlBackup($s)
        # Simple Recovery Model has a Value Property of 3
        if ($db.recoverymodel.value__ -ne 3) {
            $dt = get-date -format yyyyMMddHHmmss
            $dbtrn = new-object ('Microsoft.SqlServer.Management.Smo.Backup')
            $dbtrn.Action = 'Log'
            $dbtrn.BackupSetDescription = "Trans Log backup of " + $dbname
            $dbtrn.BackupSetName = $dbname + " Backup"
            $dbtrn.Database = $dbname
            $dbtrn.MediaDescription = "Disk"
            $dbtrn.Devices.AddDevice($bkdir + "\" + $dbname +
"_tlog_" + $dt + ".trn", 'File')
            $dbtrn.SqlBackup($s)
            }
        }

    }
```

While the best method for creating and modifying tables in SQL Server is to use Transact-SQL scripts, in some cases embedding this activity in application code is beneficial. Remote installation of application software is one good example.

Take a look at the objects, shown in Figure 7-4, used in creating tables.

As shown in Figure 7-4, the database has a `Tables` collection, which holds `Table` objects. Each `Table` object has a `Columns` collection, which holds `Column` objects. Listing 7-6 shows the complete script to define our tables, indexes, and foreign keys.

Define the `Table` object first, and then create the `Column` objects, set their properties, and add the `Column` objects to the table's `Columns` collection.

FIGURE 7-4

The SMO Database Table, Index, and Foreign Key objects

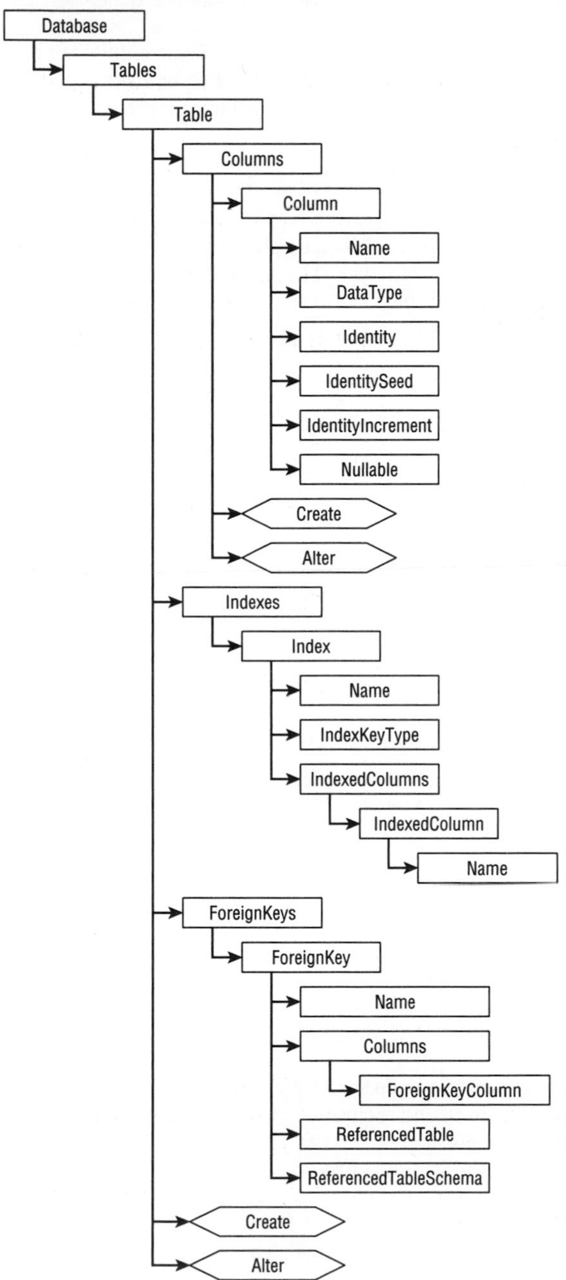

After the table and columns have been defined, the next step is to define an index and set its IndexKeyType property to indicate the index is a primary key. (Without a primary key, a foreign key to the table can't be defined.) The last step is to create a clustered index on one table to improve query performance against that table. Finally, the Create method is used to create the table.

In our example scenario, AdventureWorks has acquired another company. Their employees are being merged into the AdventureWorks HR application, but key data items need to be maintained for the short term based on their old company's records. To this end, two new tables are required.

The first table, called AcquisitionCompany, will hold the name and date the acquisition occurred, plus an identity-based key called CompanyID. (In this scenario, AdventureWorks will do this again.) The second table, called AcquisitionEmployee, contains the employee's original employee ID, original start date, number of hours available for time off this year, plus a column that indicates whether this employee earned a kind of reward called a Star Employee. The AcquisitionEmployee table also needs a column to reference the AcquisitionCompany table. These tables will be created in the HumanResources schema.

After creating the tables, the next step is to add foreign key references from AcquisitionEmployee to both the AcquisitionCompany and the existing Employee tables. Because AdventureWorks management likes the Star Employee idea, that column will be added to the existing Employee table but will be kept separate from the StarEmployee column in the AcquisitionEmployee table because the criteria are different.

Once the tables are created, the required foreign keys to the AcquisitionEmployee table can be added by creating a ForeignKey object, defining the ForeignKey columns, and adding them to the ForeignKey object and defining the referenced table and schema.

LISTING 7-6

CreateTable.ps1

```
#createtable.ps1
#Creates the Acquisition tables in the AdventureWorks database
[System.Reflection.Assembly]::LoadWithPartialName("Microsoft.SqlServer.SMO")
   | out-null

$s = new-object ("Microsoft.SqlServer.Management.Smo.Server")
"MyServer\MyInstance"

#Reference the AdventureWorks database.
$db = $s.Databases["AdventureWorks"]

#Create reusable datatype objects
$dtint = [Microsoft.SqlServer.Management.Smo.Datatype]::Int
$dtvchar100 = [Microsoft.SqlServer.Management.Smo.Datatype]::NVarChar(100)
$dtdatetm = [Microsoft.SqlServer.Management.Smo.Datatype]::DateTime
$dtbit = [Microsoft.SqlServer.Management.Smo.Datatype]::Bit

#Create the table in the HumanResources schema
$tbcomp = new-object ("Microsoft.SqlServer.Management.Smo.Table")
  ($db, "AcquisitionCompany", "HumanResources")
```

```
#Create the CompanyID column
$colcoid = new-object ("Microsoft.SqlServer.Management.Smo.Column")
  ($tbcomp, "CompanyID", $dtint)
$colcoid.Identity = $true
$colcoid.IdentitySeed = 1
$colcoid.IdentityIncrement = 1
$tbcomp.Columns.Add($colcoid)

#Create the CompanyName column
$colconame = new-object ("Microsoft.SqlServer.Management.Smo.Column")
  ($tbcomp, "CompanyName", $dtvchar100)
$colconame.Nullable = $false
$tbcomp.Columns.Add($colconame)

#Create the AcquisitionDate column
$colacqdate = new-object ("Microsoft.SqlServer.Management.Smo.Column")
  ($tbcomp, "AcquisitionDate", $dtdatetm)
$colacqdate.Nullable = $false
$tbcomp.Columns.Add($colacqdate)

#Create the Primary Key
$idxpkcompany = new-object ("Microsoft.SqlServer.Management.Smo.Index")
  ($tbcomp, "PK_AcquisitionCompany")
$idxpkcompany.IndexKeyType = "DriPrimaryKey"
$idxpkcompany.IsClustered = $true
$idxpkcompanycol = new-object
("Microsoft.SqlServer.Management.Smo.IndexedColumn")
  ($idxpkcompany, "CompanyID")
$idxpkcompany.IndexedColumns.Add($idxpkcompanycol)
$tbcomp.Indexes.Add($idxpkcompany)

#Create the table
$tbcomp.Create()

#Create the table in the HumanResources schema
$tbemp = new-object ("Microsoft.SqlServer.Management.Smo.Table")
  ($db, "AcquisitionEmployee", "HumanResources")

#Create the EmployeeID column
$colempiddt = [Microsoft.SqlServer.Management.Smo.Datatype]::Int
$colempid = new-object ("Microsoft.SqlServer.Management.Smo.Column")
  ($tbemp, "EmployeeID", $dtint)
$colempid.Nullable = $false
$tbemp.Columns.Add($colempid)

#Create the CompanyID foreign key column
$colempcolid = new-object ("Microsoft.SqlServer.Management.Smo.Column")
  ($tbemp, "CompanyID", $dtint)
$colempcolid.Nullable = $false
```

```
$tbemp.Columns.Add($colempcolid)

#Create the OriginalEmployeeID column
$colorigempid = new-object ("Microsoft.SqlServer.Management.Smo.Column")
  ($tbemp, "OriginalEmployeeID", $dtint)
$colorigempid.Nullable = $false
$tbemp.Columns.Add($colorigempid)

#Create the OriginalHireDate column
$colemporigdate = new-object ("Microsoft.SqlServer.Management.Smo.Column")
  ($tbemp, "OriginalHireDate", $dtdatetm)
$colemporigdate.Nullable = $false
$tbemp.Columns.Add($colemporigdate)

#Create the TimeOffHours column
$colemptoh = new-object ("Microsoft.SqlServer.Management.Smo.Column")
  ($tbemp, "TimeOffHours", $dtint)
$colemptoh.Nullable = $false
$tbemp.Columns.Add($colemptoh)

#Create the StarEmployee column
$colempstar = new-object ("Microsoft.SqlServer.Management.Smo.Column")
  ($tbemp, "StarEmployee", $dtbit)
$colempstar.Nullable = $false
$tbemp.Columns.Add($colempstar)

#Create the Primary Key
$idxpkemp = new-object ("Microsoft.SqlServer.Management.Smo.Index")
  ($tbemp, "PK_AcquisitionEmployee")
$idxpkemp.IndexKeyType = "DriPrimaryKey"
$idxpkempcol = new-object("Microsoft.SqlServer.Management.Smo.IndexedColumn")
  ($idxpkemp, "EmployeeID")
$idxpkemp.IndexedColumns.Add($idxpkempcol)
$tbemp.Indexes.Add($idxpkemp)

#Create the Clustered Index
$idxciemp = new-object ("Microsoft.SqlServer.Management.Smo.Index")
  ($tbemp, "CI_AcquisitionEmployee")
$idxciemp.IndexKeyType = "DriUniqueKey"
$idxciemp.IsClustered = $true
$idxciempcol = new-object("Microsoft.SqlServer.Management.Smo.IndexedColumn")
  ($idxciemp, "OriginalEmployeeID")
$idxciemp.IndexedColumns.Add($idxciempcol)
$tbemp.Indexes.Add($idxciemp)

#Create the table
$tbemp.Create()
```

```
#Connect to the HumanResources.Employee table
$tbhremp = $db.Tables | where
  {$_.Name -eq 'Employee' -and $_.Schema -eq 'HumanResources'}

#Add the StarEmployee column to the HumanResources.Employee table
$colhrempstar = new-object ("Microsoft.SqlServer.Management.Smo.Column")
  ($tbhremp, "StarEmployee", $dtbit)
$colhrempstar.Nullable = $true
$tbhremp.Columns.Add($colhrempstar)

#Alter the HumanResources.Employee table
$tbhremp.Alter()

#Define the HumanResources.Employee foreign key
$fkemp = new-object ("Microsoft.SqlServer.Management.Smo.ForeignKey")
  ($tbemp, "FK_AcqEmployee_HREmployee")
$fkcolemp = new-object("Microsoft.SqlServer.Management.Smo.ForeignKeyColumn")
  ($fkemp, "EmployeeID", "EmployeeID")
$fkemp.Columns.Add($fkcolemp)
$fkemp.ReferencedTable = "Employee"
$fkemp.ReferencedTableSchema = "HumanResources"
$fkemp.Create()

#Define the HumanResources.AcquisitionCompany foreign key
$fkco = new-object ("Microsoft.SqlServer.Management.Smo.ForeignKey")
  ($tbemp, "FK_AcqEmployee_AcqCompany")
$fkcoid = new-object ("Microsoft.SqlServer.Management.Smo.ForeignKeyColumn")
  ($fkco, "CompanyID", "CompanyID")
$fkco.Columns.Add($fkcoid)
$fkco.ReferencedTable = "AcquisitionCompany"
$fkco.ReferencedTableSchema = "HumanResources"
$fkco.Create()
```

One of the great improvements in SMO over its predecessor, DMO, is in the area of scripting. With SMO, Transact-SQL scripts can be created from objects even if they don't yet exist. Almost all maintenance dialogs in SQL Server Management Studio include a button that enables a script to be generated from the changes made in that dialog. That way, the script can be executed, rather than making the changes from the dialog, and the script can be saved for future use.

Another useful feature of scripting existing objects is the capability to generate scripts of all database objects for documentation or to put into source code control. This enables administrators to rebuild a database in the form it existed at the time the script was created, should some problem arise requiring that effort.

At any time while creating or working with objects in SMO, those objects can be scripted for archival or later use (see Figure 7-5).

FIGURE 7-5

SMO scripting objects

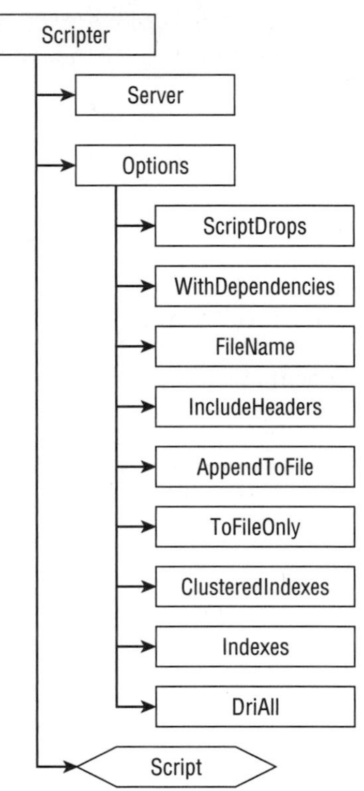

The `Server` property enables the `Scripter` object to connect to the server. The remaining properties needing to be set are in the Scripter Options collection.

The `ScriptDrops` property specifies whether the script will consist of drops for the objects or creates for the objects. If this property is set to `True`, the script will contain a `DROP` statement for each object (within an `IF` condition to ensure that it exists), but a `False` value causes the scripter to generate the `CREATE` statement for each object. The `WithDependencies` property, if true, causes the objects to be scripted in an order that respects the dependency of one scripted object on another. The `FileName` property contains the full path of the resultant script file. The `IncludeHeaders` property, when `True`, includes a comment indicating the name of the object and when the object was created in the script. The `AppendToFile` property appends the script to the end of an existing file if `True`, and overwrites the file if `False`.

By default, the scripting process sends the results to the console, so setting the `ToFileOnly` property to `True` causes the scripter to send the script only to the file specified. Setting the `ClusteredIndexes` property to `True` causes the clustered index for a table to be included in the script, and setting the `Indexes` property to `True` causes the non-clustered indexes to be included in the script. The DriAll property, when set to True, causes all objects with enforced declarative referential integrity to be included in the script.

The objects to be scripted need to be added to an array of type SqlSmoObject. Once the array has been populated with all the objects to be scripted, invoke the Script method and the script will be created. Listing 7-7 shows the script to create a T-SQL script of all tables in the AdventureWorks database.

LISTING 7-7

Scripting.ps1

```
#Script all the table objects in the AdventureWorks database

[System.Reflection.Assembly]::LoadWithPartialName("Microsoft.SqlServer.SMO")
| out-null

$s = new-object ('Microsoft.SqlServer.Management.Smo.Server')
'MyServer\MyInstance'
$db = $s.Databases['AdventureWorks']

$scrp = new-object ('Microsoft.SqlServer.Management.Smo.Scripter') ($s)
$scrp.Options.ScriptDrops = $False
$scrp.Options.WithDependencies = $True
$scrp.Options.FileName = 'c:\dbscript.sql'
$scrp.Options.IncludeHeaders = $True
$scrp.Options.AppendToFile = $True
$scrp.Options.ToFileOnly = $True
$scrp.Options.ClusteredIndexes = $True
$scrp.Options.DriAll = $True
$scrp.Options.Indexes = $True

$scrp.Script($db.Tables)
```

Data-based tasks

In the section on ADO.NET you saw an example that returned the results from a query to the user, using a DataAdapter object to fill a DataSet. This method is fine as long as there's enough memory to hold all the results of the query. If the result set is very large, though, it is better to use the ExecuteReader method of the SqlCommand object.

The following example, shown in Listing 7-8, uses the AdventureWorks2008 database to extract department employee information by DepartmentID, and creates a separate physical file for each department. The files will be text files with commas separating the columns returned. This format is easily understood by most programs that import data. The ExecuteReader method returns a DataReader object, and the columns must be retrieved from the object using the GetValue method of the DataReader, supplying the column index number to GetValue. The script sets a local variable for each of the columns retrieved for each row. Once those have been set, the script tests whether the DepartmentID value has changed. If so, a "header" row is created in a string variable ($r) and written to a file with the name of the department Name value and a .txt extension. Once the header has been written, the data row just read is written to the file.

LISTING 7-8

dept_birthdays.ps1

```
#dept_birthdays.ps1
#This script will extract information for employees by Department
#and write the results into text files named with the department name.

$cn = new-object System.Data.SqlClient.SqlConnection("Data Source=MyServer\
MyInstance;Integrated Security=SSPI;Initial Catalog=AdventureWorks2008");
$cn.Open()
$q = "SELECT d.[DepartmentID]"
$q = $q + "      ,d.[Name]"
$q = $q + "      ,p.[FirstName]"
$q = $q + "      ,p.[LastName]"
$q = $q + "      ,e.[JobTitle]"
$q = $q + "      ,e.[BirthDate]"
$q = $q + "      ,e.[SalariedFlag]"
$q = $q + "  FROM [AdventureWorks2008].[Person].[Person] p"
$q = $q + "  INNER JOIN [AdventureWorks2008].[HumanResources].[Employee] e"
$q = $q + "  ON p.[BusinessEntityID] = e.[BusinessEntityID]"
$q = $q + "  INNER JOIN [AdventureWorks2008]
.[HumanResources].[EmployeeDepartmentHistory] dh"
$q = $q + "  ON p.[BusinessEntityID] = dh.[BusinessEntityID]"
$q = $q + "  INNER JOIN [AdventureWorks2008].[HumanResources].[Department] d"
$q = $q + "  ON dh.[DepartmentID] = d. [DepartmentID]"
$q = $q + "  WHERE p.[PersonType] = 'EM'"
$q = $q + "  AND dh.[EndDate] IS NULL"
$q = $q + "  ORDER BY d.DepartmentID, p.LastName"

$cmd = new-object "System.Data.SqlClient.SqlCommand" ($q, $cn)
$cmd.CommandTimeout = 0

$dr = $cmd.ExecuteReader()
$did = ""

while ($dr.Read()) {
      $DepartmentID = $dr.GetValue(0)
      $Name = $dr.GetValue(1)
      $FirstName = $dr.GetValue(2)
      $LastName = $dr.GetValue(3)
      $JobTitle = $dr.GetValue(4)
      $BirthDate = $dr.GetValue(5)
      $SalariedFlag = $dr.GetValue(6)
if ($DepartmentID -ne $did) {
            $r = """DepartmentID"",""Name"",""FirstName"",""LastName"
            $r = $r + """,""JobTitle"",""BirthDate"",""SalariedFlag"""

            $f = $Name + ".txt"
```

```
          $r | out-file $f -append -encoding ASCII

          $did = $DepartmentID
          }
      $r = """" + $DepartmentID + """,""" + $Name + ""","""
      $r = $r + $FirstName + """,""" + $LastName + ""","""
      $r = $r + $JobTitle + """,""" + $BirthDate + """,""" + $SalariedFlag +
""""

      $f = $Name + ".txt"
      $r | out-file $f -append -encoding ASCII
      }
$dr.Close()
$cn.Close()
```

SQL Server PowerShell Extensions

With the release of SQL Server 2008, Microsoft incorporated new extensions to PowerShell specifically for working with SQL Server. The first of these is a mini-shell preconfigured with the required DLLs loaded and the providers available for use. All of the examples shown previously in this chapter run fine in standard PowerShell 1.0. The rest of the chapter focuses on the new features created for SQL Server 2008.

SQLPS.exe

SQL Server 2008 incorporates PowerShell into its management toolset. As part of Microsoft's Common Engineering Criteria, all server tools now incorporate PowerShell to enable administrators to script tasks easily.

Snap-ins to PowerShell are fairly easily achieved by writing what's called a *provider*, which is a set of tools designed to allow easy access to data. In the case of SQL Server, the provider creates a PowerShell drive that directly connects with SQL Server, and a set of cmdlets to communicate with SQL Server from PowerShell. Using the PowerShell drive, you can browse SQL Server as though it were a file system. The cmdlets enable you to run Transact-SQL commands, evaluate policies, and convert names between the characters that SQL Server supports and the more limited set of characters that PowerShell supports.

Microsoft created a special version of PowerShell (1.0) called `sqlps.exe` that includes the provider and preloads all of the DLLs that the provider requires, including the DLLs for SMO. Another difference between standard PowerShell and `sqlps.exe` is that the execution policy of PowerShell in `sqlps.exe` is set to RemoteSigned. This means that as soon as SQL Server 2008 is installed, `sqlps.exe` is ready to run scripts (on the local system, at least).

The good news, considering that PowerShell 2.0 is out (or will be soon), is that the SQL Server provider can be easily loaded into standard PowerShell. Michiel Wories developed the SQL Server provider, and in his blog post at `http://blogs.msdn.com/mwories/archive/2008/06/14/SQL2008_5F00_Powershell.aspx` he provides the script that loads it into PowerShell.

The script first loads all of the DLLs needed for SMO and the snap-ins (code and commands that extend PowerShell's capabilities), and then it loads the snap-ins. Once this is done, all of the SQL Server provider functionality is available, and this script can be run against PowerShell 1.0 or PowerShell 2.0 when it is available.

The SQL PSDrive – SQLSERVER:

Native PowerShell provides the ability to navigate not only the disk file system, but also the system registry as though it were a file system. (This is expected behavior for a shell environment, as Unix shell systems treat most everything as a file system as well.) The SQL Server provider adds a new PowerShell drive, also referred to as a PSDrive, called SQLSERVER:. The `Set-Location` cmdlet (usually aliased as `cd`) is used to change to the SQLSERVER: drive and then SQL Server can be navigated like the file system.

There are four main directories under SQLSERVER: — SQL, SQLPolicy, SQLRegistration, and DataCollection:

- The SQL folder provides access to the database engine, SQL Server Agent, Service Broker, and Database Mail, all using the various SMO DLLs.
- The SQLPolicy folder provides access to policy-based management using the DMF and Facets DLLs.
- The SQLRegistration folder enables access to the Registered Servers (and the new Central Management Server feature of SQL Server 2008).
- The DataCollection folder enables access to the Data Collector objects provided with the Management Data Warehouse feature of SQL Server 2008.

You can browse the SQLSERVER file system just like a disk file system. Issuing the command `cd SQL` (or `Set-Location SQL`) and running the `Get-ChildItem` cmdlet returns the local server and any other servers that may have been recently accessed from the PowerShell session. Changing to the local server and running `Get-ChildItem` returns the names of the SQL Server instances installed on that server. Changing to one of the instances and running `Get-ChildItem` returns the collections of objects available to that server, such as BackupDevices, Databases, Logins, and so on. Changing to the Databases collection and running `Get-ChildItem` returns the list of user databases, along with some of the database properties. The results will look something like Figure 7-6.

SQL cmdlets

The SQL Server PowerShell snap-in also provides new cmdlets specific for use with SQL Server. The majority of administrative functions are managed using SMO, and data access is managed using ADO.NET, as mentioned before, so no cmdlets were needed for these functions. Some functions are just easier using cmdlets, so they were provided. They include the following:

- Invoke-Sqlcmd
- Invoke-PolicyEvaluation
- Encode-SqlName
- Decode-SqlName
- Convert-UrnToPath

FIGURE 7-6

Navigating the SQL Server "filesystem"

```
Windows PowerShell
PS E:\Scripts> cd SQLSERVER:
PS SQLSERVER:\> cd SQL
PS SQLSERVER:\SQL> ls

MachineName
-----------
SQLTBWS

PS SQLSERVER:\SQL> cd SQLTBWS
PS SQLSERVER:\SQL\SQLTBWS> ls

Instance Name
-------------
DEFAULT
INST01
INST02

PS SQLSERVER:\SQL\SQLTBWS> cd INST01
PS SQLSERVER:\SQL\SQLTBWS\INST01> ls
Audits
BackupDevices
Credentials
CryptographicProviders
Databases
Endpoints
JobServer
Languages
LinkedServers
Logins
Mail
ResourceGovernor
Roles
ServerAuditSpecifications
SystemDataTypes
SystemMessages
Triggers
UserDefinedMessages
PS SQLSERVER:\SQL\SQLTBWS\INST01> cd Databases
PS SQLSERVER:\SQL\SQLTBWS\INST01\Databases> ls

Name                 Status     Recovery Model CompatLvl Collation                     Owner
----                 ------     -------------- --------- ---------                     -----
AdventureWorks       Normal     Full                 100 Latin1_General_CS_AS          SQLTBWS\Administrator
AdventureWorks2008   Normal     Simple               100 SQL_Latin1_General_CP1_CI_AS  SQLTBWS\Administrator
AdventureWorksDW2008 Normal     Simple               100 SQL_Latin1_General_CP1_CI_AS  SQLTBWS\Administrator
ReportServer$INST01  Normal     Full                 100 Latin1_General_CI_AS_KS_WS    SQLTBWS\Administrator
ReportServer$INST01T Normal     Simple               100 Latin1_General_CI_AS_KS_WS    SQLTBWS\Administrator
empDB
```

The first, `Invoke-Sqlcmd`, takes query text and sends it to SQL Server for processing. Rather than set up the structures in ADO.NET to execute queries, the `Invoke-Sqlcmd` cmdlet returns results from a query passed in as a parameter or from a text file, which provides a very easy way to get data out of SQL Server. It can perform either a standard Transact-SQL query or an XQuery statement, which provides additional flexibility.

The `Invoke-PolicyEvaluation` cmdlet uses the Policy-based Management feature of SQL Server 2008. It evaluates a set of objects against a policy defined for one or more servers to determine whether or not the objects comply with the conditions defined in the policy. It can also be used to reset object settings to comply with the policy, if that is needed. Lara Rubbelke has a set of blog posts on using this cmdlet at `http://sqlblog.com/blogs/lara_rubbelke/archive/2008/06/19/evaluating-policies-on-demand-through-powershell.aspx`.

The character set used by SQL Server has a number of conflicts with the character set allowed by PowerShell. For example, a standard SQL Server instance name is SQLTBWS\INST01. The backslash embedded in the name can cause PowerShell to infer a file system directory and subdirectory, because it uses that character to separate the elements of the file system. The `Encode-SqlName` cmdlet converts strings acceptable to SQL Server into strings acceptable by PowerShell. For example, the instance name SQLTBWS\INST01 would be converted by this cmdlet into SQLTBWS%5CINST01.

The Decode-SqlName cmdlet does the exact opposite of Encode-SqlName: It converts the PowerShell-acceptable string of SQLTBWS%5CINST01 back to SQLTBWS\INST01.

Because SMO uses Uniform Resource Names (URN) for its objects, a cmdlet is provided to convert those URN values to path names, which can be used in a Set-Location cmdlet — for example, to navigate through the SQL Server objects. The URN for the HumanResources.Employee table in AdventureWorks2008 on SQLTBWS\INST01 is as follows:

```
Server[@Name='SQLTBWS\INST01']\Database[@Name='AdventureWorks2008']\
Table[@Name='Employee' and @Schema='HumanResources']
```

Converting that to a path using Convert-UrnToPath would yield the following:

```
SQLSERVER:\SQL\SQLTBWS\INST01\Databases\AdventureWorks2008\
Tables\HumanResources.Employee
```

Summary

After looking at the basics of PowerShell and exploring a few ways to get some interesting information about servers, this chapter reviewed a script to provide information about each server you manage. Then it examined some of the structures in SQL Server Management Objects (SMO) and some scripts to perform basic administrative tasks. This chapter also looked at a couple of scripts to extract data from SQL Server, because that's a common request from businesspeople. Finally, this chapter took a quick look at the features in SQL Server 2008 to make PowerShell an integral part of the SQL Server toolset.

Much more can be explored with PowerShell, but this will provide a starting point. Automation enables administrators to do more in less time and provide more value to the companies that employ them. PowerShell is a powerful way to automate most everything an administrator needs to do with SQL Server.

Part II

Manipulating Data with Select

SQL is like algebra in action.

The etymology of the word "algebra" goes back to the Arabic word "al-jabr," meaning "the reunion of broken parts," or literally, "to set a broken bone." Both algebra and SQL piece together fragments to solve a problem.

I believe *select* is the most powerful word in all of computer science. Because select is so common, it's easy to take it for granted, but no keyword in any programming language I can think of is as powerful and flexible. Select can retrieve, twist, shape, join, and group data in nearly any way imaginable, and it's easily extended with the insert, update, delete (and now merge!) commands to modify data.

Part II begins by exploring the basic logical query flow and quickly digs deeper into topics such as aggregate queries, relational division, correlated subqueries, and set-difference queries. I've devoted 15 chapters to the select command and its variations because understanding the multiple options and creative techniques available with queries is critical to becoming a successful SQL Server developer, DBA, or architect.

Please don't assume that Part II is only for beginners. These 15 chapters present the core power of SQL. Part IX explores optimization strategies, and it may be tempting to go straight there for optimization ideas, but the second strategy of Smart Database Design is using good set-based code. Here are nine chapters describing how to optimize your database by writing better queries.

If SQL Server is the box, Part II is about being one with the box.

IN THIS PART

Chapter 8

Introducing Basic Query Flow

IN THIS CHAPTER

Logical flow of the query

Restricting the result set

Projecting data

Specifying the sort order

SQL is the romance language of data, but wooing the single correct answer from gigabytes of relational data can seem overwhelming until the logical flow of the query is mastered.

One of the first points to understand is that SQL is a *declarative* language. This means that the SQL query logically describes the question to the SQL Query Optimizer, which then determines the best method to physically execute the query. As you'll see in the next eight chapters, there are often many ways of stating the query, but each method could be optimized to the same query execution plan. This means you are free to express the SQL query in the way that makes the most sense and will be the easiest to maintain In some cases, one method is considered cleaner or faster than another: I'll point those instances out as well.

SQL queries aren't limited to `SELECT`. The four Data Manipulation Language (DML) commands, `SELECT`, `INSERT`, `UPDATE`, and `DELETE`, are sometimes taught as four separate and distinct commands. However, I see queries as a single structural method of manipulating data; in other words, it's better to think of the four commands as four verbs that may each be used with the full power and flexibility of the SQL.

Neither are SQL queries limited to graphical interfaces. Many SQL developers who came up through the ranks from Access and who have built queries using only the Access query interface are amazed when they understand the enormous power of the full SQL query.

This chapter builds a basic single table query and establishes the logical query execution order critical for developing basic or advanced queries. With this foundation in place, the rest of Part II develops the basic `SELECT` into what I believe is the most elegant, flexible, and powerful command in all of computing.

Understanding Query Flow

One can think about query flow in four different ways. Personally, when I develop SQL code, I imagine the query using the logical flow method. Some developers think through a query visually using the layout of SQL Server Management Studio's Query Designer. The syntax of the query is in a specific fixed order: SELECT – FROM – WHERE – GROUP BY – HAVING – ORDER BY. To illustrate the declarative nature of SQL, the fourth way of thinking about the query flow — the actual physical execution of the query — is optimized to execute in the most efficient order depending on the data mix and the available indexes.

Syntactical flow of the query statement

In its basic form, the SELECT statement tells SQL Server what data to retrieve, including which columns, rows, and tables to pull from, and how to sort the data.

Here's an abbreviated syntax for the SELECT command:

```
SELECT [DISTINCT][TOP (n)] *, columns, or expressions
  [FROM data source(s)]
    [JOIN data source
      ON condition](may include multiple joins)
  [WHERE conditions]
  [GROUP BY columns]
  [HAVING conditions]
  [ORDER BY Columns];
```

The SELECT statement begins with a list of columns or expressions. At least one expression is required — everything else is optional. The simplest possible valid SELECT statement is as follows:

```
SELECT 1;
```

The FROM portion of the SELECT statement assembles all the data sources into a result set, which is then acted upon by the rest of the SELECT statement. Within the FROM clause, multiple tables may be referenced by using one of several types of joins.

When no FROM clause is supplied, SQL Server returns a single row with values. (Oracle requires a FROM DUAL to accomplish the same thing.)

The WHERE clause acts upon the record set assembled by the FROM clause to filter certain rows based upon conditions.

Aggregate functions perform summation-type operations across the data set. The GROUP BY clause can group the larger data set into smaller data sets based on the columns specified in the GROUP BY clause. The aggregate functions are then performed on the new smaller groups of data. The results of the aggregation can be restricted using the HAVING clause.

Finally, the ORDER BY clause determines the sort order of the result set.

A graphical view of the query statement

SQL Server Management Studio includes two basic methods for constructing and submitting queries: Query Designer and Query Editor. Query Designer offers a graphical method of building a query, whereas Query Editor is an excellent tool for writing SQL code or ad hoc data retrieval because there are no graphics to get in the way and the developer can work as close to the SQL code as possible.

From SQL Server's point of view, it doesn't matter where the query originates; each statement is evaluated and processed as a SQL statement.

When selecting data using Query Designer, the SQL statements can be entered as raw code in the third pane, as shown in Figure 8-1. The bottom pane displays the results in Grid mode or Text mode and displays any messages. The Object Browser presents a tree of all the objects in SQL Server, as well as templates for creating new objects with code.

FIGURE 8-1

The Query Designer can be used to graphically create queries.

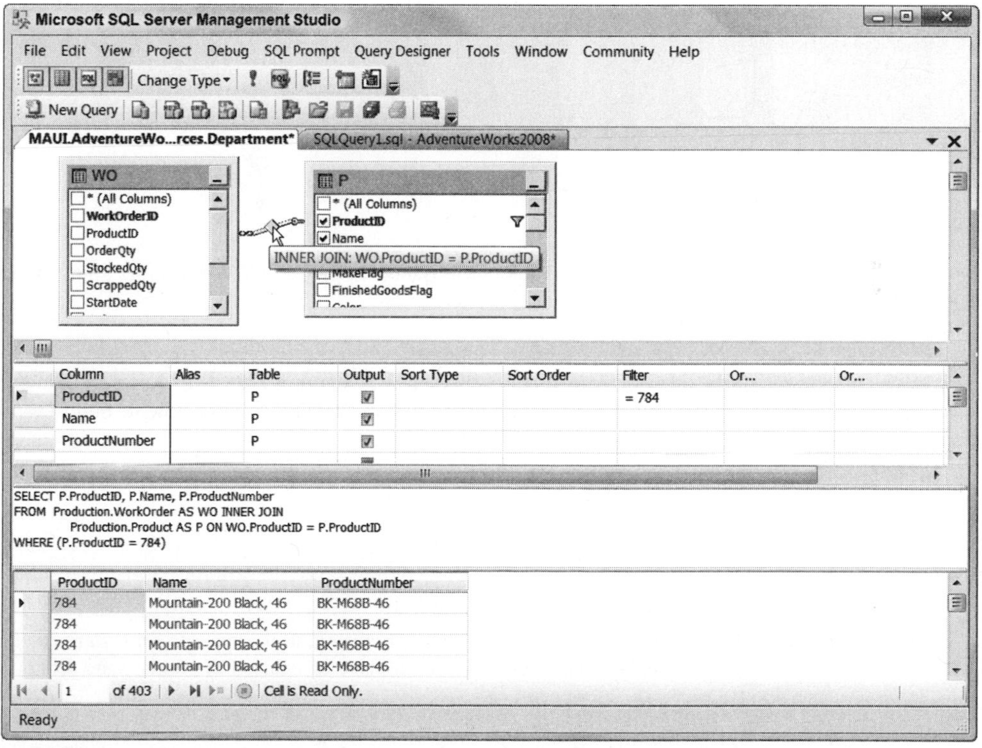

TIP **If text is selected in the Query Editor, then only the highlighted text is submitted to SQL Server when the Execute command button or the F5 key is pressed. This is an excellent way to test single SQL statements or portions of SQL code.**

TIP Though it may vary depending on the user account settings, the default database is probably the master database. Be sure to change to the appropriate user database using the database selector combo box in the toolbar, or the `USE database` command.

The best solution is to change the user's default database to a user database and avoid master altogether.

Logical flow of the query statement

The best way to think through a SQL DML statement is to walk through the query's logical flow (see Figure 8-2. Because SQL is a declarative language, the logical flow may or may not be the actual physical flow that SQL Server's query processor uses to execute the query. Nor is the logical flow the same as the query syntax. Regardless, I recommend thinking through a query in the following order.

FIGURE 8-2

A simplified view of the logical flow of the query showing how data moves through the major clauses of the SQL `select` command

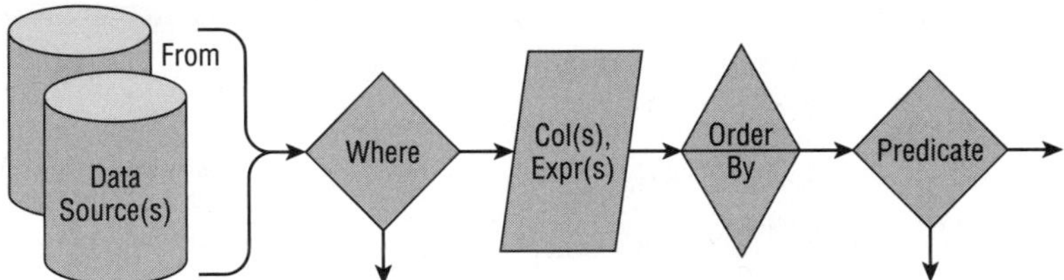

Here's a more detailed explanation of the logical flow of the query. Note that *every* step except step 4 is optional:

1. **[From]:** The query begins by assembling the initial set of data, as specified in the `FROM` portion of the `SELECT` statement. (Chapter 10, "Merging Data with Joins and Unions," and Chapter 11, "Including Data with Subqueries and CTEs," discuss how to build even the most complex `FROM` clauses.)
2. **[Where]:** The filter process is actually the `WHERE` clause selecting only those rows that meet the criteria.
3. **[Aggregations]:** SQL can optionally perform aggregations on the data set, such as finding the average, grouping the data by values in a column, and filtering the groups (see Chapter 12, "Aggregating Data").
4. **Column Expressions:** The `SELECT` list is processed, and any expressions are calculated (covered in Chapter 9, "Data Types, Expressions, and Scalar Functions," and Chapter 11, "Including Data with Subqueries and CTEs").
5. **[Order By]:** The resulting rows are sorted according to the `ORDER BY` clause.
6. **[Over]:** Windowing and ranking functions can provide a separately ordered view of the results with additional aggregate functions.
7. **[Distinct]:** Any duplicate rows are eliminated from the result set.

8. **[Top]:** After the rows are selected, the calculations are performed, and the data is sorted into the desired order, SQL can restrict the output to the top few rows.
9. **[Insert, Update, Delete]:** The final logical step of the query is to apply the data modification action to the results of the query. These three verbs are explained in Chapter 15, "Modifying Data."
10. **[Output]:** The inserted and deleted virtual tables (normally only used with a trigger) can be selected and returned to the client, inserted into a table, or serve as a data source to an outer query.
11. **[Union]:** The results of multiple queries can be stacked using a union command (see Chapter 10, "Merging Data with Joins and Unions").

As more complexity has been added to the SQL SELECT command over the years, how to think through the logical flow has also become more complex. In various sources, you'll find minor differences in how SQL MVPs view the logical flow. That's OK — it's just a way to think through a query, and this is the way I think through writing a query.

As you begin to think in terms of the SQL SELECT statement, rather than in terms of the graphical user interface, understanding the flow of SELECT and how to read the query execution plan will help you think through and develop difficult queries.

Physical flow of the query statement

SQL Server will take the SELECT statement and develop an optimized query execution plan, which may not be in the execution order you would guess (see Figure 8-3). The indexes available to the SQL Server Query Optimizer also affect the query execution plan, as explained in Chapter 64, "Indexing Strategies."

The rest of this chapter walks through the logical order of the basic query.

From Clause Data Sources

The first logical component of a typical SQL SELECT statement is the FROM clause. In a simple SQL SELECT statement, the FROM clause contains a single table. However, the FROM clause can also combine data from multiple sources and multiple types of data sources. The maximum number of tables that may be accessed within a single SQL SELECT statement is 256.

The FROM clause is the foundation of the rest of the SQL statement. In order for a table column to be in the output, or accessed in the WHERE conditions, or in the ORDER BY, it must be in the FROM clause.

Possible data sources

SQL is extremely flexible and can accept data from seven distinctly different types of data sources within the FROM clause:

- Local **SQL Server tables**
- **Subqueries** serving as derived tables, also called *subselects* or *in-line views,* are explained in Chapter 11, "Including Data with Subqueries and CTEs." Common table expressions (CTEs) are functionally similar to subqueries but may be referenced multiple times within the query.

FIGURE 8-3

The physical execution plan is very different from the syntactical order, or logical understanding, of the query.

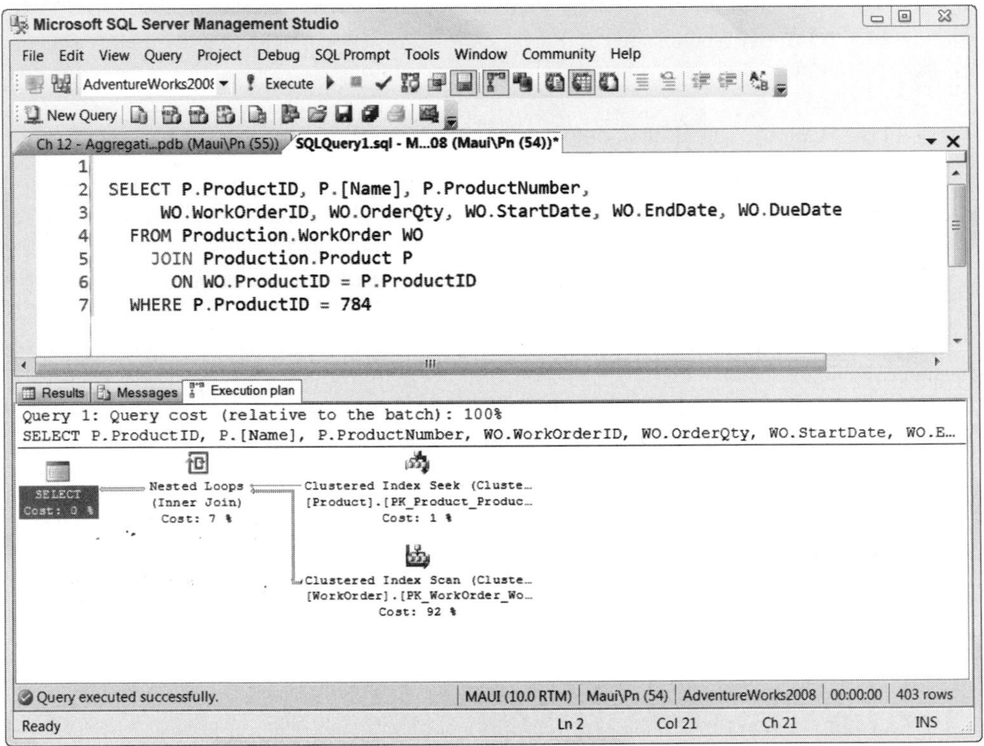

- **Views,** or stored SELECT statements, can be referenced within the FROM clause as if they were tables. Views are discussed in Chapter 14, "Projecting Data through Views."
- **Table-valued user-defined functions** return rows and columns. See Chapter 25, "Building User-Defined Functions," for more information.
- **Distributed data sources** pull in data from other SQL Server databases, other SQL Servers, other database platforms (e.g., Microsoft Access, Oracle, Foxpro), or applications (e.g., Excel) using `openquery()` and other distributed functions, as detailed in Chapter 31, "Executing Distributed Queries."
- **Full-text** search can return data sets with information about which rows contain certain words, as explained in Chapter 19, "Using Integrated Full-Text Search."
- **Pivot** creates a crosstab within the FROM clause and is covered in Chapter 12, "Aggregating Data."
- **XML** data sources using XQuery, as discussed in Chapter 18, "Manipulating XML Data."

SQL Server 2008 adds two new data sources:

- **Row constructors** build hard-coded rows using the `values()` clause, as covered in Chapter 11, "Including Data with Subqueries and CTEs."
- **Inserted and deleted** virtual tables from an insert, update, or delete can be passed to an outer query in the form of a subquery using the `output` clause.

CROSS-REF **The output clause is covered in Chapter 15, "Modifying Data." Consuming the output clause as a subquery is demonstrated in Chapter 11, "Including Data with Subqueries and CTEs."**

The `from` clause can merge data from multiple sources using several types of joins, as described in detail in Chapter 10, "Merging Data with Joins and Unions," and Chapter 11, "Including Data with Subqueries and CTEs."

Table aliases

A data source may be assigned a *table alias* within the `FROM` clause. Once the data source has an alias, it must be referred to by this new name. In some cases the data source must have an alias. The following code accesses the `Guide` table, but refers to it within the query as table `G`:

```
-- From Table [AS] Table Alias
USE CHA2;
SELECT G.lastName, G.FirstName
  FROM Guide AS G;
```

Best Practice

Using the keyword AS, to assign an alias to a column or data source, is optional and is commonly ignored. However, this practice leads to errors in the query, as seen regularly in SQL Server newsgroups. As a rule, always include the AS keyword.

ON the WEBSITE **You'll find the sample code for every chapter, and the scripts that create and populate the sample databases, on the book's website: `www.SQLServerBible.com`.**

NOTE **In SQL, the `USE` command specifies the current database. It's the code version of selecting a database from the toolbar in Management Studio.**

[Table Name]

If the name of a database object, such as a table or column name, conflicts with a SQL reserved keyword, you can let SQL know that it's the name of an object by placing it inside square brackets. Note that the square brackets are specific to SQL Server and not part of the ANSI SQL standard. The `[Order]`table in the `OBXKites` sample database is a common example of a table name that's also a keyword:

```
USE OBXKites;
SELECT OrderID, OrderDate
  FROM [Order];
```

Although it's an incredibly poor practice to include spaces within the names of database objects, it is possible nevertheless. If this is the case, square brackets are required when specifying the database object. The `Order Details` table in the `Northwind` sample database illustrates this:

```
USE Northwind;
SELECT OrderID, ProductID, Quantity
  FROM [Order Details];
```

CAUTION **The collation of the database determines its character set and sort order, but it can also affect object names within SQL statements. If the collation is case sensitive, then the object names will be case sensitive as well. For example, with a case-sensitive collation, a table created with the name `Person` is different from `person` or `PERSON`.**

Fully qualified names

The full and proper name for a table is not just the table name but what is called a *fully qualified name*, sometimes informally referred to as the *four-part name*:

```
Server.Database.Schema.Table
```

If the table is in the current database, then the server and database name are not required, so when SQL Server developers talk about a qualified table name, they usually mean a two-part table name.

Best Practice

Using the two-part name, schema, and object name is sufficient and the best practice. Including the server and database name would restrict moving code from one server to another (e.g., from development to production).

Besides just writing cleaner code, there are two specific benefits to using the qualified name:

- The same table may exist in multiple schemas. If this is the case, then the schema selected is based on the user's default schema. Qualifying the name avoids accidentally using the wrong table.
- Qualified tables names are required in order for the Query Engine to reuse the query execution plan, which is important for performance.

CROSS-REF **For more about schemas, scope, and permission issues, see Chapter 49, "Authenticating Principals," and Chapter 50, "Authorizing Securables." Query plan reuse is discussed in Chapter 65, "Query Plan Reuse."**

Where Conditions

The WHERE conditions filter the output of the FROM clause and restrict the rows that will be returned in the result set. The conditions can refer to the data within the tables, expressions, built-in SQL Server scalar functions, or user-defined functions. The WHERE conditions can also make use of several possible comparison operators and wildcards, as listed in Table 8-1. In addition, multiple WHERE conditions may be combined using Boolean AND, OR, and NOT operators.

Best Practice

One sure way to improve the performance of a client/server database is to let the Database Engine do the work of restricting the rows returned, rather than make the client application wade through unnecessary data.

TABLE 8-1

Standard Comparison Operators

Description	Operator	Example
Equals	=	Quantity = 12
Greater than	>	Quantity > 12
Greater than or equal to	>=	Quantity >= 12
Less than	<	Quantity < 12
Less than or equal to	<=	Quantity<= 12
Not equal to	<> , !=	Quantity <> 12 , Quantity != 12
Not less than	!<	Quantity !< 12
Not greater than	!>	Quantity !> 12

CAUTION **The comparison operators that include an exclamation point are not ANSI standard SQL. <> is portable; != is not.**

CROSS-REF **In addition to the standard comparison operators, which are no doubt familiar, SQL provides four special comparison operators: BETWEEN, IN, LIKE, and IS. The first three are explained in this section. Testing for nulls using the IS keyword and handling nulls are explained in Chapter 9, "Data Types, Expressions, and Scalar Functions."**

Best Practice

The best way to find a thing is to look for it, rather than to first eliminate everything it isn't. It's far easier to locate a business in a city than it is to prove that the business doesn't exist. The same is true of database searches. Proving that a row meets a condition is faster than first eliminating every row that doesn't meet that condition. In general (but not always), restating a negative WHERE condition as a positive condition will improve performance.

Using the between search condition

The BETWEEN search condition tests for values within a range. The range can be deceiving, however, because it is inclusive. For example, BETWEEN 1 and 10 would be true for 1 and 10. When using the BETWEEN search condition, the first condition must be less than the latter value because in actuality, the BETWEEN search condition is shorthand for "greater than or equal to the first value, and less than or equal to the second value."

In this example, the BETWEEN is used to select all the work orders with a quantity greater than 9 and less than 20:

```
USE AdventureWorks2008

SELECT WorkOrderID
  FROM Production.WorkOrder
  WHERE OrderQty BETWEEN 10 and 19
```

CAUTION **The BETWEEN search condition is commonly used with dates. However, BETWEEN without a time will look for the beginning of the final day, or with a time will round up the final millisecond to possibly include 12:00:00.000 of the next day. The solution is to use the following:**

```
WHERE Col >= StartDay AND Col < Ending Day + 1
```

For example,

```
WHERE SalesDate >= '6/1/2008' AND SalesDate < '7/1/2008'
```

CROSS-REF **There's actually quite a lot to consider when working with dates, all of which is covered in the next chapter, "Data Types, Expressions, and Scalar Functions."**

Comparing with a list

The WHERE condition can compare the test value against the values in a list using IN, SOME, ANY, or ALL. Each operator can also be mixed with a NOT to reverse the condition.

It Turns Out Algebra Actually *Is* Useful

As much fun as algebra class was, while we thought algebra might improve our logical minds, few of us believed we'd actually use algebra in our chosen profession.

Enter the SQL WHERE clause.

Here's the problem: If a function is applied to the test column in the WHERE clause, then SQL Server is forced to calculate that function on every row before it can filter the WHERE clause. This is a sure setup for "Gee, I don't know, it worked OK on my notebook" syndrome.

For a simple example, assume there's an index on Col1. The following WHERE clause will generate an unnecessary scan, reading every row, as every column is modified and then compared to 130:

```
SELECT Col2, Col3
  FROM table
  WHERE Col11 + 30 = 130;
```

Algebra to the rescue. Somehow figure out a way to move that function to the parameter on the right side of the "=" and off the column so that the column on the left side is unencumbered by any calculation or functions:

```
SELECT Col2, Col3
  FROM table
  WHERE Col11 = 130 - 30;
```

Now SQL Server can evaluate 130 - 30 and perform a blazingly fast index seek on the rows with 100 in Col1. Although this is a simple example, the principle is true. How you write your WHERE clauses has a significant effect on the performance of your queries.

This is only a small taste of the Query Optimizer and whether or not WHERE clause expressions are searchable arguments, known as *sargs*. Reading query execution plans and tuning queries and indexes are covered in greater detail in Chapters 63, 64, and 65.

SOME and ANY search conditions are functionally similar to IN — all are true if any value in the list is true — with three significant differences:

- SOME and ANY require a subquery. A list of literal values won't do.
- SOME and ANY are used with a mathematical operator (=, >, <, =>, etc.).
- IN, SOME, and ANY function differently when used with a NOT condition.

The AND search condition also requires a true subquery and returns a true when the search condition is true for every value in the list.

CROSS-REF **IN, SOME, ANY, and ALL are revisited in Chapter 11, "Including Data with Subqueries and CTEs." This chapter focuses on IN with a literal list.**

IN is similar to the EQUALS comparison operator, as it searches for an exact match from a list. If the value is in the list, then the comparison is true. For instance, if region data were entered into the database, the following code finds any Cape Hatteras Adventures base camps in North Carolina or West Virginia:

```
USE CHA2;
SELECT BaseCampname
  FROM dbo.BaseCamp
  WHERE Region IN ('NC', 'WV');
```

Result:

```
BaseCampName
-----------
West Virginia
Cape Hatteras
Asheville NC
```

Effectively, the IN search condition is the equivalent of multiple EQUALS comparisons ORed together:

```
USE CHA2;
SELECT BaseCampname
  FROM dbo.BaseCamp
  WHERE Region = 'NC'
    OR Region = 'WV';
```

Result:

```
BaseCampName
-----------
West Virginia
Cape Hatteras
Asheville NC
```

The IN operator may also search for a value in a list of columns. The following example searches for the text 'NC' in either the Name, City, Region, or Country columns:

```
USE CHA2;
SELECT Name
  FROM dbo.BaseCamp
  WHERE 'NC' IN (Name, City, Region, Country)
```

Result:

```
BaseCampName
-----------
Cape Hatteras
Asheville NC
```

The IN operator may be combined with NOT to exclude certain rows. For example, WHERE NOT IN ('NC', 'SC') would return all rows except those in the Carolinas:

```
USE CHA2;
SELECT BaseCampname
  FROM dbo.BaseCamp
  WHERE Region NOT IN ('NC', 'SC');
```

Result:

```
BaseCampName
-----------
FreePort
Ft Lauderdale
West Virginia
```

It's difficult to prove a negative, especially when a null value is involved. Because the meaning of null is "unknown," the value being searched for could be in the list. The following code sample demonstrates how a null in the list makes it impossible to prove that 'A' is not in the list:

```
SELECT 'IN' WHERE 'A' NOT IN ('B',NULL);
```

There's no result because the unknown null value might simply be an "A." Because SQL can't logically prove that "A" is not in the list, the WHERE clause returns a false. Anytime a NOT IN condition is mixed with a null in the list, every row will be evaluated as false.

Using the like search condition

The LIKE search condition uses wildcards to search for patterns within a string. The wildcards, however, are very different from the MS-DOS wildcards with which you may be familiar. Both the SQL and MS-DOS wildcards are shown in Table 8-2.

TABLE 8-2

SQL Wildcards

Description	SQL Wildcard	MS-DOS Wildcard	Example
Any number (zero or more) of arbitrary characters	%	*	'Able' LIKE 'A%'
One arbitrary character	_	?	'Able' LIKE 'Abl_'
One of the enclosed characters	[ ]	n/a	'a' LIKE '[a-g]' 'a' LIKE '[abcdefg]'
Match not in range of characters	[^]	n/a	'a' LIKE '[^w-z]' 'a' LIKE '[^wxyz] '

The next query uses the LIKE search condition to locate all products that begin with 'Air' optionally followed by any number of characters:

```
USE OBXKites;

SELECT ProductName
  FROM dbo.Product
  WHERE ProductName LIKE 'Air%';
```

Result:

```
ProductName
-------------------
Air Writer 36
Air Writer 48
Air Writer 66
```

The following query finds any product name beginning with a letter between a and d, inclusive:

```
SELECT ProductName
  FROM Product
  WHERE ProductName LIKE  '[a-d]%';
```

Result:

```
ProductName
--------------------------------------------------
Basic Box Kite 21 inch
Dragon Flight
Chinese 6" Kite
Air Writer 36
Air Writer 48
Air Writer 66
Competition 36"
Competition Pro 48"
Black Ghost
Basic Kite Flight
Advanced Acrobatics
Adventures in the OuterBanks
Cape Hatteras T-Shirt
```

There are two possible methods for searching for a pattern that contains a wildcard: either enclose the wildcard in square brackets or put an escape character before it. The trick to the latter workaround is that the escape character is defined within the LIKE expression.

When using the LIKE operator, be aware that the database collation's sort order determines both case sensitivity and the sort order for the range of characters. You can optionally use the keyword COLLATE to specify the collation sort order used by the LIKE operator.

Best Practice

While the LIKE operator can be very useful, it can also cause a performance hit. Indexes are based on the beginning of a column, not on phrases in the middle of the column. If you find that the application requires frequent use of the LIKE operator, you should enable full-text indexing — a powerful indexing method that can even take into consideration weighted words and variations of inflections and can return the result set in table form for joining. See Chapter 19, "Using Integrated Full-Text Search," for more details.

Multiple where conditions

Multiple WHERE conditions can be combined within the WHERE clause using the Boolean logical operators: AND, OR, and NOT. As with the mathematical operators of multiplication and division, an order of precedence exists with the Boolean logical operators: NOT comes first, then AND, and then OR:

```
SELECT ProductCode, ProductName
  FROM dbo.Product
  WHERE
      ProductName LIKE  'Air%'
    OR
      ProductCode BETWEEN '1018' AND '1020'
    AND
      ProductName LIKE '%G%';
```

Result:

```
ProductCode     ProductName
--------------- ---------------------
1009            Air Writer 36
1010            Air Writer 48
1011            Air Writer 66
1019            Grand Daddy
1020            Black Ghost
```

With parentheses, the result of the query is radically changed:

```
SELECT ProductCode, ProductName
  FROM Product
  WHERE
     (ProductName LIKE  'Air%'
    OR
      ProductCode between '1018' AND '1020')
    AND
      ProductName LIKE '%G%';
```

Result:

```
ProductCode     ProductName
--------------- ---------------------
1019            Grand Daddy
1020            Black Ghost
```

While the two preceding queries are very similar, in the first query the natural order of precedence for Boolean operators caused the AND to be evaluated before the OR. The OR included the Air Writers in the results.

The second query used parentheses to explicitly dictate the order of the Boolean operators. The OR collected the Air Writers and products with a ProductCode of 1018, 1019, or 1020. This list was then anded with products that included the letter g in their names. Only products 1019 and 1020 passed both of those tests.

Best Practice

When coding complex Boolean or mathematical expressions, explicitly stating your intentions with parentheses and detailed comments reduces misunderstandings and errors based on false assumptions.

Select...where

Surprisingly, using the WHERE clause in a SELECT statement does not require the use of a FROM clause or any data source reference at all. A SELECT statement without a FROM clause returns a single row that includes any expressions in the select's column list.

A WHERE clause on a non-table SELECT statement serves as a restriction to the entire SELECT statement. If the WHERE condition is true, the SELECT statement will function as expected:

```
SELECT 'abc' AS col
  WHERE 1>0;
```

Result:

```
col
----
abc
 (1 row(s) affected)
```

If the WHERE condition is false, the SELECT statement is still executed but it returns zero rows:

```
SELECT 'abc' AS col WHERE 1<0;
```

Result:

```
col
----

(0 row(s) affected)
```

Columns, Stars, Aliases, and Expressions

The title of this section may read like a bad tabloid headline, but in all seriousness it refers to the fact that the SQL SELECT statement will return columns in the order in which they're listed in the SELECT statement. The column may be any expression or any column in the FROM clause.

Following the FROM clause and the WHERE clause, the next logical step in the query is the list of returned expressions.

The star

The *, commonly called "star," is a special wildcard that includes all columns in their table order. If the query pulls from multiple tables, the * will include all columns from every table. Alternately, tablename.* will include only the columns from the named table.

Aliases

The name of the column in the underlying table becomes the name of the column in the result set. Optionally, the column name can be changed using a column alias.

Expressions and constants will have a blank column heading in the result set unless an alias is provided.

The AS keyword is optional, but just as with a table alias, using it is a good practice that improves the readability of the code and helps prevent errors.

To use an alias that's identical to a SQL Server keyword or that includes a space, enclose the alias in square brackets, single quotes, or double quotes. Although the square brackets are not technically required if the alias is the same as an object name (that is, table or column name), I prefer to explicitly specify that the alias is not a keyword.

The following code demonstrates adding aliases to columns:

```
SELECT ProductName AS Product,
    'abc',
    ActiveDate + 365 AS OneYearSalesDate
  FROM Product
```

Result:

```
Product                         OneYearSalesDate
-------------------------- ---- -----------------------
Basic Box Kite 21 inch     abc  2003-07-22 20:59:53.967
Dragon Flight              abc  2003-07-22 20:59:54.000
Sky Dancer                 abc  2003-07-22 20:59:54.000
...
```

The first column's name is changed from ProductName to Product by means of an alias. The second column is an expression without an alias, so it has no column name. A better practice is to name expression columns using an alias, as demonstrated in the third column.

Accidental aliases are a common source of errors. Take a careful look at the next query:

```
SELECT ProductName
    'abc',
    ActiveDate + 365 AS OneYearSalesDate
  FROM Product
```

Result:

```
Abc                        OneYearSalesDate
-------------------------- -------------------------
Basic Box Kite 21 inch     2003-07-22 20:59:53.967
Dragon Flight              2003-07-22 20:59:54.000
Sky Dancer                 2003-07-22 20:59:54.000
...
```

The second column isn't abc as in the previous query. Instead, because of a missing comma, the 'abc' in the query became an accidental alias for the first column.

What's Wrong with Select *?

Taken from my blog at www.SQLBlog.com is the following post (like an interview question, these answers reveal the mindset of the person):

Q. "What's wrong with SELECT * ?"

A. "It returns more columns than needed — wastes resources."

The interviewee is concerned about the network/systems.

A. "If you add a column it might break the app."

The interviewee is a developer.

A. "It compromises the extensibility of the database."

The interviewee is an architect type.

A. "It's hard to build a covering index for a SELECT * query"

The interviewee is a SQL PTO (Performance, Tuning & Optimization) pro.

For the many reactions, visit

http://sqlblog.com/blogs/paul_nielsen/archive/2007/12/12/what-s-wrong-with-select.aspx.

Qualified columns

A common problem with queries is that column names are duplicated in multiple tables. Including the column in the select list by column names alone will cause an "ambiguous column name" error.

Basically, SQL Server is complaining that it doesn't know to which column you're referring. Even if they contain the same exact data, SQL Server must know which column to select.

```
CREATE TABLE t1 (col1 INT);
CREATE TABLE t2 (col1 INT);

SELECT col1
  FROM t1
    CROSS JOIN t2;
```

Result:

```
Msg 209, Level 16, State 1, Line 2
Ambiguous column name 'col1'.
```

The solution, of course, is to qualify the column name by including the table:

```
SELECT t1.col1
  FROM t1
    CROSS JOIN t2;
```

CROSS-REF **The next chapter, "Data Types, Expressions, and Scalar Functions," details how to build expressions that can be used as columns or in several other places within the select statement.**

Ordering the Result Set

Logically, relational data should always be considered an unordered list. The primary key's purpose is to uniquely identify the row, not sort the table. SQL Server usually returns the data in the order of the primary key (because that's probably the clustered index), but there's no logical guarantee of that order. The only correct way to sort the results is with an ORDER BY clause.

SQL can sort by multiple columns, and the sort columns don't have to be columns that are returned by the SELECT, so there's a lot of flexibility in how the columns can be specified. Using Management Studio's Query Designer, the ORDER BY is created by selecting the sort order for the column, as shown in Figure 8-4.

Specifying the order by using column names

The best way to sort the result set is to completely spell out the ORDER BY columns:

```
USE CHA2;

SELECT FirstName, LastName
  FROM dbo.Customer
  ORDER BY LastName, FirstName;
```

FIGURE 8-4

Within Management Studio's Query Designer, you can define the sort order and sort type in the column pane. The TOP( ) predicate is set for the Query Designer inside the query's Properties page.

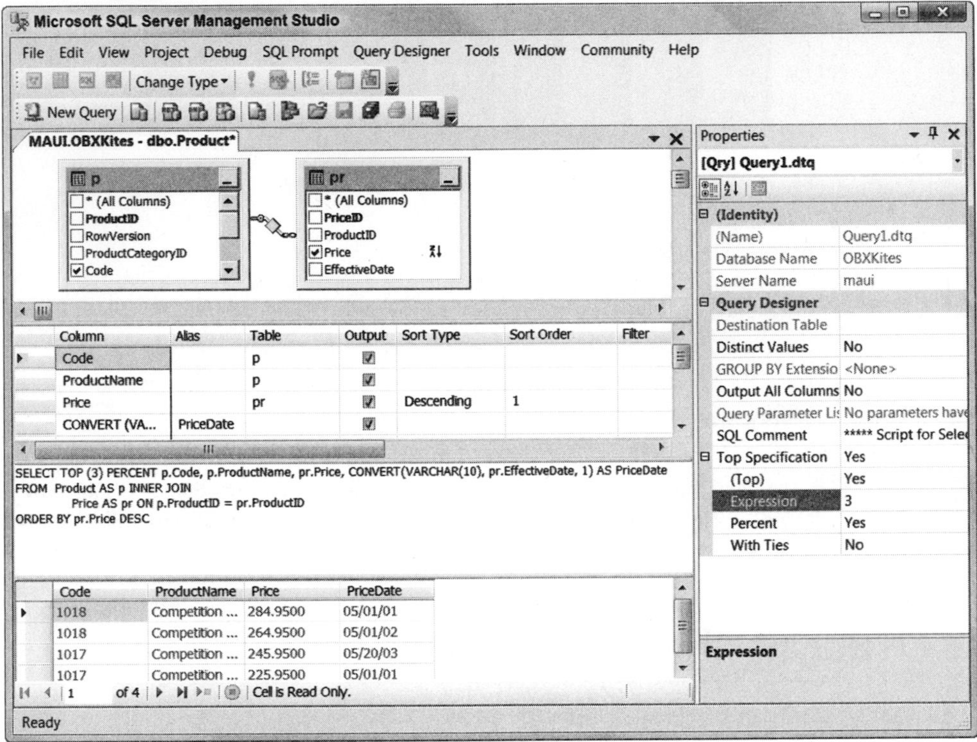

Result:

```
FirstName     LastName
------------- --------------------
Joe           Adams
Missy         Anderson
Debbie        Andrews
Dave          Bettys
...
```

NOTE `ORDER BY` **and the order of columns in the select list are completely independent.**

Specifying the order by using expressions

In the case of sorting by an expression, the entire expression can be repeated in the ORDER BY clause. This does not cause a performance hit because the SQL Server Query Optimizer is smart enough to avoid recomputing the expression:

```
SELECT LastName + ', ' + FirstName
  FROM dbo.Customer
  ORDER BY LastName + ', ' + FirstName;
```

Result:

```
FullName
----------------------
Adams, Joe
Anderson, Missy
Andrews, Debbie
Bettys, Dave
...
```

Using an expression in the ORDER BY clause can solve some headaches. For example, some database developers store product titles in two columns: one column includes the full title, and the duplicate column stores the title stripped of the leading "The." In terms of performance, such denormalization might be a good idea, but using a case expression within the ORDER BY clause will sort correctly without duplicating the title. (The full syntax for the CASE expression is covered in the Chapter 9, "Data Types, Expressions, and Scalar Functions.")

The Aesop's Fables sample database includes a list of titles. If the Title includes a leading "The," then the CASE expression removes it from the data and passes to the ORDER BY:

```
USE Aesop;
SELECT Title, Len(FableText) AS TextLength
  FROM Fable
  ORDER BY
    CASE
      WHEN Left(Title, 4) = 'The '
        THEN Stuff(Title, 1, 4, '')
      ELSE Title
    END;
```

Result:

```
FableName                          TextLength
---------------------------------- -----------
Androcles                          1370
The Ant and the Chrysalis          1087
The Ants and the Grasshopper       456
The Ass in the Lion's Skin         465
The Bald Knight                    360
```

```
The Boy and the Filberts         435
The Bundle of Sticks             551
The Crow and the Pitcher         491
...
```

Specifying the order by using column aliases

Alternatively, a column alias may be used to specify the columns used in the ORDER BY clause. This is the preferred method for sorting by an expression because it makes the code easier to read. Note that this example sorts in descending order, rather than the default ascending order:

```
SELECT LastName + ', ' + FirstName as FullName
  FROM dbo.Customer
  ORDER BY FullName DESC;
```

Result:

```
FullName
-------------
Zeniod, Kent
Williams, Larry
Valentino, Mary
Spade, Sam
...
```

An alias is allowed in the ORDER BY clause, but not the WHERE clause because the WHERE clause is logically executed prior to processing columns and expressions. The ORDER BY clause follows the assembling of the columns and aliases so it can use column aliases.

Using the column ordinal position

The ordinal number of the column (column position number) can be used to indicate the ORDER BY columns, but please don't do this. If the select columns are changed or their order changes, the sort order also changes.

One case for which it's not necessarily a horrid practice to use the ordinal number to specify the sort is for complex union queries, which are discussed in Chapter 10, "Merging Data with Joins and Unions."

The following query demonstrates sorting by ordinal position:

```
SELECT LastName + ', ' + FirstName AS FullName
  FROM dbo.Customer
  ORDER BY 1;
```

Result:

```
FullName
----------------------
Adams, Joe
```

```
Anderson, Missy
Andrews, Debbie
Bettys, Dave
...
```

Order by and collation

SQL Server's collation order is vital to sorting data. Besides determining the alphabet, the collation order also determines whether accents, case, and other alphabet properties are considered in the sort order. For example, if the collation is case sensitive, then the uppercase letters are sorted before the lowercase letters. The following function reports the installed collation options and the current collation server property:

```
SELECT * FROM fn_helpcollations();
```

Result:

```
name                    description
---------------------   -------------------------
Albanian_BIN            Albanian, binary sort
Albanian_CI_AI          Albanian, case-insensitive,
                        accent-insensitive,
                        kanatype-insensitive, width-insensitive
Albanian_CI_AI_WS       Albanian, case-insensitive,
                        accent-insensitive,
                        kanatype-insensitive, width-sensitive
...
SQL_Latin1_General_CP1_CI_AI
                        Latin1-General, case-insensitive,
                        accent-insensitive,
                        kanatype-insensitive, width-insensitive
                        for Unicode Data, SQL Server Sort Order
                        54 on Code Page 1252 for non-Unicode
                        Data
...
```

The following query reports the current server collation:

```
SELECT SERVERPROPERTY('Collation') AS ServerCollation;
```

Result:

```
ServerCollation
------------------------
SQL_Latin1_General_CP1_CI_AS
```

While the server collation setting is determined during setup, the collation property for a database or a column can be set using the COLLATE keyword. The following code changes the Family database collation so that it becomes case sensitive:

```
ALTER DATABASE Family
  COLLATE SQL_Latin1_General_CP1_CS_AS;
SELECT DATABASEPROPERTYEX('Family','Collation')
  AS DatabaseCollation;
```

Result:

```
DatabaseCollation
----------------------------------
SQL_Latin1_General_CP1_CS_AS
```

Not only can SQL Server set the collation at the server, database, and column levels, collation can even be set at the individual query level. The following query will be sorted according to the Danish collation, without regard to case or accents:

```
SELECT *
  FROM dbo.Product
  ORDER BY ProductName
    COLLATE Danish_Norwegian_CI_AI;
```

Not all queries need to be sorted, but for those that do, the `ORDER BY` clause combined with the many possible collations yields tremendous flexibility in sorting the result set.

Terminating the Statement

ANSI SQL uses a semicolon to terminate a statement. While it's been there as an option for several versions, code with semicolons was unheard of in the SQL Server community until recently. SQL Server 2005 began requiring it for some commands. Therefore, here are the rules regarding semicolons.

When semicolons are required:

- At the end of the statement preceding a common table expression (CTE)
- At the end of a MERGE statement

When not to use a semicolon:

- Between the END TRY and BEGIN CATCH
- Between the IF condition and the BEGIN
- Don't mix GO and the semicolon on the same line

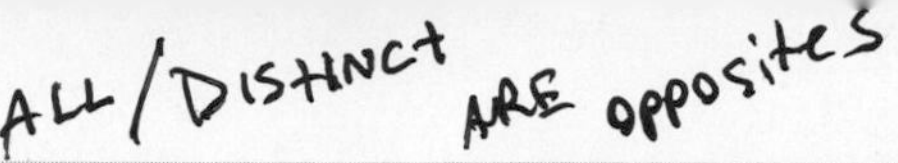

Select Distinct

The first predicate option in the SELECT command is the keyword DISTINCT, which eliminates duplicate rows from the result set of the query. The duplications are based only on the output columns, not the underlying tables. The opposite of DISTINCT is ALL. Because ALL is the default, it is typically not included.

The following example demonstrates the difference between DISTINCT and ALL. Joins are explained in Chapter 10, "Merging Data with Joins and Unions," but here the JOIN between tour and event is generating a row each time a tour is run as an event. Because this select statement returns only the tourname column, it's a perfect example of duplicate rows for the DISTINCT predicate:

```
SELECT ALL TourName
  FROM Event
    JOIN Tour
      ON Event.TourID = Tour.TourID;
```

Result:

```
TourName
---------------------------------------------------
Amazon Trek
Amazon Trek
Appalachian Trail
Appalachian Trail
Appalachian Trail
Bahamas Dive
Bahamas Dive
Bahamas Dive
Gauley River Rafting
Gauley River Rafting
Outer Banks Lighthouses
Outer Banks Lighthouses
Outer Banks Lighthouses
Outer Banks Lighthouses
Outer Banks Lighthouses
Outer Banks Lighthouses
```

With the DISTINCT predicate:

```
SELECT DISTINCT TourName
  FROM Event
    JOIN Tour
      ON Event.TourID = Tour.TourID;
```

Result:

```
TourName
-----------------------------------
Amazon Trek
Appalachian Trail
Bahamas Dive
Gauley River Rafting
Outer Banks Lighthouses
```

Whereas the first query returned 16 rows, the DISTINCT predicate in the second query eliminated the duplicate rows and returned only five unique rows.

CAUTION **SQL Server's DISTINCT is different from MS Access' distinctrow, which eliminates duplicates based on data in the source table(s), not duplicates in the result set of the query.**

Select DISTINCT functions as though a GROUP BY clause (discussed in Chapter 12, "Aggregating Data") exists on every output column.

Of course, using DISTINCT is based on the query's requirements, so there may be no choice; just be aware that depending on the size and mix of the data, there may be a performance impact.

Top ()

By definition, SELECT works with sets of data. Sometimes, however, it's only the first few rows from the set that are of interest. For these situations, SQL Server includes several ways to filter the results and find the top rows.

As mentioned earlier, SQL Server will return all the rows from the SELECT statement by default. The optional TOP() predicate tells SQL Server to return only a few rows (either a fixed number or a percentage) based upon the options specified, as shown in Figure 8-4. A variable can be passed to TOP().

NOTE **The older syntax for TOP() did not include the parentheses and did not accept a variable. The newer syntax, with the parentheses, was introduced with SQL Server 2005 and is the best practice moving forward.**

TOP() works hand-in-hand with ORDER BY. It's the ORDER BY clause that determines which rows are first. If the SELECT statement does not have an ORDER BY clause, then the TOP() predicate still works by returning an unordered sampling of the result set.

The OBXKites sample database is a good place to test the TOP() predicate. The following query finds the top 3 percent of prices in the price table. The price table allows each product to have multiple prices, according to the effective date:

```
SELECT TOP (3) PERCENT p.Code, p.ProductName, pr.Price,
    CONVERT(VARCHAR(10),pr.EffectiveDate,1) AS PriceDate
  FROM Product AS p
    JOIN Price AS pr ON p.ProductID = pr.ProductID
  ORDER BY pr.Price DESC;
```

Result:

```
ProductCode  ProductName            Price       PriceDate
------------ ---------------------- ----------  ----------
1018         Competition Pro 48"    284.9500    05/01/01
1018         Competition Pro 48"    264.9500    05/01/02
1017         Competition 36"        245.9500    05/20/03
1017         Competition 36"        225.9500    05/01/01
```

The next query locates the three lowest prices in the `price` table:

```
SELECT TOP (3) p.Code, p.ProductName, pr.Price,
    CONVERT(VARCHAR(10),pr.EffectiveDate,1) AS PriceDate
  FROM Product AS p
    JOIN Price AS  pr ON p.ProductID = pr.ProductID
  ORDER BY pr.Price;
```

Result:

```
ProductCode  ProductName            Price       PriceDate
------------ ---------------------- ----------  ----------
1044         OBX Car Bumper Sticker .7500       05/01/01
1045         OBX Car Window Decal   .7500       05/20/01
1045         OBX Car Window Decal   .9500       05/20/02
```

The query looks clean and the result looks good, but unfortunately it's wrong. If you look at the raw data sorted by price, you'll actually see three rows with a price of 95 cents. The `WITH TIES` option solves this problem, as described in the following section.

Best Practice

By the very nature of the formatting, computer-generated data tends to appear correct. Unit testing the query against a set of data with known results is the only way to check its quality.

CROSS-REF **The number of rows returned by `TOP()` may be controlled using a variable:**

```
SELECT TOP (@Variable)
```

For more details about using variables, turn to Chapter 21, "Programming with T-SQL."

The with ties option

The `WITH TIES` option is important to the `TOP()` predicate. It allows the last place to include multiple rows if those rows have equal values in the columns used in the `ORDER BY` clause. The following version of the preceding query includes the `WITH TIES` option and correctly results in five rows from a `TOP 3` predicate:

```
SELECT TOP (3) WITH TIES p.ProductCode,
    p.ProductName, pr.Price,
    CONVERT(varchar(10),pr.EffectiveDate,1) AS PriceDate
  FROM Product AS p
    JOIN Price AS  pr ON p.ProductID = pr.ProductID
  ORDER BY pr.Price;
```

Result:

```
ProductCode  ProductName            Price      PriceDate
------------ ---------------------- ---------- ----------
1044         OBX Car Bumper Sticker .7500      05/01/01
1045         OBX Car Window Decal   .7500      05/20/01
1045         OBX Car Window Decal   .9500      05/20/02
1041         Kite Fabric #6         .9500      05/01/01
1042         Kite Fabric #8         .9500      05/01/01
```

NOTE **If you are moving from Access to SQL Server, be aware that Access, by default, adds the `WITH TIES` option to the `TOP()` predicate automatically.**

NOTE **An alternative to `TOP()` is the `SET ROWCOUNT` command, which limits any DML command to affecting only *n* number of rows until it's turned off with `SET ROWCOUNT 0`. The issue is that `ROWCOUNT` isn't portable either, and it's been deprecated for `INSERT`, `UPDATE`, and `DELETE` in SQL Server 2008.**

Selecting a random row

There are times when a single random row is needed. I use this technique when populating a table with random names.

Using the `TOP(1)` predicate will return a single row, and sorting the result set by `newid()` randomizes the sort. Together they will return a random row each time the query is executed.

There is a performance cost to using `TOP(1)` and `newid()`. SQL Server has to add a `unique identifier` to every row and then sort by the `uniqueidentifier`. An elegant solution is to add a `tablesample` option to the table when randomly selecting a single row from a very large table. `Tablesample` works by randomly selecting pages within the table and then returning every row from those pages from the `from` clause:

```
SELECT TOP(1) LastName
  FROM dbo.LastNames TableSample (10 Percent)
  ORDER BY NewID();
```

Summary

A wealth of power and flexibility is hidden in the simple SELECT command.

The key to understanding the SQL query is understanding that the query is declarative — you're only phrasing a question. The Query Optimizer figures out how to execute the query, so SQL allows for some flexibility in the development style of the query.

A few of the key points from this chapter include the following:

- Think through the query in the logical flow of the query, not the syntax flow for the query.
- The FROM clause can assemble data from ten different types of data sources. Think creatively about where you can find data for your query.
- Never use SELECT *.
- Aliases are a good thing, and always use the AS.
- Be intentional about the WHERE clause. Use parentheses. Keep the expressions away from the source column.
- Never trust the sort order to the physical order of the data on the disk. If the data needs to be sorted, then use an ORDER BY.

From this introduction, the next eight chapters add incrementally more advanced features that augment the power of SELECT: incorporating complex expressions, multiple types of joins, subqueries, and groupings.

Welcome to the set-based power of SQL.

Chapter 9

Data Types, Expressions, and Scalar Functions

IN THIS CHAPTER

Working with expressions and scalar functions

Using logic within a query

Working with nulls, strings, and dates

When my son, David, was younger he built incredible monster trucks and gizmos out of K'NEX construction pieces. If you aren't familiar with K'NEX, do a Google image search and see the wild things that kids can build with it.

What makes K'NEX cool is that nearly any piece can plug into any other piece. This interconnectivity makes K'NEX flexible. In the same way, the interconnectivity of SQL expressions and functions makes SQL so flexible and powerful.

Expressions can retrieve data from a subquery, handle complex logic, convert data types, and manipulate data. If the secret to being a competent SQL database developer is mastering SQL queries, then wielding expressions and scalar functions is definitely in the arsenal.

An *expression* is any combination of constants, functions, or formulas that returns a single value. Expressions may be as simple as a hard-coded number, or as complex as a case expression that includes several formulas and functions.

Expressions may be employed in several places within the SQL syntax. Nearly anywhere a value may be used, an expression may be used instead. This includes column values, `JOIN ON` clauses, `WHERE` and `HAVING` clauses, and `ORDER BY` columns. Expressions can't be substituted for object names such as table names or column names.

Building Expressions

You can construct SQL expressions from a nearly limitless list of constants, variables, operators, and functions, as detailed in Table 9-1.

NOTE The syntax of SQL keywords is not case sensitive. The convention is to use keywords in all upper case. I sometimes will use lower case for keywords for a subquery to improve readability.

Depending on the collation setting of the server or database, database, table, and column names, and even the data itself, might be case sensitive.

TABLE 9-1

Building Expressions

Expression Components	Examples
Numeric constants	1, 2, 3, -17, -100
String literals	'LastName', 'Employee: ', 'Lifes Great!'
Dates	'1/30/1980', 'January 30, 1980', '19800130'
Mathematical operators (in order of precedence)	*, /, % (remainder), +, -
String operator (concatenation)	+
Bitwise operators (in order of precedence)	not ~, and &, or |, exclusive or ^
Columns	LastName, PrimaryKeyID
Case expressions	CASE Column1 WHEN 1 THEN 'on' ELSE 'off' END AS Status
Subqueries	(Select 3)
User-defined variables	@MyVariable
System functions	@@Error
Scalar functions	GetDate(), Radians()
User-defined functions	dbo.MyUDF()

CROSS-REF Subqueries are covered in Chapter 11, Including Data with Subqueries and CTEs. Variables are discussed in Chapter 21, Programming with T-SQL. User-defined functions are detailed in Chapter 25, Building User-Defined Functions.

Operators

While the meaning of many of these expression constants, operators, and expressions is obvious and common to other programming languages, a few deserve special mention.

The *division* mathematical operator (/) is a very common source of errors when integers are divided. This is because there is an implicit truncation of values. For instance, 17/9 will give a result of 1 although it is almost 2 (which 18/9 would yield).

The *modulo* mathematical operator (%) returns only the remainder of the division. The `floor()` (that's "deck" for sailors) and `ceiling()` mathematical functions, which return the integer rounded down or up, respectively, are related to it. The `floor()` function is the SQL Server equivalent of the BASIC `int()` function:

```
SELECT 15%4 AS Modulo,
  FLOOR(1.25) AS [Floor], CEILING(1.25) AS [Ceiling];
```

Result:

```
Modulo      Floor   Ceiling
----------- -----   -------
3           1       2
```

The + operator is used for both mathematical expressions and string concatenation. This operator is different from the Visual Basic symbol for string concatenation, the ampersand (&):

```
SELECT 123 + 456 AS Addition,
  'abc' + 'defg' AS Concatenation;

Result:
Addition      Concatenation
-----------   ------------------
579           abcdefg
```

Data from table columns and string literals may be concatenated to return custom data:

```
Use OBXKites
SELECT 'Product: ' + ProductName AS Product
  FROM Product;
Result:
Product
-------------
Product: Basic Box Kite 21 inch
Product: Dragon Flight
Product: Sky Dancer
...
```

Bitwise operators

The *bitwise* operators are useful for binary manipulation. These aren't typically used in transactional databases, but they can prove useful for certain metadata operations. For example, one way to determine which columns were updated in a trigger (code that is executed as the result of a data insert, update, or delete, as covered in Chapter 26, "Creating DML Triggers") is to inspect the `columns_updated()` function, which returns a binary representation of those columns. The trigger code can test `columns_updated()` using bitwise operations and respond to updates on a column-by-column basis.

Boolean bit operators (and, or, and not) are the basic building blocks of digital electronics and binary programming. Whereas digital-electronic Boolean gates operate on single bits, these bitwise operators work across every bit of the integer family data type (`int`, `smallint`, `tinyint`, and `bit`) values.

Boolean and

A Boolean "and" (represented by the ampersand character, &) returns a value of true only if both inputs are true (or 1 for mathematical bit operations). If either or both are false (or 0 for mathematical bit operations), then the "and" will return a value of 1, as follows:

```
SELECT 1 & 1;
Result:
1
```

Another "and" example:

```
SELECT 1 & 0;
Result:
0
```

"And"ing two integers is illustrated as follows:

```
decimal 3 = binary 011
decimal 5 = binary 101
3 AND 5
decimal 1 = binary 001


SELECT 3 & 5;
Result:
1
```

Boolean or

The Boolean `OR` operator, the vertical pipe character (|), returns true if either input is true:

```
SELECT 1 | 1;
Result:
1
```

The following `SELECT` statement combines a set (true or 1) and a cleared (false or 0) bit using the bitwise or operator:

```
SELECT 1 | 0;
Result:
1
```

`OR`ing two integers can be illustrated as follows:

```
decimal 3 = binary 011
```

```
decimal 5 = binary 101
3 OR 5
decimal  7 = binary 111


SELECT 3 | 5;
Result:
7
```

Boolean exclusive or

The "exclusive or" (XOR) bitwise operator, the carat (^), returns a value of true if either input is true, but not if both are true. The operator is shown here:

```
SELECT 1^1;
Result:
0
```

A set bit XORed with a cleared bit results in a set bit:

```
SELECT 1^0;
Result:
1
```

XORing two integers can be illustrated as follows:

```
decimal 3 = binary 011
decimal 5 = binary 101
3 OR 5
decimal  6 = binary 110
```

Bitwise not

The last bitwise operator, denoted by the tilde (~), is a bitwise NOT function. This bitwise "not" is a little different. The "not" performs a logical bit reversal for every bit in the expression. The result depends on the data length of the expression. For example, the bitwise "not" of a set bit is a cleared bit:

```
DECLARE @A BIT;
SET @A = 1;
SELECT ~@A;
Result:
0
```

The bitwise "not" is not suitable for use with Boolean expressions such as `IF` conditions. The following code, for example, is invalid:

```
SELECT * FROM Product WHERE ~(1=1);
```

Note that the "not" operator also serves as the *one's complement* operator. The system known as one's complement can be used to represent negative numbers. The one's complement form of a negative binary number is the bitwise NOT applied to it — the complement of its positive counterpart.

Case expressions

SQL Server's CASE expression is a flexible and excellent means of building dynamic expressions. If you're a programmer, no doubt you use the case command in other languages. The SQL CASE expression, however, is different. It's not used for programmatic flow of control, but rather to logically determine the value of an expression based on a condition.

Best Practice

When programmers write procedural code, it's often because part of the formula changes depending on the data. To a procedural mind-set, the best way to handle this is to loop through the rows and use multiple IF statements to branch to the correct formula. However, using a CASE expression to handle the various calculations and executing the entire operation in a single query enables SQL Server to optimize the process and make it *dramatically* faster.

Because the case expression returns an expression, it may be used anywhere in the SQL DML statement (SELECT, INSERT, UPDATE, DELETE) where an expression may be used, including column expressions, join conditions, where conditions, having conditions, in the ORDER BY, or even embedded in a longer expression. A case expression can even be used mid-expression to create a dynamic formula – very powerful.

The CASE statement has two forms, simple and searched, described in the following sections.

Simple case

With the simple CASE, the variable is presented first and then each test condition is listed. However, this version of CASE is limited in that it can perform only equal comparisons. The CASE expression sequentially checks the WHEN conditions and returns the THEN value of the first true WHEN condition.

In the following example, based on the OBXKites database, one CustomerType is the default for new customers and is set to true in the IsDefault column. The CASE expression compares the value in the default column with each possible bit setting and returns the character string 'default type' or 'possible' based on the bit setting:

```
USE OBXKites;
SELECT CustomerTypeName,
    CASE IsDefault
      WHEN 1 THEN 'default type'
      WHEN 0 THEN 'possible'
      ELSE '-'
    END AS AssignStatus
  FROM CustomerType;
```

```
Result:
CustomerTypeName             AssignStatus
--------------------------   ------------
Preferred                    possible
Wholesale                    possible
Retail                       default type
```

The CASE expression concludes with an end and an alias. In this example, the CASE expression evaluates the IsDefault column, but produces the AssignStatus column in the SQL SELECT result set.

Be careful if you use NULL in a simple CASE. This translates literally to "=NULL" and not to "IS NULL". You can get unintended results if you are not careful.

Boolean case

The Boolean form of case (called the searched case in BOL) is more flexible than the simple form in that each individual case has its own Boolean expression. Therefore, not only can each WHEN condition include comparisons other than =, but the comparison may also reference different columns:

```
SELECT
  CASE
    WHEN 1<0 THEN 'Reality is gone.'
    WHEN CURRENT_TIMESTAMP = '20051130'
      THEN 'David gets his driver''s license.'
    WHEN 1>0 THEN 'Life is normal.'
  END AS RealityCheck;
```

Following is the result of the query when executed on David's sixteenth birthday:

```
RealityCheck
--------------------------------
David gets his driver's license.
```

As with the simple case, the first true WHEN condition halts evaluation of the case and returns the THEN value. In this case (a pun!), if 1 is ever less than 0, then the RealityCheck case will accurately report 'reality is gone.' When my son turns 16, the RealityCheck will again accurately warn us of his legal driving status. If neither of these conditions is true, and 1 is still greater than 0, then all is well with reality and 'Life is normal.'

The point of the preceding code is that the searched CASE expression offers more flexibility than the simple CASE. This example mixed various conditional checks (<,=,>), and differing data was checked by the WHEN clause.

The Boolean CASE expression can handle complex conditions, including Boolean AND and OR operators. The following code sample uses a batch to set up the CASE expression (including T-SQL variables, which are explained in Chapter 21, "Programming with T-SQL"), and the CASE includes an AND and a BETWEEN operator:

```
DECLARE @b INT, @q INT;
```

```
SET @b = 2007;
SET @q = 25;

SELECT CASE
   WHEN @b = 2007 AND @q BETWEEN 10 AND 30 THEN 1
   ELSE NULL
END AS Test;
Result:
Test
---------
1
```

Working with nulls

The relational database model represents missing data using null. Technically, null means "value absent" and it's commonly understood to mean "unknown." In practice, null can indicate that the data has not yet been entered into the database or that the column does not apply to the particular row.

Because null values are unknown, the result of any expression that includes null will also have a value that is unknown. If the contents of a bank account are unknown, and its funds are included in a portfolio, then the total value of the portfolio is also unknown. The same concept is true in SQL, as the following code demonstrates. Phil Senn, a database developer, puts it this way: "Nulls zap the life out of any other value."

```
SELECT 1 + NULL;
Result:
NULL
```

Because nulls have such a devastating effect on expressions, some developers detest the use of nulls. They develop their databases so that nulls are never permitted, and column defaults supply surrogate nulls (blank, 0, or 'n/a') instead.

Other database developers argue that an unknown value should be represented by a zero or a blank just to make coding easier. I fall into the latter camp. Nulls are valuable in a database because they provide a consistent method of identifying missing data. And regardless of how missing data is represented in the database, certain types of queries will often produce nulls in the results, so it's worthwhile to write code that checks for nulls and handles them appropriately.

NOTE **An advantage to using nulls is that SQL Server's `AVG()` and `COUNT(column)` aggregate functions automatically exclude nulls from the calculation. If you're using a surrogate null (for example, I've seen IT shops use 0 or -999 to represent missing numeric data) then every aggregate query must filter out the surrogate null or the results will be less than accurate.**

Testing for null

Because null represents a missing value, there is no way to know whether a null is equal or unequal to a given value, or even to another null. Returning to the bank account example, if the balance of account 123 is missing and the balance of account 234 is missing, then it's logically impossible to say whether the two accounts have an equal or unequal balance.

Consider this simple test which proves that null does not equal null:

```
IF NULL = NULL
  SELECT '=';
ELSE
  SELECT '<> ';
```

Result:

```
<>
```

Because the = and <> operators can't check for nulls, SQL includes two special operators, `IS` and `IS NOT`, to test for equivalence to special values, as follows:

```
WHERE Expression IS NULL
```

Repeating the simple test, the `IS` search operator works as advertised:

```
IF NULL IS NULL
  SELECT 'Is';
ELSE
  SELECT 'Is Not';
Result:
Is
```

The `IS` search condition may be used in the `SELECT` statement's `WHERE` clause to locate rows with null values. Most of the Cape Hatteras Adventures customers do not have a nickname in the database. The following query retrieves only those customers with a null in the `Nickname` column:

```
USE CHA2;
SELECT FirstName, LastName, Nickname
  FROM dbo.Customer
  WHERE Nickname IS NULL
  ORDER BY LastName, FirstName;
Result:
FirstName        LastName         Nickname
------------     --------------   ----------------
Debbie           Andrews          NULL
Dave             Bettys           NULL
Jay              Brown            NULL
Lauren           Davis            NULL
...
```

The `IS` operator may be combined with `NOT` to test for the presence of a value by restricting the result set to those rows where `Nickname` is not null:

```
SELECT FirstName, LastName, Nickname
  FROM dbo.Customer
  WHERE Nickname IS NOT NULL
  ORDER BY LastName, FirstName;
```

```
Result:
FirstName       LastName        Nickname
------------    --------------  ----------------
Joe             Adams           Slim
Melissa         Anderson        Missy
Frank           Goldberg        Frankie
Raymond         Johnson         Ray
...
```

Handling nulls

When you are supplying data to reports, to end users, or to some applications, a null value will be less than welcome. Often a null must be converted to a valid value so that the data may be understood, or so the expression won't fail.

Nulls require special handling when used within expressions, and SQL includes a few functions designed specifically to handle nulls. `ISNULL()` and `COALESCE()` convert nulls to usable values, and `NULLIF()` creates a null if the specified condition is met.

Using the COALESCE() function

`COALESCE()` is not used as often as it could (some would say *should*) be, perhaps because it's not well known. It's a very cool function. `COALESCE()` accepts a list of expressions or columns and returns the first non-null value, as follows:

```
COALESCE(expression, expression, ...)
```

`COALESCE()` is derived from the Latin words *co* + *alescre*, which mean to unite toward a common end, to grow together, or to bring opposing sides together for a common good. The SQL keyword, however, is derived from the alternate meaning of the term: "to arise from the combination of distinct elements." In a sense, the `COALESCE()` function brings together multiple, differing values of unknown usefulness, and from them emerges a single valid value.

Functionally, `COALESCE()` is the same as the following case expression:

```
CASE
  WHEN expression1 IS NOT NULL THEN expression1
  WHEN expression2 IS NOT NULL THEN expression2
  WHEN expression3 IS NOT NULL THEN expression3
  ...
  ELSE NULL
END
```

The following code sample demonstrates the `COALESCE()` function returning the first non-null value. In this case, it's 1+2:

```
SELECT COALESCE(NULL, 1+NULL, 1+2, 'abc');
```

```
Result:
3
```

COALESCE() is excellent for merging messy data. For example, when a table has partial data in several columns, the COALESCE() function can help pull the data together. In one project I worked on, the client had collected names and addresses from several databases and applications into a single table. The contact name and company name made it into the proper columns, but some addresses were in Address1, some were in Address2, and some were in Address3. Some rows had the second line of the address in Address2. If the address columns had an address, then the SalesNote was a real note. In many cases, however, the addresses were in the SalesNote column. Here's the code to extract the address from such a mess:

```
SELECT COALESCE(
    Address1 + STR(13) + STR(10) + Address2,
    Address1,
    Address2,
    Address3,
    SalesNote) AS NewAddress
  FROM TempSalesContacts;
```

For each row in the TempSalesContacts table, the COALESCE() function will search through the listed columns and return the first non-null value. The first expression returns a value only if there's a value in both Address1 and Address2, because a value concatenated with a null produces a null. Therefore, if a two-line address exists, then it will be returned. Otherwise, a one-line address in Address1, Address2, or Address3 will be returned. Failing those options, the SalesNote column will be returned. Of course, the result from such a messy source table still needs to be manually scanned and verified.

Using the ISNULL() function

The most common null-handling function is ISNULL(), which is different from the IS NULL search condition. This function accepts a single expression and a substitution value. If the source is not equal to null, then the ISNULL() function passes the value on. However, if the source is null, then the second parameter is substituted for the null, as follows:

```
ISNULL(source_expression, replacement_value)
```

Functionally, ISNULL() is similar to the following case expression:

```
CASE
  WHEN source_expression IS NULL THEN replacement_value
  ELSE source_expression
END
```

The following code sample builds on the preceding queries by substituting the string ('NONE') for a null for customers without a nickname:

```
SELECT FirstName, LastName, ISNULL(Nickname,'none')
  FROM Customer
```

```
  ORDER BY LastName, FirstName;
Result:
FirstName     LastName            Nickname
------------  --------------      ----------------
Joe           Adams               Slim
Melissa       Anderson            Missy
Debbie        Andrews             none
Dave          Bettys              none
...
```

If the row has a value in the Nickname column, then that value is passed though the `ISNULL()` function untouched. However, if the nickname is null for a row, then the null is handled by the `ISNULL()` function and converted to the value none.

The `ISNULL()` function is specific to T-SQL, whereas `NULLIF()` is ANSI standard SQL.

Using the NULLIF() function

Sometimes a null should be created in place of surrogate null values. If a database is polluted with n/a, blank, or – values where it should contain nulls, then you can use the `NULLIF()` function to replace the inconsistent values with nulls and clean the database.

The `NULLIF()` function accepts two parameters. If they are equal, then it returns a null; otherwise, it returns the first parameter. Functionally, `NULLIF()` is the same as the following case expression:

```
CASE
  WHEN Expression1 = Expression2 THEN NULL
  ELSE Expression1
END
```

The following code will convert any blanks in the `Nickname` column into nulls. The first statement updates one of the rows to a blank for testing purposes:

```
UPDATE Customer
  SET Nickname = ''
  WHERE LastName = 'Adams';

SELECT LastName, FirstName,
    CASE Nickname
      WHEN '' THEN 'blank'
      ELSE Nickname
    END AS Nickname,
    NULLIF(Nickname, '') as NicknameNullIf
  FROM dbo.Customer
  WHERE LastName IN ('Adams', 'Anderson', 'Andrews')
  ORDER BY LastName, FirstName;
```

```
Result:
LastName        FirstName       Nickname        NicknameNullIf
-----------     -----------     ----------      ------------
Adams           Joe             blank           NULL
Anderson        Melissa         Missy           Missy
Andrews         Debbie          NULL            NULL
```

The third column uses a case expression to expose the blank value as "blank," and indeed the NULLIF() function converts the blank value to a null in the fourth column. To test the other null possibilities, Melissa's Nickname was not affected by the NULLIF() function, and Debbie's null Nickname value is still in place.

A common use of NULLIF() prevents divide-by-zero errors. The following expression will generate an error if the variable b is zero:

```
a / b ~~ Error if b is 0, otherwise a normal division result
```

However, you can use NULLIF() such that if the value of the b variable is 0, it will result in a NULL instead of an error, as follows:

```
a / NULLIF(b,0) ~~NULL result if b is 0, otherwise a normal division result
```

Now with a 0 as the result instead of an error, COALESCE() can be used to replace it with something more usable if needed.

Scalar Functions

Scalar functions return a single value. They are commonly used in expressions within the SELECT, WHERE, ORDER BY, GROUP, and HAVING clauses, or T-SQL code. SQL Server includes dozens of functions. This section describes the functions I find most useful.

Best Practice

Performance is as much a part of the data-schema design as it is a part of the query. Plan to store the data in the way that it will be searched by a WHERE condition, rather than depend on manipulating the data with functions at query time. While using a function in an expression in a result-set column may be unavoidable, using a function in a WHERE condition forces the function to be calculated for every row. In addition, another bottleneck is created because using a function in a WHERE clause makes it impossible for the Query Optimizer to use an index seek — it has to use a scan instead, resulting in much more I/O.

CROSS-REF **With SQL Server 2008 you can develop three types of user-defined functions, as explained in Chapter 25, "Building User-Defined Functions."**

User information functions

In a client/server environment, it's good to know who the client is. Toward that end, the following four functions are very useful, especially for gathering audit information:

- `USER_NAME()`: Returns the name of the current user as he or she is known to the database. When a user is granted access to a database, a username that is different from the server login name may be assigned. The results are affected by an `EXECUTE AS` command, in which case the username shown is that of the impersonated user.
- `SUSER_SNAME()`: Returns the login name by which the user was authenticated to SQL Server. If the user was authenticated as a member of a Windows user group, then this function still returns the user's Windows login name. The results are affected by an `EXECUTE AS` command, in which case the username shown is that of the impersonated user.
- `HOST_NAME()`: Returns the name of the user's workstation.
- `APP_NAME()`: Returns the name of the application (if set by the application itself) connected to SQL Server, as follows:

```
SELECT
  USER_NAME() AS 'User',
  SUSER_SNAME() AS 'Login',
  HOST_NAME() AS 'Workstation',
 APP_NAME() AS 'Application';
Result:
User     Login              Workstation     Application
-------  ----------------   ------------    ------------------
Dbo      NOLI\Paul          CHA2\NOLI       Management Studio
```

Date and time functions

Databases must often work with date and time data, and SQL Server includes several useful functions for that. SQL Server stores both the data and the time in a single data type. It also has types for date only, time only, and zone-aware times.

T-SQL includes several functions to return the current date and time:

- `GetDate()`: Returns the current server date and time to the nearest 3 $\frac{1}{3}$ milliseconds, rounded to the nearest value
- `CURRENT_TIMESTAMP`: The same as `GETDATE()` except ANSI standard
- `GetUTCDate()`: Returns the current server date converted to Greenwich mean time (also known as UTC time) to the nearest 3 milliseconds. This is extremely useful for companies that cross time boundaries.

New to SQL Server 2008:

- `SysDateTime()`: Returns the current server date and time to the nearest hundred nanoseconds
- `SysUTCDateTime()`: Returns the current server date converted to Greenwich mean time to the nearest hundred nanoseconds

- SYSDATETIMEOFFSET( ): Returns a DateTimeOffset value that contains the date and time of the computer on which the instance of SQL Server is running. The time zone offset is included.
- ToDateTimeOffset( ): Returns a DateTimeOffset type

The following four SQL Server date-time functions handle extracting or working with a specific portion of the date or time stored within a datetime column:

- DATEADD(date portion, number, date): Returns a new value after adding the number
- DATEDIFF(date portion, start date, end date): Returns the count of the date portion boundaries
- DateName(date portion, date): Returns the proper name for the selected portion of the datetime value or its ordinal number if the selected portion has no name (the portions for DateName( ) and DatePart( ) are listed in Table 9-2):

```
SELECT DATENAME(year, CURRENT_TIMESTAMP) AS "Year";
Result:
Year
--------
2009
```

This code gets the month and weekday name:

```
select DATENAME(MONTH,CURRENT_TIMESTAMP) as "Month",
   DATENAME(WEEKDAY,CURRENT_TIMESTAMP) As "Day"
Result
Month     Day
--------  -----------
February  Tuesday
```

This code gets the month and weekday name and displays the results in Italian:

```
Set language Italian
select DATENAME(MONTH,CURRENT_TIMESTAMP) as "Month",
   DATENAME(WEEKDAY,CURRENT_TIMESTAMP) As "Day"
Result
Month      Day
--------   -----------
Febbraio   Martedi
```

CROSS-REF **For more information about** datetime, datetime2, **and other data types, refer to Chapter 20, "Creating the Physical Database Schema."**

The following code example assigns a date of birth to Mr. Frank and then retrieves the proper names of some of the portions of that date of birth using the DateName( ) function:

```
UPDATE Guide
  SET DateOfBirth = 'September 4 1958'
  WHERE LastName = 'Frank';
```

```
RESULT:
SELECT LastName,
    DATENAME(yy,DateOfBirth) AS [Year],
    DATENAME(mm,DateOfBirth) AS [Month],
    DATENAME(dd,DateOfBirth) AS [Day],
    DATENAME(weekday, DateOfBirth) AS BirthDay
  FROM dbo.Guide
  WHERE DateOfBirth IS NOT NULL;
LastName     Year     Month          Day     BirthDay
---------    ------   -----------    -----   ----------------
Frank        1958     September      4       Thursday
```

TABLE 9-2

DateTime Portions Used by Date Functions

Portion	Abbreviation
year	yy, yyyy
quarter	qq, q
month	mm, m
dayofyear	dy, d
day	dd, d
week	wk, ww
weekday	dw
hour	hh
minute	mi, n
second	ss, s
millisecond	ms
microsecond	mcs
nanosecond	ns
TZoffset	tz

NOTE **There are two supported types: `DateTime` and `DateTime2`. `DateTime2` is new to SQL Server 2008 and represents time to a much finer granularity: within 100 nanoseconds.**

- `DatePart(date portion, date)`: Returns the ordinal number of the selected portion of the datetime value. The following example retrieves the day of the year and the day of the week as integers:

```
SELECT DATEPART(dayofyear, CURRENT_TIMESTAMP) AS DayCount;
Result:
DayCount
-----------
321

SELECT DATEPART(weekday, CURRENT_TIMESTAMP) AS DayWeek;
Result:
DayWeek
-----------
7
```

An easy way to obtain just the date, stripping off the time, is to use a couple of string functions:

```
SELECT CONVERT(char(10), CURRENT_TIMESTAMP, 112) AS "DateTime";
```

- `DateAdd(DATE PORTION, AMOUNT, BEGINNING DATE)` and `DateDiff(DATE PORTION, BEGINNING DATE, ENDING DATE)`: Performs addition and subtraction on datetime data, which databases often need to do. The `DATEDIFF()` and the `DATEADD()` functions are designed expressly for this purpose. The `DATEDIFF()` doesn't look at the complete date, only the date part being extracted:

```
select DATEDIFF(year,'september 4 2008','november 10 2009')
Result
1
select DATEDIFF(month,'september 4 2008','november 10 2009')
2
```

The following query calculates the number of years and days that my wife, Melissa, and I have been married:

```
SELECT
  DATEDIFF(yy,'19840520', CURRENT_TIMESTAMP) AS MarriedYears,
  DATEDIFF(dd,'19840520', CURRENT_TIMESTAMP) AS MarriedDays;
Result:
MarriedYears        MarriedDays
------------        -----------
17                  6390
```

The next query adds 100 hours to the current millisecond:

```
SELECT DATEADD(hh,100, CURRENT_TIMESTAMP) AS [100HoursFromNow];
Result:
100HoursFromNow
------------------------
2009-11-21 18:42:03.507
```

The following query is based on the `Family` sample database and calculates the mother's age at the birth of each child, using the `DateDiff()` function:

```
USE Family;
SELECT Person.FirstName + ' ' + Person.LastName AS Mother,
    DATEDIFF(yy, Person.DateOfBirth,
    Child.DateOfBirth) AS AgeDiff,Child.FirstName
  FROM Person
    INNER JOIN Person AS Child
      ON Person.PersonID = Child.MotherID
  ORDER By Age DESC;
```

The `DATEDIFF()` function in this query returns the year difference between `PERSON.DATEOFBIRTH`, which is the mother's birth date, and the child's date of birth. Because the function is in a column expression, it is calculated for each row in the result set:

```
Mother                AgeDiff    FirstName
--------------------- ---------- -----------
Audrey Halloway       33         Corwin
Kimberly Kidd         31         Logan
Elizabeth Campbell    31         Alexia
Melanie Campbell      30         Adam
Grace Halloway        30         James
...
```

This section discusses functions that are new to SQL Server 2008. You will take a look at the functions and then see the results of some queries.

`ToDateTimeOffset(expression, time_zone)`: Returns a `DateTimeOffset` value

The following example gets the date and time for a given time zone:

```
SELECT TODATETIMEOFFSET(CURRENT_TIMESTAMP,'-07:00');
```

Result:

```
2009-11-05 11:24:15.490 -07:00
```

String Functions

Like most modern programming languages, T-SQL includes many string-manipulation functions:

- `SUBSTRING(string, starting position, length)`: Returns a portion of a string. The first parameter is the string, the second parameter is the beginning position of the substring to be extracted, and the third parameter is the length of the string extracted:

  ```
  SELECT SUBSTRING('abcdefg', 3, 2);
  ```

  Result:

  ```
  cd
  ```

- `STUFF(string, insertion position, delete count, string inserted)`: The `STUFF()` function inserts one string into another string. The inserted string may delete a specified number of characters as it is being inserted:

  ```
  SELECT STUFF('abcdefg', 3, 2, '123');
  ```

  Result:

  ```
  ab123efg
  ```

  The following code sample uses nested `STUFF()` functions to format a U.S. social security number:

  ```
  SELECT STUFF(STUFF('123456789', 4, 0, '-'), 7, 0, '-');
  ```

  Result:

  ```
  123-45-6789
  ```

- `CHARINDEX(search string, string, starting position)`: Returns the character position of a string within a string. The third argument is optional and rarely used in practice. It defaults to 1.

  ```
  SELECT CHARINDEX('c', 'abcdefg', 1);
  ```

  Result:

  ```
  3
  ```

  The user-defined function `dbo.pTitleCase()` later in this section uses `CHARINDEX()` to locate the spaces separating words.

- `PATINDEX(pattern, string)`: Searches for a pattern, which may include wildcards, within a string. The following code locates the first position of either a `c` or a `d` in the string:

  ```
  SELECT PATINDEX('%[cd]%', 'abdcdefg');
  ```

  Result:

  ```
  3
  ```

- `RIGHT(string, count)` and `Left(string, count)`: Returns the rightmost or leftmost part of a string:

  ```
  SELECT LEFT('Nielsen',2) AS ' [Left] ',
    RIGHT('Nielsen',2) AS [Right];
  ```

  Result:

  ```
  Left     Right
  -----    ----
  Ni       en
  ```

- `LEN(string)`: Returns the length of a string:

  ```
  SELECT LEN('Supercalifragilisticexpialidocious') AS [Len];
  ```

  Result:

  ```
  Len
  -----------
  34
  ```

- `RTRIM(string)` and `LTrim(string)`: Removes leading or trailing spaces. While it's difficult to see in print, the three leading and trailing spaces are removed from the following string. They are often used together as `RTRIM(LTRIM(string)`. I adjusted the column-header lines with the remaining spaces to illustrate the functions:

  ```
  SELECT RTRIM('   middle earth   ') AS [RTrim],
   LTRIM('   middle earth   ') AS [LTrim];
  Result:
  RTrim                   LTrim
  ---------------         ---------------
  middle earth            middle earth
  ```

- `UPPER(string)` and `Lower(string)`: Converts the entire string to uppercase or lowercase. There's not much to know about these two functions, illustrated here:

  ```
  SELECT UPPER('one TWO tHrEe') AS UpperCase,
    LOWER('one TWO tHrEe') AS LowerCase;
  Result:
  UpperCase               LowerCase
  -------------           -------------
  ONE TWO THREE           one two three
  ```

- `REPLACE(string, string)`: The `Replace()` function operates as a global search and replace within a string. Using `REPLACE()` within an update DML command can quickly fix problems in the data, such as removing extra tabs or correcting string patterns. The following code sample adds apostrophes to the `LastName` column in the `OBXKITES` database's `CONTACT` table:

  ```
  USE OBXKites;

  -- Create test case by modifying one contact's last name.
  UPDATE Contact
    SET LastName = 'Adam''s'
    WHERE LastName = 'Adams';

  -- Check the modified sample data and the replacement.
  SELECT LastName, REPLACE(LastName, '''', '') AS Replaced
    FROM Contact
    WHERE LastName LIKE '%''%';
  ```

Result:

```
LastName      Replaced
------------- ------------
Adam's        Adams
```

To demonstrate the REPLACE( ) function using an update command, the next query actually changes the data in place and removes any apostrophes:

```
UPDATE Contact
  SET LastName = REPLACE(LastName, '''', '')
  WHERE LastName LIKE '%''%';

-- Show that the modification was successful.
SELECT LastName
  FROM Contact
  WHERE LastName LIKE 'Adam%';
```

Result:

```
LastName
--------------------------------------------------
Adams
```

NOTE **When working with string literals, it's generally difficult to insert a quote into the string without ending the string and causing a syntax error. SQL Server handles this situation by accepting two single quotes and converting them into one single quote within the string:**

'Life''s Great! ' is interpreted as Life's Great!

- dbo.pTitleCase(source, search, replace): T-SQL lacks a function to convert text to title case (first letter of each word in uppercase, and the remainder in lowercase). Therefore, the following user-defined function accomplishes that task:

```
CREATE FUNCTION dbo.pTitleCase (
  @StrIn NVARCHAR(MAX))
RETURNS NVARCHAR(MAX)
AS
  BEGIN;
    DECLARE
      @StrOut NVARCHAR(MAX),
      @CurrentPosition INT,
      @NextSpace INT,
      @CurrentWord NVARCHAR(MAX),
      @StrLen INT,
      @LastWord BIT;

    SET @NextSpace = 1;
    SET @CurrentPosition = 1;
```

```
        SET @StrOut = '';
        SET @StrLen = LEN(@StrIn);
        SET @LastWord = 0;

        WHILE @LastWord = 0
          BEGIN;
            SET @NextSpace =
              CHARINDEX(' ', @StrIn, @CurrentPosition + 1);
            IF  @NextSpace = 0 -- no more spaces found
              BEGIN;
                 SET @NextSpace = @StrLen;
                 SET @LastWord = 1;
              END;
            SET @CurrentWord =
              UPPER(SUBSTRING(@StrIn, @CurrentPosition, 1));
            SET @CurrentWord = @CurrentWord +
              LOWER(SUBSTRING(@StrIn, @CurrentPosition+1,
                     @NextSpace - @CurrentPosition));
            SET @StrOut = @StrOut + @CurrentWord;
            SET @CurrentPosition = @NextSpace + 1;
         END;
       RETURN @StrOut;
     END;
```

Running a user-defined function requires including the owner name in the function name:

```
SELECT dbo.pTitleCase('one TWO tHrEe') AS TitleCase;
Result:
TitleCase
------------------------
One Two Three
```

NOTE **The `dbo.pTitleCase` function does not take into consideration surnames with nonstandard capitalization, such as McDonald, VanCamp, or de Jonge. It would be inadequate to hard-code a list of exceptions. Perhaps the best solution is to store a list of exception phrases (Mc, Van, de, and so on) in an easily updateable list.**

The code for the `pTitleCase` user-defined function can be downloaded from `www.SQLServerBible.com`.

Soundex Functions

Soundex is a phonetic pattern-matching system created for the American census. Franklin Roosevelt directed the United States Bureau of Archives to develop a method of cataloguing the population that could handle variations in the spelling of similar surnames. Margaret K. Odell and Robert C. Russell developed Soundex and were awarded U.S. patents 1261167 (1918) and 1435663 (1922) for their efforts. The census filing card for each household was then filed under the Soundex method. Soundex has been applied to every census since and has been post-applied to census records back to 1880.

The purpose of Soundex is to sort similar-sounding names together, which is very useful for dealing with contact information in a database application. For example, if I call a phone bank and give them my name (Nielsen), they invariably spell it "Nelson" in the contact lookup form, but if the database uses Soundex properly, then I'll still be in the search-result list box.

For more information concerning Soundex and its history, refer to the following websites:

- `www.nara.gov/genealogy/coding.html`
- `www.amberskyline.com/treasuremaps/uscensus.html`
- `www.bluepoof.com/soundex/`

Here's how Soundex works. The first letter of a name is stored as the letter, and the following Soundex phonetic sounds are stored according to the following code:

1 = B, F, P, V

2 = C, G, J, K, Q, S, X, Z

3 = D, T

4 = L

5 = M, N

6 = R

Double letters with the same Soundex code, A, E, I, O, U, H, W, Y, and some prefixes, are disregarded. Therefore, "Nielsen" becomes "N425" via the following method:

1. The N is stored.
2. The i and e are disregarded.
3. The l sound is stored as the Soundex code 4.
4. The s is stored as the Soundex code 2.
5. The e is ignored.
6. The n is stored as the Soundex code 5.

By boiling them down to a few consonant sounds, Soundex assigns "Nielsen," "Nelson," and "Neilson" the same code: N425.

Following are additional Soundex name examples:

- Brown = B650 (r = 6, n = 5)
- Jeffers = J162 (ff = 1, r = 6, s = 2)
- Letterman = L365 (tt = 3, r = 6, m = 5)
- Nicholson = N242 (c = 2, l = 4, s = 2)
- Nickols = N242 (c = 2, l = 4, s = 2)

SQL Server includes two Soundex-related functions, `SOUNDEX()` and `DIFFERENCE()`.

Using the SOUNDEX() function

The SOUNDEX(string) function calculates the Soundex code for a string as follows:

```
SELECT SOUNDEX('Nielsen') AS Nielsen,
  SOUNDEX('Nelson') AS NELSON,
  SOUNDEX('Neilson') AS NEILSON;
```

Result:

```
Nielsen   NELSON   NEILSON
--------  -------  --------
N425      N425     N425
```

NOTE **Other, more refined, Soundex methods exist. Ken Henderson, in his book *The Guru's Guide to Transact SQL* (Addison-Wesley, 2000), provides an improved Soundex algorithm and stored procedure. If you are going to implement Soundex in a production application, I recommend exploring his version. Alternately, you can research one of the other refined Soundex methods on the websites listed previously and write your own custom stored procedure.**

There are two possible ways to add Soundex searches to a database. The simplest method is to add the SOUNDEX() function within the WHERE clause, as follows:

```
USE CHA2;
SELECT LastName, FirstName
  FROM dbo.Customer
  WHERE SOUNDEX('Nikolsen') = SOUNDEX(LastName);
```

Result:

```
LastName        FirstName
--------------  -------------------
Nicholson       Charles
Nickols         Bob
```

While this implementation has the smallest impact on the data schema, it will cause performance issues as the data size grows because the SOUNDEX() function must execute for every row in the database, and an index on the name column (if any) cannot be used with an efficient seek operation, but only with a much more expensive scan. A faster variation of this first implementation method pre-tests for names with the same first letter, thus enabling SQL Server to use any indexes to narrow the search, so fewer rows must be read and the SOUNDEX() function must be performed only for rows selected by the index:

```
SELECT LastName, FirstName
  FROM dbo.Customer
  WHERE SOUNDEX('Nikolsen') = SOUNDEX(LastName)
    AND LastName LIKE 'N%';
```

The first query executes in 37.7 milliseconds on my test server, while the improved second query executes in 6.5 milliseconds. I suspect that the performance difference would increase with more data.

The second implementation method is to write the Soundex value in a column and index it with a non-clustered index. Because the Soundex value for each row is calculated during the write, the SOUNDEX() function does not need to be called for every row read by the SELECT statement. This is the method I recommend for a database application that heavily depends on Soundex for contact searches.

The OBXKITES sample database demonstrates this method. The SoundexCode column is persisted calculated column, so it's automatically calculated for every insert and kept updated with every update. Searching for a row, or all the matching rows, based on the stored Soundex code is extremely fast.

First determine the Soundex for "Smith":

```
USE OBXKites;
SELECT SOUNDEX('Smith');
```

Result:

```
-------
S530
```

Knowing the Soundex value for "Smith," the Soundex search is now a fast index seek without ever calling the SOUNDEX() function for the row being read during the select statement:

```
SELECT LastName, FirstName, SoundexCode
  FROM Contact
  WHERE SoundexCode = 'S530';
```

Result:

```
LastName     FirstName       SoundexCode
------------ --------------  -----------
Smith        Ulisius          S530
Smith        Oscar            S530
```

Using the DIFFERENCE() Soundex function

The second SQL Server Soundex function, DIFFERENCE(), returns the Soundex difference between two strings in the form of a ranking from 1 to 4, with 4 representing a perfect Soundex match:

```
USE CHA2
SELECT LastName, DIFFERENCE('Smith', LastName) AS NameSearch
  FROM Customer
  ORDER BY Difference('Smith', LastName) DESC;
```

Result:

```
LastName      NameSearch
------------- -----------
Smythe        4
Spade         3
Zeniod        3
```

```
Kennedy        3
Kennedy        3
Quinn          2
...
Kemper         1
Nicholson      0
...
```

The advantage of the DIFFERENCE() function is that it broadens the search beyond the first letters. The problem with the function is that it wants to calculate the Soundex value for both parameters, which prevents it from taking advantage of pre-stored Soundex values.

Data-Type Conversion Functions

Converting data from one data type to another data type is often handled automatically by SQL Server. Many of those conversions are implicit, or automatic.

Conversions that are explicit require a CAST() or CONVERT() function:

- CAST(Input as data type): The ANSI standard SQL means of converting from one data type to another. Even when the conversion can be performed implicitly by SQL Server, using the CAST() function forces the desired data type.

  CAST() is actually programmed slightly differently than a standard function. Rather than separate the two parameters with a comma (as most functions do), the data passed to the CAST() function is followed by the as keyword and the requested output data type:

  ```
  SELECT CAST('Away' AS NVARCHAR(5)) AS 'Tom Hanks'
  ```

  Result:

  ```
  TOM HANKS
  ---------
  AWAY
  ```

- Another example:

  ```
  SELECT CAST(123 AS NVARCHAR(15)) AS Int2String
  ```

  Result:

  ```
  INT2STRING
  ---------------
  123
  ```

- CONVERT(datatype, expression, style): Returns a value converted to a different data type with optional formatting. The first parameter of this non-ANSI SQL function is the desired data type to be applied to the expression:

  ```
  CONVERT (data type, expression[, style])
  ```

The `style` parameter usually refers to the optional date styles listed in Table 9-3. The style is applied to the output during conversion from datetime to a character-based data type, or to the input during conversion from text to datetime. Generally, the one- or two-digit style provides a two-digit year, and its three-digit counterpart provides a four-digit year. For example, style 1 provides 01/01/03, whereas style 101 provides 01/01/2003. The styles marked with an asterisk (*) in Table 9-3 are the exceptions to this rule.

SQL Server also provides numeric formatting styles, but numeric formatting is typically the task of the user interface, not the database.

TABLE 9-3

Convert Function Date Styles

Style	Description	Format
0/100*	Default	mon dd yyyy hh:miAM (or PM)
1/101	USA	mm/dd/yy
2/102	ANSI	yy.mm.dd
3/103	British/French	dd/mm/yy
4/104	German	dd.mm.yy
5/105	Italian	dd-mm-yy
6/106	–	dd mon yy
7/107	–	mon dd, yy
8/108	–	hh:mm:ss
9 or 109*	Default+milliseconds	mon dd yyyy hh:mi:ss:mmmAM (or PM)
10 or 110	USA	mm-dd-yy
11 or 111	Japan	yy/mm/dd
12 or 112	ISO	yymmdd
13 or 113*	Europe default+milliseconds	dd mon yyyy hh:mm:ss:mmm (24h)
14 or 114	–	hh:mi:ss:mmm (24h)
20 or 120*	ODBC canonical	yyyy-mm-dd hh:mi:ss (24h)
21 or 121*	ODBC canonical + milliseconds	yyyy-mm-dd hh:mi:ss.mmm (24h)
126	ISO8601 for XML use	yyyy-mm-dd Thh:mm:ss:mmm (no spaces)
127	ISO8601 with time zone Z	yyyy-mm-ddThh:mi:ss.mmmZ
130	Kuwaiti	dd mon yyyy hh:mi:ss:mmmAM (or PM)
131	Kuwaiti	dd/mm/yy hh:mi:ss:mmmAM (or PM)

*Both styles return dates with centuries.

Best Practice

In a clean client/server design, the server provides the data in an internal format and the client application formats the data as required by the user. Unformatted data is more independent than formatted data and can be used by more applications.

The following code demonstrates the CONVERT() function:

```
SELECT  CURRENT_TIMESTAMP AS RawDate,
   CONVERT (NVARCHAR(25), CURRENT_TIMESTAMP, 100) AS Date100,
   CONVERT (NVARCHAR(25), CURRENT_TIMESTAMP, 1) AS Date1;
```

Result:

```
RawDate                           Date100                    Date1
---------------------------       ----------------------     ----------
2009-11-17 10:27:27.413           Nov 17 2001 10:27AM        11/17/01
```

An additional data-type conversion function provides a fast way to move data between text and numeric:

- STR(number, length, decimal): Returns a string from a number:

```
SELECT STR(123,6,2) AS [Str];
```

Result:

```
Str
-----
123.00
```

Server Environment Information

System functions return information about the current environment. This section covers the more commonly used system functions:

- DB_NAME(): Returns the name of the current database, as shown in the following example:

```
SELECT CURRENT_TIMESTAMP AS [Date],
  DB_NAME() AS [Database];
```

Result:

```
Date                              Database
-------------------------         -------
2009-11-15 18:38:50.250           CHA2
```

- SERVERPROPERTY(): Several useful pieces of information about the server may be determined from this function, including the following:
  - **Collation:** The collation type
  - **Edition:** Enterprise, Developer, Standard, and so on
  - **EngineEdition:** 2 = Standard, 3 = Enterprise, 4 = Express
  - **InstanceName:** Null if the default instance
  - **ProductVersion:** The version number of SQL Server
  - **ProductLevel:** "RTM" for the initial release-to-manufacturing version, "SP*n*" for service packs (*n* is the service pack number), "CTP" for Community Technology Preview versions
  - **ServerName:** The full server and instance name

  For example, the following code returns SQL Server engine edition and version information for my current instance of SQL Server:

```
SELECT
  SERVERPROPERTY ('ServerName') AS ServerName,
  SERVERPROPERTY ('Edition') AS Edition,
  SERVERPROPERTY ('ProductVersion') AS 'ProductVersion',
  SERVERPROPERTY ('ProductLevel') AS ProductLevel;
```

Result:

```
ServerName  Edition                     ProductVersion ProductLevel
----------- --------------------------- -------------- -------------
MAUI        Developer Edition (64-bit)  10.0.2520.0    SP1
```

Summary

The previous chapter introduced the basic SELECT statement and query flow. This chapter expanded the concept with expressions and calculations that can be inserted in several places within the query, significantly improving its flexibility. In subsequent chapters, you will see how expressions can receive data from subqueries and user-defined functions, further increasing the power of the query.

The next chapter continues the progression of adding capability to the query by joining data from multiple data sources.

Chapter 10

Merging Data with Joins and Unions

The introduction to this book stated that my purpose was to share the fun of developing with SQL Server. This chapter is it. Making data twist and shout, pulling an answer out of data with a creative query, replacing a few hundred lines of languishing row-by-row iterative code with a single blazingly fast, set-based SQL query — it's all pure fun and covered here.

Relational databases, by their very nature, segment data into several narrow, but long, tables. Seldom does looking at a single table provide meaningful data. Therefore, merging data from multiple tables is an important task for SQL developers. The theory behind merging data sets is *relational algebra*, as defined by E. F. Codd in 1970.

Relational algebra consists of eight relational operators:

- **Restrict:** Returns the rows that meet a certain criterion
- **Project:** Returns selected columns, or calculated data, from a data set
- **Product:** Relational multiplication that returns all possible combinations of data between two data sets
- **Union:** Relational addition and subtraction that merges two tables vertically by stacking one table above another table and lining up the columns
- **Intersection:** Returns the rows common to two data sets
- **Difference:** Returns the rows unique to one data set
- **Join:** Returns the horizontal merger of two tables, matching up rows based on common data
- **Divide:** The inverse of relational multiplication, returns rows in one data set that match every row in a corresponding data set

IN THIS CHAPTER

- Applying relational algebra
- Building scalable code with set-based queries
- Using inner, outer, complex, and Θ (theta) joins
- Merging data vertically with unions

In addition, as a method of accomplishing relational algebra, SQL has implemented the following:

- **Subqueries:** Similar to a join, but more flexible; the results of the subquery are used in place of an expression, list, or data set within an outer query.

In the formal language of relational algebra:

- A table, or data set, is a *relation* or *entity*.
- A row is a *tuple*.
- A column is an *attribute*.

However, I use the common terms of table, row, and column throughout this chapter.

Relational theory is now thirty-something and has become better defined over the years as database vendors compete with extensions, and database theorists further define the problem of representing reality within a data structure. However, E. F. Codd's original work is still the foundation of relational database design and implementation.

NOTE **To give credit where credit is due, this entire chapter is based on the work of E. F. Codd and C. J. Date. You can find a complete list of recommended resources in the Resources page on `www.SQLServerBible.com`.**

Keep in mind that joins work with more than just tables. As listed in Chapter 8, "Introducing Basic Query Flow," data sources include local SQL Server tables, subqueries/CTEs, views, table-valued user-defined functions, distributed data sources (other database tables), full-text search results, and XQueries.

The reason for writing set-based queries is more than just writing elegant code. Set-based queries scale extremely well. My last consulting contract was developing an OLTP system with a few complexities that required 35,000 transactions per second. The system was able to work at that tps rate because the database design enabled set-based queries within stored procedures. So, while this chapter may seem like it just focuses on writing queries, it's really setting you up to write better stored procedures.

Using Joins

In relational algebra, a *join* is the multiplication of two data sets followed by a restriction of the result so that only the intersection of the two data sets is returned. The whole purpose of the join is to horizontally merge two data sets and produce a new result set from the combination by matching rows in one data source to rows in the other data source, as illustrated in Figure 10-1. This section explains the various types of joins and how to use them to select data.

By merging the data using the join, the rest of the SQL `SELECT` statement, including the column expressions, aggregate groupings, and `WHERE` clause conditions, can access any of the columns or rows from the joined tables. These capabilities are the core and power of SQL.

FIGURE 10-1

A join merges rows from one data set with rows from another data set, creating a new set of rows that includes columns from both. In this diagram, the code, 101, is common to Smith and order number 1, and is used to merge the two original rows into a single result row.

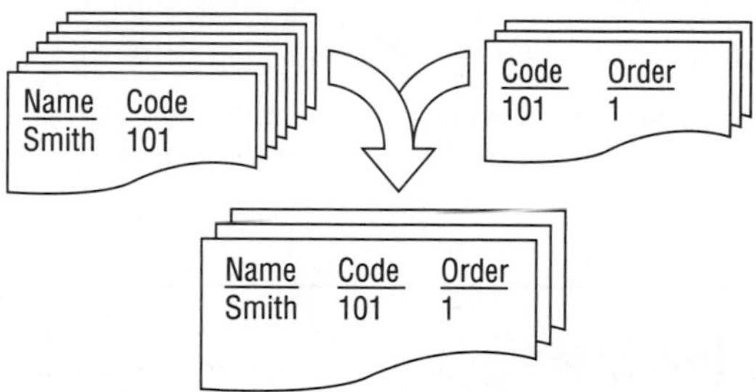

What's New with Joins and Unions?

Joins and unions are at the heart of SQL, so change here occurs slowly. The only item to watch for with joins and unions is the ANSI 89 style outer joins.

If you're upgrading from SQL Server 2000 directly to SQL Server 2008, you should be warned that ANSI 89 style outer joins (*=, =*) were removed from SQL Server with version 2005. ANSI 89 style inner joins may be a legitimate syntax, but I still don't recommend using them.

I apologize if this sounds too much like your teenager's math homework, but joins are based on the idea of intersecting data sets. As Figure 10-2 illustrates, a relational join deals with two sets of data that have common values, and it's these common values that define how the tables intersect.

FIGURE 10-2

Relational joins are based on the overlap, or common intersection, of two data sets.

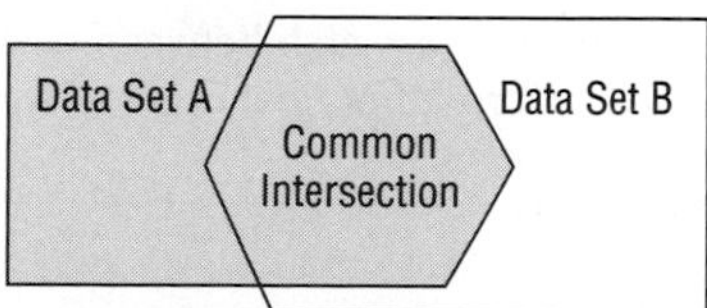

NOTE **These set diagrams are a type of Venn diagram. For more information about Venn set diagrams, visit `www.combinatorics.org/Surveys/ds5/VennEJC.html` or Wikipedia.**

The intersection simply represents the fact that some common column can connect a row from the first data set to data in the second data set. The common values are typically a primary key and a foreign key, such as these examples from the `OBXKites` sample database:

- `ContactID` between the `Contact` and `[Order]` tables
- `OrderID` between the `[Order]` and `OrderDetail` tables
- `ProductID` between the `Product` and `OrderDetail` tables

SQL includes many types of joins that determine how the rows are selected from the different sides of the intersection. Table 10-1 lists the join types (each is explained in more detail later in this section).

TABLE 10-1

Join Types

Join Type	Query Designer Symbol	Definition
Inner join		Includes only matching rows
Left outer join		Includes all rows from the left table regardless of whether a match exists, and matching rows from the right table
Right outer join		Includes all the rows from the right table regardless of whether a match exists, and matching rows from the left table
Full outer join		Includes all the rows from both tables regardless of whether a match exists
Θ (theta) join		Matches rows using a non-equal condition — the symbol shows the actual theta condition (<,>,<=,>=,<>)
Cross join	No join connection	Produces a Cartesian product — a match between each row in data source one with each row from data source two without any conditions or restrictions

Inner Joins

The *inner join* is by far the most common join. In fact, it's also referred to as a *common join*, and was originally called a *natural join* by E. F. Codd. The inner join returns only those rows that represent a match between the two data sets. An inner join is well named because it extracts only data from the inner portion of the intersection of the two overlapping data sets, as illustrated in Figure 10-3.

FIGURE 10-3

The inner join includes only those rows from each side of the join that are contained within the intersection of the two data sources.

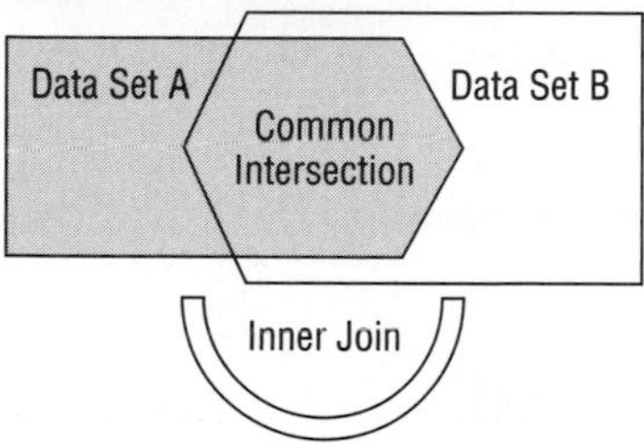

Building inner joins with the Query Designer

Inner joins are easily constructed within Management Studio using the Query Designer UI, as shown in Figure 10-4. Once both tables have been placed in the Diagram pane either using the Add Table function or by dragging the tables from the table list, the join automatically creates the required common joins based on common fields.

Any unwanted joins can be removed by selecting the join and pressing Delete. To create a new join between two tables, drag the join column from the first table to the second table. The type of join can be changed by right-clicking on the join type symbol.

The Query Designer uses a different symbol for each type of join. The symbol for an inner join, the *join diamond*, is an accurate illustration of that type of join.

Creating inner joins within SQL code

Using T- SQL code, joins are specified within the `FROM` portion of the `SELECT` statement. The keyword `JOIN` identifies the second table, and the `ON` clause defines the common ground between the two tables. The default type of join is an inner join, so the keyword `INNER` is optional. For clarity, however, I recommend always including it:

```
SELECT *
  FROM Table1
    [INNER] JOIN Table2
      ON Table1.column = Table2.column;
```

ON the WEBSITE **The sample databases and code from this chapter may be downloaded from** `www.SQLServerBible.com`.

FIGURE 10-4

Building an inner join within Management Studio's Query Designer

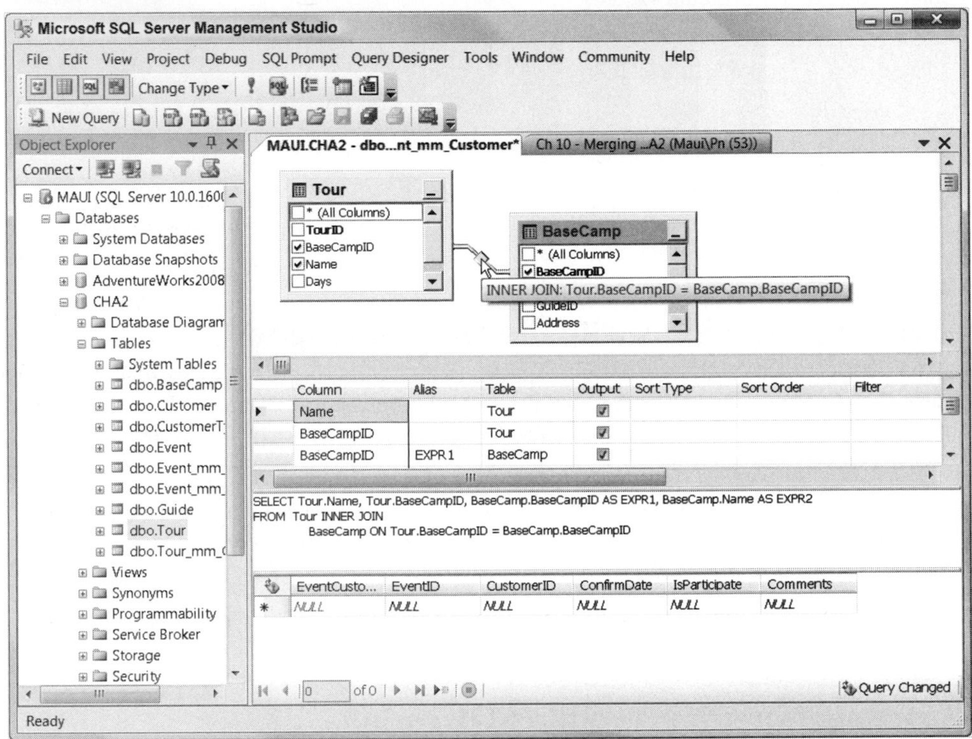

Because joins pull together data from two data sets, it makes sense that SQL needs to know how to match up rows from those sets. SQL Server merges the rows by matching a value common to both tables. Typically, a primary key value from one table is being matched with a foreign key value from the secondary table. Whenever a row from the first table matches a row from the second table, the two rows are merged into a new row containing data from both tables.

The following code sample joins the `Tour` (secondary) and `BaseCamp` (primary) tables from the Cape Hatteras Adventures sample database. The `ON` clause specifies the common data:

```
USE CHA2;

SELECT Tour.Name, Tour.BaseCampID,
    BaseCamp.BaseCampID, BaseCamp.Name
  FROM dbo.Tour
    INNER JOIN dbo.BaseCamp
      ON Tour.BaseCampID = BaseCamp.BaseCampID;
```

The query begins with the Tour table. For every Tour row, SQL Server will attempt to identify matching BaseCamp rows by comparing the BasecampID columns in both tables. The Tour table rows and BaseCamp table rows that match will be merged into a new result:

```
Tour.                    Tour.       Basecamp.   Basecamp.
TourName                 BaseCampID BaseCampID  BaseCampName
------------------------ ---------- ----------- ------------
Appalachian Trail         1          1          Ashville NC
Outer Banks Lighthouses   2          2          Cape Hatteras
Bahamas Dive              3          3          Freeport
Amazon Trek               4          4          Ft Lauderdale
Gauley River Rafting      5          5          West Virginia
```

Number of rows returned

In the preceding query, every row in both the Tour and BaseCamp tables had a match. No rows were excluded from the join. However, in real life this is seldom the case. Depending upon the number of matching rows from each data source and the type of join, it's possible to decrease or increase the final number of rows in the result set.

To see how joins can alter the number of rows returned, look at the Contact and [Order] tables of the OBXKites database. The initial row count of contacts is 21, yet when the customers are matched with their orders, the row count changes to 10. The following code sample compares the two queries and their respective results side by side:

```
USE OBXKites;

SELECT ContactCode, LastName           SELECT ContactCode, OrderNumber
  FROM dbo.Contact                       FROM dbo.Contact
  ORDER BY ContactCode;                    INNER JOIN dbo.[Order]
                                             ON [Order].ContactID
                                               = Contact.ContactID
                                         ORDER BY ContactCode;
```

Results from both queries:

```
ContactCode  LastName         ContactCode   OrderNumber
-----------  --------         -----------   -----------
101          Smith            101            1
                              101            2
                              101            5
102          Adams            102            6
                              102            3
103          Reagan           103            4
                              103            7
104          Franklin         104            8
105          Dowdry           105            9
106          Grant            106            10
107          Smith
```

```
108          Hanks
109          James
110          Kennedy
111          Williams
112          Quincy
113          Laudry
114          Nelson
115          Miller
116          Jamison
117          Andrews
118          Boston
119          Harrison
120          Earl
121          Zing
```

Joins can appear to multiply rows. If a row on one side of the join matches with several rows on the other side of the join, the result will include a row for every match. In the preceding query, some contacts (Smith, Adams, and Reagan) are listed multiple times because they have multiple orders.

Joins also eliminate rows. Only contacts 101 through 106 have matching orders. The rest of the contacts are excluded from the join because they have no matching orders.

ANSI SQL 89 joins

A join is really nothing more than the act of selecting data from two tables for which a condition of equality exists between common columns. Join conditions in the `ON` clause are similar to `WHERE` clauses. In fact, before ANSI SQL 92 standardized the `JOIN...ON` syntax, ANSI SQL 89 joins (also called *legacy style joins, old style joins*, or even *grandpa joins*) accomplished the same task by listing the tables within the `FROM` clause and specifying the join condition in the `WHERE` clause.

The previous sample join between `Contact` and `[Order]` could be written as an ANSI 89 join as follows:

```
SELECT Contact.ContactCode, [Order].OrderNumber
  FROM dbo.Contact, dbo.[Order]
  WHERE [Order].ContactID = Contact.ContactID
  ORDER BY ContactCode;
```

Best Practice

Always code joins using the ANSI 92 style. ANSI 92 joins are cleaner, easier to read, and easier to debug than ANSI 89 style joins, which leads to improved data integrity and decreases maintenance costs. With ANSI 89 style joins it's possible to get the wrong result unless it's coded very carefully. ANSI 89 style outer joins are deprecated in SQL Server 2008, so any ANSI 89 outer joins will generate an error.

Multiple data source joins

As some of the examples have already demonstrated, a `SELECT` statement isn't limited to one or two data sources (tables, views, CTEs, subqueries, etc.); a SQL Server `SELECT` statement may refer to up to 256 data sources. That's a lot of joins.

Because SQL is a declarative language, the order of the data sources is not important for inner joins. (The query optimizer will decide the best order to actually process the query based on the indexes available and the data in the tables.) Multiple joins may be combined in multiple paths, or even circular patterns (A joins B joins C joins A). Here's where a large whiteboard and a consistent development style really pay off.

The following query (first shown in Figure 10-5 and then worked out in code) answers the question "Who purchased kites?" The answer must involve five tables:

FIGURE 10-5

Answering the question "Who purchased kites?" using Management Studio's Query Designer

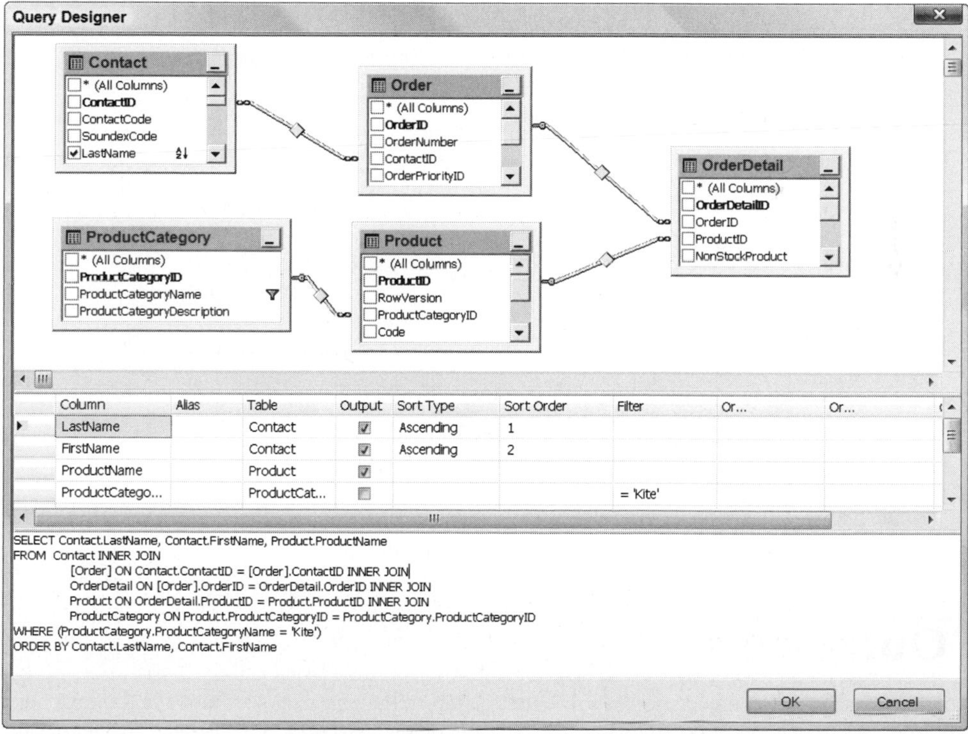

1. The `Contact` table for the "who"
2. The `[Order]` table for the "purchased"

3. The `OrderDetail` table for the "purchased"
4. The `Product` table for the "kites"
5. The `ProductCategory` table for the "kites"

The following SQL `SELECT` statement begins with the "who" portion of the question and specifies the join tables and conditions as it works through the required tables. The query that is shown graphically in Management Studio (refer to Figure 10-5) is listed as raw SQL in the following code sample. Notice how the `where` clause restricts the `ProductCategory` table rows and yet affects the contacts selected:

```
USE OBXKites;

SELECT LastName, FirstName, ProductName
  FROM dbo.Contact C
    INNER JOIN dbo.[Order] O
      ON C.ContactID = O.ContactID
    INNER JOIN dbo.OrderDetail OD
      ON O.OrderID = OD.OrderID
    INNER JOIN dbo.Product P
      ON OD.ProductID = P.ProductID
    INNER JOIN dbo.ProductCategory PC
      ON P.ProductCategoryID = PC.ProductCategoryID
  WHERE ProductCategoryName = 'Kite'
  ORDER BY LastName, FirstName;
```

Result:

```
LastName          FirstName            ProductName
----------------- -------------------- --------------
Adams             Terri                Dragon Flight
Dowdry            Quin                 Dragon Flight
...
Smith             Ulisius              Rocket Kite
```

To summarize the main points about inner joins:

- They only match rows with a common value.
- The order of the data sources is unimportant.
- They can appear to multiply rows.
- Newer ANSI 92 style is the best way to write them.

Outer Joins

Whereas an inner join contains only the intersection of the two data sets, an *outer join* extends the inner join by adding the nonmatching data from the left or right data set, as illustrated in Figure 10-6.

Outer joins solve a significant problem for many queries by including all the data regardless of a match. The common customer-order query demonstrates this problem well. If the requirement is to build a query that lists all customers plus their recent orders, only an outer join can retrieve every customer whether the customer has placed an order or not. An inner join between customers and orders would miss every customer who did not place a recent order.

CAUTION **Depending on the nullability of the keys and the presence of rows on both sides of the join, it's easy to write a query that misses rows from one side or the other of the join. I've even seen this error in third-party ISV application code. To avoid this data integrity error, know your schema well and always unit test your queries against a small data set with known answers.**

FIGURE 10-6

An outer join includes not only rows from the two data sources with a match, but also unmatched rows from outside the intersection.

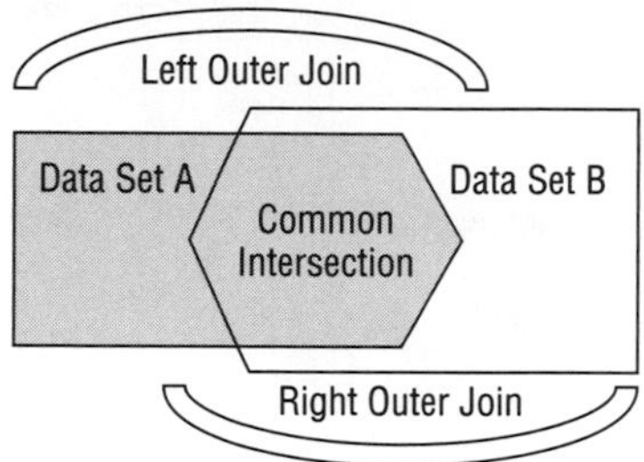

Some of the data in the result set produced by an outer join will look just like the data from an inner join. There will be data in columns that come from each of the data sources, but any rows from the outer-join table that do not have a match in the other side of the join will return data only from the outer-join table. In this case, columns from the other data source will have null values.

A Join Analogy

When I teach how to build queries, I sometimes use the following story to explain the different types of joins. Imagine a pilgrim church in the seventeenth century, segmented by gender. The men all sit on one side of the church and the women on the other. Some of the men and women are married, and some are single. Now imagine that each side of the church is a database table and the various combinations of people that leave the church represent the different types of joins.

If all the married couples stood up, joined hands, and left the church, that would be an inner join between the men and women. The result set leaving the church would include only matched pairs.

If all the men stood, and those who were married held hands with their wives and they left as a group, that would be a left outer join. The line leaving the church would include some couples and some bachelors.

Likewise, if all women and their husbands left the church, that would be a right outer join. All the bachelors would be left alone in the church.

A full outer join (covered later in this chapter) would be everyone leaving the church, but only the married couples could hold hands.

Using the Query Designer to create outer joins

When building queries using the Query Designer, the join type can be changed from the default, inner join, to an outer join via either the context menu or the properties of the join, as shown in Figure 10-7. The Query Designer does an excellent job of illustrating the types of joins with the join symbol (as previously detailed in Table 10-1).

FIGURE 10-7

The join Properties window displays the join columns, and is used to set the join condition (=, >, <, etc.) and add the left or right side of an outer join (all rows from Product, all rows from OrderDetail).

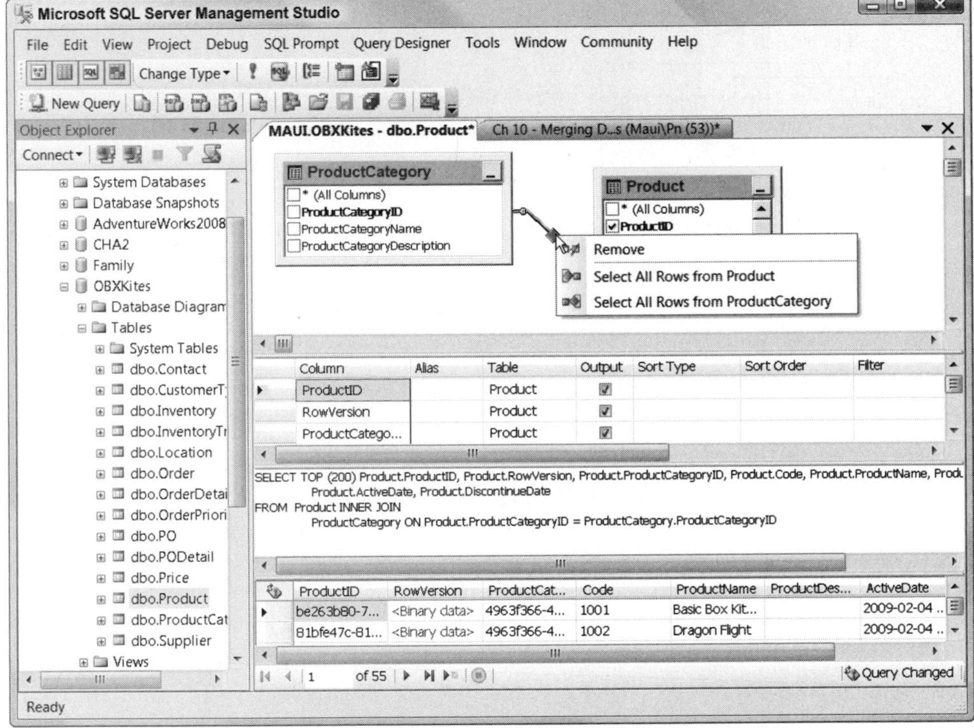

T-SQL code and outer joins

In SQL code, an outer join is declared by the keywords `LEFT OUTER` or `RIGHT OUTER` before the `JOIN` (technically, the keyword `OUTER` is optional):

```
SELECT *
  FROM Table1
    LEFT|RIGHT [OUTER] JOIN Table2
      ON Table1.column = Table2.column;
```

NOTE **Several keywords (such as `INNER`, `OUTER`, or `AS`) in SQL are optional or may be abbreviated (such as `PROC` for `PROCEDURE`). Although most developers (including me) omit the optional syntax, explicitly stating the intent by spelling out the full syntax improves the readability of the code.**

There's no trick to telling the difference between left and right outer joins. In code, left or right refers to the table that will be included regardless of the match. The outer-join table (sometimes called the *driving table*) is typically listed first, so left outer joins are more common than right outer joins. I suspect any confusion between left and right outer joins is caused by the use of graphical-query tools to build joins, because left and right refers to the table's listing in the SQL text, and the tables' positions in the graphical-query tool are moot.

Best Practice

When coding outer joins, always order your data sources so you can write left outer joins. Don't use right outer joins, and never mix left outer joins and right outer joins.

To modify the previous contact-order query so that it returns all contacts regardless of any orders, changing the join type from inner to left outer is all that's required, as follows:

```
SELECT ContactCode, OrderNumber
  FROM dbo.Contact
    LEFT OUTER JOIN dbo.[Order]
      ON [Order].ContactID = Contact.ContactID
  ORDER BY ContactCode;
```

The left outer join will include all rows from the `Contact` table and matching rows from the `[Order]` table. The abbreviated result of the query is as follows:

```
Contact.        [Order].
ContactCode      OrderNumber
--------------- -----------
101              1
101              2
...
106              10
107              NULL
108              NULL
...
```

Because contact 107 and 108 do not have corresponding rows in the `[Order]` table, the columns from the `[Order]` table return a null for those rows.

NOTE **Earlier versions of SQL Server extended the ANSI SQL 89 legacy join syntax with outer joins by adding an asterisk to the left or right of the equals sign in the `WHERE` clause condition. While this syntax worked through SQL Server 2000, it has been deprecated since SQL Server 2005. ANSI SQL 89 inner joins will still work, but outer joins *require* ANSI SQL 92 syntax.**

Having said that, SQL Server supports backward compatibility, so if the database compatibility level is set to 80 (SQL Server 2000), then the ANSI 82 style outer joins still work.

Outer joins and optional foreign keys

Outer joins are often employed when a secondary table has a foreign-key constraint to the primary table and permits nulls in the foreign key column. The presence of this optional foreign key means that if the secondary row refers to a primary row, then the primary row must exist. However, it's perfectly valid for the secondary row to refrain from referring to the primary table at all.

Another example of an optional foreign key is an order alert or priority column. Many order rows will not have an alert or special-priority status. However, those that do must point to a valid row in the order-priority table.

The OBX Kite store uses a similar order-priority scheme, so reporting all the orders with their optional priorities requires an outer join:

```
SELECT OrderNumber, OrderPriorityName
  FROM dbo.[Order]
    LEFT OUTER JOIN dbo.OrderPriority
    ON [Order].OrderPriorityID =
      OrderPriority.OrderPriorityID;
```

The left outer join retrieves all the orders and any matching priorities. The `OBXKites_Populate.sql` script sets two orders to rush priority:

```
OrderNumber OrderPriorityName
----------- -----------------
1           Rush
2           NULL
3           Rush
4           NULL
5           NULL
6           NULL
7           NULL
8           NULL
9           NULL
10          NULL
```

The adjacency pairs pattern (also called *reflexive*, *recursive*, or *self-join* relationships, covered in Chapter 17, "Traversing Hierarchies") also uses optional foreign keys. In the `Family` sample database, the `MotherID` and `FatherID` are both foreign keys that refer to the `PersonID` of the mother or father. The optional foreign key allows persons to be entered without their father and mother already in the database; but if a value is entered in the `MotherID` or `FatherID` columns, then the data must point to valid persons in the database.

CROSS-REF **Another cool twist on left outer joins is `LEFT APPLY`, used with table-valued user-defined functions. You'll find that covered in Chapter 25, "Building User-Defined Functions."**

Full outer joins

A *full outer join* returns all the data from both data sets regardless of the intersection, as shown in Figure 10-8. It is functionally the same as taking the results from a left outer join and the results from a right outer join, and unioning them together (unions are explained later in this chapter).

FIGURE 10-8

The full outer join returns all the data from both data sets, matching the rows where it can and filling in the holes with nulls.

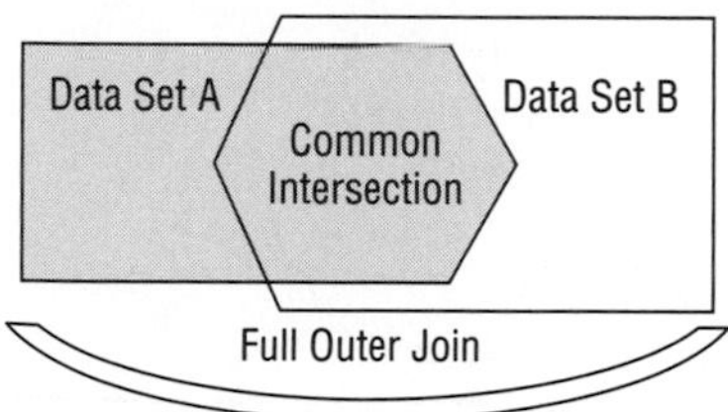

In real life, referential integrity reduces the need for a full outer join because every row from the secondary table should have a match in the primary table (depending on the optionality of the foreign key), so left outer joins are typically sufficient. Full outer joins are most useful for cleaning up data that has not had the benefit of clean constraints to filter out bad data.

Red thing blue thing

The following example is a mock-up of such a situation and compares the full outer join with an inner and a left outer join. Table `One` is the primary table. Table `Two` is a secondary table with a foreign key that refers to table `One`. There's no foreign-key constraint, so there may be some nonmatches for the outer join to find:

```
CREATE TABLE dbo.One (
  OnePK INT,
  Thing1 VARCHAR(15)
  );

CREATE TABLE dbo.Two (
  TwoPK INT,
  OnePK INT,
  Thing2 VARCHAR(15)
  );
```

The sample data includes rows that would normally break referential integrity. As illustrated in Figure 10-9, the foreign key (`OnePK`) for the plane and the cycle in table `Two` do not have a match in table `One`; and two of the rows in table `One` do not have related secondary rows in table `Two`. The following batch inserts the eight sample data rows:

```
INSERT dbo.One(OnePK, Thing1)
  VALUES (1, 'Old Thing');
```

```
INSERT dbo.One(OnePK, Thing1)
  VALUES (2, 'New Thing');
INSERT dbo.One(OnePK, Thing1)
  VALUES (3, 'Red Thing');
INSERT dbo.One(OnePK, Thing1)
  VALUES (4, 'Blue Thing');

INSERT dbo.Two(TwoPK, OnePK, Thing2)
  VALUES(1,0, 'Plane');
INSERT dbo.Two(TwoPK, OnePK, Thing2)
  VALUES(2,2, 'Train');
INSERT dbo.Two(TwoPK, OnePK, Thing2)
  VALUES(3,3, 'Car');
INSERT dbo.Two(TwoPK, OnePK, Thing2)
  VALUES(4,NULL, 'Cycle');
```

FIGURE 10-9

The Red Thing Blue Thing example has data to view every type of join.

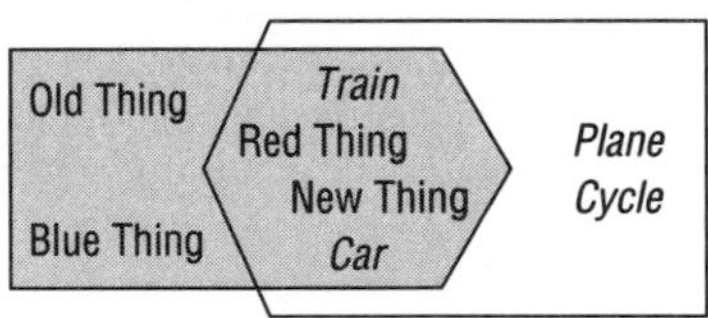

An inner join between table One and table Two will return only the two matching rows:

```
SELECT Thing1, Thing2
  FROM dbo.One
    INNER JOIN dbo.Two
      ON One.OnePK = Two.OnePK;
```

Result:

```
Thing1          Thing2
--------------- ---------------
New Thing       Train
Red Thing       Car
```

A left outer join will extend the inner join and include the rows from table One without a match:

```
SELECT Thing1, Thing2
  FROM dbo.One
    LEFT OUTER JOIN dbo.Two
      ON One.OnePK = Two.OnePK;
```

All the rows are now returned from table One, but two rows are still missing from table Two:

```
Thing1          Thing2
--------------- ---------------
Old Thing       NULL
New Thing       Train
Red Thing       Car
Blue Thing      NULL
```

A full outer join will retrieve every row from both tables, regardless of a match between the tables:

```
SELECT Thing1, Thing2
  FROM dbo.One
    FULL OUTER JOIN dbo.Two
      ON One.OnePK = Two.OnePK;
```

The plane and cycle from table Two are now listed along with every row from table One:

```
Thing1          Thing2
--------------- ---------------
Old Thing       NULL
New Thing       Train
Red Thing       Car
Blue Thing      NULL
NULL            Plane
NULL            Cycle
```

As this example shows, full outer joins are an excellent tool for finding all the data, even bad data. Set difference queries, explored later in this chapter, build on outer joins to zero in on bad data.

Placing the conditions within outer joins

When working with inner joins, a condition has the same effect whether it's in the JOIN clause or the WHERE clause, but that's not the case with outer joins:

- When the condition is in the JOIN clause, SQL Server includes all rows from the outer table and then uses the condition to include rows from the second table.
- When the restriction is placed in the WHERE clause, the join is performed and then the WHERE clause is applied to the joined rows.

The following two queries demonstrate the effect of the placement of the condition.

In the first query, the left outer join includes all rows from table One and then joins those rows from table Two where OnePK is equal in both tables and Thing1's value is New Thing. The result is all the rows from table One, and rows from table Two that meet both join restrictions:

```
SELECT Thing1, Thing2
  FROM dbo.One
    LEFT OUTER JOIN dbo.Two
```

```
        ON One.OnePK = Two.OnePK
          AND One.Thing1 = 'New Thing';
```

Result:

```
Thing1          Thing2
--------------- ---------------
Old Thing       NULL
New Thing       Train
Red Thing       NULL
Blue Thing      NULL
```

The second query first performs the left outer join, producing the same four rows as the previous query but without the AND condition. The WHERE clause then restricts that result to those rows where Thing1 is equal to New Thing1. The net effect is the same as when an inner join was used (but it might take more execution time):

```
SELECT Thing1, Thing2
  FROM dbo.One
    LEFT OUTER JOIN dbo.Two
      ON One.OnePK = Two.OnePK
  WHERE One.Thing1 = 'New Thing';
```

Result:

```
Thing1          Thing2
--------------- ---------------
New Thing       Train
```

Multiple outer joins

Coding a query with multiple outer joins can be tricky. Typically, the order of data sources in the FROM clause doesn't matter, but here it does. The key is to code them in a sequential chain. Think through it this way:

1. Grab all the customers regardless of whether they've placed any orders.
2. Then grab all the orders regardless of whether they've shipped.
3. Then grab all the ship details.

When chaining multiple outer joins, stick to left outer joins, as mixing left and right outer joins becomes very confusing very fast. Be sure to unit test the query with a small sample set of data to ensure that the outer join chain is correct.

Self-Joins

A *self-join* is a join that refers back to the same table. This type of unary relationship is often used to extract data from a *reflexive* (also called a *recursive*) relationship, such as organizational charts (employee to boss). Think of a self-join as a table being joined with a temporary copy of itself.

The `Family` sample database uses two self-joins between a child and his or her parents, as shown in the database diagram in Figure 10-10. The mothers and fathers are also people, of course, and are listed in the same table. They link back to their parents, and so on. The sample database is populated with five fictitious generations that can be used for sample queries.

FIGURE 10-10

The database diagram of the Family database includes two unary relationships (children to parents) on the left and a many-to-many unary relationship (husband to wife) on the right.

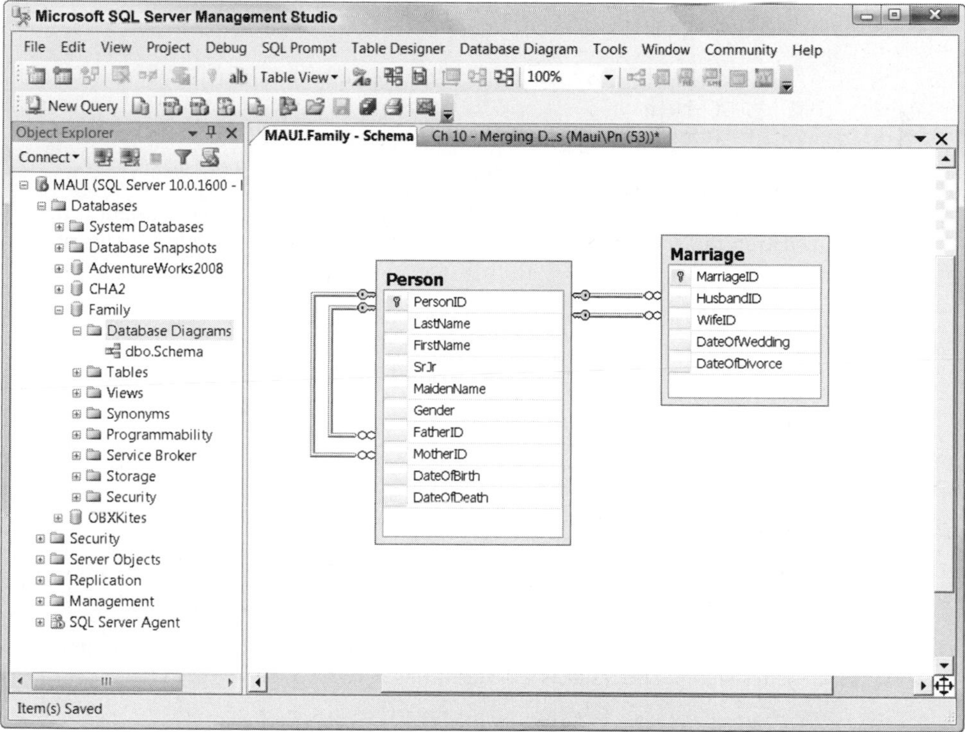

The key to constructing a self-join is to include a second reference to the table using a table alias. Once the table is available twice to the `SELECT` statement, the self-join functions much like any other join. In the following example, the `dbo.Person` table is referenced using the table alias `Mother`:

Switching over to the `Family` sample database, the following query locates the children of Audry Halloway:

```
USE Family;

SELECT Child.PersonID, Child.FirstName,
    Child.MotherID, Mother.PersonID
```

```
FROM dbo.Person AS Child
  INNER JOIN dbo.Person AS Mother
    ON Child.MotherID = Mother.PersonID
WHERE Mother.LastName = 'Halloway'
  AND Mother.FirstName = 'Audry';
```

The query uses the Person table twice. The first reference (aliased as Child) is joined with the second reference (aliased as Mother), which is restricted by the WHERE clause to only Audry Halloway. Only the rows with a MotherID that points back to Audry will be included in the inner join. Audry's PersonID is 6 and her children are as follows:

```
PersonID    FirstName       MotherID    PersonID
----------- --------------- ----------- -----------
8           Melanie         6           6
7           Corwin          6           6
9           Dara            6           6
10          James           6           6
```

While the previous query adequately demonstrates a self-join, it would be more useful if the mother weren't hard-coded in the WHERE clause, and if more information were provided about each birth, as follows:

```
SELECT CONVERT(NVARCHAR(15),C.DateofBirth,1) AS Date,
    C.FirstName AS Name, C.Gender AS G,
    ISNULL(F.FirstName + ' ' + F.LastName, ' * unknown *')
      as Father,
    M.FirstName + ' ' + M.LastName as Mother
  FROM dbo.Person AS C
    LEFT OUTER JOIN dbo.Person AS F
      ON C.FatherID = F.PersonID
    INNER JOIN dbo.Person AS M
      ON C.MotherID = M.PersonID
  ORDER BY C.DateOfBirth;
```

This query makes three references to the Person table: the child, the father, and the mother, with mnemonic one-letter aliases. The result is a better listing:

```
Date     Name     G   Father            Mother
-------- -------- --- ----------------- ---------------
5/19/22  James    M   James Halloway    Kelly Halloway
8/05/28  Audry    F   Bryan Miller      Karen Miller
8/19/51  Melanie  F   James Halloway    Audry Halloway
8/30/53  James    M   James Halloway    Audry Halloway
2/12/58  Dara     F   James Halloway    Audry Halloway
3/13/61  Corwin   M   James Halloway    Audry Halloway
3/13/65  Cameron  M   Richard Campbell  Elizabeth Campbell
...
```

CROSS-REF **For more ideas about working with hierarchies and self-joins, refer to Chapter 17, "Traversing Hierarchies."**

Cross (Unrestricted) Joins

The *cross join*, also called an *unrestricted join*, is a pure relational algebra multiplication of the two source tables. Without a join condition restricting the result set, the result set includes every possible combination of rows from the data sources. Each row in data set one is matched with every row in data set two — for example, if the first data source has five rows and the second data source has four rows, a cross join between them would result in 20 rows. This type of result set is referred to as a *Cartesian product*.

Using the `One/Two` sample tables, a cross join is constructed in Management Studio by omitting the join condition between the two tables, as shown in Figure 10-11.

FIGURE 10-11

A graphical representation of a cross join is simply two tables without a join condition.

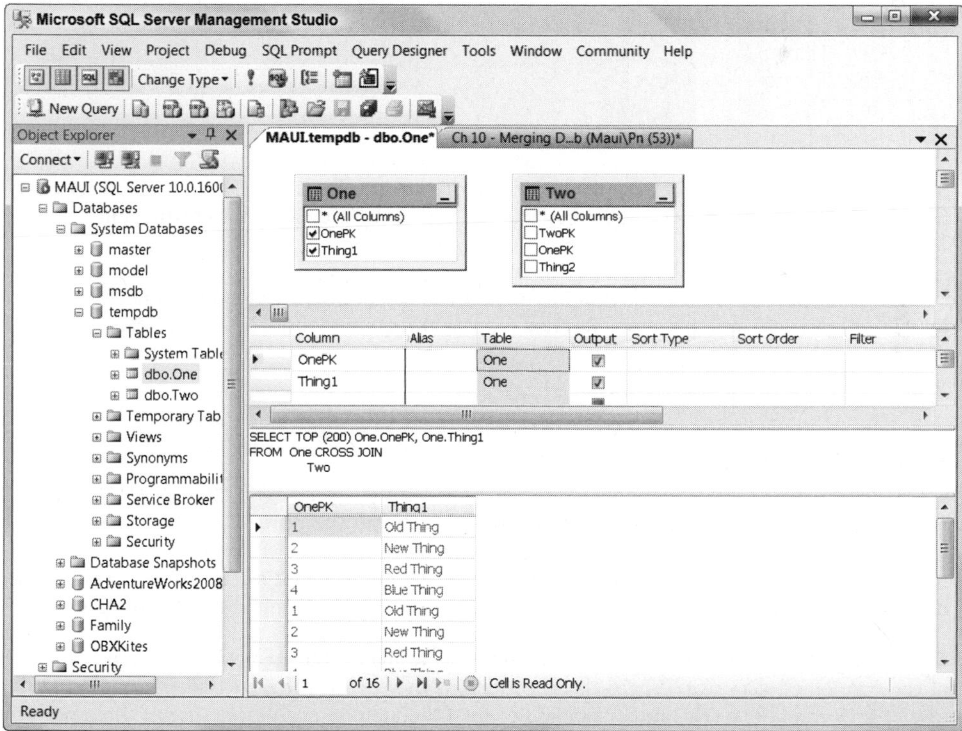

In code, this type of join is specified by the keywords `CROSS JOIN` and the lack of an `ON` condition:

```
SELECT Thing1, Thing2
  FROM dbo.One
    CROSS JOIN dbo.Two;
```

The result of a join without restriction is that every row in table One matches with every row from table Two:

```
Thing1          Thing2
--------------- ---------------
Old Thing       Plane
New Thing       Plane
Red Thing       Plane
Blue Thing      Plane
Old Thing       Train
New Thing       Train
Red Thing       Train
Blue Thing      Train
Old Thing       Car
New Thing       Car
Red Thing       Car
Blue Thing      Car
Old Thing       Cycle
New Thing       Cycle
Red Thing       Cycle
Blue Thing      Cycle
```

Sometimes cross joins are the result of someone forgetting to draw the join in a graphical-query tool; however, they are useful for populating databases with sample data, or for creating empty "pidgin hole" rows for population during a procedure.

Understanding how a cross join multiplies data is also useful when studying relational division, the inverse of relational multiplication. Relational division requires subqueries, so it's explained in the next chapter.

Exotic Joins

Nearly all joins are based on a condition of equality between the primary key of a primary table and the foreign key of a secondary table, which is why the inner join is sometimes called an *equi-join*. Although it's commonplace to base a join on a single equal condition, it is not a requirement. The condition between the two columns is not necessarily equal, nor is the join limited to one condition.

The ON condition of the join is in reality nothing more than a WHERE condition restricting the product of the two joined data sets. Where-clause conditions may be very flexible and powerful, and the same is true of join conditions. This understanding of the ON condition enables the use of three powerful techniques: Θ *(theta) joins*, *multiple-condition joins*, and *non-key joins*.

Multiple-condition joins

If a join is nothing more than a condition between two data sets, then it makes sense that multiple conditions are possible at the join. In fact, multiple-condition joins and Θ joins go hand-in-hand. Without the ability to use multiple-condition joins, Θ joins would be of little value.

If the database schema uses natural primary keys, then there are probably tables with composite primary keys, which means queries must use multiple-condition joins.

Join conditions can refer to any table in the FROM clause, enabling interesting three-way joins:

```
FROM A
  INNER JOIN B
    ON A.col = B.col
  INNER JOIN C
    ON B.col = C.col
    AND A.col = C.col;
```

The first query in the previous section, "Placing the Conditions within Outer Joins," was a multiple-condition join.

Θ (theta) joins

A theta join (depicted throughout as Θ) is a join based on a non-equal on condition. In relational theory, conditional operators (=, >, <, >=, <=, <>) are called Θ operators. While the equals condition is technically a Θ operator, it is commonly used, so only joins with conditions other than equal are referred to as Θ joins.

The Θ condition may be set within Management Studio's Query Designer using the join Properties dialog, as previously shown in Figure 10-7.

Non-key joins

Joins are not limited to primary and foreign keys. The join can match a row in one data source with a row in another data source using any column, as long as the columns share compatible data types and the data match.

For example, an inventory allocation system would use a non-key join to find products that are expected to arrive from the supplier before the customer's required ship date. A non-key join between the PurchaseOrder and OrderDetail tables with a Θ condition between PO.DateExpected and OD.DateRequired will filter the join to those products that can be allocated to the customer's orders. The following code demonstrates the non-key join (this is not in a sample database):

```
SELECT OD.OrderID, OD.ProductID, PO.POID
FROM OrderDetail AS OD
  INNER JOIN PurchaseOrder AS PO
    ON OD.ProductID = PO.ProductID
      AND OD.DateRequired > PO.DateExpected;
```

When working with inner joins, non-key join conditions can be placed in the WHERE clause or in the JOIN. Because the conditions compare similar values between two joined tables, I often place these conditions in the JOIN portion of the FROM clause, rather than the WHERE clause. The critical difference depends on whether you view the conditions as a part of creating the record set upon which the rest of the SQL SELECT statement is acting, or as a filtering task that follows the FROM clause. Either way, the query-optimization plan is identical, so use the method that is most readable and seems most logical to you. Note that when constructing outer joins, the placement of the condition in the JOIN or in the WHERE clause yields different results, as explained earlier in the section "Placing the Conditions within Outer Joins."

Asking the question, "Who are twins?" of the Family sample database uses all three exotic join techniques in the join between person and twin. The join contains three conditions. The Person.PersonID <> Twin.PersonID condition is a Θ join that prevents a person from being considered his or her own twin. The join condition on MotherID, while a foreign key, is nonstandard because it is being joined with another foreign key. The DateOfBirth condition is definitely a non-key join condition:

```
SELECT Person.FirstName + ' ' + Person.LastName AS Person,
    Twin.FirstName + ' ' + Twin.LastName AS Twin,
    Person.DateOfBirth
  FROM dbo.Person
    INNER JOIN dbo.Person AS Twin
      ON Person.PersonID <> Twin.PersonID
        AND Person.MotherID = Twin.MotherID
        AND Person.DateOfBirth = Twin.DateOfBirth;
```

The following is the same query, this time with the exotic join condition moved to the WHERE clause. Not surprisingly, SQL Server's Query Optimizer produces the exact same query execution plan for each query:

```
SELECT Person.FirstName + ' ' + Person.LastName AS Person,
    Twin.FirstName + ' ' + Twin.LastName AS Twin,
    Person.DateOfBirth
  FROM dbo.Person
    INNER JOIN dbo.Person AS Twin
      ON Person.MotherID = Twin.MotherID
        AND Person.DateOfBirth = Twin.DateOfBirth
  WHERE Person.PersonID <> Twin.PersonID;
```

```
Result:
Person          Twin            DateOfBirth
--------------- --------------- ------------------------
Abbie Halloway  Allie Halloway  1979-010-14 00:00:00.000
Allie Halloway  Abbie Halloway  1979-010-14 00:00:00.000
```

The difficult query scenarios at the end of the next chapter also demonstrate exotic joins, which are often used with subqueries.

Set Difference Queries

A query type that's useful for analyzing the correlation between two data sets is a *set difference query*, sometimes called a *left* (or *right*) *anti-semi join*, which finds the difference between the two data sets based on the conditions of the join. In relational algebra terms, it removes the divisor from the dividend, leaving the difference. This type of query is the inverse of an inner join. Informally, it's called a *find unmatched rows* query.

Set difference queries are great for locating out-of-place data or data that doesn't match, such as rows that are in data set one but not in data set two (see Figure 10-12).

FIGURE 10-12

The set difference query finds data that is outside the intersection of the two data sets.

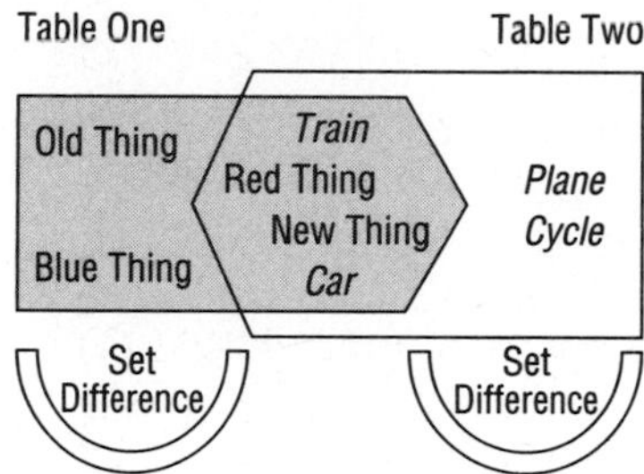

Left set difference query

A *left set difference query* finds all the rows on the left side of the join without a match on the right side of the joins.

Using the One and Two sample tables, the following query locates all rows in table One without a match in table Two, removing set two (the divisor) from set one (the dividend). The result will be the rows from set one that do not have a match in set two.

The outer join already includes the rows outside the intersection, so to construct a set difference query use an OUTER JOIN with an IS NULL restriction on the second data set's primary key. This will return all the rows from table One that do not have a match in table Two:

```
USE tempdb;

SELECT Thing1, Thing2
  FROM dbo.One
    LEFT OUTER JOIN dbo.Two
      ON One.OnePK = Two.OnePK
  WHERE Two.TwoPK IS NULL;
```

Table One's difference is as follows:

```
Thing1          Thing2
--------------- ---------------
Old Thing       NULL
Blue Thing      NULL
```

To see if the theory will fly in a real-world scenario from the OBXKites sample database, the following code is a set difference query that locates all contacts who have not yet placed an order. The Contact table is the divisor and the set difference query removes the contacts with orders (the dividend). The left outer join produces a data set with all contacts and matching orders. The WHERE condition restricts the result set to only those rows without a match in the [Order] table:

```
USE OBXKites;
SELECT Contact.LastName, Contact.FirstName
  FROM dbo.Contact
    LEFT OUTER JOIN dbo.[Order]
      ON Contact.ContactID = [Order].ContactID
  WHERE [Order].OrderID IS NULL;
```

The result is the difference between the Contact table and the [Order] table — that is, all contacts who have not placed an order:

```
LastName      FirstName
------------  ---------------
Andrews       Ed
Boston        Dave
Earl          Betty
Hanks         Nickolas
Harrison      Charlie
...
```

The set difference query could be written using a subquery (covered in the next chapter). The WHERE NOT IN condition, shown in the following example, removes the subquery rows (the divisor) from the outer query (the dividend). However, be aware that while this works logically, it doesn't perform well with a large data set.

```
SELECT LastName, FirstName
  FROM dbo.Contact
  WHERE ContactID NOT IN
    (SELECT ContactID FROM dbo.[Order])
  ORDER BY LastName, FirstName;
```

Either form of the query (LEFT OUTER JOIN or NOT IN subquery) works well, with very similar query execution plans, as shown in Figure 10-13.

Full set difference queries

I often use a modified version of this technique to clean up bad data during conversions. A *full set difference query* is the logical opposite of an inner join. It identifies all rows outside the intersection from either data set by combining a full outer join with a WHERE restriction that accepts only nulls in either primary key:

```
SELECT Thing1, Thing2
  FROM One
```

```
FULL OUTER JOIN Two
  ON One.OnePK = Two.OnePK
WHERE Two.TwoPK IS NULL
  OR One.OnePK IS NULL;
```

FIGURE 10-13

The subquery form of the set difference query is optimized to nearly the same query execution plan as the left outer join solution.

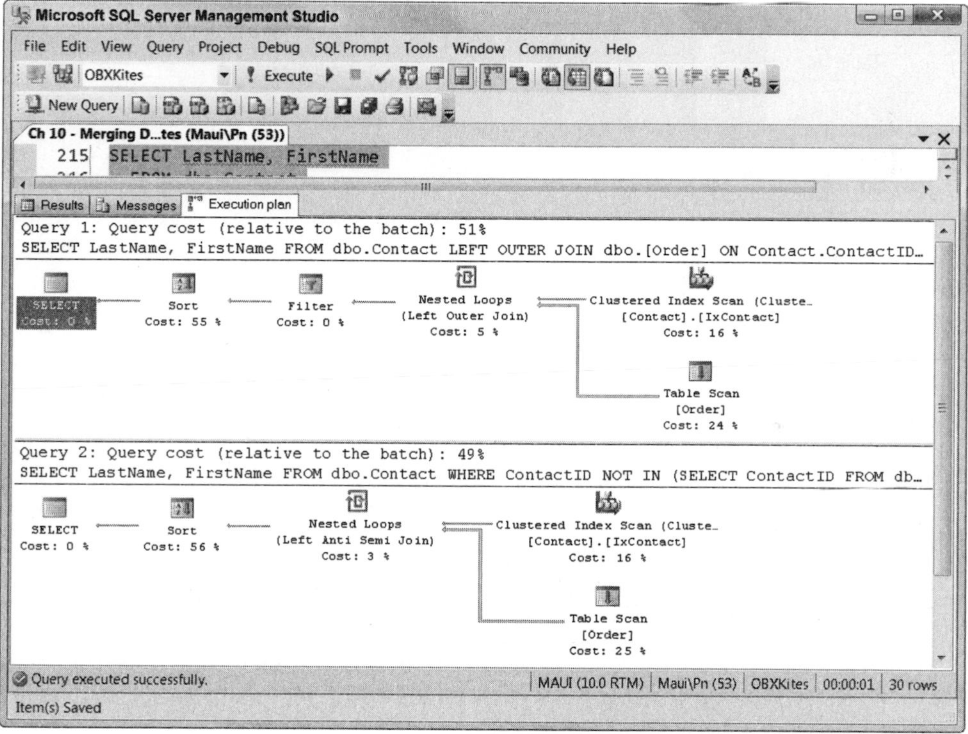

The result is every row without a match in the One and Two sample tables:

```
Thing1          Thing2
--------------- ---------------
NULL            Plane
NULL            Cycle
Blue Thing      NULL
Old Thing       NULL
```

Using Unions

The union operation is different from a join. In relational algebra terms, a union is addition, whereas a join is multiplication. Instead of extending a row horizontally as a join would, the union stacks multiple result sets into a single long table, as illustrated in Figure 10-14.

FIGURE 10-14

A union vertically appends the result of one `select` statement to the result of another `select` statement.

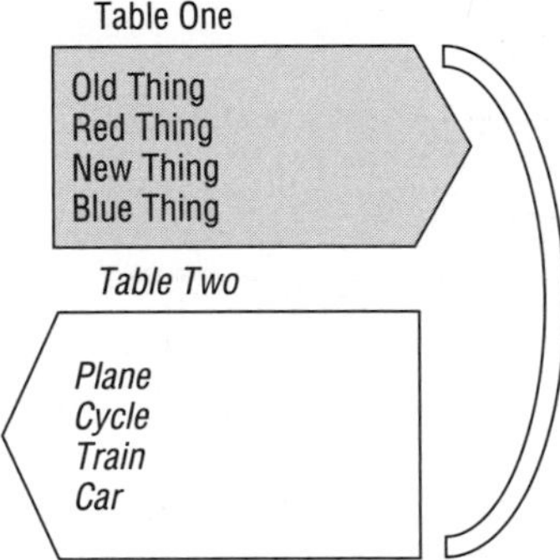

Unions come in three basic flavors: union, intersect union, and difference (or except) union.

Union [All]

The most common type of union by far is the `UNION ALL` query, which simply adds the individual `SELECT`'s results.

In the following `UNION` query, the things from table `one` and the things from table `two` are appended together into a single list. The first `SELECT` sets up the overall result, so it supplies the result set column headers. Each individual `SELECT` generates a result set for the `UNION` operation, so each `SELECT`'s individual `WHERE` clause filters data for that `SELECT`. The final `SELECT`'s `ORDER BY` then serves as the `ORDER BY` for the entire unioned results set. Note that the `ORDER BY` must refer to the columns by either the first `SELECT`'s column names, or by the ordinal position of the column:

```
SELECT OnePK, Thing1, 'from One' as Source
  FROM dbo.One
UNION ALL
SELECT TwoPK, Thing2, 'from Two'
  FROM dbo.Two
ORDER BY Thing1;
```

The resulting record set uses the column names from the first SELECT statement:

```
OnePK       Thing1          Source
----------- --------------- --------
4           Blue Thing      from One
3           Car             from Two
4           Cycle           from Two
2           New Thing       from One
1           Old Thing       from One
1           Plane           from Two
3           Red Thing       from One
2           Train           from Two
```

When constructing unions, there are a few rules to understand:

- Every SELECT must have the same number of columns, and each column must share the same data-type family with the columns in the other queries.
- The column names, or aliases, are determined by the first SELECT.
- The order by clause sorts the results of all the SELECTs and must go on the last SELECT, but it uses the column names from the first SELECT.
- Expressions may be added to the SELECT statements to identify the source of the row so long as the column is added to every SELECT.
- The union may be used as part of a SELECT into (a form of the insert verb covered in Chapter 15, "Modifying Data"), but the INTO keyword must go in the first SELECT statement.
- The basic SELECT command defaults to all rows unless DISTINCT is specified; the union is the opposite. By default, the union performs a DISTINCT; if you wish to change this behavior you must specify the keyword ALL. (I recommend that you think of the union as UNION ALL, in the same way that the you might think of top as TOP WITH TIES.)

Unions aren't limited to two tables. The largest I've personally worked with had about 90 tables (I won't try that again anytime soon). As long as the total number of tables referenced by a query is 256 or fewer, SQL Server handles the load.

Intersection union

An *intersection union* finds the rows common to both data sets. An inner join finds common rows horizontally, whereas an intersection union finds common rows vertically. To set up the intersection query, these first two statements add rows to table Two so there will be an intersection:

```
INSERT dbo.Two(TwoPK, OnePK, Thing2)
  VALUES(5,0, 'Red Thing');
INSERT dbo.Two(TwoPK, OnePK, Thing2)
  VALUES(?,?, 'Blue Thing');

SELECT Thing1
  FROM dbo.One
INTERSECT
```

```
SELECT Thing2
  FROM dbo.Two
ORDER BY Thing1;
```

Result:

```
Thing1
---------------
Blue Thing
Red Thing
```

An intersection union query is similar to an inner join. The inner join merges the rows horizontally, whereas the intersect union stacks the rows vertically. The intersect must match every column in order to be included in the result. A twist, however, is that the intersect will see null values as equal and accept the rows with nulls.

NOTE **Intersection union queries are very useful for proving that two queries give the same results. When all three queries have the same result count, the two queries must be functionally equivalent.**

Query A gives 1234 rows.

Query B gives 1234 rows.

Query A intersect Query B gives 1234 rows.

Difference union/except

The *difference union* is the union equivalent of the set difference query — it find rows in one data source that are not in the other data source.

Whereas a set difference query is interested only in the join conditions (typically the primary and foreign keys) and joins the rows horizontally, a difference union `EXCEPT` query looks at the entire row (or, more specifically, all the columns that participate in the union's `SELECT` statements).

SQL Server uses the ANSI Standard keyword `EXCEPT` to execute a difference union:

```
SELECT Thing1
  FROM dbo.One
EXCEPT
SELECT Thing2
  FROM dbo.Two
ORDER BY Thing1;
```

Result:

```
Thing1
---------------
New Thing
Old Thing
```

Summary

Merging data is the heart of SQL, and it shows in the depth of relational algebra as well as the power and flexibility of SQL. From natural joins to exotic joins, SQL is excellent at selecting sets of data from multiple data tables.

The challenge for the SQL Server database developer is to master the theory of relational algebra and the many T-SQL techniques to effectively manipulate the data. The reward is the fun.

Manipulating data with `SELECT` is the core technology of SQL Server. While joins are the most natural method of working with relational data, subqueries open numerous possibilities for creative and powerful ways to retrieve data from multiple data sources. The next chapter details the many ways you can use subqueries within a query, and introduces *common table expressions (CTEs)*, a feature new to SQL Server 2005.

Chapter 11

Including Data with Subqueries and CTEs

IN THIS CHAPTER

Understanding subquery types

Building simple and correlated subqueries

Fitting subqueries in the query puzzle

Using common table expressions (CTEs)

Solving problems with relational division

Passing data with composable SQL

SQL's real power is its capability to mix and match multiple methods of selecting data. It's this skill in fluidly assembling a complex query in code to accomplish what can't be easily done with GUI tools that differentiates SQL gurus from the wannabes. So, without hesitation I invite you to study embedded simple and correlated subqueries, derived tables, and common table expressions, and then apply these query components to solve complex relational problems such as relational division.

Methods and Locations

A *subquery* is an embedded SQL statement within an outer query. The subquery provides an answer to the outer query in the form of a scalar value, a list of values, or a data set, and may be substituted for an expression, list, or table, respectively, within the outer query. The matrix of subquery types and SELECT statement usage is shown in Table 11-1. Traditionally, a subquery may only contain a SELECT query and not a data-modification query, which explains why subqueries are sometimes referred to as *subselects*.

Five basic forms are possible when building a subquery, depending on the data needs and your favored syntax:

- **Simple subquery:** The simple subquery can be a stand-alone query and can run by itself. It is executed once, with the result passed to the outer query. Simple subqueries are constructed as normal SELECT queries and placed within parentheses.
- **Common table expression (CTE):** CTEs are a syntactical variation of the simple subquery, similar to a view, which defines the subquery at the beginning of the query using the WITH command. The CTE can then be accessed multiple times within the main query as if it were a view or derived table.

- **Correlated subquery:** This is similar to a simple subquery except that it references at least one column in the outer query, so it cannot run separately by itself. Conceptually, the outer query runs first and the correlated subquery runs once for every row in the outer query. Physically, the Query Optimizer is free to generate an efficient query execution plan.
- **Row constructor:** A `VALUES` clause or the `FROM` clause that supplies hard-coded values as a subquery
- **Composable SQL:** The ability to pass data from an `INSERT`, `UPDATE`, or `DELETE` statement's output clause to an outer query

TABLE 11-1

Subquery and CTE Usage

Outer Query Element	Subquery Returns:		
	Expression ***Subquery returns a scalar value***	List ***Subquery returns a list of values***	Data Set ***Subquery returns a multi-column data source***
Any expression e.g., `SELECT` list, `HAVING` clause, `GROUP BY`, `JOIN ON`, etc.	The subquery result is used as an expression supplying the value for the column. If the result is empty, NULL is used instead.	X	X
Derived Table `FROM` (data source) `AS ALIAS` or `WITH` *`CTE`* *This is the only location where a subquery can use a table alias*	The subquery's data set is accepted as a (one row, one column) derived table source within the outer query. If the result is empty, an empty derived table source is used.	The subquery's data set is accepted as a (one row) derived table source within the outer query.	The subquery's data set is accepted as a derived table source within the outer query.

`WHERE x`
`{=,<>,!=,>,>=,!>,<,<=,!<}`
`(subquery)`
	The `WHERE` clause is true if the test value compares true with the subquery's scalar value. If the subquery returns no result, the `WHERE` clause is not true.	X	X

TABLE 11-1 *(continued)*

Outer Query Element	Subquery Returns:		
	Expression ***Subquery returns a scalar value***	**List** ***Subquery returns a list of values***	**Data Set** ***Subquery returns a multi-column data source***
WHERE x {=,<>,!=,>,>=,!>,<,<=,!<} **ALL** (subquery)	The WHERE condition is true if the test value meets the condition for the scalar value returned by the subquery. If the subquery returns no result, the WHERE condition is not true.	The WHERE condition is true if the test value meets the condition for *every* value returned by the subquery.	X
WHERE x {=,<>,!=,>,>=,!>,<,<=,!<} **SOME|ANY** (subquery)	The WHERE condition is true if the test value meets the condition for the scalar value returned by the subquery. If the subquery returns no result, the where condition is not true.	The WHERE condition is true if the test value meets the condition for *any* value returned by the subquery.	X
WHERE x **IN | = ANY** (subquery)	The WHERE condition is true if the test value is equal to the scalar value returned by the subquery. If the subquery returns no result, the WHERE condition is not true.	The WHERE condition is true if the test value is found within the list of values returned by the subquery.	X
WHERE **EXISTS** (Subquery)	The WHERE condition is true if the subquery returns a value.	The WHERE condition is true if the subquery returns at least one value.	The WHERE condition is true if the subquery returns at least one row.

What's New with Subqueries?

Subqueries are fundamental to SQL and there's been a steady evolution of their capabilities. Significant recent improvements include the following:

- SQL Server 2005 saw the introduction of the `Apply` structure for user-defined functions and subqueries.
- With SQL Server 2008, Microsoft adds row constructors that can be used in the subquery to provide hard-coded values to the query.
- Also new with SQL server 2008 is composable SQL — a new way to plug together multiple DML statements. Anytime there's a new way to connect together different parts of the SQL query, it opens new doors for experimentation and building new queries.

It's good to see Microsoft continue to evolve and progress in critical areas such as subqueries.

Simple Subqueries

Simple subqueries are executed in the following order:

1. The simple subquery is executed once.
2. The results are passed to the outer query.
3. The outer query is executed once.

The most basic simple subquery returns a single (scalar) value, which is then used as an expression in the outer query, as follows:

```
SELECT (SELECT 3) AS SubqueryValue;
```

Result:

```
SubqueryValue
--------------
3
```

The subquery (`SELECT` 3) returns a single value of 3, which is passed to the outer `SELECT` statement. The outer `SELECT` statement is then executed as if it were the following:

```
SELECT 3 AS SubqueryValue;
```

Of course, a subquery with only hard-coded values is of little use. A useful subquery fetches data from a table, for example:

```
USE OBXKites;

SELECT ProductName
```

```
FROM dbo.Product
WHERE ProductCategoryID
  = (Select ProductCategoryID
       FROM dbo.ProductCategory
       Where ProductCategoryName = 'Kite');
```

To execute this query, SQL Server first evaluates the subquery and returns a value to the outer query (your unique identifier will be different from the one in this query):

```
Select ProductCategoryID
  FROM dbo.ProductCategory
  Where ProductCategoryName = 'Kite';
```

Result:

```
ProductCategoryID
------------------------------------
c38D8113-2BED-4E2B-9ABF-A589E0818069
```

The outer query then executes as if it were the following:

```
SELECT ProductName
  FROM dbo.Product
  WHERE ProductCategoryID
    = 'c38D8113-2BED-4E2B-9ABF-A589E0818069';
```

Result:

```
ProductName
--------------------------------------------------
Basic Box Kite 21 inch
Dragon Flight
Sky Dancer
Rocket Kite
...
```

If you think subqueries seem similar to joins, you're right. Both are a means of referencing multiple data sources within a single query, and many queries that use joins may be rewritten as queries using subqueries.

Best Practice

Use a join to pull data from two data sources that can be filtered or manipulated as a whole after the join. If the data must be manipulated prior to the join, then use a derived table subquery.

Common table expressions

The common table expression (CTE) defines what could be considered a temporary view, which can be referenced just like a view in the same query. Because CTEs may be used in the same ways that simple subqueries are used and they compile exactly like a simple subquery, I've included them in the simple subquery heading and will show example code CTEs alongside simple subqueries.

The CTE uses the `WITH` clause, which defines the CTE. Inside the `WITH` clause is the name, column aliases, and SQL code for the CTE subquery. The main query can then reference the CTE as a data source:

```
WITH CTEName (Column aliases)
AS (Simple Subquery)
SELECT...
  FROM CTEName;
```

NOTE **The `WITH` keyword not only begins a CTE, it also adds a hint to a table reference. This is why the statement before a CTE must be terminated with a semicolon — just one more reason to always terminate every statement with a semicolon.**

The following example is the exact same query as the preceding subquery, only in CTE format. The name of the CTE is `CTEQuery`. It returns the `ProductionCategoryID` column and uses the exact same SQL `Select` statement as the preceding simple subquery:

```
WITH CTEQuery (ProductCategoryID)
  AS (Select ProductCategoryID
        from dbo.ProductCategory
        Where ProductCategoryName = 'Kite')
```

(Note that a CTE by itself is an incomplete SQL statement. If you try to run the preceding code, you will get a syntax error.)

Once the CTE has been defined in the `WITH` clause, the main portion of the query can reference the CTE using its name as if the CTE were any other table source, such as a table or a view. Here's the complete example, including the CTE and the main query:

```
WITH CTEQuery (ProductCategoryID)
  AS (Select ProductCategoryID
        from dbo.ProductCategory
        Where ProductCategoryName = 'Kite')
SELECT ProductName
  FROM dbo.Product
  WHERE ProductCategoryID
    = (SELECT ProductCategoryID FROM CTEQuery);
```

To include multiple CTEs within the same query, define the CTEs in sequence prior to the main query:

```
WITH
  CTE1Name (column names)
    AS (Simple Subquery),
```

```
    CTE2Name (column names)
      AS (Simple Subquery)
  SELECT...
    FROM CTE1Name
      INNER JOIN CTE2Name
        ON ...
```

Although CTEs may include complex queries, they come with two key restrictions:

- Unlike subqueries, CTEs may not be nested. A CTE may not include another CTE.
- CTEs may not reference the main query. Like simple subqueries, they must be self-contained. However, a CTE may reference any of the CTEs defined before it, or even itself (see below).

Best Practice

Although the CTE syntax may initially appear alien, for very complex queries that reference the same subquery in multiple locations, using a CTE may reduce the amount of code and improve readability.

CROSS-REF **A CTE is really just a different syntax for a simple subquery used as a derived table, with one key exception: CTEs can recursively refer to the same table using a union, and this works great for searching an adjacency pairs pattern hierarchy. For more details on using CTEs for hierarchies, turn to Chapter 17, "Traversing Hierarchies."**

Using scalar subqueries

If the subquery returns a single value it may then be used anywhere inside the SQL `SELECT` statement where an expression might be used, including column expressions, `JOIN` conditions, `WHERE` conditions, or `HAVING` conditions.

Normal operators (+, =, between, and so on) will work with single values returned from a subquery; data-type conversion using the `CAST()` or `CONVERT()` functions may be required, however.

The example in the last section used a subquery within a `WHERE` condition. The following sample query uses a subquery within a column expression to calculate the total sales so each row can calculate the percentage of sales:

```
SELECT ProductCategoryName,
     SUM(Quantity * UnitPrice) AS Sales,
     Cast(SUM(Quantity * UnitPrice) /
         (SELECT SUM(Quantity * UnitPrice)
            FROM dbo.OrderDetail) *100)
         AS PercentOfSales
  FROM dbo.OrderDetail AS OD
    INNER JOIN dbo.Product AS P
      ON OD.ProductID = P.ProductID
    INNER JOIN dbo.ProductCategory AS PC
```

```
    ON P.ProductCategoryID = PC.ProductCategoryID
GROUP BY ProductCategoryName
ORDER BY Count(*) DESC;
```

The subquery, `SELECT SUM(Quantity * UnitPrice) from OrderDetail`, returns a value of `1729.895`, which is then passed to the outer query's `PercentageOfSales` column. The result lists the product categories, sales amount, and percentage of sales:

```
ProductCategoryName    Sales           PercentOfSales
---------------------- --------------  --------------
Kite                   1694.452500     87.891300
OBX                    64.687500       3.355300
Clothing               117.050000      6.071300
Accessory              10.530000       0.546100
Material               5.265000        0.273000
Video                  35.910000       1.862600
```

The following `SELECT` statement is extracted from the `fsGetPrice()` user-defined function in the `OBXKites` sample database. The `OBXKites` database has a `Price` table that allows each product to have a list of prices, each with an effective date. The OBX Kite store can predefine several price changes for a future date, rather than enter all the price changes the night before the new prices go into effect. As an additional benefit, this data model maintains a price history.

The `fsGetPrice()` function returns the correct price for any product, any date, and any customer-discount type. To accomplish this, the function must determine the effective date for the date submitted. For example, if a user needs a price for July 16, 2002, and the current price was made effective on July 1, 2002, then in order to look up the price the query needs to know the most recent price date using `max(effectivedate)`, where `effectivedate` is = `@orderdate`. Once the subquery determines the effective date, the outer query can look up the price. Some of the function's variables are replaced with static values for the purpose of this example:

```
SELECT @CurrPrice = Price * (1-@DiscountPercent)
  FROM dbo.Price
    INNER JOIN dbo.Product
      ON Price.ProductID = Product.ProductID
  WHERE ProductCode = '1001'
    AND EffectiveDate =
      (SELECT MAX(EffectiveDate)
        FROM dbo.Price
          INNER JOIN dbo.Product
            ON Price.ProductID = Product.ProductID
         WHERE ProductCode = '1001'
           AND EffectiveDate <= '2001/6/1');
```

Calling the function,

```
Select dbo.fGetPrice('1001','5/1/2001',NULL);
```

the subquery determines that the effective price date is January 5, 2001. The outer query can then find the correct price based on the ProductID and effective date. Once the fGetPrice() function calculates the discount, it can return @CurrPrice to the calling SELECT statement:

```
14.95
```

Using subqueries as lists

Subqueries begin to shine when used as lists. A single value, commonly a column, in the outer query is compared with the subquery's list by means of the IN operator. The subquery must return only a single column; multiple columns will fail.

The IN operator returns a value of true if the column value is found anywhere in the list supplied by the subquery, in the same way that WHERE ... IN returns a value of true when used with a hard-coded list:

```
SELECT FirstName, LastName
  FROM dbo.Contact
  WHERE HomeRegion IN ('NC', 'SC', 'GA', 'AL', 'VA');
```

A list subquery serves as a dynamic means of generating the WHERE ... IN condition list:

```
SELECT FirstName, LastName
  FROM dbo.Contact
  WHERE Region IN (Subquery that returns a list of states);
```

The following query answers the question "When OBX Kites sells a kite, what else does it sell with the kite?" To demonstrate the use of subqueries, this query uses only subqueries — no joins. All of these subqueries are simple queries, meaning that each can run as a stand-alone query.

The subquery will find all orders with kites and pass those OrderIDs to the outer query. Four tables are involved in providing the answer to this question: ProductCategory, Product, OrderDetail, and Order. The nested subqueries are executed from the inside out, so they read in the following order (explained in more detail after the query):

1. The subquery finds the one ProductCategoryID for the kites.
2. The subquery finds the list of products that are kites.
3. The subquery finds the list of orders with kites.
4. The subquery finds the list of all the products on orders with kites.
5. The outer query finds the product names.

```
SELECT ProductName
  FROM dbo.Product
  WHERE ProductID IN
    -- 4. Find all the products sold in orders with kites
    (SELECT ProductID
```

```
FROM dbo.OrderDetail
WHERE OrderID IN
-- 3. Find the Kite Orders
(SELECT OrderID  -- Find the Orders with Kites
  FROM dbo.OrderDetail
  WHERE ProductID IN
    -- 2. Find the Kite Products
    (SELECT ProductID
      FROM dbo.Product
      WHERE ProductCategoryID =
         -- 1. Find the Kite category
         (Select ProductCategoryID
           FROM dbo.ProductCategory
           Where ProductCategoryName
              = 'Kite' ) ) ) );
```

TIP **You can highlight any of these subqueries and run it as a stand-alone query in a query window by selecting just the subquery and pressing F5. Be sure to include the correct number of closing parentheses.**

Subquery 1 finds the `ProductCategoryID` for the kite category and returns a single value.

Subquery 2 uses subquery 1 as a `WHERE` clause expression subquery that returns the kite `ProductCategoryID`. Using this `WHERE` clause restriction, subquery 2 finds all products for which the `ProductCategoryID` is equal to the value returned from subquery 2.

Subquery 3 uses subquery 2 as a `WHERE` clause list subquery by searching for all `OrderDetail` rows that include any one of the `productIDs` returned by subquery 2.

Subquery 4 uses subquery 3 as a `WHERE` clause list subquery that includes all orders that include kites. The subquery then locates all `OrderDetail` rows for which the `orderID` is in the list returned by subquery 3.

The outer query uses subquery 4 as a `WHERE` clause list condition and finds all products for which the `ProductID` is in the list returned by subquery 4, as follows:

```
ProductName
--------------------------------------------------
Falcon F-16
Dragon Flight
OBX Car Bumper Sticker
Short Streamer
Cape Hatteras T-Shirt
Sky Dancer
Go Fly a Kite T-Shirt
Long Streamer
Rocket Kite
OBX T-Shirt
```

Drat! There are kites in the list. They'll have to be eliminated from the query. To fix the error, the outer query needs to find all the products WHERE:

- The ProductID is IN an order that included a kite

and

- The ProductID is NOT IN the list of kites

Fortunately, subquery 2 returns all the kite products. Adding a copy of subquery 2 with the NOT IN operator to the outer query will remove the kites from the list, as follows:

```
SELECT ProductName
  FROM dbo.Product
  WHERE ProductID IN
    -- 4. Find all the products sold in orders with kites
    (SELECT ProductID
      FROM dbo.OrderDetail
      WHERE OrderID IN
      -- 3. Find the Kite Orders
      (SELECT OrderID  -- Find the Orders with Kites
        FROM dbo.OrderDetail
        WHERE ProductID IN
          -- 2. Find the Kite Products
          (SELECT ProductID
            FROM dbo.Product
            WHERE ProductCategoryID =
               -- 1. Find the Kite category
               (Select ProductCategoryID
                 FROM dbo.ProductCategory
                 Where ProductCategoryName
                    = 'Kite'))))
        -- outer query continued
        AND ProductID NOT IN
          (SELECT ProductID
            FROM dbo.Product
            WHERE ProductCategoryID =
               (Select ProductCategoryID
                 FROM dbo.ProductCategory
                 Where ProductCategoryName
                    = 'Kite'));
```

Result:

```
ProductName
--------------------------------------------------
OBX Car Bumper Sticker
Short Streamer
```

```
Cape Hatteras T-Shirt
Go Fly a Kite T-Shirt
Long Streamer
OBX T-Shirt
```

For comparison purposes, the following queries answer the exact same question but are written with joins. The `Product` table is referenced twice, so the second reference that represents only the kites has an alias `Kite`. As with the previous subqueries, the first version of the query locates all products and the second version eliminates the kites:

```
SELECT Distinct P.ProductName
  FROM dbo.Product AS P
    JOIN dbo.OrderDetail AS OrderRow
      ON P.ProductID = OrderRow.ProductID
    JOIN dbo.OrderDetail AS KiteRow
      ON OrderRow.OrderID = KiteRow.OrderID
    JOIN dbo.Product AS Kite
      ON KiteRow.ProductID = Kite.ProductID
    JOIN dbo.ProductCategory AS PC
      ON Kite.ProductCategoryID
           = PC.ProductCategoryID
  WHERE PC.ProductCategoryName  = 'Kite';
```

The only change necessary to eliminate the kites is the addition of another condition to the `ProductCategory` join. Previously, the join was an equi-join between `Product` and `ProductCategory`. Adding a Θ-join condition of <> between the `Product` table and the `ProductCategory` table removes any products that are kites, as shown here:

```
SELECT Distinct P.ProductName
  FROM dbo.Product AS P
    JOIN dbo.OrderDetail AS OrderRow
      ON P.ProductID = OrderRow.ProductID
    JOIN dbo.OrderDetail AS KiteRow
      ON OrderRow.OrderID = KiteRow.OrderID
    JOIN dbo.Product AS Kite
      ON KiteRow.ProductID = Kite.ProductID
    JOIN dbo.ProductCategory AS PC
      ON Kite.ProductCategoryID
           = PC.ProductCategoryID
      AND P.ProductCategoryID
           <> Kite.ProductCategoryID
  Where PC.ProductCategoryName  = 'Kite';
```

Best Practice

SQL is very flexible — there are often a dozen ways to express the same question. Your choice of SQL method should be made first according to your style and to which method enables you to be readable and logically correct, and then according to performance considerations. Test the actual queries for performance but keep in mind that slow and correct beats fast and wrong every time.

Using subqueries as tables

In the same way that a view may be used in the place of a table within the `FROM` clause of a `SELECT` statement, a subquery in the form of a *derived table* can replace any table, provided the subquery has an alias. This technique is very powerful and is often used to break a difficult query problem down into smaller bite-size chunks.

Using a subquery as a derived table is an excellent solution to the aggregate-function problem. When you are building an aggregate query, every column must participate in the aggregate function in some way, either as a `GROUP BY` column or as an aggregate function (`sum()`, `avg()`, `count()`, `max()`, or `min()`). This stipulation makes returning additional descriptive information difficult. However, performing the aggregate functions in a subquery and passing the rows found to the outer query as a derived table enables the outer query to then return any columns desired.

CROSS-REF **For more information about aggregate functions and the `group by` keyword, see Chapter 12, "Aggregating Data."**

The question "How many of each product have been sold?" is easy to answer if only one column from the `Product` table is included in the result:

```
SELECT P.Code, SUM(Quantity) AS QuantitySold
  FROM dbo.OrderDetail AS OD
    JOIN dbo.Product AS P
      ON OD.ProductID = P.ProductID
  GROUP BY P.Code
  ORDER BY P.Code;
```

Result:

```
Code            QuantitySold
--------------- ---------------------------------------
1002            47.00
1003            5.00
1004            2.00
1012            5.00
...
```

The result includes P.Code, but not the name or description. Of course, it's possible to simply group by every column to be returned, but that's sloppy. The following query performs the aggregate summation in a subquery that is then joined with the Product table so that every column is available without additional work:

```
SELECT P.Code,
    P.ProductName,
    Sales.QuantitySold
  FROM dbo.Product AS P
  JOIN (SELECT ProductID, SUM(Quantity) AS QuantitySold
          FROM dbo.OrderDetail
          GROUP BY ProductID) AS Sales
    ON P.ProductID = Sales.ProductID
  ORDER BY P.Code;
```

If you use SQL Server Management Studio's Query Designer, a derived table may be added to the query. Figure 11-1 illustrates the previous query being constructed using the GUI tool.

FIGURE 11-1

Derived tables may be included within Query Designer by using the context menu and selecting Add Derived Table.

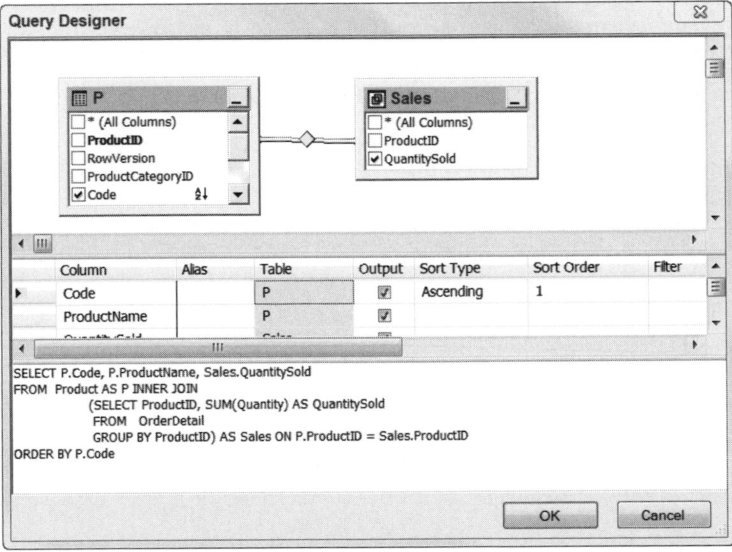

The query is fast and efficient, it provides the required aggregate data, and all the product columns can be added to the output columns. The result is as follows:

```
Code        ProductName          QuantitySold
----------- -------------------- ------------------
1002        Dragon Flight        47.00
1003        Sky Dancer           5.00
1004        Rocket Kite          2.00
1012        Falcon F-16          5.00
...
```

Another example of using a derived table to solve a problem answers the question "How many children has each mother borne?" from the `Family` sample database:

```
USE Family;
SELECT p.PersonID, p.FirstName, p.LastName, c.Children
  FROM dbo.Person AS p
    JOIN (SELECT m.MotherID, COUNT(*) AS Children
            FROM dbo.Person AS m
            WHERE m.MotherID IS NOT NULL
            GROUP BY m.MotherID) AS c
      ON p.PersonID = c.MotherID
  ORDER BY c.Children DESC;
```

The subquery performs the aggregate summation, and the columns are joined with the `Person` table to present the final results, as follows:

```
PersonID    FirstName       LastName        Children
----------- --------------- --------------- -----------
6           Audry           Halloway        4
8           Melanie         Campbell        3
12          Alysia          Halloway        3
20          Grace           Halloway        2
...
```

Row constructors

New for SQL Server 2008, row constructors provide a convenient way to supply hard-coded values directly in a subquery. The `VALUES` clause is wrapped in parentheses, as is every hard-coded row. It requires an alias and a column alias list, also in parentheses.

Row constructors can be used in the `FROM` clause and joined just like any other type of data source.

The next query creates a row constructors data source called MyRowConstructor with two columns, a and b:

```
SELECT a, b
  FROM
      (VALUES
        (1, 2),
        (3, 4),
        (5, 6),
        (7, 8),
        (9, 10)
      ) AS MyRowConstructor(a, b)
```

Result:

```
a           b
----------- -----------
1           2
3           4
5           6
7           8
9           10
```

All, some, and any

Though not as popular as IN, three other options are worth examining when using a subquery in a WHERE clause. Each provides a twist on how items in the subquery are matched with the WHERE clause's test value. ALL must be true for every value. SOME and ANY, which are equivalent keywords, must be true for some of the values in the subquery.

The next query demonstrates a simple ALL subquery. In this case, select returns true if 1 is less than every value in the subquery:

```
SELECT 'True' as 'AllTest'
  WHERE 1 < ALL
    (SELECT a
       FROM
         (VALUES
           (2),
           (3),
           (5),
           (7),
           (9)
         ) AS ValuesTable(a)
    );
```

Result:

```
AllTest
--------------
True
```

Be very careful with the ALL condition if the subquery might return a null. A null value in the subquery results will force the ALL to return a false, because it's impossible to prove that the test is true for every value in the subquery if one of those values is unknown.

In this query, the last value is changed from a 9 to null and the query no longer returns true:

```
SELECT 'True' AS 'AllTest'
  WHERE 1 < ALL
    (SELECT a
       FROM
          (VALUES
            (2),
            (3),
            (5),
            (7),
            (null)
          ) AS ValuesTable(a)
    );
```

Result (empty result set):

```
AllTest
--------------
```

The SOME and ANY conditional tests return true if the condition is met for any values in the subquery result set. For example:

```
SELECT 'True' as 'SomeTest'
  WHERE 5 = SOME
    (SELECT a
        FROM
          (VALUES
            (2),
            (3),
            (5),
            (7),
            (9)
          ) AS MyTable(a)
    );
```

Result:

```
SomeTest
--------------
True
```

The ANY and SOME conditions are similar to the in condition. In fact = ANY and = SOME are exactly like IN. ANY and SOME conditions have the extra functionality to testing for other conditional tests such as <, <=, >, =>, and <>.

Correlated Subqueries

Correlated subqueries sound impressive, and they are. They are used in the same ways that simple subqueries are used, the difference being that correlated subqueries reference columns in the outer query. They do this by referencing the name or alias of a table in the outer query, to reference the outer query. This capability to limit the subquery by the outer query makes these queries powerful and flexible. Because correlated subqueries can reference the outer query, they are especially useful for complex `WHERE` conditions.

Correlating in the where clause

The capability to reference the outer query also means that correlated subqueries won't run by themselves because the reference to the outer query would cause the query to fail. The logical execution order is as follows:

1. The outer query is executed once.
2. The subquery is executed once for every row in the outer query, substituting the values from the outer query into each execution of the subquery.
3. The subquery's results are integrated into the result set.

If the outer query returns 100 rows, then SQL Server will execute the logical equivalent of 101 queries — one for the outer query, and one subquery for every row returned by the outer query. In practice, the SQL Server Query Optimizer will likely figure out a way to perform the correlated subquery without actually performing the 101 queries. In fact, I've sometimes seen correlated subqueries outperform other query plans. If they solve your problem, then don't avoid them for performance reasons.

To explore correlated subqueries, the next few queries, based on the `Outer Banks Adventures` sample database, use them to compare the locations of customers and tour base camps. First, the following data-modification queries set up the data:

```
USE CHA2;
UPDATE dbo.BaseCamp SET Region = 'NC' WHERE BaseCampID = 1;
UPDATE dbo.BaseCamp SET Region = 'NC' WHERE BaseCampID = 2;
UPDATE dbo.BaseCamp SET Region = 'BA' WHERE BaseCampID = 3;
UPDATE dbo.BaseCamp SET Region = 'FL' WHERE BaseCampID = 4;
UPDATE dbo.BaseCamp SET Region = 'WV' WHERE BaseCampID = 5;

UPDATE dbo.Customer SET Region = 'ND' WHERE CustomerID = 1;
UPDATE dbo.Customer SET Region = 'NC' WHERE CustomerID = 2;
UPDATE dbo.Customer SET Region = 'NJ' WHERE CustomerID = 3;
UPDATE dbo.Customer SET Region = 'NE' WHERE CustomerID = 4;
UPDATE dbo.Customer SET Region = 'ND' WHERE CustomerID = 5;
UPDATE dbo.Customer SET Region = 'NC' WHERE CustomerID = 6;
UPDATE dbo.Customer SET Region = 'NC' WHERE CustomerID = 7;
UPDATE dbo.Customer SET Region = 'BA' WHERE CustomerID = 8;
UPDATE dbo.Customer SET Region = 'NC' WHERE CustomerID = 9;
UPDATE dbo.Customer SET Region = 'FL' WHERE CustomerID = 10;
```

This sample set of data produces the following matrix between customer locations and base-camp locations:

```
SELECT DISTINCT c.Region, b.Region
  FROM dbo.Customer AS c
    INNER JOIN dbo.Event_mm_Customer AS ec
      ON c.CustomerID = ec.CustomerID
    INNER JOIN dbo.Event AS e
      ON ec.EventID = e.EventID
    INNER JOIN dbo.Tour AS t
      ON e.TourID = t.TourID
    INNER JOIN dbo.BaseCamp AS b
      ON t.BaseCampID = b.BaseCampID
  WHERE c.Region IS NOT NULL
  ORDER BY c.Region, b.Region;
```

Result:

```
Customer  BaseCamp
Region    Region
-------   --------
BA        BA
BA        FL
BA        NC
FL        FL
FL        NC
FL        WV
NC        BA
NC        FL
NC        NC
NC        WV
ND        BA
ND        FL
ND        NC
NE        FL
NE        WV
NJ        FL
NJ        NC
NJ        WV
```

With this data foundation, the first query asks, "Who lives in the same region as one of our base camps?" The query uses a correlated subquery to locate base camps that share the same `Region` as the customer. The subquery is executed for every row in the `Customer` table, using the outer query's named range, `C`, to reference the outer query. If a `BaseCamp` match exists for that row, then the `EXISTS` condition is true and the row is accepted into the result set:

```
SELECT C.FirstName, C.LastName, C.Region
  FROM dbo.Customer AS C
  WHERE EXISTS
```

```
    (SELECT * FROM dbo.BaseCamp AS B
       WHERE B.Region = C.Region)
  ORDER BY C.LastName, C.FirstName;
```

The same query written with joins requires a DISTINCT predicate to eliminate duplicate rows, usually resulting in worse performance. However, it can refer to columns in every referenced table — something a correlated subquery within a WHERE EXISTS can't do:

```
SELECT DISTINCT C.FirstName, C.LastName, C.Region
  FROM Customer AS C
    INNER JOIN dbo.BaseCamp AS B
      ON C.Region = B.Region
  ORDER BY C.LastName, C.FirstName;
```

Result:

```
FirstName       LastName            Region
--------------  ------------------  ------------------
Jane            Doe                  BA
Francis         Franklin             FL
Melissa         Anderson             NC
Lauren          Davis                NC
Wilson          Davis                NC
John            Frank                NC
```

A more complicated comparison asks, "Who has gone on a tour in his or her home region?"

The answer lies in the Event_mm_Customer table — a resolution (or junction) table between the Event and Customer tables that serves to store the logical many-to-many relationships between customers and events (multiple customers may attend a single event, and a single customer may attend multiple events). The Event_mm_Customer table may be thought of as analogous to a customer's ticket to an event.

The outer query logically runs through every Event_mm_Customer row to determine whether there EXISTS any result from the correlated subquery. The subquery is filtered by the current EventID and customer RegionID from the outer query.

In an informal way of thinking, the query checks every ticket and creates a list of events in a customer's home region that the customer has attended. If anything is in the list, then the WHERE EXISTS condition is true for that row. If the list is empty, WHERE EXISTS is not satisfied and the customer row in question is eliminated from the result set:

```
USE CHA2;
SELECT DISTINCT C.FirstName, C.LastName, C.Region AS Home
  FROM dbo.Customer AS C
    INNER JOIN dbo.Event_mm_Customer AS EC
      ON C.CustomerID = EC.CustomerID
  WHERE C.Region IS NOT NULL
    AND EXISTS
         (SELECT *
```

```
                 FROM dbo.Event AS E
                   INNER JOIN dbo.Tour AS T
                     ON E.TourID = T.TourID
                   INNER JOIN dbo.BaseCamp AS B
                     ON T.BaseCampID = B.BaseCampID
                 WHERE B.Region = C.Region
                   AND E.EventID = EC.EventID);
    ORDER BY C.LastName;
```

Result:

```
FirstName LastName    Home
--------- ----------- ------
Francis   Franklin    FL
Jane      Doe         BA
John      Frank       NC
Lauren    Davis       NC
Melissa   Anderson    NC
```

The same query can be written using joins. Although it might be easier to read, the following query took 131 milliseconds, compared to only 80 milliseconds taken by the preceding correlated subquery:

```
SELECT DISTINCT C.FirstName, C.LastName, C.Region AS Home,
    T.TourName, B.Region
?PAUL: With the TourName and Region columns included, I don't think
the DISTINCT predicate does much. Consider removing.
  FROM dbo.Customer AS C
    INNER JOIN dbo.Event_mm_Customer AS EC
      ON C.CustomerID = EC.CustomerID
    INNER JOIN dbo.Event AS E
      ON EC.EventID = E.EventID
    INNER JOIN dbo.Tour AS T
      ON E.TourID = T.TourID
    INNER JOIN dbo.BaseCamp AS B
      ON T.BaseCampID = B.BaseCampID
  WHERE C.Region = B.Region
      AND C.Region IS NOT NULL
  ORDER BY C.LastName;
```

The join query has the advantage of including the columns from the `Tour` table without having to explicitly return them from the subquery. The join also lists Lauren and John twice, once for each in-region tour (and yes, the Amazon Trek tour is based out of Ft. Lauderdale):

```
FirstName LastName    Home   TourName                  Region
--------- ----------- ------ ------------------------- ------
Melissa   Anderson    NC     Outer Banks Lighthouses   NC
Lauren    Davis       NC     Appalachian Trail         NC
Lauren    Davis       NC     Outer Banks Lighthouses   NC
Jane      Doe         BA     Bahamas Dive              BA
```

```
John      Frank     NC    Appalachian Trail           NC
John      Frank     NC    Outer Banks Lighthouses NC
Francis   Franklin  FL    Amazon Trek                 FL
```

Although correlated subqueries can be mind-bending, the flexibility and potential performance gains are worth it. Make sure that the correlated subquery returns the correct answer.

Correlating a derived table using apply

A subquery used as a derived table can reference the outer query, which makes it a correlated subquery. This technique leverages the previous correlated subquery method by using the correlation in the `WHERE` clause of the derived table subquery.

Subqueries used as derived tables aren't allowed to reference the outer query if they are included in the outer query with a `JOIN`. However, the `CROSS APPLY` or `OUTER APPLY` method of including the subquery allows passing data to the subquery.

First, to set up some sample data:

```
USE tempdb;

CREATE TABLE TableA (ID INT);
INSERT INTO TableA VALUES (1);
INSERT INTO TableA VALUES (2);

CREATE TABLE TableB (ID INT);
INSERT INTO TableB VALUES (1);
INSERT INTO TableB VALUES (3);
```

The following query uses a `CROSS APPLY` to pass every row from the outer query to the derived table subquery. The subquery then filters its rows to those that match `ID`s. The `CROSS APPLY` returns every row from the outer query that had a match in the subquery. Functionally, it's the equivalent to an inner join between `TableA` and `TableB`:

```
SELECT B.ID AS Bid, A.ID AS Aid
  FROM TableB AS B
    CROSS APPLY
      (Select ID from TableA
         where TableA.ID = B.ID) AS A;
```

Result:

```
Bid         Aid
----------- -----------
1           1
```

The next query uses the same correlated derived table subquery, but changes to an `OUTER APPLY` to include all rows from the outer query. This query is the same as a left outer join between `TableA` and `TableB`:

```
SELECT B.ID AS Bid, A.ID AS Aid
  FROM TableB AS B
    OUTER APPLY
      (Select ID  from TableA
         where TableA.ID = B.ID) AS A;
```

Result:

```
ID          ID
----------- -----------
1           1
3           NULL
```

Relational Division

Recall that a cross join, discussed in the previous chapter, is relational multiplication — two data sets are multiplied to create a Cartesian product. In theory, all joins are cross joins with some type of conditional restriction. Even an inner join is the relational-multiplication product of two tables restricted to those results that match keys.

Relational division complements relational multiplication just as basic math division complements multiplication. If the purpose of relational multiplication is to produce a product set from two multiplier sets, then the purpose of relational division is to divide one data set (the *dividend data set*) by another data set (the *divisor data set*) to find the *quotient data set*, as shown in Figure 11-2. In other words, if the Cartesian product is known, and one of the multiplier data sets is known, then relational division can deduce the missing multiplier set.

FIGURE 11-2

Relational division is the inverse of relational multiplication, deducing the quotient set by dividing the dividend set by the divisor set.

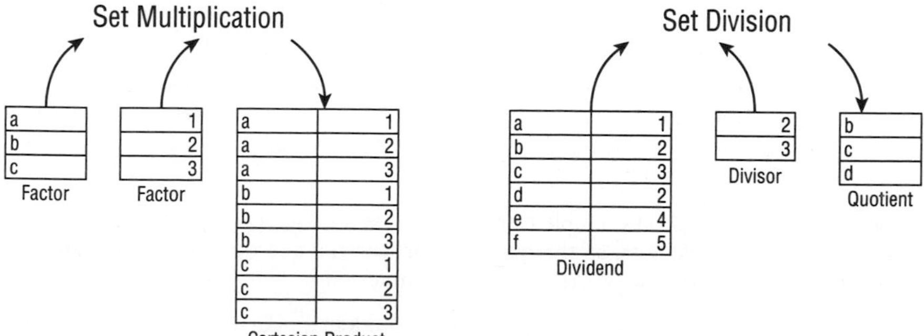

While this may sound academic, relational division can be very practical. The classic example of relational division answers the question "Which students have passed every required course?" An *exact*

relational division query would list only those students who passed the required courses and no others. A *relational division with a remainder*, also called an *approximate divide*, would list all the students who passed the required courses and include students who passed any additional courses. Of course, that example is both practical and academic.

Relational division is more complex than a join. A join simply finds any matches between two data sets. Relational division finds exact matches between two data sets. Joins/subqueries and relational division solve different types of questions. For example, the following questions apply to the sample databases and compare the two methods:

- Joins/subqueries:
  - **CHA2:** Who has ever gone on a tour?
  - **CHA2:** Who lives in the same region as a base camp?
  - **CHA2:** Who has attended any event in his or her home region?
- Exact relational division:
  - **CHA2:** Who has gone on every tour in his or her home state but no tours outside it?
  - **OBXKites:** Who has purchased every kite but nothing else?
  - **Family:** Which women (widows or divorcees) have married the same husbands as each other, but no other husbands?
- Relational division with remainders:
  - **CHA2:** Who has gone on every tour in his or her home state, and possibly other tours as well?
  - **OBXKites:** Who has purchased every kite and possibly other items as well?
  - **Family:** Which women have married the same husbands and may have married other men as well?

Relational division with a remainder

Relational division with a remainder essentially extracts the quotient while allowing some leeway for rows that meet the criteria but contain additional data as well. In real-life situations this type of division is typically more useful than an exact relational division.

The previous OBX Kites sales question ("Who has purchased every kite and possibly other items as well?") is a good one to use to demonstrate relational division. Because it takes five tables to go from contact to product category, and because the question refers to the join between `OrderDetail` and `Product`, this question involves enough complexity that it simulates a real-world relational-database problem.

The toy category serves as a good example category because it contains only two toys and no one has purchased a toy in the sample data, so the query will answer the question "Who has purchased at least one of every toy sold by OBX Kites?" (Yes, my kids volunteered to help test this query.)

First, the following data will mock up a scenario in the `OBXKites` database. The only toys are `ProductCode` 1049 and 1050. The `OBXKites` database uses unique identifiers for primary keys and therefore uses stored procedures for all inserts. The first `Order` and `OrderDetail` inserts will list the stored procedure parameters so the following stored procedure calls are easier to understand:

```
USE OBXKites;
DECLARE @OrderNumber INT;
```

The first person, ContactCode 110, orders exactly all toys:

```
EXEC pOrder_AddNew
   @ContactCode = '110',
   @EmployeeCode = '120',
   @LocationCode = 'CH',
   @OrderDate= '2002/6/1',
   @OrderNumber = @OrderNumber output;

EXEC pOrder_AddItem
   @OrderNumber = @OrderNumber,
   @Code = '1049',
   @NonStockProduct = NULL,
   @Quantity = 12,
   @UnitPrice = NULL,
   @ShipRequestDate = '2002/6/1',
   @ShipComment = NULL;

EXEC pOrder_AddItem
   @OrderNumber, '1050', NULL, 3, NULL, NULL, NULL;
```

The second person, ContactCode 111, orders exactly all toys — and toy 1050 twice:

```
EXEC pOrder_AddNew
  '111', '119', 'JR', '2002/6/1', @OrderNumber output;
EXEC pOrder_AddItem
  @OrderNumber, '1049', NULL, 6, NULL, NULL, NULL;
EXEC pOrder_AddItem
  @OrderNumber, '1050', NULL, 6, NULL, NULL, NULL;

EXEC pOrder_AddNew
  '111', '119', 'JR', '2002/6/1', @OrderNumber output;
EXEC pOrder_AddItem
  @OrderNumber, '1050', NULL, 6, NULL, NULL, NULL;
```

The third person, ContactCode 112, orders all toys plus some other products:

```
EXEC pOrder_AddNew
  '112', '119', 'JR', '2002/6/1', @OrderNumber output;
EXEC pOrder_AddItem
  @OrderNumber, '1049', NULL, 6, NULL, NULL, NULL;
EXEC pOrder_AddItem
  @OrderNumber, '1050', NULL, 5, NULL, NULL, NULL;
EXEC pOrder_AddItem
  @OrderNumber, '1001', NULL, 5, NULL, NULL, NULL;
EXEC pOrder_AddItem
  @OrderNumber, '1002', NULL, 5, NULL, NULL, NULL;
```

The fourth person, ContactCode 113, orders one toy:

```
EXEC pOrder_AddNew
  '113', '119', 'JR', '2002/6/1', @OrderNumber output;
```

```
EXEC pOrder_AddItem
  @OrderNumber, '1049', NULL, 6, NULL, NULL, NULL;
```

In other words, only customers 110 and 111 order all the toys and nothing else. Customer 112 purchases all the toys, as well as some kites. Customer 113 is an error check because she bought only one toy.

At least a couple of methods exist for coding a relational-division query. The original method, proposed by Chris Date, involves using nested correlated subqueries to locate rows in and out of the sets. A more direct method has been popularized by Joe Celko: It involves comparing the row count of the dividend and divisor data sets.

Basically, Celko's solution is to rephrase the question as "For whom is the number of toys ordered equal to the number of toys available?"

The query is asking two questions. The outer query will group the orders with toys for each contact, and the subquery will count the number of products in the toy product category. The outer query's `HAVING` clause will then compare the distinct count of contact products ordered that are toys against the count of products that are toys:

```
-- Is number of toys ordered...
SELECT Contact.ContactCode
  FROM dbo.Contact
    JOIN dbo.[Order]
      ON Contact.ContactID = [Order].ContactID
    JOIN dbo.OrderDetail
      ON [Order].OrderID = OrderDetail.OrderID
    JOIN dbo.Product
      ON OrderDetail.ProductID = Product.ProductID
    JOIN dbo.ProductCategory
      ON Product.ProductCategoryID = ProductCategory.ProductCategoryID
  WHERE ProductCategory.ProductCategoryName = 'Toy'
  GROUP BY Contact.ContactCode
  HAVING COUNT(DISTINCT Product.ProductCode) =
-- equal to number of toys available?
      (SELECT Count(ProductCode)
        FROM dbo.Product
          JOIN dbo.ProductCategory
            ON Product.ProductCategoryID
              = ProductCategory.ProductCategoryID
        WHERE ProductCategory.ProductCategoryName = 'Toy');
```

Result:

```
ContactCode
---------------
110
111
112
```

CROSS-REF **Some techniques in the previous query — namely, `group by`, `having`, and `count()` — are explained in the next chapter, "Aggregating Data."**

Exact relational division

Exact relational division finds exact matches without any remainder. It takes the basic question of relational division with remainder and tightens the method so that the divisor will have no extra rows that cause a remainder.

In practical terms it means that the example question now asks, "Who has ordered only every toy?"

If you address this query with a modified form of Joe Celko's method, the pseudocode becomes "For whom is the number of toys ordered equal to the number of toys available, and also equal to the total number of products ordered?" If a customer has ordered additional products other than toys, then the third part of the question eliminates that customer from the result set.

The SQL code contains two primary changes to the previous query. One, the outer query must find both the number of toys ordered and the number of all products ordered. It does this by finding the toys purchased in a derived table and joining the two data sets. Two, the `HAVING` clause must be modified to compare the number of toys available with both the number of toys purchased and the number of all products purchased, as follows:

```
-- Exact Relational Division
-- Is number of all products ordered...
SELECT Contact.ContactCode
  FROM dbo.Contact
    JOIN dbo.[Order]
      ON Contact.ContactID = [Order].ContactID
    JOIN dbo.OrderDetail
      ON [Order].OrderID = OrderDetail.OrderID
    JOIN dbo.Product
      ON OrderDetail.ProductID = Product.ProductID
    JOIN dbo.ProductCategory P1
      ON Product.ProductCategoryID = P1.ProductCategoryID

   JOIN
       -- and number of toys ordered
       (SELECT Contact.ContactCode, Product.ProductCode
          FROM dbo.Contact
            JOIN dbo.[Order]
              ON Contact.ContactID = [Order].ContactID
            JOIN dbo.OrderDetail
              ON [Order].OrderID = OrderDetail.OrderID
            JOIN dbo.Product
              ON OrderDetail.ProductID = Product.ProductID
            JOIN dbo.ProductCategory
              ON Product.ProductCategoryID =
                  ProductCategory.ProductCategoryID
           WHERE ProductCategory.ProductCategoryName = 'Toy'
```

```
        ) ToysOrdered

      ON Contact.ContactCode = ToysOrdered.ContactCode

    GROUP BY Contact.ContactCode

    HAVING  COUNT(DISTINCT Product.ProductCode) =
  -- equal to number of toys available?
      (SELECT Count(ProductCode)
        FROM dbo.Product
          JOIN dbo.ProductCategory
            ON Product.ProductCategoryID
              = ProductCategory.ProductCategoryID
       WHERE ProductCategory.ProductCategoryName = 'Toy')

  -- AND equal to the total number of any product ordered?
      AND COUNT(DISTINCT ToysOrdered.ProductCode) =
        (SELECT Count(ProductCode)
          FROM dbo.Product
            JOIN dbo.ProductCategory
              ON Product.ProductCategoryID
                = ProductCategory.ProductCategoryID
         WHERE ProductCategory.ProductCategoryName = 'Toy');
```

The result is a list of contacts containing the number of toys purchased (2) and the number of total products purchased (2), both equal to the number of products available (2):

```
ContactCode
---------------
110
111
```

Composable SQL

Composable SQL, also called *select from output* or *DML table source* (in SQL Server BOL), is the ability to pass data from an insert, update, or delete's output clause to an outer query. This is a very powerful new way to build subqueries, and it can significantly reduce the amount of code and improve the performance of code that needs to write to one table, and then, based on that write, write to another table.

To track the evolution of composable SQL (illustrated in Figure 11-3), SQL Server has always had DML triggers, which include the inserted and deleted virtual tables. Essentially, these are a view to the DML modification that fired the triggers. The deleted table holds the before image of the data, and the inserted table holds the after image.

Since SQL Server 2005, any DML statement that modifies data (INSERT, UPDATE, DELETE, MERGE) can have an optional OUTPUT clause that can SELECT from the virtual inserted and deleted table. The OUTPUT clause can pass the data to the client or insert it directly into a table.

CROSS-REF The inserted and deleted virtual tables are covered in Chapter 26, "Creating DML Triggers," and the output clause is detailed in Chapter 15, "Modifying Data."

In SQL Server 2008, composable SQL can place the DML statements and its OUTPUT clause in a subquery and then select from that subquery. The primary benefit of composable SQL, as opposed to just using the OUTPUT clause to insert into a table, is that OUTPUT clause data may be further filtered and manipulated by the outer query.

FIGURE 11-3

Composable SQL is an evolution of the inserted and deleted tables.

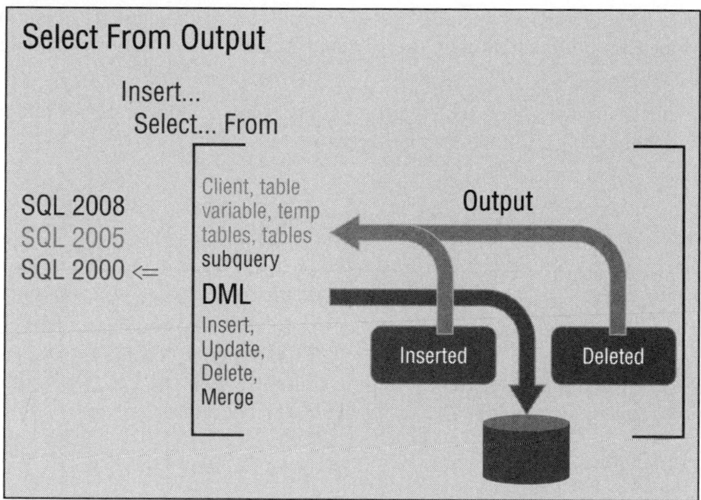

The following script first creates a table and then has a composable SQL query. The subquery has an UPDATE command with an OUTPUT clause. The OUTPUT clause passes the oldvalue and newvalue columns to the outer query. The outer query filters out TestData and then inserts it into the CompSQL table:

```
CREATE TABLE CompSQL (oldvalue varchar(50), newvalue varchar(50));

INSERT INTO CompSQL (oldvalue, newvalue )
  SELECT oldvalue, newvalue
    FROM
     (UPDATE HumanResources.Department
        SET GroupName = 'Composable SQL Test'
        OUTPUT Deleted.GroupName as 'oldvalue',
          Inserted.GroupName as 'newvalue'
        WHERE Name = 'Sales') Q;
```

```
SELECT oldvalue, newvalue
  FROM CompSQL
  WHERE newvalue <> 'TestData';
```

Result:

```
oldvalue                 newvalue
------------------------ ------------------------------
Sales and Marketing      Composable SQL Test
```

Note several restrictions on composable SQL:

- The update DML in the subquery must modify a local table and cannot be a partitioned view.
- The composable SQL query cannot include nested composable SQL, aggregate function, subquery, ranking function, full-text features, user-defined functions that perform data access, or the `textptr` function.
- The target table must be a local base table with no triggers, no foreign keys, no merge replication, or updatable subscriptions for transactional replication.

Summary

While the basic nuts and bolts of subqueries may appear simple, they open a world of possibilities, as they enable you to build complex nested queries that pull and twist data into the exact shape that is needed to solve a difficult problem. As you continue to play with subqueries, I think you'll agree that herein lies the power of SQL — and if you're still developing primarily with the GUI tools, this might provide the catalyst to move you to developing SQL using the query text editor.

A few key points from this chapter:

- Simple subqueries are executed once and the results are inserted into the outer query.
- Subqueries can be used in nearly every portion of the query — not just as derived tables.
- Correlated subqueries refer to the outer query, so they can't be executed by themselves. Conceptually, the outer query is executed and the results are passed to the correlated subquery, which is executed once for every row in the outer query.
- You don't need to memorize how to code relational division; just remember that if you need to join not on any row but every row, then relational division is the set-based solution to do the job.
- Composable SQL is useful if you need to write to multiple tables from a single transaction, but there are plenty of limitations.

The previous chapters established the foundation for working with SQL, covering the `SELECT` statement, expressions, joins, and unions, while this chapter expanded the `SELECT` with powerful subqueries and CTEs. If you're reading through this book sequentially, congratulations — you are now over the hump of learning SQL. If you can master relational algebra and subqueries, the rest is a piece of cake.

The next chapter continues to describe the repertoire of data-retrieval techniques with aggregation queries, where using subqueries pays off.

Chapter 12

Aggregating Data

The Information Architecture Principle in Chapter 2 implies that information, not just data, is an asset. Turning raw lists of keys and data into useful information often requires summarizing data and grouping it in meaningful ways. While summarization and analysis can certainly be performed with other tools, such as Reporting Services, Analysis Services, or an external tool such as SAS, SQL is a set-based language, and a fair amount of summarizing and grouping can be performed very well within the SQL `SELECT` statement.

SQL excels at calculating sums, max values, and averages for the entire data set or for segments of data. In addition, SQL queries can create cross-tabulations, commonly known as *pivot tables*.

IN THIS CHAPTER

- Calculating sums and averages
- Statistical analysis
- Grouping data within a query
- Solving aggravating aggregation problems
- Generating cumulative totals
- Building crosstab queries with the case, pivot, and dynamic methods

Simple Aggregations

The premise of an aggregate query is that instead of returning all the selected rows, SQL Server returns a single row of computed values that summarizes the original data set, as illustrated in Figure 12-1. More complex aggregate queries can slice the selected rows into subsets and then summarize every subset.

The types of aggregate calculations range from totaling the data to performing basic statistical operations.

It's important to note that in the logical order of the SQL query, the aggregate functions (indicated by the Summing function in the diagram) occur following the `FROM` clause and the `WHERE` filters. This means that the data can be assembled and filtered prior to being summarized without needing to use a subquery, although sometimes a subquery is still needed to build more complex aggregate queries (as detailed later in the "Aggravating Queries" section in this chapter.)

What's New with Query Aggregations?

Microsoft continues to evolve T-SQL's ability to aggregate data. SQL Server 2005 included the capability to roll your own aggregate functions using the .NET CLR. SQL Server 2008 expands this feature by removing the 8,000-byte limit on intermediate results for CLR user-defined aggregate functions.

The most significant enhancement to query aggregation in SQL Server 2008 is the ability to use grouping sets to further define the `CUBE` and `ROLLUP` functions with the `GROUP BY` clause.

`WITH ROLLUP` and `WITH CUBE` have been deprecated, as they are non-ISO-compliant syntax for special cases of the ISO-compliant syntax. They are replaced with the new, more powerful, syntax for `ROLLUP` and `CUBE`.

FIGURE 12-1

The aggregate function produces a single row result from a data set.

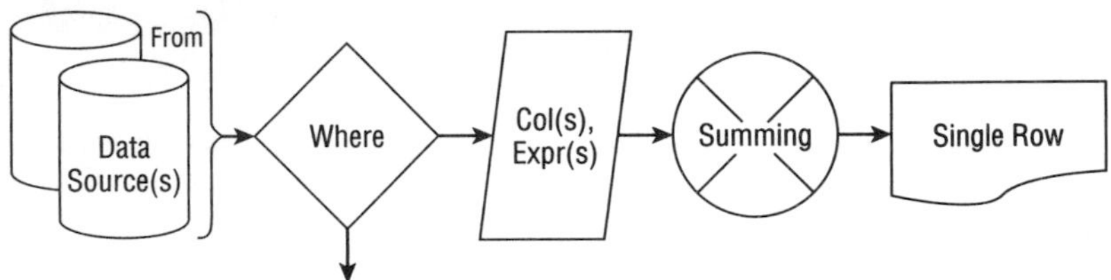

Basic aggregations

SQL includes a set of *aggregate functions*, listed in Table 12-1, which can be used as expressions in the `SELECT` statement to return summary data.

ON the WEBSITE **The code examples for this chapter use a small table called `RawData`. The code to create and populate this data set is at the beginning of the chapter's script. You can download the script from `www.SQLServerBible.com`.**

```
CREATE TABLE RawData (
  RawDataID INT NOT NULL IDENTITY PRIMARY KEY,
  Region VARCHAR(10) NOT NULL,
  Category CHAR(1) NOT NULL,
  Amount INT NULL,
  SalesDate Date NOT NULL
  );
```

TABLE 12-1

Basic Aggregate Functions

Aggregate Function	Data Type Supported	Description
`sum()`	Numeric	Totals all the non-null values in the column
`avg()`	Numeric	Averages all the non-null values in the column. The result has the same data type as the input, so the input is often converted to a higher precision, such as `avg(cast col as a float)`.
`min()`	Numeric, string, datetime	Returns the smallest number or the first datetime or the first string according to the current collation from the column
`max()`	Numeric, string, datetime	Returns the largest number or the last datetime or the last string according to the current collation from the column
`Count[_big](*)`	Any data type (row-based)	Performs a simple count of all the rows in the result set up to 2,147,483,647. The `count_big()` variation uses the `bigint` data type and can handle up to 2 ^ 63-1 rows.
`Count[_big] ([distinct]` *`column`*`)`	Any data type (row-based)	Performs a simple count of all the rows with non-null values in the column in the result set up to 2,147,483,647. The `distinct` option eliminates duplicate rows. Will not count blobs.

This simple aggregate query counts the number of rows in the table and totals the Amount column. In lieu of returning the actual rows from the `RawData` table, the query returns the summary row with the row count and total. Therefore, even though there are 24 rows in the `RawData` table, the result is a single row:

```
SELECT COUNT(*) AS Count,
    SUM(Amount) AS [Sum]
  FROM RawData;
```

Result:

```
Count       Sum
----------- -----------
24          946
```

Because SQL is now returning information from a set, rather than building a record set of rows, as soon as a query includes an aggregate function, every column (in the column list, in the expression, or in the ORDER BY) must participate in an aggregate function. This makes sense because if a query returned the total number of order sales, then it could not return a single order number on the summary row.

Because aggregate functions are expressions, the result will have a null column name. Therefore, use an alias to name the column in the results.

To demonstrate the mathematical aggregate functions, the following query produces a SUM(), AVG(), MIN(), and MAX() of the amount column. SQL Server warns in the result that null values are ignored by aggregate functions, which are examined in more detail soon:

```
SELECT SUM(Amount) AS [Sum],
    AVG(Amount) AS [Avg],
    MIN(Amount) AS [Min],
    MAX(Amount) AS [Max]
  FROM RawData ;
```

Result:

```
Sum         Avg         Min         Max
----------- ----------- ----------- -----------
946         47          11          91
Warning: Null value is eliminated by an aggregate
or other SET operation.
```

There's actually more to the COUNT() function than appears at first glance. The next query exercises four variations of the COUNT() aggregate function:

```
SELECT COUNT(*) AS CountStar,
    COUNT(RawDataID) AS CountPK,
    COUNT(Amount) AS CountAmount,
    COUNT(DISTINCT Region) AS Regions
  FROM RawData;
```

Result:

```
CountStar   CountPK     CountAmount Regions
----------- ----------- ----------- -----------
24          24          20          4
Warning: Null value is eliminated by an aggregate
or other SET operation.
```

To examine this query in detail, the first column, COUNT(*), counts every row, regardless of any values in the row. COUNT(RawDataID) counts all the rows with a non-null value in the primary key. Because primary keys, by definition, can't have any nulls, this column also counts every row. These two methods of counting rows have the same query execution plan, same performance, and same result.

The third column, COUNT(Amount), demonstrates why every aggregate query includes a warning. It counts the number of rows with an actual value in the Amount column, and it ignores any rows with a null value in the Amount column. Because there are four rows with null amounts, this COUNT(Amount) finds only 20 rows.

COUNT(DISTINCT region) is the oddball of this query. Instead of counting rows, it counts the unique values in the region column. The RawData table data has four regions: MidWest, NorthEast, South, and West. Therefore, COUNT(DISTINCT region) returns 4. Note that COUNT(DISTINCT *) is invalid; it requires a specific column.

Aggregates, averages, and nulls

Aggregate functions ignore nulls, which creates a special situation when calculating averages. A SUM() or AVG() aggregate function will not error out on a null, but simply skip the row with a null. For this reason, a SUM()/COUNT(*) calculation may provide a different result from an AVG() function. The COUNT(*) function includes every row, whereas the AVG() function might divide using a smaller count of rows.

To test this behavior, the next query uses three methods of calculating the average amount, and each method generates a different result:

```
SELECT AVG(Amount) AS [Integer Avg],
    SUM(Amount) / COUNT(*) AS [Manual Avg],
    AVG(CAST((Amount) AS NUMERIC(9, 5))) AS [Numeric Avg]
  FROM RawData;
```

Result:

```
Integer Avg   Manual Avg    Numeric Avg
------------- ------------- ----------------
47            39            47.300000
```

The first column performs the standard AVG() aggregate function and divides the sum of the amount (946) by the number of rows with a non-null value for the amount (20).

The SUM(AMOUNT)/COUNT(*) calculation in column two actually divides 946 by the total number of rows in the table (24), yielding a different answer.

The last column provides the best answer. It uses the AVG() function so it ignores null values, but it also improves the precision of the answer. The trick is that the precision of the aggregate function is determined by the data type precision of the source values. SQL Server's Query Optimizer first converts the Amount values to a numeric(9,5) data type and then passes the values to the AVG() function.

Using aggregate functions within the Query Designer

When using Management Studio's Query Designer (select a table in the Object Explorer ➪ Context Menu ➪ Edit Top 200 Rows), a query can be converted into an aggregate query using the Group By toolbar button, as illustrated in Figure 12-2.

FIGURE 12-2

Performing an aggregate query within Management Studio's Query Designer. The aggregate function for the column is selected using the drop-down box in the `Group By` column.

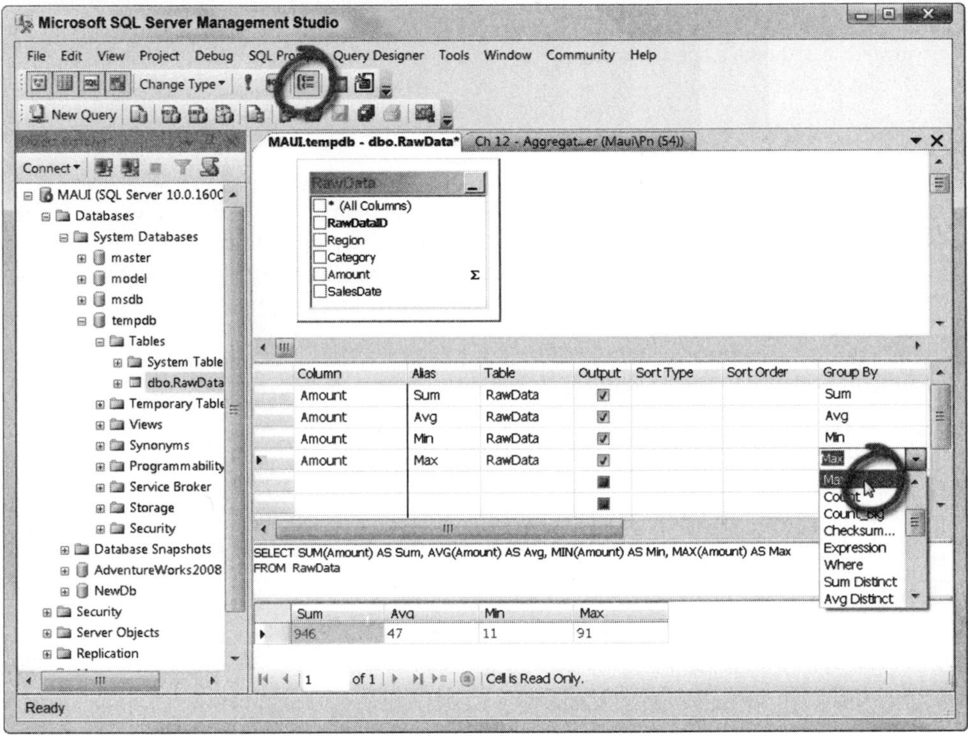

CROSS-REF **For more information on using the Query Designer to build and execute queries, turn to Chapter 6, "Using Management Studio."**

Beginning statistics

Statistics is a large and complex field of study, and while SQL Server does not pretend to replace a full statistical analysis software package, it does calculate standard deviation and variance, both of which are important for understanding the bell-curve spread of numbers.

An average alone is not sufficient to summarize a set of values (in the lexicon of statistics, a "set" is referred to as a *population*). The value in the exact middle of a population is the *statistical mean* or *median* (which is different from the average or arithmetic mean). The difference, or how widely dispersed the values are from the mean, is called the population's *variance*. For example, the populations

(1, 2, 3, 4, 5, 6, 7, 8, 9, 10) and (4, 4, 5, 5, 5, 5, 6, 6) both average to 5, but the values in the first set vary widely from the median, whereas the second set's values are all close to the median. The standard deviation is the square root of the variance and describes the shape of the bell curve formed by the population.

The following query uses the StDevP() and VarP() functions to return the statistical variance and the standard deviation of the entire population of the RawData table:

```
SELECT
    StDevP(Amount) as [StDev],
    VarP(Amount) as [Var]
  FROM RawData;
```

Result:

```
StDevP               VarP
-------------------- --------
24.2715883287435     589.11
```

To perform extensive statistical data analysis, I recommend exporting the query result set to Excel and tapping Excel's broad range of statistical functions.

The statistical formulas differ slightly when calculating variance and standard deviation from the entire population versus a sampling of the population. If the aggregate query includes the entire population, then use the StDevP() and VarP() aggregate functions, which use the *bias* or *n* method of calculating the deviation.

However, if the query is using a sampling or subset of the population, then use the StDev() and Var() aggregate functions so that SQL Server will use the unbiased or n-1 statistical method. Because GROUP BY queries slice the population into subsets, these queries should always use StDevP() and VarP() functions.

CROSS-REF **All of these aggregate functions also work with the OVER() clause; see Chapter 13, "Windowing and Ranking."**

Grouping within a Result Set

Aggregate functions are all well and good, but how often do you need a total for an entire table? Most aggregate requirements will include a date range, department, type of sale, region, or the like. That presents a problem. If the only tool to restrict the aggregate function were the WHERE clause, then database developers would waste hours replicating the same query, or writing a lot of dynamic SQL queries and the code to execute the aggregate queries in sequence.

Fortunately, aggregate functions are complemented by the GROUP BY function, which automatically partitions the data set into subsets based on the values in certain columns. Once the data set is divided into subgroups, the aggregate functions are performed on each subgroup. The final result is one summation row for each group, as shown in Figure 12-3.

A common example is grouping the sales result by salesperson. A SUM( ) function without the grouping would produce the SUM( ) of all sales. Writing a query for each salesperson would provide a SUM( ) for each person, but maintaining that over time would be cumbersome. The grouping function automatically creates a subset of data grouped for each unique salesperson, and then the SUM( ) function is calculated for each salesperson's sales. Voilà.

FIGURE 12-3

The group by clause slices the data set into multiple subgroups.

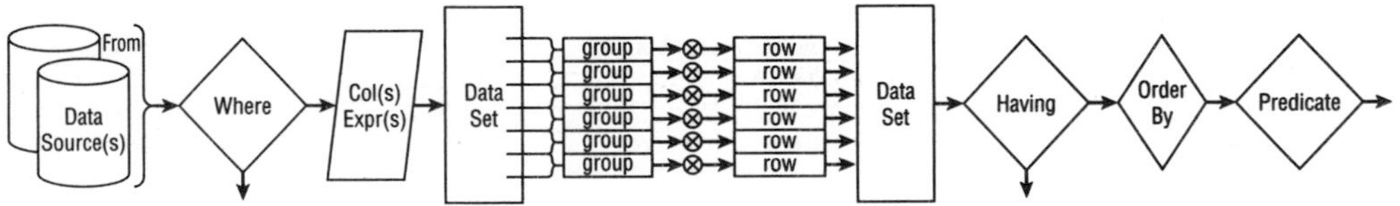

Simple groupings

Some queries use descriptive columns for the grouping, so the data used by the GROUP BY clause is the same data you need to see to understand the groupings. For example, the next query groups by category:

```
SELECT Category,
    Count(*) as Count,
    Sum(Amount) as [Sum],
    Avg(Amount) as [Avg],
    Min(Amount) as [Min],
    Max(Amount) as [Max]
  FROM RawData
  GROUP BY Category;
```

Result:

```
Category  Count    Sum      Avg      Min      Max
--------- -------- -------- -------- -------- --------
X         5        225      45       11       86
Y         15       506      46       12       91
Z         4        215      53       33       83
```

The first column of this query returns the Category column. While this column does not have an aggregate function, it still participates within the aggregate because that's the column by which the query is being grouped. It may therefore be included in the result set because, by definition, there can be only a single category value in each group. Each row in the result set summarizes one category, and the aggregate functions now calculate the row count, sum average, minimum value, and maximum value for each category.

SQL is not limited to grouping by a column. It's possible to group by an expression, but note that the exact same expression must be used in the SELECT list, not the individual columns used to generate the expression.

Nor is SQL limited to grouping by a single column or expression. Grouping by multiple columns and expressions is quite common. The following query is an example of grouping by two expressions that calculate year number and quarter from SalesDate:

```
SELECT Year(SalesDate) as [Year], DatePart(q,SalesDate) as [Quarter],
    Count(*) as Count,
    Sum(Amount) as [Sum],
    Avg(Amount) as [Avg],
    Min(Amount) as [Min],
    Max(Amount) as [Max]
  FROM RawData
  GROUP BY Year(SalesDate), DatePart(q,SalesDate);
```

Result:

```
Year   Quarter   Count   Sum   Avg   Min   Max
------ --------- ------- ----- ----- ----- -----
2009   1         6       218   36    11    62
2009   2         6       369   61    33    86
2009   3         8       280   70    54    91
2008   4         4       79    19    12    28
```

For the purposes of a GROUP BY, null values are considered equal to other nulls and are grouped together into a single result row.

Grouping sets

Normally, SQL Server groups by every unique combination of values in every column listed in the GROUP BY clause. Grouping sets is a variation of that theme that's new for SQL Server 2008. With grouping sets, a summation row is generated for each unique value in each set. You can think of grouping sets as executing several GROUP BY queries (one for each grouping set) and then combining, or unioning, the results.

For example, the following two queries produce the same result. The first query uses two GROUP BY queries unioned together; the second query uses the new grouping set feature:

```
SELECT NULL AS Category,
  Region,
  COUNT(*) AS Count,
  SUM(Amount) AS [Sum],
  AVG(Amount) AS [Avg],
  MIN(Amount) AS [Min],
  MAX(Amount) AS [Max]
FROM RawData
GROUP BY Region
```

```
UNION
SELECT Category,
  Null,
  COUNT(*) AS Count,
  SUM(Amount) AS [Sum],
  AVG(Amount) AS [Avg],
  MIN(Amount) AS [Min],
  MAX(Amount) AS [Max]
FROM RawData
GROUP BY Category;

SELECT Category,
  Region,
  COUNT(*) AS Count,
  SUM(Amount) AS [Sum],
  AVG(Amount) AS [Avg],
  MIN(Amount) AS [Min],
  MAX(Amount) AS [Max]
FROM RawData
GROUP BY GROUPING SETS (Category, Region);
```

Result (same for both queries):

```
Category Region     Count  Sum   Avg  Min  Max
-------- ---------- ------ ----- ---- ---- ----
NULL     MidWest    3      145   48   24   83
NULL     NorthEast  6      236   59   28   91
NULL     South      12     485   44   11   86
NULL     West       3      80    40   36   44
X        NULL       7      225   45   11   86
Y        NULL       12     506   46   12   91
Z        NULL       5      215   53   33   83
```

There's more to grouping sets than merging multiple GROUP BY queries; they're also used with ROLLUP and CUBE, covered later in this chapter.

Filtering grouped results

When combined with grouping, filtering can be a problem. Are the row restrictions applied before the GROUP BY or after the GROUP BY? Some databases use nested queries to properly filter before or after the GROUP BY. SQL, however, uses the HAVING clause to filter the groups. At the beginning of this chapter, you saw the simplified order of the SQL SELECT statement's execution. A more complete order is as follows:

1. The FROM clause assembles the data from the data sources.
2. The WHERE clause restricts the rows based on the conditions.
3. The GROUP BY clause assembles subsets of data.
4. Aggregate functions are calculated.

5. The HAVING clause filters the subsets of data.
6. Any remaining expressions are calculated.
7. The ORDER BY sorts the results.

Continuing with the RawData sample table, the following query removes from the analysis any grouping "having" an average of less than or equal to 25 by accepting only those summary rows with an average greater than 25:

```
SELECT Year(SalesDate) as [Year],
    DatePart(q,SalesDate) as [Quarter],
    Count(*) as Count,
    Sum(Amount) as [Sum],
    Avg(Amount) as [Avg]
  FROM RawData
  GROUP BY Year(SalesDate), DatePart(q,SalesDate)
  HAVING Avg(Amount) > 25
  ORDER BY [Year], [Quarter];
```

Result:

```
Year   Quarter   Count   Sum   Avg
------ --------- ------- ----- -----
2006   1         6       218   36
2006   2         6       369   61
2006   3         8       280   70
```

Without the HAVING clause, the fourth quarter of 2005, with an average of 19, would have been included in the result set.

Aggravating Queries

A few aspects of GROUP BY queries can be aggravating when developing applications. Some developers simply avoid aggregate queries and make the reporting tool do the work, but the Database Engine will be more efficient than any client tool. Here are four typical aggravating problems and my recommended solutions.

Including group by descriptions

The previous aggregate queries all executed without error because every column participated in the aggregate purpose of the query. To test the rule, the following script adds a category table and then attempts to return a column that isn't included as an aggregate function or GROUP BY column:

```
CREATE TABLE RawCategory (
  RawCategoryID  CHAR(1)      NOT NULL PRIMARY KEY,
  CategoryName   VARCHAR(25)  NOT NULL
  );
```

```
INSERT RawCategory (RawCategoryID, CategoryName)
  VALUES ('X', 'Sci-Fi'),
         ('Y', 'Philosophy'),
         ('Z', 'Zoology');

ALTER TABLE RawData
  ADD CONSTRAINT FT_Category
        FOREIGN KEY (Category)
          REFERENCES RawCategory(RawCategoryID);

-- including data outside the aggregate function or group by
SELECT R.Category, C.CategoryName,
    Sum(R.Amount) as [Sum],
    Avg(R.Amount) as [Avg],
    Min(R.Amount) as [Min],
    Max(R.Amount) as [Max]
  FROM RawData AS R
    INNER JOIN RawCategory AS C
      ON R.Category = C.RawCategoryID
  GROUP BY R.Category;
```

As expected, including `CategoryName` in the column list causes the query to return an error message:

```
Msg 8120, Level 16, State 1, Line 1
Column 'RawCategory.CategoryName' is invalid in the select list
because it is not contained in either an aggregate function or
the GROUP BY clause.
```

Here are three solutions for including non-aggregate descriptive columns. Which solution performs best depends on the size and mix of the data and indexes.

The first solution is to simply include the additional columns in the `GROUP BY` clause:

```
SELECT R.Category, C.CategoryName,
    Sum(R.Amount) as [Sum],
    Avg(R.Amount) as [Avg],
    Min(R.Amount) as [Min],
    Max(R.Amount) as [Max]
  FROM RawData AS R
    INNER JOIN RawCategory AS C
      ON R.Category = C.RawCategoryID
  GROUP BY R.Category, C.CategoryName
  ORDER BY R.Category, C.CategoryName;
```

Result:

```
Category CategoryName   Sum   Avg   Min   Max
-------- -------------- ----- ----- ----- -----
X        Sci-Fi         225   45    11    86
Y        Philosophy     506   46    12    91
Z        Zoology        215   53    33    83
```

Another simple solution might be to include the descriptive column in an aggregate function that accepts text, such as MIN() or MAX(). This solution returns the descriptor while avoiding grouping by an additional column:

```
SELECT Category,
    MAX(CategoryName) AS CategoryName,
    SUM(Amount) AS [Sum],
    AVG(Amount) AS [Avg],
    MIN(Amount) AS [Min],
    MAX(Amount) AS [Max]
  FROM RawData R
    JOIN RawCategory C
      ON R.Category = C.RawCategoryID
  GROUP BY Category
  ORDER BY Category,
    CategoryName
```

Another possible solution, although more complex, is to embed the aggregate function in a subquery and then include the additional columns in the outer query. In this solution, the subquery does the grunt work of the aggregate function and GROUP BY, leaving the outer query to handle the JOIN and bring in the descriptive column(s). For larger data sets, this may be the best-performing solution:

```
SELECT sq.Category, C.CategoryName,
    sq.[Sum], sq.[Avg], sq.[Min], sq.[Max]
  FROM (SELECT Category,
            Sum(Amount) as [Sum],
            Avg(Amount) as [Avg],
            Min(Amount) as [Min],
            Max(Amount) as [Max]
          FROM RawData
          GROUP BY Category ) AS sq
    INNER JOIN RawCategory AS C
      ON sq.Category = C.RawCategoryID
  ORDER BY sq.Category, C.CategoryName;
```

Which solution performs best depends on the data mix. If it's an ad hoc query, then the simplest query to write is probably the first solution. If the query is going into production as part of a stored procedure, then I recommend testing all three solutions against a full data load to determine which solution actually performs best. Never underestimate the optimizer.

Including all group by values

The GROUP BY functions occur following the where clause in the logical order of the query. This can present a problem if the query needs to report all of the GROUP BY column values even though the data needs to be filtered. For example, a report might need to include all the months even though there's no data for a given month. A GROUP BY query won't return a summary row for a group that has no data.

The simple solution is to use the GROUP BY ALL option, which includes all GROUP BY values regardless of the WHERE clause. However, it has a limitation: It only works well when grouping by a single expression. A more severe limitation is that Microsoft lists it as deprecated, meaning it will be removed from a future version of SQL Server. Nulltheless, here's an example.

Here, the fourth quarter is included in the result despite the lack of data for the fourth quarter for 2009. The GROUP BY ALL includes the fourth quarter because there is data for the fourth quarter for 2008:

```
SELECT DATEPART(qq, SalesDate) AS [Quarter],
    Count(*) as Count,
    Sum(Amount) as [Sum],
    Avg(Amount) as [Avg]
  FROM RawData
  WHERE Year(SalesDate) = 2009
  GROUP BY ALL DATEPART(qq, SalesDate);
```

Result:

```
Quarter     Count       Sum         Avg
----------- ----------- ----------- -----------
1           6           218         36
2           6           369         61
3           7           217         72
4           0           NULL        NULL
```

The real problem with the GROUP BY ALL solution is that it's dependent on data being present in the table, but outside the current Where clause filter. If the fourth quarter data didn't exist for another year other than 2009, then the query would have not listed the fourth quarter, period.

A better solution to listing all data in a GROUP BY is to left outer join with a known set of complete data. In the following case, the VALUELIST subquery sets up a list of quarters. The LEFT OUTER JOIN includes all the rows from the VALUELIST subquery and matches up any rows with values from the aggregate query:

```
SELECT ValueList.Quarter,
    Agg.[Count],
    Agg.[Sum],
    Agg.[Avg]
  FROM ( VALUES (1),
                (2),
                (3),
                (4) ) AS ValueList (Quarter)
    LEFT JOIN (SELECT DATEPART(qq, SalesDate) AS [Quarter],
                 COUNT(*) AS Count,
                 SUM(Amount) AS [Sum],
                 AVG(Amount) AS [Avg]
                FROM RawData
                WHERE YEAR(SalesDate) = 2009
                GROUP BY DATEPART(qq, SalesDate)) Agg
      ON ValueList.Quarter = Agg.Quarter
  ORDER BY ValueList.Quarter ;
```

Result:

```
Quarter     Count       Sum         Avg
----------- ----------- ----------- -----------
1           6           218         36
2           6           369         61
3           7           217         72
4           0           NULL        NULL
```

In my testing, the fixed values list solution is slightly faster than the deprecated GROUP BY ALL solution.

Nesting aggregations

Aggregated data is often useful, and it can be even more useful to perform secondary aggregations on aggregated data. For example, an aggregate query can easily SUM( ) each category and year/quarter within a subquery, but which category has the max value for each year/quarter? An obvious MAX(SUM( )) doesn't work because there's not enough information to tell SQL Server how to nest the aggregation groupings.

Solving this problem requires a subquery to create a record set from the first aggregation, and an outer query to perform the second level of aggregation. For example, the following query sums by quarter and category, and then the outer query uses a MAX( ) to determine which sum is the greatest for each quarter:

```
Select Y,Q, Max(Total) as MaxSum
  FROM ( -- Calculate Sums
         SELECT Category, Year(SalesDate) as Y,
            DatePart(q,SalesDate) as Q, Sum(Amount) as Total
          FROM RawData
          GROUP BY Category, Year(SalesDate),
            DatePart(q,SalesDate)
        ) AS sq
  GROUP BY Y,Q
  ORDER BY Y,Q;
```

If it's easier to read, here's the same query using common table expressions (CTEs) instead of a derived table subquery:

```
WITH sq AS ( -- Calculate Sums
        SELECT Category, YEAR(SalesDate) AS Y,
            DATEPART(q, SalesDate) AS Q, SUM(Amount) AS Total
          FROM RawData
          GROUP BY Category, YEAR(SalesDate), DATEPART(q, SalesDate))
SELECT Y, Q, MAX(Total) AS MaxSum
  FROM sq
  GROUP BY Y, Q;
```

Result:

```
Y           Q           MaxSum
----------- ----------- -----------
2005        4           79
2006        1           147
2006        2           215
2006        3           280
```

Including detail descriptions

While it's nice to report the MAX(SUM()) of 147 for the first quarter of 2006, who wants to manually look up which category matches that sum? The next logical step is to include descriptive information about the aggregate data. To add descriptive information for the detail columns, join with a subquery on the detail values:

```
SELECT MaxQuery.Y, MaxQuery.Q, AllQuery.Category, MaxQuery.MaxSum as MaxSum
  FROM (-- Find Max Sum Per Year/Quarter
        Select Y,Q, Max(Total) as MaxSum
          From ( -- Calculate Sums
                  select Category, Year(SalesDate) as Y,
                     DatePart(q,SalesDate) as Q, Sum(Amount) as Total
                    from RawData
                    group by Category, Year(SalesDate),
                    DatePart(q,SalesDate)) AS sq
          Group By Y,Q
          ) AS MaxQuery
  INNER JOIN (-- All Data Query
        Select Category, Year(SalesDate) as Y, DatePart(q,SalesDate) as Q,
            Sum(Amount) as Total
          From RawData
          Group By Category, Year(SalesDate), DatePart(q,SalesDate)
          ) AS AllQuery
    ON MaxQuery.Y = AllQuery.Y
      AND MaxQuery.Q = AllQuery.Q
      AND MaxQuery.MaxSum = AllQuery.Total
  ORDER BY MaxQuery.Y, MaxQuery.Q;
```

Result:

```
Y           Q           Category MaxSum
----------- ----------- -------- -----------
2008        4           Y        79
2009        1           Y        147
2009        2           Z        215
2009        3           Y        280
```

While the query appears complex at first glance, it's actually just an extension of the preceding query (in bold, with the table alias of MaxQuery.)

The second subquery (with the alias of `AllQuery`) finds the sum of every category and year/quarter. Joining `MaxQuery` with `AllQuery` on the sum and year/quarter is used to locate the category and return the descriptive value along with the detail data.

In this case, the CTE solution really starts to pay off, as the subquery doesn't have to be repeated. The following query is exactly equivalent to the preceding one (same results, same execution plan, same performance), but shorter, easier to understand, and cheaper to maintain:

```
WITH AllQuery AS
 (-- All Data Query
  SELECT   Category,
           YEAR(SalesDate) AS Y,
           DATEPART(qq, SalesDate) AS Q,
           SUM(Amount) AS Total
  FROM     RawData
  GROUP BY Category,
           YEAR(SalesDate),
           DATEPART(qq, SalesDate))
SELECT MaxQuery.Y, MaxQuery.Q, AllQuery.Category, MaxQuery.MaxSum
  FROM (-- Find Max Sum Per Year/Quarter
        Select Y,Q, Max(Total) as MaxSum
          From AllQuery
          Group By Y,Q
          ) AS MaxQuery
  INNER JOIN AllQuery
    ON MaxQuery.Y = AllQuery.Y
      AND MaxQuery.Q = AllQuery.Q
      AND MaxQuery.MaxSum = AllQuery.Total
  ORDER BY MaxQuery.Y, MaxQuery.Q;
```

Another alternative is to use the ranking functions and the `OVER()` clause, introduced in SQL Server 2005. The `Ranked` CTE refers to the `AllQuery` CTE. The following query produces the same result and is slightly more efficient:

```
WITH
AllQuery AS
 (-- All Data Query
  SELECT   Category,
           YEAR(SalesDate) AS Y,
           DATEPART(qq, SalesDate) AS Q,
           SUM(Amount) AS Total
  FROM     RawData
  GROUP BY Category,
           YEAR(SalesDate),
           DATEPART(qq, SalesDate)),
Ranked AS
 (-- All data ranked after summing
  SELECT   Category, Y, Q, Total,
           RANK() OVER (PARTITION BY Y, Q ORDER BY Total DESC) AS rn
  FROM     AllQuery)
```

```
SELECT     Y, Q, Category, Total AS MaxSum
FROM       Ranked
WHERE      rn = 1
ORDER BY   Y, Q;
```

CROSS-REF **Ranking functions and the `OVER()` clause are explained in the next chapter, "Windowing and Ranking."**

OLAP in the Park

While Reporting Services can easily add subtotals and totals without any extra work by the query, and Analysis Services builds beautiful cubes, such feats of data contortion are not exclusive to OLAP tools. The relational engine can take a lap in that park as well.

The `ROLLUP` and `CUBE` extensions to `GROUP BY` generate OLAP-type summaries of the data with subtotals and totals. The columns to be totaled are defined similarly to how grouping sets can define `GROUP BY` columns.

NOTE **The older non-ANSI standard `WITH ROLLUP` and `WITH CUBE` are deprecated. The syntax still works for now, but they will be removed from a future version of SQL Server. This section covers only the newer syntax — it's much cleaner and offers more control. I think you'll like it.**

The `ROLLUP` and `CUBE` aggregate functions generate subtotals and grand totals as separate rows, and supply a null in the `GROUP BY` column to indicate the grand total. `ROLLUP` generates subtotal and total rows for the `GROUP BY` columns. `CUBE` extends the capabilities by generating subtotal rows for every `GROUP BY` column. `ROLLUP` and `CUBE` queries also automatically generate a grand total row.

A special `GROUPING()` function is true when the row is a subtotal or grand total row for the group.

Rollup subtotals

The `ROLLUP` option, placed after the `GROUP BY` clause, instructs SQL Server to generate an additional total row. In this example, the `GROUPING()` function is used by a `CASE` expression to convert the total row to something understandable:

```
SELECT GROUPING(Category) AS 'Grouping',
    Category,
    CASE GROUPING(Category)
      WHEN 0 THEN Category
      WHEN 1 THEN 'All Categories'
    END AS CategoryRollup,
    SUM(Amount) AS Amount
  FROM RawData
  GROUP BY ROLLUP(Category);
```

Result:

```
Grouping Category CategoryRollup Amount
-------- -------- -------------- -----------
0        X        X              225
0        Y        Y              506
```

```
0         Z        Z              215
1         NULL     All Categories 946
```

The previous example had one column in the GROUP BY ROLLUP(), but just as the GROUP BY can organize by multiple columns, so can the GROUP BY ROLLUP().

The next example builds a more detailed summary of the data, with subtotals for each grouping of category and region:

```
SELECT
    CASE GROUPING(Category)
      WHEN 0 THEN Category
      WHEN 1 THEN 'All Categories'
    END AS Category,
    CASE GROUPING(Region)
      WHEN 0 THEN Region
      WHEN 1 THEN 'All Regions'
    END AS Region,
    SUM(Amount) AS Amount
  FROM RawData
  GROUP BY ROLLUP(Category, Region)
```

Result:

```
Category       Region      Amount
-------------- ----------- -----------
X              MidWest     24
X              NorthEast   NULL
X              South       165
X              West        36
Y              MidWest     38
Y              NorthEast   181
Y              South       287
Z              MidWest     83
Z              NorthEast   55
Z              South       33
Z              West        44
All Categories All Regions 946
```

But wait, there's more. Multiple columns can be combined into a single grouping level. The following query places Category and Region in parentheses inside the ROLLUP parentheses and thus treats each combination of category and region as a single group:

```
SELECT
    CASE GROUPING(Category)
      WHEN 0 THEN Category
      WHEN 1 THEN 'All Categories'
    END AS Category,
    CASE GROUPING(Region)
```

```
      WHEN 0 THEN Region
      WHEN 1 THEN 'All Regions'
    END AS Region,
    COUNT(*) AS Count
  FROM RawData
  GROUP BY ROLLUP((Category, Region))
```

Result:

```
Category       Region      Amount
-------------- ----------- -----------
X              MidWest     24
X              NorthEast   NULL
X              South       165
X              West        36
Y              MidWest     38
Y              NorthEast   181
Y              South       287
Z              MidWest     83
Z              NorthEast   55
Z              South       33
Z              West        44
All Categories All Regions 946
```

Cube queries

A *cube query* is the next logical progression beyond a rollup query: It adds subtotals for every possible grouping in a multidimensional manner — just like Analysis Services. Using the same example, the rollup query had subtotals for each category; the cube query has subtotals for each category and each reagion:

```
SELECT
    CASE GROUPING(Category)
      WHEN 0 THEN Category
      WHEN 1 THEN 'All Categories'
    END AS Category,
    CASE GROUPING(Region)
      WHEN 0 THEN Region
      WHEN 1 THEN 'All Regions'
    END AS Region,
    COUNT(*) AS Count
  FROM RawData R
  GROUP BY CUBE(Category, Region)
  ORDER BY Coalesce(R.Category, 'ZZZZ'),
    Coalesce(R.Region, 'ZZZZ')
```

Result:

```
Category       Region      Amount
-------------- ----------- -----------
X              MidWest     24
X              NorthEast   NULL
```

```
X              South        165
X              West         36
X              All Regions  225
Y              MidWest      38
Y              NorthEast    181
Y              South        287
Y              All Regions  506
Z              MidWest      83
Z              NorthEast    55
Z              South        33
Z              West         44
Z              All Regions  215
All Categories MidWest      145
All Categories NorthEast    236
All Categories South        485
All Categories West         80
All Categories All Regions  946
```

Building Crosstab Queries

Crosstab queries take the power of the previous cube query and give it more impact. Although an aggregate query can GROUP BY multiple columns, the result is still columnar and less than perfect for scanning numbers quickly. The cross-tabulation, or crosstab, query pivots the second GROUP BY column (or dimension) values counterclockwise 90 degrees and turns it into the crosstab columns, as shown in Figure 12-4. The limitation, of course, is that while a columnar GROUP BY query can have multiple aggregate functions, a crosstab query has difficulty displaying more than a single measure.

The term *crosstab query* describes the result set, not the method of creating the crosstab, because there are multiple programmatic methods for generating a crosstab query — some better than others. The following sections describe ways to create the same result.

Pivot method

Microsoft introduced the PIVOT method for coding crosstab queries with SQL Server 2005. The pivot method deviates from the normal logical query flow by performing the aggregate GROUP BY function and generating the crosstab results as a data source within the FROM clause.

If you think of PIVOT as a table-valued function that's used as a data source, then it accepts two parameters. The first parameter is the aggregate function for the crosstab's values. The second measure parameter lists the pivoted columns. In the following example, the aggregate function sums the Amount column, and the pivoted columns are the regions. Because PIVOT is part of the FROM clause, the data set needs a named range or table alias:

```
SELECT Category, MidWest, NorthEast, South, West
  FROM RawData
    PIVOT
      (SUM(Amount)
      FOR Region IN (South, NorthEast, MidWest,West)
      ) AS pt
```

FIGURE 12-4

Pivoting the second group by `group by` column creates a crosstab query. Here, the previous `group by` cube query's region values are pivoted to become the crosstab query columns.

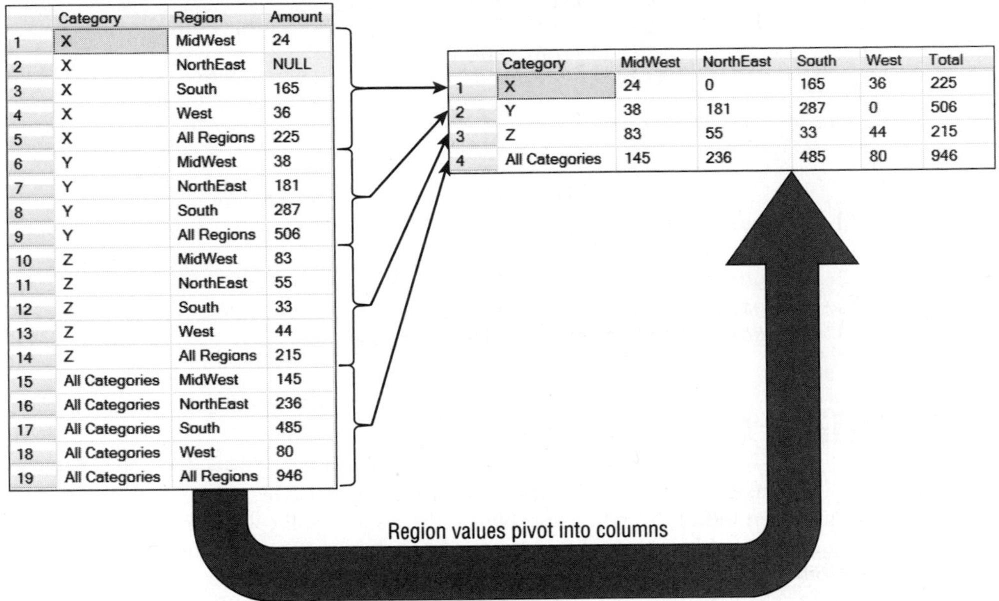

	Category	Region	Amount
1	X	MidWest	24
2	X	NorthEast	NULL
3	X	South	165
4	X	West	36
5	X	All Regions	225
6	Y	MidWest	38
7	Y	NorthEast	181
8	Y	South	287
9	Y	All Regions	506
10	Z	MidWest	83
11	Z	NorthEast	55
12	Z	South	33
13	Z	West	44
14	Z	All Regions	215
15	All Categories	MidWest	145
16	All Categories	NorthEast	236
17	All Categories	South	485
18	All Categories	West	80
19	All Categories	All Regions	946

	Category	MidWest	NorthEast	South	West	Total
1	X	24	0	165	36	225
2	Y	38	181	287	0	506
3	Z	83	55	33	44	215
4	All Categories	145	236	485	80	946

Region values pivot into columns

Result:

```
Category MidWest     NorthEast   South       West
-------- ----------- ----------- ----------- -----------
Y        NULL        NULL        12          NULL
Y        NULL        NULL        24          NULL
Y        NULL        NULL        15          NULL
Y        NULL        28          NULL        NULL
X        NULL        NULL        11          NULL
X        24          NULL        NULL        NULL
X        NULL        NULL        NULL        36
Y        NULL        NULL        47          NULL
Y        38          NULL        NULL        NULL
Y        NULL        62          NULL        NULL
Z        NULL        NULL        33          NULL
Z        83          NULL        NULL        NULL
Z        NULL        NULL        NULL        44
Z        NULL        55          NULL        NULL
X        NULL        NULL        68          NULL
X        NULL        NULL        86          NULL
Y        NULL        NULL        54          NULL
Y        NULL        NULL        63          NULL
```

```
Y        NULL        NULL        72          NULL
Y        NULL        91          NULL        NULL
Y        NULL        NULL        NULL        NULL
Z        NULL        NULL        NULL        NULL
X        NULL        NULL        NULL        NULL
X        NULL        NULL        NULL        NULL
```

The result is not what was expected! This doesn't look at all like the crosstab result shown in Figure 12-4. That's because the `PIVOT` function used every column provided to it. Because the `Amount` and `Region` are specified, it assumed that every remaining column should be used for the `GROUP BY`, so it grouped by `Category` *and* `SalesDate`. There's no way to explicitly define the `GROUP BY` for the `PIVOT`. It uses an implicit `GROUP BY`.

The solution is to use a subquery to select only the columns that should be submitted to the `PIVOT` command:

```
SELECT Category, MidWest, NorthEast, South, West
  FROM (SELECT Category, Region, Amount
          FROM RawData) sq
    PIVOT
      (SUM(Amount)
      FOR Region IN (MidWest, NorthEast, South, West)
      ) AS pt
```

Result:

```
Category MidWest     NorthEast   South       West
-------- ----------- ----------- ----------- -----------
X        24          NULL        165         36
Y        38          181         287         NULL
Z        83          55          33          44
```

Now the result looks closer to the crosstab result in Figure 12-4.

Case expression method

The `CASE` expression method starts with a normal `GROUP BY` query generating a row for each value in the `GROUP BY` column. Adding a `ROLLUP` function to the `GROUP BY` adds a nice grand totals row to the crosstab.

To generate the crosstab columns, a `CASE` expression filters the data summed by the aggregate function. For example, if the `region` is "south," then the `SUM()` will see the `amount` value, but if the `region` isn't "`south`," then the `CASE` expression passes a `0` to the `SUM()` function. It's beautifully simple.

The `CASE` expression has three clear advantages over the `PIVOT` method, making it easier both to code and to maintain:

- The `GROUP BY` is explicit. There's no guessing which columns will generate the rows.
- The crosstab columns are defined only once.
- It's easy to add a grand totals row.

The CASE expression method's query execution plan is identical to the plan generated by the PIVOT method:

```
SELECT CASE GROUPING(Category)
      WHEN 0 THEN Category
      WHEN 1 THEN 'All Categories'
    END AS Category,
    SUM(CASE WHEN Region = 'MidWest' THEN Amount ELSE 0 END)
       AS MidWest,
    SUM(CASE WHEN Region = 'NorthEast' THEN Amount ELSE 0 END)
       AS NorthEast,
    SUM(CASE WHEN Region = 'South' THEN Amount ELSE 0 END)
       AS South,
    SUM(CASE WHEN Region = 'West' THEN Amount ELSE 0  END)
       AS West,
    SUM(Amount) AS Total
  FROM RawData
  GROUP BY RollUp (Category)
  ORDER BY Coalesce(Category, 'ZZZZ')
```

Result:

```
Category        MidWest  NorthEast  South  West  Total
--------------- -------- ---------- ------ ----- ------
X               24       0          165    36    225
Y               38       181        287    0     506
Z               83       55         33     44    215
All Categories  145      236        485    80    946
```

Dynamic crosstab queries

The rows of a crosstab query are automatically dynamically generated by the aggregation at runtime; however, in both the PIVOT method and the CASE expression method, the crosstab columns (region in this example) must be hard-coded in the SQL statement.

The only way to create a crosstab query with dynamic columns is to determine the columns at execution time and assemble a dynamic SQL command to execute the crosstab query. While it could be done with a cursor, the following example uses a multiple-assignment variable SELECT to create the list of regions in the @SQLStr. A little string manipulation to assemble the pivot statement and an sp_executesql command completes the job:

```
DECLARE @SQLStr NVARCHAR(1024)

SELECT @SQLStr = COALESCE(@SQLStr + ',', '') + [a].[Column]
  FROM (SELECT DISTINCT Region AS [Column]
          FROM RawData) AS a

SET @SQLStr = 'SELECT Category, ' + @SQLStr
  + ' FROM (Select Category, Region, Amount from RawData) sq '
```

```
  + ' PIVOT (Sum (Amount) FOR Region IN ('
  + @SQLStr + ')) AS pt'

PRINT @SQLStr
EXEC sp_executesql @SQLStr
```

Result:

```
SELECT Category, MidWest,NorthEast,South,West FROM (Select
Category, Region, Amount from RawData) sq   PIVOT (Sum (Amount)
FOR Region IN (MidWest,NorthEast,South,West)) AS pt

Category MidWest     NorthEast   South       West
-------- ----------- ----------- ----------- -----------
X        24          NULL        165         36
Y        38          181         287         NULL
Z        83          55          33          44
```

CROSS-REF **This example is only to demonstrate the technique for building a dynamic crosstab query. Anytime you're working with dynamic SQL, be sure to guard against SQL injection, which is discussed in Chapter 29, "Dynamic SQL and Code Generation."**

CROSS-REF **An Analysis Services cube is basically a dynamic crosstab query on steroids. For more about designing these high-performance interactive cubes, turn to Chapter 71, "Building Multidimensional Cubes with Analysis Services."**

Unpivot

The inverse of a crosstab query is the UNPIVOT command, which is extremely useful for normalizing denormalized data. Starting with a table that looks like the result of a crosstab, the UNPIVOT command will twist the data back to a normalized list. Of course, the UNPIVOT can only normalize the data supplied to it, so if the pivoted data is an aggregate summary, that's all that will be normalized. The details that created the aggregate summary won't magically reappear.

The following script sets up a table populated with crosstab data:

```
IF OBJECT_ID('Ptable') IS NOT NULL
  DROP TABLE Ptable
go

SELECT Category, MidWest, NorthEast, South, West
  INTO PTable
  FROM (SELECT Category, MidWest, NorthEast, South, West
          FROM (SELECT Category, Region, Amount
                  FROM RawData) sq
            PIVOT
              (SUM(Amount)
              FOR Region IN (MidWest, NorthEast, South, West)
              ) AS pt
        ) AS Q
```

```
SELECT *
  FROM PTable
```

Result:

```
Category MidWest     NorthEast   South       West
-------- ----------- ----------- ----------- -----------
X        24          NULL        165         36
Y        38          181         287         NULL
Z        83          55          33          44
```

The UNPIVOT command can now pick apart the Ptable data and convert it back into a normalized form:

```
SELECT *
  FROM PTable
    UNPIVOT
      (Measure
       FOR Region IN
           (South, NorthEast, MidWest, West)
       ) as sq
```

Result:

```
Category Measure     Region
-------- ----------- ------------
X        165         South
X        24          MidWest
X        36          West
Y        287         South
Y        181         NorthEast
Y        38          MidWest
Z        33          South
Z        55          NorthEast
Z        83          MidWest
Z        44          West
```

Cumulative Totals (Running Sums)

There are numerous reasons for calculating cumulative totals, or running sums, in a database, such as account balances and inventory quantity on hand, to name only two. Of course, it's easy to just pump the data to a reporting tool and let the report control calculate the running sum, but those calculations are then lost. It's much better to calculate the cumulative total in the database and then report from consistent numbers.

Cumulative totals is one area that defies the norm for SQL. As a rule, SQL excels at working with sets, but calculating a cumulative total for a set of data is based on comparing individual rows, so an iterative row-based cursor solution performs much better than a set-based operation.

Correlated subquery solution

First, here's the set-based solution. The correlated subquery sums every row, from the first row to every row in the outer query. The first row sums from the first row to the first row. The second row sums from the first row to the second row. The third row sums from the first row to the third row, and so on until the hundred thousandths row sums from the first row to the hundred thousandths row.

For a small set this solution works well enough, but as the data set grows, the correlated subquery method becomes exponentially slower, which is why whenever someone is blogging about this cool solution, the sample code tends to have a `top(100)` in the `SELECT`:

```
USE AdventureWorks2008;
SET NoCount NOCOUNT ON;

SELECT OuterQuery.SalesOrderIdD, OuterQuery.TotalDue,
  (Select sumSELECT SUM(InnerQuery.TotalDue)
     From FROM Sales.SalesOrderHeader AS InnerQuery
     Where WHERE InnerQuery.SalesOrderID
        <= OuterQuery.SalesOrderID ) as AS CT
  FROM Sales.SalesOrderHeader AS OuterQuery
  ORDER BY OuterQuery.SalesOrderID;
```

On Maui (my Dell 6400 notebook), the best time achieved for that query was 2 minutes, 19 seconds to process 31,465 rows. Youch!

T-SQL cursor solution

With this solution, the cursor fetches the next row, does a quick add, and updates the value in the row. Therefore, it's doing more work than the previous `SELECT` — it's writing the cumulative total value back to the table.

The first couple of statements add a `CumulativeTotal` column and make sure the table isn't fragmented. From there, the cursor runs through the update:

```
USE AdventureWorks;
SET NoCount ON;

ALTER TABLE Sales.SalesOrderHeader
  ADD CumulativeTotal MONEY NOT NULL
  CONSTRAINT dfSalesOrderHeader DEFAULT(0);

ALTER INDEX ALL ON Sales.SalesOrderHeader
  REBUILD WITH (FILLFACTOR = 100, SORT_IN_TEMPDB = ON);


DECLARE
  @SalesOrderID INT,
  @TotalDue MONEY,
  @CumulativeTotal MONEY = 0;
```

```
DECLARE cRun CURSOR STATIC
  FOR
    SELECT SalesOrderID, TotalDue
      FROM Sales.SalesOrderHeader
      ORDER BY SalesOrderID;
OPEN cRun;
-- prime the cursor
FETCH cRun INTO @SalesOrderID, @TotalDue;
WHILE @@Fetch_Status = 0
  BEGIN;
    SET @CumulativeTotal += @TotalDue;

    UPDATE Sales.SalesOrderHeader
      SET CumulativeTotal = @CumulativeTotal
      WHERE SalesOrderID = @SalesOrderID;
    -- fetch next
    FETCH cRun INTO @SalesOrderID, @TotalDue;
  END;

CLOSE cRun;
DEALLOCATE cRun;

go --

SELECT SalesOrderID, TotalDue, CumulativeTotal
  FROM Sales.SalesOrderHeader
  ORDER BY OrderDate, SalesOrderID;

go --

ALTER TABLE Sales.SalesOrderHeader
  DROP CONSTRAINT dfSalesOrderHeader;
ALTER TABLE Sales.SalesOrderHeader
  DROP COLUMN CumulativeTotal;
```

The T-SQL cursor with the additional update functionality pawned the set-based solution with an execution time of 15 seconds! w00t! That's nearly a magnitude difference. Go cursor!

Multiple assignment variable solution

Another solution was posted on my blog (`http://tinyurl.com/ajs3tr`) in response to a screencast I did on cumulative totals and cursors.

The multiple assignment variable accumulates data in a variable iteratively during a set-based operation. It's fast — the following multiple assignment variable solves the cumulative total problem in about one second:

```
DECLARE @CumulativeTotal MONEY = 0

UPDATE Sales.SalesOrderHeader
```

```
SET @CumulativeTotal=CumulativeTotal
      =@CumulativeTotal+ISNULL(TotalDue, 0)
```

With SQL Server 2008, the multiple assignment variable seems to respect the `order by` cause, so I'm cautiously optimistic about using this solution. However, it's not documented or supported by Microsoft, so if the order is critical, and it certainly is to a cumulative totals problem, then I recommend the T-SQL cursor solution. If you do choose the multiple assignment variable solution, be sure to test it thoroughly with every new service pack.

Summary

SQL Server excels in aggregate functions, with the proverbial rich suite of features, and it is very capable of calculating sums and aggregates to suit nearly any need. From the simple `COUNT()` aggregate function to the complex dynamic crosstab query and the new `PIVOT` command, these query methods enable you to create powerful data analysis queries for impressive reports. The most important points to remember about aggregation are as follows:

- Aggregate queries generate a single summary row, so every column has to be an aggregate function.
- There's no performance difference between `COUNT(*)` and `COUNT(pk)`.
- Aggregate functions, such as `COUNT(column)` and `AVG(column)`, ignore nulls, which can be a good thing, and a reason why nulls make life easier for the database developer.
- `GROUP BY` queries divide the data source into several segmented data sets and then generate a summary row for each group. For `GROUP BY` queries, the `GROUP BY` columns can and should be in the column list.
- In the logical flow of the query, the `GROUP BY` occurs after the `FROM` clause and the `WHERE` clause, so when coding the query, get the data properly selected and then add the `GROUP BY`.
- Complex aggregations (e.g., nested aggregations) often require CTEs or subqueries. Design the query from the inside out — that is, design the aggregate subquery first and then add the outer query.
- `GROUP BY`'s `ROLLUP` and `CUBE` option have a new syntax, and they can be as powerful as Analysis Service's cubes.
- There are several way to code a crosstab query. I recommend using a `GROUP BY` and `CASE` expressions, rather than the `PIVOT` syntax.
- Dynamic crosstabs are possible only with dynamic SQL.
- Calculating cumulative totals (running sums) is one of the few problems best solved by a cursor.

The next chapter continues working with summary data using the windowing and ranking technology of the `OVER()` clause.

Chapter 13

Windowing and Ranking

Have you ever noticed the hidden arrow in the FedEx logo? Once you know that it's there, it's obvious, but in an informal poll of FedEx drivers, not one of them was aware of the arrow. Sometimes, just seeing things in a different perspective can help clarify the picture.

That's what SQL's windowing and ranking does — the windowing (using the `over()` clause) provides a new perspective on the data. The ranking functions then use that perspective to provide additional ways to manipulate the query results.

Windowing and ranking are similar to the last chapter's aggregate queries, but they belong in their own chapter because they work with an independent sort order separate from the query's `order by` clause, and should be thought of as a different technology than traditional aggregate queries.

IN THIS CHAPTER

- **Creating an independent sort of the result set**
- **Grouping result sets**
- **Calculating ranks, row numbers, and ntiles**

Windowing

Before the ranking functions can be applied to the query, the window must be established. Even though the SQL query syntax places these two steps together, logically it's easier to think through the window and then add the ranking function.

Referring back to the logical sequence of the query in Chapter 8, "Introducing Basic Query Flow," the `OVER()` clause occurs in the latter half of the logical flow of the query in step 6 after the column expressions and `ORDER BY` but before any verbs (`OUTPUT`, `INSERT`, `UPDATE`, `DELETE`, or `UNION`).

What's New with Windowing and Ranking?

The functionality was introduced in SQL Server 2005, and I had hoped it would be expanded for 2008. Windowing and ranking hold so much potential, and there's much more functionality in the ANSI SQL specification, but unfortunately, there's nothing new with windowing and ranking in SQL Server 2008.

NOTE **All the examples in this chapter use the** `AdventureWorks2008` **sample database.**

The Over() clause

The `OVER()` clause creates a new window on the data — think of it as a new perspective, or independent ordering, of the rows — which may or may not be the same as the sort order of the `ORDER BY` clause. In a way, the windowing capability creates an alternate flow to the query with its own sort order and ranking functions, as illustrated in Figure 13-1. The results of the windowing and ranking are passed back into the query before the `ORDER BY` clause.

FIGURE 13-1

The windowing and ranking functions can be thought of as a parallel query process with an independent sort order.

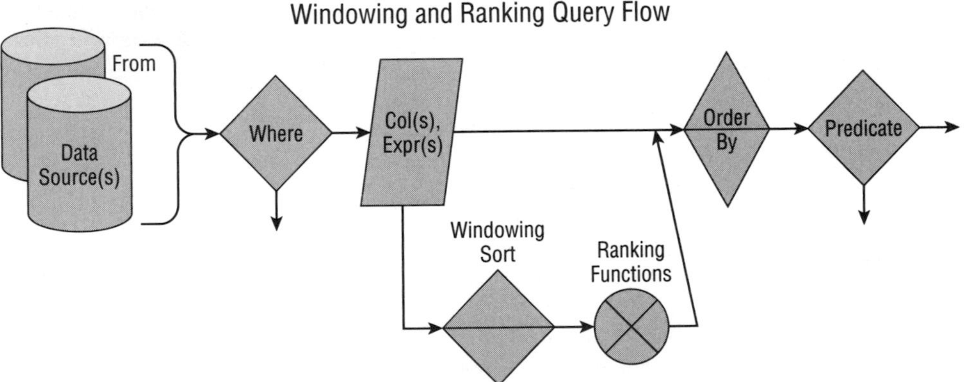

The complete syntax `OVER(ORDER BY columns)`. The columns may be any available column or expression, just like the `ORDER BY` clause; but unlike the `ORDER BY` clause, the `OVER()` clause won't accept a column ordinal position, e.g., `1, 2`. Also, like the `ORDER BY` clause, it can be ascending (`asc`), the default, or descending (`desc`); and it can be sorted by multiple columns.

The window's sort order will take advantage of indexes and can be very fast, even if the sort order is different from the main query's sort order.

In the following query, the OVER( ) clause creates a separate view to the data sorted by OrderDate (ignore the ROW_NUMBER( ) function for now):

```
USE AdventureWorks2008;

SELECT ROW_NUMBER() OVER(ORDER BY OrderDate) as RowNumber,
    SalesOrderID, OrderDate
  FROM Sales.SalesOrderHeader
  WHERE SalesPersonID = 280
  ORDER BY RowNumber;
```

Result (abbreviated, and note that OrderDate does not include time information, so the results might vary within a given date):

```
RowNumber            SalesOrderID OrderDate
-------------------- ------------ -----------------------
1                    43664        2001-07-01 00:00:00.000
2                    43860        2001-08-01 00:00:00.000
3                    43866        2001-08-01 00:00:00.000
4                    43867        2001-08-01 00:00:00.000
5                    43877        2001-08-01 00:00:00.000
```

Partitioning within the window

The OVER( ) clause normally creates a single sort order, but it can divide the windowed data into partitions, which are similar to groups in an aggregate GROUP BY query. This is dramatically powerful because the ranking functions will be able to restart with every partition.

The next query example uses the OVER( ) clause to create a sort order of the query results by OrderDate, and then partition the data by YEAR( ) and MONTH( ). Notice that the syntax is the opposite of the logical flow — the PARTITION BY goes before the ORDER BY within the OVER( ) clause:

```
SELECT ROW_NUMBER()
      OVER(Partition By
            Year(OrderDate),
            Month(OrderDate)
           ORDER BY OrderDate) as RowNumber,
    SalesOrderID, OrderDate
  FROM Sales.SalesOrderHeader
  WHERE SalesPersonID = 280
  ORDER BY OrderDate;
```

Result (abbreviated):

```
RowNumber            SalesOrderID OrderDate
-------------------- ------------ -----------------------
1                    43664        2001-07-01 00:00:00.000
1                    43860        2001-08-01 00:00:00.000
2                    43866        2001-08-01 00:00:00.000
3                    43867        2001-08-01 00:00:00.000
```

```
4                    43877       2001-08-01 00:00:00.000
5                    43894       2001-08-01 00:00:00.000
6                    43895       2001-08-01 00:00:00.000
7                    43911       2001-08-01 00:00:00.000
1                    44109       2001-09-01 00:00:00.000
1                    44285       2001-10-01 00:00:00.000
1                    44483       2001-11-01 00:00:00.000
2                    44501       2001-11-01 00:00:00.000
```

As expected, the windowed sort (in this case, the RowNumber column) restarts with every new month.

Ranking Functions

The windowing capability (the OVER() clause) by itself doesn't create any query output columns; that's where the *ranking functions* come into play:

- row_number
- rank
- dense_rank
- ntile

Just to be explicit, the ranking functions all require the windowing function.

All the normal aggregate functions — SUM(), MIN(), MAX(), COUNT(*), and so on — can also be used as ranking functions.

Row number() function

The ROW_NUMBER() function generates an on-the-fly auto-incrementing integer according to the sort order of the OVER() clause. It's similar to Oracle's RowNum column.

The row number function simply numbers the rows in the query result — there's absolutely no correlation with any physical address or absolute row number. This is important because in a relational database, row position, number, and order have no meaning. It also means that as rows are added or deleted from the underlying data source, the row numbers for the query results will change. In addition, if there are sets of rows with the same values in all ordering columns, then their order is undefined, so their row numbers may change between two executions even if the underlying data does not change.

One common practical use of the ROW_NUMBER() function is to filter by the row number values for pagination. For example, a query that easily produces rows 21–40 would be useful for returning the second page of data for a web page. Just be aware that the rows in the pages may change — typically, this grabs data from a temp table.

It would seem that the natural way to build a row number pagination query would be to simply add the OVER() clause and ROW_NUMBER() function to the WHERE clause:

```
SELECT ROW_NUMBER() OVER(ORDER BY OrderDate, SalesOrderID) as
RowNumber, SalesOrderID
  FROM Sales.SalesOrderHeader
  WHERE SalesPersonID = 280
```

```
        AND ROW_NUMBER() OVER(ORDER BY OrderDate, SalesOrderID)
        Between 21 AND 40
      ORDER BY RowNumber;
```

Result:

```
Msg 4108, Level 15, State 1, Line 4
Windowed functions can only appear in the SELECT or ORDER BY clauses.
```

Because the WHERE clause occurs very early in the query processing — often in the query operation that actually reads the data from the data source — and the OVER() clause occurs late in the query processing, the WHERE clause doesn't yet know about the windowed sort of the data or the ranking function. The WHERE clause can't possibly filter by the generated row number.

There is a simple solution: Embed the windowing and ranking functionality in a subquery or common table expression:

```
SELECT RowNumber, SalesOrderID, OrderDate, SalesOrderNumber
  FROM (
    SELECT ROW_NUMBER() OVER(ORDER BY OrderDate, SalesOrderID) as
    RowNumber, *
      FROM Sales.SalesOrderHeader
      WHERE SalesPersonID = 280
     ) AS Q
  WHERE RowNumber BETWEEN 21 AND 40
  ORDER BY RowNumber;
```

Result:

```
RowNumber       SalesOrderID OrderDate               SalesOrderNumber
--------------- ------------ ----------------------- ------------------
21              45041        2002-01-01 00:00:00.000 SO45041
22              45042        2002-01-01 00:00:00.000 SO45042
23              45267        2002-02-01 00:00:00.000 SO45267
24              45283        2002-02-01 00:00:00.000 SO45283
25              45295        2002-02-01 00:00:00.000 SO45295
26              45296        2002-02-01 00:00:00.000 SO45296
27              45303        2002-02-01 00:00:00.000 SO45303
28              45318        2002-02-01 00:00:00.000 SO45318
29              45320        2002-02-01 00:00:00.000 SO45320
30              45338        2002-02-01 00:00:00.000 SO45338
31              45549        2002-03-01 00:00:00.000 SO45549
32              45783        2002-04-01 00:00:00.000 SO45783
33              46025        2002-05-01 00:00:00.000 SO46025
34              46042        2002-05-01 00:00:00.000 SO46042
35              46052        2002-05-01 00:00:00.000 SO46052
36              46053        2002-05-01 00:00:00.000 SO46053
37              46060        2002-05-01 00:00:00.000 SO46060
38              46077        2002-05-01 00:00:00.000 SO46077
39              46080        2002-05-01 00:00:00.000 SO46080
40              46092        2002-05-01 00:00:00.000 SO46092
```

The second query in this chapter, in the "Partitioning within the Window" section, showed how grouping the sort order of the window generated row numbers that started over with every new partition.

Rank() and dense_rank() functions

The `RANK()` and `DENSE_RANK()` functions return values as if the rows were competing according to the windowed sort order. Any ties are grouped together with the same ranked value. For example, if Frank and Jim both tied for third place, then they would both receive a `rank()` value of 3.

Using sales data from `AdventureWorks2008`, there are ties for least sold products, which makes it a good table to play with `RANK()` and `DENSE_RANK()`. `ProductID`'s 943 and 911 tie for third place and `ProductID`'s 927 and 898 tie for fourth or fifth place depending on how ties are counted:

```
-- Least Sold Products:
SELECT ProductID, COUNT(*) as 'count'
  FROM Sales.SalesOrderDetail
  GROUP BY ProductID
  ORDER BY COUNT(*);
```

Result (abbreviated):

```
ProductID   count
----------- -----------
897         2
942         5
943         6
911         6
927         9
898         9
744         13
903         14
...
```

Examining the sales data using windowing and the `RANK()` function returns the ranking values:

```
SELECT ProductID, SalesCount,
    RANK() OVER (ORDER BY SalesCount) as 'Rank',
    DENSE_RANK() OVER(Order By SalesCount) as 'DenseRank'
  FROM (SELECT ProductID, COUNT(*) as SalesCount
          FROM Sales.SalesOrderDetail
          GROUP BY ProductID
        ) AS Q
   ORDER BY 'Rank';
```

Result (abbreviated):

```
ProductID   SalesCount  Rank                 DenseRank
----------- ----------- -------------------- --------------------
897         2           1                    1
942         5           2                    2
943         6           3                    3
911         6           3                    3
927         9           5                    4
```

```
898          9          5                4
744          13         7                5
903          14         8                6
...
```

This example perfectly demonstrates the difference between RANK() and DENSE_RANK(). RANK() counts each tie as a ranked row. In this example, Product IDs 943 and 911 both tie for third place but consume the third and fourth row in the ranking, placing ProductID 927 in fifth place.

DENSE_RANK() handles ties differently. Tied rows only consume a single value in the ranking, so the next rank is the next place in the ranking order. No ranks are skipped. In the previous query, ProductID 927 is in fourth place using DENSE_RANK().

Just as with the ROW_NUMBER() function, RANK() and DENSE_RANK() can be used with a partitioned OVER() clause. The previous example could be partitioned by product category to rank product sales with each category.

Ntile() function

The fourth ranking function organizes the rows into *n* number of groups, called *tiles*, and returns the tile number. For example, if the result set has ten rows, then NTILE(5) would split the ten rows into five equally sized tiles with two rows in each tile in the order of the OVER() clause's ORDER BY.

If the number of rows is not evenly divisible by the number of tiles, then the tiles get the extra row. For example, for 74 rows and 10 tiles, the first 4 tiles get 8 rows each, and tiles 5 through 10 get 7 rows each. This can skew the results for smaller data sets. For example, 15 rows into 10 tiles would place 10 rows in the lower five tiles and only place five tiles in the upper five tiles. But for larger data sets — splitting a few hundred rows into 100 tiles, for example — it works great.

This rule also applies if there are fewer rows than tiles. The rows are not spread across all tiles; instead, the tiles are filled until the rows are consumed. For example, if five rows are split using NTILE(10), the result set would not use tiles 1, 3, 5, 7, and 9, but instead show tiles 1, 2, 3, 4, and 5.

A common real-world example of NTILE() is the percentile scoring used in college entrance exams.

The following query first calculates the AdventureWorks2008 products' sales quantity in the subquery. The outer query then uses the OVER() clause to sort by the sales count, and the NTILE(100) to calculate the percentile according to the sales count:

```
SELECT ProductID, SalesCount,
    NTILE(100) OVER (ORDER BY SalesCount) as Percentile
  FROM (SELECT ProductID, COUNT(*) as SalesCount
          FROM Sales.SalesOrderDetail
          GROUP BY ProductID
        ) AS Q
  ORDER BY Percentile DESC;
```

Result (abbreviated):

```
ProductID   SalesCount  Percentile
----------- ----------- --------------------
712         3382        100
870         4688        100
921         3095        99
```

```
    873          3354         99
    707          3083         98
    711          3090         98
    922          2376         97

...

    830          33           5
    888          39           5
    902          20           4
    950          28           4
    946          30           4
    744          13           3
    903          14           3
    919          16           3
    911          6            2
    927          9            2
    898          9            2
    897          2            1
    942          5            1
    943          6            1
```

Like the other three ranking functions, NTILE() can be used with a partitioned OVER() clause. Similar to the ranking example, the previous example could be partitioned by product category to generate percentiles within each category.

Aggregate Functions

SQL query functions all fit together like a magnificent puzzle. A fine example is how windowing can use not only the four ranking functions — ROW_NUMBER(), RANK(), DENSE_RANK(), and NTILE() — but also the standard aggregate functions: COUNT(*), MIN(), MAX(), and so on, which were covered in the last chapter.

I won't rehash the aggregate functions here, and usually the aggregate functions will fit well within a normal aggregate query, but here's an example of using the SUM() aggregate function in a window to calculate the total sales order count for each product subcategory, and then, using that result from the window, calculate the percentage of sales orders for each product within its subcategory:

```
SELECT ProductID, Product,  SalesCount,
  NTILE(100) OVER (ORDER BY SalesCount)  as Percentile,
  SubCat,
  CAST(CAST(SalesCount AS NUMERIC(9,2))
    / SUM(SalesCount) OVER(Partition BY SubCat)
    * 100 AS NUMERIC (4,1)) AS PercOfSubCat
  FROM (SELECT P.ProductID, P.[Name] AS Product,
          PSC.NAME AS SubCat, COUNT(*) as SalesCount
          FROM Sales.SalesOrderDetail AS SOD
            JOIN Production.Product AS P
              ON SOD.ProductID = P.ProductID
```

```
            JOIN Production.ProductSubcategory PSC
              ON P.ProductSubcategoryID = PSC.ProductSubcategoryID
          GROUP BY PSC.NAME, P.[Name], P.ProductID
        ) Q
    ORDER BY Percentile DESC
```

Result (abbreviated):

```
ProductID Product                 SalesCount  Percentile SubCat          PercOfSubCat
--------- ----------------------- ----------- ---------- --------------- ------------
870       Water Bottle - 30 oz.   4688        100        Bottles and Cages       55.6
712       AWC Logo Cap            3382        100        Caps                   100.0
921       Mountain Tire Tube      3095        99         Tires and Tubes         17.7
873       Patch Kit/8 Patches     3354        99         Tires and Tubes         19.2
707       Sport-100 Helmet, Red   3083        98         Helmets                 33.6
711       Sport-100 Helmet, Blue  3090        98         Helmets                 33.7
708       Sport-100 Helmet, Black 3007        97         Helmets                 32.8
922       Road Tire Tube          2376        97         Tires and Tubes         13.6
878       Fender Set - Mountain   2121        96         Fenders                100.0
871       Mountain Bottle Cage    2025        96         Bottles and Cages       24.0
...
```

Summary

Windowing — an extremely powerful technology that creates an independent sort of the query results — supplies the sort order for the ranking functions which calculate row numbers, ranks, dense ranks, and n-tiles. When coding a complex query that makes the data twist and shout, creative use of windowing and ranking can be the difference between solving the problem in a single query or resorting to temp tables and code.

The key point to remember is that the `OVER()` clause generates the sort order for the ranking functions.

This chapter wraps up the set of chapters that explain how to query the data. The next chapters finish up the part on select by showing how to package queries into reusable views, and add insert, update, delete, and merge verbs to queries to modify data.

(In case you haven't checked yet and still need to know: The hidden arrow in the FedEx logo is between the E and the X.)

Chapter 14

Projecting Data Through Views

A *view* is the saved text of a SQL SELECT statement that may be referenced as a data source within a query, similar to how a subquery can be used as a data source — no more, no less. A view can't be executed by itself; it must be used within a query.

Views are sometimes described as "virtual tables." This isn't an accurate description because views don't store any data. Like any other SQL query, views merely refer to the data stored in tables.

With this in mind, it's important to fully understand how views work, the pros and cons of using views, and the best place to use views within your project architecture.

IN THIS CHAPTER

- Planning views wisely
- Creating views with Management Studio or DDL
- Updating through views
- Performance and views
- Nesting views
- Security through views
- Synonyms

Why Use Views?

While there are several opinions on the use of views, ranging from total abstinence to overuse, the Information Architecture Principle (from Chapter 2, "Smart Database Design") serves as a guide for their most appropriate use. The principle states that "*information ... must be ... made readily available in a usable format for daily operations and analysis by individuals, groups, and processes ...*"

Presenting data in a more useable format is precisely what views do best.

Based on the premise that views are best used to increase data integrity and ease of writing ad hoc queries, and not as a central part of a production application, here are some ideas for building ad hoc query views:

- Use views to denormalize or flatten complex joins and hide any surrogate keys used to link data within the database schema. A well-designed view invites the user to get right to the data of interest.
- Save complex aggregate queries as views. Even power users will appreciate a well-crafted aggregate query saved as a view.

Best Practice

Views are an important part of the abstraction puzzle; I recommend being intentional in their use. Some developers are enamored with views and use them as the primary abstraction layer for their databases. They create layers of nested views, or stored procedures that refer to views. This practice serves no valid purpose, creates confusion, and requires needless overhead. The best database abstraction layer is a single layer of stored procedures that directly refer to tables, or sometimes user-defined functions (see Chapter 28, "Building out the Data Abstraction Layer").

Instead, use views only to support ad hoc queries and reports. For queries that are run occasionally, views perform well even when compared with stored procedures.

Data within a normalized database is rarely organized in a readily available format. Building ad hoc queries that extract the correct information from a normalized database is a challenge for most end-users. A well-written view can hide the complexity and present the correct data to the user.

- Use aliases to change cryptic column names to recognizable column names. Just as the SQL `SELECT` statement can use column or table aliases to modify the names of columns or tables, these features may be used within a view to present a more readable record set to the user.
- Include only the columns of interest to the user. When columns that don't concern users are left out of the view, the view is easier to query. The columns that are included in the view are called *projected columns*, meaning they project only the selected data from the entire underlying table.
- Plan generic, dynamic views that will have long, useful lives. Single-purpose views quickly become obsolete and clutter the database. Build the view with the intention that it will be used with a `WHERE` clause to select a subset of data. The view should return all the rows if the user does not supply a `WHERE` restriction. For example, the `vEventList` view returns all the events; the user should use a `WHERE` clause to select the local events, or the events in a certain month.
- If a view is needed to return a restricted set of data, such as the next month's events, then the view should calculate the next month so that it will continue to function over time. Hard-coding values such as a month number or name would be poor practice.
- If the view selects data from a range, then consider writing it as a user-defined function (see Chapter 25, "Building User-Defined Functions"), which can accept parameters.
- Consolidate data from across a complex environment. Queries that need to collect data from across multiple servers are simplified by encapsulating the union of data from multiple servers within a view. This is one case where basing several reports, and even stored procedures, on a view improves the stability, integrity, and maintainability of the system.

Using Views for Column-Level Security

One of the basic relational operators is projection — the ability to expose specific columns. One primary advantage of views is their natural capacity to project a predefined set of columns. Here's where theory becomes practical. A view can project columns on a need-to-know basis and hide columns that are sensitive (e.g., payroll and credit card data), irrelevant, or confusing for the purpose of the view.

SQL Server supports column-level security, and it's a powerful feature. The problem is that ad hoc queries made by users who don't understand the schema very well will often run into security errors. I recommend implementing SQL Server column-level security, and then also using views to shield users from ever encountering the security. Grant users read permission from only the views, and restrict access to the physical tables (see Chapter 50, "Authorizing Securables").

I've seen databases that only use views for column-level security without any SQL Server–enforced security. This is woefully inadequate and will surely be penalized by any serious security audit.

The goal when developing views is two-fold: to enable users to get to the data easily and to protect the data from the users. By building views that provide the correct data, you are preventing erroneous or inaccurate queries and misinterpretation.

CROSS-REF **There are other advanced forms of views.**

***Distributed partition views*, or *federated databases*, divide very large tables across multiple smaller tables or separate servers to improve performance. The partitioned view then spans the multiple tables or servers, thus sharing the query load across more disk spindles. These are covered in Chapter 68, "Partitioning."**

***Indexed views* are a powerful feature that actually materializes the data, storing the results of the view in a clustered index on disk, so in this sense it's not a pure view. Like any view, it can select data from multiple data sources. Think of the indexed view as a covering index but with greater control — you can include data from multiple data sources, and you don't have to include the clustered index keys. The index may then be referenced when executing queries, regardless of whether the view is in the query, so the name is slightly confusing.**

CROSS-REF **Because designing an indexed view is more like designing an indexing structure than creating a view, I've included indexed views in Chapter 64, "Indexing Strategies."**

The Basic View

Using SQL Server Management Studio, views may be created, modified, executed, and included within other queries, using either the Query Designer or the DDL code within the Query Editor.

Creating views using the Query Designer

Because a view is nothing more than a saved SQL SELECT statement, the creation of a view begins with a working SELECT statement. Any SQL SELECT statement, as long as it's a valid SQL SELECT statement (with a few minor exceptions), can be cut and pasted from nearly any other tool into a view.

Within SQL Server Management Studio, views are listed in their own node under each database.

The New View command in the context menu launches the Query Designer in a mode that creates views, as shown in Figure 14-1.

FIGURE 14-1

Creating a view in Management Studio's Query Designer

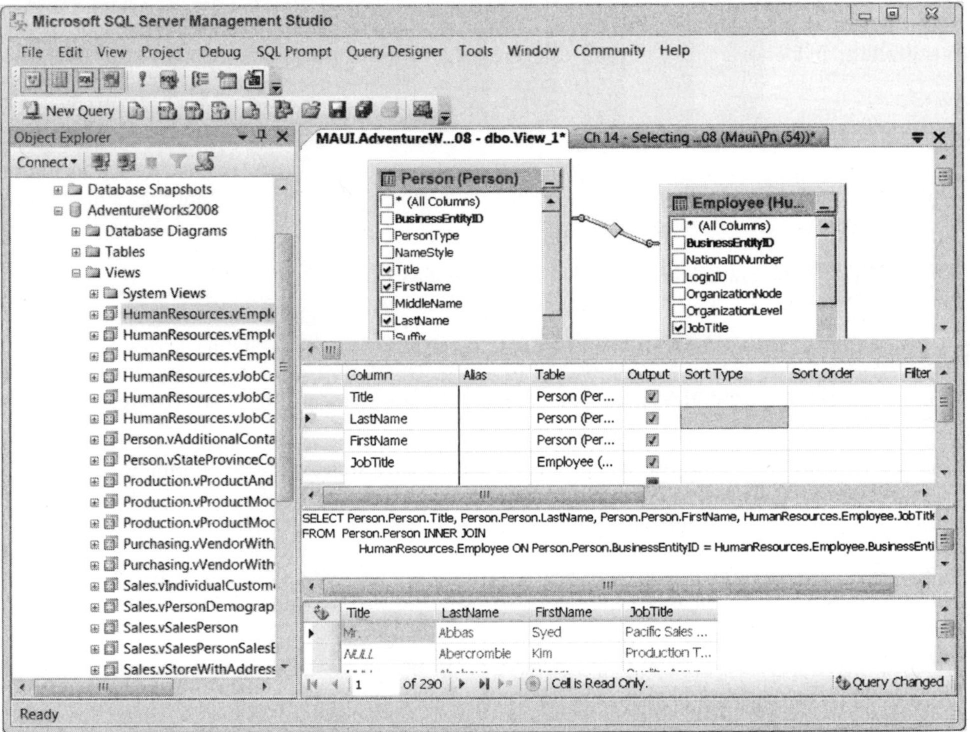

The View Designer mode functions within Management Studio's Query Designer, which is also used to query tables. The actual SQL code for the view is displayed or edited in the SQL pane. Columns may be added to the view by using the Diagram pane, the Grid pane, or the SQL pane. The Add Table feature, available in the context menu or toolbar, can add tables, other views, synonyms, and table-valued functions.

Tables or other views can be added to the new view by dragging them to the Diagram pane from the Object Explorer or using the Add Table context menu option.

There's a toolbar button and a context menu item to add a derived table to the view, but all it does is slightly modify the `from` clause to create a placeholder for the subquery. The SQL for the subquery is then manually entered in the SQL pane.

The Verify SQL Syntax button in the toolbar verifies only the SQL syntax; it does not verify the names of tables, views, or columns in the SQL `SELECT` statement.

To test the view's SQL `SELECT` statement within Query Designer, use the Execute SQL button or F5. This will run the `SELECT` statement by itself, without creating the view.

The Save toolbar button actually runs the script to create the view in the database. Note that the view must be a valid, error-free SQL `SELECT` statement in order to be saved.

CROSS-REF **For more details on using the Query Designer, refer to Chapter 6, "Using Management Studio."**

Once the view is created, several tasks may be performed on the view using Object Explorer's view context menu:

- **Redesign the view:** Opens the Query Designer tool with the view's `SELECT` statement.
- **Select top n rows:** Opens the Query Editor with a `SELECT` statement referencing the view. The number of rows selected can be modified in Management Studio's options.
- **Edit top n rows:** Opens the Query Designer with a `SELECT` statement referencing the view, with only the results pane visible, and executes the view.
- **Script the view:** Management Studio can script the DDL statements to `CREATE`, `ALTER`, or `DROP` the view, as well as sample DML statements referencing the view.
- **View dependencies:** This option can be very important because views, by definition, reference other data sources, and are often referenced themselves.
- **Full-text indexes:** A full-text index (covered in Chapter 19, "Using Integrated Full-Text Search") can be created and managed based on data selected by the view.
- **Policies:** Apply and manage policy-based management policies for the view.
- **Rename/Delete the view:** The view may also be renamed or dropped by selecting it and pressing Rename or Delete, respectively.
- **Properties:** Opens the properties dialog with pages for security permissions and extended properties.

Double-clicking the view opens its subnodes: columns, triggers (instead of tasks), indexes (indexed views), and statistics.

Creating views with DDL code

Views may be managed using the Query Editor by executing SQL scripts with the *data definition language (DDL)* commands: CREATE, ALTER, and DROP. The basic syntax for creating a view is as follows:

```
CREATE VIEW schemaname.ViewName [(Column aliases)]
AS
SQL Select Statement;
```

For example, to create the view vEmployeeList in code, the following command would be executed in a query window:

```
USE AdventureWorks2008
Go

CREATE VIEW dbo.vEmployeeList
AS
  SELECT P.BusinessEntityID, P.Title, P.LastName,
      P.FirstName, E.JobTitle
    FROM Person.Person P
      INNER JOIN HumanResources.Employee E
        ON P.BusinessEntityID = E.BusinessEntityID
```

As with creating any object, the create command must be the only command in the batch.

NOTE **Although I'm generally opposed to Hungarian notation (tblTablename, intIntegerColumn, etc.) for database objects, I prefer to preface views with a lowercase v, simply to keep them separate in data source listings, but, to be honest, most database developers do not preface views with a v.**

The view name must be unique in the database. Attempting to create a view with a name shared by any other object will generate an error.

Executing views

Technically, a view by itself cannot be executed. A view can only patiently wait to be referenced by a SQL query.

A query (SELECT, INSERT, UPDATE, DELETE, or MERGE) can include the view as a data source, and that query can be executed. As illustrated in Figure 14-2, a view is useful only as a data source within a query. You can think of a view as nothing more than a placeholder for a saved SELECT statement.

The following SELECT statement references the vEmployeeList view:

```
SELECT BusinessEntityID, LastName, FirstName, JobTitle
  FROM dbo.vEmployeeList
```

FIGURE 14-2

When the query that references a view is submitted to SQL Server, the query parser picks the query apart and replaces the name of the view with the view's `select` statement.

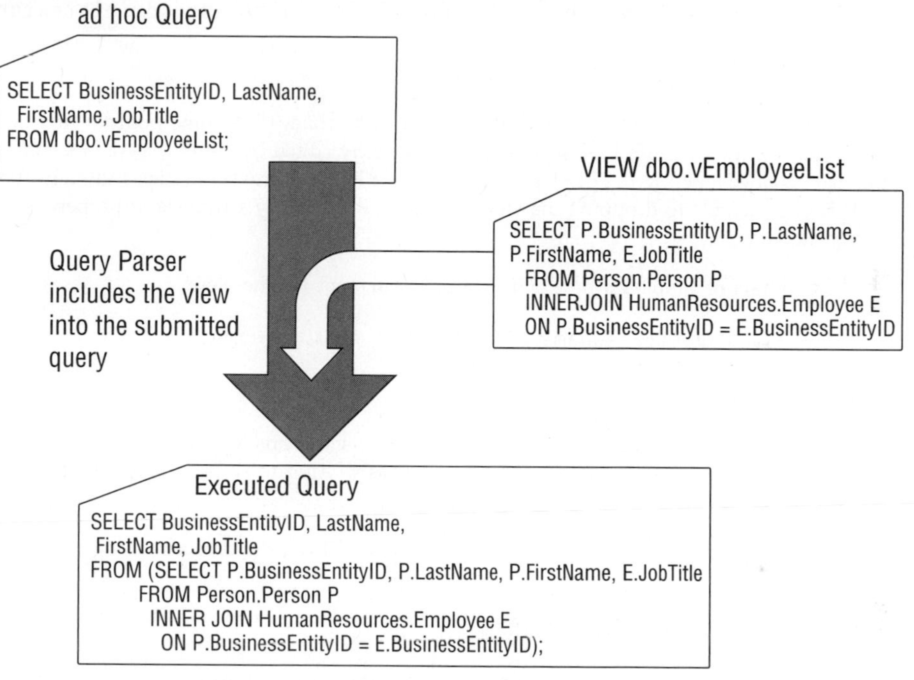
ad hoc Query
SELECT BusinessEntityID, LastName,
FirstName, JobTitle
FROM dbo.vEmployeeList;
VIEW dbo.vEmployeeList
SELECT P.BusinessEntityID, P.LastName,
P.FirstName, E.JobTitle
FROM Person.Person P
INNERJOIN HumanResources.Employee E
ON P.BusinessEntityID = E.BusinessEntityID
Query Parser
includes the view
into the submitted
query
Executed Query
SELECT BusinessEntityID, LastName,
FirstName, JobTitle
FROM (SELECT P.BusinessEntityID, P.LastName, P.FirstName, E.JobTitle
FROM Person.Person P
INNER JOIN HumanResources.Employee E
ON P.BusinessEntityID = E.BusinessEntityID);

Result (abbreviated):

```
BusinessEntityID LastName     FirstName   JobTitle
---------------- ------------ ----------- ----------------------
1                Sánchez      Ken         Chief Executive Officer
2                Duffy        Terri       Vice President of Engineering
3                Tamburello   Roberto     Engineering Manager
4                Walters      Rob         Senior Tool Designer
```

When views are referenced from ad hoc queries, a `WHERE` condition is typically added to filter the data from the view:

```
SELECT BusinessEntityID, LastName, FirstName, JobTitle
  FROM dbo.vEmployeeList
  WHERE JobTitle = 'Database Administrator';
```

Result:

```
BusinessEntityID LastName     FirstName   JobTitle
---------------- ------------ ----------- ------------------------
270              Ajenstat     Françoi     Database Administrator
271              Wilson       Dan         Database Administrator
```

Altering and dropping a view

It's likely that the view's SELECT statement will need to be changed at some point in time. Once a view has been created, the SQL SELECT statement may be easily edited by using the ALTER command. Altering the view changes the saved SELECT statement while keeping any properties and security settings in place. This is preferable to dropping the view, losing all the security settings and properties, and then recreating the view.

The ALTER command supplies a new SQL SELECT statement for the view:

```
ALTER SchemaName.ViewName
AS
SQL Select Statement;
```

Management Studio can automatically generate an ALTER statement from an existing view. In Object Explorer, select the view and then choose Script View as ➪ Alter to ➪ New Query Editor Window from the context menu.

If the view is no longer needed, it can be completely erased from the database using the DROP command:

```
DROP VIEW SchemaName.ViewName;
```

Within a script that is intended to be executed several times, the following code can drop and recreate the view:

```
IF OBJECT_ID('vEmployeeList') IS NOT NULL
  DROP VIEW dbo.vEmployeeList
Go
CREATE VIEW SchemaName.ViewName
AS
SQL Select Statement;
```

Just to reiterate, views don't contain any data, so there's no danger that dropping a view will cause any data loss. However, applications, reports, and other objects might depend on the view, and dropping the view might break something else. For more about viewing dependencies within SQL Server, see the section "Nesting Views" later in this chapter.

A Broader Point of View

The basic mechanics of creating a view and selecting data from the view are pretty straightforward, but views have their own particular nuances — topics such as sorting data, updating data through a view, and nesting views several levels deep. This section examines views from a broader point of view.

Column aliases

The column aliases option is rarely used. With syntax similar to the column list for a common table expression, the view's column list renames every output column just as if every column had those alias names in the SELECT statement. The view's column list names override any column names or column aliases in the view's SELECT statement.

The following query alters the vEmployeeList view so that the result columns become ID, Last, First, and Job:

```
ALTER VIEW dbo.vEmployeeList (ID, Last, First, Job)
AS
  SELECT P.BusinessEntityID,
      P.LastName, P.FirstName, E.JobTitle
    FROM Person.Person P
      INNER JOIN HumanResources.Employee E
        ON P.BusinessEntityID = E.BusinessEntityID
GO

SELECT *
  FROM dbo.vEmployeeList
```

Result (abbreviated):

```
ID          Last        First       Job
----------------------- ----------- ------------------------------
1           Sánchez     Ken         Chief Executive Officer
2           Duffy       Terri       Vice President of Engineering
3           Tamburello  Roberto     Engineering Manager
4           Walters     Rob         Senior Tool Designer
```

Order by and views

Views serve as data sources for other queries and don't support sorting the data within the view. To sort data from a view, include the ORDER BY clause in the query referencing the view. For example, the following code selects data from the vEmployeeList view and orders it by LastName, FirstName. The ORDER BY clause is not a part of vEmployeeList , but it is applied to the view by the executing SQL statement:

```
SELECT *
  FROM dbo.vEmployeeList
  ORDER BY LastName, FirstName
```

Result:

```
BusinessEntityID LastName     FirstName   JobTitle
---------------- ------------ ----------- -----------------------
285              Abbas        Syed        Pacific Sales Manager
38               Abercrombie  Kim         Production Technician - WC60
211              Abolrous     Hazem       Quality Assurance Manager
121              Ackerman     Pilar       Shipping and Receiving
                                          Supervisor
```

If the view includes a TOP predicate, then the view is allowed to include an ORDER BY — without the ORDER BY, the top would be meaningless. However, this ORDER BY clause serves *only* to define which rows qualify for the TOP predicate. The only way to logically guarantee sorted results is to define the ORDER BY clause in the executing query.

WARNING **SQL Server 2000, and some service packs of SQL Server 2005, had a bug (yes, I call it a bug) in the Query Optimizer that would allow an ORDER BY in a view using a top 100 percent predicate. This behavior was never documented or officially supported. However, in SQL Server 2008, this error was corrected and the top 100 percent with an ORDER BY trick will not sort the result.**

A source of confusion is that Management Studio's Query Designer allows views to have sorted columns, and it adds the top 100 percent trick to the view. That is a SQL Server 2008 bug.

View restrictions

Although a view can contain nearly any valid SELECT statement, a few basic restrictions do apply:

- Views may not include the SELECT INTO option that creates a new table from the selected columns. SELECT INTO fails if the table already exists and it does not return any data, so it's not a valid view:

  ```
  SELECT * INTO Table
  ```

- Views may not refer to a temporary table (one with a # in the name) or a table variable (preceded with an @), because these types of tables are very transient.
- The OPTION clause, which gives table or query hints for the entire query, is not allowed.
- The tablesample table option, which can randomly select pages, is not allowed within a view.
- Views may not contain compute or compute by columns. Instead, use standard aggregate functions and groupings. (Compute and compute by are obsolete and are included for backward compatibility only.)

Nesting views

Because a view is nothing more than a SQL SELECT statement, and a SQL SELECT statement may reference any data source, views may reference other views. Views referred to by other views are sometimes called *nested views*.

The following view uses vEmployeeList and adds a WHERE clause to restrict the results to the smartest and best-looking employees:

```
CREATE VIEW dbo.vEmployeeListDBA
AS
  SELECT BusinessEntityID, LastName, FirstName, JobTitle
    FROM dbo.vEmployeeList AS vE
    WHERE JobTitle = 'Database Administrator';
```

In this example, the view vEmployeeList is nested within vEmployeeListDBA. Another way to express the relationship is to say that vEmployeeListDBA depends on vEmployeeList.

Dependencies from other objects in SQL Server can be easily viewed using Object Explorer's view context menu ➪ View Dependencies. Figure 14-3 shows the Object Dependencies dialog for a nested view.

FIGURE 14-3

The dependency chain for nested views is easily seen in the Object Dependencies dialog. Here, the vEmployeeListDBA includes the nested view vEmployeeList, which in turn is based on the Employee table, and so on.

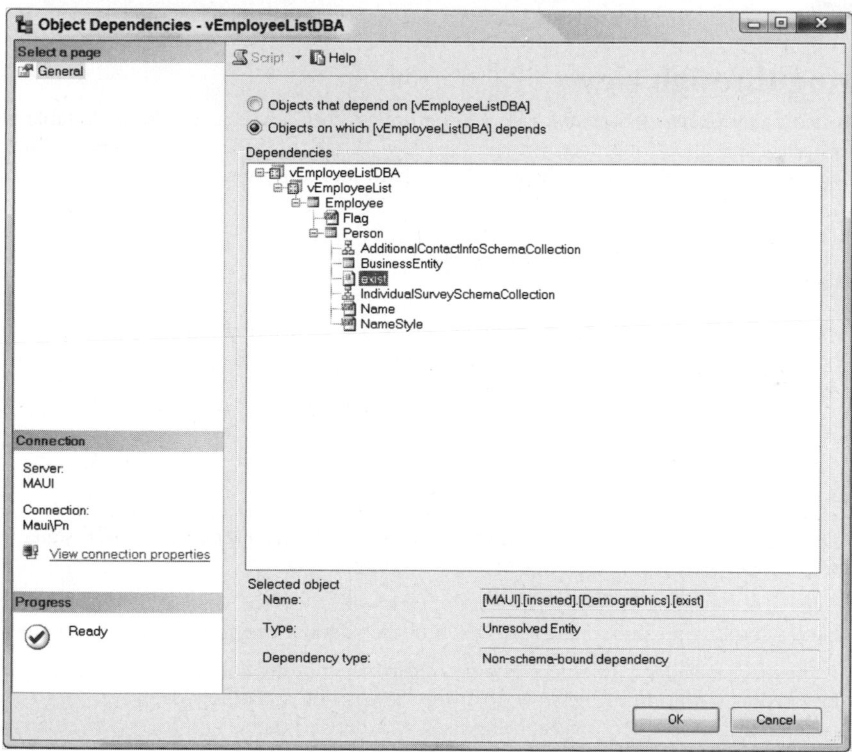

From code dependencies may be seen using the sys.dm_sql_referencing_entities()function. For example, the following query would indicate whether any other SQL Server object referenced vEmployeeList:

```
SELECT *
  FROM sys.dm_sql_referencing_entities
    ('dbo.vEmployeeList, 'Object')
```

Best Practice

While there may be a good reason for nesting views to support power users who build ad hoc queries, I don't recommend nesting views as a general practice. They're just too difficult to diagnose and maintain. I've seen development shops that build their production abstraction layer with nested views several layers deep. It performs poorly and is very difficult to modify.

CROSS-REF **For other options to nesting subselects within outer queries, see Chapter 11, "Including Data with Subqueries and CTEs."**

Updating through views

One of the main complaints concerning views is that unless the view is a simple single table view, it's difficult to update the underlying data through the view. While the SQL Server Query Optimizer can update through some complex views, there are some hard-and-fast limitations.

Best Practice

I don't recommend designing an application around updatable views. Views are best used as an abstraction layer for ad hoc queries and reports, not for power users to update data, and certainly not for forms, websites, or client applications to update the database.

Any of the following factors may cause a view to be non-updatable:

- Only one table may be updated. If the view includes joins, then the `UPDATE` statement that references the view must change columns in only one table.
- Aggregate functions or `GROUP BY`s in the view will cause the view to be non-updatable. SQL Server couldn't possibly determine which of the summarized rows should be updated.
- If the view includes a subquery as a derived table, and any columns from the subquery are exposed as output from the view, then the view is not updateable. However, aggregates are permitted in a subquery that is being used as a derived table, so long as any columns from the aggregate subquery are not in the output columns of the view.
- If the view includes the `WITH CHECK OPTION`, the `INSERT` or `UPDATE` operation must meet the view's `WHERE`-clause conditions.

CROSS-REF **Of course, the other standard potential difficulties with updating and inserting data still apply. Chapter 16, "Modification Obstacles," discusses in more detail potential troubles with modifying data.**

CROSS-REF **One way to work around non-updatable views is to build an `INSTEAD OF` trigger that inspects the modified data and then performs a legal `UPDATE` operation based on that data. Chapter 26, "Creating DML Triggers," explains how to create an `INSTEAD OF` trigger.**

Views and performance

Views have an undeserved reputation for poor performance. I think the reason for this belief is based on several factors:

- Views are often used by power users who submit ad hoc SQL. In earlier versions of SQL Server, ad hoc SQL didn't perform as well as stored procedures.
- Views are often used by power users who use front-end UI applications to select and browse data. Some of these applications opened the connections and held locks, causing all sorts of performance problems.
- Views are often used by power users who find useful data in a view and then build new views on top of views. These nested views might contain a horribly complex view several layers deep that kills performance, while the top-level view appears to be a simple, easy view.

Let me put the myth to rest: Well-written views will perform well. The reason to limit views to ad hoc queries and reports isn't for performance, but for extensibility and control.

Alternatives to Views

Besides views, SQL Server offers several technologies to build an abstraction layer around the data. Stored procedures are generally my first choice when exposing any data to the outside world. User-defined functions offer several benefits, and inline table-valued user-defined functions are very similar to views but with parameters. Chapter 21 discuss T-SQL, stored procedures, and functions.

If you are using views to support ad hoc queries, as I suggest you do, you may also want to explore providing Analysis Services cubes for those users who need to perform complex explorations of the data. Cubes *pre-aggregate*, or summarize, the data along multiple dimensions. The user may then browse the cube and compare the different data dimensions. For the developer, providing one cube can often eliminate several queries or reports.

Chapter 71, ''Building Multidimensional Cubes with Analysis Services,'' explains how to create cubes.

Locking Down the View

Views are designed to control access to data. There are several options that protect the data or the view.

The `WITH CHECK OPTION` causes the `WHERE` clause of the view to check the data being inserted or updated through the view in addition to the data being retrieved. In a sense, it makes the `WHERE` clause a two-way restriction.

The `WITH CHECK OPTION` is useful when the view should limit inserts and updates with the same restrictions applied to the `WHERE` clause.

Unchecked data

To understand the need for the WITH CHECK OPTION, it's important to first understand how views function without the CHECK OPTION. The following view will generate a list of tours for the Cape Hatteras base camp:

```
USE CHA2;

CREATE VIEW dbo.vCapeHatterasTour
AS
SELECT TourName, BaseCampID
   FROM dbo.Tour
   WHERE BaseCampID = 2;
go
SELECT TourName, BaseCampID FROM dbo.vCapeHatterasTour;

TourName                       BaseCampID
----------------------------- -----------
Outer Banks Lighthouses        2
```

If the Ashville base camp adds a Blue Ridge Parkway Hike tour and inserts it through the view without the CHECK OPTION, the INSERT is permitted:

```
INSERT dbo.vCapeHatterasTour (TourName, BaseCampID)
   VALUES ('Blue Ridge Parkway Hike', 1);
(1 row(s) affected)
```

The INSERT worked, and the new row is in the database, but the row is not visible through the view because the WHERE clause of the view filters out the inserted row. This phenomenon is called *disappearing rows*:

```
SELECT TourName, BaseCampID FROM dbo.vCapeHatterasTour;

TourName                       BaseCampID
----------------------------- -----------
Outer Banks Lighthouses        2
```

If the purpose of the view were to give users at the Cape access to their tours alone, then the view failed. Although they can see only the Cape's tours, they successfully modified another base camp's tours. The WITH CHECK OPTION would have prevented this fault.

Protecting the data

A view with a WHERE clause and the WITH CHECK OPTION can protect the data from undesired inserts and updates.

The following code will back out the previous INSERT and redo the same scenario, but this time the view will include the WITH CHECK OPTION:

```
DELETE dbo.vCapeHatterasTour
   WHERE TourName = 'Blue Ridge Parkway Hike';
```

```
go
ALTER VIEW dbo.vCapeHatterasTour
   AS
   SELECT TourName, BaseCampID
      FROM dbo.Tour
      WHERE BaseCampID = 2
   WITH CHECK OPTION;
go
INSERT dbo.vCapeHatterasTour (TourName, BaseCampID)
   VALUES ('Blue Ridge Parkway Hike', 1);

Server: Msg 550, Level 16, State 1, Line 1
The attempted insert or update failed because the target view either
specifies WITH CHECK OPTION or spans a view that specifies WITH CHECK
OPTION and one or more rows resulting from the operation did not qualify
under the CHECK OPTION constraint.
The statement has been terminated.
```

This time the INSERT failed and the error message attributed the cause to the WITH CHECK OPTION in the view, which is exactly the effect desired.

Some developers employ views and the WITH CHECK OPTION as a way of providing row-level security — a technique called *horizontally positioned views*. As in the base camp view example, they create a view for each department, or each sales branch, and then give users security permission to the view that pertains to them. While this method does achieve row-level security, it also has a high maintenance cost.

CROSS-REF **For the application, row-level security can be designed using user-access tables and stored procedures, as demonstrated in Chapter 52, "Row-Level Security," but views can help enforce row-level security for ad hoc queries.**

Within Management Studio's View Designer, the WITH CHECK OPTION can be enforced within the View Properties form. There are actually two properties that must be enabled. The first is (Update Using View Rules), which prohibits Management Studio and MDAC from decoding the view and directly accessing the underlying tables. Only when (Update Using View Rules) is enabled can the second option, WITH CHECK OPTION, be enabled.

Protecting the view

Three options protect views from data schema changes and prying eyes. These options are simply added to the CREATE command and applied to the view, in much the same way that the WITH CHECK OPTION is applied.

Database code is fragile and tends to break when the underlying data structure changes. Because views are nothing more than stored SQL SELECT queries, changes to the referenced tables may break the view.

Creating a view with schema binding locks the underlying tables to the view and prevents changes, as demonstrated in the following code sample:

```
CREATE TABLE dbo.Test (
   [Name] NVARCHAR(50)
```

```
    );
go

CREATE VIEW dbo.vTest
WITH SCHEMABINDING
AS
SELECT [Name] FROM dbo.Test;
go

ALTER TABLE Test
   ALTER COLUMN [Name] NVARCHAR(100);
```

Result:

```
Msg 5074, Level 16, State 1, Line 1
The object 'vTest' is dependent on column 'Name'.
Msg 4922, Level 16, State 9, Line 1
ALTER TABLE ALTER COLUMN Name failed because one
or more objects access this column.
```

Some restrictions apply to the creation of schema-bound views. The SELECT statement must include the schema name for any referenced objects, and SELECT all columns (*) is not permitted (but that last requirement shouldn't bother anyone who follows best practices, says Hugo the Tech Editor).

Within Management Studio's View Designer, the WITH SCHEMA BINDING option can be enabled within the View Properties page.

When the schema underlying a view (that is not schema bound) does change, it will likely break the view. If this happens, to repair the view, either recreate it or run the sp_refreshview system stored procedure.

Encrypting the view's select statement

The WITH ENCRYPTION option is another security feature. When views or stored procedures are created, the text can be retrieved through the sys.sql_modules and sys.syscomments system views. The code is therefore available for viewing. The view may contain a WHERE condition that should be kept confidential, or there may be some other reason for encrypting the code. The WITH ENCRYPTION option encrypts the code in the system tables, hides them from sys.sql_modules and sys.syscomments, and prevents anyone from viewing the original code.

In the following code example, the text of the view is inspected within sys.sql_modules, the view is encrypted, and sys.sql_modules is again inspected (as expected, the SELECT statement for the view is then no longer readable):

```
SELECT definition
   FROM sys.sql_modules
   WHERE object_id = OBJECT_ID(N'dbo.vTest');
```

The result is the text of the vText view:

```
definition
-----------------------------
CREATE VIEW vTest
WITH SCHEMABINDING
AS
SELECT [Name] FROM dbo.Test;
```

The following ALTER command rebuilds the view WITH ENCRYPTION:

```
ALTER VIEW vTest
WITH ENCRYPTION
AS
SELECT [Name] FROM dbo.Test;
```

Be careful with this option. Once the code is encrypted, Management Studio can no longer produce a script to alter the view, and will instead generate this message:

```
/****** Encrypted object is not transferable,
and script cannot be generated. ******/
```

In addition, be aware that the encryption affects replication. An encrypted view will not be published.

Application metadata

The front-end application or data access layer may request schema information, called *meta-data*, along with the data when querying SQL Server. Typically, SQL Server returns schema information for the underlying tables, but the WITH VIEW METADATA option tells SQL Server to return schema information about the view, rather than the tables referenced by the view. This prohibits someone from learning about the table's schema and is useful when the view's purpose is to hide sensitive columns.

Using Synonyms

Views are sometimes employed to hide cryptic database schema names. Synonyms are similar to views, but they are more limited. Whereas views can project columns, assign column aliases, and build data using joins and subqueries, synonyms can only assign alternative names to tables, views, and stored procedures.

Synonyms are primarily used to simplify complex object names, particularly with lengthy schema names. A synonym can change HumanResources.EmployeeDepartmentHistory into EmpHist. Which would you rather type 100 times?

Synonyms are part of the SQL standard and are used frequently by Oracle DBAs. Note that Oracle includes both private and public synonyms. SQL Server synonyms are only public. Even though they were introduced to SQL Server with version 2005, I've seen very little acceptance or use of synonyms in the SQL community.

Schemas enhance security and help prevent SQL injection attacks. The hacker needs to guess the schema name as well as the table name. Little Bobby Tables (a standard DBA joke: `http://xkcd.com/327/`) would need to know `myschema.students`. Giving the table `myschema.students` an easy to guess synonym would defeat the purpose of using the schema to prevent SQL injection.

Synonyms can be managed using Object Explorer, or `CREATE` and `DROP` DDL commands.

Summary

Views are nothing more than stored SQL `SELECT` queries. There's no magic in a view. Any valid SQL `SELECT` statement may be saved as a view, including subqueries, complex joins, and aggregate functions.

Views are great for simplifying a complex schema and presenting a more useful picture of the data for power users writing ad hoc queries and reports. Views can simplify complex aggregate queries and hide nasty joins. Any well-planned abstraction layer should include views. My only caution is to not push the view too far. Don't expect to sort data in a view, and don't make views the pillar of the front-end application or website. However, for those who detest views, I suggest that a view is infinitely better than an ad hoc SQL statement that directly hits a table without any abstraction layer.

The previous chapters have discussed retrieving data using the powerful `SELECT` statement. Views store the `SELECT` statement for ad hoc queries. The next chapter continues the discussion of `SELECT`, extending its power by adding data modification verbs.

Chapter 15

Modifying Data

IN THIS CHAPTER

Inserting data from expressions, other result sets, and stored procedures

Updating and deleting data

Mastering the new merge command

Exposing inserted and deleted tables to the DML

Things change. Life moves on. Because the purpose of a database is to accurately represent reality, the data must change along with reality. For SQL programmers, that means inserting, updating, and deleting rows — using the basic data manipulation language (DML) commands. However, these operations aren't limited to writing single rows of data. Working with SQL means thinking in terms of data sets. The process of modifying data with SQL draws on the entire range of SQL Server data-retrieval capabilities — the powerful `SELECT`, joins, full-text searches, subqueries, and views.

This chapter is all about modifying data within SQL Server using the `INSERT`, `UPDATE`, `DELETE`, and `MERGE` SQL commands. Modifying data raises issues that need to be addressed, or at least considered. Inserting surrogate primary keys requires special methods. Table constraints may interfere with the data modification. Referential integrity demands that some `DELETE` operations cascade to other related tables. This chapter will help you understand these concerns and offer some ways to deal with them. Because these potential obstacles affect `INSERT`, `UPDATE`, `MERGE`, and, to some degree, `DELETE`, they are addressed in their own sections after the sections devoted to the individual commands.

CROSS-REF **The ACID database properties (atomic, consistent, isolated, and durable) are critical to the modification of data. For many databases, SQL Server's default transactional control is sufficient. However, misapplied transaction locking and blocking represents one of the top four causes of poor performance. Chapter 66, "Managing Transactions, Locking, and Blocking," digs into SQL Server's architecture and explains how data modifications occur within transactions to meet the ACID requirements, and how SQL Server manages data locks.**

Best Practice

The SQL INSERT, UPDATE, DELETE, and MERGE commands are really verb extensions of the basic SELECT command. The full potential of the SELECT command lies within each data-modification operation. Even when modifying data, you should think in terms of sets, rather than single rows.

Data-modification commands may be submitted to SQL Server from any one of several interfaces. This chapter is concerned more with the strategy and use of the INSERT, UPDATE, DELETE, and MERGE commands than with the interface used to submit a given command to SQL Server.

What's New in Data Modification?

This is an area in which SQL Server 2008 has a few significant new T-SQL features:

- **Row constructors:** Insert multiple rows with a single INSERT...VALUES statement
- **Merge:** Set-based command that can insert, update, or delete for matching or non-matching rows
- **Composable SQL:** Builds on SQL Server 2005's OUTPUT clause and can pass the result of the OUTPUT clause to an outer query. Composable SQL is covered in Chapter 11, "Including Data with Subqueries and CTEs."

SQL Server Management Studio offers two interfaces for submitting SQL commands: Query Designer and Query Editor. If you love a visual UI, then Query Designer may work for a while, but you should migrate to Query Editor to enjoy the richness of T-SQL. I do all my development work exclusively in Query Editor.

CROSS-REF **For more details on using Management Studio's Query Designer and Query Editor, see Chapter 6, "Using Management Studio."**

Inserting Data

SQL offers six forms of INSERT and SELECT/INTO as the primary methods of inserting data (as shown in Table 15-1). The most basic method simply inserts a row of data, while the most complex builds a data set from a complex SELECT statement and creates a table from the result.

Each of these INSERT forms is useful for a unique task, often depending on the source of the data being inserted.

TABLE 15-1

Insert Forms

Insert Form	Description
INSERT/VALUES	Inserts one or more rows of values; commonly used to insert data from a user interface
INSERT/SELECT	Inserts a result set; commonly used to manipulate sets of data
INSERT/EXEC	Inserts the results of a stored procedure; used for complex data manipulation
INSERT/DEFAULT VALUES	Creates a new row with all defaults; used for pre-populating pigeonhole data rows
SELECT/INTO	Creates a new table from the result set of a SELECT statement
MERGE	Combines inserting, updating, and deleting data in a single statement

CROSS-REF **SQL Server complements the SQL `INSERT` commands with other tools to aid in moving large amounts of data or performing complex data conversions. The venerable Bulk Copy Wizard and the Copy Database Wizard are introduced in Chapter 44, "Transferring Databases." The Copy Database Wizard actually creates a simple Integration Services package. Chapter 37, "Performing ETL with Integration Services," details Integration Services, a very powerful tool that can move and manipulate large sets of data between/among nearly any data sources.**

When inserting new data, if the table has surrogate keys, then primary key values must be generated to identify the new rows. While identity columns and GUIDs both make excellent primary keys, each requires special handling during the insertion of rows. This section describes how to create identity-column values and GUIDs.

Inserting simple rows of values

The simplest and most direct method of inserting data is the `INSERT/VALUES` method. Until SQL Server 2008, `INSERT...VALUES` was limited to inserting a single row, but SQL Server is now compliant with the ANSI standard and can include row constructors — inserting multiple rows in a single `INSERT...VALUES` statement:

```
INSERT [INTO] schema.table [(columns, ...)]
  VALUES (value,...), (value,...), ... ;
```

Building an `INSERT...VALUES` statement is mostly straightforward, although you do have a few options. The `INTO` keyword is optional and is commonly ignored. The key to building an `INSERT` statement is getting the columns listed correctly and ensuring that the data type of the value is valid for the inserted column.

When the values are inserted into a new row, each value corresponds to an insert column. The insert columns may be in any order — the order of the columns within the table is irrelevant — as long as the insert columns and the value columns in the SQL INSERT command are in the same order.

CROSS-REF **As with every chapter that includes code, the file** Ch 15 - Modifying Data.sql **on** www.SQLServerBible.com **contains all the sample code for this chapter. Additional examples of data-modification statements may be found in any of the sample database "populate" scripts, or in the stored procedures of the** OBXKites **sample database.**

The following INSERT commands reference the columns in varying order, inserting one row and then multiple rows:

```
USE CHA2

INSERT INTO dbo.Guide (FirstName, LastName)
  VALUES ('Tammie', 'Commer');
INSERT INTO dbo.Guide (LastName, FirstName, Qualifications)
  VALUES
  ('Smith', 'Dan', 'Diver, Whitewater Rafting'),
  ('Jeff', 'Davis', 'Marine Biologist, Diver');
```

The following SELECT command verifies the insert:

```
SELECT GuideID, LastName, FirstName, Qualifications
  FROM dbo.Guide;
```

Result (your result may differ depending on the data loaded into the database):

```
GuideID  LastName    FirstName    Qualifications
-------- ----------  -----------  -----------------------------
1        Smith       Dan          Diver, Whitewater Rafting
2        Davis       Jeff         Marine Biologist, Diver
3        Commer      Tammie       NULL
```

Not every column in the table has to be listed, but if a column appears, then a value has to be available for the INSERT command. The first INSERT statement in the previous sample code omitted the Qualifications column. The INSERT operation worked nonetheless and inserted a NULL into the omitted column.

If the Qualifications column had a default constraint, then the default value would have been inserted instead of the NULL. When a column has both no default and a NOT NULL constraint, and no value is provided in the INSERT statement, the INSERT operation will fail. (For more information about inserting defaults and nulls, see the section "Potential Data-Modification Obstacles" later in this chapter.)

It's possible to explicitly force the INSERT of a default without knowing the default value. If the keyword DEFAULT is provided in the value-column list, then SQL Server will store the default value for the column. This is a good practice because it documents the intention of the code, rather than leaving the code blank and assuming the default. The insert-column list is required when using row constructors to insert multiple rows.

Explicitly listing the columns is a good idea. It prevents an error if the table schema changes, and it helps document the insert. However, the insert-column list is optional. In this case, the values are inserted into the table according to the order of the columns in the table (ignoring an identity column). It's critical that every table column receive valid data from the value list. Omitting a column in the value list causes the INSERT operation to fail.

You learned earlier that when the columns are explicitly listed within the INSERT/VALUES command, an identity column can't receive a value. Similarly, the identity column is also ignored in the value list when the columns are assumed. The rest of the values are in the same order as the columns of the Guide table, as follows:

```
INSERT Guide
  VALUES ('Jones', 'Lauren',
      'First Aid, Rescue/Extraction','19590625','200104415');
```

To view the inserted data, the following SELECT command pulls data from the Guide table:

```
SELECT GuideID, LastName, FirstName, Qualifications
  FROM dbo.Guide;
```

Result:

```
GuideID  LastName   FirstName   Qualifications
-------- ---------- ----------- ----------------------------
1        Smith      Dan         Diver, Whitewater Rafting
2        Davis      Jeff        Marine Biologist, Diver
3        Commer     Tammie      NULL
4        Jones      Lauren      First Aid, Rescue/Extraction
```

So far in the sample code, values have been hard-coded string literals. Alternately, the value could be returned from an expression. This is useful when a data type requires conversion, or when data need to be altered, calculated, or concatenated:

```
INSERT dbo.Guide (FirstName, LastName, Qualifications)
  VALUES ('Greg', 'Wilson',
          'Rock Climbing' + ', ' + 'First Aid');
```

The next SELECT statement verifies Greg's insert:

```
SELECT GuideID, LastName, FirstName, Qualifications
  FROM dbo.Guide;
```

Result:

```
GuideID  LastName   FirstName   Qualifications
-------- ---------- ----------- ----------------------------
1        Smith      Dan         Diver, Whitewater Rafting
2        Davis      Jeff        Marine Biologist, Diver
3        Commer     Tammie      NULL
4        Jones      Lauren      First Aid, Rescue/Extraction
```

```
5        Wilson     Greg        Rock Climbing, First Aid
(5 row(s) affected)
```

When the data to be inserted, usually in the form of variables sent from the user interface, is known, inserting using the INSERT...VALUES form is the best insert method.

Typically, to reference values from a data source, the INSERT...SELECT is used, but an INSERT...VALUES can include a scalar subquery as one of the values.

Inserting a result set from select

Data may be moved and massaged from one result set into a table by means of the INSERT...SELECT statement. The real power of this method is that the SELECT command can pull data from nearly anywhere and reshape it to fit the current needs. It's this flexibility that the INSERT...SELECT statement exploits. Because SELECT can return an infinite number of rows, this form can insert an infinite number of rows.

Of course, the full power of the SELECT can be used to generate rows for the insert. The SELECT can include any clause except ORDER BY. A simplified form of the syntax is as follows:

```
INSERT [INTO] schema.Table [(columns, ...)]
  SELECT columns
    FROM data sources
    [WHERE conditions];
```

As with the INSERT...VALUES statement, the data columns must line up and the data types must be valid. If the optional insert columns are ignored, then every table column (except an identity column) must be populated in the table order.

The following code sample uses the OBXKites database. It selects all the guides from the Cape Hatteras Adventures database and inserts them into the OBXKites Contact table. The name columns are pulled from the Guide table, while the company name is a string literal (note that the Guide table is specified by means of a three-part name, database.schema.table):

```
Use OBXKites
-- Using a fresh copy of OBXKites without population

INSERT dbo.Contact (FirstName, LastName, ContactCode, CompanyName)
  SELECT FirstName, LastName, GuideID, 'Cape Hatteras Adv.'
    FROM CHA2.dbo.Guide;
```

To verify the insert, the following SELECT statement reads the data from the Contact table:

```
SELECT FirstName as First, LastName AS Last, CompanyName
  FROM dbo.Contact;
```

Result:

```
First     Last      CompanyName
--------- --------- ----------------------
Dan       Smith     Cape Hatteras Adv.
```

```
Jeff      Davis    Cape Hatteras Adv.
Tammie    Commer   Cape Hatteras Adv.
Lauren    Jones    Cape Hatteras Adv.
Greg      Wilson   Cape Hatteras Adv.

(5 row(s) affected)
```

The key to using the INSERT/SELECT statement is selecting the correct result set. It's a good idea to run the SELECT statement by itself to test the result set prior to executing the insert. Measure twice, cut once.

Inserting the result set from a stored procedure

The INSERT...EXEC form of the INSERT operation pulls data from a stored procedure and inserts it into a table. Behind these inserts are the full capabilities of T-SQL. The basic function is the same as that of the other insert forms. The columns have to line up between the INSERT columns and the stored-procedure result set. Here's the basic syntax of the INSERT...EXEC command:

```
INSERT [INTO] schema.Table [(Columns)]
  EXEC StoredProcedure Parameters;
```

Be careful, though, because stored procedures can easily return multiple record sets, in which case the INSERT attempts to pull data from each of the result sets, and the columns from every result set must line up with the insert columns.

CROSS-REF **For more about programming stored procedures, refer to Chapter 24, "Developing Stored Procedures."**

The following code sample builds a stored procedure that returns the first and last names of all guides from both the Cape Hatteras Adventures database and Microsoft's Northwind sample database from SQL Server 2000. Next, the code creates a table as a place to insert the result sets. Once the stored procedure and the receiving table are in place, the sample code performs the INSERT...EXEC statement:

```
Use CHA2;

CREATE PROC ListGuides
AS
  SET NOCOUNT ON;
  -- result set 1
  SELECT  FirstName, LastName
    FROM dbo.Guide;
  -- result set 1
  SELECT  FirstName, LastName
    FROM Northwind.dbo.Employees;
  RETURN;
```

When the ListGuides stored procedure is executed, two result sets should be produced:

```
Exec ListGuides;
```

Result:

```
FirstName                 LastName
------------------------- -------------------------
Dan                       Smith
Jeff                      Davis
Tammie                    Commer
Lauren                    Jones
Greg                      Wilson

FirstName  LastName
---------- --------------------
Nancy      Davolio
Andrew     Fuller
Janet      Leverling
Margaret   Peacock
Steven     Buchanan
Michael    Suyama
Robert     King
Laura      Callahan
Anne       Dodsworth
```

The following DDL command creates a table that matches the structure of the procedure's result sets:

```
CREATE TABLE dbo.GuideSample
  (FirstName VARCHAR(50),
  LastName VARCHAR(50),
  CONSTRAINT PK_GuideSample PRIMARY KEY (FirstName, LastName) );
```

With the situation properly set up, here's the INSERT...EXEC command:

```
INSERT dbo.GuideSample (FirstName, LastName)
  Exec ListGuides;
```

A SELECT command can read the data and verify that fourteen rows were inserted:

```
SELECT FirstName, LastName
  FROM dbo.GuideSample;
```

Result:

```
FirstName            LastName
-------------------- --------------------
Dan                  Smith
Jeff                 Davis
Tammie               Commer
```

```
Lauren          Jones
Wilson          Greg
Nancy           Davolio
Andrew          Fuller
Janet           Leverling
Margaret        Peacock
Steven          Buchanan
Michael         Suyama
Robert          King
Laura           Callahan
Anne            Dodsworth
```

INSERT/EXEC does require more work than INSERT/VALUES or INSERT/SELECT, but because the stored procedure can contain complex logic, it's the most powerful of the three.

The INSERT...EXEC and SELECT...INTO forms will not insert data into table variables. Table variables are covered in Chapter 21, "Programming with T-SQL."

Creating a default row

SQL includes a special form of the INSERT command that creates a single new row with only default values. The only parameter of the new row is the table name. Data and column names are not required. The syntax is very simple, as shown here:

```
INSERT schema.Table DEFAULT VALUES;
```

I have never used this form of INSERT in any real-world applications. It could be used to create "pigeon hole" rows with only keys and null values, but I don't recommend that design.

Creating a table while inserting data

The last method of inserting data is a variation on the SELECT command. The INTO select option takes the results of a SELECT statement and creates a new table containing the results. SELECT...INTO is often used during data conversions and within utilities that must dynamically work with a variety of source-table structures. The full syntax includes every SELECT option. Here's an abbreviated syntax to highlight the function of the INTO option:

```
SELECT Columns
  INTO NewTable
  FROM DataSources
  [WHERE conditions];
```

The data structure of the newly created table might be less of an exact replication of the original table structure than expected because the new table structure is based on a combination of the original table and the result set of the SELECT statement. String lengths and numerical digit lengths may change. If the SELECT...INTO command is pulling data from only one table and the SELECT statement contains no data-type conversion functions, then there's a good chance that the table columns and null settings will remain intact. However, keys, constraints, and indexes will be lost.

SELECT...INTO is a bulk-logged operation, similar to BULK INSERT and BULK COPY. Bulk-logged operations may enable SQL Server to quickly move data into tables by minimally recording the bulk-logged operations to the transaction log (depending on the database's recovery model). Therefore, the database options and recovery model affect SELECT...INTO and the other bulk-logged operations.

CROSS-REF **For more about BULK INSERT and BULK COPY, refer to Chapter 30, "Performing Bulk Operations." For details on recovery models, refer to Chapter 41, "Recovery Planning."**

The following code sample demonstrates the SELECT/INTO command as it creates the new table GuideList by extracting data from Guide (some results abridged):

```
USE CHA2;

-- sample code for setting the bulk-logged behavior
ALTER DATABASE CHA2 SET RECOVERY BULK_LOGGED;

-- the select/into statement
SELECT LastName, FirstName
  INTO dbo.GuideList
  FROM dbo.Guide
  ORDER BY Lastname, FirstName;
```

The sp_help system stored procedure can display the structure of a table. Here it is being used to verify the structure that was created by the SELECT/INTO command:

```
EXEC sp_help GuideList;
```

Result (some columns abridged):

```
Name         Owner    Type         Created_datetime
------------ -------- ------------ -----------------------
GuideList    dbo      user table   2001-08-01 16:30:02.937


Column_name       Type       Length    Prec  Scale Nullable
----------------- ---------- --------- ----- ----- --------
GuideID           int        4         10    0      no
LastName          varchar    50                     no
FirstName         varchar    50                     no
Qualifications    varchar    2048                   yes
DateOfBirth       datetime    8                     yes
DateHire          datetime    8                     yes

Identity        Seed     Increment   Not For Replication
--------------- -------- ----------- ---------------------
GuideID         1        1           0

RowGuidCol
----------------------------
No rowguidcol column defined.
```

```
Data_located_on_filegroup
---------------------------
PRIMARY

The object does not have any indexes.

No constraints have been defined for this object.

No foreign keys reference this table.

No views with schema binding reference this table.
```

The following insert adds a new row to test the identity column created by the SELECT/INTO:

```
INSERT Guidelist (LastName, FirstName, Qualifications)
  VALUES('Nielsen', 'Paul', 'trainer');
```

To view the data that was inserted using the SELECT/INTO command and the row that was just added with the INSERT/VALUES command, the following SELECT statement extracts data from the GuideList table:

```
SELECT GuideID, LastName, FirstName
  FROM dbo.GuideList;
```

Result:

```
GuideID     LastName     FirstName
----------- ------------ --------------------------
12          Nielsen      Paul
7           Atlas        Sue
11          Bistier      Arnold
3           Commer       Tammie
2           Davis        Jeff
10          Fletcher     Bill
5           Greg         Wilson
4           Jones        Lauren
1           Smith        Dan
```

In this case, the SELECT/INTO command retained the column lengths and null settings. The identity column was also carried over to the new table, although this may not always be the case. I recommend that you build tables manually, or at least carefully check the data structures created by SELECT/INTO.

SELECT/INTO can serve many useful functions:

- If zero rows are selected from a table, then SELECT/INTO will create a new table with only the data schema (though with the limitations listed earlier).
- If SELECT reorders the columns, or includes the cast() function, then the new table will retain the data within a modified data schema.

- When combined with a UNION query, SELECT/INTO can combine data from multiple tables vertically. The INTO goes in the first SELECT statement of a UNION query.
- SELECT/INTO is especially useful for denormalizing tables. The SELECT statement can pull from multiple tables and create a new flat-file table.

CAUTION **Note one caveat concerning SELECT/INTO and development style: The SELECT/INTO statement should not replace the use of joins or views. When the new table is created, it's a snapshot in time — a second copy of the data. Databases containing multiple copies of old data sets are a sure sign of trouble. If you need to denormalize data for ad hoc analysis, or to pass to a user, then creating a view is likely a better alternative.**

Developing a Data Style Guide

There are potential data troubles that go beyond data types, nullability, and check constraints. Just as MS Word's spelling checker and grammar checker can weed out the obvious errors but also create poor (or libelous) literature, a database can protect against only gross logical errors. Publishers use manuals of style and style guides for consistency. For example, should Microsoft be referred to as MS, Microsoft Corp., or Microsoft Corporation in a book or article? The publisher's chosen style manual provides the answer.

Databases can also benefit from a data style guide that details your organization's preferences about how data should be formatted. Do phone numbers include parentheses around the area codes? Are phone extensions indicated by "x." or "ext."?

One way to begin developing a style guide is to spend some time just looking at the data and observing the existing inconsistencies. Then, try to reach a consensus about a common data style. *The Chicago Manual of Style* is a good source for ideas. There's no magical right or wrong style — the goal is simply data consistency.

Updating Data

SQL's UPDATE command is an incredibly powerful tool. What used to take dozens of lines of code with multiple nested loops now takes a single statement. Even better, SQL is not a true command language — it's a declarative language. The SQL code is only describing to the Query Optimizer what you want to do. The Query Optimizer then develops a cost-based, optimized query execution plan to accomplish the task. It determines which tables to fetch and in which order, how to merge the joins, and which indexes to use. It does this based on several factors, including the current data-population statistics, the indexes available and how they relate to the data population within the table, and table sizes. The Query Optimizer even considers current CPU performance, memory capacity, and hard-drive performance when designing the plan. Writing code to perform the update row by row could never result in that level of optimization.

Updating a single table

The UPDATE command in SQL is straightforward and simple. It can update one column of one row in a table, or every column in every row in the updated table, but the optional FROM clause enables that table to be part of a complete complex data source with all the power of the SQL SELECT.

Here's how the UPDATE command works:

```
UPDATE schema.Table
  SET column = expression,
    column = value...
  [FROM  data sources]
  [WHERE conditions];
```

The UPDATE command can update multiple rows, but only one table. The SET keyword is used to modify data in any column in the table to a new value. The new value can be a hard-coded string literal, a variable, an expression, or even another column from the data sources listed in the FROM portion of the SQL UPDATE statement.

CROSS-REF **For a comprehensive list of expression possibilities, see Chapter 9, "Data Types, Expressions, and Scalar Functions."**

The WHERE clause is vital to any UPDATE statement. Without it, the entire table is updated. If a WHERE clause is present, then only the rows not filtered out by the WHERE clause are updated. Be sure to check and double-check the WHERE clause. Again, measure twice, cut once.

The following sample UPDATE resembles a typical real-life operation, altering the value of one column for a single row. The best way to perform a single-row update is to filter the UPDATE operation by referencing the primary key:

```
USE CHA2;

UPDATE dbo.Guide
  SET Qualifications = 'Spelunking, Cave Diving,
First Aid, Navigation'
  Where GuideID = 6;
```

The following SELECT statement confirms the preceding UPDATE command:

```
SELECT GuideID, LastName, Qualifications
  FROM dbo.Guide
  WHERE GuideID = 6;
```

Result:

```
GuideID     LastName               Qualifications
----------- ---------------------- ---------------
6           Bistier                Spelunking, Cave Diving,
                                      First Aid, Navigation
```

Performing global search and replace

Cleaning up bad data is a common database developer task. Fortunately, SQL includes a REPLACE() function, which when combined with the UPDATE command can serve as a global search and replace. I've used this to remove extra tabs from data.

In the following example, which references the Family sample database, every occurrence of "ll" in the LastName column is updated to "qua":

```
Use Family;

Update Person
  Set LastName = Replace(LastName, 'll', 'qua');
```

The following SELECT statement examines the result of the REPLACE() function:

```
Select LastName from Person;
```

Result (abbreviated):

```
lastname
---------------
Haquaoway
Haquaoway
Miquaer
Miquaer
Haquaoway
...
```

Referencing multiple tables while updating data

A more powerful function of the SQL UPDATE command is setting a column to an expression that can refer to the same column, other columns, or even other tables.

While expressions are certainly available within a single-table update, expressions often need to reference data outside the updated table. The optional FROM clause enables joins between the table being updated and other data sources. Only one table can be updated, but when the table is joined to the corresponding rows from the joined tables, the data from the other columns is available within the UPDATE expressions.

One way to envision the FROM clause is to picture the joins merging all the tables into a new super-wide result set. Then the rest of the SQL statement sees only that new result set. While that is what's happening in the FROM clause, the actual UPDATE operation is functioning not on the new result set, but only on the declared UPDATE table.

The following query uses the FROM clause to access the Contact and Order tables. The JOIN limits the query to only those contact rows that have placed orders. The UPDATE command updates only the Contact table:

```
USE OBXKites
```

```
UPDATE dbo.Contact
  SET IsCustomer = 1
  FROM dbo.Contact AS C
    JOIN dbo.[Order] AS O
      ON C.ContactID = O.ContactID
```

CAUTION **The UPDATE FROM syntax is a T-SQL extension and not standard ANSI SQL 92. If the database will possibly be ported to another database platform in the future, then use a subquery to select the correct rows:**

```
UPDATE dbo.Contact
  SET IsCustomer = 1
  WHERE ContactID
    IN (SELECT ContactID
          FROM dbo.[Order])
```

For a real-life example, suppose all employees will soon be granted a generous across-the-board raise (OK, so it's not a real-life example) based on department, length of service in the position, performance rating, and length of time with the company. If the percentage for each department is stored in the Department table, SQL can adjust the salary for every employee with a single UPDATE statement by joining the Employee table with the Department table and pulling the Department raise factor from the joined table. Assume the formula is as follows:

```
2 + (((Years in Company * .1) + (Months in Position * .02)
  + ((PerformanceFactor * .5 ) if over 2))
  * Department RaiseFactor)
```

The sample code sets up the scenario by creating a couple of tables and populating them with test data:

```
USE tempdb

CREATE TABLE dbo.Dept (
   DeptID INT IDENTITY
              NOT NULL
              PRIMARY KEY,
   DeptName VARCHAR(50) NOT NULL,
   RaiseFactor NUMERIC(4, 2)
  )

CREATE  TABLE dbo.Employee (
   EmployeeID INT IDENTITY
                  NOT NULL
                  PRIMARY KEY,
   DeptID INT FOREIGN KEY REFERENCES Dept,
   LastName VARCHAR(50) NOT NULL,
   FirstName VARCHAR(50) NOT NULL,
   Salary NUMERIC(9,2) NOT NULL,
   PerformanceRating NUMERIC(4,2) NOT NULL,
   DateHire DATE NOT NULL,
```

```
    DatePosition DATE NOT NULL
   )

INSERT dbo.Dept (DeptName, RaiseFactor)
  VALUES ('Engineering', 1.2),
         ('Sales', .8),
         ('IT', 2.5),
         ('Manufacturing', 1.0) ;

INSERT dbo.Employee (DeptID, LastName, FirstName,
        Salary, PerformanceRating, DateHire, DatePosition)
  VALUES (1, 'Smith', 'Sam', 54000, 2.0, '19970101', '19970101'),
         (1, 'Nelson', 'Slim', 78000, 1.5, '19970101', '19970101'),
         (2, 'Ball', 'Sally', 45000, 3.5, '19990202', '19990202'),
         (2, 'Kelly', 'Jeff', 85000, 2.4, '20020625', '20020625'),
         (3, 'Guelzow', 'Jo', 120000, 4.0, '19991205', '19991205'),
         (3, 'Ander', 'Missy', 95000, 1.8, '19980201', '19980201'),
         (4, 'Reagan', 'Sam', 75000, 2.9, '20051215', '20051215'),
         (4, 'Adams', 'Hank', 34000, 3.2, '20080501', '20080501');
```

When developing complex queries, I work from the inside out. The first step performs the date math; it selects the data required for the raise calculation, assuming June 25, 2009, is the effective date of the raise, and ensures the performance rating won't count if it's only 1:

```
SELECT EmployeeID, Salary,
    CAST(CAST(DATEDIFF(d, DateHire, '20090625')
          AS DECIMAL(7, 2)) / 365.25 AS INT)
      AS YrsCo,
    CAST(CAST(DATEDIFF(d, DatePosition, '20090625')
          AS DECIMAL(7, 2)) / 365.25
          * 12 AS INT)
      AS MoPos,
    CASE WHEN Employee.PerformanceRating >= 2
           THEN Employee.PerformanceRating
           ELSE 0
    END AS Perf,
    Dept.RaiseFactor
  FROM dbo.Employee
    JOIN dbo.Dept
      ON Employee.DeptID = Dept.DeptID
```

Result:

```
EmployeeID  Salary      YrsCo MoPos  Perf   RaiseFactor
----------- ---------- ----- ------ ------ -------------
1           54000.00    12    149    2.00   1.20
2           78000.00    12    149    0.00   1.20
3           45000.00    10    124    3.50   0.80
```

```
4           85000.00  7    84    2.40   0.80
5           120000.00 9    114   4.00   2.50
6           95000.00  11   136   0.00   2.50
7           75000.00  4    42    2.90   1.00
8           34000.00  1    13    3.20   1.00
```

The next step in developing this query is to add the raise calculation. The simplest way to see the calculation is to pull the values already generated from a subquery:

```
SELECT EmployeeID,  Salary,
    (2 + ((YearsCompany * .1) + (MonthPosition * .02)
     + (Performance * .5)) * RaiseFactor) / 100 AS EmpRaise
  FROM (SELECT EmployeeID, FirstName, LastName, Salary,
            CAST(CAST(DATEDIFF(d, DateHire, '20090625') AS
            DECIMAL(7, 2)) / 365.25 AS INT) AS YearsCompany,
            CAST(CAST(DATEDIFF(d, DatePosition, '20090625') AS
            DECIMAL(7, 2)) / 365.25 * 12 AS INT) AS MonthPosition,
            CASE WHEN Employee.PerformanceRating >= 2
                 THEN Employee.PerformanceRating
                 ELSE 0
            END AS Performance, Dept.RaiseFactor
          FROM dbo.Employee
            JOIN dbo.Dept
              ON Employee.DeptID = Dept.DeptID) AS SubQuery
```

Result:

```
EmployeeID  Salary       EmpRaise
----------- ------------ ---------------
1           54000.00     0.082160000
2           78000.00     0.070160000
3           45000.00     0.061840000
4           85000.00     0.048640000
5           120000.00    0.149500000
6           95000.00     0.115500000
7           75000.00     0.046900000
8           34000.00     0.039600000
```

The last query was relatively easy to read, but there's no logical reason for the subquery. The query could be rewritten combining the date calculations and the case expression into the raise formula:

```
SELECT EmployeeID, Salary,
    (2 +
    -- years with company
    + ((CAST(CAST(DATEDIFF(d, DateHire, '20090625')
         AS DECIMAL(7, 2)) / 365.25 AS INT) * .1)
    -- months in position
    + (CAST(CAST(DATEDIFF(d, DatePosition, '20090625')
         AS DECIMAL(7, 2)) / 365.25 * 12 AS INT) * .02)
```

```
    -- Performance Rating minimum
    + (CASE WHEN Employee.PerformanceRating >= 2
            THEN Employee.PerformanceRating
          ELSE 0
      END * .5))
    -- Raise Factor
     * RaiseFactor) / 100 AS EmpRaise
  FROM dbo.Employee
    JOIN dbo.Dept
      ON Employee.DeptID = Dept.DeptID
```

It's easy to verify that this query gets the same result, but which is the better query? From a performance perspective, both queries generate the exact same query execution plan. When considering maintenance and readability, I'd probably go with the second query carefully formatted and commented.

The final step is to convert the query into an `UPDATE` command. The hard part is already done — it just needs the `UPDATE` verb at the front of the query:

```
UPDATE Employee
  SET Salary = Salary *
    (1 + ((2
    -- years with company
    + ((CAST(CAST(DATEDIFF(d, DateHire, '20090625')
        AS DECIMAL(7, 2)) / 365.25 AS INT) * .1)
    -- months in position
    + (CAST(CAST(DATEDIFF(d, DatePosition, '20090625')
        AS DECIMAL(7, 2)) / 365.25 * 12 AS INT) * .02)
    -- Performance Rating minimum
    + (CASE WHEN Employee.PerformanceRating >= 2
            THEN Employee.PerformanceRating
          ELSE 0
      END * .5))
    -- Raise Factor
     * RaiseFactor) / 100 ))
  FROM dbo.Employee
    JOIN dbo.Dept
      ON Employee.DeptID = Dept.DeptID
```

A quick check of the data confirms that the update was successful:

```
SELECT FirstName, LastName, Salary
  FROM dbo.Employee
```

Result:

```
FirstName    LastName      Salary
------------ ------------- -----------
Sam          Smith         58436.64
```

```
Slim          Nelson        83472.48
Sally         Ball          47782.80
Jeff          Kelly         89134.40
Jo            Guelzow       137940.00
Missy         Anderson      105972.50
Sam           Reagan        78517.50
Hank          Adams         35346.40
```

The final step of the exercise is to clean up the sample tables:

```
DROP TABLE dbo.Employee, dbo.Dept;
```

This sample code pulls together techniques from many of the previous chapters: creating and dropping tables, CASE expressions, joins, and date scalar functions, not to mention the inserts and updates from this chapter. The example is long because it demonstrates more than just the UPDATE statement. It also shows the typical process of developing a complex UPDATE, which includes the following:

1. **Checking the available data:** The first SELECT joins employee and dept, and lists all the columns required for the formula.
2. **Testing the formula:** The second SELECT is based on the initial SELECT and assembles the formula from the required rows. From this data, a couple of rows can be hand-tested against the specs, and the formula verified.
3. **Performing the update:** Once the formula is constructed and verified, the formula is edited into an UPDATE statement and executed.

The SQL UPDATE command *is* powerful. I have replaced terribly complex record sets and nested loops that were painfully slow and error-prone with UPDATE statements and creative joins that worked well, and I have seen execution times reduced from hours to a few seconds. I cannot overemphasize the importance of approaching the selection and updating of data in terms of data sets, rather than data rows.

Deleting Data

The DELETE command is dangerously simple. In its basic form, it deletes all the rows from a table. Because the DELETE command is a row-based operation, it doesn't require specifying any column names. The first FROM is optional, as are the second FROM and the WHERE conditions. However, although the WHERE clause is optional, it is the primary subject of concern when you're using the DELETE command. Here's an abbreviated syntax for the DELETE command:

```
DELETE [FROM] schema.Table
  [FROM data sources]
  [WHERE condition(s)];
```

Notice that everything is optional except the actual DELETE command and the table name. The following command would delete all data from the Product table — no questions asked and no second chances:

```
DELETE
  FROM OBXKites.dbo.Product;
```

SQL Server has no inherent "undo" command. Once a transaction is committed, that's it. That's why the WHERE clause is so important when you're deleting.

By far, the most common use of the DELETE command is to delete a single row. The primary key is usually the means of selecting the row:

```
USE OBXKites;
DELETE FROM dbo.Product
  WHERE ProductID = 'DB8D8D60-76F4-46C3-90E6-A8648F63C0F0';
```

Referencing multiple data sources while deleting

There are two techniques for referencing multiple data sources while deleting rows: the double FROM clause and subqueries.

The UPDATE command uses the FROM clause to join the updated table with other tables for more flexible row selection. The DELETE command can use the exact same technique. When using this method, the first optional FROM can make it look confusing. To improve readability and consistency, I recommend that you omit the first FROM in your code.

For example, the following DELETE statement ignores the first FROM clause and uses the second FROM clause to join Product with ProductCategory so that the WHERE clause can filter the DELETE based on the ProductCategoryName. This query removes all videos from the Product table:

```
DELETE dbo.Product
  FROM dbo.Product
  JOIN dbo.ProductCategory
    ON Product.ProductCategoryID
      = ProductCategory.ProductCategoryID
  WHERE ProductCategory.ProductCategoryName = 'Video';
```

The second method looks more complicated at first glance, but it's ANSI standard and the preferred method. A correlated subquery actually selects the rows to be deleted, and the DELETE command just picks up those rows for the delete operation. It's a very clean query:

```
DELETE FROM dbo.Product
  WHERE EXISTS
    (SELECT *
       FROM dbo.ProductCategory AS pc
       WHERE pc.ProductCategoryID = Product.ProductCategoryID
         AND pc.ProductCategoryName = 'Video');
```

It terms of performance, both methods generate the exact same query execution plan.

CAUTION **As with the UPDATE command's FROM clause, the DELETE command's second FROM clause is not an ANSI SQL standard. If portability is important to your project, then use a subquery to reference additional tables.**

Cascading deletes

Referential integrity (RI) refers to the idea that no secondary row foreign key should point to a primary row primary key unless that primary row does in fact exist. This means that an attempt to delete a primary row will fail if a foreign-key value somewhere points to that primary row.

CROSS-REF **For more information about referential integrity and when to use it, turn to Chapter 3, "Relational Database Design," and Chapter 20, "Creating the Physical Database Schema."**

When implemented correctly, referential integrity will block any delete operation that would result in a foreign key value without a corresponding primary key value. The way around this is to first delete the secondary rows that point to the primary row, and then delete the primary row. This technique is called a *cascading delete*. In a complex database schema, the cascade might bounce down several levels before working its way back up to the original row being deleted.

There are two ways to implement a cascading delete: manually with triggers or automatically with *declared referential integrity (DRI)* via foreign keys.

Implementing cascading deletes manually is a lot of work. Triggers are significantly slower than foreign keys (which are checked as part of the query execution plan), and trigger-based cascading deletes usually also handle the foreign key checks. While this was commonplace a decade ago, today trigger-based cascading deletes are very rare and might only be needed with a very complex nonstandard foreign key design that includes business rules in the foreign key. If you're doing that, then you're either very new at this or very, very good.

Fortunately, SQL Server offers cascading deletes as a function of the foreign key. Cascading deletes may be enabled via Management Studio, in the Foreign Key Relationship dialog, or in SQL code.

The sample script that creates the Cape Hatteras Adventures version 2 database (CHA2_Create.sql) provides a good example of setting the cascade-delete option for referential integrity. In this case, if either the event or the guide is deleted, then the rows in the event-guide many-to-many table are also deleted. The ON DELETE CASCADE foreign-key option is what actually specifies the cascade action:

```
CREATE TABLE dbo.Event_mm_Guide (
  EventGuideID
    INT IDENTITY NOT NULL PRIMARY KEY,
  EventID
    INT NOT NULL
    FOREIGN KEY REFERENCES dbo.Event ON DELETE CASCADE,
  GuideID
    INT NOT NULL
    FOREIGN KEY REFERENCES dbo.Guide ON DELETE CASCADE,
  LastName
```

```
    VARCHAR(50) NOT NULL,
  )
  ON [PRIMARY];
```

As a caution, cascading deletes, or even referential integrity, are not suitable for every relationship. It depends on the permanence of the secondary row. If deleting the primary row makes the secondary row moot or meaningless, then cascading the delete makes good sense; but if the secondary row is still a valid row after the primary row is deleted, then referential integrity and cascading deletes would cause the database to break its representation of reality.

As an example of determining the usefulness of cascading deletes from the `Cape Hatteras Adventures` database, consider that if a tour is deleted, then all scheduled events for that tour become meaningless, as do the many-to-many schedule tables between event and customer, and between event and guide. Conversely, a tour must have a base camp, so referential integrity is required on the `Tour.BaseCampID` foreign key. However, if a base camp is deleted, then the tours originating from that base camp might still be valid (if they can be rescheduled to another base camp), so cascading a base-camp delete down to the tour is not a reasonable action. If RI is on and cascading deletes are off, then a base camp with tours cannot be deleted until all tours for that base camp are either manually deleted or reassigned to other base camps.

Alternatives to physically deleting data

Some database developers choose to completely avoid deleting data. Instead, they build systems to remove the data from the user's view while retaining the data for safekeeping (like `dBase][` did) . This can be done in several different ways:

- A logical-delete `bit` flag, or nullable `MomentDeleted` column, in the row can indicate that the row is deleted. This makes deleting or restoring a single row a straightforward matter of setting or clearing a bit. However, because a relational database involves multiple related tables, there's more work to it than that. All queries must check the logical-delete flag and filter out logically deleted rows. This means that a bit column (with extremely poor selectivity) is probably an important index for every query. While SQL Server 2008's new filtered indexes are a perfect fit, it's still a performance killer.
- To make matters worse, because the rows still physically exist in SQL Server, and SQL Server's declarative referential integrity does not know about the logical-delete flag, custom referential integrity and cascading of logical delete flags are also required. Restoring, or undeleting, cascaded logical deletes can become a nightmare.
- The cascading logical deletes method is complex to code and difficult to maintain. This is a case of complexity breeding complexity, and I no longer recommend this method.
- Another alternative to physically deleting rows is to archive the deleted rows in an archive or audit table. This method is best implemented by an `INSTEAD OF` trigger that copies the data to the alternative location and then physically deletes the rows from the production database.
- This method offers several advantages. Data is physically removed from the database, so there's no need to artificially modify `SELECT` queries or index on a bit column. Physically removing the data enables SQL Server referential integrity to remain in effect. In addition, the database is not burdened with unnecessary data. Retrieving archived data remains relatively straightforward and can be easily accomplished with a view that selects data from the archive location.

CROSS-REF Chapter 53, "Data Audit Triggers," details how to automatically generate the audit system discussed here that stores, views, and recovers deleted rows.

Merging Data

An *upsert* operation is a logical combination of an insert and an update. If the data isn't already in the table, the upsert inserts the data; if the data is already in the table, then the upsert updates with the differences. Ignoring for a moment the new MERGE command in SQL Server 2008, there are a few ways to code an upsert operation with T-SQL:

- The most common method is to attempt to locate the data with an IF EXISTS; and if the row was found, UPDATE, otherwise INSERT.
- If the most common use case is that the row exists and the UPDATE was needed, then the best method is to do the update, and if @@RowCount = 0, then the row was new and the insert should be performed.
- If the overwhelming use case is that the row would be new to the database, then TRY to INSERT the new row; if a unique index blocked the INSERT and fired an error, then CATCH the error and UPDATE instead.

All three methods are potentially obsolete with the new MERGE command. The MERGE command is very well done by Microsoft — it solves a complex problem well with a clean syntax and good performance.

First, it's called "merge" because it does more than an upsert. Upsert only inserts or updates; merge can be directed to insert, update, and delete all in one command.

In a nutshell, MERGE sets up a join between the source table and the target table, and can then perform operations based on matches between the two tables.

To walk through a merge scenario, the following example sets up an airline flight check-in scenario. The main work table is FlightPassengers, which holds data about reservations. It's updated as travelers check in, and by the time the flight takes off, it has the actual final passenger list and seat assignments. In the sample scenario, four passengers are scheduled to fly SQL Server Airlines flight 2008 (Denver to Seattle) on March 1, 2008. Poor Jerry, he has a middle seat on the last row of the plane — the row that doesn't recline:

```
USE tempdb;

-- Merge Target Table
CREATE TABLE FlightPassengers (
   FlightID INT NOT NULL
                IDENTITY
                PRIMARY KEY,
   LastName VARCHAR(50) NOT NULL,
   FirstName VARCHAR(50) NOT NULL,
   FlightCode CHAR(6) NOT NULL,
   FlightDate DATE NOT NULL,
   Seat CHAR(3) NOT NULL
```

```
  );

INSERT FlightPassengers
         (LastName, FirstName, FlightCode, FlightDate, Seat)
  VALUES ('Nielsen', 'Paul', 'SS2008', '20090301', '9F'),
         ('Jenkins', 'Sue', 'SS2008', '20090301', '7A'),
         ('Smith', 'Sam', 'SS2008', '20090301', '19A'),
         ('Nixon', 'Jerry', 'SS2008', '20090301', '29B');
```

The day of the flight, the check-in counter records all the passengers as they arrive, and their seat assignments, in the CheckIn table. One passenger doesn't show, a new passenger buys a ticket, and Jerry decides today is a good day to burn an upgrade coupon:

```
-- Merge Source table
CREATE TABLE CheckIn (
   LastName VARCHAR(50),
   FirstName VARCHAR(50),
   FlightCode CHAR(6),
   FlightDate DATE,
   Seat CHAR(3)
  );

INSERT CheckIn (LastName, FirstName, FlightCode, FlightDate, Seat)
  VALUES ('Nielsen', 'Paul', 'SS2008', '20090301', '9F'),
         ('Jenkins', 'Sue', 'SS2008', '20090301', '7A'),
         ('Nixon', 'Jerry', 'SS2008', '20090301', '2A'),
         ('Anderson', 'Missy', 'SS2008', '20090301', '4B');
```

Before the MERGE command is executed, the next three queries look for differences in the data. The first set-difference query returns any no-show passengers. A LEFT OUTER JOIN between the FlightPassengers and CheckIn tables finds every passenger with a reservation joined with their CheckIn row if the row is available. If no CheckIn row is found, then the LEFT OUTER JOIN fills in the CheckIn column with nulls. Filtering for the null returns only those passengers who made a reservation but didn't make the flight:

```
-- NoShows
SELECT F.FirstName + ' ' + F.LastName AS Passenger, F.Seat
  FROM FlightPassengers AS F
    LEFT OUTER JOIN CheckIn AS C
      ON C.LastName = F.LastName
         AND C.FirstName = F.FirstName
         AND C.FlightCode = F.FlightCode
         AND C.FlightDate = F.FlightDate
  WHERE C.LastName IS NULL
```

Result:

```
Passenger                    Seat
---------------------------- -------
Sam Smith                    19A
```

The walk-up check-in query uses a LEFT OUTER JOIN and an IS NULL in the WHERE clause to locate any passengers who are in the CheckIn table but not in the FlightPassenger table:

```
-- Walk Up CheckIn
SELECT C.FirstName + ' ' + C.LastName AS Passenger, C.Seat
  FROM CheckIn AS C
    LEFT OUTER JOIN FlightPassengers AS F
      ON C.LastName = F.LastName
         AND C.FirstName = F.FirstName
         AND C.FlightCode = F.FlightCode
         AND C.FlightDate = F.FlightDate
  WHERE F.LastName IS NULL
```

Result:

```
Passenger                    Seat
---------------------------- -------
Missy Anderson               4B
```

The last difference query lists any seat changes, including Jerry's upgrade to first class. This query uses an inner join because it's searching for passengers who both had previous seat assignments and now are boarding with a seat assignment. The query compares the seat columns from the FlightPassenger and CheckIn tables using a not equal comparison, which finds any passengers with a different seat than previously assigned. Go Jerry!

```
-- Seat Changes
SELECT C.FirstName + ' ' + C.LastName AS Passenger, F.Seat AS
    'previous seat', C.Seat AS 'final seat'
  FROM CheckIn AS C
    INNER JOIN FlightPassengers AS F
      ON C.LastName = F.LastName
         AND C.FirstName = F.FirstName
         AND C.FlightCode = F.FlightCode
         AND C.FlightDate = F.FlightDate
         AND C.Seat <> F.Seat
  WHERE F.Seat IS NOT NULL
```

Result:

```
Passenger                    previous seat  final seat
---------------------------- -------------- ----------
Jerry Nixon                  29B            2A
```

CAUTION **For another explanation of set difference queries, flip over to Chapter 10, "Merging Data with Joins and Unions."**

With the scenario's data in place and verified with set-difference queries, it's time to merge the check-in data into the FlightPassenger table.

The first section of the merge query identifies the target and source tables and how they relate. Following the table definition, there's an optional clause for each match combination, as shown in this simplified syntax:

```
MERGE TargetTable
  USING SourceTable
    ON join conditions
  [WHEN Matched
    THEN DML]
  [WHEN NOT MATCHED BY TARGET
    THEN DML]
  [WHEN NOT MATCHED BY SOURCE
    THEN DML]
```

Applying the MERGE command to the airline check-in scenario, there's an appropriate action for each match combination:

- If the row is in both FlightPassengers (the target) and CheckIn (the source), then the target is updated with the CheckIn table's seat column.
- If the row is present in CheckIn (the source) but there's no match in FlightPassenger (the target), then the row from CheckIn is inserted into FlightPassenger. Note that the data from the source table is gathered by the INSERT command using INSERT...VALUES.
- If the row is present in FlightPassenger (the target), but there's no match in CheckIn (the source), then the row is deleted from FlightPassenger. Note that the DELETE command deletes from the target and does not require a WHERE clause because the rows are filtered by the MERGE command.

Here's the complete working MERGE command for the scenario:

```
MERGE FlightPassengers F
  USING CheckIn C
  ON C.LastName = F.LastName
    AND C.FirstName = F.FirstName
    AND C.FlightCode = F.FlightCode
    AND C.FlightDate = F.FlightDate
  WHEN Matched
    THEN UPDATE
          SET F.Seat = C.Seat
  WHEN NOT MATCHED BY TARGET
    THEN INSERT (FirstName, LastName, FlightCode, FlightDate, Seat)
          VALUES (FirstName, LastName, FlightCode, FlightDate, Seat)
  WHEN NOT MATCHED BY SOURCE
    THEN DELETE ;
```

The next query looks at the results of the MERGE command, returning the finalized passenger list for SQL Server Airlines flight 2008:

```
SELECT FlightID, FirstName, LastName, FlightCode, FlightDate, Seat
  FROM FlightPassengers
```

Result:

```
FlightID   FirstName   LastName  FlightCode   FlightDate Seat
---------- ----------- --------- ------------ ---------- ----
1          Paul        Nielsen   SS2008       2009-03-01 9F
2          Sue         Jenkins   SS2008       2009-03-01 7A
4          Jerry       Nixon     SS2008       2009-03-01 2A
5          Missy       Anderson  SS2008       2009-03-01 4B
```

MERGE has a few specific rules:

- It must be terminated by a semicolon.
- The rows must match one-to-one. One-to-many matches are not permitted.
- The join conditions must be deterministic, meaning they are repeatable.

Returning Modified Data

SQL Server can optionally return the modified data as a data set for further use. This can be useful to perform more work on the modified data, or to return the data to the front-end application to eliminate an extra round-trip to the server.

The OUTPUT clause can access the inserted and deleted virtual tables, as well as any data source referenced in the FROM clause, to select the data to be returned. Normally used only by triggers, inserted and deleted virtual tables contain the before and after views to the transaction. The deleted virtual table stores the old data, and the inserted virtual table stores the newly inserted or updated data.

For more examples of the inserted and deleted table, turn to Chapter 26, "Creating DML Triggers."

Returning data from an insert

The INSERT command makes the inserted virtual table available. The following example, taken from earlier in this chapter, has been edited to include the OUTPUT clause. The inserted virtual table has a picture of the new data being inserted and returns the data:

```
USE CHA2;
INSERT dbo.Guidelist (LastName, FirstName, Qualifications)
  OUTPUT Inserted.*
  VALUES('Nielsen', 'Paul','trainer');
```

Result:

```
GuideID    LastName    FirstName    Qualifications   DateOfBirth   DateHire
---------- ----------- ------------ ---------------- ------------- --------
12         Nielsen     Paul         trainer          NULL          NULL
```

Best Practice

An excellent application of the OUTPUT clause within an INSERT is returning the values of newly created surrogate keys. The identity_scope() function returns the last single identity inserted, but it can't return a set of new identity values. There is no function to return the GUID value just created by a newsequentialid() default. However, the OUTPUT clause returns sets of new surrogate keys regardless of their data type. You can almost think of the INSERT...OUTPUT as a scope_GUID() function or a set-based scope_identity().

Returning data from an update

The OUTPUT clause also works with updates and can return the before and after picture of the data. In this example, the deleted virtual table is being used to grab the original value, while the inserted virtual table stores the new updated value. Only the Qualifications column is returned:

```
USE CHA2;
UPDATE dbo.Guide
  SET Qualifications = 'Scuba'
  OUTPUT Deleted.Qualifications as OldQuals, Inserted.Qualifications as
  NewQuals Where GuideID = 3;
```

Result:

```
OldQuals                NewQuals
----------------------- --------------------------
NULL                    Scuba
```

Returning data from a delete

When deleting data, only the deleted table has any useful data to return:

```
DELETE dbo.Guide
  OUTPUT Deleted.GuideID, Deleted.LastName, Deleted.FirstName
  WHERE GuideID = 3;
```

Result:

```
GuideID     LastName        FirstName
----------- --------------- -------------
5           Wilson          Greg
```

Returning data from a merge

The MERGE command can return data using the OUTPUT clause as well. A twist is that the MERGE command adds a column, $action, to identify whether the row was inserted, updated, or deleted from the target table. The next query adds the OUTPUT clause to the previous MERGE command:

```
MERGE FlightPassengers F
  USING CheckIn C
  ON C.LastName = F.LastName
    AND C.FirstName = F.FirstName
    AND C.FlightCode = F.FlightCode
    AND C.FlightDate = F.FlightDate
  WHEN MATCHED
    THEN UPDATE
          SET F.Seat = C.Seat
  WHEN NOT MATCHED BY TARGET
    THEN INSERT (FirstName, LastName, FlightCode, FlightDate, Seat)
          VALUES (FirstName, LastName, FlightCode, FlightDate, Seat)
  WHEN NOT MATCHED BY SOURCE
    THEN DELETE
  OUTPUT
    deleted.FlightID, deleted.LastName, Deleted.Seat,
    $action,
    inserted.FlightID, inserted.LastName, inserted.Seat ;
```

Result:

```
FlightID  LastName  Seat  $action  FlightID  LastName  Seat
--------- --------- ----- -------- --------- --------- ----
NULL      NULL      NULL  INSERT   5         Anderson  4B
1         Nielsen   9F    UPDATE   1         Nielsen   9F
2         Jenkins   7A    UPDATE   2         Jenkins   7A
3         Smith     2A    DELETE   NULL      NULL      NULL
4         Nixon     29B   UPDATE   4         Nixon     2A
```

Returning data into a table

For T-SQL developers, the OUTPUT clause can return the data for use within a batch or stored procedure. The data is received into a user table, temp table, or table variable, which must already have been created. Although the syntax may seem similar to the INSERT...INTO syntax, it actually functions very differently.

In the following example, the OUTPUT clause passes the results to a @DeletedGuides table variable:

```
DECLARE @DeletedGuides TABLE (
  GuideID INT NOT NULL PRIMARY KEY,
  LastName VARCHAR(50) NOT NULL,
  FirstName VARCHAR(50) NOT NULL
  );

DELETE dbo.Guide
  OUTPUT Deleted.GuideID, Deleted.LastName, Deleted.FirstName
  INTO @DeletedGuides
  WHERE GuideID = 2;
```

Interim result:

```
(1 row(s) affected)
```

Continuing the batch ...

```
SELECT GuideID, LastName, FirstName FROM @DeletedGuides;
```

Result:

```
(1 row(s) affected)
GuideID     LastName   FirstName
----------- ---------- ----------------
2           Frank      Ken
```

CROSS-REF **An advance use of the OUTPUT clause, called *composable DML*, passes the output data to an outer query, which can then be used in an INSERT command. For more details, refer to Chapter 11, "Including Data with Subqueries and CTEs."**

Summary

Data retrieval and data modification are primary tasks of a database application. This chapter examined the workhorse INSERT, UPDATE, DELETE, and MERGE DML commands and described how you can use them to manipulate data.

Key points in this chapter include the following:

- There are multiple formats for the INSERT command depending on the data's source: INSERT...VALUES, INSERT...SELECT, INSERT...EXEC, and INSERT...DEFAULT.
- INSERT...VALUES now has row constructors to insert multiple rows with a single INSERT.
- INSERT...INTO creates a new table and then inserts the results into the new table.
- UPDATE always updates only a single table, but it can use an optional FROM clause to reference other data sources.
- Using DELETE without a WHERE clause is dangerous.
- The new MERGE command pulls data from a source table and inserts, updates, or deletes in the target table depending on the match conditions.
- INSERT, UPDATE, DELETE, and MERGE can all include an optional OUTPUT clause that can select data from the query or the virtual inserted and deleted tables. The result of the OUTPUT clause can be passed to the client, inserted into a table, or passed to an outer query.

This chapter explained data modifications assuming all goes well, but in fact several conditions and situations can conspire to block the INSERT, UPDATE, DELETE, or MERGE. The next chapter looks at the dark side of data modification and what can go wrong.

Chapter 16

Modification Obstacles

IN THIS CHAPTER

Avoiding and solving complex data-modification problems

Primary keys, foreign keys, inserts, updates, and deletes

Deleting duplicate rows

Nulls and defaults

Trigger issues

Updating with views

Some newsgroup postings ask about how to perform a task or write a query, but another set of postings ask about troubleshooting the code when there is some problem. Typically, SQL Server is working the way it is supposed to function, but someone is having trouble getting past what's perceived to be an obstacle.

This chapter surveys several types of potential obstacles and explains how to avoid them. In nearly every case, the obstacle is understood — it's really a safety feature and SQL Server is protecting the data by blocking the insert, update, or delete.

As Table 16-1 illustrates, INSERT and UPDATE operations face more obstacles than DELETE operations because they are creating new data in the table that must pass multiple validation rules. Because the DELETE operation only removes data, it faces fewer possible obstacles.

Data Type/Length

Column data type/length may affect INSERT and UPDATE operations. One of the first checks the new data must pass is that of data type and data length. Often, a data-type error is caused by missing or extra quotes. SQL Server is particular about implicit, or automatic, data-type conversion. Conversions that function automatically in other programming languages often fail in SQL Server, as shown in the following example:

```
USE OBXKites;
DECLARE @ProblemDate DATETIME = '20090301';

INSERT dbo.Price (ProductID, Price, EffectiveDate)
  VALUES ('6D37553D-89B1-4663-91BC-0486842EAD44',
    @ProblemDate, '20020625');
```

TABLE 16-1

Potential Data Modification Obstacles

Potential Problem	Insert Operation	Update Operation	Delete Operation
Data Type/Length	X	X	
Primary Key Constraint and Unique Constraint	X	X	
Duplicate Rows		X	X
Foreign Key Constraint	X	X	X
Unique Index	X	X	
Not Null and No Default	X	X	
Check Constraint	X	X	
Instead of Trigger	X	X	X
After Trigger	X	X	X
Non-Updatable Views	X	X	X
Views with Check Option	X	X	
Security	X	X	X

Result:

```
Msg 257, Level 16, State 3, Line 3
Implicit conversion from data type datetime to money is not allowed.
Use the CONVERT function to run this query.
```

The problem with the preceding code is that a DATETIME variable is being inserted into a money data type column. For most data type conversions, SQL server handles the conversion implicitly; however, conversion between some data types requires using the cast() or convert() function.

CROSS-REF **For more details about data types and tables, refer to Chapter 20, "Creating the Physical Database Schema." Data-type conversion and conversion scalar functions are discussed in Chapter 9, "Data Types, Expressions, and Scalar Functions."**

Primary Key Constraint and Unique Constraint

Both primary key constraints and unique constraints may affect INSERT and UPDATE operations. While this section explicitly deals with primary keys, the same is true for unique indexes.

Primary keys, by definition, must be unique. Attempting to insert a primary key that's already in use will cause an error. Technically speaking, updating a primary key to a value already in use also causes an error, but surrogate primary keys (identity columns and GUIDs) should never need to be updated; and a good natural key should rarely need updating. Candidate keys should also be stable enough that they rarely need updating.

Updating a primary key may also break referential integrity, causing the update to fail. In this case, however, it's not a primary-key constraint that's the obstacle, but the foreign-key constraint that references the primary key.

CROSS-REF **For more information about the design of primary keys, foreign keys, and many of the other constraints mentioned in this chapter, refer to Chapter 3, "Relational Database Design." For details on creating constraints, turn to Chapter 20, "Creating the Physical Database Schema."**

One particular issue related to inserting is the creation of surrogate key values for the new rows. SQL Server provides two excellent means of generating surrogate primary keys: *identity columns* and *GUIDs*. Each method has its pros and cons, and its rules for safe handling.

NOTE **Every table should have a primary key. If the primary key is the same data used by humans to identify the item in reality, then it's a *natural key*, e.g., ssn, vehicle vin, aircraft tail number, part serial number.**

The alternative to the natural key is the *surrogate key*, surrogate meaning artificial or a stand-in replacement. For databases, a surrogate key means an artificial, computer-generated value is used to uniquely identify the row. SQL Server supports *identity columns* and *globally unique identifiers (GUIDs)* as surrogate keys.

Identity columns

SQL Server automatically generates incrementing integers for identity columns at the time of the insert and any SQL `INSERT` statement normally can't interfere with that process by supplying a value for the identity column.

The fact that identity columns refuse to accept inserted integers can be a serious issue if you're inserting existing data with existing primary key values that must be maintained because they are referenced by secondary tables. The solution is to use the `IDENTITY_INSERT` database option. When set to `ON` it temporarily turns off the identity column and permits the insertion of data into an identity column. This means that the insert has to explicitly provide the primary-key value. The `IDENTITY_INSERT` option may only be set `ON` for one table at a time within a database. The following SQL batch uses the `IDENTITY_INSERT` option when supplying the primary key:

```
USE CHA2;

-- attempt to insert into an identity column
INSERT dbo.Guide (GuideID, FirstName, LastName)
  VALUES (10, 'Bill', 'Fletcher');
```

Result:

```
Server: Msg 544, Level 16, State 1, Line 1
Cannot insert explicit value for identity column in table
'Guide' when IDENTITY_INSERT is set to OFF.
```

CROSS-REF **The sample database for this book can be downloaded from the book's website: www.sqlserverbible.com.**

The next step in the batch sets the IDENTITY_INSERT option and attempts some more inserts:

```
SET IDENTITY_INSERT Guide ON;

INSERT Guide (GuideID, FirstName, LastName)
  VALUES (100, 'Bill', 'Mays');

INSERT dbo.Guide (GuideID, FirstName, LastName)
  VALUES (101, 'Sue', 'Atlas');
```

To see what value the identity column is now assigning, the following code re-enables the identity column, inserts another row, and then selects the new data:

```
SET IDENTITY_INSERT Guide OFF;

INSERT Guide ( FirstName, LastName)
  VALUES ( 'Arnold', 'Bistier');

SELECT GuideID, FirstName, LastName
  FROM dbo.Guide;
```

Result:

```
GuideID     FirstName     LastName
----------- ------------- ------------------------
1           Dan            Smith
2           Jeff           Davis
3           Tammie         Commer
4           Lauren         Jones
5           Greg           Wilson
100         Bill           Mays
101         Sue            Atlas
102         Arnold         Bistier
```

As this code demonstrates, manually inserting a GuideID of "101" sets the identity column's next value to "102."

Another potential problem when working with identity columns is determining the value of the identity that was just created. Because the new identity value is created with SQL Server at the time of the insert, the code causing the insert is unaware of the identity value. The insert works fine; the perceived problem occurs when the code inserts a row and then tries to display the row on a user-interface grid within an application, because the code is unaware of the new data's database-assigned primary key.

SQL Server provides four methods for determining the identity value:

- @@IDENTITY: This venerable global variable returns the last identity value generated by SQL Server for any table, connection, or scope. If another insert takes place between the time of your insert and the time when you check @@IDENTITY, @@IDENTITY will return not your insert, but the last insert. For this reason, don't use @@IDENTITY; it's only there for backward compatibility.

- SCOPE_IDENTITY ( ): This system function, introduced in SQL Server 2000, returns the last generated identity value within the scope of the calling batch or procedure. I recommend using this method, as it is the safest way to determine the identity value you last generated.
- IDENT_CURRENT (TABLE): This function, also introduced in SQL Server 2000, returns the last identity value per table. While this option seems similar to SCOPE_IDENTITY( ), IDENT_CURRENT( ) returns the identity value for the given table regardless of inserts to any other tables that may have occurred. This prevents another insert, buried deep within a trigger, from affecting the identity value returned by the function.
- OUTPUT clause: The INSERT, UPDATE, DELETE, and MERGE commands can include an OUTPUT clause that can select from the inserted and deleted virtual tables. Using this data, any data modification query can return the inserted identity values.

Globally unique identifiers (GUIDs)

Globally unique identifiers (GUIDs) are sometimes, and with great debate, used as primary keys. A GUID can be the best choice when you have to generate unique values at different locations (i.e., in replicated scenarios), but hardly ever otherwise.

With regard to the insertion of new rows, the major difference between identity columns and GUIDs is that GUIDs are generated by the SQL code or by a column default, rather than automatically generated by the engine at the time of the insert. This means that the developer has more control over GUID creation.

There are five ways to generate GUID primary key values when inserting new rows:

- The NEWID( ) function can create the GUID in T-SQL code prior to the INSERT.
- The NEWID( ) function can create the GUID in client code prior to the INSERT.
- The NEWID( ) function can create the GUID in an expression in the INSERT command.
- The NEWID( ) function can create the GUID in a column default.
- The NEWSEQUENTIALID( ) function can create the GUID in a column default. This is the only method that avoids the page split performance issues with GUIDs. If you must use a GUID, then I strongly recommend using NEWSEQUENTIALID( ) .

The following sample code demonstrates various methods of generating GUID primary keys during the addition of new rows to the ProductCategory table in the OBXKites database. The first query simply tests the NEWID( ) function:

```
USE OBXKites;
Select NewID();
```

Result:

```
5CBB2800-5207-4323-A316-E963AACB6081
```

The next three queries insert a GUID, each using a different method of generating the GUID:

```
--  GUID from Default (the columns default is NewID())
INSERT dbo.ProductCategory
  (ProductCategoryID, ProductCategoryName)
```

```
  VALUES (DEFAULT, 'From Default');

-- GUID from function
INSERT dbo.ProductCategory
    (ProductCategoryID, ProductCategoryName)
  VALUES (NewID(), 'From Function');

-- GUID in variable
DECLARE @NewGUID UniqueIdentifier;
SET @NewGUID = NewID();

INSERT dbo.ProductCategory
    (ProductCategoryID, ProductCategoryName)
  VALUES (@NewGUID, 'From Variable');
```

To view the results of the previous three methods of inserting a GUID, the following `SELECT` statement is filtered to those rows that are `like 'From %'`:

```
SELECT ProductCategoryID, ProductCategoryName
 FROM dbo.ProductCategory
   WHERE ProductCategoryName like 'From %';
```

Result:

```
ProductCategoryID                    ProductCategoryName
------------------------------------ ----------------------
25894DA7-B5BB-435D-9540-6B9207C6CF8F From Default
393414DC-8611-4460-8FD3-4657E4B49373 From Function
FF868338-DF9A-4B8D-89B6-9C28293CA25F From Variable
```

This `INSERT` statement uses the `NEWID()` function to insert multiple GUIDs:

```
INSERT dbo.ProductCategory
    (ProductCategoryID, ProductCategoryName)
   Select NewID(), LastName
     From CHA2.dbo.Guide;
```

The following `SELECT` statement retrieves the new GUIDs:

```
SELECT ProductCategoryID, ProductCategoryName
 FROM dbo.ProductCategory;
```

Result:

```
ProductCategoryID                    ProductCategoryName
------------------------------------ --------------------
1B2BBE15-B415-43ED-BCA2-293050B7EFE4 Kite
23FC5D45-8B60-4800-A505-D2F556F863C9 Accessory
3889671A-F2CD-4B79-8DCF-19F4F4703693 Video
...
```

```
5471F896-A414-432B-A579-0880757ED097 Fletcher
428F29B3-111B-4ECE-B6EB-E0913A9D34DC Atlas
E4B7D325-8122-48D7-A61B-A83E258D8729 Bistier
```

The final GUID insert example features my recommended method, `NEWSEQUENTIALID()`. The function is defined as the default for the primary key column. Three rows are inserted and then selected:

```
USE tempdb;

CREATE TABLE GUIDtable (
  GUIDtableID UNIQUEIDENTIFIER NOT NULL
    DEFAULT (NewSequentialID())
    PRIMARY KEY,
  Col1 CHAR(1),
  );

INSERT GUIDtable (Col1)
  VALUES ('a'),
   ('b'),
   ('c');

SELECT GUIDtableID, Col1
  FROM GUIDtable;
```

Result:

```
GUIDtableID                          Col1
------------------------------------ ----
748040E1-210D-DE11-8196-002170BF2EB9 a
758040E1-210D-DE11-8196-002170BF2EB9 b
768040E1-210D-DE11-8196-002170BF2EB9 c
```

SQL Server provides the flexibility of two excellent candidates for surrogate key generation. Whether the database relies on identity columns or GUIDs may be based on other factors. Either way, there are multiple methods for inserting new rows. You, as the SQL developer or DBA, are in control.

NOTE **If a column has a unique index (even if it's not a key), then attempting to insert a new value, or an update to a new value that's already in use, will fail.**

Typically, the entire transaction, including all the inserted or updated rows, will fail. However, there's an index option, `IGNORE DUP KEY`, that enables the transaction to succeed with only a warning, and just skips any duplicate rows. This should only be used for staging tables in a scenario where an external application may accidentally include the same data more than once.

Deleting Duplicate Rows

A common question on the newsgroups is "How can I delete a single row when I don't have a primary key?"

NOTE **<rant>The first order of business is to question why the table doesn't have a primary key. Without a primary key, it's not a legitimate table. My beef with SQL is that it even allows a table without a primary key. Horrors! One reason I like policy-based management is that it can be configured to require a primary key on every table. As soon as the duplicates are deleted, be sure to apply a primary key to the table.</rant>**

Fortunately, there are several methods to clean up duplicate data. The following sections include the windowing, surrogate key, and `SELECT DISTINCT INTO` methods.

To experiment with duplicate data, the following script sets up a poorly designed (no primary key) table and inserts some duplicate data:

```
USE tempdb ;
go

CREATE TABLE DupsNoPK (
   Col1 INT NULL,
   Col2 CHAR(5) NULL
  );
go

-- Insert multiple dup rows (can be executed mulitple times)
INSERT DupsNoPK (Col1, Col2)
  VALUES  (1, 'abc'),
          (2, 'abc'),
          (2, 'abc'),
          (2, 'abc'),
          (7, 'xyz'),
          (7, 'xyz') ;
```

To verify that the table does in fact have duplicate data, the following query uses a `GROUP BY` and `HAVING` clause to return only the duplicated rows, with a count of the number of duplicates:

```
SELECT Col1, Col2, COUNT(*) AS DupCount
  FROM DupsNoPK
  GROUP BY Col1, Col2
  HAVING COUNT(*) > 1;
```

Result:

```
Col1        Col2  DupCount
----------- ----- -----------
2           abc   3
7           xyz   2
```

Deleting duplicate rows using windowing

Of the three methods to remove duplicate rows, this method is the most straightforward because it doesn't need to alter the table or generate a second table.

The key to this method is using the windowing's OVER() clause with a ROW_NUMBER() function and a partition. The partition will begin renumbering with every new partition. Set the OVER() clause to PARTITION BY every column to be checked for duplicate data. In this case, every column is being checked.

Running the windowing query first shows how it applies the row number:

```
SELECT Col1, Col2,
    ROW_NUMBER() OVER (PARTITION BY Col1, Col2 ORDER BY Col1) AS rn
  FROM DupsNoPK
```

Result:

```
Col1        Col2  rn
----------- ----- --------------------
1           abc   1
2           abc   1
2           abc   2
2           abc   3
7           xyz   1
7           xyz   2
```

Every duplicate row has an rn value of greater than 1, so it's now easy to delete the duplicates:

```
WITH DupsNumbered
AS (
SELECT Col1, Col2,
    ROW_NUMBER() OVER (PARTITION BY Col1, Col2 ORDER BY Col1) AS rn
  FROM DupsNoPK
)
DELETE DupsNumbered
  WHERE rn > 1;
```

The next SELECT tests the effect of the windowing remove duplicates query:

```
SELECT Col1, Col2
  FROM DupsNoPK;
```

Result:

```
Col1        Col2
----------- -----
1           abc
2           abc
7           xyz
```

Deleting duplicate rows using a surrogate key

A traditional method of removing duplicate rows uses a surrogate key to uniquely identify each row. This means the table itself must be altered to add the surrogate key column.

Assuming the DupsNoPK table is reset with the original rows, the following script applies an IDENTITY surrogate key and looks at the altered table:

```
ALTER TABLE dbo.DupsNoPK
ADD
  PK INT IDENTITY
         NOT NULL
         CONSTRAINT PK_DupsNoPK PRIMARY KEY;

SELECT *
  FROM DupsNoPK;
```

Result:

```
Col1        Col2  PK
----------- ----- -----------
1           abc   74
2           abc   75
2           abc   76
2           abc   77
7           xyz   78
7           xyz   79
```

To search and destroy the duplicate data, the next query finds and deletes all the rows with matching Col1 and Col2 data but higher primary key values:

```
DELETE DupsNoPK
  WHERE EXISTS ( SELECT *
                  FROM DupsNoPK AS D1
                  WHERE D1.Col1 = DupsNoPK.Col1
                    AND D1.Col2 = DupsNoPK.Col2
                    AND D1.PK > DupsNoPK.PK );


SELECT *
  FROM DupsNoPK;
```

Result:

```
Col1        Col2  PK
----------- ----- -----------
1           abc   74
2           abc   77
7           xyz   79
```

Deleting duplicate rows using select distant into

The third method of removing duplicate data may seem crude, but if the goal is to remove duplicates while creating a new table — perhaps as part of an ETL process — it may be the best choice.

A SELECT DISTINCT will automatically pass the data through a filter that eliminates duplicate rows. The INTO option causes the results of the select to be placed into a new table instead of going to the client application. Mix the two options together and you have an instant duplicate row remover.

Again, assuming the DupsNoPK table is reset with its original duplicate data, the following query generates a new table without duplicates and then examines the contents of the new table:

```
SELECT distinct Col1, Col2 INTO NoDups
  FROM DupsNoPK;

SELECT Col1, Col2
  FROM NoDups;
```

Result:

```
Col1        Col2
----------- -----
1           abc
2           abc
7           xyz
```

Foreign Key Constraints

Foreign keys may affect INSERT, UPDATE, and DELETE commands by blocking those operations. Inserting a new secondary table row with a foreign key value that doesn't match an existing primary key will cause the secondary row insert to fail.

In the following insert example, the ProductCategoryID supplied does not exist in the ProductCategory table. This causes the foreign key constraint to block the INSERT operation, as the error message indicates:

```
-- Foreign Key: Insert Obstacle
INSERT Product (ProductID, Code,
    ProductCategoryID, ProductName)
  VALUES ('9562C1A5-4499-4626-BB33-E5E140ACD2AC',
    '999'
    'DB8D8D60-76F4-46C3-90E6-A8648F63C0F0',
    'Basic Box Kite 21"');
```

Result:

```
Server: Msg 547, Level 16, State 1, Line 1
INSERT statement conflicted with COLUMN FOREIGN KEY
constraint 'FK__Product__Product__7B905C75'.
The conflict occurred in database 'OBXKites',
table 'ProductCategory', column 'ProductCategoryID'.
The statement has been terminated.
```

Note that because every GUID is unique, the GUIDs you use on your system will be different.

Foreign key constraints can also block updates to either the primary or the secondary table. If the primary key is updated and a foreign key is pointed to that primary key, then the update will fail.

In the following sample code, the update is blocked because the secondary table update is trying to set the foreign key, ProductCategoryID, to a value that does not exist in the ProductCategory table:

```
-- Foreign Key: Secondary table Update Obstacle
UPDATE Product
  SET ProductCategoryID =
    'DB8D8D60-76F4-46C3-90E6-A8648F63C0F0'
  WHERE ProductID = '67804443-7E7C-4769-A41C-3DD3CD3621D9';
```

Result:

```
Server: Msg 547, Level 16, State 1, Line 1
UPDATE statement conflicted with COLUMN FOREIGN KEY
Constraint 'FK__Product__Product__7B905C75'.
The conflict occurred in database 'OBXKites',
table 'ProductCategory', column 'ProductCategoryID'.
The statement has been terminated.
```

If foreign keys are pointing to a primary key, updating the primary key to a new value has the same effect as deleting a primary table row with an existing secondary table row referring to it. In both cases the error is caused not by the primary key but by the foreign key referencing the primary key.

In the following code, the error is generated not by the ProductCategory table, even though it is the table being updated, but by the Product table. This is because the Product table has both the row and the foreign key reference constraint that will be violated if the primary key value no longer exists:

```
-- Foreign Key: Primary table Update Obstacle
UPDATE ProductCategory
  SET ProductCategoryID =
    'DB8D8D60-76F4-46C3-90E6-A8648F63C0F0'
  WHERE ProductCategoryID =
    '1B2BBE15-B415-43ED-BCA2-293050B7EFE4';
```

Result:

```
Server: Msg 547, Level 16, State 1, Line 1
UPDATE statement conflicted with COLUMN REFERENCE constraint
'FK__Product__Product__7B905C75'. The conflict occurred
in database 'OBXKites', table 'Product',
column 'ProductCategoryID'.
The statement has been terminated.
```

CROSS-REF **For more information about creating unique index constraints, refer to Chapter 20, "Creating the Physical Database Schema."**

Null and Default Constraints

Column nullability and defaults may affect INSERT and UPDATE operations. An INSERT or UPDATE operation can send one of four possible values to a table column: data values, null, default, or nothing at all. The table column can be configured with a default value and nullability.

Table 16-2 indicates the result of the operation according to the column configuration, and the new value to be inserted or updated. For example, if the column properties are set so that the column has a default and does not accept nulls (see the far-right column) and the SQL insert or update sends a null, then the result is an error.

TABLE 16-2

Data Modifications, Defaults, and Nulls

	Column Properties			
	No default, allow null	No default, not allow null	Has default, allow null	Has default, not allow null
SQL Sent:	**Result:**			
data	data	data	data	data
null	null	error	null	error
default	null	error	default	default
nothing sent	null	most common error	default	default

By far, the most common error in the table is submitting nothing when no default exists and nulls are not permitted.

CROSS-REF **For more information about dealing with nulls when retrieving data, see Chapter 9, "Data Types, Expressions, and Scalar Functions."**

Check Constraints

Check constraints may affect INSERT and UPDATE operations.

Each table column may have multiple check constraints. These are fast Boolean operations that determine whether the update will pass or fail.

The following check constraint permits Dr. Johnson's insert but blocks Greg's insert (note that the check constraint is already applied to the database by the `Create_CHA2.sql` script):

```
USE CHA2;
go
ALTER TABLE dbo.Guide ADD CONSTRAINT
  CK_Guide_Age21 CHECK (DateDiff(yy,DateOfBirth, DateHire)
    >= 21);
```

The following query inserts Dr. Johnson's data. Because she was 26 years old at the time of hire, her row is accepted by the check constraint:

```
INSERT Guide(LastName, FirstName,
    Qualifications, DateOfBirth, DateHire)
  VALUES ('Johnson', 'Mary',
           'E.R. Physician', '19710114', '19970601');
```

Greg, conversely, was only 18 at the time he applied, so his insert is rejected by the check constraint:

```
INSERT Guide (LastName, FirstName,
    Qualifications, DateOfBirth, DateHire)
  VALUES ('Franklin', 'Greg',
    'Guide', '19831212', '20020101');
```

Result:

```
Server: Msg 547, Level 16, State 1, Line 1
INSERT statement conflicted with TABLE CHECK constraint
'CK_Guide_Age21'.
The conflict occurred in database 'CHA2', table 'Guide'.
The statement has been terminated.
```

Instead of Triggers

`INSTEAD OF` triggers may affect `INSERT`, `UPDATE`, and `DELETE` operations.

Triggers are special stored procedures that are attached to a table and fire when certain data-modification operations hit that table. Two types of triggers exist: `INSTEAD OF` and `AFTER`. They differ both in their timing and in how they handle the data-modification operation.

An `INSTEAD OF` trigger always causes the `INSERT`, `UPDATE`, or `DELETE` operation to be canceled. The SQL command submitted to SQL Server is discarded by the `INSTEAD OF` trigger; the code within the `INSTEAD OF` trigger is executed *instead of* the submitted SQL command, hence the name. The `INSTEAD OF` trigger might be programmed to repeat the requested operation so that it looks like it went through, or it could do something else altogether.

The problem with the `INSTEAD OF` trigger is that it reports back "*n* row(s) affected" when in fact nothing is written to the database. There is no error warning because the `INSTEAD OF` trigger works properly; however, the operation doesn't go through.

In the following code sample, the InsteadOfDemo trigger causes the INSERT operation to disappear into thin air:

```
USE CHA2;
go

CREATE TRIGGER InsteadOfDemo
ON Guide
INSTEAD OF INSERT
AS
  Print 'Instead of trigger demo';
```

With the INSTEAD OF trigger in place, the following query inserts a test row:

```
INSERT Guide(lastName, FirstName,
    Qualifications, DateOfBirth, DateHire)
  VALUES ('Jamison', 'Tom',
    'Biologist, Adventurer', '19560114', '19990109');
```

Result:

```
Instead of trigger demo
(1 row(s) affected)
```

The INSERT operation appears to have worked, but is the row in the table?

```
SELECT GuideID
  FROM Guide
  WHERE LastName = 'Jamison';
```

Result:

```
GuideID
-----------

(0 row(s) affected)
```

CROSS-REF **Building triggers is explained in detail in Chapter 26, "Creating DML Triggers." The flow of data-modification transactions and the timing of triggers are also discussed in Chapter 66, "Managing Transactions, Locking, and Blocking."**

Note that the sample code for this chapter drops the InsteadOfDemo trigger before moving on.

After Triggers

AFTER triggers may affect INSERT, UPDATE, and DELETE operations.

AFTER triggers are often used for complex data validation. These triggers can roll back, or undo, the insert, update, or delete if the code inside the trigger doesn't like the operation in question. The code can then do something else, or it can just fail the transaction. However, if the trigger doesn't explicitly ROLLBACK the transaction, the data-modification operation will go through as originally intended. Unlike INSTEAD OF triggers, AFTER triggers normally report an error code if an operation is rolled back.

As Chapter 66, "Managing Transactions, Locking, and Blocking," discusses in greater detail, every DML command implicitly occurs within a transaction, even if no BEGIN TRANSACTION command exists. The AFTER trigger takes place after the modification but before the implicit commit, so the transaction is still open when the AFTER trigger is fired. Therefore, a transaction ROLLBACK command in the trigger will roll back all pending transactions.

This code sample creates the AfterDemo AFTER trigger on the Guide table, which includes the RAISERROR and ROLLBACK TRANSACTION commands:

```
USE CHA2;

CREATE TRIGGER AfterDemo
ON Guide
AFTER INSERT, UPDATE
AS
  Print 'After Trigger Demo';
  -- logic in a real trigger would decide what to do here
  RAISERROR ('Sample Error', 16, 1 );
  ROLLBACK TRAN;
```

With the AFTER trigger applied to the Guide table, the following INSERT will result:

```
INSERT Guide(lastName, FirstName,
    Qualifications, DateOfBirth, DateHire)
  VALUES ('Harrison', 'Nancy',
    'Pilot, Sky Diver, Hang Glider,
      Emergency Paramedic', '19690625', '20000714');
```

Result:

```
After Trigger Demo
Server: Msg 50000, Level 16, State 1,
    Procedure AfterDemo, Line 7
Sample Error
```

A SELECT searching for Nancy Harrison would find no such row because the AFTER trigger rolled back the transaction.

Note that the sample code in the file for this chapter drops the AfterDemo trigger so that the code in the remainder of the chapter will function.

Non-Updateable Views

Non-updateable views may affect INSERT, UPDATE, and DELETE operations.

Several factors will cause a view to become non-updateable. The most common causes of non-updateable views are aggregate functions (including DISTINCT), group bys, and joins. If the view includes other nested views, any nested view that is non-updateable will cause the final view to be non-updateable as well.

The view vMedGuide, created in the following sample code, is non-updateable because the DISTINCT predicate eliminates duplicates, making it impossible for SQL to be sure which underlying row should be updated:

```
CREATE VIEW dbo.vMedGuide
AS
SELECT DISTINCT GuideID, LastName, Qualifications
  FROM dbo.Guide
  WHERE Qualifications LIKE '%Aid%'
  OR Qualifications LIKE '%medic%'
  OR Qualifications LIKE '%Physician%';
```

To test the updateability of the view, the next query attempts to perform an UPDATE command through the view:

```
UPDATE dbo.vMedGuide
  SET Qualifications = 'E.R. Physician, Diver'
  WHERE GuideID = 1;
```

Result:

```
Server: Msg 4404, Level 16, State 1, Line 1
View or function 'dbo.vMedGuide' is not updatable
because the definition contains the DISTINCT clause.
```

CROSS-REF **For more information about creating views and a more complete list of the causes of non-updateable views, refer to Chapter 14, "Projecting Data Through Views."**

Views With Check Option

Views WITH CHECK OPTION may affect INSERT and UPDATE operations.

Views can cause two specific problems, both related to the WITH CHECK OPTION. A special situation called *disappearing rows* occurs when rows are returned from a view and then updated such that they no longer meet the WHERE clause's requirements for the view. The rows are still in the database but they are no longer visible in the view.

CROSS-REF **For more about disappearing rows, the WITH CHECK OPTION, and their implications for security, refer to Chapter 14, "Projecting Data Through Views."**

Adding the WITH CHECK OPTION to a view prohibits disappearing rows, but causes another problem. A view that includes the WITH CHECK OPTION will apply the WHERE clause condition to both data being retrieved through the view and data being inserted or updated through the view. If the data being inserted or updated will not be retrievable through the view after the insert or update of the operation, the WITH CHECK OPTION will cause the data-modification operation to fail.

The following code sample modifies the previous view to add the WITH CHECK OPTION and then attempts two updates. The first update passes the WHERE clause requirements. The second update would remove the rows from the result set returned by the view, so it fails:

```
ALTER VIEW dbo.vMedGuide
AS
SELECT GuideID, LastName, Qualifications
  FROM dbo.Guide
  WHERE Qualifications LIKE '%Aid%'
  OR Qualifications LIKE '%medic%'
  OR Qualifications LIKE '%Physician%'
WITH CHECK OPTION;
```

The following queries test the views WITH CHECK OPTION. The first one will pass because the qualifications include `Physician´, but the second query will fail:

```
UPDATE dbo.vMedGuide
  SET Qualifications = 'E.R. Physician, Diver'
  WHERE GuideID = 1;

UPDATE dbo.vMedGuide
  SET Qualifications = 'Diver'
  WHERE GuideID = 1;
```

Result:

```
Server: Msg 550, Level 16, State 1, Line 1
The attempted insert or update failed because the target
view either specifies WITH CHECK OPTION or spans a view
that specifies WITH CHECK OPTION and one or more rows
resulting from the operation did not qualify
under the CHECK OPTION constraint.
The statement has been terminated.
```

Calculated Columns

A related issue to non-updateable views involves updating calculated columns. Essentially, a calculated column is a read-only generated value. Just like non-updateable views, attempting to write to a calculated column will block the data-modification statement.

To demonstrate how a calculated column can block an insert or update, the following code builds a table with a calculated column and inserts a couple of sample rows:

```
USE tempdb;

CREATE TABLE CalcCol (
  ID INT NOT NULL IDENTITY PRIMARY KEY,
```

```
    Col1 CHAR(2),
    Col2 CHAR(2),
    Calc AS Col1 + Col2
    );

INSERT CalcCol (Col1,Col2)
  VALUES ('ab', 'cd'),
         ('12', '34');

 SELECT Col1, Col2, Calc
   FROM CalcCol;
```

Result:

```
Col1 Col2 Calc
---- ---- ----
ab   cd   abcd
12   34   1234
```

The last SELECT proved that the Calc column did indeed calculate its contents. The next query attempts to write into the Calc column and generates an error:

```
INSERT CalcCol (Col1, Col2, Calc)
  VALUES ('qw', 'er', 'qwer')
```

Result:

```
Msg 271, Level 16, State 1, Line 1
The column "Calc" cannot be modified because it is either
a computed column or is the result of a UNION operator.
```

Security Constraints

Security may affect INSERT, UPDATE, and DELETE operations.

A number of security settings and roles can cause any operation to fail. Typically, security is not an issue during development; but for production databases, security is often paramount. Documenting the security settings and security roles will help you solve data-modification problems caused by security.

Best Practice

Every data-modification obstacle is easily within the SQL developer's or DBA's ability to surmount. Understanding SQL Server and documenting the database, as well as being familiar with the database schema, stored procedures, and triggers, will prevent most data-modification problems.

Summary

Having read through this exhaustive list of potential obstacles, the question is, are these obstacles a problem or is it good that SQL Server behaves like this?

Clearly, the answer is yes, it is good. Most of these issues involve constraints that enforce some type of integrity (see Chapter 3, "Relational Database Design," and Chapter 20, "Creating the Physical Schema"). A well-architected database requires keys, constraints, and security. The real value of this chapter isn't learning about problems, but how to work with SQL Server the way it is supposed to work.

One last critical point: If your database doesn't have these constraints in place — to make data modification easier — that's just plain wrong.

This concludes a nine-chapter study on using the `SELECT` command, and its `INSERT`, `UPDATE`, and `DELETE` variations, to manipulate data. The next part moves beyond the traditional relational data types and discusses working with spatial data, hierarchies, full-text search, BLOBs, and XML.

Part III

Beyond Relational

The database world has grown in the past few years to data types that were once considered outside the realm of the traditional database. Websites and corporate applications require storing and searching of media, geography, XML, full-text, and hierarchies data. SQL Server 2008 is up for the job.

Part III covers storing, searching, and retrieving five types of beyond relational data. Some of these data types require unique forms of table design and very different means of selecting the data. It may not look at all like SQL, but it's SQL Server.

If SQL Server is the box, then Part III is all about retooling the box into a more friendly, inclusive type of box that holds all sorts of data.

IN THIS PART

Chapter 17

Traversing Hierarchies

IN THIS CHAPTER

Hierarchical patterns

Hierarchical user-defined functions (UDFs)

Recursive CTE queries

Materialized lists

HierarchyID data type

Traditionally, SQL has had a hard time getting along with data that doesn't fit well into a relational grid, and that includes hierarchical data. The lack of an elegant solution became obvious when working with family trees, bills of materials, organizational charts, layers of jurisdictions, or modeling O-O class inheritance. At best, the older methods of handling hierarchies were more of a clumsy work-around than a solution.

The problems surrounding hierarchical data involve modeling the data, navigating the tree, selecting multiple generations of ancestors or descendents, or manipulating the tree — i.e., moving portions of the tree to another location or inserting items. When the requirements demand a many-to-many relationship, such as a bill of materials, the relationships become even more complex.

New query methods, new data types, and a better understanding of hierarchical information by the SQL community have coalesced to make this an area where SQL Server offers intelligent, scalable solutions to hierarchical problems.

Is managing hierarchical data as easy as `SELECT * FROM too`? No. Hierarchies still don't fit the traditional relational model so it takes some work to understand and code a database that includes a hierarchy.

The initial question when working with hierarchical data is how to store the hierarchy, as hierarchies aren't natural to the relational model. There are several possibilities to choose from. In this chapter I'll explain three techniques (there are other methods but this chapter focuses on three), each with its own unique pros and cons:

- **Adjacency list:** By far, the most popular method
- **Materialized path:** My personal favorite method
- **HierarchyID:** Microsoft's new method

What's New with Hierarchies?

SQL Server 2005 introduced ANSI SQL 99's recursive common table expressions (CTEs), which lessened the pain of querying hierarchies modeled using the adjacency list pattern. Recursive CTEs are simpler and often faster than the SQL Server 2000 methods of writing a user-defined function to iteratively query each level.

The big news for SQL Server 2008 is the `HierarchyID` data type — a fast, compact CLR data type with several methods for querying and managing hierarchies.

Hierarchies are common in the real world, which is why they are so important for database design and development. The word hierarchy comes from the Greek and was first used in English in 1880 to describe the order of angels. I highly recommend you take the time to read the Wikipedia article on hierarchies — fascinating stuff.

Simple hierarchies only have a one parent to many children relationship and may be modeled using any of the three techniques. Examples of simple hierarchies include the following:

- Organizational charts
- Object-oriented classes
- Jurisdictions
- Taxonomy, or a species tree
- Network marketing schemes
- File system directory folders

More complex hierarchies, referred to in the mathematics world as *graphs*, involve multiple cardinalities and can only be modeled using variations of the adjacency list pattern:

- **Genealogies:** A child may have multiple parent relationships.
- **Bill of materials:** An assembly may consist of multiple sub-assemblies or parts, and the assembly may be used in multiple parent assemblies.
- **Social Network Follows:** A person may follow multiple other people, and multiple people may follow the person.
- **Complex organizational charts:** An employee may report to one supervisor for local administration duties and another supervisor for technical issues on a global scale.

This chapter walks through the three aforementioned patterns (adjacency lists, materialized paths, and `HierarchyID`s) for storing hierarchical data and presents several ways of working with the data for each pattern. For each method, I present the tasks in the flow that make the most sense for that method.

NOTE **It's possible that some hierarchies have more than one top node. For example, a jurisdiction hierarchy with countries, states, counties, and cities could have multiple country nodes at the top. This pattern is sometimes referred to as a hierarchical *forest* (with many trees.)**

NOTE **Because the material for this chapter exceeds the allotted page count, you can find several additional code examples in the chapter script file, which you can download from** `www.sqlserverbible.com`.

Adjacency List Pattern

The traditional pattern used to model hierarchical data is the *adjacency list pattern*, informally called the *self-join pattern*, which was presented by Dr. Edgar F. Codd. The adjacency list pattern stores both the current node's key and its immediate parent's key in the current node row. (This chapter refers to the two data elements in the data pair as *current node* and *parent node*.)

The most familiar example of the adjacency list pattern is a simple organizational chart like the one in the `AdventureWorks2008` sample database, partially illustrated in Figure 17-1.

In a basic organizational chart, there's a one-to-many relationship between employees who play the role of supervisor, and employees who report to supervisors. Supervisors may have multiple employees reporting to them, but every employee can have only one supervisor. An employee may both be a supervisor and report to another supervisor.

The adjacency lists pattern handles this one-to-many relationship by storing the parent node's primary key in the current node. This allows multiple current nodes to point to a single parent node.

In the case of the basic organizational chart, the employee is the current node, and the manager is the parent node. The employee's row points to the employee's manager by storing the manager's ID in the employee's `ManagerID` column.

FIGURE 17-1

Jean Trenary and her crew are the able Information Service Department at AdventureWorks.

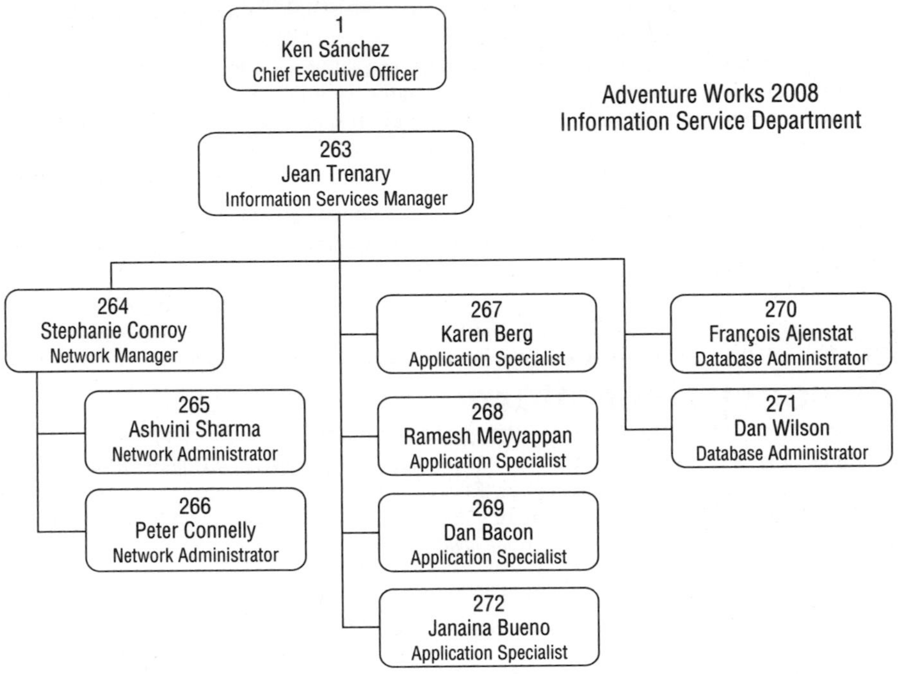

The next query result shows the data from the Information Service Department:

```
BusinessEntityID                                         ManagerID
      Name                JobTitle                              Manager
----- ------------------- ----------------------------- ----- -------------
263   Jean Trenary        Information Services Manager 1      Ken Sánchez
264   Stephanie Conroy    Network Manager              263    Jean Trenary
267   Karen Berg          Application Specialist       263    Jean Trenary
268   Ramesh Meyyappan    Application Specialist       263    Jean Trenary
269   Dan Bacon           Application Specialist       263    Jean Trenary
270   François Ajenstat   Database Administrator       263    Jean Trenary
271   Dan Wilson          Database Administrator       263    Jean Trenary
272   Janaina Bueno       Application Specialist       263    Jean Trenary
265   Ashvini Sharma      Network Administrator        264    Stephanie Conroy
266   Peter Connelly      Network Administrator        264    Stephanie Conroy
```

To examine one row from the employee perspective, Karen Berg's `BusinessEntityID` (PK) is 264. Her `ManagerID` is 263. That's the `BusinessEntityID` for Jean Trenary, so Karen reports to Jean.

From the supervisor's point of view, his `BusinessEntityID` is stored in each of his direct report's rows in the `ManagerID` column. For example, Jean Trenary's `BusinessEntityID` is 263, so 263 is stored in the `ManagerID` column of everyone who reports directly to her.

To maintain referential integrity, the `ManagerID` column has a foreign key constraint that refers to the `BusinessEntityID` column (the primary key) in the same table, as shown in Figure 17-2. The `ManagerID` column allows nulls so that the top person of the organization chart can report to no one.

FIGURE 17-2

The Employee table has a foreign key reference from the ManagerID column to the same table's primary key. That's why this pattern is often called the *self-join pattern.*

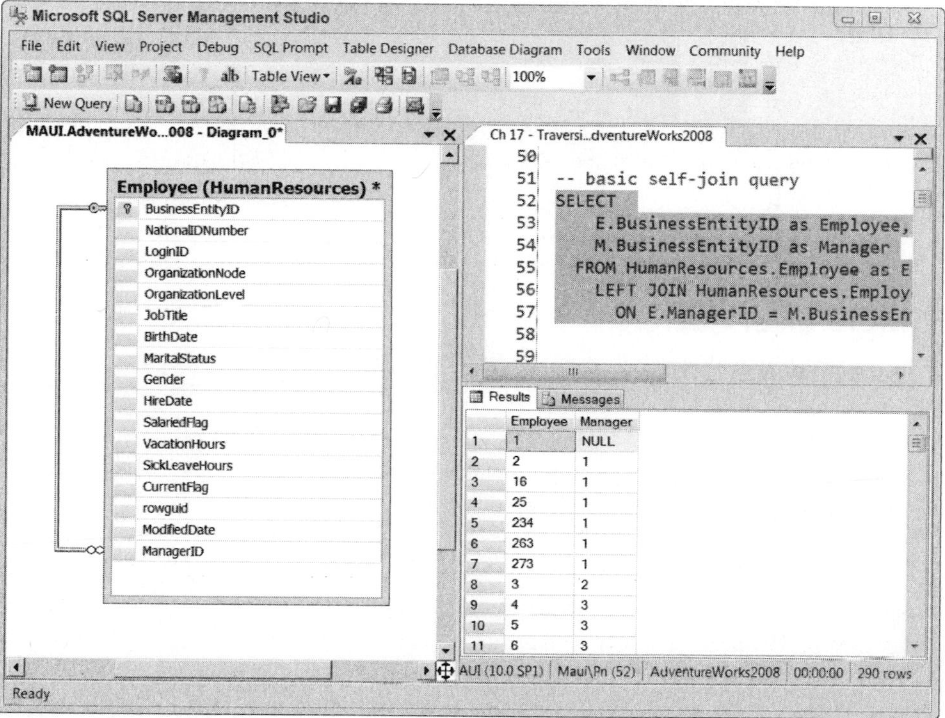

Restoring AdventureWorks2008's Adjacency List

With the advent of the HierarchyID data type in SQL Server 2008, Microsoft removed the adjacency list pattern from AdventureWorks2008 and replaced it with HierarchyID. The following script repairs AdventureWorks2008 and readies the database for experimentation with the adjacency list pattern:

```
ALTER TABLE HumanResources.Employee
 ADD ManagerID INT
 CONSTRAINT FK_AdjPairs
   FOREIGN KEY(ManagerID)
     REFERENCES HumanResources.Employee(BusinessEntityID);
GO
-- Update new ManagerID Column using join condition to match
UPDATE E
  SET ManagerID = M.BusinessEntityID
  FROM HumanResources.Employee AS E
    JOIN HumanResources.Employee AS M
      ON M.OrganizationNode = E.OrganizationNode.GetAncestor(1);
CREATE INDEX IxParentID
  ON HumanResources.Employee
    (ManagerID)
```

AdventureWorks2008 is now ready for some adjacency list fun with Ken Sánchez, the CEO; Jean Trenary, the IT Manager; and François Ajenstat, the DBA.

Single-level queries

The simplest hierarchical task is to match every node with a direct connection one level up the hierarchy. In this case, it means listing all AdventureWorks2008 employees and their supervisor.

The crux of the query is the self-join between two instances of the employee table represented in the LEFT OUTER JOIN between the employee's (E) ManagerID column and the manager's (M) BusinessEntityID column. There's still one physical employee table, but the query contains two references to the table and joins the two table references together, i.e., the query is joining the table back to itself.

Notice that because it's an outer join, an employee without a manager (i.e., the CEO) will still show up in the result list:

```
-- basic self-join query
SELECT
    E.BusinessEntityID as Employee,
    M.BusinessEntityID as Manager
  FROM HumanResources.Employee as E
   LEFT OUTER JOIN HumanResources.Employee as M
      ON E.ManagerID = M.BusinessEntityID;
```

Result (abbreviated):

```
Employee    Manager
----------- -----------
1           Null
2           1
16          1
25          1
234         1
273         1
3           2
4           3
...
```

Of course, listing integers isn't very useful. The next query adds some meat to the bones and fleshes out the data into a readable result set:

```
-- Employees and their Direct Supervisors
SELECT E.BusinessEntityID AS EmpID,
       EP.FirstName + ' ' + EP.LastName AS EmpName, E.JobTitle AS EmpTitle,
       E.ManagerID AS [MgrID],
       MP.FirstName + ' ' + MP.LastName AS MgrName, M.JobTitle AS MgrTitle
  FROM HumanResources.Employee AS E           -- the employee
    JOIN Person.Person AS EP                  -- the employee's contact info
      ON E.BusinessEntityID = EP.BusinessEntityID
    LEFT OUTER JOIN HumanResources.Employee AS M  -- the mgr(if there is one)
      ON E.ManagerID = M.BusinessEntityID
    LEFT JOIN Person.Person AS MP            -- the manager's contact info
      ON M.BusinessEntityID = MP.BusinessEntityID
  ORDER BY E.ManagerID , E.BusinessEntityID;
```

The abbreviated result is shown in Figure 17-3.

FIGURE 17-3

Results from the query showing every employee and his manager.

Results | Messages

	EmpID	EmpName	EmpTitle	MgrID	MgrName	MgrTitle
1	1	Ken Sánchez	Chief Executive Officer	NULL	NULL	NULL
2	2	Terri Duffy	Vice President of Engineering	1	Ken Sánchez	Chief Executive Officer
3	16	David Bradley	Marketing Manager	1	Ken Sánchez	Chief Executive Officer
4	25	James Hamilton	Vice President of Production	1	Ken Sánchez	Chief Executive Officer
5	234	Laura Norman	Chief Financial Officer	1	Ken Sánchez	Chief Executive Officer
6	263	Jean Trenary	Information Services Manager	1	Ken Sánchez	Chief Executive Officer
7	273	Brian Welcker	Vice President of Sales	1	Ken Sánchez	Chief Executive Officer
8	3	Roberto Tamburello	Engineering Manager	2	Terri Duffy	Vice President of Engineering
9	4	Rob Walters	Senior Tool Designer	3	Roberto Tamburello	Engineering Manager
10	5	Gail Erickson	Design Engineer	3	Roberto Tamburello	Engineering Manager

The reverse of "find all managers," which searches one level up the hierarchy query, is searching down the hierarchy. This query uses a downward looking join to locate every employee who has direct reports. The key to understanding this query is the self-join between the `Employee` table as `M`, representing the managers, and the `Employee` as `E`, representing the employees:

```
-- Every Manager and their direct Reports
SELECT M.BusinessEntityID AS 'MgrID',
       MP.FirstName + ' ' + MP.LastName AS 'MgrName',
       M.JobTitle AS 'MgrTitle',
       E.BusinessEntityID AS 'EmpID',
       EP.FirstName + ' ' + EP.LastName AS 'EmpName',
       E.JobTitle AS EmpTitle
  FROM HumanResources.Employee AS M  -- the manager
    JOIN Person.Person AS MP         -- the manager's contact info
      ON M.BusinessEntityID = MP.BusinessEntityID
    JOIN HumanResources.Employee AS E  -- the direct report
      ON E.ManagerID = M.BusinessEntityID
    JOIN Person.Person AS EP           -- the manager's contact info
      ON E.BusinessEntityID = EP.BusinessEntityID
  ORDER BY M.BusinessEntityID
```

The result is shown in Figure 17-4.

FIGURE 17-4

Results of the query showing every manager and his direct reports.

Results | Messages

	MgrID	MgrName	MgrTitle	EmpID	EmpName	EmpTitle
1	1	Ken Sánchez	Chief Executive Officer	2	Terri Duffy	Vice President of Engineering
2	1	Ken Sánchez	Chief Executive Officer	16	David Bradley	Marketing Manager
3	1	Ken Sánchez	Chief Executive Officer	25	James Hamilton	Vice President of Production
4	1	Ken Sánchez	Chief Executive Officer	234	Laura Norman	Chief Financial Officer
5	1	Ken Sánchez	Chief Executive Officer	263	Jean Trenary	Information Services Manager
6	1	Ken Sánchez	Chief Executive Officer	273	Brian Welcker	Vice President of Sales
7	2	Terri Duffy	Vice President of En...	3	Roberto Tam...	Engineering Manager
8	3	Roberto Ta...	Engineering Manager	4	Rob Walters	Senior Tool Designer

The last adjacency list single-level query performs a count of each manager's direct reports. Here, the work is being done in the subquery, which groups by the `ManagerID` column and counts the number or rows for each `ManagerID`:

```
-- Everyone who has Direct Reports w/count
SELECT M.BusinessEntityID as ID,
       MP.FirstName + ' ' + MP.LastName AS Manager,
       M.JobTitle,
       C.DirectReports
  FROM HumanResources.Employee AS M   -- the manager
    JOIN Person.Person AS MP          -- the manager's contact info
      ON M.BusinessEntityID = MP.BusinessEntityID
    JOIN (SELECT ManagerID, COUNT(*) AS DirectReports
            FROM HumanResources.Employee
```

```
            WHERE ManagerID IS NOT NULL
            GROUP BY ManagerID) AS C
        ON M.BusinessEntityID = C.ManagerID;
    ORDER BY Manager
```

Result (abbreviated):

```
ID   Manager              JobTitle                  DirectReports
---- -------------------- ------------------------- -------------
222  A. Scott Wright      Master Scheduler                      4

287  Amy Alberts          European Sales Manager                3
47   Andrew Hill          Production Supervisor - WC10          7
192  Brenda Diaz          Production Supervisor - WC40         12
273  Brian Welcker        Vice President of Sales               3
228  Christian Kleinerman Maintenance Supervisor                4
...
```

Subtree queries

The preceding queries work well with one level. If you need to return all the nodes for two levels, then you could add another self-join. As the number of levels needed increases, the queries become complex and the query is fixed to a certain number of levels. A continuing parade of self-joins is not the answer.

SQL queries should be able to handle any amount of data, so an adjacency list subtree query should be able to handle any number of levels. There are two solutions to the subtree problem when using the adjacency model: a recursive CTE or a looping user-defined function.

Recursive CTE down the hierarchy

The most direct solution to the subtree problem is the recursive common table expression, introduced in SQL Server 2005. This variant of the CTE (the basic CTE is covered in Chapter 11, "Including Data with Subqueries and CTEs") uses a `UNION ALL` and two `SELECT` statements.

The first `SELECT` statement defines the anchor node from which the recursion will start, i.e., the top of the subtree. When the recursion starts, the row(s) returned by this query are added to the CTE.

The second `SELECT` defines how rows are recursively added to the result set. This `SELECT` statement joins with the CTE itself — similar to the earlier self-join — and uses the `UNION ALL` to add the rows to the output of the CTE. The key is that the second `SELECT` will continue to self-join through the layers of the hierarchy until no more rows are found.

The loop stops executing when no more data is returned from the recursive step of the CTE. The first example focuses on the recursive nature of the CTE. The first `SELECT` in the CTE locates the employee with a `ManagerID` of null, which should be the top of the hierarchy. The name of the CTE is `OrgPath`, so when the second select joins with `OrgPath` it can find all the related nodes. The CTE continues to execute the second `SELECT` for every level of the hierarchy until the hierarchy ends:

```
-- Find all - Recursive CTE down the OrgChart
-- All employees who report to the CEO
-- simple query
```

```
WITH OrgPath (BusinessEntityID, ManagerID, lv)
AS (
   -- Anchor
      SELECT BusinessEntityID, ManagerID, 1
        FROM HumanResources.Employee
        WHERE ManagerID IS NULL -- should only be EmployeeID 1

    -- Recursive Call
    UNION ALL
      SELECT E.BusinessEntityID, E.ManagerID, lv + 1
        FROM HumanResources.Employee AS E
          JOIN OrgPath
            ON E.ManagerID = OrgPath.BusinessEntityID
    )
SELECT BusinessEntityID, ManagerID, lv
  FROM OrgPath
  ORDER BY Lv, BusinessEntityID
  OPTION (MAXRECURSION 20);
```

Result (abbreviated):

```
BusinessEntityID ManagerID   lv
---------------- ----------- -----------
1                NULL        1
2                1           2
16               1           2
25               1           2
234              1           2
273              1           2
...
```

Because you join to the CTE in the recursive section of the CTE, you can use columns from this iteration to calculate the level in the hierarchy. In the previous query, the `Lv` column is calculated using the `lv` column from the previous iteration + 1. Thus, each iteration is given a sequential level number.

If the adjacency list data had a cyclic error (A reports to B, who reports to C, who reports to A), then the recursive query could run forever, in which case the `maxrecursion` option limits the levels of recursion.

CAUTION **If the recursive CTE hits the `maxrecursion` limit and there's still data yet unprocessed, it will raise a 530, level 16 error, so even if the requirement is to return five levels of the hierarchy, `option(maxrecursion 5)` will return an error. Horrors!**

A solution is to use a `WHERE` clause in the second `SELECT`:

```
WHERE Lv <= 3
```

This will safely limit the second query to return the first four levels of the hierarchy without throwing an error.

The next query extends the previous recursive CTE by adding joins to flesh out the data. It also uses a different anchor node — Jean Trenary, Adventure Works' IT Manager:

```
-- Find Subtree - Recursive CTE
-- All employees who report to IT Manager
-- full query with joins
WITH OrgPath (BusinessEntityID, ManagerID, lv)
AS (
   -- Anchor
      SELECT BusinessEntityID, ManagerID, 1
        FROM HumanResources.Employee
        WHERE BusinessEntityID = 263 -- Jean Trenary - IS Manager
    -- Recursive Call
    UNION ALL
      SELECT E.BusinessEntityID, E.ManagerID, lv + 1
        FROM HumanResources.Employee AS E
          JOIN OrgPath
            ON E.ManagerID = OrgPath.BusinessEntityID
    )
SELECT Lv, Emp.BusinessEntityID,
    C.FirstName + ' ' + C.LastName AS [Name],
    Emp.JobTitle,
    OrgPath.ManagerID,
    M.FirstName + ' ' + M.LastName AS [Manager]
  FROM HumanResources.Employee AS Emp
    JOIN OrgPath
      ON Emp.BusinessEntityID = OrgPath.BusinessEntityID
    JOIN Person.Person AS C
      ON C.BusinessEntityID = Emp.BusinessEntityID
    LEFT JOIN Person.Person AS M
      ON Emp.ManagerID = M.BusinessEntityID
  ORDER BY Lv, BusinessEntityID
  OPTION (MAXRECURSION 20);
```

Result (abbreviated):

```
    BusinessEntityID                                        ManagerID
Lv       Name                 JobTitle                            Manager
--- ----- ------------------ ---------------------------- ----- -------------
1   263   Jean Trenary       Information Services Manager 1     Ken Sánchez
2   264   Stephanie Conroy   Network Manager              263   Jean Trenary
2   267   Karen Berg         Application Specialist       263   Jean Trenary
2   268   Ramesh Meyyappan   Application Specialist       263   Jean Trenary
2   269   Dan Bacon          Application Specialist       263   Jean Trenary
2   270   François Ajenstat  Database Administrator       263   Jean Trenary
2   271   Dan Wilson         Database Administrator       263   Jean Trenary
2   272   Janaina Bueno      Application Specialist       263   Jean Trenary
3   265   Ashvini Sharma     Network Administrator        264   Stephanie Conroy
3   266   Peter Connelly     Network Administrator        264   Stephanie Conroy
...
```

User-defined function down the hierarchy

SQL Server 2005's recursive CTE is not the only way to skin a hierarchy. Before 2005, hierarchies were handled with stored procedures or user-defined functions that looped through the hierarchy layers adding each layer as a set to a temp table or table variable — effectively doing the same thing as a CTE but with T-SQL.

The following multiple-statement table-valued user-defined function accepts an `EmployeeID` as a parameter. The function returns this employee and all the employees below them in the organization tree. The function definition includes the structure for the returned table variable, called `@Tree`. The function populates `@Tree`, first inserting the anchor node, the employee for the `EmployeeID` passed to the function.

CROSS-REF **This method jumps ahead a bit, using an advanced programming feature of SQL Server to solve the hierarchical problem. For more information about one of my personal favorite features of SQL Server, see Chapter 25, "Building User-Defined Functions."**

The `WHILE` loop continues to `INSERT INTO @tree` the next hierarchy level until no more rows are found (`@@rowcount > 0`).

Even though this is a loop, it's still performing nice set-based inserts, one for every hierarchy level. If the hierarchy has a million nodes and is nine levels deep, then nine set-based inserts complete the entire task from top to bottom:

```
-- User-Defined Functions for Navigating Adjacency list
CREATE FUNCTION dbo.OrgTree
  (@BusinessEntityID INT)
  RETURNS
    @Tree TABLE (BusinessEntityID INT, ManagerID INT, Lv INT)
AS
BEGIN
  DECLARE @LC INT = 1
  -- insert the top level (anchor node)
  INSERT @Tree (BusinessEntityID, ManagerID, Lv)
    SELECT BusinessEntityID, ManagerID, @LC
      FROM HumanResources.Employee AS E    -- the employee
      WHERE BusinessEntityID = @BusinessEntityID
   -- Loop through each lower levels
  WHILE @@RowCount > 0
    BEGIN
        SET @LC = @LC + 1
        -- insert the Next level of employees
        INSERT @Tree (BusinessEntityID, ManagerID, Lv)
          SELECT NextLevel.BusinessEntityID,
                 NextLevel.ManagerID, @LC
            FROM HumanResources.Employee AS NextLevel
              JOIN @Tree AS CurrentLevel
                ON CurrentLevel.BusinessEntityID
                   = NextLevel.ManagerID
            WHERE CurrentLevel.Lv = @LC - 1
```

```
      END
    RETURN
  END; -- end of function
```

A table-valued function returns a result set so it's called in the FROM clause. The following query returns AdventureWorks2008's entire organizational chart:

```
-- test UDF
-- find all
-- simple query
SELECT * FROM dbo.OrgTree(1);
```

Result (abbreviated):

```
BusinessEntityID ManagerID   Lv
---------------- ----------- -----------
1                NULL        1
2                1           2
16               1           2
25               1           2
234              1           2
263              1           2
...
```

Best Practice

The recursive CTE in this case is about twice as fast as the user-defined function. However, the function can include more variations of code, so it's useful to know both methods.

Just as with the recursive CTE, it's easy to expand the query and include the data necessary for a human-readable result set. Just like the previous recursive CTE example, this query finds only the subtree of those who work for Jean Trenary in the IT dept:

```
-- find subtree
-- all who work in IT
-- full query with joins
SELECT Lv, Emp.BusinessEntityID, Emp.JobTitle,
    C.FirstName + ' ' + C.LastName AS [Name],
    OrgTree.ManagerID,
    M.FirstName + ' ' + M.LastName AS [Manager]
  FROM HumanResources.Employee AS Emp
    JOIN dbo.OrgTree (263) -- Jean Trenary, IT Manager
      ON Emp.BusinessEntityID = OrgTree.BusinessEntityID
    JOIN Person.Person AS C
```

```
      ON C.BusinessEntityID = Emp.BusinessEntityID
    LEFT JOIN Person.Person AS M
      ON Emp.ManagerID = M.BusinessEntityID
  ORDER BY Lv, BusinessEntityID;
```

Result (abbreviated):

```
    BusinessEntityID                                        ManagerID
Lv          Name               JobTitle                           Manager
--- ----- ---------------- --------------------------- ----- -------------
1   263   Jean Trenary      Information Services Manager 1      Ken Sánchez
2   264   Stephanie Conroy  Network Manager             263    Jean Trenary
2   267   Karen Berg        Application Specialist      263    Jean Trenary
2   268   Ramesh Meyyappan  Application Specialist      263    Jean Trenary
2   269   Dan Bacon         Application Specialist      263    Jean Trenary
2   270   François Ajenstat Database Administrator      263    Jean Trenary
2   271   Dan Wilson        Database Administrator      263    Jean Trenary
2   272   Janaina Bueno     Application Specialist      263    Jean Trenary
3   265   Ashvini Sharma    Network Administrator       264    Stephanie Conroy
3   266   Peter Connelly    Network Administrator       264    Stephanie Conroy
...
```

A nice feature of the table-valued user-defined function is that it can be called from the `CROSS APPLY` (new in SQL Server 2005), which executes the function once for every row in the outer query. Here, the `CROSS APPLY` is used with the function to generate an extensive list of every report under every `BusinessEntityID` from `HumanResources.Employee`:

```
-- using Cross Apply to report all node under everyone
SELECT E.BusinessEntityID, OT.BusinessEntityID, OT.Lv
  FROM HumanResources.Employee AS E
    CROSS APPLY dbo.OrgTree(BusinessEntityID) AS OT;
```

The next query builds on the previous query, adding a `GROUP BY` to present a count of the number of reports under every manager. Because it explodes out every manager with its complete subtree, this query returns not 290 rows, but 1,308:

```
-- Count of All Reports
SELECT E.BusinessEntityID, COUNT(OT.BusinessEntityID)-1 AS ReportCount
  FROM HumanResources.Employee E
    CROSS APPLY dbo.OrgTree(BusinessEntityID) OT
  GROUP BY E.BusinessEntityID
  HAVING COUNT(OT.BusinessEntityID) > 1
  ORDER BY COUNT(OT.BusinessEntityID) DESC;
```

Result (abbreviated):

```
BusinessEntityID BusinessEntityID Lv
---------------- ---------------- -----------
1                1                1
1                2                2
1                16               2
1                25               2
1                234              2
...
```

Recursive CTE looking up the hierarchy

The previous adjacency list subtree queries all looked down the hierarchical tree. Searching up the tree returns the path from the node in question to the top of the hierarchy — for an organizational chart, it would return the chain of command from the current node to the top of the organizational chart. The technical term for this search is an *ancestor search*.

The queries to search up the hierarchy are similar to the downward-looking queries, only the direction of the join is modified. The following queries demonstrate the modification.

This query returns François the DBA's chain of command to the CEO using a recursive CTE:

```
-----------------------------------
-- Adjacency list
-- navigating up the tree

-- Recursive CTE
WITH OrgPathUp (BusinessEntityID, ManagerID, lv)
AS (
   -- Anchor
      SELECT BusinessEntityID, ManagerID, 1
        FROM HumanResources.Employee
        WHERE BusinessEntityID = 270 -- François Ajenstat the DBA

    -- Recursive Call
    UNION ALL
      SELECT E.BusinessEntityID, E.ManagerID, lv + 1
        FROM HumanResources.Employee AS E
          JOIN OrgPathUp
            ON OrgPathUp.ManagerID = E.BusinessEntityID
    )
SELECT Lv, Emp.BusinessEntityID,
    C.FirstName + ' ' + C.LastName AS [Name],
    Emp.JobTitle
  FROM HumanResources.Employee Emp
    JOIN OrgPathUp
      ON Emp.BusinessEntityID = OrgPathUp.BusinessEntityID
    JOIN Person.Person AS C
      ON C.BusinessEntityID = Emp.BusinessEntityID
    LEFT JOIN Person.Person AS M
      ON Emp.ManagerID = M.BusinessEntityID
  ORDER BY Lv DESC, BusinessEntityID
  OPTION (MAXRECURSION 20);
```

Result:

```
    BusinessEntityID
Lv        Name                JobTitle
--- ----- ------------------ ---------------------------
3   1     Ken Sánchez         Chief Executive Officer
2   263   Jean Trenary        Information Services Manager
1   270   François Ajenstat  Database Administrator
```

Searching up the hierarchy with a user-defined function

Modifying the recursive CTE to search up the hierarchy to find the chain of command, instead of search down the hierarchy to find the subtree, was as simple as changing the join criteria. The same is true for a user-defined function. The next function searches up the hierarchy and is called for François the DBA. The modified join is shown in bold:

```
-- Classic UDF
CREATE FUNCTION dbo.OrgTreeUP
  (@BusinessEntityID INT)
  RETURNS @Tree TABLE (BusinessEntityID INT, ManagerID INT, Lv INT)
AS
BEGIN
  DECLARE @LC INT = 1
  -- insert the starting level (anchor node)
  INSERT @Tree (BusinessEntityID, ManagerID, Lv)
    SELECT BusinessEntityID, ManagerID, @LC
      FROM HumanResources.Employee AS E     -- the employee
      WHERE BusinessEntityID = @BusinessEntityID
   -- Loop through each lower levels
  WHILE @@RowCount > 0
    BEGIN
        SET @LC = @LC + 1
        -- insert the Next level of employees
        INSERT @Tree (BusinessEntityID, ManagerID, Lv)
          SELECT NextLevel.BusinessEntityID,
               NextLevel.ManagerID, @LC
            FROM HumanResources.Employee AS NextLevel
              JOIN @Tree AS CurrentLevel
                ON NextLevel.BusinessEntityID
                   = CurrentLevel.ManagerID
            WHERE CurrentLevel.Lv = @LC - 1
      END
    RETURN
  END;

go

-- calling the Function
-- chain of command up from François
SELECT * FROM dbo.OrgTreeUp(270);  -- François Ajenstat the DBA
```

Result :

```
BusinessEntityID ManagerID   Lv
---------------- ----------- -----------
270              263         1
263              1           2
1                NULL        3
```

Is the node an ancestor?

A common programming task when working with hierarchies is answering the question, Is node A in node B subtree? In practical terms, it's asking, "Does François, the DBA, report to Jean Trenary, the IT manager?"

Using an adjacency list to answer that question from an adjacency list is somewhat complicated, but it can be done by leveraging the subtree work from the previous section.

Answering the question "Does employee 270 report to node 263?" is the same question as "Is node 270 an ancestor of node 263?" Both questions can be expressed in SQL as, "Is the ancestor node in current node's the ancestor list?" The `OrgTreeUp()` user-defined function returns all the ancestors of a given node, so reusing this user-defined function is the simplest solution:

```
SELECT 'True'
  WHERE 263 -- 263: Jean Trenary
    IN (SELECT BusinessEntityID FROM OrgTreeUp(270));
            -- 270: François Ajenstat the DBA
Result:
-------
True
```

Determining the node's level

Because each node only knows about itself, there's no inherent way to determine the node's level without scanning up the hierarchy. Determining a node's level requires either running a recursive CTE or user-defined function to navigate up the hierarchy and return the column representing the level.

Once the level is returned by the recursive CTE or user-defined function, it's easy to update a column with the `lv` value.

Reparenting the adjacency list

As with any data, there are three types of modifications: inserts, updates, and deletes. With a hierarchy, inserting at the bottom of the node is trivial, but inserting into the middle of the hierarchy, updating a node to a different location in the hierarchy, or deleting a node in the middle of the hierarchy can be rather complex.

The term used to describe this issue is *reparenting* — assigning a new parent to a node or set of nodes. For example, in `AdventureWorks2008`, IT Manager Jean Trenary reports directly to CEO Ken Sánchez, but what if a reorganization positions the IT dept under Terri Duffy, VP of Engineering? How many of the nodes would need to be modified, and how would they be updated? That's the question of reparenting the hierarchy.

Because each node only knows about itself and its direct parent node, reparenting an adjacency list is trivial. To move the IT dept under the VP of Engineering, simply update Jean Trenary's `ManagerID` value:

```
UPDATE HumanResources.Employee
  SET ManagerID = 2 -- Terri Duffy, Vice President of Engineering
  WHERE BusinessEntityID = 263; -- Jean Trenary IT Manager
```

Deleting a node in the middle of the hierarchy is potentially more complex but is limited to modifying *n* nodes, where *n* is the number of nodes that have the node being deleted as a parent. Each node under the node to be deleted must be reassigned to another node. By default, that's probably the deleted node's ManagerID.

Indexing an adjacency list

Indexing an adjacency list pattern hierarchy is rather straightforward. Create a non-clustered index on the column holding the parent node ID. The current node ID column is probably the primary key and the clustered index and so will be automatically included in the non-clustered index. The parent ID index will gather all the subtree values by parent ID and perform fast index seeks.

The following code was used to index the parent ID column when the adjacency list pattern was restored to AdventureWorks2008 at the beginning of this chapter:

```
CREATE INDEX IxParentID
  ON HumanResources.Employee
    (ManagerID);
```

If the table is very wide (over 25 columns) and large (millions of rows) then a non-clustered index on the primary key and the parent ID will provide a narrow covering index for navigation up the hierachy.

Cyclic errors

As mentioned earlier, every node in the adjacency list pattern knows only about itself and its parent node. Therefore, there's no SQL constraint than can possibly test for or prevent a cyclic error.

If someone plays an April Fools Day joke on Jean Trenary and sets her ManagerID to, say, 270, so she reports to the DBA (gee, who might have permission to do that?), it would introduce a cyclic error into the hierarchy:

```
UPDATE HumanResources.Employee
 SET ManagerID = 270 -- François Ajenstat the DBA
 WHERE BusinessEntityID = 263 -- Jean Trenary IT Manager
```

The cyclic error will cause the OrgTree function to loop from Jean to François to Jean to François forever, or until the query is stopped. Go ahead and try it:

```
SELECT 'True'
  WHERE 270 -- François Ajenstat the DBA
    IN (SELECT BusinessEntityID FROM OrgTree(263));
```

Now set it back to avoid errors in the next section:

```
UPDATE HumanResources.Employee
  SET ManagerID = 1 - the CEO
  WHERE BusinessEntityID = 263 -- Jean Trenary IT Manager
```

To locate cyclic errors in the hierarchy, a stored procedure or function must navigate both up and down the subtrees of the node in question and use code to detect and report an out-of-place duplication. Download the latest code to check for cyclic errors from www.sqlserverbible.com.

Adjacency list variations

The basic adjacency list pattern is useful for situations that include only a one-parent-to-multiple-nodes relationship. With a little modification, an adjacency list can also handle more, but it's not sufficient for most serious production database hierarchies. Fortunately, the basic data-pair pattern is easily modified to handle more complex hierarchies such as bills of materials, genealogies, and complex organizational charts.

Bills of materials/multiple cardinalities

When there's a many-to-many relationship between current nodes and parent nodes, an associative table is required, similar to how an associative table is used in any other many-to-many cardinality model. For example, an order may include multiple products, and each product may be on multiple orders, so the `order detail` table serves as an associative table between the order and the product.

The same type of many-to-many problem commonly exists in manufacturing when designing schemas for bills of materials. For example, part a23 may be used in the manufacturing of multiple other parts, and part a23 itself might have been manufactured from still other parts. In this way, any part may be both a child and parent of multiple other parts.

To build a many-to-many hierarchical bill of materials, the bill of materials serves as the adjacency table between the current part(s) and the parent parts(s), both of which are stored in the same `Parts` table, as shown in Figure 17-5.

The same pattern used to navigate a hierarchy works for a bill of materials system as well — it just requires working through the `BillOfMaterials` table.

The following query is similar to the previous subtree recursive CTE. If finds all the parts used to create a given assembly — in manufacturing this is commonly called a *parts explosion report*. In this instance, the query does a parts explosion for Product 777 — Adventure Works' popular Mountain-100 bike in Black with a 44" frame:

```
WITH PartsExplosion (ProductAssemblyID, ComponentID, lv, Qty)
AS (
   -- Anchor
      SELECT ProductID, ProductID, 1, CAST(0 AS DECIMAL (8,2))
        FROM Production.Product
        WHERE ProductID = 777 --  Mountain-100 Black, 44

    -- Recursive Call
    UNION ALL
      SELECT BOM.ProductAssemblyID, BOM.ComponentID, lv + 1, PerAssemblyQty
        FROM PartsExplosion CTE
          JOIN (SELECT *
                  FROM Production.BillOfMaterials
                  WHERE EndDate IS NULL
                  ) AS BOM
             ON CTE.ComponentID = BOM.ProductAssemblyID
    )
SELECT lv, PA.NAME AS 'Assembly', PC.NAME AS 'Component',
```

```
        CAST(Qty AS INT) as Qty
FROM PartsExplosion AS PE
  JOIN Production.Product AS PA
    ON PE.ProductAssemblyID = PA.ProductID
  JOIN Production.Product AS PC
    ON PE.ComponentID = PC.ProductID
ORDER BY Lv, ComponentID ;
```

FIGURE 17-5

The bill of materials structure in AdventureWorks uses an adjacency table to store which parts (ComponentID) are used to manufacture which other parts (ProductAssembyID).

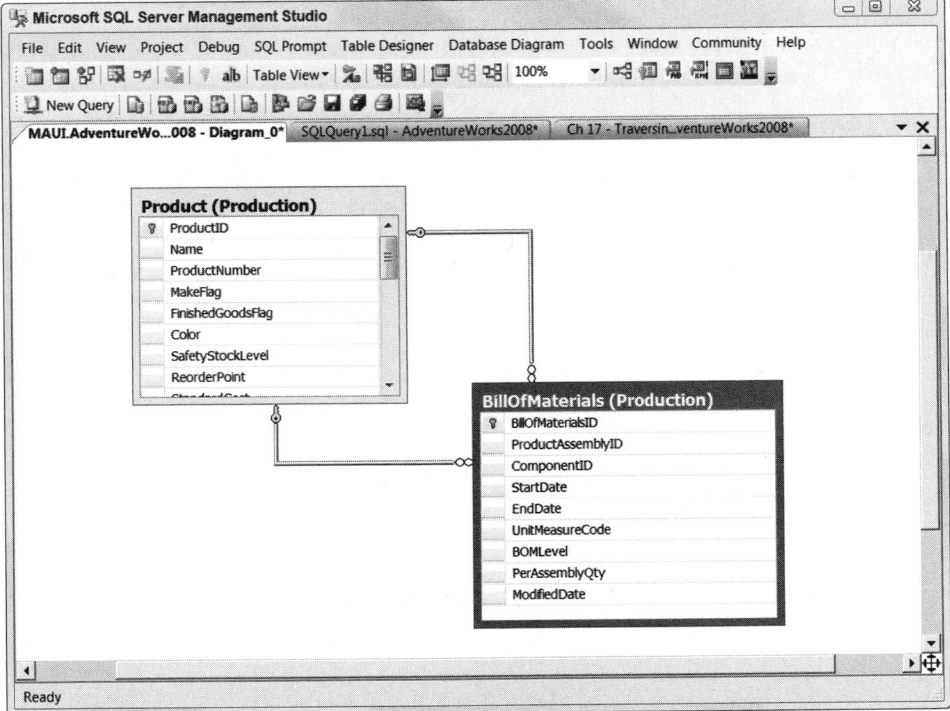

The result is a complete list of all the parts required to make a mountain bike:

```
lv   Assembly                         Component                    Qty
---- -------------------------------- ---------------------------- ----
1    Mountain-100 Black, 44           Mountain-100 Black, 44       0
2    Mountain-100 Black, 44           HL Mountain Seat Assembly    1
2    Mountain-100 Black, 44           HL Mountain Frame - Black,44 1
```

```
2     Mountain-100 Black, 44          HL Headset                  1
2     Mountain-100 Black, 44          HL Mountain Handlebars      1
2     Mountain-100 Black, 44          HL Mountain Front Wheel     1
2     Mountain-100 Black, 44          HL Mountain Rear Wheel      1
...
4     Chain Stays                     Metal Sheet 5               1
4     Handlebar Tube                  Metal Sheet 6               1
4     BB Ball Bearing                 Cup-Shaped Race             2
4     BB Ball Bearing                 Cone-Shaped Race            2
4     HL Hub                          HL Spindle/Axle             1
4     HL Hub                          HL Spindle/Axle             1
4     HL Hub                          HL Shell                    1
4     HL Hub                          HL Shell                    1
4     HL Fork                         Steerer                     1
5     Fork End                        Metal Sheet 2               1
5     Blade                           Metal Sheet 5               1
5     Fork Crown                      Metal Sheet 5               1
5     Steerer                         Metal Sheet 6               1
```

Adjacency list pros and cons

The adjacency list pattern is common and well understood, with several points in its favor:

- Reparenting is trivial.
- It's easy to manually decode and understand.

On the con side, the adjacency list pattern has these concerns:

- Consistency requires additional care and manual checking for cyclic errors.
- Performance is reasonable, but not as fast as the materialized list or `hierarchyID` when retrieving a subtree. The adjacency list pattern is hindered by the need to build the hierarchy if you need to navigate or query related nodes in a hierarchy. This needs to be done iteratively using either a loop in a user-defined function or a recursive CTE. Returning data though a user-defined function also presents some overhead.

The Materialized-Path Pattern

The materialized-path pattern is another excellent method to store and navigate hierarchical data. Basically, it stores a denormalized, comma-delimited representation of the list of the current node's complete ancestry, including every generation of parents from the top of the hierarchy down to the current node. A common materialized path is a file path:

```
c:\Users\Pn\Documents\SQLServer2009Bible\AuthorReview\Submitted
```

François Ajenstat, the DBA, has a hierarchy chain of command that flows from Ken Sánchez (ID: 1) the CEO, to Jean Trenary (ID: 263) the IT Manager, and then down to François (ID: 270). Therefore, his materialized path would be as follows:

```
1, 263, 270
```

The following scalar user-defined function generates the materialized path programmatically:

```
CREATE FUNCTION dbo.MaterializedPath
  (@BusinessEntityID INT)
  RETURNS VARCHAR(200)
AS
BEGIN
  DECLARE @Path VARCHAR(200)
  SELECT @Path = ''
  -- Loop through Hierarchy
  WHILE @@RowCount > 0
    BEGIN
      SELECT @Path
         = ISNULL(RTRIM(
             CAST(@BusinessEntityID AS VARCHAR(10)))+ ',','')
             + @Path
      SELECT @BusinessEntityID = ManagerID
        FROM Humanresources.Employee
        WHERE BusinessEntityID = @BusinessEntityID
    END
  RETURN @Path
END;
```

Executing the function for François Ajenstat (ID:270) returns his materialized path:

```
Select dbo.MaterializedPath(270) as MaterializedPath
```

Result:

```
MaterializedPath
----------------------
1,263,270,
```

Because the materialized path is stored as a string, it may be indexed, searched, and manipulated as a string, which has its pros and cons. These are discussed later in the chapter.

Modifying AdventureWorks2008 for Materialized Path

The following script modifies AdventureWorks2008 and builds a materialized path using the previously added ManagerID data and the newly created MaterializedPath user-defined function:

```
ALTER TABLE HumanResources.Employee
  ADD MaterializedPath VARCHAR(200);
```

continued

continued

```
Go

UPDATE HumanResources.Employee
  SET MaterializedPath = dbo.MaterializedPath(BusinessEntityID);

CREATE INDEX IxMaterializedPath
  ON HumanResources.Employee
    (MaterializedPath);

SELECT BusinessEntityID, ManagerID, MaterializedPath
  FROM HumanResources.Employee;
```

Result (abbreviated):

```
BusinessEntityID ManagerID   MaterializedPath
---------------- ----------- -------------------
1                NULL        1,
2                1           1,2,
3                2           1,2,3,
4                3           1,2,3,4,
5                3           1,2,3,5,
6                3           1,2,3,6,
7                3           1,2,3,7,
8                7           1,2,3,7,8,
9                7           1,2,3,7,9,
...
263              1           1,263,
264              263         1,263,264,
265              264         1,263,264,265,
266              264         1,263,264,266,
267              263         1,263,267,
268              263         1,263,268,
269              263         1,263,269,
270              263         1,263,270,
...
```

The way the tasks build on each other for a materialized path are very different from the flow of tasks for an adjacency list; therefore, this section first explains subtree queries. The flow continues with ancestor checks and determining the level, which is required for single-level queries.

NOTE **Enforcing the structure of the hierarchy — ensuring that every node actually has a parent — is a bit oblique when using the materialized-path method. However, one chap, Simon Sabin (SQL Server MVP in the U.K., all-around good guy, and technical editor for this chapter) has an ingenious method. Instead of explaining it here, I'll direct you to his excellent website:** `http://sqlblogcasts.com/blogs/simons/archive/2009/03/09/Enforcing-parent-child-relationship-with-Path-Hierarchy-model.aspx`

Subtree queries

The primary work of a hierarchy is returning the hierarchy as a set. The adjacency list method used similar methods for scanning up or down the hierarchy. Not so with materialized path. Searching down a materialized path is a piece of cake, but searching up the tree is a real pain.

Searching down the hierarchy with materialized path

Navigating down the hierarchy and returning a subtree of all nodes under a given node is where the materialized path method really shines.

Check out the simplicity of this query:

```
SELECT BusinessEntityID, ManagerID, MaterializedPath
  FROM HumanResources.Employee
  WHERE MaterializedPath LIKE '1,263,%'
```

Result:

```
BusinessEntityID ManagerID   MaterializedPath
---------------- ----------- ------------------------
263              1           1,263,
264              263         1,263,264,
265              264         1,263,264,265,
266              264         1,263,264,266,
267              263         1,263,267,
268              263         1,263,268,
269              263         1,263,269,
270              263         1,263,270,
271              263         1,263,271,
272              263         1,263,272
```

That's all it takes to find a node's subtree. Because the materialized path for every node in the subtree is just a string that begins with the subtree's parent's materialized path, it's easily searched with a `LIKE` function and a `%` wildcard in the `WHERE` clause.

It's important that the `LIKE` search string includes the comma before the `%` wildcard; otherwise, searching for `1,263%` would find `1,2635`, which would be an error, of course.

Searching up the hierarchy with materialized path

Searching up the hierarchy means searching for the all the ancestors, or the chain of command, for a given node. The nice thing about a materialized path is that the full list of ancestors is right there in the materialized path. There's no need to read any other rows.

Therefore, to get the parent nodes, you need to parse the materialized path to return the IDs of each parent node and then join to this set of IDs to get the parent nodes.

The trick is to extract it quickly. Unfortunately, SQL Server lacks a simple split function. There are two options: build a CLR function that uses the C# split function or build a T-SQL scalar user-defined function to parse the string.

A C# CLR function to split a string is a relatively straightforward task:

```
using Microsoft.SqlServer.Server;
using System.Data.SqlClient;
using System;using System.Collections;

public class ListFunctionClass
{
[SqlFunction(FillRowMethodName = "FillRow",

TableDefinition = "list nvarchar(max)")]
public static IEnumerator ListSplitFunction(string list)
{

string[] listArray = list.Split(new char[] {','});

Array array = listArray;

return array.GetEnumerator();
}

public static void FillRow(Object obj, out String sc)
{

sc = (String)obj;
}
}
```

NOTE **Adam Machanic, SQL Server MVP and one of the sharpest SQL Server programmers around, went on a quest to write the fastest CLR split function possible. The result is posted on** SQLBlog.com **at** http://tinyurl.com/dycmxb.

But I'm a T-SQL guy, so unless there's a compelling need to use CLR, I'll opt for T-SQL. There are a number of T-SQL string-split solutions available. I've found that the performance depends on the length of the delimited strings. Erland Sommerskog's website analyzes several T-SQL split solutions: http://www.sommarskog.se/arrays-in-sql-2005.html.

Of Erland's solutions, the one I prefer for shorter length strings such as these is in the ParseString user-defined function:

```
-- up the hierarchy
-- parse the string

CREATE
-- alter
FUNCTION dbo.ParseString (@list varchar(200))
   RETURNS @tbl TABLE (ID INT) AS
BEGIN
   -- code by Erland Sommarskog
   -- Erland's Website: http://www.sommarskog.se/arrays-in-sql-2005.html
```

```
      DECLARE @valuelen   int,
              @pos        int,
              @nextpos    int

      SELECT @pos = 0, @nextpos = 1

      WHILE @nextpos > 0
      BEGIN
         SELECT @nextpos = charindex(',', @list, @pos + 1)
         SELECT @valuelen = CASE WHEN @nextpos > 0
                                 THEN @nextpos
                                 ELSE len(@list) + 1
                            END - @pos - 1
         INSERT @tbl (ID)
            VALUES (substring(@list, @pos + 1, @valuelen))
         SELECT @pos = @nextpos
      END
     RETURN
   END

   go --

   SELECT ID
     FROM HumanResources.Employee
       CROSS APPLY dbo.ParseString(MaterializedPath)
       WHERE BusinessEntityID = 270

   go --

   DECLARE @MatPath VARCHAR(200)

   SELECT @MatPath = MaterializedPath
     FROM HumanResources.Employee
     WHERE BusinessEntityID = 270

   SELECT E.BusinessEntityID, MaterializedPath
     FROM dbo.ParseString(@MatPath)
       JOIN HumanResources.Employee E
         ON ParseString.ID = E.BusinessEntityID
     ORDER BY MaterializedPath
```

Is the node in the subtree?

Because the materialized-path pattern is so efficient at finding subtrees, the best way to determine whether a node is in a subtree is to reference the WHERE-like subtree query in a WHERE clause, similar to the adjacency list solution:

```
-- Does 270 work for 263
SELECT 'True'
  WHERE 270 IN
    (SELECT BusinessEntityID
       FROM HumanResources.Employee
       WHERE MaterializedPath LIKE '1,263,%')
```

Determining the node level

Determining the current node level using the materialized-path pattern is as simple as counting the commas in the materialized path. The following function uses CHARINDEX to locate the commas and make quick work of the task:

```
CREATE FUNCTION MaterializedPathLevel
  (@Path VARCHAR(200))
  RETURNS TINYINT
AS
BEGIN
  DECLARE
    @Position TINYINT = 1,
    @Lv TINYINT = 0;

  WHILE @Position >0
    BEGIN;
      SET @Lv += 1;
      SELECT @Position = CHARINDEX(',', @Path, @Position + 1 );
    END;
  RETURN @Lv - 1
END;
```

Testing the function:

```
SELECT dbo.MaterializedPathLevel('1,20,56,345,1010')
  As Level
```

Result:

```
Level
------------------
6
```

A function may be easily called within an update query, so pre-calculating and storing the level is a trivial process. The next script adds a Level column, updates it using the new function, and then takes a look at the data:

```
ALTER TABLE HumanResources.Employee
  ADD Level TINYINT

UPDATE HumanResources.Employee
  SET Level = dbo.MaterializedPathLevel(MaterializedPath)
```

```
SELECT BusinessEntityID, MaterializedPath, Level
  FROM HumanResources.Employee
```

Result (abbreviated):

```
BusinessEntityID MaterializedPath   Level
---------------- ------------------ -------
1                1,                 1
2                1,2,               2
3                1,2,3,             3
4                1,2,3,4,           4
5                1,2,3,5,           4
6                1,2,3,6,           4
7                1,2,3,7,           4
8                1,2,3,7,8,         5
9                1,2,3,7,9,         5
10               1,2,3,7,10,        5
```

Storing the level can be useful; for example, being able to query the node's level makes writing single-level queries significantly easier. Using the function in a persisted calculated column with an index works great.

Single-level queries

Whereas the adjacency list pattern was simpler for doing single-level queries, rather than returning complete subtrees, the materialized-path pattern excels at returning subtrees, but it's more difficult to return just a single level. Although neither solution excels at returning a specific level in a hierarchy on its own, it is possible with the adjacency pattern but requires some recursive functionality. For the materialized-path pattern, if the node's level is also stored in table, then the level can be easily added to the `WHERE` clause, and the queries become simple.

This query locates all the nodes one level down from the CEO. The CTE locates the `MaterializedPath` and the `Level` for the CEO, and the main query's join conditions filter the query to the next level down:

```
-- Query Search 1 level down
WITH CurrentNode(MaterializedPath, Level)
  AS
  (SELECT MaterializedPath, Level
     FROM HumanResources.Employee
     WHERE BusinessEntityID = 1)
SELECT BusinessEntityID, ManagerID, E.MaterializedPath, E.Level
  FROM HumanResources.Employee E
    JOIN CurrentNode C
      ON E.MaterializedPath LIKE C.MaterializedPath + '%'
    AND E.Level = C.Level + 1
```

Result:

```
BusinessEntityID ManagerID   MaterializedPath  Level
---------------- ----------- ----------------- -------
16               1           1,16,             2
2                1           1,2,              2
234              1           1,234,            2
25               1           1,25,             2
263              1           1,263,            2
273              1           1,273,            2
```

An advantage of this method over the single join method used for finding single-level queries for the adjacency list pattern is that this method can be used to find any specific level, not just the nearest level.

Locating the single-level query up the hierarchy is the same basic outer query, but the CTE/subquery uses the up-the-hierarchy subtree query instead, parsing the materialized path string.

Reparenting the materialized path

Because the materialized-path pattern stores the entire tree in the materialized path value in each node, when the tree is modified by inserting, updating, or deleting a node, the entire affected subtree must have its materialized path recalculated.

Each node's path contains the path of its parent node, so if the parent node's path changes, so do the children. This will propagate down and affect all descendants of the node being changed.

The brute force method is to reexecute the user-defined function that calculates the materialized path. A more elegant method, when it applies, is to use the `REPLACE` T-SQL function.

Indexing the materialized path

Indexing the materialized path requires only a non-clustered index on the materialized path column. Because the level column is used in some searches, depending on the usage, it's also a candidate for a non-clustered index. If so, then a composite index of the level and materialized path columns would be the best-performing option.

Materialized path pros and cons

There are some points in favor of the materialized-path pattern:

- The strongest point in its favor is that in contains the actual references to every node in its hierarchy. This gives the pattern considerable durability and consistency. If a node is deleted or updated accidentally, the remaining nodes in its subtree are not orphaned. The tree can be reconstructed. If Jean Trenary is deleted, the materialized path of the IT department employees remains intact.

- The materialized-path pattern is the only pattern that can retrieve an entire subtree with a single index seek. It's wicked fast.
- Reading a materialized path is simple and intuitive. The keys are there to read in plain text.

On the down side, there are a number of issues, including the following:

- The key sizes can become large; at 10 levels deep with an integer key, the keys can be 40–80 bytes in size. This is large for a key.
- Constraining the hierarchy is difficult without the use of triggers or complex check constraints. Unlike the adjacency list pattern, you cannot easily enforce that a parent node exists.
- Simple operations like "get me the parent node" are more complex without the aid of helper functions.
- Inserting new nodes requires calculating the materialized path, and reparenting the materialized path requires recalculating the materialized paths for every node in the affected subtree. For an OLTP system this can be a very expensive operation and lead to a large amount of contention. Offloading the maintenance of the hierarchy to a background process can alleviate this. An option is to combine adjacency and path solutions; one provides ease of maintenance and one provides performance for querying.

The materialized path is my favorite hierarchy pattern and the one I use in Nordic (my SQL Server object relational façade) to store the class structure.

Using the New HierarchyID

For SQL Server 2008, Microsoft has released a new data type targeted specifically at solving the hierarchy problem. Working through the materialized-path pattern was a good introduction to `HierarchyID` because `HierarchyID` is basically a binary version of materialized path.

`HierarchyID` is implemented as a CLR data type with CLR methods, but you don't need to enable CLR to use `HierarchyID`. Technically speaking, the CLR is always running. Disabling the CLR only disables installing and running user-programmed CLR assemblies.

To jump right into the `HierarchyID`, this first query exposes the raw data. The `OrganizationalNode` column in the `HumanResources.Employee` table is a `HierarchyID` column. The second column simply returns the binary data from `OrganizationalNode`. The third column, `HierarchyID.ToString()` uses the `.ToString()` method to converrt the `HierarchyID` data to text. The column returns the values stored in a caluculated column that's set to the `.getlevel()` method:

```
-- View raw HierarchyID Data
SELECT E.BusinessEntityID, P.FirstName + ' ' + P.LastName as 'Name',
    OrganizationNode, OrganizationNode.ToString() as 'HierarchyID.ToString()',
OrganizationLevel
  FROM HumanResources.Employee E
```

```
    JOIN Person.Person P
      ON E.BusinessEntityID = P.BusinessEntityID
Result (abbreviated):
BusinessEntityID OrganizationNode  HierarchyID.ToString()  OrganizationLevel
---------------- ----------------- ----------------------- -------------------
1                0x                /                       0
2                0x58              /1/                     1
16               0x68              /2/                     1
25               0x78              /3/                     1
234              0x84              /4/                     1
263              0x8C              /5/                     1
273              0x94              /6/                     1
3                0x5AC0            /1/1/                   2
17               0x6AC0            /2/1/                   2
```

In the third column, you can see data that looks similar to the materialized path pattern, but there's a significant difference. Instead of storing a delimited path of ancestor primary keys, `HierarchyID` is intended to store the relative node position, as shown in Figure 17-6.

FIGURE 17-6

The AdventureWorks Information Services Department with HierarchyID nodes displayed

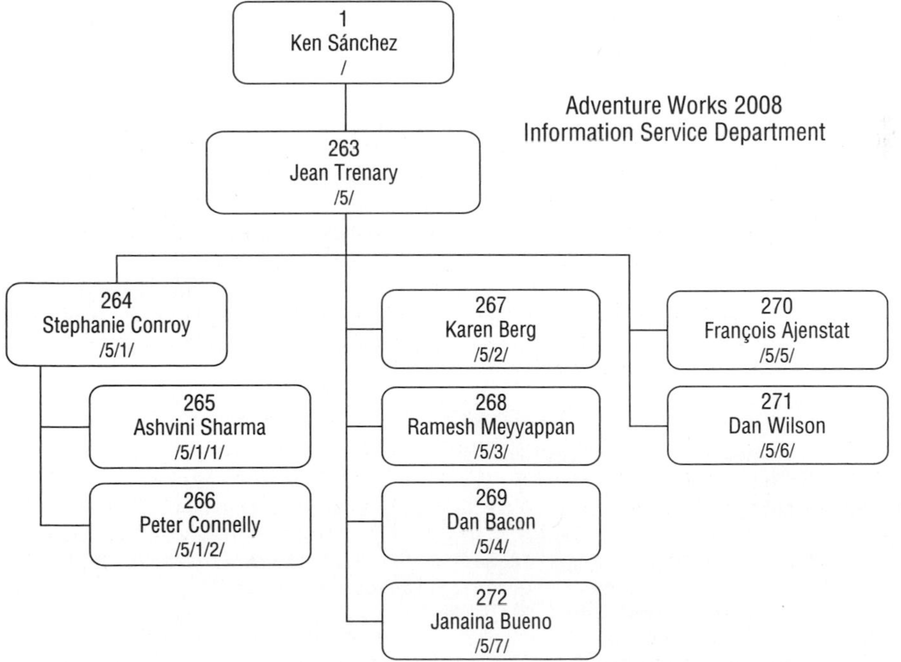

Walking through a few examples in this hierarchy, note the following:

- The CEO is the root node, so his HierarchyID is just /.
- If all the nodes under Ken were displayed, then Jean would be the fifth node. Her relative node position is the fifth node under Ken, so her HierarchyID is /**5**/.
- Stephanie is the first node under Jean, so her HierarchyID is /5/**1**/.
- Ashivini is the first node under Stephanie, so his node is /5/1/**1**/.

Selecting a single node

Even though HierarchyID stores the data in binary, it's possible to filter by a HierarchyID data type column in a WHERE clause using the text form of the data:

```
SELECT E.BusinessEntityID, P.FirstName + ' ' + P.LastName as 'Name', E.JobTitle
  FROM HumanResources.Employee E
    JOIN Person.Person P
      ON E.BusinessEntityID = P.BusinessEntityID
  WHERE OrganizationNode = '/5/5/'
Result:
BusinessEntityID  Name                     JobTitle
----------------- ------------------------ ----------------------------
270               François Ajenstat        Database Administrator
```

Scanning for ancestors

Searching for all ancestor nodes is relatively easy with HierarchyID. There's a great CLR method, IsDescendantOf(), that tests any node to determine whether it's a descendant of another node and returns either true or false. The following WHERE clause tests each row to determine whether the @EmployeeNode is a descendent of that row's OrganizationNode:

```
WHERE @EmployeeNode.IsDescendantOf(OrganizationNode) = 1
```

The full query returns the ancestor list for François. The script must first store François' HierarchyID value in a local variable. Because the variable is a HierarchyID, the IsDescendantOf() method may be applied. The fourth column displays the same test used in the WHERE clause:

```
DECLARE @EmployeeNode HierarchyID

SELECT @EmployeeNode = OrganizationNode
  FROM HumanResources.Employee
  WHERE OrganizationNode = '/5/5/' -- François Ajenstat the DBA

SELECT E.BusinessEntityID, P.FirstName + ' ' + P.LastName as 'Name', E.JobTitle,
    @EmployeeNode.IsDescendantOf(OrganizationNode) as Test
  FROM HumanResources.Employee E
    JOIN Person.Person P
      ON E.BusinessEntityID = P.BusinessEntityID
  WHERE @EmployeeNode.IsDescendantOf(OrganizationNode) = 1
```

Result:

```
BusinessEntityID Name                JobTitle                      Test
---------------- ------------------- ----------------------------- ---
1                Ken Sánchez         Chief Executive Officer         1
263              Jean Trenary        Information Services Manager    1
270              François Ajenstat   Database Administrator          1
```

Performing a subtree search

The IsDescendantOf() method is easily flipped around to perform a subtree search locating all descendants. The trick is that either side of the IsDescendantOf() method can use a variable or column. In this case the variable goes in the parameter and the method is applied to the column. The result is the now familiar AdventureWorks Information Service Department:

```
DECLARE @ManagerNode HierarchyID

SELECT @ManagerNode = OrganizationNode
  FROM HumanResources.Employee
  WHERE OrganizationNode = '/5/' -- Jean Trenary - IT Manager

SELECT E.BusinessEntityID, P.FirstName + ' ' + P.LastName as 'Name',
    OrganizationNode.ToString() as 'HierarchyID.ToString()',
    OrganizationLevel
  FROM HumanResources.Employee E
    JOIN Person.Person P
      ON E.BusinessEntityID = P.BusinessEntityID
  WHERE OrganizationNode.IsDescendantOf(@ManagerNode) = 1
```

Result:

```
BusinessEntityID Name               HierarchyID.ToString() OrganizationLevel
---------------- ------------------ ---------------------- -----
263              Jean Trenary           /5/                 1
264              Stephanie Conroy       /5/1/               2
265              Ashvini Sharma         /5/1/1/             3
266              Peter Connelly         /5/1/2/             3
267              Karen Berg             /5/2/               2
268              Ramesh Meyyappan       /5/3/               2
269              Dan Bacon              /5/4/               2
270              François Ajenstat      /5/5/               2
271              Dan Wilson             /5/6/               2
272              Janaina Bueno          /5/7/               2
```

Single-level searches

Single-level searches were presented first for the adjcency list pattern because they were the simpler searches. For HierarchyID searches, a single-level search is more complex and builds on the previous searches. In fact, a single-level HierarchyID search is really nothing more than an IsDescendantOf() search with the organizational level filter in the WHERE clause.

The following script adds the level to the WHERE cause of the previous script and finds only those members of the Information Servies Department who report directly to Jean:

```
DECLARE
  @ManagerNode HierarchyID,
  @ManagerLevel INT

SELECT @ManagerNode = OrganizationNode, @ManagerLevel = OrganizationLevel
  FROM HumanResources.Employee
  WHERE OrganizationNode = '/5/' -- Jean Trenary - IT Manager

SELECT E.BusinessEntityID, P.FirstName + ' ' + P.LastName as 'Name',
    OrganizationNode, OrganizationNode.ToString() as 'HierarchyID.ToString()',
OrganizationLevel
  FROM HumanResources.Employee E
    JOIN Person.Person P
      ON E.BusinessEntityID = P.BusinessEntityID
  WHERE OrganizationNode.IsDescendantOf(@ManagerNode) = 1
    AND OrganizationLevel = @ManagerLevel + 1
Result:
BusinessEntityID Name                HierarchyID.ToString() OrganizationLevel
---------------- ------------------- ---------------------- -------------
264              Stephanie Conroy        /5/1/                  2
267              Karen Berg              /5/2/                  2
268              Ramesh Meyyappan        /5/3/                  2
269              Dan Bacon               /5/4/                  2
270              François Ajenstat       /5/5/                  2
271              Dan Wilson              /5/6/                  2
272              Janaina Bueno           /5/7/                  2
```

Inserting new nodes

Inserting the root node into a HierarchyID hierarchy must start with the binary root node. The getroot() method returns a root node value.

Inserting additional nodes into HierarchyID's relative node position hierarchy first requires determining which nodes are already there. The GetDescendant() method can be used to generate the next node position.

You can download additional hierarchical sample code from www.sqlserverbible.com.

Performance

The HierarchyID data type is a compact data type optimized for storing relative node postion. As such, it takes less space than a character-based materialized path.

The HierarchyID node column should be indexed, which will aid subtree-type searches. There are specific Query Optimizer optimizations for indexing and HierarchyID, but I have found that materialized path is still slightly faster than HierarchyID.

If the searches are primarily along a specific level, then another index keyed by level column and the `HierarchyID` node column will be of use. However, I've found that this type of search is rarely used in the production hierarchies I've worked with.

HierarchyID pros and cons

The new `HierarchyID` is not without controversy. It's new and gets plenty of press and demo time, but I'm not sure it's a problem that needed another solution.

On the pro side, `HierarchyID` has the following advantage:

- It's faster than the adjacency list pattern.

On the con side:

- `HierarchyID` *embeds data within a binary data type so it's more difficult to navigate and diagnose.*
- *Storing only the relative node position is risky. If a node is moved or deleted without very careful coding, it can be nearly impossible to correct the orphaned nodes. Adjacency list and materialized path both store the actual primary keys values, so they are both more robust than* `HierarchyID`.

NOTE **Although Microsoft intends the `HierarchyID` to use a relative node postion, the contents of the data type accept any numeric values up to 45 bytes per node position (space between the /n/.) There's no reason why you can't insert a primary key instead of the relative node postion. It won't be as compact, but it will be more robust.**

Summary

Hierarchical data can present a challenge if you're not armed with patterns and solutions, but knowing the possible patterns and having several navigational methods in your toolset will increase the odds that your next hierarchical data project will be successful.

Adjacency pairs is the most common hierarchy solution, as it's easy to work with and well understood. Unless your requirement is very high performance when searching for all ancestors, stick with the known solution.

If the hierarchy is the crux of the database and most functions use the hierarchy in some way, then go with the materialized-path solution. My Nordic software navigates the class hierarchy in nearly every query, so I tested the three patterns with a million-node hierarchy. For searching a subtree of descendents, materialized path was slightly faster than `HierarchyID`. For finding all ancestors, materialized path was significantly faster than `HierarchyID`. Both easily beat the adjacency list pattern.

The next chapter continues with the theme of working with non-relational data and looks at SQL Server's new spatial data types.

Chapter 18

Manipulating XML Data

There has been a significant increase in the popularity and usage of XML in the past few years. XML is becoming widely accepted as the preferred format for exchanging and publishing information. Almost all modern applications seem to be touching XML in one way or another. They either generate XML for consumption by other applications or components, or they consume the XML produced by others. This chapter closely examines the XML capabilities of SQL Server 2008

XML is seen everywhere today. Knowingly or unknowingly, every application deals with XML in one way or another. For example, .NET applications use XML files to store configuration information. ASP.NET web pages are XML documents. Almost all modern websites generate and publish information as XML feeds (RDF, RSS, ATOM, OPML, etc.).

Changing application architectures in recent years contributed to the widespread acceptance of XML. Service-oriented architecture (SOA) promotes the usage of XML Web Services. AJAX (Asynchronous JavaScript and XML) has become a basic requirement of every web application today. XHTML has become the default standard for every web page.

To support the changing data processing requirements, Microsoft has added XML processing capabilities to SQL Server starting from SQL Server 2000. The XML support in SQL Server 2000 was very much limited. SQL Server 2005 added significant improvements to the XML processing capabilities, and SQL Server 2008 enhanced it further.

SQL Seconr's own usage of XML in a number of core components shows the level of acceptance XML is getting inside SQL Server. A few examples are given here:

- SSRS (SQL Server Reporting Services) stores report definitions as XML documents.
- SSSB (SQL Server Service Broker) exchanges messages in XML format.

IN THIS CHAPTER

Understanding the XML data type

Creating and using XML columns and variables

Loading XML documents from disk files

Understanding XPath and XQuery

Generating XML documents using FOR XML

Performing XML data modification

Handling XML namespaces

Shredding XML using OPENXML

Creating and using XML Schema Collections

Working with XML indexes

XML best practices

- SSIS (SQL Server Integration Services) stores the SSIS packages as XML documents and supports XML configuration files.
- DDL triggers use XML format for exchanging event information.

This chapter discusses the XML processing capabilities of SQL Server 2008 in detail.

What's New for XML in SQL Server 2008?

SQL Server 2008 adds a number of enhancements to the XML processing capabilities of the previous versions.

Improved Schema Validation Capabilities

- Added support for "lax" validation
- Added full support for `date`, `time`, and `dateTime` data types, including preservation of time zone information
- Improved support for union and list types. Allows creating unions of list types and lists of union types.

Enhancements to XQuery Support

- Added support for the "let" clause in `FLWOR` operations

DML Language Enhancements

- XML Data Type's `modify()` method now accepts XML data type variables in the XML DML expressions: `insert` and `replace value of`.

XML Processing in SQL Server 2008

The XML processing capabilities of SQL Server 2008 may be classified into three broad categories:

- Capability to generate XML documents
- Capability to query XML documents
- Capability to validate XML documents

Generating XML documents

Today, a large number of applications publish and exchange information in XML format. One of the most common examples is a website that publishes RSS or ATOM feeds. Applications that expose or consume XML Web Services need to generate XML documents containing the information to be exchanged. Web applications that support the AJAX programming model need to generate and serve information in XML format.

Most of the time, the data being exchanged in XML format by these applications comes from one or more databases. A major part of the data may come from one or more relational tables and the rest may come from some unstructured data storage. Some component or module has to take the responsibility for building the required XML document from the source data.

In the past, the responsibility for building the XML documents was handled by the application layer. The application might execute a stored procedure that returns one or more result sets, and it could build the desired XML document using a set of XML API functions exposed by the application programming language.

The first version of SQL Server shipped with XML generation capabilities is SQL Server 2000. SQL Server 2000 introduced a new T-SQL clause `FOR XML`, which transforms the results of a `SELECT` query to an XML stream. This new feature removed the burden of building XML documents at the application layer. Instead of returning tabular result sets to the client application, SQL Server could serve XML streams using the `FOR XML` clause.

SQL Server 2000's `FOR XML` clause offers a different level of control over the structure of the output XML document through the additional directives `AUTO`, `RAW`, and `EXPLICIT`.

When used with `AUTO` and `RAW`, `FOR XML` generates an XML document that contains an XML element for each row in the result set. While they have a simpler syntax and are quite easy to use, they provide very little control over the structure of the output XML document. `EXPLICIT`, on the contrary, provides a great extent of control over the output XML structure, but has a much more complex syntax and most people find it very hard to use.

SQL Server 2005 introduced a new directive, `PATH`, that has a simpler syntax and powerful customization capabilities. Almost all customization requirements that were possible only with `EXPLICIT` in SQL Server 2000 are now possible with `PATH`.

SQL Server's `FOR XML` clause, along with the `RAW`, `AUTO`, `PATH`, and `EXPLICIT` directives can generate XML documents to serve almost all XML generation requirements. A detailed explanation of `FOR XML`, along with several examples, is given in the section "FOR XML" later in this chapter.

Querying XML documents

Almost all applications that exchange information in XML format need to have a module or component capable of extracting information from the XML markup.

For example, an RSS reader desktop application might need to extract channel and item information from the XML document before it can be displayed in the UI element. A client application that calls a Web Service to retrieve a weather forecast or stock price needs to parse the XML result document and extract the required pieces of information.

Many of these applications might decide to store the information received in one or more relational tables. A Web Service that accepts sales order information from customers is one such example. The Web Service might send the order information to a stored procedure that stores the information in a set of relational tables.

Applications that run on SQL Server versions prior to 2000 do the XML parsing at the application layer. They parse XML documents and extract the required values, which are then sent to the database as parameters. Applications that deal with a variable number of values (like sales orders) either call the stored procedure once for each line (which is very bad for performance) or pass all the information in a single stored procedure call as a delimited string (which adds considerable string parsing overhead at the stored procedure level).

Microsoft shipped SQL Server 2000 with a very powerful XML processing function, `OPENXML()`, that is capable of shredding an XML document into a result set. Applications that run on SQL Server 2000 could pass entire XML documents to a SQL Server stored procedure without bothering to parse the XML document at the application layer. Applications that deal with a variable number of parameters, like sales or purchase orders, could make use of this XML processing capability of SQL Server and send all the information in an XML document with a single stored procedure call.

A typical call to `OPENXML()` includes a system stored procedure call to prepare an XML document handle, a call to `OPENXML()` to retrieve the result set, and another call to a system stored procedure to release the document handle. Because of this specific requirement — a system stored procedure call before and after the `OPENXML()` call — `OPENXML()` can neither be called from a function nor used in a set-based operation. For example, to read information from an XML formatted string stored in a SQL Server column, a `WHILE` loop is required, because `OPENXML()` can process only one XML document at a time. Before and after processing each document, calls to system stored procedures to initialize and release the document handle are necessary.

SQL Server 2005 introduced the native XML data type. An XML data type can store a complete XML document or a fragment. The XML data type supports XQuery, a language designed to query XML documents. The introduction of XQuery made querying information from XML documents much easier. XQuery is lightweight, very powerful, much easier to use compared to `OPENXML()`, and it can be used in a set-based operation or can be called from a function.

SQL Server is equipped with powerful XML querying capabilities. A database developer can perform almost every XML parsing/shredding requirement using XQuery or `OPENXML()`, both of which are discussed in detail in this chapter.

Validating XML documents

One of the basic requirements of any serious application is a set of robust validation processes applied on information being exchanged. A well-written piece of code would ideally validate all the input parameters before performing the actual processing for which it was created. Usually, correct validation of parameters protects the application and database from logical and data errors. It also helps to protect the data from malicious attempts such as SQL injection.

When information is exchanged in XML format, a more rigid validation is needed because the chances of invalid values are greater in the case of an XML document. An application passing the value "thirty" to the `@age` parameter of a stored procedure (`@age INT`) would receive a conversion error right away, as SQL Server will perform an implicit data type validation. The developer writing the stored procedure does not need to perform validations such as ensuring that all integer parameters are valid integer values. The developer might only need to perform validations specific to the business logic, such as a range validation on the age of an employee to ensure that it is within the accepted range (e.g., 18 to 65).

The story will be different in the case of an XML parameter. SQL Server may not be able to detect a possible error in an XML document such as "`<Employee age="who knows"/>`" because the attribute `@age` is not associated with a data type and SQL Server does not know how to validate it. This indicates that XML documents might need much more validation than non-XML parameters. For example:

- There are times when the elements in the XML document should follow a certain order. An application that parses the XML document sequentially might require that the `OrderDate` element should precede the `ExpectedShippingDate` element to validate the shipping date based on the order date.
- Structure of the XML should be validated. For example, an application might expect the employee address under the `employee` element, and the zip code as an attribute of the `address` element.
- Certain elements may be optional and certain elements mandatory.
- Certain elements may appear more than once and others may be allowed only once.
- Data type validations may be needed. For example, age should be an integer value.
- Restrictions might be needed on the accepted range of values, such as age of an employee should be between 18 and 65.
- Certain values may follow specific formats. For example, an application might require phone numbers to be in the format of (999) 999-9999, or social security numbers must be 999-99-9999.

XSD (XML Schema Definition Language) is a W3C recommended language used for describing and validating XML documents. Based on the structure, format, and validation rules required by an application, an XSD schema can be created and a schema validator can then validate XML documents against the rules defined in the schema document.

Microsoft added XSD validation support in SQL Server 2005 and extended it further in SQL Server 2008. SQL Server stores an XML schema as XML `SCHEMA COLLECTION` objects. XML schema collections are SQL Server objects just like tables, views, constraints, and so on. An XML schema collection can be created from the definition of an XML schema.

An XML column, variable, parameter, or return value of a function can be associated with a specific XML schema collection. XML data type values that are bound to an XML schema collection are called *typed XML*. The other flavor of XML (not bound to an XML schema collection) is called *untyped XML*.

SQL Server validates typed XML values against the rules defined in the XML schema collection. When a new value is assigned to a typed XML variable or column, or the value is modified by a DML operation (insert, update, or delete), SQL Server will validate the new value against the schema and the operation will succeed only if the new value passes the validation.

Support of XSD schemas is a powerful addition to the XML processing capabilities of SQL Server. A good combination of the capabilities to generate, query, and validate XML documents makes SQL Server the right platform for building applications that handle structured and unstructured data.

Sample Tables and Data

To explain and demonstrate the XML processing capabilities of SQL Server 2008, this chapter presents a number of code snippets. To make the examples and the underlying data more comprehensible, a fixed set of sample tables and sample data is used throughout the examples presented in this chapter. The sample tables include tables for storing `Customer`, `Item`, and Order information.

Here's a script to create sample tables:

```
IF OBJECT_ID('Customers','U') IS NOT NULL DROP TABLE Customers
CREATE TABLE Customers (
    CustomerID INT IDENTITY PRIMARY KEY,
    CustomerNumber VARCHAR(20),
    Name VARCHAR(40),
    Phone VARCHAR(15),
    Street VARCHAR(40),
    City VARCHAR(20),
    State VARCHAR(10),
    Zip VARCHAR(10) )
GO
IF OBJECT_ID('Items','U') IS NOT NULL DROP TABLE Items
CREATE TABLE Items (
    ItemID INT IDENTITY PRIMARY KEY,
    ItemNumber VARCHAR(20),
    ItemDescription VARCHAR(40) )
GO
IF OBJECT_ID('OrderHeader','U') IS NOT NULL DROP TABLE OrderHeader
CREATE TABLE OrderHeader (
    OrderID INT IDENTITY PRIMARY KEY,
    OrderNumber VARCHAR(20),
    OrderDate DATETIME,
    CustomerID INT )
GO
IF OBJECT_ID('OrderDetails','U') IS NOT NULL DROP TABLE OrderDetails
CREATE TABLE OrderDetails (
    OrderDetailID INT IDENTITY PRIMARY KEY,
    OrderID INT,
    ItemID INT,
    Quantity INT,
    Price MONEY )
IF OBJECT_ID('OrderXML','U') IS NOT NULL DROP TABLE OrderXML
CREATE TABLE OrderXML (OrderID INT, ItemData XML)
GO
```

Here's a script to insert sample data:

```
-- Populate Customer Table
INSERT INTO Customers (
    CustomerNumber, Name, Phone, Street,
```

```
    City, State, Zip )
SELECT
    'J001', 'Jacob Sebastian', '(999) 999-9999', '401, Jacobs Street',
    'New York', 'NY', '12345'

-- Populate Items Table
INSERT INTO Items (ItemNumber, ItemDescription)
SELECT 'D001','DELL XPS 1130 Laptop'
UNION ALL
SELECT 'Z001','XBOX 360 Console'

-- Create order "SO101"
INSERT INTO OrderHeader( OrderNumber, OrderDate, CustomerID )
SELECT 'SO101','2009-01-23',1
-- Add Line Items
INSERT INTO OrderDetails (OrderID, ItemID, Quantity, Price)
SELECT 1, 1, 1, 900
UNION ALL
SELECT 1, 2, 1, 200

-- Create order "SO102"
INSERT INTO OrderHeader( OrderNumber, OrderDate, CustomerID )
SELECT 'SO102','2009-01-24',1
-- Add Line Items
INSERT INTO OrderDetails (OrderID, ItemID, Quantity, Price)
SELECT 2, 1, 1, 900

-- And finally, some XML data
INSERT INTO OrderXML (OrderID, ItemData) SELECT 1, '
    <Order OrderID="1">
        <Item ItemNumber="D001" Quantity="1" Price="900"/>
        <Item ItemNumber="Z001" Quantity="1" Price="200"/>
    </Order>'

INSERT INTO OrderXML (OrderID, ItemData) SELECT 2, '
    <Order OrderID="2">
        <Item ItemNumber="D001" Quantity="1" Price="900"/>
    </Order>'
```

These sample tables and sample data will be used for the examples presented in this chapter. You can download them from www.sqlserverbible.com.

XML Data Type

The most significant addition to the XML capabilities of SQL Server is the introduction of the XML native data type released with SQL Server 2005. XML data can store a complete XML document or a fragment. The XML data type can be used like other native SQL Server data types. SQL Server supports creating tables with XML columns, and allows declaring XML variables and using them as parameters and return values.

XQuery is a W3C-recommended language created to query and format XML documents. XQuery can be used to query XML documents just like a SQL query is used to retrieve information from relational tables. The XML data type implements a limited subset of the XQuery specification and a T-SQL query can use XQuery to retrieve information from XML columns or variables.

XQuery is built into the Relational Engine of SQL Server, and the Query Optimizer can build query plans that contain relational query operations as well as XQuery operations. Results of XQuery operations can be joined with relational data, or relational data can be joined with XQuery results. SQL Server supports creating special types of indexes on XML columns to optimize XQuery operations.

XML Schema Definition (XSD) is another W3C-recommended language created for describing and validating XML documents. XSD supports creating very powerful and complex validation rules that can be applied to XML documents to verify that they are fully compliant with the business requirements. The XML data type supports XSD validation and is explained later in this chapter.

The XML data type supports a number of methods, listed here:

- `value()`
- `exist()`
- `query()`
- `modify()`
- `nodes()`

Each of these methods is explained in detail later in this chapter.

Typed and untyped XML

As mentioned earlier, support for XSD schema validation is implemented in SQL Server in the form of XML schema collections. An XML schema collection can be created from an XML schema definition. XML columns or variables can be bound to an XML schema collection. An XML column or variable that is bound to an XML schema collection is known as typed XML.

When a typed XML value is modified, SQL Server validates the new value against the rules defined in the XML schema collection. The assignment or modification operation will succeed only if the new value passes the validations defined in the XML schema collection.

Typed XML has a number of advantages over untyped XML columns or variables. The most important benefit is that the validation constraints are always respected. The content of a typed XML document is always valid as per the schema with which it is associated.

With typed XML, SQL Server has better knowledge of the XML document (structure, data types, and so on) and can generate a more optimized query plan. Because SQL Server has complete knowledge of the data types of elements and attributes, storage of typed XML can be made significantly more compact than untyped XML.

Static type checking is possible with typed XML documents, and SQL Server can detect, at compile time, if an XQuery expression on a typed XML document is mistyped. Stored procedures or functions that accept typed XML parameters are protected from receiving invalid XML documents, as SQL Server will perform implicit validation of the XML value against the schema collection before accepting the parameter value.

Creating and using XML columns

The XML data type can be used like other native SQL Server data types in most cases. (Note that there are exceptions, however. For example, an XML column cannot be added as a column to a regular index or used in a comparison operation.) A table can be created with one or more XML columns, or XML columns can be added to an existing table. VARCHAR/NVARCHAR/VARBINARY/TEXT/NTEXT columns can be altered to XML data type columns if all the existing values are well-formed XML values.

Entire XML documents can be retrieved as part of a SELECT query, or specific information can be extracted from within the XML documents. The following example shows a SELECT query that selects a column from a table and a value from the XML document stored in each row:

```
DECLARE @t TABLE (OrderID INT,OrderData XML )
INSERT INTO @t(OrderID, OrderData)
SELECT 1,
    '<CustomerNumber>1001</CustomerNumber>
    <Items>
        <Item ItemNumber="1001" Quantity="1" Price="950"/>
        <Item ItemNumber="1002" Quantity="1" Price="650" />
    </Items>'

SELECT
    OrderID,
    OrderData.value('CustomerNumber[1]','CHAR(4)') AS CustomerNumber
FROM @t
/*
OrderID     CustomerNumber
----------- --------------
1           1001
*/
```

The code might get a little more complex if the query needs to retrieve more than one element from the XML document stored in each row. Such a query needs to generate more than one row against each row stored in the base table. The nodes() method of the XML data type can be used to obtain an accessor to each element within the XML document. The XML element collection returned by the nodes() method can be joined with the base table using the CROSS APPLY operator as shown in the following example:

```
DECLARE @t TABLE (OrderID INT,OrderData XML )
INSERT INTO @t(OrderID, OrderData)
SELECT 1,
    '<CustomerNumber>1001</CustomerNumber>
     <Items>
        <Item ItemNumber="1001" Quantity="1" Price="950"/>
```

```
        <Item ItemNumber="1002" Quantity="1" Price="650" />
    </Items>'

SELECT
    OrderID,
    o.value('@ItemNumber','CHAR(4)') AS ItemNumber,
    o.value('@Quantity','INT') AS Quantity,
    o.value('@Price','MONEY') AS Price
FROM @t
CROSS APPLY OrderData.nodes('/Items/Item') x(o)
/*
OrderID     ItemNumber Quantity    Price
----------- ---------- ----------- ---------------------
1           1001       1           950.00
1           1002       1           650.00
*/
```

The preceding examples use the `value()` method exposed by the XML data type. XML data type methods are explained in detail later in this section.

Declaring and using XML variables

Just like other SQL Server native data types, XML variables can be created and used in T-SQL batches, stored procedures, functions, and so on. The following example demonstrates a few different ways an XML variable can be declared:

```
-- Declare an XML variable
DECLARE @x XML

-- Declare a TYPED XML Variable
DECLARE @x XML(CustomerSchema)

-- Declare a TYPED XML DOCUMENT Variable
DECLARE @x XML(DOCUMENT CustomerSchema)

-- Declare a TYPED XML CONTENT variable
DECLARE @x XML(CONTENT CustomerSchema)
```

The first example creates an untyped XML variable, and the second example creates a typed one. The third example creates a `DOCUMENT` type variable, and the last one creates a `CONTENT` type variable. `DOCUMENT` and `CONTENT` types are explained later in this chapter.

There is a slight difference in the way that an XQuery expression needs to be written for an XML variable versus an XML column. While working with an XML variable, the query will always process only one document at a time. However, while working with an XML column, more than one XML document may be processed in a single batch operation. Because of this, the `CROSS APPLY` operator is required while running such a query on an XML column (as demonstrated in the previous example).

What follows is the version of the prior query that operates on an XML variable:

```
DECLARE @x XML
SELECT @x = '
<CustomerNumber>1001</CustomerNumber>
 <Items>
    <Item ItemNumber="1001" Quantity="1" Price="950"/>
    <Item ItemNumber="1002" Quantity="1" Price="650" />
 </Items>'

SELECT
 o.value('@ItemNumber','CHAR(4)') AS ItemNumber,
 o.value('@Quantity','INT') AS Quantity,
 o.value('@Price','MONEY') AS Price
FROM @x.nodes('/Items/Item') x(o)

/*
ItemNumber Quantity    Price
---------- ----------- ---------------------
1001       1           950.00
1002       1           650.00
*/
```

An XML variable may be initialized by a static XML string, from another XML or VARCHAR/NVARCHAR/VARBINARY variable, from the return value of a function, or from the result of a FOR XML query. The following example shows how to initialize an XML variable from the result of a FOR XML query:

```
DECLARE @x XML
SELECT @x = (
    SELECT OrderID
    FROM OrderHeader
    FOR XML AUTO, TYPE)
```

XML variables can also be initialized from an XML file, as demonstrated later in the section "Loading XML Documents from Disk Files."

Using XML parameters and return values

Typed and untyped XML parameters can be passed to a stored procedure as INPUT as well as OUTPUT parameters. XML parameters can be used as arguments as well as the return value of scalar functions or in result columns of table-valued functions.

When a function returns an XML data type value, XML data type methods can be directly called on the return value, as shown in the following example:

```
-- Create a function that returns an XML value
CREATE FUNCTION GetOrderInfo(
    @OrderID INT
) RETURNS XML
```

```
AS
BEGIN
    DECLARE @x XML
    SELECT @x = (
        SELECT OrderID, CustomerID
        FROM OrderHeader
        WHERE OrderID = @OrderID
        FOR XML PATH(''),ROOT('OrderInfo'))
    RETURN @x
END
GO

-- Call the function and invoke the value() method
SELECT dbo.GetOrderInfo(1).value('(OrderInfo/CustomerID)[1]','INT')
    AS CustomerID
/*
CustomerID
-----------
1
*/
```

Loading/querying XML documents from disk files

The capability to load XML documents from disk files is one of the very interesting XML features available with SQL Server. This is achieved by using the BULK row set provider for OPENROWSET. The following example shows how to load the content of an XML file into an XML variable:

```
/*The sample code below assumes that a file named "items.xml"
exists in folder c:\temp with the following content.

<Items>
  <Item ItemNumber="1001" Quantity="1" Price="950"/>
  <Item ItemNumber="1002" Quantity="1" Price="650" />
</Items>
*/

DECLARE @xml XML
SELECT
    @xml = CAST(bulkcolumn AS XML)
FROM OPENROWSET(BULK 'C:\temp\items.xml', SINGLE_BLOB) AS x

SELECT
    x.value('@ItemNumber','CHAR(4)') AS ItemNumber,
    x.value('@Quantity','INT') AS Quantity,
    x.value('@Price','MONEY') AS Price
FROM @xml.nodes('/Items/Item') i(x)
```

```
/*
ItemNumber Quantity    Price
---------- ----------- ---------------------
1001       1           950.00
1002       1           650.00
*/
```

OPENROWSET(BULK...[filename, option]) can even query the data in the file directly without loading it to a table or variable. It can also be used as the source of an INSERT/UPDATE operation. The following example queries the XML file directly:

```
SELECT
    x.value('@ItemNumber','CHAR(4)') AS ItemNumber,
    x.value('@Quantity','INT') AS Quantity,
    x.value('@Price','MONEY') AS Price
FROM (
    SELECT CAST(bulkcolumn AS XML) AS data
    FROM OPENROWSET(BULK 'C:\temp\items.xml', SINGLE_BLOB)
    AS x
) a
CROSS APPLY data.nodes('/Items/Item') i(x)

/*
ItemNumber Quantity    Price
---------- ----------- ---------------------
1001       1           950.00
1002       1           650.00
*/
```

To use the OPENROWSET(BULK..) option, the user should have ADMINISTRATOR BULK OPERATIONS permission.

Limitations of the XML data type

Though the XML data type comes with a number of very interesting capabilities, it has a number of limitations as well. However, the limitations are not really "limiting," considering the extensive set of functionalities provided by the data type.

The stored representation of an XML data type instance cannot exceed 2 GB. The term "stored representation" is important in the preceding statement, because SQL Server converts XML data type values to an internal structure and stores it. This internal representation takes much less space than the textual representation of the XML value. The following example demonstrates the reduction in size when a value is stored as an XML data type value:

```
DECLARE @EmployeeXML XML, @EmployeeText NVARCHAR(500)

SELECT @EmployeeText = '
```

```
<EmployeeInfo>
    <EmployeeName>Jacob</EmployeeName>
    <EmployeeName>Steve</EmployeeName>
    <EmployeeName>Bob</EmployeeName>
</EmployeeInfo>'

SELECT DATALENGTH(@EmployeeText) AS StringSize
/*
StringSize
-----------
284
*/

SELECT @EmployeeXML = @EmployeeText
SELECT DATALENGTH(@EmployeeXML) AS XMLSize
/*
XMLSize
-----------
109
*/
```

The stored representation of the XML data type value is different and much more optimized than the textual representation and the limit of 2 GB is on the stored representation. It indicates that an XML data type column may be able to store XML documents containing more than 2 * 1024 * 1024 * 1024 VARCHAR characters.

Unlike other data types, XML data type values cannot be sorted or used in a group by expression. They cannot be used in a comparison operation. However, they can be used with the IS NULL operator to determine if the value is NULL. XML data type columns cannot be used in the key of an index. They can only be used in the INCLUDED column of an index.

NOTE **To facilitate faster querying and searching over XML columns, SQL Server supports a special type of index called an XML index. XML indexes are different from regular indexes and are discussed later in this chapter.**

Understanding XML Data Type Methods

The XML data type supports a number of methods that allow various operations on the XML document. The most common operations needed on an XML document might be reading values from elements or attributes, querying for specific information, or modifying the document by inserting, updating, or deleting XML elements or attributes. The XML data type comes with a number of methods to support all these operations.

Any operation on an XML document is applied on one or more elements or attributes at a specific location. To perform an operation, the location of the specific element or attribute has to be specified.

XPath

XPath is used for locating XML elements and attributes within an XML document and navigating through the XML tree. Every element and attribute within an XML document has a unique "path." For example:

```
'<Items>
   <ItemNumber>1003</ItemNumber>
   <ItemNumber>1004</ItemNumber>
</Items>'
```

In the preceding example, the path to the first `ItemNumber` element is `/Items/ItemNumber[1]` and the second is `/Items/ItemNumber[2]`. Each element and attribute within an XML document can be uniquely identified and processed using an XPath expression.

All the XML data type methods accept XPath expressions to specify the target element or attribute on which the given operation needs to be performed.

value()

One of the most useful methods exposed by the XML data type is the `value()` method. It is used to retrieve scalar values from an XML document as a relational column. It takes an XQuery expression and evaluates it to a single node, casts the results to the specified SQL Server data type, and returns the value. Here is an example:

```
DECLARE @x XML
SELECt @x = '<Order OrderID="1" OrderNumber="SO101" />'

SELECT
    @x.value('(Order/@OrderID)[1]','INT') AS OrderID,
    @x.value('(Order/@OrderNumber)[1]','CHAR(5)') AS OrderNumber

/*
OrderID     OrderNumber
----------- -----------
1           SO101
*/
```

The `value()` method accepts an XPath expression pointing to the element or attribute to read data from. It also specifies the data type of the result column.

nodes()

The `nodes()` method returns a row set representation of the XML document. An XQuery operation can be performed on each node returned by the nodes() method. This is useful when information has to be retrieved from all the nodes matching a specific expression. Here is an example:

```
DECLARE @x XML
SELECT @x = '
```

```
    <Items>
      <ItemNumber>1001</ItemNumber>
      <ItemNumber>1002</ItemNumber>
    </Items>'

SELECT
    x.value('.','CHAR(4)') AS ItemNumber
FROM @x.nodes('/Items/ItemNumber') o(x)

/*
ItemNumber
----------
1001
1002
*/
```

The preceding query returns an accessor to all the `ItemNumber` elements in the XML document and applies the `value()` method on each node.

Both of the preceding examples demonstrate how to read information from XML variables. There is a slight difference between the way the query has to be written for XML variables and XML columns. That's because when working with an XML variable, only one XML document is processed at a time; but when working with an XML column, several XML documents need to be processed in a single batch. This is usually achieved by using the `CROSS APPLY` operator. The following example is a modified version of the preceding query that reads information from an XML column:

```
SELECT
    OrderID,
    x.value('@ItemNumber','CHAR(4)') AS ItemNumber
FROM OrderXML
CROSS APPLY ItemData.nodes('/Order/Item') o(x)

/*
OrderID     ItemNumber
----------- ----------
1           D001
1           Z001
2           D001
*/
```

The `CROSS APPLY` operator joins each node returned by the `nodes()` method with the table, and the `value()` method reads the `ItemNumber` value from each element returned by the `nodes()` method.

exist()

The `exist()` method checks whether an element or attribute specified by a given XPath expression exists in the document. The following query uses the `exist()` method to filter rows that have a specific item number:

```
SELECT
    OrderID
```

```
FROM OrderXML
WHERE ItemData.exist('/Order/Item[@ItemNumber = "Z001"]') = 1

/*
OrderID
-----------
1
*/
```

The `exist()` method returns true (1) if an element or attribute with the specified XPath expression exists in the XML document.

query()

The `query()` method takes an XQuery expression and evaluates it to a list of XML elements that can be accessed and processed further.

This method supports a subset of the XQuery 1.0 specification and allows querying the XML document, just like a relational database is queried using a SQL query. XQuery is very powerful and supports a number of operators and functions. XQuery is discussed later in this chapter under the section "Understanding XQuery and FLWOR operations."

modify()

The `modify()` method is used to perform XML DML operations on an XML document. It allows inserting, updating, or deleting XML elements or attributes within an XML document. A detailed discussion on the `modify()` method is given later in this chapter in the section "Performing XML Data Modification."

Joining XML nodes with relational tables

SQL Server has extended the Relational Engine with XQuery capabilities. This offers a number of advantages — for example, the query processor can evaluate relational and XQuery operations in a single query. A single query plan is created with relational and XQuery operations, and results of a relational query can be joined with XQuery results and vice versa.

A T-SQL Developer can take advantage of this and write T-SQL queries that join XML nodes with relational columns. The following code demonstrates a basic example:

```
SELECT
    oh.OrderID,
    c.Name AS Customer,
    i.ItemDescription AS Item,
    x.value('@Quantity','INT') AS Quantity,
    x.value('@Price','MONEY') AS Price
FROM OrderHeader oh
INNER JOIN OrderXML ox ON
    ItemData.value('(Order/@OrderID)[1]','INT') = oh.OrderID
CROSS APPLY ItemData.nodes('/Order/Item') o(x)
```

```
INNER JOIN Customers c ON c.CustomerID = oh.CustomerID
INNER JOIN Items i ON
    i.ItemNumber = x.value('@ItemNumber','CHAR(4)')

/*
OrderID Customer             Item                     Quantity   Price
------- -------------------- ------------------------ ---------- ------
1       Jacob Sebastian      DELL XPS 1130 Laptop     1          900.00
1       Jacob Sebastian      XBOX 360 Console         1          200.00
2       Jacob Sebastian      DELL XPS 1130 Laptop     1          900.00
*/
```

The preceding example joins the `OrderHeader` table with the `OrderXML` table and this join is between a relational column and an XML node. Again, another join is established between the `Items` table and the `Item` elements returned by the `nodes()` method.

Another way to write this query is to embed the join operators as part of the XQuery expression itself. The following example demonstrates this:

```
SELECT
    oh.OrderID,
    c.Name AS Customer,
    i.ItemDescription AS Item,
    x.value('@Quantity','INT') AS Quantity,
    x.value('@Price','MONEY') AS Price
FROM OrderHeader oh
INNER JOIN Customers c ON c.CustomerID = oh.CustomerID
CROSS JOIN OrderXML
CROSS JOIN Items i
CROSS APPLY ItemData.nodes('
    /Order[@OrderID=sql:column("oh.OrderID")]
    /Item[@ItemNumber=sql:column("i.ItemNumber")]') o(x)

/*
OrderID Customer             Item                     Quantity   Price
------- -------------------- ------------------------ ---------- ------
1       Jacob Sebastian      DELL XPS 1130 Laptop     1          900.00
1       Jacob Sebastian      XBOX 360 Console         1          200.00
2       Jacob Sebastian      DELL XPS 1130 Laptop     1          900.00
*/
```

The capability to join relational tables with XML nodes opens up a wide variety of possibilities to perform join operations between relational and XML data.

Using variables and filters in XQuery expressions

SQL Server allows only string literals as XQuery expressions. The following is illegal in SQL Server 2008:

```
DECLARE @node VARCHAR(100)
SELECT @node = '/Order/Item')
```

```
SELECT
 /* columns here */
FROM OrderXML
CROSS APPLY ItemData.nodes(@node) o(x)
```

Although you might want to use such an expression, it won't work; I see this in XML forums all the time. Don't make the same mistake. There are two common scenarios in which one might need to use variables in XQuery expressions:

- To apply filters on the value of elements or attributes; for example, to retrieve the nodes with itemnumber = "Z001" or OrderID = "1"
- To retrieve the value of an element or attribute that is not known in advance, such as in cases where the name of the element or attribute is passed as an argument

SQL Server allows using variables as part of an XQuery expression using the `sql:variable()` function. The following example uses a variable to filter an item number from the XML node:

```
DECLARE @ItemNumber CHAR(4)
SELECT @ItemNumber = 'D001'

SELECT
    x.value('@ItemNumber','CHAR(4)') AS ItemNumber,
    x.value('@Quantity','INT') AS Quantity,
    x.value('@Price','MONEY') AS Price
FROM OrderXML
CROSS APPLY ItemData.nodes('
    /Order/Item[@ItemNumber=sql:variable("@ItemNumber")]'
    ) o(x)

/*
ItemNumber Quantity    Price
---------- ----------- ---------------------
D001       1           900.00
D001       1           900.00
*/
```

Returning the values of elements or attributes not known in advance is a little trickier. This can be achieved by using the XQuery function `local-name()` and by matching it with the value of the given variable:

```
DECLARE @Att VARCHAR(50)
SELECT @Att = 'ItemNumber'

SELECT
    x.value('@*[local-name()=sql:variable("@Att")][1]',
        'VARCHAR(50)') AS Value
FROM OrderXML
CROSS APPLY ItemData.nodes('/Order/Item') o(x)

/*
```

```
Value
--------------------------------------------------
D001
Z001
D001
*/
```

The preceding example retrieves the value of an attribute that is not known in advance. The name of the attribute is stored in a variable and the XQuery function `local-name()` is used to match the name of the attribute with the variable.

Supporting variables as part of XQuery expressions greatly extends the power and flexibility of XQuery programming possibilities within T-SQL.

Accessing the parent node

Most of the time, a query retrieving information from an XML document needs to access information from nodes at different levels in the XML tree. The easiest way to achieve this may be by using the parent node accessor, as shown in the following example:

```
SELECT
    x.value('../@OrderID','INT') AS OrderID,
    x.value('@ItemNumber','CHAR(4)') AS ItemNumber,
    x.value('@Quantity','INT') AS Quantity,
    x.value('@Price','MONEY') AS Price
FROM OrderXML
CROSS APPLY ItemData.nodes('/Order/Item') o(x)

/*
OrderID     ItemNumber Quantity    Price
----------- ---------- ----------- ---------------------
1           D001       1           900.00
1           Z001       1           200.00
2           D001       1           900.00
*/
```

The preceding example uses the parent node accessor (..) to retrieve the `OrderID` attribute. While this syntax is pretty simple and easy to use, it may not be good in terms of performance. When the parent node accessor is used, the XQuery processor needs to go backward to read the parent node information while processing each row, which might slow down the query.

The following example demonstrates a more optimized way of writing the preceding query using `CROSS APPLY`:

```
SELECT
    h.value('@OrderID','INT') AS OrderID,
    x.value('@ItemNumber','CHAR(4)') AS ItemNumber,
    x.value('@Quantity','INT') AS Quantity,
    x.value('@Price','MONEY') AS Price
```

```
FROM OrderXML
CROSS APPLY ItemData.nodes('/Order') o(h)
CROSS APPLY h.nodes('Item') i(x)

/*
OrderID     ItemNumber Quantity    Price
----------- ---------- ----------- ---------------------
1           D001       1           900.00
1           Z001       1           200.00
2           D001       1           900.00
*/
```

The first CROSS APPLY operator used in the preceding query retrieves an accessor to the Order element, and the second CROSS APPLY returns an accessor to each Item element. This eliminates the need to use the parent node accessor in the query to read information from the Order element.

The parent node accessor may be fine with small tables and small XML documents, but it is not recommended for large XML documents or tables. A better way of accessing the parent node is by using the CROSS APPLY approach demonstrated in the preceding example.

Generating XML Output Using FOR XML

FOR XML is a row set aggregation function that returns a one-row, one-column result set containing an NVARCHAR(MAX) value. The TYPE directive can be used along with FOR XML to produce XML data type output instead of NVARCHAR(MAX).

FOR XML can be used with the AUTO, RAW, PATH and EXPLICIT directives to achieve different levels of control over the structure and format of the XML output.

FOR XML AUTO

FOR XML AUTO is one of the easiest options available to generate XML output from results of a SELECT query. It returns XML output having nested XML elements. Though it is easy to use and has a simple syntax, FOR XML AUTO does not provide much control over the structure of the XML output.

FOR XML AUTO, as the name suggests, "automatically" identifies the element names, hierarchies, and so on, based on the table name, aliases, and joins used in the query. The following example demonstrates a basic use of FOR XML AUTO:

```
SELECT OrderNumber, CustomerID
FROM OrderHeader
FOR XML AUTO
/*
<OrderHeader OrderNumber="SO101" CustomerID="1" />
<OrderHeader OrderNumber="SO102" CustomerID="1" />
*/
```

The element name is determined based on the name or alias of the table. In the preceding example, an element named `OrderHeader` is created because the name of the table is `OrderHeader`. By adding an alias to the table name, a different element name can be generated:

```
SELECT OrderNumber, CustomerID
FROM OrderHeader o
FOR XML AUTO

/*
<o OrderNumber="SO101" CustomerID="1" />
<o OrderNumber="SO102" CustomerID="1" />
*/
```

These examples produce XML fragments, and not valid XML documents. A valid XML document can have only one top-level element. A root element can be added to the output of a `FOR XML AUTO` query by specifying the `ROOT` directive.

The `ROOT` directive takes an optional argument that specifies the name of the root element. If this argument is not specified, the name of the top-level element will always be "root." The following example adds a top-level element named `SalesOrder` to the XML output:

```
SELECT OrderNumber, CustomerID
FROM OrderHeader
FOR XML AUTO, ROOT('SalesOrder')
/*
<SalesOrder>
  <OrderHeader OrderNumber="SO101" CustomerID="1" />
  <OrderHeader OrderNumber="SO102" CustomerID="1" />
</SalesOrder>
*/
```

If the query has more than one table, `FOR XML AUTO` will generate hierarchical XML output based on the joins used in the query. The example given here joins the `Order` table with the `Customers` table:

```
SELECT
    [Order].OrderNumber, [Order].OrderDate,
    Customer.CustomerNumber, Customer.Name
FROM OrderHeader [Order]
INNER JOIN Customers Customer ON [Order].CustomerID = Customer.CustomerID
FOR XML AUTO

/*
<Order OrderNumber="SO101" OrderDate="2009-01-23T00:00:00">
  <Customer CustomerNumber="J001" Name="Jacob Sebastian" />
</Order>
*/
```

By default, FOR XML AUTO generates elements for each row, and values are generated as attributes. This behavior can be changed by specifying the ELEMENTS directive, which forces SQL Server to generate values as attributes:

```
SELECT
    [Order].OrderNumber, [Order].OrderDate,
    Customer.CustomerNumber, Customer.Name
FROM OrderHeader [Order]
INNER JOIN Customers Customer ON [Order].CustomerID = Customer.CustomerID
FOR XML AUTO, ELEMENTS

/*
<Order>
  <OrderNumber>SO101</OrderNumber>
  <OrderDate>2009-01-23T00:00:00</OrderDate>
  <Customer>
    <CustomerNumber>J001</CustomerNumber>
    <Name>Jacob Sebastian</Name>
  </Customer>
</Order>
*/
```

A FOR XML query returns a result set with one row and one column containing an NVARCHAR(MAX) value. The TYPE directive can be used to request SQL Server to return an XML data type value, instead of NVARCHAR(MAX). The TYPE directive is explained in this chapter. FOR XML AUTO can be used with additional directives such as XSINIL, XMLDATA, and XMLSCHEMA, each of which is covered in detail later in this chapter.

FOR XML RAW

FOR XML RAW is very similar to FOR XML AUTO, differing from it in only a couple of ways. One of the basic differences between FOR XML AUTO and FOR XML RAW is that the former doesn't allow altering the name of the elements. FOR XML AUTO always generates XML elements based on the name of the table or alias.

Conversely, FOR XML RAW generates elements named <row> by default, and allows customizing it. An optional element name can be specified with the RAW directive and SQL Server will generate the elements with the specified name:

```
SELECT OrderNumber, CustomerID
FROM OrderHeader
FOR XML RAW('Order')
/*
<Order OrderNumber="SO101" CustomerID="1" />
<Order OrderNumber="SO102" CustomerID="1" />
*/
```

Another difference worth noticing is that FOR XML AUTO generates a top-level element for each table used in the query. FOR XML RAW generates only one top-level element for each row in the query result:

```
SELECT
 OrderNumber, CustomerNumber
FROM OrderHeader o
INNER JOIN Customers c ON o.CustomerID = c.CustomerID
FOR XML RAW('Order')
/*
<Order OrderNumber="SO101" CustomerNumber="J001" />
<Order OrderNumber="SO102" CustomerNumber="J001" />
*/
```

If the preceding query were executed with FOR XML AUTO, it would create a top-level element for the order information and a child element for the customer information. If the ELEMENTS directive is specified, SQL Server will create child elements for each column instead of attributes.

Like the AUTO directive, RAW also supports an optional ROOT directive that generates a root element with the specified name. If the root name is not specified, a top-level element named <root> will be created:

```
SELECT OrderNumber, CustomerID
FROM OrderHeader
FOR XML RAW('Order'), ROOT('Orders')
/*
<Orders>
  <Order OrderNumber="SO101" CustomerID="1" />
  <Order OrderNumber="SO102" CustomerID="1" />
</Orders>
*/
```

FOR XML RAW can also be used with additional directives such as XSINIL, XMLDATA, and XMLSCHEMA, covered in detail later in this chapter.

FOR XML EXPLICIT

FOR XML EXPLICIT is the most powerful clause available to generate XML output. It can generate very complex XML structures and offers a great deal of control over the output structure. However, most people find it too complicated to use.

To use FOR XML EXPLICIT, each row should have two mandatory columns: Tag and Parent. The data should be such that a hierarchical relationship is established between the rows using Tag and Parent. Other columns should be named in a certain format that provides some additional metadata information.

The following FOR XML EXPLICIT query generates an XML document with nested elements up to two levels:

```
SELECT
    1 AS Tag,
```

```
    NULL AS Parent,
    CustomerNumber AS 'Customer!1!CustNo',
    NULL AS 'LineItems!2!ItemNo',
    NULL AS 'LineItems!2!Qty'
FROM OrderHeader o
INNER JOIN Customers c ON o.CustomerID = c.CustomerID
    AND o.OrderID = 1
UNION ALL
SELECT
    2 AS Tag,
    1 AS Parent,
    NULL,
    i.ItemNumber,
    o.Quantity
FROM Items i
INNER JOIN OrderDetails o ON i.ItemID = o.ItemID
    AND o.OrderID = 1
FOR XML EXPLICIT

/*
<Customer CustNo="J001">
  <LineItems ItemNo="D001" Qty="1" />
  <LineItems ItemNo="Z001" Qty="1" />
</Customer>
*/
```

The results of the query without the FOR XML EXPLICIT clause look like the following:

```
Tag    Parent    Customer!1!CustNo    LineItems!2!ItemNo    LineItems!2!Qty
------ --------- -------------------- --------------------- ---------------
1      NULL      J001                 NULL                  NULL
2      1         NULL                 D001                  1
2      1         NULL                 Z001                  1
```

Essentially, to run a FOR XML EXPLICIT query, SQL Server needs data in a format similar to the one given above. Tag and Parent are mandatory columns and they should maintain a valid parent-child (hierarchical) relationship. There should be at least one more additional column to run a FOR XML EXPLICIT query successfully.

The XML generator will read the results of the query and identify the hierarchy of the XML document based on the hierarchical relationship specified by Tag and Parent columns. The name of each column specifies the name of its parent element, its position in the hierarchy, and the name of the attribute. LineItems!2!Qty indicates that the value should apply to an attribute named Qty under the LineItems element at hierarchy level two.

Due to this complex structuring requirement of the query results, most people feel that FOR XML EXPLICIT is overly complex. However, on the positive side, it is very powerful and offers a number of XML generation capabilities that no other FOR XML directive offers.

FOR XML EXPLICIT allows creating XML documents to satisfy almost every complex customization requirement. The trick is to generate a result set with the required hierarchical relationship, and the XML output will be generated accordingly.

As shown in the preceding example, the names of the columns can be used to pass important metadata information to SQL Server. The previous example demonstrated a three-part column-naming convention that specified the element name, tag number, and attribute name. An optional fourth part can be used to control a number of aspects of the XML generation process.

By default, FOR XML EXPLICIT generates values as attributes. The ELEMENTS directive can be used to instruct SQL Server to generate a given column as an element. The ELEMENTS directive can be specified along with each column. The following example demonstrates a slightly modified version of the previous query that generates a customer number as an element:

```
SELECT
    1 AS Tag,
    NULL AS Parent,
    CustomerNumber AS 'Customer!1!CustNo!ELEMENT',
    NULL AS 'LineItems!2!ItemNo',
    NULL AS 'LineItems!2!Qty'
FROM OrderHeader o
INNER JOIN Customers c ON o.CustomerID = c.CustomerID
    AND o.OrderID = 1
UNION ALL
SELECT
    2 AS Tag,
    1 AS Parent,
    NULL,
    i.ItemNumber,
    o.Quantity
FROM Items i
INNER JOIN OrderDetails o ON i.ItemID = o.ItemID
    AND o.OrderID = 1
FOR XML EXPLICIT
/*
<Customer>
  <CustNo>J001</CustNo>
  <LineItems ItemNo="D001" Qty="1" />
  <LineItems ItemNo="Z001" Qty="1" />
</Customer>
*/
```

FOR XML EXPLICIT processes rows in the same order as that returned by the SELECT query. If the data in the output should appear in a specific order, then the order clause should be specified in the SELECT query. Sometimes, it can happen that the order should be done on a column that is not needed in the output XML.

This might be a little tricky. Because the final output is generated by a series of queries that uses UNION ALL, the sort operation can be applied only on a column that already exists in the query results. However, often the column or expression to be used for the ordering might not be required in the XML output.

FOR XML EXPLICIT supports another directive, HIDE, that can be applied on columns that should be excluded from the final output. A column or expression that a query needs for sorting of the final results can be marked as HIDE and will be excluded from the XML output.

An example might best explain this. The example demonstrated earlier in this section generated XML output with information taken from only one order. The next example tries to generate an XML document with information from all the orders in the sample database. It attempts to generate XML output as follows:

```
<Orders>
  <Order CustNo="J001" OrderNo="S0101">
    <LineItems ItemNo="D001" Qty="1" />
    <LineItems ItemNo="Z001" Qty="1" />
  </Order>
  <Order CustNo="J001" OrderNo="S0102">
    <LineItems ItemNo="D001" Qty="1" />
  </Order>
</Orders>
```

Just as with RAW and AUTO, EXPLICIT supports the ROOT directive to generate a top-level element. The following example shows a slightly modified version of the previous query that has a ROOT clause and the filter for order ID removed:

```
SELECT
    1 AS Tag,
    NULL AS Parent,
    CustomerNumber AS 'Order!1!CustNo',
    OrderNumber AS 'Order!1!OrderNo',
    NULL AS 'LineItems!2!ItemNo',
    NULL AS 'LineItems!2!Qty'
FROM OrderHeader o
INNER JOIN Customers c ON o.CustomerID = c.CustomerID
UNION ALL
SELECT
    2 AS Tag,
    1 AS Parent,
    NULL,
    NULL,
    i.ItemNumber,
    o.Quantity
FROM Items i
INNER JOIN OrderDetails o ON i.ItemID = o.ItemID
FOR XML EXPLICIT, ROOT('Orders')
/*
<Orders>
  <Order CustNo="J001" OrderNo="S0101" />
  <Order CustNo="J001" OrderNo="S0102">
    <LineItems ItemNo="D001" Qty="1" />
    <LineItems ItemNo="Z001" Qty="1" />
```

```
    <LineItems ItemNo="D001" Qty="1" />
  </Order>
</Orders>
*/
```

Though the root element is correctly added, the XML output is not in the required structure. In fact, the information given is incorrect, because it shows that all three line items belong to Order SO102.

This behavior is caused by the fact that the XML generator consumes rows in the same order as they are returned by the `SELECT` query. To generate the results in the correct order, the `SELECT` query should contain an `ORDER BY` clause that controls the order of the rows in the result set.

The following example shows a new version of the query that generates a column just for the purpose of sorting. It then uses the `HIDE` directive to instruct SQL Server that the column should not be included in the XML output:

```
SELECT
    1 AS Tag,
    NULL AS Parent,
    CustomerNumber AS 'Order!1!CustNo',
    OrderNumber AS 'Order!1!OrderNo',
    REPLACE(STR(OrderID,4) + STR(0,4),' ','0') AS 'Order!1!Sort!HIDE',
    NULL AS 'LineItems!2!ItemNo',
    NULL AS 'LineItems!2!Qty'
FROM OrderHeader o
INNER JOIN Customers c ON o.CustomerID = c.CustomerID
UNION ALL
SELECT
    2 AS Tag,
    1 AS Parent,
    NULL,
    NULL,
    REPLACE(STR(OrderID,4) + STR(OrderDetailID,4),' ','0'),
    i.ItemNumber,
    o.Quantity
FROM Items i
INNER JOIN OrderDetails o ON i.ItemID = o.ItemID
ORDER BY 'Order!1!Sort!HIDE'
FOR XML EXPLICIT, ROOT('Orders')
/*
<Orders>
  <Order CustNo="J001" OrderNo="SO101">
    <LineItems ItemNo="D001" Qty="1" />
    <LineItems ItemNo="Z001" Qty="1" />
  </Order>
  <Order CustNo="J001" OrderNo="SO102">
    <LineItems ItemNo="D001" Qty="1" />
  </Order>
</Orders>
*/
```

That query could produce the correct result because of the ORDER BY clause present in the query. The ORDER BY clause ensures that the first row is the order header information for SO101 and that the next two rows contain order detail information for the same order. Again, it ensures that the next row is order header information for SO102, followed by the order detail information of the same order. The query returns the following result set (column names abridged for space):

```
Tag  Parent CustNo OrderNo Sort!HIDE ItemNo Qty
---- ------ ------ ------- --------- ------ ----
1    NULL   J001   S010    00010000  NULL   NULL
2    1      NULL   NULL    00010001  D001   1
2    1      NULL   NULL    00010002  Z001   1
1    NULL   J001   S010    00020000  NULL   NULL
2    1      NULL   NULL    00020003  D001   1
```

As clearly apparent from the example, the ORDER BY clause has arranged the rows in the correct order using the arbitrary sort column. This result set is consumed by the XML generator and the output XML is generated in the correct order.

One of the most common problems that people face with FOR XML EXPLICIT is ordering. It will be helpful in such cases to run the query without the FOR XML clause and inspect the output to ensure that the rows are in the correct order.

FOR XML EXPLICIT supports a few more interesting directives, such as XML, XMLTEXT, and CDATA. The XML directive behaves very similarly to the ELEMENT directive. The only difference is that ELEMENT entitizes XML tags and XML preserves the XML tags:

```
SELECT
    1 AS Tag,
    NULL AS Parent,
    '<Info about="XML"/>' AS 'MyData!1!!ELEMENT'
FOR XML EXPLICIT
/*
ELEMENT directive encodes XML tags
<MyData>&lt;Info about="XML"/&gt;</MyData>
*/
SELECT
    1 AS Tag,
    NULL AS Parent,
    '<Info about="XML"/>' AS 'MyData!1!!XML'
FOR XML EXPLICIT
/*
XML directive preserves XML tags
<MyData>
  <Info about="XML" />
</MyData>
*/
```

The XMLTEXT directive wraps the column content in a single tag and integrates it with the rest of the document:

```
SELECT
    1 AS Tag,
    NULL AS Parent,
```

```
    '<Info about="XML"/>' AS 'MyData!1!!XMLTEXT'
FOR XML EXPLICIT
/*
<MyData about="XML"></MyData>
*/
```

The CDATA directive wraps the value within a CDATA block in the output XML document. EXPLICIT is the only directive that can generate a CDATA section:

```
SELECT
    1 AS Tag,
    NULL AS Parent,
    '<Info about="XML"/>' AS 'MyData!1!!CDATA'
FOR XML EXPLICIT
/*
<MyData><![CDATA[<Info about="XML"/>]]></MyData>
*/
```

The ID, IDREF, and IDREFS directives can be used to create intra-document links.

Another helpful directive that FOR XML EXPLICIT supports is ELEMENTXSINIL. The behavior of this directive is very similar to the XSINIL directive supported by AUTO and RAW. It is explained in the section "XSINIL Directive" later in this chapter.

FOR XML PATH

FOR XML PATH was introduced in SQL Server 2005. It is a lightweight alternative to FOR XML EXPLICIT. FOR XML PATH is as powerful as FOR XML EXPLICIT and as simple as FOR XML AUTO and RAW.

The previous section demonstrated the complexity of using a FOR XML EXPLICIT query. FOR XML PATH has a simple syntax and supports generating almost all XML document structures previously possible only with FOR XML EXPLICIT.

The true power of FOR XML PATH can be experienced when the XML structure is complex and has a multi-level hierarchy. It may be interesting to compare the complexity of code needed to produce the same XML document using FOR XML EXPLICIT and FOR XML PATH.

The following example shows a sample XML document that will be generated using FOR XML PATH and FOR XML EXPLICIT to see the extent of the simplicity that FOR XML PATH provides to the SQL programmer:

```
<Orders>
  <Order OrderNumber="SO102">
    <Customer CustomerNumber="J001" />
    <LineItems>
      <Item ItemNo="D001" Qty="1" />
    </LineItems>
  </Order>
</Orders>
```

The preceding XML document contains information about a sales order. The following example shows the FOR XML EXPLICIT code needed to produce the preceding output:

```
SELECT
    1 AS Tag,
    NULL AS Parent,
    OrderNumber AS 'Order!1!OrderNumber',
    NULL AS 'Customer!2!CustomerNumber',
    NULL AS 'LineItems!3!',
    NULL AS 'Item!4!ItemNo',
    NULL AS 'Item!4!Qty'
FROM OrderHeader oh
WHERE OrderID = 2
UNION ALL
SELECT
    2 AS Tag,
    1 AS Parent,
    NULL,
    c.CustomerNumber,
    NULL, NULL, NULL
FROM OrderHeader oh
INNER JOIN Customers c ON oh.CustomerID = c.CustomerID
    AND OrderID = 2
UNION ALL
SELECT
    3 AS Tag,
    1 AS Parent,
    NULL,
    NULL,
    NULL, NULL, NULL
UNION ALL
SELECT
    4 AS Tag,
    3 AS Parent,
    NULL, NULL, NULL,
    i.ItemNumber, od.Quantity
FROM OrderDetails od
INNER JOIN Items i ON i.ItemID = od.ItemID
    AND od.OrderID = 2
FOR XML EXPLICIT,ROOT('Orders')
/*
<Orders>
  <Order OrderNumber="SO102">
    <Customer CustomerNumber="J001" />
    <LineItems>
      <Item ItemNo="D001" Qty="1" />
    </LineItems>
  </Order>
</Orders>
*/
```

The following example shows the FOR XML PATH query needed to produce the same XML output:

```
SELECT
    oh.OrderNumber AS '@OrderNumber',
    c.CustomerNumber AS 'Customer/@CustomerNumber',
    i.ItemNumber AS 'LineItems/Item/@ItemNo',
    od.Quantity AS 'LineItems/Item/@Qty'
FROM OrderHeader oh
INNER JOIN Customers c ON oh.CustomerID = c.CustomerID
    AND OrderID = 2
INNER JOIN OrderDetails od ON od.OrderID = oh.OrderID
INNER JOIN Items i ON i.ItemID = od.ItemID
FOR XML PATH('Order'),ROOT('Orders')
/*
<Orders>
  <Order OrderNumber="SO102">
    <Customer CustomerNumber="J001" />
    <LineItems>
      <Item ItemNo="D001" Qty="1" />
    </LineItems>
  </Order>
</Orders>
*/
```

The amount of simplicity and power that comes with FOR XML PATH is apparent from the preceding example. The true power comes from the fact that FOR XML PATH allows generating deep hierarchies based on the column name. The column name LineItems/Item/@Qty creates an Item element with a Qty attribute under LineItems. An attribute is created by prefixing the name with an @ sign:

```
SELECT
    CustomerID AS '@CustomerID',
    OrderNumber AS 'OrderNumber'
FROM OrderHeader
FOR XML PATH('Order'), ROOT('Orders')
/*
<Orders>
  <Order CustomerID="1">
    <OrderNumber>SO101</OrderNumber>
  </Order>
  <Order CustomerID="1">
    <OrderNumber>SO102</OrderNumber>
  </Order>
</Orders>
*/
```

FOR XML PATH supports a number of special characters to achieve different XML formatting requirements. For example, a "mixed" type element (an element that has a text value as well as attributes) can be created by naming a column with an asterisk ("*"), as shown in the following example:

```
SELECT
    CustomerID AS '@CustomerID',
```

```
    OrderNumber AS '*'
FROM OrderHeader
FOR XML PATH('Order'), ROOT('Orders')
/*
<Orders>
  <Order CustomerID="1">SO101</Order>
  <Order CustomerID="1">SO102</Order>
</Orders>
*/
```

The same result can be obtained by using the special column name indicators `data()`, `node()`, or `text()`.

The `data()` indicator can also be used to generate a space-separated list of values by making the `PATH` name empty:

```
SELECT
    ItemNumber AS 'data()'
FROM Items
FOR XML PATH(''), ROOT('Items')
/*
<Items>D001 Z001</Items>
*/
```

Using the `text()` indicator along with empty `PATH` name will generate a similar string, but without spaces between the values:

```
SELECT
    ItemNumber AS 'text()'
FROM Items
FOR XML PATH(''), ROOT('Items')
/*
<Items>D001Z001</Items>
*/
```

Finally, a comment can be generated using the special column name indicator `comment()` along with `FOR XML PATH`:

```
SELECT
    'Order Number' AS 'comment()',
    OrderNumber,
    'Customer ID' AS 'comment()',
    CustomerID
FROM OrderHeader WHERE OrderID = 1
FOR XML PATH(''), ROOT('Orders')
/*
<Orders>
  <!--Order Number-->
  <OrderNumber>SO101</OrderNumber>
  <!--Customer ID-->
```

```
    <CustomerID>1</CustomerID>
  </Orders>
  */
```

FOR XML PATH is both powerful and easy to use. It offers a great deal of control over the structure of the output document. Most operations previously possible only with complex FOR XML EXPLICIT queries are now possible with FOR XML PATH.

TYPE directive

A FOR XML query returns a result set with one row and one column containing an NVARCHAR(MAX) value. The TYPE directive can be used to request SQL Server to return an XML data type value, instead of NVARCHAR(MAX). FOR XML queries can take advantage of the TYPE directive in a number of ways.

FOR XML AUTO and RAW are relatively simple to use, but they provide very little control over the structure of the XML result. The TYPE directive can be used to write nested FOR XML queries with FOR XML AUTO and RAW, which offers greater control over the structure of the XML output.

For example, the following XML output cannot be achieved with FOR XML AUTO or RAW without using a nested FOR XML query:

```
<SalesOrder OrderNumber="SO101">
  <Customer CustomerNumber="J001" Name="Jacob Sebastian"/>
  <Items>
    <Item ItemNumber="D001" Quantity="1" Price="900.0000" />
    <Item ItemNumber="Z001" Quantity="1" Price="200.0000" />
  </Items>
</SalesOrder>
```

The following example shows a nested FOR XML AUTO query that generates the preceding XML output:

```
SELECT
    SalesOrder.OrderNumber,
    SalesOrder.OrderDate,
    ( SELECT CustomerNumber, Name
        FROM Customers Customer
        FOR XML AUTO, TYPE ),
    ( SELECT ItemNumber, Quantity, Price FROM
        (
            SELECT
                i.ItemNumber,
                o.Quantity,
                o.Price
            FROM Items i
            INNER JOIN OrderDetails o ON i.ItemID = o.ItemID
            WHERE OrderID = 1
        ) Item
        FOR XML AUTO, ROOT('Items'),TYPE )
```

```
FROM OrderHeader SalesOrder
WHERE OrderID = 1
FOR XML AUTO
```

Because the TYPE directive generates an XML data type value, instead of NVARCHAR(MAX), the result of a FOR XML query that uses the TYPE directive can be used as input for other XML operations. The following example demonstrates this:

```
SELECT
    (
        SELECT OrderID, CustomerID
        FROM OrderHeader
        FOR XML AUTO, TYPE
    ).value('(OrderHeader/@OrderID)[1]','INT') AS OrderID
/*
OrderID
-----------
1
*/
```

The inner query in the preceding example returns an XML data type value and hence it is possible to invoke XML data type methods such as value() or query() on the FOR XML query result.

XSINIL Directive

Let us look at two examples:

Example 1:

```
<Employee>
 <FirstName>Jacob</FirstName>
<Employee>
```

Example 2:

```
<Employee>
 <FirstName>Jacob</FirstName>
 <HireDate xsi:nil="true" />
<Employee>
```

Example 3:

```
<Employee>
 <FirstName>Jacob</FirstName>
 <HireDate >1900-01-01</HireDate>
</Employee>
```

By default, FOR XML does not include columns with NULL values in the XML output. Some applications might need to process missing values different from NULL values. Those applications might require that an XML element be present in the XML document, even if the value is NULL. FOR XML supports a special directive, XSINIL, that helps to achieve this. XSINIL is applicable only to elements, and can be used only with the ELEMENTS directive. When XSINIL is specified, FOR XML generates an empty element for any column that has a NULL value:

```
SELECT
    OrderNumber, CustomerID, NULL AS CustomerPhone
FROM OrderHeader [Order]
FOR XML AUTO, ELEMENTS XSINIL

/*
<Order xmlns:xsi="http://www.w3.org/2001/XMLSchema-instance">
  <OrderNumber>SO101</OrderNumber>
  <CustomerID>1</CustomerID>
  <CustomerPhone xsi:nil="true" />
</Order>
*/
```

Note that an empty CustomerPhone element is created in the preceding example, along with a special attribute xsi:nil set to "true". It signals the XML parser that the element has a NULL value.

Generating XML Schema information

FOR XML AUTO and RAW provide very little control over the structure of the XML document. The document is usually structured based on the tables, columns, and joins used in the SELECT query. Because the structure of the XML document is based on the order of the columns in the select list and the way joins are applied in the query, it is important to tell any applications that consume the XML result about the structure of the XML document.

An XML document is usually described using a *schema*. SQL Server can generate an XML or XDR (XML Data Reduced) schema along with the query results of a FOR XML AUTO or RAW query.

FOR XML EXPLICIT and PATH are usually used to generate XML documents as per a given structure or schema; hence, support for generating schema information is not available with these options.

An XDR schema can be generated along with the output by specifying the XMLDATA directive as part of the FOR XML query:

```
SELECT
    OrderNumber, CustomerID
FROM OrderHeader [Order]
FOR XML AUTO, XMLDATA
```

Similarly, the XMLSCHEMA directive can be used to generate an XML schema describing the output XML document:

```
SELECT
    OrderNumber, CustomerID
FROM OrderHeader [Order]
FOR XML AUTO, XMLSCHEMA
```

A client application that processes the XML output will read the inline schema information before processing the XML document and understand the structure of the XML document. An optional target namespace can be specified along with the XMLSCHEMA directive. If a target namespace is specified, the XML output will be generated with a target namespace declaration:

```
SELECT
    OrderNumber, CustomerID
FROM OrderHeader [Order]
FOR XML AUTO, XMLSCHEMA('urn:some-namespace')
```

Generating XML namespaces

XML uses namespaces to resolve ambiguity between elements or attributes referring to different contexts. All programming languages use some kind of operators to resolve ambiguity. T-SQL uses table aliases to resolve ambiguity — for example, "employee.name" is differentiated from "department.name." .NET uses namespaces to avoid conflicts between objects inherited from different libraries.

Similarly, XML documents use namespaces to avoid conflicts between elements or attributes with the same name. A FOR XML query can generate an XML document that contains one or more namespace declarations. The following code demonstrates an example that generates an XML document with a namespace declaration:

```
;WITH XMLNAMESPACES(
    'http://www.sqlserverbible.com/orders' AS ord
)
SELECT
    CustomerID AS '@CustomerID',
    OrderNumber AS 'data()'
FROM OrderHeader
FOR XML PATH('Order'),ROOT('Orders')
/*
<Orders xmlns:ord="http://www.sqlserverbible.com/orders">
  <Order CustomerID="1">SO101</Order>
  <Order CustomerID="1">SO102</Order>
</Orders>
*/
```

A default namespace declaration can be added by using the DEFAULT clause along with the namespace declaration:

```
;WITH XMLNAMESPACES(
    DEFAULT 'http://www.sqlserverbible.com/orders'
)
SELECT
    CustomerID AS '@CustomerID',
    OrderNumber AS 'data()'
FROM OrderHeader
FOR XML PATH('Order'),ROOT('Orders')
/*
```

```
<Orders xmlns="http://www.sqlserverbible.com/orders">
  <Order CustomerID="1">SO101</Order>
  <Order CustomerID="1">SO102</Order>
</Orders>
*/
```

The following example demonstrates how to generate elements with multiple namespaces:

```
;WITH XMLNAMESPACES(
    'http://www.sqlserverbible.com/customers' AS cust,
    'http://www.sqlserverbible.com/orders' AS ord
)
SELECT
    OrderNumber AS 'ord:OrderNumber',
    CustomerID AS 'cust:CustomerID'
FROM OrderHeader WHERE OrderID = 1
FOR XML PATH(''),ROOT('Orders')
/*
<Orders xmlns:ord="http://www.sqlserverbible.com/orders"
        xmlns:cust="http://www.sqlserverbible.com/customers">
  <ord:OrderNumber>SO101</ord:OrderNumber>
  <cust:CustomerID>1</cust:CustomerID>
</Orders>
*/
```

An element can be associated with a namespace by specifying a *colonized name* as the element name (a name that contains a namespace name and element name separated by a colon).

`WITH XMLNAMESPACES` offers a very easy way to generate XML output with namespace declarations. XML documents can be created with one or more namespace declarations.

Understanding XQuery and FLWOR operations

XQuery is a W3C recommended language created for querying XML documents. In a simplified sense, one could say that "XQuery is to XML what SQL is to a relational database."

The `query()` method of the `XML` data type implements a subset of XQuery specifications and provides a very extensive set of functionalities that enables performing a number of interesting operations on XML documents.

Simple queries

The basic usage of the `query()` method is to retrieve one or more XML nodes from the given XML document. The result of the `query()` method is always an `XML` data type value:

```
SELECT
    ItemData.query('/Order/Item')
FROM OrderXML
```

```
/*
<Item ItemNumber="D001" Quantity="1" Price="900" />
<Item ItemNumber="Z001" Quantity="1" Price="200" />
<Item ItemNumber="D001" Quantity="1" Price="900" />
*/
```

The query() method takes an XQuery expression that can be customized to locate and retrieve specific nodes matching a given condition:

```
SELECT
    ItemData.query('/Order/Item[@ItemNumber="D001"]')
FROM OrderXML
/*
<Item ItemNumber="D001" Quantity="1" Price="900" />
<Item ItemNumber="D001" Quantity="1" Price="900" />
*/
```

The result of the query() method can be used as input for other operations, such as the example given here:

```
SELECT
    OrderID,
    ItemData.query('
        count(/Order/Item)
    ').value('.','INT') AS LineCount
FROM OrderXML
/*
OrderID     LineCount
----------- -----------
1           2
2           1
*/
```

This example used the XQuery count() method to retrieve the number of Item elements in each row. The query() method always returns an XML data type value; hence, the value() method is used to retrieve an INT value from it.

FLWOR operation

The true power of XQuery comes with the FLWOR operation, which is pronounced like "flower" and stands for FOR LET WHERE ORDER BY and RETURN. A FLWOR operation enables querying or transforming XML documents. It can be used either to extract specific information from an XML document or to restructure the XML document and return a completely new XML value.

A basic FLWOR query using FOR and RETURN is shown in the following example:

```
DECLARE @x XML
SELECT @x = '
    <Items>
      <ItemNumber>1003</ItemNumber>
```

```
        <ItemNumber>1004</ItemNumber>
      </Items>'

  SELECT
      @x.query('
          for $item in Items/ItemNumber
          return $item ')

  /*
  <ItemNumber>1003</ItemNumber>
  <ItemNumber>1004</ItemNumber>
  */
```

WHERE and ORDER BY can be specified to filter and sort the output:

```
  DECLARE @x XML
  SELECT @x = '
      <Items>
        <ItemNumber>1003</ItemNumber>
        <ItemNumber>1004</ItemNumber>
        <ItemNumber>1001</ItemNumber>
        <ItemNumber>2007</ItemNumber>
        <ItemNumber>3009</ItemNumber>
        <ItemNumber>4005</ItemNumber>
      </Items>'

  SELECT
      @x.query('
          for $item in Items/ItemNumber
          where $item[. < "2000"]
          order by $item
          return $item ')

  /*
  <ItemNumber>1001</ItemNumber>
  <ItemNumber>1003</ItemNumber>
  <ItemNumber>1004</ItemNumber>
  */
```

The WHERE condition in the preceding XQuery expression filters the nodes for ItemNumber less than 2000. The ORDER BY clause then orders the nodes by ItemNumber.

A FLWOR operation can be used to completely restructure an XML document, as demonstrated here:

```
  DECLARE @x XML
  SELECT @x = '
  <Item ItemNumber="D001" Quantity="1" Price="900" />
  <Item ItemNumber="Z001" Quantity="1" Price="200" />'
```

```
SELECT
    @x.query('
        for $item in Item
        return
            <ItemNumber>
                {data($item/@ItemNumber)}
            </ItemNumber> ')
/*
<ItemNumber>D001</ItemNumber>
<ItemNumber>Z001</ItemNumber>
*/
```

The preceding example transforms the `ItemNumber` attributes to elements and produces a completely different XML document. Complex `FLWOR` operations can be applied on an XML document to achieve very complex transformation requirements.

What's new for XQuery in SQL Server 2008

SQL Server 2008 adds support for the `let` clause in `FLWOR` operations. The `let` clause allows declaring and using inline variables within the XQuery expression used in a `FLWOR` query:

```
DECLARE @x XML
SELECT @x = '
<Item ItemNumber="D001" Quantity="2" Price="900" />
<Item ItemNumber="Z001" Quantity="3" Price="200" />'

SELECT
    @x.query('
        for $item in Item
        let $itm := $item/@ItemNumber
        let $tot := $item/@Quantity * $item/@Price
        return
            <Item>
                <ItemNumber>{data($itm)}</ItemNumber>
                <TotalPrice>{data($tot)}</TotalPrice>
            </Item>
        ')
/*
<Item>
  <ItemNumber>D001</ItemNumber>
  <TotalPrice>1800</TotalPrice>
</Item>
<Item>
  <ItemNumber>Z001</ItemNumber>
  <TotalPrice>600</TotalPrice>
</Item>
*/
```

The XQuery expression in the preceding example declares two inline variables using the `let` clause: `$itm` and `$tot`. These variables are initialized within the XQuery expression and used to generate custom XML nodes.

The `let` clause reduces the complexity of `FLWOR` operations by enabling complex expressions to be translated into variables.

Understanding XQuery Functions

The XQuery specification has defined a number of XQuery functions, many of which have been implemented by SQL Server. This section briefly examines the XQuery functions supported by SQL Server 2008.

String functions

String functions are one of the most commonly used set of functions in any language. SQL Server 2008 supports the following XQuery string functions:

- `string()`
- `concat()`
- `substring()`
- `contains()`
- `string-length()`

The `string()` function is a data accessor function that returns the string value from an element or attribute. The `concat()` function joins two string values, and the `substring()` function returns a substring from a given value, starting at a specified position and having a specified length. The `string-length()` function returns the length of a given string value. Finally, the `contains()` function accepts two string values and returns true if the second value is a substring of the first value.

Numeric and aggregate functions

SQL Server 2008 supports the following XQuery aggregate functions. These functions can be used to perform aggregate operations over the nodes of an XML document:

- `min()`
- `max()`
- `count()`
- `sum()`
- `avg()`

Support for the following XQuery numeric functions is implemented in SQL Server 2008:

- `ceiling()`
- `floor()`
- `round()`

The functionality exposed by each of these functions is self-explanatory. All these functions exist in T-SQL as well, and the T-SQL versions of these functions provide the same functionality as the XQuery versions (except that the T-SQL function is applied on relational rows, whereas the XQuery version is applied on XML nodes).

Other functions

SQL Server 2008 supports a few more XQuery functions that may be less commonly used, but are still worth a mention here:

- **Data accessor function:** `data()`
- **Boolean functions:** `not()`, `true()`, and `false()`
- **Sequence functions:** `empty()`, `distinct-values()`, and `id()`
- **Node functions:** `number()`, `local-name()`, and `namespace-uri()`
- **Context functions:** `last()` and `position()`
- **QName functions:** `expanded-QName()`, `local-name-from-QName()` and `namespace-uri-from-QName`
- **SQL Server XQuery extension functions:** `sql:variable()` and `sql:column()`

The XQuery implementation of SQL Server 2008 still does not support user-defined functions (UDFs), recommended by the XQuery specification. Future versions of SQL Server might add support for user-defined functions within XQuery expressions, and the addition of XQuery UDFs will provide more programming power to the T-SQL developer.

Performing XML Data Modification

The `modify()` method of the `XML` data type can be used to perform DML operations on XML documents. It allows performing insert, update, and delete operations on XML variables or columns.

The `insert`, `replace value of`, and `delete` instructions are used with the `modify()` method to perform `INSERT`, `UPDATE`, and `DELETE` operations on XML documents. Each of these operations has its own syntax and is briefly explained in the following sections.

Insert operation

A new element or attribute can be inserted into an XML document by using the `modify()` method with the `insert` command. A basic example demonstrating an `insert` operation is given here:

```
DECLARE @x XML
SELECT @x = '<SalesOrder OrderNumber="SO101"/>'

DECLARE @CustomerID INT
SELECT @CustomerID = 1
SET @x.modify('
        insert element CustomerID {sql:variable("@CustomerID")}
        as last into (SalesOrder)[1]
    ')

SELECT @x
/*
<SalesOrder OrderNumber="SO101">
  <CustomerID>1</CustomerID>
</SalesOrder>
*/
```

Update operation

The `modify()` method can be used with `replace value of` command to modify the value of elements or attributes. The following example changes the value of the `CustomerID` element:

```
DECLARE @x XML
SELECT @x = '
<SalesOrder OrderNumber="SO101">
  <CustomerID>1</CustomerID>
</SalesOrder>'

DECLARE @CustomerID INT
SELECT @CustomerID = 2

SET @x.modify('
        replace value of (SalesOrder/CustomerID/text())[1]
        with sql:variable("@CustomerID")
    ')

SELECT @x

/*
<SalesOrder OrderNumber="SO101">
  <CustomerID>1</CustomerID>
</SalesOrder>
*/
```

Delete operation

The modify() method can be used with the delete instruction to remove an element or attribute from a given XML document. The following example deletes the CustomerID element from the XML document:

```
DECLARE @x XML
SELECT @x = '
<SalesOrder OrderNumber="SO101">
  <CustomerID>1</CustomerID>
</SalesOrder>'

SET @x.modify('
        delete (SalesOrder/CustomerID)[1]
    ')

SELECT @x
/*
<SalesOrder OrderNumber="SO101" />
*/
```

What's new for XML DML operations in SQL Server 2008

SQL Server 2005's implementation of the modify() method does not support XML variables with the insert instruction. With SQL Server 2005, it is not possible to insert an XML value into an XML document. A possible workaround is to cast the XML value to VARCHAR/NVARCHAR and perform an insert operation. However, in such a case, SQL Server will encode the XML tags within the VARCHAR/NVARCHAR value, which may not be the desired result most of the time.

SQL Server 2008 enhanced the modify() method to support XML variables with the insert command. The following code snippet shows an example:

```
DECLARE @doc XML, @val XML
SELECT @doc = '
<SalesOrder OrderNumber="SO101">
  <CustomerID>1</CustomerID>
</SalesOrder>'

SELECT @val = '
<Items>
    <Item ItemNumber="Z001" Quantity="1" Price="900"/>
</Items>'

SET @doc.modify('
        insert sql:variable("@val")
        as last into (SalesOrder)[1]
    ')

SELECT @doc
```

```
/*
<SalesOrder OrderNumber="SO101">
  <CustomerID>1</CustomerID>
  <Items>
    <Item ItemNumber="Z001" Quantity="1" Price="900" />
  </Items>
</SalesOrder>
*/
```

Note that the syntax of the `insert` command is slightly different when an XML value is being inserted.

Handling Namespaces

XML uses namespaces to disambiguate elements and attributes. If the XML document contains namespace declarations, then the XQuery expressions for querying or modifying the XML document should also contain the required namespace declarations to identify and access the correct XML nodes.

The `WITH NAMESPACES` directive can be used to declare the XML namespaces and refer to them in the XQuery expressions following the declaration:

```
DECLARE @x XML
SELECT @x = '
<SalesOrder xmlns="http://www.sqlserverbible.com/order"
    xmlns:cust="http://www.sqlserverbible.com/customer">
  <OrderID>1</OrderID>
  <cust:CustomerID>10001</cust:CustomerID>
</SalesOrder>'

;WITH XMLNAMESPACES(
    DEFAULT 'http://www.sqlserverbible.com/order',
    'http://www.sqlserverbible.com/customer' AS cust
)
SELECT
    @x.value('(SalesOrder/OrderID)[1]','INT') AS OrderID,
    @x.value('(SalesOrder/cust:CustomerID)[1]','INT') AS CustomerID

/*
OrderID     CustomerID
----------- -----------
1           10001
*/
```

The `WITH XMLNAMESPACES` directive simplifies namespace declaration, as the namespaces can be declared once and then reused in the XQuery expression that follows the declaration.

Shredding XML Using OPENXML()

OPENXML(), released along with SQL Server 2000, was the first XML shredding function added to SQL Server. OPENXML() is very powerful and is the only option available to shred XML documents (from T-SQL) in SQL Server 2000. SQL Server 2005 added support for XQuery, which is a better choice over OPENXML() in most cases. SQL Server 2008 enhanced the XQuery functionalities further by adding support for "let" clause in FLWOR operations.

The following example shows a basic OPENXML() function call:

```
DECLARE @hdoc INT
DECLARE @xml VARCHAR(MAX)
SET @xml ='
<SalesOrder OrderNumber="SO101">
  <Items>
    <Item ItemNumber="D001" Quantity="1" Price="900.0000" />
    <Item ItemNumber="Z001" Quantity="1" Price="200.0000" />
  </Items>
</SalesOrder>'

-- Step 1: initialize XML Document Handle
EXEC sp_xml_preparedocument @hdoc OUTPUT, @xml

-- Step 2: Call OPENXML()
SELECT * FROM OPENXML(@hdoc, '/SalesOrder/Items/Item')
WITH (
    OrderNumber CHAR(5) '../../@OrderNumber',
    ItemNumber CHAR(4) '@ItemNumber',
    Quantity INT '@Quantity',
    Price MONEY '@Price'
)

-- Step 3: Free document handle
exec sp_xml_removedocument @hdoc

/*
OrderNumber ItemNumber Quantity    Price
----------- ---------- ----------- ---------------------
SO101       D001       1           900.00
SO101       Z001       1           200.00
*/
```

As is apparent from the preceding example, a call to OPENXML() is always a three-step process. Before the function can be called, a document handle for the current XML document should be created and initialized. This handle should be passed to the OPENXML() function call as an argument. Finally, the handle has to be released to free system resources used for the operation.

The system stored procedure `xp_xml_preparedocument` takes an optional fourth argument that accepts the namespace declarations. If the XML document contains namespace declarations, this parameter can be used to specify the namespaces declared in the XML document. The following example shows how to do this:

```
DECLARE @hdoc INT
DECLARE @xml VARCHAR(MAX)
SET @xml ='
<itm:Items xmlns:itm="http://www.sqlserverbible.com/items">
    <itm:Item ItemNumber="D001" Quantity="1" Price="900.0000" />
    <itm:Item ItemNumber="Z001" Quantity="1" Price="200.0000" />
</itm:Items>'

-- Step 1: initialize XML Document Handle
EXEC sp_xml_preparedocument
    @hdoc OUTPUT,
    @xml,
    '<itm:Items xmlns:itm="http://www.sqlserverbible.com/items"/>'

-- Step 2: Call OPENXML()
SELECT * FROM OPENXML(@hdoc, 'itm:Items/itm:Item')
WITH (
    ItemNumber CHAR(4) '@ItemNumber',
    Quantity INT '@Quantity',
    Price MONEY '@Price'
)

-- Step 3: Free document handle
exec sp_xml_removedocument @hdoc

/*
ItemNumber Quantity    Price
---------- ----------- ---------------------
D001       1           900.00
Z001       1           200.00
*/
```

Because `OPENXML()` needs a three-step process to shred each XML document, it is not suitable for set-based operations. It cannot be called from a scalar or table-valued function. If a table has an XML column, and a piece of information is to be extracted from more than one row, with `OPENXML()` a `WHILE` loop is needed. Row-by-row processing has significant overhead and will typically be much slower than a set-based operation. In such cases, XQuery will be a better choice over `OPENXML()`.

Using `OPENXML()` may be expensive in terms of memory usage too. It uses the MSXML parser internally, using a COM invocation, which may not be cheap. A call to `xp_xml_preparedocument` parses the XML document and stores it in the internal cache of SQL Server. The MSXML parser uses one-eighth of the total memory available to SQL Server. Every document handle initialized by `xp_xml_prepare` document should be released by calling the `xp_xml_releasedocument` procedure to avoid memory leaks.

XSD and XML Schema Collections

XSD (XML Schema Definition) is a W3C-recommended language for describing and validating XML documents. SQL Server supports a subset of the XSD specification and can validate XML documents against XSD schemas.

SQL Server implements support for XSD schemas in the form of XML schema collections. An XML SCHEMA COLLECTION is a SQL Server database object just like tables or views. It can be created from an XML schema definition. Once a schema collection is created, it can be associated with an XML column or variable. An XML column or variable that is bound to a schema collection is called *typed XML*. SQL Server strictly validates typed XML documents when the value of the column or variable is modified either by an assignment operation or by an XML DML operation (insert/update/delete).

Creating an XML Schema collection

An XML schema collection can be created with CREATE XML SCHEMA COLLECTION statement. It creates a new XML schema collection with the specified name using the schema definition provided.

The following example shows an XML schema that describes a customer information XML document and implements a number of validation rules:

```
CREATE XML SCHEMA COLLECTION CustomerSchema AS '
<xs:schema xmlns:xs="http://www.w3.org/2001/XMLSchema">
  <xs:element name="Customer">
    <xs:complexType>
      <xs:attribute name="CustomerID" use="required">
        <xs:simpleType>
          <xs:restriction base="xs:integer">
            <xs:minInclusive value="1"/>
            <xs:maxInclusive value="9999"/>
          </xs:restriction>
        </xs:simpleType>
      </xs:attribute>
      <xs:attribute name="CustomerName" use="optional">
        <xs:simpleType>
          <xs:restriction base="xs:string">
            <xs:maxLength value="40"/>
          </xs:restriction>
        </xs:simpleType>
      </xs:attribute>
    </xs:complexType>
  </xs:element>
</xs:schema>'
GO
```

This schema defines a top-level element "Customer" with two attributes: CustomerID and CustomerNumber. CustomerID attribute is set to mandatory by using the use attribute. A restriction of minimum value and maximum value is applied on the customerID attribute. The CustomerNumber attribute is set to optional by setting the use attribute to optional. A restriction is applied on the length of this attribute.

Creating typed XML columns and variables

Once the schema collection is created, typed XML columns and variables can be created that are bound to the schema collection. The following example creates a typed XML variable:

```
DECLARE @x XML(CustomerSchema)
```

Similarly, a typed XML column can be created as follows:

```
-- Create a table with a TYPED XML column
CREATE TABLE TypedXML(
    ID INT,
    CustomerData XML(CustomerSchema))
```

Typed XML columns can be added to existing tables by using the ALTER TABLE ADD statement:

```
-- add a new typed XML column
ALTER TABLE TypedXML ADD Customer2 XML(CustomerSchema)
```

Typed XML parameters can be used as input and output parameters of stored procedures. They can also be used as input parameters and return values of scalar functions.

Performing validation

When a value is assigned to a typed XML column or variable, SQL Server will perform all the validations defined in the schema collection against the new value being inserted or assigned. The insert/assignment operation will succeed only if the validation succeeds. The following code generates an error because the value being assigned to the CustomerID attribute is outside the range defined for it:

```
DECLARE @x XML(CustomerSchema)
SELECT @x = '<Customer CustomerID="19909" CustomerName="Jacob"/>'
/*
Msg 6926, Level 16, State 1, Line 2
XML Validation: Invalid simple type value: '19909'. Location: /*:Cus-
tomer[1]/@*:
CustomerID
*/
```

SQL Server will perform the same set of validations if a new value is being assigned or the existing value is modified by using XML DML operations (insert/update/delete).

An existing untyped XML column can be changed to a typed XML column by using the ALTER TABLE ALTER COLUMN command. SQL Server will validate the XML values stored in each row for that column, and check if the values validate successfully against the schema collection being bound to the column. The ALTER COLUMN operation will succeed only if all the existing values are valid as per the rules defined in the schema collection. The same process happens if a typed XML column is altered and the column is bound to a different schema collection. The operation can succeed only if all the existing values are valid as per the rules defined in the new schema collection.

XML DOCUMENT and CONTENT

A typed XML column or variable can accept two flavors of XML values: DOCUMENT and CONTENT. DOCUMENT is a complete XML document with a single top-level element. CONTENT usually is an XML fragment and can have more than one top-level element. Depending upon the requirement, a typed XML column or variable can be defined as DOCUMENT or CONTENT when it is bound with the schema collection.

The following code snippet shows examples of XML variables declared as DOCUMENT and CONTENT.

```
-- XML Document
DECLARE @x XML(DOCUMENT CustomerSchema)
SELECT @x = '<Customer CustomerID="1001" CustomerName="Jacob"/>'

-- XML Content
DECLARE @x XML(CONTENT CustomerSchema)
SELECT @x = '
<Customer CustomerID="1001" CustomerName="Jacob"/>
<Customer CustomerID="1002" CustomerName="Steve"/>'
```

If a content model is not specified, SQL Server assumes CONTENT when creating the typed XML column or variable.

Altering XML Schema collections

There are times when you might need to alter the definition of a given schema collection. This can usually happen when the business requirement changes or you need to fix a missing or incorrect validation rule.

However, altering schema collections is a big pain in SQL Server. Once created, the definition of a schema cannot be altered. The schema demonstrated earlier in this section defines customer name as an optional attribute. If the business requirement changes and this attribute has to be made mandatory, that will be a lot of work.

Because the definition of a schema collection cannot be altered, if a new schema definition is wanted, the existing schema collection should be dropped by executing the DROP XML SCHEMA COLLECTION statement.

Note that a schema collection cannot be dropped unless all the references are removed. All columns bound to the given schema collection should be dropped, changed to untyped XML, or altered and bound to another schema collection before dropping the schema collection. Similarly, any XML parameters or return values that refer to the schema collection in stored procedures or functions should be removed or altered as well.

What's in the "collection"?

An XML schema collection can contain multiple schema definitions. In most production use cases, it will likely have only one schema definition, but it is valid to have more than one schema definition in a single schema collection.

When a schema collection contains more than one schema definition, SQL Server will allow XML values that validate with any of the schema definitions available within the schema collection.

For example, a feed aggregator that stores valid RSS and ATOM feeds in a single column can create a schema collection containing two schema definitions, one for RSS and one for ATOM. SQL Server will then allow both RSS and ATOM feeds to be stored in the given column. The following XML schema collection defines two top-level elements, `Customer` and `Order`:

```
CREATE XML SCHEMA COLLECTION CustomerOrOrder AS '
<xs:schema xmlns:xs="http://www.w3.org/2001/XMLSchema">
  <xs:element name="Customer">
    <xs:complexType>
      <xs:attribute name="CustomerID"/>
       <xs:attribute name="CustomerName"/>
     </xs:complexType>
  </xs:element>
  <xs:element name="Order">
    <xs:complexType>
      <xs:attribute name="OrderID"/>
      <xs:attribute name="OrderNumber"/>
    </xs:complexType>
  </xs:element>
</xs:schema>'
GO
```

A typed XML column or variable bound to this schema collection can store a `Customer` element, an `Order` element or both (if the XML column or variable is defined as `CONTENT`). The following sample code presents an example to demonstrate this.

```
-- XML Document
DECLARE @x XML(CustomerOrOrder)
SELECT @x = '<Customer CustomerID="1001" CustomerName="Jacob"/>'
SELECT @x = '<Order OrderID="121" OrderNumber="10001"/>'

SELECT @x = '
<Customer CustomerID="1001" CustomerName="Jacob"/>
<Order OrderID="121" OrderNumber="10001"/>'
```

A new schema definition can be added to an existing schema collection by using the `ALTER XML SCHEMA COLLECTION ADD` statement:

```
ALTER XML SCHEMA COLLECTION CustomerOrOrder ADD '
<xs:schema xmlns:xs="http://www.w3.org/2001/XMLSchema">
  <xs:element name="Item">
    <xs:complexType>
      <xs:attribute name="ItemID"/>
      <xs:attribute name="ItemNumber"/>
    </xs:complexType>
  </xs:element>
</xs:schema>'
GO
```

Before creating or altering an XML schema collection, it is important to check whether a schema collection with the given name exists. XML schema collections are stored in a set of internal tables and are accessible through a number of system catalog views. Sys.xml_schema_collections can be queried to determine whether a given XML schema collection exists:

```
IF EXISTS(
    SELECT name FROM sys.xml_schema_collections
    WHERE schema_id = schema_id('dbo') AND name = 'CustomerSchema'
) DROP XML SCHEMA COLLECTION CustomerSchema
```

What's new in SQL Server 2008 for XSD

SQL Server 2008 added a number of enhancements to the XSD implementation of the previous version. The XSD implementation of date, time, and dateTime data types required time zone information in SQL Server 2005, so a date value should look like 2009-03-14Z or 2009-03-14+05:30, where the z and +05:30 indicates the time zone. This requirement has been removed in SQL Server 2008. The XSD processor now accepts date, time, and dateTime values with or without time zone information.

Though the date, time, and dateTime data type implementation in SQL Server 2005 required time zone information, the XML document did not preserve it. It normalized the value to a UTC date/time value and stored it. SQL Server 2008 added enhancements to preserve the time zone information. If the date, time, or dateTime value contains time zone information, then SQL Server 2008 preserves it.

Unions and lists are two powerful data models of XSD. Union types are simple types created with the union of two or more atomic types. List types are simple types that can store a space-delimited list of atomic values. Both of these types supported only atomic values in their implementation in SQL Server 2005. SQL Server 2008 enhanced these types so that lists of union types and unions of list types can be created.

Lax validation is the most important addition to the XSD validation in SQL Server 2008. In SQL Server 2005, wildcard elements could be validated either with "skip" (does not validate at all) or "strict" (performs a strict, or full, validation). SQL Server 2008 added "lax" validation whereby the schema processor performs the validation only if the declaration for the target namespace is found in the schema collection.

This chapter provides only a brief overview of the XSD implementation in SQL Server. Detailed coverage of all the XSD features is beyond the scope of this chapter.

Understanding XML Indexes

SQL Server does not allow an XML column to be part of a regular index (SQL Index). To optimize queries that extract information from XML columns, SQL Server supports a special type of index called an XML index. The query processor can use an XML index to optimize XQuery, just like it uses SQL indexes to optimize SQL queries.

SQL Server supports four different types of XML indexes. Each XML column can have a *primary* XML index and three different types of *secondary* XML indexes.

A primary XML index is a clustered index created in document order, on an internal table known as a *node table*. It contains information about all tags, paths, and values within the XML instance in each row. A primary XML index can be created only on a table that already has a clustered index on the primary key. The primary key of the base table is used to join the XQuery results with the base table. The primary XML index contains one row for each node in the XML instance. The query processor will use the primary XML index to execute every query, except for cases where the whole document is retrieved.

Just like SQL indexes, XML indexes should be created and used wisely. The size of a primary XML index may be around three times the size of the XML data stored in the base table, although this may vary based on the structure of the XML document. Document order is important for XML, and the primary XML index is created in such a way that document order and the structural integrity of the XML document is maintained in the query result.

If an XML column has a primary XML index, three additional types of secondary XML indexes can be created on the column. The additional index types are `PROPERTY`, `VALUE`, and `PATH` indexes. Based upon the specific query requirements, one or more of the index types may be used. Secondary indexes are non-clustered indexes created on the internal node table.

A `PATH` XML index is created on the internal node table and indexes the path and value of each XML element and attribute. `PATH` indexes are good for operations in which nodes with specific values are filtered or selected.

A `PROPERTY` XML index is created on the internal node table and contains the primary key of the table, the path to elements and attributes, and their values. The advantage of a `PROPERTY` XML index over a `PATH` XML index is that it helps to search multi-valued properties in the same XML instance.

A `VALUE` XML index is just like the `PATH` XML index, and contains the value and path of each XML element and attribute (instead of path and value). `VALUE` indexes are helpful in cases where wildcards are used in the path expression.

XML indexes are a great addition to the XML capabilities of SQL Server. Wise usage of XML indexes helps optimize queries that use XQuery to fetch information from XML columns.

XML Best Practices

SQL Server comes with a wide range of XML-related functionalities, and the correct usage of these functionalities is essential for building a good system. A feature may be deemed "good" only if it is applied on an area where it is really required. If not, it might result in unnecessary overhead or add unwanted complexity to an otherwise simpler task.

- XML should be used only where it is really required. Using XML where relational data would best be suited is not a good idea. Similarly, using a relational model where XML might run better won't produce the desired results.
- XML is good for storing semi-structured or unstructured data. XML is a better choice if the physical order of values is significant and the data represents a hierarchy. If the values are valid XML documents and need to be queried, storing them on an XML column will be a better choice over `VARCHAR`, `NVARCHAR`, or `VARBINARY` columns.

- If the structure of the XML documents is defined, using typed XML columns will be a better choice. Typed XML columns provide better metadata information and allow SQL Server to optimize queries running over typed XML columns. Furthermore, typed XML provides storage optimization and static type checking.
- Creating a primary XML index and a secondary XML index (or more, depending on the workload) might help improve XQuery performance. An XML primary index usually uses up to three times the storage space than the data in the base table. This indicates that, just like SQL indexes, XML indexes also should be used wisely. Keep in mind that a full-text index can be created on an XML column. A wise combination of a full-text index with XML indexes might be a better choice in many situations.
- Creating property tables to promote multi-valued properties from the XML column may be a good idea in many cases. One or more property tables may be created from the data in an XML column, and these tables can be indexed to improve performance further.
- Two common mistakes that add a lot of overhead to XQuery processing are usage of wildcards in the path expression and using a parent node accessor to read information from upper-level nodes.
- Using specific markups instead of generic markups will enhance performance significantly. Generic markups do not perform well and do not allow XML index lookups to be done efficiently.
- Attribute-centric markup is a better choice than element-centric markup. Processing information from attributes is much more efficient than processing information from elements. Attribute-centric markups take less storage space than element-centric markups, and the evaluation of predicates is more efficient because the attribute's value is stored in the same row as its markup in the primary XML index.
- An in-place update of the `XML` data type gives better performance in most cases. If the update operation requires modifying the value of one or more elements or attributes, it is a better practice to modify those elements and attributes using XML DML functions, rather than replace the whole document.
- Using the `exist()` method to check for the existence of a value is much more efficient than using the `value()` method. Parameterizing XQuery and XML DML expressions is much more efficient than executing dynamic SQL statements.

Summary

SQL Server 2008 is fully equipped with a wide range of XML capabilities to support the XML processing requirements needed by almost every modern application. SQL Server 2008 added a number of enhancements to the XML features supported by previous versions. Key points to take away from this chapter include the following:

- SQL Server 2008 is equipped with a number of XML processing capabilities, including support for generating, loading, querying, validating, modifying, and indexing XML documents.
- The `XML` data type can be used to store XML documents. It supports the following methods: `value()`, `exist()`, `query()`, `modify()`, and `nodes()`.

- An XML data type column or variable that is associated with a schema collection is called *typed XML*. SQL Server validates typed XML columns and variables against the rules defined in the schema.
- The OPENROWSET() function can be used with the BULK row set provider to load an XML document from a disk file.
- XML output can be generated from the result of a SELECT query using FOR XML. FOR XML can be used with the AUTO, RAW, EXPLICIT, and PATH directives to achieve different levels of control over the structure and format of the XML output.
- The query() method of the XML data type supports XQuery FLWOR operations, which allow complex restructuring and manipulation of XML documents. SQL Server 2008 added support for the let clause in FLWOR operations.
- The XML data type supports XML DML operations through the modify() method. It allows performing insert, update, and delete operations on XML documents.
- SQL Server 2008 added support for inserting an XML data type value into another XML document.
- WITH XMLNAMESPACES can be used to process XML documents that have namespace declarations.
- SQL Server supports XSD in the form of XML schema collections. SQL Server 2008 added a number of enhancements to the XSD support available with previous versions. These enhancements include full support for the date, time, and dateTime data types, support for lax validation, support for creating unions of list types and lists of union types, etc.
- SQL Server supports a special category of indexes called *XML indexes* to index XML columns. A primary XML index and up to three secondary indexes (PATH, VALUE, and PROPERTY) can be created on an XML column.

Chapter 19

Using Integrated Full-Text Search

IN THIS CHAPTER

- Setting up full-text index catalogs with Management Studio or T-SQL code
- Maintaining full-text indexes
- Using full-text indexes in queries
- Performing fuzzy word searches
- Searching text stored in binary objects
- Full-text search performance

Several years ago I wrote a word search for a large database of legal texts. For word searches, the database parsed all the documents and built a word-frequency table as a many-to-many association between the word table and the document table. It worked well, and word searches became lightning-fast. As much fun as writing your own word search can be, fortunately, you have a choice.

SQL Server includes a structured word/phrase indexing system called Full-Text Search. More than just a word parser, Full-Text Search actually performs linguistic analysis by determining base words and word boundaries, and by conjugating verbs for different languages. It runs circles around the simple word index system that I built.

ANSI Standard SQL uses the `LIKE` operator to perform basic word searches and even wildcard searches. For example, the following code uses the `LIKE` operator to query the Aesop's Fables sample database:

```
USE Aesop;

SELECT Title
  FROM Fable
  WHERE Fabletext LIKE '%Lion%'
    AND Fabletext LIKE '%bold%';
```

Result:

```
Title
-------------------------------------------
The Hunter and the Woodman
```

The main problem with performing SQL Server `WHERE...LIKE` searches is the slow performance. Indexes are searchable from the beginning of the word, so searching for `LIKE 'word%'` is fast, but `LIKE '%word%'` is terribly slow. Searching for strings within a string can't use the b-tree structure of an index to perform a fast index seek so it must perform a table scan instead, as demonstrated in Figure 19-1. It's like looking for all the instances of "Paul" in the telephone book. The phone book isn't indexed by first name, so each page must be scanned.

FIGURE 19-1

Filtering by a `where` clause value that begins with a wildcard is not "sargable" — that is, not a searchable argument — so it forces the Query Optimizer to use a full scan.

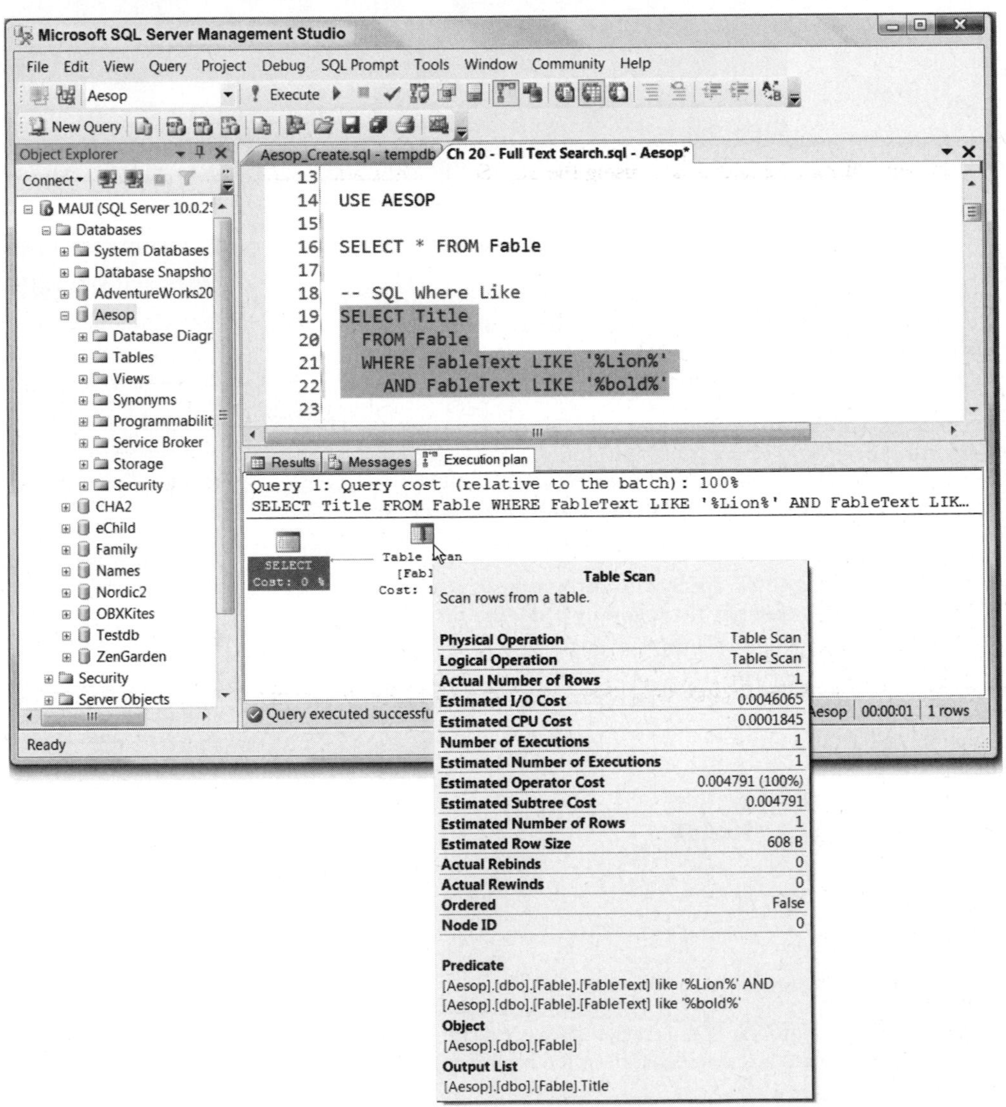

Basically, Integrated Full-Text Search (iFTS) extends SQL Server beyond the traditional relational data searches by building an index of every significant word and phrase. In addition, the full-text search engine adds advanced features such as the following:

- Searching for one word near another word
- Searching with wildcards
- Searching for inflectional variations of a word (such as *run*, *ran*, *running*)
- Weighting one word or phrase as more important to the search than another word or phrase
- Performing fuzzy word/phrase searches
- Searching character data with embedded binary objects stored with SQL Server
- Using Full-Text Search in the `WHERE` clause or as a data source like a subquery

Full-Text Search must be installed with the instance of SQL Server. If it's not installed on your instance, it may be added later using the SQL Server Installation Center (see Chapter 4, "Installing SQL Server 2008").

What's New with Full-Text Search?

The history of Full-Text Search began in late 1998 when Microsoft reengineered one of its search engines (Site Server Search — designed for websites) to provide search services for SQL Server 7. The engine was called MSSearch, and it also provided search services to Exchange Content Indexing and SharePoint Portal Server 2001. I liked Full-Text Search when it was first introduced back in SQL Server 7, and I'm glad that it's still here and Microsoft is continuing to invest in it.

Microsoft continued to improve iFTS's performance and scalability with SQL Server 2000 and SQL Server 2005. Also, in case you didn't follow the evolution of Full-Text Search back in SQL Server 2005, Microsoft worked on bringing Full-Text Search closer to industry standards:

- The list of *noise words* was renamed to the industry standard term of *stoplist*.
- The many set-up stored procedures were simplified into normal DDL `CREATE`, `ALTER`, and `DROP` commands.

With SQL Server 2008, the old stored procedure methods of setting up Full-Text Search are deprecated, meaning they will be removed in a future version.

SQL 2008 Integrated Full-Text Search (iFTS) is the fourth-generation search component for SQL Server, and this new version is by far the most scalable and feature-rich. SQL 2008 iFTS ships in the Workgroup, Standard, and Enterprise versions of SQL Server.

With SQL Server 2008, SQL Server is no longer dependent on the indexing service of Windows. Instead, it is now fully integrated within SQL Server, which means that the SQL Server development team can advance Full-Text Search features without depending on a release cycle.

continued

continued

The integration of FTS in the SQL engine should also result in better performance because the Query Optimizer can make an informed decision whether to invoke the full-text engine before or after applying non-FTS filters.

Minor enhancements include the following:

- A number of new DMVs expose the workings of iFTS
- Forty new languages
- Noise words management with T-SQL using `create fulltext stoplist`
- Thesaurus stored in system table and instance-scoped

CROSS-REF **All the code samples in this chapter use the Aesop's Fables sample database. The `Aesop_Create.sql` script will create the database and populate it with 25 of Aesop's fables. The database create script as well as the chapter code can be downloaded from `www.sqlserverbible.com`.**

NOTE **Integrated Full-Text Search is not installed by default by SQL Server 2008 Setup. The option is under the Database Engine Services node. To add Integrated Full-Text Search to an existing instance, use the Programs and Features application in the Control Panel to launch SQL Server Setup in a mode that allows changing the SQL Server components.**

NOTE **Microsoft is less than consistent with the naming of Integrated Full-Text Search. Management Studio and Books Online sometimes call it only Full-Text Search or Full-Text Indexing. In this chapter I use Integrated Full-Text Search or iFTS. If I use a different term it's only because the sentence is referring to a specific UI command in Management Studio.**

Configuring Full-Text Search Catalogs

A *full-text search catalog* is a collection of full-text indexes for a single SQL Server database. Each catalog may store multiple full-text indexes for multiple tables, but each table is limited to only one catalog. Typically, a single catalog will handle all the full-text searches for a database, although dedicating a single catalog to a very large table (one with over one million rows) will improve performance.

Catalogs may index only user tables (not views, temporary tables, table variables, or system tables).

Creating a catalog with the wizard

Although creating and configuring a full-text search catalog with code is easy, the task is usually done once and then forgotten. Unless the repeatability of a script is important for redeploying the project, the Full-Text Indexing Wizard is sufficient for configuring full-text search.

The wizard may be launched from within Management Studio's Object Explorer. With a table selected, use the context menu and select Full-Text Index ➪ Define Full-Text Index.

The Full-Text Indexing Wizard starts from a selected database and table and works through multiple steps to configure the full-text catalog, as follows:

1. Select a unique index that full-text can use to identify the rows indexed with full-text. The primary key is typically the best choice for this index; however, any non-nullable, unique, single-column index is sufficient. If the table uses composite primary keys, another unique index must be created to use full-text search.
2. Choose the columns to be full-text indexed, as shown in Figure 19-2. Valid column data types are character data types (`char`, `nchar`, `varchar`, `nvarchar`, `text`, `ntext`, and `xml`) and binary data types (`binary`, `varbinary`, `varbinary(max)`, and the deprecated `image`). (Indexing binary images is an advanced topic covered later in this chapter.) You may need to specify the language used for parsing the words, although the computer default will likely handle this automatically.

   Full-text search can also read documents stored in `binary`, `varbinary`, `varbinary(max)`, and `image` columns. Using full-text search with embedded BLOBs (binary large objects) is covered later in this chapter.

FIGURE 19-2

Any valid columns are listed by the Full-Text Indexing Wizard and may be selected for indexing.

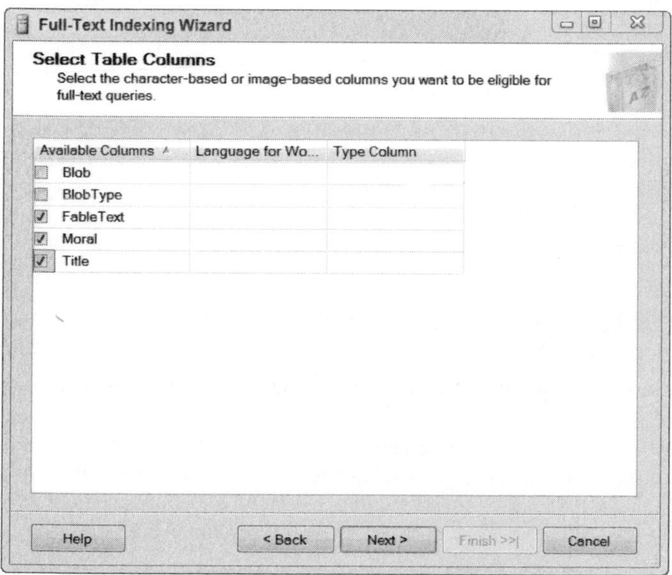

3. Enable change tracking if desired. This will automatically update the catalog when the data changes. The Automatic option means that Change Tracking is enabled and automatically updated. The Manual option means that updates are manual but change tracking is still enabled. Change Tracking can also be completely disabled.
4. Select a catalog or opt to create a new catalog. The stoplist may also be selected.

5. Skip creating a population schedule; there's a better way to keep the catalog up-to-date. (The strategies for maintaining a full-text index are discussed later in the chapter.)
6. Click Finish.

When the wizard is finished, if Change Tracking was selected in step 3, then the Start full population check box was also automatically selected, so Full-Text Search should begin a population immediately and iFTS will be set to go as soon as all the data is indexed. Depending on the amount of data in the indexed columns, the population may take a few seconds, a few minutes, or a few hours to complete.

If Change Tracking was disabled, then the iFTS indexes are empty and need to be populated. To initially populate the catalog, right-click on the table and select Full-Text Index Table ⇨ Enable Full-Text Index, and then Full-Text Index Table ⇨ Start Full Population from the context menu. This directs SQL Server to begin passing data to Full-Text Search for indexing.

Creating a catalog with T-SQL code

To implement full-text search using a method that can be easily replicated on other servers, your best option is to create a SQL script. Creating a catalog with code means following the same steps as the Full-Text Indexing Wizard. Creating full-text catalogs and indexes uses normal DDL `CREATE` statements. The following code configures a full-text search catalog for the Aesop's Fables sample database:

```
USE AESOP;

CREATE FULLTEXT CATALOG AesopFT;

CREATE FULLTEXT INDEX ON dbo.Fable(Title, Moral, Fabletext)
KEY INDEX FablePK ON AesopFT
WITH CHANGE_TRACKING AUTO;
```

Use the `alter fulltext index` command to change the full-text catalog to manually populate it.

Pushing data to the full-text index

Full-text indexes are different from data engine clustered and non-clustered indexes that are updated as part of the ACID transaction (see Chapter 66, "Managing Transactions, Locking, and Blocking" for details on ACID transactions). Full-text indexes are updated only when the Database Engine passes new data to the full-text engine. That's both a benefit and a drawback. On the one hand, it means that updating the full-text index doesn't slow down large-text updates. On the other hand, the full-text index is not real-time in the way SQL Server data is. If a user enters a résumé and then searches for it using full-text search before the full-text index has been updated, then the résumé won't be found.

Every full-text index begins empty, and if data already exists in the SQL Server tables, then it must be *pushed* to the full-text index by means of a *full population*. A full population re-initializes the index and passes data for all rows to the full-text index. A full population may be performed with Management Studio or T-SQL code. Because the data push is driven by SQL Server, data is sent from one table at a time regardless of how many tables might be full-text indexed in a catalog. If the full-text index is created for an empty SQL Server table, then a full population is not required.

Two primary methods of pushing ongoing changes to a full-text index exist:

- **Incremental populations:** An incremental population uses a timestamp to pass any rows that have changed since the last population. This method can be performed manually from Management Studio or by means of T-SQL code or scheduled as a SQL Server Agent job (typically, each evening). Incremental population requires a `rowversion` (`timestamp`) column in the table.

  Incremental populations present two problems. First, a built-in delay occurs between the time the data is entered and the time the user can find the data using full-text search. Second, incremental populations consolidate all the changes into a single process that consumes a significant amount of CPU time during the incremental change. In a heavily used database, the choice is between performing incremental populations each evening and forcing a one-day delay each time or performing incremental populations at scheduled times throughout the day and suffering performance hits at those times.

- **Change tracking and background population (default):** SQL Server can watch for data changes in columns that are full-text indexed and then send what is effectively a single-row incremental population every time a row changes. While this method seems costly in terms of performance, in practice, the effect is not noticeable. The full-text update isn't fired by a trigger, so the update transaction doesn't need to wait for the data to be pushed to the full-text index. Instead, the full-text update occurs in the background slightly behind the SQL DML transaction. The effect is a balanced CPU load and a full-text index that appears to be near real-time.

  Change tracking can also be configured to require manual pushes of only the changed data.

Best Practice

If the database project incorporates searching for words within columns, use full-text search with change tracking and background population. It's the best overall way to balance search performance with update performance.

Maintaining a catalog with Management Studio

Within Management Studio, the iFTS catalogs are maintained with the right-click menu for each table. The menu offers the following maintenance options under Full-Text Index Table:

- **Define Full-Text Indexing on Table:** Launches the Full-Text Indexing Wizard to create a new catalog as described earlier in the chapter
- **Enable/Disable Full-Text Index:** Turns iFTS on or off for the catalog
- **Delete Full-Text Index:** Drops the selected table from its catalog
- **Start Full Population:** Initiates a data push of all rows from the selected SQL Server table to its full-text index catalog

- **Start Incremental Population:** Initiates a data push of rows that have changed since the last population in the selected table from SQL Server to the full-text index
- **Stop Population:** Halts any currently running full-text population push
- **Track Changes Manually:** Enables Change Tracking but does not push any data to the index
- **Track Changes Automatically:** Performs a full or incremental population and then turns on change tracking so that SQL Server can update the index
- **Disable Change Tracking:** Temporarily turns off change tracking
- **Apply Tacked Changes:** Pushes updates of rows that have been flagged by change tracking to the full-text index as the changes occur
- **Update Index:** Pushes an update of all rows that change tracking has flagged to the full-text index
- **Properties:** Launches the Full-Text Search Property page, which can be used to modify the catalog for the selected table

Maintaining a catalog in T-SQL code

Each of the previous Management Studio iFTS maintenance commands can be executed from T-SQL code. The following examples demonstrate iFTS catalog-maintenance commands applied to the Aesop's Fables sample database:

- Full population:

  ```
  ALTER FULLTEXT INDEX ON Fable START FULL POPULATION;
  ```

- Incremental population:

  ```
  ALTER FULLTEXT INDEX ON Fable START Incremental POPULATION
  ```

- Remove a full-text catalog:

  ```
  DROP FULLTEXT INDEX ON dbo.Fable
  DROP FULLTEXT CATALOG AesopFT
  ```

Word Searches

Once the catalog is created, iFTS is ready for word and phrase queries. Word searches are performed with the `CONTAINS` keyword. The effect of `CONTAINS` is to pass the word search to the iFTS component with SQL Server and await the reply. Word searches can be used within a query in one of two ways, `CONTAINS` or `CONTAINSTABLE`.

The Contains function

`CONTAINS` operates within the `WHERE` clause, much like a `WHERE IN(subquery)`. The parameters within the parentheses are passed to the iFTS engine, which returns an "include" or "omit" status for each row.

The first parameter passed to the iFTS engine is the column name to be searched, or an asterisk for a search of all columns from one table. If the FROM clause includes multiple tables, then the table must be specified in the CONTAINS parameter. The following basic iFTS searches all indexed columns for the word "Lion":

```
USE Aesop;
SELECT Title
  FROM Fable
  WHERE CONTAINS (Fable.*,'Lion');
```

The following fables contain the word "Lion" in either the fable title, moral, or text:

```
Title
--------------------------------------------------
The Dogs and the Fox
The Hunter and the Woodman
The Ass in the Lion's Skin
Androcles
```

NOTE **Integrated Full-Text Search is not case sensitive. Even if the server is configured for a case-sensitive collation, iFTS will accept column names regardless of the case.**

The ContainsTable function

Not only will iFTS work within the WHERE clause, but the CONTAINSTABLE function operates as a table or subquery and returns the result set from the full-text search engine. This SQL Server feature opens up the possibility of powerful searches.

CONTAINSTABLE returns a result set with two columns. The first column, Key, identifies the row using the unique index that was defined when the catalog was configured.

The second column, Rank, reports the ranking of the rows using values from 1 (low) to 1000 (high). There is no high/median/low range or fixed range to the rank value; the rank compares the row with other rows only with regard to the following factors:

- The frequency/uniqueness of the word in the table
- The frequency/uniqueness of the word in the column

Therefore, a rare word will be ranked as statistically more important than a common word.

Because rank is only a relative ranking, it's useful for sorting the results, but never assume a certain rank value indicates significance and thus filter by a rank value in the WHERE clause.

The same parameters that define the iFTS for CONTAINS also define the search for CONTAINSTABLE. The following query returns the raw data from the iFTS engine:

```
SELECT *
  FROM CONTAINSTABLE (Fable, *, 'Lion');
```

Result:

```
KEY         RANK
----------- -----------
3           86
4           80
20          48
14          32
```

The key by itself is useless to a human, but joining the CONTAINSTABLE results with the Fable table, as if CONTAINSTABLE were a derived table, enables the query to return the Rank and the fable's Title, as follows:

```
SELECT Fable.Title, FTS.Rank
  FROM Fable
    INNER JOIN CONTAINSTABLE (Fable, *, 'Lion') AS FTS
    ON Fable.FableID = FTS.[KEY]
  ORDER BY FTS.Rank DESC;
```

Result:

```
Title                              Rank
---------------------------------- -----------
Androcles                          86
The Ass in the Lion's Skin         80
The Hunter and the Woodman         48
The Dogs and the Fox               32
```

A fourth CONTAINSTABLE parameter, top *n* limit, reduces the result set from the full-text search engine much as the SQL SELECT TOP predicate does. The limit is applied assuming that the result set is sorted descending by rank so that only the highest ranked results are returned. The following query demonstrates the top *n* limit throttle:

```
SELECT Fable.Title, FTS.Rank
  FROM Fable
    INNER JOIN CONTAINSTABLE (Fable, *, 'Lion', 2) AS FTS
    ON Fable.FableID = FTS.[KEY]
  ORDER BY FTS.Rank DESC;
```

Result:

```
Title                              Rank
---------------------------------- -----------
Androcles                          86
The Ass in the Lion's Skin         80
```

The advantage of using the top *n* limit option is that the full-text search engine can pass less data back to the query. It's more efficient than returning the full result set and then performing a SQL TOP in the SELECT statement. It illustrates the principle of performing the data work at the server instead of the client. In this case, the full-text search engine is the server process and SQL Server is the client process.

Advanced Search Options

Full-text search is powerful, and you can add plenty of options to the search string. The options described in this section work with CONTAINS and CONTAINSTABLE.

Multiple-word searches

Multiple words may be included in the search by means of the OR and AND conjunctions. The following query finds any fables containing both the word "Tortoise" and the word "Hare" in the text of the fable:

```
SELECT Title
  FROM Fable
  WHERE CONTAINS (FableText,'Tortoise AND Hare');
```

Result:

```
Title
--------------------------------------------------
The Hare and the Tortoise
```

One significant issue pertaining to the search for multiple words is that while full-text search can easily search across multiple columns for a single word, it searches for multiple words only if those words are in the same column. For example, the fable "The Ants and the Grasshopper" includes the word "thrifty" in the moral and the word "supperless" in the text of the fable itself. But searching for "thrifty and supperless" across all columns yields no results, as shown here:

```
SELECT Title
  FROM Fable
  WHERE CONTAINS (*,' "Thrifty AND supperless" ');
```

Result:

```
(0 row(s) affected)
```

Two solutions exist, and neither one is pretty. The query can be reconfigured so that the AND conjunction is at the WHERE-clause level, rather than within the CONTAINS parameter. The problem with this solution is performance. The following query requires two remote scans to the full-text search engine:

```
SELECT Title
  FROM Fable
  WHERE CONTAINS (*,'Thrifty')
    AND CONTAINS(*,'supperless')
```

Result:

```
Title
--------------------------------------------------
The Ants and the Grasshopper
```

The other solution to the multiple-column search problem consists of adding an additional column to hold all the text to be searched and duplicating the data from the original columns to a `FullTextSearch` column within an after trigger or using a persisted computed column. This solution is not smooth either. It duplicates data and costs performance time during inserts and updates. The crux of the decision regarding how to solve the multiple-column search is the conflict between fast reads and fast writes — OLAP versus OLTP.

Searches with wildcards

Because the full-text search engine has its roots in Windows Index and was not a SQL Server–developed component, its wildcards use the standard DOS conventions (asterisk for a multi-character wildcard, and double quotes) instead of SQL-style wildcards and SQL single quotes.

The other thing to keep in mind about full-text wildcards is that they work only at the end of a word, not at the beginning. Indexes search from the beginning of strings, as shown here:

```
SELECT Title
  FROM Fable
  WHERE CONTAINS (*,' "Hunt*" ');
```

Result:

```
Title
--------------------------------------------------
The Hunter and the Woodman
The Ass in the Lion's Skin
The Bald Knight
```

Phrase searches

Full-text search can attempt to locate full phrases if those phrases are surrounded by double quotes. For example, to search for the fable about the boy who cried wolf, searching for "Wolf! Wolf!" does the trick:

```
SELECT Title
  FROM Fable
  WHERE CONTAINS (*,' "Wolf! Wolf!" ');
```

Result:

```
Title
--------------------------------------------------
The Shepherd's Boy and the Wolf
```

Word-proximity searches

When searching large documents, it's nice to be able to specify the proximity of the search words. Full-text search implements a proximity switch by means of the `NEAR` option. The relative distance between the words is calculated, and, if the words are close enough (within about 30 words, depending on the size of the text), then full-text search returns a `true` for the row.

The story of Androcles, the slave who pulls the thorn from the lion's paw, is one of the longer fables in the sample database, so it's a good test sample.

The following query attempts to locate the fable "Androcles" based on the proximity of the words "pardoned" and "forest" in the fable's text:

```
SELECT Title
  FROM Fable
  WHERE CONTAINS (*,'pardoned NEAR forest');
```

Result:

```
Title
--------------------------------------------------
Androcles
```

The proximity switch can handle multiple words. The following query tests the proximity of the words "lion," "paw," and "bleeding":

```
SELECT Title
  FROM Fable
  WHERE CONTAINS (*,'lion NEAR paw NEAR bleeding');
```

Result:

```
Title
--------------------------------------------------
Androcles
```

The proximity feature can be used with `CONTAINSTABLE`; the `RANK` indicates relative proximity. The following query ranks the fables that mention the word "life" near the word "death" in order of proximity:

```
SELECT Fable.Title, FTS.Rank
  FROM Fable
    INNER JOIN CONTAINSTABLE (Fable, *,'life NEAR death') AS FTS
    ON Fable.FableID = FTS.[KEY]
  ORDER BY FTS.Rank DESC;
```

Result:

```
Title                             Rank
--------------------------------- -----------
The Serpent and the Eagle         7
The Eagle and the Arrow           1
The Woodman and the Serpent       1
```

Word-inflection searches

The full-text search engine can actually perform linguistic analysis and base a search for different words on a common root word. This enables you to search for words without worrying about number or tense. For example, the inflection feature makes possible a search for the word "flying" that finds a row containing the word "flew." The language you specify for the table is critical in a case like this. Something else to keep in mind is that the word base will not cross parts of speech, meaning that a search for a noun won't locate a verb form of the same root. The following query demonstrates inflection by locating the fable with the word "flew" in "The Crow and the Pitcher":

```
SELECT Title
  FROM Fable
  WHERE CONTAINS (*,'FORMSOF(INFLECTIONAL,fly)');
```

Result:

```
Title
--------------------------------------------------
The Crow and the Pitcher
The Bald Knight
```

Thesaurus searches

The full-text search engine has the capability to perform thesaurus lookups for word replacements as well as synonyms. To configure your own thesaurus options, edit the thesaurus file. The location of the thesaurus file is dependent on your language, and server.

The thesaurus file for your language will follow the naming convention TS*XXX*.xml, where *XXX* is your language code (e.g., ENU for U.S. English, ENG for U.K. English, and so on). You need to remove the comment lines from your thesaurus file. If you edit this file in a text editor, then there are two sections or nodes to the thesaurus file: an *expansion node* and a *replacement node*. The expansion node is used to expand your search argument from one term to another argument. For example, in the thesaurus file, you will find the following expansion:

```
<expansion>
  <sub>Internet Explorer</sub>
    <sub>IE</sub>
    <sub>IE5</sub>
</expansion>
```

This will convert any searches on "IE" to search on "IE" or "IE5" or "Internet Explorer."

The replacement node is used to replace a search argument with another argument. For example, if you want the search argument *sex* interpreted as *gender*, you could use the replacement node to do that:

```
<replacement>
     <pat>sex</pat>
     <sub>gender</sub>
</replacement>
```

The pat element (sex) indicates the pattern you want substituted by the sub element (gender).

A FREETEXT query will automatically use the thesaurus file for the language type. Here is an example of a generational query using the Thesaurus option:

```
SELECT * FROM TableName WHERE CONTAINS(*,'FORMSOF(Thesaurus,"IE")');
```

This returns matches to rows containing IE, IE5, and Internet Explorer.

Variable-word-weight searches

In a search for multiple words, relative weight may be assigned, making one word critical to the search and another word much less important. The weights are set on a scale of 0.0 to 1.0.

The ISABOUT option enables weighting, and any hit on the given word allows the rows to be returned, so it functions as an implied Boolean OR operator.

The following two queries use the weight option with CONTAINSTABLE to highlight the differences among the words "lion," "brave," and "eagle" as the weighting changes. The query will examine only the FableText column to prevent the results from being skewed by the shorter lengths of the text found on the title and moral columns. The first query weights the three words evenly:

```
SELECT Fable.Title, FTS.Rank
  FROM Fable
    INNER JOIN CONTAINSTABLE
     (Fable, FableText,
        'ISABOUT (Lion weight (.5),
         Brave weight (.5),
         Eagle weight (.5))') AS FTS
    ON Fable.FableID = FTS.[KEY]
    ORDER BY Rank DESC;
```

Result:

```
Title                              Rank
---------------------------------  --------
Androcles                          92
The Eagle and the Fox              85
The Hunter and the Woodman         50
The Serpent and the Eagle          50
The Dogs and the Fox               32
The Eagle and the Arrow            21
The Ass in the Lion's Skin         16
```

When the relative importance of the word "eagle" is elevated, it's a different story:

```
SELECT Fable.Title, FTS.Rank
  FROM Fable
    INNER JOIN CONTAINSTABLE
     (Fable, FableText,
```

```
        'ISABOUT (Lion weight (.2),
         Brave weight (.2),
         Eagle weight (.8))') AS FTS
    ON Fable.FableID = FTS.[KEY]
    ORDER BY Rank DESC;
```

Result:

```
Title                                Rank
------------------------------------ -----------
The Eagle and the Fox                102
The Serpent and the Eagle            59
The Eagle and the Arrow              25
Androcles                            25
The Hunter and the Woodman           14
The Dogs and the Fox                 9
The Ass in the Lion's Skin           4
```

When all the columns participate in the full-text search, the small size of the moral and the title make the target words seem relatively more important within the text. The next query uses the same weighting as the previous query but includes all columns (*):

```
SELECT Fable.Title, FTS.Rank
  FROM Fable
    INNER JOIN CONTAINSTABLE
     (Fable, *,
        'ISABOUT (Lion weight (.2),
         Brave weight (.2),
         Eagle weight (.8))') AS FTS
    ON Fable.FableID = FTS.[KEY]
    ORDER BY Rank DESC;
```

Result:

```
Title                                Rank
------------------------------------ -----------
The Wolf and the Kid                 408
The Hunter and the Woodman           408
The Eagle and the Fox                102
The Eagle and the Arrow              80
The Serpent and the Eagle            80
Androcles                            25
The Ass in the Lion's Skin           23
The Dogs and the Fox                 9
```

The ranking is relative, and is based on word frequency, word proximity, and the relative importance of a given word within the text. "The Wolf and the Kid" does not contain an eagle or a lion, but two factors favor bravado. First, "brave" is a rarer word than "lion" or "eagle" in both the column and the table. Second, the word "brave" appears in the moral as one of only 10 words. So even though "brave" was weighted less, it rises to the top of the list. It's all based on word frequencies and statistics (and sometimes, I think, the phase of the moon!).

Fuzzy Searches

While the CONTAINS predicate and CONTAINSTABLE-derived table perform exact word searches, the FREETEXT predicate expands on the CONTAINS functionality to include *fuzzy*, or approximate, full-text searches from free-form text.

Instead of searching for two or three words and adding the options for inflection and weighting, the fuzzy search handles the complexity of building searches that make use of all the full-text search engine options, and tries to solve the problem for you. Internally, the free-form text is broken down into multiple words and phrases, and the full-text search with inflections and weighting is then performed on the result.

Freetext

FREETEXT works within a WHERE clause just like CONTAINS, but without all the options. The following query uses a fuzzy search to find the fable about the big race:

```
SELECT Title
  FROM Fable
  WHERE FREETEXT
   (*,'The tortoise beat the hare in the big race');
```

Result:

```
Title
--------------------------------------------------
The Hare and the Tortoise
```

FreetextTable

Fuzzy searches benefit from the FREETEXT-derived table that returns the ranking in the same way that CONTAINSTABLE does. The two queries shown in this section demonstrate a fuzzy full-text search using the FREETEXT-derived table. Here is the first query:

```
SELECT Fable.Title, FTS.Rank
  FROM Fable
    INNER JOIN FREETEXTTABLE
      (Fable, *, 'The brave hunter kills the lion') AS FTS
      ON Fable.FableID = FTS.[KEY]
  ORDER BY Rank DESC;
```

Result:

```
Title                              Rank
---------------------------------- -----------
The Hunter and the Woodman         257
The Ass in the Lion's Skin         202
The Wolf and the Kid               187
Androcles                          113
```

```
The Dogs and the Fox                100
The Goose With the Golden Eggs      72
The Shepherd's Boy and the Wolf     72
```

Here is the second query:

```
SELECT Fable.Title, FTS.Rank
  FROM Fable
    INNER JOIN FREETEXTTABLE
      (Fable, *, 'The eagle was shot by an arrow') AS FTS
      ON Fable.FableID = FTS.[KEY]
  ORDER BY Rank DESC;
```

Result:

```
Title                               Rank
----------------------------------- -----------
The Eagle and the Arrow             288
The Eagle and the Fox               135
The Serpent and the Eagle           112
The Hunter and the Woodman          102
The Father and His Two Daughters    72
```

Performance

SQL Server 2008's full-text search engine performance is several orders of magnitude faster than previous versions of SQL Server. However, you still might want to tune your system for optimal performance.

- iFTS benefits from a very fast subsystem. Place your catalog on its own controller, preferably its own RAID 10 array. A sweet spot exists for SQL iFTS on eight-way servers. After a full or incremental population, force a master merge, which will consolidate all the shadow indexes into a single master index, by issuing the following command:

  ```
  ALTER FULLTEXT CATALOG catalog_name REORGANIZE;
  ```

- You can also increase the maximum number of ranges that the gathering process can use. To do so, issue the following command:

  ```
  EXEC sp_configure 'max full-text crawl range', 32;
  ```

Summary

SQL Server indexes are not designed for searching for words in the middle of a column. If the database project requires flexible word searches, then Integrated Full-Test Search (iFTS) is the perfect solution, even though it requires additional development and administrative work.

- iFTS requires configuring a catalog for each table to be searched.
- iFTS catalogs are not populated synchronously within the SQL Server transaction. They are populated asynchronously following the transaction. The recommended method is using Change Tracking, which can automatically push changes as they occur.
- `CONTAINS` is used within the `WHERE` clause and performs simple word searches, but it can also perform inflectional, proximity, and thesaurus searches.
- `CONTAINSTABLE` functions like `CONTAINS` but it returns a data set that can be referenced in a `FROM` clause.
- `FREETEXT` and `FREETEXTTABLE` essentially turn on every advanced feature of iFTS and perform a fuzzy word search.

As you read through this "Beyond Relational" part of the book, I hope you're getting a sense of the breadth of data SQL Server can manage. The next chapter concludes this part with Filestream, a new way to store large BLOBs with SQL Server.

Part IV

Developing with SQL Server

Part II of this book was all about writing set-based queries. Part III extended the `select` command to data types beyond relational. This part continues to expand on `select` to provide programmable flow of control to develop server-side solutions; and SQL Server has a large variety of technologies to choose from to develop server-side code — from the mature T-SQL language to .NET assemblies hosted within SQL Server.

This part opens with DDL commands (`create`, `alter`, and `drop`), and progresses through 10 chapters of Transact-SQL that build on one another into a crescendo with the data abstraction layer and dynamic SQL. The final chapter fits CLR programming into the picture.

So, unleash the programmer within and have fun. There's a whole world of developer possibilities with SQL Server 2005.

If SQL Server is the box, then Part IV is all about thinking inside the box, and moving the processing as close to the data as possible.

IN THIS PART

Chapter 20

Creating the Physical Database Schema

IN THIS CHAPTER

Creating the database files

Creating tables

Creating primary and foreign keys

Configuring constraints

Creating the user data columns

Documenting the database schema

Creating indexes

The longer I work with databases, the more I become convinced that the real magic is the physical schema design. No aspect of application development has more potential to derail an application or enable it to soar than the physical schema — not even indexing. (This idea is crucial to my view of Smart Database Design as expressed in Chapter 2, "Data Architecture".)

The primary features of the application are designed at the data schema level. If the data schema supports a feature, then the code will readily bring the feature to life; but if the feature is not designed in the tables, then the client application can jump through as many hoops as you can code and it will never work right.

The logical database schema, discussed in Chapter 3, "Relational Database Design," is a necessary design step to ensure that the business requirements are well understood. However, a logical design has never stored nor served up any data.

In contrast, the physical database schema is an actual data store that must meet the Information Architecture Principle's call to make information "readily available in a usable format for daily operations and analysis by individuals, groups, and processes." It's the physical design that meets the database objectives of usability, scalability, integrity, and extensibility.

This chapter first discusses designing the physical database schema and then focuses on the actual implementation of the physical design:

- Creating the database files
- Creating the tables
- Creating the primary and foreign keys
- Creating the data columns
- Adding data-integrity constraints

- Creating indexes (although indexes can be easily added or modified after the physical schema implementation)

CROSS-REF While this is the chapter entitled "Creating the Physical Database Schema," it's actually just the core chapter of 10 chapters that encompass the design and creation of databases.

This chapter focuses on the syntax of creating the database. However, Chapter 3, "Relational Database Design," discusses how to design a logical schema.

Similarly, while this chapter covers the syntax and mechanics of creating indexes, Chapter 64, "Indexing Strategies," explores how to fine-tune indexes for performance.

Part III, "Beyond Relational," has three chapters related to database design. Chapters 17–19, discuss modeling and working with data that's not traditionally thought of as relational: hierarchical data, spatial data, XML data, full-text searches, and storing BLOBs using Filestream.

Implementation of the database often considers partitioning the data, which is covered in Chapter 68, "Partitioning."

And whereas this chapter focuses on building relational databases, Chapter 70, "BI Design," covers creating data warehouses.

What's New with the Physical Schema?

SQL Server 2008 supports several new data types, and an entirely new way of storing data in the data pages — *sparse columns*. Read on!

Designing the Physical Database Schema

If there's one area where I believe the SQL Server community is lacking in skills and emphasis, it's translating a logical design into a decent physical schema.

When designing the physical design, the design team should begin with a clean logical design and/or well-understood and documented business rules, and then brainstorm until a simple, flexible design emerges that performs excellently, is extensible and flexible, has appropriate data integrity, and is usable by all those who will consume the data. I firmly believe it's not a question of compromising one database attribute for another; all these goals can be met by a well-designed elegant physical schema.

Translating the logical database schema into a physical database schema may involve the following changes:

- Converting complex logical designs into simpler, more agile table structures
- Converting logical many-to-many relationships to two physical one-to-many relationships with an associative, or junction, table
- Converting logical composite primary keys to surrogate (computer-generated) single-column primary keys
- Converting the business rules into constraints or triggers, or, better yet, into data-driven designs

Logical to physical options

Every project team develops the physical database schema drawing from these two disciplines (logical data modeling and physical schema design) in one of the following possible combinations:

- A logical database schema is designed and then implemented without the benefit of physical schema development. This plan is a sure way to develop a slow and unwieldy database schema. The application code will be frustrating to write and the code will not be able to overcome the performance limitations of the design.
- A logical database schema is developed to ensure that the business requirements are understood. Based on the logical design, the database development team develops a physical database schema. This method can result in a fast, usable schema.

  Developing the schema in two stages is a good plan if the development team is large enough and one team is designing and collecting the business requirements and another team is developing the physical database schema. Make sure that having a completed logical database schema does not squelch the team's creativity as the physical database schema is designed.
- The third combination of logical and physical design methodologies combines the two into a single development step as the database development team develops a physical database schema directly from the business requirements. This method can work well providing that the design team fully understands logical database modeling, physical database modeling, and advanced query design.

The key task in designing a physical database schema is brainstorming multiple possible designs, each of which meets the user requirements and ensures data integrity. Each design is evaluated based on its simplicity, performance of possible query paths, flexibility, and maintainability.

Refining the data patterns

The key to simplicity is refining the entity definition with a lot of team brainstorming so that each table does more work — rearranging the data patterns until an elegant and simple pattern emerges. This is where a broad repertoire of database experience aids the design process.

Often the solution is to view the data from multiple angles, finding the commonality between them. Users are too close to the data and they seldom correctly identify the true entities. What a user might see as multiple entities a database design team might model as a single entity with dynamic roles.

Combining this quest for simplicity with some data-driven design methods can yield normalized databases with higher data integrity, more flexibility and agility, and dramatically fewer tables.

Designing for performance

A normalized logical database design without the benefit of physical database schema optimization will perform poorly, because the logical design alone doesn't consider performance. Issues such as lock contention, composite keys, excessive joins for common queries, and table structures that are difficult to update are just some of the problems that a logical design might bring to the database.

Designing for performance is greatly influenced by the simplicity or complexity of the design. Each unnecessary complexity requires additional code, extra joins, and breeds even more complexity.

One particular decision regarding performance concerns the primary keys. Logical database designs tend to create composite meaningful primary keys. The physical schema can benefit from redesigning these as single-column surrogate (computer-generated) keys. The section on creating primary keys later in this chapter discusses this in more detail.

Responsible denormalization

A popular myth is that the primary task of translating a logical design into a physical schema is denormalization. Denormalization, purposefully breaking the normal forms, is the technique of duplicating data within the data to make it easier to retrieve. Interestingly, the Microsoft Word spell checker suggests replacing "denormalization" with "demoralization." Within the context of a transactional, OLTP database, I couldn't agree more.

CROSS-REF **Normalization is described in Chapter 3, "Relational Database Design."**

Some examples of denormalizing a data structure, including the customer name in an `[Order]` table would enable retrieving the customer name when querying an order without joining to the `Customer` table. Or, including the `CustomerID` in a `ShipDetail` table would enable joining directly from the `ShipDetail` table to the `Customer` table while bypassing the `OrderDetail` and `[Order]` tables. Both of these examples violate the normalization because the attributes don't depend on the primary key.

Some developers regularly denormalize portions of the database in an attempt to improve performance. While it might seem that this would improve performance because it reduces the number of joins, I have found that in practice the additional code (procedures, triggers, constraints, etc.) required to keep the data consistent, or to renormalize data for use in set-based queries, actually costs performance. In my consulting practice, I've tested a normalized design vs. a denormalized design several times. In every case the normalized design was about 15% faster than the denormalized design.

Best Practice

There's a common saying in the database field: "Normalize 'til it hurts, then denormalize 'til it works." Poppycock! That's a saying of data modelers who don't know how to design an efficient physical schema. I never denormalize apart from the two cases identified as responsible denormalization.

- Denormalize aggregate data — such as account balances, or inventory on hand quantities within OLTP databases — for performance even though such data could be calculated from the inventory transaction table or the account transaction ledger table. These may be calculated using a trigger or a persisted computed column.
- If the data is not original and is primarily there for OLAP or reporting purposes, data consistency is not the primary concern. For performance, denormalization is a wise move.

The architecture of the databases, and which databases or tables are being used for which purpose, are the driving factors in any decision to denormalize a part of the database.

If the database requires both OLTP and OLAP, the best solution might just be to create a few tables that duplicate data for their own distinct purposes. The OLTP side might need its own tables to maintain the data, but the reporting side might need that same data in a single, wide, fast table from which it can retrieve data without any joins or locking concerns. The trick is to correctly populate the denormalized data in a timely manner.

CROSS-REF **Indexed views are basically denormalized clustered indexes. Chapter 64, "Indexing Strategies," discusses setting up an indexed view. Chapter 70, "BI Design," includes advice on creating a denormalized reporting database and data warehouse.**

Designing for extensibility

Maintenance over the life of the application will cost significantly more than the initial development. Therefore, during the initial development process you should consider as a primary objective making it as easy as possible to maintain the physical design, code, and data. The following techniques may reduce the cost of database maintenance:

- Enforce a strong T-SQL based abstraction layer.
- Always normalize the schema.
- Data-driven designs are more flexible, and therefore more extensible, than rigid designs.
- Use a consistent naming convention.
- Avoid data structures that are overly complex, as well as unwieldy data structures, when simpler data structures will suffice.
- Develop with scripts instead of using Management Studio's UI.
- Enforce the data integrity constraints from the beginning. Polluted data is a bear to clean up after even a short time of loose data-integrity rules.
- Develop the core feature first, and once that's working, then add the bells and whistles.
- Document not only how the procedure works, but also why it works.

Creating the Database

The database is the physical container for all database schemas, data, and server-side programming. SQL Server's database is a single logical unit, even though it may exist in several files.

Database creation is one of those areas in which SQL Server requires little administrative work, but you may decide instead to fine-tune the database files with more sophisticated techniques.

The Create DDL command

Creating a database using the default parameters is very simple. The following data definition language (DDL) command is taken from the `Cape Hatteras Adventures` sample database:

```
CREATE DATABASE CHA2;
```

The `CREATE` command will create a data file with the name provided and a `.mdf` file extension, as well as a transaction log with an `.ldf` extension.

Of course, more parameters and options are available than the previous basic `CREATE` command suggests. By default, the database is created as follows:

- **Default collation:** Server collation
- **Initial size:** A data file of 3 MB, and a transaction log of 1 MB
- **Location:** The data file and transaction log default location is determined during setup and can be changed in the Database Settings page of the Server Properties dialog.

While these defaults might be acceptable for a sample or development database, they are sorely inadequate for a production database. Better alternatives are explained as the `CREATE DATABASE` command is covered.

Using the Object Explorer, creating a new database requires only that the database name be entered in the New Database form, as shown in Figure 20-1. Use the New Database... menu command from the Databases node's context menu to open the New Database form.

FIGURE 20-1

The simplest way to create a new database is by entering the database name in Object Explorer's New Database page.

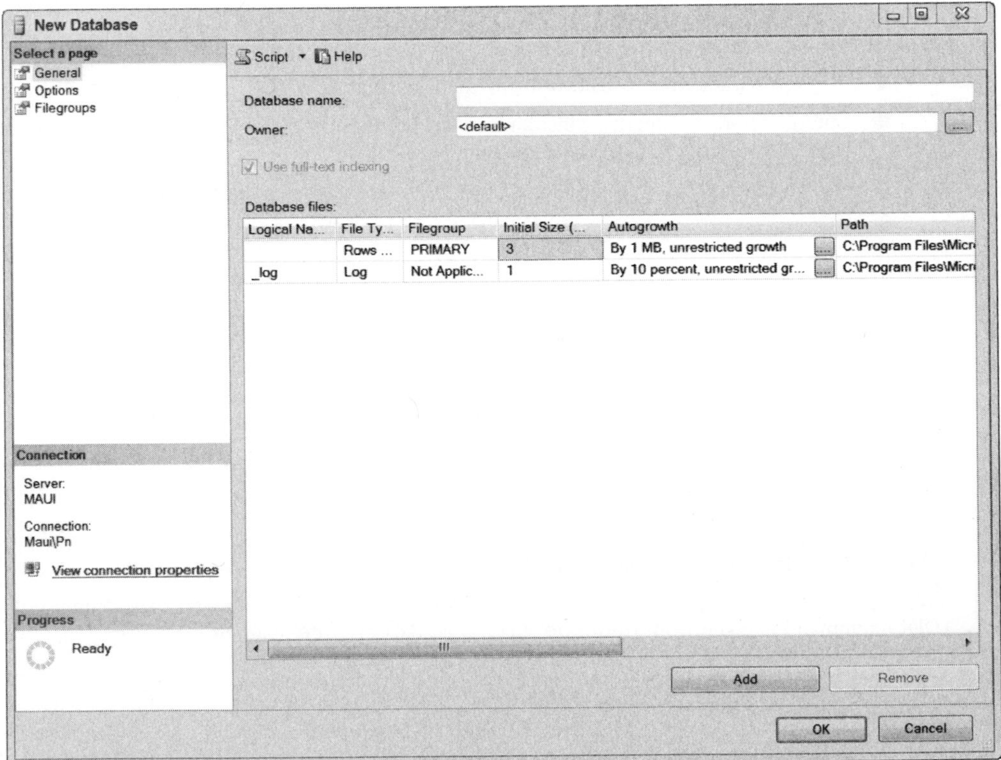

The New Database page includes several individual subpages — the General, Options, and Filegroups pages, as shown in Table 20-1. For existing databases, the Files, Permissions, Extended Properties, Mirroring, and Log Shipping pages are added to the Database Properties page (not shown).

TABLE 20-1

Database Property Pages

Page	New Database	Existing Database
General	Create new database, setting the name, owner, collation, recovery model, full-text indexing, and data file properties	View (read-only) general properties: name, last back-up, size, collation
Files	n/a	View and modify database owner, collation, recovery model, full-text indexing, and database files
Filegroups	View and modify filegroup information	View and modify filegroup information
Options	View and modify database options such as auto shrink, ANSI settings, page verification method, and single-user access	View and modify database options such as auto shrink, ANSI settings, page verification method, and single-user access
Permissions	n/a	View and modify server roles, users, and permissions. See Chapter 50, ''Authorizing Securables,'' for more details.
Extended Properties	n/a	View and modify extended properties
Mirroring	n/a	View and configure database mirroring, covered in Chapter 47, ''Mirroring''
Transaction Log Shipping	n/a	View and configure database mirroring, covered in Chapter 46, ''Log Shipping''

Database-file concepts

A database consists of two files (or two sets of files): the data file and the transaction log. The data file contains all system and user tables, indexes, views, stored procedures, user-defined functions, triggers, and security permissions. The write-ahead transaction log is central to SQL Server's design. All updates to the data file are first written and verified in the transaction log, ensuring that all data updates are written to two places.

CAUTION **Never store the transaction log on the same disk subsystem as the data file. For the sake of the transactional-integrity ACID properties and the recoverability of the database, it's critical that a failing disk subsystem not be able to take out both the data file and the transaction file.**

The transaction log contains not only user writes but also system writes such as index writes, page splits, table reorganizations, and so on. After one intensive update test, I inspected the log using Lumigent's Log Explorer and was surprised to find that about 80 percent of all entries represented system activities, not user updates. Because the transaction file contains not only the current information but also all updates to the data file, it has a tendency to grow and grow.

CROSS-REF **Administering the transaction log involves backing up and truncating it as part of the recovery plan, as discussed in Chapter 41, "Recovery Planning." How SQL Server uses the transaction log within transactions is covered in Chapter 66, "Managing Transactions, Locking, and Blocking."**

Configuring file growth

Prior to SQL Server version 7, the data files required manual size adjustment to handle additional data. Fortunately, for about a decade now, SQL Server can automatically grow thanks to the following options (see Figure 20-2):

- **Enable Autogrowth:** As the database begins to hold more data, the file size must grow. If autogrowth is not enabled, an observant DBA will have to manually adjust the size. If autogrowth is enabled, SQL Server automatically adjusts the size according to one of the following growth parameters:
  - **In percent:** When the data file needs to grow, this option will expand it by the percent specified. Growing by percent is the best option for smaller databases. With very large files, this option may add too much space in one operation and hurt performance while the data file is being resized. For example, adding 10 percent to a 5GB data file will add 500MB; writing 500MB could take a while.
  - **In megabytes:** When the data file needs to grow, this option will add the specified number of megabytes to the file. Growing by a fixed size is a good option for larger data files.

Best Practice

The default setting is to grow the data file by 1 MB. Autogrow events require database locks, which severely impact performance. Imagine a database that grows by a couple of gigabytes. It will have to endure 2,048 tiny autogrow events. On the other hand, a large autogrowth event will consume more time.

The best solution is to turn autogrow off and manually increase the file size during the database maintenance window. However, if that's not expedient, then I recommend setting Autogrow to a reasonable mid-size growth. For my open-source O/R DBMS product, Nordic, I set both the initial size and the autogrow to 100MB.

- **Maximum file size:** Setting a maximum size can prevent the data file or transaction log file from filling the entire disk subsystem, which would cause trouble for the operating system.

The maximum size for a data file is 16 terabytes, and log files are limited to 2 terabytes. This does not limit the size of the database because a database can include multiple files.

FIGURE 20-2

With Management Studio's New Database form, a new database is configured for automatic file growth and a maximum size of 20GB.

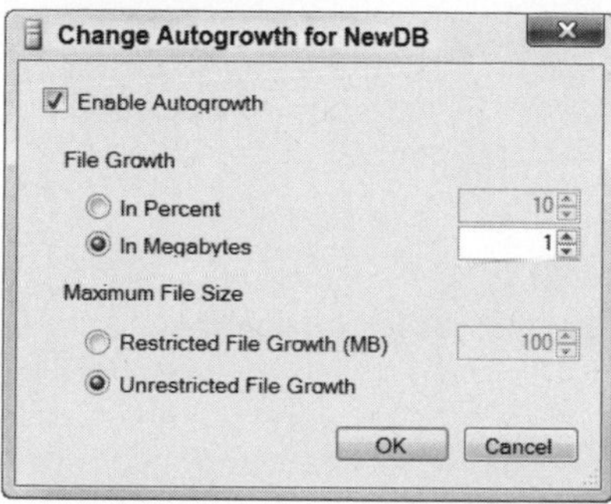

Automatic file growth can be specified in code by adding the file options to the `CREATE DATABASE` DDL command. File size can be specified in kilobytes (KB), megabytes (MB), gigabytes (GB), or terabytes (TB). Megabytes is the default. File growth can be set to a size or a percent. The following code creates the `NewDB` database with an initial data-file size of 10MB, a maximum size of 200GB, and a file growth of 10MB. The transaction log file is initially 5MB, with a maximum size of 10GB and a growth of 100MB:

```
CREATE DATABASE NewDB
ON
PRIMARY
  (NAME = NewDB,
    FILENAME = 'c:\SQLData\NewDB.mdf',
      SIZE = 10MB,
      MAXSIZE = 200Gb,
      FILEGROWTH = 100)
LOG ON
  (NAME = NewDBLog,
    FILENAME = 'd:\SQLLog\NewDBLog.ldf',
      SIZE = 5MB,
      MAXSIZE = 10Gb,
      FILEGROWTH = 100);
```

CROSS-REF **All the code in this chapter and all the sample databases are available for download from the book's website, `www.sqlserverbible.com`. In addition, there are extensive queries using the catalog views that relate to this chapter.**

If autogrowth is not enabled, then the files require manual adjustment if they are to handle additional data. File size can be adjusted in Management Studio by editing it in the database properties form.

TIP **An easy way to determine the files and file sizes for all databases from code is to query the `sys.database_files` catalog view.**

The file sizes and growth options can be adjusted in code with the ALTER DATABASE DDL command and the MODIFY FILE option. The following code sets NewDB's data file to manual growth and sets the size to 25MB:

```
ALTER DATABASE NewDB
  MODIFY FILE
    (Name = NewDB,
    SIZE = 25MB,
    MAXSIZE = 2Gb,
    FILEGROWTH = 0);
```

TIP **To list the databases using code, query the sys.databases catalog view.**

Best Practice

Many DBAs detest the default autogrowth settings because the database is locked during an autogrowth. Growing by 1MB per growth is probably far too small and will cause frequent interruptions. Another common error is to set the autogrowth to a percentage. As the database grows, so will the growth size. For serious production databases the best solution is to monitor the data size and manually grow the database, but leave autogrowth on as a safety factor.

Using multiple files

Both the data file and the transaction log can be stored on multiple files for improved performance and to allow for growth. Any additional, or *secondary*, data files have an .ndf file extension by default. If the database uses multiple data files, then the first, or *primary*, file will contain the system tables.

While it does not enable control over the location of tables or indexes, this technique does reduce the I/O load on each disk subsystem. SQL Server attempts to balance the I/O load by splitting the inserts among the multiple files according to the free space available in each file. As SQL Server balances the load, rows for a single table may be split among multiple locations. If the database is configured for automatic growth, all of the files will fill up before SQL Server increases the size of the files.

Creating a database with multiple files

To create a database with multiple files using Management Studio, add the filename to the file grid in the Files page of the Database Properties dialog (see Figure 20-3).

To create a database with multiple data files from code, add the file locations to the CREATE DATABASE DDL command using the ON option:

```
CREATE DATABASE NewDB
ON
PRIMARY
```

FIGURE 20-3

Creating a database with multiple files using SQL Server Management Studio

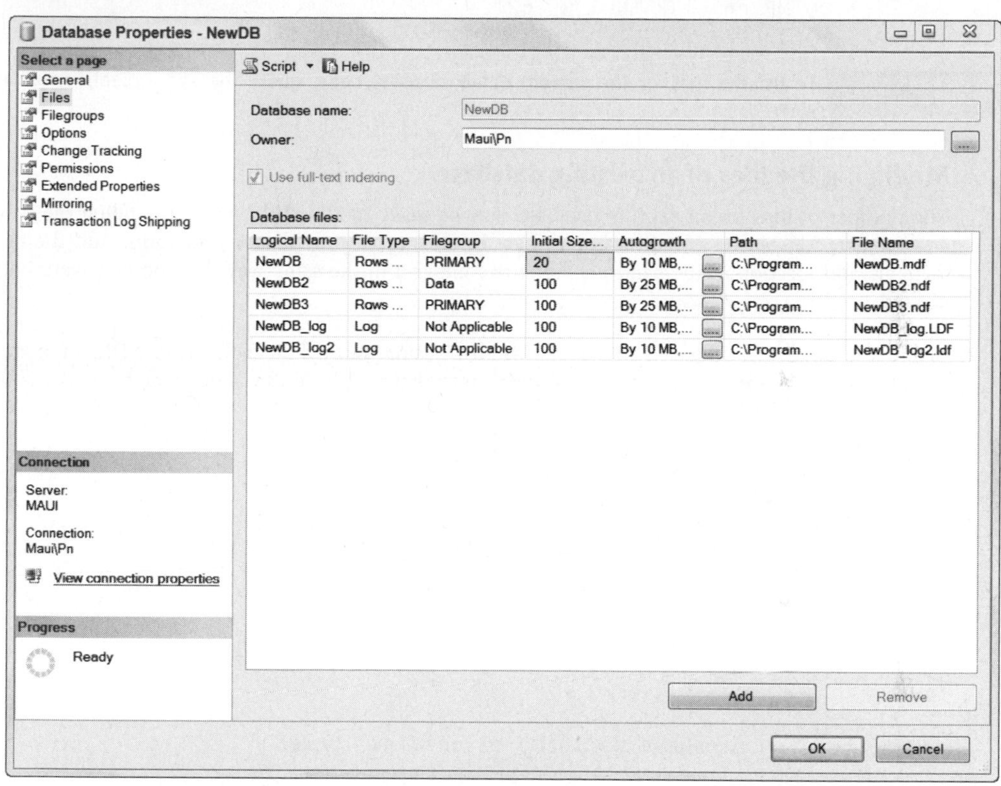


```
    (NAME = NewDB,
      FILENAME = 'e:\SQLData\NewDB.mdf'),
    (NAME = NewDB2,
      FILENAME = 'f:\SQLData\NewDB2.ndf')
  LOG ON
    (NAME = NewDBLog,
      FILENAME = 'g:\SQLLog\NewDBLog.ldf'),
    (NAME = NewDBLog2,
      FILENAME = 'h:\SQLLog\NewDBLog2.ldf');
```

Result:

```
The CREATE DATABASE process is allocating
  0.63 MB on disk 'NewDB'.
The CREATE DATABASE process is allocating
  1.00 MB on disk 'NewDB2'.
```

```
The CREATE DATABASE process is allocating
  1.00 MB on disk 'NewDBLog'.
The CREATE DATABASE process is allocating
  1.00 MB on disk 'NewDBLog2'.
```

To list the files for the current database using code, query the `sys.databases` catalog view.

Modifying the files of an existing database

The number of files for an existing database may be easily modified. If the data is filling the drive, another data file can be added to the database by adding it to the database file grid. Add the new filename and location to the database properties file grid in the same way that the files were initially created.

In code, a file can be added to an existing database using the `ALTER DATABASE` DDL command and the `ADD FILE` option. The file syntax is identical to that used to create a new database. The following code adds a third file to `NewDB`:

```
ALTER DATABASE NewDB
  ADD FILE
    (NAME = NewDB3,
      FILENAME = 'i:\SQLData\NewDB3.ndf',
      SIZE = 10MB,
      MAXSIZE = 2Gb,
      FILEGROWTH = 20);
```

Result:

```
Extending database by 10.00 MB on disk 'NewDB3'.
```

If a file is no longer desired because the disk subsystem is being retired or designated for another use, one of the data or transaction log files can be deleted by shrinking the file using `DBCC ShrinkFile` and then deleting it in Management Studio by selecting the file and pressing Delete.

Using T-SQL code, remove additional files with the `ALTER DATABASE REMOVE FILE` DDL command. The following code removes the data file added earlier:

```
DBCC SHRINKFILE (NewDB3, EMPTYFILE)
ALTER DATABASE NewDB
  REMOVE FILE NewDB3;
```

Result:

```
DbId FileId CurrentSize MinimumSize UsedPages EstimatedPages
---- ------ ----------- ----------- --------- --------------
12   5      1280        1280        0         0
```

The file `NewDB3` has been removed.

Planning multiple filegroups

A *filegroup* is an advanced means of organizing the database objects. By default, the database has a single filegroup — the *primary* filegroup. By configuring a database with multiple filegroups, new objects (tables, indexes, and so on) can be created on a specified filegroup. This technique can support two main strategies:

- Using multiple filegroups can increase performance by separating heavily used tables or indexes onto different disk subsystems.
- Using multiple filegroups can organize the backup and recovery plan by containing static data in one filegroup and more active data in another filegroup.

Best Practice

Create a single secondary filegroup, I call mine "Data," and set it as the default filegroup. This leaves the primary filegroup dedicated for system objects.

Creating a database with filegroups

To add filegroups to a database using Management Studio, open the Database Properties page from Object Explorer. On the Filegroups page, add the new logical filegroup. Then, on the Files page, you can add the new file and select the filegroup for the new file in the combo box.

Using T-SQL, you can specify filegroups for new databases using the Filegroups option. The following code creates the NewDB database with two data filegroups:

```
CREATE DATABASE NewDB
ON
PRIMARY
  (NAME = NewDB,
    FILENAME = 'd:\SQLData\NewDB.mdf',
      SIZE = 50MB,
      MAXSIZE = 5Gb,
      FILEGROWTH = 25MB),
FILEGROUP Data DEFAULT
  (NAME - NewDBData,
    FILENAME = 'e:\SQLData\NewDBData.ndf',
      SIZE = 100MB,
      MAXSIZE = 50Gb,
      FILEGROWTH = 100MB)
LOG ON
  (NAME = NewDBLog,
    FILENAME = 'f:\SQLLog\NewDBLog.ndf',
      SIZE = 100MB,
      MAXSIZE = 25Gb,
      FILEGROWTH = 25MB);
```

Modifying filegroups

Filegroups are easily modified in a manner similar to how files are modified. Using Management Studio, new filegroups may be added, files may be added or removed from a filegroup, and a filegroup may be removed if it is empty. Emptying a filegroup is more difficult than shrinking a file. If there's data in the filegroup, shrinking a file will only move the data to another file in the filegroup. The tables and indexes must be dropped from the filegroup before the filegroup can be deleted.

With Query Editor and T-SQL code, you can add or drop filegroups using the `ALTER DATABASE ADD FILEGROUP` or `ALTER DATABASE REMOVE FILEGROUP` commands, respectively, much as you would use the `ADD` or `REMOVE FILE` command.

Dropping a database

A database may be removed from the server by selecting the database in Object Explorer and selecting Delete from the context menu.

In code, you can remove a database with the DDL `DROP DATABASE` command:

```
DROP DATABASE NewDB;
```

There is no undo.

Creating Tables

Like all relational databases, SQL Server is table-oriented. Once the database is created, the next step is to create the tables. A SQL Server database may include up to 2,147,483,647 objects, including tables, so there's effectively no limit to the number of tables you can create.

Designing tables using Management Studio

If you prefer working in a graphical environment, Management Studio provides two primary work surfaces for creating tables, both of which you can use to create new tables or modify existing ones:

- The Table Designer tool (see Figure 20-4) lists the table columns vertically and places the column properties below the column grid.
- The Database Designer tool (see Figure 20-5) is more flexible than the Table Designer form in that it can display foreign-key constraints as connections to other tables.

CROSS-REF **Chapter 6, "Using Management Studio," explains how to launch and navigate these tools.**

Each of these tools presents a graphical design of the table. Once the design is complete, Management Studio generates a script that applies the changes to the database. When modifying an existing table, often the script must save the data in a temporary table, drop several items, create the new tables, and reinsert the data.

FIGURE 20-4

Developing the Contact table in the OBXKites sample database using Management Studio's Table Designer

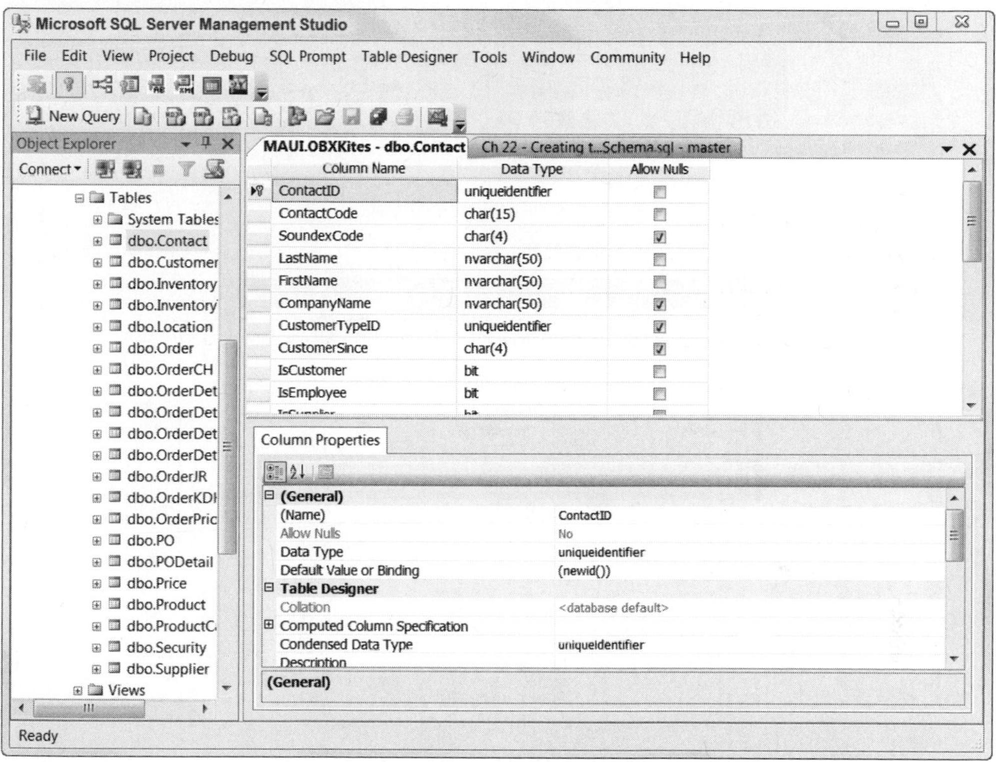

Table Designer displays only the column name and data type (with length), and allows nulls in the column grid. While these are the main properties of a column, I personally find it annoying to have to select each column in order to inspect or change the rest of the properties.

Each data type is explained in detail later in this chapter. For some data types, the `length` property sets the data length, while other data types have fixed lengths. Nulls are discussed in the section "Creating User-Data Columns," later in this chapter.

Once an edit is made to the table design, the Save Change Script toolbar button is enabled. This button displays the actual code that the Table Designer will run if the changes are saved. In addition, the Save Change Script button can save the script to a `.sql` file so the change can be repeated on another server.

CROSS-REF **For more details about using the Table Designer and Database Designer, see Chapter 6, "Using Management Studio."**

FIGURE 20-5

Developing the Customer table in the CHA2 sample database using Management Studio's Database Designer

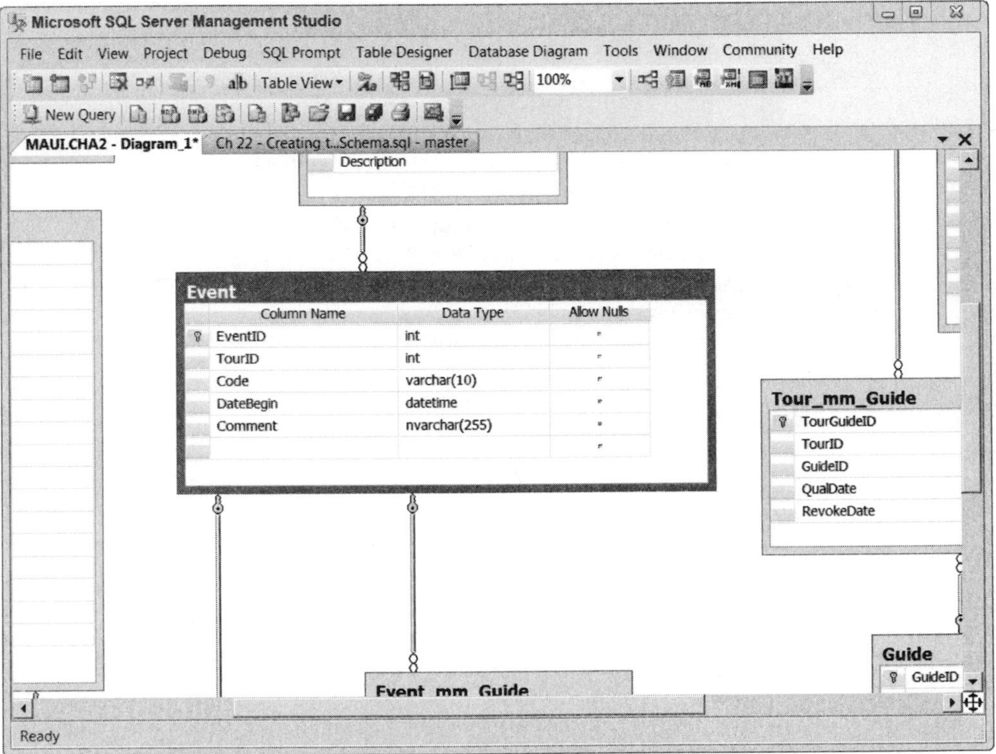

Working with SQL scripts

If you are developing a database for mass deployment or repeatable installations, the benefits of developing the database schema in scripts become obvious:

- All the code is in one location. Working with SQL scripts is similar to developing an application with VB.NET or C#.
- The script may be stored in Solutions as a Project using the Solution Explorer. In addition, scripts can be stored in Microsoft SourceSafe or another change-management system.
- If a database master script contains all the code necessary to generate the database, then the most current version of the database may be installed without running change scripts or restoring a backup.
- An installation that is a fresh new database, as opposed to a backup or detached database, is beneficial for testing because it won't have any residual data.

Working with scripts does have its drawbacks, however:

- The T-SQL commands may be unfamiliar and the size of the script may become overwhelming.
- If the foreign-key constraints are embedded within the table, the table-creation order is very picky. If the constraints are applied after the tables are created, the table-creation order is no longer a problem; however, the foreign keys are distanced from the tables in the script.
- Changes to the database schema must be made using `ALTER` scripts, which are either integrated into the master script or carefully executed in the correct order.
- Management Studio database diagrams are not part of the script.

The T-SQL commands for working with objects, including tables, are `CREATE`, `ALTER`, and `DROP`. The following `CREATE TABLE` DDL command from the Outer Banks Kite Store sample database creates the `ProductCategory` table. The table name, including the name of the owner (`dbo`), is provided, followed by the table's columns. The final code directs SQL Server to create the table `ON` the `Data` filegroup:

```
CREATE TABLE dbo.ProductCategory (
  ProductCategoryID UNIQUEIDENTIFIER NOT NULL
    ROWGUIDCOL DEFAULT (NEWID()) PRIMARY KEY NONCLUSTERED,
  ProductCategoryName NVARCHAR(50) NOT NULL,
  ProductCategoryDescription NVARCHAR(100) NULL
  )
  ON [Data];
```

TIP **To list the tables for the current database using code, query the `sys.objects` catalog view, filtering for `type_desc = 'USER_TABLE'`.**

Best Practice

I consider the schema to be code, and as such it should be handled as code and checked into a version control system. I *never* develop using the graphic user interfaces in Management Studio. I strictly develop using T-SQL scripts.

CROSS-REF **For extensive examples of building databases and tables with scripts, you can reference this book's sample databases, which are all developed with scripts and are available on `www.sqlserverbible.com`.**

Schemas

A schema is an object that exists purely to own database objects, most likely to segment a large database into manageable modules, or to implement a segmented security strategy.

In previous versions of SQL Server, objects were owned by users. Or rather, objects were owned by schema-objects that were the same as the user-owners, but no one spoke in those terms. In SQL Server 2005, the concepts of users and schema were separated. Users could no longer own objects.

Typically, and by default, objects are owned by the `dbo` schema. The schema name is the third part of the four-part name:

```
Server.database.schema.object;
```

When using custom schemas, other than `dbo`, every query has to specify the schema. That's not a bad thing, because using a two-part name improves performance, but always typing a long schema is no fun.

Best Practice

Creating objects in a schema other than `dbo` can improve security. Getting the correct schema is one more obstacle that helps prevent SQL injection.

To list the schema for the current database using code, query the `sys.schemas` catalog view.

Column names

SQL Server is very liberal with table and column names, allowing up to 128 Unicode characters and spaces, as well as both uppercase and lowercase letters. Of course, taking advantage of that freedom with wild abandon will be regretted later when typing the lengthy column names and having to place brackets around columns with spaces. It's more dangerous to discuss naming conventions with programmers than it is to discuss politics in a mixed crowd. Nevertheless, here's my two cents.

There is a debate over whether table names should be singular or plural. The plural camp believes that a table is a set of rows, just like object-oriented classes, and as such should be named with a plural name. The reasoning often used by this camp is, "A table of customers is a set of customers. Sets include multiple items, so the table should be named the Customers table, unless you only have one customer, in which case you don't need a database."

From my informal polling, however, the singular-name view is held by about three-fourths of SQL Server developers. These developers hold that the customer table is the customer set, rather than the set of customers. A set of rows is not called a *rows set*, but a *row set,* and because tables are generally discussed as singular items, saying "the `Customer` table" sounds cleaner than "the `Customers` table."

Most (but not all) developers would agree that consistency is more important than the naming convention itself.

Personally, I think that developers choose their naming conventions as a way to distance themselves from sloppy designs they've had to work with in the past. Having worked on poorly designed flat-file databases with plural names, I slightly prefer singular names.

Best Practice

Consistency is the database developer's holy grail. The purpose of naming conventions, constraints, referential integrity, relational design, and even column data type is to bring order and consistency to the data we use to model reality. When faced with a database decision, asking "Which choice is the most consistent?" is a good step toward a solution.

Another issue involving differences in naming is the use of underscores to indicate words within the name. For example, some IT shops insist that the order-detail table be named `ORDER_DETAIL`. Personally, I avoid underscores except in many-to-many resolution tables. Studies have shown that the use of mixed case, such as in the name `OrderDetail`, is easier to read than all lowercase or all uppercase words.

However, studies have also shown that using the underscore is the most readable, and some experts hold firmly to that position.

Here are the database-naming conventions I use when developing databases:

- Use singular table names with no numbers, and a module prefix if useful.
- For many-to-many resolution tables, use `table_mm_table`.
- Set all names in mixed case (`MixedCase`) with no underscores or spaces.
- For the primary key, use the table name + `ID`. For example, the primary key for the `Customer` table is `CustomerID`.
- Give foreign keys the same name as their primary key unless the foreign key enforces a reflexive/recursive relationship, such as `MotherID` referring back to `PersonID` in the `Family` sample database, or the secondary table has multiple foreign keys to the same primary key, such as the many-to-many reflexive relationship in the `Material` sample database (`BillofMaterials.MaterialID` to `Material.MaterialID` and `BillofMaterials.SourceMaterialID` to `Material.MaterialID`).
- Avoid inconsistent abbreviations.
- Organize a large complex database with schemas.
- Use consistent table and column names across all databases. For example, always use `LastName` followed by `FirstName`.

Filegroups

Apart from the columns, the only information normally supplied when a table is being created is the name. However, the table can be created on a specific filegroup if the database has multiple filegroups.

The OBX Kites database uses two filegroups for data organization purposes. All data that is modified on a regular basis goes into the `Primary` filegroup. This filegroup is backed up frequently. Data that is rarely modified (such as the order priority lookup codes) goes into the `Static` filegroup:

```
CREATE TABLE OrderPriority (
  OrderPriorityID UNIQUEIDENTIFIER NOT NULL
    ROWGUIDCOL DEFAULT (NEWID()) PRIMARY KEY NONCLUSTERED,
  OrderPriorityName NVARCHAR (15) NOT NULL,
  OrderPriorityCode NVARCHAR (15) NOT NULL,
  Priority INT NOT NULL
  )
  ON [Static];
```

Creating Keys

The primary and foreign keys are the links that bind the tables into a working relational database. I treat these columns as a domain separate from the user's data column. The design of these keys has a critical effect on the performance and usability of the physical database.

The database schema must transform from a theoretical logical design into a practical physical design, and the structure of the primary and foreign keys is often the crux of the redesign. Keys are very difficult to modify once the database is in production. Getting the primary keys right during the development phase is a battle worth fighting.

Primary keys

The relational database depends on the primary key — the cornerstone of the physical database schema. The debate over natural (understood by users) versus surrogate (auto-generated) primary keys is perhaps the biggest debate in the database industry.

A physical-layer primary key has two purposes:

- To uniquely identify the row
- To serve as a useful object for a foreign key

SQL Server implements primary keys and foreign keys as constraints. The purpose of a constraint is to ensure that new data meets certain criteria, or to block the data-modification operation.

A primary-key constraint is effectively a combination of a unique constraint (not a null constraint) and either a clustered or non-clustered unique index.

The surrogate debate: pros and cons

There's considerable debate over natural vs. surrogate keys. Natural keys are based on values found in reality and are preferred by data modelers who identify rows based on what makes them unique in reality. I know SQL Server MVPs who hold strongly to that position. But I know other, just as intelligent, MVPs who argue that the computer-generated surrogate key outperforms the natural key, and who use `int identity` for every primary key.

The fact is that there are pros and cons to each position.

A *natural key* reflects how reality identifies the object. People's names, automobile VIN numbers, passport numbers, and street addresses are all examples of natural keys.

There are pros and cons to natural keys:

- Natural keys are easily identified by humans. On the plus side, humans can easily recognize the data. The disadvantage is that humans want to assign meaning into the primary key, often creating "intelligent keys," assigning meaning to certain characters within the key.
- Humans also tend to modify what they understand. Modifying primary key values is troublesome. If you use a natural primary key, be sure to enable cascading updates on every foreign key that refers to the natural primary key so that primary key modifications will not break referential integrity.
- Natural keys propagate the primary key values in every generation of the foreign keys, creating composite foreign keys, which create wide indexes and hurt performance. In my presentation on "Seven SQL Server Development Practices More Evil Than Cursors," number three is composite primary keys.
- The benefit is that it is possible to join from the bottom secondary table to the topmost primary table without including every intermediate table in a series of joins. The disadvantage is that the foreign key becomes complex and most joins must include several columns.
- Natural keys are commonly not in any organized order. This will hurt performance, as new data inserted in the middle of sorted data creates page splits.

A *surrogate key* is assigned by SQL Server and typically has no meaning to humans. Within SQL Server, surrogate keys are identity columns or globally unique identifiers.

By far, the most popular method for building primary keys involves using an identity column. Like an auto-number column or sequence column in other databases, the identity column generates consecutive integers as new rows are inserted into the database. Optionally, you can specify the initial seed number and interval.

Identity columns offer three advantages:

- Integers are easier to manually recognize and edit than GUIDs.
- Integers are obviously just a logical value used to number items. There's little chance humans will become emotionally attached to any integer values. This makes it easy to keep the primary keys hidden, thus making it easier to refactor if needed.
- Integers are small and fast. The performance difference is less today than it was in SQL Server 7 or 2000. Since SQL Server 2005, it's been possible to generate GUIDs sequentially using the `newsequentialid()` function as the table default. This solves the page split problem, which was the primary source of the belief that GUIDs were slow.

Here are the disadvantages to identity columns:

- Because the scope of their uniqueness is only tablewide, the same integer values are in many tables. I've seen code that joins the wrong tables still return a populated result set because there was matching data in the two tables. GUIDs, on the other hand, are globally unique. There is no chance of joining the wrong tables and still getting a result.

- Designs with identity columns tend to add surrogate primary keys to every table in lieu of composite primary keys created by multiple foreign keys. While this creates small, fast primary keys, it also creates more joins to navigate the schema structure.

Database design layers

Chapter 2, "Data Architecture," introduced the concept of database layers — the business entity (visible) layer, the domain integrity (lookup) layer, and the supporting entities (associative tables) layer. The layered database concept becomes practical when designing primary keys. To best take advantage of the pros and cons of natural and surrogate primary keys, use these rules:

- **Domain Integrity (lookup) layer:** Use natural keys — short abbreviations work well. The advantage is that the abbreviation, when used as a foreign key, can avoid a join. For example, a state table with surrogate keys might refer to Colorado as StateID = 6. If 6 is stored in every state foreign key, it would always require a join. Who's going to remember that 6 is Colorado? But if the primary key for the state lookup table stored "CO" for Colorado, most queries wouldn't need to add the join. The data is in the lookup table for domain integrity (ensuring that only valid data is entered), and perhaps other descriptive data.
- **Business Entity (visible) layer:** For any table that stores operational data, use a surrogate key, probably an identity. If there's a potential natural key (also called a *candidate key*), it should be given a unique constraint/index.
- **Supporting (associative tables) layer:** If the associative table will never serve as the primary table for another table, then it's a good idea to use the multiple foreign keys as a composite primary key. It will perform very well. But if the associative table is ever used as a primary table for another table, then apply a surrogate primary key to avoid a composite foreign key.

Creating primary keys

In code, you set a column as the primary key in one of two ways:

- Declare the primary-key constraint in the `CREATE TABLE` statement. The following code from the `Cape Hatteras Adventures` sample database uses this technique to create the `Guide` table and set `GuideID` as the primary key with a clustered index:

```
CREATE TABLE dbo.Guide (
  GuideID INT IDENTITY NOT NULL PRIMARY KEY,
  LastName  VARCHAR(50) NOT NULL,
  FirstName  VARCHAR(50) NOT NULL,
  Qualifications  VARCHAR(2048) NULL,
  DateOfBirth  DATETIME NULL,
  DateHire  DATETIME NULL
  );
```

A problem with the previous example is that the primary key constraint will be created with a randomized constraint name. If you ever need to alter the key with code, it will be much easier with an explicitly named constraint:

```
CREATE TABLE dbo.Guide (
  GuideID INT IDENTITY NOT NULL
```

```
    CONSTRAINT PK_Guide PRIMARY KEY (GuideID),
  LastName  VARCHAR(50) NOT NULL,
  FirstName  VARCHAR(50) NOT NULL,
  Qualifications  VARCHAR(2048) NULL,
  DateOfBirth  DATETIME NULL,
  DateHire  DATETIME NULL
  );
```

- Declare the primary-key constraint after the table is created using an ALTER TABLE command. Assuming the primary key was not already set for the Guide table, the following DDL command would apply a primary-key constraint to the GuideID column:

```
ALTER TABLE dbo.Guide ADD CONSTRAINT
  PK_Guide PRIMARY KEY(GuideID)
  ON [PRIMARY];
```

CROSS-REF **The method of indexing the primary key (clustered vs. non-clustered) is one of the most important considerations of physical schema design. Chapter 64, "Indexing Strategies," digs into the details of index pages and explains the strategies of primary key indexing.**

TIP **To list the primary keys for the current database using code, query the** sys.objects **and** sys.key_constraints **catalog views.**

Identity column surrogate primary keys

Identity-column values are generated at the database engine level as the row is being inserted. Attempting to insert a value into an identity column or update an identity column will generate an error unless set insert_identity is set to true.

CROSS-REF **Chapter 16, "Modification Obstacles," includes a full discussion about the problems of modifying data in tables with identity columns.**

The following DDL code from the Cape Hatteras Adventures sample database creates a table that uses an identity column for its primary key (the code listing is abbreviated):

```
CREATE TABLE dbo.Event (
  EventID INT IDENTITY NOT NULL
    CONSTRAINT PK_Event PRIMARY KEY (EventID),
  TourID INT NOT NULL FOREIGN KEY REFERENCES dbo.Tour,
  EventCode VARCHAR(10) NOT NULL,
  DateBegin DATETIME NULL,
  Comment NVARCHAR(255)
  )
  ON [Primary];
```

Setting a column, or columns, as the primary key in Management Studio is as simple as selecting the column and clicking the primary-key toolbar button. To build a composite primary key, select all the participating columns and press the primary-key button.

CROSS-REF **To enable you to experience sample databases with both surrogate methods, the** Family, Cape Hatteras Adventures, **and** Material Specification **sample databases use identity columns, and the** Outer Banks Kite Store **sample database uses unique identifiers. All the chapter code and sample databases may be downloaded from** www.sqlserverbible.com.

Using uniqueidentifier surrogate primary keys

The uniqueidentifier data type is SQL Server's counterpart to .NET's globally unique identifier (GUID, pronounced GOO-id or gwid). It's a 16-byte hexadecimal number that is essentially unique among all tables, all databases, all servers, and all planets. While both identity columns and GUIDs are unique, the scope of the uniqueness is greater with GUIDs than identity columns, so while they are grammatically incorrect, GUIDs are more unique than identity columns.

GUIDs offer several advantages:

- A database using GUID primary keys can be replicated without a major overhaul. Replication will add a unique identifier to every table without a uniqueidentifier column. While this makes the column globally unique for replication purposes, the application code will still be identifying rows by the integer primary key only; therefore, merging replicated rows from other servers causes an error because there will be duplicate primary key values.
- GUIDs discourage users from working with or assigning meaning to the primary keys.
- GUIDs are more unique than integers. The scope of an integer's uniqueness is limited to the local table. A GUID is unique in the universe. Therefore, GUIDs eliminate join errors caused by joining the wrong tables but returning data regardless, because rows that should not match share the same integer values in key columns.
- GUIDs are forever. The table based on a typical integer-based identity column will hold only 2,147,483,648 rows. Of course, the data type could be set to bigint or numeric, but that lessens the size benefit of using the identity column.
- Because the GUID can be generated by either the column default, the SELECT statement expression, or code prior to the SELECT statement, it's significantly easier to program with GUIDs than with identity columns. Using GUIDs circumvents the data-modification problems of using identity columns.

The drawbacks of unique identifiers are largely performance based:

- Unique identifiers are large compared to integers, so fewer of them fit on a page. As a result, more page reads are required to read the same number of rows.
- Unique identifiers generated by NewID(), like natural keys, are essentially random, so data inserts will eventually cause page splits, hurting performance. However, natural keys will have a natural distribution (more Smiths and Wilsons, fewer Nielsens and Shaws), so the page split problem is worse with natural keys.

The Product table in the Outer Banks Kite Store sample database uses a uniqueidentifier as its primary key. In the following script, the ProductID column's data type is set to uniqueidentifier. Its nullability is set to false. The column's rowguidcol property is set to true, enabling replication to detect and use this column. The default is a newly generated uniqueidentifier. It's the primary key, and it's indexed with a non-clustered unique index:

```
CREATE TABLE dbo.Product (
  ProductID UNIQUEIDENTIFIER NOT NULL
    ROWGUIDCOL DEFAULT (NEWSEQUNTIALID())
    PRIMARY KEY CLUSTERED,
```

```
ProductCategoryID UNIQUEIDENTIFIER NOT NULL
  FOREIGN KEY REFERENCES dbo.ProductCategory,
ProductCode CHAR(15) NOT NULL,
ProductName NVARCHAR(50) NOT NULL,
ProductDescription NVARCHAR(100) NULL,
ActiveDate DATETIME NOT NULL DEFAULT GETDATE(),
DiscountinueDate DATETIME NULL
)
ON [Static];
```

There are two primary methods of generating `Uniqueidentifiers` (both actually generated by Windows), and multiple locations where one can be generated:

- The `NewID()` function generates a `Uniqueidentifier` using several factors, including the computer NIC code, the MAC address, the CPU internal ID, and the current tick of the CPU clock. The last six bytes are from the node number of the NIC card.

  The versatile `NewID()` function may be used as a column default, passed to an insert statement, or executed as a function within any expression.

- `NewsequentialID()` is similar to `NewID()`, but it guarantees that every new `uniqueidentifier` is greater than any other `uniqueidentifier` for that table.

  The `NewsequntialID()` function can be used only as a column default. This makes sense because the value generated is dependent on the greatest `Uniqueidentifier` in a specific table.

Best Practice

The `NewsequentialID()` function, introduced in SQL Server 2005, solves the page-split clustered index problem.

Creating foreign keys

A secondary table that relates to a primary table uses a foreign key to point to the primary table's primary key. *Referential integrity (RI)* refers to the fact that the references have integrity, meaning that every foreign key points to a valid primary key. Referential integrity is vital to the consistency of the database. The database must begin and end every transaction in a consistent state. This consistency must extend to the foreign-key references.

CROSS-REF **Read more about database consistency and the ACID principles in Chapter 2, "Data Architecture," and Chapter 66, "Managing Transactions, Locking, and Blocking."**

SQL Server tables may have up to 253 foreign key constraints. The foreign key can reference primary keys, unique constraints, or unique indexes of any table except, of course, a temporary table.

It's a common misconception that referential integrity is an aspect of the primary key. It's the foreign key that is constrained to a valid primary-key value, so the constraint is an aspect of the foreign key, not the primary key.

Declarative referential integrity

SQL Server's *declarative referential integrity (DRI)* can enforce referential integrity without writing custom triggers or code. DRI is handled inside the SQL Server engine, which executes significantly faster than custom RI code executing within a trigger.

SQL Server implements DRI with foreign key constraints. Access the Foreign Key Relationships form, shown in Figure 20-6, to establish or modify a foreign key constraint in Management Studio in three ways:

- Using the Database Designer, select the primary-key column and drag it to the foreign-key column. That action will open the Foreign Key Relationships dialog.
- In the Object Explorer, right-click to open the context menu in the *DatabaseName* ➪ Tables ➪ *TableName* ➪ Keys node and select New Foreign Key.
- Using the Table Designer, click on the Relationships toolbar button, or select Table Designer ➪ Relationships. Alternately, from the Database Designer, select the secondary table (the one with the foreign key), and choose the Relationships toolbar button, or Relationship from the table's context menu.

FIGURE 20-6

Use Management Studio's Foreign Key Relationships form to create or modify declarative referential integrity (DRI).

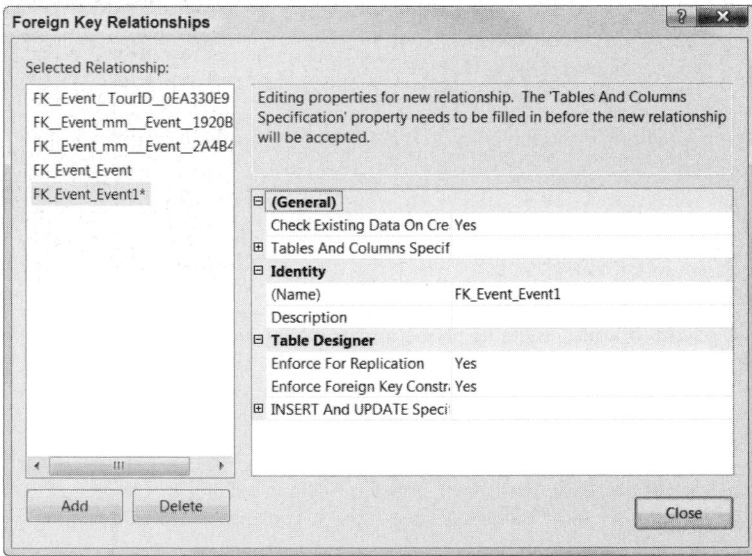

Several options in the Foreign Key Relationships form define the behavior of the foreign key:

- Enforce for Replication
- Enforce Foreign Key Constraint

- Enforce Foreign Key Constraint
- Delete Rule and Update Rule (Cascading delete options are described later in this section)

Within a T-SQL script, you can declare foreign key constraints by either including the foreign key constraint in the table-creation code or applying the constraint after the table is created. After the column definition, the phrase FOREIGN KEY REFERENCES, followed by the primary table, and optionally the column(s), creates the foreign key, as follows:

```
ForeignKeyColumn FOREIGN KEY REFERENCES PrimaryTable(PKID)
```

The following code from the CHA sample database creates the tour_mm_guide many-to-many junction table. As a junction table, tour_mm_guide has two foreign key constraints: one to the Tour table and one to the Guide table. For demonstration purposes, the TourID foreign key specifies the primary-key column, but the GuideID foreign key simply points to the table and uses the primary key by default:

```
CREATE TABLE dbo.Tour_mm_Guide (
  TourGuideID INT
    IDENTITY
    NOT NULL
    PRIMARY KEY NONCLUSTERED,
  TourID INT
    NOT NULL
    FOREIGN KEY REFERENCES dbo.Tour(TourID)
    ON DELETE CASCADE,
  GuideID INT
    NOT NULL
    FOREIGN KEY REFERENCES dbo.Guide
    ON DELETE CASCADE,
  QualDate DATETIME NOT NULL,
  RevokeDate DATETIME NULL
  )
  ON [Primary];
```

Some database developers prefer to include foreign key constraints in the table definition, while others prefer to add them after the table is created. If the table already exists, you can add the foreign key constraint to the table using the ALTER TABLE ADD CONSTRAINT DDL command, as shown here:

```
ALTER TABLE SecondaryTableName
  ADD CONSTRAINT ConstraintName
    FOREIGN KEY (ForeignKeyColumns)
    REFERENCES dbo.PrimaryTable (PrimaryKeyColumnName);
```

The Person table in the Family database must use this method because it uses a reflexive relationship, also called a *unary* or *self-join* relationship. A foreign key can't be created before the primary key exists. Because a reflexive foreign key refers to the same table, that table must be created prior to the foreign key.

This code, copied from the family_create.sql file, creates the Person table and then establishes the MotherID and FatherID foreign keys:

```
CREATE TABLE dbo.Person (
  PersonID  INT NOT NULL PRIMARY KEY NONCLUSTERED,
  LastName  VARCHAR(15) NOT NULL,
  FirstName  VARCHAR(15) NOT NULL,
  SrJr  VARCHAR(3) NULL,
  MaidenName VARCHAR(15) NULL,
  Gender CHAR(1) NOT NULL,
  FatherID INT NULL,
  MotherID INT NULL,
  DateOfBirth  DATETIME  NULL,
  DateOfDeath  DATETIME  NULL
  );
go
ALTER TABLE dbo.Person
  ADD CONSTRAINT FK_Person_Father
    FOREIGN KEY(FatherID) REFERENCES dbo.Person (PersonID);
ALTER TABLE dbo.Person
  ADD CONSTRAINT FK_Person_Mother
    FOREIGN KEY(MotherID) REFERENCES dbo.Person (PersonID);
```

TIP **To list the foreign keys for the current database using code, query the `sys.foreign_key_columns` catalog view.**

Optional foreign keys

An important distinction exists between optional foreign keys and mandatory foreign keys. Some relationships require a foreign key, as with an `OrderDetail` row that requires a valid order row, but other relationships don't require a value — the data is valid with or without a foreign key, as determined in the logical design.

In the physical layer, the difference is the nullability of the foreign-key column. If the foreign key is mandatory, the column should not allow nulls. An optional foreign key allows nulls. A relationship with complex optionality requires either a check constraint or a trigger to fully implement the relationship.

The common description of referential integrity is "no orphan rows" — referring to the days when primary tables were called *parent files* and secondary tables were called *child files*. Optional foreign keys are the exception to this description. You can think of an optional foreign key as "orphans are allowed, but if there's a parent it must be the legal parent."

Best Practice

Although I've created databases with optional foreign keys, there are strong opinions that this is a worst practice. My friend Louis Davison argues that it's better to make the foreign key not null and add a row to the lookup table to represent the Does-Not-Apply value. I see that as a surrogate lookup and would prefer the null.

Cascading deletes and updates

A complication created by referential integrity is that it prevents you from deleting or modifying a primary row being referred to by secondary rows until those secondary rows have been deleted. If the primary row is deleted and the secondary rows' foreign keys are still pointing to the now deleted primary keys, referential integrity is violated.

The solution to this problem is to modify the secondary rows as part of the primary table transaction. DRI can do this automatically for you. Four outcomes are possible for the affected secondary rows selected in the Delete Rule or Update Rule properties of the Foreign Key Relationships form. Update Rule is meaningful for natural primary keys only:

- **No Action:** The secondary rows won't be modified in any way. Their presence will block the primary rows from being deleted or modified.

  Use No Action when the secondary rows provide value to the primary rows. You don't want the primary rows to be deleted or modified if secondary rows exist. For instance, if there are invoices for the account, don't delete the account.
- **Cascade:** The delete or modification action being performed on the primary rows will also be performed on the secondary rows.

  Use Cascade when the secondary data is useless without the primary data. For example, if Order 123 is being deleted, all the order details rows for Order 123 will be deleted as well. If Order 123 is being updated to become Order 456, then the order details rows must also be changed to Order 456 (assuming a natural primary key).
- **Set Null:** This option leaves the secondary rows intact but sets the foreign key column's value to null. This option requires that the foreign key is nullable.

  Use Set Null when you want to permit the primary row to be deleted without affecting the existence of the secondary. For example, if a class is deleted, you don't want a student's rows to be deleted because the student's data is valid independent of the class data.
- **Set Default:** The primary rows may be deleted or modified and the foreign key values in the affected secondary rows are set to their column default values.

  This option is similar to the Set Null option except that you can set a specific value. For schemas that use surrogate nulls (e.g., empty strings), setting the column default to '' and the Delete Rule to Set Default would set the foreign key to an empty string if the primary table rows were deleted.

CROSS-REF **Cascading deletes, and the trouble they can cause for data modifications, are also discussed in the section "Foreign Key Constraints" in Chapter 16, "Modification Obstacles."**

Within T-SQL code, adding the `ON DELETE CASCADE` option to the foreign key constraint enables the cascade operation. The following code, extracted from the `OBXKites` sample database's `OrderDetail` table, uses the cascading delete option on the `OrderID` foreign key constraint:

```
CREATE TABLE dbo.OrderDetail (
  OrderDetailID UNIQUEIDENTIFIER
    NOT NULL
    ROWGUIDCOL
    DEFAULT (NEWID())
    PRIMARY KEY NONCLUSTERED,
```

```
OrderID UNIQUEIDENTIFIER
  NOT NULL
  FOREIGN KEY REFERENCES dbo.[Order]
    ON DELETE CASCADE,
ProductID UNIQUEIDENTIFIER
  NULL
  FOREIGN KEY REFERENCES dbo.Product,
```

CROSS-REF **Chapter 23, "T-SQL Error Handling," shows how to create triggers that handle custom referential integrity and cascading deletes for nonstandard data schemas or cross-database referential integrity.**

Creating User-Data Columns

A user-data column stores user data. These columns typically fall into two categories: columns users use to identify a person, place, thing, event, or action, and columns that further describe the person, place, thing, event, or action.

SQL Server tables may have up to 1,024 columns, but well-designed relational-database tables seldom have more than 25, and most have only a handful.

Data columns are created during table creation by listing the columns as parameters to the `CREATE TABLE` command. The columns are listed within parentheses as column name, data type, and any column attributes such as constraints, nullability, or default value:

```
CREATE TABLE TableName (
ColumnName DATATYPE Attributes,
ColumnName DATATYPE Attributes
);
```

Data columns can be added to existing tables using the `ALTER TABLE ADD` *`columnname`* command:

```
ALTER TABLE TableName
  ADD ColumnName DATATYPE Attributes;
```

An existing column may be modified with the `ALTER TABLE ALTER COLUMN` command:

```
ALTER TABLE TableName
  ALTER COLUMN ColumnName
    NEWDATATYPE Attributes;
```

TIP **To list the columns for the current database using code, query the `sys.objects` and `sys.columns` catalog views.**

Column data types

The column's data type serves two purposes:

- It enforces the first level of data integrity. Character data won't be accepted into a `datetime` or `numeric` column. I have seen databases with every column set to `nvarchar` to ease data entry. What a waste. The data type is a valuable data-validation tool that should not be overlooked.
- It determines the amount of disk storage allocated to the column.

Character data types

SQL Server supports several character data types, listed in Table 20-2.

TABLE 20-2

Character Data Types

Data Type	Description	Size in Bytes
`Char(n)`	Fixed-length character data up to 8,000 characters long using collation character set	Defined length * 1 byte
`Nchar(n)`	Unicode fixed-length character data	Defined length * 2 bytes
`VarChar(n)`	Variable-length character data up to 8,000 characters long using collation character set	1 byte per character
`VarChar(max)`	Variable-length character data up to 2GB in length using collation character set	1 byte per character
`nVarChar(n)`	Unicode variable-length character data up to 8,000 characters long using collation character set	2 bytes per character
`nVarChar(max)`	Unicode variable-length character data up to 2GB in length using collation character set	2 bytes per character
`Text`	Variable-length character data up to 2,147,483,647 characters in length *Warning: Deprecated*	1 byte per character
`nText`	Unicode variable-length character data up to 1,073,741,823 characters in length *Warning: Deprecated*	2 bytes per character
`Sysname`	A Microsoft user-defined data type used for table and column names that is the equivalent of `nvarchar(128)`	2 bytes per character

Unicode data types are very useful for storing multilingual data. The cost, however, is the doubled size. Some developers use `nvarchar` for all their character-based columns, while others avoid it at all costs. I recommend using Unicode data when the database might use foreign languages; otherwise, use `char`, `varchar`, or `text`.

Numeric data types

SQL Server supports several numeric data types, listed in Table 20-3.

Best Practice

When working with monetary values, be very careful with the data type. Using `float` or `real` data types for money will cause rounding errors. The data types `money` and `smallmoney` are accurate to one hundredth of a U.S. penny. For some monetary values, the client may request precision only to the penny, in which case `decimal` is the more appropriate data type.

TABLE 20-3

Numeric Data Types

Data Type	Description	Size in Bytes
`Bit`	1 or 0	1 bit
`Tinyint`	Integers from 0 to 255	1 byte
`Smallint`	Integers from -32,768 to 32,767	2 bytes
`Int`	Integers from -2,147,483,648 to 2,147,483,647	4 bytes
`Bigint`	Integers from -2 ^ 63 to 2 ^ 63-1	8 bytes
`Decimal` or `Numeric`	Fixed-precision numbers up to -10 ^ 38 + 1	Varies according to length
`Money`	Numbers from -2 ^ 63 to 2 ^ 63, accuracy to one ten-thousandths (.0001)	8 bytes
`SmallMoney`	Numbers from -214,748.3648 through +214,748.3647, accuracy to ten thousandths (.0001)	4 bytes
`Float`	Floating-point numbers ranging from -1.79E + 308 through 1.79E + 308, depending on the bit precision	4 or 8 bytes
`Real`	Float with 24-bit precision	4 bytes

Date/Time data types

Traditionally, SQL Server stores both the date and the time in a single column using the `datetime` and `smalldatetime` data types, described in Table 20-4. With SQL Server 2008, Microsoft released several new date/time data types, making life much easier for database developers.

Some programmers (non-DBAs) choose character data types for date columns. This can cause a horrid conversion mess. Use the `IsDate()` function to sort through the bad data.

Other data types

Other data types, listed and described in Table 20-5, fulfill the needs created by unique values, binary large objects, and variant data.

TABLE 20-4

Date/Time Data Types

Data Type	Description	Size in Bytes
`Datetime`	Date and time values from January 1, 1553 (beginning of the Julian calendar), through December 31, 9999, accurate to three milliseconds	8 bytes
`Smalldatetime`	Date and time values from January 1, 1900, through June 6, 2079, accurate to one minute	4 bytes
`DateTime2()`	Date and time values January 1, 0001 through December 31, 9999 (Gregorian calendar), variable accuracy from .01 seconds to 100 nanoseconds	6–8 bytes depending on precision
`Date`	Date and time values January 1, 0001 through December 31, 9999 (Gregorian calendar)	3 bytes
`Time(2)`	Time values, variable accuracy from .01 seconds to 100 nanoseconds	3–5 bytes depending on precision
`Datetimeoffset`	Date and time values January 1, 0001 through December 31, 9999 (Gregorian calendar), variable accuracy from .01 seconds to 100 nanoseconds, includes embedded time zone	8–10 bytes depending on precision

TABLE 20-5

Other Data Types

Data Type	Description	Size in Bytes
`Timestamp` or `Rowversion`	Database-wide unique random value generated with every update based on the transaction log LSN value	8 bytes
`Uniqueidentifier`	System-generated 16-byte value	16 bytes
`Binary(n)`	Fixed-length data up to 8,000 bytes	Defined length
`VarBinary(max)`	Fixed-length data up to 8,000 bytes	Defined length
`VarBinary`	Variable-length binary data up to 8,000 bytes	Bytes used
`Image`	Variable-length binary data up to 2,147,483,647 bytes *Warning: Deprecated*	Bytes used
`Sql_variant`	Can store any data type up to 2,147,483,647 bytes	Depends on data type and length

Calculated columns

A calculated column is powerful in that it presents the results of a predefined expression the way a view (a stored SQL SELECT statement) does, but without the overhead of a view. Calculated columns also improve data integrity by performing the calculation at the table level, rather than trusting that each query developer will get the calculation correct.

By default, a calculated column doesn't actually store any data; instead, the data is calculated when queried. However, since SQL Server 2005, calculated columns may be optionally persisted, in which case they are calculated when entered and then sorted as regular, but read-only, row data. They may even be indexed. Personally, I've replaced several old triggers with persisted, indexed, calculated columns with great success. They're easy, and fast.

The syntax simply defines the formula for the calculation in lieu of designating a data type:

```
ColumnName as Expression
```

The OrderDetail table from the OBXKites sample database includes a calculated column for the extended price, as shown in the following abbreviated code:

```
CREATE TABLE dbo.OrderDetail (
...
  Quantity NUMERIC(7,2) NOT NULL,
  UnitPrice MONEY NOT NULL,
  ExtendedPrice AS Quantity * UnitPrice Persisted,
...
  )
  ON [Primary];
Go
```

Sparse columns

New for SQL Server 2008, sparse columns use a completely different method for storing data within the page. Normal columns have a predetermined designated location for the data. If there's no data, then some space is wasted. Even nullable columns use a bit to indicate the presence or absence of a null for the column.

Sparse columns, however, store nothing on the page if no data is present for the column for that row. To accomplish this, SQL Server essentially writes the list of sparse columns that have data into a list for the row (5 bytes + 2–4 bytes for every sparse column with data). If the columns usually hold data, then sparse columns actually require more space than normal columns. However, if the majority of rows are null (I've heard a figure of 50%, but I'd rather go much higher), then the sparse column will save space.

Because sparse columns are intended for columns that infrequently hold data, they can be used for very wide tables — up to 30,000 columns.

To create a sparse column, add the SPARSE keyword to the column definition. The sparse column must be nullable:

```
CREATE TABLE Foo (
  FooPK INT NOT NULL IDENTITY PRIMARY KEY,
  Name VARCHAR(25) NOT NULL,
  ExtraData VARCHAR(50) SPARSE NULL
);
```

Worst Practice

Any table design that requires sparse columns is a horrible design. A different pattern, probably a super-type subtype pattern, should be used instead. Please don't ever implement a table with sparse columns. Anyone who tells you they need to design a database with sparse columns should get a job flipping burgers. Don't let them design your database.

Column constraints and defaults

The database is only as good as the quality of the data. A constraint is a high-speed data-validation check or business-logic check performed at the database-engine level. Besides the data type itself, SQL Server includes five types of constraints:

- **Primary key constraint:** Ensures a unique non-null key
- **Foreign key constraint:** Ensures that the value points to a valid key
- **Nullability:** Indicates whether the column can accept a null value
- **Check constraint:** Custom Boolean constraint
- **Unique constraint:** Ensures a unique value

SQL Server also includes the following column option:

- **Column Default:** Supplies a value if none is specified in the `INSERT` statement

The column default is referred to as a type of constraint on one page of SQL Server Books Online, but is not listed in the constraints on another page. I call it a column option because it does not constrain user-data entry, nor does it enforce a data-integrity rule. However, it serves the column as a useful option.

Column nullability

A null value is an unknown value; typically, it means that the column has not yet had a user entry.

CROSS-REF **Chapter 9, "Data Types, Expressions, and Scalar Functions," explains how to define, detect, and handle nulls.**

Whether or not a column will even accept a null value is referred to as the nullability of the column and is configured by the `null` or `not null` column attribute.

New columns in SQL Server default to `not null`, meaning that they do not accept nulls. However, this option is normally overridden by the connection property `ansi_null_dflt_on`. The ANSI standard is to default to null, which accepts nulls, in table columns that aren't explicitly created with a not null option.

Best Practice

Because the default column nullability differs between ANSI SQL and SQL Server, it's best to avoid relying on the default behavior and explicitly declare null or not null when creating tables.

The following code demonstrates the ANSI default nullability versus SQL Server's nullability. The first test uses the SQL Server default by setting the database ANSI NULL option to false, and the ANSI_NULL_DFLT_OFF connection setting to ON:

```
USE TempDB;
EXEC sp_dboption 'TempDB', ANSI_NULL_DEFAULT, 'false';
SET ANSI_NULL_DFLT_OFF ON;
```

The NullTest table is created without specifying the nullability:

```
CREATE TABLE NullTest(
  PK INT IDENTITY,
  One VARCHAR(50)
  );
```

The following code attempts to insert a null:

```
INSERT NullTest(One)
  VALUES (NULL);
```

Result:

```
Server: Msg 515, Level 16, State 2, Line 1
Cannot insert the value NULL into column 'One',
table 'TempDB.dbo.NullTest';
column does not allow nulls. INSERT fails.
The statement has been terminated.
```

Because the nullability was set to the SQL Server default when the table was created, the column does not accept null values. The second sample will rebuild the table with the ANSI SQL nullability default:

```
EXEC sp_dboption 'TempDB', ANSI_NULL_DEFAULT, 'true';
SET ANSI_NULL_DFLT_ON ON;

DROP TABLE NullTest;

CREATE TABLE NullTest(
  PK INT IDENTITY,
```

```
One VARCHAR(50)
);
```

The next example attempts to insert a null:

```
INSERT NullTest(One)
  VALUES (NULL);
```

Result:

```
(1 row(s) affected)
```

Managing Optional Data

Databases attempt to model reality. In reality, sometimes there's standard data that for one reason or another doesn't apply to a specific object. Some people don't have a suffix (e.g., Jr. or Sr.). Some addresses don't have a second line. Some orders are custom jobs and don't have part numbers.

Sometimes the missing data is only temporarily missing and it will be filled in later. A new customer supplies her name and e-mail address, but not her street address. A new order doesn't yet have a closed date, but will have one later. Every employee will eventually have a termination date.

The usual method for handling optional or missing data is with a nullable column. Nulls are controversial at best. Some database modelers use them constantly, while other believe that nulls are evil. Even the meaning of null is debated, with some claiming null means unknown, others saying null means the absence of data.

When the bits hit the hard drive, there are three possible solutions for representing optional data in a database. Rather than debate the merits of each option, this is an opportunity to apply the database objectives from Chapter 2, "Data Architecture":

- **Nullable columns:** These use a consistent bit to represent the fact that the column is missing data.
- **Surrogate nulls:** These use a data flag (e.g., "na", "n/a", empty string, -99) to represent the missing data. While popular with data modelers who want to avoid nulls and left outer joins, this solution has several problems.

  Real data is being used to represent missing data, so every query must filter out the missing data correctly. Using surrogate nulls for date/time columns is particularly messy. Surrogate nulls in a numeric aggregate must be filtered out (nulls handle this automatically). Over time, surrogate nulls tend to become less consistent as more users or developers employ differing values for the surrogate null.
- **Absent rows:** This solution removes the optional data column from the main table and places it in another supertype/subtype table. If the data does not apply to a given row, that row is not inserted into the subtype table, hence the name missing row. While this

continued

continued

completely eliminates nulls and surrogate nulls from the database and sounds correct in theory, it presents a host of practical difficulties.

Queries are now very complex to code correctly. Left outer joins are required to retrieve or even test for the presence of data in the optional data column. This can create data integrity issues if developers use the wrong type of join; and it kills performance, as SQL Server has to read from multiple tables and indexes to retrieve data for a single entity.

Inserts and updates have to parse out the columns to different tables.

Creating Indexes

Indexes are the bridge from a query to the data. Without indexes, SQL Server must scan and filter to select specific rows — a dog slow process at best. With the right indexes, SQL Server screams.

SQL Server uses two types of indexes: *clustered indexes*, which reflect the logical sort order of the table, and *non-clustered indexes*, which are additional b-trees typically used to perform rapid searches of non-key columns. The columns by which the index is sorted are referred to as the *key columns*.

Within the Management Studio's Object Explorer, existing indexes for each table are listed under the *DatabaseName* ➪ Tables ➪ *TableName* ➪ Indexes node. Every index property for new or existing indexes may be managed using the Index Properties page, shown in Figure 20-7. The page is opened for existing indexes by right-clicking on the index and choosing Properties. New indexes are created from the context menu of the Indexes node under the selected table.

CAUTION **While this chapter covers the syntax and mechanics of creating indexes, Chapter 64, "Indexing Strategies," explores how to design indexes for performance.**

Using Management Studio, indexes are visible as nodes under the table in Object Explorer. Use the Indexes context menu and select New Index to open the New Index form, which contains four pages:

- *General* index information includes the index name, type, uniqueness, and key columns.
- Index *Options* control the behavior of the index. In addition, an index may be disabled or re-enabled.
- *Included Columns* are non-key columns used for covering indexes.
- The *Storage* page places the index on a selected filegroup.
- The *Spatial* page has configuration options specific to indexes for the spatial data type.
- The *Filter* page is for SQL Server 2008's new `WHERE` clause option for indexes.

When opening the properties of an existing index, the Index Properties form also includes two additional pages:

- The *Fragmentation* page displays detailed information about the health of the index.
- *Extended Properties* are user-defined additional properties.

FIGURE 20-7

Every index option may be set using Management Studio's Index Properties page.

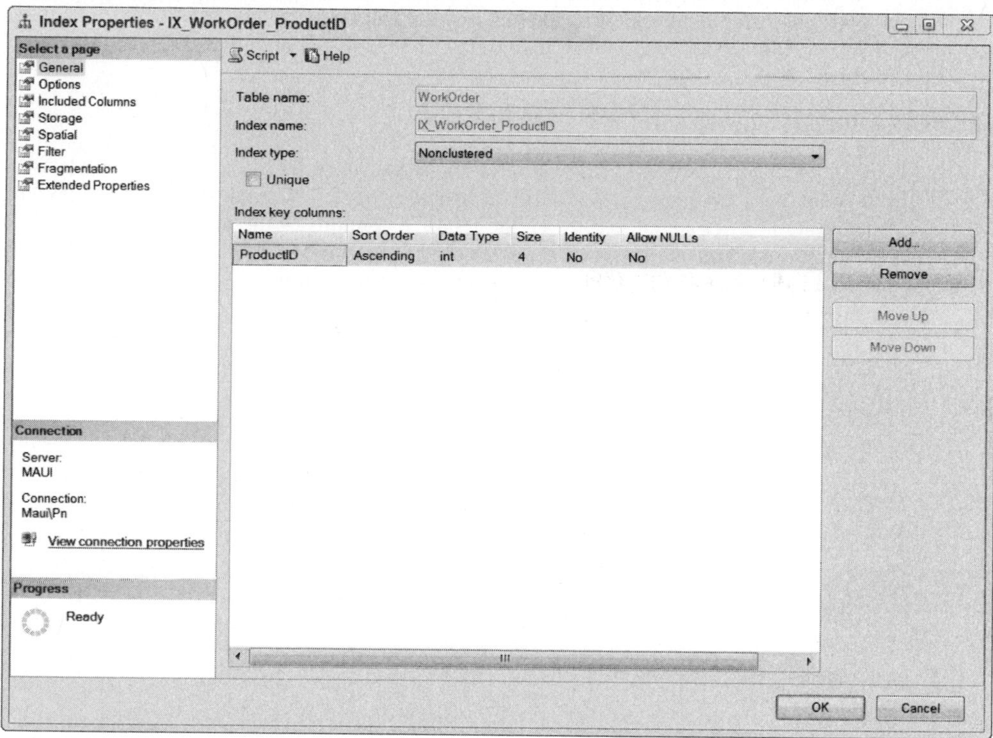

Changes made in the Index Properties page may be executed immediately using the OK button or scheduled or scripted using the icons at the top of the page.

Indexes are created in code with the `CREATE INDEX` command. The following command creates a clustered index named `IxOrderID` on the `OrderID` foreign key of the `OrderDetail` table:

```
CREATE CLUSTERED INDEX IxOrderID
  ON dbo.OrderDetail (OrderID);
```

TIP **To retrieve fascinating index information from T-SQL code, use the following functions and catalog views:** `sys.indexes`, `sys.index_columns`, `sys.stats`, `sys.stats_columns`, `sys.dm_db_index_physical_stats`, `sys.dm_index_operational_stats`, `sys.indexkey_property`, **and** `sys.index_col`.

By default a clustered index is created automatically when the primary key constraint is created.

To remove an index use the DROP INDEX command with both the table and index name:

```
DROP INDEX OrderDetail.IxOrderID;
```

CROSS-REF **Indexes, once created, do not automatically maintain their efficiency. Updates can fragment the index and affect the index page's fill factor. While this chapter mentions index maintenance, Chapter 42, "Maintaining the Database," details the administrative requirements for index performance.**

Composite indexes

A *composite index* is a clustered or non-clustered index that includes multiple key columns. Most non-clustered indexes are composite indexes. If you use SQL Server Management Studio's Index Properties form, composite indexes are created by adding multiple columns to the index in the General page. When creating a composite index with code, it must be declared in a CREATE INDEX DDL statement after the table is created. The following code sample creates a composite clustered index on the Guide table in the CHA2 database:

```
CREATE CLUSTERED INDEX IxGuideName
   ON dbo.Guide (LastName, FirstName);
```

The order of the columns in a composite index is important. In order for a search to take advantage of a composite index it must include the index columns from left to right. If the composite index is lastname, firstname, a search for firstname will not use the index, but a search for lastname, or lastname and firstname, will.

CROSS-REF **SQL Server can index words within columns using Integrated Full-Text Search, covered in Chapter 19, "Using Integrated Full-Text Search."**

Primary keys

A primary key can be initially defined as a clustered or non-clustered index. However, in order for the index type to be changed, the primary key constraint must be dropped and recreated — a painful task if numerous foreign keys are present or the table is replicated. For more information on designing primary keys, please see the section "Primary keys," earlier in this chapter and Chapter 3, "Relational Database Design."

Filegroup location

If the database uses multiple named filegroups, the index may be created on a certain filegroup with the ON *filegroupname* option:

```
CREATE NONCLUSTERED INDEX IndexName
  ON Table (Columns)
ON filegroupname;
```

This option is useful for spreading the disk I/O throughput for very heavily used databases. For example, if a web page is hit by a zillion users per minute, and the main page uses a query that involves two tables and three indexes, and several disk subsystems are available, then placing each table and index on its own disk subsystem will improve performance. Remember that a clustered index must be in the same location as the table because the clustered index pages and the data pages are merged.

CROSS-REF **The physical location of tables and indexes may be further configured using filegroups and partitioning. For more details on table and index partitioning, refer to Chapter 68, "Partitioning."**

Index options

SQL Server 2008 indexes may have several options, including uniqueness, space allocation, and performance options.

Unique indexes

A UNIQUE INDEX option is more than just an index with a unique constraint; index optimizations are available to unique indexes. A primary key or a unique constraint automatically creates a unique index.

In Management Studio, a unique index is created by checking the Unique option in the General page of the Index Properties form.

In code, an index is set as unique by adding the UNIQUE keyword to the index definition, as follows:

```
CREATE UNIQUE INDEX OrderNumber
  ON [Order] (OrderNumber);
```

Include columns

SQL Server 2005 added the capability to include non-key columns in the leaf level of non-clustered indexes. These non-sorted columns are great for defining covering indexes. Multiple columns may be included, and included columns can be added in the Index Properties dialog or with code:

```
CREATE INDEX ixGuideCovering
  ON dbo.Guide (LastName, FirstName)
  INCLUDE (Title)
```

Filtered indexes

New for SQL Server 2008, filtered indexes enable DBAs to create indexes that include less than the entire table's worth of data. Essentially, a WHERE clause is added to the index definition. These are perfect for highly tuned covering indexes. Filtered indexes can be configured in the Filter page of the Management Studio's Index Properties dialog, or using T-SQL. The following DDL statement creates a filtered non-clustered index that includes only the work orders that are active. Older work orders are ignored by the index:

```
CREATE INDEX IxActiveProduction
  ON Production.WorkOrders (WorkOrderID, ProductID)
  WHERE Status = 'Active'
```

Index fill factor and pad index

An index needs a little free space in the tree so that new entries don't require restructuring of the index. When SQL Server needs to insert a new entry into a full page, it splits the page into two pages and writes two half-full pages back to the disk. This causes three performance problems: the page split itself, the new pages are no longer sequential, and less information is on each page so more pages must be read to read the same amount of data.

Because the index is a balanced tree (b-tree), each page must hold at least two rows. The fill factor and the pad index affect both the intermediate pages and the leaf node, as described in Table 20-6.

TABLE 20-6

Fill Factor and Pad Index

Fill Factor	Intermediate Page(s)	Leaf Node
0	One free entry	100% full
1–99	One free entry or ≤ fill factor if pad index	≤ Fill factor
100	One free entry	100% full

The fill factor only applies to the detail, or leaf, node of the index, unless the `PAD INDEX` option is applied to the fill factor. The `PAD INDEX` option directs SQL Server to apply the looseness of the fill factor to the intermediate levels of the b-tree as well.

Best Practice

The best fill factor depends on the purpose of the database and the type of clustered index. If the database is primarily for data retrieval, or the primary key is sequential, a high fill factor will pack as much as possible in an index page. If the clustered index is nonsequential (such as a natural primary key), then the table is susceptible to page splits, so use a lower page fill factor and defragment the pages often.

CROSS-REF **The index's fill factor will slowly become useless as the pages fill and split. The maintenance plan must include periodic re-indexing to reset the fill factor. Chapter 42, "Maintaining the Database," includes information on how to maintain indexes.**

Using Management Studio, the fill factor is set in the Index Properties Options page. In T-SQL code, include the fill factor and index pad options after the `CREATE INDEX` command. The following code example creates the `OrderNumber` index with 15 percent free space in both the leaf nodes and the intermediate pages:

```
CREATE NONCLUSTERED INDEX IxOrderNumber
  ON dbo.[Order] (OrderNumber)
  WITH FILLFACTOR = 85, PAD_INDEX = ON;
```

Limiting index locks and parallelism

The locking behavior of queries using the index may be controlled using the ALLOW_ROW_LOCKS and ALLOW_PAGE_LOCKS options. Normally these locks are allowed.

Index sort order

SQL Server can create the index as a descending index.

Any query using an ORDER BY clause will still be sorted ascending unless the query's ORDER BY specifically states DESC.

The ASC or DESC option follows the column name in the CREATE INDEX DDL command.

The Ignore Dup Key index option

The IGNORE_DUPLICATE_KEY option doesn't affect the index, but rather how the index affects data modification operations later.

Normally, transactions are atomic, meaning that the entire transaction either succeeds or fails as a logical unit. However, the IGNORE_DUPLICATE_KEY option directs INSERT transactions to succeed for all rows accepted by the unique index, and to ignore any rows that violate the unique index.

This option does not break the unique index. Duplicates are still kept out of the table, so the consistency of the database is intact, but the atomicity of the transaction is violated. Although this option might make importing a zillion questionable rows easier, I personally don't like any option that weakens the ACID (atomic, consistent, isolated, durable) properties of the database.

The following command is the same as the previous CREATE UNIQUE INDEX command, but with the IGNORE_DUPLICATE_KEY option:

```
CREATE UNIQUE INDEX OrderNumber
  ON [Order] (OrderNumber)
  WITH IGNORE_DUP_KEY = ON
```

The Drop Existing index option

The DROP EXISTING option directs SQL Server to drop the current index and rebuild the new index from scratch. This may cause a slight performance improvement over rebuilding every index if the index being rebuilt is a clustered index and the table also has nonclustered indexes, because rebuilding a clustered index forces a rebuild of any non-clustered indexes.

The Statistics Norecompute index option

The SQL Server Query Optimizer depends on data-distribution statistics to determine which index is most significant for the search criteria for a given table. Normally, SQL Server updates these statistics automatically. However, some tables may receive large amounts of data just prior to being queried, and the statistics may be out of date. For situations that require manually initiating the statistics update, the STATISTICS NORECOMPUTE = ON index option disables automatic statistics, but for nearly all indexes this option should be ignored.

Sort in tempdb

The `SORT_IN_TEMPDB = ON` option modifies the index-creation method by forcing it to use `tempdb` as opposed to memory. If the index is routinely dropped and recreated, this option may shorten the index-creation time. For most indexes, this option is neither required nor important.

Disabling an index

An index may be temporarily disabled, or taken offline, using the Use Index check box in the Index Properties ➪ Options page. Using T-SQL, to disable an index use the `ALTER INDEX` DDL command with the `DISABLE` option:

```
ALTER INDEX [IxContact] ON [dbo].[Contact] DISABLE
```

During some intensive data import operations, it's faster to drop the index and recreate it than to update the index with every newly inserted row. The benefit of disabling an index is that the metadata for the index is maintained within the database, rather than depending on the code to recreate the correct index.

CAUTION **Disabling a clustered index effectively disables the table.**

To re-enable an index, use the `ALTER INDEX... REBUILD WITH` command:

```
ALTER INDEX [PKContact0BC6C43E]
  ON [dbo].[Contact]
  REBUILD WITH
  ( PAD_INDEX  = OFF,
    STATISTICS_NORECOMPUTE  = OFF,
    ALLOW_ROW_LOCKS  = ON,
    ALLOW_PAGE_LOCKS  = ON,
    SORT_IN_TEMPDB = OFF,
    ONLINE = OFF )
```

Summary

The logical database schema often requires tweaking in order to serve as a physical schema. It's in the nitty-gritty details of the physical-database schema that the logical design takes shape and becomes a working database within the restrictions of the data types, keys, and constraints of the database product. Knowing the table-definition capabilities of SQL Server means that you can implement some project features at the server-constraint level, rather than in T-SQL code in a trigger or stored procedure.

A few key points about creating the physical schema:

- DDL code is like any other source code. Write it in script form and keep it under source code control.
- Be careful with autogrowth.

- Set up a separate filegroup for user tables and set it as the default filegroup, and keep user tables off the primary filegroup.
- Natural keys are good for lookup tables. Use surrogate keys for the other tables.
- Constraints are faster and more reliable than application code. Always enforce the database rules with constraints.
- Indexes are easy to create but complex to design, as covered in Chapter 64, "Indexing Strategies."

Within this part of the book, "Developing with SQL Server," this chapter has provided the code to build the physical schema. From here, the rest of this part continues the development discussion, with several more chapters of T-SQL and a chapter of .NET, and key development ideas.

Chapter 21

Programming with T-SQL

IN THIS CHAPTER

- **The basics of T-SQL and batches**
- **Working with local variables**
- **Controlling the flow of the batch**
- **Exploring SQL Server objects with code**
- **Working with temporary tables and table variables**
- **Using multiple assignment variable select statements**

Standard SQL Data Manipulation Language (DML) commands — `SELECT`, `INSERT`, `UPDATE`, and `DELETE` — only modify or return data. SQL DML lacks both the programming structure to develop procedures and algorithms, and the database-specific commands to control and tune the server. To compensate, each full-featured database product must complement the SQL standard with some proprietary SQL language extension.

Transact-SQL, better known as T-SQL, is Microsoft's implementation of SQL plus its collection of extensions to SQL. The purpose of T-SQL is to provide a set of procedural and administrative tools for the development of a transactional database.

T-SQL is often thought of as synonymous with stored procedures. In reality it's much more than that, which is why this chapter is about T-SQL and the next chapter covers stored procedures. It may be employed in several different ways within a SQL Server client/server application:

- T-SQL is used within expressions as part of DML commands (`INSERT`, `UPDATE`, and `DELETE`) submitted by the client process.
- It is used within blocks of code submitted to SQL Server from a client as a batch or script.
- T-SQL functions are used as expressions within check constraints.
- T-SQL code is used within batches of code that have been packaged within SQL Server as stored procedures, functions, or triggers.

Truth be told, this book has been covering T-SQL programming since Chapter 8, "Introducing Basic Query Flow." The DML commands are the heart of T-SQL. This chapter merely adds the programmatic elements required to develop server-side procedural code. The language features explained in this chapter are the foundation for developing stored procedures, user-defined functions, and triggers.

What's New with T-SQL Programming?

Microsoft has steadily enhanced Transact-SQL. SQL Server 7 saw unique identifiers, SQL Server 2000 added user-defined functions, and SQL Server 2005 added common table expressions. SQL Server 2008 adds a few juicy new features as well: Topping the list are table-valued parameters and the new user-defined table type, which radically improves how client applications can send complex transactions to SQL Server. In addition, variables may be initialized when they're declared, and there's a new shortcut for incrementing variables and columns.

Transact-SQL Fundamentals

T-SQL is designed to add structure to the handling of sets of data. Because of this, it does not provide several language features that application development needs. If you do a lot of application programming development, you'll find that T-SQL is in many ways the exact opposite of how you think when programming in VB, C#, Java, or any other structured development language.

Best Practice

SQL Server 2005 added the capability to create stored procedures, functions, and triggers using .NET and the common language runtime. Nevertheless, T-SQL is the native language of SQL Server, and it remains the best choice for any data-oriented task.

T-SQL batches

A *query* is a single SQL DML statement, and a *batch* is a collection of one or more T-SQL statements. The entire collection is sent to SQL Server from the front-end application as a single unit of code.

SQL Server parses the entire batch as a unit. Any syntax error will cause the entire batch to fail, meaning that none of the batch will be executed. However, the parsing does not check any object names or schemas because a schema may change by the time the statement is executed.

Terminating a batch

A SQL script file or a Query Analyzer window may contain multiple batches. If this is the case, a batch-separator keyword terminates each batch. By default, the batch-separator keyword is `GO` (similar to how the Start button is used to shut down Windows). The batch-separator keyword must be the only keyword in the line. You can add a comment after the `GO`.

The batch separator is actually a function of SQL Server Management Studio and SQLCMD, not SQL Server. It can be modified in the Query Execution page by selecting Tools ➪ Options, but I don't recommend creating a custom batch separator (at least not for your friends).

Because the GO batch terminator tells Management Studio's Query Editor to send the batch to the connected SQL Server, it can be used to submit the batch multiple times. The following script demonstrates this poor man's cursor:

```
PRINT 'I'm a batch.';
go 5 -- will execute 5 times
```

Result:

```
Beginning execution loop
I'm a batch.
I'm a batch.
I'm a batch.
I'm a batch.
I'm a batch.
Batch execution completed 5 times.
```

Terminating a batch kills all local variables, temporary tables, and cursors created by that batch.

DDL commands

Some T-SQL DDL commands, such as CREATE PROCEDURE, are required to be the only command in the batch. Very long scripts that create several objects often include numerous GO batch terminators. Because SQL Server evaluates syntax by the batch, using GO throughout a long script also helps locate syntax errors.

Switching databases

Interactively, the current database is indicated in the Query Editor toolbar and can be changed there. In code, the current database is selected with the USE command. You can insert USE within a batch to specify the database from that point on:

```
USE CHA2;
```

It's a good practice to explicitly specify the correct database with the USE command, rather than assume that the user will select the correct database prior to running the script.

At the end of scripts, I tend to add a USE tempdb database, so Query Editor windows aren't kept parked in the development database.

Executing batches

A batch can be executed in several ways:

- A complete SQL script (including all the batches in the script) may be executed by opening the .sql file with SQL Server Management Studio's SQL Editor and pressing F5, clicking the "! Execute" toolbar button, pressing Ctrl+E, or selecting Query ➪ Execute.
- Selected T-SQL statements may be executed within SQL Server Management Studio's SQL Editor by highlighting those statements and pressing F5, clicking the "! Execute" toolbar button, pressing Ctrl+E, or selecting Query ➪ Execute.

- An application can submit a T-SQL batch using ADO or ODBC for execution.
- A SQL script may be executed by running the SQLCMD command-line utility and passing the SQL script file as a parameter.
- The SQLCMD utility has several parameters and may be configured to meet nearly any command-line need.

T-SQL formatting

Throughout this book, T-SQL code has been formatted for readability; this section specifies the details of formatting T-SQL code.

Statement termination

The ANSI SQL standard is to place a semicolon (;) at the end of each command in order to terminate it. When programming T-SQL, the semicolon is optional. Most other database products (including Access) do require semicolons.

There are a few rules about using the semicolon:

- Don't place one after an `END TRY`.
- Don't place one after an `IF` or `WHILE` condition.
- You must place one before any CTE.
- A statement terminator is required following a `MERGE` command.

Best Practice

As a best practice and for improved readability, I recommend using the semicolon. In future versions of SQL Server this may become a requirement, so making the change now may pay off later.

Line continuation

T-SQL commands, by their nature, tend to be long. I have written production queries with multiple joins and subqueries that were a few pages long. I like that T-SQL ignores spaces and end-of-line returns. This smart feature means that long lines can be continued without a special line-continuation character, which makes T-SQL code significantly more readable.

Comments

T-SQL accepts both simple comments and bracketed comments within the same batch. The simple comment begins with two hyphens and concludes with an end-of-line:

```
-- This is a simple comment
```

Simple comments may be embedded within a single SQL command:

```
SELECT FirstName, LastName      -- selects the columns
  FROM Persons                  -- the source table
  WHERE LastName LIKE 'Hal%';   -- the row restriction
```

Management Studio's Query Editor can apply or remove simple comments to all selected lines. Select either Edit ➪ Advanced ➪ Comment Selection (Ctrl+K, Ctrl+C) or Edit ➪ Advanced ➪ Uncomment Selection (Ctrl+K, Ctrl+U), respectively.

Bracketed comments begin with /* and conclude with */. These comments are useful for commenting out a block of lines such as a code header or large test query:

```
/*
Order table Insert Trigger
Paul Nielsen
ver 1.0 July 21, 2006
Logic: etc.
ver 1.1: July 31, 2006, added xyz
*/
```

A benefit of bracketed comments is that a large multi-line query within the comments may be selected and executed without altering the comments.

A GO batch terminator inside a bracketed comment block will terminate the batch, and the statements after the GO will be executed as a new non-commented batch.

Variables

Every language requires variables to temporarily store values in memory. T-SQL variables are created with the DECLARE command. The DECLARE command is followed by the variable name and data type. The available data types are similar to those used to create tables, with the addition of the table and cursor. The deprecated text, ntext, and image data types are only available for table columns, and not for variables. Multiple comma-separated variables can be declared with a single DECLARE command.

Variable default and scope

The scope, or application and duration, of the variable extends only to the current batch. Newly declared variables default to NULL and must be initialized if you want them to have a value in an expression. Remember that null added with a value yields null.

New for SQL Server 2008 is the ability to initialize a variable to a value while declaring it, which saves an extra line of code:

```
DECLARE @x INT = 0;
```

The following script creates two test variables and demonstrates their initial value and scope. The entire script is a single execution, even though it's technically two batches (separated by a GO), so the results of the three SELECT statements appear at the conclusion of the script:

```
DECLARE @Test INT ,
        @TestTwo NVARCHAR(25);
SELECT @Test, @TestTwo;

SET @Test = 1;
SET @TestTwo = 'a value';
SELECT @Test, @TestTwo ;
GO

SELECT @Test AS BatchTwo, @TestTwo;
```

Result of the entire script:

```
----------- -------------------------
NULL        NULL

(1 row(s) affected)


----------- -------------------------
1           a value

(1 row(s) affected)

Msg 137, Level 15, State 2, Line 2
Must declare the scalar variable "@Test".
```

The first SELECT returns two NULL values. After the variables have been initialized, they properly return the sample values. When the batch concludes (due to the GO terminator), so do the variables. Error message 137 is the result of the final SELECT statement.

Variables are local in scope and do not extend to other batches or called stored procedures.

Using the set and select commands

Both the SET command and the SELECT command can assign the value of an expression to a variable. The main difference between the two is that a SELECT can retrieve data from a data source (e.g., table, subquery, or view) and can include the other SELECT clauses as well (e.g., FROM, WHERE), whereas a SET is limited to retrieving data from expressions. Both SET and SELECT can include functions. Use the simpler SET command when you only need to assign a function result or constant to a variable and don't need the Query Optimizer to consider a data source.

A detailed exception to the preceding paragraph is when a SET command uses a scalar subquery that accesses a data source. This is a best practice if you want to ensure that the variable is set to NULL if no rows qualify, and that you get an error if more than one row qualifies.

Of course, a SELECT statement may retrieve multiple columns. Each column may be assigned to a variable. If the SELECT statement retrieves multiple rows, then the values from the last row are stored in the variables. No error will be reported.

The following SQL batch creates two variables and initializes one of them. The SELECT statement will retrieve 32 rows, ordered by PersonID. The PersonID and the LastName of the *last person* returned by the SELECT will be stored in the variables:

```
USE Family;
DECLARE @TempID INT,
        @TempLastName VARCHAR(25);
SET @TempID = 99;
SELECT
    @TempID = PersonID,
    @TempLastName = LastName
  FROM Person
  ORDER BY PersonID;
SELECT @TempID, @TempLastName;
```

Result:

```
----------- -------------------------
Campbell
```

CAUTION **The preceding code demonstrates a common coding mistake. Never use a SELECT to populate a variable unless you're sure that it will return only a single row.**

If no rows are returned from the SELECT statement, the SELECT does not affect the variables. In the following query, there is no person with a PersonID of 100, so the SELECT statement does not affect either variable:

```
DECLARE @TempID INT,
        @TempLastName VARCHAR(25);
SET @TempID = 99;
SELECT @TempID = PersonID,
    @TempLastName = LastName
  FROM Person
  WHERE PersonID = 100
  ORDER BY PersonID;
SELECT @TempID, @TempLastName;
```

The final SELECT statement reports the value of @TempID and @TempLastName, and indeed they are still 99 and NULL, respectively. The first SELECT did not alter its value:

```
----------- -------------------------
NULL
```

Incrementing variables

T-SQL finally has the increment variable feature, which saves a few keystrokes when coding and certainly looks cleaner and more modern.

The basic idea is that an operation and equals sign will perform that function on the variable. For example, the code

```
SET @x += 5;
```

is the logical equivalent of

```
SET @x = @x + 5
```

The next short script walks through addition, subtraction, and multiplication using the new variable increment feature:

```
DECLARE @x INT = 1

SET @x += 5
SELECT @x

SET @x -=3
SELECT @x

SET @x *= 2
SELECT @x
```

Result (of whole batch):

```
-----------
6

-----------
3

-----------
6
```

Conditional select

Because the `SELECT` statement includes a `WHERE` clause, the following syntax works well, although those not familiar with it may be confused:

```
SELECT @Variable = expression WHERE BooleanExpression;
```

The `WHERE` clause functions as a conditional `IF` statement. If the Boolean expression is true, then the `SELECT` takes place. If not, the `SELECT` is performed but the `@Variable` is not altered in any way because the `SELECT` command has no effect.

Using variables within SQL queries

One of my favorite features of T-SQL is that variables may be used with SQL queries without having to build any complex dynamic SQL strings to concatenate the variables into the code. Dynamic SQL still has its place, but the single value can simply be modified with a variable.

Anywhere an expression can be used within a SQL query, a variable may be used in its place. The following code demonstrates using a variable in a `WHERE` clause:

```
USE OBXKites;

DECLARE @ProductCode CHAR(10);
SET @Code = '1001';

SELECT ProductName
  FROM Product
  WHERE Code = @ProductCode;
```

Result:

```
Name
--------------------------------------------------
Basic Box Kite 21 inch
```

Debugging T-SQL

When a syntax error is found, the Query Editor will display the error and the line number of the error within the batch. Double-clicking on the error message will place the cursor near the offending line.

Often the error won't occur at the exact word that is reported as the error. The error location reported simply reflects how far SQL Server's parser got before it detected the error. Usually the actual error is somewhere just before or after the reported error. Nevertheless, the error messages are generally close.

SQL Server 2008 brings back the T-SQL debugger, which is great for debugging variables, and flow of control, but it can't help when debugging a query.

Most of the debugging I need to do involves checking the contents of a temp table or table variable to see the output of a query. Inserting a SELECT command and running the batch up to that SELECT command works well for my purposes.

My other debugging technique is to double-check the source data. Seriously. More than half the time when I don't get what I expect from a T-SQL query or batch, the problem is not the code, but the data. SQL is basically asking a question of the data and returning the result. If the data isn't what you thought it was, then neither will the answer be what you expected. This is why I'm such a stickler for unit testing using a small set of sample data.

Multiple assignment variables

A *multiple assignment variable*, sometimes called an *aggregate concatenation*, is a fascinating method that appends a variable to itself using a SELECT statement and a subquery.

This section demonstrates a real-world use of multiple assignment variables, but because it's an unusual use of the SELECT statement, here it is in its basic form:

```
SELECT @variable = @variable + d.column
  FROM datasource;
```

Each row from the derived table is appended to the variable, changing the vertical column in the underlying table into a horizontal list.

This type of data retrieval is quite common. Often a vertical list of values is better reported as a single comma-delimited horizontal list than as a subreport or another subheading level several inches long. A short horizontal list is more readable and saves space.

The following example builds a list of departments in the AdventureWorks2008 sample database from the HumanResources.Department table:

```
USE AdventureWorks2008;

Declare @MAV VARCHAR(max)

SELECT @MAV = Coalesce(@MAV + ', ' + Name, Name)
  FROM (select name from HumanResources.Department) D
  order by name

Select @MAV
```

Result:

```
------------------
Changed Name, Document Control, Engineering, Executive, Facilities and
 Maintenance, Finance, Human Resources, Information Services, Marketing,
 Production, Production Control, Purchasing, Quality Assurance, Research
 and Development, Sales, Shipping and Receiving
```

The problem with multiple assignment variables is that Microsoft is vague about their behavior. The order of the denormalized data isn't guaranteed, but queries do seem to respond to the ORDER BY clause. It's not documented in BOL but it has been documented in MSKB article Q287515. It performs very well, but I'm cautious about using it when the result is order dependent.

NOTE **The multiple assignment variable may be used with an UPDATE command to merge multiple rows during the update. For more details, turn back to Chapter 12, "Aggregating Data."**

An alternate method of denormalizing a list is the XML PATH method:

```
Select [text()] =  Name + ','
  FROM (select distinct name from HumanResources.Department) D
  order by Name
  FOR XML PATH('')
```

For more details on XML, see Chapter 18, "Manipulating XML Data."

Procedural Flow

At first glance, it would appear that T-SQL is weak in procedural-flow options. While it's less rich than some other languages, it suffices. The data-handling Boolean extensions — such as EXISTS, IN, and CASE — offset the limitations of IF and WHILE.

If

This is your grandfather's IF. The T-SQL IF command determines the execution of *only* the next single statement — one IF, one command. In addition, there's no THEN and no END IF command to terminate the IF block:

```
IF Condition
  Statement;
```

In the following script, the IF condition should return a false, preventing the next command from executing:

```
IF 1 = 0
  PRINT 'Line One';
PRINT 'Line Two';
```

Result:

```
Line Two
```

NOTE **The IF statement is not followed by a semicolon; in fact, a semicolon will cause an error. That's because the IF statement is actually a prefix for the following statement; the two are compiled as a single statement.**

Begin/end

An IF command that can control only a single command is less than useful. However, a BEGIN/END block can make multiple commands appear to the IF command as the next single command:

```
IF Condition
  Begin;
    Multiple lines;
  End;
```

I confess: Early one dreary morning a couple of years ago, I spent an hour trying to debug a stored procedure that always raised the same error no matter what I tried, only to realize that I had omitted the BEGIN and END, causing the RAISERROR to execute regardless of the actual error condition. It's an easy mistake to make.

If exists()

While the IF command may seem limited, the condition clause can include several powerful SQL features similar to a WHERE clause, such as IF EXISTS() and IF...IN().

The IF EXISTS() structure uses the presence of any rows returned from a SQL SELECT statement as a condition. Because it looks for any row, the SELECT statement should select all columns (*). This method is faster than checking an @@rowcount >0 condition, because the total number of rows isn't required. As soon as a single row satisfies the IF EXISTS(), the query can move on.

The following example script uses the IF EXISTS() technique to process orders only if any open orders exist:

```
USE OBXKITES;
IF EXISTS(SELECT * FROM [ORDER] WHERE Closed = 0)
  BEGIN;
    PRINT 'Process Orders';
  END;
```

There is effectively no difference between SELECT * or selecting a column. However, selecting all columns enables SQL Server to select the best column from an index and might, in some situations, be slightly faster.

If/else

The optional ELSE command defines code that is executed only when the IF condition is false. Like IF, ELSE controls only the next single command or BEGIN/END block:

```
IF Condition
  Single line or begin/end block of code;
ELSE
  Single line or begin/end block of code;
```

While

The WHILE command is used to loop through code while a condition is still true. Just like the IF command, the WHILE command determines the execution of only the following single T-SQL command. To control a full block of commands, BEGIN/END is used.

Some looping methods differ in the timing of the conditional test. The T-SQL WHILE works in the following order:

1. The WHILE command tests the condition. If the condition is true, WHILE executes the following command or block of code; if not, it skips the following command or block of code and moves on.
2. Once the following command or block of code is complete, flow of control is returned to the WHILE command.

The following short script demonstrates using the WHILE command to perform a loop:

```
DECLARE @Temp INT;
SET @Temp = 0;

WHILE @Temp < 3
  BEGIN;
    PRINT 'tested condition' + STR(@Temp);
    SET @Temp = @Temp + 1;
  END;
```

Result:

```
tested condition        0
tested condition        1
tested condition        2
```

The CONTINUE and BREAK commands enhance the WHILE command for more complex loops. The CONTINUE command immediately jumps back to the WHILE command. The condition is tested as normal.

The BREAK command immediately exits the loop and continues with the script as if the WHILE condition were false. The following pseudocode (not intended to actually run) demonstrates the BREAK command:

```
CREATE PROCEDURE MyLife()
AS
WHILE Not @@Eyes2blurry = 1
  BEGIN;
    EXEC Eat;
    INSERT INTO Book(Words)
      FROM Brain(Words)
      WHERE Brain.Thoughts
        IN('Make sense', 'Good Code', 'Best Practice');
    IF @SciFi_Eureka = 'On'
      BREAK;
   END;
```

Goto

Before you associate the T-SQL GOTO command with bad memories of 1970s-style spaghetti-BASIC, this GOTO command is limited to jumping to a label within the same batch or procedure, and is rarely used for anything other than jumping to an error handler at the close of the batch or procedure.

The label is created by placing a colon after the label name:

```
LabelName:
```

The following code sample uses the GOTO command to branch to the ErrorHandler: label, bypassing the 'more code':

```
GOTO ErrorHandler;
Print 'more code';
ErrorHandler:
Print 'Logging the error';
```

Result:

```
Logging the error
```

Examining SQL Server with Code

One of the benefits of using SQL Server is the cool interface it offers to develop and administer the database. Management Studio is great for graphically exploring a database; T-SQL code, while more complex, exposes even more detail within a programmer's environment.

Dynamic Management Views

Introduced in SQL Server 2005, dynamic management views (DMVs) offer a powerful view into the structure of SQL Server and the databases, as well as the current SQL Server status (memory, IO, etc.).

As an example of using DMVs, the next query looks at three DMVs concerning objects and primary keys:

```
SELECT s.NAME + '.' + o2.NAME AS 'Table', pk.NAME AS 'Primary Key'
  FROM sys.key_constraints AS pk
    JOIN sys.objects AS o
      ON pk.OBJECT_ID = o.OBJECT_ID
    JOIN sys.objects AS o2
      ON o.parent_object_id = o2.OBJECT_ID
    JOIN sys.schemas AS s
      ON o2.schema_id = s.schema_id;
```

Result:

```
Table                      Primary Key
-------------------        -------------------------------------
dbo.ErrorLog               PK_ErrorLog_ErrorLogID
Person.Address             PK_Address_AddressID
Person.AddressType         PK_AddressType_AddressTypeID
dbo.AWBuildVersion         PK_AWBuildVersion_SystemInformationID
Production.BillOfMaterials PK_BillOfMaterials_BillOfMaterialsID
Production.Document        UQ__Document__F73921F730F848ED
```

CROSS-REF **A complete listing of all the DMVs and sample queries can be found on** `www.SQLServerBible.com`.

The Microsoft SQL Server 2008 System Views Map (a 36″ x 36″ `.pdf` **file) can be downloaded from** `http://tinyurl.com/dbbw78`**. If it changes, I'll keep a link on my website,** `www.SQLServerBible.com`**. I keep a copy of this document on my desktop.**

sp_help

`Sp_help`, and its variations, return information regarding the server, the database, objects, connections, and more. The basic `sp_help` lists the available objects in the current database; the other variations provide detailed information about the various objects or settings.

Adding an object name as a parameter to `sp_help` returns additional appropriate information about the object:

```
USE OBXKites;
EXEC sp_help Price;
```

The result here is seven data sets of information about the `Price` table:

- Name, creation date, and owner
- Columns
- Identity columns
- Row GUID columns
- FileGroup location
- Indexes
- Constraints

System functions

A system function, sometimes called a global variable, returns information about the current system or connection status.

System functions can't be created. There's a fixed set of system functions, all beginning with two @ signs (the more significant ones are listed in Table 21-1). The most commonly used global variables are `@@NestLevel`, `@@Rowcount`, `@@ServerName`, and `@@Version`. The system functions are slowly being replaced by DMV information.

TABLE 21-1

System Functions

System Function	Returns	Scope
`@@DateFirst`	The day of the week currently set as the first day of the week; 1 represents Monday, 2 represents Tuesday, and so on. For example, if Sunday is the first day of the week, `@@DateFirst` returns a 7.	Connection
`@@Error`	The error value for the last T-SQL statement executed	Connection
`@@Fetch_Status`	The row status from the last `cursor fetch` command	Connection
`@@LangID`	The language ID used by the current connection	Connection
`@@Language`	The language, by name, used by the current connection	Connection
`@@Lock_TimeOut`	The lock timeout setting for the current connection	Connection
`@@Nestlevel`	Current number of nested stored procedures	Connection

TABLE 21-1 *(continued)*

System Function	Returns	Scope
@@ProcID	The stored procedure identifier for the current stored procedure. This can be used with sys.objects to determine the name of the current stored procedure, as follows: `SELECT name FROM sys.objects WHERE object_id = @@ProcID;`	Connection
@@RemServer	Name of the login server when running remote stored procedures	Connection
@@RowCount	Number of rows returned by the last T-SQL statement	Connection
@@ServerName	Name of the current server	Server
@@ServiceName	SQL Server's Windows service name	Server
@@SPID	The current connection's server-process identifier — the ID for the connection	Connection
@@TranCount	Number of active transactions for the current connection	Connection
@@Version	SQL Server edition, version, and service pack	Server

Temporary Tables and Table Variables

Temporary tables and table variables play a different role from standard user tables. By their temporary nature, these objects are useful as a vehicle for passing data between objects or as a short-term scratch-pad table intended for very temporary work.

Local temporary tables

A temporary table is created the same way as a standard user-defined table, except the temporary table must have a pound, or hash, sign (#) preceding its name. Temporary tables are actually created on the disk in tempdb:

```
CREATE TABLE #ProductTemp (
  ProductID INT PRIMARY KEY
  );
```

A temporary table has a short life. When the batch or stored procedure that created it ends, the temporary table is deleted. If the table is created during an interactive session (such as a Query

Editor window), it survives only until the end of that session. Of course, a temporary table can also be normally dropped within the batch.

The scope of a temporary table is also limited. Only the connection that created the local temporary table can see it. Even if a thousand users all create temporary tables with the same name, each user will only see his or her own temporary table. The temporary table is created in `tempdb` with a unique name that combines the assigned table name and the connection identifier. Most objects can have names up to 128 characters in length, but temporary tables are limited to 116 so that the last 12 characters can make the name unique. To demonstrate the unique name, the following code creates a temporary table and then examines the name stored in `sys.objects`:

```
SELECT name
  FROM tempdb.sys.objects
  WHERE name LIKE'#Pro%';
```

Result (shortened to save space; the real value is 128 characters wide):

```
name
-------------------------------------------------------------
#ProductTemp__________________________________000000000002D
```

Despite the long name in `sys.objects`, SQL queries still reference any temporary tables with the original name.

Global temporary tables

Global temporary tables are similar to local temporary tables but they have a broader scope. All users can reference a global temporary table, and the life of the table extends until the last session accessing the table disconnects.

To create a global temporary table, begin the table name with two pound signs, e.g., *##TableName*. The following code sample tests to determine whether the global temporary table exists, and creates one if it doesn't:

```
IF NOT EXISTS(
  SELECT * FROM tempdb.sys.objects
    WHERE name = '##TempWork')
CREATE TABLE ##TempWork(
  PK INT PRIMARY KEY,
  Col1 INT
  );
```

When a temporary table is required, it's likely being used for a work in progress. Another alternative is to simply create a standard user table in `tempdb`. Every time the SQL Server is restarted, it dumps and rebuilds `tempdb`, effectively clearing the alternative temporary worktable.

Table variables

Table variables are similar to temporary tables. The main difference, besides syntax, is that table variables have the same scope and life as a local variable. They are only seen by the batch, procedure, or function that creates them. To be seen by called stored procedures, the table variables must be passed in as table-valued parameters, and then they are read-only in the called routine.

The life span of a table variable is also much shorter than a temp table. Table variables cease to exist when the batch, procedure, or function concludes. Table variables have a few additional limitations:

- Table variables may not be created by means of the `select * into` or `insert into @tablename exec` table syntax.
- Table variables may not be created within functions.
- Table variables are limited in their allowable constraints: no foreign keys or check constraints are allowed. Primary keys, defaults, nulls, and unique constraints are OK.
- Table variables may not have any dependent objects, such as triggers or foreign keys.

Table variables are declared as variables, rather than created with SQL DDL statements. When a table variable is being referenced with a SQL query, the table is used as a normal table but named as a variable. The following script must be executed as a single batch or it will fail:

```
DECLARE @WorkTable TABLE (
  PK INT PRIMARY KEY,
  Col1 INT NOT NULL);

INSERT INTO @WorkTable (PK, Col1)
  VALUES ( 1, 101);

SELECT PK, Col1
  FROM @WorkTable;
```

Result:

```
PK          Col1
----------- -----------
            101
```

Memory vs. Disk; Temp Tables vs. Table Variables

A common SQL myth is that table variables are stored in memory. They're not. They exist in `tempdb` just like a temporary table. However, the life span of a table variable (as well as that of most temporary tables) is such that it's extremely unlikely that it would every actually be written to disk. The truth is that the table variable lives in `tempdb` pages in memory.

continued

continued
So if the difference isn't memory vs. disk, how do you choose between using a temp table or a table variable? Size and scope.

Rule of thumb: If the temp space will hold more than about 250 rows, then go with a temp table, otherwise choose a table variable. The reason is because temp tables have the overhead of statistics, whereas table variables do not. This means that for more data, the temp table's statistics can help the Query Optimizer choose the best plan. Of course, one always has to consider the overhead of maintaining the statistics.

Table variables don't have statistics, so they save on the overhead; but without statistics, the Query Optimizer always assumes the table variable will result in one row, and may therefore choose a poor plan if the table variable contains a lot of data.

Scope is the other consideration. If the temp space must be visible and updatable by called routines, then you'll have to choose a temp table.

Summary

T-SQL extends the SQL query with a set of procedural commands. While it's not the most advanced programming language, T-SQL gets the job done. T-SQL batch commands can be used in expressions, or packaged as stored procedures, user-defined functions, or triggers.

A few key points to remember from this chapter:

- The batch terminator, `GO`, is only a Query Editor command, and it can send the batch multiple times when followed by a number.
- DDL commands (`CREATE`, `ALTER`, `DROP`) must be the only command in the batch.
- Ctrl+K+C converts the current lines to comments, and Ctrl+K+U uncomments the lines.
- `IF` only controls execution of the next line, unless it is followed by a `BEGIN...END` block.
- Variables can now be incremented with +=.
- If the temporary space needs to hold more than 250 rows, then use a temp table; otherwise, use a table variable.

The next chapter moves into a technology fraught with negative passion. "Cursors are evil!" is a rallying call for most of the SQL community. But rather than just echo the common sentiment, I'll show you when cursors should be used, and how to refactor cursors into set-based operations.

Chapter 22

Kill the Cursor!

IN THIS CHAPTER

- Iterating through data
- Strategically avoiding cursors
- Refactoring cursors to a high-performance set-based solution
- Measuring cursor performance

SQL excels at handling sets of rows. However, the current database world grew out of the old ISAM files structures, and the vestige of looping through data one row at a time remains in the form of the painfully slow SQL cursor.

The second tier of Smart Database Design (a framework for designing high-performance systems, covered in Chapter 2) is developing set-based code, rather than iterative code.

How slow are cursors? In my consulting practice, the most dramatic cursor-to-set-based refactoring that I've worked on involved three nested cursors and about a couple hundred nested stored procedures that ran nightly taking seven hours. Reverse engineering the cursors and stored procedures, and then developing the query took me about three weeks. The query was three pages long and involved several case subqueries, but it ran in 3–5 seconds.

When testing a well-written cursor against a well-written set-based solution, I have found that the set-based solutions usually range from three to ten times faster than the cursors.

Why are cursors slow? *Very* hypothetically, let's say I make a cool million from book royalties. A cursor is like depositing the funds at the bank one dollar at a time, with a million separate transactions. A set-based transaction deposits the entire million in one transaction. OK, that's not a perfect analogy, but if you view cursors with that type of mindset, you'll be a better database developer.

While there are legitimate reasons to use a cursor (and I'll get to those), the most common reason is that programmers with a procedural background feel more comfortable thinking in terms of loops and pointers than set-based relational algebra.

SQL cursors also appear deceptively tunable. Programmers see the long list of cursor options and assume it means the cursor can be tweaked for high performance. The types of cursors have names such as fast forward, dynamic, and scrollable.

CROSS-REF **SQL Server cursors are server-side cursors, which are different from client-side ADO cursors. The SQL Server cursor occurs inside the server before any data is ever sent to the client. Client-side cursors are frequently used to scroll through the rows in an ADO record set within the application to populate a grid or combo box. ADO cursors are covered in Chapter 32, "Programming with ADO.NET."**

While this chapter explains how to iterate through data using a cursor, my emphasis is clearly on strategically identifying the few appropriate uses of a cursor, but exterminating unnecessary cursors by refactoring them with set-based code.

Anatomy of a Cursor

A cursor is essentially a pointer to a single row of data. A `WHILE` loop is used to cycle through the data until the cursor reaches the end of the data set. SQL Server supports the standard ANSI SQL-92 syntax and an enhanced T-SQL cursor syntax, which offers additional options.

The five steps to cursoring

A cursor creates a result set from a `SELECT` statement and then fetches a single row at a time. The five steps in the life of a cursor are as follows:

1. Declaring the cursor establishes the type and behavior of the cursor and the `SELECT` statement from which the cursor will pull data. Declaring the cursor doesn't retrieve any data; it only sets up the `SELECT` statement. This is the one case in which `DECLARE` doesn't require an ampersand as a prefix for a variable.

   A SQL-92 cursor is declared using `CURSOR FOR` (this is only the basic syntax):

   ```
   DECLARE CursorName [CursorOptions] CURSOR
     FOR Select Statement;
   ```

   The enhanced T-SQL cursor is very similar:

   ```
   DECLARE CursorName CURSOR [CursorOptions]
     FOR Select Statement;
   ```

2. Opening the cursor retrieves the data and fills the cursor:

   ```
   OPEN CursorName;
   ```

3. Fetching moves to the next row and assigns the values from each column returned by the cursor into a local variable, or to the client. The variables must have been previously declared:

   ```
   FETCH [Direction] CursorName [INTO @Variable1, @Variable2, ...];
   ```

   By default, `FETCH` moves to the next row; however, `FETCH` can optionally move to the prior, first, or last row in the data set. `FETCH` can even move an absolute row position in the result set, or move forward or backward a relative *n* number of rows. The problem with these options is that row position is supposed to be meaningless in a relational database. If the code must move to specific positions to obtain a correct logical result, then there's a major flaw in the database design.

4. Closing the cursor releases the data locks but retains the SELECT statement. The cursor can be opened again at this point (CLOSE is the counterpart to OPEN):

```
Close CursorName;
```

5. Deallocating the cursor releases the memory and removes the definitions of the cursor (DEALLOCATE is the counterpart to CREATE):

```
DEALLOCATE CursorName;
```

These are the five basic commands required to construct a cursor. Wrap the FETCH command with a method to manage the iterative loops and the cursor code is a basic, but working, cursor.

Managing the cursor

Because a cursor fetches a single row, T-SQL code is required to repeatedly fetch the next row. To manage the looping process, T-SQL offers two cursor-related system functions that provide cursor status information.

The @@cursor_rows system function returns the number of rows in the cursor. If the cursor is populated asynchronously, then @@cursor_rows returns a negative number.

Essential to developing a cursor is the @@fetch_status system function, which reports the state of the cursor after the last FETCH command. This information is useful to control the flow of the cursor as it reaches the end of the result set. The possible @@fetch_status values indicate the following:

- **0:** The last FETCH successfully retrieved a row.
- **-1:** The last FETCH failed by reaching the end of the result set, trying to fetch prior to a row before the beginning of the result set, or the fetch simply failed.
- **-2:** The last row fetched was not available; the row has been deleted.

Combining @@fetch_status with the WHILE command builds a useful loop for moving through the rows. Typically, the batch will include step 3 — the FETCH — twice.

The first FETCH primes the cursor with two important results. Priming the cursor places data from the first row into the variables so that the action part of the cursor loop can be placed early in the WHILE loop. Priming the cursor also sets up the @@fetch_status system function for the first iteration of the WHILE command.

The second FETCH command occurs within the WHILE loop, fetching the second row and every following row through to the end of the cursor.

The WHILE loop examines the @@Fetch_Status global variable to determine whether the cursor is done.

In the following example cursor loop, a row is inserted and deleted so that you can test how data changes affect the different types of cursors:

```
Use AdventureWorks2008;

-- setup sample row for deleted row cursor test
DELETE Production.Location
  WHERE Name like 'Paul%';
INSERT Production.Location (Name, CostRate, Availability)
  VALUES ('PaulsTest', 1, 1);

-- set-up variables
DECLARE
  @LocationID SMALLINT,
  @LocationName VARCHAR(50),
  @CostRate SMALLMONEY,
  @Availability DECIMAL(8,2);

-- Step 1 / Declare the Cursor
     -- alternative cursor types:
     -- STATIC | KEYSET | DYNAMIC | FAST_FORWARD
DECLARE cLocation CURSOR STATIC
  FOR SELECT LocationID, Name, CostRate, Availability
        FROM Production.Location
        ORDER BY Name;

-- Step 2 / Open the Cursor
OPEN cLocation;

-- Step 3 / Prime the Cursor
FETCH cLocation
  INTO @LocationID,
       @LocationName,
       @CostRate,
       @Availability;

-- set-up the print output
PRINT '@@Fetch_Status   LocationID  Name ';
PRINT '--------------   ----------  ----------------------';

WHILE @@Fetch_Status  <> -1 -- = 0
  BEGIN; -- while loop

  -- perform some work with the data
  -- but only if row actually found
  IF @@Fetch_Status = 0
     BEGIN;
       PRINT CAST(@@Fetch_Status as CHAR(10))
             + '       ' + CAST(@LocationID as CHAR(10))
```

```
                + ' ' + @LocationName;
        END;

      IF @@Fetch_Status = -2 PRINT 'Hit Deleted Row';

      -- Step 3 / Iterating through the cursor
      FETCH cLocation
        INTO @LocationID,
             @LocationName,
             @CostRate,
             @Availability;

      -- Insert and delete rows during cursor run
      -- for cursor type testing
      IF @LocationID = 40
        BEGIN;
           INSERT Production.Location (Name, CostRate, Availability)
             VALUES ('PaulsINSERT', 1, 1);
           DELETE Production.Location
             WHERE Name = 'PaulsTest';
        END;
      END; -- while loop

    PRINT '';
    PRINT 'Final @@Fetch_Status: ' + Cast(@@Fetch_Status as char(2));

    -- Step 4 / Close
    CLOSE cLocation;

    -- Step 5 / Deallocate
    DEALLOCATE cLocation;
```

Watching the cursor

In SQL Server 2008, there are three ways to observe the cursor in action:

- Step through the cursor WHILE loop using the new T-SQL debugger. The T-SQL debugger is covered in Chapter 6, "Using Management Studio," and there's a screencast demonstrating the debugger on www.sqlserverbible.com.
- Use SQL Profiler to watch the T-SQL statements. Select the T-SQL / SQL:StmtCompleted event. There are cursor events listed in SQL Profiler, but they apply to ADO cursors, not T-SQL server-side cursors. SQL Profiler is explained in Chapter 56, "Tracing and Profiling."
- Insert simple PRINT and SELECT statements to display the cursor progress to the client, as shown in the previous example.

Cursor options

Focusing on the enhanced T-SQL cursor, SQL Server supports four basic types of cursors — their differences lie in how they store the data set as the cursor is working with the data.

To test these cursor types, change the option in the previous code sample and watch for inserted and deleted rows:

- **Static:** Copies all the data into `tempdb` and the cursor iterates over the copy of the data. Any changes (inserts, updates, or deletes) to the real data are not seen by the cursor. This type of cursor is generally the fastest.
- **Keyset:** Only the minimum number of columns needed to identify the rows in the correct order are copied to `tempdb`. The cursor walks through the data by internally joining the keyset table in `tempdb` with the real data. Updates and deletes are seen by the cursor, but not inserts. This is the only cursor type that experiences deleted rows as `@@fetch_status = −2`, so be sure to test for deleted rows.

  Keyset cursors, compared to static cursors, write less to `tempdb` when creating the cursor set, but they must perform most of the cursor `SELECT` statement for every fetch. Therefore, if the `SELECT` statement used to define the cursor references several data sources, avoid keyset cursors.
- **Dynamic:** The cursor iterates over the original real data. All changes are seen by the cursor without any special handling of the changes. If a row is inserted after the cursor location, then the cursor will see that row when the cursor reaches the new row. If a row is deleted, then the cursor will simply not see the row when it reaches where the row had been.
- **Fast_Forward:** This is the "high-performance" cursor option introduced in SQL Server 2000. Basically, it's a read-only, forward-only dynamic cursor.

While there are numerous options I'm purposely ignoring in this chapter, two others worth mentioning are:

- **Forward_only:** The cursor may move only to the next row using `FETCH` [next].
- **Scroll:** The cursor may move to any row in any direction using any `FETCH` option — first, last, prior, next, relative, or absolute.

NOTE **Some developers, having heard that cursors are slow, propose to replace the cursor with a manual `while` loop. This technique, which I call a *surrogate cursor*, is still nothing more than a row-by-row iteration, and accomplishes nothing toward optimization and performance.**

Update cursor

Because the cursor is already iterating through the data set, SQL Server knows which row is the current row. The cursor pointer can be referenced within a SQL `UPDATE` or `DELETE` command's `WHERE` clause to manipulate the correct data.

The cursor `DECLARE` command's `FOR UPDATE` option enables updating using the cursor. Specific columns may be listed; or, if no columns are listed, then any column may be updated:

```
DECLARE cDetail CURSOR
  FOR SELECT DetailID
      FROM Detail
```

```
WHERE AdjAmount IS NULL
FOR UPDATE OF AdjAmount;
```

Within the cursor loop, after the row has been fetched, a DML command may include the cursor within the `WHERE` clause using the `CURRENT OF` syntax. The following example, from the `KilltheCursor.sql` script, references the `cDetail` cursor:

```
UPDATE Detail
  SET AdjAmount = @SprocResult
  WHERE CURRENT OF cDetail;
```

CAUTION **You would think that the update cursor would have a performance advantage when iterating through rows and updating them. In testing, however, Hugo Kornelis (this book's primary tech editor) and I have found that the update cursor is actually slightly slower than other cursor options.**

There are more cursor options, but if you're that deep into a writing a cursor, you've gone too far.

Cursor scope

Because cursors tend to be used in the most convoluted situations, understanding cursor scope is important. The scope of the cursor determines whether the cursor lives only in the batch in which it was created or extends to any called procedures. The scope can be configured as the cursor is declared:

```
DECLARE CursorName CURSOR Local | Global
  FOR Select Statement;
```

The default cursor scope is set at the database level with the `cursor_default` option:

```
ALTER DATABASE Family SET CURSOR_DEFAULT LOCAL;
```

The current cursor scope is important to the execution of the procedure. To examine the current default setting, use the database property's examine function:

```
SELECT DATABASEPROPERTYEX('Family', 'IsLocalCursorsDefault');
```

Result:

```
1
```

Cursors and transactions

When compared with set-based solutions, cursors seem to have the edge with locking. Some argue that a million-row, set-based update transaction might lock the entire table, whereas performing the same update within a cursor would lock a single row at a time, so while the cursor might take several times longer, at least it's not blocking other transactions. You can decide where you fall in this particular debate.

NOTE **Executing set-based queries in controlled batches of rows — for example, 1,000 rows per set-based batch — is another way to manage the locking issues presented by very large transactions. This can be done using `Set RowCount` (but it's deprecated) or by windowing and ranking's `row_number()`function.**

Regarding locking, one technique that is sometimes used to improve the performance of cursors is to wrap the entire cursor within a logical transaction. There are pros and cons to this solution. While it will improve the cursor by as much as 50 percent because less locks need to be taken and released, the penalty is the blocking caused by coarser granularity and longer life span of the locks in the transaction.

Cursor Strategies

Most SQL Server developers would agree that cursors should be avoided, unless they are required, which begs the question, "When are cursors the best solution?"

In that spirit, here are the four "Paul Approved" specific situations when using a cursor is the right solution:

- **Iterating over a stored procedure:** When a stored procedure must be executed several times, once for each row or value, and the stored procedure can't be refactored into a set-based solution, or it's a system stored procedure, then a cursor is the right way to iteratively call the stored procedure.
- **Iterating over DDL code:** When DDL code must be dynamically executed multiple times, using a cursor is the appropriate solution.

  For example, in several places in the Nordic code (my O/R DBMS, available on CodePlex.com), it's necessary to iterate over multiple rows or columns, generating a dynamic SQL statement for each row or column. For instance, each `IsSearchable` column must be inserted into the `SearchWordList` table as a separate row, so a cursor selects each `IsSearchable` column and a dynamic SQL statement performs the insert.

  This type of technique can also be used for automating admin tasks. However, as with the problem of denormalizing a list, if the DDL order is not important, such as when generating the `updated()`portions of the AutoAudit triggers (see Chapter 53, "Data Audit Triggers"), then the multiple-assignment variable solution performs best.
- **Cumulative Totals/Running Sums:** While there are set-based solutions, a cursor is the best-performing solution in these cases because it only has to add the next row's value to the cumulative value. See Chapter 12, "Aggregating Data," for a complete cursor solution to this type of problem.
- **Time-Sensitive Data:** Some time-sensitive problems, depending on the database design, can benefit by using a cursor to determine the duration between events. Like the cumulative totals problem, time-sensitive data requires comparing the current row with the last row. Although there are possible set-based solutions, in some cases I've seen cursors perform better than set-based solutions.

  For example, if a table holds manufacturing data using a row for every process event, then a cursor might be required to analyze the time difference between manufacturing events, or to identify the previous event that caused a problem in the current events.

It's important to note that a difficult problem or one with complex logic is not a justified reason for resorting to a cursor.

Refactoring Complex-Logic Cursors

A cursor that's wrapped around a complex-logic problem is often considered the most difficult cursor to kill. The difficulty arises when the logic includes multiple formulas, variable amounts, and multiple exceptions.

I have found three techniques useful when refactoring an iterative solution into a set-based solution:

- Embed the logic into a user-defined function.
- Break up the solution into multiple set-based queries.
- Use case expressions to embed variable logic, and even dynamic formulas, into the query.

Testing a Complex-Logic Problem

Imagine a billing situation with multiple billing formulas and multiple exceptions. Here are the business rules for the sample complex-logic cursor.

Variable Formula:

- **1 — Normal:** BaseRate * Amount * ActionCode's BaseMultiplier
- **2 — Accelerated Rate Job:** BaseRate * Amount * Variable Acceleration Rate
- **3 — Prototype Job:** Amount * ActionCode's BaseMultiplier

Exceptions:

- If there's an executive override on the order, then ignore the ActionCode's BaseMultiplier.
- If the transaction occurs on a weekend, then multiply the adjusted amount by an additional 2.5.
- Premium clients receive a 20% discount to their adjusted rate.
- The adjusted rate is zero if the client is a pro bono client.

That's it: three formulas and four exceptions. Typically, that's enough to justify writing a cursor . . . but is it?

The CursorTest script sets up the preceding problem and then tests it with several possible options, including several cursor types, a surrogate cursor, and the three set-based methods for refactoring a complex cursor against a progressively growing set of data. You can see the results in Figure 22-1.

continued

continued

FIGURE 22-1

Cursors fail to scale, as demonstrated by the results of the CursorTest performance test. The vertical scale indicates the time to complete the formula for all the rows ranging from 0 to 35000 milliseconds. The horizontal scale (1-10) indicates the size of the data. Each iteration adds the same amount of data.

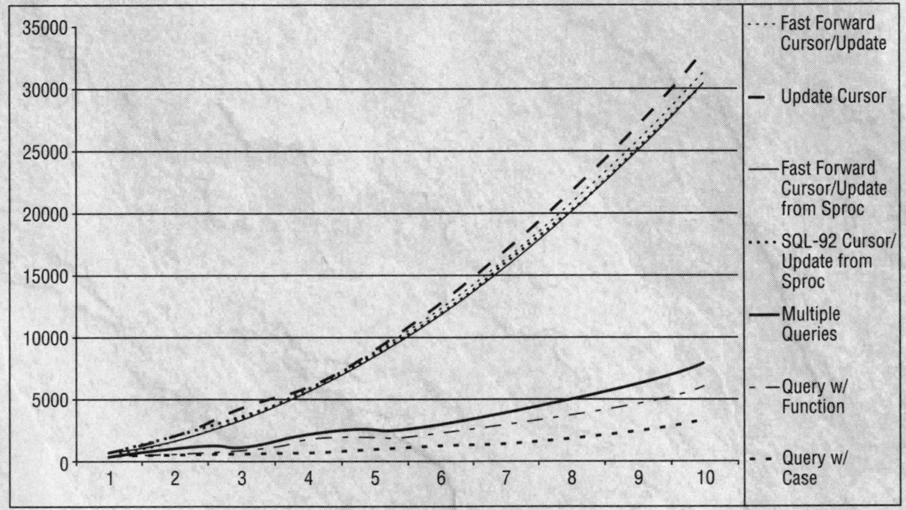

If you want to examine the code for this test, test it, and tweak it for yourself, download the `CursorTest.sql` script from `www.sqlserverbible.com`.

Update query with user-defined function

This solution appears surprisingly simplistic, but looks can be deceiving. This solution hides all the logic within the user-defined formula. Although it would appear that SQL Server calls the function for every row of the query, embedding the function within an `UPDATE` DML statement has its benefits. Examining the query execution plan shows that the Query Optimizer can sometimes incorporate the function's logic within the query plan and generate an excellent set-based solution. Here's an example from the `CursorTest` script:

```
UPDATE dbo.Detail
  SET AdjAmount = dbo.fCalcAdjAmount(DetailID)
  WHERE AdjAmount IS NULL;
```

Multiple queries

The second set-based method uses an individual query for each formula and exception. The WHERE clauses of the queries restrict their operation to only those rows that require their respective formula or exception.

This solution introduces a data-driven database design component. The acceleration rate is supplied as a data-driven value from the Variable table using a scalar subquery, and the exceptions are handled using data-driven joins to the ClientType and DayofWeekMultiplier tables:

```
UPDATE dbo.Detail
  SET AdjAmount = BaseRate * Amount
  FROM Detail
    JOIN ActionCode
      ON Detail.ActionCode = ActionCode.ActionCode
    JOIN [Order]
    ON [Order].OrderID = Detail.OrderID
  WHERE (Formula = 1 OR Formula = 3 )AND ExecOverRide = 1
    AND AdjAmount IS NULL;
UPDATE dbo.Detail
  SET AdjAmount = BaseRate * Amount * BaseMultiplier
  FROM Detail
    JOIN ActionCode
      ON Detail.ActionCode = ActionCode.ActionCode
    JOIN [Order]
    ON [Order].OrderID = Detail.OrderID
  WHERE Formula = 1 AND ExecOverRide = 0
    AND AdjAmount IS NULL;

-- 2-Accelerated  BaseRate * Amount * Acceleration Rate
UPDATE dbo.Detail
  SET AdjAmount = BaseRate * Amount * (SELECT Value
                                        FROM dbo.Variable
                                          WHERE Name = 'AccRate');
  FROM Detail
    JOIN ActionCode
      ON Detail.ActionCode = ActionCode.ActionCode
    JOIN [Order]
    ON [Order].OrderID = Detail.OrderID
  WHERE Formula = 2
    AND AdjAmount IS NULL;

-- 3-Prototype    Amount * ActionCode's BaseMultiplier
UPDATE dbo.Detail
  SET AdjAmount = Amount * BaseMultiplier
  FROM Detail
    JOIN ActionCode
      ON Detail.ActionCode = ActionCode.ActionCode
```

```
    JOIN [Order]
    ON [Order].OrderID = Detail.OrderID
  WHERE Formula = 3 AND ExecOverRide = 0
    AND AdjAmount IS NULL;

-- Exceptions
-- WeekEnd Adjustment
UPDATE dbo.Detail
  SET AdjAmount *= Multiplier
  FROM Detail
    JOIN [Order]
      ON [Order].OrderID = Detail.OrderID
    JOIN DayOfWeekMultiplier DWM
      ON CAST(DatePart(dw,[Order].TransDate) as SMALLINT) =
DWM.DayOfWeek;

    -- Client Adjustments
UPDATE dbo.Detail
  SET AdjAmount *= Multiplier
  FROM Detail
    JOIN [Order]
      ON [Order].OrderID = Detail.OrderID
    JOIN Client
      ON [Order].ClientID = Client.ClientID
    Join ClientType
      ON Client.ClientTypeID = ClientType.ClientTypeID;
```

Query with case expression

The third refactoring strategy uses a CASE expression and data-driven values to solve complexity within a single query. The CASE expression's power derives from the fact that it incorporates flexible logic within a single query.

Data-driven values and formulas are also incorporated into the query using joins to connect the base row with the correct lookup values. Data-driven designs also reduce maintenance costs because values can be easily changed without programming alterations.

In this example, the CASE expression selects the correct formula based on the values within the ActionCode table. The executive override is hard-coded into the CASE expression, but with a little work that too could be data driven.

As with the multiple query solution, the acceleration rate and exceptions are data driven:

```
UPDATE dbo.Detail
SET AdjAmount = DWM.Multiplier * ClientType.Multiplier *
  CASE
    WHEN ActionCode.Formula = 1 AND
ExecOverRide = 0
      THEN BaseRate * Amount * BaseMultiplier
```

```
    WHEN (ActionCode.Formula = 1 OR ActionCode.Formula = 3 )
AND ExecOverRide = 1
      THEN BaseRate * Amount
    WHEN ActionCode.Formula = 2
      THEN BaseRate * Amount * (SELECT Value
                                 FROM dbo.Variable
                                 WHERE Name = 'AccRate')
    WHEN (Formula = 3 AND ExecOverRide = 0)
      THEN Amount * BaseMultiplier
  END
FROM Detail
  JOIN ActionCode
    ON Detail.ActionCode = ActionCode.ActionCode
  JOIN [Order]
    ON [Order].OrderID = Detail.OrderID
  JOIN Client
    ON [Order].ClientID = Client.ClientID
  Join ClientType
    ON Client.ClientTypeID = ClientType.ClientTypeID
  JOIN DayOfWeekMultiplier DWM
    ON CAST(DatePart(dw,[Order].TransDate) as SMALLINT) = DWM.DayOfWeek
WHERE AdjAmount IS NULL;
```

Summary

To quote another book author and MVP, my friend Bill Vaughn, "Cursors are evil!" — perhaps not the greatest evil in database development, but Bill has a point.

When an optimization improves performance by a magnitude of time (e.g., hours to minutes, minutes to seconds), that's when the job is fun. As shown earlier, cursors have their place, but I've never seen any business requirements that couldn't be solved with a set-based query. There's no better way to optimize a stored procedure than to find one that has an unnecessary cursor. When you're looking for low-hanging fruit, cursors are about the juiciest you can find.

The next chapter continues the theme of developing smarter T-SQL code by adding error handling to the mix.

Chapter 23

T-SQL Error Handling

So an atom goes into a bar and says to the barkeeper, "Hey, I think I've lost an electron."

"Are you sure?" asks the barkeep.

"Of course, in fact, I'm positive."

Lame, I know, but it's my favorite geek joke; I couldn't help it. Back to SQL, despite our best efforts, any application can lose an electron every once in a while — the trick is to handle it in a positive way.

Of course, all robust programming languages provide some method for trapping, logging, and handling errors. In this area, T-SQL has a sad history (almost as sad as that joke), but it's made significant progress with SQL Server 2005.

There are two distinctly different ways to code error handling with SQL Server:

- Legacy error handling is how it's been done since the beginning of SQL Server, using `@@error` to see the error status of the previous SQL statement.
- Try/catch was introduced in SQL Server 2008, bringing SQL Server into the 21st century.

IN THIS CHAPTER

Legacy Error Handling

Historically, T-SQL error handling has been tedious at best. I'd prefer to not even include this legacy method of handling errors, but I'm sure you'll see it in old code, so it must be covered.

What's New with Error Handling?

Unfortunately, there is nothing new in 2008 when it comes to error handling. However, when performing code reviews for third-party software vendors, I rarely see production code with any error handling, much less the improved `try...catch`, which was introduced in SQL Server 2005. So, from an adoption standpoint, it may as well be new.

The basic error information system functions, such as `@@error` and `@@rowcount`, contain the status for the previous T-SQL command in the code. This means that the legacy method of error handling must examine T-SQL's system functions and handle the error after each SQL statement that might potentially encounter an error.

@@error system function

The `@@error` system function will contain the integer error code for the previous T-SQL statement. A `0` indicates success.

The difficulty is that `@@error`, unlike other languages that hold the last error in a variable until another error occurs, is updated for every command, so even testing its value updates it.

The following code sample attempts to update the primary key to a value already in use. This violates the foreign key constraint and generates an error. The two `print` commands demonstrate how `@@error` is reset by every T-SQL command. The first `print` command displays the success or failure of the update.

The second `print` command (results in bold) displays the success or failure of the previous `print` command:

```
USE Family;
UPDATE Person
  SET PersonID = 1
  Where PersonID = 2;
Print @@error;
Print @@error;
```

Result:

```
Msg 2627, Level 14, State 1, Line 2
Violation of PRIMARY KEY constraint 'PK__Person__AA2FFB847F60ED59'.
Cannot insert duplicate key in object 'dbo.Person'.
The statement has been terminated.
2627
0
```

The solution to the "last error status" problem is to save the error status to a local variable. This solution retains the error status so it may be properly tested and then handled. The following batch uses @err as a temporary error variable:

```
USE Family;
DECLARE @err INT;

UPDATE Person
  SET PersonID = 1
  Where PersonID = 2
SET @err = @@error;

IF @err <> 0
  BEGIN
    -- error handling code
    PRINT @err;
  END;
```

Result:

```
Msg 2627, Level 14, State 1, Line 2
Violation of PRIMARY KEY constraint 'PK__Person__AA2FFB847F60ED59'.
Cannot insert duplicate key in object 'dbo.Person'.
The statement has been terminated.
2627
```

@@rowcount system function

Another way to determine whether the query was a success is to check the number of rows affected. Even if no error was generated, it's possible that the data didn't match and the operation failed, which might indicate a data, logic, or business rule problem. The @@rowCount system function is useful for checking the effectiveness of the query.

The reset issue that affects @@error also affects @@rowcount.

The following batch uses @@rowcount to check for rows updated. The failure results from the incorrect WHERE clause condition. No row with PersonID = 100 exists. @@rowcount is used to detect the query failure:

```
USE FAMILY;
UPDATE Person
  SET LastName = 'Johnson'
  WHERE PersonID = 100;

IF @@rowCount = 0
  BEGIN
    -- error handling code
    PRINT 'no rows affected';
  END;
```

Result:

```
no rows affected
```

To capture both the @@error and the @@rowcount functions, use a SELECT statement with two variables:

```
SELECT @err = @@error, @rcount = @@rowcount
```

Raiserror

To return custom error messages to the calling procedure or front-end application, use the RAISERROR command. Two forms for RAISERROR exist: a legacy simple form and the recommended complete form.

The simple raiserror form

The simple form, which dates from the Sybase days, passes only a hard-coded number and message. The severity level is always passed back as 16 — user error severe:

```
RAISERROR ErrorNumber ErrorMessage;
```

For example, this code passes back a simple error message:

```
RAISERROR 5551212 'Unable to update customer.';
```

Result:

```
Msg 5551212, Level 16, State 1, Line 1
'Unable to update customer.'
```

NOTE **The simple form is deprecated and will be removed in a future version of SQL Server. I don't recommend writing new code using this form — it's included here only in case you see this form in legacy code.**

The improved raiserror form

The improved form (introduced back in SQL Server 7) incorporates the following four useful features into the RAISERROR command:

- Specifies the severity level
- Dynamically modifies the error message
- Uses serverwide stored messages
- May optionally log the error to the event log

The syntax for the improved RAISERROR adds parameters for the severity level, state (seldom used), and message-string arguments:

```
RAISERROR (
  message or number, severity, state, optional arguments
  ) WITH LOG;
```

Error severity

Windows has established standard error-severity codes, listed in Table 23-1. The other severity codes are reserved for Microsoft's use. In any case, the severity code you'll use for your RAISERROR will almost always be 16.

TABLE 23-1

Available Severity Codes

Severity Code	Description
10	Status message: Does not raise an error, but returns a message, such as a PRINT statement
11–13	No special meaning
14	Informational message
15	Warning message: Something may be wrong
16	Critical error: The procedure failed

Adding variable parameters to messages

The error message can be a fixed-string message or the error number of a stored message. Either type can work with optional arguments.

The arguments are substituted for placeholders within the error message. While several types and options are possible, the placeholders I find useful are %s for a string and %i for a signed integer. The following example uses one string argument:

```
RAISERROR ('Unable to update %s.', 14, 1, 'Customer');
```

Result:

```
Msg 50000, Level 14, State 1, Line 1
Unable to update Customer.
```

Stored messages

The RAISERROR command can also pull a message from the sys.messages system view. Message numbers 1–50,000 are reserved for Microsoft. Higher message numbers are available for user-defined messages. The benefit of using stored messages is that all messages are forced to become consistent and numbered.

Note that with sys.messages stored messages, the message-number scheme is serverwide. If two vendors, or two databases, use overlapping messages, then no division exists between databases, and there's no solution beyond recoding all the error handling on one of the projects. The second issue is that when migrating a database to a new server, the messages must also be moved.

The sys.messages table includes columns for the message_id, text, severity, and whether the error should be logged. However, the severity of the RAISERROR command is used instead of the severity from the sys.messages table, so sys.messages.severity is moot.

To manage messages in code, use the sp_addmessage system stored procedure:

```
EXEC sp_addmessage 50001, 16, 'Unable to update %s';
```

For database projects that may be deployed in multiple languages, the optional @lang parameter can be used to specify the language for the error message.

If the message already exists, then a replace parameter must be added to the system stored procedure call, as follows:

```
EXEC sp_addmessage 50001, 16,
  'Update error on %s', @replace = 'replace';
```

To view the existing custom messages, select from the sys.messages system view:

```
SELECT *
  FROM sys.messages
  WHERE message_id > 50000;
```

Result:

```
message_id  language_id severity is_event_logged text
----------- ----------- -------- --------------- -----------------------
50001       1033        16       0               Unable to update %s
```

To move messages between servers, do one of the following:

- Save the script that was originally used to load the messages.
- Use the Transfer Error Messages Task in Integration Services.
- Use the following query to generate a script that adds the messages:

```
SELECT 'EXEC sp_addmessage, '
    + CAST(message_id AS VARCHAR(7))
    + ', ' + CAST(severity AS VARCHAR(2))
    + ', ''' + [text] +  ''';'
  FROM sys.messages
  WHERE message_id > 50000;
```

Result:

```
-----------------------------------------------------------
EXEC sp_addmessage, 50001, 16, 'Unable to update %s';
```

To drop a message, use the sp_dropmessage system stored procedure with the error number:

```
EXEC sp_dropmessage 50001;
```

Logging the error

Another advantage of using the improved form of the RAISERROR command is that it can log the error to the Windows Application event log and the SQL Server event log.

The downside to logging to the Application event log is that it's stored on individual workstations. While the Application event log is a great place to log front-end "unable to connect" errors, it's an inconvenient place to store database errors.

To specify that an event should be logged from the RAISERROR command, add the WITH LOG option:

```
RAISERROR ('Unable to update %s.', 14, 1, 'Customer')
  WITH LOG
```

Result:

```
Server: Msg 50000, Level 14, State 1, Line 1
Unable to update Customer.
```

To view errors in the Application event log (see Figure 23-1), select Control Panel ➪ Administrative Tools ➪ Event Viewer. An Event Viewer is also located in Control Panel ➪ Administrative Tools.

FIGURE 23-1

A SQL Server raiserror error in the Windows Application event log. Notice that the server and database name are embedded in the error data.

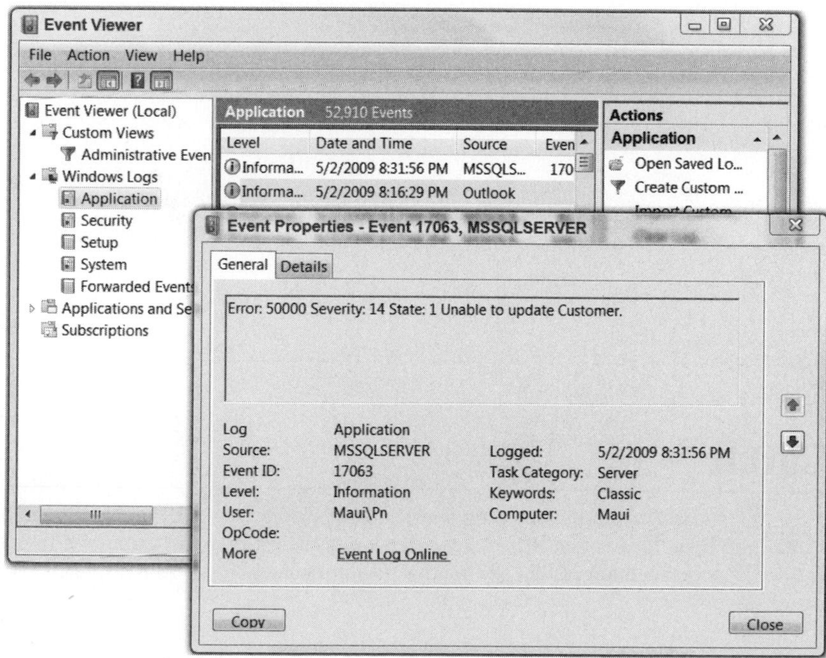

SQL Server log

SQL Server also maintains a series of log files. Each time SQL Server starts, it creates a new log file. Six archived copies of the last log files are retained, for a total of seven log files. Management Studio's Object Explorer in the Management ➪ SQL Server Logs node lists the logs. Double-clicking a log opens SQL Server's very cool Log File Viewer, shown in Figure 23-2. It's worth exploring, as it has a filter and search capabilities.

FIGURE 23-2

Viewing an error in the SQL Server log using Management Studio

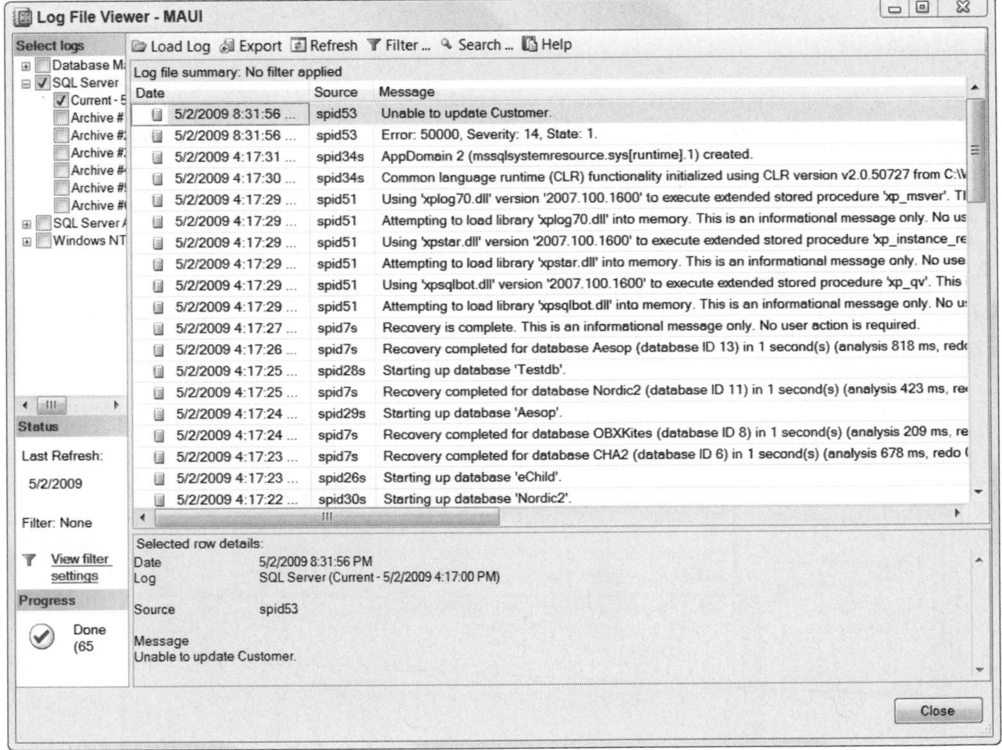

Try...Catch

TRY...CATCH is a standard method of trapping and handling errors that .NET programmers have enjoyed for years. The basic idea is that if SQL Server encounters any errors when it tries to execute a block of code, it will stop execution of the TRY block and immediately jump to the CATCH block to handle the error:

```
BEGIN TRY
```

```
    <SQL code>;
END TRY
BEGIN CATCH
    <error handling code>;
END CATCH;
```

If the TRY block of code executes without any error, then the CATCH code is never executed, and execution resumes after the CATCH block:

```
BEGIN TRY
  SELECT 'Try One';
  RAISERROR('Simulated Error', 16, 1);
  Select 'Try Two';
END TRY
BEGIN CATCH
  SELECT 'Catch Block';
END CATCH;
SELECT 'Post Try';
```

Result:

```
---------
Try One

------------
Catch Block

-----------
Post Try

(1 row(s) affected)
```

Walking through this example, SQL Server executes the TRY block until the RAISERROR's simulated error, which sends the execution down to the CATCH block. The entire CATCH block is executed. Following execution of the CATCH block, execution continues with the next statement, SELECT 'Post Try'.

NOTE **The T-SQL compiler treats the END TRY ... BEGIN CATCH combination as a single contiguous command. Any other statements, a batch terminator (go), or a statement terminator (;) between these two commands will cause an untrapped error. END TRY must be followed immediately by a BEGIN CATCH.**

Catch block

When an error does occur, the best way to trap and handle it is in the CATCH blocks. Within the CATCH block, you want to do the following:

1. If the batch is using logical transactions (BEGIN TRAN/COMMIT TRAN), then, depending on the error and situation, the error handler might need to roll back the transaction. If this is

the case, I recommend rolling back the transaction as the first action so that any locks the transaction might be holding are released.

CROSS-REF **For more details on transactions and error handling, including a discussion on doomed transactions and the `xact_state()` function, please refer to Chapter 66, "Managing Transactions, Locking, and Blocking."**

2. If the error is one that the stored procedure logic detects, and it's not a SQL Server error, then raise the error message so that the user or front-end application is informed.
3. Optionally, log the error to an error table.
4. Terminate the batch. If it's a stored procedure, user-defined function, or trigger, then terminate it with a `RETURN` command.

When an error occurs in the `TRY` block and execution is passed to the `CATCH` block, the error information is also passed to the `CATCH` block. The information may be examined using the error functions listed in Table 23-2. These functions are designed specifically for the `CATCH` block. Outside a `CATCH` block, they will always return a `null` value.

TABLE 23-2

Catch Functions

Error Function	Returns
`Error_Message()`	The text of the error message
`Error_Number()`	The number of the error
`Error_Procedure()`	The name of the stored procedure or trigger in which the error occurred
`Error_Severity()`	The severity of the error
`Error_State()`	The state of the error
`Error_Line()`	The line number within the batch or stored procedure that generated the error
`Xact_State()`	Whether the transaction can be committed (see Chapter 66)

These `CATCH` functions retain the error information of the error that fired the `CATCH` block. They may be called multiple times and still retain the error information.

The following sample demonstrates a `CATCH` block using the `CATCH` functions and a `RAISERROR` to report the error to the client. The contents of the error functions are being passed to variables so a custom error string can be assembled for the `RAISERROR`:

```
BEGIN CATCH

    DECLARE
```

```
        @Error_Severity INT,
        @Error_State INT,
        @Error_Number INT,
        @Error_Line INT,
        @Error_Message VARCHAR(245);

    SELECT
        @Error_Severity = ERROR_SEVERITY(),
        @Error_State = ERROR_STATE(),
        @Error_Number = ERROR_NUMBER(),
        @Error_Line = ERROR_LINE(),
        @Error_Message = ERROR_MESSAGE();

    RAISERROR ('Msg %d, Line %d: %s',
        @Error_Severity,
        @Error_State,
        @Error_Number,
        @Error_Line,
        @Error_Message);

  RETURN @Error_Number;

END CATCH;
```

Nested try/catch and rethrown errors

Any error (or RAISERROR event) will bubble up through every layer of stored procedures until it's caught by a try/catch block or it reaches the client. Visualizing the call stack — the stack of procedures that have executed or called other stored procedures — it's possible for lower level, or nested, stored procedures to use this principle to send, or rethrow, errors to higher-level stored procedures in the call stack.

Try/catch blocks can easily be nested even if the nesting is unintentional. If one stored procedure calls another stored procedure and both procedures are well written, with try/catch blocks, then not only are the stored procedures nested, but the try/catch blocks are nested too.

In the following example, the TopProc will execute, or call, the CalledProc. A divide by zero error in CalledProc causes the code to jump to the CATCH block. The catch block will issue a RAISERROR.

The TopProc will receive the error that was raised by the CalledProc. It sees the error as any other type of error and therefore jumps down to its CATCH block. The RAISERROR in the TopProc is executed, and it too raises an error. This time the raised error is seen by the client, in this case Management Studio:

```
CREATE PROC TopProc
AS
BEGIN TRY
  EXEC CalledProc
```

```
END TRY
BEGIN CATCH
  RAISERROR ('TopProc Raiserror',16,1)
END CATCH

GO

CREATE PROC CalledProc
AS
BEGIN TRY
  SELECT 3/0
END TRY
BEGIN CATCH
  RAISERROR ('CalledProc Raiserror',16,1)
END CATCH

Go

EXEC TopProc
```

Result:

```
Msg 50000, Level 16, State 1, Procedure TopProc, Line 7
TopProc Raiserror
```

T-SQL Fatal Errors

If T-SQL encounters a fatal error, then the batch will immediately abort without giving you the opportunity to test `@@Error`, handle the error, or correct the situation.

Fatal errors are rare enough that they shouldn't pose much of a problem. Generally, if the code works once, then it should continue to work unless the schema is changed or SQL Server is reconfigured. The most common fatal errors are those caused by the following:

- Data-type incompatibilities
- Unavailable SQL Server resources
- SQL Server advanced settings that are incompatible with certain tasks
- Missing objects or misspelled object names

For a list of most of the fatal error messages, run the following query:

```
SELECT message_id, severity, language_id, text
  FROM master.sys.messages
  WHERE language_id = 1033   -- US English
  AND severity >= 19
  ORDER BY severity, message_id;
```

`Try...Catch` does a good job of handling typical day-to-day user errors, such as constraint-violation errors. Nevertheless, to be safe, front-end application developers should also include error-handling code in their programs.

Summary

Error handling — perhaps it's the developer's equivalent of the DBA's backup command, yet it adds a sense of polish and finish to any stored procedure. Any production T-SQL code should have error handling, no question about it. It's easy.

Key points about T-SQL error handling:

- Legacy error handling uses `@@error` and `@@rowcount` to determine whether an error occurred in the previous statement. The values must be checked after every DML statement by saving them to local variables.
- `RAISERROR` can send errors toward the client and log errors.
- Try/catch blocks are the right way to handle errors. On any error in the `TRY` block, execution jumps to the `CATCH` block.
- Error functions in the `CATCH` block return information about the last error.

Next on the agenda: All the T-SQL query and programming pieces finally come together as stored procedures.

Chapter 24

Developing Stored Procedures

Of all the possible SQL Server bad practices, I believe the worst is ad hoc SQL. The solution: stored procedures. Here's why.

Chapter 2, "Data Architecture," presented six databases objectives and the notion that with careful design and development, all six could be achieved. Architecting the database with stored procedures is critical to achieving five of the six objectives (all but availability):

- **Extensibility:** Using stored procedures is the best means of abstracting, or decoupling, the database. A stored procedure API contract will encapsulate the database and provide it with long-term extensibility.
- **Performance:** A well-written stored procedure is the fastest possible SQL Server code, it keeps the execution of data-centric code close to the data, and it's easier to index tune a database with stored procedures.
- **Usability:** It's easier for application programmers to make a stored procedure call and consume the result than it is to write ad hoc SQL.
- **Data Integrity:** A stored procedure developed by the database developer is less likely to contain data integrity errors, and easier to unit test, than ad hoc SQL code.
- **Security:** Locking down the tables and providing access only through stored procedures is a standard best practice for database development.

Of these five, extensibility is the most compelling reason to use stored procedures. I've personally witnessed too many IT shops and ISVs that have a nightmare database they wish they could fix, but without an abstraction layer, it seems too scary to manage. As a result, they spend 10 times more building out additional code, adding extra databases, or losing business because they can't adapt.

IN THIS CHAPTER

Stored procedures aren't mysterious. All the features of T-SQL queries and batches are in full force. In the same way that a view is a SQL query saved under a view name, a stored procedure is a batch that has been stored with a name so it can be easily called, and its query execution plan saved in memory (see Figure 24-1).

FIGURE 24-1

Stored procedures keep the code inside the box, protecting the abstraction layer and keeping the data execution close to the data.

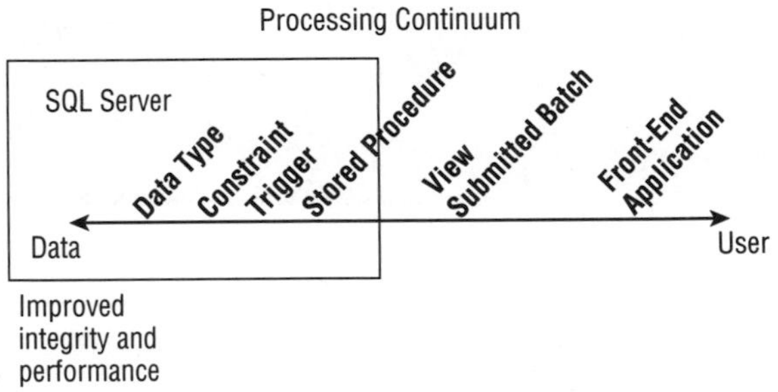

To write an efficient stored procedure, don't start with this chapter. A well-written stored procedure is based on a well-written batch (see Chapter 23) consisting of well-written, set-oriented SQL queries (see Chapters 8 through 21). This chapter explains how to pull together the batch and wrap it as a stored procedure.

What's New with Stored Procedures?

SQL Server 2008 adds user-defined table types and table-valued parameters (my number two favorite new feature) to T-SQL. These radically improve how a client application can pass a complex transaction to SQL Server. Previously, the only options were to pass in a comma-delimited list using a `varchar(max)` parameter, pass in an XML variable, or make multiple calls to stored procedures.

Stored procedures are highly dependent on the objects they call. SQL Server 2008 provides enhanced ways to view these dependencies.

Managing Stored Procedures

The actual management of stored procedures is simple compared to the logic within them. Once you know the basic facts and syntax, managing stored procedures shouldn't present any problems.

Create, alter, and drop

Stored procedures are managed by means of the data definition language (DDL) commands: CREATE, ALTER, and DROP.

CREATE must be the first command in a batch; the termination of the batch ends the creation of the stored procedure. The following example creates a very simple stored procedure that retrieves data from the ProductCategory table in the OBXKites database:

```
USE OBXKites;
go

CREATE PROCEDURE dbo.CategoryList
AS
SELECT ProductCategoryName, ProductCategoryDescription
  FROM dbo.ProductCategory;

go
```

As this chapter progresses, more features will be added to the CategoryList example stored procedure.

Dropping a stored procedure removes it from the database. Altering a stored procedure replaces the entire existing stored procedure with new code. When modifying a stored procedure, altering it is preferable to dropping and recreating it, because the latter method removes any permissions.

Of course, stored procedures may be created, altered, or dropped using Object Explorer, but I strongly suggest that stored procedures be managed using scripts (.sql files) that may be checked into a version control system.

Executing a stored procedure

When calling a stored procedure within a SQL batch, the EXECUTE command executes the stored procedure with a few special rules. EXECUTE is typically coded as EXEC.

If the stored-procedure call is the first line of a batch (and if it's the only line, then it's also the first line), the stored-procedure call doesn't require the EXEC command. However, including it anyway won't cause any problems and it prevents an error if the code is cut and pasted later.

The following two-system stored procedure calls demonstrate the use of the EXEC command within a batch:

```
sp_help;
EXEC sp_help;
```

CROSS-REF **This section covers the batch aspects of EXEC. You can find more details about using the EXECUTE command in Chapter 29, "Dynamic SQL and Code Generation."**

Returning a record set

If a stored procedure is a saved batch, then whatever a batch can do, a stored procedure can do. Just as a batch returns a record set from a SQL SELECT query, a stored procedure also returns a record set from a query.

Referring back to the stored procedure that was created in the preceding section, when the CategoryList stored procedure is executed, the query within the stored procedure returns all rows from the productcategory table:

```
EXEC dbo.CategoryList;
```

Result (abridged):

```
ProductCategoryName   ProductCategoryDescription
--------------------- ------------------------------
Accessory             kite flying accessories
Book                  Outer Banks books
Clothing              OBX t-shirts, hats, jackets
...
```

Compiling stored procedures

Compiling a stored procedure is an automatic process. Stored procedures compile and are stored in memory the first time they are executed. Rather more accurately, SQL Server develops query execution plans for the queries and code within the stored procedures, and these query execution plans are stored in memory.

CROSS-REF **For more details about query execution plans and how they're stored in memory, refer to Chapter 65, "Query Plan Reuse."**

Stored procedure encryption

When the stored procedure is created, its text is saved in a system table. The text is not stored for the execution of the stored procedure, but only so that it may be retrieved later if it needs to be modified.

The sp_helptext system stored procedure will extract the original text of the stored procedure:

```
EXEC sp_helptext 'dbo.CategoryList';
```

Result:

```
Text
-------------------------------------------
CREATE PROCEDURE  CategoryList
AS
SELECT ProductCategoryName, ProductCategoryDescription
  FROM dbo.ProductCategory;
```

If the stored procedure is created with the WITH ENCRYPTION option, the stored procedure text is not directly readable. It's common practice for third-party vendors to encrypt their stored procedures. The following ALTER command stores the CategoryList procedure with WITH ENCRYPTION and then attempts to read the code:

```
ALTER PROCEDURE dbo.CategoryList
WITH ENCRYPTION
AS
SELECT ProductCategoryName, ProductCategoryDescription
  FROM dbo.ProductCategory;
go
EXEC sp_helptext 'dbo.CategoryList';
```

Result:

```
The text for object 'dbo.CategoryList' is encrypted.
```

System stored procedures

The basic SQL syntax includes only DML, DDL, and DCL commands. For other admin tasks, Microsoft adds system stored procedures stored in the `master` database. But with every version of SQL Server, Microsoft moves more of these tasks from system stored procedures into standard SQL. Specifically, the `ALTER` command is becoming more powerful with every version.

To make these procedures available to all databases, special rules govern the scope of system stored procedures. Any procedures beginning with `sp_` in the `master` database can be executed from any database. If a name conflict exists between a system stored procedure and a stored procedure in the local user database, the system stored procedure in the local database is executed.

Best Practice

When creating stored procedures, use a consistent naming convention other than `sp_` to name your stored procedures. Using `sp_` can only cause name conflicts and confusion. I sometimes add the `p` prefix to the names of stored procedures, but even no prefix is better than `sp_`.

Using stored procedures within queries

Stored procedures are typically executed with the `EXEC` command or submitted by the client application, but a stored procedure can be used within the `FROM` portion of a query if the stored procedure is called from within an `openquery()` function.

`Openquery()` is a distributed query function that sends a pass-through query to an external data source for remote execution. When the `openquery()` function includes a stored procedure, it simply submits the stored procedure to the local server.

CROSS-REF **The `openquery()` function is explained in more detail in Chapter 31, "Executing Distributed Queries."**

Because the result set of the stored procedure is returned via a function being used by a data source in the FROM clause of the SELECT statement, a WHERE clause can further reduce the output of the stored procedure.

While this technique enables the use of stored procedures within a SELECT statement, it's not as optimized as the technique of passing any row restrictions to the stored procedure for processing within the stored procedure. The only benefit of using openquery() is that it enables a complex stored procedure to be called from within an ad hoc query.

For the purpose of the following code, assume that a linked server connection has been established to the local server with the name NOLI:

```
SELECT * FROM OpenQuery(
  MAUINOLI,
  'EXEC OBXKites.dbo.pProductCategory_Fetch;')
  WHERE ProductCategoryDescription Like '%stuff%';
```

Result:

```
ProductCategoryName    ProductCategoryDescription
---------------------- ----------------------------------
OBX                     OBX stuff
Toy                     Kids stuff
```

Best Practice

If you need to call complex code within a SELECT statement, using openquery() to call a stored procedure works, but the syntax is a bit bizarre. A better method is to use a CASE expression or create a user-defined function.

Executing remote stored procedures

Two methods exist for calling a stored procedure located on another server: a four-part name reference and a distributed query. Both methods require that the remote server be a linked server. Stored procedures may only be *called* remotely; they may not be *created* remotely.

The remote stored procedure may be executed by means of the four-part name:

```
server.database.schma.procedurename
```

For example, the following code adds a new product category to the OBXKites database on Noli's (my development server) second instance of SQL Server:

```
EXEC [MAUINoli\SQL2COPENHAGEN].OBXKites.dbo.pProductCategory_AddNew
  'Food', 'Eatables';
```

Alternately, the OpenQuery( ) function can be used to call a remote stored procedure:

```
OpenQuery(linked server name, 'exec 'EXEC stored procedure;')
```

The next code sample executes the pCustomerType_Fetch stored procedure in the default database for the user login being used to connect to MAUI\COPENHAGENNoli\SQL2. If the default database is incorrect, a three-part name can be used to point to the correct database.

```
SELECT CustomerTypeName, DiscountPercent, [Default]
  FROM OPENQUERY(
    [MAUI\COPENHAGENNoli\SQL2], 'EXEC OBXKites.dbo.pCustomerType_Fetch;');
```

Result:

```
CustomerTypeName    DiscountPercent Default
------------------- --------------- -------
Preferred           10              0
Retail              00              1
Wholesale           15              0
```

As with any other distributed query, the Distributed Transaction Coordinator service must be running if the transaction updates data in more than one server.

Passing Data to Stored Procedures

A stored procedure is more useful when it can be manipulated by parameters. The CategoryList stored procedure created previously returns all the product categories, but a procedure that performs a task on an individual row requires a method for passing the row ID to the procedure.

SQL Server stored procedures may have numerous input and output parameters (SQL Server 2005 increased the number of parameters from 1,024 to 2,100 to be exact).

Input parameters

You can add input parameters that pass data to the stored procedure by listing the parameters after the procedure name in the CREATE PROCEDURE command. Each parameter must begin with an @ sign, and becomes a local variable within the procedure. Like local variables, the parameters must be defined with valid data types. When the stored procedure is called, the parameter must be included (unless the parameter has a default value).

The following code sample creates a stored procedure that returns a single product category. The @CategoryName parameter can accept Unicode character input up to 35 characters in length. The value passed by means of the parameter is available within the stored procedure as the variable @CategoryName in the WHERE clause:

```
USE OBXKites;
```

```
go
CREATE PROCEDURE dbo.CategoryGet (
  @CategoryName NVARCHAR(35)
  )
AS
SELECT ProductCategoryName, ProductCategoryDescription
  FROM dbo.ProductCategory
  WHERE ProductCategoryName = @CategoryName;
go
```

When the following code sample is executed, the Unicode string literal 'Kite' is passed to the stored procedure and substituted for the variable in the WHERE clause:

```
EXEC dbo.CategoryGet N'Kite';
```

Result:

```
ProductCategoryName    ProductCategoryDescription
---------------------- -----------------------------------
Kite                   a variety of kites, from simple to
                       stunt, to Chinese, to novelty kites
```

If multiple parameters are involved, the parameter name can be specified in any order, or the parameter values listed in order. If the two methods are mixed, then as soon as the parameter is provided by name, all the following parameters must be as well.

The next four examples each demonstrate calling a stored procedure and passing the parameters by original position and by name:

```
EXEC Schema.StoredProcedure
  @Parameter1 = n,
  @Parameter2 = 'n';

EXEC Schema.StoredProcedure
  @Parameter2 = 'n',
  @Parameter1 = n;

EXEC Schema.StoredProcedure n, 'n';

EXEC Schema.StoredProcedure n, @Parameter2 = 'n';
```

Parameter defaults

You must supply every parameter when calling a stored procedure, unless that parameter has been created with a default value. You establish the default by appending an equal sign and the default to the parameter, as follows:

```
CREATE PROCEDURE Schema.StoredProcedure (
  @Variable DataType = DefaultValue
  )
```

The following code, extracted from the OBXKites sample database, demonstrates a stored procedure default. If a product category name is passed in this stored procedure, the stored procedure returns only the selected product category. However, if nothing is passed, the NULL default is used in the WHERE clause to return all the product categories:

```
CREATE PROCEDURE dbo.pProductCategory_Fetch2
  @Search NVARCHAR(50) = NULL
-- If @Search = null then return all ProductCategories
-- If @Search is value then try to find by Name
AS
  SET NOCOUNT ON;
  SELECT ProductCategoryName, ProductCategoryDescription
    FROM dbo.ProductCategory
    WHERE ProductCategoryName = @Search
      OR @Search IS NULL;
  IF @@RowCount = 0
    BEGIN;
    RAISERROR(
      'Product Category ''%s" Not Found.',14,1,@Search);
    END;
```

The first execution passes a product category:

```
EXEC dbo.pProductCategory_Fetch2 'OBX';
```

Result:

```
ProductCategoryName    ProductCategoryDescription
---------------------- ----------------------------------
OBX                    OBX stuff
```

When pProductCategory_Fetch executes without a parameter, the @Search parameter's default of NULL allows the WHERE clause to evaluate to true for every row, as follows:

```
EXEC dbo.pProductCategory_Fetch2;
```

Result:

```
ProductCategoryName    ProductCategoryDescription
---------------------- ----------------------------------
Accessory              kite flying accessories
Book                    Outer Banks books
Clothing                OBX t-shirts, hats, jackets
Kite                    a variety of kites, from simple to
                        stunt, to Chinese, to novelty kites
Material                Kite construction material
OBX                     OBX stuff
Toy                     Kids stuff
Video                   stunt kite contexts and lessons,
                        and Outer Banks videos
```

Table-valued parameters

New to SQL Server 2008 are *table-valued parameters (TVPs)*. The basic idea is that a table can be created and populated in the client application or T-SQL and then passed, as a table variable, into a stored procedure or user-defined function. This is no small thing. Chapter 1, "The World of SQL Server," listed TVPs as my favorite new feature for developers and the number two top new feature overall.

In every complex application I've worked on, there's been a requirement that a complex transaction be passed to the database — orders and order details, flights and flight legs, or an object and a dynamic set of attributes. In each case, the complete transaction includes multiple types of items.

Without considering TVPs, there are three traditional ways to solve the problem of how to pass multiple types of items in a transaction to SQL Server — none of them particularly elegant:

- Pass each item in a separate stored procedure call — `AddNewOrder`, `AddNewOrderDetails` — repeatedly for every item, and then `CloseNewOrder`. This method has two primary problems. First, it's very chatty, with multiple trips to the server. Second, if the client does not complete the transaction, a process on the server must clean up the remains of the unfinished transaction.
- Package the entire transaction at the client into XML, pass the XML to SQL Server, and shred the XML into the relational tables. This solution is significantly cleaner than the first method, but there's still the extra work of shredding the data in the server.
- Concatenate any data that includes multiple rows into a comma-delimited string and pass that as a `varchar(max)` parameter into the stored procedure. Like the XML solution, this method does achieve a single stored procedure call for the complex transaction, but it involves even more coding complexity than the XML method and will prove to be difficult to maintain.

Table-valued parameters provide a fourth alternative. A table can be created in ADO.NET 3.5 or in T-SQL and passed into a SQL Server stored procedure or user-defined function.

The following script creates a test order, order detail scenario:

```
USE tempdb;

Create Table dbo.Orders(
  OrderID INT NOT NULL IDENTITY
    Constraint OrdersPK Primary Key,
  OrderDate DateTime,
  CustomerID INT
  );

Create Table dbo.OrderDetails(
  OrderID INT NOT NULL
    Constraint OrderDetailsFKOrders References Orders,
  LineNumber SmallInt NOT NULL,
  ProductID INT
  );
```

NOTE **The chapter file, which may be downloaded from `www.sqlserverbible.com`, includes both the XML solution (not printed here) and the TVP solution (listed here).**

The first step is to define a table type in SQL Server for consistency when creating the TVP:

```
CREATE TYPE OrderDetailsType AS Table (
  LineNumber INT,
  ProductID INT,
  IsNew BIT,
  IsDirty BIT,
  IsDeleted BIT
  );
```

Once the table type is created, it can be seen in Object Explorer in the Database ➪ Programmability ➪ Types ➪ User-Defined Table Types node.

With the table type established, the stored procedure can now be created that references the table type. The table must be defined as the table type name with the READONLY option. The TVP parameter will look like a table variable inside the stored procedure.

Code can reference the data as a normal other data source except that it's read-only. Some have criticized this as a major drawback. I don't see it that way. If I want to modify the data and return it, I think the best way is to return the data as a selected result set.

Here's the stored procedure. It simply returns the data from the TVP so it's easy to see the TVP in action:

```
CREATE
  --alter
PROC OrderTransactionUpdateTVP (
  @OrderID INT OUTPUT,
  @CustomerID INT,
  @OrderDate DateTime,
  @Details as OrderDetailsType READONLY
  )
AS
SET NoCount ON ;
  Begin Try
    Begin Transaction;
    -- If @OrderID is NULL then it's a new order, so Insert Order
    If @OrderID IS NULL
      BEGIN;
        Insert Orders(OrderDate, CustomerID)
          Values (@OrderDate, @CustomerID);
          -- Get OrderID value from insert
        SET @OrderID = Scope_Identity();
      END;

      -- Test view of the data
      SELECT * FROM @Details ;

      Commit Transaction;
  End Try
```

```
    Begin Catch;
      RollBack;
    End Catch
  RETURN;
```

To test table-valued parameters, the following script creates a table variable as the previously defined table type, populates it using the new row constructers, and then calls the stored procedure:

```
Declare @OrderID INT;

DECLARE @DetailsTVP as OrderDetailsType;

INSERT @DetailsTVP (LineNumber,ProductID,IsNew,IsDirty,IsDeleted)
  VALUES
    (5, 101, -1, -1, 0),
    (2, 999,  0, -1, 0),
    (3, null, 0,  0, 0);

exec OrderTransactionUpdateTVP
  @OrderID = @OrderID Output ,
  @CustomerID = '78',
  @OrderDate = '2008/07/24',
  @Details = @DetailsTVP;
```

Result:

```
LineNumber  ProductID   IsNew IsDirty IsDeleted
----------- ----------- ----- ------- ---------
5           101         1     1       0
2           999         0     1       0
3           NULL        0     0       0
```

I've already converted some of my software to TVP and have found that not only does the TVP syntax make sense and simplify a nasty problem with an elegant solution, but TVPs are fast. Under the covers, TVPs leverage SQL Server's bulk insert technology, which is by far the fastest way to move data into SQL Server.

Returning Data from Stored Procedures

SQL Server provides five means of returning data from a stored procedure. A batch can return data via a `SELECT` statement or a `RAISERROR` command. Stored procedures inherit these from batches and add output variables and the `RETURN` command. And, the calling stored procedure can create a table that the called stored procedure populates.

This section walks through the methods added by stored procedures and clarifies their scope and purpose.

Output parameters

Output parameters enable a stored procedure to return data to the calling client procedure. The keyword `OUTPUT` is required both when the procedure is created and when it is called. Within the stored procedure, the output parameter appears as a local variable. In the calling procedure or batch, a variable must have been created to receive the output parameter. When the stored procedure concludes, its current value is passed to the calling procedure's local variable.

Although output parameters are typically used solely for output, they are actually two-way parameters.

Best Practice

Output parameters are useful for returning single units of data when a whole record set is not required. For returning a single row of information, using output parameters is blazingly faster than preparing a record set.

The next code sample uses an output parameter to return the product name for a given product code from the `Product` table in the `OBXKites` sample database. To set up for the output parameter:

1. The batch declares the local variable `@ProdName` to receive the output parameter.
2. The batch calls the stored procedure, using `@ProdName` in the `EXEC` call to the stored procedure.
3. Within the stored procedure, the `@ProductName` output parameter/local variable is created in the header of the stored procedure. The initial value is `NULL` until it is initialized by code.
4. Inside the stored procedure, the `SELECT` statement sets `@ProductName` to '`Basic Box Kite 21 inch`', the product name for the product code '`1001`'.
5. The stored procedure finishes and execution is passed back to the calling batch. The value is transferred to the batch's local variable, `@ProdName`.
6. The calling batch uses the `PRINT` command to send `@ProdName` to the user.

This is the stored procedure:

```
USE OBXKites;
go
CREATE PROC dbo.GetProductName (
  @ProductCode CHAR(10),
  @ProductName VARCHAR(25) OUTPUT
  )
AS
SELECT @ProductName = ProductName
  FROM dbo.Product
  WHERE Code = @ProductCode;
RETURN;
```

This is the calling batch:

```
USE OBXKites;
DECLARE @ProdName VARCHAR(25);
EXEC dbo.GetProductName '1001', @ProdName OUTPUT;
PRINT @ProdName;
```

Result:

```
Basic Box Kite 21 inch
```

Unit Testing

I combine agile development with unit testing when designing and developing a database, using three scripts:

- **Create:** The first script includes all the DDL code and creates the database, tables, and all stored procedures and functions.
- **Sample:** The second script includes the sample data in the form of INSERT...VALUES statements and is used to load the data for unit testing.
- **ProcTest:** The last script executes every procedure, checking the output against what is expected from the sample data.

Sequentially executing the three scripts unit tests every procedure.

Using the Return Command

A RETURN command unconditionally terminates the procedure and returns an integer value to the calling batch or client. Technically, a return can be used with any batch, but it can only return a value from a stored procedure or a function.

When calling a stored procedure, the EXEC command must use a local integer variable if the returned status value is to be captured:

```
EXEC @LocalVariable = StoredProcedureName;
```

I've seen stored procedures in production at different companies that use the return code for everything from success/failure, to the number of rows processed, to the @@error code. Personally, I prefer to use the return code for success/failure, and pass back any other data in parameters, or RAISERROR. The most important consideration is that the database is 100% consistent in the use of RETURN.

The following basic stored procedure returns a success or failure status, depending on the parameter:

```
CREATE PROC dbo.IsItOK (
  @OK VARCHAR(10)
  )
AS
IF @OK = 'OK'
  BEGIN;
  RETURN 0;
  END;
ELSE
  BEGIN;
  RETURN -100;
  END;
```

The calling batch:

```
DECLARE @ReturnCode INT;
EXEC @ReturnCode = dbo.IsItOK 'OK';
PRINT @ReturnCode;
EXEC @ReturnCode = dbo.IsItOK 'NotOK';
PRINT @ReturnCode;
```

Result:

```
0
-100
```

Path and scope of returning data

Any stored procedure has five possible methods of returning data (SELECT, RAISERROR, external table, OUTPUT parameters, and RETURN). Deciding which method is right for a given stored procedure depends on the quantity and purpose of the data to be returned, and the scope of the method used to return the data. The return scope for the five methods is as follows:

- Selected record sets are passed to the calling stored procedure. If the calling stored procedure consumes the result set (e.g., INSERT...EXEC) then the result set ends there. If the calling stored procedure does not consume the result set, then it is passed up to the next calling stored procedure or client.
- RETURN values, and OUTPUT parameters are all passed to local variables in the immediate calling procedure or batch within SQL Server.
- RAISERROR is passed to the calling stored procedure and will continue to bubble up until it is trapped by a TRY...CATCH or it reaches the client application.

If SQL Server Management Studio (the client application) executes a batch that calls stored procedure A, which then calls stored procedure B, there are multiple ways procedure B can pass data back to procedure A or to the client application, as illustrated in Figure 24-2.

FIGURE 24-2

The path and scope of return methods differ among the five possible methods of returning data.

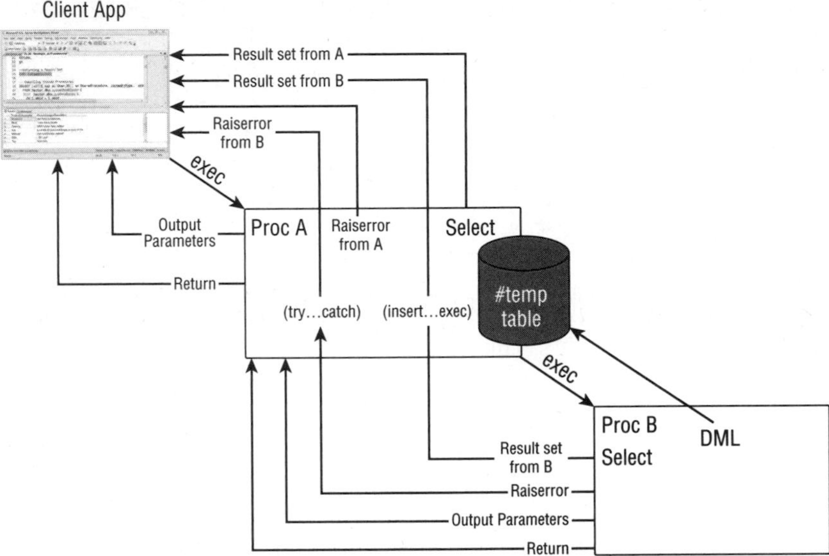

Best Practice

With every returned record set, SQL Server will, by default, also send a message stating the number of rows affected or returned. Not only is this a nuisance, but I have found in my informal testing that it can slow a query by up to 17 percent depending on the query's complexity.

Therefore, get into the habit of beginning every stored procedure with the following code:

```
CREATE PROC MyProc
AS
  SET NOCOUNT ON;
```

Summary

Using stored procedures is a way to save and optimize batches. Stored procedures are compiled and stored in memory the first time they are executed. No method is faster at executing SQL commands, or more popular for moving the processing close to the data. Like a batch, a stored procedure can return a record set by simply executing a `SELECT` command.

The next chapter covers user-defined functions, which combine the benefits of stored procedures with the benefits of views at the cost of portability.

Chapter 25

Building User-Defined Functions

IN THIS CHAPTER

Creating scalar functions

Replacing views with inline table-valued functions

Using complex code within multi-statement table-valued functions to generate a result set

SQL Server 2000 introduced user-defined functions (UDFs), and the SQL Server community was initially slow to adopt them. Nevertheless, UDFs were my personal favorite new feature in SQL Server 2000, and I still use them frequently.

The community discovered that UDFs can be used to embed complex T-SQL logic within a query, and problems that were impossible or required cursors could now be solved with UDFs. The result is that UDFs have become a favorite tool in the toolbox of any serious SQL Server database developer.

The benefits of UDFs can be easily listed:

- UDFs can be used to embed complex logic within a query. This is huge. I've solved several nasty problems using user-defined functions.
- UDFs can be used to create new functions for complex expressions.
- UDFs offer the benefits of views because they can be used within the `FROM` clause of a `SELECT` statement or an expression, and they can be schema-bound. In addition, user-defined functions can accept parameters, whereas views cannot.
- UDFs offer the benefits of stored procedures because they are compiled and optimized in the same way.

The chief argument against developing with user-defined functions has to do with potential performance issues if they're misused. Any function, user-defined or system that must be executed for every row in a `WHERE` clause will cripple performance (see the sidebar on algebra in Chapter 8, "Introducing Basic Query Flow.")

User-defined functions come in three distinct types (as shown in Figure 25-1.) Management Studio groups inline table-valued functions with multi-statement table-valued functions:

- Scalar functions that return a single value

- Inline table-valued functions similar to views
- Multi-statement table-valued functions that build a result set with code

New in 2008

User-defined functions haven't changed much since they were introduced in SQL Server 2000. If you're upgrading to SQL Server 2008 directly from SQL Server 2000, then it's worth knowing that the APPLY keyword, covered later in this chapter, was added in SQL Server 2005.

Microsoft system functions are changing. When they were introduced in SQL Server 2000, system functions were all prefixed with a double colon, such as ::fn_SystemFunction. The double colon has been deprecated and will be disabled in a future version of SQL Server. Instead, system functions are now in the sys. schema — for example, sys.fn_SystemFunction.

FIGURE 25-1

Management Studio's Object Explorer lists all the user-defined functions within a database, organized by table-valued and scalar-valued.

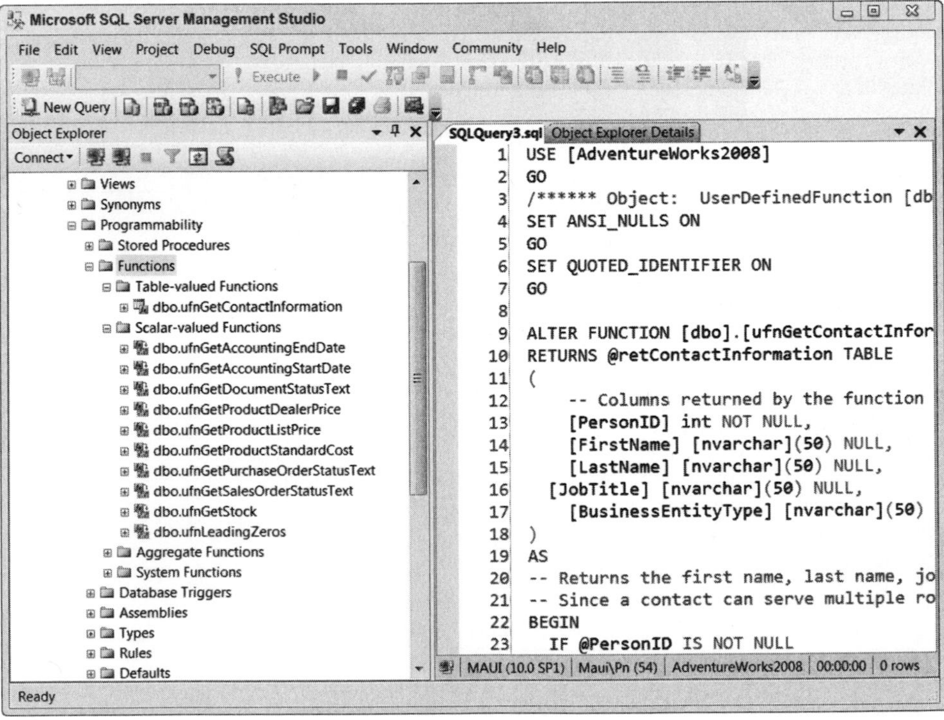

Andrew Novick, who regularly presents about UDFs at user groups and SQL conferences, has compiled a great resource of sample UDFs. His website is `www.novicksoftware.com`**.**

Scalar Functions

A *scalar function* is one that returns a single specific value. The function can accept multiple parameters, perform a calculation, and then return a single value. For example, a scalar function could accept three parameters, perform a calculation, and return the answer.

Within the code of a scalar function, the value is passed back through the function by means of a `RETURN` command. Every possible codepath in the user-defined function should conclude with a `RETURN` command.

Scalar user-defined functions may be used within any expressions in SQL Server, even expressions within check constraints (although I don't recommend scalar function within check constraints because that extends the duration of the transaction and it is difficult to locate and maintain later).

Limitations

The scalar function must be deterministic, meaning it must repeatedly return the same value for the same input parameters. For this reason, nondeterministic functions — such as `newid()` and `rand()` — are not allowed within scalar functions. Writing a UDF to return a random row is out of the question.

User-defined scalar functions are not permitted to update the database or call `DBCC` commands, with the single exception that they may update table variables. They cannot return BLOB (binary large object) data such as `text`, `ntext`, `timestamp`, and `image` data-type variables, nor can they return table variables or `cursor` data types. For error handling, UDFs may not include `TRY...CATCH` or `RAISERROR`.

A user-defined function may call other user-defined functions nesting up to 32 levels deep, or it can call itself recursively up to 32 levels deep before it blows up.

Creating a scalar function

User-defined functions are created, altered, or dropped with the same DDL commands used for other objects, although the syntax is slightly different to allow for the return value:

```
CREATE FUNCTION FunctionName (InputParameters)
RETURNS DataType
AS
BEGIN;
  Code;
  RETURN Expression;
END;
```

The input parameters include a data-type definition and may optionally include a default value similar to stored procedure parameters (parameter = default). Function parameters differ from stored procedure parameters in that even if the default is desired, the parameter is still required to call the function. Parameters with defaults don't become optional parameters. To request the default when calling the function, pass the keyword DEFAULT to the function.

The following user-defined scalar function performs a simple mathematical function. The second parameter includes a default value:

```
CREATE FUNCTION dbo.fsMultiply (@A INT, @B INT = 3)
RETURNS INT
AS
BEGIN;
   RETURN @A * @B;
END;
go

SELECT dbo.fsMultiply (3,4),
       dbo.fsMultiply (7, DEFAULT);
```

Result:

```
----------- -----------
12          21
```

NOTE **While I'm not a stickler for naming conventions (as long as they're consistent), I can understand the practice of prefacing user-defined functions with an f.**

For a more complex scalar user-defined function, the fGetPrice function from the OBXKites sample database returns a single result via an output parameter. It's just a variation of the pGetPrice stored procedure. Both the stored procedure and function determine the correct price for any given date and for any customer discount. Because the task returns a single value, calculating the price is a prime candidate for a scalar user-defined function. As a function, it can be plugged into any query, whereas a stored procedure is more difficult to use as a building block in other code.

The function uses the same internal code as the stored procedure, except that the @CurrPrice is passed back through the final RETURN instead of an output variable. The function uses a default value of NULL for the contact code. Here is the code for the fsGetPrice user-defined scalar function:

```
CREATE FUNCTION fsGetPrice (
  @Code CHAR(10),
  @PriceDate DATETIME,
  @ContactCode CHAR(15) = NULL)
RETURNS MONEY
AS
BEGIN;
  DECLARE @CurrPrice MONEY ;
  DECLARE @DiscountPercent NUMERIC (4,2);
     -- set the discount percent
```

```
    -- if no customer lookup then it's zilch discount
  SELECT @DiscountPercent = CustomerType.DiscountPercent
    FROM dbo.Contact
      JOIN dbo.CustomerType
        ON contact.CustomerTypeID =
            CustomerType.CustomerTypeID
    WHERE ContactCode = @ContactCode;
  IF @DiscountPercent IS NULL
    SET @DiscountPercent = 0;
  SELECT @CurrPrice = Price * (1-@DiscountPercent)
    FROM dbo.Price
       JOIN dbo.Product
         ON Price.ProductID = Product.ProductID
    WHERE Code = @Code
      AND EffectiveDate =
        (SELECT MAX(EffectiveDate)
           FROM dbo.Price
             JOIN dbo.Product
               ON Price.ProductID = Product.ProductID
           WHERE Code = @Code
             AND EffectiveDate <= @PriceDate);
    RETURN @CurrPrice;
END;
```

Calling a scalar function

Scalar functions may be used anywhere within any expression that accepts a single value. User-defined scalar functions must always be called by means of at least a two-part name (owner.name). The following script demonstrates calling the `fGetPrice()` function within `OBXKites`:

```
USE OBXKites;
SELECT dbo.fsGetPrice('1006',CURRENT_TIMESTAMP,DEFAULT),
       dbo.fsGetPrice('1001','5/1/2001',NULL);
```

Result:

```
--------------------- ---------------------
125.9500              14.9500
```

CROSS-REF **The user-defined scalar function `dbo.fTitleCase` is created in Chapter 9, "Data Types, Expressions, and Scalar Functions," and is available on `www.sqlserverbible.com`.**

Inline Table-Valued Functions

The second type of user-defined function, the inline table-valued function, is very similar to a view. Both are wrapped for a stored `SELECT` statement. An inline table-valued user-defined function retains the benefits of a view, and adds parameters. As with a view, if the `SELECT` statement is updateable, then the function will be updateable.

Creating an inline table-valued function

The inline table-valued user-defined function has no BEGIN/END body. Instead, the SELECT statement is returned as a virtual table:

```
CREATE FUNCTION FunctionName (InputParameters)
RETURNS Table
AS
RETURN (Select Statement);
```

The following inline table-valued user-defined function is functionally equivalent to the vEventList view created in Chapter 14, "Projecting Data Through Views."

```
USE CHA2;
go
CREATE FUNCTION ftEventList ()
RETURNS Table
AS
RETURN(
SELECT dbo.CustomerType.Name AS Customer,
   dbo.Customer.LastName, dbo.Customer.FirstName,
   dbo.Customer.Nickname,
   dbo.Event_mm_Customer.ConfirmDate, dbo.Event.Code,
   dbo.Event.DateBegin, dbo.Tour.Name AS Tour,
   dbo.BaseCamp.Name, dbo.Event.Comment
   FROM dbo.Tour
      INNER JOIN dbo.Event
         ON dbo.Tour.TourID = dbo.Event.TourID
      INNER JOIN dbo.Event_mm_Customer
         ON dbo.Event.EventID = dbo.Event_mm_Customer.EventID
      INNER JOIN dbo.Customer
         ON dbo.Event_mm_Customer.CustomerID
               = dbo.Customer.CustomerID
      LEFT OUTER JOIN dbo.CustomerType
         ON dbo.Customer.CustomerTypeID
               = dbo.CustomerType.CustomerTypeID
      INNER JOIN dbo.BaseCamp
         ON dbo.Tour.BaseCampID = dbo.BaseCamp.BaseCampID);
```

Calling an inline table-valued function

To retrieve data through ftEventList, call the function within the FROM portion of a SELECT statement:

```
SELECT LastName, Code, DateBegin
  FROM dbo.ftEventList();
```

Result (abridged):

```
LastName     Code       DateBegin
------------ ---------- ---------------------------
Anderson     01-003     2001-03-16 00:00:00.000
Brown        01-003     2001-03-16 00:00:00.000
Frank        01-003     2001-03-16 00:00:00.000
```

...

Using parameters

An advantage of inline table-valued functions over views is the function's ability to include parameters within the pre-compiled SELECT statement. Views, conversely, do not include parameters, and restricting the result at runtime is typically achieved by adding a WHERE clause to the SELECT statement that calls the view.

The following examples compare adding a restriction to the view to using a function parameter. The following view returns the current price list for all products:

```
USE OBXKites;
go

CREATE VIEW vPricelist
AS
SELECT P.Code, Price.Price
  FROM dbo.Price
    JOIN dbo.Product P
      ON Price.ProductID = P.ProductID
  WHERE EffectiveDate =
      (SELECT MAX(EffectiveDate)
        FROM dbo.Price
        WHERE ProductID = P.ProductID
          AND EffectiveDate <= CURRENT_TIMESTAMP);
```

To retrieve the current price for a single product, the calling SELECT statement adds a WHERE-clause restriction when calling the view:

```
SELECT *
  FROM vPriceList
  WHERE = '1001';
```

Result:

```
Code            Price
--------------- ---------------------
1001            14.9500
```

SQL Server internally creates a new SQL statement from vPricelist and the calling SELECT statement's WHERE-clause restriction and then generates a query execution plan.

In contrast, a function allows the restriction to be passed as a parameter to the SQL SELECT statement:

```
CREATE FUNCTION dbo.ftPriceList (
  @Code CHAR(10) = Null, @PriceDate DateTime)
RETURNS Table
AS
RETURN(
SELECT Code, Price.Price
  FROM dbo.Price
    JOIN dbo.Product P
      ON Price.ProductID = P.ProductID
  WHERE EffectiveDate =
      (SELECT MAX(EffectiveDate)
        FROM dbo.Price
        WHERE ProductID = P.ProductID
          AND EffectiveDate <= @PriceDate)
    AND (Code = @Code
      OR @Code IS NULL)
 );
```

If the function is called with default code, then the price for the entered date is returned for all products:

```
SELECT * FROM dbo.ftPriceList(DEFAULT, '20020220');
```

Result:

```
Code            Price
--------------- ---------------------
1047            6.9500
1049            12.9500
...
```

If a product code is passed in the first input parameter, then the pre-compiled SELECT statement within the function returns the single product row:

```
SELECT * FROM dbo.ftPriceList('1001', '2/20/2002');
```

Result:

```
Code            Price
--------------- --------------
1001            14.9500
```

Correlated user-defined functions

The APPLY command may be used with a table-valued user-defined function so that the UDF accepts a different parameter value for each corresponding row being processed by the main query.

Back in the SQL Server 2000 days, not having this capability was a serious limitation that caused me a considerable amount of time to work around, so I'm pleased to see that Microsoft added the APPLY function in SQL Server 2005.

The APPLY command has two forms. The most common form, the CROSS APPLY, has a confusing name because it operates more like an inner join than a cross join. The CROSS APPLY command will join data from the main query with any table-valued data sets from the user-defined function. If no data is returned from the UDF, then the row from the main query is also not returned, as shown in the following example:

```
USE CHA2;
go
CREATE FUNCTION ftEventList2 (@CustomerID INT)
RETURNS Table
AS
RETURN(
SELECT dbo.CustomerType.Name AS Customer,
   dbo.Customer.LastName, dbo.Customer.FirstName,
   dbo.Customer.Nickname,
   dbo.Event_mm_Customer.ConfirmDate, dbo.Event.Code,
   dbo.Event.DateBegin, dbo.Tour.Name AS Tour,
   dbo.BaseCamp.Name, dbo.Event.Comment
   FROM dbo.Tour
      INNER JOIN dbo.Event
         ON dbo.Tour.TourID = dbo.Event.TourID
      INNER JOIN dbo.Event_mm_Customer
         ON dbo.Event.EventID = dbo.Event_mm_Customer.EventID
      INNER JOIN dbo.Customer
         ON dbo.Event_mm_Customer.CustomerID
               = dbo.Customer.CustomerID
      LEFT OUTER JOIN dbo.CustomerType
         ON dbo.Customer.CustomerTypeID
               = dbo.CustomerType.CustomerTypeID
      INNER JOIN dbo.BaseCamp
         ON dbo.Tour.BaseCampID = dbo.BaseCamp.BaseCampID
  WHERE Customer.CustomerID = @CustomerID
 );

SELECT C.LastName, Code, DateBegin, Tour
  FROM Customer C
    CROSS APPLY ftEventList2(C.CustomerID)
  ORDER BY C.LastName;
```

Result:

```
LastName        Code       DateBegin               Tour
--------------- ---------- ----------------------- ------------------------
Anderson        01-003     2001-03-16 00:00:00.000 Amazon Trek
Anderson        01-006     2001-07-03 00:00:00.000 Bahamas Dive
```

```
Anderson      01-016    2001-11-16 00:00:00.000 Outer Banks Lighthouses
Andrews       01-015    2001-11-05 00:00:00.000 Amazon Trek
Andrews       01-012    2001-09-14 00:00:00.000 Gauley River Rafting
Andrews       01-014    2001-10-03 00:00:00.000 Outer Banks Lighthouses
Bettys        01-013    2001-09-15 00:00:00.000 Gauley River Rafting
Bettys        01-015    2001-11-05 00:00:00.000 Amazon Trek
...
```

The second form, the OUTER APPLY command, operates much like a left outer join. With this usage, rows from the main query are included in the result set regardless of whether the virtual table returned by the user-defined function is empty.

Creating functions with schema binding

All three types of user-defined functions may be created with the significant added benefit of schema binding. Views may be schema bound; in this way, UDFs are like views — both can be schema bound. This is one reason why you might choose a UDF over a stored procedure, as stored procedures cannot be schema bound. Schema binding prevents the altering or dropping of any object on which the function depends. If a schema-bound function references TableA, then columns may be added to TableA, but no existing columns can be altered or dropped, and neither can the table itself.

To create a function with schema binding, add the option after RETURNS and before AS during function creation, as shown here:

```
CREATE FUNCTION FunctionName (Input Parameters)
RETURNS DataType
WITH SCHEMA BINDING
AS
BEGIN;
  Code;
  RETURNS Expression;
END;
```

Schema binding not only alerts the developer that the change will may affect an object, it prevents the change. To remove schema binding so that changes can be made, ALTER the function so that schema binding is no longer included.

Multi-Statement Table-Valued Functions

The multi-statement table-valued user-defined function combines the scalar function's ability to contain complex code with the inline table-valued function's ability to return a result set. This type of function creates a table variable and then populates it within code. The table is then passed back from the function so that it may be used within SELECT statements.

The primary benefit of the multi-statement table-valued user-defined function is that complex result sets may be generated within code and then easily used with a SELECT statement. This enables you to build complex logic into a query and solve problems that would otherwise be very difficult to solve without a cursor.

The APPLY command may be used with multi-statement table-valued user-defined functions in the same way that it's used with inline user-defined functions.

Creating a multi-statement table-valued function

The syntax to create the multi-statement table-valued function is very similar to that of the scalar user-defined function:

```
CREATE FUNCTION FunctionName (InputParamenters)
RETURNS @TableName TABLE (Columns)
AS
BEGIN;
  Code to populate table variable
  RETURN;
END;
```

The following process builds a multi-statement table-valued user-defined function that returns a basic result set:

1. The function first creates a table variable called @Price within the CREATE FUNCTION header.
2. Within the body of the function, two INSERT statements populate the @Price table variable.
3. When the function completes execution, the @Price table variable is passed back as the output of the function.

The ftPriceAvg function returns every price in the Price table and the average price for each product:

```
USE OBXKite;
go

CREATE FUNCTION ftPriceAvg()
RETURNS @Price TABLE
  (Code CHAR(10),
    EffectiveDate DATETIME,
    Price MONEY)
AS
  BEGIN;
    INSERT @Price (Code, EffectiveDate, Price)
      SELECT Code, EffectiveDate, Price
        FROM Product
          JOIN Price
            ON Price.ProductID = Product.ProductID;

    INSERT @Price (Code, EffectiveDate, Price)
      SELECT Code, Null, Avg(Price)
        FROM Product
          JOIN Price
            ON Price.ProductID = Product.ProductID
```

```
        GROUP BY Code;
    RETURN;
  END;
```

Calling the function

To execute the function, refer to it within the FROM portion of a SELECT statement. The following code retrieves the result from the ftPriceAvg function:

```
SELECT *
  FROM dbo.ftPriceAvg();
```

Result:

```
Code   EffectiveDate             Price
------ ------------------------- --------
1001   2001-05-01 00:00:00.000   14.9500
1001   2002-06-01 00:00:00.000   15.9500
1001   2002-07-20 00:00:00.000   17.9500
```

CAUTION **Multi-statement table-valued user-defined functions use tempdb to pass the table variable to the calling query. For many applications this is not a concern, but for high-transaction applications I recommend focusing on the performance of the UDF and, if possible, incorporating the code directly into the calling stored procedure.**

Summary

User-defined functions expand the capabilities of SQL Server objects and open a world of flexibility within expressions and the SELECT statement.

The big ideas from this chapter:

- Scalar user-defined functions return a single value and must be deterministic.
- Inline table-valued user-defined functions are very similar to views, and return the results of a single SELECT statement.
- Multi-statement table-valued user-defined functions use code to populate a table variable, which is then returned.
- The APPLY function can be used to pass data to an inline table-valued UDF or a multi-statement table-valued UDF from the outer query, similar to how a correlated subquery can receive data from the outer query.

T-SQL code can be packaged in stored procedures, user-defined functions, and triggers. The next chapter delves into triggers, specialized T-SQL procedures that fire in response to table-level events.

Chapter 26

Creating DML Triggers

IN THIS CHAPTER

Creating instead of and after triggers

Using the transaction's data within the trigger

Integrating multiple triggers

Building a delete trigger to enforce a single-row delete

Triggers are special stored procedures attached to table events. They can't be directly executed; they fire only in response to an INSERT, UPDATE, or DELETE event on a table. In the same way that attaching code to a form or control event in Visual Basic or Access causes that code to execute on the form or control event, triggers fire on table events. Users can't bypass a trigger; and unless the trigger sends a message to the client, the end-user is unaware of the trigger.

Developing triggers involves several SQL Server topics. Understanding transaction flow and locking, T-SQL, and stored procedures is a prerequisite for developing smooth triggers. Triggers contain a few unique elements and require careful planning, but they provide rock-solid execution of complex business rules and data validation.

Trigger Basics

SQL Server triggers fire once per data-modification operation, not once per affected row. This is different from Oracle, which can fire a trigger once per operation, or once per row. While this may seem at first glance to be a limitation, being forced to develop set-based triggers actually helps ensure clean logic and fast performance.

Triggers may be created for the three table events that correspond to the three data-modification commands: INSERT, UPDATE, and DELETE.

Best Practice

Triggers extend the duration of a transaction, which can lead to locking and blocking problems for high-transaction systems. For data integrity, sometimes a trigger is the best solution, but be aware of the potential performance impact. If the processing can be performed in the abstraction layer with 100 percent certainty, then I'd rather see the code there than in a trigger. If the abstraction layer isn't enforced 100 percent of the time, then the code must exist in a trigger.

SQL Server has two kinds of transaction triggers: *instead of* triggers and *after* triggers. They differ in their purpose, timing, and effect, as detailed in Table 26-1.

CROSS-REF **Database triggers fire on data definition language (DDL) commands —** `CREATE`, `ALTER`, `DROP` **— and are useful for auditing server or database schema changes. For more details, see Chapter 27, "Creating DDL Triggers."**

TABLE 26-1

Trigger Type Comparison

	`Instead of` Trigger	`After` Trigger
DML statement	Simulated but not executed	Executed, but can be rolled back in the trigger
Timing	Before PK and FK constraints	After the transaction is complete, but before it is committed
Number possible per table event	One	Multiple
May be applied to views?	Yes	No
Nested?	Depends on server option	Depends on server option
Recursive?	No	Depends on database option

Transaction flow

Developing triggers requires understanding the overall flow of the transaction; otherwise, conflicts between constraints and triggers can cause designing and debugging nightmares.

Every transaction moves through the various checks and code in the following order:

1. `IDENTITY INSERT` check
2. Nullability constraint

3. Data-type check
4. INSTEAD OF trigger execution. If an INSTEAD OF trigger exists, then execution of the DML stops here. INSTEAD OF triggers are not recursive. Therefore, if the INSERT trigger executes another DML command, then the INSTEAD OF trigger will be ignored the second time around (recursive triggers are covered later in this chapter).
5. Primary-key constraint
6. Check constraints
7. Foreign-key constraint
8. DML execution and update to the transaction log
9. AFTER trigger execution
10. Commit transaction (for more details on commits, see Chapter 66, "Managing Transactions, Locking, and Blocking")

Based on SQL Server's transaction flow, note a few key points about developing triggers:

- An AFTER trigger occurs after all constraints. Because of this, it can't correct data, so the data must pass any constraint checks, including foreign-key constraint checks.
- An INSTEAD OF trigger can circumvent foreign-key problems, but not nullability, data-type, or identity-column problems.
- An AFTER trigger can assume that the data has passed all the other built-in data-integrity checks.
- The AFTER trigger occurs before the DML transaction is committed, so it can roll back the transaction if the data is unacceptable.

Creating triggers

Triggers are created and modified with the standard DDL commands, CREATE, ALTER, and DROP, as follows:

```
CREATE TRIGGER Schema.TriggerName ON Schema.TableName
AFTER | INSTEAD OF [Insert, Update, (and or) Delete]
AS
Trigger Code;
```

The trigger can be fired for any combination of insert, update, or delete events.

Prior to SQL Server 2000, SQL Server had AFTER triggers only. Because no distinction between AFTER and INSTEAD OF was necessary, the old syntax created the trigger FOR INSERT, UPDATE, or DELETE. To ensure that the old FOR triggers will still work, AFTER triggers can be created by using the keyword FOR in place of AFTER.

Although I strongly recommend that triggers be created and altered using scripts and version control, you can view and modify triggers using Management Studio's Object Explorer, as shown in Figure 26-1.

FIGURE 26-1

Object Explorer will list all triggers for any table and may be used to modify the trigger using the context menu.

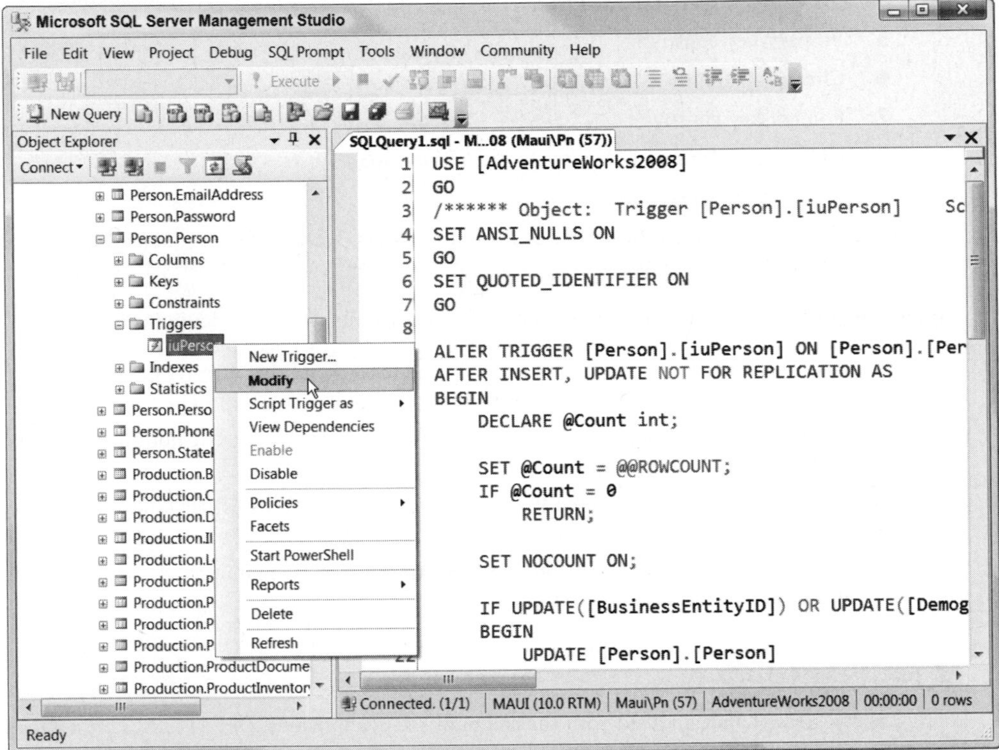

After triggers

A table may have several AFTER triggers for each of the three table events. AFTER triggers may be applied to tables only, not to views.

The traditional trigger is an AFTER trigger that fires after the modification implied by the statement is complete, but before the statement ends and before the transaction is committed. AFTER triggers are useful for the following:

- Complex data validation
- Enforcing complex business rules
- Writing data-audit trails
- Maintaining modified date columns
- Enforcing custom referential-integrity checks and cascading deletes

Best Practice

When planning triggers, consider the most likely path. If the trigger verifies data that will nearly always be accepted, then an AFTER trigger is the best route. That's because the work is completed and the trigger is merely a check.

For inserts, updates, or deletes that are rarely accepted, use an INSTEAD OF trigger, which doesn't actually perform the DML statement's work prior to the trigger's execution.

When you are learning a new programming language, the first program you write is traditionally a "hello world" application that does nothing more than compile the program and prove that it runs by printing "hello world." The following AFTER trigger simply prints 'In the After Trigger' when the trigger is executed:

```
USE Family;

CREATE TRIGGER dbo.TriggerOne ON dbo.Person
AFTER INSERT
AS
PRINT 'In the After Trigger';
```

With the AFTER trigger enforced, the following code inserts a sample row:

```
INSERT dbo.Person(PersonID, LastName, FirstName, Gender)
  VALUES (50, 'Ebob', 'Bill','M');
```

Result:

```
In the After Trigger

(1 row(s) affected)
```

The INSERT worked and the trigger printed its own version of the "hello world" message.

Instead of triggers

INSTEAD OF triggers execute "instead of" (as a substitute for) the submitted transaction, so that the submitted transaction does not occur. It's as if the presence of an INSTEAD OF trigger signals the submitted transaction to be ignored by SQL Server.

As a substitution procedure, each table is limited to only one INSTEAD OF trigger per table event. In addition, INSTEAD OF triggers may be applied to views as well as tables.

Don't confuse INSTEAD OF triggers with BEFORE triggers or before update events. They're not the same. A BEFORE trigger, if such a thing existed in SQL Server, would not interfere with the submitted DML statement execution unless code in the trigger executed a transaction rollback.

INSTEAD OF triggers are useful when it's known that the DML statement firing the trigger will always be rolled back and some other logic will be executed *instead of* the DML statement. For example:

- When the DML statement attempts to update a non-updatable view, the INSTEAD OF trigger updates the underlying tables instead.
- When the DML statement attempts to directly update an inventory table, an INSTEAD OF trigger updates the inventory transaction table instead.
- When the DML statement attempts to delete a row, an INSTEAD OF trigger moves the row to an archive table instead.

The following code creates a test INSTEAD OF trigger and then attempts to INSERT a row:

```
CREATE TRIGGER dbo.TriggerTwo ON dbo.Person
INSTEAD OF INSERT
AS
PRINT 'In the Instead of Trigger';
go

INSERT dbo.Person(PersonID, LastName, FirstName, Gender)
  VALUES (51, 'Ebob', '','M');
```

Result:

```
In the Instead of Trigger

(1 row(s) affected)
```

The result includes the INSTEAD OF trigger's "hello world" declaration and a report that one row was affected. However, selecting personID 51 will prove that no rows were in fact inserted:

```
SELECT LastName
  FROM dbo.Person
  WHERE PersonID = 51;
```

Result:

```
LastName
---------------

(0 row(s) affected)
```

The INSERT statement worked as if one row were affected, although the effect of the INSERT statement was blocked by the INSTEAD OF trigger. The PRINT command was executed instead of the rows being inserted. In addition, the AFTER trigger is still in effect, but its PRINT message failed to print.

Trigger limitations

Given their nature (code attached to tables), triggers have a few limitations. The following SQL commands are not permitted within a trigger:

- CREATE, ALTER, or DROP database
- RECONFIGURE
- RESTORE database or log
- DISK RESIZE
- DISK INIT

Disabling triggers

A user's DML statement can never bypass a trigger, but a system administrator can temporarily disable it, which is better than dropping it and then recreating it if the trigger gets in the way of a data-modification task.

WARNING **Disabling a trigger can only be done for the entire database, not just for the current connection or the current user; this makes disabling a trigger an extremely dangerous instrument. Think twice before making any attempt to bypass an instrument that is used to guard data integrity!**

To temporarily turn off a trigger, use the ALTER TABLE DDL command with the ENABLE TRIGGER or DISABLE TRIGGER option:

```
ALTER TABLE schema.TableName ENABLE or DISABLE TRIGGER
  schema.TriggerName;
```

For example, the following code disables the INSTEAD OF trigger (TriggerOne on the Person table):

```
ALTER TABLE dbo.Person
  DISABLE TRIGGER TriggerOne;
```

To view the enabled status of a trigger, use the OBJECTPROPERTY() function, passing to it the object ID of the trigger and the ExecIsTriggerDisabled option:

```
SELECT OBJECTPROPERTY(
  OBJECT_ID('TriggerOne'),'ExecIsTriggerDisabled');
```

Listing triggers

Because triggers tend to hide in the table structure, the following query lists all the triggers in the database based on the sys.triggers catalog view:

```
SELECT Sc.name + '.' + Ob.name as [table],
  Tr.Name as [trigger],
    CASE (Tr.is_instead_of_trigger )
    WHEN 0 THEN 'after'
    WHEN 1 THEN 'instead of'
  END AS type,
  CASE (Tr.is_disabled)
    WHEN 0 THEN 'enabled'
    WHEN 1 THEN 'disabled'
```

```
END AS status
FROM sys.triggers Tr
  JOIN sys.objects Ob
    ON Tr.parent_id = Ob.object_id
  JOIN sys.schemas Sc
    ON Ob.schema_id = Sc.schema_id
WHERE Tr.Type = 'TR' and Tr.parent_class = 1
ORDER BY Sc.name + '.' + Ob.name, Tr.Name
```

Result:

```
table                          trigger               type        status
------------------------------ --------------------- ----------- ---------
HumanResources.Employee        dEmployee             instead of  enabled
Person.Person                  iuPerson              after       enabled
Production.WorkOrder           iWorkOrder            after       enabled
Production.WorkOrder           uWorkOrder            after       enabled
Purchasing.PurchaseOrderDetail iPurchaseOrderDetail  after       enabled
Purchasing.PurchaseOrderDetail uPurchaseOrderDetail  after       enabled
Purchasing.PurchaseOrderHeader uPurchaseOrderHeader  after       enabled
Purchasing.Vendor              dVendor               instead of  enabled
Sales.SalesOrderDetail         iduSalesOrderDetail   after       enabled
Sales.SalesOrderHeader         uSalesOrderHeader     after       enabled
```

Triggers and security

Only users who are members of the `sysadmin` fixed server role, or are in the `dbowner` or `ddldmin` fixed database roles, or are the tables' owners, have permission to create, alter, drop, enable, or disable triggers.

Code within the trigger is executed assuming the security permissions of the owner of the trigger's table.

Working with the Transaction

A DML `INSERT`, `UPDATE`, or `DELETE` statement causes a trigger to fire. It's important that the trigger has access to the changes being caused by the DML statement so that it can test the changes or handle the transaction. SQL Server provides four ways for code within the trigger to determine the effects of the DML statement. The first two methods are the `update()` and `columns_updated()` functions, which may be used to determine which columns were potentially affected by the DML statement. The other two methods use `deleted` and `inserted` images, which contain the before and after data sets.

Determining the updated columns

SQL Server provides two methods for detecting which columns are being updated. The first is the `UPDATE()` function, which returns `true` for a single column if that column is affected by the DML transaction:

```
IF UPDATE(ColumnName)
```

An INSERT affects all columns, and an UPDATE reports the column as affected if the DML statement addresses the column. The following example demonstrates the UPDATE() function:

```
ALTER TRIGGER dbo.TriggerOne ON dbo.Person
AFTER INSERT, UPDATE
AS
IF Update(LastName)
  BEGIN;
  PRINT 'You might have modified the LastName column';
  END;
ELSE
  BEGIN;
  PRINT 'The LastName column is untouched.';
  END;
```

With the trigger looking for changes to the LastName column, the following DML statement will test the trigger:

```
UPDATE dbo.Person
  SET LastName = 'Johnson'
  WHERE PersonID = 25;
```

Result:

```
You might have modified the LastName column
```

This function is generally used to execute data checks only when needed. There's no reason to test the validity of column A's data if column A isn't updated by the DML statement. However, the UPDATE() function will report the column as updated according to the DML statement alone, not the actual data. Therefore, if the DML statement modifies the data from 'abc' to 'abc', then the UPDATE() will still report it as updated.

The columns_updated() function returns a bitmapped varbinary data type representation of the columns updated (again, according to the DML statement). If the bit is true, then the column is updated. The result of columns_updated() can be compared with integer or binary data by means of any of the bitwise operators to determine whether a given column is updated.

The columns are represented by right-to-left bits within left-to-right bytes. A further complication is that the size of the varbinary data returned by columns_updated() depends on the number of columns in the table.

The following function simulates the actual behavior of the columns_updated() function. Passing the column to be tested and the total number of columns in the table will return the column bitmask for that column:

```
CREATE FUNCTION dbo.GenColUpdated
  (@Col INT, @ColTotal INT)
RETURNS INT
AS
BEGIN;
```

```
-- Copyright 2001 Paul Nielsen
-- This function simulates the Columns_Updated() behavior
DECLARE
  @ColByte INT,
  @ColTotalByte INT,
  @ColBit INT;

  -- Calculate Byte Positions
  SET @ColTotalByte =  1 + ((@ColTotal-1) /8);
  SET @ColByte = 1 + ((@Col-1)/8);
  SET @ColBit = @Col - ((@ColByte-1) * 8);

  RETURN Power(2, @ColBit + ((@ColTotalByte-@ColByte) * 8)-1);
END;
```

To use this function, perform a bitwise AND (&) between columns_updated() and GenColUpdated(). If the bitwise and is equal to GenColUpdated(), then the column in question is indeed updated:

```
...
If COLUMNS_UPDATED()& dbo.GenColUpdated(@ColCounter,@ColTotal) =
@ColUpdatedTemp
```

Inserted and deleted logical tables

SQL Server enables code within the trigger to access the effects of the transaction that caused the trigger to fire. The inserted and deleted logical tables are read-only images of the data. Think of them as views to the transaction log.

The deleted table contains the rows before the effects of the DML statement, and the inserted table contains the rows after the effects of the DML statement, as shown in Table 26-2.

TABLE 26-2

Inserted and Deleted Tables

DML Statement	Inserted Table	Deleted Table
Insert	Rows being inserted	Empty
Update	Rows in the database after the update	Rows in the database before the update
Delete	Empty	Rows being deleted

The inserted and deleted tables have a limited scope. Stored procedures called by the trigger will not see the inserted or deleted tables. The SQL DML statement that originated the trigger can see the inserted and deleted triggers using the OUTPUT clause.

CROSS-REF For more details on the OUTPUT clause, refer to Chapter 15, "Modifying Data."

The following example uses the inserted table to report any new values for the LastName column:

```
ALTER TRIGGER TriggerOne ON Person
AFTER UPDATE
AS
SET NOCOUNT ON;
IF Update(LastName)
  SELECT 'You modified the LastName column to '
    + Inserted.LastName;
  FROM Inserted;
```

With TriggerOne implemented on the Person table, the following update will modify a LastName value:

```
UPDATE Person
  SET LastName = 'Johnson'
  WHERE PersonID = 32;
```

Result:

```
--------------------------------------------------
You modified the LastName column to Johnson
 (1 row(s) affected)
```

Developing multi-row-enabled triggers

Many triggers I see in production are not written to handle the possibility of multiple-row INSERT, UPDATE, or DELETE operations. They take a value from the inserted or deleted table and store it in a local variable for data validation or processing. This technique checks only one of the rows affected by the DML statement — a serious data integrity flaw. I've also seen databases that use cursors to step through each affected row. This is the type of slow code that gives triggers a bad name.

Best Practice

Because SQL is a set-oriented environment, every trigger must be written to handle DML statements that affect multiple rows. The best way to deal with multiple rows is to work with the inserted and deleted tables with set-oriented operations.

A join between the inserted table and the deleted or underlying table will return a complete set of the rows affected by the DML statement. Table 26-3 lists the correct join combinations for creating multi-row-enabled triggers.

TABLE 26-3

Multi-Row-Enabled FROM Clauses

DML Type	FROM Clause
`Insert`	`FROM Inserted`

`Update`	`FROM Inserted`
	`INNER JOIN Deleted`
	`ON Inserted.PK = Deleted.PK`

`Insert, Update`	`FROM Inserted`
	`LEFT OUTER JOIN Deleted`
	`ON Inserted.PK = Deleted.PK`

`Delete`	`FROM Deleted`

The following trigger sample alters `TriggerOne` to look at the `inserted` and `deleted` tables:

```
ALTER TRIGGER TriggerOne ON Person
AFTER UPDATE
AS
SELECT D.LastName + ' changed to ' + I.LastName
  FROM Inserted AS I
    INNER JOIN Deleted AS D
      ON I.PersonID = D.PersonID;
GO

UPDATE Person
  SET LastName = 'Carter'
  WHERE LastName = 'Johnson';
```

Result:

```
-------------------------------------------
Johnson changed to Carter
Johnson changed to Carter
(2 row(s) affected)
```

The following `AFTER` trigger, extracted from the `Family` sample database, enforces a rule that not only must the `FatherID` point to a valid person (that's covered by the foreign key), the person must be male:

```
CREATE TRIGGER Person_Parents
ON Person
AFTER INSERT, UPDATE
AS
```

```
IF UPDATE(FatherID)
  BEGIN;
    -- Incorrect Father Gender
    IF EXISTS(
         SELECT *
           FROM Person
             INNER JOIN Inserted
               ON Inserted.FatherID = Person.PersonID
           WHERE Person.Gender = 'F');
      BEGIN;
        ROLLBACK;
        RAISERROR('Incorrect Gender for Father',14,1);
        RETURN;
     END;
  END;
```

Multiple-Trigger Interaction

Without a clear plan, a database that employs multiple triggers can quickly become disorganized and extremely difficult to troubleshoot.

Trigger organization

In SQL Server 6.5, each trigger event could have only one trigger, and a trigger could apply only to one trigger event. The coding style that was required to develop such limited triggers lingers on. However, since version 7, SQL Server allows multiple AFTER triggers per table event, and a trigger can apply to more than one event. This enables more flexible development styles.

Having developed databases that include several hundred triggers, I recommend organizing triggers not by table event, but by the trigger's task, including the following:

- Data validation
- Complex business rules
- Audit trail
- Modified date
- Complex security

CROSS-REF **To see a complete audit trail trigger, see Chapter 53, "Data Audit Triggers."**

Nested triggers

Trigger nesting refers to whether a trigger that executes a DML statement will cause another trigger to fire. For example, if the Nested Triggers server option is enabled, and a trigger updates TableA, and TableA also has a trigger, then any triggers on TableA will also fire, as demonstrated in Figure 26-2.

FIGURE 26-2

The Nested Triggers configuration option enables a DML statement within a trigger to fire additional triggers.

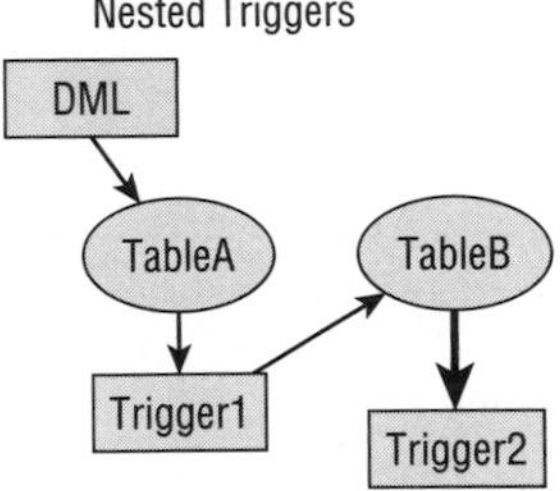

By default, the Nested Triggers option is enabled. Use the following configuration command to disable trigger nesting:

```
EXEC sp_configure 'Nested Triggers', 0;
RECONFIGURE;
```

If the database is developed with extensive server-side code, then it's likely that a DML will fire a trigger, which will call a stored procedure, which will fire another trigger, and so on.

SQL Server triggers have a limit of 32 levels of recursion. Don't blindly assume that nested triggers are safe. Test the trigger's nesting level by printing the `Trigger_NestLevel()` value, so you know how deep the triggers are nesting. When the limit is reached, SQL Server generates a fatal error.

Recursive triggers

A recursive trigger is a unique type of nested `AFTER` trigger. If a trigger executes a DML statement that causes itself to fire, then it's a recursive trigger (see Figure 26-3). If the database recursive triggers option is off, then the recursive iteration of the trigger won't fire. (Note that nested triggers is a server option, whereas recursive triggers is a database option.)

A trigger is considered recursive only if it directly fires itself. If the trigger executes a stored procedure that then updates the trigger's table, then that is an indirect recursive call, which is not covered by the recursive-trigger database option.

Recursive triggers are enabled with the `ALTER DATABASE` command:

```
ALTER DATABASE DatabaseName SET RECURSIVE_TRIGGERS ON | OFF ;
```

Practically speaking, recursive triggers are very rare. I've needed to write a recursive trigger only for production.

One example that involves recursion is a `ModifiedDate` trigger. This trigger writes the current date and time to the modified column for any row that's updated. Using the `OBXKites` sample database, this script first adds a `Created` and `Modified` column to the product table:

```
USE OBXKites;

ALTER TABLE dbo.Product
  ADD
    Created SmallDateTime NOT NULL DEFAULT CURRENT_TIMESTAMP,
    Modified SmallDateTime NOT NULL DEFAULT CURRENT_TIMESTAMP;
```

FIGURE 26-3

A recursive trigger is a self-referencing trigger — one that executes a DML statement that causes itself to be fired again.

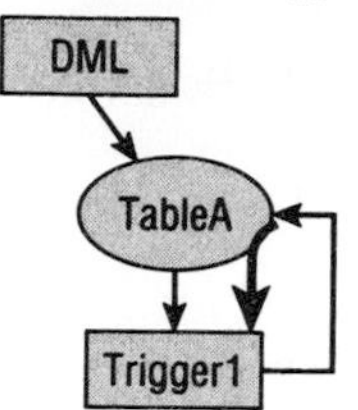

The issue is that if recursive triggers are enabled, then this trigger might become a runaway trigger. Then, after 32 levels of recursion, it will error out.

The trigger in the following example prints the `Trigger_NestLevel()` level. This is very helpful for debugging nested or recursive triggers, but it should be removed when testing has finished. The second `if` statement prevents the `Created` and `Modified` date from being directly updated by the user. If the trigger is fired by a user, then the nest level is 1.

The first time the trigger is executed, the `UPDATE` is executed. Any subsequent executions of the trigger `RETURN` because the trigger nest level is greater than 1. This prevents runaway recursion. Here's the trigger DDL code:

```
CREATE TRIGGER Products_ModifiedDate ON dbo.Product
AFTER UPDATE
AS
IF @@ROWCOUNT = 0
  RETURN;

If Trigger_NestLevel() > 1
  Return;

SET NOCOUNT ON;

PRINT TRIGGER_NESTLEVEL();

If (UPDATE(Created) or UPDATE(Modified))
```

```
Begin;
  Raiserror('Update failed.', 16, 1);
  ROLLBACK;
  Return;
End;

-- Update the Modified date
UPDATE Product
  SET Modified = CURRENT_TIMESTAMP
  WHERE EXISTS
    (SELECT *
     FROM Inserted AS i
     WHERE i.ProductID = Product.ProductID);
```

To test the trigger, the next UPDATE command will cause the trigger to update the Modified column. The SELECT command returns the Created and Modified date and time:

```
UPDATE PRODUCT
  SET [Name] = 'Modified Trigger'
  WHERE Code = '1002';

SELECT Code, Created, Modified
  FROM Product
  WHERE Code = '1002';
```

Result:

```
Code   Created                  Modified
------ ------------------------ ------------------------
1002   2009-01-25 10:00:00.000  2009-06-25 12:02:31.234
```

Recursive triggers are required for replicated databases.

Instead of and after triggers

If a table has both an INSTEAD OF trigger and an AFTER trigger for the same event, then the following sequence is possible:

1. The DML statement initiates a transaction.
2. The INSTEAD OF trigger fires in place of the DML.
3. If the INSTEAD OF trigger executes DML against the same table event, then the process continues.
4. The AFTER trigger fires.

Multiple after triggers

If the same table event has multiple `AFTER` triggers, then they will all execute. The order of the triggers is less important than it may at first seem.

Every trigger has the opportunity to `ROLLBACK` the transaction. If the transaction is rolled back, then all the work done by the initial transaction and all the triggers are rolled back. Any triggers that had not yet fired won't fire because the original DML is aborted by the `ROLLBACK`.

Nevertheless, it is possible to designate an `AFTER` trigger to fire `first` or `last` in the list of triggers. I recommend doing this only if one trigger is likely to roll back the transaction and, for performance reasons, you want that trigger to execute before other demanding triggers. Logically, however, the order of the triggers has no effect.

The `sp_settriggerorder` system stored procedure is used to assign the trigger order using the following syntax:

```
sp_settriggerorder
  @triggername = 'TriggerName',
  @order = 'first' or 'last' or 'none',
  @stmttype = 'INSERT' or 'UPDATE' or 'DELETE'
```

The effect of setting the trigger order is not cumulative. For example, setting `TriggerOne` to `first` and then setting `TriggerTwo` to `first` does not place `TriggerOne` in second place. In this case, `TriggerOne` returns to being unordered.

Transaction-Aggregation Handling

Triggers can maintain denormalized aggregate data.

A common example of this is an inventory system that records every individual transaction in an `InventoryTransaction` table, calculates the inventory quantity on hand, and stores the calculated quantity-on-hand in the `Inventory` table for performance.

CROSS-REF **Index views are another excellent solution to consider for maintaining aggregate data. They're documented in Chapter 64, "Indexing Strategies."**

To protect the integrity of the `Inventory` table, implement the following logic rules when using triggers:

- The quantity on hand in the `Inventory` table should not be updatable by any process other than the inventory transaction table triggers. Any attempt to directly update the `Inventory` table's quantity should be recorded as a manual adjustment in the `InventoryTransaction` table.
- Inserts in the `InventoryTransaction` table should write the current on-hand value to the `Inventory` table.
- The `InventoryTransaction` table should not allow updates. If an error is inserted into the `InventoryTransaction` table, an adjusting entry should be made to correct the error.

The OBXKites database includes a simplified inventory system. To demonstrate transaction-aggregation handling, the following triggers implement the required rules. The first script creates a sample valid inventory item for test purposes:

```
USE OBXKites;

DECLARE
  @ProdID UniqueIdentifier,
  @LocationID UniqueIdentifier;

SELECT @ProdID = ProductID
  FROM dbo.Product
  WHERE Code = 1001;
SELECT @LocationID= LocationID
  FROM dbo.Location
  WHERE LocationCode = 'CH';

INSERT dbo.Inventory (ProductID, InventoryCode, LocationID)
  VALUES (@ProdID,'A1', @LocationID);

SELECT P.Code, I.InventoryCode, I.QuantityOnHand
  FROM dbo.Inventory AS I
    INNER JOIN dbo.Product AS P
      ON I.ProductID = P.ProductID;
```

Result:

```
Code            InventoryCode   QuantityOnHand
--------------- --------------- --------------
1001            A1              0
```

The inventory-transaction trigger

The inventory-transaction trigger performs the aggregate function of maintaining the current quantity-on-hand value in the Inventory table. With each row inserted into the InventoryTransaction table, the trigger updates the Inventory table. The JOIN between the Inserted image table and the Inventory table enables the trigger to handle multiple-row inserts:

```
CREATE TRIGGER InvTrans_Aggregate
ON dbo.InventoryTransaction
AFTER Insert
AS

UPDATE dbo.Inventory
  SET QuantityOnHand += i.Value
  FROM dbo.Inventory AS Inv
    INNER JOIN Inserted AS i
      ON Inv.InventoryID = i.InventoryID;

Return;
```

The next batch tests the InvTrans_Aggregate trigger by inserting a transaction and observing the InventoryTransaction and Inventory tables:

```
INSERT InventoryTransaction (InventoryID, Value)
  SELECT InventoryID, 5
    FROM dbo.Inventory
    WHERE InventoryCode = 'A1';

INSERT InventoryTransaction (InventoryID, Value)
  SELECT InventoryID, -3
    FROM dbo.Inventory
    WHERE InventoryCode = 'A1';

INSERT InventoryTransaction (InventoryID, Value)
  SELECT InventoryID, 7
    FROM dbo.Inventory
    WHERE InventoryCode = 'A1';
```

The following query views the data within the InventoryTransaction table:

```
SELECT i.InventoryCode, it.Value
  FROM dbo.InventoryTransaction AS it
    INNER JOIN dbo.Inventory AS i
      ON i.InventoryID
         = it.InventoryID;
```

Result:

```
InventoryCode   Value
--------------- ------
A1              5
A1              -3
A1              7
```

The InvTrans_Aggregate trigger should have maintained a correct quantity-on-hand value through the inserts to the InventoryTransaction table. Indeed, the next query proves the trigger functioned correctly:

```
SELECT p.Code, i.InventoryCode, i.QuantityOnHand
  FROM dbo.Inventory AS i
    INNER JOIN dbo.Product AS p
      ON i.ProductID = p.ProductID;
```

Result:

```
Code            InventoryCode   QuantityOnHand
--------------- --------------- --------------
1001            A1              9
```

The inventory trigger

The quantity values in the Inventory table should never be directly manipulated. Every quantity adjustment must go through the InventoryTransaction table. However, some users will want to make manual adjustments to the Inventory table. The gentlest solution to the problem is to use server-side code to perform the correct operations regardless of the user's method:

1. An inventory instead of trigger must redirect direct updates intended for the Inventory table, converting them into inserts in the InventoryTransaction table, while permitting the InvTrans_Aggregate trigger to update the Inventory table.
2. The inserts into the InventoryTransaction table then update the Inventory table, leaving the correct audit trail of inventory transactions.

As a best practice, the trigger must accept multiple-row updates. The goal is to undo the original DML UPDATE command while keeping enough of the data to write the change as an INSERT to the InventoryTransaction table:

```
CREATE TRIGGER Inventory_Aggregate
ON Inventory
INSTEAD OF UPDATE
AS
-- Redirect direct updates
If Update(QuantityOnHand)
  BEGIN;
    UPDATE dbo.Inventory
      SET QuantityOnHand = d.QuantityOnHand
      FROM Deleted AS d
        INNER JOIN dbo.Inventory AS i
          ON i.InventoryID = d.InventoryID;

     INSERT dbo.InventoryTransaction
       (Value, InventoryID)
       SELECT
        i.QuantityOnHand - Inv.QuantityOnHand,
        Inv.InventoryID
          FROM dbo.Inventory AS Inv
            INNER JOIN Inserted AS i
              ON Inv.InventoryID = i.InventoryID;
  END;
```

To demonstrate the trigger, the following UPDATE attempts to change the quantity on hand from 9 to 10. The new Inventory_Aggregate trigger traps the UPDATE and resets the quantity on hand back to 9, but it also writes a transaction of +1 to the InventoryTransaction table. (If the InventoryTransaction table had transaction type and comment columns, then the transaction would be recorded as a manual adjustment by user X.) The InventoryTransaction table's InvTrans_Aggregate trigger sees the INSERT and properly adjusts the Inventory .QuantityOnHand to 10:

```
-- Trigger Test
```

```
UPDATE dbo.Inventory
  SET QuantityOnHand = 10
  WHERE InventoryCode = 'A1';
```

Having performed the manual adjustment, the following query examines the InventoryTransaction table:

```
SELECT i.InventoryCode, it.Value
  FROM dbo.InventoryTransaction AS it
    INNER JOIN dbo.Inventory AS i
      ON i.InventoryID
         = it.InventoryID;
```

Sure enough, the manual adjustment of 1 has been written to the InventoryTransaction table:

```
InventoryCode   Value
--------------- --------------------------------
A1              5
A1              -3
A1              7
A1              1
```

As the adjustment was being inserted into the InventoryTransaction table, the InvTrans_Aggregate trigger posted the transaction to the Inventory table. The following query double-checks the QuantityOnHand for inventory item 'A1':

```
SELECT p.Code, i.InventoryCode, i.QuantityOnHand
  FROM dbo.Inventory AS i
    INNER JOIN dbo.Product AS p
      ON i.ProductID = p.ProductID;
```

Result:

```
Code            InventoryCode   QuantityOnHand
--------------- --------------- --------------
1001            A1              10
```

Summary

Triggers are a key feature of client/server databases. It is the trigger that enables the developer to create complex custom business rules that are strongly enforced at the Database Engine level. SQL Server has two types of triggers: INSTEAD OF triggers and AFTER triggers.

Key takeaways about triggers:

- INSTEAD OF triggers cancel the firing DML statement and do something else *instead of* the original DML statement.

- Triggers extend the lock duration, so try to place the code in the abstraction layer before it goes into the trigger.
- Triggers fire once per DML statement, not once per row, so be certain the trigger is set-based and can handle multiple rows well.
- Use the inserted and deleted virtual tables to access the data being modified by the DML statement.
- Logic in triggers can quickly become a rat's nest of code — ad hoc SQL firing a trigger, which calls a stored procedure, which updates two tables, which fires two triggers, one of which updates another table, and so on. This type of system is very expensive to maintain or refactor.

The previous five chapters presented T-SQL programming and described how to package the code within stored procedures, user-defined functions, and triggers. The next chapter, "Creating DDL Triggers," continues the discussion about triggers.

Chapter 27

DDL Triggers

IN THIS CHAPTER

Sometimes the difference between an endless search to identify the problem and readily solving the problem is as simple as knowing what changed. DDL triggers are perfect for auditing server-level and database changes.

Why devote a whole chapter to DDL triggers when the material only takes a few pages? Because I'm convinced every database, development, test, or production, should have a schema audit DDL trigger.

A *trigger* is code that executes as the result of some action. DML triggers fire as the result of DML code — an `INSERT`, `UPDATE`, `DELETE`, or `MERGE` statement. DDL triggers fire as the result of some server-level or database schema–level event — typically data definition language (DDL) code — a `CREATE`, `ALTER`, or `DROP` statement. DML triggers respond to data changes, and DDL triggers respond to schema changes.

Just like DML triggers, DDL triggers can execute T-SQL code and can rollback the event. DML triggers can see into the data transaction using the inserted and deleted tables. Because DDL triggers can respond to so many types of events and commands, the command that fired the trigger and other appropriate information about the event is passed to the trigger in XML using the `EventData()` function.

What's New with DDL Triggers

Introduced in SQL Server 2005, DDL triggers were extended to include logon triggers with SQL Server 2005 SP2. For SQL Server 2008, DDL triggers are a bit more fleshed out and slightly easier to code:

- More trappable events — especially system stored procedures that work like DDL code
- EventData() XML schema is more readily available

Policy-Based Management, new in SQL Server 2008, leverages DDL triggers to enforce policies, so you can be assured that DDL triggers reflect a technology that's here to stay.

Many of the reasons for using a DDL trigger can now be accomplished with more consistency across multiple servers using Policy-Based Management (PBM). For more about PBM see Chapter 40, "Policy-Based Management."

Chapter 54, "Schema Audit Triggers," is a sister chapter to this one that shows how to implement DDL triggers to record every schema change to a database.

Managing DDL Triggers

DDL triggers are easy to manage because they are managed using normal DDL. The most significant factor when developing a DDL trigger is the scope of the trigger — deciding which server- or database-level events will fire a trigger.

Creating and altering DDL triggers

DDL triggers are created or altered using syntax similar to working with DML triggers. The location of the trigger, specified by the ON clause, is either ALL SERVER or DATABASE — literally, the term is DATABASE, not the name of the database. The following code creates a database-level DDL trigger:

```
CREATE TRIGGER SchemaAudit
ON DATABASE
FOR DDL_Database_Level
AS
code
```

Server-level events are a superset of database-level events. They include all database level events. The next example shows a server-level DDL trigger:

```
CREATE TRIGGER SchemaAudit
ON ALL SERVER
```

```
FOR DDL_Server_Level
WITH Options
AS
code
```

Using Management Studio, database triggers are listed under the database's Programmability node in Object Explorer. Server triggers are listed under Server Objects in Object Explorer. Database triggers can be scripted using Object Explorer, but not modified as easily as other programmability objects such as stored procedures. The context menu for DDL triggers does not offer the ➪ modify, or ➪ script to alter options that a stored procedure's context menu includes.

To list the database DDL triggers using code, query the `sys.triggers` and `sys.events` catalog views. Server triggers are found at `sys.server_triggers` and `sys.server_trigger_events`.

Trigger scope

There are dozens of events that can potentially fire a DDL trigger — one for every DDL type of action that can be executed on the server or database. These events are categorized into a hierarchy using event groups. Creating a DDL trigger for an event group will cause the DDL trigger to fire for every event in that group.

DDL triggers can be fired by individual events, such as `create_table`, `create_login`, or `alter_view`. This can be the perfect scope for trapping the specific event. There are 136 server/database-level events, and 33 server-only level events. The full list of DDL events is listed in Books Online — search for "DDL Events."

With so many events, it's sometimes (often) useful to develop a DDL trigger that spans multiple events. Fortunately, Microsoft has combined multiple similar events into a well-designed logical hierarchy of event groups. The "DDL Event Groups" page in Books Online clearly shows the whole hierarchy.

The top, or root, of the hierarchy is the `ddl_events` group, which includes every possible event. The next level has two groups: `ddl_server_level_events` and `ddl_database_level_events`. Each of these groups includes several subgroups and events. Chances are good that when you need to write a DDL trigger, there's a group that matches exactly with the types of events you want to handle.

The following code creates three DDL triggers to demonstrate DDL trigger scope. The first DDL trigger handles all server-level events:

```
CREATE TRIGGER DDL_Server_Level_Sample
ON ALL SERVER
FOR DDL_SERVER_LEVEL_EVENTS
AS
Set NoCount ON
Print 'DDL_Server_Level_Sample DDL Trigger'
```

The second DDL trigger fires for all database-level events:

```
USE tempdb

CREATE TRIGGER DDL_Database_Sample
```

```
ON DATABASE
FOR DDL_DATABASE_LEVEL_EVENTS
AS
Set NoCount ON
Print 'DDL_Database_Sample DDL Trigger'
```

The third DDL trigger traps only `create table` commands:

```
CREATE TRIGGER DDL_Create_Table_Sample
ON DATABASE
FOR Create_Table
AS
Set NoCount ON
Print 'DDL_Create_Table_Sample DDL Trigger'
```

With these three DDL triggers installed, the next few DDL commands demonstrate DDL trigger scope. Creating a new database is a server-level event:

```
Create database Testdb
```

Result:

```
DDL_Server_Level_Sample DDL Trigger
```

Creating a new table will fire the `create table` DDL trigger as well as the general database DDL events trigger:

```
create table Test (col1 INT)
```

Result:

```
DDL_Database_Sample DDL Trigger
DDL_Create_Table_Sample DDL Trigger
```

Dropping the table fires the general database DDL event trigger, but not the specific `create table` event trigger:

```
drop table Test
```

Result:

```
DDL_Database_Sample DDL Trigger
```

DDL triggers and security

The DDL trigger creation options, `ENCRYPTION` and `EXECUTE AS`, both ensure the security of system-level auditing triggers. The following DDL trigger will be encrypted when stored:

```
CREATE TRIGGER DDL_DDL_Level_Sample
ON ALL SERVER
WITH ENCRYPTION
FOR DDL_EVENTS
AS
code
```

As with stored procedures, triggers can be executed under a different security context. Instead of the user who issued the DDL command that caused the DDL trigger to fire, the trigger can execute as one the following security contexts:

- **Caller:** Executes as the person executing the DDL command that fires the DDL trigger
- **Self:** Executes as the person who created the DDL trigger
- **'login_name':** Executes as a specific login

Enabling and disabling DDL triggers

DDL triggers can be turned on and off. This is good because DBAs need an easy way to disable DDL triggers that roll back any schema changes. The following code disables and then enables the `DDL_Create_Table_Sample` trigger:

```
DISABLE TRIGGER DDL_Create_Table_Sample
ON DATABASE;

ENABLE TRIGGER DDL_Create_Table_Sample
ON DATABASE;
```

Removing DDL triggers

Typically, removing an object in SQL Server requires nothing more than a `DROP` command. Because DDL triggers can exist on either the database or server level, slightly more code is required. Also, because of their dual lives (residing in either the database or server), DDL triggers aren't listed in `sys.objects`, nor can their presence be detected using `object_id()`. DDL triggers are listed in `sys.server_triggers` and `sys.triggers` DMVs :

```
IF EXISTS (SELECT *
             FROM sys.server_triggers
             WHERE Name = 'DDL_Server_Level_Sample')
  DROP TRIGGER DDL_Server_Level_Sample ON ALL SERVER

IF EXISTS (SELECT *
             FROM sys.triggers
             WHERE Name = 'DDL_Database_Sample')
  DROP TRIGGER DDL_Database_Sample ON DATABASE
```

Developing DDL Triggers

The code in the trigger is normal T-SQL code. In some way, a DDL trigger is easier to write than a DML trigger because DDL triggers always fire for a single event, whereas DML triggers must handle events with multiple affected rows involving the base table, and the `inserted` and `deleted` virtual tables. The complexity of the DDL trigger results from the fact that the data about the event is in XML.

EventData()

DDL triggers can respond to so many different events that they need some method of capturing data about the event that caused them to fire. DML triggers have the `inserted` and `deleted` virtual tables; DDL triggers have the `EventData()` function. This function returns XML-formatted data about the event. The XML schema varies according to the type of event captured. Note that parts of the XML schema are case sensitive.

Using the `EventData()` function to populate an XML variable, the trigger can use XQuery to investigate the values. Use the XQuery `Value()` method to extract the data from the XML.

The XML schema for event data is at `C:\Program Files\Microsoft SQL Server\100\Tools\Binn\schemas\sqlserver\2006\11\events\events.xsd`

Alternatively, the event schema is published at `http://schemas.microsoft.com/sqlserver`.

The following code example creates a DDL trigger that reads `EventData()` into an XML variable and then selects from the variable to display the data:

```
CREATE TRIGGER DDLTrigger
ON DATABASE
FOR CREATE_TABLE
AS
Set NoCount ON

    DECLARE @EventData XML = EventData()

    SELECT
      @EventData.value
        ('data(/EVENT_INSTANCE/SchemaName)[1]','VARCHAR(50)') as
        'Schema',
      @EventData.value
        ('data(/EVENT_INSTANCE/ObjectName)[1]', 'VARCHAR(50)') as
        'Object',
      @EventData.value
        ('data(/EVENT_INSTANCE/EventType)[1]', 'VARCHAR(50)') as
        'EventType'
```

With the DDL triggers in place, the next comamnd creates a table, which fires the trigger, which examines `EventData`'s XML, and returns the values to the client:

```
CREATE TABLE Test (Col1 INT)
```

Result:

```
Schema               Object      EventType
-------------------- ----------- --------------------
dbo                  Test        CREATE_TABLE
```

For more on XML and working with XQuery, see Chapter 18, "Manipulating XML Data."

Preventing database object changes

DDL triggers can execute code, including executing a transaction rollback command. Such a trigger could prohibit anyone from making server- or database-level changes.

The following code is a simple example of a rollback DDL trigger blocking any stored procedures from being altered in the database:

```
CREATE TRIGGER NoTouchDaProc
ON DATABASE
FOR ALTER_PROCEDURE, DROP_PROCEDURE
AS
Set NoCount ON
Raiserror ('These Procs may not be altered or dropped!',16,1)
Rollback
```

To test the DDL trigger, the next few commands attempt to modify the procedure so it won't print "SQL Rocks!":

```
DROP PROC QuickProc
```

Result:

```
Msg 50000, Level 16, State 1, Procedure NoTouchDaProc, Line 6
These Procs may not be altered or dropped!
Msg 3609, Level 16, State 2, Procedure QuickProc, Line 3
  The transaction ended in the trigger. The batch has been aborted.
```

And

```
ALTER PROC QuickProc
AS
Print 'Oracle Rocks!'
```

Result:

```
Msg 50000, Level 16, State 1, Procedure NoTouchDaProc, Line 6
These Procs may not be altered or dropped!
Msg 3609, Level 16, State 2, Procedure QuickProc, Line 3
The transaction ended in the trigger. The batch has been aborted.
```

With DDL triggers, you can write your own system to prevent object changes that disagree with your shop's policies, but a more strategic solution might be to use SQL Server 2008's new policy-based management feature, documented in Chapter 40, ''Policy-Based Management.''

Summary

DDL triggers provide a safety net — a way to track every change to the schema. The event model that can be tracked is comprehensive and the data available to the trigger using the `EventData()` function and XML is dynamic and complete. Without a doubt, DDL triggers serve their purpose well.

Highlights from this chapter are as follows:

- Server-level DDL triggers can trap any event and are seen in Object Explorer under the Server Objects ➪ Triggers node.
- Database-level DDL triggers exist in the user database, can only fire for database-level events, and are listed in Object Explorer in the [*Database*] ➪ Programmability ➪ Database Triggers node.
- DDL Triggers can fire for any specific DDL event, or for DDL Event Groups — a hierarchy of DDL events.
- Because DDL triggers can fire for such a broad range of events, the `EventData()` function returns XML data about the event.

The next chapter continues the theme of developing with SQL Server with the critical concepts of building out the abstraction layer.

Chapter 28

Building Out the Data Abstraction Layer

IN THIS CHAPTER

- Buying database extensibility
- Building CRUD stored procedures
- Searching stored procedures

I recently blogged the question, "*Why use stored procedures?*" (`http://tinyurl.com/ohauye`) and received a firestorm of replies. I invite you to add your view to the replies — let's attempt the most replies on SQLBlog.com.

My post is based on the discussion of extensibility presented in Chapter 2, "Data Architecture," and makes the point that the abstraction layer should be as permanent as the data it encapsulates. The only effective data abstraction layer is T-SQL.

One of the talks I give at conferences is "7 SQL Server development practices more evil than cursors." What's the number one worst development practice on my list? Ad-hoc SQL, because it violates the abstraction layer and creates a brittle database.

There are many good reasons for wrapping the database in a protective layer of stored procedures:

- **Extensibility:** It's far easier to modify the database when there's a consistent contract to access the database.
- **Usability:** It's far easier for application developers to call a set of stored procedure API calls that return the correct result set than for them to write correct SQL queries.
- **Integrity:** The goal is to get the correct answer to the question. Stored procedures written by database developers will include better queries than ad-hoc SQL written by application developers.
- **Performance:** Moving the lookups and validation closer to the data improves performance.
- **Security:** The best security (tighter control, reduced surface area, limits SQL injection) passes all database access through stored procedures and blocks any direct access to the tables.

The basic idea is that a contract, or API agreement, drives development on both the database and the client side. If the database developers want to refactor the database to increase performance or integrity or add new features that don't change the API, then they are free to do so without affecting any other code. If the application needs a new feature that affects the API, then both sides need to agree on the change and can work on the modification independently until both are ready for integration testing.

CRUD Stored Procedures

Generally speaking, the data abstraction layer needs an interface for each table for each of the following tasks:

- Searching for multiple rows
- Fetching a single row
- Inserting new data
- Updating existing data
- Deleting existing data

Each of these stored procedures should include data validation, transaction control, and error handling.

For lookup tables, some choose to build a more dynamic solution that allows a single set of stored procedures to work against multiple tables by making the table name a parameter and dynamically building the `FROM` clause within the stored procedure.

For examples of these stored procedures, please download the latest version of the `OBXKites` sample database from `www.sqlserverbible.com`.

I'm also considering developing an AutoCRUD utility that will code-gen CRUD stored procedures. If you'd like to use such a utility, please e-mail me at `pauln@sqlserverbible.com`.

Best Practice

When designing the data abstraction layer, avoid using a CRUD matrix approach — CRUD being a list of create, retrieve, update, and delete functions for every table. A data abstraction layer — that is, a set of sprocs for every table — will tend to lock in the schema to that set of sprocs. Instead, design the data abstraction layer as a set of logical contracts that deal with business entities and tasks, even though the contract may involve multiple underlying tables.

For example, design a single interface that involves the inventory, order, and shipping tables. Decreasing the inventory count for an item might involve updating the count field, triggering a reorder, and updating a physical capacity table. You want to ensure that one contract does it all.

Google-Style Search Procedure

Of the standard data abstraction layer stored procedures, the most interesting one is the search stored procedure. This Google-style search comes from Nordic (New Object/Relational Design) version 2.09 — my CodePlex.com project that transforms SQL Server into an object database. It works very well even against millions of rows. Of course, this is a work in progress, so please get the newest version from CodePlex.com or SQLServerBible.com.

The goal of the Google-style search is to enable users to enter as many search words as desired in any order and then find the best results. I've had a lot of fun designing this search routine.

The common solution is to use dynamic SQL to generate a complex `WHERE` clause. This solution instead splits the `@SearchString` words entry into a set-based list and stores the search words in a table variable. The table variable is then joined with several data sources — names, object code, and a list of data extracted from searchable columns. Each time a row is found it's added to the `#Results` table. As the row is found multiple times, its `hits` counter is incremented. At the end, the rows with the most hits are sorted to the top of the list. This search also handles class, workflow state, and association filters, which are shown toward the end of the listing:

```
Create
-- alter
PROC SearchObjects
  (@ClassID INT,
   @StateID INT = NULL,
   @SearchString VARCHAR(500) = NULL,
   @AssocMMID INT = NULL,
   @HASAssoc BIT = 0)
 --  WITH recompile
AS

  CREATE TABLE #Results (
    ObjectID INT NOT NULL PRIMARY KEY ,
    Hits TINYINT NULL
  ) ;

  CREATE TABLE #Classes (ClassID INT)
  INSERT #Classes
      SELECT ClassID
        FROM dbo.SubClassesID(@ClassID)

  DECLARE @SQL NVARCHAR(MAX)

  SET NoCount ON

  IF @SearchString = ''
    SET @SearchString = NULL

  --------------------------------------------------------
  -- All in class search
```

```
IF @SearchString IS NULL AND @StateID IS NULL
    INSERT #Results (ObjectID, Hits)
       SELECT top(1000) o.ObjectID, 1
            FROM Object o
              JOIN #Classes c
                ON o.ClassID = c.ClassID
            --  LEFT JOIN dbo.State s
            --     ON o.StateID = s.StateID
            -- WHERE o.ClassID IN (SELECT ClassID FROM
                 dbo.SubClassesID(@ClassID))

-------------------------------------------------------
-- All in class / state search
IF @SearchString IS NULL AND @StateID IS NOT NULL
    INSERT #Results (ObjectID, Hits)
      SELECT top(1000) o.ObjectID, 1
        FROM Object o
          JOIN #Classes c
            ON o.ClassID = c.ClassID
        --  JOIN dbo.State s
        --     ON o.StateID = s.StateID
        WHERE o.StateID = @StateID

-------------------------------------------------------
-- save search string

IF @SearchString IS NOT NULL
  BEGIN
    DECLARE @User SYSNAME
    SET @User = SUSER_SNAME()
    -- upsert
    UPDATE dbo.SearchHistory
      SET LastViewDate = GETDATE()
      WHERE SearchString = @SearchString
        AND [User] = @User
    IF @@RowCount = 0
      -- rewrite as MERGE
      INSERT dbo.SearchHistory ([User], SearchString, LastViewDate)
        VALUES (@User, @SearchString, GETDATE())

    -------------------------------------------------------
    -- Object Code Exact match / first word entry /
    -- regardless of class / state / associations / anything

    IF Exists(SELECT * FROM dbo.Object WHERE ObjectCode = @SearchString)
      BEGIN
        EXEC SearchObjects_ObjectCode @SearchString
        RETURN
      END
```

```
--------------------------------------------------------
-- Parse out multiple search words
DECLARE @SearchWords TABLE
  (Word VARCHAR(50))

INSERT @SearchWords (Word)
    SELECT String
      FROM dbo.String2Set(LTRIM(RTRIM(@SearchString)))

-- Exact Name2 Match - 1 points
-- should be a merge
INSERT #Results (ObjectID, Hits)
SELECT ObjectID, 1
  FROM @SearchWords W
    JOIN dbo.Object O
      ON O.Name2 = W.Word
    JOIN #Classes C
      ON O.ClassID = C.ClassID
--  GROUP BY ObjectID

-- Exact Name1 Match - 1 points
MERGE #Results AS R
    USING (
            SELECT ObjectID--, COUNT(*) as Hits
              FROM @SearchWords W
                JOIN dbo.Object O
                  ON O.Name1 = W.Word
                JOIN #Classes C
                  ON O.ClassID = C.ClassID
             -- GROUP BY ObjectID
            ) as S
    ON R.ObjectID = S.ObjectID
    WHEN Matched
      THEN UPDATE
            SET Hits += R.Hits
    WHEN NOT MATCHED BY TARGET
      THEN INSERT (ObjectID, Hits)
            VALUES(ObjectID, 1);

  -- Name1 Soundex - 1 point
  MERGE #Results AS R
    USING (
            SELECT ObjectID
              FROM @SearchWords W
                JOIN dbo.Object O
                  ON O.Name1Soundex = Soundex(W.Word)
                JOIN #Classes C
                  ON O.ClassID = C.ClassID) as S
```

```
      ON R.ObjectID = S.ObjectID
      WHEN Matched
        THEN UPDATE
               SET Hits = R.Hits + 1
      WHEN NOT MATCHED BY TARGET
        THEN INSERT (ObjectID, Hits)
               VALUES(ObjectID, 1);

     -- Name2 Soundex - 1 point
    MERGE #Results AS R
      USING (
              SELECT ObjectID
                FROM @SearchWords W
                  JOIN dbo.Object O
                    ON O.Name2Soundex = Soundex(W.Word)
                  JOIN #Classes C
                    ON O.ClassID = C.ClassID) as S
      ON R.ObjectID = S.ObjectID
      WHEN Matched
        THEN UPDATE
               SET Hits = R.Hits + 1
      WHEN NOT MATCHED BY TARGET
        THEN INSERT (ObjectID, Hits)
               VALUES(ObjectID, 1);

    -- Exact Seachable Column Match - 1 point per hit
    MERGE #Results AS R
      USING (
              SELECT ObjectID, COUNT(*) as Hits
                FROM SearchWordList SWL
                  JOIN @SearchWords W
                    ON SWL.Word = W.Word
                  JOIN #Classes C
                    ON O.ClassID = C.ClassID
                 GROUP BY ObjectID) as S
      ON R.ObjectID = S.ObjectID
      WHEN Matched
        THEN UPDATE
               SET Hits = R.Hits + S.Hits
      WHEN NOT MATCHED BY TARGET
        THEN INSERT (ObjectID, Hits)
               VALUES(ObjectID, 1);

END  -- @SearchString IS NOT NULL

---------------------------------------------------------
-- apply filters

IF @StateID IS NOT NULL
```

```
    DELETE #Results
      WHERE ObjectID IN
         (SELECT ObjectID FROM dbo.Object WHERE StateID <> @StateID)

  IF @AssocMMID IS NOT NULL AND @HASAssoc = 0
    DELETE #Results
      WHERE ObjectID NOT IN
        (SELECT ObjectID
          FROM Association A
            JOIN AssociationMatrix AM
              ON A.AssociationMatrixID = AM.AssociationMatrixID
            JOIN dbo.ClassStateAssociationMatrix CSAM
              ON AM.AssociationMatrixID = CSAM.AssociationMatrixID
          WHERE AM.AssociationMatrixMasterID = @AssocMMID)

  IF @AssocMMID IS NOT NULL AND @HASAssoc = 1
    DELETE #Results
      WHERE ObjectID IN
        (SELECT ObjectID
          FROM Association A
            JOIN AssociationMatrix AM
              ON A.AssociationMatrixID = AM.AssociationMatrixID
            JOIN dbo.ClassStateAssociationMatrix CSAM
              ON AM.AssociationMatrixID = CSAM.AssociationMatrixID
          WHERE AM.AssociationMatrixMasterID = @AssocMMID)

  -- Return Results
  SELECT TOP 1000 o.ObjectID, c.ClassID, c.ClassName, s.StateID,
      s.StateName, o.ObjectCode, o.Name1, o.Name2,
      '(' + Cast(r.Hits as VARCHAR(9)) + ') '
          + IsNull(dbo.SearchDetails(o.ObjectID),'') AS Descript,
      o.Created, o.Modified,
      o.Version
    FROM #Results r
      JOIN dbo.Object o
        ON r.ObjectID = o.ObjectID
      JOIN dbo.Class c
        ON o.ClassID = c.ClassID
      LEFT JOIN dbo.State s
        ON o.StateID = s.StateID
    WHERE r.Hits > (Select max(Hits) /2 FROM #Results)
    ORDER BY r.Hits DESC, ObjectCode

RETURN
```

The real point of this procedure isn't the cool way it searches multiple locations for multiple words, but that the API is very stable. I have refactored the search stored procedure dozens of times, sometimes even changing the table structures, without ever having to alter the .NET client code.

Summary

The data abstraction layer is a key component of your database architecture plan and it plays a major role in determining the future extensibility and maintenance costs of the database. Even when it seems that the cost of developing a data abstraction layer and refactoring the existing application code to hit the data abstraction layer instead of tables might be prohibitively expensive, savvy IT or product managers understand that in the long run it will save money — and their job.

Chapter 29

Dynamic SQL and Code Generation

IN THIS CHAPTER

- Executing dynamic SQL
- Parameterized queries
- The risk of SQL injection
- Generating stored procedures
- Alternatives to dynamic SQL

Folks laugh when they hear that my favorite project is based on the notion that T-SQL is a great language for code generation. Nordic (New Object/Relational Design) is essentially a code-generation tool that uses dynamic SQL to create tables, stored procedures, and views. T-SQL works rather well for code generation, thank you.

The term *dynamic SQL* has a couple of differing definitions. Some say it describes any SQL query submitted by a client other than a stored procedure. That's not true. SQL submitted from the client is better known as ad-hoc SQL.

It's more accurate to say that dynamic SQL describes any SQL DML statement assembled dynamically at runtime as a string and then submitted.

Dynamic SQL is very useful for several tasks:

- Multiple possible query criteria can be dynamically assembled into custom `FROM`, `WHERE`, and `ORDER BY` clauses for flexible queries.
- Code can respond to the schema of the database and generate appropriate triggers, CRUD stored procedures, and views.
- Dynamic code can auto-generate very consistent stored procedures.

However, note the following issues when developing dynamic SQL:

- Dynamic SQL that includes user entries in `WHERE` clauses can be open to SQL injection attacks.
- Poorly written dynamic SQL queries often include extra table references and perform poorly.
- T-SQL code that generates T-SQL code can be tricky to debug.

Executing Dynamic SQL

The EXECUTE command, or EXEC for short, creates a new instance of the batch as if it were a batch submitted from some client to the server. While the EXECUTE command is normally used to call a stored procedure, it can also be used to execute a T-SQL query or batch:

```
EXEC[UTE] ('T-SQL batch');
```

For example, the following EXEC command executes a simple SELECT statement:

```
USE Family;
EXEC ('SELECT LastName FROM Person WHERE PersonID = 12;');
```

Result:

```
LastName
---------------
Halloway
```

The security context of executing code should be considered when working with the EXECUTE command. You can control which user account the Database Engine uses to validate permissions on objects that are referenced by the module. The following code uses the EXECUTE AS syntax to execute the query as the user Joe:

```
Use OBXKites
EXECUTE AS 'Joe' select * from Products
```

Another aspect of the EXECUTE command is the capability to execute the code at a linked server, instead of at the local server. The code is submitted to the linked server and the results are returned to the local server:

```
EXECUTE ('Code') AT MAUI/SYDNEY;
```

sp_executeSQL

Another method of executing dynamic SQL is to use the sp_executesql system stored procedure. It offers greater compatibility with complex SQL queries than the straight EXECUTE command. In several situations I have found that the EXECUTE command failed to execute the dynamic SQL, but sp_executesql worked flawlessly:

```
EXEC sp_Executesql
  'T-SQL query',
  'Parameters Definition',
  Parameter, Parameter... ;
```

Parameterized queries

Sometimes it's easier to create queries based on a number of parameters because it usually avoids the need for concatenating strings. The query and the definition must be Unicode strings.

Parameters provide optimization. If the T-SQL query has the same parameters for each execution, then these parameters can be passed to sp_executesql so the SQL query plan can be stored, and future executions will be optimized. The following example executes the same query from the Person table in the Family database, but this example uses parameters (the N before the parameters is necessary because sp_executesql requires Unicode strings):

```
EXEC sp_executesql
  N'SELECT LastName
      FROM Person
      WHERE PersonID = @PersonSelect;',
  N'@PersonSelect INT',
  @PersonSelect = 12;
```

Result:

```
LastName
---------------
Halloway
```

Developing dynamic SQL code

Building a dynamic SQL string usually entails combining a SELECT column's literal string with a more fluid FROM clause and WHERE clause. While any part of the query can be dynamic, normally the SELECT @columns is not.

Once the SQL string is complete, the SQL statement is executed by means of the sp_executesql command. The example that follows builds both custom FROM and WHERE clauses based on the user's requirements.

Within the batch, the NeedsAnd bit variable tracks the need for an And separator between WHERE clause conditions. If the product category is specified, then the initial portion of the SELECT statement includes the required joins to fetch the ProductCategory table. The WHERE clause portion of the batch examines each possible user criterion. If the user has specified a criterion for that column, then the column, with its criterion, is added to the @SQLWhere string.

Real-world dynamic SQL sometimes includes dozens of complex options. The following code listing uses three possible columns for optional user criteria:

```
USE OBXKites;

DECLARE
  @SQL NVARCHAR(1024),
  @SQLWhere NVARCHAR(1024),
  @NeedsAnd BIT,

-- User Parameters
  @ProductName VARCHAR(50),
  @ProductCode VARCHAR(10),
  @ProductCategory VARCHAR(50);

-- Initialize Variables
SET @NeedsAnd = 0;
SET @SQLWhere = '';
```

```
-- Simulate User's Requirements
SET @ProductName = NULL;
SET @ProductCode = 1001;
SET @ProductCategory = NULL;

-- Assembly Dynamic SQL

-- Set up initial SQL Select
IF @ProductCategory IS NULL
  SET @SQL = 'Select ProductName from Product';
ELSE
  SET @SQL = 'Select ProductName
              from Product
                Join ProductCategory
                  on Product.ProductCategoryID
                    = ProductCategory.ProductCategoryID';

-- Build the Dynamic Where Clause
IF @ProductName IS NOT NULL
  BEGIN;
    SET @SQLWhere = 'ProductName = ' + @ProductName;
    SET @NeedsAnd = 1;
  END;

 IF @ProductCode IS NOT NULL
  BEGIN;
    IF @NeedsAnd = 1
      SET @SQLWhere = @SQLWhere + ' and ';
    SET @SQLWhere = 'Code = ' + @ProductCode;
    SET @NeedsAnd = 1;
  END;

IF @ProductCategory IS NOT NULL
  BEGIN;
    IF @NeedsAnd = 1
      SET @SQLWhere = @SQLWhere + ' and ';
    SET @SQLWhere = 'ProductCategory = ' + @ProductCategory;
    SET @NeedsAnd = 1;
  END;

-- Assemble the select and the where portions of the dynamic SQL
IF @SQLWhere <> ''
  SET @SQL = @SQL + ' where ' + @SQLWhere + ';';

~~Use this for testing and debug use only.
PRINT @SQL;
EXEC sp_executesql @SQL
```

The results shown are both the printed text of the dynamic SQL and the data returned from the execution of the dynamic SQL statement:

```
Select ProductName from Product where Code = 1001;
Name
-----------------------------------------------------
Basic Box Kite 21 inch
```

Code generation

The following example may seem a bit complex, but it's a great real-world demonstration of T-SQL code generation. It's from the Nordic database and this is the piece of code that actually generates the stored procedures and views for each class. This procedure is called every time a new class or attribute is added or changed.

A few points in the code worth noting:

- + CHAR(13) + CHAR(10) are added to the generated code to make it more readable.
- The columns (attributes) are built up in the @SQLStr variable first, then the dynamic FROM clause is added.
- A cursor is used to iterate through the columns and tables to build up the custom stored procedure and view.
- The @SQLStr is assembled once and the @GenStr is modified to first create the view and then create the stored procedure.
- The dynamic SQL variables @SQLStr and @GenStr are both declared as NVARCHAR(MAX).
- Any custom columns are automatically enclosed in square brackets to avoid any syntax errors.

Here's the code:

```
-- Gen Class
CREATE
-- alter
PROC dbo.GenClass
  (@ClassName NVARCHAR(50))
AS
  SET NoCount ON

  EXEC IncVersion 'Class Design'

  DECLARE @GenStr NVARCHAR(MAX),
    @SQLStr NVARCHAR(MAX),
    @ClassStr NVARCHAR(MAX),
    @CurrentClass CHAR(100),
```

```
  @CurrentAttrib CHAR(100)

-- SET @ClassName = REPLACE(@ClassName, ' ', '')

-- data from Object Table
SET @SQLStr = 'SELECT o.ObjectID, o.ClassID, c.ClassName, o.StateID, '
  + CHAR(13) + CHAR(10)
  + ' sc.ClassName + '':'' + StateName as [State],'
  + CHAR(13) + CHAR(10)
  + ' ObjectCode as [Object:ObjectCode], Name1 as [Object:Name1],
      Name2 as [Object:Name2],'
  + CHAR(13) + CHAR(10) + ' NULL as [Object:Description],' + CHAR(13)
  + CHAR(10)
  + ' o.Created as [Object:Created], o.Modified as [Object:Modified],
     o.Version as [Object:Version] '
  + CHAR(13) + CHAR(10)

    -- Walk through custom attributes
DECLARE cAttributes CURSOR FAST_FORWARD
  FOR SELECT REPLACE(ClassName, ' ', ''), AttributeName
        FROM dbo.Attributes(@ClassName)
OPEN cAttributes
  -- prime the cursor
FETCH cAttributes INTO @CurrentClass, @CurrentAttrib
WHILE @@Fetch_Status = 0
  BEGIN
    SET @SQLStr = @SQLStr + '   , CC' + RTRIM(@CurrentClass) + '.'
      + RTRIM(@CurrentAttrib) + ' as [' + RTRIM(@CurrentClass) + ':'
      + RTRIM(@CurrentAttrib) + ']' + CHAR(13) + CHAR(10)
     -- fetch next
    FETCH cAttributes INTO @CurrentClass, @CurrentAttrib
  END
CLOSE cAttributes
DEALLOCATE cAttributes

      -- FROM base metadata tables
SET @SQLStr = @SQLStr + ' FROM dbo.Object AS o' + CHAR(13) + CHAR(10)
  + '   JOIN dbo.Class AS c' + CHAR(13) + CHAR(10)
  + '     ON o.ClassID = c.ClassID' + CHAR(13) + CHAR(10)
  + '   LEFT JOIN dbo.State AS s' + CHAR(13) + CHAR(10)
  + '     ON o.StateID = s.StateID' + CHAR(13) + CHAR(10)
  + '   LEFT JOIN dbo.Class AS sc' + CHAR(13) + CHAR(10)
  + '     ON s.ClassID = sc.ClassID' + CHAR(13) + CHAR(10)

    -- FROM dynamic classes
DECLARE cClasses CURSOR FAST_FORWARD
        -- Set Difference Query
  FOR SELECT REPLACE(ClassName, ' ', '')
```

```
          FROM SuperClasses(dbo.GetClassID(@ClassName))
          ORDER BY ClassID DESC
  OPEN cClasses
  FETCH cClasses INTO @CurrentClass  -- prime the cursor
  WHILE @@Fetch_Status = 0
    BEGIN
      SET @SQLStr = @SQLStr + ' JOIN dbo.Obj'
        + RTRIM(@CurrentClass) + ' CC'
        + RTRIM(@CurrentClass) + CHAR(13) + CHAR(10)
        + '    ON o.ObjectID = CC'
        + RTRIM(@CurrentClass) + '.ObjectID' + CHAR(13) + CHAR(10)
      FETCH cClasses INTO @CurrentClass  -- fetch next
    END
  CLOSE cClasses

  DEALLOCATE cClasses

  -- Drop and Create View
  SET @GenStr = 'IF OBJECT_ID(''v' + RTRIM(REPLACE(@ClassName, ' ', ''))
    + ''')' + ' IS NOT NULL DROP VIEW dbo.v'
    + RTRIM(REPLACE(@ClassName, ' ', ''))

  EXEC sp_executesql @GenStr

  SET @GenStr = 'CREATE VIEW dbo.v'
          + RTRIM(REPLACE(@ClassName, ' ', ''))
          + CHAR(13) + CHAR(10)
          + ' AS ' + CHAR(13) + CHAR(10) + @SQLStr

  EXEC sp_executesql @GenStr

      -- Standard Where Clause
  SET @SQLStr = @SQLStr + CHAR(13) + CHAR(10)
    + ' WHERE o.ObjectID = @ObjectID -- weirdness aboundeth'

      -- Drop and Create Proc
  SET @GenStr = 'IF OBJECT_ID(''p' + RTRIM(REPLACE(@ClassName, ' ', ''))
               + ''')' + ' IS NOT NULL DROP PROC dbo.p'
               + RTRIM(REPLACE(@ClassName, ' ', ''))

  EXEC sp_executesql @GenStr

  SET @GenStr = 'CREATE PROC dbo.p'
    + RTRIM(REPLACE(@ClassName, ' ', ''))
    + ' (@ObjectID INT) AS SET NoCount ON ' + @SQLStr

  EXEC sp_executesql @GenStr

RETURN
```

For additional examples of code generation, I recommend walking through the AutoAudit utility — it's all code-generation that creates triggers, views, and user-defined functions. You can download the latest version from CodePlex.com.

Preventing SQL Injection

SQL injection is a hacker technique that appends SQL code to a parameter that is later executed as dynamic SQL. What makes SQL injection so dangerous is that anyone with access to the organization's website who can enter data into a text field can attempt an SQL injection attack. There are several malicious techniques that involve appending code or modifying the WHERE clause. Before learning how to prevent it, it's important to understand how it works, as the following sections explain.

Appending malicious code

Adding a statement terminator, another SQL command, and a comment, a hacker can pass code into the execute string. For example, if the parameter passed in is

```
123'; Delete OrderDetail --
```

the parameter, including the delete DDL command, placed within a dynamic SQL string would execute as a batch:

```
SELECT *
  FROM Customers
  WHERE CustomerID = '123'; Delete OrderDetail --'
```

The statement terminator ends the intended code and the delete command looks to SQL Server like nothing more than the second line in the batch. The quotes would normally cause a syntax error, but the comment line solves that problem for the hacker. The result? An empty OrderDetail table.

Other popular appended commands include running xp_commandshell or setting the sa password.

Or 1=1

Another SQL injection technique is to modify the WHERE clause so that more rows are selected than intended.

If the user enters the following string into the user text box:

```
123' or 1=1 --
```

then the 1=1 (always true) condition is injected into the WHERE clause. The injected hyphens comment out the closing quote:

```
SELECT *
  FROM Customers
  WHERE CustomerID = '123' or 1=1 --'
```

With every row selected by the SQL statement, what happens next depends on how the rest of the system handles multiple rows. Regardless, it's not what should happen.

Password? What password?

Another creative use of SQL injection is to comment out part of the intended code. Suppose the user enters the following in the web form:

```
UserName: Joe' --
Password : who cares
```

The resulting SQL statement might read as follows:

```
SELECT USerID
  FROM Users
  WHERE UserName = 'Joe' --' AND Password = 'who cares'
```

The comment in the username causes SQL Server to ignore the rest of the WHERE clause, including the password condition.

Preventing SQL Server injection attacks

Several development techniques can prevent SQL injection:

- Use EXECUTE AS and carefully define the roles so that statements don't have permission to drop tables.
- Use DRI referential integrity to prevent deleting primary table rows with dependent secondary table rows.
- Never let user input mixed with dynamic SQL in a web form execute as submitted SQL. Always pass all parameters through a stored procedure.
- Check for and reject parameters that include statement terminators, comments, or xp_.
- Test your database using the SQL injection techniques described above.

SQL injection is a real threat. If your application is exposed to entry from the Internet and you haven't taken steps to prevent SQL injection, it's only a matter of time before your database is attacked.

Best Practice

For a flexible search procedure in Nordic, I've started using a new practice of parsing and joining. Rather than build a dynamic SQL WHERE clause, I allow the application to pass in a multiple-word search string. This is parsed into a table with each word becoming a row. The search table is then joined with the various data points that can be searched. For an example of this technique, turn back to Chapter 28, "Building Out the Data Abstraction Layer," or download the latest version of Nordic from CodePlex.com.

Summary

Writing dynamic SQL is definitely taking your game to a higher level. Code that creates code. Cool. Remember to always be aware of whether or not the parameters can be used to enable SQL injection.

A few key points from this chapter:

- Build up the `@SQLStr` variable from the inside out — start with the dynamic list and then append the `SELECT` prolog.
- If the `WHERE` clause is dynamic, chances are good the `FROM` clause will be also.
- When writing dynamic SQL, add a `PRINT` statement to output the `@SQLStr` variable during development. It makes debugging much easier.
- Use `sp_executesql`.
- If there's a different way to make the code flexible, such as the parse and join method mentioned in the best practice, do that instead of dynamic SQL.
- All the standard database integrity features (e.g., foreign keys) help defend against SQL injection.
- Always think like a hacker. Where can an SQL injection string be used to alter the intention of the code?
- Dynamic SQL is not necessarily ad-hoc SQL. Never permit ad-hoc SQL to your database.

This concludes a ten-chapter discussion on T-SQL development that began with "what is a batch" and progressed to the point of code-generating batches. If you're up to writing code-generating code in T-SQL, you're doing well as a SQL Server database developer. I congratulate you.

Part V

Data Connectivity

As much as I'd like to think that Management Studio is the ultimate UI and there's no need for any other interface to SQL Server, the truth is that SQL Server needs to connect to nearly any possible data conduit.

Other than Chapter 5, "Client Connectivity," all the code so far has occurred inside SQL Server. Part V focuses on myriad ways that data can be brought into and synchronized with SQL Server.

Some of the connectivity technologies are well known and familiar technologies like the simple but mighty bulk insert, distributed queries and linked servers, ADO.NET, replication, and Microsoft Access.

Other connectivity technologies are newer. Integration services replaced DTA with SQL Server 2005. Service Broker was also introduced with SQL Server 2005. LINQ and Synch are new with SQL Server 2008.

If SQL Server is the box, then this part busts out of the box and pumps data in and out of SQL Server.

IN THIS PART

Chapter 30

Bulk Operations

Often, DBAs need to load copious amounts of data quickly — whether it's a nightly data load or a conversion from comma-delimited text files. When a few hundred megabytes of data need to get into SQL Server in a limited time frame, a bulk operation is the way to get the heavy lifting done.

XML's popularity may be growing, but its file sizes seem to be growing even faster. XML's data tags add significant bloat to a data file, sometimes quadrupling the file size or more. For very large files, IT organizations are sticking with CSV (also known as comma-delimited) files. For these old standby files, the best way to insert that data is a bulk operation.

In SQL Server, bulk operations pump data directly to the data file according to the following models:

- **Simple recovery model:** No problem with recovery; the transaction log is used for current transactions only.
- **Bulk-logged recovery model:** No problem with recovery; the bulk operation transaction bypasses the log, but then the entire bulk operation's data is still written to the log. One complication with bulk-logged recovery is that if bulk operations are undertaken, point-in-time recovery is not possible for the time period covered by the transaction log. To regain point-in-time recovery, the log has to be backed up. As extent allocations are logged for bulk operations, a log backup after bulk operations will contain *all* the pages from extents that have been added, which results in a large transaction log backup.
- **Full recovery model:** In full recovery model, bulk operations are not performed; the engine does full logging of inserts. To restart the transaction log recoverability process, following the bulk operation, perform a complete backup, and restart the transaction logs.

IN THIS CHAPTER

CROSS-REF For more details on recovery models and how to set them, see Chapter 41, "Recovery Planning." Details on the transaction log are covered in Chapter 66, "Managing Transactions, Locking, and Blocking."

Technically, the `SELECT INTO` syntax is also a bulk-logged operation, and it too bypasses the transaction log. `SELECT INTO` creates a table from the results of a `SELECT` statement; it is discussed in Chapter 15, "Modifying Data."

Bulk insert operations are normally one step of an ETL (extract-transform-load) nightly process. While developing these ETL processes in T-SQL is perfectly acceptable, Integration Services is a strong alternative, and it includes bulk operations. For more details about developing Integration Services solutions, see Chapter 37, "Performing ETL with Integration Services."

CAUTION `Bulk insert` is extremely fast, and I've had good success using it in production environments. My one word of caution is that the data must be clean. Variations in data type, irregular columns, and missing columns will cause trouble.

Bulk operations can be performed with a command prompt using BCP (a command-prompt utility to copy data to and from SQL Server), within T-SQL using the `BULK INSERT` command, or using Integration Services.

Bulk Insert

The `BULK INSERT` command can be used within any T-SQL script or stored procedure to import data into SQL Server. The parameters of the command specify the table receiving the data, the location of the source file, and the options.

To test the `BULK INSERT` command, use the `Address.csv` file that's part of the build script to load the `AdventureWorks` sample database. It's probably already on your hard drive or it can be downloaded from MSDN. The 4MB file has 19,614 rows of address data — that's small by ETL norms.

The following batch bulk inserts from the `Address.csv` file in the `AdventureWorks` directory into the `AWAddress` table:

```
Use Tempdb;

CREATE TABLE AWAddressStaging (
  ID INT,
  Address VARCHAR(500),
  City    VARCHAR(500),
  Region  VARCHAR(500),
  PostalCode VARCHAR(500),
  GUID VARCHAR(500),
  Updated DATETIME
  );
```

```
BULK INSERT AWAddressStaging
  FROM 'C:\Program Files\Microsoft SQL Server\90\Tools\Samples\
          AdventureWorks OLTP\Address.csv'
  WITH (FIRSTROW = 1,ROWTERMINATOR ='\n');
```

On my Dell notebook, the BULK INSERT completes in less than a half-second.

The first thing to understand about BULK INSERT is that every column from the source table is simply inserted directly into the destination table using a one-to-one mapping. The first column from the source file is dumped into the first column of the destination table. Each column lines up. If there are too many columns in the destination table, then it will fail. However, if there are not enough columns in the destination table, then BULK INSERT will work, as the extra data is placed into the bit bucket and simply discarded.

CROSS-REF **The BULK INSERT command won't accept a string concatenation or variable in the FROM parameter, so if you're assembling the string of the file location and the filename, then you need to assemble a dynamic SQL statement to execute the BULK INSERT. Building and executing dynamic SQL is covered in Chapter 29, "Dynamic SQL and Code Generation," which contains many examples.**

Best Practice

Because BULK INSERT is dependent on the column position of both the source file and the destination table, it is best practice to use a view as an abstraction layer between the BULK INSERT command and the table. If the structure of either the source file or the destination table is altered, then modifying the view can keep the BULK INSERT running without having to change the other object's structure.

Another best practice is to BULK INSERT the data into a staging table, check the data, and then perform the rest of the transformations as you merge the data into the permanent tables. As long as you don't mind copying the data twice, this works well.

Bulk Insert Options

In practice, I've always needed to use some options when using BULK INSERT:

- **Field Terminator** specifies the character used to delimit or separate columns in the source file. The default, of course, is a comma, but I've also seen the pipe character (|) used in production.
- **Row Terminator** specifies the character that ends a row in the source file. '\n' means end of row and is the typical setting. However, files from mainframes or other systems sometimes don't use a clean end of line. In these cases, use a hex editor to view the actual end of line characters and specify the row terminator in hex. For example, a hex value of '0A' is coded as follows:

```
ROWTERMINATOR =  '0x0A'
```

- **FirstRow** is useful when specifying whether the incoming file has column headers. If the file does have column headers, then use this option to indicate that the first row of data is actually the second row of the file.
- **TabLock** places an exclusive lock on the entire table and saves SQL Server the trouble of having to lock the table's data pages being created. This option can dramatically improve performance, but at the cost of blocking data readers during the bulk insert. If the bulk insert is part of an ETL into a staging table, then there's no problem, but if it's a bulk insert into a production system with potential users selecting data, then this might not be a good idea. Multiple bulk-import streams can potentially block each other. To prevent this, SQL Server provides a special internal lock, called a bulk-update (BU) lock. To get a BU lock, you need to specify the `TABLOCK` option with each bulk-import stream without blocking other bulk-import streams.
- **Rows per Batch** tells SQL Server to insert *n* number of rows in a single batch, rather than the entire file. Tweaking the batch size can improve performance. I've found that beginning with 100 and then experimenting to find the best size for the particular set of data works best. This helps performance because the logging is done less often. Too many rows, however, often exceed memory cache and may create waits. In my experience, 2,000 rows is often the best number.
- **Max Errors** specifics how many rows can fail before the bulk insert fails. Depending on the business requirement for the data, you may need to set this to zero.
- The **Errorfile** option points to a file that will collect any rows not accepted by the bulk insert operation. This is a great idea and should be used with every `BULK INSERT` command in production.

Other options, which I've never needed in production, include `Check_Constraints`, `CodePage`, `DataFileType`, `Fire_Triggers`, `KeepIdentity`, `KeepNulls`, `Kilobytes_per_batch`, and `Order`. (The best practice of bulk inserting into a staging table and then performing the ETL merge into the permanent tables makes these commands less useful.)

Best Practice

`BULK INSERT` handles columns in the order they appear in the source comma-delimited file, and the columns must be in the same order in the receiving SQL table. Bulk inserting into a view provides a data abstraction layer so that any changes in column order won't break the `BULK INSERT` code.

When developing a `BULK INSERT` statement, it's generally useful to open the source file using Excel and examine the data. Excel often reformats data, so it's best not to save files in Excel. Sorting the data by the columns can help find data formatting anomalies.

BCP

BCP, short for bulk copy program (or bulk copy Porsche — a reference among DBAs to its speed), is a command-line variation of bulk operations. BCP differs from BULK INSERT in that it is command-line executed and can import or export data. It uses many of the same options as BULK INSERT. The basic syntax is as follows:

```
BCP destination table  direction datafile options
```

For the destination, use the server name along with the complete three-part name (server and database.schema.object). For a complete listing of the syntax, just type **BCP** at the command prompt.

Because this is an external program, it needs authorization to connect to SQL Server. You have two options: Use the -P password option and hard-code your password into the batch file script, or omit the -P, in which case it will prompt for a password. Neither is a very good option. You can also use integrated security, which is usually considered the best practice.

NOTE **For straightforward ETL operations, I prefer using T-SQL and BULK INSERT. For complex ETL loads, Integration Services is great. To be frank, I have little use for automating ETL processes using DOS batch scripts and BCP, although Powershell may make a believer of me yet.**

Summary

This chapter explained a specific T-SQL command: BULK INSERT. Bulk operations provide the additional horsepower needed to import massive amounts of data by ignoring the transaction log and pumping the data directly to the table. The downside is that it complicates the recovery plan. The best way to perform a bulk operation is with the BULK INSERT T-SQL command.

The next chapter continues the theme of moving data with a personal favorite of mine, distributed queries — when one SQL Server instance executes a query against a second SQL Server instance.

Chapter 31

Executing Distributed Queries

IN THIS CHAPTER

Data is seldom in one place. In today's distributed world, most new projects enhance, or at least connect to, existing data. That's not a problem; SQL Server can read and write data to most other data sources. Heterogeneous joins can even merge SQL Server data with an Excel spreadsheet.

SQL Server offers several methods for accessing data external to the current database. From simply referencing another local database to executing pass-through queries that engage an Oracle server, SQL Server can handle it.

Distributed Query Concepts

Linking to an external data source is nothing more than configuring the name of the linked server, along with the necessary location and login information, so that SQL Server can access data on the linked server.

Linking is a one-way configuration, as illustrated in Figure 31-1. If Server A links to Server B, then it means that Server A knows how to access and log into Server B. As far as Server B is concerned, Server A is just another user.

If linking a server is a new concept to you, then it could easily be confused with registering a server in Management Studio. As illustrated in Figure 31-1, Management Studio is only communicating with the servers as a client application. Linking the servers enables SQL Server instance A to communicate directly with SQL Server instance B.

Links can be established in Management Studio or with T-SQL code (which could, of course, be created by configuring the link in Management Studio and then generating a script.) The latter has the advantage of repeatability in case a rebuild is necessary, although building the links in code requires more steps.

Best Practice

While SQL Server can handle the technical problems of querying external data, if the two systems are in fact two separate applications, then directly accessing an external data store will likely violate the principle of encapsulation; and coupling the two data stores reduces the flexibility of the architecture. In many IT shops this practice would not be approved. Instead, consider using a middle tier that communicates with each of the two databases.

New in 2008

The syntax and feature set remain the same in SQL Server 2008, but the internal buffer space for distributed queries has been increased for improved performance. Also, the transaction semantics of `INSERT . . . EXECUTE` against a loopback linked server have changed (from not supported to supported as long as MARS is not enabled on the connection).

FIGURE 31-1

A linked server is a one-way direct connection and is not dependent on Management Studio registering the servers. In this diagram, SQL Server instance A sees SQL Server instance B as a linked server, so A can access B's data.

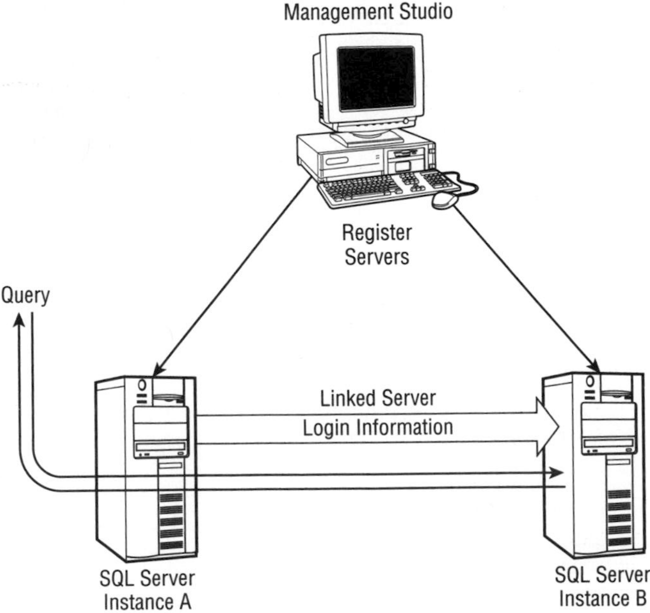

A linked server can be a SQL server or any other data source with either an OLE DB provider or ODBC drivers. Distributed queries can select data and modify it (INSERT, UPDATE, DELETE), according to the features of the OLE DB provider or ODBC driver.

SQL Server queries can reference external data by referring to the preconfigured linked server or specifying the link in the query code.

NOTE **In this chapter, I refer to the two data sources as *local* and *external*. Other descriptions of distributed queries might refer to the same two servers as local and remote, or sending and receiving.**

In a sense, linking to an external data source only moves declaring the link from the query code to a server administration task. Because queries can refer to the named link without concern for the location or security particulars of the link, queries that use linked servers are more portable and easier to maintain than queries that declare the external data source in the query code. If the database is moved to a new server, then once the database administrator creates the appropriate links, the queries will work without modification.

In the case of a distributed query, SQL Server is the client process receiving the results from the external data source. Distributed queries can either pull the data into SQL Server for processing or pass the query to the external data source for processing.

CROSS-REF **There's more than one way to distribute data. You might want to consider replication (see Chapter 36, "Replicating Data") or setting up a standby server as a reporting server (see Chapter 46, "Log Shipping").**

Accessing a Local SQL Server Database

When you access a second database on a single server, the same SQL Server engine processes the data. Therefore, although the data is outside the local database, the query is not actually a distributed query.

A SQL Server query may access another database on the same server by referring to the remote stored procedure, table, or view using the three parts of the four-part name. The complete four-part name is the full address of the object:

```
Server.Database.Schema.Object
```

Because the database is on the same server, the server name is optional. Typically, the tables are in the database owner schema (dbo). If that's the case, then dbo can be assumed:

```
USE CHA2;
SELECT LastName, FirstName
  FROM OBXKites.dbo.Contact;
```

Result (abbreviated):

```
LastName     FirstName
------------ ------------
Adams        Terri
```

```
Andrews      Ed
...
```

The schema can be assumed to be dbo and ignored by just leaving the schema empty. The following query is functionally equivalent to the previous query, but does not specify the schema:

```
SELECT LastName, FirstName
  FROM OBXKites..Contact;
```

CROSS-REF **The code listings in this chapter are also in the `ch31.sql` script file. In addition, the Cape Hatteras Adventures conversion script (`CHA2_Convert.sql`) uses distributed queries exclusively to convert the data from Access and Excel to SQL Server.**

Linking to External Data Sources

SQL Server is also capable of establishing a link to any other data source that is ODBC- or OLE DB-compatible. The link can be created using Management Studio or T-SQL code.

Linking to SQL Server with Management Studio

A link to another SQL Server can be established by means of Management Studio or code. Within Management Studio's Object Explorer, linked servers are listed under the Server Objects node. Selecting Linked Servers ➪ context menu ➪ New Linked Server opens the New Server Properties form (see Figure 31-2).

Selecting the server

In the General tab of the Linked Server Properties form, enter the name of the external SQL Server in the Linked Server field, and click the SQL Server button in the Server Type section. To link to a named instance of SQL Server, enter the instance name as ***server\instance*** without square brackets. In Figure 31-2, the linked server is MAUI\COPENHAGEN.

SQL Server 2008 can link to any other SQL Server 2000, 2005, or 2008 instance, or to a SQL Server 7 server, but SQL Server 2008 won't link to a SQL Server 6.5 server without going through an OBDC driver.

Configuring the logins

The whole point of linked servers is to enable local users to run queries that access data from other data sources. If the external data source is SQL Server, then it will require some type of user authentication, which is accomplished via mapping logins, or for those local users whose logins are not mapped, via setting the default behavior.

The login map will either pass the user along without translating the login name if the Impersonate option is checked, or translate any user's login to a remote login and password if the Impersonate option is not checked. Of course, on the external server, the login must be a valid login and must have been granted security rights in order for the link to be effective.

FIGURE 31-2

The Linked Server Properties form

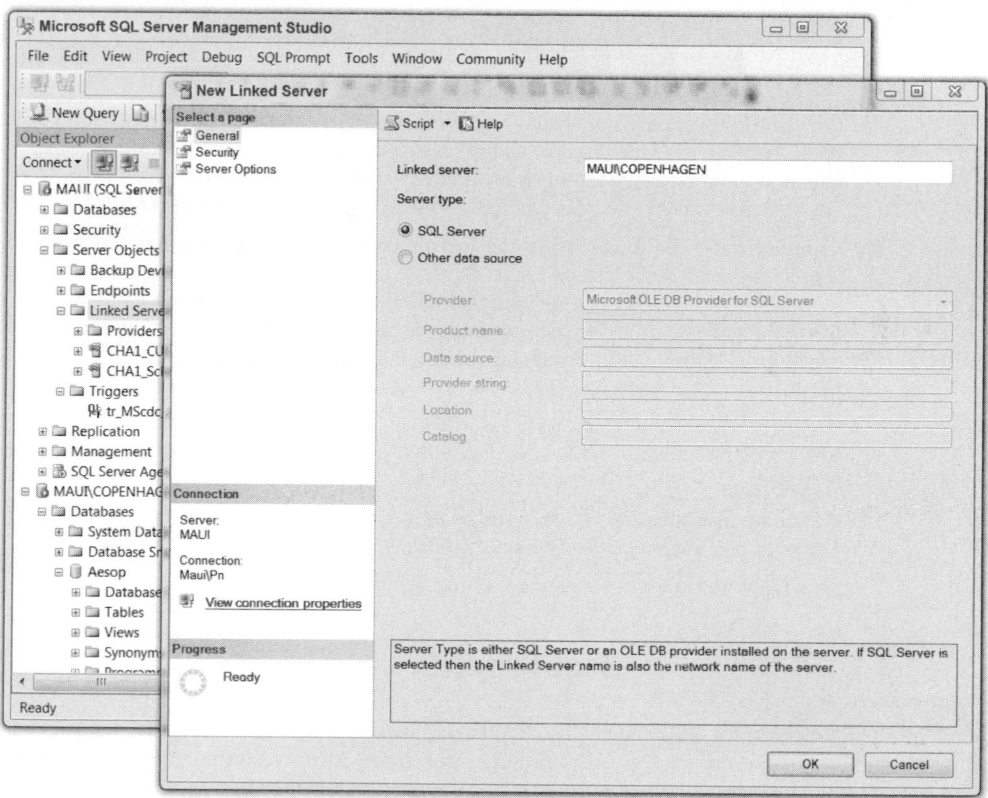

The default connection options for a user not mapped are as follows:

- **Connection — Not be made:** Restricts the ability to run distributed queries to those users in the user mapping list. If a user not on the user mapping list attempts to run a distributed query, then that user will receive the following error:

```
Server: Msg 7416, Level 16, State 1, Line 1
Access to the remote server is denied
  because no login-mapping exists.
```

- **Connection — Be made without using a security context:** This option is for non–SQL Server external data sources and is not useful for SQL Server. SQL Server will attempt to connect as the user SQL without a password. If a user not on the user mapping list attempts to run a distributed query, then that user will receive the following error:

```
OLE DB provider "SQLNCLI10" for linked server "MAUI\COPENHAGEN"
```

```
  returned message "Invalid authorization specification".
Msg 7399, Level 16, State 1, Line 1
The OLE DB provider "SQLNCLI10" for linked server "MAUI\COPENHAGEN"
  reported an error. Authentication failed.
Msg 7303, Level 16, State 1, Line 1
Cannot initialize the data source object of OLE DB provider
  "SQLNCLI10" for linked server "MAUI\COPENHAGEN".
```

For security purposes, connecting without using a security context is the default method when creating the linked server using Management Studio. It won't work with this method, which is the intention. You must manually change it to a security context method that will work — most likely the next method — using the login's current security context.

- **Connection — Be made using the login's current security context:** When the local SQL Server connects to the external SQL Server, it can delegate security, meaning that the local SQL Server will connect to the external SQL Server using the local user's login. Using this method is similar to listing the user and selecting the Impersonate option except that this uses security delegation, and to pass the security context, the login must be the exact same account, not just the same login and password. If an account is deleted, creating a new account with the same name and password isn't sufficient.

  The user's rights and roles for the distributed query will be those assigned at the external SQL Server.

  To use security delegation, every server must run Windows 2000 or greater, and both Kerberos and Active Directory must be enabled.

  This is the default when creating the link using T-SQL code.

Best Practice

For most SQL Server–to–SQL Server distributed queries, the local login's security context is the best linked-server security option because it preserves the user's identity and conforms to the SQL Server security plan. If the infrastructure doesn't support Kerberos and Active Directory, then map the users.

- **Connection — Be made using this security context:** The final option simply assigns every non-mapped local user to a hard-coded external SQL Server login. While this may be the simplest method and might be useful when connecting to simpler data sources like Access or Excel, it's a risk because it allows every local user the same access to the external data source. Be careful hard-coding security contexts; this method won't pass a security audit, and it would certainly exclude the external SQL Server from achieving C2-level security certification. There's no good reason to use this method when connecting to another SQL Server.

Configuring the options

The third tab in the Linked Server Properties form, Server Options, presents the following options, which control how SQL Server expects to receive data from the external SQL Server:

- **Collation Compatible:** Set this option to `true` if the two servers, databases, columns, and queries are using the same collation (character set and sort order).

- **Data Access:** If set to `false`, this option disables distributed queries to the external server.
- **RPC:** If this option is set to `true`, remote procedure calls may be made to the external server.
- **RPC Out:** If this option is set to `true`, remote procedure calls may be made from the external server.
- **Use Remote Collation:** If this option is set to `true`, distributed queries will use the collation of the external SQL Server, rather than that of the local server.
- **Collation Name:** Specifies a collation for distributed queries. This option cannot be chosen if collation compatibility is set.
- **Connection Timeout:** The connection timeout in milliseconds. A value of 0 means to use the default value set with `sp_configure`.
- **Query Timeout:** The distributed query timeout in milliseconds. A value of 0 means to use the default value set with `sp_configure`.
- **Publisher:** The local server is a replication publisher.
- **Distributor:** The local server is a replication distributor.
- **Lazy Schema Validation:** When set, does not pre-validate the schema for distributed queries.
- **Enable Promotion of Distributed Transactions:** Uses DTC for remote stored procedure calls.

Once the link is properly established, a table listing will likely be available in the Catalogs ➪ Database ➪ Tables node under the linked server. The tables listed will be those of the login's default database.

Deleting a linked server in Management Studio will also delete all security-login mappings.

Linking to SQL Server with T-SQL

Management Studio handles the connection and the login information in a single form. However, if you choose to establish a linked server with T-SQL code, then the server connection and the login information are handled by separate commands.

Establishing the link

To configure the server link with code, use the `sp_addlinkedserver` system stored procedure. If the link is being made to another SQL Server, and the name of the other SQL Server instance is acceptable as the name for the link, then only two parameters are required: the linked server name and the server product. The following command creates a link to the `COPENHAGEN` instance on my notebook, `MAUI`.

Note that `sp_addlinkedserver` doesn't actually establish the link: It merely records information SQL Server can use to establish the link later. It doesn't even try to check whether a server with the supplied name exists and can be accessed.

Here's an example:

```
EXEC sp_addlinkedserver
  @server = 'MAUI\COPENHAGEN',
  @srvproduct = 'SQL Server';
```

NOTE **If you run these scripts, then you'll need to change the SQL Server instance names to match your configuration.**

To link to another SQL Server instance using a linked server name other than the SQL Server instance name, two parameters are added. The `provider` parameter must specify 'SQLNCLI', and the `@datasrc` (data source) parameter passes the actual SQL Server instance name of the linked server. The `@srvproduct` (server product) parameter is left blank. The `@server` parameter will be the name by which the linked server will be known. The example links to the `COPENHAGEN` instance on `MAUI`, but the linked server will be referred to as `Yonder` in queries:

```
EXEC sp_addlinkedserver
  @server = 'Yonder',
  @datasrc = 'MAUI\COPENHAGEN',
  @srvproduct = '',
  @provider='SQLNCLI';
```

TIP **The catalog view, `sys.servers`, lists the servers, including linked servers. The system stored procedure, `sp_linkedservers`, also returns information about linked servers:**

```
SELECT [name], product, provider, data_source
  FROM sys.servers
  WHERE is_linked = 1;
```

To drop an existing linked server, which only severs the link and does not affect the external server, use the `sp_dropserver` system stored procedure:

```
EXEC sp_dropserver @server = 'Yonder';
```

If any login mappings exist for the linked server, they too will be dropped.

Distributed security and logins

In Management Studio, the security issue is broken down into two parts: login mapping and what to do with non-mapped logins. T-SQL uses the `sp_addlinkedsrvlogin` system stored procedure to handle both parts, as follows:

```
EXEC sp_addlinkedsrvlogin
  @rmtsrvname = 'rmtsrvname',
  @useself = 'useself', (default True)
  @locallogin = 'locallogin', (default Null)
  @rmtuser = 'rmtuser', (default Null)
  @rmtpassword = 'rmtpassword' (default Null);
```

If the linked server was added using T-SQL instead of Management Studio, then the security option for non-mapped logins is already configured to use the login's current security context.

If the `@locallogin` is `null`, then the setting applies to all non-mapped users. The `@useself` option is the same as impersonate.

The following stored procedure call enables the `SQL2008VPC\Pn` login to access the `SQL2008VPC\London` server as the `sa` user with the password `P@s$w0rd`:

```
EXEC sp_addlinkedsrvlogin
  @rmtsrvname = 'MAUI\COPENHAGEN',
  @useself = 'FALSE',
  @locallogin = 'MAUI\Pn',
  @rmtuser = 'sa',
  @rmtpassword = 'P@s$w0rd';
```

The next example sets all non-mapped users to connect using their own security context (the recommended option). The local user is `null`, so this linked server login applies to all non-mapped users. The `@useself` option is not specified, so the default setting, `true`, will apply, causing the users to use their local security context. This is the default setting, so you'll only need this code if you want to return to the default setting:

```
EXEC sp_addlinkedsrvlogin
  @rmtsrvname = 'MAUI\COPENHAGEN';
```

The third example will prevent all non-mapped users from executing distributed queries. The second parameter, `@useself`, is set to `false`, and the mapping user login and password are left as `null`:

```
EXEC sp_addlinkedsrvlogin 'SQL2008VPC\London', 'false';
```

The catalog view, `sys.linked_logins`, lists the logins. The system stored procedure, `sp_helplinkedsrvlogin`, also returns information about linked logins:

```
SELECT ls.[Name], dp.[Name]
  FROM sys.servers ls
    JOIN sys.linked_logins ll
      ON ls.server_id = ll.server_id
   JOIN sys.database_principals dp
     ON ll.local_principal_id = dp.principal_id
  WHERE Is_Linked = 1;
```

To drop a linked server login, use the `sp_droplinkedsrvlogin` system stored procedure:

```
EXEC sp_droplinkedsrvlogin
  @rmtsrvname = 'rmtsrvname', (no default)
  @locallogin = 'locallogin'  (no default);
```

The following code example will remove the `SQL2008VPC\Pn` login that's mapped to `SQL2008VPC\London`:

```
EXEC sp_droplinkedsrvlogin
  @rmtsrvname = 'SQL2008VPC\London',
  @locallogin = 'SQL2008VPC\Pn';
```

To remove the non-mapped user's default mapping, run the same procedure but specify a `null` local login, as follows:

```
EXEC sp_droplinkedsrvlogin 'SQL2008VPC\London', NULL;
```

Linked server options

The linked server options shown in the Server Options tab of the Linked Server Properties form may be set in code using the sp_serveroption system stored procedure. The procedure must be called once for each option setting:

```
EXEC sp_serveroption
  @server = 'server',
  @optname = 'option_name',
  @optvalue = 'option_value';
```

The options are the same as those in the form (but in lowercase for case-sensitive collation, and in some cases spelled slightly differently) with the addition of lazy schema validation, which disables the checking of the table schema for distributed queries. You may want to use lazy schema validation when you're sure of the schema but want to reduce network overhead.

TIP **The catalog view, sys.servers, returns the linked server's options. The system stored procedure, sp_helpserver, also returns information about linked servers:**

```
SELECT *
  FROM sys.servers
  WHERE Is_Linked = 1;
```

Linking with non–SQL Server data sources

If the external data source isn't SQL Server, then SQL Server can likely still access the data. It depends on the availability and the features of the ODBC drivers or OLE DB providers. SQL Server uses OLE DB for external data, and several OLE DB providers are included with SQL Server. If for some reason OLE DB isn't available for the external data source, then use the "Microsoft OLE DB Provider for ODBC Drivers" provider. Nearly every data-source type has an ODBC driver.

NOTE **Besides the connection information listed in BOL in the sp_addlinkedserver (Transact-SQL) page, a *great* list of connection strings for dozens of databases, to be used with the ODBC data source, can be found at www.connectionstrings.com.**

To set up the linked server, either with code or via Management Studio, a data source (or location) and possibly a provider string to supply additional information are required, in addition to the name of the linked server, the provider name, and the product name. Some common data-source settings are listed in Table 31-1.

NOTE **Microsoft and Oracle don't cooperate with each other when developing drivers. Therefore, if connecting with Oracle is an important part of your application, then I recommend using a high-performance third-party driver.**

As two examples of linking to non–SQL Server data sources, the Cape Hatteras Adventures sample database uses distributed queries to pull data from both Access and Excel. The sample database models a typical small business that is currently using Access and Excel to store its customer list and schedule.

TABLE 31-1

Other Common Data Source Settings

Link to	OLE DB Provider	Provider Name	Data Source
ODBC data source	Microsoft OLE DB Provider for ODBC	`MSDASQL`	System DSN of the ODBC data source (Alternately, Provider string = ODBC connection string)
MS Access	Microsoft OLE DB Provider for Jet	`Microsoft.Jet.OLEDB.4.0`	Database File Location
Excel	Microsoft OLE DB Provider for Jet	`Microsoft.Jet.OLEDB.4.0`	Spreadsheet File Location (also req. Provider string = "Excel 5.0"
Oracle	Microsoft OLE DB Provider for Oracle	`MSDAORA`	SQL*Net alias for Oracle database
Oracle v8 +	Oracle Provider for OLE DB	`OraOLEDB.Oracle`	Alias for the Oracle database

As of this writing, Microsoft had still not yet released an x64-bit version of `Microsoft.Jet.OLEDB.4.0`, making working with distributed queries to Access or Excel difficult at best.

Linking to Excel

The code samples used in this section are taken directly from the `CHA2_Convert.sql` script, which moves the data from the old version 1 (Access and Excel) to version 2 (SQL Server). The Cape Hatteras Adventures folks have been keeping their tour schedule in Excel, as shown in Figure 31-3.

Within Excel, each spreadsheet page and named range appears as a table when accessed from an external data provider. Within Excel, the named ranges are set up by means of the Insert ➪ Name ➪ Define menu command. Excel's Define Name dialog is used to create new named ranges and to edit the existing named ranges. The `CHA1_Schedule` spreadsheet has five named ranges (as shown in Figure 31-4), which overlap much like SQL Server views. Each of the five named ranges appears as a table when SQL Server links to the spreadsheet. SQL Server will automatically pick up on column headers and use them as column names. SQL Server can `SELECT`, `INSERT`, `UPDATE`, and `DELETE` rows just as if this table were a SQL Server table.

The following code sample sets up the Excel spreadsheet as a linked server:

```
EXEC sp_addlinkedserver
  @server = 'CHA1_Schedule',
  @provider = 'Microsoft.Jet.OLEDB.4.0',
```

```
@datasrc = 'C:\SQLServerBible\CHA1_Schedule.xls',
@provstr = 'Excel 5.0';
```

Excel spreadsheets are not multi-user spreadsheets. SQL Server can't perform a distributed query that accesses an Excel spreadsheet while that spreadsheet is open in Excel.

Linking to MS Access

Not surprisingly, SQL Server links easily to MS Access databases. SQL Server uses the OLE DB Jet provider to connect to Jet and request data from the MS Access `.mdb` file.

FIGURE 31-3

Prior to the conversion to SQL Server, the Cape Hatteras Adventures company was managing its tour schedule in the CHA1_Schedule.xls spreadsheet.

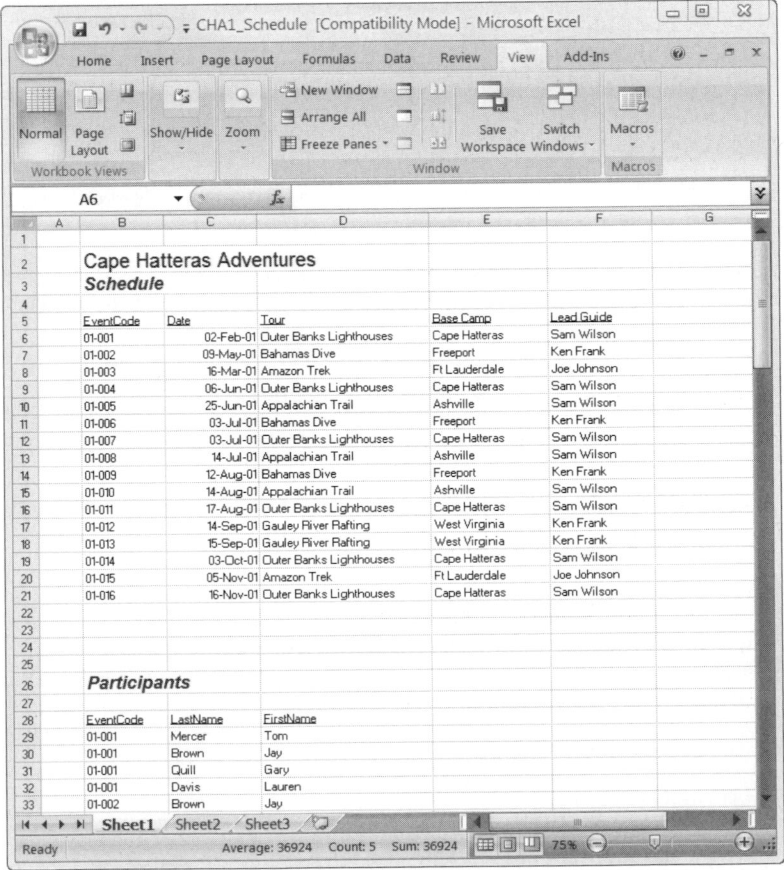

FIGURE 31-4

Tables are defined within the Excel spreadsheet as named ranges. The CHA1_Schedule spreadsheet has five named ranges.

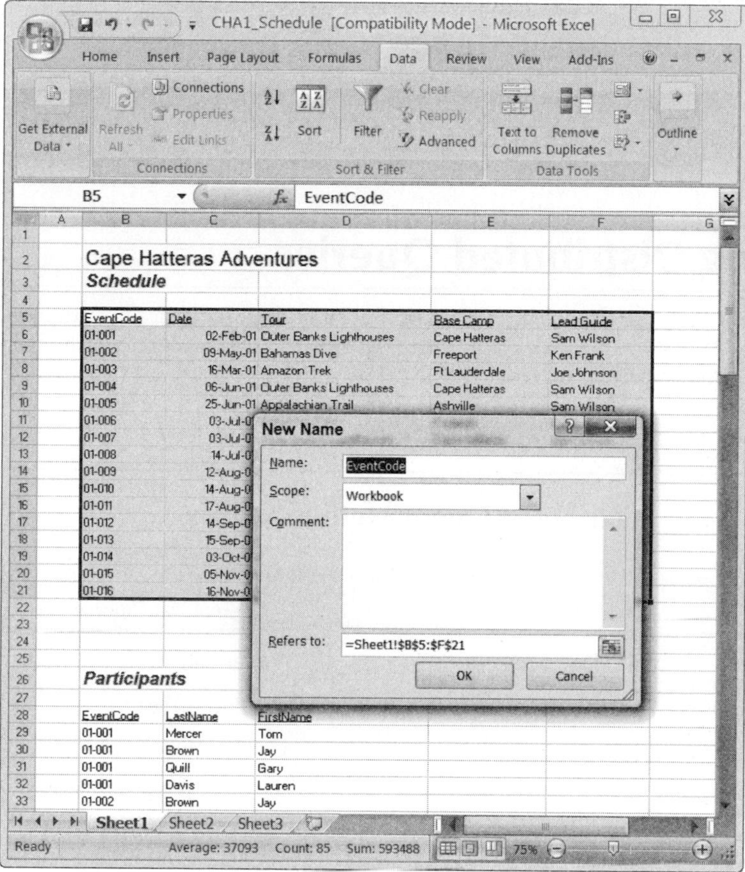

Because Access is a database, there's no trick to preparing it for linking, as there is with Excel. Each Access table will appear as a table under the Linked Servers node in Management Studio.

The Cape Hatteras Adventures customer/prospect list was stored in Access prior to upsizing the database to SQL Server. The following code from the `CHA2_Convert.sql` script links to the `CHA1_Customers.mdb` Access database so SQL Server can retrieve the data and populate the SQL Server tables:

```
EXEC sp_addlinkedserver
  'CHA1_Customers',
```

```
    'Access 2003',
    'Microsoft.Jet.OLEDB.4.0',
    'C:\SQLServerBible\CHA1_Customers.mdb';
```

If you are having difficulty with a distributed query, one of the first places to check is the security context. Excel expects that connections do not establish a security context, so the non-mapped user login should be set to no security context:

```
EXEC sp_addlinkedsrvlogin
  @rmtsrvname = 'CHA1_Schedule',
  @useself  = 'false';
```

Developing Distributed Queries

Once the link to the external data source is established, SQL Server can reference the external data within queries. Table 31-2 shows the four basic syntax methods that are available, which differ in query-processing location and setup method.

TABLE 31-2

Distributed Query Method Matrix

Link Setup	Query-Execution Location	
	Local SQL Server	External Data Source (Pass-Through)
Linked Server	Four-part name	Four-part name `OpenQuery()`
Ad Hoc Link Declared in the Query	`OpenDataSource()`	`OpenRowSet()`

Distributed queries and Management Studio

Management Studio doesn't supply a graphic method for initiating a distributed query. There's no way to drag a linked server or remote table into the Query Designer. However, the distributed query can be entered manually in the SQL pane and then executed as a query.

Using the Query Editor, the name of the linked server can be dragged from the Object Explorer to the Query Editor.

Distributed views

Views are saved SQL `SELECT` statements. While I don't recommend building a client/server application based on views, they are useful for ad hoc queries. Because most users (and even developers) are unfamiliar with the various methods of performing distributed queries, wrapping a distributed query inside a view might be a good idea.

Local-distributed queries

A local-distributed query sounds like an oxymoron, but it's a query that pulls the external data into SQL Server and then processes the query at the local SQL Server. Because the processing occurs at the local SQL Server, local-distributed queries use T-SQL syntax and are sometimes called T-SQL distributed queries.

Using the four-part name

If the data is in another SQL Server, then a complete four-part name is required:

```
Server.Database.Schma.ObjectName
```

The four-part name may be used in any SELECT or data-modification query. On my writing computer is a second instance of SQL Server called [SQL2008RC0\London]. The object's owner name is required if the query accesses an external SQL Server.

The following query retrieves the Person table from the SQL2 instance:

```
SELECT LastName, FirstName
  FROM [SQL2008RC0\London].Family.dbo.Person;
```

Result:

```
LastName        FirstName
--------------- ---------------
Halloway        Kelly
Halloway        James
```

When performing an INSERT, UPDATE, or DELETE command as a distributed query, either the four-part name or a distributed query function must be substituted for the table name. For example, the following SQL code, extracted from the CHA2_Convert.sql script that populates the CHA2 sample database, uses the four-part name as the source for an INSERT command. The query retrieves base camps from the Excel spreadsheet and inserts them into SQL Server:

```
INSERT BaseCamp(Name)
  SELECT DISTINCT [Base Camp]
    FROM CHA1_Schedule...[Base_Camp]
    WHERE [Base Camp] IS NOT NULL;
```

If you've already executed CHA2_Convert.sql and populated your copy of CHA2, then you may want to re-execute CHA2_Create.sql in order to start with an empty database.

As another example of using the four-part name for a distributed query, the following code updates the Family database on the second SQL Server instance:

```
UPDATE [SQL2008RC0\London].Family.dbo.Person
  SET LastName = 'Wilson'
  WHERE PersonID = 1;
```

OpenDataSource()

Using the OpenDataSource() function is functionally the same as using a four-part name to access a linked server, except that the OpenDataSource() function defines the link within the function instead of referencing a pre-defined linked server. While defining the link in code bypasses the linked server requirement, if the link location changes, then the change will affect every query that uses OpenDataSource(). In addition, OpenDataSource() won't accept variables as parameters.

The OpenDataSource() function is substituted for a server in the four-part name and may be used within any DML statement.

The syntax for the OpenDataSource() function seems simple enough:

```
OPENDATASOURCE ( provider_name, init_string )
```

However, there's more to it than the first appearance betrays. The init string is a semicolon-delimited string containing several parameters (the exact parameters used depend on the external data source and are not described here; see Books Online for a full overview). The potential parameters within the init string include data source, location, extended properties, connection timeout, user ID, password, and catalog. The init string must define the entire external data-source connection, and the security context, within a function. No quotes are required around the parameters within the init string. The common error committed in building OpenDataSource() distributed queries is mixing the commas and semicolons.

If OpenDataSource() is connecting to another SQL Server using Windows authentication, then authentication delegation via Kerberos security is required.

A relatively straightforward example of the OpenDataSource() function is using it as a means of accessing a table within another SQL Server instance:

```
SELECT FirstName, Gender
  FROM OPENDATASOURCE(
        'SQLOLEDB',
        'Data Source=SQL2008VPC\London;User ID=Joe;Password=j'
        ).Family.dbo.Person;
```

Result:

```
FirstName       Gender
--------------- ------
Adam            M
Alexia          F
```

The following example of a distributed query that uses OpenDataSource() references the Cape Hatteras Adventures sample database. Because an Access location contains only one database and the tables don't require the owner to specify the table, the database and owner are omitted from the four-part name:

```
SELECT ContactFirstName, ContactLastName
  FROM OPENDATASOURCE(
    'Microsoft.Jet.OLEDB.4.0',
```

```
'Data Source =
     C:\SQLServerBible\CHA1_Customers.mdb'
  )...Customers;
```

Result:

```
ContactFirstName    ContactLastName
------------------- --------------------
Neal                Garrison
Melissa             Anderson
Gary                Quill
```

To illustrate using OpenDataSource() in an update query, the following query example will update any rows inside the CHA1_Schedule.xls Excel 2000 spreadsheet. A named range was previously defined as Tours '=Sheet1!$E$5:$E$24', which now appears to the SQL query as a table within the data source. Rather than update an individual spreadsheet cell, this query performs an UPDATE operation that affects every row in which the tour column is equal to Gauley River Rafting and updates the Base Camp column to the value Ashville.

The distributed SQL Server query will use OLE DB to call the Jet engine, which will open the Excel spreadsheet file. Because the spreadsheet is opened by a user, the file is now unavailable to anyone else. Excel is a single-user database. The OpenDataSource() function supplies only the server name in a four-part name; as with Access, the database and owner values are omitted:

```
UPDATE OpenDataSource(
    'Microsoft.Jet.OLEDB.4.0',
    'Data Source=C:\SQLServerBible\CHA1_Schedule.xls;
    User ID=Admin;Password=;Extended properties=Excel 5.0'
    )...Tour
  SET [Base Camp] = 'Ashville'
  WHERE Tour = 'Gauley River Rafting';
```

Figure 31-5 illustrates the query execution plan for the distributed UPDATE query, beginning at the right with a Remote Scan operation that returns all 19 rows from the Excel named range. The data is then processed within SQL Server. The details of the Remote Update logical operation reveal that the distributed UPDATE query actually updated only two rows.

To complete the example, the following query reads from the same Excel spreadsheet and verifies that the update took place. Again, the OpenDataSource() function is only pointing the distributed query to an external server:

```
SELECT *
  FROM OpenDataSource(
    'Microsoft.Jet.OLEDB.4.0',
    'Data Source=C:\SQLServerBible\CHA1_Schedule.xls;
    User ID=Admin;Password=;Extended properties=Excel 5.0'
    )...Tour
  WHERE Tour = 'Gauley River Rafting';
```

FIGURE 31-5

The query execution plan for the distributed query using OpenDataSource()

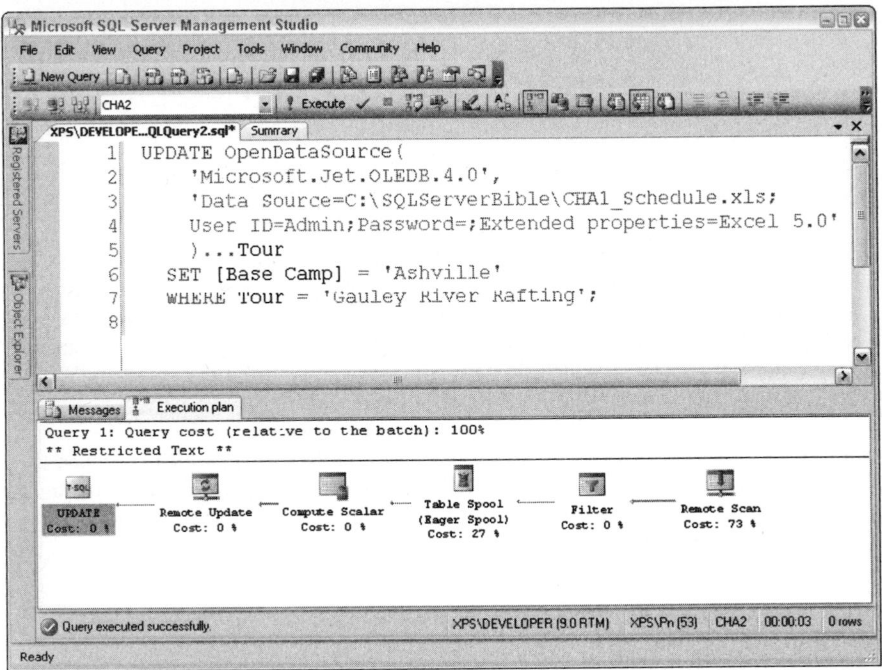

Result:

```
Base Camp        Tour
---------------- ----------------------
Ashville         Gauley River Rafting
Ashville         Gauley River Rafting
```

Pass-through distributed queries

A pass-through query executes a query at the external data source and returns the result to SQL Server. The primary reason for using a pass-through query is to reduce the amount of data being passed from the server (the external data source) and the client (SQL Server). Rather than pull a million rows into SQL Server so that it can use 25 of them, it may be better to select those 25 rows from the external data source.

Be aware that the pass-through query will use the query syntax of the external data source. If the external data source is Oracle or Access, then PL/SQL or Access SQL must be used in the pass-through query.

In the case of a pass-through query that modifies data, the remote data type determines whether the update is performed locally or remotely:

- When another SQL Server is being updated, the remote SQL Server will perform the update.
- When non–SQL Server data is being updated, the data providers determine where the update will be performed. Often, the pass-through query merely selects the correct rows remotely. The selected rows are returned to SQL Server, modified inside SQL Server, and then returned to the remote data source for the update.

Two forms of local distributed queries exist, one for linked servers and one for external data sources defined in the query; likewise, two forms of explicitly declaring pass-through distributed queries exist as well. OpenQuery() uses an established linked server, and OpenRowSet() declares the link within the query.

Using the four-part name

If the distributed query is accessing another SQL Server, then the four-part name becomes a *hybrid distributed query method*. Depending on the FROM clause and the WHERE clause, SQL Server will attempt to pass as much of the query as possible to the external SQL Server to improve performance.

When building a complex distributed query using the four-part name, it's difficult to predict how much of the query SQL Server will pass through. I've seen SQL Server take a single query and depending on the WHERE clause, the whole query was passed through, each table became a separate pass-through query, or only one table was passed through.

OpenQuery()

For pass-through queries, the OpenQuery() function leverages a linked server, so it's the easiest to develop. It also handles changes in server configuration without changing the code.

The OpenQuery() function is used within the SQL DML statement as a table. The function accepts only two parameters: the name of the linked server and the pass-through query. The next query uses OpenQuery() to retrieve data from the CHA1_Schedule Excel spreadsheet:

```
SELECT *
  FROM OPENQUERY(CHA1_Schedule,
    'SELECT * FROM Tour WHERE Tour = "Gauley River Rafting"');
```

Result:

```
Tour                          Base Camp
----------------------------  ----------------------------
Gauley River Rafting          Ashville
Gauley River Rafting          Ashville
```

The OpenQuery() pass-through query requires almost no processing by SQL Server. The Remote Scan returns exactly two rows to SQL Server. The WHERE clause is executed by the Jet engine as it reads from the Excel spreadsheet.

In the next example, the OpenQuery() requests the Jet engine to extract only the two rows requiring the update. The actual UPDATE operation is performed in SQL Server, and the result is written back to the external data set. In effect, the pass-through query is performing only the SELECT portion of the UPDATE command:

```
UPDATE OPENQUERY(CHA1_Schedule,
   'SELECT * FROM Tour WHERE Tour = "Gauley River Rafting"')
  SET [Base Camp] = 'Ashville';
```

OpenRowSet()

The OpenRowSet() function is the pass-through counterpart to the OpenDataSet() function. Both require the remote data source to be fully specified in the distributed query. OpenRowSet() adds a parameter to specify the pass-through query:

```
SELECT ContactFirstName, ContactLastName
  FROM OPENROWSET ('Microsoft.Jet.OLEDB.4.0',
  'C:\SQLServerBible\CHA1_Customers.mdb'; 'Admin';'',
  'SELECT * FROM Customers WHERE CustomerID = 1');
```

Result:

```
ContactFirstName    ContactLastName
------------------- ----------------------
Tom                  Mercer
```

Best Practice

Of the four distributed-query methods, the best option is the OpenQuery() function. With OpenQuery(), you have specific control over which data will be processed where. In addition, it has the advantage of predefined links, making the query more robust if the server configuration changes.

To perform an update using the OpenRowSet() function, use the function in place of the table being modified. The following code sample modifies the customer's last name in an Access database. The WHERE clause of the UPDATE command is handled by the pass-through portion of the OpenRowSet() function:

```
UPDATE OPENROWSET ('Microsoft.Jet.OLEDB.4.0',
  'C:\SQLServerBible\CHA1_Customers.mdb'; 'Admin';'',
  'SELECT * FROM Customers WHERE CustomerID = 1')
  SET ContactLastName = 'Wilson';
```

Distributed Transactions

Transactions are key to data integrity. If the logical unit of work includes modifying data outside the local SQL server, then a standard transaction is unable to handle the atomicity of the transaction. If a failure should occur in the middle of the transaction, then a mechanism must be in place to roll back the partial work; otherwise, a partial transaction will be recorded and the database will be left in an inconsistent state.

CROSS-REF **Chapter 66, "Managing Transactions, Locking, and Blocking," explores the ACID properties of a database and transactions.**

Distributed Transaction Coordinator

SQL Server uses the Distributed Transaction Coordinator (DTC) to handle multiple server transactions, commits, and rollbacks. The DTC service uses a two-phase commit scheme for multiple server transactions. The two-phase commit ensures that every server is available and handling the transaction by performing the following steps:

1. Each server is sent a "prepare to commit" message.
2. Each server performs the first phase of the commit, ensuring that it is capable of committing the transaction.
3. Each server replies when it has finished preparing for the commit.
4. Only after every participating server has responded positively to the "prepare to commit" message is the actual commit message sent to each server.

If the logical unit of work only involves reading from the external SQL Server, then the DTC is not required. Only when remote updates are occurring is a transaction considered a distributed transaction.

The Distributed Transaction Coordinator is a separate service from SQL Server. DTC is started or stopped with the SQL Server Service Manager.

Only one instance of DTC runs per server regardless of how many SQL Server instances may be installed or running on that server. The actual service name is `msdtc.exe`, and it consumes only about 2.5 MB of memory.

DTC must be running when a distributed transaction is initiated or the transaction will fail.

Developing distributed transactions

Distributed transactions are similar to local transactions with a few extensions to the syntax:

```
SET xact_abort on;
BEGIN DISTRIBUTED TRANSACTION;
```

In case of error, the `xact_abort` connection option will cause the current transaction, rather than only the current T-SQL statement, to be rolled back. The `xact_abort ON` option is required for any distributed transactions accessing a remote SQL Server and for most other OLE DB connections as well; but if `xact_abort ON` is not in the code, then SQL Server will automatically convert the transaction to `xact_abort ON` as soon as a distributed query is executed.

The `BEGIN DISTRIBUTED TRANSACTION` command, which determines whether the DTC service is available, is not strictly required. If a transaction is initiated with only `BEGIN TRAN`, then the transaction is escalated to a distributed transaction, and DTC is checked as soon as a distributed query is executed. It's considered a better practice to use `BEGIN DISTRIBUTED TRANSACTION` so that DTC is checked at the beginning of the transaction. When DTC is not running, an 8501 error is raised automatically:

```
Server: Msg 8501, Level 16, State 3, Line 7
MSDTC on server 'SQL2008RC0' is unavailable.
```

The following example demonstrates a distributed transaction between the local SQL Server and the second instance:

```
USE Family;
SET xact_abort on;
BEGIN DISTRIBUTED TRANSACTION;

  UPDATE Person
    SET LastName = 'Johnson2'
    WHERE PersonID = 10;

  UPDATE [Noli\SQL2].Family.dbo.Person
    SET LastName = 'Johnson2'
    WHERE PersonID = 10;

COMMIT TRANSACTION;
```

FIGURE 31-6

Component Services includes a list of current DTC transactions.

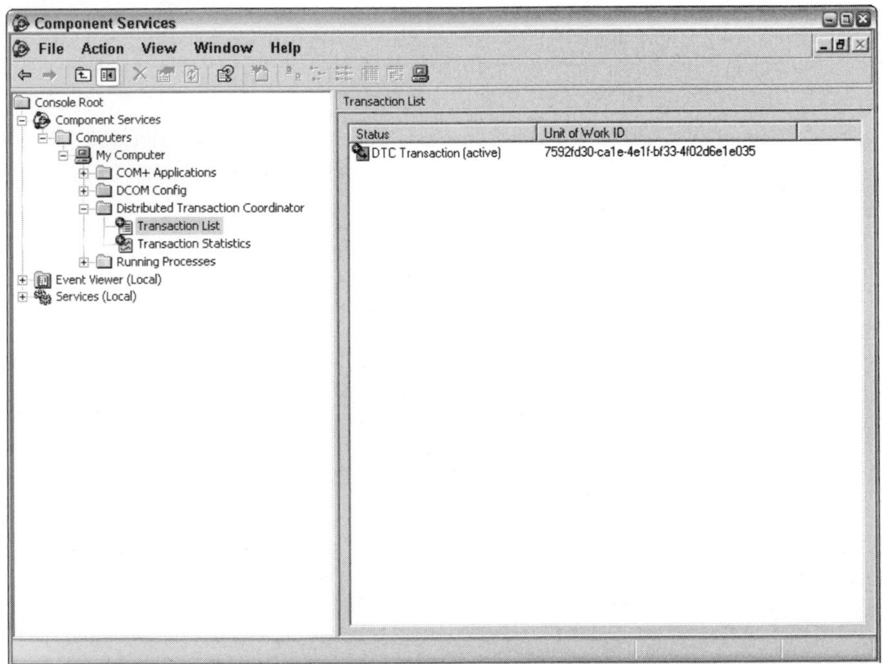

Rolling back a nested SQL Server local transaction rolls back all pending transactions. However, DTC uses true nested transactions, and rolling back a DTC transaction will roll back only the current transaction (this is different from a normal local transaction, which rolls back every pending transaction level).

Monitoring distributed transactions

As a separate service, Distributed Transaction Coordinator activity can be viewed from within the Windows operating system by selecting Control Panel ➪ Administrative Tools ➪ Component Services. Component Services provides both a list of current pending distributed transactions (see Figure 31-6) and an overview of DTC statistics (see Figure 31-7).

FIGURE 31-7

The current and accumulated count of distributed transactions as viewed in Component Services. The statistics begin at 0 when DTC is restarted.

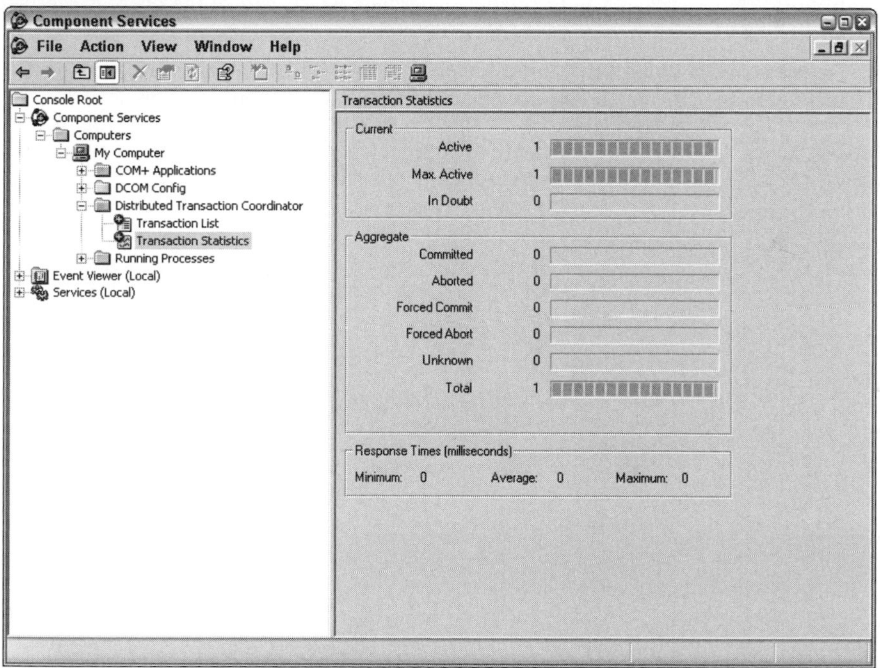

If a distributed transaction is having difficulty, it will likely be aborted. However, if the transaction is marked "In Doubt," forcibly committing, aborting, or forgetting the transaction using the context menu in Component Services may resolve the transaction.

Summary

Enterprise data tends to involve multiple platforms and locations. SQL Server's ability to leverage OLE DB and ODBC to perform distributed queries is a key factor in the success of many database projects, and knowing how to build distributed queries well is a necessary component in the database developer's skill set.

Major highlights from this chapter include the following:

- Linked servers are all about security. I strongly recommend passing the user's security context to the remote server.
- Queries using the four-part name or `OpenQuery()` with linked servers are pre-configured and are a better practice than hard-coding the connection security information in a `OpenDataSource()` or `OpenRowSet()`.
- Four-part name queries give SQL Server the choice of where the query is executed, but `OpenQuery()` enables you to carefully determine which part of the query is executed remotely and which part is executed locally.
- Scripting the creation of the linked servers as a repeatable process is far better than creating them with the UI, even if you document the linked server configuration.

The next chapter in this group of Data Connectivity chapters digs into ADO.NET, a standard in connecting to SQL Server from applications.

Chapter 32

Programming with ADO.NET 3.5

IN THIS CHAPTER

Understanding ADO and ADO.NET 3.5

Visual Studio 2008 usability features for ADO.NET 3.5

Building applications with ADO.NET 3.5

Unless data can be moved in and out of the database, there is no need for the database, the database administrator, or the database developer. In this chapter, the focus moves away from the database and into the application layer to examine one of the most important and useful SQL Server data access technology genealogies: the ActiveX Data Objects (ADO) family. The newest member, ADO.NET 3.5, is a suite of managed technologies capable of interacting with many relational database management systems (RDBMSs). Of course, SQL Server 2008 is a close relative to ADO.NET 3.5 in the family of Microsoft technologies. It is reasonable — and correct — to expect that they share a special relationship. As you will see, the underlying interface between ADO.NET application code and SQL Server is optimized.

This chapter covers ADO and ADO.NET, with special attention given to the new concepts and features introduced in ADO.NET version 3.5. The first new bit of information to learn is that the technologies are not mutually exclusive. Both ADO and ADO.NET are available to the Visual Studio 2008 programmer. Both have a place in the programmer's toolkit, and it will prove useful to know how ADO and ADO.NET technologies differ. This chapter compares and contrasts ADO and ADO.NET as an aid in making good development decisions. It also illuminates the fundamental shift that occurs between ADO.NET 2.0 and ADO.NET 3.5 because these sweeping changes are keys to getting the most not only from SQL Server 2008, but also from previous releases of SQL Server.

This chapter provides information on the Visual Studio 2008 IDE features that aid in developing and debugging data access solutions that employ ADO and ADO.NET. There isn't room to discuss all the similarities between Visual Studio and SQL Server Management Studio, though they are many and welcome. This chapter covers only Visual Studio's capabilities to assist in the development of ADO and ADO.NET data access methods within applications.

CROSS-REF **Readers new to Visual Studio will find much of the material in Chapter 6, "Using Management Studio," and in Part 10, "Business Intelligence," of interest as a good introduction to the user interface shared between SQL Server 2008 and Visual Studio 2008.**

An Overview of ADO.NET

In keeping with the Microsoft data access tradition, ADO.NET 3.5 builds on the existing data access technology base. Since the introduction of SQL Server v1.1, this tradition has shown some common threads of evolution. Each generation has made creating a connection between the application and the data easier than the last, and each has provided greater flexibility and improved features. The improvements have consistently moved in step with leading contemporary design goals, such as host-based computing, client/server, n-tier, service-oriented architecture (SOA), or Web Services, at any given time in the evolution. Each iteration of the data access technology has attempted to repair the problems of its predecessors in important areas, such as support for referential integrity, performance, and application stability.

With each release of SQL Server, the oldest surviving data access technologies tend to be left behind as newer technologies are integrated. Only rarely are data access changes revolutionary. SQL Server 2008 is no exception.

The original or "classic" ADO is showing its age and vulnerability. It is not supported by the SQL Native Client (SNAC or SQLNCLI). Although Microsoft documentation tends to use the awkward SQLNCLI acronym to refer to this new API, Microsoft folks (in presentations) and the user community in general are much more likely to use the SNAC acronym (pronounced like "snack").

ADO is shipped with the Microsoft Data Access Component (MDAC) libraries. Furthermore, ADO will be able to access SQL Server 2008 databases. However, the new features of SQL Server 2008 will not be available with ADO, such as the new data types or the user-defined types. New applications should not be written with ADO. Instead, plan how applications now using ADO and the underlying Component Object Model (COM) technology will be upgraded or replaced. In a future release of SQL Server, ADO and COM will no longer be supported.

This chapter describes the steps to undertake to begin preparing for that eventuality. The installed base of ADO-based applications is simply too large for ADO to change or disappear at this time or anytime soon. Certainly, the best practice is to develop new applications under the service-oriented architecture (SOA) model using ADO.NET 3.5. However, it's still necessary to understand both ADO and previous ADO.NET technologies in addition to ADO.NET 3.5 in order to support and maintain existing applications while building the next generation of applications.

ADO brought unprecedented speed and flexibility in data access and data manipulation to the Windows development platform. Beginning with ADO and the COM-based OLEDB interfaces that ADO employs, developers acquired the ability to access heterogeneous data sources — from documents to databases — with a single consistent methodology. ADO abstracted the powerful yet complex COM components and OLEDB interfaces to a simple and friendly object model that enabled large numbers of programmers and web developers to build successful applications.

ADO

Even today, ADO remains a COM-based data access technology. It's important to realize that Object Linking and Embedding components (COM-based OLEDB) have been around since the earliest days of the Microsoft Windows platform. Much has changed since that time. Most notably, the COM specifications were published, and, more recently, data access has moved away from the OS layer and into the common language runtime (CLR) space. However, much remains the same. As fast as the database world is changing, it took a very long time for that early vision of OLE and COM to be accepted by the developer community, and only then did it reach maturity. It is hoped that the software life cycle for .NET will not be as steep or as long and will enjoy a much longer ride at its pinnacle. While Microsoft is making assurances that the COM binary standard will be around through Vista and the next version of the Windows OS, Windows 7, the likelihood that it will begin descending into obscurity sometime thereafter is real. The movement toward XML-based data transfer is safely beyond critical mass. This leaves COM and the original ADO to play only a legacy role.

As one convincing signal of that progression, with ADO.NET 3.5, Microsoft is recommending that the high-level ADO data access implementation of COM be accessed only through the ADO primary interop assembly (PIA) (`ADODB.dll`). Figure 32-1 shows how this assembly exposes the unmanaged COM components into the managed .NET environment. The ADO code remains essentially ADO code, but through the PIA it will be managed by the CLR, rather than at the operating system layer. This will not mandate large changes in legacy implementations of ADO, though some changes will be necessary. Nor does it mean that current ADO implementations will be much different from before when written in .NET. It will still be necessary to specify a valid OLEDB data provider in the ADO connection string, for example, and to understand the interfaces and requirements of each of those data providers. Conversely, constructors and garbage collection, security, and runtime type checking (courtesy of the .NET Framework) come into play.

FIGURE 32-1

Unmanaged ADO interfaces with the native MDAC services to access the database.

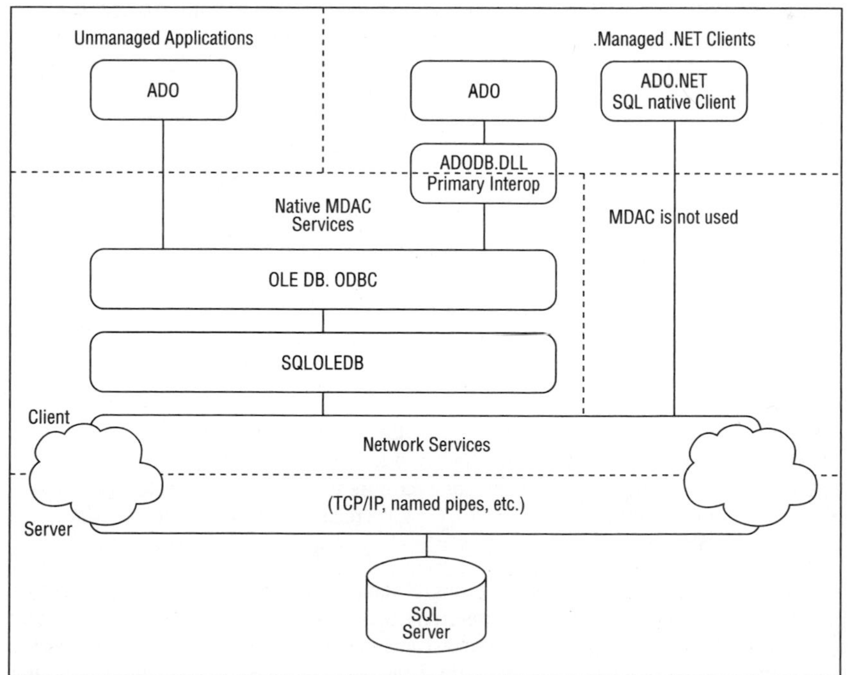

Application problems could result in operating system instability in this model. With SQL Server 2008, ADO uses the `adodb.dll` PIA to provide continued support for ADO application code while realizing the safety of a managed .NET Framework client. The SQL Native Client (SNAC) is optimized for SQL Server access because it communicates directly through the Network services.

Migrating code to ADO.NET 3.5 is the development goal. To ease the transition, use the provided primary interop assembly. For example, a phased approach to upgrading applications to ADO.NET can be pursued. A reasonable scenario is to first migrate ADO applications to the `adodb.dll`, requiring minimal code changes. Applications gradually become modified to move state away from the database and into .NET data sets or XML streams. Once state is possible at the client, the door is open for caching and data maintenance at the client, as well as disconnected service-oriented architectures. The result is more reliable applications.

TIP **Thoughtful planning is necessary in moving ADO applications to the .NET Framework. Microsoft has done a good job of making topics regarding moving from ADO to ADO.NET available on the Internet. Microsoft's journal for developers, *MSDN*, published a very useful two-part article by John Papa, "Migrating from ADO to ADO.NET," in July and August of 2004. These articles and many other articles from this informative and in-depth magazine are available free online at** `http://msdn.microsoft.com/msdnmag/default.aspx`**. The URL to part one of "Migrating from ADO to ADO.NET" is** `http://msdn.microsoft.com/msdnmag/issues/04/07/DataPoints/default.aspx`**. The URL for part two is** `http://msdn.microsoft.com/msdnmag/issues/04/08/DataPoints/default.aspx`**. Readers can also find very useful information about moving from ADO to ADO.NET by searching the Microsoft Developer's Network (MSDN) online library at** `http://msdn.microsoft.com/en-us/library/default.asp`**.**

Finally, be sure to consult SQL Server Books Online when planning a migration from ADO to ADO.NET. The Books Online article "Updating an Application to SQL Native Client from MDAC" lists many potential problems that can be avoided if identified early in the migration design. If you have an application that is already using SQL Server 2005, then the article "Updating an Application to SQL Server 2008 Native Client from SQL Server 2005 Native Client" will be very useful because it describes differences in behavior between the SQL Server 2008 Native Client and earlier versions of the SQL Server Native Client.

Since ADO's introduction, it hasn't been necessary to be an advanced COM or OLEDB programmer to support, maintain, and enhance existing ADO-based applications. It will continue to be useful to have a high level of insight into COM and OLEDB to support and debug many ADO issues. Most ADO experience and knowledge can be useful when working with ADO.NET. After all, ADO is the basis on which ADO.NET is built. Likewise, OLEDB is the foundation of ADO. Understanding OLEDB can also prove useful when working with ADO or ADO.NET.

OLEDB

The key to OLEDB is found in the consumer and provider metaphor used to describe the technology. OLEDB is a method for connecting data from data providers to applications that consume the data. Well-defined steps must be completed to create some common ground between the variety of data providers and the consumer. OLEDB is a COM CoType or related group of COM interfaces that is described in a discoverable hierarchy, qualified by properties and controlled by events.

Generally, OLEDB tries to deliver rows and columns of data to consumers. Some providers are not well suited to such descriptions. The CoType hierarchy provides a ladder on which different types of data can ascend from unknown sources to the consumer, beginning at different rungs on the ladder yet coalescing at the point of delivery, known as the `CoCreateInstance` CoType. Each rung of this conceptual ladder can be thought of as a consumer of the rung below it, and a provider to the rung above it. These transitions are collectively known as *interfaces*. All interfaces inherit from the primordial `IUnknown` interface. This shows how the components are useful and reusable in that each CoType is similar in form even if very different in function. This is easily borne out if the structural similarities among the ADO objects are considered. At the simplest level, each has properties and methods, and participates in a member hierarchy.

CROSS-REF **Readers desiring more details on CoTypes and OLEDB in general might want to consult "Introduction to OLEDB Programming," located in the MSDN library at** `http://msdn.microsoft.com/en-us/library/ms714272(VS.85).aspx`. **CoTypes are discussed throughout this multi-chapter conceptual reference.**

The number of OLEDB CoTypes is fairly large. What is useful and quite powerful in OLEDB is the ability to express and transfer all provided data to the consumer in the simple terms of a data value, its length, and distinguishing properties such as a status. Ideally, the status is good data (`DBPROPSTATUS_OK`), but the status may also indicate a null value or that the value is bad and by what criteria it is deemed bad among other states.

OLEDB, as with all of the COM components, is not programming language dependent. This makes it an ideal low-level architecture for the high-level languages that are used to implement ADO. The low-level specifications are able to remain the same while the ADO object model can be expressed in VB, C#, scripting languages such as VBScript and JScript, and languages capable of entering the low-level specification space, such as C++.

OLEDB is a rich programming solution designed to enable database technology to handle data from database and non-database sources in record sets or streams. ADO makes OLEDB available and useful to developers in a way that makes meeting those overarching deadlines and delivery schedules possible. That said, it is not the final data access solution.

ADODB primary interop assembly

COM and .NET are compatible technologies. .NET assemblies can be used in COM application code, and COM components can be used in .NET code. .NET assemblies can be marshaled by COM wrappers. The COM wrapper must implement the core set of COM interop assemblies. An interop assembly is essentially metadata — or type definitions — for the COM components expressed in managed code.

CROSS-REF **For additional details on the interoperability of COM and .NET components, see the Microsoft Patterns and Practices white paper "Microsoft .NET/COM Migration and Interoperability" at** `http://msdn.microsoft.com/en-us/library/ms978506.aspx`.

A primary interop assembly (PIA) is designated by the original owner of a COM object. The PIA is the recommended interop assembly to be used in the .NET Framework when exposing a COM object in managed code. Microsoft provides such a digitally signed PIA for ADO in Visual Studio .NET: `adodb.dll`. Microsoft recommends that only this assembly be used for ADO when used in .NET code. As shown in Figure 32-2, the reference for the `adodb` primary interop assembly is selected from the list of .NET references when adding to a Visual Studio project, rather than adding a reference to the ADO component on the COM tab of the Add Reference dialog.

One final consideration when using ADO in Visual Studio 2008 and with ADO.NET 3.5 is that the SNAC does not provide ADO support. This means that the ADO application will rely on MDAC components to access SQL Server. ADO.NET is supported in the SNAC and shouldn't require coordination with the complex web of MDAC libraries and components.

FIGURE 32-2

Selecting the adodb.dll as a .NET reference in a Visual Studio project

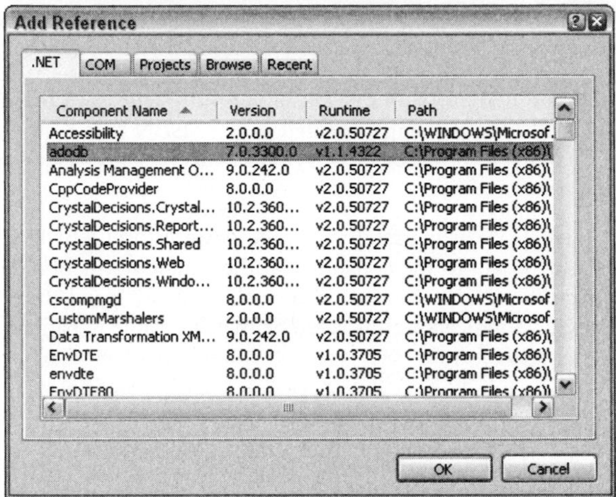

MDAC is becoming a part of the various Microsoft operating systems and will no longer be versioned or released apart from the operating systems. A specially installed MDAC is not used in any of the examples in this chapter. The MDAC drivers used are those provided with Windows XP SP2, Windows XP x64, Windows Server 2003 R2 Standard, and Windows Server 2003 R2 Enterprise x64 editions. It is unlikely that Microsoft will announce any future versioned releases to the MDAC libraries. Perhaps the best place to monitor MDAC changes in the future will be in OS releases, service packs, and patch documentation. Similarly, MDAC version compatibility should be verified through regression testing whenever a Microsoft-provided change is applied to the operating system.

SNAC is a completely separate API from MDAC. The SNAC is designed to simplify the task of keeping SQL Server clients updated in lock-step with the server. When SQL clients must rely on MDAC components, an update to MDAC is necessary to ensure client and database compatibility; otherwise, problems and failures for other application components running on the client can arise. It follows that MDAC changes that are necessary for other application components can create problems with the SQL Server connectivity. With SNAC, the SQL client is contained in a single `.dll` file. The risks of introducing a SNAC change to the application server are low compared to the risks of introducing an MDAC change.

CROSS-REF **Another place to watch for changes to MDAC and SNAC is the Data Access and Storage Developer Center at** `http://msdn.microsoft.com/en-us/data/default.aspx`**. One informative document that can be found there is the current Microsoft "Data Access Technologies Road Map" vision at** `http://msdn.microsoft.com/en-us/library/ms810810.aspx`**.**

The ADO object model

Thus far, this chapter has provided a handle on ADO's place in the .NET world and ADO's OLEDB infrastructure, as well as how to implement ADO in the .NET Framework. Now consider where ADO fits — or more appropriately doesn't fit — into the ADO.NET grand scheme. One of the design goals of ADO.NET has been to provide all the capabilities of good old ADO. At a minimum, ADO is the role model for ADO.NET. ADO.NET 1.*x* came up a bit short in meeting the design features of ADO, so the adoption of .NET was impeded in the data access space.

With the ADO.NET 3.5 release and SQL Server 2008, the full feature set of ADO is combined with the independence and safety of the .NET Framework and the promise of XML. Not that there isn't some work to be done before ADO is completely bested by the new kid, especially in terms of performance. Understanding this progression from ADO to ADO.NET 3.5 is best accomplished by comparing the object models of the two. To adequately complete the comparison, consider the features and components of the ADO object model. This will build a foundation for reviewing what is new and what is improved in ADO.NET as the chapter progresses.

ADO isn't just a wrapper over OLEDB. It provides real value to the developer and has several advantages over previous database access methods. The following list describes those advantages originated by ADO:

- **Independently created objects:** With ADO it is no longer necessary to thread through a hierarchy of objects. The developer creates only the objects needed, thus reducing memory requirements while increasing application speed and decreasing the lines of code needed.
- **Batch updating:** Instead of sending one change to the server, they can be collected in local memory and sent at one time. Using this feature improves application performance (because the data provider can perform the update in the background) and reduces network load.
- **Stored procedures:** These procedures reside on the server as part of the database manager. They are used to perform specific tasks on the data set. ADO uses stored procedures with in/out parameters and return values.
- **Multiple cursor types:** Cursors point to the data currently in play and can be manifested as client-side cursors and server-side cursors.

NOTE **It's important to distinguish between application code cursors and T-SQL cursors. Client-side application cursors have little of the performance and contention issues of T-SQL cursors. Server-side cursors, particularly when updateable, can negatively affect the database almost to the degree that T-SQL cursors can be problematic. See Chapter 22, "Kill the Cursor!" for more information on cursors.**

- **Returned row limits:** This enables information retrieval limited to the amount of data actually needed to meet the user's request.
- **Multiple record-set objects:** Works with multiple record sets returned by stored procedures or batch processing.
- **Free threaded objects:** This feature enhances web server performance by enabling the server to perform multiple tasks.

Like all OLEDB components, ADO uses COM. ADO provides a dual interface: a program ID of `ADODB` for local operations and a program ID of `ADOR` for remote operations. The ADO library itself is free-threaded, even though the registry shows it as using the apartment-threaded model. The thread safety of ADO depends on the OLEDB provider that is used. In other words, if a Microsoft provider such as the Open Database Connectivity (ODBC) OLEDB provider is used, then no problems should be expected. If a third-party OLEDB provider is used, then it may be necessary to check the vendor's documentation before assuming that ADO is thread-safe (a requirement for using ADO over an Internet or intranet connection).

NOTE Open Database Connectivity (ODBC) is a technology for connecting applications to databases that has been in use longer than OLEDB. Unlike OLEDB, ODBC is designed for connecting only to RDBMS sources. The ODBC driver is included in the SNAC, however.

A small set of objects is used to work with ADO. Table 32-1 lists these objects and describes how to use them. Most of these object types have a counterpart in predecessor technologies that Microsoft has introduced, although the level of ADO-object functionality is much greater than that offered by previous technologies and, as demonstrated next, the potential usability for more recent technologies such as ADO.NET and XML transcends even ADO.

TABLE 32-1

ADO-Object Overview

Object	Description
Connection	A `connection` object defines the connection with the OLEDB provider. Use this object to perform tasks such as beginning, committing, and rolling back transactions. There are also methods for opening or closing the connection and for executing commands.
Error	ADO creates an error object as part of the `connection` object. The `error` object provides additional information about errors raised by the OLEDB provider. A single `error` object can contain information about more than one error. Each object is associated with a specific event, such as committing a transaction.
Command	A `command` object performs a task using a `connection` or `recordset` object. Even though commands can be executed as part of the `connection` or `recordset` object, the `command` object is much more flexible and enables the definition output parameters.
Parameter	The `parameter` object defines a single parameter for a command. A parameter modifies the result of a stored procedure or query. `Parameter` objects can provide input, output, or both.
Recordset	The `recordset` object contains the result of a query, and a cursor for choosing individual elements within the returned table.
Record	A record is a single row of data. It can stand alone or be derived from a record set.
Field	A `field` object contains a single column of data contained in a record or recordset object. In other words, a field can be thought of as a single column in a table; it contains one type of data for all the records associated with a record set.
Stream	When a data provider is not able to easily express the value and length of the data as a record set with discrete fields, as is the case for large text, BLOB, or document data, the data may be sent to the consumer via the stream object.
Property	Some OLEDB providers will need to extend the standard ADO object. Property objects represent one way to do this. A property object contains attribute, name, type, and value information.

There are also four object collections in ADO: Errors, Parameters, Fields, and Properties. Note that these collections are containers for child objects in the ADO model. There are no collections at the root of the object model, and the model is never more than two levels deep. The structure is consistent and simple, always with the following progression: Parent Object → Collection of dependent objects → Child Object

OLEDB data providers

Even when ADO is used through the provided .NET primary interop assembly, all data access will occur through one of the available OLEDB COM data providers. A *data provider* manages the connection between the client and the DBMS using a number of objects. Of course, this means that a data provider requires a source of information and must define the specifics for creating that connection. Generally, a provider is database specific or provides a means for configuring a specific database. Figure 32-3 shows a typical list of database providers. Some of the providers on the list are quite specialized.

FIGURE 32-3

A typical list of database providers

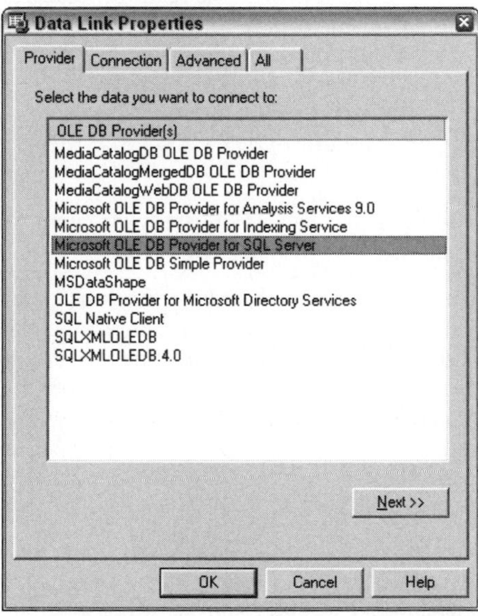

The source of an OLEDB object is known as a *provider*. Consequently, ADO also relies on data providers as a source of data. Even in this day of the .NET Framework, the number of OLEDB providers — each specialized to a particular data source — is greater than at any time in the past. One nice thing about OLEDB is that the same provider works with any Visual Studio programming language.

Generally, especially for SQL Server developers, it's better to use the SQL Server–specific provider. Even though other general-purpose providers will work, Microsoft has optimized the SQL Server provider for use with SQL Server. The performance advantages of using the SQL Server provider over using a general-purpose provider are well known.

TIP **To find out which OLEDB providers are available on a particular machine, create a new text file and rename it to include an extension of ".udl" (e.g., `temp.udl` — the name is not important, only the extension). Open the file to see a dialog similar to the one shown in Figure 32-3 showing all the OLEDB providers installed locally on that computer.**

Mapping data types

When working exclusively within SQL Server, the challenge with data types amounts to choosing the right type for a given data-storage need. However, when moving the data from the DBMS through a data provider to a client, several layers of transition occur. For some DBMSs this is an extreme problem because the general providers supplied with OLEDB don't support many special data types. For all providers, the cost of data type conversions as data propagates through those layers is significant. These problems of data typing are additional reasons to use the SQL Server–specific OLEDB data providers when working with ADO.

When using data found in a SQL Server table in a client application, the provider must map the data from a type that SQL Server understands to a type that the client application understands. Fortunately for SQL Server developers, the ADO mapping for the SQLOLEDB provider is relatively straightforward. Table 32-2 shows how the SQL Server provider maps ADO data types. One problem occurs when ADO uses the same data type to represent two or three SQL Server data types when the application requires subtle differences to appear in the user interface. The complete set of SQL Server 2008 data types is exposed in the SQL Native Client. ADO is only aware of the SQL Server 2000 data types and will not be able to handle the new types, such as `XML` or a `varchar(max)`, discussed later in this chapter.

Table 32-2 shows the SQL Server 2008 data types and the equivalent ADO data types, along with the data type conversion that the .NET Framework will conduct for each ADO data type.

The comments in Table 32-2 touch on the most significant problems that can occur in the mapping of data between ADO and SQL Server. It is important to also consider data-conversion errors. According to Microsoft, all nondirect data translations are subject to data loss. For example, neither the provider nor SQL Server will complain if an eight-byte number is converted into a four-byte number, but obviously there is a potential for data loss. In addition, some types cannot be converted to other types. For example, it's impossible to convert an `adBinary` data type into an `adSmallInt` data type. In this situation, the development environment would complain. The sort order of SQL character data types is, by default, different from the sort order of .NET data types.

The .NET Framework adds another level of conversion and potential conversion errors to the ADO implementation. ADO data types are specified within ADO objects. The .NET Framework will convert those data types to valid .NET data types implicitly when they are used outside of the ADO objects in the code. This conversion should happen without the need for explicit data conversion type casting, although it is good programming practice to ensure that data is always of the type expected. The developer must remain vigilant for data type conversion problems when programming ADO, even in the .NET Framework. Using the .NET data types that support null values may provide relief for conversion problems with many applications. There seems to be no perfect solution to this problem short of environment coding standards that mandate consistent best practice programming techniques for all programmers in the environments, and rigorous testing.

Best Practice

To avoid unexpected data type conversions at assignment, ADO data types can be assigned using explicit casting to the desired data type.

TABLE 32-2

SQL Server to ADO/ADO.NET Data Mapping

SQL Server Data Type	ADO Data Type (.NET Framework Data Type)	Notes
`Bigint`	`adBigInt` (`int64`)	The `bigint` data-type value ranges from `-2^63` (-9,223,372,036,854,775,807) through `2^63-1` (9,223,372,036,854,775,807). This value is only available for SQL Server 2000, but the OLEDB provider will still try to send it to SQL Server 7.0 and older systems, and data loss will result. Use the `adBigInt` type only when necessary and then with caution.
`Binary`	`adBinary` (`byte[]`)	ADO uses the same data-type equivalence for both `binary` and `timestamp`.
`Bit`	`adBoolean` (`Int16`)	While this data transfer always works, conceptual differences exist between the two. For example, a `bit` can have values of `1`, `0`, or `NULL`, whereas an `adBoolean` always has either a `true` or `false` value.
`Char`	`adChar` (`string`)	ADO uses the same data-type equivalence for `char`, `varchar`, and `text` data types. The .NET Framework uses Unicode (UTF-16) to represent all character data.
`Date`		0001-01-01 through 9999-12-31. Three bytes storage; is not time zone offset aware or daylight saving time aware.
`Datetime`	`adDBTimeStamp` (`DateTime`)	The default precision for the `Datetime` data type in SQL Server is 3.33 milliseconds.
`Datetime2`		0001-01-01 through 9999-12-31. Six bytes storage for precision less than 3, 7 bytes for precisions 4 and 5, 8 bytes for all other precisions.
`Datetimeoffset`		0001-01-01 through 9999-12-31. Ten bytes storage.
`Decimal`	`adNumeric` (`Decimal`)	ADO uses the same data-type equivalence for both `decimal` and `numeric` data types.

continued

TABLE 32-2 *(continued)*

SQL Server Data Type	ADO Data Type (.NET Framework Data Type)	Notes
`Float`	`adDouble` (`Double`)	
`Hierarchyid`		
`Image`	`adVarbinary` (`byte[]`)	This data type can be so large that it won't fit in memory. The lack of memory can cause provider errors and possibly only a partial retrieval. When this happens, the developer must write a custom routine to retrieve the data in pieces. ADO uses the same data-type equivalence for `image`, `tinyint`, and `varbinary`.
`Int`	`adInteger` (`Int32`)	–2,147,483648 to 2,147,483647. Storage of 4 bytes.
`Money`	`adCurrency` (`Decimal`)	ADO uses the same data-type equivalence for `money` and `smallmoney`.
`Nchar`	`adWChar` (`string`)	ADO uses the same data-type equivalence for `nchar`, `ntext`, `nvarchar`, and `sysname`. The .NET Framework uses Unicode (UTF-16) to represent all character data.
`Ntext`	`adWChar` (`string`)	This data type can be so large that it won't fit in memory. The lack of memory can cause provider errors and possibly a partial retrieval. When this happens, the developer must write a custom routine to retrieve the data in pieces. ADO uses the same data-type equivalence for `nchar`, `ntext`, `nvarchar`, and `sysname`. The .NET Framework uses Unicode (UTF-16) to represent all character data.
`Numeric`	`adNumeric` (`decimal`)	ADO uses the same data-type equivalence for both `decimal` and `numeric` data types.
`Nvarchar`	`adWChar` (`string`)	ADO uses the same data-type equivalence for `nchar`, `ntext`, `nvarchar`, and `sysname`. The .NET Framework uses Unicode (UTF-16) to represent all character data.
`NvarChar(MAX)`	`None (string)`	SQL Server 2008 provides the same data-type equivalence for what was previously `Nvarchar` if less than or equal to 8 KB, and `text` if greater than 8 KB. The .NET Framework uses Unicode (UTF-16) to represent all character data.

continued

TABLE 32-2 *(continued)*

SQL Server Data Type	ADO Data Type (.NET Framework Data Type)	Notes
Real	adSingle (Single)	
Smalldatetime	adTimeStamp (DateTime)	
Smallint	adSmallInt (Int16)	–32,768 to 32,767. Storage of 2 bytes.
Smallmoney	adCurrency (Decimal)	ADO uses the same data-type equivalence for money and smallmoney.
sql_variant	adVariant (object)	This data type can contain any of a number of primitive data types, such as smallint, float, and char. It can't contain larger data types such as text, ntext, and image. The adVariant type maps to the OLEDB DBTYPE_VARIANT data type and is only usable with SQL Server 2000. Be careful when using this data type because it can produce unpredictable results. Even though OLEDB provides complete support for it, ADO doesn't.
Sysname	adWChar (string)	ADO uses the same data-type equivalence for nchar, ntext, nvarchar, and sysname. The .NET Framework uses Unicode (UTF-16) to represent all character data.
Table		
Text	adChar (string)	This data type can be so large that it won't fit in memory. The lack of memory can cause provider errors and possibly a partial retrieval. When this happens, the developer must write a custom routine to retrieve the data in pieces. ADO uses the same data-type equivalence for char, varchar, and text data types. The .NET Framework uses Unicode (UTF-16) to represent all character data.
Time		An integer from 0 to 7. Specifies the fractional part of the seconds. 00:00:00.0000000 to 12:59:59.9999999. Five bytes storage.
Timestamp	adBinary (byte[])	ADO uses the same data-type equivalence for both binary and timestamp.

continued

TABLE 32-2 (continued)

SQL Server Data Type	ADO Data Type (.NET Framework Data Type)	Notes
`Tinyint`	`adTinyInt (byte)`	0 to 255. Storage of 1 byte.
`Uniqueidentifier`	`adGUID (Guid)`	The data provider supports a string GUID, not a true GUID. This means that when an actual GUID is needed, the code must explicitly convert it into a GUID data structure.
`Varbinary`	`adVarbinary (byte[])`	ADO uses the same data-type equivalence for `image` and `varbinary`.
`Varbinary(MAX)`	`none (byte[])`	SQL Server 2008 provides the same data-type equivalence for what was previously `varbinary` if less than or equal to 8 KB, and `image` if greater than 8 KB.
`Varchar`	`adChar (string)`	ADO uses the same data-type equivalence for `char`, `varchar`, and `text`. The .NET Framework uses Unicode (UTF-16) to represent all character data.
`Varchar(MAX)`	`None (string)`	SQL Server 2008 provides the same data-type equivalence for what was previously `varchar` if less than or equal to 8 KB, and `text` if greater than 8 KB. The .NET Framework uses Unicode (UTF-16) to represent all character data.

ADO and scripting

ADO often appears in scripts of various types. Because ADO relies on COM technology, any scripting language capable of creating an object can probably use ADO to retrieve data from a database. Using scripts to perform small tasks makes sense because they can easily be modified if necessary and they are quick to write. Be aware that scripting facilities such as the Windows Script Component can be created and referenced from VB.NET or C#, and the Windows Scripting Host runs ADO as a COM component only. Interoperability with .NET does not apply.

.NET code is compiled to IL. Because the compilation to IL must happen at some point before runtime, the concept of late binding is not available to .NET code. Conversely, script-based ADO, such as that used in the Windows Scripting Host 5.6, a SQL Server 2000 DTS ActiveX script step, or a pre .NET ASP page, requires late binding. Late binding simply means that the COM object referenced is created at runtime and is identifiable by the use of the `CreateObject()`function. Therefore, to use ADO in scripts, MDAC must be installed on any machine that will execute scripts. In contrast, ADO.NET will be fully supported by the SQL Native Client and will not require MDAC. This important new distinction with ADO.NET 2.0 (and subsequently ADO.NET 3.5) is covered in greater detail later in this chapter.

Of course, scripting languages don't provide the robust interactive environment found in programming languages such as C# or Visual Basic or even ASP.NET. It may be necessary to restrict the use of scripts to small tasks such as calling on a stored procedure to perform some task automatically or to retrieve the result of a data query for onscreen display.

Microsoft makes a point of demonstrating the flexibility of ADO with several languages, including Java, JavaScript, VBScript, and the new XML-based Windows Script Component available in Visual Studio 2005 as well as 2008.

ADO.NET

It's somewhat confusing that ADO.NET inherits the ADO part of its name from the original ADO. ADO is the acronym for ActiveX Data Objects. ActiveX is a clear signal that the topic is `IUnknown` and COM. `IUnknown` is the prototype for all COM classes. In its raw form it indicates that the calling module needs to know nothing about a called object and the caller will still be able to statefully interact with the called module. While deep down in the bowels of .NET there still exists COM programmability, the whole point of the .NET Framework and the common language runtime (CLR) is the shift away from the limitations of the COM code execution environment and toward consistency in the object-oriented class model. `IUnknown` means there is no need to know anything about a class to instantiate and use the class. The .NET Framework signifies that the system assemblies and the base classes will be reliably consistent types. In short, there is little that is COM-based ADO in ADO.NET from a technical perspective.

Only from a functional perspective is ADO.NET a natural progression from ADO. A new technology was required to overcome the limitations of ADO performance and scalability — a technology that provided the developer with a variety of execution options. ADO.NET was designed to both overcome ADO limitations and leverage the developer's ADO skills. The basic objects of ADO are found in ADO.NET. Commands executed on connections to data providers are used in ADO.NET with only slight differences from the commands executed on connections to data providers used with ADO. However, with ADO.NET, developers have greater control over how the data will be retrieved and manipulated. Execution can be asynchronous and batched. Results can be elegantly stored and manipulated at the application, disconnected from the database. Alternately, results can as easily be streamed as binary data or as XML.

Many developers labor under the misconception that ADO.NET is simply the upgrade to ADO. ADO was developed to support client/server applications and presupposes that the user and the data will both remain connected to the application for the lifetime of an execution cycle. At the risk of oversimplifying the difference, ADO held state in the data source and ADO.NET is built to be able to maintain state disconnected from the database. One advantage for .NET is that there is no requirement that the database remain connected to the application for the complete execution cycle. In part, this design goal is realized because XML technology is fundamental to ADO.NET. To a larger degree, state is managed in the ADO.NET application layer by the local application cache known as the `DataSet` class. In ADO.NET 2.0 and later, state management is further extended with asynchronous command execution and *Multiple Active Result Sets (MARS)*.

The following sections describe ADO.NET objects, keeping ADO objects in perspective, and point out the new features in the ADO.NET 3.5 release. In other words, the discussion builds on the ADO information presented earlier in this chapter as ADO.NET concepts are introduced. ADO.NET is a managed object model with functional capabilities much like the classic ADO, yet designed to enable more scalable applications, particularly in the disconnected environments found in many n-tier, SOA, Web Services, and ASP.NET applications.

The ADO.NET object model

The ADO.NET object model is different from the object model used by ADO. It is more complex yet undeniably richer. The most striking difference is the in-memory data cache known as the `DataSet`. This ADO.NET object can be divided into two components: the `DataSet` and the data provider. A data provider is used for connecting the application to a database, executing commands and returning the results to the application. The results that are returned to the application are either processed directly or placed into a DataSet.

ADO.NET provides many data providers in order to access the many types of data sources such as Microsoft SQL Server, Access, Excel, and others. These and other data providers are very lightweight and create a very thin layer between application source code and the data source. This provides great performance without giving up functionality. The data provider contains the classes that create the connection, issue commands, handle the data reader, and provide data-adapter support. The `connection` provides the conduit for database communications. The `command` enables the client to request information from the database server through the `data adapter`. In addition to providing data, the data adapter also enables the client cache to synchronize or update back to the data source. The `data reader` is a one-way, read-only method of viewing data in ADO. The `data adapter` provides the real-time connection support normally associated with live data connections.

The `DataSet` is a special object that contains one or more tables. The data in the `DataSet` is retrieved from the data source through the provider and stored in the application work space. The data can be manipulated and constrained at the application. The `DataSet` is a disconnected subset of the data from the data source defined by the provider properties. The data provider properties include the `Connection`, `Command`, `DataReader`, and `DataAdapter` objects. Each of these objects also has capabilities not found in an ADO provider. For example, a `DataAdapter` can actually handle more than one connection and one set of rules.

As with many managed objects, enumerators are used to access the various objects within these main objects in application code. The DataSet is the representation of information within the database. It contains two collections: `DataTableCollection` and `DataRelationCollection`. The `DataTableCollection` contains the columns and rows of the table, along with any constraints imposed on that information. The `DataRelationCollection` contains the relational information used to create the `DataSet`.

Table 32-3 provides an overview of the most frequently used ADO.NET data classes.

NOTE **Visual Studio 2008 provides a `TableAdapter`, which is a single-table data collection that can be used in application code much like an ADO.NET 3.5 `DataSet`. The `TableAdapter` is significantly easier for the developer to create and manipulate than the underlying ADO.NET 3.5 data components when only one table is needed at the application. The `TableAdapter` is not derived from the `System.Data.DataSet` class, as are all other `DataSets`. In fact, `TableAdapters` are not even part of the .NET Framework. They are a level of abstraction provided by Visual Studio 2008. All `TableAdapters` inherit from `System.Component.ComponentModel`. This means that they are fully integrated with the Visual Studio tools, such as the Data Grid. In addition, the base class for a `TableAdapter` can be any of the .NET providers that expose a `DataTable` class. The base class is specified when the `TableAdapter` is created. `TableAdapters` are type-safe and include all properties and methods necessary to connect to a data source, retrieve the table's data, and update the data source. You can find more information about the `TableAdapter` on the MSDN website: `http://msdn.microsoft.com/en-us/library/7zt3ycf2.aspx`.**

TABLE 32-3

ADO.NET 3.5 Class Overview

Class Type	Description
Connection	Creates the physical connection between the DBMS and a `DataAdapter`, `DataReader`, or `factory`. The `Connection` object also includes logic that optimizes the use of connections within the distributed application environment.
ProviderFactory	Implemented in ADO.NET 2.0. Each .NET provider implements a `ProviderFactory` class, each of which derives from the common base class `DBProviderFactory`. The `factory` class includes methods for creation of provider-specific ADO.NET components in a generic code style. The idea behind the `ProviderFactory` is to enable the developer to write generic code that can use a provider determined at runtime. The possible providers a factory can use are stored in the `machine.config` file.
Command	Defines an action to perform on the DBMS, such as adding, deleting, or updating a record. The `DataAdapter` includes the command objects required to query, delete, insert, and edit records.
Parameter	A parameter to a command
Error	The error or warning information returned from the database. For SQL Server this includes the error number, the severity, and the text for the error.
Exception	The application exception when ADO.NET encounters an error. The `Error` class is created by the `Exception` class. The `Exception` class is used in ADO.NET try-catch error handling.
DataAdapter	Translates the data from the data provider source into the in-memory `DataSet` or `DataReader`. The `DataAdapter` performs all queries, translates data from one format to another, and performs table mapping. One `DataAdapter` can manage one database relation. The result collection can have any level of complexity. The `DataAdapter` is also responsible for issuing requests for new connections and terminating connections after it obtains the data.
DataReader	Provides a live connection to the database. However, it only provides a means of reading the database. In addition, the `DataReader` cursor works only in the forward direction. This is the object to use to perform a fast retrieval of a local table when there is no need to update the database. The `DataReader` blocks subsequent `DataAdapters` and associated `Connection` objects, so it's important to close the `DataReader` immediately after using it.

continued

TABLE 32-3 *(continued)*

Class Type	Description
DataSet	Contains a local copy of the data retrieved by one or more `DataAdapters`. The `DataSet` uses a local copy of the data, so the connection to the database isn't live. A user makes all changes to the local copy of the database, and then the application requests an update. (Updates can occur in batch mode or one record at a time.) The `DataSet` maintains information about both the original and the current state of each modified row. If the original row data matches the data on the database, then the `DataAdapter` makes the requested update. If not, then the `DataAdapter` returns an error, which the application must handle. `DataSets` may be typed or untyped in ADO.NET. They are defined in the `System.Data` namespace; and they are not provider specific. Only the `DataAdapter` classes are associated with the provider.
Transaction	Implemented in ADO.NET 2.0. The ADO.NET transaction is, by default, a lightweight transactional container for a single data source. If the ADO code enlists another data source in the transaction, then the transaction will transparently escalate to a distributed or multi-phase transaction, with no additional coding required by the developer.

Managed providers

Five managed providers are included in ADO.NET 3.5:

- **OracleClient:** The Microsoft provider for the Oracle database version 8.1.7 and later. This provider requires that the Oracle client be installed.
- **OleDb:** The bridge provider for using OLEDB providers in ADO.NET
- **SqlClient:** The Microsoft provider for SQL Server 7.0 and later. Just as the OLEDB provider directly connects SQL Server and ADO, the SQLClient uses a private protocol for direct connection to SQL Server from ADO.NET.
- **SqlServerCe:** The Microsoft provider for SQL Server CE mobile edition
- **ODBC:** An API used to access data in a relational or indexed sequential access method or database. Supported in SQL Server through the SQL Server Native Client ODBC driver.

As noted, the `OracleClient` provider requires co-installation of the Oracle client. The OLEDB.NET provider relies on MDAC components for some functionality. `SqlClient` and `SqlServerCe` are contained in the SQL Native Client library.

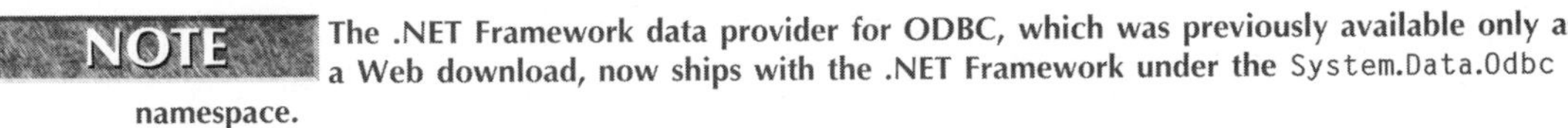

The .NET Framework data provider for ODBC, which was previously available only as a Web download, now ships with the .NET Framework under the `System.Data.Odbc` namespace.

While ADO.NET 1.*x* used the shared MDAC architecture, it did not have a single object that was instantiated to create a command, a data reader, or a data adapter. It supported several per-provider, class-specific objects contained in different libraries that performed these tasks. It was necessary for the developer to select the namespace appropriate to the application. The selected namespace aligned with a specific provider.

When working with SQL Server, that meant using the objects that Microsoft had optimized for native SQL Server use, including `SqlConnection`, `SqlCommand`, `SqlDataReader`, and `SqlDataAdapter`.

These provider-specific classes are still supported. When the data source is SQL Server, the provider-specific classes will be optimized and therefore are preferred. Better performance should be expected from any of the per-provider classes. In addition, there is a common base class alternative with ADO.NET 3.5 that you should consider for use on new projects. In an environment that must support multiple RDBMS data sources, the common class may require fewer lines of code than duplicating the same logic with each provider. However, the likelihood that coding with the common base class will require some per-provider customizations is quite high.

Table 32-4 shows a cross-reference of `System.Data.Common` classes and the provider-specific classes available for each of the class types listed previously in Table 32-3.

TABLE 32-4

ADO.NET 3.5 Class Reference by Namespace

Class Type (from Table 32-3)	System.Data. Common	System.Data. SQLClient	System.Data. OracleClient	System.Data. OleDb	System.Data. Odbc
Connection	DbConnection	SqlConnection	OracleConnection	OleDbConnection	OdbcConnection
ProviderFactory	DbProviderFactory	SqlClientFactory	OracleClientFactory	OleDbFactory	OdbcFactory
Command	DbCommand	SqlCommand	OracleCommand	OleDbCommand	OdbcCommand
Parameter	DbParameter	SqlParameter	OracleParameter	OleDbParameter	OdbcParameter
Error	None	SqlError	None	OleDbError	None
Exception	DbException	SqlException	OracleException	OleDbException	OdbcException
DataAdapter	DbDataAdapter	SqlDataAdapter	OracleDataAdapter	OleDbDataAdapter	OdbcDataAdapter
DataReader	DbDataReader	SqlDataReader	OracleDataReader	OleDbDataReader	OdbcDataReader
Transaction	DbTransaction	SqlTransaction	OracleTransaction	OleDbTransaction	OdbcTransaction

NOTE **When working with other RDBMS data sources in ADO.NET 1.1, the developer had to use a separate but parallel set of ADO.NET provider classes for each provider. Included with the .NET Framework 1.1 were the classes of the `System.Data.OleDb` namespace, the `System.Data.Odbc` namespace, and the `OracleClient` namespace. Developers could also write custom providers; and third-party sources made other provider namespaces available. The same Interfaces used by Microsoft to create the included provider classes can be used to create custom providers.**

Introduced in ADO.NET 2.0, the `System.Data.Common` namespace contains a base class to write provider-independent (often termed *generic*) code. The provider is defined and accessed through the `DbProviderFactory` class in this model. The provider components are `DbConnection`,

DbCommand, DbDataReader, and DbDataAdapter. The factory model creates the capability to specify not only the connection string, but also the provider in the application's configuration file, the registry, another structure, or even user input readable at the time the connection class is instantiated. It is called a factory because of the capability to construct instances of provider-specific classes automatically. The factory-created classes are inherited by a factory class in the SQLClient or any other provider-specific classes. In theory, the result is simplified and provider-agnostic code from the developer's perspective.

In many cases it may be possible to achieve that coding objective with the System.Data.Common classes. Applications that must be able to run on multiple database platforms are prime candidates for generic ADO.NET. In reality, each specific provider needs extensions to the base model, so the base class is probably not completely usable by any .NET providers without some references to provider-specific classes in the developer's code. Consequently, common base class coding may be more complex than using the provider-specific namespaces at this time. Undoubtedly, the common base class' usability will continue to evolve in future releases of ADO.NET. It is conceivable that the provider-specific classes derived from the common base class model may even fall out of favor in the future. For now, it may be wise for all but the most adventurous developers to proceed with some caution into the generic coding model.

NOTE **For additional details on the common base class and the DBPProviderFactory, see the MSDN white papers "Generic Coding with the ADO.NET 2.0 Base Classes and Factories," by Bob Beauchemin, at http://msdn.microsoft.com/en-us/library/ms379620.aspx, and "Writing Generic Data Access Code in ASP.NET 2.0 and ADO.NET 2.0," by Dr. Shahram Khosravi, at http://msdn.microsoft.com/en-us/library/ms971499.aspx. While these articles refer to ADO.NET 2.0, they still apply to ADO.NET 3.5 because the foundations and principles are the same.**

The managed database providers for ADO.NET incorporate a certain level of intelligence not found in the ADO version of the same providers. For example, the .NET providers make better use of database connections. They make and break connections as necessary to ensure optimal use of server and client resources. The differences between an unmanaged provider and a managed provider can easily be categorized into four areas:

- **Object Access Technique:** An unmanaged provider will use a COM progID to access required objects. When working with a managed provider, the application relies on a command class. The command class may still access the COM progID, but the command class hides access details from the developer, which makes development faster and less prone to error. It also enables streamlining of the SQL client data access and the possibility that the ADO.NET code will have the same look and feel regardless of whether the underlying access is via a COM ProgID.
- **Data Result Handling:** The unmanaged provider relies on the Parameter objects of the Command, along with the Recordset and Stream objects provided by ADO, to present the data within the application. The managed equivalents include the Parameter, DataSet, DataTable, and DataReader classes, along with the ExecuteReader, ExecutePageReader, ExecuteNonQuery, and ExecuteScalar methods of the command class and the XML stream. The unmanaged COM interface always incurs the overhead of converting SQL data types to COM data types. The managed providers have the distinct advantage here again because of the XML-based transport stream.

- **Data Updates:** Because the unmanaged environment uses a live connection, resources are in constant use and the user must have a connection to the database. In addition, the developer spends plenty of time creating the commands by hand. The managed environment uses connections only as needed to actually transfer data, so resource usage is more efficient and the user doesn't need a connection at all times. As shown later in the chapter, the managed environment also provides other automation techniques, including the `CommandBuilder` method.
- **Data-Transfer Format:** The unmanaged environment uses binary data transfer. The managed-data provider relies solely on XML for data transfer in ADO.NET 1.*x*. Distributed applications in ADO.NET 2.0 and higher can also be transferred using binary serialization, with a remarkable improvement in size and throughput over XML in cases where remoting is appropriate. Remoting provides improved performance and interoperability in interprocess communication between .NET applications. If either the source or the target of a data transfer is not a .NET application, then XML will provide a standards-based method to transfer data, which requires much less code and therefore lower maintenance cost than unmanaged transfer methods.

The differences in data-transfer methods between the managed XML and unmanaged data providers require close examination. The XML data-transfer format used by a managed provider is better suited to SOA and the Internet because it enables data transfer through firewalls that normally block binary data transfers. However, XML is a bulkier data-transfer method and isn't secure. In the past, it may have been enticing to use ADO for local database needs and ADO.NET for distributed applications because of the obvious size and performance penalties inherent in XML and the illusory security value of binary over ASCII bits flying over the private network. The ADO.NET 3.5 binary serialization option provides a performance advantage to remote streams and thereby helps reduce the often poorly founded temptation to continue to support both ADO and ADO.NET.

SQL Native Client

With SQL Server 2008 and ADO.NET 3.5, access to SQL Server does not rely on MDAC. Instead, the `SQLClient` is contained in a single `.dll` known as the SQL Native Client. The SQL Native Client is expected to resolve the well-known consistency issues in the distribution of updates through the massive MDAC file set, and improve security by limiting the number of interfaces — or surface area — exposed. The proprietary .NET-to-SQL Server access protocols, as well as OLEDB and ODBC interfaces to SQL Server and the traditional native interfaces to SQL Server, are contained in the SQL Native Client.

The SQL Native Client can only be used to access SQL Server 7.0 and later. While it would be nice to say that the SQL Native Client is the only way to access SQL Server, that idea remains elusive. For example, SQLXML is not integrated in the SQL Native Client. SQLXML is a method through which SQL Server exposes the functionality of XML inside the .NET Framework. In all likelihood, many .NET Framework applications will have dependencies on both MDAC and the SQL Native Client. After all, one of the selling points for .NET is heterogeneous data sources. The monolithic SQL Native Client should simplify maintenance and security of the contained interfaces, but it does not appear that there will be a noticeable difference in how applications interact with SQL Server. Similarly, it is likely that ODBC, OleDB, and in particular ADO, access will continue to be problematic to whatever extent the SQL Native Client is dependent on MDAC components.

CROSS-REF Introduced in SQL Server 2005, SQLXML is updated to version 4.0 in SQL Server 2008. While not integrated into the SQL Native Client provider, SQLXML is supported in the .NET Framework through the OLEDB-based SQLXMLOLED provider. Chapter 18, "Manipulating XML Data," offers more information on working with XML in SQL.

Data types

ADO.NET uses XML to move data from the database to the application. This is not XML as in the XML data type, but XML as in the actual carrier of all SQL data, just as TDS is the native binary carrier of SQL data from SQL Server. XML can support all data types without prejudice because XML is a stream of bits. Visual Studio applications, conversely, rely on managed data types to represent onscreen data. In other words, XML adds yet another translation layer to the mix. ADO.NET moves the data in and out of the database on an XML stream. Then it must unpackage the XML stream into the desired flavor of relational data results at the application. All of the data restrictions, oddities, and problems that were discussed earlier regarding ADO also apply to the data provided to the application by ADO.NET. Consequently, developers must consider the same problems, such as data loss and compatibility issues, during development.

Fortunately, the managed environment provides good marshaling for data types used in database management. Using ADO.NET may introduce a small performance penalty to transport the inherently bloated XML stream and to package and unpackage that stream, but it is unlikely that the managed environment will introduce data-translation problems. In fact, the expectation is that in the near future, ADO.NET's XML-based I/O performance will be as good as ADO's binary transport method. ADO.NET uses .NET Framework data types, rather than defining its own data types, as was the case with ADO. This should immediately help curb the proliferation of data type conversion errors at runtime.

One particularly compelling reason to favor ADO.NET over ADO, even in the short term, is ADO.NET's better support for SQL Server's data types, such as `XML`, `VARCHAR(MAX)`, `VARBINARY(MAX)`, the new date and time data types, the new spatial data types, and any CLR user-defined data types.

The `XML` data type that can be stored in SQL Server 2005 and 2008 should not be confused with the XML stream that ADO.NET uses to transport data. The `XML` data type is supported by the `System.Data.SQLTypes SqlXml` data type in ADO.NET 3.5. The `XML` data type can be used to store XML documents and XML document fragments. ADO.NET 3.5 supports reading this data type through the `XmlReader` class. Unlike other SQL Server 2005 and 2008 data types, `XML` is not validated in ADO.NET but at the SQL server. This means that the `XML` data type has some risk of raising errors during the `DataAdapter`'s update method — when changes are sent back to the database — that would not be expected for other primitive data types. SQLXML 4.0 provides the richest client-side support for the `XML` data type, including its own set of data access components. Recall that SQLXML 4.0 is not provided as part of ADO.NET 2.0 or higher.

CLR user-defined data types deserve a special mention here. In order to use a CLR user-defined data type (UDT) in .NET code, a structurally consistent version of the assembly that defines the data type must be available — not only on the database server, but also on the application server. There is a small amount of flexibility in the requirements. It is not necessary that the assembly be a strongly named match on the server and at the application, only that the structure of the type be identically defined at both locations.

This requirement makes sense. The system-defined primitive data types — `int`, `char`, `bit`, and so on — must exist at both locations. The difference lies in the logistics required to keep a custom feature such as the UDT synchronized at all tiers, compared to the comparatively static primitive types. A UDT that is used only on the SQL Server is likely to be of little real value, and a UDT that is deployed in a production environment is likely to be somewhat fragile because of this awkward requirement. Careful deployment planning is necessary when using UDTs in ADO.NET 3.5 applications.

CROSS-REF **For a complete discussion on creating and deploying CLR user-defined data types, see** **Chapter 9, "Data Types, Expressions, and Scalar Functions."**

DataAdapters and DataSets

Until this point in the chapter, ADO and ADO.NET have been shown to be very different technologies despite the similarities in their names and a common purpose. The core of ADO is the `Recordset`. To modify data through a recordset, it is necessary to either use a server API cursor that stays in the database or write code that sends updates back to the database once the changes are identified. Both methods have proven to be fragile because of concurrency and contention issues, and both can require a hefty chunk of code. To work with multiple `Recordsets`, it is necessary to create multiple connections and juggle the `Recordsets` in code or pull multiple `Recordsets` from the database as a collection and work with them one at a time. Similarly, both methods have proven to be rigid and can require a hefty chuck of often repetitive code.

The primary in-memory data store of ADO.NET is the `DataSet`. The `DataAdapter` is used to connect the data source and the in-memory data store. Starting with ADO.NET 2.0, the `DataSet` is more powerful than ever.

The `DataSet` is disconnected from the database in order to reduce database contention, thereby opening the door to highly scalable applications. The code required to either fill the `DataSet` from the database or update the database from the `DataSet` is minimal.

The `DataAdapter` populates the `DataSet` with a stream of data from the database, and handles any inserts, updates, or deletes that must be propagated back to the database.

`DataSet` queries can reference multiple `DataTables` within the `DataSet`, and enforcement of defined relationships and data types occurs seamlessly at the moment data is modified in the `DataSet`.

Index optimizations in ADO.NET 3.5 have enabled the size of the `DataSet` cache to increase significantly, and performance has improved considerably over ADO.NET 1.*x*. A `DataSet` populated with a relatively small amount of data may not realize benefits from these index optimizations. As the `DataSet` grows larger, the optimizations become more important.

NOTE **Visual Studio 2008 is well integrated with ADO.NET 3.5 classes. ADO.NET is already a remarkably easy to use technology. Many features of the Visual Studio UI simplify ADO.NET usage even further. For example, a `DataSet` can be bound to a control simply by dragging and dropping the DataSet on the control at design time. In addition, using the `DataAdapter` Wizard and the `DataSet` Wizard at design time will produce a typed DataSet and the code to populate it.**

Using the CommandBuilder method will automatically create the UPDATE, INSERT, and DELETE commands used by the DataAdapter to maintain the database based on the SELECT statement used to fill the DataSet: one line of code to generate three database operations.

Binary serialization functionality in ADO.NET 3.5 also allows those larger DataSets to be propagated out of the database and between tiers of the application much faster. This feature is most useful in .NET remoting situations whereby different components of the same application do not suffer the complexity and performance penalties when decoding the binary data stream.

By default, the DataReader class uses a read-only, forward-only cursor. The DataReader object is able to offer a connected behavior or to enable disconnected mode operation for applications. A user can download data from the company database while using an Internet (or other) connection. In the disconnected mode, the data is then available for viewing offline (but not for direct modification at the database because the connection to the database is lost). While perhaps more interesting for the DataReader per se than the DataTable, ADO.NET 3.5 also provides methods to fill a DataTable from a DataReader or a database-connected DataAdapter. Increased flexibility and reduction in lines of code required by these refinements to the DataTable class are two more reasons to consider ADO.NET over ADO.

One drawback to programmatically making a DataSet from a DataReader is that the DataSet will not be typed. One advantage of typed data sets is an opportunity for better performance by not forcing any more implicit data-conversion layers or any more complex translations than necessary in .NET. Another advantage is more readable code. For example, to locate and use a column in a DataTable of an untyped DataSet, the code would look like the following:

```
City = dsOrder.Tables[n].Rows[n].ItemArray.GetValue(1).ToSTring()
```

Using an ADO.NET typed DateSet, the code is considerably friendlier:

```
City = dsOrder.Invoice[0].Name;
```

Clearly, the reference to the typed DataSet is more concise.

An ADO Recordset object has the advantage of requiring less code to access an individual value. In addition, note that the field can be accessed by name when using a Recordset object — the DataSet or stand-alone DataTable offers an integer item indexed value that must be derived from the field's position within the data result. The typed DataSet is the readability winner hands down. Using ADO.NET offers other significant advantages that may not be readily identified if an "ADO is better" attitude is allowed to cloud the picture.

Starting in ADO.NET 2.0, ADO.NET provides the capability to return Multiple Active Result Sets (MARS) for SQL Server 2005 and SQL Server 2008. MARS is easily understood as a mechanism for pooling sessions in a similar manner to how connections have been pooled for quite some time in ADO technologies. While there are still many reasons to create multiple connections, in some cases, such as when multiple queries must maintain transactional consistency, a MARS connection can provide that transactional consistency and offer performance benefits without the need for a two-phase transaction riding on multiple connections. SELECT statements can be interleaved as desired when the provider is MARS-enabled. When inserts, updates, or deletes occur on a MARS-enabled connection, serialization of DML and SELECT statements will occur. The MARS behavior is not enabled by default in SQL Server 2005 and 2008. To enable the functionality, specify MultipleActiveResultSets =true in the connection string.

NOTE **Even though MARS is not enabled by default, overhead is involved in all connections in order to support MARS. Microsoft has stated that setting `MultipleActiveResultSets =False` will not eliminate this MARS-related overhead. Possibly the only reason to ever set MARS off is to ensure an error condition when more than one query is submitted on a connection.**

ADO does provide remote connectivity features, but like all other COM-based technologies, it uses the Distributed Component Object Model (DCOM) as the basis for data exchange across a remote network. This means that the connection-port number changes often and that the data itself is in binary form. One benefit of this approach is that few crackers and hackers have the knowledge required to peek at the data (assuming they can unscramble it after locating it). The disadvantages include an inability to leverage ADO.NET 3.5–specific features, the high technical cost of transferring binary data, and web server firewall support. Good firewall design keeps ports closed and restricts binary data.

NOTE **Simply stated, DCOM is COM when the components must communicate on the network. With DCOM, the components use RPC to communicate. In practice, security and integration with the network protocol stack render DCOM a different technology from COM, even though they serve a similar purpose. Readers seeking more details on DCOM should refer to Microsoft's 1996 white paper titled "DCOM Technical Overview," at `http://msdn.microsoft.com/en-us/library/ms809340.aspx`.**

ADO.NET gets around the firewall problems by using XML to transfer the data using Hypertext Transport Protocol (HTTP) or some other appropriate data transfer technology. The data is in ASCII format and relies on a single port for data transfers. Many other tools in the developer's toolkit rise above ADO.NET to better secure XML on the wire, such as SSL encryption and signing, certificate exchange, and the self-contained Web Services Security protocol in environments where text on the wire is a security issue.

A host of additional enhancements are available in ADO.NET 3.5. It would be prudent for the developer community to pay attention to whether actual behavior matches expectations. Some enhancements are made possible by the new features of 2008 and are covered throughout this book. Some of the more interesting .NET enhancements include the following:

- **LINQ:** Introduces query capabilities directly into the .NET Framework programming languages. Query operations are expressed in the query language itself and not as string literals imbedded in the application code.
- **LINQ to SQL:** Provides support for queries against an object model that is mapped to the data structures of a Microsoft SQL Server database without an intermediate conceptual model. Tables are represented by separate classes that are tightly coupled to the object model of the database. LINQ to SQL translates the language-integrated queries in the object model into T-SQL and sends those statements to the database for execution. The reverse happens when the database returns the query results to the application.
- **LINQ to DataSet:** Provides LINQ capabilities for disconnected data stored in a DataSet.
- **SQL Server 2008 SqlClient:** Several new features have been added that support the new enhancements to SQL Server 2008.
  - As discussed previously, new Date and Time data types have been added to SQL Server 2008.
  - Table-valued parameters provide the ability to marshal multiple rows of data from a client application to SQL Server without requiring multiple round-trips to the database server.

- Whereas SQL Server 2005 restricted the size of UDTs to 8 KB, this restriction has been removed in SQL Server 2008.
- SQL Server performance metrics are exposed in the programming interface as properties of the connection.

CROSS-REF **Four important extensions to ADO.NET can be used in server-side CLR on SQL Server:** `SQLContext`, `SqlPipe`, `SqlTriggerContext`, **and** `SqlDataRecord`.

ADO.NET in Visual Studio 2008

There was some concern within the SQL Server DBA community when Microsoft announced that SQL Server's Enterprise Manager would be moving into Visual Studio in Visual Studio 2005. That seems to have been a misunderstanding. SQL Server Management Studio has found its way into the common Visual Studio graphical interface, but they remain separate products sharing little more than a common look and feel.

A complete description of the Visual Studio integrated development environment (IDE) is beyond the scope of this chapter. Fortunately, details of the IDE are well covered in the Microsoft Visual Studio documentation. This section examines the IDE components that are particularly important for the development of successful applications that use ADO.NET 3.5.

Server Explorer

It's a smart bet that each ADO.NET 3.5 project will begin with the Server Explorer. The programmer will either add a data connection or select an existing data connection when an ADO.NET 3.5 project is created. A new data connection can be defined using the Data Source Configuration Wizard from the Data menu item or in Server Explorer by selecting Add Connection from the context menu of the Data Connections icon.

In addition to managing database connections, Server Explorer provides other useful database tools. Database metadata diagramming, access, and generation capabilities are available to the developer from Server Explorer. While the database components exposed by Server Explorer do not provide support identical to Management Studio's Object Explorer, they are quite similar. In some cases, Server Explorer is better than Management Studio. For example, not only can database objects be created, viewed, and modified from Server Explorer, but typed `DataSets` and `DataTables` can be created just by dropping tables from Server Explorer onto the `DataSet` at design time.

Programming purists might object to this easy drag-and-drop approach to coding, but developers shouldn't discount the real performance and consistency benefits of typed data sets, which are often derided in part because of the tedium and precision required to code a typed `DataSet`. Developers and DBAs with a shortage of time and a wealth of workload will appreciate the help. Everyone stands a much improved chance of meeting those ever-shortening project deadlines when the Visual Studio helpers are used.

NOTE **Server Explorer functionality is accessible programmatically through the** `ServiceController` **namespace. This can provide elegant, high-level access to automated actions such as starting and stopping services.**

Debugging ADO.NET

Interactively debugging application code in Visual Studio is straightforward and elegant. ADO.NET code is specialized to the data source. It is of unquestionable benefit to be able to include not only the application code, but also T-SQL code executing on the data source in the debugging session. Getting the debugger to step into T-SQL code is somewhat painful. To be able to step into database code while debugging an application in Visual Studio, all of the following conditions must be met:

- Allow SQL/CLR Debugging must be enabled on the data connection in Server Explorer.
- Enable SQL Server Debugging must be checked on the Debug tab of the project's Properties dialog in Solution Explorer.
- Visual Studio's Remote Components Setup must have been run on the SQL Server machine if the SQL Server is not running on the same OS instance as Visual Studio.
- Additionally, if SQL Server and Visual Studio are not on the same computer, and either SQL Server or Visual Studio is running on Windows XP with the Internet firewall, then the firewall must be configured to allow remote debugging. On the Visual Studio machine, this would involve adding `devenv.exe` to the white list and opening port 135. On the SQL Server machine, `sqlservr.exe` must be added and port 135 opened.
- If server-side CLR components are to be debugged, then it is necessary to install and configure the Visual Studio Remote Debug Monitor on the SQL Server 2008 machine.
- If the remote SQL Server is a SQL Server 7 or SQL Server 2000 instance, then it is necessary to configure DCOM on the SQL Server to allow remote debugging using the `dcomcnfg.exe` utility. The procedure varies by operating system. Refer to the DCOM documentation or to the Microsoft Visual Studio documentation for complete details.
- The Visual Studio documentation on debugging is outstanding. Complete information on how to use the debugging tools, including what is installed on a SQL Server when remote debugging is enabled, is available.

Debugging T-SQL code causes all managed connections on the database server instance to stop while the developer is stepping through a stored procedure or function. All resource locks will also persist according to the normal concurrency configuration for the SQL Server. Essentially, this means that debugging T-SQL code on a busy SQL Server is to be avoided. By extension, it should almost go without saying that using the Visual Studio debugger on a production SQL Server is sure to cause more problems than it might solve.

Application tracing

Once the application has been moved to production, tools such as Server Explorer and the Visual Studio debugger facilities are of little use. There are runtime tools such as the Windows debugger and SQL Profiler that can identify problems that inevitably surface only in the production environment. SQL Profiler is an excellent tool for performance tuning and troubleshooting at the SQL Server. Many readers may be familiar with the ODBC runtime tracing capability. While ODBC trace is exceptionally verbose and anything but lightweight, it identifies error conditions and connectivity problems down to the application statement level. Furthermore, it is possible to employ ODBC trace even in the production environment when necessary. Visual Studio languages have offered various types of debug build-only assertion capabilities for some time. The .NET Framework offers a diagnostics alternative that is usable in both debug and release builds in the `System.Diagnostics.Trace` namespace.

It's up to developers to instrument their application by adding trace points during development. By default, every .NET application domain — the basic unit of isolation in the CLR — contains a `DefaultTraceListener`, and can contain other listeners in its collection. Normally the role of the trace listener is to direct trace output to a file or the event log. A .NET application developer can define trace points at method calls or even metrics such as performance counters throughout the application's code.

Trace switches can also be defined by the developer to produce various levels of trace output during runtime, depending on the value of the trace switch. Trace switches can be set at runtime within the `app.config` file. Under favorable run conditions, tracing can be disabled. If problems occur, then tracing can be enabled at a level appropriate for capturing information for a given problem.

CROSS-REF **Among the wealth of information available on the Internet about trace instrumentation with the .NET Framework is a very good MSDN magazine article by Jon Fancet, "Powerful Instrumentation Options in .NET Let You Build Manageable Apps with Confidence," at** `http://msdn.microsoft.com/en-us/magazine/cc300488.aspx`**, and an excellent MSDN white paper by Bob Beauchemin, "Tracing Data Access," at** `http://msdn.microsoft.com/en-us/library/ms971550.aspx`**.**

Beginning with ADO.NET 2.0, trace instrumentation is extended by Microsoft to include built-in trace points in the ADO.NET assemblies, the SQL Native Client `.dll`, and the other .NET providers. ADO.NET 2.0 introduced built-in tracing functionality that is supported by all the .NET data providers for SQL Server, Oracle, OLEDB, and ODBC, and even the ADO.NET DataSet and SQL Server 2005 network protocols.

Tracing is not an ADO.NET-specific feature, but Microsoft providers in ADO.NET 2.0 and later can take advantage of generalized tracing and instrumentation APIs.

Tracing data access API calls can help diagnose problems such as schema mismatch between client and database, incorrect SQL, invalid programming logic, and database availability.

Application Building Basics

This discussion of ADO.NET 3.5 would not be complete without a look at the code techniques that have been covered thus far in this chapter. This section provides code that uses the `adodb.dll` .NET primary interop assembly to interact with SQL Server, code that uses the `SqlClient` to perform equivalent operations, and code that demonstrates access through the SQL Native Client using the common base classes. As stated previously, the ADO and ADO.NET technologies are fundamentally different yet do similar work. The code is presented to show how different interactions with the database are completed by each technology.

Little space is given here to matters of graphical interface design, XML, or remoting in the .NET Framework. Windows Forms design, ASP.NET, SOA, and remoting are extensive subjects that require more space than the *SQL Server 2008 Bible* can allocate. Instead, shown here are the methods needed to move data in and out of the data source and how to work with the ADO.NET components. The purpose is to see how easily and elegantly data can be moved in and out of the data access layer. What is done with that data above the data access layer is best left to the developer's imagination.

With that said, the coding style used here is intended only to permit a straightforward view of a particular method. How ADO.NET is used in .NET Framework programming depends largely on usage requirements and the established coding practices within a given development environment.

The first activity in any ADO.NET project is to connect to the data source(s) that will be used to develop the project using the Server Explorer.

CROSS-REF **Sample code for this chapter is available on the *SQL Server 2008 Bible* website at** `www.sqlserverbible.com`. **The code uses a console application to show the techniques that follow.**

Connecting to SQL Server

The easiest way to create a connection is to run the Data Source Configuration Wizard. From the Visual Studio Data menu, launch the wizard by selecting Add New Data Source, or view the data sources associated with an existing application project by selecting the Show Data Sources menu option.

It is easy to programmatically define a connection string. The connection string is a set of name-value pairs. One slight confusion in defining connection strings is that they can be somewhat different for each .NET provider, and the ADO connection is different still.

TIP **With .NET Framework 2.0 and later, connection strings are more flexible than in the past. For example, an** `ADODB.dll` **provider connection string or a SNAC connection string allow the SQL Server to be called a "Data Source" or a "Server."**

It is possible to define the connection string based on values stored in the file system or in the registry or specified by a user. If the common base class is used, then it is possible to define both the provider used and the connection string in the `app.config` file.

What's new in ADO.NET 3.5

This section covers what's new in ADO.NET 3.5.

LINQ

One of the major new features to ADO.NET 3.5 is LINQ (Language Integrated Query). LINQ is a welcome new advancement in query technology that introduces query facilities and capabilities directly into the .NET Framework 3.0 programming languages.

The goal of LINQ is to fill the gap between two completely different spheres, that of data and that of objects. For example, developers up until now have had to learn completely different querying technologies or languages, depending on the source of data, such as SQL databases and XML documents. LINQ bridges this gap by making a query a first-class construct in .NET. Instead of writing inline SQL to query a SQL database or using XQuery or XPath to query an XML document, developers can now write queries against strongly typed objects using standard query operators and keywords.

The additional benefit of this is that now there is compile-time syntax checking and IntelliSense, providing improved developer productivity. Because of LINQ integration into Visual Studio, developers can write queries in either C# or Visual Basic that can query SQL databases, ADO.NET DataSets, XML documents, and even an in-memory collection of objects. Anything that implements and supports the `IEnumerable` or `IEnumerable<T>` interfaces can be queried using LINQ.

CROSS-REF **Chapter 34, "LINQ," is completely dedicated to LINQ and LINQ technologies.**

Table-valued parameters

Table-valued parameters are a new parameter type in SQL Server 2008 that enable developers to send multiple rows of data to a stored procedure or function. They are declared by using user-defined table types and have the benefit of not requiring the creation of temporary tables or passing in a bunch of parameters.

In essence, table-valued parameters are an easy way to funnel multiple rows of data from the application to SQL Server in a single trip. An added value is that table-valued parameters are strongly typed, and structure validation is automatic. Moreover, the only limitation to the size of a table-valued parameter is the amount of server memory.

For example, the following illustrates how to add rows of data to a table-valued parameter from a data reader:

```
Dim cmd As New SqlCommand("usp_AddEmployees", conn)
cmd.CommandType = CommandType.StoredProcedure
Dim tvp As SqlParameter = cmd.Parameters.AddWithValue( _
    "@tvpNewEmployees", dataReader)
tvp.SqlDbType = SqlDbType.Structured
```

Likewise, a SQL parameter can be configured to insert data using a table-valued parameter as follows:

```
Dim cmd AS New SqlCommand(strInsert, conn)
Dim tvp As SqlParameter = cmd.Parameters.AddWithValue( _
    "@tvpNewEmployees", addedEmps)
tvp.SqlDbType = SqlDbType.Structured
tvp.TypeName = "@EmployeeTableType"
```

From the SQL side, a table type needs to be created that defines the table structure. That new table type can then be used in a routine (stored procedure or function, for example).

Keep in mind that table-valued parameters are for input. Using the `OUTPUT` keyword won't work; it is not supported and data cannot be returned. In addition, a name type for the table-value parameter must be specified as part of the `SqlParameter`. This is done using the `TypeName` property.

From an application perspective, the SqlClient provider supports populating table-valued parameters via several options. A developer can use a `DataTable`, a `DbDataReader`, or a generic list (`System.Collections.Generic.IList<SqlDataRecord>`).

Stored procedures vs. parameterized/ad-hoc queries

"Is it better to use stored procedures or parameterized/ad-hoc queries?" is an age-old debate. Everyone has an opinion on this topic — a topic that has caused watercoolers everywhere to boil over from the heated discussions among developers gathered around them. First, you need to understand the difference between the two options.

Ad-hoc SQL is any query sent to SQL Server as opposed to calling stored procedures. Not all ad-hoc queries are parameterized. This differs from dynamic SQL in that dynamic SQL is any code-generated SQL regardless of whether it is generated in the client or in a stored procedure.

What I want to stress here is that when dealing with SQL on the client side, a developer has several options, and some are better than others. First and foremost, use stored procedures whenever possible. The following .NET code calls a stored procedure, which also utilizes a parameter:

```
Dim tConnStr = "connectioninfo"

Using conn As New SqlConnection(tConnStr)
    Dim cmd As New SqlCommand("uspGetEmployeeInfo", conn)
    cmd.CommandType = CommandType.StoredProcedure
    conn.Open()

    Dim param As New SqlParameter("@EmployeeID", SqlDbType.Int)
    With param
        .IsNullable = True
        .Direction = ParameterDirection.Input
        .Value = 5
    End With

    cmd.Parameters.Add(param)

    Dim rdr As SqlDataReader = cmd.ExecuteReader
    If rdr.HasRows Then
    rdr.Read()

    End If

End Using
```

Why use stored procedures? There are several reasons. First, they create an abstraction layer between the database and the application. By creating this layer, changes to the database (schema changes, new DB technology, tuning) have much less chance of breaking the application. The application should have no knowledge of the physical shape of the database at all. This enables the database experts to work their tuning/indexing/relationship magic without breaking the application.

The second reason is security. SQL injection attacks are much less common and easier to prevent when using stored procedures. This is because, as stated earlier, ad-hoc queries require that the underlying database objects be exposed.

However, if you need to use ad-hoc queries, make sure that the SQL is used with parameters, as shown in the example that follows, as this helps lessen the likelihood of an injection attack:

```
Dim tConnStr = "connectioninfo"

Using conn As New SqlConnection(tConnStr)
    Dim cmd As New SqlCommand("SELECT EmployeeID, ManagerID, _    Title,
HireDate, BirthDate FROM HumanResources.Employee WHERE _ EmployeeID =
@EmployeeID", conn)
    cmd.CommandType = CommandType.Text
    conn.Open()
```

```
        Dim param As New SqlParameter("@EmployeeID", SqlDbType.Int)
        With param
            .IsNullable = True
            .Direction = ParameterDirection.Input
            .Value = 5
        End With

        cmd.Parameters.Add(param)

        Dim rdr As SqlDataReader = cmd.ExecuteReader
        If rdr.HasRows Then
            rdr.Read()

        End If
    End Using
```

I cannot stress enough the importance of using stored procedures and parameterized queries (whether it's with stored procedures or ad-hoc queries). However, by using stored procedures, the likelihood of breaking the application when the database schema changes is drastically reduced; and it is hard to tune a database when the SQL is embedded in the application.

There must be a layer of abstraction between the application and the database. When designing a database, many developers forget that there are two layers to the process — physical and logical. Many developers create the database and then begin to code directly against the physical layer. Because there is now no layer of abstraction, they lose many of the benefits described earlier.

CROSS-REF For more information on SQL generation and dynamic SQL, see Chapter 29 "Dynamic SQL and Code Generation," as well as Chapter 63, "Interpreting Query Execution Plans."

Data adapters

The Data Source Configuration Wizard offers opportunities to specify tables, views, stored procedures, and functions that are to be used to create the `DataSet` and to create a typed `DataSet`. Alternately, the `DataSet` can be added and specified by adding a data set to the project in Solution Explorer. Using this method, the Dataset Designer will be opened for the project.

The Dataset Designer enables either the toolbox or Server Explorer to be used to source and identify the application's `DataSet`. The Dataset Designer tool is another great way to ensure that only typed data sets are created. The programming purist can even type out the definition for a typed data set if so desired, although there seems to be scant justification for this technique.

Recall that a typed `DataSet` can prevent runtime data conversion errors from sneaking into the code. If the intention is to use an untyped `DataSet`, then there is no reason to use the Dataset Designer. Simply declare a new, empty `DataSet` in-line, before it is filled from the specified `DataAdapter`:

```
'populate an untyped dataset from a SqlDataAdapter
Dim daScrapReasons As SqlDataAdapter = _
        New SqlDataAdapter(sSQLScrapReasons, cnADONET2)
```

```
'create an untyped dataset
Dim dsWOWithScrap As New DataSet

'fill the DataSet from the Adapter
daScrapReasons.Fill(dsWOWithScrap, "ScrapReason")
```

If the developer opts for the typed data set, then the Table Adapter Configuration Wizard can be used to create a TableAdapter for each table in the specified DataSet. The wizard is launched from the context menu of the Dataset Designer design surface. Within this wizard, the programmer can select database tables or specify queries and stored procedures from which to populate the table adapter(s). Once the table population is defined, the wizard willingly creates the INSERT, UPDATE, and DELETE SQL commands that will be executed when the DataAdapter.Update method is called on the data set. These commands can be viewed and edited as desired in the Properties pane of the adapter. The code generated by the design surface can also be viewed. Editing this code is not recommended, as changes may cause incorrect behavior. Any custom changes will be lost if the DataSet or TableAdapter is regenerated by the wizard.

DataReaders and Recordsets

ADO Recordsets can be processed as Server API cursors or as client cursors. On the client side, the Recordsets can be used after the database connection is closed, but it is completely up to the developer to determine if and how the data can be modified and propagated back to the database:

```
'A record set from an ADO server side cursor
Dim rsADOWOWithScrap As New ADODB.Recordset
rsADOWOWithScrap.CursorLocation = CursorLocationEnum.adUseServer

rsADOWOWithScrap.Open(sSQLWOWithScrap, cnADO,_
                      CursorTypeEnum.adOpenForwardOnly, _
                      LockTypeEnum.adLockReadOnly)
'A disconnected recordset from an ADO client cursor
Dim cmdADOWOWithScrap1 As New ADODB.Command
Dim rsADOWOWithScrap1 As New ADODB.Recordset
cmdADOWOWithScrap1.CommandText = sSQLWOWithScrap
cmdADOWOWithScrap1.CommandType = _
                    CommandTypeEnum.adCmdText
rsADOWOWithScrap1.CursorType = _
                    CursorTypeEnum.adOpenStatic
rsADOWOWithScrap1.LockType = _
                    LockTypeEnum.adLockBatchOptimistic
rsADOWOWithScrap1.CursorLocation = _
                    CursorLocationEnum.adUseClient
cmdADOWOWithScrap1.ActiveConnection = cnADO
rsADOWOWithScrap1 = cmdADOWOWithScrap1.Execute
```

The ADO.NET DataReader is a forward-only client cursor. It can be loaded into a DataTable if needed. The DataAdapter includes methods to insert, update, and delete data from the DataSet's DataTable back to the database.

Streams

Data can be streamed in and out of the database as XML or in binary format. Streams can be somewhat difficult to work with because of their transient nature. Generally, a stream can be consumed once and then it disappears:

```
Dim bfBINWOWithScrap As New Binary.BinaryFormatter
Dim msXMLWOWithScrap As New MemoryStream()
Dim msBINWOWithScrap As New MemoryStream()

'get XML streamfrom dataset
bfBINWOWithScrap.Serialize(msXMLWOWithScrap, _
                           dsBINWOWithScrap)
```

Typically, XML streams are used in .NET Framework AppDomains and to move data in service-oriented settings. Binary streams are most frequently used in scenarios where remoting between AppDomains is appropriate. Intimate knowledge of the data is necessary to serialize (that is, meaningfully write to disk) a binary stream. The XML stream includes metadata information and can be serialized by any receiver that is able to manipulate XML.

Asynchronous execution

In some cases, a query or procedure needs time to execute at the database, and the application can do other useful work while the query completes. In spite of the somewhat restrictive rules regarding when asynchronous execution can be used, the capability provides increased flexibility, as shown in the following code:

```
Dim rdrAsyncScrapCountInit As IAsyncResult = _
             cmdScrapCount.BeginExecuteReader

'do some other work

Dim rdrAsyncScrapCount As SqlDataReader = _
  cmdScrapCount.EndExecuteReader(rdrAsyncScrapCountInit)
```

The database connection will support only one asynchronous query at a time. This means that from the application or mid-tier, multiple connections might be required. From server-side CLR, asynchronous queries are not supported in ADO.NET 3.5.

Using a single database value

An application is often interested in a single column or perhaps a few columns from a single row. With ADO, the options are to execute a query and return the value into a `Recordset` that is one-column wide and one-row long, or to execute a command with output parameters defined in the command's parameters collection. The single value or single row into a `Recordset` is well known to be the least scalable because of the overhead required to build and tear down the `Recordset` repeatedly. Therefore, in ADO, the preference should always go to using the parameters collection:

```
paramscrapWOCount = _
  cmdScrapWOByProduct.CreateParameter("ScrapWOCount", _
```

```
                                        DataTypeEnum.adInteger, _
                                        ParameterDirectionEnum.adParamOutput)
            cmdScrapWOByProduct.Parameters.Append(paramscrapWOCount)
            cmdScrapWOByProduct.Parameters.Item("ProductName").Value =
      sProductName
```

With ADO.NET, the options are greater and the preference less obvious. The value can be returned into a DataTable of one row in length. This method could be advantageous in some scenarios where the data point is used in concert with other DataTables in the DataSet. In addition, the ExecuteWithNoQuery method could be used to populate variables via the parameters collection when multiple columns from a single row are of interest; or the ExecuteScalar method could be used for cases when only a single value will be needed:

```
            Dim iScrapWOCount As Integer = _
                  cmdScrapCount.ExecuteScalar()
```

or

```
            cmdScrapCountByProduct.Parameters.Add("@ScrapWOCount", _
                                     SqlDbType.Int).Direction = _
                                     ParameterDirection.Output
            cmdScrapCountByProduct.ExecuteNonQuery()
```

Data modification

When a change is made to data in the .NET application, the change must be moved to the database. This can be done within a pessimistic concurrency model or an optimistic concurrency model. The concurrency model is actually a mechanism to aid the developer in deciding whether to use a disconnected ADO.NET DataClass (under the optimistic concurrency model) or a connected method (under the pessimistic model) to read and write to the database.

NOTE **The pessimistic concurrency model is useful when data is bulk loaded or when DML queries (INSERT, UPDATE, or DELETE SQL statements) or input parameters are used within an ExecuteNonQuery statement. The optimistic concurrency model is useful when it is desirable for the application to take specific steps such as retrying or writing to a failure log when a data modification operation fails.**

Updating a DataSet requires nothing more than value assignment within .NET. Any or all rows in a DataSet can be inserted, deleted, or updated. When a data row is changed within a DataSet, the row is marked as changed. Running the Update method of the DataAdapter will cause the INSERT, UPDATE, and DELETE commands defined in the DataAdapter to be executed on the database using the DataAdapter's data. It is possible that another user has changed a data point between the time it was read to a DataAdapter and the time that data was written back to the database. In such a case, if the insert fails, then the code must determine whether a concurrency error has occurred. This is typically done with a timestamp column or by comparing the original values in the DataSet with the current values in the database when an UPDATE method is executed. It is the developer's responsibility to determine the correct resolution for such concurrency collisions.

In ADO.NET 1.1, the INSERT, UPDATE, and DELETE commands processed by the Update method could be automatically generated by the Table Adapter Configuration Wizard. The generated statements would compare every column of the table in the `DataSet` with the corresponding database column using a .NET concurrency option named `CompareAllSearchableValues`. The resulting statements were unruly, performed poorly, and made it difficult to detect and resolve collisions.

The preferred method is to use stored procedures even for the commands in the `DataAdapter`. With ADO.NET 3.5, stored procedures can be created using the wizard, although they are not particularly good procedures. Different concurrency options other than `CompareAllSearchableValues` can also be specified. Alternatives include `CompareRowVersion`, which checks for changes in the primary key and the row version, and `OverwriteChanges`, which checks only the primary key to determine whether a collision has occurred. The options are getting better, but the preferred method is still to write custom SQL commands for `DataAdapters` and to use stored procedures, rather than embed SQL statements in the application code.

Binding to controls

In the true spirit of reducing lines of code, the only thing necessary to bind data to a control in Visual Studio 2008 is to drag the data component onto the control and voilà! A bound data control is created. To make things look nice, it is almost a certainty that more layout design will be needed, but that takes us out of ADO.NET programming and into the business of form design.

Summary

This chapter compared ADO and ADO.NET and discussed the advantages and limitations of one over the other at some length. Admittedly, the bias has been one in favor of ADO.NET. While it was perhaps less compelling to use ADO.NET 1.*x* than good old ADO in some scenarios, this chapter tried to show that, in fact, ADO.NET 3.5 offers the most complete high-level data access technology from Microsoft to date. This chapter discussed the following:

- The differences between ADO and ADO.NET
- Usability features in Visual Studio 2008
- New ADO.NET 3.5 features
- SQL Server 2008 SQL Native Client features

With an understanding of Visual Studio 2008 and the new ADO.NET 3.5 features, you are ready for the next chapter, which discusses the Sync Framework.

Chapter 33

Sync Framework

The Microsoft Sync Framework is a robust, comprehensive yet user-friendly synchronization platform providing synchronization capabilities between two distinct data sources. It also enables developers to create and include sync capabilities in their applications.

The overall goal of the Sync Framework is to enable synchronization between two peers such as two SQL Server databases or a Microsoft SQL Server Compact database client and another data source. It was created when Microsoft perceived the need among developers to synchronize data sources without having to require a DBA to create SQL Server publishers, publications, and subscriptions using replication.

One of the components of the Sync Framework is Sync Services, which provides a powerful yet flexible API that enables developers to create applications that provide offline and collaboration capabilities, which can enhance their applications, as well as services or mobile devices.

Because Sync Services is part of the Microsoft Sync Framework, any database that uses Sync Services can also participate in the exchange of information with other data sources supported by the Sync Framework, including file systems and Web Services or even custom data stores. While it is not integrated into SQL Server Management Studio, the Sync Framework and Sync Services is part of the SQL Server 2008 installation and can be used with all SQL Server versions and editions.

This chapter begins by providing an overview of the Microsoft Sync Framework and discussing some of its fundamentals, and then dives into the core functionality of Microsoft Sync Services.

IN THIS CHAPTER

Sync Framework example

The best way to understand the Microsoft Sync Framework is to see it in action. So before we dive into any technical mumbo jumbo (I'm starting a new trend; "mumbo jumbo" is the new technical term for really cool technical stuff), let's dive right into an example.

If you have not installed synchronization services as part of your SQL Server 2008 installation, then rerun setup (it is an optional feature at the bottom of the Shared Features section), or download the appropriate Sync Framework. Version 2.0 can be found at `www.microsoft.com/downloads/details.aspx?FamilyId=109DB36E-CDD0-4514-9FB5-B77D9CEA37F6&displaylang=en`.

This file is a zip file that contains, and installs, the following:

- Microsoft Sync Framework Runtime v2.0
- Microsoft Sync Framework SDK v2.0
- Microsoft Sync Framework Services v2.0
- Microsoft Sync Framework Services for ADO.NET v3.0

This example also assumes that you have the SQL Server `AdventureWorks` databases installed. These databases are installed as part of the Microsoft SQL Server installation. They are not installed by default, so if you do not have them, rerun the SQL Server installation and select the Sample Databases feature.

Once everything has been installed, start Visual Studio 2008 and create a new Windows Forms application. It does not matter if you create a VB.NET or C# project, but this example will be using C#. On the New Project dialog, make sure that .NET Framework 3.5 is selected. This example names the project "SyncFrameworkDemo," but feel free to name the project whatever suits you.

Once the project has been created, the first thing that needs to be done is to add a local data cache. Right-click on the project (it will be called SyncFrameworkDemo) in Solution Explorer and select Add ➪ New Item from the context menu. This will open the Add New Item dialog.

In the Add New Item dialog, select the Data category tab, and then select the Local Database Cache template. Name the data cache "DataCache" and click Add.

Clicking Add will open the Configuration Data Synchronization dialog. This dialog serves several purposes. As it states near the top of the dialog, this is where a connection to a remote database is either created or selected, and the client connection is created. The client connection is the local database where cached tables are used for synchronization.

This dialog is also where the tables are selected to be included in the synchronization and cached locally. If any connections have been previously created, they can be selected in the Server connection drop-down. Otherwise, click the New button next to Server connection, which enables you to define a connection to the remote database.

You can also click the New button next to Client connection to define the connection to the client data cache. Expand the Advanced section to view advanced configuration items, such as synchronization transactions. For this example, no changes will be made to these items.

Once connections have been defined, this dialog should look like Figure 33-1.

FIGURE 33-1

The Configure Data Synchronization dialog

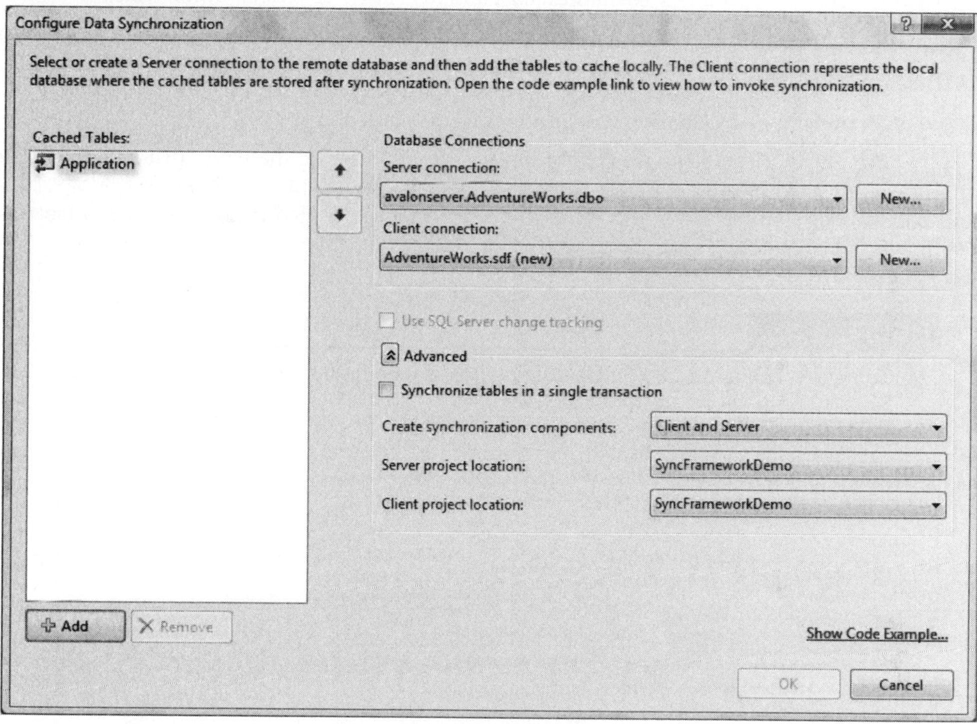

Once the connections to the server and the client have been created, tables can now be selected. To do this, click the Add button below the Cached Tables list. This will open the dialog shown in Figure 33-2.

The Configure Tables dialog enables you to select the tables to be included in the client-side cache. Think about this for a minute. When dealing with Sync Services, you need to consider where this functionality will more than likely be used. In a real-world scenario, you would probably see Sync Services used in applications that run on laptops, but you might also see Sync Services running on tablets or PDAs — devices that really don't have a lot of storage capabilities. For this reason, you don't want to select every single table. You want to select only the tables that are practical for the application.

In this example I have connected to the `AdventureWorks` database, which has just over 70 tables. For this example, only the `HumanResources.Employee` table will be used. Notice that prior to selecting any tables, the information on the right is grayed out. As you select a table, the options on the right are enabled, providing the capability to define synchronization properties per table.

- Data to download: "New and incremental changes after first synchronization" retrieves records from the server that have been modified since the last time data was synchronized. The entire table is downloaded the first time synchronization is called. "Entire table each time" drops the local table and replaces it with the version on the server.

- Compare updates using: This option enables you to select the column name in the selected table that is used to track when the last update of a record was made. Any column in the table that is defined as a `datetime` or `timestamp` data type will appear in this list. You can also choose to let a new column called `LastEditDate` be created in the table.
- Compare inserts using: Enables you to select the column name in the selected table that is used to track when new records are added to the table. Any column in the table that is defined as a `datetime` or `timestamp` data type will appear in this list. You can also choose to let a new column called CreationDate be created in the table.
- Move deleted items to: Enables you to pick the table on the server that will be used to store deleted records. If a table named *`tablename`*`_Deleted` or *`tablename`*`_Tombstone` already exists on the server, that table will be used for the deleted items; otherwise, a table named *`tablename`*`_Tombstone` will be created.

FIGURE 33-2

The Configure Tables for Offline Use dialog box is where you select tables.

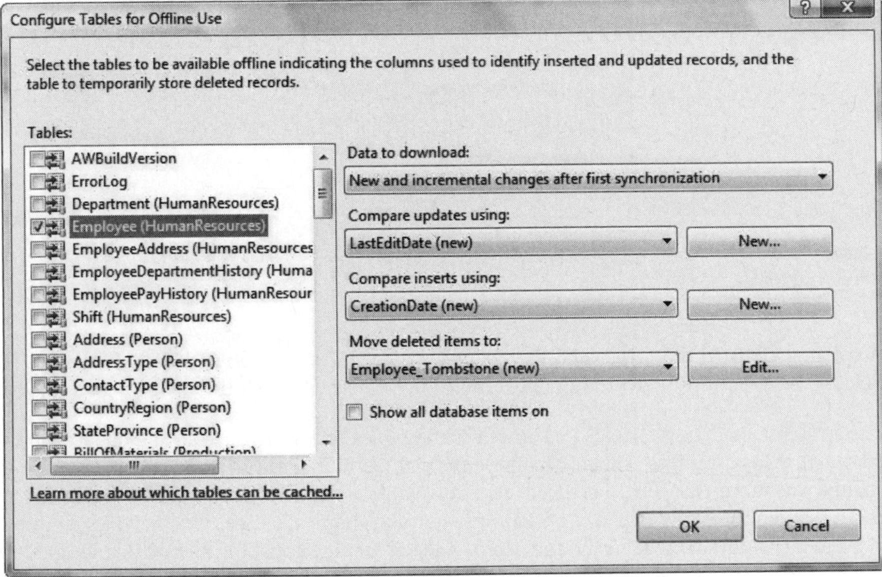

After you have selected the tables you want to cache, click OK. This will bring you back to the Configuration Data Synchronization dialog with the tables you selected listed under the Cached Tables section. Click OK on this dialog.

A small dialog will appear informing you that it needs to update the server, giving you the option to save SQL scripts to be used later if needed. By default, both of these options are selected. Click OK on this dialog.

The wizard will then create the local database cache (.sdf), create the selected tables inside that database, and then copy over the records for each of those tables. Once all of the data is copied over, the next step in the wizard will appear, asking you which of the selected tables in the database cache should be included in the dataset, as shown in Figure 33-3.

FIGURE 33-3

Use this dialog box to choose which objects sets you want included in your dataset.

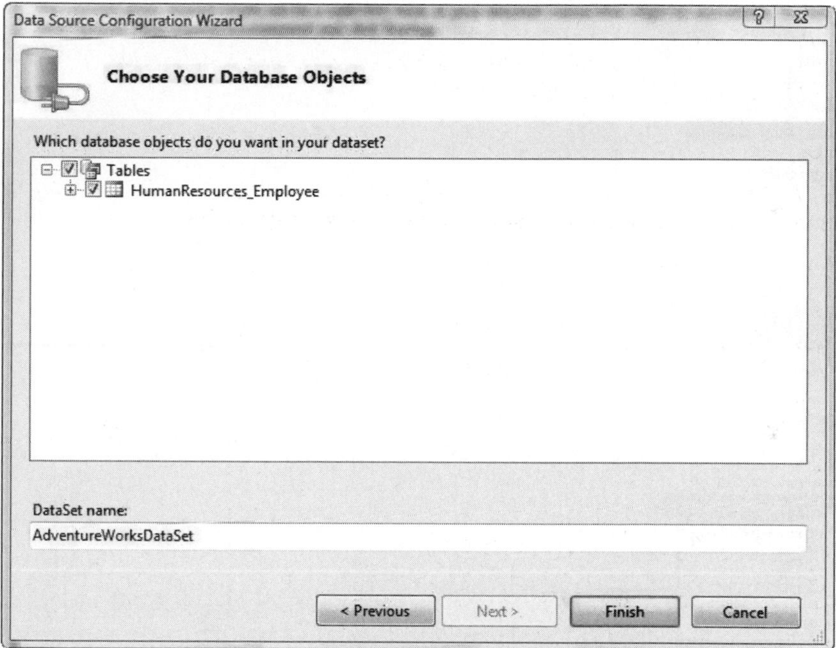

Select all of the tables in this dialog and click Finish. The dataset is then created with the selected tables.

At this point, your Solution Explorer should look like Figure 33-4, containing the client database cache, the appropriate references, SQL scripts, and a blank form called Form1. From here it is time to start writing code to synchronize the local cache with the main database and vice versa. Luckily, Microsoft makes this really easy — very little code is required to get synchronization working.

In the Visual Studio IDE, make sure that the Data Sources Explorer bar is displayed. If it is not, then select Show Data Sources from the Data menu. The Data Sources Explorer bar will open on the left side of the IDE by default.

Open form1 in design view; and in the Data Sources Explorer (see Figure 33-5), select the `Human_Resources_Employee` table, ensuring that the DataGridView option is selected from the drop-down menu. Drag the Employee table onto the form.

FIGURE 33-4

Check your Solution Explorer for the client database cache, the appropriate references, SQL scripts, and a blank form.

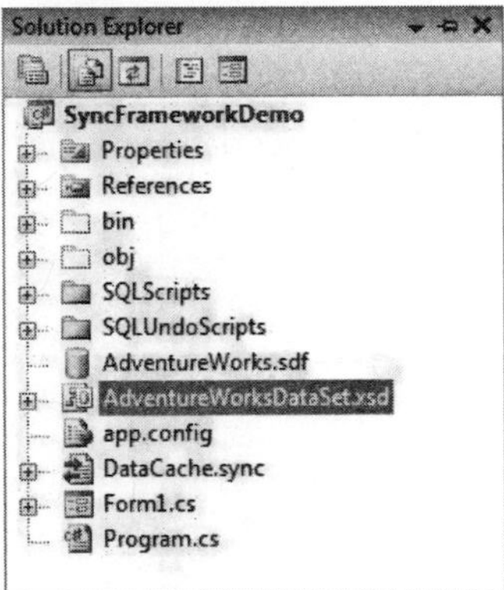

FIGURE 33-5

The Data Sources Explorer lets you select the DataGridView.

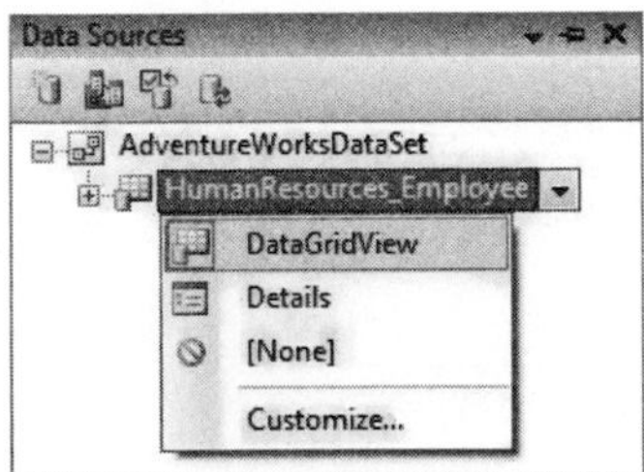

Here is where it gets cool. Visual Studio automatically creates the data grid and navigation controls for you. Not only that, it also creates a ton of the code behind the form as well, such as saving and loading of the data. How awesome is that! Visual Studio will automatically place the navigation bar at the top of the form, and randomly place the grid below that. Select the grid on the form, and in the properties of that grid set the `Dock` property to `Fill`. This will ensure that the grid fills the rest of the form and even expand with the form as it is resized. Notice that the navigation bar has most of the button functionality needed to work with the grid, such as add, delete, and save.

As the form sits now, it really can't do any synchronization. It can and will load the data and save the data back to the cache if any changes are made and the Save button on the navigation bar is clicked. Go ahead and run the application as is. Notice that the data is loaded when the form loads. While this is nice, it can also be a nuisance. For example, the `SalesOrderHeader` table contains roughly 31,500 records. That might take a moment to load. However, what if there were 100,000 records or more? From a user-experience standpoint, you really don't want the application, or any form for that matter, to take a long time to display while it loads a ton of data.

The next steps, therefore, are going to implement synchronization logic and change when the loading of the data takes place. The really neat part about this is that it takes only a few lines of code to do all of this. Sweet.

The first thing that needs to be done is to add a couple of buttons to the navigation bar. Again, this is really easy. Simply click on the navigation bar next to the Save button and a new object placeholder will appear with a drop-down arrow. When the arrow is selected, a list of objects appears that can be added to the navigation bar, as shown in Figure 33-6. For this example, select the top option, Button. This will be the button that loads the data when clicked. Add another button for the synchronization.

FIGURE 33-6

A list of objects can be added to the navigation bar.

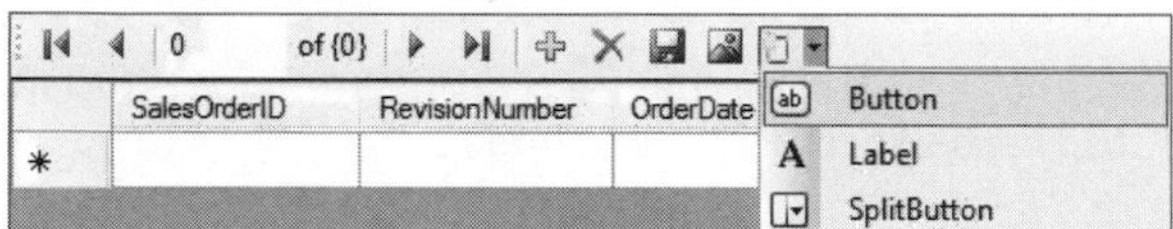

To make things easy, rename the first button from toolStripButton1 to "btnLoadData" and set its `Text` property to `Load Data`. Rename the second button to "btnSync" and set its `Text` property to `Sync Data`. Setting the `Text` property will display the text when you hover the mouse over each button.

Double-click the first button, which will open the code behind the form and create the `Click()` event for this button. This event will not contain code, but the code we do want is in the load event of the form. Therefore, find the Form1_Load event and copy and paste the following line of code from the form load event to the btnLoadData click event:

```
this.humanResources_EmployeeTableAdapter.Fill(
this.adventureWorksDataSet.HumanResources_Employee);
```

This line of code was placed in the load event of the form by Visual Studio when the controls were placed on the form. Moving this line of code from the load event to the click event of the button will speed up the loading of the form.

Go ahead and test what you currently have by saving all the changes and running the project. From the Debug menu, select Start Debugging. When the form opens, it will show an empty grid. Click the Load Data button. After a couple of seconds the grid should populate with all of the employee records. Remember that the data is coming from the local cache (the .sdf).

Close the form. The next step is to add the sync functionality. Once again, this is easy. Referring to Figure 33-1, notice that the bottom right-hand corner of that form contains a link named Show Code Example. That is exactly what is needed for this example, so in Visual Studio open the Solution Explorer and double-click `DataCache.sync`. This will open the Configure Data Synchronization dialog shown in Figure 33-1. Click the Show Code Example link. The Code Example dialog will be displayed, showing a fragment of code that can actually be used. Simply click the Copy Code to Clipboard button. This copies the displayed code to the Windows clipboard. Close the Code Example dialog, and then close the Configure Data Synchronization dialog.

With the synchronization code on the clipboard, go back to the project form and double-click on the Data Sync button, which will open the code behind the form and create the `Click()` event for this button. In the `Click()` event for the DataSync button, paste the code from the Windows clipboard into this event. The `Click()` event should now look like the following:

```
private void SyncData_Click(object sender, EventArgs e)
{
    // Call SyncAgent.Synchronize() to initiate the synchronization
process.
    // Synchronization only updates the local database, not your
    // project's data source.
    DataCacheSyncAgent syncAgent = new DataCacheSyncAgent();
    Microsoft.Synchronization.Data.SyncStatistics syncStats =
syncAgent.Synchronize();

    // TODO: Reload your project data source from the local database
(for example, call the TableAdapter.Fill method).

}
```

Not quite done, because the code that does the actual merge to the local cache needs to be added. Right below the `TODO` comment in the code, add the following line:

```
this.adventureWorksDataSet.Merge(
humanResources_EmployeeTableAdapter.GetData());
```

With that, your first sync example is done and ready to test. Run the project again and click the Load Data button. With the data loaded, keep the form open and open SQL Server Management Studio and the data server where the source data resides. Open the `AdventureWorks` database, and in the Tables node, right-click on the `HumanResources.Employee` table and select Open Table from the context menu.

To test synchronization, within SSMS (SQL Server Management Studio) change the Title of one of the employees. For example, change the Title for EmployeeID 2 from "Marketing Assistant" to "Marketing Director."

Now go back to the project form and click the Sync Data button. The title "Marketing Assistant" in the local cache will also change to "Marketing Director." Try to sync in the other direction by changing some data on the form. Make sure you click the Save button so that the data is saved back to the cache. Now click the Sync Data button.

Requery the source data and you will see that it has not been changed. This is because, by default, synchronization is only one direction; from the source to the client. To fix this and set synchronization to bi-directional is a really easy change. In the Solution Explorer, right-click on the `DataCache.sync` and select View Code from the context menu. What you will see is the following:

```
public partial class DataCacheSyncAgent {

    partial void OnInitialized(){
    }
}
```

Within the `OnInitialized()` method, add the following statement:

```
HumanResources_Employee.SyncDirection =
Microsoft.Synchronization.Data.SyncDirection.Bidirectional;
```

This statement simply tells the synchronization agent to sync both ways, not just up or down. Now try the change again. Start the application, load the data, make a change on the client, save the changes, and then click the Sync Data button. Then, go back to the source data and verify that the data on the server reflects the change or changes made on the client.

One last note for this example: Bi-directional sync can be tricky. What if both the client and the server update the same record? Who wins, and how does sync handle this?

Luckily, synchronization provides a way to take care of this. Any and all conflicts automatically raise an `ApplyChangesFailed` event. This can be accomplished by adding a method to the `SyncProvider` partial class. In the same class to which you added code earlier, add the following below the `OnInitialized` method:

```
void DataCache_ApplyChangeFailed(object sender,
Microsoft.Synchronization.Data.ApplyChangeFailedEventArgs e)
{
    DataTable cc = e.Conflict.ClientChange;
    DataTable sc = e.Conflict.ServerChange;

    if ((System.DateTime)(cc.Rows[0]["ModifiedDate"]) >=
(System.DateTime)(sc.Rows[0]["ModifiedDate"]))
    {
        e.Action = Microsoft.Synchronization.Data.ApplyAction
.RetryWithForceWrite;
    }
}
```

In this method, the `ModifiedDate` on the server is compared to the `ModifiedDate` on the client. If the client `ModifiedDate` is later than the `ModifiedDate` on the server, then the server record is forcefully updated with that of the client.

To test this, run the project and modify a record on the client and save it. Next, modify the same record on the server. Click the Sync Data button. Because the server record was modified later, this will win the synchronization battle. Had the client date been later than the server date, the client would have won the synchronization battle and updated the server.

This example is a very simple demonstration of how the Sync Framework and synchronization works. Obviously, additional business logic can be placed in many areas to provide additional sync capabilities or to satisfy business rules, but it should give you a good idea of how powerful and flexible the Sync Framework is and how easy it is to use.

Keep in mind that SQL Server 2008 introduces change tracking. This is a lightweight and very thin solution that provides a very robust change tracking mechanism for applications. While this chapter does not cover SQL Server change tracking specifically, it would be worth your while to understand change tracking and how it can be used in your environment.

So with that introduction, it is time to get into the nitty-gritty. We begin with a brief overview of the Sync Framework before diving into some of its great technologies.

Sync Framework overview

The Microsoft Sync Framework is a very broad and wide-ranging synchronization platform that enables developers to architect and develop applications targeted toward offline and collaboration scenarios. It would be quite narrow-minded to think that this technology can be used only in applications, however, because included in the list of uses for offline and collaboration scenarios are services and mobile devices, and each of these is a prime target for synchronization technology. The Sync Framework allows for the building of systems that integrate any application to any data store by using any protocol over any network. How sweet is that!

Also data is not limited to information stored in databases. Data also comes in the form of files. The Microsoft Sync Framework enables business applications to share documents to guarantee that all team members receive the necessary data.

The Sync Framework contains the following technologies:

- **Sync Framework core components:** Used to create sync providers for any type of data store
- **Microsoft Sync Services for ADO.NET:** Used to sync databases for offline and joint scenarios
- **Metadata Storage Services:** Used to store sync metadata
- **Sync Services for File Systems:** Used to sync file system files and folders
- **Sync Services for FeedSync:** Used to sync RSS and Atom feeds with a local data store

At least 25 pages could be written on each one of these technologies, but due to space constraints Metadata Storage Services, Sync Services for File Systems, and Sync Services for FeedSync will not be covered in this chapter. Plenty of information, though, can be found on Microsoft's MSDN site at `http://msdn.microsoft.com/en-us/library/cc307159.aspx`.

The rest of this chapter provides an overview of the Sync Framework core components, a discussion of the Sync architecture and synchronization fundamentals, as well as a good discussion of Sync Services for ADO.NET 2.0.

Sync architecture

The Microsoft Sync Framework architecture enables the flow of data between many devices and services by using a set of building blocks that incorporate all of the synchronization functionality, such as the data store and transfer systems. These building blocks are the essential components that make up the synchronization runtime, metadata services, and synchronization providers.

During synchronization, the sync runtime drives and controls synchronization between the providers. It is the job of the metadata services to process and store metadata that is used by the providers.

For example, Figure 33-7 illustrates a simple high-level architecture of the Microsoft Sync Framework in which synchronization is attained by exposing a provider interface from a data store to a synchronization object.

This example is quite simple, in that it is illustrating a synchronization between a single data store and a controlling application such as a mobile device and a Microsoft SQL Server database.

FIGURE 33-7

A simple high-level architecture

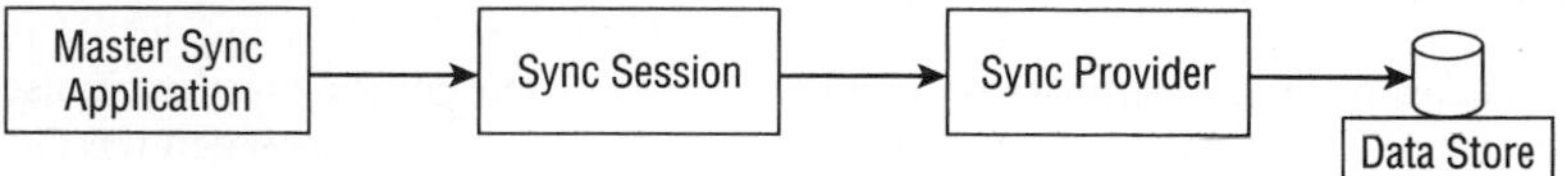

FIGURE 33-8

An architecture of multiple data stores synchronizing with a single controlling application, with each data store using its own synchronization provider

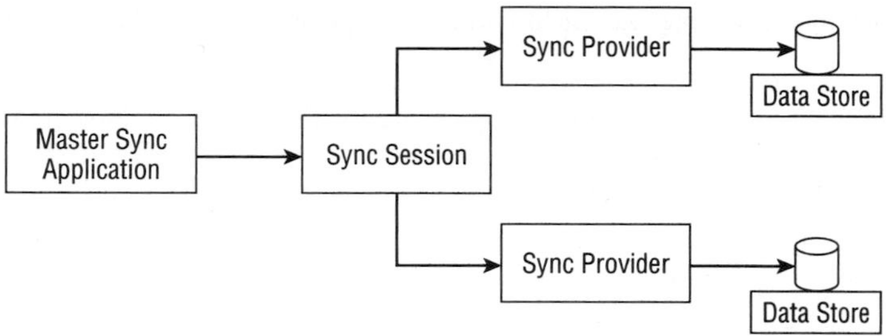

However, the Sync Framework is much more flexible and interoperable than that. For example, the illustration shown in Figure 33-8 shows multiple data stores synchronizing with a single controlling application, with each data store using its own synchronization provider. This is important because the two data stores could be two completely different and unique types of data stores.

In both scenarios, the sync session connects to both sync providers. It then makes appropriate API calls to determine what changes have been made and what changes need to be applied. Again, this information is supplied by the metadata services.

The sync runtime has the primary responsibility of driving and managing synchronization. This includes starting and hosting the sync process, and disposing of the session when synchronization is complete.

The runtime also controls all communication with the client application, including status, conflicts, and any errors. The runtime initiates and begins synchronization for the client application by making requests through the sync session to the sync providers.

The role of the metadata service is to manage synchronization metadata. The metadata service has the sole responsibility of understanding the details of the metadata, thereby freeing the application and provider from needing to understand items such as the structure of the data. By assisting the application in this way, it allows for maximum flexibility when designing applications. It also provides improved synchronization performance by enabling the other components to focus on what they excel at.

The sync provider is the main integration point into the Sync Framework, as it contains a layer that shields the runtime from the complexities of the data store. In terms of a provider, the sync provider is the component that enables synchronization between data stores. The great thing about the Sync

Framework is that each provider can be different, in that one provider does not really care about the other types of data stores or providers. This is all handled by the sync session. When a synchronization session takes place, data between a source data store and a destination data store are exchanged by connecting a source provider with a destination provider.

As synchronization takes place, the destination provider supplies its current state to the sync session. At that point, it accepts a list of changes from the source, detects any conflicts between the data it just received and its own data, and then applies any changes to its own data store.

Sync knowledge

A term that you should remember when working with the Sync Framework is the concept of sync *knowledge*. Knowledge is metadata. It is the information that the Sync Framework algorithms use to utilize change enumeration and conflict detection. The metadata describes each and every change that has been or will be applied to a data store via synchronization or applied directly. Thus, knowledge assists in the following:

- **Change enumeration:** The process of resolving changed items — that is, resolving which items have been changed on the source data store that have not been applied to the destination data store (thus, the destination data store does not have knowledge of the source data store changes).
- **Conflict detection:** The process of obtaining synchronization conflicts. A synchronization conflict happens when an operation was made by one data store and knowledge of that change was not transferred to the other data store.

Now, with that in mind, it is important to understand that neither an application nor a synchronization provider uses sync knowledge directly. Nor should it. That is the job of the Sync Framework. The Sync Framework will call the necessary methods to initiate operations for them.

However, it is also important to understand how sync knowledge works, so this section briefly describes sync knowledge operations and how they are used to enumerate and send the changes, as well as detect conflicts.

There are four synchronization knowledge operations:

- **Contains:** Used in both change enumeration and conflict detection, this operation checks whether the data store that owns the specified data has applied the changes. This is determined by looking at the specified item version of a knowledge object.
- **Project:** Creates a new knowledge object containing the same changes as the original knowledge object. This new object is based on one or more item IDs or a change unit ID. No other items are included.
- **Exclude:** This is the exact opposite of the Project operation. The new knowledge object includes knowledge about everything except the specified item.
- **Union:** Creates a new knowledge object that includes the same changes within at least one or both of the original knowledge objects.

These operations are critical in determining synchronization state. For example, what happens when a synchronization is interrupted or there is a failure in applying changes? What about when a synchronization knowledge object needs to be filtered or restricted?

That is where these operations come in. The Sync Framework uses these operations to provide itself with the appropriate knowledge necessary to conduct change enumeration and apply the changes.

Change enumeration takes place when the destination provider sends current knowledge of the destination data store to the source provider. The source provider then goes through all of the items in the source data store and determines whether the destination knowledge has the same version of the item contained in the source store. If it does not, then the items are batched and sent to the destination provider.

Changes are sent from the source provider to the destination provider in batches. Each batch contains metadata that describes each change in the batch (added by the provider) and current knowledge of the source data store, which will then be used to detect conflicts.

Think of this as two types of knowledge: *made-with* knowledge and *learned* knowledge. When the batch is created, it is created with current knowledge of the source data store. When those changes are applied at the destination, the conflicts are logged and tracked by the current knowledge. Therefore, made-with knowledge can determine what was known when the changes were made, and learned knowledge is what is learned after the changes are applied.

These two types of knowledge are extremely useful when detecting conflicts. When conflicts arise, the Sync Framework looks at two things. First, is the change a conflict with the current version of the item stored in the destination data store? Second, is the destination version of the item superseded by the current version, thus making the change obsolete?

When the version of the item stored in the destination data store is not contained in the knowledge of the source data store, then there is a change conflict. If the current version is found in the knowledge of the destination data store, then the change is obsolete. Simple as that.

Once the changes have been received by the destination and the conflicts detected, the changes are applied to the destination data store. This is accomplished by modifying the learned knowledge of the change batch with things that happen at the destination. The knowledge of the destination data store is then replaced with an updated version that is calculated by the Sync Framework.

Note two things here: The Sync Framework will use the `Exclude` operator to remove any conflicts that are not detected or resolved. Also, a recoverable error for each change is set by the Sync Framework if there is an interruption or cancellation of the synchronization, or if there are digital rights management (DRM) issues such as locked objects.

Sync fundamentals

One of the key terms when dealing with synchronization is *replica*. A replica is, in essence, a full or partial copy of the data source. The key to understanding replication is that two basic but essential components are used. These components have been discussed previously:

- The synchronization session
- The sync providers

In simple terms, synchronization takes place when an application creates a synchronization session, passing to it both a source provider and a destination provider. The session then manages the exchange of data between the source data store and destination data store by determining changes at both the source and the destination.

In terms of the provider, it has already been stated that the provider is the mechanism that contains metadata and knowledge for the replica, as well as for each item being synchronized. It is the provider that actually performs the transfer of the data in and out of the replica. The provider has two other primary responsibilities as well: It itemizes all the changes when the provider is acting as a source, and it detects conflicts when it is acting as a destination. These two responsibilities are important to ensure that the right (correct) data is transferred to and from the replica.

Synchronization takes place by using the following algorithm (uni-directional):

1. The application creates a synchronization session.
2. The sync session obtains current destination knowledge and sends it to the source provider.
3. The source provider itemizes changes not present in destination knowledge.
4. The source provider sends changes to the sync session.
5. The sync session detects conflicts and applies changes to the destination via the destination provider.

Two-way synchronization is accomplished by simply executing two one-way synchronizations.

The Sync Framework can use *managed code* and *unmanaged code* to perform synchronizations. However, the way in which sessions are managed differs between the two. Managed code uses the `SyncOrchestrator` class, whose sole responsibility is to initiate and control synchronization sessions.

When using unmanaged code, the application must use the `ISyncSession` interface. This interface controls a synchronization session between providers.

This is important because developers can create their own providers, which necessitates a fair amount of work. Thus, the approach of using managed code or unmanaged code when developing a provider must be taken into consideration.

Sync services for ADO.NET 2.0

With an understanding of the Sync Framework now under your belt, it is time to discuss Sync Services for ADO.NET 2.0. Earlier in the chapter it was mentioned that Sync Services provides a very powerful yet flexible API that enables developers to build applications for offline and collaboration scenarios.

The need to support remote and mobile users grows increasingly every day and is becoming more important for many organizations. As this need grows, so does the need to provide these users with the same data they have access to when they are working in the office. This presents a problem because in many cases these users are using a laptop, PDA, or smartphone, and remote access usually means connecting via a VPN or some other method.

There are several serious downsides to this approach:

- **Data access speeds:** When users are in the office, they have direct access to the company's high-speed and reliable network. Remote users do not have this luxury. They use either wireless or broadband connection, which can be slow and unreliable depending on the connection strength.

- **Scalability:** More remote users means fewer available resources on existing servers (and more cost to purchase additional hardware), and more data being transferred (thus, a slower connection).
- **More points of failure:** In a remote scenario, users are relying on several components to access information. Not just the SQL Server, but their VPN solution, as well as how they are connecting (wireless, etc.). If any one of these items fails, then users cannot gain access to their information.
- **Network requirements:** Imagine an individual who is constantly on the go as part of his or her job. Reliable access to data can be difficult or nearly impossible due to dropped connections and bad service areas.
- **Data persistence:** Every piece of data that the client wants to access must be downloaded to the client; and because there is no way to cache the data, the same data could potentially be downloaded multiple times.

Necessity facilitates invention. Sync Services is not new, but Sync Services for ADO.NET 2.0 provides new capabilities to overcome all of these downsides and enable remote workers access to their data through *occasionally connected applications*. Occasionally connected applications enable remote users to access their data at all times and in all places. Continuous access to data, how sweet is that? The user has real-time access to the data because the data is local, not remote. This is where data synchronization comes in.

Sync Services enables synchronization of data between two distinct sources of data such as databases. Data synchronization is the ability to transfer information from one data store to another data store on a periodic basis, such as from a client database (e.g., a SQL Server Compact 3.5 database) to a server database (Microsoft SQL Server). There are several advantages to data synchronization:

- It removes the need for constant network connection.
- Access to the data is limited only by the speed of the client device.

Because the data is stored locally, the user has continuous access to all of the information stored on the local device and can access the data as quickly as the device can operate. No lag time, performance, or reliability issues trying to access data remotely. Thus, access to the data is much faster and more reliable.

Sync Services is part of the Microsoft Sync Framework. As stated earlier in the chapter, Sync Services provides an easy-to-use API that enables developers to create and distribute applications that require offline data access and collaboration. The API is extremely flexible; developers can use as much or as little of the API components as needed to meet their application requirements. Because Sync Services is part of the Sync Framework, any database that uses Sync Services is able to share and exchange information with other data sources that are also using Sync Services.

What's new in Sync Services 2.0

The following list describes the new features and capabilities in Microsoft Sync Services 2.0 and Synchronization Services for ADO.NET 1.1 (SP1) and 2.0:

- **Peer-to-peer synchronization:** Part of the API, this enables applications to engage in collaboration.
- **Sync Services inclusion in the Microsoft Sync Framework:** Sync Services now requires `Microsoft.Synchronization.dll`.

- **Device Synchronization:** Provides synchronization capabilities between a server database and SQL Server Compact 3.5 databases on devices
- **SQL Server change tracking:** Available in SQL Server 2008, this provides a way to track changes, either via manual synchronization commands or using the synchronization adapter builder.
- **SQL Server 2008 data types:** New data types in SQL Server 2008 are supported.
- **Synchronization process tracing:** Provides the capability to trace and troubleshoot issues that can be hard to identify.

The following two sections briefly describe offline and collaboration scenarios in a synchronization environment.

Offline scenarios

More and more applications that are being developed today fit into the two-tier, *n*-tier, and serviced-based architecture category, and Sync Services for ADO.NET 2.0 fits perfectly into these environments. This match is due to a very flexible Sync Services API for client and server synchronization that provides a powerful set of components to enable the synchronizing of data between data services and a local data store, whereas previously the solution included the replication of the database and its schema.

The technology world is also seeing an increase in mobile applications that run on portable devices or mobile devices. As stated earlier, the downside to mobile applications is that they (and the applications that run on them) do not have a reliable connection to the source data, so the need to access the data locally is becoming increasingly important. It would also be nice to be able to do some form of synchronization if and when a stable and reliable connection to the central server and data source were available.

This is where Sync Services comes in. The Sync Services API provides a powerful yet friendly synchronization platform, simply because it is modeled after the ADO.NET data access APIs, which enables the building of occasionally connected applications as an extension of building always-connected applications.

It might be helpful at this point to highlight the differences between Sync Services and other technologies that are designed to be incorporated into the occasionally connected environment. While there are a few, the two most common are as follows:

- **RDA (remote data access):** Used to synchronize a SQL Server Compact 3.5 database with other editions of SQL Server
- **Merge replication:** Used to synchronize different editions of SQL Server, including SQL Server Compact 3.5

While these technologies are extremely useful and fulfill many needs, they are primarily focused on Microsoft database technologies. Table 33-1 briefly compares these options in order to help you determine which technology is appropriate for the type of application you want to build and the environment in which the application will be used.

A few words about this list. First, RDA supports incremental uploads. Downloads are done via a snapshot that updates the client data. Second, if you have done any merge replication, then you know that it has a built-in conflict-resolution solution. Not so with Sync Services. It provides a mechanism for building a custom solution for resolving conflicts, meaning the capability is there but you need to build it yourself.

TABLE 33-1

Comparing RDA, Merge Replication, and Sync Services

Feature	RDA	Merge Replication	Sync Services
Sync using services	No	No	Yes
Heterogeneous database support	No	No	Yes
Incremental change tracking	No	Yes	Yes
Detect and resolve conflicts	No	Yes	Yes
Create data views on the client	No	No	Yes
Initialize schema and data automatically	Yes	Yes	Yes
Large dataset support	Yes	Yes	Yes
Transmit schema changes automatically	No	Yes	No
Automatically repartition data	No	Yes	No
Use on devices	Yes	Yes	Yes

Also keep in mind that the Sync Services architecture for client and server synchronization is asymmetric, meaning that change tracking is built into the client database. Incremental changes on the server can be downloaded, but they must be tracked by the programmer.

In determining which path to take when looking at a data synchronization solution, it helps to consider some of the concepts behind these technologies. For example, not many developers really work with SQL Server replication technology. That is usually a DBA function and is primarily designed to keep SQL Server databases in sync with each other.

RDA itself is a great technology, but it is somewhat inferior to Sync Services. A SQL Server Compact 3.5 technology, it is simply intended to provide applications with the capability to access data from a remote SQL Server database and store it locally. RDA uses a push/pull method to propagate data changes to and from the SQL Server Compact database.

However, the Microsoft MSDN Books Online document clearly states the following:

> Because of design limitations, remote data access (RDA) will be removed in a future release. If you are currently using RDA, you should consider transitioning to Microsoft Synchronization Services for ADO.NET. If you were planning to use RDA in a new application, you should instead consider merge replication or Synchronization Services. Note that Synchronization Services is available for both desktop and mobile devices.

Sync Services is a richer programming model that includes many features also found in merge replication technology. It is superior to RDA and, unlike replication, it is targeted toward developers who want the power and flexibility to access the client data that is based on a server database or another data source.

And unlike RDA, Sync Services is not limited to just SQL Server databases, as it includes support for heterogeneous databases. Sync Services also allows for synchronization over services such as WCF (Windows Communication Foundation).

So, it boils down to the following. Use Sync Services if the following apply:

- The application needs to synchronize with non-SQL Server databases.
- The application needs separate components to enable synchronization over different transports or services.
- The need to replicate a schema and its data from one database to another database is not a requirement.
- You want to replicate data without the administrative overhead of merge replication, but with the core merge engine functionality.
- The capability to architect and develop a really cool multi-tier or serviced-based synchronization application is extremely appealing.

Okay, so I threw in that last one just for the fun of it, but it is really cool.

This section wraps up with a discussion of the architecture and classes needed for offline scenario synchronization such as two-tier, *n*-tier, and service-based architecture.

Sync Services is flexible enough to provide multiple synchronization types, including the following:

- **Snapshot and download-only:** Used to store and update reference data. Changes made to data on the server are downloaded to the client during synchronization. Snapshot synchronization does a complete refresh of the data every time the client is synchronized. Download-only synchronization downloads only the changes that have occurred since the last synchronization.
- **Upload only:** Used to insert data on a client. Changes made to the client (such as inserts) are uploaded to the server during synchronization.
- **Bi-directional:** Used for data that can be updated on both the client and the server.

When synchronizing, Sync Services uses the following classes:

- Microsoft.Synchronization.Data.dll
- Microsoft.Synchronization.Data.SqlServerCe.dll
- Microsoft.Synchronization.Data.Server.dll

The Synchronization Agent, Synchronization tables, and Synchronization Groups are found in `Microsoft.Synchronization.Data.dll`.

The Client Synchronization Provider is found in `Microsoft.Synchronization.Data.SqlServerCe.dll`.

The Server Synchronization Provider and Synchronization Adapters are in `Microsoft.Synchronization.Data.Server.dll`.

When working with two-tier applications, all of the Sync Services DLLs are located on the client. For *n*-tier applications, `Microsoft.Synchronization.Data.dll` and `Microsoft.Synchronization.Data.Server.dll` are located on a separate computer that provides a synchronization service.

The following three illustrations show how the components map to a set of Sync Services classes. Note the existence of a client database, a server database, and Sync Services classes.

The client database in a Sync Services application is a SQL Server Compact 3.5 database. The server database can be any database that is supported by an available ADO.NET adapter. Out of the box, Sync Services provides the capability to track changes in the client database. This infrastructure is enabled the first time any table is synchronized using any method other than snapshot synchronization.

Figure 33-9 shows a standard two-tier architecture. All of the items shown in the figure correspond to a Sync Services class, except for the two databases. In a two-tier architecture, a direct connection between the server and the client is required.

FIGURE 33-9

A standard two-tier architecture

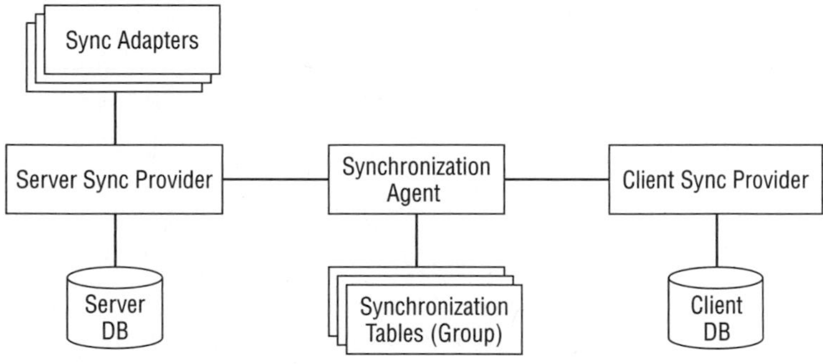

An *n*-tier architecture (see Figure 33-10) is similar to a two-tier architecture with the additional requirement of a proxy and service, as well as a transport mechanism whose responsibility it is to facilitate communication between the client and server databases.

An *n*-tier architecture is becoming more commonplace simply because it does not require the constant connection between server and client, and it provides a more flexible architecture.

Figure 33-11 illustrates a service-based architecture. This differs from the previous two examples in that it does not include a server database and corresponding synchronization providers and adapters. Rather, in a service-based architecture, the application needs to communicate with the Synchronization Agent through a custom proxy and custom service, such as WCF (Windows Communication Foundation).

The thing to keep in mind is that the custom proxy and custom service must provide the same functionality that the synchronization provider and adapter would provide, such as enumerating synchronization changes.

FIGURE 33-10

An *n*-tier architecture

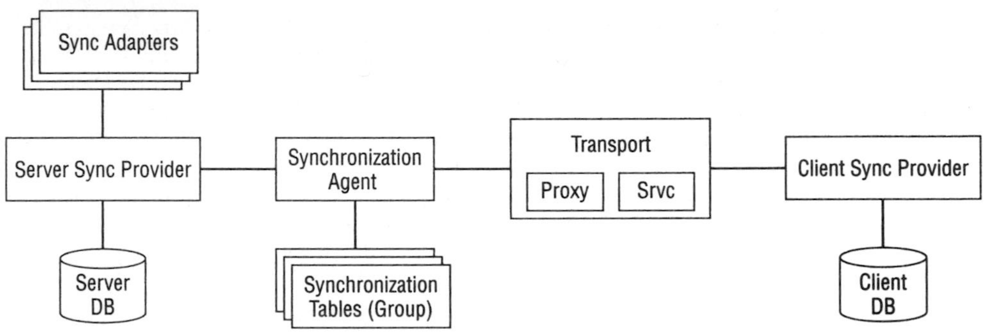

FIGURE 33-11

A simple service-based architecture

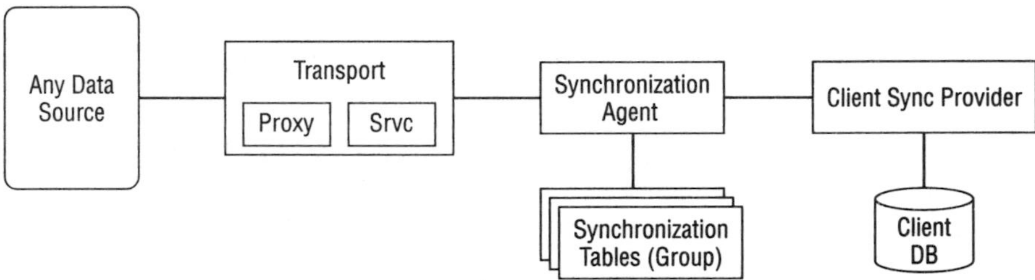

The common theme in each of these examples is the existence of the Sync Services classes: SyncAgent, DbServerSyncProvider, SqlCeClientSyncProvider, SyncAdapter, SyncTable, and SyncGroup. Here is a quick review of the roles and responsibilities of each of these classes. The Synchronization Agent has the following responsibilities:

- Enumerate through each table being synchronized
- Call the client synchronization provider, retrieving and applying changes at the client database
- Call the server synchronization provider, retrieving and applying changes at the client database

The Client Synchronization Provider is responsible for the following:

- Store information on the client about tables that are enabled for synchronization
- Obtain changes that occurred on the client since the last synchronization
- Detect conflict changes
- Apply changes to the client

The Server Synchronization Provider has similar responsibilities to the Client Synchronization Provider, but obviously performs all of its necessary actions on the server.

Several other items are highlighted in the figure above that need to be discussed here. First, a synchronization table is defined for each table that is included for synchronization. The responsibility of a synchronization table is to store settings about the table, such as the synchronization direction.

Second, once a synchronization table is defined, it is added to a synchronization group. The purpose of the synchronization group is to provide the means of ensuring reliable synchronization changes to all of the synchronization tables in the group. Thus, all the changes are applied in a transaction and are synchronized as a unit, or a whole, not individually. If a change from one of the tables in the group fails, then all of the changes are rolled back, and the group is applied again during the next synchronization.

The final section in this chapter discusses collaboration scenarios in a peer-to-peer synchronization architecture.

Collaboration scenarios

Sync Services for ADO.NET 2.0 provides the capability to perform peer-to-peer synchronization — each peer can synchronize with any other peer, and that peer can synchronize with any other peer. And all of this can take place without the need to go through a central repository or data store. This is what makes this architecture so good for collaboration scenarios. Peer-to-peer synchronization can also be used when applications do not have a reliable network connection for offline synchronization.

This section first provides an overview of peer-to-peer synchronization, and then discusses its architecture.

Like the offline synchronization scenarios, a comparison between Sync Services and other technologies might be useful here. Table 33-2 highlights the main features of Sync Services and peer-to-peer transactional replication that will be helpful in determining when to use which technology for building applications.

TABLE 33-2

Comparing Sync Services to Transactional Replication

Feature	Peer-to-Peer Transactional Replication	Sync Services
Synchronize using services	No	Yes
Synchronize with other types of data stores	No	Yes
Incremental change tracking	Yes	Yes
Conflict detection and resolution	Yes	Yes
Support large datasets	Yes	Yes
Automatically initialize schema and data	Yes	No
Automatically propagate schema changes	Yes	No

When tracking incremental changes, Sync Services uses *net change tracking* for peer-to-peer synchronization. This means that the latest version is synchronized and all changes to a given row are applied in order at each peer.

Peer-to-peer synchronization can be compared in many ways to a combination of offline data-set technology and replication. Sync Services provides a programming model like that of offline datasets but with a feature set like that of replication. As stated in the previous section, replication is a database administrator function, but via Sync Services, developers can have the same synchronization support through the many available synchronization classes, enabling developers to synchronize with other data store types.

Like the offline scenario, the choice between using peer-to-peer transaction replication versus using Sync Services for peer-to-peer synchronization, it comes down to need. Peer-to-peer transactional replication is more of an administrator responsibility, but it does provide a highly available and scalable system and requires almost no coding.

Sync Services, however, is for developers. It allows for synchronization of different transports or services, and provides synchronization capabilities with data sources other than a database. Sync Services is the mechanism for moving beyond just replicating schema and data from one database to another.

From an architecture standpoint, the peer-to-peer scenario has each peer containing its own application code and Sync Services code to initiate and facilitate synchronization. This functionality is provided via the Sync Services peer-to-peer API. During a typical synchronization, a pair of peers is synchronized.

For example, given a scenario in which three peers need to be synchronized, synchronization could take place like this: Peer1 and peer2 are synchronized, then peer1 and peer3, and then finally peer2 and peer3. In each synchronization, one peer acts as the local peer, and one peer acts as the remote peer.

However, this scenario might seem a bit redundant, as it is not necessary for each and every peer to be synchronized. In the earlier example, peer1 and peer2 could be synchronized, then peer2 and peer3. Peer1 and peer3 would be synchronized via peer2.

As for the components used in a peer-to-peer synchronization, Figures 33-12 and 33-13 show which components are used in a two-tier and *n*-tier architecture, respectively.

FIGURE 33-12

A two-tier architecture in peer-to-peer synchronization

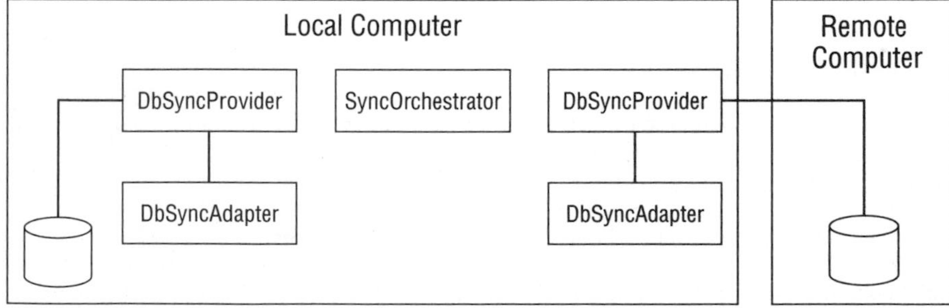

FIGURE 33-13

An *n*-tier architecture in peer-to-peer synchronization with a proxy

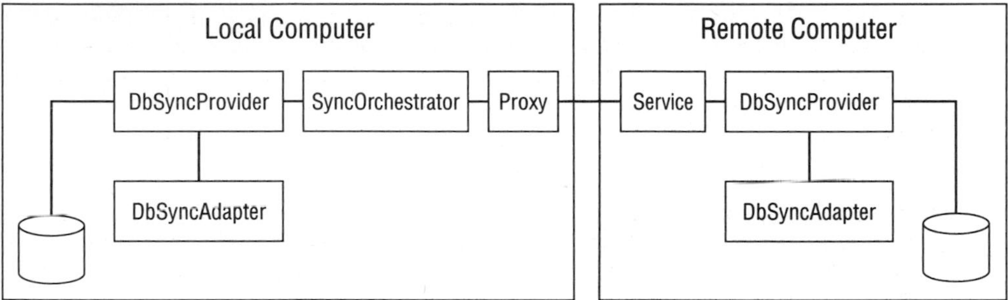

In a two-tier architecture, all the services exist on the local peer, as shown in Figure 33-12.

In an *n*-tier architecture, a proxy and service are also introduced, and some of the services reside on the remote computer, as shown in Figure 33-13.

The *n*-tier architecture requires a service and a transport system which provides communication between a proxy on the local computer and a service on the remote computer. The difference between peer-to-peer and client-server synchronization is that the proxy is not part of the Sync Framework API. This proxy must be written by the developer and must be derived from the `KnowledgeSyncProvider` class.

The `SyncOrchestrator` in a peer-to-peer synchronization is responsible for the following:

- Storing table information on the peer
- Applying incremental changes to the peer database
- Detecting conflict changes
- Assisting applications in obtaining changes that occurred on the peer since the last synchronization

By now it should be fairly clear that using Sync Services for ADO.NET 2.0 provides a very powerful yet flexible synchronization mechanism. There are many options to consider. What makes Sync Services great is simply how comprehensive it is for building offline and collaboration applications.

Summary

This chapter provided a look at the Microsoft Sync Framework and Sync Services for ADO.NET 2.0. The chapter began by providing a brief and simple example demonstrating how easy it is to use this great technology. It then jumped feet first into first an overview, and then the architecture, of the Sync Framework.

That discussion was followed by an overview and architectural discussion about one of the Sync Framework components, Sync Services, and why it should be considered when architecting offline solutions.

Chapter 34

LINQ

IN THIS CHAPTER

Overview and history of LINQ

Understanding LINQ

LINQ standard query operators

Syntax options

LINQ to SQL

LINQ to XML

LINQ to Dataset

LINQ to Entities

Let's get right to the point. I often see code like this:

```
string ConnectionString = @"Data Source=(local);
Initial Catalog = Adventureworks;UID=username;PWD=password";
using (SqlConnection conn = new
SqlConnection(ConnectionString))
{
    conn.Open();
    SqlCommand cmd = conn.CreateCommand();
    cmd.CommandType = CommandType.Text;
    cmd.CommandText = "SELECT LastName, FirstName,
MidleName FROM Person.Contact";
    using (SqlDataReader rdr = cmd.ExecuteReader())
    {
        // do something
    }
}
```

Maybe you have also seen code like this or have even done it yourself, but at some point in your career one of the two have happened. Given the preceding code, ask yourself two questions. First, will it compile when run? Second, if so, will it run successfully? Set aside for a minute the fact that there is no `WHERE` clause and ignore the lack of encapsulation. That is not the intent of this example. What is important are the two questions.

First, yes, it will compile. Second, when it runs it will fail. It will fail because the column "MidleName" should actually be "MiddleName." The problem is that you need to run the program in order to catch this. Even worse, if your program does error, where do you look? (That is, the developer was unaware that the column name was misspelled.) Debugging an error such as this is time consuming and unproductive. Equally, the example is "unfriendly" on several levels. First, two languages are being combined, in this case, C# and T-SQL. The problem is that the T-SQL language is not understood in the context of .NET.

Another nuisance is the fact that there is a different set of technologies for the different data sources (SQL databases, XML, collections, in-memory objects, and so on) that developers work with on a daily basis. For example, you typically use ADO.NET to work with databases, but you might use XQuery, XPath, or some of the XML classes built into the .NET Framework to work with XML.

Those are the two issues: Because queries against data are often written as strings embedded in code, the result is no compile-time checking or IntelliSense support, as well as difficulty debugging; and multiple technologies (different query languages) for different data sources (SQL, XML, etc.).

Wouldn't it be nice if there were a way to solve both of these issues? Even better, wouldn't it be nice if there were a way to solve both of these issues with a single technology?

Luckily, there is an answer: Microsoft LINQ. This chapter provides a brief history and overview of LINQ, and then looks at the different LINQ providers, including examples that demonstrate how to use them.

LINQ Overview

Before looking at LINQ's current incarnation, it would be wise to first look at its history. Microsoft LINQ has been in the works for well over five years. LINQ (and other LINQ providers such as LINQ to SQL) has roots that extend to previous projects, which have been growing and evolving for quite some time.

LINQ goes all the way back to a previous Microsoft project named C-Omega (or C). C-Omega, in its fullness, really contained more than what shows up in LINQ, as it contained functionality that truly experimented with using integrated queries (a mix of C# and other query languages such as SQL and XQuery). C was initially released to the public as a preview in 2004, and it quickly caught the attention of other Microsoft people (such as Anders Hejlsberg) who then took that same concept to C# and other languages.

Yet, as good as C-Omega was, LINQ now contains a lot of what C contained, plus many additional features and functionality. It could be said that LINQ "leapfrogged" over C. Those familiar with Microsoft's ORM history know that LINQ to SQL is not Microsoft's first endeavor at object-relational mapping. The roots of LINQ to SQL can actually be traced to something called *ObjectSpaces* dating back to 2001. In simple terms, ObjectSpaces is a set of data access APIs that enable data to be treated as objects, regardless of the source of the data.

This story has both a happy ending and a sad ending. The sad ending is that ObjectSpaces was never officially released, simply because ObjectSpaces depended on WinFS and when Microsoft made the announcement that WinFS would not make it into the first release of Windows Vista, that was the end of ObjectSpaces. Happily, however, Microsoft learned a ton about ORM from ObjectSpaces and applied that knowledge to LINQ to SQL, the result being a well thought-out and solid ORM product. Is it the ORM product to end all ORM products? No, but even for a first release, LINQ to SQL is surely nothing to sneeze at.

In the same category is a product called *Nordic*, developed by Paul Nielsen, which is a T-SQL-based O/R DBMS façade. It is a nice utility that uses code-gen to emulate an object-database. It includes polymorphism, inheritance, inheritable workflow states, and inheritable complex expressions. Moreover, according to Paul, it's fast. This nice tool can be found on CodePlex at `www.codeplex.com/Nordic`.

What Is LINQ?

LINQ stands for language-integrated query. In essence, this means that developers have at their disposal a query language integrated directly into their .NET programming of choice (such as C# and Visual Basic), giving them general-purpose query capabilities.

LINQ is a standard, unified query experience across different data sources, built directly into your .NET-supported programming language. LINQ brings powerful query facilities to the .NET Framework languages, such as C# and VB.NET. Microsoft accomplished this by turning query set operations, transforms, and constructs into high-level concepts (on the same level of classes and objects) within the .NET Framework. LINQ makes a query a first-class construct within C# and Visual Basic.

Moreover, LINQ addresses the very large mismatch between programming languages and data sources such as databases, XML, and in-memory objects. The entire goal of LINQ is to make the interaction between objects and data sources easier and simpler, enabling developers to interact with the different data sources (such as SQL and XML), because there is a disconnect between the data sources and the programming languages that communicate with (that is, work with) each of them.

As stated earlier, LINQ is a "unified" query experience. This means that it unifies data access regardless of the source of data. Simply stated, LINQ bridges the gap between the world of data and the world of programming.

Prior to LINQ, developers had to learn different technologies to query different data sources. No more! LINQ gives developers a new way of querying different types of data using strongly typed queries common across many different data sources. The result is improved developer productivity along with LINQ-specific IntelliSense in the Visual Studio IDE and compile-time error checking!

That's right. Because developers are now working with data in an object-oriented fashion, they are also working in a strongly typed environment. The benefits of this include compile-time error checking, not runtime error checking. In addition, developers can now write queries using Visual Studio's IntelliSense, driving the experience toward a more declarative programming model.

Because LINQ makes a query a first-class construct within the programmer's development language, developers can now write and execute queries against strongly typed objects using keywords, or operators. These keywords, called *standard query operators*, are discussed in the next section.

Who should use LINQ? The real question is who *shouldn't* use LINQ? LINQ is targeted toward application developers who want a new way to query data using strongly typed queries and strongly typed results. It is for developers seeking commonality across a number of different data sources, including but not limited to relational databases. It is for developers who want improved productivity — and who like using really cool technology.

Standard Query Operators

Standard query operators are essentially methods that form the LINQ pattern. They provide the query capabilities, including filtering, projection, sorting, and more. A large portion of these methods that make up the standard query operators operate on sequences, objects that have implemented the `IEnumerable<T>` or `IQueryable<T>` interface. These two interfaces are what provide the querying and iteration for queries over a non-generic collection.

There are two sets of standard query operators that implement the two interfaces mentioned above. The key to remember when working with the standard query operators is that regardless of the set, each method of the standard query operators is a static member of the `Enumerable` and `Queryable` classes, meaning they can be called using either static method syntax or instance method syntax.

The standard query operators also vary in their execution timing. This timing depends on the results of the query. Whether a sequence of values is returned or a singleton value is returned determines when the query is executed. Methods are executed immediately if they return a singleton value; otherwise, the query execution is deferred and an enumerable object is returned if the method returns a sequence.

Table 34-1 lists the 53 standard query operators, grouped according to their functionality.

Query expression syntax

To understand the flow of LINQ query syntax, compare it to standard T-SQL syntax. If you have written any T-SQL, you know the basic T-SQL query syntax and how it is written. For instance, a simple query looks like the following:

```
SELECT FirstName, LastName
FROM Person.Contact
```

TABLE 34-1

Standard Query Operators

Functionality	Standard Query Operator	Description
Sorting	`OrderBy`	Sorts values in ascending order
	`OrderByDescending`	Sorts values in descending order
	`ThenBy`	Applies a secondary sort in ascending order
	`ThenByDescending`	Applies a secondary sort in descending order
	`Reverse`	Sorts the elements of a collection in reverse order
Set	`Distinct`	Removes duplicate values from a collection
	`Except`	Returns the differences between two sets (elements in one collection that do not exist in a second collection)
	`Intersect`	Returns the matches between two sets (elements that appear in two separate collections)
	`Union`	Returns the union of two sets (unique elements that appear in either of two collections)

continued

TABLE 34-1 *(continued)*

Functionality	Standard Query Operator	Description
Filtering	`OfType`	Selects values from a sequence based on their ability to be cast to a specified type
	`Where`	Selects values from a sequence based on a predicate function
Quantifier	`All`	Determines whether all the elements in a sequence meet a condition
	`Any`	Determines whether any of the elements in a sequence meet a condition
	`Contains`	Determines whether a sequence contains a specified element
Projection	`Select`	Projects values based on a transform function
	`SelectMany`	Projects sequences of values based on a transform function and then combines them into a single sequence
Partitioning	`Skip`	Skips elements up to a specified position in a sequence
	`SkipWhile`	Skips elements based on a predicate function until an element does not satisfy the condition
	`Take`	Takes elements up to a specified position in a sequence
	`TakeWhile`	Takes elements based on a predicate function until an element does not satisfy the condition
Join	`Join`	Joins two sequences based on key selector functions
	`GroupJoin`	Joins two sequences based on key selector, grouping the matches for each element
Grouping	`GroupBy`	Groups elements that share a common attribute
	`ToLookup`	Inserts elements into a `Lookup(TKey, TElement)`
Generation	`DefaultIfEmpty`	Replaces an empty collection with a default singleton collection
	`Empty`	Returns an empty collection
	`Range`	Generates a collection that contains a sequence of numbers
	`Repeat`	Generates a collection that contains one repeated value
Equality	`SequenceEqual`	Determines whether two sequences are equal by comparing elements in a pair-wise manner

continued

TABLE 34-1 *(continued)*

Functionality	Standard Query Operator	Description
Element	`ElementAt`	Returns the element at a specified index in a collection
	`ElementAtOrDefault`	Returns the element at the specified index in a collection, or the first element that satisfies a condition
	`First`	Returns the first element of a collection, or the first element that satisfies a condition
	`FirstOrDefault`	Returns the first element of a collection, or the first element that satisfies a condition. A default value is returned if the specified element does not exist.
	`Last`	Returns the last element of a collection or the last element that satisfies a condition
	`LastOrDefault`	Returns the last element of a collection or the last element that satisfies a condition. A default value is returned if the specified element does not exist in the collection.
	`Single`	Returns the only element of a collection or the only element that satisfies a condition
	`SingleOrDefault`	Returns the only element of a collection or the only element that satisfies a condition. A default value is returned if the specified element does not exist in the collection.
Conversion	`AsEnumerable`	Returns the input types as `IEnumerable(T)`
	`AsQueryable`	Converts a generic `IEnumerable` to a generic `IQueryable`
	`Cast`	Casts the elements of a collection to a specified type
	`OfType`	Filters values based on their ability to be cast to a specified type
	`ToArray`	Converts a collection to an array. Forces query execution.
	`ToDictionary`	Puts elements into a `Dictionary(TKey, TValue)`. Forces query execution.
	`ToList`	Converts a collection to a `List(T)`. Forces query execution.
	`ToLookup`	Puts elements into a `Lookup(TKey, TValue)`as a one-to-many dictionary. Forces query execution.

continued

TABLE 34-1 (continued)

Functionality	Standard Query Operator	Description
Concatenation	Concat	Concatenates two sequences into a single sequence
Aggregation	Aggregate	Performs a custom aggregation operation on the values of a collection
	Average	Calculates the average value of a collection of values
	Count	Counts the elements in a collection; optionally, only those elements that satisfy a predicate expression
	LongCount	Counts the elements in a large collection; optionally, only those elements that satisfy a predicate expression
	Max	Determines the maximum value in a collection
	Min	Determines the minimum value in a collection
	Sum	Calculates the sum of the values in a collection

This example queries the `Person.Contact` table in the AdventureWorks database and returns the `FirstName` and `LastName` columns for each row in the table. Because that's so simple, the following example adds a secondary table, and then applies a filter and a sort:

```
SELECT E.EmployeeID,C.FirstName, C.LastName
FROM Person.Contact AS C
INNER JOIN HoumanResources.Employee AS E ON C.ContactID = E.ContactID
WHERE E.EmployeeID < 100
ORDER BY C.LastName
```

This is the syntax with which all T-SQL developers are familiar. At the very minimum, the query begins with a `SELECT` clause, which specifies the columns you want to be returned by the query, followed by a `FROM` clause, which lists the tables and/or views containing the columns identified in the `SELECT` clause.

The query could include one or more joins such as an `INNER JOIN` or `OUTER JOIN`, followed by some filtering using the `WHERE` clause and possibly a `GROUP BY` or `HAVING` clause, and quite possibly some ordering using the `ORDER BY` clause.

How many developers have really stopped to think about how SQL Server processes these queries? Does it execute the query from top to bottom, starting with the `SELECT` clause and working its way down? One might assume that, but that is not how a query is processed in SQL Server at all. SQL Server logically processes a query in the order indicated here by the number in parentheses:

```
(8)  SELECT
(9)  TOP
(1)  FROM
(3)  JOIN
(2)  ON
```

```
(4)  WHERE
(5)  GROUP BY
(6)  WITH
(7)  HAVING
(10) ORDER BY
```

Notice that the FROM clause is processed first, while the SELECT clause is processed almost last. Any clause that is not specified in the query is simply skipped by the query processing engine. This information is important because it points out the similarities between LINQ query syntax and how SQL Server processes a query.

CROSS-REF **For more information on SQL logical query flow, please see Chapter 8, "Introducing Basic Query Flow."**

In a LINQ query, the first clause is the FROM clause, which specifies the source of the data, and it must end with either a SELECT clause or a GROUP clause. The first clause, called a *generator*, defines where the data will be coming from when the query is executed. It also specifies the range variable that is used as a reference for each element in the data source. For example, the following uses LINQ to return a list of the directories in the root of a hard drive:

```
DirectoryInfo di = new DirectoryINfo("C:\\");

var query =
    from dir in di.GetDirectories()
    order by di.Name
    select new { dir.Name };

foreach (var item in query)
    Console.WriteLine(item.Name);
```

In this example, the first statement creates a new instance of the DirectoryInfo class. This is what is used to retrieve a list of the directories.

The second statement is the LINQ statement. The variable var is the query variable. This variable does not store actual result data. The results are produced during the iteration of the query, which is done in the foreach loop. When the foreach statement executes, the query results are returned during each iteration in the variable item.

Whereas the LINQ query and the T-SQL query are executed similarly, the T-SQL query syntax is a bit different. In T-SQL, the query would be executed internally following the steps described earlier. With LINQ, the query does not need to go through the rewriting process.

In the next example, the LINQ query uses the same syntax to query data from the Contact table in the AdventureWorks database in SQL Server:

```
var query =
    from c in Contact
    where c.FirstName.StartsWith("S")
    orderby c.LastName
    select c;
```

Notice in this query that the syntax is exactly the same as the first query. An additional WHERE clause has been added, but syntactically it is the same. This is what is great about LINQ. Similar query expressions can be written against two completely different sources of data.

Query syntax and method syntax

LINQ has the ability to write queries using both query syntax and method syntax. The examples shown so far have used query syntax, which is writing the query as a query expression, as follows:

```
IEnumberable<string> query =
    from c in Contact
    where c.FirstName.StartsWith("S")
    select c;
```

This declarative syntax is easy to read and understand, but developers also have the option of writing queries using method syntax. When a LINQ query is compiled, the query expression is translated into method syntax because the .NET CLR (common language runtime) doesn't understand query syntax. Thus, at compile time, query expressions are translated into method calls because this is what the CLR understands.

The following shows the previous query written using method syntax:

```
    IEnumberable<string> query = contact.Where(c =>
c.FirstName.StartsWith("S"));
```

For clarification, take a look at a couple more examples. This first example adds an additional filter to the previous example:

```
IEnumberable<string> query =
    from c in Contact
    where c.FirstName.StartsWith("S")
    && c.LastName.StartsWith("A")

    select c;
```

Here is the same query in method syntax:

```
    IEnumberable<string> query = contact.Where(a =>
a.FirstName.StartsWith("S") && a.LastName.StartsWith("A"));
```

Just to complicate things a bit more, this next example adds an OrderBy clause:

```
IEnumberable<string> query =
    from c in Contact
    where c.FirstName.StartsWith("S")
    && c.LastName.StartsWith("A")
    order by c.LastName
    select c;
```

The preceding query written using method syntax is as follows:

```
IEnumberable<string> query = contact.Where(c =>
    c.FirstName.StartsWith("S") && c.LastName.StartsWith("A"))
    .OrderBy(c => c.LastName);
```

The output of both queries is identical.

Choosing a query syntax

As you have seen, although there are syntactical differences between query syntax and method syntax, execution is essentially the same. However, the .NET CLR does not understand query syntax, so it is translated into method syntax anyway. The CLR understands method calls, so query expressions are translated into method syntax (method calls) and executed as such.

Although there is no semantic difference between method syntax and query syntax, I recommended that developers use query syntax whenever possible, as it is easier to read, understand, and maintain.

Now that you have a good understanding of LINQ, the standard query operators, and LINQ query expressions, the rest of this chapter focuses on the LINQ providers and offers detailed examples of each, beginning with LINQ to SQL.

LINQ to SQL

LINQ to SQL is part of ADO.NET which provides a run-time infrastructure for mapping relational data as objects. In essence, it is an ORM (object-relational mapping) framework that enables the direct 1-to-1 mapping of a SQL Server database and its objects to .NET classes without losing the ability to query.

One of most important things that developers need to understand when working with LINQ to SQL is the `DataContext` class. The `DataContext` is the main medium through which objects are retrieved from the database and changes are resubmitted. The `DataContext` is much like an ADO.NET connection in that it is initialized with a connection string.

The `DataContext` has the responsibility of converting objects, which means that because LINQ to SQL deals with objects, the `DataContext` converts the objects into SQL queries, as well as reassembling the results back into queryable objects.

The `DataContext` has several overloads, one of which is just a simple connection string specifying the connection information, as shown here:

```
DataContext db = new DataContext("Initial Catalog=AdventureWorks; ↩
    Integrated Security=sspi");
```

It is recommended, however, that you use strongly typed `DataContexts`. This is as simple as creating a new class that inherits from the `DataContext` class:

```
[Database(Name = "AdventureWorks")]
public class AdventureWorks : DataContext
{
    public AdventureWorks(string connection) : base(connection) {}
}
```

Here, the strongly typed DataContext is given the same name as the database to use — in this case, the AdventureWorks (2005 and 2008) database. Therefore, no database needs to be specified in the connection string.

In the preceding example, the [Database] attribute is applied to any strongly typed DataContext declaration. This attribute is optional, but when it is used a Name property must also be used to supply the name of the database to which you are mapping. This attribute maps the database in the Name property to your entity class.

With the DataContext created, the next step is to create mappings to the specific objects. Database tables are represented by entity classes in LINQ to SQL. An *entity class* is a normal class annotated with a specific tag that maps that class to a specific table in the database.

The Table attribute, part of the System.Data.Linq.Mapping namespace, maps an entity class to a database table or view. This attribute has a single property, Name, which specifies the name of the relational table or view.

In the following example, the Table attribute is applied to a class to define a mapping between the Person.Contact table in the AdventureWorks database and a class named Contact:

```
[Table(Name="Person.Contact")]
public class Contact
{
    //
}
```

Once the table is mapped to an entity class, table columns must be mapped to class properties. This is accomplished by applying the Column attribute, which maps a database table column to a member of an entity class, as shown here:

```
[Column(DbType="nvarchar(50) not null")]
public string FirstName
```

Several properties are commonly applied with this attribute, including the following:

- Name: The name of the table column
- DbType: Database type of the column
- IsPrimaryKey: Specifies that the associated column is the primary key of the corresponding table
- IsDbGenerated: Specifies that the associated column auto-generates its values
- CanBeNull: Specifies that the associated column can contain null values

So far, the connection has been defined via the DataContext, and the table and column mappings have been defined. When this is all put together, it looks like the following:

```
public class AdventureWorks : DataContext
{
    public AdventureWorks(string connection) : base(connection) {}
    public Table<Contact> Contact;
}
```

```
[Table(Name="Person.Contact")]
public class Contact
{
    [Column(DbType="nvarchar(50) not null")]
    public string FirstName
}
```

To help this sink in, this section offers a couple of examples. The first example applies the mappings manually, and the second example illustrates an easier way.

Example 1: Manually applying the mappings

For this first example, follow these steps:

1. Create a new Visual Studio C# Windows project.
2. Add a reference to the `System.Data.Linq` component.
3. On the form, add a button and a list box.
4. Add a new class to the project and name it `AdventureWorks`.
5. Open the new class and replace all the code that is there with the following code. (Because I named my project LINQ, the namespace is called LINQ. Be sure to change the namespace name if you named your project something different.)

```
using System.Data.Linq;
using System.Data.Linq.Mapping;
using System.Data;
using System.Collections.Generic;
using System.Reflection;
using System.Linq;
using System.Linq.Expressions;
using System.ComponentModel;
using System;


namespace LINQ
{
    [Database(Name = "AdventureWorks")]
    public class AdventureWorks : DataContext
    {
        public AdventureWorks(string connection) : base(connection)
        {
        }

        public Table<Contacts> Contact;
    }

    [Table(Name="Person.Contact")]
    public class Contacts
    {
        [Column(DbType = "int not null", IsDbGenerated = true,
IsPrimaryKey = true)]
```

```
            public int ContactID;

            [Column(DbType = "nvarchar(8)")]
            public string Title;

            [Column(DbType = "nvarchar(50)")]
            public string FirstName;

            [Column(DbType = "nvarchar(50)")]
            public string MiddleName;

            [Column(DbType = "nvarchar(50)")]
            public string LastName;

            [Column(DbType = "nvarchar(50)")]
            public string EmailAddress;

            [Column(DbType = "int")]
            public int EmailPromotion;

            [Column(DbType = "bit")]
            public byte NameStyle;
        }
    }
```

This code first defines the DataContext class. The next section of code defines a class that maps that class to the Person.Contact table (in SQL Server 2005) as well as maps several columns from the table to members of the class.

Note some of the properties used in the Column attribute applied to the ContactID member. The ContactID column in the Person.Contact table is a primary key column that auto-generates its IDs. Thus, in order for LINQ to support this and recognize this functionality, the IsDbGenerated and IsPrimaryKey properties need to be used.

6. In the Click event of the button on the form, add the following code:

```
AdventureWorks db = new AdventureWorks("Data Source=ServerName;
Initial Catalog=AdventureWorks;Integrated Security=sspi");

        var query =
            from con in db.Contact
            where con.FirstName.StartsWith("S")
            select con;

        foreach (var cont in query)
            listBox1.Items.Add(cont.FirstName);
```

7. Compile the project to ensure that there are no errors, and then run it. When the form displays, press the button. The list box should be populated with the first name of all contacts whose first name begins with the letter S.

Prior to moving on to the next example, let's take a closer look at this one. The class created earlier used LINQ to SQL to define the mapping between the relational data and the class. On the form, an instance of the class was created, and a LINQ query was created and used, employing a few of the standard query operators. The query was then iterated over, at which point the data was returned to the application.

The thing to pay attention to here is the query itself. As the query was typed, IntelliSense displayed the column names of the table, as well as a list of the available standard query operators and methods. This is LINQ in all its glory! Equally, notice that the syntax used to retrieve relational data is exactly the same as what was used to query the directories on the local drive in the example shown earlier.

This first example demonstrated how to create the mapping classes manually in order to provide a good understanding of how the mapping works. However, there is an easier way.

Example 2: The easy way

For this second example, follow these steps:

1. In Visual Studio, right-click the project in the Solution Explorer and select Add ➪ New Item.
2. When the Add New Item dialog appears, select the LINQ to SQL Classes item from the list of templates. Name it `AWDB.dbml` and click OK.

   A LINQ to SQL designer page will open in the Visual Studio environment. This object-relational designer provides a visual surface for creating LINQ to SQL entity classes and relationships based on database objects. In essence, this is where the object model is defined that maps database objects within an application.
3. The empty design surface represents a `DataContext` that is ready to be configured. From here, open the Server Explorer and, if necessary, create a connection to the AdventureWorks database. Once that is created, database objects can be dragged onto the designer.
4. For this example, drag the `Person.Contact` table onto the designer and then save the project. Next, modify the code behind the button on the form to look like the following:

   ```
   AWDBDataContext db = new AWDBDataContext();
   var query =
       from con in db.Contacts
       where con.FirstName.StartsWith("S")
       select con;

   foreach (var cont in query)
       listBox1.Items.Add(cont.FirstName);
   ```

   The only thing that changes is the first line; everything else remains the same. Run the project and click the button. The list box will be populated with the same data presented in the first example.
5. Before moving on, however, a few things need to be highlighted. In the Solution Explorer, expand the AWDB node. Underneath that node are two files: `AWDB.dbml.layout` and `AWDB.designer.cs`. The layout file simply contains the layout information for the designer. If you open this file you will see that it is simply an XML file.

   The important file is the `designer.cs` file. Open this file and notice that it looks very similar to the file manually created in the first example. It contains a bit more information than the one you manually created earlier, but overall it is the same.

One of the differences between the two examples is that connection string information needed to be passed in the first example, whereas no connection information needed to be passed in the second example. This is because the Server Explorer connection information was automatically saved and added to the project's resource file when the OR mapping was created. In the `designer.cs` file, the `DataContext` class contains the following:

```
public AWDBDataContext() :
    base(global::LINQ.Properties.Settings.Default
.AdventureWorksConnectionString,   mappingSource)
{
OnCreated();
}
```

Right-click on the line `AdventureWorksConnectionString` and select Go To Definition, which will take you to where the connection string is defined in the project settings. Notice that the `AWDBDataContext` has several overloads, which enables different connection information to be passed to the `DataContext`.

Much more could be said about LINQ to SQL, but this should provide a solid foundation for understanding how it works. Your homework assignment for this section is to add more tables to the designer, look at their relationships, and modify the LINQ query to utilize the relationships (hint: use the `JOIN` operator).

LINQ to SQL and Stored Procedures

A few words on using LINQ to SQL and stored procedures. I am a firm believer in using stored procedures for several reasons:

- They provide a layer of abstraction.
- They provide increased maintainability.
- They enable performance improvement through database query optimizations.

The great thing about LINQ is that it supports accessing data by calling and executing stored procedures. For example, given the following stored procedure:

```
CREATE PROCEDURE [dbo].[uspGetSalesOrderDetail]
@SalesOrderID [int]
AS
BEGIN
SET NOCOUNT ON;

SELECT      SalesOrderDetailID,
    OrderQty,
```

continued

continued

```
    ProductID,
    UnitPrice,
    LineTotal
FROM Sales.SalesOrderDetail
WHERE SalesOrderID = @SalesOrderID

END;
```

Calling a stored procedure is as simple as the following:

```
var query = db.uspGetSalesOrderDetail(43659)

foreach (SalesOrderDetailResult salesOrderDetail in query)
{
    //do something
}
```

However, while using stored procedures does have its advantages, it is still an individual call as to when and where stored procedures are appropriate. For example, if I know that a query will always return a single row (and maybe only few columns), then I may forgo using a stored procedure in that case. If I have a complex T-SQL query, then I will more than likely use a stored procedure.

My recommendation is to experiment and find what works best given the scenario in your application. Using stored procedures provides certain benefits, such as those listed earlier, but not all scenarios need stored procedures; and as you become familiar with LINQ and LINQ to SQL, you will find what works best in each situation.

LINQ to XML

I love XML. The fact that it is entirely possible to query XML using LINQ just rocks my world. It is an excellent form of moving and storing data. Those who have used other technologies to query XML know that it can be somewhat difficult and cumbersome. LINQ to XML is heaven sent. This section introduces LINQ to XML and demonstrates how easy it is to create and query XML using LINQ to XML.

The component that gives LINQ to XML its power is the `System.Xml.Linq` namespace, and its corresponding classes. These classes provide the capability to work with XML with ease, leaving behind the need to work with complex and cumbersome technologies such as the DOM and XQuery.

Table 34-2 describes the 19 classes contained in the `System.Xml.Linq` namespace that enable developers to easily work with XML.

TABLE 34-2

LINQ to XML Classes

Class	Description
XAttribute	Represents an XML attribute
XCData	Represents a CDATA text node
XComment	Represents an XML comment
XContainer	An abstract base class representing nodes that have child nodes
XDeclaration	Represents an XML declaration
XDocument	Represents an XML document
XDocumentType	Represents an XML DTD
XElement	Represents an XML element
XName	Represents the name of an XML element or attribute
Xnamespace	Represents an XML namespace
XNode	An abstract class representing nodes of an XML element tree
XNodeDocumentOrderComparer	Provides mechanisms for node comparisons regarding their order within the XML document
XNodeEqualityComparer	Provides mechanisms for node comparisons regarding their equality value
XObject	An abstract class representing XNodes and XAttributes
XObjectChange	The event type when an XObject event is raised
XObjectChangeEventArgs	Provides information and data for the Changing and Changed events
XObjectChangeEventHandler	The method that handles the XObject's Changed and Changing events
XProcessingInstruction	Represents an XML processing instruction
XText	Represents an XML text node

LINQ to XML example

Create a new Visual Studio project. On the form, add a text box and two buttons. Set the properties of the text box so that it is multi-line and has a vertical scroll bar. Behind button1, add the following code:

```
XDocument riders = new XDocument
    (new XDeclaration("1.0", "utf-8", "yes"),
    new XComment("Riders for the year 2008"),
    new XElement("Riders",
        new XElement("Rider",
            new XAttribute("Residence", "Florida"),
            new XElement("Name", "Ricky Carmich ael"),
            new XElement("Class", "450"),
            new XElement("Brand", "Suzuki"),
            new XElement("Sponsors",
                new XElement("Name", "Makita")
                )
              ),
        new XElement("Rider",
            new XAttribute("Residence", "California"),
            new XElement("Name", "Chad Reed"),
            new XElement("Class", "450"),
            new XElement("Brand", "Yamaha"),
            new XElement("Sponsors",
                new XElement("Name", "ProTaper")
                )
              ),
        new XElement("Rider",
            new XAttribute("Residence", "Mississippi"),
            new XElement("Name", "Kevin Windham"),
            new XElement("Class", "450"),
            new XElement("Brand", "Honda"),
            new XElement("Sponsors",
                new XElement("Name", "Factory Connection")
                )
              ),
          new XElement("Rider",
              new XAttribute("Residence", "Florida"),
            new XElement("Name", "James Stewart"),
            new XElement("Class", "450"),
            new XElement("Brand", "Kawasaki"),
            new XElement("Sponsors",
                new XElement("Name", "Renthal")
                )
            )
        )
      );

textBox1.Text = riders.ToString();
```

Be sure to add the appropriate reference to `System.XML.Linq` in your form prior to running the project:

```
using System.XML.Linq;
```

Before running the project, take a look at the code. Notice that several of the classes were used to create and define the XML. For example, the `XDocument` class was used to create an XML document. As well, the `XElement` and `XAttribute` classes were used to define the attributes and elements of the XML document.

Run the project and click button1 when the form displays. The text box on the form will display the following XML:

```
<!--Riders for the year 2008-->
<Riders>
  <Rider Residence="Florida">
    <Name>Ricky Carmichael</Name>
    <Class>450</Class>
    <Brand>Suzuki</Brand>
    <Sponsors>
      <Name>Makita</Name>
    </Sponsors>
  </Rider>
  <Rider Residence="California">
    <Name>Chad Reed</Name>
    <Class>450</Class>
    <Brand>Yamaha</Brand>
    <Sponsors>
      <Name>ProTaper</Name>
    </Sponsors>
  </Rider>
  <Rider Residence="Mississippi">
    <Name>Kevin Windham</Name>
    <Class>450</Class>
    <Brand>Honda</Brand>
    <Sponsors>
      <Name>Factory Connection</Name>
    </Sponsors>
  </Rider>
  <Rider Residence="Florida">
    <Name>James Stewart</Name>
    <Class>450</Class>
    <Brand>Kawasaki</Brand>
    <Sponsors>
      <Name>Renthal</Name>
    </Sponsors>
  </Rider>
</Riders>
```

Isn't that much easier than using the DOM?

What about querying XML? Open Notepad or another text editor and type in the following:

```
<Employees>
  <Employee id="1" Dept="0001">
    <Name>Scott</Name>
    <Address>
      <Street>555 Main St.</Street>
      <City>Wellington</City>
      <State>FL</State>
    </Address>
    <Title>All Things Techy</Title>
    <HireDate>02/05/2007</HireDate>
    <Gender>M</Gender>
  </Employee>
  <Employee id="2" Dept="0005">
    <Name>Steve</Name>
    <Address>
      <Street>444 Main St.</Street>
      <City>Snahomish</City>
      <State>WA</State>
    </Address>
    <Title>Mr. SciFi</Title>
    <HireDate>05/14/2002</HireDate>
    <Gender>M</Gender>
  </Employee>
  <Employee id="3" Dept="0004">
    <Name>Joe</Name>
    <Address>
      <Street>222 Main St.</Street>
      <City>Easley</City>
      <State>SC</State>
    </Address>
    <Title>All Things Bleeding Edge</Title>
    <HireDate>07/22/2004</HireDate>
    <Gender>M</Gender>
  </Employee>
</Employees>
```

Save this file as `Employees.xml`. Next, add the following code behind button2 :

```
    XElement employees =
        XElement.Load("Employees.xml");
textBox1.Text = employees.Element("Employee").ToString();
```

Run the project again and click button2. The text box will be filled with the first employee from the XML document, as shown here:

```
<Employee id="1" Dept="0001">
  <Name>Scott</Name>
```

```
  <Address>
    <Street>555 Main St.</Street>
    <City>Wellington</City>
    <State>FL</State>
  </Address>
  <Title>All Things Techy</Title>
  <HireDate>02/05/2007</HireDate>
  <Gender>M</Gender>
</Employee>
```

However, another way to return the first employee is to use the `First()` property to manually select the first `employee` element:

```
employees.Elements("Employee").First()
```

Another alternative is to use the `ElementAt()` method to specify which element to return:

```
employees.Elements("Employee").ElementAt(0)
```

Yet another method is to use a LINQ query expression:

```
XElement empnum2 = (from emp in employees.Elements("Employee")
                    where (int)emp.Attribute("id") == 2
                    select emp).ElementAt(0);
```

This example uses a LINQ query expression to query the XML document, using the attribute `"id"` as a filter. In this example, the `ElementAt()` method is used to return the first element that matches the specified criteria.

This next example uses a LINQ query expression to query the XML document and return the values of all the `Name` elements for each employee. To get that information, the `descendants()` method is used to return a collection of all descendants for the selected element:

```
IEnumerable<string> empNames =
   from emp in employees.Descendants("Name")
   orderby emp.Value
   select emp.Value;

foreach (string name in empNames)
   listBox1.Items.Add(name);
```

When run, this example returns the following:

```
Joe
Scott
Steve
```

Traversing XML

Traversing XML in an XML tree using LINQ to XML is quite simple. Just use the methods of the `XElement` and `XAttribute` classes as necessary. Basically, the `Elements` and `Element` methods provide all of the element children of an `XContainer` (an `XElement` or `XDocument`) object. Using the `XName` object, such as `Element(XName)`, one can return elements of that specific `XName`.

For example, using the XML document used in the previous example, one can "walk the XML tree," as shown here:

```
employees.Element("Employees").Element("Employee")
employees.Element("Employees").Element("Employee")
.Element("Name")
```

The same can be accomplished with attributes as well. The following illustrates how to walk an XML tree to get to a specific attribute:

```
employees.Elements("Employee").ElementAt(1).Attribute("id")
```

The thing to remember is that the `Nodes()`, `Elements()`, `Element(Name)`, and `Elements(Name)` methods provide the foundation and basic functionality of XML tree navigation.

LINQ to DataSet

Most, if not all, .NET developers are familiar with the concept of a `DataSet` because it is one of the most frequently used components in ADO.NET. A `DataSet` is a representation of the tables and relationships found in a database, exposing a hierarchical object model made of objects such as tables, rows, columns, constraints, and relationships.

The `Dataset` itself is extremely flexible and powerful. It provides the capability for applications to efficiently work with a subset of data found in a database and to manipulate the data as needed by the application, all while in a disconnected state.

Yet, with all the flexibility there has not been, up to this point, a means or method for querying data contained within the `DataSet` (other than the few methods on the `DataTable` class such as `Select`, `GetParentRow`, and `GetChildRow`). This is where LINQ and LINQ to `DataSet` come in. With the querying power of LINQ, LINQ to `DataSet` provides developers with a full set of query capabilities to quickly and easily query the contents of a `DataSet`.

An illustration of how easy it is to query a `DataSet` using LINQ to DataSet follows.

Querying a DataSet using LINQ to DataSet

First, create a new Visual Studio project. Make sure that the project includes references to both the `System.Core` and `System.Data.DataSetExtension` namespaces. On the form, place a button, a text box, and a list box. Add the following `using` statement to the code as well:

using System.Data.SqlClient;

Anyone who has worked with a DataSet is intimately familiar with how to populate it using the SqlDataAdapter. The following example uses the SqlDataAdapter to populate a DataSet with data from the Person.Contact table then use a LINQ query expression to query the DataSet.

Add the following code to the Click event of the button:

```
try
{
    //first, populate the dataset
    DataSet ds = new DataSet();

    string connectionInfo = "Data Source=SERVERNAME;Initial
Catalog=AdventureWorks;Integrated Security=sspi";

    SqlDataAdapter da = new SqlDataAdapter("select pc.ContactID,
pc.FirstName, pc.MiddleName, pc.LastName, pc.EmailAddress from
Person.Contact pc", connectionInfo);

    da.TableMappings.Add("Table", "Contact");

    da.Fill(ds);

    DataTable dt = ds.Tables["Contact"];

    textBox1.Text = ds.Tables[0].Rows.Count.ToString();

    //now query it for specific people
    var con = from contact in dt.AsEnumerable()
              where contact.Field<string>("FirstName")
              .StartsWith("S")
              select new { ContactID = contact.Field<int>
             ("ContactID"),
                           FirstName = contact.Field<string>
                           ("FirstName"),
                           MiddleName =
contact.Field<string>("MiddleName"),
                           LastName = contact.Field<string>
                           ("LastName"),
                           Email = contact.Field<string>
                           ("EmailAddress")};

    foreach (var cont in con)
        listBox1.Items.Add(cont.ContactID.ToString() + "   " +
            cont.FirstName + "   " +
            cont.MiddleName + "   " +
            cont.LastName + "   " +
            cont.Email);

}
```

```
    catch (Exception ex)
    {
        MessageBox.Show(ex.Message);
    }
```

Compile the project to ensure there are no errors, and then run it. When the form opens, click the button. The text box will display the total number of records contained in the DataSet. The list box will fill with all the contacts from the DataSet whose first name begins with the letter S.

Note a couple of things here:

- The DataSet is not a typed DataSet because the Field() method is used to access the column values of the DataRow.
- The LINQ query itself. Like the others before it in this chapter, the syntax follows the same pattern as the other queries. The only difference is the data source.
- The use of the AsEnumerable() method. This method returns an IEnumerable object, which in this case enables you to iterate over the data in the DataTable.

The next example does two things. One, it uses a typed DataSet. Two, it adds a second table to the DataSet that illustrates how to use a LINQ query to query data from two tables.

Add a new item to the solution, this time adding a DataSet. In the Add New Item dialog, select Data from the list of Categories, and then select DataSet from the list of Templates. Name the DataSet ContactDS.xsd and click OK.

The DataSet Designer will display in the Visual Studio IDE. The DataSet Designer is a visual tool for creating and editing typed DataSets and the individual items that make up DataSets. The DataSet Designer provides developers with a visual depiction of the objects contained in the DataSets.

In the Dataset Designer, drag and drop the Contact and Employee tables from the Server Explorer. Next, modify the code behind the button as follows:

```
try
{
    ContactsDS ds = new ContactsDS();

    string connectionInfo = "Data Source=SERVERNAME;Initial
Catalog=AdventureWorks;Integrated Security=sspi";

    SqlDataAdapter da = new SqlDataAdapter("select * from Person
.Contact; select * from HumanResources.Employee;", connectionInfo);

    da.TableMappings.Add("Table", "Contact");
    da.TableMappings.Add("Table1", "Employee");

    da.Fill(ds);

    textBox1.Text = "contact table has " + ds.Tables[0].Rows.Count
.ToString() + " records, and employee table has " +
```

```
ds.Tables[1].Rows.Count.ToString() + " records.";

    var query =
        from con in ds.Contact
        join emp in ds.Employee
        on con.ContactID equals emp.ContactID
        where con.FirstName.StartsWith("S")
        select new
        {
            ContactID = con.ContactID,
            FirstName = con.FirstName,
            LastName = con.LastName,
            EMail = con.EmailAddress,
            EmpID = emp.EmployeeID,
            IDNum = emp.NationalIDNumber,
            HireDate = emp.HireDate
        };

    foreach (var cont in query)
        listBox1.Items.Add(cont.ContactID.ToString() + "   " +
            cont.FirstName + "   " +
            cont.LastName + "   " +
            cont.EMail + "   " +
            cont.EmpID + "   " +
            cont.IDNum + "   " +
            cont.HireDate.ToString());

}
catch (Exception ex)
{
    MessageBox.Show(ex.Message);
}
```

Compile the project to ensure there are no coding errors, and then run it. When the form displays, click the button. The text box will display a message indicating the number of records returned in each table. The list box will then display a combination of contact and employee data for all contacts whose first name begins with the letter S.

Before moving on to the last example, consider what the code is doing. In many ways it is very similar to the previous example, but several things are different:

- This example uses a typed `DataSet`.
- Two tables are being populated, not just one.
- Because a typed `DataSet` is being used, it's no longer necessary to use the `Field<>` method. Instead, it employs a direct mapping to the tables and columns and the use of IntelliSense.
- The LINQ query expression uses the `join` standard query operator to join the `Contact` table and the `Employee` table.

One more comment about the prior example. Because a typed DataSet was used, the DataSet itself contains the relationship information. This can be visually seen on the DataSet Designer. If a typed dataset had not been used, then the relationship would have to be defined programmatically using the DataRelation class.

Data binding with LINQ to DataSet

This section describes how to use LINQ to DataSet to do data binding. This example is similar to the first, in that it uses an untyped DataSet, but this is not the focus of the example because a typed DataSet can still be used. The important thing to learn from this example is how to do data binding using LINQ to DataSet.

For this example, open the form in design view. From the toolbox, drag and drop a DataGridView control onto the form. Place another button on the form and enter the following code in its Click event:

```
try
{
    DataSet ds = new DataSet();

    string connectionInfo = "Data Source=SERVERNAME;Initial
Catalog=AdventureWorks;Integrated Security=sspi";

    SqlDataAdapter da = new SqlDataAdapter("select pc.ContactID,
pc.FirstName, pc.MiddleName, pc.LastName, pc.EmailAddress from
Person.Contact pc", connectionInfo);

    da.TableMappings.Add("Table", "Contact");

    da.Fill(ds);

    DataTable dt = ds.Tables["Contact"];

    textBox1.Text = ds.Tables[0].Rows.Count.ToString();

    IEnumerable<DataRow> contact =
        from con in dt.AsEnumerable()
        where con.Field<string>("FirstName").StartsWith("S")
        orderby con.Field<string>("LastName")
        select con;

    DataTable partialTable = contact.CopyToDataTable<DataRow>();

    DataView dv = new DataView(partialTable);
    dataGridView1.DataSource = dv;

}
catch (Exception ex)
{
    MessageBox.Show(ex.Message);
}
```

This example populates a DataSet with all the data from the Contacts table and then queries the DataSet using a LINQ query. The query returns an enumeration of DataRow objects that is used to populate a DataTable via the CopyToDataTable() method. Once the DataTable is populated, a new DataView is created and populated with the data in the DataTable. The DataView is then assigned to the DataSource property of the DataGridView.

Another option for binding would have been to bind the DataTable directly to the DataGridView, as follows:

```
dataGridView1.DataSource = partialTable;
```

However, the DataView provides additional capabilities such as sorting and filtering data that is stored in a DataTable.

Additionally, the data can be bound by implicitly binding data to controls, by implementing the IListSource interface. This interface enables an object to return a list that is bindable to a data source, as shown here:

```
var query =
    from c in contact
    where c.Field<string>("FirstName").StartsWith("S")
    orderby c.Field<string>("LastName")
    select c;

dataGridView1.DataSource = query;
```

Likewise, the following can be done:

```
BindingSource bindsrc = new BindingSource();
bindsrc.DataSrouce = query;
dataGridView1.DataSource = bindsrc;
```

Implicit binding is available because the Table<T> and DataQuery<T> classes have been updated to implement the IListSource interface.

All of these examples populated the initial DataSet with all of the records from the Contacts table. This was done by design to illustrate the querying capabilities of LINQ to DataSet.

LINQ to Entities

When talking about LINQ to Entities, the discussion must also discuss the ADO.NET Entity Framework. This is because LINQ to Entities is the part of the ADO.NET Entity Framework that provides the LINQ query capabilities.

That statement then begs the question, what is the difference between LINQ to SQL and LINQ to Entities? In the LINQ to SQL section, it was stated that LINQ to SQL is an object-relational mapping framework that enables the direct 1-to-1 mapping of SQL Server database objects to .NET classes, where the database closely resembles the application model.

LINQ to Entities is more than a simple ORM tool. The ADO.NET Entity Framework and LINQ to Entities enable developers to work against a conceptual model that offers more flexible mapping, which provides the capability to utilize a wider degree of variance from the underlying data source.

What determines whether a project should use LINQ to SQL or LINQ to Entities/Entity Framework? You should use LINQ to SQL when you want the following:

- A rapid development cycle
- An ORM solution and a 1:1 data/object model mapping
- Optimized performance through stored procedures and compiled queries
- To generate your own CLR classes versus using generated classes or deriving from base classes

In contrast, LINQ to Entities and the Entity Framework should be used when the following apply:

- Your application targets different database engines in addition to Microsoft SQL Server
- Your physical database structure could be significantly different from your object model. That means you still want the benefits of an ORM but your classes may or may not map 1:1 with your database schema.
- You want to optimize performance through stored procedures and compiled queries
- The LINQ query should work in a database vendor–neutral manner
- You want to define application domain models to be used as the basis for a persistence layer

This section introduces LINQ to Entities and the Entity Framework and illustrates by example how easy it is to create entities and query them using LINQ.

Everything needed to use LINQ to Entities and the Entity Framework is installed with Visual Studio 2008 SP1, which can be downloaded from the following location:

```
www.microsoft.com/downloads/details.aspx?FamilyId=FBEE1648-7106-44A7-
9649-6D9F6D58056E&displaylang=en
```

Creating and querying entities using LINQ

After installing the service pack, create a new Visual Studio C# Windows forms project. When the project is loaded, add a new item to it. In the Add New Item dialog you will notice a new item in the list of templates called ADO.NET Entity Data Model. This Entity Data Model provides the capability to define domain models for an application. Select the ADO.NET Entity Data Model template, name it `AdventureWorks.edmx`, and then click OK.

The Entity Data Model wizard begins. The first screen of the wizard provides the capability to define the model contents. The model can be created from scratch, by selecting Empty Model, or generated from a database, by selecting Generate from Database. By default, Generate from Database is selected, so ensure that this option is selected and click Next.

The next step of the wizard defines the data connection. If a connection has previously been defined, you can select it from the drop-down menu. If not, click the New Connection button and define a connection in the Connection Properties dialog. You are also asked at this step whether or not you want to store sensitive connection information in the connection string. The connection string information is stored in the application configuration file (`app.config`) and is used by the `ObjectContext` to connect to the database. Excluding the sensitive data (such as password information) from the connection string requires that the information be set in the application code. Including the sensitive data includes it in clear text in the `app.config`. For production environments, it is recommended that sensitive information be excluded from the connection string. For the purposes of this example, select the option to include the sensitive information in the connection string.

Once the connection has been defined, click Next.

The next step of the wizard enables you to select the objects to be included in the model. Objects such as tables, views, and stored procedures can be selected for inclusion. For this example, select the `Person.Contact`, `HumanResources.Employee`, `Sales.Customer`, and `Sales.SalesOrderHeader` tables.

In addition, it is at this step of the wizard that the model namespace must be entered. It defaults to a value, but it is good to verify that there is a value. By default, it takes the object name entered when the ADO.NET Entity Data Model template was selected, which in this example is AdventureWorks, and then adds the word "Model" to the end. Thus, the namespace should default to `AdventureWorksModel` in this example. Click Finish.

The wizard then builds the Entity Data Model based on the objects and selections in the wizard. When it is complete, the Entity Data Model Designer opens in the Visual Studio IDE.

This process is very familiar to the LINQ to SQL example shown earlier. The difference is that with LINQ to SQL, the database objects were added in the model *after* the designer was created. With the Entity Framework, a wizard walks the developer through the steps of selecting which objects to include in the model *prior* to creating the designer and model.

When the creation of the model is complete, a new node appears in the Solution Explorer. The node is called `AdventureWorks.edmx` and it has a child file, which is the `Designer` file called `AdventureWorks.Designer.cs`.

Opening the `.edmx` file opens the visual model designer that was created at the end of the wizard. Our focus here is the `Designer.cs` file. Opening that file displays some code that should look very familiar. The `Designer.cs` file contains the `DataContext` and all the necessary object mappings to the database. For example, one of the first lines that should look familiar is the creation of a class that inherits from the `DataContext`:

```
public partial class AdventureWorksEntities :
global::System.Data.Objects.ObjectContext
```

Also different is the way tables are defined. Instead of applying the `[Table]` attribute, as done in LINQ to SQL, this class inherits from the `EntityObject` class, which is the base class for entity types that are generated via the Entity Data Model tools, as shown here:

```
public partial class Employee :
global::System.Data.Objects.DataClasses.EntityObject
```

The class is also attributed with several attributes, such as AdmEntityTypeAttribute, which indicates that the class represents an entity type:

```
[global::System.Data.Objects.DataClasses.EdmEntityTypeAttribute
(NamespaceName="AdventureWorksModel", Name="Employee")]
[global::System.Runtime.Serialization.DataContractAttribute
(IsReference=true)]
[global::System.Serializable()]
public partial class Employee :
global::System.Data.Objects.DataClasses.EntityObject
```

Also different is the way in which columns are defined and mapped. Instead of using the [Column] attribute, as done in LINQ to SQL, columns are attributed with the EdmScalarProperty Attribute, which indicates that the property represents a scalar property:

```
[global::System.Data.Objects.DataClasses.EdmScalarPropertyAttribute
(EntityKeyProperty=true, IsNullable=false)]
[global::System.Runtime.Serialization.DataMemberAttribute()]
public int EmployeeID
```

Another important item to look at is the set of relationship attributes. The EdmRelationship Attribute is used to define a relationship between two entity types (in this case, Contacts and Employees) based on an association in the conception model:

```
[assembly: global::System.Data.Objects.DataClasses
.EdmRelationshipAttribute("AdventureWorksModel",
"FK_Employee_Contact_ContactID", "Contact",
global::System.Data.Metadata.Edm.RelationshipMultiplicity.One,
typeof(EF.Contact), "Employee",
global::System.Data.Metadata.Edm.RelationshipMultiplicity.Many,
typeof(EF.Employee))]
```

With that background, it is time to focus on the front end. Open the form in design view and place a list box and a button on the form. In the Click event of the button, add the following code:

```
AdventureWorksEntities awe = new AdventureWorksEntities();

var query =
    from emp in awe.Contact
    where emp.FirstName.StartsWith("S")
    select emp;

foreach (var empl in query)
    listBox1.Items.Add(empl.LastName);
```

By now this code should look very familiar. It looks almost exactly like the LINQ to SQL code. The first line creates an instance of the AdventureWorksEntities class, followed by a LINQ query expression. The query is then iterated through and the results displayed in the list box.

Compile the project and then run it. When the form displays, click the button. The list box will display results, some of which are shown here:

```
Agcaoili
Jacobson
Altamirano
Alvarado
Appelbaum
Ayers
...
```

Querying multiple tables using LINQ to Entities and the Entity Framework

This chapter closes with one last example that illustrates how to query multiple tables using LINQ to Entities and the Entity Framework.

Place another button the form, and in the Click event add the following code:

```
AdventureWorksEntities awe = new AdventureWorksEntities();

var query =
    from cus in awe.Customer
    where cus.CustomerID == 2
    select cus;

foreach (var cust in query)
{
    listBox1.Items.Add(cust.CustomerID);
    foreach (var ord in cust.SalesOrderHeader)
        listBox1.Items.Add("    " + ord.OrderDate);
}
```

This example begins like the previous example, but the `foreach` loops are different. The LINQ query returns a single record, where the CustomerID column in the `Sales` table is 2. In the `foreach` loop, that same CustomerID is written to the list box, and then a secondary loop loops through the orders for that customerID.

Compile the application and run it. When the form displays, click button2. The list box displays the CustomerID, but it does not display the sales order header rows for that customer. That is because the query fetched the customer but it did not fetch the orders. Because the Entity Framework did not know how the orders were going to be used, it did not want to automatically bring back information that was not needed.

To fix that, the orders can be explicitly loaded for that specific customer by adding the following highlighted line of code to the first `foreach` loop:

```
foreach (var cust in query)
{
    listBox1.Items.Add(cust.CustomerID);
```

```
        cust.SalesOrderHeader.Load();
        foreach (var ord in cust.SalesOrderHeader)
            listBox1.Items.Add("    " + ord.OrderDate);
}
```

When the foreach is executed, it will execute the query to return the customers, but not the orders. When the Load() statement is executed, it will create a separate query and return the orders for that customer.

Run the project again and click button2. This time the list box will display the order dates for CustomerID 2:

```
2
   8/1/2002
   11/1/2002
   2/1/2003
   5/1/2003
   8/1/2003
   11/1/2003
   2/1/2004
   5/1/2004
```

The preceding query is OK if the goal is to load only orders for some of the customers (for example, when selecting a customer from a list), but in this case there exists a loop that will bring back every order for every customer. Therefore, instead of executing multiple queries, a request can be made to only pull back all of the orders with the customer in the initial query, as follows:

```
var query =
    from cus in awe.Customer.Include("SalesOrderHeader")
    where cus.CustomerID == 2
    select cus;
```

When the application is run again, the results displayed in the text box are the same as the previous query.

The goal of these two examples is to illustrate how easy LINQ to Entities and the Entity Framework are to access SQL Server and query entities. With all that was shown in this chapter, it should be very apparent how flexible yet powerful LINQ is for querying different data sources such as XML, DataSets, and Entities.

Your homework assignment for this section is to create a new EF model. This time, however, in the wizard use an empty model, add one or more tables to it, and then write a LINQ query to query the data.

Summary

The purpose of this chapter was to provide an overview of LINQ and the different LINQ providers, and show by example how powerful, flexible, and efficient they are in accessing the different types of data sources.

In this chapter you learned what LINQ is and how to use LINQ to query data from different data sources, such as XML, entities, and databases, using LINQ's powerful standard query operators.

Chapter 35

Asynchronous Messaging with Service Broker

IN THIS CHAPTER

Defining a work queue

Queuing messages

Managing conversations

Service Broker is a powerful yet simple work queue system that can be used to add asynchronous messaging and work queues to a database abstraction layer to provide high scalability, and it is essential in any SOA data store architecture.

If you've ever built a table to hold work to be done, such as orders to be processed by a Materials Requirement Planning system, then you've built a work queue. In one application Service Broker is just that — a high-performance, wide-payload work queue integrated into SQL Server with DDL and monitoring capabilities.

Service Broker can also be used to pass messages with guaranteed secure delivery between work queues, which opens up a world of possibilities.

Because Service Broker is essentially just a SQL Server table, it includes all the cool transactional and back-up capabilities inherent to SQL Server. This is what sets Service Broker apart from other queuing technologies, such as Microsoft Message Queuing (MSMQ).

The queue contains a single, wide column for the message body, which is OK because the message will typically contain a single XML file or fragment or SOAP message as the payload.

Service Broker is not enabled by default so the first specific step to working with Service Broker is to turn it on using the `ALTER DATABASE` command:

```
ALTER DATABASE AdventureWorks SET ENABLE_BROKER;
```

What's New with Service Broker?

Service Broker was introduced with much fanfare in SQL Server 2005. For SQL Server 2008, there are a few slight enhancements: Conversations may now have an assigned priority; there are new DMVs for monitoring Service Broker; there's a new Service Broker Statistics Report; and Management Studio can now auto-generate some Service Broker scripts.

Configuring a Message Queue

Service Broker uses a messaging or dialog metaphor, but there's much more to Service Broker than just the messages. The Service Broker objects must be defined in the following order:

1. *Message types* define the legal requirements of the message.
2. *Contracts* define the agreement between the initiating service and the target, including the message type, the queue, and the services.
3. *Queues* hold the lists of messages.
4. *Services* communicate with the queue and either send or receive messages as the initiating service or the target service, respectively.

Other than defining the message type as XML and naming the objects, there isn't much complexity to setting up a Service Broker database. That's because the data definition language, or DDL, does all the work; Service Broker is a message-agnostic work queue that's serving as an infrastructure for the messages. There's more work in placing messages on and taking messages off the queue.

Because Service Broker is integrated within SQL Server, the objects are created using the familiar create DDL commands.

The first step in creating a Service Broker queue is to define a message type and a contract that uses that message type:

```
CREATE MESSAGE TYPE HelloWorldMessage
  VALIDATION = WELL_FORMED_XML ;
CREATE CONTRACT HelloWorldContract
  ( HelloWorldMessage SENT BY INITIATOR);
```

The initiator and target queues are also simply created using DDL:

```
CREATE QUEUE [dbo].[TargetQueue] ;
CREATE QUEUE [dbo].[InitiatorQueue] ;
```

Likewise, the initiator and target services are also defined using DDL. Both services are associated with a queue, and the receiving, or target, service specifies that it can receive messages from a contract:

```
CREATE SERVICE InitiatorService
    ON QUEUE [dbo].[InitiatorQueue];
GO

CREATE SERVICE TargetService
    ON QUEUE [dbo].[TargetQueue]
    (HelloWorldContract);
```

With the Service Broker objects created, you'll be able to see them listed under the Object Explorer Service Broker node.

Working with Conversations

With the Service Broker object created, messages can be placed into the queue or received from the queue. Messages exist as part of a conversation that can be divided into conversation groups.

Sending a message to the queue

The following code creates a conversation using a `conversationhandle` GUID. The `BEGIN CONVERSATION` command opens the conversation, and the `SEND` command actually places the message into the queue:

```
BEGIN TRANSACTION ;

DECLARE @message XML ;
SET @message = N'<message>Hello, World!</message>' ;

DECLARE @conversationHandle UNIQUEIDENTIFIER ;

BEGIN DIALOG CONVERSATION @conversationHandle
    FROM SERVICE [InitiatorService]
    TO SERVICE 'TargetService'
    ON CONTRACT [HelloWorldContract]
    WITH ENCRYPTION = OFF, LIFETIME = 1000 ;

SEND ON CONVERSATION @conversationHandle
  MESSAGE TYPE [HelloWorldMessage]
  (@message) ;

END CONVERSATION @conversationHandle ;

COMMIT TRANSACTION ;
To view the message in the queue, select from the queue table as if it
were a normal relational table:
SELECT CAST(message_body as nvarchar(MAX)) from [dbo].[TargetQueue]
```

Receiving a message

The RECEIVE command will retrieve and remove the oldest message from the queue. Use RECEIVE within a transaction so that if something goes wrong, the receive can be rolled back and the message will still be in the queue. Service Broker is not a trigger that can code when a message is placed on the queue; some code must run to extract the message. To accomplish this, Microsoft added a new option to the WAIT FOR command, enabling it to wait for a message in the queue. Without this option, the code would have to run a loop to continuously check for a new message. The following routine within a stored procedure will wait for a message and then receive the top message from the queue:

```
USE AdventureWorks ;
GO

-- Process all conversation groups.
WHILE (1 = 1)
  BEGIN

  DECLARE @conversation_handle UNIQUEIDENTIFIER,
        @conversation_group_id  UNIQUEIDENTIFIER,
        @message_body XML,
        @message_type_name NVARCHAR(128);

  BEGIN TRANSACTION ;

-- Get next conversation group.

  WAITFOR(
    GET CONVERSATION GROUP @conversation_group_id FROM
    [dbo].[TargetQueue]), TIMEOUT 500 ;

  -- If there are no more conversation groups, roll back the
  -- transaction and break out of the outermost WHILE loop.

  IF @conversation_group_id IS NULL
  BEGIN
      ROLLBACK TRANSACTION ;
      BREAK ;
  END ;

      -- Process all messages in the conversation group. Notice
      -- that all processing occurs in the same transaction.

      WHILE 1 = 1
      BEGIN

          -- Receive the next message for the conversation group.
          -- Notice that the receive statement includes a WHERE
          -- clause to ensure that the messages received belong to
          -- the same conversation group.
```

```
            RECEIVE
              TOP(1)
              @conversation_handle = conversation_handle,
              @message_type_name = message_type_name,
              @message_body =
              CASE
                  WHEN validation = 'X' THEN CAST(message_body AS XML)
                  ELSE CAST(N'<none/>' AS XML)
              END
            FROM [dbo].[TargetQueue]
            WHERE conversation_group_id = @conversation_group_id ;

            -- If there are no more messages, or an error occurred,
            -- stop processing this conversation group.

            IF @@ROWCOUNT = 0 OR @@ERROR <> 0 BREAK;

            -- Show the information received.

            SELECT 'Conversation Group Id' = @conversation_group_id,
                  'Conversation Handle' = @conversation_handle,
                  'Message Type Name' = @message_type_name,
                  'Message Body' = @message_body ;


            -- If the message_type_name indicates that the message is
            -- an error or an end dialog message, end the
            -- conversation.

            IF @message_type_name
='http://schemas.microsoft.com/SQL/ServiceBroker/EndDialog'
              OR @message_type_name
='http://schemas.microsoft.com/SQL/ServiceBroker/Error'
            BEGIN
              END CONVERSATION @conversation_handle ;
            END ;

      END; -- Process all messages in conversation group.

     -- Commit the receive statements and the end conversation
     -- statement.

     COMMIT TRANSACTION ;

END ; -- Process all conversation groups.

use tempdb;;
```

Service Broker can handle complex message groups, such as multiple line items of an order that may not appear consecutively in the queue due to other messages being received simultaneously. The conversation group can be used to select out the related messages.

Monitoring Service Broker

While Management Studio has no visibility in the activity of a queue, nor summary page reports for the queue object, you can select directly from the queue or select a `count()`. In addition, there are database catalog views to shed light on the queue:

* `sys.dm_broker_activated_tasks`
* `sys.dm_broker_connections`
* `sys.dm_broker_forwarded_messages`
* `sys.dm_broker_queue_monitors`

SQL Trace/Profiler has a Broker event class with 10 Service Broker–related events that can be traced.

Summary

Service Broker is one of those technologies that provides no benefit "out of the box." Unless you make the effort to architect the database using Service Broker, it offers no advantage. However, if you do take the time to design the database using Service Broker, you'll see significant scalability benefits, as Service Broker queues buffer the workload.

The next chapter continues the progression through SQL Server technologies and discusses ADO.NET 2.0 and its powerful methods for connectivity.

Chapter 36

Replicating Data

Replication is an optional native SQL Server 2008 component that is used to copy data and other database objects from one database or server to another.

Replication is used for many purposes, listed here in order from most popular to rarely used:

- Offloading reporting from an OLTP server to a reporting server
- Data consolidation — for example, consolidating branch office data to a central server
- Data distribution — for example, distributing data from a central server to a set of member servers to improve read performance
- Disaster recovery — replication can be used to keep a DR (disaster recovery) server synchronized with the main server, and clients can be manually redirected to the DR with minimal interruption
- Synchronizing data with a central server and a mobile sales force
- Synchronizing data with handheld devices (such as PDAs and smartphones)

Replication processes can be made to be highly scalable, and typically can synchronize data between servers/databases with acceptable latency. *Latency* reflects the lag of time between when data is sent (replicated) from the source server and received at the destination server.

Replication is not the only way to move data between servers. There are several alternatives, each with its own pros and cons:

- bcp utility
- SSIS

IN THIS CHAPTER

Replication concepts

Configuring replication

- Distributed transactions
- Triggers
- Copy Database Wizard
- Backup and restore
- Log shipping and database mirroring

Bulk copy program (bcp) is a command-line tool that can be used to send tabular data to the file system, and from there to a remote server. While it can be scripted, it is slower than replication processes, requires significant work to set up, and the DBA/developer needs to ensure that all objects are in place on the destination server. For example, all tables, views, stored procedures, and functions need to be on the destination server. There is no provision for change tracking. In other words, bcp can't tell what has changed in the data, and only sends the changes to the destination server. The solution requires change tracking — a way to determine what has been inserted/updated/deleted on the source server. These may involve using Change Data Capture or the Change Tracking features in SQL 2008.

SSIS can be thought of as a programmatic interface to a high-performance bcp utility. It can be faster than bcp. As with bcp, it requires that the DBA/developer place all objects on the destination server, and there is no provision for change tracking.

Distributed transactions normally involve using MS DTC (Microsoft Distributed Transaction Coordinator). With a distributed transaction, the transaction is committed on the source server, then on the destination server, and then the application can do the next unit of work. (This is sometimes called a *split write*.) The application has to be configured to use distributed transactions, and the network connection must be stable and have ample bandwidth; otherwise, the transactions will fail. With distributed transactions, only changes are "replicated." The DBA/developer needs to place all tables (along with the initial data), stored procedures, views, and functions on the destination server.

Triggers are very similar to distributed transactions. With distributed transactions, all application code (for example, stored procedures, and sometimes ADO.NET code) must be rewritten for the distributed transactions. With triggers, the "replication" logic is incorporated on the trigger. And like distributed transactions, only changes are "replicated." The DBA/developer needs to place all tables (along with the initial data), stored procedures, views, and functions on the destination server. There is also overhead with using triggers, especially over a network.

The Copy Database Wizard will move or copy a database from one server to another. It is intended for a single use move or copy. In the move mode, you can only move the database one time. In the copy mode, the database can be copied multiple times if you specify the options to delete the database and the database files that might exist on the destination server.

Backup and restore will copy the entire database to the destination server. The level of granularity possible for the preceding options are tables (bcp, SSIS) and transactions (triggers, distributed transactions).

Backup and restore, log shipping, database mirroring, and the Copy Database Wizard "replicate" entire databases. As the name suggests, backup and restore involves backing up the database on the source server and restoring it on the destination server. This option is not scalable for large databases, and the database must go offline while the database is being restored. It is not a good option in environments with real-time data requirements, as the data becomes progressively out of date until the latest backup is restored on the destination server.

Log shipping is continuous backup and restore. The log is backed up on the source server and applied to a previously restored database backup on the destination server. Log shipping is not considered to be scalable, especially for large databases or large numbers of databases. The database on the destination server is not accessible with log shipping. There are options to make it accessible, but it will be in read-only mode, and users need to be kicked off when the next log is ready to be applied.

Database mirroring is continuous log shipping. Changes to the database transaction log are continually shipped from the source server to the destination server. The database on the destination server will be inaccessible while being mirrored. There are two modes of database mirroring: high performance and high safety. With high safety, application writes on the source server are not committed on the source server until they are also committed on the destination server. This can cause increased latency for all writes on the destination server, which may make database mirroring not a good fit for your particular requirements. High-performance mode does not have this problem, as changes occurring on the source server are applied to the destination server asynchronously. However, the high-performance option is only available on the Enterprise Edition of SQL Server 2005 and SQL Server 2008.

What's New with Replication?

There are several new features in SQL Server 2008 replication:

- Integration with database mirroring. If you have a remote distributor, you can configure your publisher on your principal to failover to your mirror without having to reinitialize your subscribers.
- Much faster snapshot delivery on Windows 2008 servers
- A new Wizard for deploying nodes in a peer-to-peer topology. For more information, consult `http://msdn.microsoft.com/en-us/library/dd263442.aspx`.
- Conflict detection in peer-to-peer replication
- Ability to make schema changes in peer-to-peer replication without having to stop all users from using the topology while changes are deployed.

Replication Concepts

SQL Server replication operates according to a publishing metaphor. There can be three types of servers in a replication topology:

- **Publisher:** The source server
- **Distributor:** For transactional replication and peer-to-peer replication, the distributor is where the changes are stored until they are replicated to the destination server. For merge replication, the distributor is merely a repository for replication process history. Changes and historical information are stored in a database called the *distribution database*.
- **Subscriber:** The destination server

Types of replication

Based on the publishing metaphor, SQL Server 2008 offers five basic types of replication, each serving a different purpose:

- **Snapshot replication:** A point-in-time image of database objects (a snapshot) is copied from the source server to the destination server. This image generation and deployment can be scheduled at whatever interval makes sense for your requirements; however, it is best used when the majority of your data seldom changes, and when it does, it changes at the same time.
- **Transactional replication:** Transactions occurring on the source server are asynchronously captured and stored in a repository (called a *distribution database*) and then applied, again asynchronously, on the destination server.
- **Oracle publishing:** This is a variant of transactional replication. Instead of SQL Server being the source server, an Oracle server is the source server, and changes are replicated from the Oracle server to SQL Server. This SQL Server can be the final destination for the Oracle server's data, or it can act as a gateway, and changes can be replicated downstream to other SQL Servers, or other RDBMs. Oracle publishing is only available on SQL Server Enterprise Edition and above.
- **Peer-to-peer replication:** Another variant of transactional replication that is used to replicate data to one or more nodes. Each node can publish data to member nodes in a peer-to-peer replication topology. Should one node go offline, changes occurring on the offline node and the other member servers will be synchronized when that node comes back online. Changes are replicated bi-directionally, so a change occurring on Node A will be replicated to Node B, and changes occurring on Node B will be replicated to Node A. Peer-to-peer replication is an Enterprise Edition–only feature that is scalable to approximately 10 nodes, but your results may vary depending on your replicated workload, your hardware, and your available bandwidth.
- **Merge replication:** As the name indicates, merge replication is used to merge changes occurring on the destination server with changes occurring on the source server, and vice versa. It is highly scalable to hundreds if not thousands of destination servers. With merge replication, there is a central clearinghouse for changes that determines which changes go where. With peer-to-peer replication, any member node in the topology can assume the clearinghouse role.

Replication agents

As you might imagine, a lot of work is required to move data between the various servers in the publishing metaphor. To do so, SQL Server replication makes use of three agents:

- **Snapshot agent:** Generates the tabular and schema data or schemas for the objects you wish to replicate. The tables and schema data, and related replication metadata, is frequently referred to as the *snapshot*. The snapshot agent is used by all replication types. The snapshot agent writes the tabular/schema data to the file system.
- **Distribution agent:** Used by snapshot replication to apply the snapshot on the subscribers, and used by transactional replication to apply the snapshot on the subscriber and to replicate subsequent changes occurring on the publisher to the subscriber.

- **Merge agent:** Detects changes that have occurred on the publisher and the subscriber since the last time these agents ran and merges them together to form a consistent set on both the publisher and the subscriber. In some cases, the same primary key value will be assigned on the publisher and one or more subscribers between runs of the merge agent (called a *sync*). When the merge agent runs it detects this conflict and logs it to conflict tables that can be viewed using the conflict viewer. With merge replication, the data that is in conflict will persist on the publisher and the subscriber by default. For example, if a primary key value of 1,000 for a table is assigned on the publisher, and then the same value is assigned on the same table on the subscriber, when the merge agent runs it will log the conflict, but keep the publisher's values for the row with a PK (primary key) of 1,000 on the publisher, and keep the subscriber's values for the row with a PK of 1,000 on the subscriber.

  Merge replication has a rich set of features to handle conflicts, including one that skips changes to different columns occurring on the same row between publisher and subscriber. This is termed *column-level conflict tracking*. For example, a change to John Smith's home phone number occurring on the publisher and his cell phone number occurring on the subscriber would be merged to have both changes persisting on both the publisher and subscriber. By default, merge replication uses row-level conflict tracking that might result in the change to John Smith's home phone number being updated on both the publisher and the subscriber, but his cell phone change being rolled back, with this conflict and the conflicting values being logged to the conflict tables.

Best Practice

A single server can serve as both the publisher and the distributor and even as the subscriber. An excellent configuration for experimenting with replication is a server with multiple SQL Server instances. However, when performance is an issue, a dedicated distributor server is the best plan. This remote distributor can act as a distributor for multiple publishers; in fact, you can configure this remote distributor to have a separate distribution database for each publisher.

The publisher server organizes multiple articles (an article is a data source: a single table, view, function, or stored procedure) into a publication. You may find that you get better performance by grouping large articles (tables) into their own publication. The distributor server manages the replication process. The publisher can initiate the subscription and push data to the subscriber server, or the subscriber can set up the subscription and pull the subscription from the publisher.

Transactional consistency

The measure of *transactional consistency* is the degree of synchronization between two replicated servers. As the lag time between synchronizations increases, transactional consistency decreases. If the data is identical on both servers most of the time, transactional consistency is said to be high. Conversely, a replication system that passes changes every two weeks by e-mail has low transactional consistency.

Configuring Replication

Using wizards is the simplest way to implement replication. Developers and DBAs generally avoid wizards because they have limited features, but implementing replication without wizards requires numerous calls to arcane stored procedures and is a tedious and painful process prone to user errors.

Before configuring replication, it is important to understand the limitations of various SQL Server editions. For example, SQL Server Express can only act as a subscriber, and the number of subscribers each edition can have is limited. For example, the Standard Edition can only have five subscribers, the Web 25 subscribers. Merge replication can only be used to replicate to subscribers with same version or lower. For example, you can't have a SQL Server 2005 publisher merge replicating to SQL Server 2008 subscribers; however, a SQL Server 2008 publisher can replicate to a SQL Server 2005 subscriber. Merge replication is the only replication type that can replicate to SQL Server CE subscribers.

Creating a publisher and distributor

To enable a server as a publisher you must first configure it as a subscriber. While you can configure the publisher with a local or remote distributor, it is recommended that you configure the distributor first, before creating your first publication. This way, if there is a problem, it will be easier to troubleshoot.

The following steps walk you through the process of creating your first distributor:

1. Connect to the server that will be acting as your publisher/distributor or remote distributor using SQL Server Management Studio. You need to use the SQL Server 2008 version of SQL Server Management Studio for this.
2. Once you have connected, right-click on the replication folder and select the menu option Configure Distribution.

NOTE **If you do not see the Configure Distribution option, either your SQL Server edition is SQL Server Express or you do not have the replication components installed. To install the replication components, you need to run Setup again.**

3. After clicking through the initial splash screen, you will have the option to select which server you should use as your distributor: either the local server or a remote server. If you are using a remote server, you need to ensure that the remote server is already configured as a distributor. Because this is a local distributor, select the default option and click Next.
4. You will be prompted for a folder to serve as the default location where the snapshot agent deposits the snapshot. Select a different location if the default folder does not have adequate space for your snapshots, or if you want to minimize I/O contention. The snapshot generation process is an I/O-intensive process during snapshot generation. You do have the option to select a snapshot folder or share for each publication when you create it, so the snapshot folder location is not of critical importance.
5. Once you have selected the location for your snapshot folder or snapshot share, click Next. The Distribution Database dialog enables you to name your distribution database and select folders where the database data and log files will reside.

Best Practice

If you have a large number of subscribers, or you are replicating over a WAN, you should use a share for your snapshot folder, or use FTP along with pull subscribers (you will configure FTP server details when you create your publication). With pull subscribers, the merge or distribution agent or process runs on the subscriber. With push subscribers, the distribution and merge agents run on the publisher/distributor or distributor. If you are using push subscribers with a remote distributor, your snapshot folder must also be configured as a snapshot share. It is not a good security practice to use the Admin shares (i.e., C$), but rather a share name that hides the path of the actual physical snapshot folder location, and does not require the distribution or merge agents to run under an account that has rights to access the snapshot share.

Best Practice

Optimal configuration of a distributor or a distribution server is on a 64-bit server with ample RAM and RAID 10 drives. The distributor server will be I/O and network bound, so the more RAM available for caching and the greater the available network bandwidth, the greater the throughput of your transactional replication solution. Merge replication is CPU and network bound, so these best practices do not apply for it.

6. Click Next to enable the publishers that you wish to use this distributor. If this is a local publisher/distributor, your publisher will already be selected. If not, you need to click the Add button if you want to enable other publishers to use this distributor.
7. Click Next to assign a distributor password. This allows remote publishers to use this distributor as their distributor.
8. Click Next, Next again, and Finish to complete the creation of your distributor.

To configure a publisher to use a remote distributor, follow these steps:

1. Connect to the publisher using SQL Server Management Studio, right-click on the Replication folder, and select Configure Distribution.
2. When you get to the option to select which server you wish to use as your distributor, select the "Use the following server as the Distributor" option.
3. Click the Add button and enter the connection information to connect to the remote distributor. You will be prompted for the password you configured to access the remote distributor.
4. Click Next, Next again, and Finish.

Your remote distributor is now ready to use.

Creating a snapshot/transactional publication

Once a distributor is set up for your server, you can create your publications. A publication is defined as a collection of articles, where an article is an item to be published. An article in SQL Server can be a table, a view, an indexed view, a user-defined function, or even a stored procedure or its execution. If you choose to replicate the execution of a stored procedure, the stored procedure call will be executed on the subscriber.

For example, if you fire a stored procedure that updates 10,000 rows on a table, this table is replicated, and the execution of the stored procedure is executed, only the stored procedure call will be executed. If the replication of the stored procedure execution was not replicated, 10,000 update statements would have to be replicated by the publisher, through the distributor to the subscriber. As you can imagine, there are considerable benefits to doing this.

Typically tables are published, but views can also be published. You just need to ensure that the base tables referenced by the views are also published.

To create a publication, execute the following steps:

1. Connect to your publisher using SQL Server Management Studio, and expand the Replication folder, then right-click on the local publication folder and select New Publication.
2. After clicking through the initial splash screen, select the database you wish to replicate from the Publication Databases section.
3. Click Next. In the Replication Types dialog that appears, select the replication type you wish to use. You will then get a dialog entitled Articles, from which you can select the type of objects you wish to replicate.
4. Expand each object type tree and select the articles you wish to replicate. For example, if you wish to replicate tables, expand the table tree and select the individual tables you wish to replicate. You can elect to replicate all tables by selecting the check box next to the table tree. You also have the option to replicate only a subset of the columns in tables you are replicating.

NOTE **If you see a table with what appears to be a red circle with a slash through it next to the table, this table does not have a primary key and you will be unable to replicate it in a transactional publication. Snapshot and merge replication allow you replicate tables without primary keys.**

If you highlight a table and then click the article properties drop-down box, you can configure options regarding how the table will be replicated to the subscriber. For example, you can replicate user triggers, include foreign key dependencies, and determine what will happen if a table with the same name already exists on the subscriber. The options are as follows:

- Drop the subscriber table
- Do nothing
- Keep the table, but delete all of its data
- Keep the table, but delete all of the data that meets your filtering criteria (covered in the next step)

5. Once you have selected the objects you wish to replicate, click Next. The Filter Table Rows dialog will appear. From here, you can configure filtering criteria that sends only a subset of the rows to the subscriber. For example, if you were replicating a table with a state column,

you may decide that the subscriber should have only rows from California. To enable that, you would click the Add button, select the table in the drop-down box in the "Select table to filter option," click the State column in the "Complete the filter statement" section, and then add the state value. In code, it might look like this:

```
SELECT <published_columns> FROM [dbo].[SalesStaff] WHERE [State]='CA'
```

This would ensure that the subscriber only receives data and changes from sales staff when the value of `State` is `CA`.

6. Once you have enabled your filters, click Next. The next dialog is Snapshot Agent, which controls two snapshot options:
   - Create a snapshot immediately and keep the snapshot available to initialize subscriptions.
   - Schedule the Snapshot Agent to run at the following times.

   The first option generates the snapshot immediately; and every replicated change that occurs in the publication is not only replicated to the subscriber, but also added to the snapshot files. This is a great option when you have to deploy a lot of snapshots frequently, but it does add a constant load to your publisher. The second option to schedule the snapshot agent generates a snapshot on a schedule, so the snapshot files are updated each time you run the snapshot agent. Changes not in the snapshot have to be stored in the distribution agent, which may mean extra storage requirements on the distributor. For most DBAs/developers, it is not a good practice to enable these options.
7. Click Next to configure Agent Security. This option allows you to select the security context you wish your replication agents to run under. By default, SQL Server runs the replication agents under the same account under which the SQL Server agent account runs.

CAUTION **This is not considered to be a good security practice, as buffer overflow, worm attacks, or Trojan attacks might be able to hijack the replication agent and run commands with the same security context as the SQL Server Agent on the publisher, distributor, or subscriber. This dialog enables you to control which account the replication agent is going to run under; ideally, this will be an account with as few rights as possible on the publisher, distributor, or subscriber. Figure 36-1 illustrates this dialog.**

8. Click the Security Settings button to display the Snapshot Agent Security dialog shown in Figure 36-2. From here, you can enter the Windows or SQL Server Agent account under which you wish the snapshot agent to run. If you choose a Windows account, it needs to be added using the following syntax: *DomainName\AccountName*.
9. Once you have selected the agents you wish to use, click OK, and then Next to exit the Agent Security dialog.
10. The next dialog is the Wizard Actions dialog. This enables you to create the publication immediately, create a script to create the publication, or both. Once you have made your selection, click Next. In the Complete the Wizard dialog that appears, you can name your publication.
11. Once you have given your publication a name, click Finish to create it.

After you have created your publication, you can now create one or more subscriptions to it.

FIGURE 36-1

The Agent Security dialog

FIGURE 36-2

The Snapshot Agent Security dialog

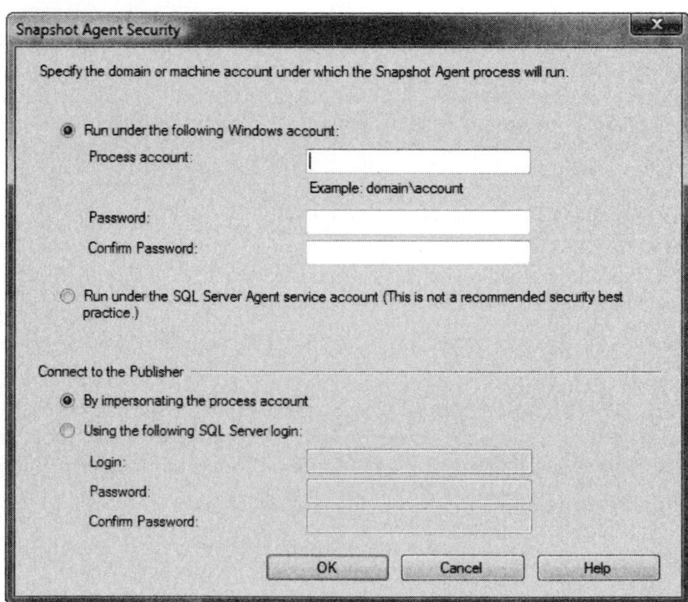

Creating a push subscription to a transactional/snapshot publication

The previous two sections discussed the two ways of replicating data, a push and a pull. This section focuses on how to create push subscriptions to transactional and snapshot publications:

1. Connect to your publisher in SQL Server Management Studio and expand the Replication folder and the Local Publications folder.
2. Locate your publication, right-click on it, and select New Subscriptions. Click Next to exit the splash screen.
3. In the Publication dialog, ensure that the publication you wish to create a subscription to is highlighted. If it is not already selected, do so now; you may have to expand other databases to find it. Once your publication is highlighted, click Next.
4. In the distribution Agent Location dialog, accept the default, which is Run all agents on the Distributor, *MySQLServerName* (push subscriptions), where *MySQLServerName* is the name of your publisher.
5. Click Next to advance to the Subscribers dialog. All subscribers currently enabled will appear in this dialog. If your subscriber does not appear, then click the Add Subscriber button. Note that this button is a drop-down button that enables you to create SQL Server and Non-SQL Server Subscribers. You can create subscriptions to SQL Servers, as well as Oracle and DB2 subscribers using this wizard. With the replication stored procedures it is possible to replicate to any ODBC level 2 compliant and above data source.

CROSS-REF **For more information on how to replicate to Oracle and DB2 subscribers, please refer to this link:** `http://msdn.microsoft.com/en-us/library/ms188360.aspx`.

6. After clicking the Add Subscriber button, you are prompted to connect to your Subscriber. This dialog looks very similar to the Connect to SQL Server dialogs you are familiar with from connecting to SQL Server. Once you have added the subscriber, you will be able to select the subscription database. Select it in the drop-down box, and then click Next.
7. The Distribution Agent Security dialog will appear. This is similar to the Snapshot Agent Security dialog. Enter the account under which you wish the distribution agent to run. You can also specify the accounts you wish to use to connect to the distributor and subscriber here.
8. Click OK when you have completed the setup of these accounts.
9. Click Next to advance to the Synchronization Schedule dialog. From here, you can set a schedule. The default is Run Continuously, which means that the agent will always be running in the case of transactional replication (this setting has no effect on snapshot publications). If you wish to run your distribution agent on a schedule, click the drop-down button and define a schedule or have the agent run on demand. If you select the option to run the agent on demand, then you have to run the agent either through Replication Monitor, by running the job for the distribution agent, or by expanding the publication, locating the subscriber, right-clicking on it, and selecting View Synchronization Status and then clicking the Start button.
10. Click Next to advance to the Initialize Subscriptions dialog. The options are to initialize, which means the snapshot will be applied at the subscriber, or not to initialize, which means that

you need to put all the required objects in place. This includes all tables, the data, stored procedures, functions, and views, as well as replication stored procedures.

a. To create the replication stored procedures, use the command `sp_scriptpublication customprocs 'PublicationName'` in your publication database. The stored procedures will appear in the results pane. Copy them into the query window and run them in your subscription database. Under most circumstances the best choice is to select the initialize option.

b. If you do select the initialize option, two selections are available in the drop-down list: At First Synchronization and Immediately. At first synchronization means the snapshot will be generated when the distribution agent runs. Immediately means the snapshot will be generated and applied on the subscriber when you complete the dialog.

11. Click Next to advance to the Wizard options. Here you can specify whether you want the snapshot created immediately, scripted, or both.
12. Click Finish to complete the dialog and create your subscription.

Creating a pull subscription to a transactional/snapshot publication

Creating a pull subscription is very similar to creating a push subscription. The following steps show you how:

1. Connect to your subscriber using SQL Server Management Studio, expand the Replication folder, and then right-click the Local Subscriptions folder.
2. Select New Subscriptions, and click Next at the splash screen. In the drop-down box, select your publisher, and then expand your publication database and select your publication.
3. Click Next. In the Distribution Agent location dialog, select "Run each agent at its Subscriber (pull subscriptions)" and click Next.
4. Click the check box next to your subscriber, and select your subscription database on the right side of the screen. Click Next to advance to the Distribution Agent Security dialog.
5. Select the security context you wish the binary to run under, and choose the account you want to use to connect to the subscriber. This account should be in the dbo_owner role on the subscriber.
6. Click Next. In the Synchronization Schedule dialog, choose how frequently you want the subscriber to connect. The options are to run continuously, run on demand, or run on a schedule.
7. Click Next to continue to the Initialize Subscriptions dialog. The options are to initialize your subscription immediately, at first synchronization, or not to initialize your subscription at all (by not selecting the initialize check box). Follow the notes in Creating a Push Subscription for more details on this option.
8. Click Next to advance to the Wizard options. Here you can specify whether you want the snapshot created immediately, scripted, or both.
9. Click Finish to complete the dialog and create your subscription.

Creating a peer-to-peer topology

To create a peer-to-peer topology you must be running the Enterprise Edition of SQL Server. Create a transactional replication publication, and once you have completed the publication creation, right-click on the publication in the Local Publications folder. In the Subscription Options tab, ensure that Allow Peer-to-Peer Subscriptions is set to true. Click OK.

Once this is done, follow these steps to set up a peer-to-peer topology:

1. Return to the publication, right-click on the publication again, and this time select Configure Peer-to-Peer Topology. Click Next at the splash screen.
2. In the Publication dialog that appears, select your publication database and publication. These should be highlighted.
3. Click Next to launch the Configure Topology dialog. Right-click and select Add a New Peer Node.
4. Enter your subscriber name, select the appropriate authentication type, and click Next. You will then be prompted for a database and Peer Originator ID. Choose 2 for the Originator ID; the publisher will have an Originator ID of 1.
5. Right-click the database icon in the center of the Configure Topology dialog, and select Connect to All Displayed Nodes. Click Next. This launches the Log Agent Security dialog.
6. Select a security context under which the Log Reader Agent will run, and click Next. This launches the Distributor Security dialog.
7. Select an account under which the Distribution Agent should run and how the Distribution Agent should connect to the Subscriber. You need to repeat this for each node in the topology. Click Next. This launches the New Peer Initialization dialog. You will need to restore the publication database on each of the peers or place the tables and related replication metadata in place.
8. Click Next and then Finish to complete the peer-to-peer topology configuration.

Creating a merge publication

Creating merge publications is very similar to creating transactional or snapshot publications. Follow these steps to create a merge publication:

1. Connect to your publisher in SQL Server Management Studio, expand the Replication folder, and right-click on the Local Publications folder. Select New Publication and click Next.
2. Select the database you wish to merge replicate, and click Next in the Publication Database dialog.
3. For Publication Type, select Merge publication and click Next.
4. For Subscriber types, select the type of SQL Server to which you are replicating. It is possible to select multiple subscriber types; for example, you can replicate to SQL 2005 and SQL 2008 publishers.
5. Click Next to Advance to the Articles dialog. From here, you can choose what you wish to replicate — for example, tables, views, stored procedures, or functions. If you expand a table, you will notice that you have the option to select or deselect columns that you wish to

replicate. The Article Properties button enables you to control how tables will be replicated (for example, you can choose to replicate user indexes). Click Next. The Article Issues dialog will then warn you that a unique identifier (GUID) column will be added to all tables you are indexing.

6. Click Next to advance to the Filter Rows dialog. Merge replication is designed to only replicate a subset of the data to the subscriber. Part of the reason for this is because merge replication is frequently used over low bandwidth lines, such as over a phone line or the Internet. By filtering rows you can minimize the amount of data that is sent to your subscriber. You can also use join filters. Basically, join filters extend a filter you place on a table to all the other tables that have foreign key relationships on the filtered column. Consider the `SalesTerritory` table in the `AdventureWorks2008` database. It is joined to the `SalesOrderHeader` table by `TerritoryID`, and the `SalesOrderHeaderTable` is joined to the `SalesOrderDetail` table by the `SalesOrderID` column. If you filter on the `TerritoryID`, subscribers would only get the related data for a particular `TerritoryID`.

   To use join filters, click the Add button in the Filter Table Rows dialog and select Automatically Generate Filters, or click the Add Filter button and select the tables and rows you want to filter on. You then have the option to click the Add Button again and select Add Join to Extend the Selected Filter. You can also filter on Host_Name() and USER_NAME(), both of which can be overridden by the Merge Agent (HostName and PublisherLogin, respectively).

7. Once you have created your filters, click Next to launch the Snapshot Agent dialog; in most cases you will want to accept the default. Click Next to launch the Snapshot Security Agent dialog and set the appropriate accounts for your Snapshot Agent.

8. Click Next to advance to the Snapshot Options dialog, where you can either generate your publication or script it out. Click Next to name your publication and then click Finish. When your publication has been created, click Close.

Creating merge replication subscriptions is almost identical to creating subscriptions to transactional and snapshot publications. There are two differences.

The first is that there is a Subscription Type dialog. This controls conflicts. Conflicts arise when an attempt is made to update a row that has been deleted on the subscriber between syncs, or the same primary key value is assigned on the publisher and subscriber between syncs. The Subscription Type dialog controls how conflicts are resolved. For example, you can assign a value of 75% to your subscriber. This means that the subscriber change will remain on the publisher unless another subscriber with a higher priority syncs that row at a later point in time. In this case, the subscriber with a higher priority will replace the value that came from the lower priority subscriber.

The other subscription type is Client, which means that the first value to the publisher will win any conflicts.

The other difference is that you will be able to add a value for hostname that supplies a value to your filter.

Web synchronization

One other feature of merge replication is web synchronization. Merge replication is frequently used to replicate to servers in branch offices over WANs or the Internet. To reduce the exposure of SQL Servers to viruses, worms, Trojan horses, and hackers, Microsoft created web synchronization, whereby the subscriber connects to a web server over port 80 or port 443 and an ISAPI filter redirects traffic to a SQL

Server. While most firewall administrators are reluctant to open port 1433 (the TCP/IP port that SQL Server listens on), they have no problem leaving port 80 or 443 open.

To configure web synchronization, execute the following steps:

1. Connect to your publisher using SQL Server Management Studio, and expand the Replication and Local Publications folders.
2. Right-click your publication and select Configure Web Synchronization. Click Next.
3. Specify whether your subscribers are running SQL Server or SQL CE and select Next.
4. Enter the name of the web server and choose to either create a new virtual directory or use an existing one. You will receive a prompt to accept the copying of an ISAPI extension that will process your web synchronization. Click Yes, and then Next to launch a dialog for Authentication Access. I recommend that you use Basic Authentication.
5. For the domain, enter the name of the domain as it appears on the certificate; for the realm, enter the name of your fully qualified domain name as it appears on your certificate. After clicking Next, the Directory Access dialog appears.
6. Select an account or a group here that will be used to connect to your snapshot share. This group should have read rights to access the snapshot share.
7. Click Next to advance to the Snapshot Share Access dialog. Enter the name of the snapshot share as a `UNC: \\MyServerName\ShareName`. The share must pre-exist.
8. Click Next. If you have not already configured a publication to use this share as its snapshot folder, you will get a prompt telling you that the share is empty. Ensure that this is the share you want to use and click Next to continue to the Complete the Wizard dialog.
9. Confirm your choices and click Finish.

After the Web Configuration Wizard completes, you will get a success or failure report. The latter report enables you to determine which component failed and to rerun the wizard to correct those portions.

Summary

Replication is a complex and powerful feature of SQL Server, and fully describing it could easily take a book by itself. Using the wizards and dialogs that Microsoft has written into Management Studio greatly simplifies the process of configuring and deploying replication.

Key points from this chapter include the following:

- Replication can be a good fit for your data distribution needs.
- Replication uses a publisher — distributor — subscriber metaphor.
- Transactional replication is one-way replication by default and the fastest and most popular replication method.
- Peer-to-peer replication is bi-directional transactional replication, and an Enterprise Edition–only feature.
- Merge replication is a best fit for bi-directional replication, especially when the publisher and subscribers are occasionally or frequently offline.

The next chapter continues the data connectivity theme with Microsoft's BI solution for moving data: Integration Services.

Chapter 37

Performing ETL with Integration Services

Integration Services is most commonly described as an extract-transform-load (ETL) tool. ETL tools are traditionally associated with preparing data for warehousing, analysis, and reporting, but Integration Services represents a step beyond the traditional role. It is really a robust programming environment that happens to be good at data and database-related tasks.

Many prospective users have been intimidated by the Integration Services learning curve, sticking to the Transact-SQL that they know instead of investigating a more powerful ETL tool. This has made traditional SQL approaches one of the largest competitors of Integration Services, but those who take the time to understand this tool will find several advantages:

- Simple, fast methods for moving large quantities of data, minimizing database load, and batching data into destination tables to keep blocking and transaction log sizes down
- The capability to chain together many tasks, with complete control over ordering and error and exception handling. Many tasks can be executed in parallel.
- Connections to read or write most any type of data without special programming or linked server calls
- Common data and database management tasks are implemented without the need to write code; a .NET scripting environment is available for more custom tasks, plus Integration Services is fully extensible with custom assemblies.
- Resulting packages are as manageable as the situation requires, with several deployment, configuration, auditing, restart, and logging options.

While careful coding in SQL or other languages can approach the same core functionality as Integration Services, most projects require significant effort and end

IN THIS CHAPTER

up with minimal exception handling — often something like "stop and send me an e-mail if there is a problem." One colleague recently received 8,000 e-mails over a two-day period from such a data loading system.

Integration Services enables you to avoid many of the tedious details and spend more time building robust applications. It also excels at identifying problems and performing recovery operations within the application itself. Many of the Integration Services features, such as error row redirection, complex precedence constraints, data conversion, and fuzzy lookup, are well suited to recovering from data problems, rather than ignoring or failing on them. There is nothing better than building a system integration application that one seldom even thinks about.

New in 2008

Look throughout this chapter for new features added in SQL Server 2008, including enhanced ADO.NET connectivity, upgrade of the scripting environment to use Visual Studio Tools for Applications (VSTA), enhanced lookup functionality, including cache creation and tuning, and the new Data Profiling task. Additionally, the Integration Services runtime environment has been made more scalable through increased parallelism.

Design Environment

One of the best ways to understand Integration Services is to understand its design environment. Begin by opening a new Integration Services project within the Business Intelligence Development Studio. The Integration Services template is located in the Business Intelligence folder. The window that appears should look similar to what is shown in Figure 37-1.

Beyond the ever-present Solution Explorer and Properties panes, several panes and tabs are used in building a package (use the View menu to display any missing panes):

- **Connection Managers pane:** Connection managers are pointers to files, databases, and so on, that are used to provide context for the execution of tasks placed on the design surface. For example, an Execute SQL task requires a database connection.
- **Toolbox:** The toolbox provides a list of tasks that can be dragged onto the design surface. The list of available tasks varies according to the active tab in the main pane.
- **Control Flow tab:** This is the primary design surface on which tasks are placed, configured, and ordered by connecting tasks with precedence arrows.
- **Data Flow tab:** One of the tasks that can be configured on the Control Flow tab is a Data Flow task, used to move and transform data. The Data Flow tab is used to configure Data Flow tasks; think of it as a Properties window on steroids.
- **Event Handlers tab:** Events are exposed for the overall package and each task within it. Tasks are placed here to execute for any event, such as `OnError` or `OnPreExecute`.

- **Package Explorer tab:** This tab lists all the package's elements in a single tree view. This can be helpful for discovering configured elements not always obvious in other views, such as event handlers and scoped variables.

FIGURE 37-1

The Control Flow tab of Integration Services' design environment

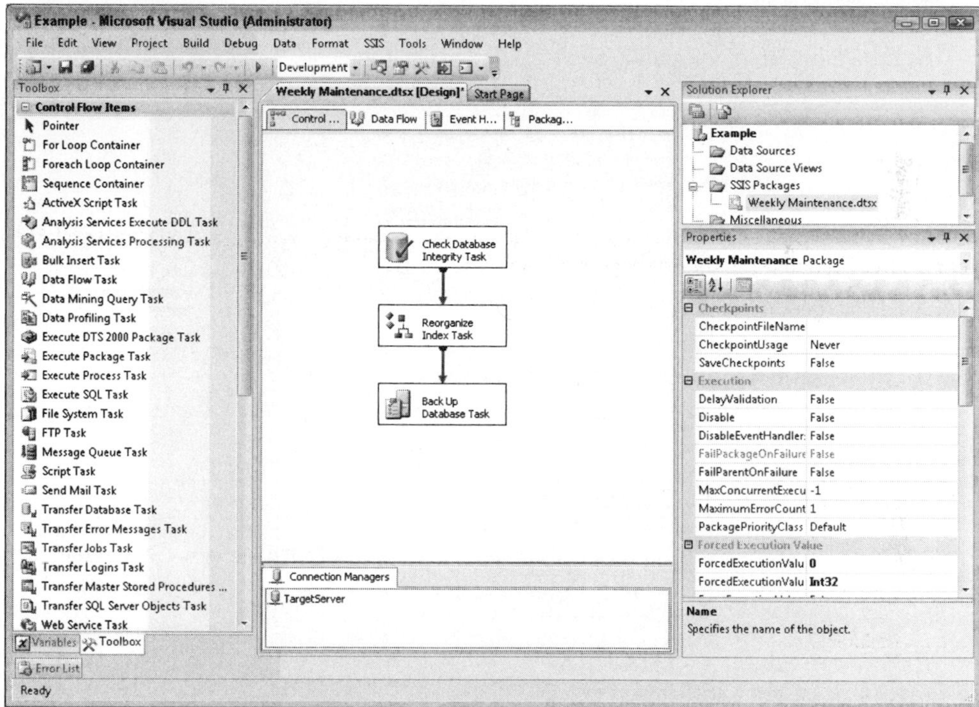

The package runs by executing Control Flow tasks, beginning with tasks that have no incoming precedence constraints (arrows). As each task completes, the next task executes based on the precedence constraints until all tasks are complete. Refer to Figure 37-1 for an example of three tasks sequenced by two such arrows. While the tasks in this example are ordered for serial execution, many combinations are possible (see the section "Control Flow Precedence" later in this chapter).

For users of Data Transformation Services (DTS) in SQL 7.0 and SQL 2000, this approach to building a package will be familiar, but why the Data Flow tab?

Each data flow is a single task on the Control Flow tab; drill down (e.g., via a double-click) to view a single data flow's configuration on the Data Flow tab (see Figure 37-2). Note that it does not contain tasks but data sources, destinations, and transformations. The arrows between the boxes are not precedence indicators but data inputs and outputs that determine how data flows from source to destination.

Unlike DTS, in which transformations happen in a single step as data is read from a source and written to a destination, Integration Services enables several transformations to be used between reading and writing data. Data flows can come from several sources, and they can be split and merged, and written to several destinations within the confines of a single Data Flow task. Because the transformations occur without reading and writing the database at every step, well-designed data flows can be surprisingly fast.

FIGURE 37-2

The Data Flow tab of Integration Services' design environment

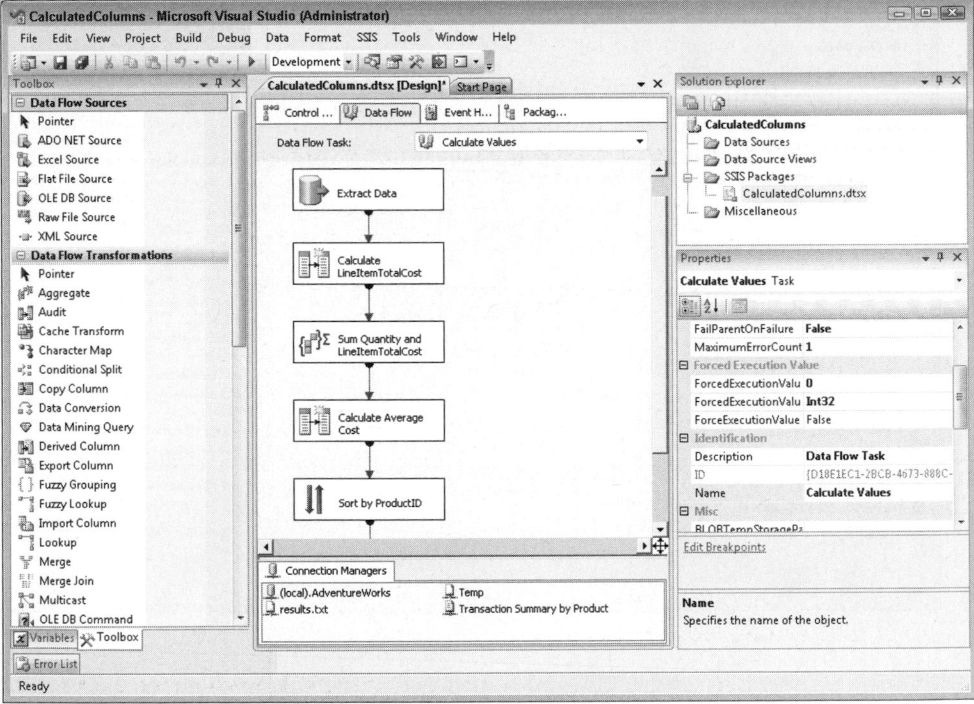

Connection managers

A *connection manager* is a wrapper for the connection string and properties required to make a connection at runtime. Once the connection is defined, it can be referenced by other elements in the package without duplicating the connection definition, thus simplifying the management of this information and configuration for alternate environments.

Create a new connection manager by right-clicking in the Connection Managers pane or by choosing the New option when configuring a task that requires a connection manager. When right-clicking, notice that several of the more popular connection types are listed directly on the menu, but additional connection types are available by choosing the New Connection option.

Each connection type has an editor dialog and properties that appear in the Properties pane, both of which vary according to the connection type. Each of the two lists may contain properties not available in the other. For example, the connection timeout can be set only in the OLE DB editor, while the delay validation property must be set in the Properties pane.

Variables

As with all proper programming environments, Integration Services provides variables to control execution, pass around values, and so on. Right-click the design surface and choose Variables to show the Variables pane. Notice that along with Name, Data Type, and Value columns, the Scope column indicates at which level in the package hierarchy the variable is visible.

Variables with package scope (scope equals the package name) are visible everywhere, whereas variables scoped to a task or event handler are visible only within that object. Variables scoped to a container are visible to the container and any objects it contains.

By default, the Variables pane displays only variables whose scope matches the currently selected object or one of its parents. For example, clicking on the design surface will select the package object and display only the variables scoped at the package level, but selecting a Control Flow task will show variables for both the selected task and the package (the task's parent). Alternately, the full variable list can be displayed by selecting the Show All Variables button on the pane's toolbar.

Create a new variable by first selecting the object to provide the scope and then click the Variable pane's Add Variable toolbar button. Once created, set the variable's name, data type, and value. Note that you cannot change a variable's scope without deleting and recreating it.

In addition to scope, each variable has a namespace, which by default is either `User` or `System`. You can change the namespace for user-created variables, but there is very little that you can change (only the occasional value) for system namespace variables. The namespace is used to fully qualify a variable reference. For example, a variable called `MyVar` in the user namespace is referred to as `@[User::MyVar]`.

Variable usage

Variable values can be manually set via the Variables pane, but their values can also come from a number of other sources, including the following:

- Variable values can be provided at runtime via the `/SET` switch on the `dtexec` utility (or equivalent dialog of the `dtexecui` utility).
- Variable values can be entered as expressions, which are evaluated at runtime. Enter the expression by clicking the Expression ellipses on the variable's Properties pane, and then use the Expression Builder to enter the appropriate formula. Be sure to set the `EvaluateAsExpression` property to `True` to cause the contents of the variable to be evaluated as a formula.
- `For` and `Foreach` container tasks can set a variable to contain a simple numeric sequence, each file in a directory on disk, each node in an XML document, and items from other lists and collections.
- Query results can provide variable values, either as an individual value or an entire result set.
- Scripts can read and/or set variable values.

Among the many places for variables to be used, property expressions are one of the most useful, as nearly any task property can be determined at runtime based on an expression. This enables variables to control everything from the text of a query to the enabling/disabling of a task.

Expressions

Expressions are used throughout Integration Services to calculate values used in looping, splitting data streams, setting variable values, and setting task properties. The language used to define an expression is a totally new syntax, resembling a cross between C# and Transact-SQL. Fortunately, an Expression Builder is available in many places where an expression can be entered. Some of the key themes include the following:

- Variables are referred to by prefixing them with an @, and can be qualified by namespace, making `@[User::foo]` the fully qualified reference to the user variable `foo`. Columns are referred to by their name, and can be qualified by their source name, making `[RawFileSource].[Customer Name]`the fully qualified reference to the `Customer Name` column read from the `RawFileSource`. Square brackets are optional for names with no embedded spaces or other special characters.
- Operators are very C-like, including == (double equal signs) for equality tests, prefix of an exclamation mark for `not` (for example, `!>` and `!=`), `&&` for logical `AND`, `||` for logical `OR`, and `?` for conditional expressions (think `IIf()` function). For example, `@[User::foo] == 17 && CustomerID < 100` returns `true` if the variable `foo` equals `17 AND` the `CustomerID` column is less than 100.
- String constants are enclosed in double quotes, and special characters are C-like backslash escape sequences, such as `\n` for new line and `\t` for tab.
- The `cast` operator works by describing the target type in parentheses immediately before the value to be converted. For example, `(DT_I4)"193"` will convert the string "193" to a four-byte integer, whereas `(DT_STR,10,1252)@[User::foo]`converts the value of the user variable `foo` to a 10-character string using codepage 1252. The codepage has no default, so everyone will learn the number of their favorite codepage.
- Functions mostly come from the Transact-SQL world, including the familiar date (`GETDATE()`, `DATEADD()`, `YEAR()`), string (`SUBSTRING()`, `REPLACE()`, `LEN()`), and mathematical (`CEILING()`, `SIGN()`) entries. Details do differ from standard T-SQL, however, so use the Expression Builder or Books Online to check availability and syntax.

NOTE **A codepage, not to be confused with a locale identifier, maps character representations to their corresponding codes. Two good sources for codepage references are** `www.i18nguy.com/unicode/codepages.html` **and** `www.microsoft.com/typography/unicode/cscp.htm`.

Configuring elements

A large number of elements work together in a functioning Integration Services package, including Control Flow tasks, task precedence, and data flow components. This section describes the concepts and settings common to each area. Later, this chapter describes the functions and unique properties for individual elements.

Control flow

Work flow for both the Control Flow and Event Handler tabs is configured by dragging control flow elements (tasks and/or containers) onto the design surface, configuring each element's properties, and then setting execution order by connecting the items using precedence constraints. Each item can be configured using the overlapping sets of properties in the Properties pane and the Editor dialog. Right-click an item and choose Edit to invoke its Editor, which presents multiple pages (content varies according to the type of task).

All editors include an Expressions page that enables many of the configurable properties to be specified by expressions, rather than static values. You can view and modify existing expression assignments directly on the page, or you can click the ellipses next to an expression to launch the Expression Builder. You can add additional expression assignments by clicking the ellipses in the top line of the expressions page, launching the Property Expressions Editor, shown in Figure 37-3. Choose the property to be set in the left column, and then enter the expression in the right column, pressing the ellipses to use the Expression Builder if desired.

FIGURE 37-3

Property Expressions Editor

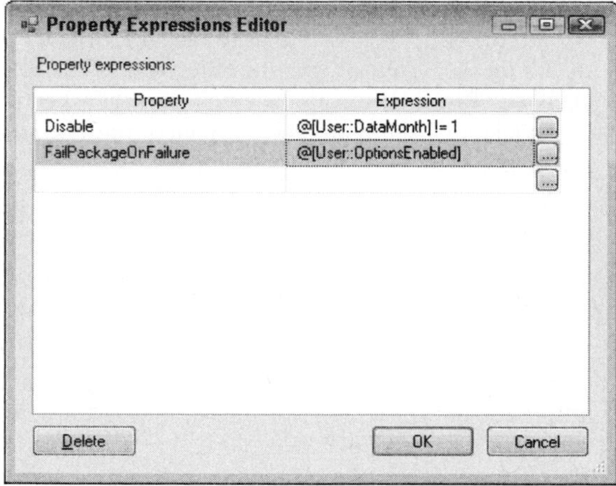

While many of the properties available vary by item, several are available across all items, including packages, containers, and individual tasks. These common properties include the following:

- **DelayValidation:** Normally, each task in a package is validated before beginning execution to avoid unnecessary partial runs (such as waiting 20 minutes to discover that the last step's filename was mistyped). Set this property to `true` to delay validation until the task actually runs. This option is useful for tasks that reference objects that don't exist when the package starts, but that will exist by the time the task executes.
- **Disable:** When set to `true`, the task will not execute. This option is also available from the context menu's Disable/Enable toggle. Note how disabled tasks display in a darker color.

- **DisableEventHandler:** This keeps event handlers from executing for the current task, although event handlers for parent objects (e.g., containers, packages) still execute.
- Error handling properties are best considered as a group:
  - **FailPackageOnFailure:** When set to `true`, the entire package fails when the individual item fails. The default is `false`.
  - **FailParentOnFailure:** When set to `true`, the parent container fails when the individual task fails. If a task is not explicitly included in a container (e.g., `For Loop`, `Foreach Loop`, or `Sequence`), then it is implicitly wrapped in an invisible `TaskHost` container, which acts as the parent. The default is `false`.
  - **MaximumErrorCount:** Maximum number of errors a task or container can see before failing itself. The default is 1, so the first error encountered will fail the task.

  Because of the default settings that apply at the package, container, and task levels, any task that fails will cause its container to fail, which in turn will fail the package, all based on the `MaximumErrorCount`. This is true regardless of any failure branches defined by precedence constraints. You can increase the `MaximumErrorCount` on a task to allow error branching to succeed.

  Given this behavior, where do the "FailOn" properties fit in? Consider a container with two tasks, one that is expected to fail in certain cases (call it "Try") and another that will recover from the expected failure but is not itself expected to fail (call it "Recover"). The container's `MaximumErrorCount` must be increased to allow the "Recover" to be reached when "Try" fails, but this has the side effect of ignoring failures in "Recover"! Use the `FailPackageOnFailure` property on "Recover" to stop the entire package when the task fails, or `FailParentOnFailure` to take the failure precedence branch from the container when "Recover" fails.
- **LoggingMode:** This property defaults to `UseParentSetting` so that logging can be defined for the entire package at once, but individual items can also be enabled or disabled.
- Transactions can be used to ensure that a sequence of operations, such as changes to multiple tables, either succeed or fail together. The following properties control transactions in a package:
  - **IsolationLevel:** Specifies the isolation level of a transaction as one of the following: `Unspecified`, `Chaos`, `ReadUncommitted`, `ReadCommitted`, `RepeatableRead`, `Serializable`, or `Snapshot`. The default is `Serializable`.
  - **TransactionOption:** This property offers three options: `NotSupported` (the item will not participate in a transaction), `Supported` (if a parent container requires a transaction, then this item will participate), and `Required` (if a parent container has not started a transaction, then this container will start one).

  Once begun by a parent container, all child items can participate in that transaction by specifying a `TransactionOption` setting of either `Supported` or `Required`.

Control flow precedence

As described earlier, precedence constraints determine the order in which tasks will execute. Select any task or container to expose its precedence constraint arrow, and then drag that arrow to the task that should follow it, repeating until all items are appropriately related. Any unconstrained task will be run at the discretion of the runtime engine in an unpredictable and often parallel ordering. Each constraint defaults to an "On Success" constraint, which can be adjusted by double-clicking the constraint to reveal the Precedence Constraint Editor, shown in Figure 37-4.

FIGURE 37-4

Precedence Constraint Editor

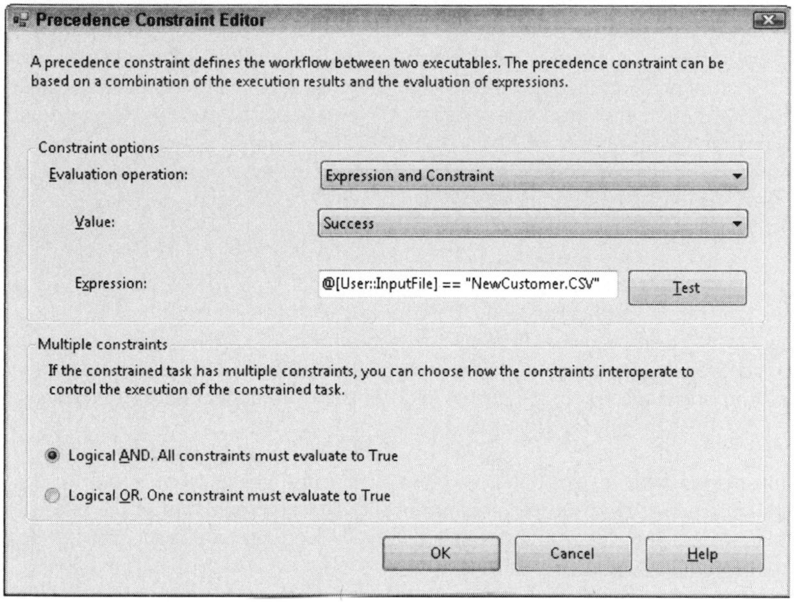

The upper half of the editor, "Constraint options," determines when the constraint should fire. It relies on two evaluation operation concepts:

- **Constraint:** How the previous item completed — Success, Failure, or Completion (Completion being any outcome, either success or failure)
- **Expression:** The evaluation of the entered expression, which must resolve to either true or false

These concepts are combined as four separate options — constraint, expression, expression and constraint, expression or constraint — enabling very flexible constraint construction. For example, consider a task that processes a previously loaded table of data and counts the successfully processed rows. The processing task could have two outgoing paths: a success path indicating that the task was successful and that the processed rowcount matches the loaded rowcount, and a failure path indicating that either the task failed or the rowcounts don't match.

The lower half of the editor, labeled "Multiple constraints," determines how the downstream tasks should deal with multiple incoming arrows. If logical `AND` is chosen (the default), then all the incoming constraints must fire before the task can execute. If logical `OR` is chosen, then any incoming constraint firing will cause the task to execute. Logical `AND` is the most frequently used behavior, but logical

OR is useful for work flows that split apart and then rejoin. For example, control can split when an upstream task has both success and failure branches, but the failure branch needs to rejoin the normal processing once the error has been resolved. Using a logical AND at the merge point would require both the success and the failure branches to execute before the next task could run, which cannot happen by definition. Logical AND constraints are presented visually as solid lines, whereas logical OR constraints are dotted lines.

The arrows that represent precedence constraints provide other visual clues as to the type of constraint. Green arrows denote a success constraint, red a failure constraint, and blue a completion constraint. Constraints that use an expression include an f(x) icon. There is no visual queue to distinguish between `Constraint AND expression` versus `Constraint OR expression`, so it is best to double-check the Precedence Constraint Editor when an f(x) is displayed. For example, a green arrow with an f(x) displayed could fire even if the preceding task had failed, given the expression had been satisfied and the `Constraint OR expression` option was chosen.

Data flow

Unlike other tasks that can be configured in the control flow, a Data Flow task does not show an Editor dialog in response to an edit request. Instead, it switches to the Data Flow tab to view/configure the task details. Each component appearing on the design surface can in turn be configured in the Properties pane, by a component-specific editor dialog, and, for many components, by an advanced editor as well.

Each data flow must begin with at least one Data Flow source, and generally ends with one or more Data Flow destinations, providing a source and sink for the data processed within the task. Between source and destination, any number of transformations may be configured to sort, convert, aggregate, or otherwise change the data.

Out of each source or transformation, a green Data Flow path arrow is available to be connected to the next component. Place the next component on the design surface and connect it to the path before attempting to configure the new component, as the path provides necessary meta-data for configuration. Follow a similar process for the red error flow for any component that has been configured to redirect error rows.

Use the Data Flow Path Editor to view/configure paths as necessary, double-clicking on a path to invoke its editor. The editor has three pages:

- **General:** For name, description, and annotation options. While the default annotations are usually adequate, consider enabling additional annotations for more complex flows with intertwined paths.
- **Metadata:** Displays metadata for each column in the Data Flow path, including data type and source component. This information is read-only, so adjust upstream components as necessary to make changes, or use a Data Conversion transformation to perform necessary conversions.
- **Data Viewers:** Allows different types of Data Viewers to be attached to the path for testing and debugging.

Because a data flow occurs within a single Control Flow task, any component that fails will cause the task to fail.

Event handlers

Event handlers can be defined for a long list of possible events for any Control Flow task or container. Use them for custom logging, error handling, common initialization code, and a variety of other tasks. If a handler is not defined for a given item when an event fires, then Integration Services will search parent containers up to the package level looking for a corresponding event handler to use instead. It is this "inheritance" that makes event handlers useful, enabling a single handler to be built once and then used repeatedly over many tasks and containers.

To construct an event handler, switch to the Event Handlers tab and choose the Control Flow item (Executable) in the upper-left drop-down list and the event in the upper-right list. Then click the hotlink on the design surface to initialize the event. Build the logic within the handler as if it were just another control flow.

Executing a package in development

As portions of a package are completed, they can be tested by running the package within the development environment. Right-click a package in the Solution Explorer and choose Execute Package to start the package in debug mode. Packages run in debug mode display progress within the designer environment, with tasks and components changing from white (not yet run) to yellow (running) to green or red (completed with success or failure, respectively).

CAUTION **There are other convenient methods for executing a package from within Business Intelligence Development Studio, but you must ensure that the correct object executes. Selecting Start Debugging from the menu, keyboard (F5), or toolbar can be very convenient, but ensure that the package to be executed has been "Set as Startup Object" by right-clicking on that package in the Solution Explorer. In addition, solutions that contain more than one project may execute unexpected actions (such as deploying an Analysis Services database) regardless of startup object/project settings before beginning to debug the selected package. Even in development, inadvertently starting a six-hour data load or stepping on a cube definition can be quite painful.**

Once the debug run begins, an Execution Results tab appears displaying the execution trace, including detailed messages and timing for each element of the package. When the package completes, it remains in debug mode to enable variables and state information to be reviewed. To return to design mode, choose the Stop button on the Debug toolbar, or choose Stop Debugging from the Debug menu (Shift+F5).

You can set breakpoints on any task, container, or the package by right-clicking on the object and selecting Edit Breakpoints. The Set Breakpoints dialog (see Figure 37-5) enables a breakpoint to be set on any event associated with that object. PreExecute and PostExecute events are common choices; selecting an object and pressing F9 is a shortcut for toggling the PreExecute event breakpoint. Optionally, instead of breaking at every execution (Always), a breakpoint can be ignored until the nth execution (Hit count equals), any time at or after the nth execution (Hit count greater than or equal to), or ignored except for the nth, 2nth, etc., execution (Hit count multiple).

While execution is suspended at a breakpoint, use the Locals window to view the current values of variables. You can also check the Output window for useful messages and warnings, and the Progress tab for details on run history across all tasks.

The analogue to the breakpoint for data flows is the Data Viewer. Double-click on a data path of interest to add a viewer. Then, during a debug run, package execution will be suspended when the Data

Viewer has been populated with data. Choose the Go or Detach buttons on the Data Viewer to resume execution.

FIGURE 37-5

Set Breakpoints dialog

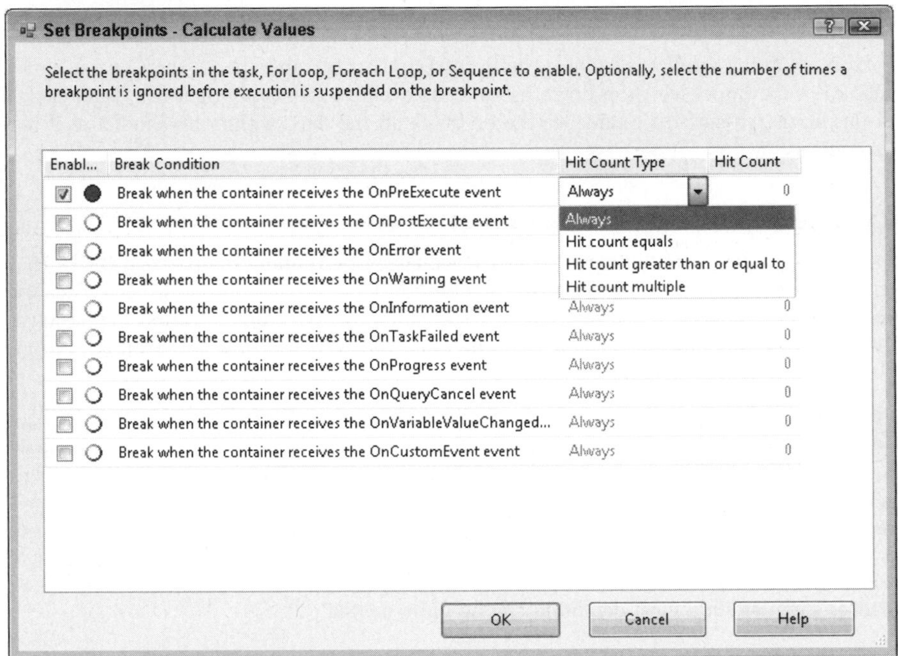

Breakpoints can also be placed in the code of a Script task. Open the script, set a breakpoint on the line of interest, and Integration Services will stop in the script debugger at the appropriate place.

Integration Services Package Elements

This section describes in detail the individual elements that can be used in constructing an Integration Services package. For general concepts and common properties, review the earlier sections of this chapter.

Connection managers

A connection manager is a wrapper for the connection string and properties required to make a connection at runtime. Once the connection is defined, it can be referenced by other elements in the package without duplicating the connection definition. This simplifies the management of this information and configuration for alternate environments.

Database

Defining database connections through one of the available connection managers requires setting a few key properties:

- **Provider:** The driver to be used in accessing the database
- **Server:** The server or filename containing the database to be accessed
- **Initial Catalog:** The default database in a multi-database source
- **Security:** Database authentication method and any username/password required

The first choice for accessing databases is generally an OLE DB connection manager using one of the many native providers, including SQL Server, Oracle, Jet (Access), and a long list of other source types. Other database connection managers include the following:

The key to most Integration Services packages is speed. ADO.NET has more capabilities, but in most cases that is not what you are after. Most developers prefer OLE DB for that reason.

- **ADO:** Provides ADO abstractions (such as command, recordset) on top of the OLE DB provider. ADO is not used by Integration Services built-in elements, but it could be required by custom tasks written to the ADO interface.
- **ADO.NET:** Provides ADO.NET abstractions (such as named parameters, data reader, data set) for the selected database connection. While not as fast as using OLE DB, an ADO.NET connection can execute complex parameterized scripts, provide an in-memory recordset to a Foreach loop, or support custom tasks written using C# or VB.NET.
- **ODBC:** Allows a connection manager to be configured based on an ODBC DSN. This is useful when OLE DB or .NET providers are not available for a given source (e.g., Paradox).
- **OLE DB:** The OLE DB connection manager is generally the preferred database connection due to its raw speed. It provides methods for basic parameter substitution but falls short of ADO.NET's flexibility.
- **Analysis Services:** When accessing an existing Analysis Services database, this connection manager is equivalent to an OLE DB connection using the Analysis Services 10.0 provider. Alternately, an Analysis Services database in the same solution can be referenced — a useful feature for packages being developed in support of a new database. If one of the older OLAP providers is needed for some reason, it can be accessed via the OLE DB connection manager.
- **SQL Server Mobile:** Allows a connection to mobile database `.SDF` files

As individual tasks execute, a connection described by the connection manager is opened and closed for each task. This default setting safely isolates tasks, keeping prior tasks from tweaking the connection of subsequent tasks. If you would like to keep the same connection between tasks, then set the `RetainSameConnection` property to `True`. With appropriate care, this allows a session to be shared between tasks for the manual control of transactions, the passing of temp tables, and so on.

File

Remember that every file or folder referenced needs to be available not only at design time, but after a package is deployed as well. Consider using Universal Naming Convention (UNC) paths for global information or package configurations (see "Maintainable Packages," later in this chapter) to adjust names and locations for specific target servers. UNC is a method of identifying a path so that it can be accessed from anywhere on the network a package may be run; it takes the form of `\\servername\sharename\path\file.ext`. The many file configuration managers are listed here:

- **Flat File:** Presents a text file as if it were a table, with locale and header options. The file can be in one of four formats:
  - **Delimited:** File data is separated by column (e.g., comma) and row delimiters (e.g.,{CR}{LF}).
  - **Fixed Width:** File data has known sizes without column or row delimiters. When opened in Notepad, such a file appears as if all data is on a single line.
  - **Ragged Right:** File data is interpreted using fixed width for all columns except the last, which is terminated by the row delimiter.

  Only files that use the delimited format are able to interpret zero-length strings as null.
- **Multiple Flat Files:** Same as the Flat File connection manager, but it allows multiple files to be selected, either individually or using wildcards. Data then appears as a single large table to Integration Services elements.
- **File:** Identifies a file or folder in the file system without specifying content. Such file pointers are used by several elements with Integration Services, including the file system and FTP tasks for file manipulation and the Execute SQL task to identify the file from which a SQL statement should be read. The usage type (Create file, Existing file, Create folder, Existing folder) ensures that the correct type of file pointer is created.
- **Multiple Files:** Same as the file connection manager, but it allows multiple files to be selected, either individually or using wildcards
- **Excel:** Identifies a file containing a group of cells that can be interpreted as a table (0 or 1 header rows, data rows below without row or column gaps)

Special

Beyond Database and File connection managers, several other types are provided:

- **Cache:** Defines a data cache location. The cache is first populated using the Cache transform and then used by Lookup transforms within Data Flow tasks. The cache is a write once, read many data store: All the data to be included in the cache must be written by a single Cache transform but can then be used by many Lookup transforms. Configuring the connection manager requires that index columns be selected, so it is often easiest to use the New button from within the Cache transform to create the connection manager, as it provides the column meta-data.

  Configure the connection manager by marking the columns that will be used to look up rows in the Columns tab. Mark the first column in the lookup as index position 1, the second as 2, and so on. The lookups performed on a cache must use all of the marked columns and no others to find the row. By default, the cache is created in memory and is available only in the current package. Make the cache available on disk for use by subsequent packages by enabling file cache on the General tab and identifying the `.CAW` file to be used to store the cached data.
- **FTP:** Defines a connection to an FTP server. For most situations, entering the server name and credentials is sufficient to define the connection. This is used with the FTP task to move and remove files or create and remove directories using FTP.

- **HTTP:** Defines a connection to a Web Service. Enter the URL of the WSDL (Web Service Definition) for the Web Service in question — for example, `http://MyServer/reportserver/reportservice.asmx?wsdl` points to the WSDL for Reporting Services on MyServer. Used with the Web Service task to access Web Service methods.
- **MSMQ:** Defines a connection to a Microsoft Message Queue; used in conjunction with a Message Queue task to send or receive queued messages.
- **SMO:** Specifies the name and authentication method to be used with Database Transfer tasks (Transfer Objects, Transfer Logins, etc.).
- **SMTP:** Specifies the name of the Simple Mail Transfer Protocol Server for use with the Send Mail task. Older SMTP server versions may not support all the commands necessary to send e-mail from Integration Services.
- **WMI:** Defines a server connection for use with Windows Management Instrumentation tasks, which enable logged and current event data to be collected.

Control flow elements

The Control Flow tab provides an environment for defining the overall work flow of the package. The following elements are the building blocks of that work flow.

Containers

Containers provide important features for an Integration Services package, including iteration over a group of tasks and isolation for error and event handling.

In addition to containers, the Integration Services Designer will also create task groups. Define a group by selecting a number of Control Flow items, right-clicking one of the selected items, and choosing Group. This encloses several tasks in a group box that can be collapsed into a single title bar. Note, however, that this group has no properties and cannot participate in the container hierarchy — in short, it is a handy visual device that has no effect on how the package executes.

The containers available are as follows:

- **TaskHost:** This container is not visible in a package, but implicitly hosts any task that is not otherwise enclosed in a container. Understanding this default container helps understand error and event handler behaviors.
- **Sequence:** This simply contains a number of tasks without any iteration features, but it provides a shared event and error-handling context, allows shared variables to be scoped to the container level instead of the package level, and enables the entire container to be disabled at once during debugging.
- **For Loop:** This container provides the advantages of a Sequence container but runs the tasks in the container as if the tasks were in a C# for loop. For example, given an integer variable `@LoopCount`, assigning the For Loop properties `InitExpression` to `@LoopCount=0`, `EvalExpression` to `@LoopCount<3`, and `AssignExpression` to `@LoopCount=@LoopCount+1` will execute the contents of the container three times, with `@LoopCount` containing the values `(0,1,2)` on each successive iteration.

- **Foreach Loop:** This container provides iteration over the contents of the container based on various lists of items:
  - **File:** Each file in a wildcarded directory command
  - **Item:** Each item in a manually entered list
  - **ADO:** Each row in a variable containing an ADO recordset or ADO.NET data set
  - **ADO.NET Schema Rowset:** Each item in the schema rowset
  - **Nodelist:** Each node in an XPath result set
  - **SMO:** List of server objects (such as jobs, databases, file groups)

  Describe the list to be iterated on the Collection page, and then map each item being iterated over to a corresponding variable. For example, a File loop requires a single string variable mapped to index 0, but an ADO loop requires *n* variables for *n* columns, with indexes 0 through n-1.

Control flow tasks

Tasks that can be included in control flow are as follows:

- **ActiveX Script:** Enables legacy VB and Java scripts to be included in Integration Services. New scripts should use the Script task instead. Consider migrating legacy scripts where possible because this task will not be available in future versions of SQL Server.
- **Analysis Services Execute DDL:** Sends Analysis Services Scripting Language (ASSL) scripts to an Analysis Services server to create, alter, or process cube and data mining structures. Often such scripts can be created using the Script option in SQL Server Management Studio.
- **Analysis Services Processing Task:** Identifies an Analysis Services database, a list of objects to process, and processing options
- **Bulk Insert:** Provides the fastest mechanism to load a flat file into a database table without transformations. Specify source file and destination table as a minimum configuration. If the source file is a simple delimited file, then specify the appropriate row and column delimiters; otherwise, create and specify a format file that describes the layout of the source file. Error rows cannot be redirected, but rather cause the task to fail.
- **Data Flow:** Provides a flexible structure for loading, transforming, and storing data as configured on the Data Flow tab. See the section "Data Flow Components," later in this chapter for the components that can be configured in a Data Flow task.
- **Data Profiling:** Builds an XML file to contain an analysis of selected tables. Available analyses include null ratio, column length for string columns, statistics for numeric columns, value distribution, candidate keys, and inter-column dependencies. Open the resulting file in the Data Profile Viewer to explore the results. Alternately, the analysis results can be sent to an XML variable for programmatic inspection as part of a data validation regimen.

  Configure by setting the destination and file overwrite behavior on the General page. Select profiles to run either by pressing the Quick Profile button to select many profiles for a single table or by switching to the Profile Requests page to add profiles for one or more tables individually. Add a new profile request manually by clicking the Profile Type pull-down list on the first empty row.

- **Data Mining Query:** Runs prediction queries against existing, trained data mining models. Specify the Analysis Services database connection and mining structure name on the Mining Model tab. On the Build Query tab, enter the DMX query, using the Build New Query button to invoke the Query Builder if desired. The DMX query can be parameterized by placing parameter names of the form `@MyParamName` in the query string. If parameters are used, then map from the parameter name (without the @ prefix) to a corresponding variable name on the Parameter Mapping tab. Results can be handled by sending them either to variable(s) on the Result Set tab and/or to a database table on the Output tab:
  - Single-row result sets can be stored directly into variables on the Result Set tab by mapping each Result (column) Name returned by the query to the corresponding target variable, choosing the Single Row result type for each mapping.
  - Multiple-row result sets can be stored in a variable of type `Object` for later use with a Foreach loop container or other processing. On the Result Set tab, map a single Result Name of 0 (zero) to the object variable, with a result type of Full Result Set.
  - Independent of any variable mappings, both single-row and multiple-row result sets can be sent to a table by specifying the database connection and table name on the Output tab.
- **Execute DTS 2000 Package:** Enables legacy DTS packages to be executed as part of the Integration Services work flow. Specify the package location, authentication information, and DTS-style Inner/Outer variable mappings. Optionally, once the package is identified, it can be loaded as part of the Integration Services package. Additional downloads are required in SQL Server 2008 to enable DTS package execution; see Books Online for details.
- **Execute Package:** Executes the specified Integration Services package, enabling packages to be broken down into smaller, reusable pieces. Invoking a child package requires substantial overhead, so consider the number of invocations per run when considering child packages. For example, one or two child packages per file or table processed is probably fine, but one package per row processed is probably not. The child package will participate in a transaction if the Execute Package task is configured to participate. Variables available to the Execute Package task can be used by the child package by creating a "parent package variable" configuration in the child package, mapping each parent package variable to a locally defined package variable as needed.
- **Execute Process:** Executes an external program or batch file. Specify the program to be run in the `Executable` property, including the extension (e.g., `MyApp.exe`), and the full path if the program is not included in the computer's `PATH` setting (e.g., `C:\stuff\MyApp.exe`). Place any switches or arguments that would normally follow the program name on the command line in the `Arguments` property. Set other execution time parameters as appropriate, such as `WorkingDirectory` or `SuccessValue` so Integration Services knows if the task succeeded. The `StandardInputVariable` property allows the text of a variable to be supplied to applications that read from `StdIn` (e.g., `find` or `grep`). The `StandardOutputVariable` and `StandardErrorVariable` properties enable the task's normal and error messages to be captured in variables.

- **Execute SQL:** Runs a SQL script or query, optionally returning results into variables. On the General page of the editor, set the `ConnectionType` and `Connection` properties to specify which database the query will run against. `SQLSourceType` specifies how the query will be entered:
  - **Direct Input:** Enter into the `SQLStatement` property by typing in the property page, pressing the ellipses to enter the query in a text box, pressing the Browse button to read the query from a file into the property, or pressing the Build Query button to invoke the Query Builder.
  - **File connection:** Specify a file that the query will be read from at runtime.
  - **Variable:** Specify a variable that contains the query to be run.

  A query can be made dynamic either by using parameters or by setting the `SQLStatement` property using the Expressions page of the editor. Using expressions is slightly more complicated but much more flexible, as parameter use is limited — only in the `WHERE` clause and, with the exception of ADO.NET connections, only for stored procedure executions or simple queries. If parameters are to be used, then the query is entered with a marker for each parameter to be replaced, and then each marker is mapped to a variable via the Parameter Mapping page. Parameter markers and mapping vary according to connection manager type:

  - **OLE DB:** Write the query leaving a ? to mark each parameter location, and then refer to each parameter using its order of appearance in the query to determine a name: 0 for the first parameter, 1 for the second, and so on.
  - **ODBC:** Same as OLE DB, except parameters are named starting at 1 instead of 0
  - **ADO:** Write the query using ? to mark each parameter location, and specify any non-numeric parameter name for each parameter. For ADO, it is the order in which the variables appear on the mapping page (and not the name) that determines which parameter they will replace.
  - **ADO.NET:** Write the query as if the parameters were variables declared in Transact-SQL (e.g., `SELECT name FROM mytable WHERE id = @ID`), and then refer to the parameter by name for mapping.

  The `ResultSet` property (General page) specifies how query results are returned to variables:

  - **None:** Results are not captured.
  - **Single row:** Results from a singleton query can be stored directly into variables. On the Result Set tab, map each result name returned by the query to the corresponding target variable. As with input parameters, result names vary according to connection manager type. OLE DB, ADO, and ADO.NET connections map columns by numeric order starting at 0. ODBC also allows numeric mapping but starts at 1 for the first column. In addition, OLE DB and ADO connections allow columns to be mapped by column name instead of number.
  - **Full result set:** Multiple-row result sets are stored in a variable of type `Object` for later use with a Foreach loop container or other processing. On the Result Set tab, map a single result name of 0 (zero) to the object variable, with a result type of Full Result Set.
  - **XML:** Results are stored in an XML DOM document for later use with a Foreach loop container or other processing. On the Result Set tab, map a single result name of 0 (zero) to the object variable, with a result type of Full Result Set.

- **File System Task:** Provides a number of file (copy, delete, move, rename, set attributes) and folder (copy, create, delete, delete content, move) operations. Source and destination files/folders can be specified by either a File connection manager or a string variable that contains the path. Remember to set the appropriate usage type when configuring a File connection manager (e.g., Create folder vs. Existing folder). Set the `OverwriteDestination` or `UseDirectoryIfExists` properties to obtain the desired behavior for preexisting objects.
- **FTP:** Supports a commonly used subset of FTP functionality, including send/receive/delete files and create/remove directories. Specify the server via an FTP connection manager. Any remote file/path can be specified via either direct entry or a string variable that contains the file/path. A local file/path can be specified via either a File connection manager or a string variable that contains the file/path. Wildcards are accepted in filenames. Use `OverWriteFileAtDest` to specify whether target files can be overwritten, and `IsAsciiTransfer` to switch between ASCII and binary transfer modes.
- **Message Queue:** Sends or receives queued messages via MSMQ. Specify the message connection, send or receive, and the message type.

New in 2008

Script tasks and script components now use the Visual Studio Tools for Applications (VSTA) development environment. This enables C# code to be used in addition to the Visual Basic code supported by SQL Server 2005. Scripts also have full access to Web and other assembly references, compared to the subset of .NET assemblies available in SQL Server 2005.

- **Script:** This task allows either Visual Basic 2008 or Visual C# 2008 code to be embedded in a task. Properties include the following:
  - **ScriptLanguage:** Choose which language to use to create the task. Once the script has been viewed/edited, this property becomes read-only.
  - **ReadOnlyVariables/ReadWriteVariables:** List the read and read/write variables to be accessed within the script, separated by commas, in these properties. Attempting to access a variable not listed in these properties results in a run-time error. Entries are case sensitive, so `myvar` and `MyVar` are considered different variables, although using the new Select Variables dialog will eliminate typos.
  - **EntryPoint:** Name of the class that contains the entry point for the script. There is normally no reason to change the default name (ScriptMain). It generates the following code shell:

```
Public Class ScriptMain
   Public Sub Main()
            '
            ' Add your code here
            Dts.TaskResult = Dts.Results.Success
   End Sub
End Class
```

At the end of execution, the script must return `Dts.TaskResult` as either success or failure to indicate the outcome of the task. Variables can be referenced through the `Dts.Variables` collection. For example, `Dts.Variables("MyVar").Value` exposes the value of the `MyVar` variable. Be aware that the collection is case sensitive, so referencing `"myvar"` will not return the value of `"MyVar"`. The `Dts` object exposes several other useful members, including the `Dts.Connections` collection to access connection managers, `Dts.Events.Fire` methods to raise events, and the `Dts.Log` method to write log entries. See "Interacting with the Package in the Script Task" in SQL Server 2008 Books Online for additional details.

- **Send Mail:** Sends a text-only SMTP e-mail message. Specify the SMTP configuration manager and all the normal e-mail fields (To, From, etc.). Separate multiple addresses by commas (not semicolons). The source of the message body is specified by the `MessageSourceType` property: `Direct Input` for entering the body as text in the `MessageSource` property, `File Connection` to read the message from a file at runtime, or `Variable` to use the contents of a string variable as the message body. Attachments are entered as pipe-delimited file specs. Missing attachment files cause the task to fail.
- **Transfer Database:** Copies or moves an entire database between SQL Server instances. Choose between the faster `DatabaseOffline` method (which detaches, copies files, and reattaches the databases) or the slower `DatabaseOnline` (which uses SMO to create the target database). Identify the source and destination servers via SMO connection managers. For the `DatabaseOnline` method, specify the source and destination database names, and the path for each destination file to be created. The `DatabaseOnline` method requires the same information, plus a *network share path* for each source and destination file, as the copy must move the physical files. Specifying UNC paths for the network share path is the most general, but packages that are running on one of the servers can reference local paths for that server. Using the `DatabaseOnline` method requires that any objects on which the database depends, such as logins, be in place before the database is transferred.
- **Transfer Error Messages:** Transfers custom error messages (ala `sp_addmessage`) from one server to another. Identify the source and destination servers via SMO connection managers and the list of messages to be transferred.
- **Transfer Jobs:** Copies SQL Agent jobs from one SQL Server instance to another. Identify the source and destination servers via SMO connection managers and the list of messages to be transferred. Any resources required (e.g., databases) by the jobs being copied must be available to successfully copy.
- **Transfer Logins:** Copies logins from one SQL Server instance to another. Identify the source and destination servers via SMO connection managers and the list of logins to be transferred. The list may consist of selected logins, all logins on the source server, or all logins that have access to selected databases (see the `LoginsToTransfer` property in the Task dialog).
- **Transfer Master Stored Procedures:** Copies any custom stored procedures from the master database on one server to the master database on another server. Identify the source and destination servers via SMO connection managers, and then select to either copy all custom stored procedures or individually mark the procedures to be copied.
- **Transfer Objects:** Copies any database-level object from one SQL Server instance to another. Identify the source and destination servers via SMO connection managers and the database on each server. For each type of object, select to either copy all such objects or to individually identify which objects to transfer, and then enable copy options (e.g., `DropObjectsFirst`, `CopyIndexes`, etc.).

- **Web Service:** Executes a Web Service call, storing the output in either a file or a variable. Specify an HTTP connection manager and a local file in which to store WSDL information. If the HTTP connection manager points directly at the WSDL file (e.g., `http://MyServer/MyService/MyPage.asmx?wsdl` for the `MyService` Web Service on `MyServer`), then use the Download WSDL button to fill the local copy of the WSDL file; otherwise, manually retrieve and create the local WSDL file. Setting `OverwriteWSDLFile` to `true` will store the latest Web Service description into the local file each time the task is run.

  Once connection information is established, switch to the Input page to choose the service and method to execute, and then enter any parameters required by the chosen method. The Output page provides options to output to either a file, as described by a File connection manager, or a variable. Take care to choose a variable with a data type compatible with the result the Web Service will return.
- **WMI Data Reader:** Executes a Windows Management Instrumentation (WQL) query against a server to retrieve event log, configuration, and other management information. Select a WMI connection manager and specify a WQL Query (e.g., `SELECT * FROM win32_ntlogevent WHERE logfile = 'system' AND timegenerated > '20080911'` for all system event log entries since 9/11/2008) from direct input, a file containing a query, or a string variable containing a query. Choose an output format by setting the `OutputType` property to "Data table" for a comma-separated values list, "Property name and value" for one comma-separated name/property combination per row with an extra newline between records, or "Property value" for one property value per row without names. Use `DestinationType` and `Destination` to send the query results to either a file or a string variable.
- **WMI Event Watcher:** Similar to a WMI data reader but instead of returning data, the task waits for a WQL specified event to occur. When the event occurs or the task times out, the SSIS task events `WMIEventWatcherEventOccurred` or `WMIEventWatcherEventTimeout` can fire, respectively. For either occurrence, specify the action (log and fire event or log only) and the task disposition (return success, return failure, or watch again). Set the task timeout (in seconds) using the `Timeout` property, with 0 specifying no timeout.
- **XML:** Performs operations on XML documents, including comparing two documents (diff), merging two documents, applying diff output (diffgram) to a document, validating a document against a DTD, and performing XPath queries or XSLT transformations. Choose a source document as direct input, a file, or a string variable, and an output as a file or a string variable. Set other properties as appropriate for the selected `OperationType`.

Maintenance Plan tasks

Maintenance Plan tasks provide the same elements that are used to build maintenance plans for use in custom package development. Tasks use an ADO.NET connection manager to identify the server being maintained, but any database selected in the connection manager is superseded by the databases identified within each Maintenance Plan task. Any questions about what a particular task does can be answered by pressing the View T-SQL button on the maintenance task.

CROSS-REF **For more information about database maintenance, see Chapter 42, "Maintaining the Database."**

The available tasks are as follows:

- **Back Up Database:** Creates a native SQL backup of one or more databases
- **Check Database Integrity:** Performs a DBCC `CHECKDB`

- **Execute SQL Server Agent Job:** Starts the selected SQL Agent job via the `sp_start_job` stored procedure
- **Execute T-SQL Statement:** A simplified SQL-Server-only statement execution. It does not return results or set variables: Use the Execute SQL task for more complex queries.
- **History Cleanup:** Trims old entries from backup/restore, maintenance plan, and SQL Agent job history
- **Maintenance Cleanup:** Prunes old maintenance plan, backup, or other files
- **Notify Operator:** Performs an `sp_notify_operator`, sending a message to selected on-duty operators defined on that SQL Server
- **Rebuild Index:** Issues an `ALTER INDEX REBUILD` for each table, indexed view, or both in the selected databases
- **Reorganize Index:** Uses `ALTER INDEX ... REORGANIZE` to reorganize either all or selected indexes within the databases chosen. It optionally compacts large object data.
- **Shrink Database:** Performs a DBCC `SHRINKDATABASE`
- **Update Statistics:** Issues an `UPDATE STATISTICS` statement for column, index, or all statistics in the selected databases

Data flow components

This section describes the individual components that can be configured within a Data Flow task: sources of data for the flow, destinations that output the data, and optional transformations that can change the data in between. See the "Data Flow" section earlier in this chapter for general information about configuring a Data Flow task.

Sources

Data Flow sources supply the rows of data that flow through the Data Flow task. Right-clicking a source on the design surface reveals that each source has two different editing options: Edit (basic) and Show Advanced Editor, although in some cases the basic Edit option displays the Advanced Editor anyway. The common steps to configuring a source are represented by the pages of the basic editor:

- **Connection Manager:** Specify the particular table, file(s), view, or query that will provide the data for this source. Several sources will accept either a table name or a query string from a variable.
- **Columns:** Choose which columns will appear in the data flow. Optionally, change the default names of the columns in the data flow.
- **Error Output:** Specify what to do for each column should an error occur. Each type of error can be ignored, cause the component to fail (default), or redirect the problem row to an error output. Truncation errors occur when a string is longer than the destination allows, "Error" errors catch all other types of failures. Don't be confused by the "Description" column; it is not another type of error, but merely provides a description of the context under which the error could occur.

The advanced editor provides the same capabilities as the basic editor in a different format, plus much finer control over input and output columns, including names and data types. When the rows sent to the data flow are already sorted, they can be marked as such using the advanced editor. On the

Input and Output Properties tab, choose the top node of the tree and set the IsSorted property to true. Then select each of the output (data flow) columns that make up the sort and enter a SortKeyPosition value, beginning with 1 and incrementing by 1 for each column used in sorting. To mark a column as sorted descending, specify a negative SortKeyPosition. For example, giving the Date and Category columns SortKeyPosition values of -1 and 2, respectively, will mark the Date descending and the Category ascending.

The available sources are as follows:

- **OLE DB:** The preferred method of reading database data. It requires an OLE DB connection manager.
- **ADO.NET:** Uses an ADO.NET connection manager to read database data, either by identifying a database object or entering a query to execute.
- **Flat File:** Requires a Flat File connection manager. Delimited files translate zero-length strings into null values for the data flow when the RetainNulls property is true.
- **Excel:** Uses an Excel connection manager and either a worksheet or named ranges as tables. A SQL command can be constructed using the Build Query button that selects a subset of rows. Data types are assigned to each column by sampling the first few rows, but can be adjusted using the advanced editor.
- **Raw:** Reads a file written by the Integration Services Raw File destination (see the following "Destinations" section) in a preprocessed format, making this a very fast method of retrieving data, often used when data processed by one stage of a package needs to be stored and reused by a later stage. Because the data has already been processed once, no error handling or output configuration is required. The input filename is directly specified without using a connection manager.
- **XML:** Reads a simple XML file and presents it to the data flow as a table, using either an inline schema (a header in the XML file that describes the column names and data types) or an XSD (XML Schema Definition) file. The XML source does not use a connection manager; instead, specify the input filename and then either specify an XSD file or indicate that the file contains an inline schema. (Set the UseInlineSchema property to true or select the check box in the basic editor).
- **Script:** A script component can act as a source, destination, or transformation of a data flow. Use a script as a source to generate test data or to format a complex external source of data. For example, a poorly formatted text file could be read and parsed into individual columns by a script. Start by dragging a script transform onto the design surface, choosing Source from the pop-up Select Script Component Type dialog. On the Inputs and Outputs page of the editor, add as many outputs as necessary, renaming them as desired. Within each output, define columns as appropriate, carefully choosing the corresponding data types. On the Script page of the editor, list the read and read/write variables to be accessed within the script, separated by commas, in the ReadOnlyVariables and ReadWriteVariables properties, respectively. Click the Edit Script button to expose the code itself, and note that the primary method to be coded overrides CreateNewOutputRows, as shown in this simple example:

```
Public Overrides Sub CreateNewOutputRows()
    'Create 20 rows of random integers between 1 and 100
    Randomize()
    Dim i As Integer
```

```
        For i = 1 To 20
            Output0Buffer.AddRow()
            Output0Buffer.RandomInt = CInt(Rnd() * 100)
        Next
    End Sub
```

This example works for a single output with the default name `Output 0` containing a single integer column `RandomInt`. Notice how each output is exposed as `name+"buffer"` and embedded spaces are removed from the name. New rows are added using the `AddRow` method and columns are populated by referring to them as output properties. An additional property is exposed for each column with the suffix `_IsNull` (e.g., `Output0Buffer.RandomInt_IsNull`) to mark a value as `NULL`.

Reading data from an external source requires some additional steps, including identifying the connection managers that will be referenced within the script on the Connection Managers page of the editor. Then, in the script, additional methods must be overridden: `AcquireConnections` and `ReleaseConnections` to open and close any connections, and `PreExecute` and `PostExecute` to open and close any record sets, data readers, and so on (database sources only). Search for the topic "Extending the Data Flow with the Script Component" in SQL Server Books Online for full code samples and related information.

Destinations

Data Flow destinations provide a place to write the data transformed by the Data Flow task. Configuring destinations is similar to configuring sources, including both basic and advanced editors, and the three common steps:

- **Connection Manager:** Specify the particular table, file(s), view, or query to which data will be written. Several destinations will accept a table name from a variable.
- **Columns:** Map the columns from the data flow (input) to the appropriate destination columns.
- **Error Output:** Specify what to do should a row fail to insert into the destination: ignore the row, cause the component to fail (default), or redirect the problem row to error output.

The available destinations are as follows:

- **OLE DB:** Writes rows to a table, view, or SQL command (ad hoc view) for which an OLE DB driver exists. Table/view names can be selected directly in the destination or read from a string variable, and each can be selected with or without *fast load*. Fast load can decrease runtime by an order of magnitude or more depending on the particular data set and selected options. Options for fast load are as follows:
  - **Keep identity:** When the target table contains an identity column, either this option must be chosen to allow the identity to be overwritten with inserted values (ala `SET IDENTITY_INSERT ON`) or the identity column must be excluded from mapped columns so that new identity values can be generated by SQL Server.
  - **Keep nulls:** Choose this option to load null values instead of any column defaults that would normally apply.
  - **Table lock:** Keeps a table-level lock during execution

- **Check constraints:** Enables CHECK constraints (such as a valid range on an integer column) for inserted rows. Note that other types of constraints, including UNIQUE, PRIMARY KEY, FOREIGN KEY, and NOT NULL cannot be disabled. Loading data with CHECK constraints disabled will result in those constraints being marked as "not trusted" by SQL Server.
- **Rows per batch:** Specifying a batch size provides a hint to building the query plan, but it does not change the size of the transaction used to put rows in the destination table.
- **Maximum insert commit size:** Similar to the BatchSize property of the Bulk Insert task (see "Control flow tasks" earlier in the chapter), the maximum insert commit size is the largest number of rows included in a single transaction. The default value is very large (maximum integer value), allowing most any load task to be committed in a single transaction.

- **SQL Server:** This destination uses the same fast-loading mechanism as the Bulk Insert task but is restricted in that the package must execute on the SQL Server that contains the target table/view. Speed can exceed OLE DB fast loading in some circumstances.
- **ADO.NET:** Uses an ADO.NET connection manager to write data to a selected table or view
- **DataReader:** Makes the data flow available via an ADO.NET DataReader, which can be opened by other applications, notably Reporting Services, to read the output from the package.
- **Flat File:** Writes the data flow to a file specified by a Flat File connection manager. Because the file is described in the connection manager, limited options are available in the destination: Choose whether to overwrite any existing file and provide file header text if desired.
- **Excel:** Sends rows from the data flow to a sheet or range in a workbook using an Excel connection manager. Note that versions of Excel prior to 2007 can handle at most 65,536 rows and 256 columns of data, the first row of which is consumed by header information. Excel 2007 format supports 1,048,576 rows and 16,384 columns. Strings are required to be Unicode, so any DT_STR types need to be converted to DT_WSTR before reaching the Excel destination.
- **Raw:** Writes rows from the data flow to an Integration Services format suitable for fast loads by a raw source component. It does not use a connection manager; instead, specify the AccessMode by choosing to supply a filename via direct input or a string variable. Set the WriteOption property to an appropriate value:
  - **Append:** Adds data to an existing file, assuming the new data matches the previously written format
  - **Create always:** Always start a new file
  - **Create once:** Creates initially and then appends on subsequent writes. This is useful for loops that write to the same destination many times in the same package.
  - **Truncate and append:** Keeps the existing file's meta-data, but replaces the data.

  Raw files cannot handle BLOB data, which excludes any of the large data types, including text, varchar(max), and varbinary(max).
- **Recordset:** Writes the data flow to a variable. Stored as a recordset, the object variable is suitable for use as the source of a Foreach loop or other processing within the package.

- **SQL Server Compact:** Writes rows from the data flow into a SQL Mobile database table. Configure by identifying the SQL Server Mobile connection manager that points to the appropriate `.SDF` file, and then enter the name of the table on the Component Properties tab.
- **Dimension Processing and Partition Processing:** These tasks enable the population of Analysis Services cubes without first populating the underlying relational data source. Identify the Analysis Services connection manager of interest, choose the desired dimension or partition, and then select a processing mode:
  - **Add/Incremental:** Minimal processing required to add new data
  - **Full:** Complete reprocess of structure and data
  - **Update/Data-only:** Replaces data without updating the structure
- **Data Mining Model Training:** Provides training data to an existing data mining structure, thus preparing it for prediction queries. Specify the Analysis Services connection manager and the target mining structure in that database. Use the Columns tab to map the training data to the appropriate mining structure attributes.
- **Script:** A script can also be used as a destination, using a similar process to that already described for using a script as a source. Use a script as a destination to format output in a manner not allowed by one of the standard destinations. For example, a file suitable for input to a COBOL program could be generated from a standard data flow. Start by dragging a script component onto the design surface, choosing Destination from the pop-up Select Script Component Type dialog. Identify the input columns of interest and configure the script properties as described previously. After pressing the Edit Script button to access the code, the primary routine to be coded is named after the Input name with a `_ProcessInputRow` suffix (e.g., `Input0_ProcessInputRow`). Note the row object passed as an argument to this routine, which provides the input column information for each row (e.g., `Row.MyColumn` and `Row.MyColumn_IsNull`). Connection configuration and preparation is the same as described in the source topic. Search for the topic "Extending the Data Flow with the Script Component" in SQL Server Books Online for full code samples and related information.

Transformations

Between the source and the destination, transformations provide functionality to change the data from what was read into what is needed. Each transformation requires one or more data flows as input and provides one or more data flows as output. Like sources and destinations, many transformations provide a way to configure error output for rows that fail the transformation. In addition, many transformations provide both a basic and an advanced editor to configure the component, with normal configurations offered by the basic editor when available.

The standard transformations available in the Data Flow task are as follows:

- **Aggregate:** Functions rather like a `GROUP BY` query in SQL, generating Min, Max, Average, and so on, on the input data flow. Due to the nature of this operation, Aggregate does not pass through the data flow, but outputs only aggregated rows. Begin on the Aggregations tab by selecting the columns to include and adding the same column multiple times in the bottom pane if necessary. Then, for each column, specify the output column name (Output Alias), the operation to be performed (such as Group by, Count ...), and any comparison flags for determining value matches (e.g., Ignore case). For columns being distinct counted, performance hints can be supplied for the exact number (Distinct Count Keys) or an approximate number

(Distinct Count Scale) of distinct values that the transform will encounter. The scale ranges are as follows:

- **Low:** Approximately 500,000 values
- **Medium:** Approximately 5,000,000 values
- **High:** Approximately 25,000,000 values

Likewise, performance hints can be specified for the Group By columns by expanding the Advanced section of the Aggregations tab, entering either an exact (Keys) or an approximate (Keys Scale) count of different values to be processed. Alternately, you can specify performance hints for the entire component, instead of individual columns, on the Advanced tab, along with the amount to expand memory when additional memory is required.

- **Audit:** Adds execution context columns to the data flow, enabling data to be written with audit information about when it was written and where it came from. Available columns are ExecutionInstanceGUID, PackageID, PackageName, VersionID, ExecutionStartTime, MachineName, UserName, TaskName, and TaskID.
- **Cache:** Places selected columns from a data flow into a cache for later use by a Lookup transform. Identify the Cache connection manager and then map the data flow columns into the cache columns as necessary. The cache is a write once, read many data store: All the data to be included in the cache must be written by a single Cache transform but can then be used by many Lookup transforms.
- **Character Map:** Allows strings in the data flow to be transformed by a number of operations: Byte reversal, Full width, Half width, Hiragana, Katakana, Linguistic casing, Lowercase, Simplified Chinese, Traditional Chinese, and Uppercase. Within the editor, choose the columns to be transformed, adding a column multiple times in the lower pane if necessary. Each column can then be given a destination of a New column or In-place change (replaces the contents of a column). Then choose an operation and the name for the output column.
- **Conditional Split:** Enables rows of a data flow to be split between different outputs depending on the contents of the row. Configure by entering output names and expressions in the editor. When the transform receives a row, each expression is evaluated in order, and the first one that evaluates to true will receive that row of data. When none of the expressions evaluate to true, the default output (named at the bottom of the editor) receives the row. Once configured, as data flows are connected to downstream components, an Input Output Selection pop-up appears, and the appropriate output can be selected. Unmapped outputs are ignored and can result in data loss.
- **Copy Column:** Adds a copy of an existing column to the data flow. Within the editor, choose the columns to be copied, adding a column multiple times in the lower pane if necessary. Each new column can then be given an appropriate name (Output Alias).
- **Data Conversion:** Adds a copy of an existing column to the data flow, enabling data type conversions in the process. Within the editor, choose the columns to be converted, adding a column multiple times in the lower pane if necessary. Each new column can then be given an appropriate name (Output Alias) and data type. Conversions between code pages are not allowed. Use the advanced editor to enable locale-insensitive fast parsing algorithms by setting the `FastParse` property to `true` on each output column.
- **Data Mining Query:** Runs a DMX query for each row of the data flow, enabling rows to be associated with predictions, such as the likelihood that a new customer will make a purchase or the probability that a transaction is fraudulent. Configure by specifying an Analysis Services

connection manager, choosing the mining structure and highlighting the mining model to be queried. On the Query tab, click the Build New Query button and map columns in the data flow to the columns of the model (a default mapping is created based on column name). Then specify the columns to be added to the data flow in the lower half of the pane (usually a prediction function) and give the output an appropriate name (Alias).

- **Derived Column:** Uses expressions to generate values that can either be added to the data flow or replace existing columns. Within the editor, construct Integration Services expressions to produce the desired value, using type casts to change data types as needed. Assign each expression to either replace an existing column or be added as a new column. Give new columns an appropriate name and data type.
- **Export Column:** Writes large object data types (`DT_TEXT`, `DT_NTEXT`, or `DT_IMAGE`) to file(s) specified by a filename contained in the data flow. For example, large text objects could be extracted into different files for inclusion in a website or text index. Within the editor, specify two columns for each extract defined: a large object column and a column containing the target filename. A file can receive any number of objects. Set Append/Truncate/Exists options to indicate the desired file create behavior.
- **Fuzzy Grouping:** Identifies duplicate rows in the data flow using exact matching for any data type and/or fuzzy matching for string data types (`DT_STR` and `DT_WSTR`). Configure the task to examine the key columns within the data flow that identify a unique row. Several columns are added to the output as a result of this transform:
  - **Input key** (`default name _key_in`): A sequential number assigned to identify each input row
  - **Output key** (`default name _key_out`): The Input key of the row this row matches (or its own Input key if not a duplicate). One way to cull the duplicate rows from the data flow is to define a downstream conditional split on the condition `[_key_in] == [_key_out]`.
  - **Similarity score** (`default name _score`): A measure of the similarity of the entire row, on a scale of 0 to one, to the first row of the set of duplicates.
  - **Group Output** (`default name <column>_clean`): For each key column selected, this is the value from the first row of the set of duplicates (that is, the value from the row indicated by `_key_out`).
  - **Similarity Output (default name _Similarity_<column>):** For each key column selected, this is the similarity score for that individual column versus the first row of the set of duplicates.

  Within the editor, specify an OLE DB connection manager, where the transform will have permissions to create a temporary table. Then configure each key column by setting its Output, Group Output, and Similarity Output names. In addition, set the following properties for each column:

  - **Match Type:** Choose between Fuzzy and Exact Match types for each string column (non-string data types always match exactly).
  - **Minimum Similarity:** Smallest similarity score allowed for a match. Leaving fuzzy match columns at the default of 0 enables similarity to be controlled from the slider on the Advanced tab of the editor.

- **Numerals:** Specify whether leading or trailing numerals are significant in making comparisons. The default of Neither specifies that leading and training numerals are not considered in matches.
- **Comparison Flags:** Choose settings appropriate to the type of strings being compared.

- **Fuzzy Lookup:** Similar to the Lookup transform, except that when an exact lookup fails, a fuzzy lookup is attempted for any string columns (DT_STR and DT_WSTR). Specify an OLE DB connection manager and table name where values will be looked up, and a new or existing index to be used to cache fuzzy lookup information. On the Columns tab, specify a join between the data flow and the reference table, and which columns from the reference table will be added to the data flow. On the Advanced tab, select the similarity required for finding a match: The lower the number the more liberal the matches become. In addition to the specified columns added to the data flow, match meta-data is added as follows:
  - **_Similarity:** Reports the similarity between all of the values compared
  - **_Confidence:** Reports the confidence level that the chosen match was the correct one compared to other possible matches in the lookup table
  - **_Similarity_<column name>:** Similarity for each individual column

  The advanced editor has settings of `MinimumSimilarity` and `FuzzyComparisonFlags` for each individual column.

- **Import Column:** Reads large object data types (DT_TEXT, DT_NTEXT, or DT_IMAGE) from files specified by a filename contained in the data flow, adding the text or image objects as a new column in the data flow. Configure in the advanced editor by identifying each column that contains a filename to be read on the Input Columns tab. Then, on the Input and Output Properties tab, create a new output column for each filename column to contain the contents of the files as they are read, giving the new column an appropriate name and data type. In the output column properties, note the grayed-out `ID` property, and locate the properties for the corresponding input (filename) column. Set the input column's `FileDataColumnID` property to the output column's `ID` value to tie the filename and contents columns together. Set the `ExpectBOM` property to `true` for any `DT_NTEXT` data being read that has been written with byte-order marks.

- **Lookup:** Finds rows in a database table or cache that match the data flow and includes selected columns in the data flow, much like a join between the data flow and a table or cache. For example, a product ID could be added to the data flow by looking up the product name in the master table. Note that all lookups are case sensitive regardless of the collation of the underlying database. Case can be effectively ignored by converting the associated text values to a single case before comparison (e.g., using the `UPPER` function in a derived column expression).

  The Lookup transform operates in three possible modes:
  - **No cache:** Runs a query against the source database for each lookup performed. No cache is kept in memory in order to minimize the number of database accesses, but each lookup reflects the latest value stored in the database.
  - **Full cache:** Populates an in-memory cache from either the database or a Cache connection manager (see Cache transform and connection manager descriptions earlier in this chapter) and relies solely on that cache for lookups during execution. This minimizes the disk accesses required but may exceed available memory for very large data sets, which can

dramatically reduce performance. Because no error message appears as performance degrades, it is useful to monitor resource usage while processing sample datasets to determine whether the cache size will work for the range of data sizes expected in production uses.

- **Partial cache:** Populates an in-memory cache with a subset of the data available from the database, and then issues queries against the database for any values not found within the in-memory cache. This method provides a compromise between speed and available memory. Whenever possible, this mode should be used with a query that fills the cache with the most likely rows encountered. For example, many warehousing applications are more likely to access values recently added to the database.

Start the lookup transform configuration process by selecting the cache mode and the connection type for Full Cache transforms. The most common handling of rows with no matching entries is to "Redirect rows to no match output" for further processing, but the context may require one of the other options. On the Connections page, choose the connection manager containing the reference data, and the table or query to retrieve that data from (for database connections). Usually, the best choice is a query that returns only the columns used in the lookup, which avoids reading and storing unused columns.

On the Columns tab, map the join columns between the data flow and the reference table by dragging and dropping lines between corresponding columns. Then check the reference table columns that should be added to the data flow, adjusting names as desired in the bottom pane.

The Advanced tab provides an opportunity to optimize memory performance of the Lookup transform for Partial Cache mode, and to modify the query used for row-by-row lookups. Set the size for in-memory caching based on the number of rows that will be loaded — these values often require testing to refine. "Enable cache for rows with no matching entries" enables data from row-by-row lookups that fail to be saved in the in-memory cache along with the data originally read at the start of the transform, thus avoiding repeated database accesses for missing values. Review the custom query to ensure that the row-by-row lookup statement is properly built.

- **Merge:** Combines the rows of two sorted data flows into a single data flow. For example, if some of the rows of a sorted data flow are split by an error output or Conditional Split transform, then they can be merged again. The upstream sort must have used the same key columns for both flows, and the data types of columns to be merged must be compatible. Configure by dragging two different inputs to the transform and mapping columns together in the editor. See the Union All description later in this list for the unsorted combination of flows.
- **Merge Join:** Provides SQL join functionality between data flows sorted on the join columns. Configure by dragging the two flows to be joined to the transform, paying attention to which one is connected to the left input if a left outer join is desired. Within the editor, choose the join type, map the join columns, and choose which columns are to be included in the output.
- **Multicast:** Copies every row of an input data flow to many different outputs. Once an output has been connected to a downstream component, a new output will appear for connection to the next downstream component. Only the names of the output are configurable.
- **OLE DB Command:** Executes a SQL statement (such as `UPDATE` or `DELETE`) for every row in a data flow. Configure by specifying an OLE DB connection manager to use when executing the command, and then switch to the Component Properties tab and enter the SQL statement using question marks for any parameters (e.g., `UPDATE MyTable SET Col1 = ? WHERE`

Col2=?). On the Column Mappings tab, associate a data flow column with each parameter in the SQL statement.

- **Percentage Sampling:** Splits a data flow by randomly sampling the rows for a given percentage. For example, this could be used to separate a data set into training and testing sets for data mining. Within the editor, specify the approximate percentage of rows to allocate to the selected output, while the remaining rows are sent to the unselected output. If a sampling seed is provided, the transform will always select the same rows from a given data set.
- **Pivot:** Denormalizes a data flow, similar to the way an Excel pivot table operates, making attribute values into columns. For example, a data flow with three columns, Quarter, Region, and Revenue, could be transformed into a data flow with columns for Quarter, Western Region, and Eastern Region, thus pivoting on Region.
- **Row Count:** Counts the number of rows in a data flow and places the result into a variable. Configure by populating the VariableName property.
- **Row Sampling:** Nearly identical to the Percentage Sampling transform, except that the approximate number of rows to be sampled is entered, rather than the percentage of rows
- **Script:** Using a script as a transformation enables transformations with very complex logic to act on a data flow. Start by dragging a script component onto the design surface, choosing Transformation from the pop-up Select Script Component Type dialog. Within the editor's Input Columns tab, mark the columns that will be available in the script, and indicate which will be ReadWrite versus ReadOnly. On the Inputs and Outputs tab, add any output columns that will be populated by the script above and beyond the input columns.

  On the Script page of the editor, list the read and read/write variables to be accessed within the script, separated by commas, in the ReadOnlyVariables and ReadWriteVariables properties, respectively. Click the Edit Script button to expose the code itself, and note that the primary method to be coded overrides <inputname>_ProcessInputRow, as shown in this simple example:

```
Public Overrides Sub Input0_ProcessInputRow _
   (ByVal Row As Input0Buffer)
    'Source system indicates missing dates with old values,
    'replace those with NULLs. Also determine if given time
    'is during defined business hours.
    If Row.TransactionDate < #1/1/2000# Then
        Row.TransactionDate_IsNull = True
        Row.PrimeTimeFlag_IsNull = True
    Else
        'Set flag for prime time transactions
        If Weekday(Row.TransactionDate) > 1 _
        And Weekday(Row.TransactionDate) < 7 _
        And Row.TransactionDate.Hour > 7 _
        And Row.TransactionDate.Hour < 17 Then
            Row.PrimeTimeFlag = True
        Else
            Row.PrimeTimeFlag = False
        End If
    End If
End Sub
```

This example uses one ReadWrite input (TransactionDate) and one output (PrimeTimeFlag), with the input name left with the default of Input 0. Each column is exposed as a property of the Row object, as is the additional property with the suffix _IsNull to test or set the column value as NULL. The routine is called once for each row in the data flow.

- **Slowly Changing Dimension:** Compares the data in a data flow to a dimension table, and, based on the roles assigned to particular columns, maintains the dimension. This component is unusual in that it does not have an editor; instead, a wizard guides the steps to define column roles and interactions with the dimension table. At the conclusion of the wizard, several components are placed on the design surface to accomplish the dimension maintenance task.
- **Sort:** Sorts the rows in a data flow by selected columns. Configure by selecting the columns to sort by. Then, in the lower pane, choose the sort type, the sort order, and the comparison flags appropriate to the data being sorted.
- **Term Extraction:** Builds a new data flow based on terms it finds in a Unicode text column (DT_WSTR or DT_NTEXT). This is the training part of text mining, whereby strings of a particular type are used to generate a list of commonly used terms, which is later used by the Term Lookup component to identify similar strings. For example, the text of saved RSS documents could be used to find similar documents in a large population. Configure by identifying the column containing the Unicode text to be analyzed. If a list of terms to be excluded has been built, then identify the table and column on the Exclusions tab. The Advanced tab controls the extraction algorithm, including whether terms are single words or phrases (articles, pronouns, etc., are never included), the scoring algorithm, minimum frequency before extraction, and maximum phrase length.
- **Term Lookup:** Provides a "join" between a Unicode text column (DT_WSTR or DT_NTEXT) in the data flow and a reference table of terms built by the Term Extraction component. One row appears in the output data flow for each term matched. The output data flow also contains two columns in addition to the selected input columns: Term and Frequency. Term is the noun or noun phrase that was matched and Frequency is the number of occurrences in the data flow column. Configure the transform by specifying the OLE DB connection manager and table that contains the list of terms. Use the Term Lookup tab to check the input columns that should be passed through to the output data flow, and then map the input Unicode text column to the Term column of the reference table by dragging and dropping between those columns in the upper pane.
- **Union All:** Combines rows from multiple data flows into a single data flow, assuming the source columns are of compatible types. Configure by connecting as many data flows as needed to the component. Then, using the editor, ensure that the correct columns from each data flow are mapped to the appropriate output column.
- **Unpivot:** Makes a data flow more normalized by turning columns into attribute values. For example, a data flow with one row for each quarter and a column for revenue by region could be turned into a three-column data flow: Quarter, Region, and Revenue.

Maintainable and Manageable Packages

Integration Services enables applications to be created with relatively little effort, which is a great advantage from a development perspective, but can be a problem if quickly developed systems are deployed without proper planning. Care is required to build maintainable and manageable applications regardless of the implementation. Fortunately, Integration Services is designed with many features that support long-term maintainability and manageability.

Designing before developing is especially important when first getting started with Integration Services, as practices established early are often reused in subsequent efforts, especially logging, auditing, and overall structure. Perhaps the key advantage to developing with Integration Services is the opportunity to centralize everything about a data processing task in a single place, with clear precedence between steps, and opportunities to handle errors as they occur. Centralization greatly increases maintainability compared to the traditional "script here, program there, stored procedure somewhere else" approach. Other topics to consider during design include the following:

- Identify repeating themes for possible package reuse. Many tasks that repeat the same activities on objects with the same metadata are good candidates for placing in reused subpackages.
- Appropriate logging strategies are the key to operational success. When an error occurs, who will be responsible for noticing and how will they know? For example, how will someone know whether a package was supposed to run but did not for some reason? What level of logging is appropriate? (More is not always better; too many irrelevant details mask true problems.) What kinds of environment and package state information will be required to understand why a failure has occurred after the fact? (For more information about logging, see the next section.)
- Auditing concepts may be useful for both compliance and error-recovery operations. What type of information should be associated with data created by a package? If large quantities of information are required, then consider adding the details to an *audit* or *lineage log*, adding only an ID to affected records. Alternately, the Audit transform described earlier in this chapter can be used to put audit information on each row.
- For packages that run on multiple servers or environments, what configuration details change for those environments? Which storage mode (registry, SQL, XML, etc.) will be most effective at distributing configuration data? (See the "Package configurations" section later in this chapter.)
- Determine how to recover from a package failure. Will manual intervention be required before the package can run again? For example, a package that loads data may be able to use transactions to ensure that rerunning a package does not load duplicate rows.
- Consider designing checkpoint restartable logic for long-running packages. (See the "Checkpoint restart" section later in this chapter.)
- Determine the most likely failure points in a package. What steps will be realistically taken to address a failure? Add those steps to the package if possible, using error data flows and task constraints now to avoid labor costs later.

Good development practices help increase maintainability as well. Give packages, tasks, components, and other visible objects meaningful names. Liberal use of annotations to note non-obvious meanings and motivations will benefit future developers, too. Finally, use version-control software to maintain a history of package and related file versions.

Logging

Because many packages are destined for unattended operation, generating an execution log is an excellent method for tracking operations and collecting debug information. To configure logging for a package, right-click on the package design surface and choose Logging. On the Providers and Logs tab, add a provider for each output type that will be logged (multiple are allowed). On the Details tab, specify the events for which log entries will be written; the advanced view, shown in Figure 37-6, also allows selecting which columns will be included in each event's log entry.

FIGURE 37-6

Advanced view of the Logging Details tab

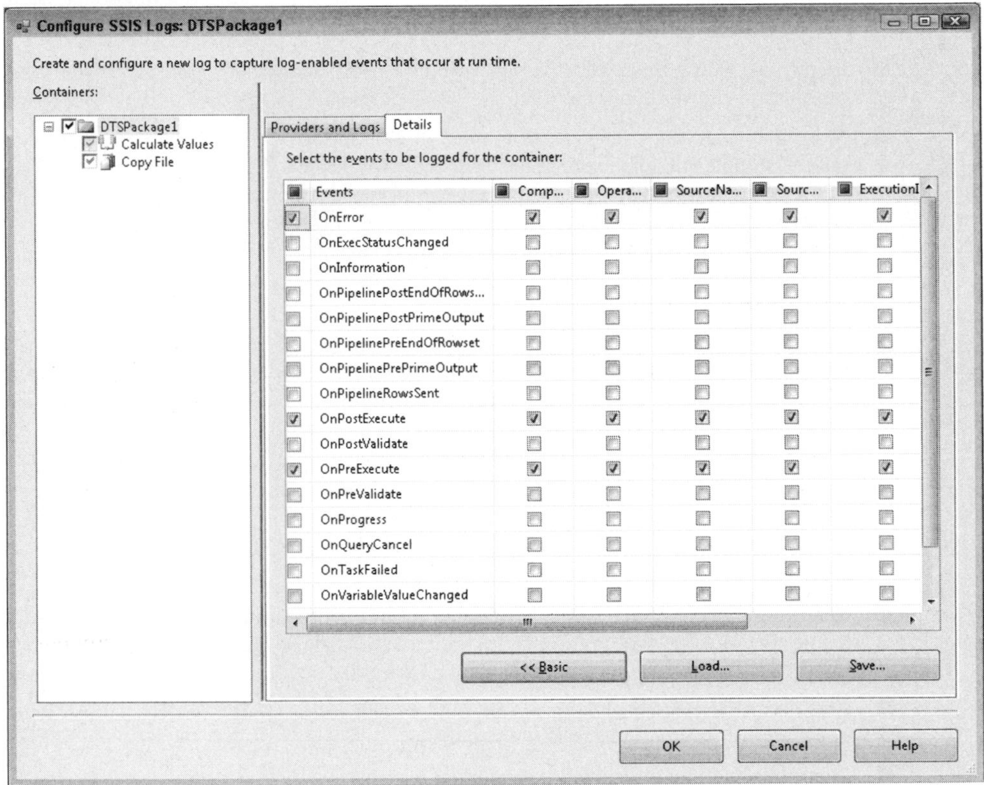

The tree view in the left pane represents the container hierarchy of the package. The check boxes correspond to each object's `LoggingMode` property: clear for Disabled, a black check for Enabled, and a gray check for `UseParentSetting` (logging settings inherited from the parent). By default, all objects inherit from the package settings. Highlighting an item in the tree displays the details for that object in the current tab. Note that providers can only be configured for the package, and any object with `UseParentSetting` will have its options grayed out in deference to its parents' settings.

The standard log providers are as follows:

- **Text File:** Writes a comma-separated-value text file. Configure with an appropriate File connection manager.
- **SQL Profiler:** Writes a `.TRC` file that can be viewed in the Profiler application. This can be a useful option when viewed with other trace or performance information within Profiler. Configure with an appropriate File connection manager.
- **SQL Server:** Writes log entries to the `dbo.sysssislog` table in the database indicated by the associated OLE DB connection manager. Any database can be chosen to host this table. If the table does not exist, then it will be created on first use.
- **Event Log:** Writes log entries to the Windows application event log on the computer that executes the package. No configuration is required.
- **XML File:** Writes an `.XML` file. Configure with an appropriate File connection manager.

Once a useful set of event/column combinations has been constructed, it can be saved as a template and reloaded on other packages.

Package configurations

Package configurations make it easier to move packages between servers and environments, providing a way to set properties within the package based on environment-specific configurations. For example, the server names and input directories might change between the development and production environments.

Right-click on the package design surface and choose Package Configurations to setup/modify configurations. The configurations shown are applied to the package in the order listed. To add a new configuration, ensure that configurations are enabled and click Add to start the Package Configuration Wizard. Choose the desired Configuration Type (storage location). There are essentially three categories to consider:

- **Registry and Environment Variable:** These types can hold a single property only.
- **XML File and SQL Server Table:** Each of these configuration types can hold any number of property settings.
- **Parent Package Variable:** Allows access to the contents of a single variable from the calling package.

Most configuration types allow the storage location to be identified either directly or via an environment variable. The environment variable approach can be useful when the storage location (such as file directory) must change between environments. Once the configuration type and location are specified, the Select Properties to Export option enables the properties that will change between environments to be chosen. Complete the wizard by reviewing the selections and giving the configuration a name.

Configurations can be reused between packages if the names of the objects containing the properties to be set are the same between packages. For example, packages that use the same names for their connection managers could share a configuration that sets server or filenames. To share a configuration in a subsequent package, choose the same configuration type, and then specify the same storage location (e.g., XML filename) as the initial package. When prompted by a dialog warning that the configuration already exists, select Reuse Existing.

Checkpoint restart

Enabling checkpoint restart allows a package to restart without rerunning tasks that already completed successfully. Note the following basic rules about restart points:

- Only Control Flow tasks define restart points — a Data Flow task is viewed as a single unit of work regardless of the number of components it contains.
- Any transaction in progress is rolled back on failure, but the restart point may not coincide with a transaction boundary, so unexpected results can occur.
- Any loop containers are started over from the first iteration.
- The configuration used on restart is saved in the checkpoint file, rather than the current configuration file.

Enable checkpoints by setting the package properties:

- **CheckpointFilename:** Name of the file in which checkpoint information should be saved
- **CheckpointUsage:** Set to either `IfExists` (starts at the beginning of the package if no file exists or at the restart point if the checkpoint file exists) or `Always` (fails if the checkpoint file does not exist).
- **SaveCheckPoints:** Set to `True`.

In addition, the `FailPackageOnFailure` property must be set to `True` for the package and every task or container that can act as a restart point.

Deploying Packages

The Business Intelligence Development Studio is an excellent environment for designing and debugging Integration Services packages, but it is not an efficient method for routinely executing packages. Without installing a package on a server, it can execute without the development overhead by using `dtexec/dtexecui`. You can run `dtexecui` from the command line, or you can choose the Execute Package Utility from the Start menu, and specify the desired execution options. Then either choose the Execute button or switch to the Command Line page to copy the appropriate `dtexec` command-line switches.

Conversely, installing packages on the target SQL Server(s) makes sense when a package will be reused. Once installed, a package is known to the Integration Services service, which in turn can be connected to SQL Server Management Studio for tracking and monitoring. Integration Services also caches the components executed by packages to reduce startup time.

Installing packages

Creating a deployment utility enables the installation of all the packages in a project on a target server. Configure the utility by right-clicking on the project (not the package) in the Solution Explorer and choosing Properties. Navigate to the Deployment Utility page of the resulting dialog and set the value of `CreateDeploymentUtility` to `True`. Review the settings for `DeploymentOutputPath` indicating where the install package will be written relative to the project directory, and the setting of `AllowConfigurationChanges`, which enables configuration values to be adjusted as part of the install process. Save the property changes, and then right-click on the project and choose Build to create the install package.

Once the deployment utility has been created, double-click the package manifest (*<project name>*`.SSISDeploymentManifest`) to start the package installation. Given a network connection to the target server and adequate permissions, the installation can be run from any machine.

In addition, individual packages can be installed on a server using SQL Server Management Studio. Log on to the target server and connect the local instance of Integration Services in the Object Explorer. On either the File System or msdb nodes, right-click and choose Import Package. Note that the source package can be stored either as a file or as a SQL Server (msdb) package. Similar functionality is available from the `dtutil` command-line utility.

Executing packages

Once installed on the target server, a package can be executed in several ways:

- Locate the installed package in SQL Server Management Studio, right-click, and choose Run Package, which in turn invokes `dtexecui` for the selected package.
- Run the `dtexecui` utility, which enables the full array of execution options to be selected. It also displays the command-line switches to use with the `dtexec` command-line utility.
- From a SQL Agent Job step, choose the step type as SQL Server Integration Services Package, and the package source as SSIS Package Store.

The execution method and location that you choose can have a profound effect on performance and reporting. Execution using `dtexec/dtexecui` can offload package processing from the SQL Server when run on another server or workstation. These options also default to providing verbose feedback during execution, which can be useful in tracking progress or understanding errors. However, consider network traffic that may be introduced by this scenario. For example, loading a series of data files from a file server to the SQL Server via a workstation can double the network load (every file must move from the file server to the workstation, and then again from the workstation to the SQL Server) compared to running the package on the SQL Server.

Running a package via the SQL Agent causes the package to execute on the SQL Server, which tends to minimize network load, but this can be a problem if the SQL Server does not have adequate resources to accommodate the often memory-hungry package.

Summary

Integration Services is a capable environment for building applications that move large quantities of data efficiently and for sequencing multi-step processing with error handling. Management features such as easy installation, auditing and logging facilities, and environment-specific configurations make Integration Services applications easy to live with once developed.

Many organizations have written reams of Transact-SQL and programmed custom applications to address tasks that Integration Services handles with ease. For those willing to make a small investment in learning the Integration Services environment, the cost savings and performance gains can be truly stunning.

The best way to get started is to choose a small project and dive in. Like any programming environment, the first application won't be perfect, but soon you'll wonder how you ever lived without Integration Services.

Chapter 38

Access as a Front End to SQL Server

Access was originally conceived as a standalone desktop database product, combining in one file a relational database engine (Jet) as well as user interface objects, such as forms, reports, macros, designers, and a VBA coding environment. Its very name, Access, denoted one of its most powerful features: the ability to easily incorporate data originating from heterogeneous data sources. When Access was introduced, installable ISAM drivers were used primarily for linking to the prevailing desktop databases, such as Paradox, dBase, and FoxPro, or to Lotus and Excel spreadsheets. An ODBC installable ISAM enables connecting to many server-based database systems, such as SQL Server and Oracle, and additional drivers have been added to connect to Microsoft Exchange Server data and to HTML tables. In Access 2003, Windows SharePoint Services support was added, which enabled linking to SharePoint lists, allowing them to be queried and updated as if they were standard relational tables.

Access 2007 introduced a new version of the Jet database engine, ACE, which is designed to support Access-specific features but is 100% backward compatible with Jet. When it comes to the mechanics of working with SQL Server, the underlying architecture is fundamentally the same as it was in Jet, so regardless of which version of Access you are using, the techniques for working with SQL Server data described in this chapter apply, except where otherwise noted. The Access 2007 user interface is designed to make working in the Access environment more intuitive for information workers, providing a more Excel-like experience in datasheet view, introducing powerful new filtering, sorting, and totaling features, along with improved designers for forms and reports.

CROSS-REF **For more in-depth information and ideas for getting the most out of using Access 2007 as a front end for your SQL Server data, see the Microsoft Office Access Vision white paper,** `http://office.microsoft.com/en-us/access/HA102133061033.aspx`.

IN THIS CHAPTER

Access–SQL Server use case scenarios

Migrating from Access to SQL Server

Designing your Access front end

Connecting to SQL Server

Monitoring and troubleshooting

Ad hoc querying and reporting

Access–SQL Server Use Case Scenarios

Using Access as a front end to SQL Server can be an optimal solution for a wide variety of business problems, often delivering the best return on investment while meeting the business requirements. The following are several scenarios in which Access has proven to be effective:

- The business problem does not warrant the expense of a full-fledged, end-to-end .NET solution.
- You want to empower users to solve their own problems. For example, executives and power users want to access server data to run their own analytics and create ad hoc reports.
- You need to deliver a solution in a time frame that does not allow for a lengthy development process.
- You work in an agile, iterative programming environment, and Access enables you to deliver prototypes quickly.
- Your application exists behind the corporate firewall where users are authenticated by Windows.
- You use Access as part of a hybrid application, such as a customer-facing web application created in ASP.NET with a data maintenance component that uses Access.
- You work with heterogeneous data from different vendors or data stores. For example, customer data is stored in relational SQL Server tables, while internal data may be stored in SharePoint lists. Access makes it simple to create data entry forms and reports based on queries that join this heterogeneous data.

Access projects or ODBC linked tables?

Access project files, also called ADPs or .adp files, provide an alternative to using the Access database engine by allowing an Access application to connect to the tables in a SQL Server database using OLE DB as an alternative to the Jet engine, which connects to SQL Server using ODBC. Because ADPs do not use a local database engine, they also do not support the use of local Access tables.

ADPs also provide visual designers for creating database objects in SQL Server. However, these features can become outdated as new versions of SQL Server are released. Microsoft recommends the use of Access databases with ODBC linked tables to connect to SQL Server data, which gives you the best performance in most situations and the widest set of features. For creating server-side objects, Microsoft recommends that you use a version of SQL Server that contains SQL Server Management Studio.

NOTE **If you are an Access developer who does not have access to one of the full versions of SQL Server, the SQL Server Developer Edition, which is priced at $49 U.S., contains all of the features and functionality of the Enterprise Edition. It has all the designers and tools you need to create and secure your server-side data objects, although there are some licensing restrictions.**

Migrating from Access to SQL Server

Successful Access database applications outlive their usefulness for a variety of reasons, and at some point you may decide that it's time to upgrade to a server database. Or perhaps your application has become indispensable to the business, and you need server-side features such as security, support for larger numbers of concurrent users, and reliability.

Migrating to SQL Server is not a panacea for problems that may have existed in the original Access application. In fact, the exact opposite is often true. It is not uncommon for a straight port of an Access application to run much more slowly when the data is in SQL Server. The Access Jet/ACE database engine and the SQL Server database engine are quite different, and what worked well in your Access application can cause problems when the data is moved to the server. Performance problems are magnified, not reduced, when server and network overhead are added to the mix.

You need to diagnose and thoroughly understand any problems with your Access application before you dive into migrating. Often issues like database corruption and poor performance can be fixed by taking simple measures to solve the problem in Access, removing the need to do a migration at all. In other cases, a complete rewrite from the ground up is required. Thoroughly understanding the problem will help you make the right decision, saving you time and money.

Once the decision is made, migrating data is actually the easiest and least complicated part of the process.

Resources for Migrating from Access to SQL Server

Rather than rewrite it all, some great resources are already available that will help you plan and implement a migration:

- Microsoft Access or SQL Server: What's Right in Your Organization? `http://download.microsoft.com/download/a/4/7/a47b7b0e-976d-4f49-b15d-f02ade638ebe/SQLAccessWhatsRight.doc`
- The SQL Server Migration Assistant for Access (SSMA Access) starter videos and FAQ `www.microsoft.com/sqlserver/2005/en/us/migration-access-learning.aspx`
- Move Access data to a SQL Server database by using the Upsizing Wizard `http://office.microsoft.com/en-us/access/HA102755371033.aspx?pid=CH101759711033`
- Use the Upsizing Wizard (Access 2003) `http://office.microsoft.com/en-us/access/HP052730091033.aspx`
- SQL Server Integration Services (SQL Server 2008 Books Online) `http://msdn.microsoft.com/en-us/library/ms141026.aspx`
- Microsoft Access to SQL Server Upsizing Center (resources from FMS, Inc.) `www.fmsinc.com/Consulting/sqlserverupsizing.aspx`

Designing Your Access Front End

When creating an Access application that connects to SQL Server, use the same general design principles that you would if you were creating a web application. Here are a few general suggestions:

- Fetch only needed data. Do not link to large tables or views.
- Perform data processing on the server, not the client.
- Normalize your database and create appropriate indexes.
- Do not use `SELECT *` without a `WHERE` clause, or allow users to do so. Create query-by-form user interfaces that force users to select criteria that reduce the size of result sets.
- Populate form elements such as list boxes and combo boxes when a user clicks on the control, not when the form loads. Otherwise, if you have a bound form with six combo boxes, then Access must run seven concurrent queries when the form opens.
- Take advantage of local Jet/ACE storage to cache static data that rarely changes.
- For editing data, create browse forms populated with read-only data. When the user selects a row to edit, load it read/write in a separate form.
- When creating reports, use pass-through queries to execute stored procedures, views, or user-defined functions that process aggregate data on the server.
- Do not use Access expressions or functions in queries. The function must run once for every row retrieved, slowing down processing. If you want to format the data, do so using expressions bound to form or report controls.
- If you want users to be able to create their own ad hoc queries without negatively impacting OLTP operations, create a separate set of "reporting tables" that they can query instead of the tables used in production. Reporting tables can be refreshed in the background or on demand.

CROSS-REF **If you want to maximize the performance and scalability of your Access–SQL Server applications, or just want a deeper understanding of the interactions between Access and SQL Server, the white paper "Optimizing Microsoft Office Access Applications Linked to SQL Server" (`http://msdn.microsoft.com/en-us/library/bb188204.aspx`) is indispensable. Many pitfalls can be avoided by understanding how Access interacts with SQL Server, freeing you to create rich Access client applications quickly and easily while treading lightly on your SQL Server.**

Connecting to SQL Server

There are several ways you can interact with SQL Server data from an Access client application:

- Through linked tables and views in the user interface
- Programmatically using VBA/ADO
- Using pass-through queries to bypass the Jet/ACE database engine. Pass-through queries are written in Transact-SQL and are passed directly to SQL Server without being syntax checked or parsed by Jet/ACE or ODBC. They always return read-only data.

Linking to tables and views

When you connect to a SQL Server database using the Access user interface, a wizard loads, prompting you for information about the ODBC database to which you want to connect. You have the option to import the data into a new table in the current Access database, or to link to the data source by creating a linked table. The wizard then asks you to select an ODBC driver (see Figure 38-1). If you are using SQL Server 2008, choose the SQL Server Native Client 10.0 driver.

FIGURE 38-1

Use the External Data tab on the ribbon to access the ODBC Administrator and specify a DSN to connect to SQL Server.

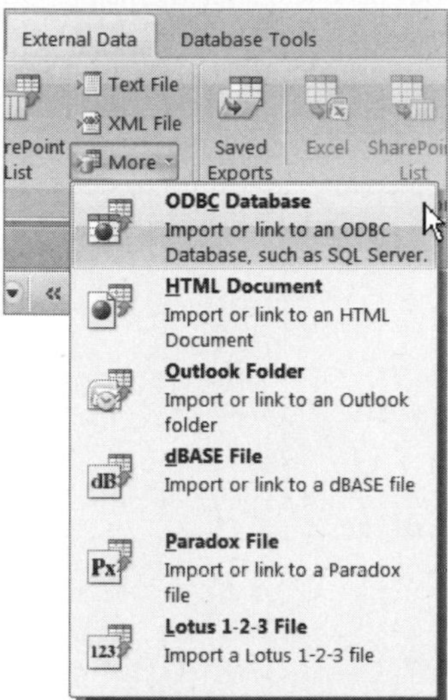

You are then prompted for additional information, such as the database name. Once the DSN is created, Access displays a list of tables to which you can link. You can then select one or more tables, which are displayed in the Access user interface using the underscore character to separate the schema name from the object name. For example, Sales.SalesOrderHeader will be displayed as Sales_SalesOrderHeader. If you are linking to a view, you will be prompted to designate a primary key, which Access requires in order for the view to be updatable.

Using DSNs to link to SQL Server tables is fine for quick-and-dirty linking, but DSNs are difficult to manage, so for applications you deploy to your users you may prefer to link using VBA code. There are several advantages to this:

- You can prompt the user for specific connection information, such as the name of a server or database.
- If you are using SQL logins, you can prompt for user credentials to avoid storing them on the local machine.
- You do not need to worry about copying or maintaining DSNs on different machines.

When you link to a SQL Server table in Access, Access caches connection information and metadata. If you make schema changes in SQL Server, the cached metadata will be invalid, and subsequent attempts to open the linked table will fail. A common technique to avoid this fate is to delete all links when you close the Access application, and relink tables on startup.

NOTE **When writing VBA code in Access, ADO (ActiveX Data Objects) is the preferred object model for working with SQL Server. However, the DAO (Data Access Objects) object model is more efficient and full-featured for working with Access objects, and tables linked to SQL Server are Access objects. So although you could use ADOX code to create links, the code presented in this chapter uses DAO.**

The DAO object model enables you to manipulate tables using the `DAO.Database` and `DAO.TableDef` objects. The following VBA function takes input parameters for the name of the linked table as it will appear in Access (you can specify any legal Access object name here), the name of the source table in SQL Server, and an ODBC connection string. The code checks to see if the linked table already exists in the local database's `TableDefs` collection; if it does, it deletes it and refreshes the collection. The code then creates a new `TableDef` object, using the connection string to connect to SQL Server and specifying the source table. The code appends the new `TableDef` to the `TableDefs` collection:

```
Public Function LinkTableDAO( _
    LinkedTableName As String, _
    SourceTableName As String, _
    ConnectionString As String) As Boolean

    ' Links or re-links a single table.
    ' Returns True or False based on Err value.

    Dim db As DAO.Database
    Dim tdf As DAO.TableDef

 On Error Resume Next
    Set db = CurrentDb

    ' Check to see if the table link already exists;
    ' if so, delete it
    Set tdf = db.TableDefs(LinkedTableName)
    If Err.Number = 0 Then
        db.TableDefs.Delete LinkedTableName
        db.TableDefs.Refresh
    Else
        ' Ignore error and reset
        Err.Number = 0
    End If

    Set tdf = db.CreateTableDef(LinkedTableName)
    ' Set the Connect and SourceTableName
    ' properties to establish the link
    tdf.Connect = ConnectionString
```

```
        tdf.SourceTableName = SourceTableName
        ' Append to the database's TableDefs collection
        db.TableDefs.Append tdf

        LinkTableDAO = (Err = 0)
    End Function
```

Caching data in local tables using pass-through queries

You can also easily create a routine to cache data in local tables that can be used as the source for combo boxes or other controls. Data can be refreshed when the application starts up, or on demand.

A pass-through query is not parsed or processed by Access or ODBC. It is passed directly to SQL Server for processing, which means it must be written using valid Transact-SQL syntax. Pass-through queries have a Returns Records property that you must set to Yes if you expect a result set.

To create a pass-through query in the Access 2007 user interface, execute the following steps:

1. Select the Create tab on the Ribbon.
2. Click the Query Design option in the Other section on the far right of the Ribbon.
3. When the Query Designer loads, click close.
4. At the far left, click SQL and type in your Transact-SQL `SELECT` statement.

You can also manipulate pass-through queries in code using a `DAO.QueryDef` object. The following procedure takes the name of the saved query that you want to modify, the SQL statement, the connection string, and a Boolean indicating whether the `QueryDef` will return records or not. The code sets the various properties of the `QueryDef` object:

```
Public Sub PassThroughFixup( _
  strQdfName As String, _
  strSQL As String, _
  strConnect As String, _
  fRetRecords As Boolean = True)

    Dim db As DAO.Database
    Dim qdf As DAO.QueryDef

    Set db = CurrentDb
    Set qdf = db.QueryDefs(strQdfName)
    If Len(strSQL) > 0 Then
        qdf.SQL = strSQL
    End If
    If Len(strConnect) > 0 Then
        qdf.Connect = strConnect
    End If
    qdf.ReturnsRecords = fRetRecords
    qdf.Close
    Set qdf = Nothing
End Sub
```

Once you have specified the Transact-SQL statement for the pass-through query, it can be used as the record source for a form or report, or invoked from another query. To insert the result set from a pass-through query directly into a local table, create an Access append (INSERT) query that uses the pass-through query as its data source:

```
INSERT INTO [LocalTableName] ( ColumnName )
SELECT ColumnName
FROM [NameOfPassThroughQuery];
```

You can invoke the whole process from VBA code, which can run on startup or on demand. The following routine uses the Execute method of the DAO.Database object to delete data from an existing table and then execute an Access append query to insert the refreshed data:

```
Public Sub RefreshLocal()
    Dim db As DAO.Database

    Set db = CurrentDb

    ' Delete existing data
    db.Execute "DELETE * FROM LocalTableName"

    ' Run the append query
    db.Execute "AppendFromPassthroughQuery"
End Sub
```

Extending the power of pass-through queries using table-valued parameters (TVPs)

Table-valued parameters (TVPs) are useful for marshalling multiple rows of data from a client application to SQL Server without requiring multiple round-trips or special server-side logic for processing the data. Normally you would work with TVPs directly in Transact-SQL code, or by using either ADO.NET or SQL Server Native Client objects. In ADO.NET, the SqlParameter class has been extended to take a DataTable object as a value. The SQL Server Native Client OLE DB API accomplishes the same thing by leveraging the COM IRowset interface along with a new implementation that allows buffering.

The downside for Access developers is that the ADO API has not been updated to support TVPs directly through ADO Parameter objects. Unless you want to program directly against the SQL Server Native Client API by declaring and calling API functions, that leaves you with a single option: pass-through queries running Transact-SQL, which you can modify programmatically using a DAO QueryDef object.

You've seen how pass-through queries can return data, but that feature is not available with TVPs — you must set the ReturnsRecords property to No or Access will raise an error. Unfortunately, this means that you will be unable to return any information whatsoever through the pass-through query mechanism. You will thus be unable to determine whether a transaction succeeded, get error information, or retrieve new identity values for inserted data. You need to devise other methods of determining the success or failure of the operation. In addition, you need to test and debug your Transact-SQL syntax using SQL Server Management Studio. The following example is extracted from the white paper "Using SQL Server 2008 Table-valued Parameters in Access 2007." See http://msdn.microsoft.com/en-us/library/dd721896.aspx.

The first step is to create the table-valued parameter type in SQL Server. This is the structure that holds the rows:

```
Use Northwind
GO
CREATE TYPE dbo.CategoryTableType AS TABLE
     ( CategoryName nvarchar(15), CategoryDescription ntext )
GO
```

Then you create the stored procedure that takes the new table type as an input parameter. Even though Access can't process the output parameter shown here, the assumption is that you can use the same stored procedure with clients that can, such as SqlClient. Note also that `SET NOCOUNT ON` is the first statement in the body of the stored procedure (this is important for client applications that cannot process multiple result sets, such as Access):

```
CREATE PROCEDURE dbo.usp_InsertCategory
(@tvpNewCategories dbo.CategoryTableType READONLY,
@ReturnMessage nvarchar(255) = NULL OUTPUT)

AS
SET NOCOUNT ON
BEGIN TRY
BEGIN TRAN
INSERT INTO dbo.Categories (CategoryName, Description)
SELECT CategoryName, CategoryDescription FROM @tvpNewCategories
IF @@ROWCOUNT = 0
RAISERROR ('No Categories inserted.', 16, 1)
COMMIT
SELECT @ReturnMessage='Categories inserted.';
END TRY

BEGIN CATCH
IF @@TRANCOUNT > 0
ROLLBACK
SELECT @ReturnMessage = ERROR_MESSAGE() +
' Severity=' + CAST(ERROR_SEVERITY() AS nvarchar(2))
END CATCH
GO
```

In Access, create a pass-through query and set the `ReturnsRecords` property to No. You can test by pasting the following Transact-SQL statements into the SQL pane of the query window and setting the Connect property to a valid connection string or DSN:

```
DECLARE @ReturnMessage nvarchar(255)
DECLARE @catType CategoryTableType
INSERT INTO @catType
EXEC ('
SELECT ''Organic'', ''Organically grown produce and grains''
SELECT ''Conventional'', ''Non-organically grown produce and grains''
```

```
SELECT ''Irish'', ''Mrs. O''''Leary''''s creamery products''
')
EXEC dbo.usp_InsertCategory @catType, @ReturnMessage OUTPUT;
SELECT @ReturnMessage as ReturnMessage
```

You need to handle the string processing in your VBA code to avoid syntax errors with apostrophes and single quotes using the VBA Replace function. Packaging up the multiple rows in your VBA code requires a fair amount of work, but the added efficiency of processing multiple rows at once may be worth it for some scenarios.

Monitoring and Troubleshooting

A major cause of query performance degradation is that a query involving very large tables can require that all of the data from one or more tables be downloaded to the client. This occasionally happens, even when joins or criteria appear to limit the result set to a small number of records, if the Access database engine determines that it cannot submit the entire query to SQL Server in one call. Instead, it submits multiple queries which sometimes request all of the rows in a table, and then it combines or filters data on the client.

If any of the criteria in a query require local processing, such as invoking Access expressions or VBA functions, then even single-call queries that should return only selected rows can require all of the rows in the table to be returned for local processing of the criteria. There are two tools you can use to monitor and troubleshoot the commands that Access is submitting to SQL Server: SQL Server Profiler and ODBC Trace.

SQL Server Profiler is indispensable for understanding the interaction between your Access front end and SQL Server. Selecting a Profiler template that shows Transact-SQL statements being processed by the server enables you to analyze the commands that Access is submitting. SQL Server Profiler is described in detail in Chapter 56, "Tracing and Profiling." You can also enable ODBC Trace to log queries submitted to any ODBC data source, which is useful for tracing Access database engine behavior.

CROSS-REF **The most comprehensive information describing how Access interacts with SQL Server — and how to work with SQL Server Profiler and ODBC Trace — is contained in the white paper "Optimizing Microsoft Office Access Applications Linked to SQL Server," which can be found at** `http://msdn.microsoft.com/en-us/library/bb188204.aspx`.

Ad Hoc Querying and Reporting

If you are familiar only with earlier versions of Access, Access 2007 may come as a surprise. The user interface has been completely rewritten with the goal of making Access easier to use for business users who are not developers or database professionals. When you launch Access 2007 for the first time, you will see a link to the Guide to the Access 2007 User Interface, or you can launch it directly from `http://office.microsoft.com/en-us/access/HA100398921033.aspx`. The remainder of this section assumes that you are familiar with the basic features of the new user interface, and jumps directly into using them to access SQL Server data.

Access 2007 makes it extremely easy for power users to create their own queries and reports, and with a minimal amount of time and effort a developer can quickly cobble together forms and reports using the built-in wizards and toolbars. For more comprehensive solutions, download one of the Access templates from the Access download center. Although Access 2007 is optimized around the Access Database Engine (ACE), you can easily switch the data store to SQL Server, as discussed earlier in this chapter.

Pre-aggregating data on the server

In many situations it will not be desirable for users to link directly to tables. In those situations, you can create views or stored procedures to filter or pre-aggregate data so that users do not have to create queries involving joins or aggregate functions. If you have large tables, you can also create separate "reporting tables" and export data from the base tables at regular intervals. In some situations you might want to export data to an Access database engine table, which is easily done from Access by using append queries or by importing into new tables. If your database is locked down and the base tables are not directly accessible, then exporting data to a separate database or invoking stored procedures from pass-through queries are also options.

Sorting and filtering data

Access 2007 introduces context-sensitive sorting and filtering, which can be a powerful tool for users who are unaccustomed to writing queries.

Once the tables or views are linked in Access, you can open them in datasheet view and work with the data interactively using the right-click menus and the Ribbon, which is shown in Figure 38-2.

FIGURE 38-2

Filtering and sorting options are on the Home tab of the Ribbon.

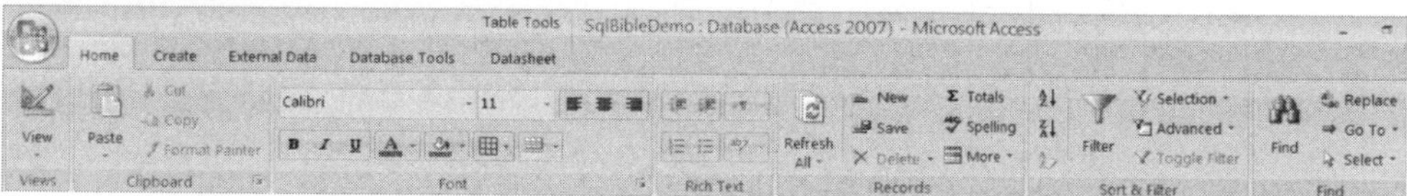

However, instead of using the Ribbon, it's often easier to use the right-click menus to access sorting and filtering. Figure 38-3 shows how you can quickly sort the Sales.vSalesPersonSalesByFiscalYears view from `AdventureWorks2008` in datasheet view after right-clicking on the column head SalesTerritory.

When filtering text data, the actual value is loaded into the filter options, as shown in Figure 38-4. You can further refine the filter with partial string values. For example, you could specify "Tool" in the Does Not Begin With dialog, which loads if that option is selected in the far-right fly-out menu.

Filtering on numbers enables you to specify several different operators, as shown in Figure 38-5. Operators such as Not Equals are different in Access and SQL Server, although these differences are transparent to the user querying the data.

FIGURE 38-3

Right-clicking on a column shows options for sorting as well as formatting columns. You can also drag the vertical lines separating the columns to resize or hide them.

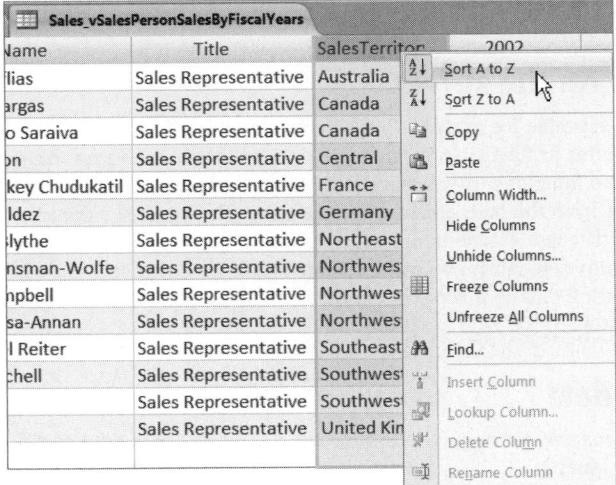

FIGURE 38-4

Filtering options for text fields include being able to specify parts of strings, not just whole words.

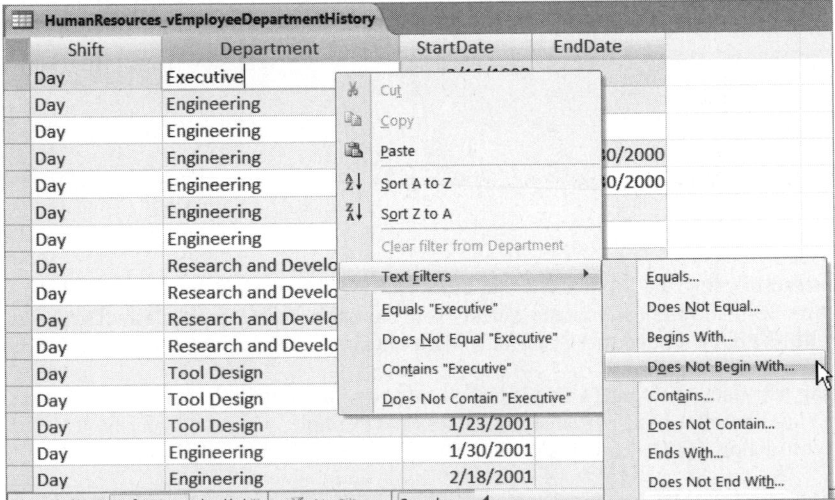

FIGURE 38-5

Specifying numeric filters in the Access UI masks syntax differences between Access and Transact-SQL.

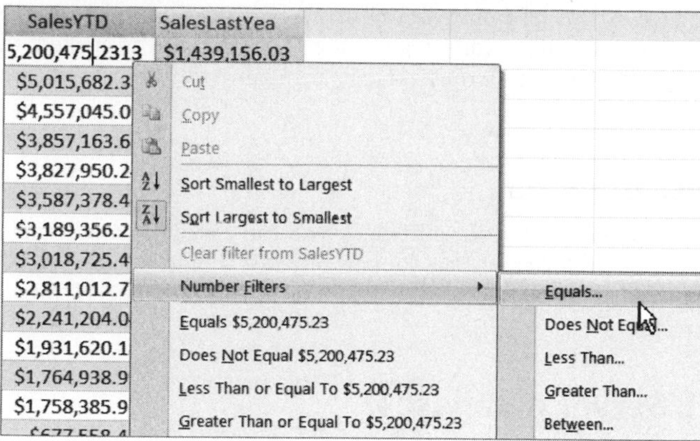

Filtering on dates is especially powerful. Not only do you get the usual operators, but you also can specify quarters or months, as shown in Figure 38-6.

FIGURE 38-6

Filtering on date values is simple, flexible, and powerful.

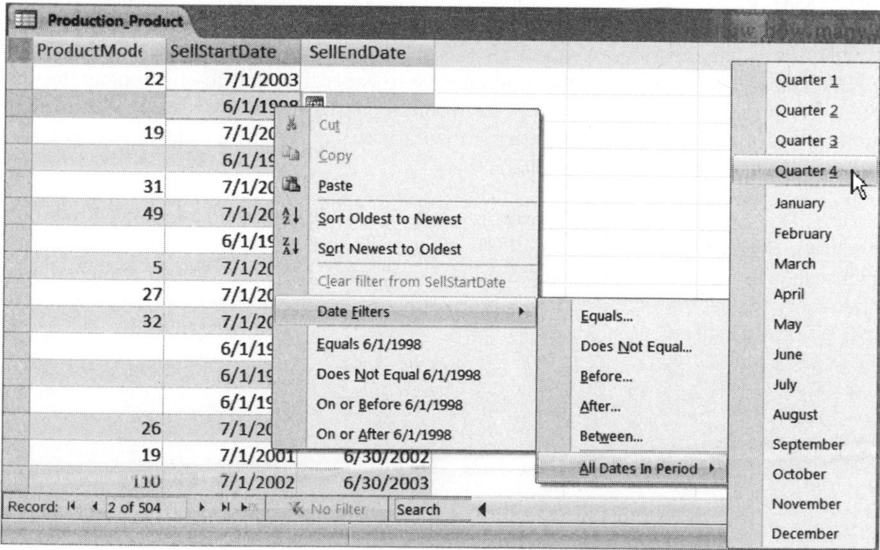

Creating forms and reports

Access makes it easy for users to create forms and reports based on linked tables or views by selecting the table or view in the Access database window and selecting one of the wizards or templates on the Create toolbar Ribbon. You can also expose read-only data returned by stored procedures by creating pass-through queries that call them, as described earlier. Once the form or report is created, the Format Ribbon automatically loads, enabling you to format controls manually or choose from a variety of AutoFormats.

Exporting and publishing data

Another powerful feature in Access 2007 is the ease with which you can export data, not only from datasheet view but also from reports. The External Data Ribbon provides a graphical user interface to save or export reports to formats such as Excel, PDF, XPS, .RTF, XML, text files, and HTML. You can also move the data to SharePoint lists.

Managing your SQL Server databases

Even if you choose not to expose Access functionality and features to your end users for security or performance reasons, Access can be tremendously useful as an administrative tool for managing the databases on a SQL Server instance. A single Access front end can contain links to tables, views, information schema views, and other objects in multiple databases. Behind a firewall or on a secured share where there is little risk of penetration, Access can provide a handy supplement to the SQL Server UI tools.

Summary

For DBAs and line-of-business users who simply want to create their own ad hoc queries and reports, Access 2007 can provide a quick, low-cost alternative to expensive, end-to-end programmed applications that could take months or years to develop. Such solutions can augment existing .NET or Reporting Services applications, or they can empower users to work with the intuitive, built-in Access Ribbon features for sorting, filtering, and manipulating data.

For scenarios that require more control over user behavior and increased scalability, VBA code and pass-though queries enable developers to create secure, efficient Access applications, often in much less time than would be required using Visual Studio. Access has long been wrongly maligned as a “toy,” when the reality is that, correctly used, it is potentially one of the most powerful and useful tools in any developer or DBA’s toolbox.

Part VI

Enterprise Data Management

This part is about the enterprise DBA role.

The project isn't done when the production database goes live. A successful database requires preventive maintenance (tune-ups) and corrective maintenance (diligent recovery planning).

The Information Architecture Principle introduced in Chapter 1 presented the idea that information must be secured and made readily available for daily operations by individuals, groups, and processes, both today and in the future.

While SQL Server is more automated than ever before, and Microsoft sometimes makes the error of presenting SQL Server as the database that doesn't require a DBA, the truth is that it takes diligent work to keep a production database up 24 hours a day, 7 days a week, 365 days a year.

If SQL Server is the box, Part VI is about making sure the box holds its shape, day after day.

IN THIS PART

Chapter 39

Configuring SQL Server

IN THIS CHAPTER

SQL Server has a plethora of configuration options. The difficulty in mastering them lies in the fact that they are spread across three levels:

- Server-level options generally configure how the server works with hardware, and determine the database defaults.
- Database-level options determine the behavior of the database, and set the connection-level defaults.
- Connection-level options determine the current behaviors within the connection or current procedure.

Several of the configuration options overlap or simply set the default for the level immediately below. This chapter pulls these three configuration levels into a single unified understanding of how they relate to and affect each other. This chapter does not cover every single SQL Server configuration option but it covers most of them that I think are important. If you are a SQL Server beginner, you may find that some of the configuration options are advanced and you may not need them immediately.

Setting the Options

Whether you choose to adjust the properties from SQL Server Management Studio's graphical tool or from code is completely up to you, but not every property is available from Management Studio using the graphical interface. While the graphical interface has the advantage of being easy to use, and walks you through easily understood dialogs that prompt for the possible options in a pick-and-choose format, it lacks the repeatability of a T-SQL script run as a query.

TIP **To view miscellaneous information about the computer system while configuring SQL Server, query the** `sys.dm_os_sys_info` **dynamic management view.**

New in SQL Server 2008 Configuration

SQL Server 2008 offers many new configuration options, such as `backup compression default` and `filestream access level`, that give the SQL DBA much more control in configuring SQL Server 2008.

The configuration options `set working set size`, `open objects`, and `locks` are still present in the `sp_configure` stored procedure, but their functionality is unavailable in SQL Server 2008. These options have no effect.

Configuring the server

The server-level configuration options control server-wide settings, such as how SQL Server interacts with hardware, how it multi-threads within Windows, and whether triggers are permitted to fire other triggers. When configuring the server, keep in mind the goals of configuration: consistency and performance.

Graphically, many of the server options may be configured within the Server Properties page, which you can open by right-clicking a server in the console tree and choosing Properties from the context menu. The General tab in Management Studio's SQL Server Properties dialog (see Figure 39-1) reports the versions and environment of the server.

The same information is available to code. For example, the version may be identified with the `@@VERSION` global variable:

```
select @@VERSION;
```

Result:

```
Microsoft SQL Server 2008 (RTM) - 10.0.1600.22 (Intel X86)
        Jul  9 2008 14:43:34
        Copyright (c) 1988-2008 Microsoft Corporation
        Enterprise Edition on Windows NT 5.2 <X86> (Build 3790: Service
Pack 2)
```

The first line of the preceding result includes the product version of SQL Server. In this example, the SQL Server product version is 10.0.1600.22. The last line of the result can be confusing. It reports the edition of SQL Server. In this example, it is SQL Server 2008 Enterprise Edition, but the service pack reported in the last line is the Windows service pack level and not the SQL Server service pack level. In this example, it is SP2 for Windows Server 2003. That is one of the reasons why I don't like to use the `SELECT @@VERSION` command. Instead, I prefer to use the `SERVERPROPERTY` system function to determine the information. The advantage of this method is that the function may be used as an expression within a `SELECT` statement. The following example uses the `SERVERPROPERTY` function to return the SQL Server product version, product level, and edition:

```
SELECT
SERVERPROPERTY('ProductVersion') AS ProductVersion,
SERVERPROPERTY('ProductLevel') AS ProductLevel,
SERVERPROPERTY('Edition') AS Edition;
```

FIGURE 39-1

The General tab of Management Studio's Server Properties dialog

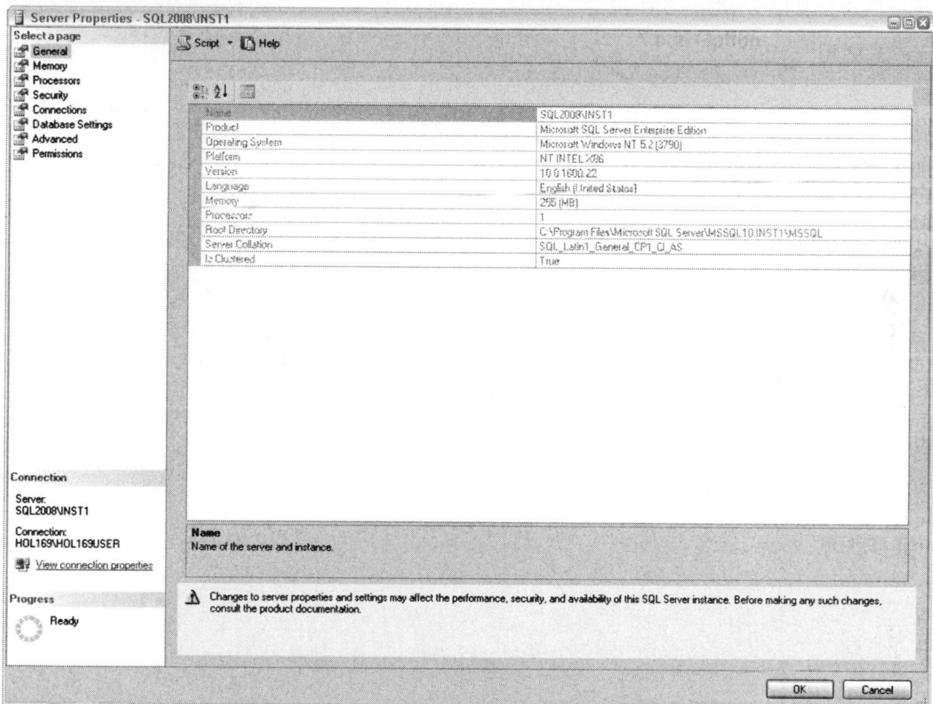

Result:

```
ProductVersion  ProductLevel Edition
10.0.1600.22  RTM  Enterprise Edition
```

In the preceding result, the `ProductVersion` indicates the SQL Server product version number. The `ProductLevel` indicates the SQL Server product level. At the time of writing this chapter, we did not have any service packs for SQL Server 2008 and the product level is `RTM` (Release to Manufacturing). If a SQL Server service pack is installed, the product level will indicate the service pack level too. For example, if you run the preceding command against your SQL Server 2005 SP3 instance, the `ProductLevel` will return SP3. The `Edition` indicates the SQL Server edition.

NOTE **Many of the configuration properties do not take effect until SQL Server is restarted, so the General tab in the SQL Server Properties (Configure) dialog box displays the current running values.**

Within code, many of the server properties are set by means of the `sp_configure` system stored procedure. When executed without any parameters, this procedure reports the current settings, as in the following code (word-wrap adjusted to fit on the page):

```
EXEC sp_configure;
```

Result:

```
name                              minimum   maximum      config_value
run_value
------------------------------ --------- ----------- ------------
allow updates                     0         1            0            0
backup compression default        0         1            0            0
clr enabled                       0         1            0            0
cross db ownership chaining       0         1            0            0
default language                  0         9999         0            0
filestream access level           0         2            2            2
max text repl size (B)            -1        2147483647   65536        65536
nested triggers                   0         1            1            1
remote access                     0         1            1            1
remote admin connections          0         1            0            0
remote login timeout (s)          0         2147483647   20           20
remote proc trans                 0         1            0            0
remote query timeout (s)          0         2147483647   600          600
server trigger recursion          0         1            1            1
show advanced options             0         1            0            0
user options                      0         32767        0            0
```

NOTE **You can always discover the minimum and maximum values for a particular configuration option by running the `sp_configure` command with the option, but without any value. For example, run**

```
EXEC sp_configure 'remote login timeout';
```

and you'll discover that the `remote login timeout` configuration option can have any value in the range of 0 to 2,147,483,647.

The extended stored procedure `xp_msver` reports additional server and environment properties:

```
EXEC xp_msver;
```

Result:

```
Index  Name                   Internal_Value Character_Value
1      ProductName            NULL           Microsoft SQL Server
2      ProductVersion         655360         10.0.1600.22
3      Language               1033           English (United States)
4      Platform               NULL           NT INTEL X86
5      Comments               NULL           SQL
6      CompanyName            NULL           Microsoft Corporation
7      FileDescription        NULL           SQL Server Windows NT
8      FileVersion            NULL           2007.0100.1600.022
((SQL_PreRelease).080709-1414 )
9      InternalName           NULL           SQLSERVR
10     LegalCopyright         NULL           Microsoft Corp. All
```

```
rights reserved.
11      LegalTrademarks              NULL          Microsoft SQL Server is
a registered trademark of Microsoft Corporation.
12      OriginalFilename             NULL          SQLSERVR.EXE
13      PrivateBuild                 NULL          NULL
14      SpecialBuild                 116588544     NULL
15      WindowsVersion               393281542     5.2 (3790)
16      ProcessorCount               1             1
17      ProcessorActiveMask          1             00000001
18      ProcessorType                586           PROCESSOR_INTEL_PENTIUM
19      PhysicalMemory               2046          2046 (2145845248)
20      Product ID                   NULL          NULL
```

The information returned by `sp_configure` is settable, but the information returned by `xp_msver` is not.

Configuring the database

The database-level options configure the current database's behavior regarding ANSI compatibility and recovery.

Most database options can be set in Management Studio within the Database Properties page, which you can access by right-clicking a database in the console tree and choosing Properties from the context menu. The Options tab is shown in Figure 39-2.

The database configuration options can be set using T-SQL `ALTER DATABASE SET` options. The following example sets the `AdventureWorks2008` database to single-user mode to obtain exclusive access:

```
ALTER DATABASE AdventureWorks2008 SET SINGLE_USER;
```

View database configuration options using the `sys.databases` catalog view or the `DATABASEPROPERTYEX()` function. The following example returns all the database properties of the `AdventureWorks2008` database:

```
SELECT * FROM sys.databases WHERE name = 'AdventureWorks2008';
```

Do not use the `sp_dboption` system stored procedure, as it will be removed in the next version of SQL Server.

Configuring the connection

Many of the connection-level options configure ANSI compatibility or specific connection-performance options.

Connection-level options are very limited in scope. If the option is set within an interactive session, then the setting is in force until it's changed or the session ends. If the option is set within a stored procedure, then the setting persists only for the life of that stored procedure.

FIGURE 39-2

Management Studio's Database Properties Options tab can be used to configure the most common database properties

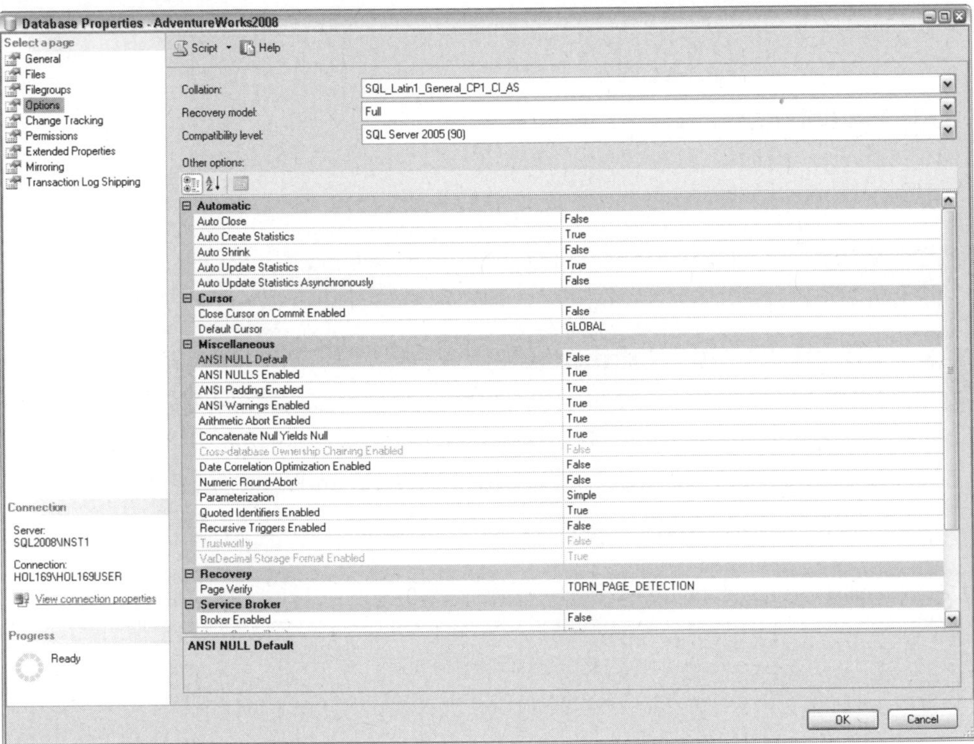

The connection-level options are typically configured by means of the SET command. The following code configures how SQL Server handles nulls within this current session:

```
SET ANSI_NULLS OFF;
```

Result:

```
Command(s) completed successfully.
```

Connection properties can also be checked by means of the SessionProperty() function:

```
Select SESSIONPROPERTY ('ANSI_NULLS');
```

Result:

```
0
```

Management Studio allows you to set several query properties. You can review and set these properties for current queries by clicking the Query menu and then Query Options. For all future connections, review and set the properties by clicking the Tools menu and then Options. Figure 39-3 shows an example of the ANSI settings that SQL Server will use to run the queries.

To view current settings of connection-level options, query the `sys.dm_exec_connections` **dynamic management view.**

FIGURE 39-3

The ANSI settings that SQL Server uses to run your queries

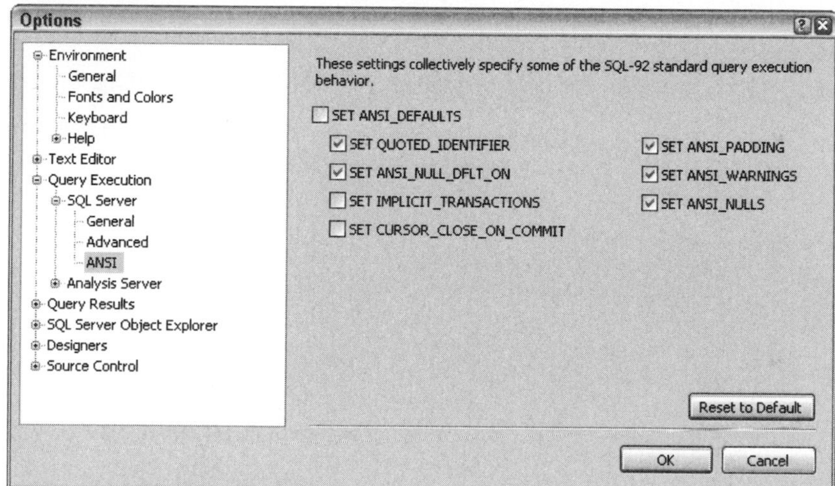

Configuration Options

Because so many similar configuration options are controlled by different commands and at different levels (server, database, connection), this section organizes the configuration options by topic, rather than command or level.

Displaying the advanced options

As with many operations, displaying advanced options can be achieved using several methods. One method is to query the `sys.configurations` catalog view as shown here:

```
SELECT   name, minimum, maximum, value, value_in_use
FROM     sys.configurations
WHERE    is_advanced = 1
ORDER BY name;
```

The preceding example will display all the SQL Server advanced options. To display all the options, comment the WHERE clause. Another method to display the advanced options is to turn on the show advanced options configuration, as follows:

```
EXEC sp_configure 'show advanced options', 1;
RECONFIGURE;
```

NOTE **After a configuration setting is changed with sp_configure, the RECONFIGURE command causes the changes to take effect. If you don't run RECONFIGURE, then the config_value field will still show the change, but the change won't appear in the run_value field, even if you restart the service. Some configuration changes take effect only after SQL Server is restarted.**

After you enable the advanced option display, you can use the sp_configure command to display a list of all of the options:

```
EXEC sp_configure;
```

Result (with advanced options enabled):

```
name                                minimum     maximum     config_value
run_value
----------------------------------- ----------- ----------- ------------
-----------
access check cache bucket count     0           16384       0            0
access check cache quota            0           2147483647  0            0
Ad Hoc Distributed Queries          0           1           0            0
affinity I/O mask                   -2147483648 2147483647  0            0
affinity64 I/O mask                 -2147483648 2147483647  0            0
affinity mask                       -2147483648 2147483647  0            0
affinity64 mask                     -2147483648 2147483647  0            0

Agent XPs                           0           1           1            1
allow updates                       0           1           0            0
awe enabled                         0           1           0            0
backup compression default          0           1           0            0
blocked process threshold (s)       0           86400       0            0
c2 audit mode                       0           1           0            0
clr enabled                         0           1           0            0
common criteria compliance enabled  0           1           0            0
cost threshold for parallelism      0           32767       5            5
cross db ownership chaining         0           1           0            0
cursor threshold                    -1          2147483647  -1           -1
Database Mail XPs                   0           1           0            0
default full-text language          0           2147483647  1033
1033
default language                    0           9999        0            0
default trace enabled               0           1           1            1
disallow results from triggers      0           1           0            0
EKM provider enabled                0           1           0            0
```

```
filestream access level          0       2           2           2
fill factor (%)                  0       100         0           0
ft crawl bandwidth (max)         0       32767       100         100

ft crawl bandwidth (min)         0       32767       0           0
ft notify bandwidth (max)        0       32767       100         100

ft notify bandwidth (min)        0       32767       0           0
index create memory (KB)         704     2147483647  0           0
in-doubt xact resolution         0       2           0           0
lightweight pooling              0       1           0           0
locks                            5000    2147483647  0           0
max degree of parallelism        0       64          0           0
max full-text crawl range        0       256         4           4
max server memory (MB)           16      2147483647  2147483647
2147483647
max text repl size (B)           -1      2147483647  65536
65536
max worker threads               128     32767       0           0
media retention                  0       365         0           0
min memory per query (KB)        512     2147483647  1024
1024
min server memory (MB)           0       2147483647  0           0
nested triggers                  0       1           1           1
network packet size (B)          512     32767       4096
4096
Ole Automation Procedures        0       1           0           0
open objects                     0       2147483647  0           0
optimize for ad hoc workloads    0       1           0           0
PH timeout (s)                   1       3600        60          60
precompute rank                  0       1           0           0
priority boost                   0       1           0           0
query governor cost limit        0       2147483647  0           0
query wait (s)                   -1      2147483647  -1          -1
recovery interval (min)          0       32767       0           0
remote access                    0       1           1           1
remote admin connections         0       1           0           0
remote login timeout (s)         0       2147483647  20          20
remote proc trans                0       1           0           0
remote query timeout (s)         0       2147483647  600
600
Replication XPs                  0       1           0           0
scan for startup procs           0       1           0           0
server trigger recursion         0       1           1           1
set working set size             0       1           0           0
show advanced options            0       1           1           1
SMO and DMO XPs                  0       1           1           1
SQL Mail XPs                     0       1           0           0
transform noise words            0       1           0           0
```

```
two digit year cutoff                    1753       9999       2049
2049
user connections                         0          32767      0          0
user options                             0          32767      0          0
xp_cmdshell                              0          1          0          0
```

NOTE **The key difference between the preceding two methods to display advanced options is that the `sys.configurations` catalog view only displays the configurations. The `show advanced options` configuration not only controls the display of advanced options through `sp_configure` system stored procedure, it also controls whether these advanced options can be changed.**

Start/Stop configuration properties

The startup configuration properties, described in Table 39-1, control how SQL Server and the processes are launched.

Startup parameters

You use the startup parameters with the SQL Server services. The startup parameters are passed as parameters to the SQL Server program when the SQL Server service is started. Although you can add startup parameters from the Services console, I highly recommend using the SQL Server Configuration Manager, shown in Figure 39-4. One of the main reasons has to do with minimizing downtime. The Configuration Manager allows you to add startup parameters with the SQL Server service still running. You can restart the service during a maintenance window and minimize downtime. Also, the Configuration Manager is the only method for a SQL Server failover clustering instance, as it is a cluster-aware tool, whereas the Services console is not.

TABLE 39-1

Start/Stop Configuration Properties

Property	Level*	Graphic Control	Code Option
AutoStart SQL Server	S	Configuration Manager, or Services Console	-
AutoStart SQL Server Agent	S	Configuration Manager, or Services Console	-
AutoStart MS DTC	S	Services Console	-
Scan for startup procs	S	-	`EXEC sp_configure 'scan for startup procs'`

* The configuration level refers to Server, Database, or Connection.

FIGURE 39-4

Add startup parameters to the SQL Server service to change its behavior

To add the startup parameters in SQL Server Configuration Manager:

1. Open SQL Server Configuration Manager from Start ➪ Programs ➪ Microsoft SQL Server 2008 ➪ Configuration Tools ➪ SQL Server Configuration Manager.
2. Click SQL Server Services under SQL Server Configuration Manager.
3. Right-click the SQL Server service (on the right-hand side) to which you want to add startup parameters and select the Advanced tab.
4. On the Advanced tab, in the Startup Parameters box, type the startup parameters separated by semicolons (refer to Figure 39-4).

Besides the standard master database location parameters, two parameters are particularly useful:

- `-m`: Starts SQL Server in single-user mode. This is required to restore the master database.
- `-f`: Used to start up with a minimal configuration

Additional startup parameters are as follows:

- `-d`: Used to include the full path of the master database file, with no spaces between the `d` and the path
- `-l`: Used to include the full path of the master database log file, with no spaces between the `l` and the path

- -e: Used to include the full path of the SQL Server error log file, with no spaces between the e and the path
- -c: Starts SQL Server so that it is not running as a Windows service
- -x : Allows maximum performance by disabling monitoring features. Because the monitoring features are disabled, your ability to troubleshoot performance and functional problems will be greatly reduced.
- -g: Specifies virtual memory (in MB) available to SQL Server for memory allocations within the SQL Server process, but outside the SQL Server memory pool (extended procedure .dll files, the OLE DB providers referenced by distributed queries, and automation objects referenced in Transact-SQL statements)
- -n: Disables logging to the Windows application log
- -s: Used to start a named instance of SQL Server. The instance name follows directly after the s, with no spaces in between.
- -Ttrace#: Enables trace-specific flags by trace flag number. Refer to the SQL Server 2008 Books Online topic "Trace Flags" for documented trace flags. I do not recommend using trace flags for an extended period of time. I usually use trace flags for troubleshooting SQL Server issues and then remove them once the issue is resolved. Also, never use undocumented trace flags, as they can cause more damage, rather than assist you in solving any issue.
- -h: Assuming your hardware allows you to add physical memory without restarting the server, use this option to enable SQL Server to immediately begin using the hot-add memory. This is only available on SQL Server Enterprise Edition and can be used on 64-bit SQL Server and 32-bit SQL Server with AWE enabled.

Startup stored procedures

SQL Server can be configured to scan for a startup stored procedure every time the SQL Server starts — similar to how Microsoft DOS operating systems scan for the autoexec.bat file when they boot up. All the startup procedures need to be in the master database but there is no limit on the number of startup procedures. The key is to remember that each startup procedure will consume one worker thread while executing it. To mark an existing stored procedure to execute automatically when SQL Server starts, use the sp_procoption system stored procedure as follows:

```
EXEC sp_procoption @ProcName = 'ExistingSP',
              @OptionName = 'startup',
              @OptionValue = 'on';
```

You use the same sp_procoption system stored procedure to stop a stored procedure from executing at SQL Server startup:

```
EXEC sp_procoption @ProcName = 'ExistingSP',
              @OptionName = 'startup',
              @OptionValue = 'off';
```

Although you can individually mark a stored procedure for automatic execution at SQL Server startup, you can further control the execution of all the startup stored procedures by using the scan for startup procs configuration option. If this option is set to 1, SQL Server scans for and runs all stored procedures marked for automatic execution at startup. The default value of this option is 0, which skips automatic execution of startup stored procedures. The `scan for startup procs` configuration option is automatically set to 1 when you execute `sp_procoption` to mark the first stored procedure for automatic execution, and is set to 0 when you unmark the last stored procedure for automatic execution. The following code can be used to skip automatic execution for all startup stored procedures:

```
EXEC sp_configure 'scan for startup procs', 0;
RECONFIGURE;
```

Memory-configuration properties

SQL Server can either dynamically request memory from the operating system or consume a fixed amount of memory. These settings can be configured on the SQL Server Properties Memory tab, shown in Figure 39-5, or from code by means of the `sp_configure` stored procedure.

FIGURE 39-5

Memory tab of Management Studio's SQL Server Properties dialog

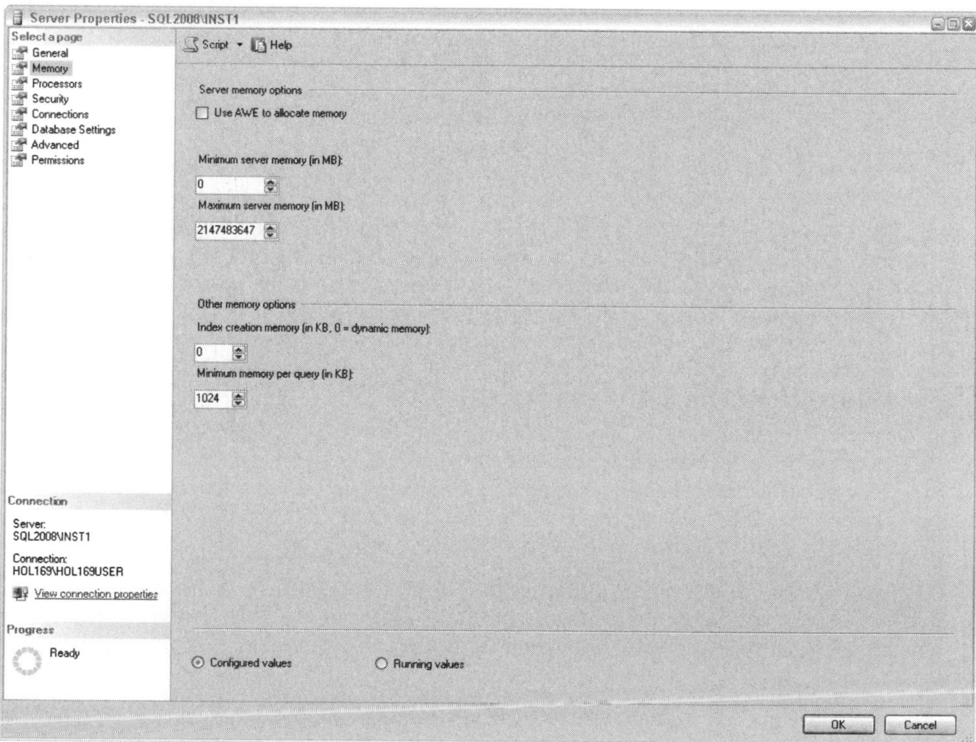

The memory-configuration properties, listed in Table 39-2, control how SQL Server uses and allocates memory.

TABLE 39-2

Memory-Configuration Properties

Property	Level*	Graphic Control	Code Option
Dynamic Memory Minimum	S	Management Studio	`EXEC sp_configure 'min server memory'`
Dynamic Memory Maximum	S	Management Studio	`EXEC sp_configure 'max server memory'`
Fixed Memory Size	S	Management Studio	`EXEC sp_configure 'min server memory'` and `EXEC sp_configure 'max server memory'`
Minimum Query Memory	S	Management Studio	`EXEC sp_configure 'min memory per query'`
Query Wait	S	Management Studio	`EXEC sp_configure 'query wait'`
AWE Enabled	S	Management Studio	`EXEC sp_configure 'AWE Enabled'`
Index Create Memory	S	Management Studio	`EXEC sp_configure 'index create memory'`

* The configuration level refers to Server, Database, or Connection.

NOTE **The configuration options `set working set size`, `open objects`, and `locks` are still present in the `sp_configure` stored procedure, but their functionality is unavailable in Microsoft SQL Server 2008. These options have no effect. Do not use them in new development work, as they may be removed in future SQL Server versions.**

Dynamic memory

If SQL Server is set to use memory dynamically, then SQL Server's memory can grow or be reduced as needed within the minimum and maximum constraints based on the physical memory available and the workload. The goal is to have enough memory available while avoiding Windows needing to swap pages from memory to the virtual-memory support file (`pagefile.sys`).

The minimum-memory property prohibits SQL Server from reducing memory below a certain point and hurting performance, but it does not guarantee that SQL Server will immediately allocate the minimum amount of memory at startup. The minimum simply means that once SQL Server memory has reached that point, it will not reduce memory below it.

The maximum-memory setting prevents SQL Server from growing to the point where it contends with the operating system, or other applications, for memory. If the maximum is set too low, then performance will suffer.

Multiple SQL Server instances do not cooperate when requiring memory. In servers with multiple instances, it's highly possible for two busy instances to contend for memory and for one to become memory-starved. Reducing the maximum-memory property for each instance can prevent this from happening.

From T-SQL code, the minimum- and maximum-memory properties are set by means of the `sp_configure` system stored procedure. It's an advanced option, so it can be changed only if the `show advanced options` property is on:

```
EXEC sp_configure 'show advanced options', 1;
RECONFIGURE;
```

NOTE **The** `show advanced options` **property needs to be enabled only if it is not already turned on. Once it is turned on, you can change the advanced options and then reset it to the default value of 0.**

The following code sets the min-memory configuration to 1GB:

```
EXEC sp_configure 'min server memory', 1024;
RECONFIGURE;
```

Result:

```
Configuration option 'min server memory (MB)'
   changed from 0 to 1024.
Run the RECONFIGURE statement to install.
```

This code sets the max-memory configuration to 4GB:

```
EXEC sp_configure 'max server memory', 4096;
RECONFIGURE;
```

Result:

```
Configuration option 'max server memory (MB)'
   changed from 2147483647 to 4096.
Run the RECONFIGURE statement to install.
```

Fixed memory

Instead of dynamically consuming memory, SQL Server may be configured to request a fixed amount of memory from the operating system. To set a fixed amount of memory from code, set the minimum- and maximum-memory properties to the same value. The following code sets the SQL Server memory to a fixed memory of 6144MB:

```
EXEC sp_configure 'show advanced options', 1;
RECONFIGURE;
EXEC sp_configure 'min server memory', 6144;
RECONFIGURE;
EXEC sp_configure 'max server memory', 6144;
RECONFIGURE;
```

Although calculating memory cost, polling the environment, and requesting memory may seem as if they would require overhead, you aren't likely to see any performance gains from switching from dynamic to fixed memory. The primary purpose of using fixed memory is to configure a dedicated SQL Server computer to use a fixed amount of memory after the value is reached.

Minimum query memory

At times, the SQL Server team amazes me with the level of detailed control it passes to DBAs. SQL Server will allocate the required memory for each query as needed. The `min memory per query` option sets the minimum threshold for the memory (in KB) used by each query. While increasing this property to a value higher than the default 1MB may provide slightly better performance for some queries, there is no reason to override SQL Server automatic memory control and risk causing a memory shortage. If you insist on doing so, however, here's how — the following code increases the minimum query memory to 2MB:

```
EXEC sp_configure 'show advanced options', 1;
RECONFIGURE;
EXEC sp_configure 'min memory per query', 2048;
RECONFIGURE;
```

Query wait

If the memory is unavailable to execute a large query, SQL Server will wait for the estimated amount of time necessary to execute the query times 25 and then time out.

Usually, you don't need to change the `query wait` time, but if you have a valid reason to change this option, you can either use Management Studio or TSQL-code. In Management Studio, set the `query wait` option by entering the value in the "query wait" box in the Server Properties Advanced tab (refer to Figure 39-9 later in this chapter).

The following code specifies that every query will either start executing within 20 seconds or time out:

```
EXEC sp_configure 'show advanced options', 1;
RECONFIGURE;
EXEC sp_configure 'query wait', 20;
RECONFIGURE;
```

Note that to revert to the default wait time of the estimated execution time times 25, you must specify the query wait time as -1.

AWE enabled

On 32-bit operating systems, SQL Server is normally restricted to the standard 2GB physical-memory limit (or 3GB if the `/3GB` switch is used in `boot.ini`). On 64-bit operating systems, the `awe enabled` option is ignored even though it is present in the `sp_configure` stored procedure.

SQL Server x86 Standard, Enterprise, and Developer Editions, when running on Windows Server 2003 or 2008 Enterprise or Datacenter Editions, can use up to 64GB of physical memory if SQL Server is configured to address the Address Windowing Extensions (AWE) API. The AWE-enabled property turns on AWE memory addressing within SQL Server:

```
EXEC sp_configure 'show advanced options', 1;
RECONFIGURE;
EXEC sp_configure 'awe enabled', 1;
RECONFIGURE;
```

NOTE **The Windows privilege `LOCK PAGES IN MEMORY` must be granted to the SQL Server service account before enabling awe. A system administrator can use the Windows Group Policy tool (`gpedit.msc`) to enable this privilege for the SQL Server service account.**

NOTE **The SQL Server instance must be restarted in order for the `awe enabled` option to take effect. If the `awe enabled` option is configured successfully, then the SQL Server error log file will include an "Address Windowing Extensions enabled" message when the SQL Server restarts.**

Index create memory

The amount of memory SQL Server uses to perform sorts when creating an index is generally self-configuring. However, you can control it by using `sp_configure` to hard-code a certain memory footprint (in KB) for index creation. For example, the following code sets the memory used to create an index to 8MB:

```
EXEC sp_configure 'show advanced options', 1;
RECONFIGURE;
EXEC sp_configure 'index create memory', 8096;
RECONFIGURE;
```

Processor-configuration properties

You can use the processor-configuration properties (listed in Table 39-3) to control how SQL Server uses multi-processor computers.

TABLE 39-3

Processor-Configuration Properties

Property	Level*	Graphic Control	Code Option
Processors Used	S	Management Studio	`EXEC sp_configure 'affinity mask'`
Maximum Worker Threads	S	Management Studio	`EXEC sp_configure 'max worker threads'`
Boost SQL Server Priority on Windows	S	Management Studio	`EXEC sp_configure 'priority boost'`
Use Windows NT Fibers	S	Management Studio	`EXEC sp_configure 'lightweight pooling'`
Number of processors for parallel execution of queries	S	Management Studio	`EXEC sp_configure 'max degree of parallelism'`
Minimum query plan threshold for parallel execution	S	Management Studio	`EXEC sp_configure 'cost threshold for parallelism'`

* The configuration level refers to Server, Database, or Connection.

The Processors tab (see Figure 39-6) of the SQL Server Properties page determines how SQL Server will use multi-processor computers. Most of these options are moot in a single-processor server.

FIGURE 39-6

The Processors tab shows the processors available on the system and enables you to set how SQL Server uses them

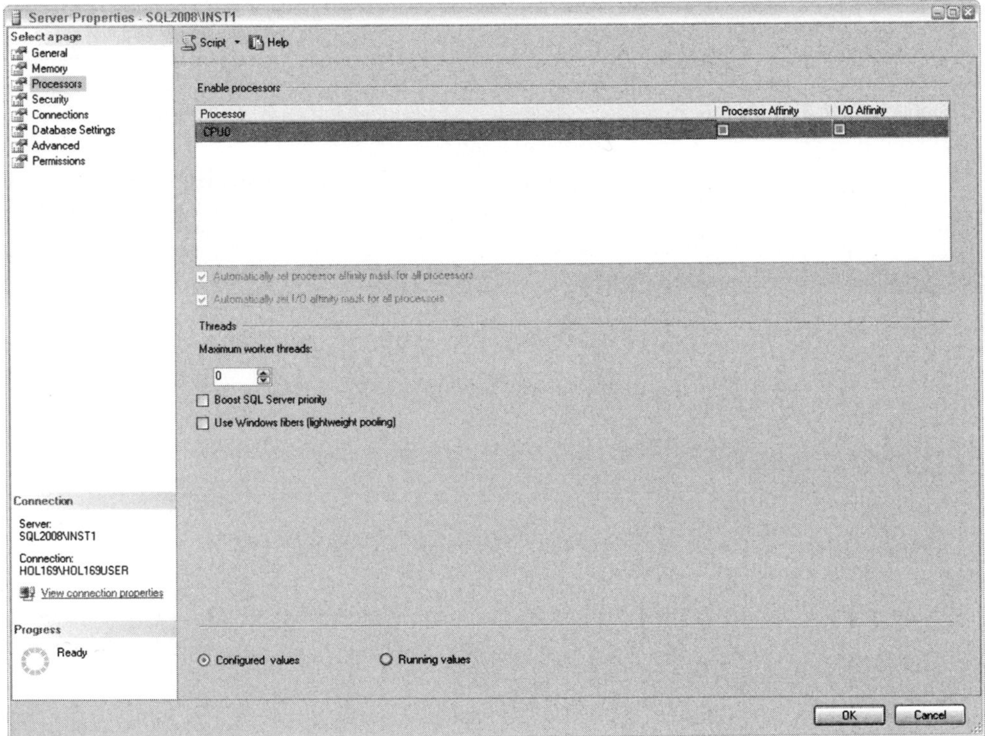

Processor affinity

In a multi-CPU server, the operating system can move processes to CPUs as the load requires. The SQL Server *processor affinity*, or the relationship between a task and a CPU, can be configured on a per-CPU basis. By enabling the affinity between SQL Server and a CPU, you make that CPU available to SQL Server, but it is not dedicated to SQL Server. Therefore, while a CPU can't be forced to run SQL Server, it can be segmented from SQL Server.

SQL Server supports processor affinity by means of two affinity mask configuration options: `affinity mask` (also referred to as CPU affinity mask) and `affinity I/O mask`. The `affinity mask` configuration option enables you to specify which CPUs on a multi-processor computer are to be used to run threads from SQL Server. The `affinity I/O mask` configuration option enables you to specify which CPUs are configured to run SQL Server threads related to I/O operations. These two configuration options give you the ability to allocate particular CPUs for disk I/O processing and particular CPUs for non-disk-related CPU requirements.

The affinity mask is a bitmap whereby the rightmost bit specifies the lowest-order CPU(0), the next rightmost bit specifies the next lowest-order CPU(1), and so on. A one-byte (eight bits) mask covers 8 CPUs in a multi-processor server, a two-byte mask covers up to 16 CPUs, a three-byte mask covers up to 24 CPUs, and a four-byte mask covers up to 32 CPUs. A one bit specifies that the corresponding CPU is allocated, and a zero bit specifies that the corresponding CPU is not allocated.

When you are configuring the affinity mask option, you must use it in conjunction with the affinity I/O mask. I recommend against enabling the same CPU for both affinity mask and affinity I/O mask configuration options. The bit corresponding to each CPU should be one of the following:

- 0 for both the `affinity mask` and `affinity I/O mask` options
- 1 for the `affinity mask` and 0 for the `affinity I/O mask` option
- 0 for the `affinity mask` and 1 for the `affinity I/O mask` option

For example, suppose that on an 8-CPU system you want to allocate CPUs 0, 1, 2, and 3 for processing SQL Server threads, CPUs 4 and 5 for disk I/O processing, and CPUs 6 and 7 for other non-SQL Server activities. This means the last four bits will be one for the `affinity mask` bitmap (00001111), which is 15 in decimal, and the fifth and sixth bits will be one for the `affinity I/O mask` (00110000), which is 48 in decimal:

```
EXEC sp_configure 'show advanced options', 1;
RECONFIGURE;
EXEC sp_configure 'affinity mask', 15;
RECONFIGURE;
EXEC sp_configure 'affinity I/O mask', 48;
RECONFIGURE;
```

The `affinity mask` setting takes effect immediately without requiring a restart of the SQL Server service, whereas the `affinity I/O mask` setting takes effect only after restarting the SQL Server service.

NOTE **The default value of 0 for the `affinity mask` option indicates that all the processors on the server are available for processing SQL Server threads. The default value of 0 for the `affinity I/O mask` option indicates that any CPUs that are eligible to process SQL Server threads are available for disk I/O processing.**

In Management Studio, processor affinity is configured by means of the check boxes in the Server Properties Processors tab (refer to Figure 39-6).

NOTE **Affinity support for SQL Servers with 33 to 64 processors is available only on 64-bit SQL Servers and requires the additional use of the `affinity64 mask` and `affinity64 I/O mask` configuration options.**

Max worker threads

SQL Server is a multi-threaded application, meaning that it can execute on multiple processors concurrently for increased performance. Multi-threaded applications also allow more efficient use of a single processor, because this allows another task to execute while a task waits for a process that doesn't use the CPU to finish. The threads are designed as follows:

- A thread for each network connection
- A thread to handle database checkpoints
- Multiple threads to handle user requests. When SQL Server is handling a small number of connections, a single thread is assigned to each connection. However, as the number of connections grows, a pool of threads handles the connections more efficiently.

Depending on the number of connections and the percentage of time those connections are active (versus idle), making the number of worker threads less than the number of connections can force connection pooling, conserve memory, and improve performance.

In Management Studio, the `max worker threads` option is set by typing or selecting a value in the Maximum Worker Threads box in the Server Properties Processor tab (refer to Figure 39-6).

From code, the maximum number of worker threads is set by means of the `sp_configure` stored procedure and the `max worker threads` option. For example, the following code sets the `max worker threads` to 128:

```
EXEC sp_configure 'show advanced options', 1;
RECONFIGURE;
EXEC sp_configure 'max worker threads', 128;
RECONFIGURE;
```

The SQL Server service must be restarted for the `max worker threads` setting to take effect.

Best Practice

On SQL Server 2005 and SQL Server 2008, the default value of 0 for the `max worker threads` property provides the best performance of SQL Server. This default value indicates that SQL Server will automatically determine the correct number of active worker threads based on user requests.

If you do need to change the default value, then I recommend not setting the `max worker threads` option to a small value, which might prevent enough threads from servicing incoming client requests in a timely manner and could lead to "thread starvation." Conversely, don't set the `max worker threads` option to a large value, which wastes memory, because each active thread consumes 512KB on 32-bit servers and up to 4MB on 64-bit servers.

TIP **To view information about the connections established to an instance of SQL Server, query the `sys.dm_exec_connections` dynamic management view. This information includes statistics about each of the databases, connections by both local and remote users, and details about each connection.**

Priority boost

Different processes in Windows operate at different priority levels, ranging from 0 to 31. The highest priorities are executed first and are reserved for the operating-system processes. Typically, Windows scheduling priority-level settings for applications are 4 (low), 7 (normal), 13 (high), and 24 (real-time). By default, SQL Server installs with a Windows scheduling priority level of 7. The default value of `priority boost` gives SQL Server enough CPU resources without adversely affecting other applications.

Best Practice

In almost all cases, it is recommended to leave the `priority boost` option to the default value of 0. Raising the priority of SQL Server may drain essential operating system and networking functions, resulting in a poorly performing SQL Server; and in some cases it may even result in a SQL Server shutdown. If you do change the priority boost from 0 to 1, then be sure to test it thoroughly and evaluate all other performance-tuning opportunities first.

If you still insist on changing the `priority boost` configuration option, you can use either Management Studio or T-SQL code. In Management Studio, `priority boost` is set to 1 by checking the Boost SQL Server priority checkbox in the Server Properties Processor tab (refer to Figure 39-6 earlier in this chapter).

Using T-SQL code, the following command sets the `priority boost` option to `1`. This will set the Windows scheduling priority level to 13 (high):

```
EXEC sp_configure 'show advanced options', 1;
RECONFIGURE;
EXEC sp_configure 'priority boost', 1;
RECONFIGURE;
```

The SQL Server service must be restarted for the `priority boost` option to take effect.

Lightweight pooling

You can use the `lightweight pooling` option for multi-processing servers to reduce the overhead of frequently switching processes among the CPUs.

Best Practice

For most SQL Servers, the default value of 0 for the `lightweight pooling` configuration option offers the best performance. In fact, changing the value from 0 to 1 may result in decreased performance. If you do change `lightweight pooling` to 1, then be sure to test it thoroughly and evaluate all other performance-tuning opportunities first.

If you still insist on changing the `lightweight pooling` configuration option, you can use either Management Studio or T-SQL code. In Management Studio, `lightweight pooling` can be set to 1 (default is 0) by checking the Use Windows Fibers (lightweight pooling) check box in the Server Properties Processor tab (refer to Figure 39-6 earlier in this chapter).

In code, set the `lightweight pooling` option as follows:

```
EXEC sp_configure 'show advanced options', 1;
RECONFIGURE;
EXEC sp_configure 'lightweight pooling', 1;
RECONFIGURE;
```

The SQL Server service must be restarted for the `lightweight pooling` option to take effect.

NOTE **The need for the `lightweight pooling` option is reduced by improved context switching in Microsoft Windows Server 2003 and 2008.**

The `lightweight pooling` and `clr enabled` configuration options are mutually exclusive. You can use one of the two options: `lightweight pooling` or `clr enabled`.

Parallelism

On a multi-processor server, SQL Server detects the best number of processors that can be used to run a single statement for each parallel plan. The `max degree of parallelism` configuration option can be used to limit the number of processors used in a parallel plan execution.

SQL Server's Query Optimizer is a cost-based optimizer, which means it chooses a plan that returns the results in a reasonable amount of time with a reasonable resource cost. SQL Server always considers a serial plan first. If this serial plan costs less than the `cost threshold for parallelism` value, then no parallel plan is generated. The `cost threshold for parallelism` option refers to the cost of the query in seconds on a specific hardware configuration. If the cheapest serial plan costs more than the `cost threshold for parallelism`, then a parallel plan is produced. The parallel plan cost is compared with the serial plan cost and the cheaper one is chosen.

Complex queries benefit the most from parallelism, as generating a parallel query execution plan, synchronizing the parallel query, and terminating the query all require additional overhead. To determine whether a query is using parallelism, view the query execution plan in Management Studio. A symbol shows the merger of different parallel query execution threads.

NOTE **The default value of the `max degree of parallelism` option is 0, which tells SQL Server to use all the available processors.**

In Management Studio, the `max degree of parallelism` option can be set by entering the maximum number of processors to be used in a parallel plan in the Max Degree of Parallelism box in the Server Properties Advanced tab (see Figure 39-9, later in the chapter).

The following code sets the `max degree of parallelism` option to 4:

```
EXEC sp_configure 'show advanced options', 1;
RECONFIGURE;
GO
EXEC sp_configure 'max degree of parallelism', 4;
RECONFIGURE;
```

Best Practice

The default value of 0 for the `max degree of parallelism` option works well for SQL Servers that have up to eight processors. The performance of the SQL Server can actually degrade if more than eight processors are used in a parallel plan. I recommend changing the `max degree of parallelism` option on SQL Servers that have more than eight processors from the default value of 0 to 8 or less.

For servers that have NUMA configured, `max degree of parallelism` should not exceed the number of CPUs assigned to each NUMA node.

For servers that have hyperthreading enabled, `max degree of parallelism` should not exceed the number of physical processors.

Although a parallel query execution plan can be much faster, there is a point at which the parallel query execution becomes inefficient and can even extend the execution time. For example, parallel queries performing small joins and aggregations on small data sets might be inefficient; and due to different degrees of parallelism chosen at execution time, response times for one query can be different depending on resource availability such as CPU and memory.

Paul recommends setting the `max degree of parallelism` option to 1 for OLTP workloads. I don't agree 100%, but certain applications do need `max degree of parallelism` set to 1 — for example, the `max degree of parallelism` option is set to "1" during the configuration of BizTalk Server for the SQL Server instance(s) that host the BizTalk Server MessageBox database(s). As per BizTalk's documentation, changing this to anything other than 1 can have a significant negative impact on the BizTalk Server stored procedures and performance. With this in mind, I recommend checking with your application vendor for any best practices for the `max degree of parallelism` option. If you are unable to contact the vendor or you are using an in-house application, then you may want to test different values of the `max degree of parallelism` option to see which value offers the maximum performance gains.

If you find that setting the `max degree of parallelism` option to 1 or any low value works best for your workload, I recommend changing the option back to 0 (or 8 if you have more than eight CPUs) when you are performing database maintenance tasks such as index creation, index rebuild, and checkdb, as doing so will speed up these tasks if they can leverage more CPUs. You can change the `max degree of parallelism` option without needing to restart SQL Server.

While these server-tuning options can affect performance, performance begins with the database schema, queries, and indexes. No amount of server tuning can overcome poor design and development.

NOTE **The default value of the `cost threshold for parallelism` option works well for most SQL Servers. Change the default value only after performing thorough testing and considering other performance-tuning opportunities.**

If you insist on changing the default value of the `cost threshold for parallelism` option, then you can use either Management Studio or T-SQL code. In Management Studio, the `cost threshold` for parallelism option can be set by entering the desired value in the Cost Threshold for Parallelism box in the Server Properties Advanced tab (refer to Figure 39-9, later in the chapter).

The following code sets the cost threshold for parallelism option to 30 seconds:

```
EXEC sp_configure 'show advanced options', 1;
RECONFIGURE;
EXEC sp_configure 'cost threshold for parallelism', 30;
RECONFIGURE;
```

Security-configuration properties

The security-configuration properties, shown in Table 39-4, are used to control the security features of SQL Server.

The same security-configuration options established during the installation are again presented in the Security tab of the Server Properties page (see Figure 39-7), so the configuration may be adjusted after installation.

Server authentication mode

The two server authentication modes are exactly the same as those presented during SQL Server installation:

- **Windows Authentication mode:** This uses Windows Authentication to validate connections.
- **SQL Server and Windows Authentication mode:** This uses both SQL and Windows Authentication to validate connections.

TABLE 39-4

Security-Configuration Properties

Property	Level*	Graphic Control	Code Option
Server Authentication Mode	S	Management Studio	-
Security Audit Level	S	Management Studio	-
C2 Audit Tracing	S	Management Studio	EXEC sp_configure 'c2 audit mode'
Common Criteria Compliance	S		EXEC sp_configure 'common criteria compliance enabled'
Cross Database Ownership Chaining	S D	Management Studio	EXEC sp_configure 'cross db ownership chaining' ALTER DATABASE xxx SET DB_CHAINING {ON | OFF}

* The configuration level refers to Server, Database, or Connection.

NOTE During installation, if you select SQL Server and Windows Authentication mode, you are prompted for a *sa* password. When you select Windows Authentication mode, the sa account gets a random strong password, unknown to the user. When you change to SQL Server and Windows Authentication mode, the sa account is disabled. You need to enable the sa account and then change the sa password in order to use the account.

FIGURE 39-7

Security tab of Management Studio's SQL Server Properties dialog

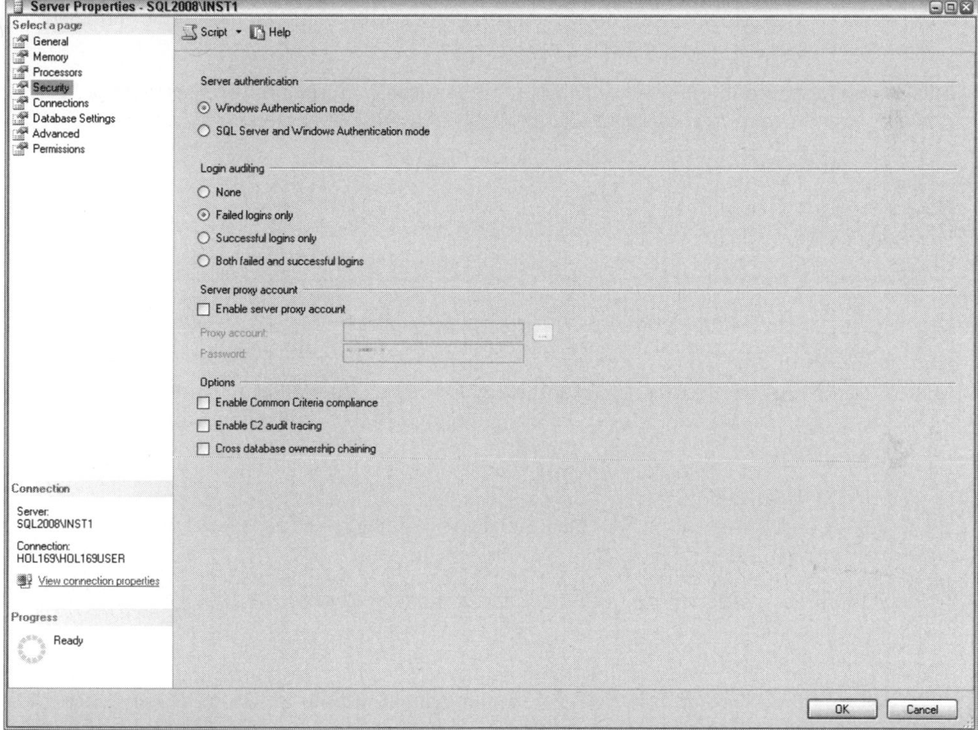

Security-audit level

The login auditing options configure the level of user-login auditing performed by SQL Server. You can choose one of the following four login auditing options (refer to Figure 39-7):

- None
- Failed logins only
- Successful logins only
- Both failed and successful logins

Based on the setting, SQL Server will record every successful or failed user login attempt to the Windows application log and the SQL Server log. The SQL Server service must be restarted in order for the login auditing options to take effect.

C2 audit tracing

C2 auditing is a U.S. government standard for monitoring database security. SQL Server supports C2 auditing. To configure SQL Server for C2 auditing, enable the `c2 audit mode` option. Enabling the `c2 audit mode` option configures the SQL Server to all security-related events. You can find all the events by browsing through them in SQL Server Profiler.

NOTE **By default, a trace file (C2 audit log) is stored in the default SQL Server data directory. The trace file rolls over automatically when it reaches 200MB. This continues until the data drive fills up or C2 auditing is turned off.**

In Management Studio, the `c2 audit mode` option can be turned on by selecting the "Enable C2 audit tracing" box in the Server Properties Security tab (refer to Figure 39-7).

In code, turn on the `c2 audit mode` option as follows:

```
EXEC sp_configure 'show advanced options', 1;
RECONFIGURE;
EXEC sp_configure 'c2 audit mode', 1;
RECONFIGURE;
```

The SQL Server service must be restarted for the `c2 audit mode` option to take effect.

The C2 auditing mode has been superseded by Common Criteria Compliance. Common Criteria Compliance can be enabled only with code, using the `sp_configure` system stored procedure:

```
EXEC sp_configure 'show advanced options', 1;
RECONFIGURE;
EXEC sp_configure 'common criteria compliance enabled', 1;
RECONFIGURE;
```

The SQL Server service must be restarted in order for the `common criteria compliance enabled` option to take effect.

CROSS-REF **In addition to enabling the option, you also must download and run a script from the Microsoft SQL Server Common Criteria website at** `www.microsoft.com/sql/commoncriteria/certifications.mspx`.

Cross-database ownership chaining

By default, all database objects, such as tables, views, and stored procedures, have owners. When an object references another object, an ownership chain is formed. When the same user owns the source object and the target object, SQL Server checks permission on the source objects, and not on the target objects.

Cross-database ownership chaining occurs when the source object depends on objects in another database. Cross-database ownership chaining works in the same way as ownership chaining in a database, except that an unbroken ownership chain is based on all the object owners being mapped to the same login account. If your application uses more than one database and it calls objects from one database that is based on objects in another database, then cross-database chaining is used. If the source object in the source database and the target object in the target database are owned by the same login, SQL Server does not check permissions on the target objects.

The `cross db ownership chaining` option enables control of the cross-database ownership chaining for all databases. By default, the `cross db ownership chaining` option is turned off (0), which ensures maximum security. If you turn this option on (1), then database owners and members of the `db_ddladmin` or the `db_owners` database roles can create objects that are owned by other users. These objects can potentially target objects in other databases, so you must fully trust these users with data in all databases.

In Management Studio, cross-database ownership chaining can be turned on by checking the "Cross database ownership chaining" option in the Server Properties Security tab.

In code, use the following to turn on cross-database ownership chaining:

```
EXEC sp_configure 'cross db ownership chaining', 1;
RECONFIGURE;
```

When the `cross db ownership chaining` option is turned off (0), cross database ownership chaining can be controlled at the database level with the `SET DB_CHAINING` option of the `ALTER DATABASE` command.

CROSS-REF **For more information about locking down SQL Server's security, refer to the chapters in Part VII, "Security."**

Connection-configuration properties

The connection-configuration properties, shown in Table 39-5, are used to set connection options in SQL Server.

The Server Properties Connections tab (see Figure 39-8) sets connection-level properties, including defaults, number of connections permitted, and timeout settings.

Maximum concurrent user connections

The `user connections` option is used to specify the maximum number of simultaneous user connections allowed on SQL Server. This option is self-configuring; SQL Server automatically adjusts the maximum number of user connections as needed, up to a maximum of 32,767 connections.

NOTE **The default for the `user connections` option is zero, which means unlimited user connections are allowed. For most SQL Servers, this default value works best. If you change this option, don't set the value too high, as each connection has overhead regardless of whether the connection is being used. However, don't set this option to a small value such as 1 or 2, which might prevent administrators from connecting to administer the SQL Server. The Dedicated Admin Connection can always connect.**

TABLE 39-5

Connection-Configuration Properties

Property	Level*	Graphic Control	Code Option
Max Concurrent User Connections	S	Management Studio	`EXEC sp_configure 'user connections'`
Query Cost Governor	CS	Management Studio	`EXEC sp_configure 'query governor cost limit'` `SET QUERY_GOVERNOR_COST_LIMIT 15`
Permit Remote Server Connections	S	Management Studio	`EXEC sp_configure 'remote access'`
Remote Login Timeout	S	Management Studio	`EXEC sp_configure 'remote login timeout'`
Remote Query Timeout	S	Management Studio	`EXEC sp_configure 'remote query timeout'`
Enforce DTC	S	Management Studio	`EXEC sp_configure 'remote proc trans'`
Network Packet Size	S	Management Studio	`EXEC sp_configure 'network packet size'`

* The configuration level refers to Server, Database, or Connection.

The maximum concurrent `user connections` option should probably not be set to a given number of users because applications often open several connections to SQL Server. For example, ODBC- and ADO-based applications open a connection for every connection object in code — possibly as many as one for every form, list box, or combo box. Access tends to open at least two connections.

In Management Studio, the `user connections` configuration option can be set by typing a value from 0 through 32767 in the "Max number of concurrent connections" box in the Server Properties Connections tab (refer to Figure 39-8).

The following code sets the maximum number of `user connections` to 10240:

```
EXEC sp_configure 'show advanced options', 1;
RECONFIGURE;
GO
EXEC sp_configure 'user connections', 10240;
RECONFIGURE;
```

The SQL Server service must be restarted in order for the `user connections` option to take effect.

FIGURE 39-8

Connections tab of Management Studio's SQL Server Properties dialog

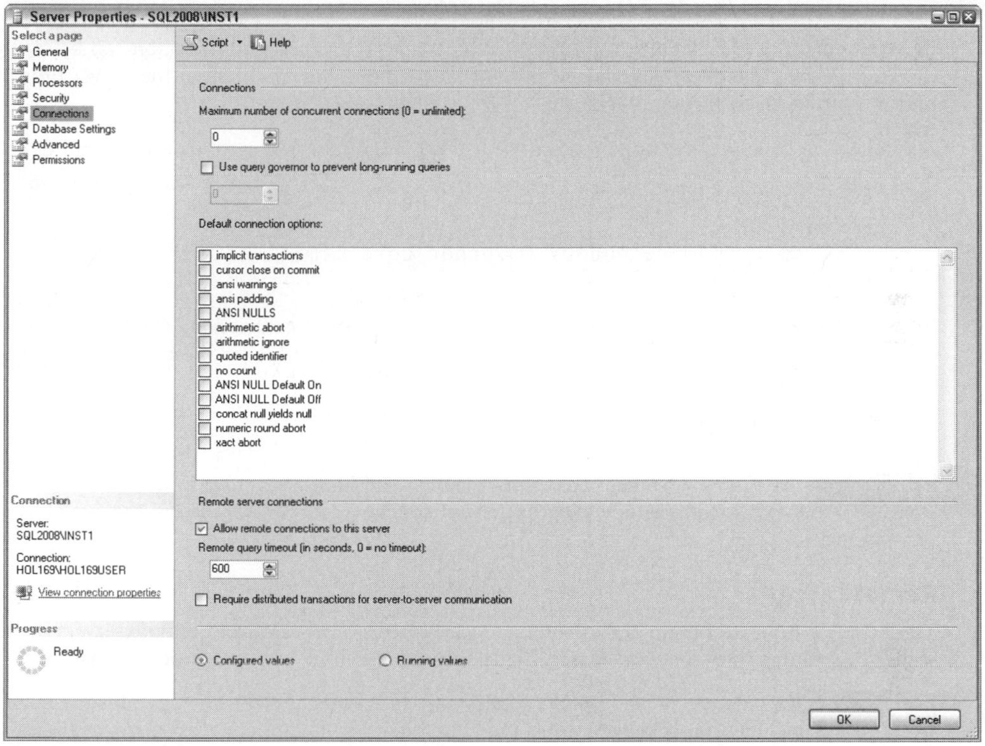

To determine the maximum number of simultaneous user connections allowed on a SQL Server instance using code, examine the value in the @@ MAX_CONNECTIONS global variable. The number returned is neither the actual number of connections nor the configured value — it is the maximum number allowed:

```
SELECT @@MAX_CONNECTIONS;
```

Result:

```
-----------
32767
```

Query governor cost limit

In the same way that a small gas-engine governor controls the top speed of the engine, the *query governor* limits the queries that SQL Server will run according to the estimated query cost on a specific hardware configuration. If a user submits a query that exceeds the limit set by the query governor, then SQL

Server will not execute it. By default, the query governor cost limit option is set to 0. This value allows all queries to execute, no matter how long they will take.

NOTE **The `query governor cost limit` option will not abort queries with an estimated duration of less than the limit but a longer actual duration.**

In Management Studio, the `query governor cost limit` configuration option can be set by typing the limit in the "Use query governor to prevent long-running queries" box in the Server Properties Connections tab (refer to Figure 39-8).

The following code sets the `query governor cost limit` to 300 seconds for the entire server:

```
EXEC sp_configure 'show advanced options', 1;
RECONFIGURE;
EXEC sp_configure 'query governor cost limit', 300;
RECONFIGURE;
```

In code, the query governor can also be changed for the current connection. The following code overrides the currently configured `query governor cost limit` value for the current connection and sets it to 15 seconds:

```
SET QUERY_GOVERNOR_COST_LIMIT 15;
```

TIP **The `query governor cost limit` option can be used to stop long-running queries before they start, thereby helping to prevent system resources from being consumed by these long-running queries.**

Remote access

The `remote access` option allows running local stored procedures from remote servers or remote stored procedures from the local server. By default, the `remote access` option is enabled.

NOTE **The `remote access` option applies only to servers added using `sp_addserver` and is included for backward compatibility. Using this feature is not recommended, as it will be removed in the next version of Microsoft SQL Server. Use the `sp_addlinkedserver` feature instead.**

To disallow `remote access`, uncheck the "Allow remote connections to this server" check box in Management Studio in the Server Properties Connections tab (refer to Figure 39-8) or set the `remote access` option to `0` in code:

```
EXEC sp_configure 'remote access', 0;
RECONFIGURE;
```

The SQL Server service must be restarted in order for the `remote access` option to take effect.

Remote login timeout

The `remote login timeout` configuration option specifies the number of seconds to wait before returning from a failed attempt to connect to a remote SQL Server. The default value for `remote login timeout` is 20 seconds.

In Management Studio, set the `remote login timeout` option by entering the new timeout, in seconds, in the "Remote login timeout" box in the Server Properties Advanced tab (refer to Figure 39-9 later in the chapter).

The following code changes the default value of 20 to 30:

```
EXEC sp_configure 'remote login timeout', 30;
RECONFIGURE;
```

To cause an indefinite wait, you can change the value for the `remote login timeout` option to 0.

Remote query timeout

The `remote query timeout` option sets the number of seconds SQL Server will wait on a remote query before assuming it failed and generating a timeout error. The default value of 600 seconds (10 minutes) seems sufficient for executing a remote query:

```
EXEC sp_configure 'remote query timeout', 600;
RECONFIGURE;
```

In Management Studio, you can set the `remote query timeout` option by entering the desired time in the "Remote query timeout (in seconds, 0 = no timeout)" box in the Server Properties Connections tab (refer to Figure 39-8).

Enforce DTC

When updating multiple servers within a transaction (logical unit of work), SQL Server can enforce dual-phase commits using the Microsoft Distributed Transaction Coordinator.

From code, the Enforce DTC property is enabled by setting the `remote proc trans` option to 1:

```
EXEC sp_configure 'remote proc trans', 1;
RECONFIGURE;
```

In Management Studio, the `remote proc trans` option can be set by checking the "Require distributed transactions for server-to-server communication" box in the Server Properties Connections tab (refer to Figure 39-8).

NOTE **We don't recommend using this feature in new development work, as it will be removed in the next version of Microsoft SQL Server. Plan to modify applications that currently use this feature, and use the `sp_addlinkedserver` feature instead.**

CROSS-REF **Transactions are explained in Chapter 66, "Managing Transactions, Locking, and Blocking."**

Network packet size

Packets are blocks of information sent over the network to transfer requests and results between clients and servers. The network packet size may be changed from its default of 4KB by means of the `network packet size` option. However, very rarely should network packet size need reconfiguring. Consider this property a fine-tuning tool and use it only when the data being passed tends to greatly exceed the default size, such as large text or image data.

In Management Studio, the `network packet size` option can be set by entering the new size (in bytes) in the "Network packet size" box in the Server Properties Advanced tab (refer to Figure 39-9 later in the chapter).

FIGURE 39-9

Advanced tab of Management Studio's SQL Server Properties dialog

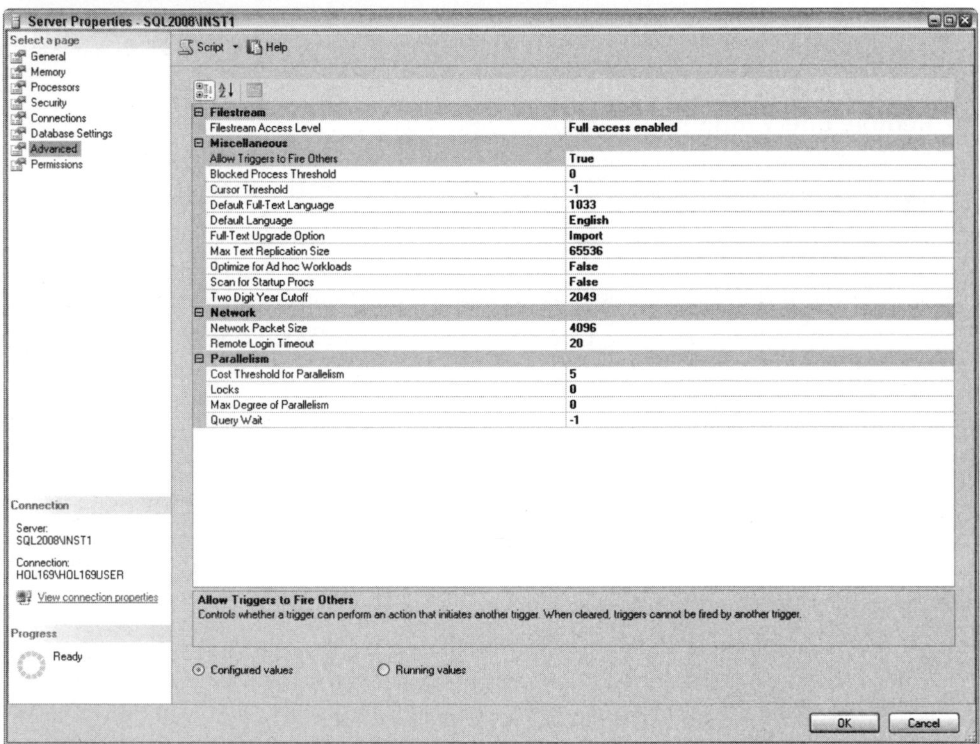

The following code sets the network packet size to 2KB:

```
EXEC sp_configure 'network packet size', 2048;
RECONFIGURE;
```

TIP **The** `sys.dm_exec_connections` **dynamic management view contains information about the network packet size (the column named** `net_packet_size`) **used for information and data transfer.**

Advanced server-configuration properties

The advanced server-configuration properties, shown in Table 39-6, enable you to set advanced SQL Server configuration options.

The Advanced tab of Management Studio's Server Properties dialog (see Figure 39-9) is used to view or modify these settings.

TABLE 39-6

Advanced Server-Configuration Properties

Property	Level*	Graphic Control	Code Option
Filestream Access Level	S	Management Studio	EXEC sp_configure 'filestream access level'
Extensible Key Management	S	-	EXEC sp_configure 'EKM provider enabled'
Default Full-text Language	S	Management Studio	EXEC sp_configure 'default full-text language'
Default Language	S	Management Studio	EXEC sp_configure 'default language'
Two-Digit Year Cutoff	S	Management Studio	EXEC sp_configure 'two digit year cutoff'
Max Text Replication Size	S	Management Studio	EXEC sp_configure 'max text repl size'

* The configuration level refers to Server, Database, or Connection.

Filestream access level

SQL Server 2008 introduces a new feature called Filestream that enables the storing of structured data in the database, and the storing of associated unstructured (i.e., BLOB) data such as text documents, images, and videos directly in the NTFS file system. By default, Filestream is not enabled. You can enable it during the SQL Server 2008 installation in the Database Engine Configuration page of the setup. You can also enable the Filestream feature after installation using the SQL Server Configuration Manager as follows:

1. Open SQL Server Configuration Manager from Start ➪ Programs ➪ Microsoft SQL Server 2008 ➪ Configuration Tools ➪ SQL Server Configuration Manager.
2. Click SQL Server Services under SQL Server Configuration Manager.
3. Right-click the SQL Server service (on the right-hand side) for which you want to enable Filestream and select Properties.
4. Click the Filestream tab (see Figure 39-10) and select the "Enable Filestream for Transact-SQL access" check box.

   If you want to read and write Filestream data from Windows, select the "Enable Filestream for file I/O streaming access" check box. Enter the name of the Windows share in which the Filestream data will be stored in the "Windows Share Name" box.

   If you want to allow remote clients to access the Filestream data stored on this share, select "Allow remote clients to have streaming access to Filestream data."
5. Click Apply.

FIGURE 39-10

Enable the Filestream feature using SQL Server Configuration Manager

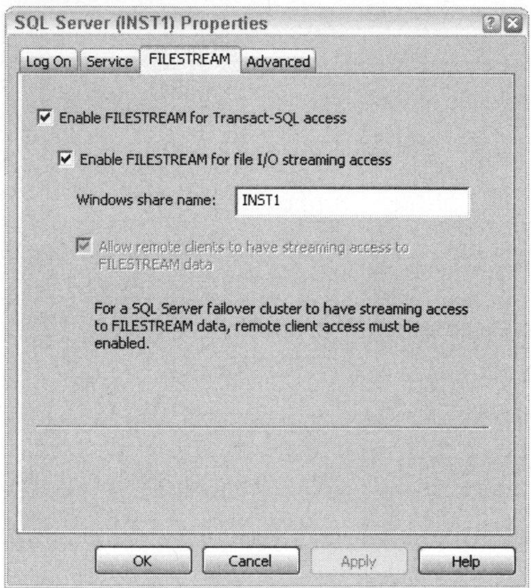

After enabling Filestream during setup or by using SQL Server Configuration Manager, the next step is to configure it in SQL Server using the `filestream_access_level` configuration option. The possible Filestream access settings are as follows:

- **0:** Disable Filestream support for this SQL Server instance
- **1:** Enable Filestream for Transact-SQL access only
- **2:** Enable Filestream for Transact-SQL and Win32 streaming access

The following example configures Filestream for both Transact-SQL and Win32 streaming access:

```
EXEC sp_configure 'filestream_access_level', 2;
RECONFIGURE;
```

Extensible Key Management

The Extensible Key Management (EKM) feature in SQL Server 2008 enables third-party EKM and hardware security module vendors to register their devices in SQL Server. This capability makes it possible for DBAs to use third-party EKM products along with SQL Server's built-in encryption.

NOTE **The EKM feature is available only on Enterprise, Developer, and Evaluation editions of SQL Server 2008. Trying to enable this option on other editions will result in an error. By default, the EKM feature is** `0 (OFF)` **for all editions.**

Use the following to turn the EKM feature ON in code:

```
EXEC sp_configure 'show advanced options', 1;
RECONFIGURE;
EXEC sp_configure 'EKM provider enabled', 1;
RECONFIGURE;
```

Default full-text language

The default language for full-text index columns can be set using the default full-text language configuration option. Linguistic analysis of full-text indexed data varies according to the language of the data.

NOTE **The default value for the default full-text language option is the language of the SQL Server instance. In addition, the default value set by this option only applies when no language is indicated in the CREATE or ALTER FULLTEXT INDEX statement.**

In Management Studio, the default full-text language configuration option can be set by specifying the local identifier (lcid) for the language you want, as listed in the sys.fulltext_languages table in the "Default full-text language" box in the Server Properties Advanced tab (refer to Figure 39-9).

The following example sets the default full-text language option to U.S. English using T-SQL code:

```
EXEC sp_configure 'show advanced options', 1;
RECONFIGURE;
EXEC sp_configure 'default full-text language', 1033;
RECONFIGURE;
```

In this case, the value of 1033 refers to U.S. English. You need to change this value only when you need to support something other than the default system language.

CROSS-REF **Many of the language settings in SQL Server rely on a *locale identifier (LCID)*. You can find a list of common LCID values at** http://krafft.com/scripts/deluxe-calendar/lcid_chart.htm.

CROSS-REF **The details of full-text search are discussed in Chapter 19, "Using Integrated Full-Text Search."**

Default language

The default language for all newly created logins can be set in both Management Studio and code using the default language configuration option. The default language is used both for messages from the server and for formatting dates. It can be overridden by the CREATE LOGIN or ALTER LOGIN statement.

In Management Studio, set the default language configuration option by selecting the language from the "Default language" drop-down list in the Server Properties Advanced tab (refer to Figure 39-9).

From code, set the `default language` configuration option by specifying the unique language ID of the language you want, as listed in the `sys.syslanguages` table. For example, to set the default language to British English, first query the `sys.syslanguages` table to get the language ID for British English. Then use the language ID as shown here:

```
EXEC sp_configure 'default language', 23;
RECONFIGURE;
```

The language for a session can be changed during the session with the `SET LANGUAGE` statement.

Two-digit-year cutoff

The two-digit-year cutoff converts a two-digit year to a four-digit year based on the values supplied. The default time span for SQL Server is 1950–2049, which represents a cutoff year of 2049. If the two-digit year falls on or after the first value (default 50), then it is interpreted as being in the twentieth century. If it falls on or before the second value (default 49), then it is interpreted as being in the twenty-first century. For example, 01/01/69 is interpreted as 01/01/1969, and 01/01/14 is interpreted as 01/01/2014.

In Management Studio, the `two digit year cutoff` configuration option can be set by specifying an integer that represents the cutoff year in the "Two digit year cutoff" box in the Server Properties Advanced tab (refer to Figure 39-9).

The following code sets the `two digit year cutoff` to 2041:

```
EXEC sp_configure 'show advanced options', 1;
RECONFIGURE;
EXEC sp_configure 'two digit year cutoff', 2041;
RECONFIGURE;
```

Best Practice

Use four-digit date formats to avoid ambiguity with dates. To maintain backward compatibility, leave the default setting for the `two digit year cutoff` configuration option.

Max text replication size

By default, text or image data greater than 65536 bytes (64KB) cannot be added to a replicated column or a captured column. The `max text repl size` option applies to transactional replication and the Change Data Capture feature. This option does not apply to snapshot and merge replication. The maximum size of 65536 bytes is configurable using `max text repl size` configuration option.

In Management Studio, the `max text repl size` configuration option can be set by specifying maximum size in the "Max text replication size" box in the Server Properties Advanced tab (refer to Figure 39-9).

The following code sets the max text repl size to 131072 (128KB):

```
EXEC sp_configure 'max text repl size', 131072;
RECONFIGURE;
```

CROSS-REF **The details of replication and change data capture are discussed in Chapter 36, "Replicating Data," and Chapter 60, "Change Data Capture" respectively.**

Configuring database auto options

Five database-configuration options determine the automatic behaviors of SQL Server databases, as described in Table 39-7. In Management Studio, they are all set in the Options tab of the Database Properties page (refer to Figure 39-2 earlier in this chapter).

Auto close

Auto close directs SQL Server to release all database resources (cached data pages, compiled stored procedures, saved query execution plans) when all users exit the database and all processes are complete. This frees memory for other databases. Although this option improves performance slightly for other databases, reloading the database takes longer, as will recompiling the procedures and recalculating the query execution plans, once the database is again opened by a SQL Server when a user accesses the database again.

If the database is used regularly, do not enable auto close. If the database is used occasionally, then auto close might be appropriate to save memory.

Many front-end client applications repeatedly open and close a connection to SQL Server. Setting auto close ON in this type of environment is a sure way to kill SQL Server performance.

TABLE 39-7

Index-Configuration Properties

Property	Level*	Graphic Control	Code Option
Auto Close	D	Management Studio	ALTER DATABASE <DB Name> SET auto_close
Auto Shrink	D	Management Studio	ALTER DATABASE <DB Name> SET auto_shrink
Auto Create Statistics	D	Management Studio	ALTER DATABASE <DB NAME> SET auto_create_statistics
Auto Update Statistics	D	Management Studio	ALTER DATABASE <DB NAME> SET auto_update_statistics
Auto Update Statistics Asynchronously	D	Management Studio	ALTER DATABASE <DB Name> SET auto_update_statistics_async

* The configuration level refers to Server, Database, or Connection.

The following code sets auto close on for the AdventureWorks2008 sample database:

```
ALTER DATABASE AdventureWorks2008 SET AUTO_CLOSE ON;
```

Best Practice

In general, don't enable auto close for production SQL Server databases. However, in some situations, you may have hundreds or even thousands of databases with archived data that are never all used at the same time. For these situations you may benefit from having auto close on for some or even all databases. By default, auto close is enabled only for SQL Server Express Edition; it is off for all other editions.

Auto shrink

If the database has more than 25 percent free space, then this option causes SQL Server to perform a data and log file shrink operation. This option also causes the transaction log to shrink after it's backed up.

Performing a file shrink is a costly operation because several pages must be moved within the file. Plus, it's very probable that the files later have to grow again (another costly operation), causing file fragmentation at the OS level. This option also regularly checks the status of the data pages to determine whether they can be shrunk.

CROSS-REF **Shrinking the data and transaction log files is discussed in detail in Chapter 41, "Recovery Planning."**

The following example sets the auto shrink option to OFF for the AdventureWorks2008 sample database:

```
ALTER DATABASE AdventureWorks2008 SET AUTO_SHRINK OFF;
```

Best Practice

I have seen a few customers cause severe SQL Server performance degradation by setting the auto shrink option on. I highly recommended not enabling auto shrink for production SQL Server databases.

Auto create statistics

Data-distribution statistics are a key factor in how the SQL Server Query Optimizer creates query execution plans. This option directs SQL Server to automatically create statistics for any columns for which statistics could be useful. The default for this option is set to ON.

To set auto create statistics ON for AdventureWorks2008 sample database in code, do the following:

```
ALTER DATABASE AdventureWorks2008 SET AUTO_CREATE_STATISTICS ON;
```

Auto update statistics

SQL Server's cost-based Query Optimizer uses statistics to choose the most efficient plan for retrieving or updating data. Hence, out-of-date data-distribution statistics aren't very useful. The AUTO_UPDATE_STATISTICS database option causes statistics to be recomputed every time a specified number of rows in the table changes. The default for this option is set to on, which is best practice and works for most environments.

However, based on the row changes, sometimes the statistics may be updated too frequently, other times too infrequently, and sometimes automatically updating the statistics may cause a delay just when you don't want it. To avoid these situations, you can disable the AUTO_UPDATE_STATISTICS database option and schedule jobs to recompute statistics during low traffic or maintenance. In some environments, DBAs schedule jobs to manually compute the statistics, and keep the AUTO_UPDATE_STATISTICS option on as a failsafe measure in case many more rows change than normal. The following code example sets the auto update statistics option on for the AdventureWorks2008 sample database:

```
ALTER DATABASE AdventureWorks2008 SET AUTO_UPDATE_STATISTICS ON;
```

Auto update statistics asynchronously

When a query triggers an AUTO_UPDATE_STATISTICS event, the query waits until the updated statistics can be used. This can cause unpredictable query response times. Beginning with SQL Server 2005, a database option called AUTO_UPDATE_STATISTICS_ASYNC enables you to update the statistics asynchronously. By default, this option is off. If the AUTO_UPDATE_STATISTICS_ASYNC database option is enabled, then SQL Server performs the automatic update of statistics in the background. The query that causes the automatic statistics does not need to wait for the statistics to be updated and proceeds with the old statistics. This may result in a less efficient query plan but the query response times are predictable. Queries that start after the statistics are updated will use those statistics.

The following code enables the AUTO_UPDATE_STATISTICS_ASYNC option for the AdventureWorks2008 sample database:

```
ALTER DATABASE AdventureWorks2008 SET AUTO_UPDATE_STATISTICS_ASYNC ON;
```

NOTE **The AUTO_UPDATE_STATISTICS_ASYNC database option is dependent on the AUTO_UPDATE_STATISTICS option. Therefore, you need to ensure that the AUTO_UPDATE_STATISTICS option is ON and then enable AUTO_UPDATE_STATISTICS_ASYNC. Like any SQL Server configuration, you need to thoroughly test this option to determine whether your SQL Server applications benefit from it.**

CROSS-REF **Query execution plans rely heavily on data-distribution statistics, covered in more detail in Chapter 64, "Indexing Strategies."**

Cursor-configuration properties

The cursor-configuration properties, shown in Table 39-8, are used to control cursor behavior in SQL Server.

TIP **To view information about the open cursors in various databases, query the sys.dm_exec_cursors dynamic management view.**

TABLE 39-8

Cursor-Configuration Properties

Property	Level*	Graphic Control	Code Option
Cursor Threshold	S	Management Studio	`EXEC sp_configure 'cursor threshold'`
Cursor Close on Commit	SDC	Management Studio	`ALTER DATABASE <DB Name> SET cursor_close_on_commit`
Cursor Default	D	Management Studio	`ALTER DATABASE <DB Name> SET cursor_default`

* The configuration level refers to Server, Database, or Connection.

For information about cursor concepts, writing, and avoiding cursors, refer to Chapter 22, "Kill the Cursor!"

Cursor threshold

The `cursor threshold` property sets the number of rows in a cursor set before the cursor keysets are generated asynchronously. The Query Optimizer estimates the number of rows that will be returned from the result set. If the estimated number of rows is greater than the `cursor threshold`, then the cursor is generated asynchronously; otherwise, it is generated synchronously, causing a delay because the query has to wait until all the rows are fetched. Every cursor keyset will be generated asynchronously if the `cursor threshold` property is set to `0`.

The default of `-1` causes all keysets to be generated synchronously, which is OK for smaller keysets. For larger cursor keysets, though, this may be a problem.

In Management Studio, the `cursor threshold` option can be set to the desired value in the "Cursor threshold" box in the Server Properties Advanced tab (refer to Figure 39-9).

When you are working with cursors, the following code will permit synchronous cursor keysets for cursors of up to 10,000 rows:

```
EXEC sp_configure 'show advanced options', 1;
RECONFIGURE;
EXEC sp_configure 'cursor threshold', 10000;
RECONFIGURE;
```

Cursor close on commit

This property will close an open cursor after a transaction is committed when set to `ON`. If it is set to `OFF` (the default), then cursors remain open across transactions until a `close cursor` statement is issued.

The CURSOR_CLOSE_ON_COMMIT option can be set from Management Studio and code at the server, database, and connection level. In Management Studio, the CURSOR_CLOSE_ON_COMMIT option can be turned on at the various levels as follows:

- **Server level:** Check the "cursor close on commit" checkbox in the Server properties Connections tab (refer to Figure 39-8).
- **Database level:** Select True for the "cursor close on commit enabled" box in the Database Properties Options tab (refer to Figure 39-2).
- **Connection level:** To set this property for current queries, click the Query menu ➪ Query Options ➪ Execution ➪ ANSI and check the SET CURSOR_CLOSE_ON_COMMIT check box. To set this property for all future connections, click the Tools menu ➪ Options ➪ Query Execution ➪ ANSI and check the SET CURSOR_CLOSE_ON_COMMIT check box.

To set CURSOR_CLOSE_ON_COMMIT in code, do the following:

- Server level

```
EXEC sp_configure 'user options', 4;
RECONFIGURE;
```

- Database level (example to set the option on for the AdventureWorks2008 sample database)

```
ALTER DATABASE AdventureWorks2008 SET CURSOR_CLOSE_ON_COMMIT ON;
```

- Connection level

```
SET CURSOR_CLOSE_ON_COMMIT ON;
```

Cursor default

This property will make each cursor local to the object that declared it when set to local. When it is set to global (the default), the cursor's scope can be extended outside the object that created it.

In Management Studio, the CURSOR_DEFAULT option can be set to the desired scope in the "Default cursor" box in the Database Properties Options tab (refer to Figure 39-2).To set the cursor default for the AdventureWorks2008 sample database to LOCAL in code, do the following:

```
ALTER DATABASE AdventureWorks2008 SET CURSOR_DEFAULT LOCAL;
```

SQL ANSI–configuration properties

The SQL ANSI–configuration properties, shown in Table 39-9, are used to set ANSI behavior in SQL Server.

The connection default properties (there are several) affect the environment of batches executed within a connection. Most of the connection properties change SQL Server behavior so that it complies with the ANSI standard. Because so few SQL Server installations modify these properties, it's much safer to modify them in code at the beginning of a batch than to set them at the server or database level.

TABLE 39-9

SQL ANSI–Configuration Properties

Property	Level*	Graphic Control	Code Option
ANSI Defaults	C	Management Studio	`SET ANSI_DEFAULTS`
ANSI Null Behavior	SDC	Management Studio	`ALTER DATABASE <DB Name> SET ANSI_NULL_DFLT_OFF` `SET ANSI_NULL_DFLT_ON`
ANSI Nulls	SDC	Management Studio	`ALTER DATABASE <DB Name> SET ANSI_NULLS`
ANSI Padding	SDC	Management Studio	`ALTER DATABASE <DB Name> SET ANSI_PADDING`
ANSI Warnings	SDC	Management Studio	`ALTER DATABASE <DB Name> SET ANSI_WARNINGS`
Arithmetic Abort	SDC	Management Studio	`ALTER DATABASE <DB Name> SET arithabort`
Arithmetic Ignore	SC	-	`SET ARITHIGNORE`
Numeric Round Abort	SDC	Management Studio	`ALTER DATABASE <DB Name> SET NUMERIC_ROUNDABORT{ON | OFF}`
Null Concatenation	SDC	Management Studio	`ALTER DATABASE <DB Name> SET CONCAT_NULL_YIELDS_NULL`
Use Quoted Identifier	SD	Management Studio	`ALTER DATABASE <DB Name> SET QUOTED_IDENTIFIER`

* The configuration level refers to Server, Database, or Connection.

For example, T-SQL requires a `begin transaction` to start a logical unit of work. Oracle assumes a `begin transaction` is at the beginning of every batch. If you prefer to work with implicit (non-stated) transactions, then you're safer setting the implicit transaction connection property at the beginning of your batch. For these reasons, I recommend leaving the connection properties at the default values and setting them in code if needed.

The SQL ANSI-configuration settings are set at three levels: server, database and connection, as indicated in Table 39-9. The `sp_configure` system stored procedure has the "user options" setting that allows manipulation of server-wide ANSI settings and it works across databases. The `ALTER DATABASE` command can be used to set the default database setting for ANSI. Connection-level settings are performed with the `SET` command and they override the default database setting.

In Management Studio, the ANSI settings can be enabled (`ON`) at the three levels as follows:

- **Server level:** In the Server properties Connections tab (refer to Figure 39-8), check the boxes for the ANSI settings that you want to enable.
- **Database level:** In the Database Properties Options tab (refer to Figure 39-2 above), enable the ANSI settings.

- **Connection level:** Click the Query menu ➪ Query Options ➪ Execution ➪ ANSI, and then check the boxes for the ANSI settings that you want to enable.

NOTE For backward compatibility, the `sp_dboption` stored procedure is also available, but using this procedure is not recommended because it will be removed in future versions of SQL Server.

You can change the default ANSI database settings in model system database and then the defaults will be changed for all future databases.

The database setting for ANSI overwrites the server setting, and the connection setting overwrites the server and database setting.

ANSI defaults

SQL Server provides the `SET ANSI_DEFAULTS` command to manage a group of SQL Server settings. When `SET ANSI_DEFAULTS` is enabled, it provides the following settings (explained later in this section):

- `SET ANSI_NULLS`
- `SET ANSI_NULL_DFLT_ON`
- `SET ANSI_PADDING`
- `SET ANSI_WARNINGS`
- `SET CURSOR_CLOSE_ON_COMMIT`
- `SET IMPLICIT_TRANSACTIONS`
- `SET QUOTED_IDENTIFIER`

To set `ANSI_DEFAULTS` in code, do the following:

```
SET ANSI_DEFAULTS ON;
```

ANSI null default

The `ANSI_NULL_DEFAULT` setting controls the default nullability. This setting is used when a `NULL` or `NOT_NULL` is not explicitly specified when creating a table. The default database setting for `ANSI_NULL_DEFAULT` is `OFF`.

To set the `ANSI_NULL_DEFAULT` option to `ON` for the `AdventureWorks2008` sample database in code, do the following:

```
ALTER DATABASE AdventureWorks2008 SET ANSI_NULL_DEFAULT ON;
```

If the `ANSI_NULL_DEFAULT` option is not set at the database level, you can set the nullability of new columns using the `SET ANSI_NULL_DFLT_ON` and `SET ANSI_NULL_DFLT_OFF` commands. `SET ANSI_NULL_DFLT_ON` can be enabled to allow null values at the connection level:

```
SET ANSI_NULL_DFLT_ON ON;
```

`SET ANSI_NULL_DFLT_OFF` can be enabled to not allow null values at the connection level:

```
SET ANSI_NULL_DFLT_OFF ON;
```

To enable ANSI_NULL_DFLT_ON at the server level in code, do the following:

```
EXEC sp_configure 'user options', 1024;
RECONFIGURE;
```

The following enables ANSI_NULL_DFLT_OFF at the server level:

```
EXEC sp_configure 'user options', 2048;
RECONFIGURE;
```

NOTE **You cannot set both the SET ANSI_NULL_DFLT_ON and the SET ANSI_NULL_DFLT_OFF commands to ON at the same time. Either one can be ON and the other can be OFF or both can be OFF.**

ANSI NULLs

The ANSI_NULLS connection setting is used to determine comparison evaluations. When set to ON, all comparisons to a null value will evaluate to UNKNOWN. When set to OFF, the comparison to a null value will evaluate to true if both values are NULL. The default database setting for ANSI_NULLS is OFF.

The following enables ANSI_NULLS at the connection level:

```
SET ANSI_NULLS ON;
```

If SET ANSI_NULLS is not specified, then the settings of ANSI_NULLS of the current database apply. To enable ANSI_NULLS for the AdventureWorks2008 sample database in code, do the following:

```
ALTER DATABASE AdventureWorks2008 SET ANSI_NULLS ON;
```

The following enables ANSI_NULLS at the server level:

```
EXEC sp_configure 'user options', 32;
RECONFIGURE;
```

NOTE **The ANSI_NULLS option is deprecated and will always be ON in a future version of SQL Server.**

ANSI padding

The ANSI_PADDING connection setting affects only newly created columns. When set to ON, data stored in char, varchar, binary, and varbinary data types will retain any padded zeros to the left of variable binary numbers, and any padded spaces to the right or left of variable-length characters. When set to OFF, all leading and trailing blanks and zeros are trimmed. The default database setting for ANSI_PADDING is OFF.

The following enables ANSI_PADDING in code at the connection level:

```
SET ANSI_PADDING ON;
```

If SET ANSI_PADDING is not specified, then the settings of ANSI_PADDING of the current database apply. The following enables ANSI_PADDING for the AdventureWorks2008 sample database:

```
ALTER DATABASE AdventureWorks2008 SET ANSI_PADDING ON;
```

This enables ANSI_PADDING at the server level in code:

```
EXEC sp_configure 'user options', 16;
RECONFIGURE;
```

The ANSI_PADDING option is deprecated and will always be ON in a future version of SQL Server.

ANSI warnings

The ANSI_WARNINGS connection setting is used to handle ANSI errors and warnings such as arithmetic overflow, divide-by-zero and null values appearing in aggregate functions. The default database setting for ANSI_WARNINGS is OFF. When this setting is OFF, no warnings are raised when null values appear in aggregate functions, and null values are returned when divide-by-zero occurs and overflow errors occur. When the setting is ON, the query is aborted and errors are raised when arithmetic overflow errors and divide-by-zero occurs.

To set ANSI_WARNINGS in code at the connection level:

```
SET ANSI_WARNINGS ON;
```

If SET ANSI_WARNINGS is not specified, then the settings of ANSI_WARNINGS of the current database apply. The following enables ANSI_WARNINGS for the AdventureWorks2008 sample database:

```
ALTER DATABASE AdventureWorks2008 SET ANSI_WARNINGS ON;
```

Use the following to enable ANSI_WARNINGS at the server level in code:

```
EXEC sp_configure 'user options', 8;
RECONFIGURE;
```

Arithmetic abort

The ARITHABORT connection setting is used to handle query termination if arithmetic errors such as data overflow or divide-by-zero occurs. The default database setting for ARITHABORT is OFF.

What exactly is terminated also depends on the ANSI_WARNINGS setting. Table 39-10 explains the behavior based on the values of ANSI_WARNINGS and ARITHABORT.

To set ARITHABORT in code at the connection level:

```
SET ARITHABORT ON;
```

If ARITHABORT is not specified, then the settings of the current database apply. To enable ARITHABORT for AdventureWorks2008 sample database in code, do the following:

```
ALTER DATABASE AdventureWorks2008 SET ARITHABORT ON;
```

The following enables ARITHABORT at the server level:

```
EXEC sp_configure 'user options', 64;
RECONFIGURE;
```

TABLE 39-10

ANSI_WARNINGS and ARITHABORT Behavior

ARITHABORT	ANSI_WARNINGS	Behavior
ON	ON	Query is aborted
ON	OFF	Batch is aborted or transaction is rolled back
OFF	ON	Query is aborted
OFF	OFF	No warning is raised and null is returned

Arithmetic ignore

The ARITHIGNORE connection setting is used to control whether an error message is returned from arithmetic overflow or divide-by-zero errors. To abort the query, you need to use the ARITHABORT setting. Both ARITHABORT and ARITHIGNORE can be set to ON but ARITHABORT takes precedence over ARITHIGNORE. To set ARITHIGNORE in code, use the following:

```
SET ARITHIGNORE ON;
```

The following enables ARITHIGNORE at the server level:

```
EXEC sp_configure 'user options', 128;
RECONFIGURE;
```

Numeric round abort

The NUMERIC_ROUNDABORT connection setting is used to control the behavior of numeric decimal-precision-rounding errors in process. When NUMERIC_ROUNDABORT is set to ON and ARITHABORT is set to ON, an error is generated and no result is returned if the numeric-decimal precision is lost in an expression value. Loss of numeric-decimal precision can occur when a value with fixed precision is stored in a column or variable with less precision.

If ARITHABORT is set to OFF and NUMERIC_ROUNDABORT is set to ON, a warning appears and null is returned. When NUMERIC_ROUNDABORT is set to OFF, the process will proceed without errors or warnings, and the result is rounded down to the precision of the object in which the number is being stored. The default database setting for NUMERIC_ROUNDABORT is OFF.

To set NUMERIC_ROUNDABORT in code at the connection level:

```
SET NUMERIC_ROUNDABORT ON;
```

If NUMERIC_ROUNDABORT is not specified, then the settings of the current database apply. The following enables NUMERIC_ROUNDABORT for the AdventureWorks2008 sample database:

```
ALTER DATABASE AdventureWorks2008 SET NUMERIC_ROUNDABORT ON;
```

To enable NUMERIC_ROUNDABORT at the server level in code, do the following:

```
EXEC sp_configure 'user options', 8192;
RECONFIGURE;
```

Concatenation null yields null

The CONCAT_NULL_YIELDS_NULL setting is used to control the behavior of the result when concatenating a string with a null. When set to ON, any string concatenated with a null will result in a null. When set to OFF, any string concatenated with a null will result in the original string, ignoring the null. The default database setting for CONCAT_NULL_YIELDS_NULL is OFF.

The following sets CONCAT_NULL_YIELDS_NULL at the connection level:

```
SET CONCAT_NULL_YIELDS_NULL ON;
```

If CONCAT_NULL_YIELDS_NULL is not specified, then the settings of the current database apply. The following enables CONCAT_NULL_YIELDS_NULL for the AdventureWorks2008 sample database:

```
ALTER DATABASE AdventureWorks2008 SET CONCAT_NULL_YIELDS_NULL ON;
```

The following enables CONCAT_NULL_YIELDS_NULL at the server level:

```
EXEC sp_configure 'user options', 4096;
RECONFIGURE;
```

Use quoted identifier

The QUOTED_IDENTIFIER setting enables you to refer to an identifier, such as a column name, by enclosing it within double quotes. When set to ON, identifiers can be delimited by double quotation marks. When set to OFF, identifiers cannot be placed in quotation marks and must not be keywords. The default database setting for QUOTED_IDENTIFIER is OFF.

This sets QUOTED_IDENTIFIER to ON at the connection level:

```
SET QUOTED_IDENTIFIER ON;
```

If QUOTED_IDENTIFIER is not specified, then the settings of the current database apply. To enable QUOTED_IDENTIFIER for the AdventureWorks2008 sample database, use the following:

```
ALTER DATABASE AdventureWorks2008 SET QUOTED_IDENTIFIER ON;
```

This enables QUOTED_IDENTIFIER at the server level:

```
EXEC sp_configure 'user options', 256;
RECONFIGURE;
```

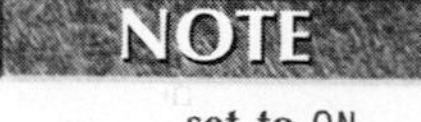

When dealing with indexes on computed columns and indexed views, four of these defaults (ANSI_NULLS, ANSI_PADDING, ANSI_WARNINGS, and QUOTED_IDENTIFIER) must be set to ON.

Trigger configuration properties

The trigger configuration properties, shown in Table 39-11, are used to control trigger behavior in SQL Server.

Trigger behavior can be set at both the server and database levels.

TABLE 39-11

Trigger Configuration Properties

Property	Level*	Graphic Control	Code Option
Allow Nested Triggers	S	Management Studio	`EXEC sp_configure 'nested triggers'`
Recursive Triggers	D	Management Studio	`ALTER DATABASE <DB Name> SET recursive_triggers`

* The configuration level refers to Server, Database, or Connection.

Nested triggers

A trigger is a small stored procedure that is executed on an `insert`, `update`, or `delete` operation on a table. Triggers are nested when a trigger performs an action that initiates another trigger, which can initiate another trigger, and so on. Triggers can be nested up to 32 levels. The `nested triggers` server configuration option can be used to control whether `AFTER` triggers can be nested triggers.

In Management Studio, the `nested trigger` option can be set by selecting True (default) or False in the "Allow Triggers to Fire Others" option in the Server Properties Advanced tab (refer to Figure 39-9).

To turn `nested triggers OFF` in code, do the following:

```
EXEC sp_configure 'nested triggers', 0;
RECONFIGURE;
```

`INSTEAD OF` triggers can be nested regardless of the setting of this option.

Recursive triggers

If the code in the trigger inserts, updates, or deletes the same table again, then the trigger causes itself to be executed again. Recursion can also occur if the code in the trigger fires and performs an action that causes a trigger on another table to fire. This second trigger performs an action that causes an update to occur on the original table, which causes the original trigger to fire again. Recursive behavior is enabled or disabled by the recursive trigger database option. By default, the `RECURSIVE_TRIGGERS` option is set to `OFF`.

In Management Studio, the recursive triggers option can be enabled by selecting True in the "Recursive Triggers Enabled" option in the Database Properties Options tab (refer to Figure 39-2).

The following sets the recursive triggers option `ON` in the `AdventureWorks2008` sample database in T-SQL code:

```
ALTER DATABASE AdventureWorks2008 SET RECURSIVE_TRIGGERS ON;
```

CROSS-REF **The server property `nested triggers` and the database property `recursive triggers` are often confused with each other. Refer to Chapter 26, "Creating DML Triggers," for a complete explanation, including coverage of how triggers can call other triggers and how these properties control trigger behavior.**

Database-state-configuration properties

The database-state-configuration properties, shown in Table 39-12, are available in SQL Server. These configurations are mostly used when a DBA is performing maintenance on the database.

The state of the database can be set with the `ALTER DATABASE` command. The `sp_dboption` command is also available for backward compatibility. However, using the `sp_dboption` command it is not recommended because it will be removed in future versions of SQL Server.

Database-access level

The database-access-configuration options are used to set the state of the database. When the database is offline, no access to the database is allowed.

To set `AdventureWorks2008` sample database to an `OFFLINE` state in code, do the following:

```
ALTER DATABASE AdventureWorks2008 SET OFFLINE;
```

TABLE 39-12

Database-State-Configuration Properties

Property	Level*	Graphic Control	Code Option
Database OffLine	D	Management Studio	ALTER DATABASE <DB Name> SET OFFLINE
Database OnLine	D	Management Studio	ALTER DATABASE <DB Name> SET ONLINE
Emergency	D	-	ALTER DATABASE <DB Name> SET EMERGENCY
Read-Only	D	Management Studio	ALTER DATABASE <DB Name> SET READ_ONLY
Restricted Access — Members of db_owner, dbcreator, or sysadmin	D	Management Studio	ALTER DATABASE <DB Name> SET RESTRICTED_USER
Restricted Access — Single user	D	Management Studio	ALTER DATABASE <DB Name> SET SINGLE_USER
Multi User	D	Management Studio	ALTER DATABASE <DB Name> SET MULTI_USER
Compatibility Level	D	Management Studio	ALTER DATABASE <DB NAME> SET COMPATIBILITY_LEVEL

* The configuration level refers to Server, Database, or Connection.

To revert this change and make the AdventureWorks2008 database online and available, do the following:

```
ALTER DATABASE AdventureWorks2008 SET ONLINE;
```

You may encounter a situation in which the database is inaccessible and you do not have a backup. To access the database regardless of online/offline state, members of the sysadmin role can put the database in EMERGENCY mode. Once in EMERGENCY mode, the database is in read-only mode and is accessible only by members of the sysadmin role. To put the AdventureWorks2008 sample database in EMERGENCY mode in code, do the following:

```
ALTER DATABASE AdventureWorks2008 SET EMERGENCY;
```

The READ_ONLY database-state settings are used to allow only selects from the database. READ_ONLY cannot take effect if any users are in the database. To reset the database to a normal read-and-write state, the READ_WRITE database setting is used.

To set the AdventureWorks2008 sample database to a READ_ONLY state in code, do the following:

```
ALTER DATABASE AdventureWorks2008 SET READ_ONLY;
```

The restricted access database-state settings are also available. The three restricted access levels are single_user, restricted_user, and multi_user states. These settings control which users are allowed to access the database. The SINGLE_USER setting is appropriate when you are doing database maintenance. The RESTRICTED_USER setting allows database access only to users in the db_owner, dbcreator, and sysadmin roles. The MULTI_USER setting is used to set the database in the normal operating state.

The following sets the AdventureWorks2008 sample database to SINGLE_USER access:

```
ALTER DATABASE AdventureWorks2008 SET SINGLE_USER;
```

To revert the preceding setting and set the AdventureWorks2008 database access to MULTI_USER access, do the following:

```
ALTER DATABASE AdventureWorks2008 SET MULTI_USER;
```

Compatibility level

In SQL Server, the database-compatibility level can be set to 80 (SQL Server 2000), 90 (SQL Server 2005), or 100 (SQL Server 2008). When a database is upgraded to SQL Server 2008 from any earlier version of SQL Server, the database retains its existing compatibility level. Setting the database-compatibility level to a level lower than 100 may be necessary if you are upgrading the Database Engine and still need to maintain the behavior of an earlier version of SQL Server.

NOTE **The compatibility level option does not provide full backward compatibility. It is mainly intended to enable new reserved words to be used in tables, and to retain some (very limited) changed behavior. Refer to SQL Server Books Online for a full overview.**

To set the compatibility level of the AdventureWorks2008 sample database to 100 (SQL Server 2008) in code, do the following:

```
ALTER DATABASE AdventureWorks2008 SET COMPATIBILITY_LEVEL = 100;
```

TABLE 39-13

Recovery-Configuration Properties

Property	Level*	Graphic Control	Code Option
Recovery Model	D	Management Studio	`ALTER DATABASE <DB Name> SET RECOVERY`
Page Verify	D	Management Studio	`ALTER DATABASE <DB Name> SET PAGE_VERIFY`
Media Retention	S	Management Studio	`EXEC sp_configure 'media retention'`
Backup Compression	S	Management Studio	EXEC sp_configure 'backup compression default'
Recovery Interval	S	Management Studio	`EXEC sp_configure 'recovery interval'`

* The configuration level refers to Server, Database, or Connection.

New in 2008

In SQL Server 2008, the `ALTER DATABASE` syntax shown in the sample code replaces the `sp_dbcmptlevel` stored procedure for setting the database compatibility level

To view the compatibility level of SQL Server, query the compatibility_level column in the `sys.databases` **catalog view.**

Recovery-configuration properties

The recovery-configuration properties, shown in Table 39-13, are used to set recovery options in SQL Server.

The recovery options determine how SQL Server handles transactions and the transaction log, and how the transaction log is backed up.

Recovery model

SQL Server 2008 uses a recovery model to configure several settings that work together to control how the transaction log behaves regarding file growth and recovery possibilities. The three recovery model options are as follows:

- **Simple:** The transaction log contains only transactions that are not yet written to the data file. This option does not provide up-to-the-minute recovery.

- **Bulk-Logged:** The transaction log contains all DML operations, but bulk insert operations are only marked, not logged.
- **Full:** The transaction log contains all changes to the data file. This option provides the greatest recovery potential.

CROSS-REF **Chapter 41, "Recovery Planning," focuses on recovery planning and operations in detail.**

In code, set the recovery option with the `ALTER DATABASE SET RECOVERY` command.

In Management Studio, the recovery model can be changed by selecting Simple, Bulk-logged, or Full in the Recovery Model drop-down list in the Database Properties Options tab (refer to Figure 39-2).

To set the recovery mode in the `AdventureWorks2008` sample database to Bulk-Logged in code, do the following:

```
ALTER DATABASE AdventureWorks2008 SET RECOVERY BULK_LOGGED;
```

Page Verify

Even though SQL Server works with 8KB data pages, the operating system I/O writes in 512-byte sectors. Therefore, it's possible that a failure might occur in the middle of a data-page write, resulting in only some of the 512-byte sectors to be written to disk. This is known as a *torn page*. You can have SQL Server tell you if a torn page occurs by using the `PAGE_VERIFY` database option.

The `PAGE_VERIFY` database option can be set to one of the following values:

- `CHECKSUM`: This is the default level for `PAGE_VERIFY`. With this option, SQL Server calculates a checksum over the contents of each page and stores the value in the page header when a page is written to disk. When the page is read from disk, the checksum is recalculated and compared to the original checksum value.
- `TORN_PAGE_DETECTION`: This option instructs SQL Server to toggle a bit on each 512-byte sector with each write operation. If all the sectors were written to disk, then all the detection bits should be identical. If, on recovery, any of the bits are different, then SQL Server can detect the torn-page condition and mark the database as suspect.
- `NONE`: With this option, database page writes will not generate a `CHECKSUM` or `TORN_PAGE_DETECTION` value.

To change the `PAGE_VERIFY` option, you can either use Management Studio or T-SQL code. In Management Studio, `PAGE_VERIFY` can be changed by selecting `CHECKSUM`, `TORN_PAGE_DETECTION`, or `NULL` in the Page Verify box in the Database Properties Options tab (refer to Figure 39-2).

Using T-SQL code, the following command can be used to set the `PAGE_VERIFY` option for `AdventureWorks2008` sample database to `TORN_PAGE_DETECTION`:

```
ALTER DATABASE AdventureWorks2008 SET PAGE_VERIFY TORN_PAGE_DETECTION;
```

TIP **To view the `PAGE_VERIFY` option for the database, query the `page_verify_option_desc` column in the `sys.databases` catalog view.**

Media retention

The `media retention` option is used to set the number of days to retain each backup set. The default value for `media retention` is 0 days. This option helps protect backups from being overwritten until the specified number of days has elapsed.

In Management Studio, the `media retention` server configuration option can be set by entering the number of days to retain each backup media in the "Default backup media retention (in days)" box in the Server Properties Database Settings tab (see Figure 39-11).

FIGURE 39-11

The Database Settings tab of Management Studio's Server Properties

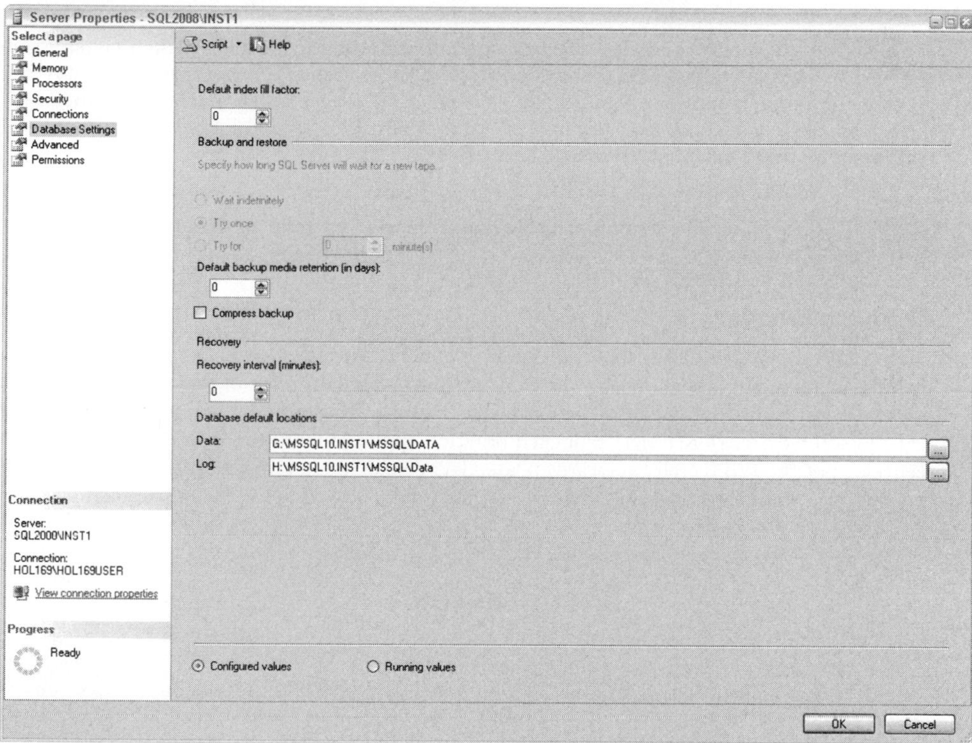

To set `media retention` to 10 days in code, do the following:

```
EXEC sp_configure 'show advanced options', 1;
RECONFIGURE;
EXEC sp_configure 'media retention', 10;
RECONFIGURE;
```

Backup compression

Backup compression is a new feature introduced in SQL Server 2008 Enterprise Edition. Although this feature is supported only in Enterprise Edition, every SQL Server 2008 edition can restore a compressed backup.

In Management Studio, to compress new backups by default, set `backup compression default` by checking the Compress Backup check box in the Server Properties Database Settings tab (refer to Figure 39-11).

To set `backup compression default` in code, do the following:

```
EXEC sp_configure 'backup compression default', 1
RECONFIGURE
```

NOTE **After installation, new backups are uncompressed by default. Backup compression can greatly reduce backup size and backup restore time. This improvement is not free, however. Backup compression significantly increases CPU usage, which may impact other operations on the server. Hence, I recommend testing this feature thoroughly to understand the pros and cons before implementing it in your production SQL Server.**

CROSS-REF **For more information about backup compression, refer to Chapter 41, "Recovery Planning."**

Recovery interval

The `recovery interval` server configuration option controls when SQL Server issues checkpoints for each database. A checkpoint flushes dirty pages from the buffer cache of the database to disk. Checkpoints are performed when SQL Server estimates that the recovery time will be longer than the specified `recovery interval`. The estimated duration applies only to the `REDO` (roll forward) phase of the recovery, not the `UNDO` (roll backward) phase. The default value for this option is `0`, which implies that this option is automatically configured by SQL Server.

Best Practice

Leave the `recovery interval` option at the default value of `0`. If you do change the `recovery interval`, then be sure to test it thoroughly and evaluate all other performance-tuning opportunities first.

If you insist on changing the `recovery interval` option, you can use either Management Studio or T-SQL code. In Management Studio, the `recovery interval` server configuration option can be set by entering the maximum number of minutes per database to recover databases in the "Recovery interval (minutes)" box in the Server Properties Database Settings tab (refer to Figure 39-11).

Using T-SQL code, the following command sets the `recovery interval` server configuration option to five minutes:

```
EXEC sp_configure 'show advanced options', '1';
RECONFIGURE;
EXEC sp_configure 'recovery interval', 5;
RECONFIGURE;
```

Summary

Configuration options are important for compatibility, performance tuning, and controlling the connection. The configuration options are set at the server, database, and connection level. Most of the options can be set from Management Studio, and all of them can be configured with code.

Continuing with SQL Server administration tasks, the next chapter focuses on managing policies.

Chapter 40

Policy-Based Management

IN THIS CHAPTER

Declarative management

Exploring facet properties

Defining policies

Enforcing policies

Recently I was on a virtual panel with SQL Server MVPs Steve Wynkop and Chris Shaw (of SSWUG.org fame) discussing what's new with SQL Server 2008. I said the top new developer feature is table-valued parameters, and the top DBA feature is Policy-Based Management (affectionately called PBM). This surprised Chris because he expected me to focus on only developer features, and he wanted to say that PBM was the top new feature. Sorry to steal your thunder, Chris.

But it's true. For SQL Server operations, PBM has the potential to radically alter how DBAs do their job, advance the consistency and quality of the operations up a few levels, and significantly ease managing hundreds of servers.

I'll put it in print here: *If you're an operational DBA and you don't get excited about PBM, then you should consider flipping burgers instead.* (And as a DB dev type, I don't usually get very excited about an admin feature.)

So, with that introduction, what is PBM?

Traditionally, applying and enforcing server and database settings and configurations across multiple SQL Servers has been a mash-up of log books, checklists, jobs, DDL triggers, scripts, and good ideas on the whiteboard that were never actually implemented.

PBM changes all that by making policies *declarative* — in fact, during its early life, PBM was called Declarative Management Framework.

SQL is a declarative language, meaning that SQL commands don't state how the query should be solved. SQL describes the question, and the Query Optimizer figures out how to solve the query.

Similarly, PBM abstracts the management intent, meaning the policies, from the procedural implementation. As the DBA, you define what the system should be and then let SQL Server figure out how to achieve it. Policy checking can be automated, and the results logged.

SQL Server 2008 focuses on automating policy checking for a single SQL Server instance. But users can build multi-server solutions quite easily using PowerShell scripts and agent jobs.

What's New with Policy-Based Management?

Of course, everything is new with PBM — it's a new feature — but there's more to the story. In SQL Server 2008, PBM replaces the Surface Area Configuration (SAC) tool that SQL Server 2005 introduced. With SQL Server 2005, Microsoft installed SQL Server in a locked-down state — with a minimum exposed surface area configuration. Any setting that could be turned off was turned off. The SAC tool was a pretty slick and easy way to check the server settings and enable features.

PBM is considerably more complicated than the old SAC tool. One of SQL Server's strengths has always been the scalability of the experience — it's usable by the occasional, accidental DBA as well as by the professional, experienced DBA. I contend that SAC was very useful for the web developers who also serve as the DBA 30 minutes a month. They're never going to learn PBM, and probably never going to read this chapter, but the SAC tool was easy to find and easy to use. PBM is far superior to SAC in every way; SAC was just really easy to use.

The demise of SAC aside, Policy-Based Management is brilliant. Without a doubt, PBM is the right direction for SQL Server management and it's the right tool for the professional DBA today.

It's worth mentioning that there is more to PBM than meets the eye. PBM is actually a down-payment technology that Microsoft can build on. I expect to see great things being done in SQL 11 to leverage PBM.

Defining Policies

Policies may be defined interactively in Management Studio, loaded in from XML, or defined with either T-SQL code or APIs. There are three types of PBM objects. In a sense they function as three levels, with one *policy* built from *conditions*, which are built out of *facets*:

- **74 Management facets**, defined only by Microsoft, are collections of properties that represent a management dimension. For example, the table facet has 34 specific properties that can be checked about a table. Examples of common facets include logins, a server, a linked server, or an index. Inside each facet are anywhere from a handful to dozens of properties, which can be referred to by a condition.
- **Health conditions**, defined by the DBA, based on one facet, are the desired states, or values, in terms of facet properties.

- **Policies**, defined by the DBA, based on one health condition, declare how and upon what object (server, database, etc.) the health condition should be enforced.

The UI for Policy-Based Management is in Management Studio's Object Explorer under the Management node, as shown in Figure 40-1. Most of the PBM tasks are found in the PBM node context menus.

Management facets

A brilliant-cut diamond has 58 facets. Policy-Based Management has 74 management facets; fortunately, a condition can be built with only one facet. The easiest way to see all the facets is to open the Facets node under Management ➪ Policy Management, as shown in Figure 40-1.

FIGURE 40-1

Policy-Based Management's policies, conditions, and facets are found in Object Explorer under the Management node.

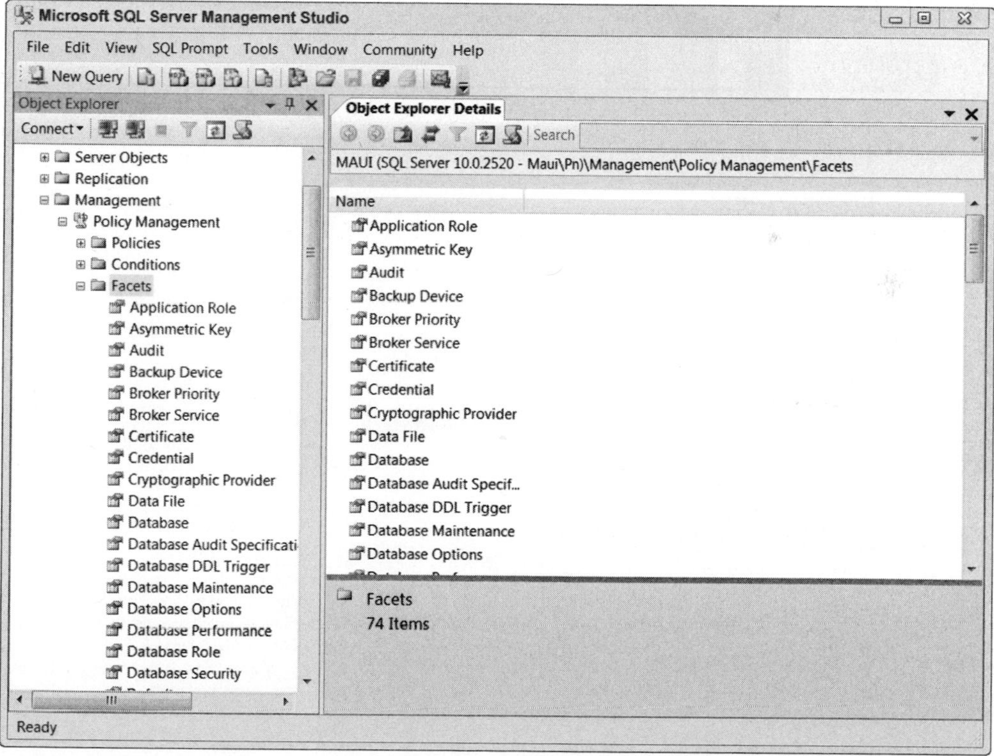

In database design terminology, there's a many-to-many relationship between SQL Server object types and properties. For example, database facet properties apply only to databases, but the name facet property (there's only one property) can apply to 19 different types of SQL Server objects, ranging from ApplicationRoles to XmlSchemaCollections, including databases.

The Facet collection is the associative table between SQL Server object types and properties.

A facet may be opened by double-clicking it or by using the Property command in its context menu. The Facet Properties dialog, shown in Figure 40-2, has three pages:

- **General:** Describes the property, lists the type of SQL Server objects to which the facet properties may apply, and lists the facet's properties.
- **Dependent Policies:** Lists the policies that use any dependent conditions of the facet.
- **Dependent Conditions:** Lists the conditions that use any property of the facet.

The last two pages are not without purpose. There may potentially be a very large number of conditions and policies; the dependent policies and conditions pages are very useful for quickly tracking down a condition or policy.

It's worth spending some time browsing the facets and exploring the properties of each one, available from the facet's context menu.

FIGURE 40-2

The Facet Properties' General page lists of all the facet properties and their descriptions. In this case, it's showing the properties for the database facet.

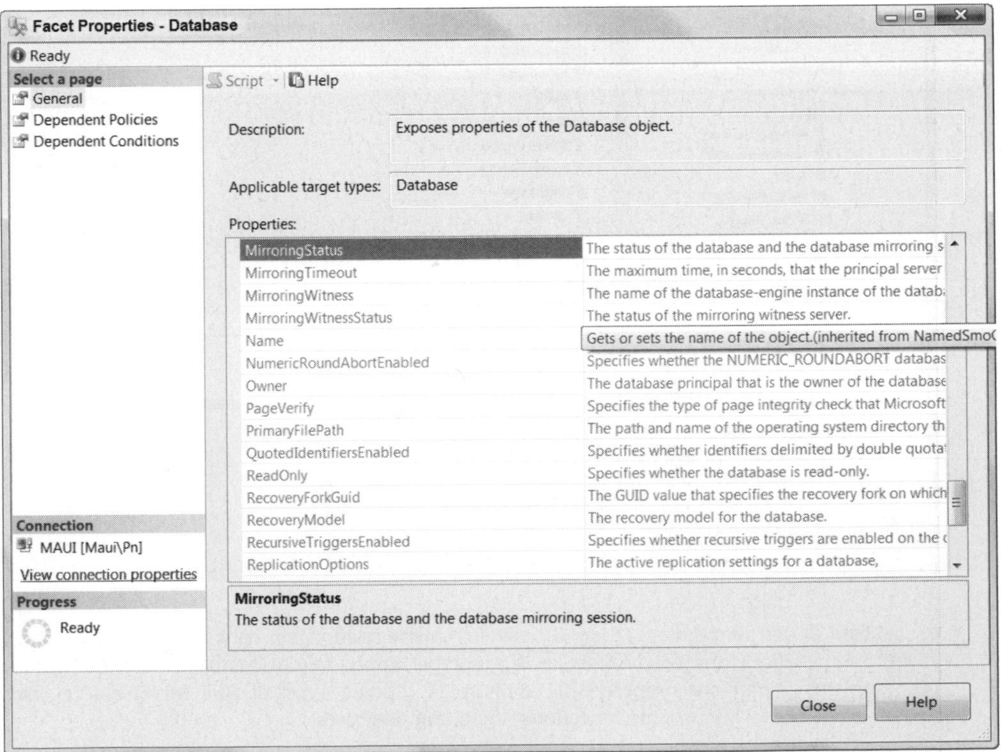

The Object Explorer ➪ Management ➪ Policy Management ➪ Facets context menu also includes New Condition and New Policy. The only difference between these context menu items and New Condition under Conditions, or New Policy under Policies, is that when the new condition or policy is opened from the facet node, it pre-selects the facet in the drop-down selection box (not terribly important but nice).

There's not much to be gained by just looking at facets, as their purpose is to be evaluated by conditions, but it's important to be intimately familiar with the breadth of facets and their properties to realize the types of policies that may be declared and enforced by SQL Server.

Because the facet collection is actually a many-to-many relationship between properties and object types, it makes sense that there should be a way to see all the facets and properties that apply to any given object. Indeed, every object in Object Explorer that can have PBM applied has a Facet menu option in its context menu. Open the View Facets dialog (shown in Figure 40-3) and it presents a drop-down box to select a facet from the list of facets that applies to the object, and a list of applicable properties. If the object is an example of what you want, the View Facets dialog can even export the current state to a new policy. Very cool.

FIGURE 40-3

The View Facets dialog, opened from any object's context menu, presents a browsable UI of every facet and property that can apply to that type of object, and can export a new policy to match the current object's settings.

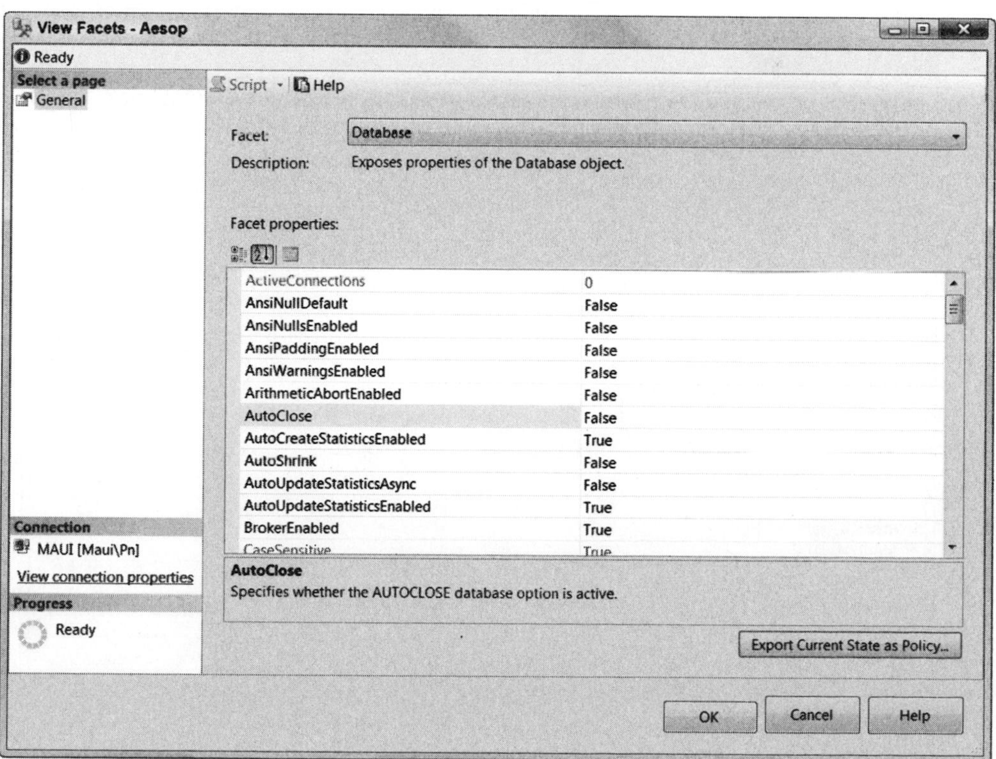

Health conditions

Conditions are the second step in the chain, providing the logical connection between facet properties and policies. Most of the key policy design decisions are made while creating conditions.

To begin building a new condition, use either the Object Explorer Management ➪ Policy Management ➪ Facets ➪ Database context menu, or the Management ➪ Policy Management ➪ Conditions context menu and choose New Condition.

An existing condition may be opened by double-clicking the condition or by using the Property command in its context menu.

A condition may have multiple expressions, but each condition is based on only one facet, so every property in all the expressions in a condition must belong to the same facet.

Condition expressions use facet properties in Boolean expressions that can be evaluated as true or false. The expression consists of a facet property, a comparison operator (such as =, `!=`, `in`, `not in`, `like`, `not like`), and a value.

To construct a condition that tests a database's autoshrink property, the expression would use the database facet and the `@AutoShrink` property, as shown in Figure 40-4. In this case, the full expression is as follows:

```
@AutoShrink = False
```

FIGURE 40-4

This condition includes an expression that tests the database facet's @AutoShrink. The condition will evaluate as true if @AutoShrink = false.

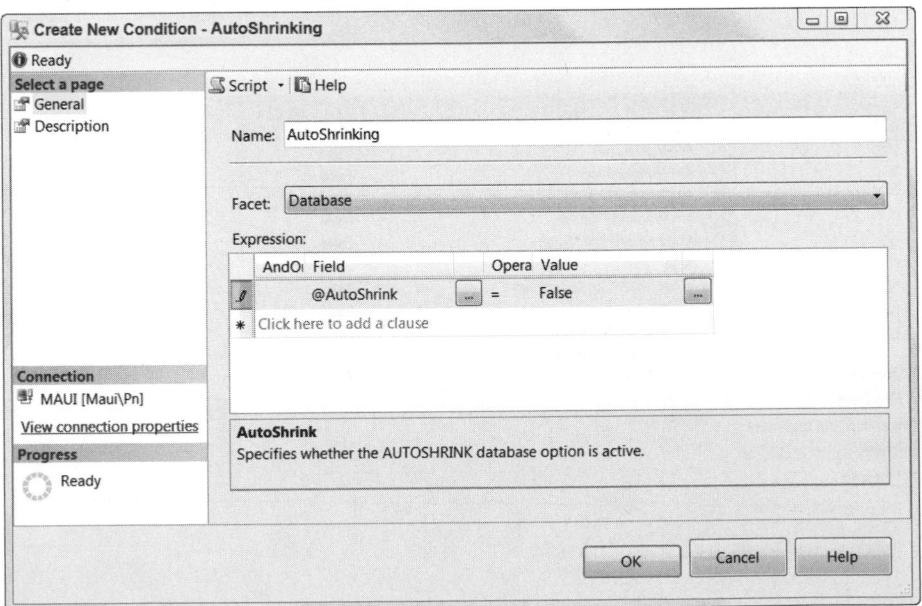

Best Practice

Think of condition expressions as positive statements. Instead of thinking "No database should be set to autoshrink," think "All databases should have autoshrink set to false."

The ellipses button under Field and Value headings opens the Advanced Edit dialog, shown in Figure 40-5. The Cell value is typically a property, a function, or a literal value; however, it is possible to build more advanced expressions that reference DMV or system tables.

A condition may include multiple expressions, in which case the AndOr column defines how they are evaluated.

Best Practice

In the entire policy design scheme, the only place that allows multiples is when designing multiple expressions within a single condition. Therefore, if every expression should indeed be tested, then encapsulating multiple expressions in a single condition can reduce the number of conditions and policies.

FIGURE 40-5

The Advanced Edit dialog is used to create each side of the expression. In this case it shows the left side of the AutoShrink expression.

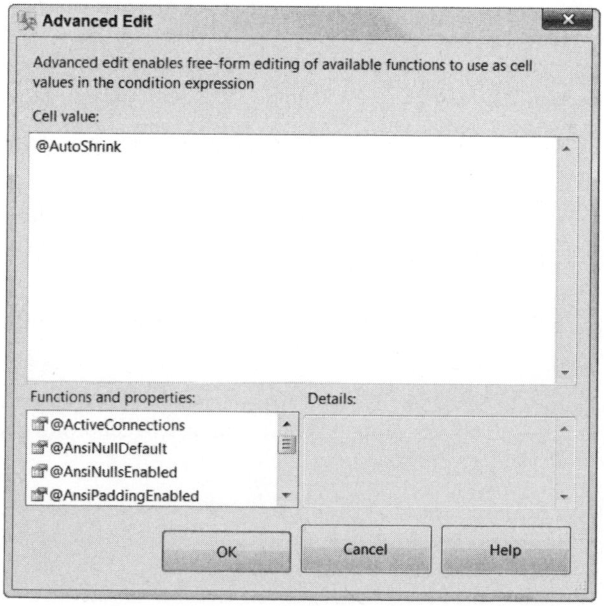

Advanced Edit

Advanced edit enables free-form editing of available functions to use as cell values in the condition expression

Cell value:

@AutoShrink

Functions and properties:

@ActiveConnections
@AnsiNullDefault
@AnsiNullsEnabled
@AnsiPaddingEnabled

Details:

OK Cancel Help

The open condition's description page may be used to record a description of the condition, and the dependent policies page lists the policies based on the condition.

Once the condition is created, it may be enforced by one or more policies.

To programmatically view the created conditions, query the dbo.syspolicy_conditions view in the MSDB database:

```
select * from msdb.dbo.syspolicy_conditions
```

To build advanced conditions that check factors other than the built-in facets, look into the `executeSQL()` **and** `executeWMI()` **functions.**

Policies

If the facet property is the skeleton and the condition the brain, then the policy is the muscle. Policies define how and where the condition is applied and enforced.

A new policy is created using the New Policy menu item in Object Explorer's Management ➪ Policy Management ➪ Facets context menu, or in Management ➪ Policy Management ➪ Policies ➪ Database context menu. The Open Policy dialog, shown in Figure 40-6, has a General page and a Description page.

An existing policy may be opened by double-clicking the policy or by using the Property command in its context menu.

The General page has four key selections. The first is the condition — a policy may check only a single condition. The ellipses will open the condition.

The second selection, targets, defines which objects will be tested. The options vary depending on the type of object to which the facets apply.

Evaluation mode is the third key selection. There are four evaluation modes for a policy:

- **On Demand:** The policy is evaluated only manually. There's no schedule or automatic testing or enforcement.
- **On Schedule:** The policy is evaluated and any violations are logged but not corrected.
- **On Change - Log Only:** The policy is evaluated when the facet is changed, and violations are logged.
- **On Change - Prevent:** The policy is evaluated when the facet is changed, and violations are rolled back immediately.

Every facet may be set to On Demand or On Schedule, but On Change is limited. PBM relies on DDL eventing to do Check On Change, and not all objects support DDL eventing. The following query reports which execution modes are available for which facets:

```
SELECT name as Facet,
    Max(CASE WHEN execution_mode & 0 = 0 Then 1 else 0 End)
      as 'On Demand',
    Max(CASE WHEN execution_mode & 4 = 4 Then 1 else 0 End)
      as 'On Schedule',
    Max(CASE WHEN execution_mode & 2 = 2 Then 1 else 0 End)
      as 'On Change Log Only',
    Max(CASE WHEN execution_mode & 1 = 1 Then 1 else 0 End)
      as 'On Change Prevent'
  FROM msdb.dbo.syspolicy_management_facets
  GROUP BY name
  ORDER BY name
```

FIGURE 40-6

Viewing a policy. This policy enforces the AutoShrinking condition for every database on demand.

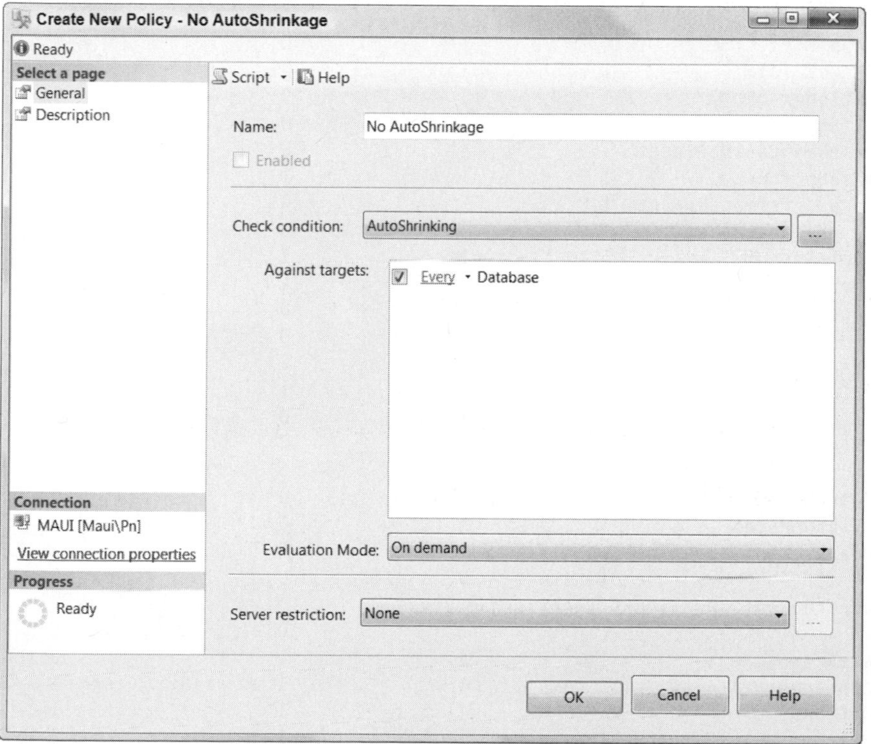

Result:

```
Facet                  On Demand  On Schedule On Change Log Only On Change Prevent
--------------------- ----------- ----------- ----------------- -----------------
ApplicationRole             1           1            1                 1
AsymmetricKey               1           1            1                 1
Audit                       1           1            0                 0
BackupDevice                1           1            0                 0
BrokerPriority              1           1            0                 0
BrokerService               1           1            0                 0
Certificate                 1           1            0                 0
Credential                  1           1            0                 0
CryptographicProvider       1           1            0                 0
Database                    1           1            0                 0
DatabaseAuditSpecification  1           1            0                 0
DatabaseDdlTrigger          1           1            0                 0
DatabaseRole                1           1            1                 1
DataFile                    1           1            0                 0
Default                     1           1            0                 0
Endpoint                    1           1            1                 1
FileGroup                   1           1            0                 0
FullTextCatalog             1           1            0                 0
FullTextIndex               1           1            0                 0
FullTextStopList            1           1            0                 0
IDatabaseMaintenanceFacet   1           1            0                 0
IDatabaseOptions            1           1            1                 0
IDatabasePerformanceFacet   1           1            0                 0
IDatabaseSecurityFacet      1           1            0                 0
ILoginOptions               1           1            1                 1
IMultipartNameFacet         1           1            1                 1
INameFacet                  1           1            0                 0
Index                       1           1            0                 0
IServerAuditFacet           1           1            0                 0
IServerConfigurationFacet   1           1            1                 0
IServerInformation          1           1            0                 0
IServerPerformanceFacet     1           1            0                 0
IServerSecurityFacet        1           1            0                 0
IServerSettings             1           1            0                 0
IServerSetupFacet           1           1            0                 0
ISurfaceAreaConfigurationForAnalysisServer
                            1           0            0                 0
ISurfaceAreaConfigurationForReportingServices
                            1           0            0                 0
ISurfaceAreaFacet           1           1            1                 0
ITableOptions               1           1            1                 1
IUserOptions                1           1            1                 1
IViewOptions                1           1            1                 1
LinkedServer                1           1            0                 0
LogFile                     1           1            0                 0
Login                       1           1            0                 0
MessageType                 1           1            0                 0
```

```
PartitionFunction              1    1    0    0
PartitionScheme                1    1    0    0
PlanGuide                      1    1    0    0
RemoteServiceBinding           1    1    0    0
ResourceGovernor               1    1    0    0
ResourcePool                   1    1    1    1
Rule                           1    1    0    0
Schema                         1    1    1    1
Server                         1    1    0    0
ServerAuditSpecification       1    1    0    0
ServerDdlTrigger               1    1    0    0
ServiceContract                1    1    0    0
ServiceQueue                   1    1    0    0
ServiceRoute                   1    1    0    0
Statistic                      1    1    0    0
StoredProcedure                1    1    1    1
SymmetricKey                   1    1    0    0
Synonym                        1    1    0    0
Table                          1    1    0    0
Trigger                        1    1    0    0
User                           1    1    0    0
UserDefinedAggregate           1    1    0    0
UserDefinedDataType            1    1    0    0
UserDefinedFunction            1    1    1    1
UserDefinedTableType           1    1    0    0
UserDefinedType                1    1    0    0
View                           1    1    0    0
WorkloadGroup                  1    1    1    1
XmlSchemaCollection            1    1    0    0
```

The fourth key selection on the General page is Server Restriction. This option may be used to define the target servers based on criteria.

CAUTION **PBM actually generates DDL triggers that enforce the policy and roll back DDL operations that don't comply with it. Don't manually delete or edit these DDL triggers. In addition, servers that use PBM must have nested triggers enabled.**

PBM also generates agent jobs for policy automation. They shouldn't be deleted either.

To programmatically view the created policies, query the `dbo.syspolicy_policies` view in the `MSDB` database:

```
select * from msdb.dbo.syspolicy_policies
```

Policies may be exported to XML and imported using the Policy context menu.

Evaluating Policies

Of course, policies would be purely academic if they never actually executed and evaluated any objects.

As described in the preceding section, policies may be set for On Schedule, On Demand, On Change, or Log Only.

Policies must be enabled using their context menu. On demand policies may not be enabled.

For policies set to On Demand, the policies may be evaluated for any object by selecting Policies ➪ Evaluate from the object's context menu. This opens the Evaluate Polices dialog for the object, shown in Figure 40-7.

FIGURE 40-7

All the policies that can be run on demand for an object can be selected and evaluated using the Evaluate Polices dialog.

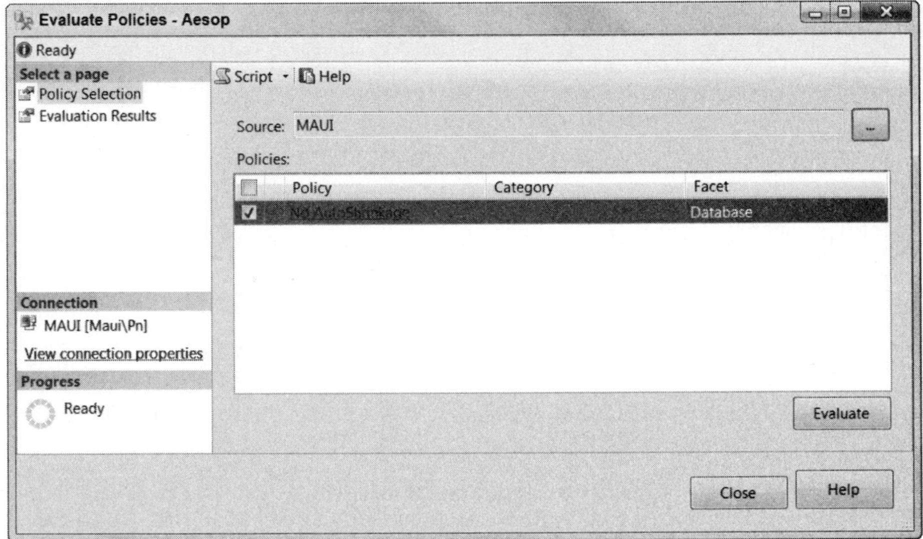

Outcome of the policy evaluations are displayed in the Evaluation Results page, as shown in Figure 40-8.

The current state of any object regarding all policies regardless of their execution mode may be seen in the View Policies dialog. You can find this dialog in any object's context menu under Policies ➪ View.

Within the View Policies dialog, the history for any policy evaluation for the object may be seen using the log viewer by clicking on the View History link in the policy row. Policy evaluation can also be seen in the Windows event log and the SQL Server event log.

Use the following to view a history of policy execution queries:

```
msdb.dbo.syspolicy_policy_execution_history_details
```

FIGURE 40-8

Here, the Aesop database passes the No AutoShrinkage policy and is declared to be in good health.

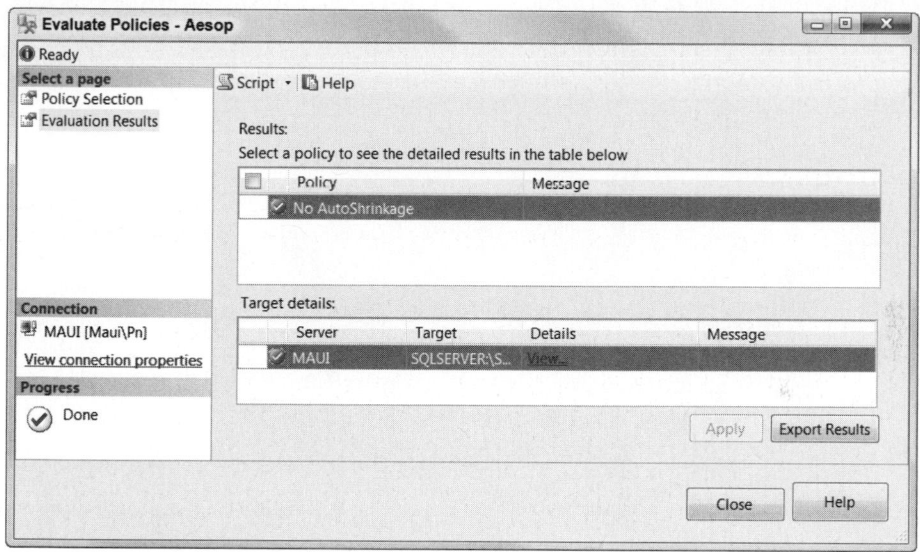

Use this to view exception queries:

```
msdb.dbo.syspolicy_policy_execution_history
```

PBM health is also well integrated into Management Studio's object listings. The Object Explorer Details page has an optional column to display the policy health of any object.

NOTE **PBM requires SQL Agent to be running on the central monitoring server. Be sure that the SQL Agent service is set to start automatically and that its service account password won't expire.**

Summary

If you're an operational DBA, policies will change your world. IT database operations will be more consistent, and your life should become smoother. Indeed, Policy-Based Management is a completely new animal, and it will take some time to build up a set of good conditions and policies; but when it's all put together, it will have been worth it.

The next chapter continues the thread of database administration with the nuts and bolts of backup and restore.

Chapter 41

Recovery Planning

IN THIS CHAPTER

- Understanding the recovery models
- Backing up user databases
- Understanding and working with the transaction log
- Recovering a lost database, a lost system database, or the entire server

The foundation for this book, the Information Architecture Principle (introduced in Chapter 2), puts into words the reason why there must be a solid recovery plan.

Information is an organizational asset, and, according to its value and scope, must be organized, inventoried, secured, and made readily available in a usable format for daily operations and analysis by individuals, groups, and processes, both today and in the future.

It goes without writing that for information to be "readily available . . . both today and in the future," regardless of hardware failure, catastrophes, or accidental deletion, there has to be a plan B.

Obviously, this is an imperfect world and bad things do happen to good people. Since you're bothering to read this chapter, I'll be honest and agree that doing backups isn't very exciting. In some jobs excitement means trouble, and this is one of them. To a good DBA, being prepared for the worst means having a sound recovery plan that has been tested more than once.

Consistent with the flexibility found in other areas of SQL Server, there are multiple ways to perform a backup, each suited to a different purpose. SQL Server offers three recovery models, which help organize the backup options and simplify database administration.

This chapter discusses the concepts that support the recovery effort, which entail both backup and restoration. It seems foolish to study backup without also learning about how restoration completes the recovery.

CROSS-REF **Recovery planning is not an isolated topic. Transactional integrity (Chapter 66) is deeply involved in the theory behind a sound recovery plan. Once the recovery strategy is determined, it's often implemented within a maintenance plan (Chapter 42). Because recovery is actually a factor of availability, the high availability of log shipping (Chapter 46), database mirroring (Chapter 47), and failover clustering (Chapter 48) is also a factor in recovery planning.**

While backups tend to be boring, restores tend to occur when people are excited. For this reason, it makes sense to be as familiar with restoration as with backup. Without restoring a backup, there is no way to determine whether the backup is good and can be used when it is really needed.

What's New in SQL Server Recovery?

Backup compression is introduced in SQL Server 2008 Enterprise Edition. This is one of the most frequently requested features and I am happy that this is released now. Although this feature is supported only in Enterprise Edition, every SQL Server 2008 edition can restore a compressed backup.

The following backup commands are no longer available in SQL Server 2008:

- `BACKUP LOG WITH NO_LOG`
- `BACKUP LOG WITH TRUNCATE_ONLY`

There is no replacement for these options in SQL Server 2008. These statements were used in previous versions of SQL Server to manually force the transaction log to be truncated without taking a backup. These options broke the log chain and the database was not protected from media failure until the next full or differential log backup.

A new feature has been added to rebuilding SQL Server 2008 system databases. The system databases used for rebuilding the local system databases do not come from the original installation media and are located locally in the \BINN\Templates folder and setup.exe in the 100\Setup Bootstrap\Release folder.

Recovery Concepts

The concept of database recovery is based on the D in the transactional-integrity ACID properties — transactional *durability*. Durability means that a transaction, once committed, regardless of hardware failure, must be persistent.

SQL Server accomplishes transactional durability with a write-ahead transaction log. Every transaction is written to the transaction log prior to being written to the data file. This provides a few benefits to the recovery plan:

- The transaction log ensures that every transaction can be recovered up to the very last moment before the server stopped.
- The transaction log permits backups while transactions are being processed.
- The transaction log reduces the impact of a hardware failure because the transaction log and the data file may be placed on different disk subsystems.

The strategy of a recovery plan should be based on the organization's tolerance level, or *pain level*, for lost transactions. Recovery-plan tactics involve choosing among the various backup options, generating a backup schedule, and off-site storage.

SQL Server backup and recovery are very flexible, offering three recovery models from which to choose. The transaction log can be configured, based on your recovery needs, according to one of the following recovery models:

- **Simple:** No transaction log backups
- **Bulk-logged:** The bulk-logged recovery model minimally logs bulk operations, although fully logging other transactions.
- **Full:** All transactions are logged.

In addition, SQL Server offers the following backup options:

- **Full:** Complete backup of all data
- **Differential:** Backup of all data pages modified since the last full backup
- **Partial:** Backup of primary filegroup, every read/write filegroup, and any optionally specified read-only files
- **Transaction log:** Backup of all transactions in the log
- **File or filegroup:** Backup of all the data in the file or filegroup
- **File differential:** Backup of all data pages modified since the last file or filegroup backup
- **Copy-only:** Backup of all the data without affecting the overall backup and restore procedures for the database

NOTE **Backing up the database may not be the only critical backup you have to perform. If the database-security scheme relies on Windows authentication, backing up the Windows users is important as well. The point is that the SQL Server recovery plan must fit into a larger IT recovery plan.**

Because SQL Server backups are very flexible, they can handle any backup-to-file ratio. A single backup instance can be spread across several backup files, creating a *backup set*. Conversely, a single backup set can contain multiple backup instances.

Restoration always begins with a full backup. Differential and transaction log backups then restore the transaction that occurred after the full backup.

Recovery Models

The recovery model configures SQL Server database settings to accomplish the type of recovery required for the database, as detailed in Table 41-1. The key differences among the recovery models involve how the transaction log behaves and which data is logged.

While the durability of the transaction is configurable, the transaction log is still used as a write-ahead transaction log to ensure that each transaction is atomic. In case of system failure, the transaction log is used by SQL Server to roll back any uncommitted transactions, as well as to complete any committed transactions.

TABLE 41-1

SQL Server Recovery Models

Recovery Model	Description	Transaction Atomicity	Transaction Durability	Bulk-Copy Operations (SELECT INTO and BULK INSERT)
Simple	Transaction log is continuously truncated on checkpoints	Yes	No, can restore only to the last full or differential backup	Minimally logged — high performance
Bulk-Logged	Bulked operations are minimally logged and all other transactions are fully logged. Minimal logging logs only the information required to recover the transaction but does not allow point-in-time recovery.	Yes	Maybe, can restore only to the last full or differential backup, or to the last transaction-log backup if no bulk-copy operations have been performed	Minimally logged — high performance
Full	All transactions are logged and stored until transaction-log backup	Yes	Yes, can restore up to the point of recovery	Slower than simple or bulk-logged

Simple recovery model

The simple recovery model is suitable for databases that require that each transaction be atomic, but not necessarily durable. The simple recovery model directs SQL Server to truncate, or empty, the transaction log on checkpoints. The transaction log will keep a transaction until it's confirmed in the data file, but after that point the space may be reused by another transaction in a round-robin style. This is the reason why the simple recovery model does not support transaction log backup.

A simple recovery model has the benefit of keeping the transaction log small, at the cost of potentially losing all transactions since the last full or differential backup. Choosing the simple recovery model is the equivalent of setting the `truncate log on checkpoint` database option to `true` in SQL Server 7.0.

A recovery plan based on a simple recovery model might perform full backups once a week and differential backups every weeknight, as shown in Figure 41-1. The full backup copies the entire database, and the differential backup copies all changes that have been made since the last full backup.

When restoring from a simple recovery plan:

1. Restore the most recent full backup.
2. Restore the most recent (optional) single differential backup.

FIGURE 41-1

A typical recovery plan using the simple recovery model includes only full and differential backups.

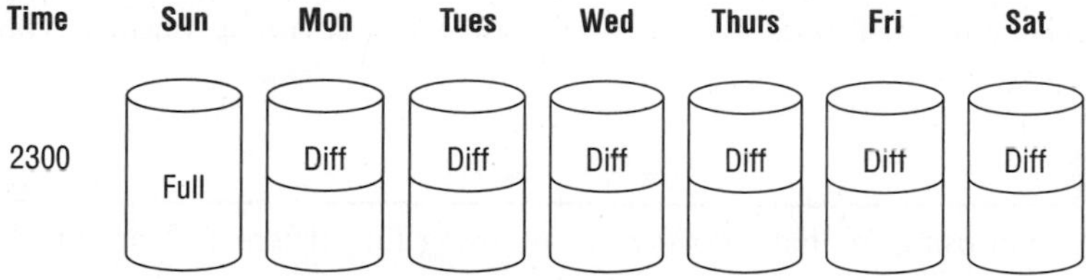

Best Practice

Simple recovery is mostly used for test and development databases or databases containing mostly read-only data. Simple recovery should not be used where loss of data since the last full or differential backup is unacceptable. In these cases, the full recovery model is recommended. The full recovery model is also a requirement for database mirroring and log shipping.

The full recovery model

The full recovery model offers the most robust recovery plan. Under this model all transactions, including bulk-logged operations, are fully logged in the transaction log. Even system functions such as index creation are fully logged. The primary benefit of this model is that every committed transaction in the database can be restored right up to the point when failure occurred.

Best Practice

Use the full recovery model for production user databases where data loss since the last full or differential backup is unacceptable. While it will run on a single-drive system, the transaction log should be located on a fault-tolerant disk subsystem physically separate from the data files to ensure a high level of transactional durability.

The trade-off for this high level of transactional integrity is a certain amount of performance:

- Bulk-logged and select-into operations will be slower. If the database doesn't import data using these methods, this is a moot point.

- Depending on the database activities, the transaction log may be huge. This can be controlled by performing regular transaction log backups. If copious drive space is available, this too is a moot point.
- Backing up and restoring the transaction log will take longer than it does with the other recovery models. However, in a crisis, restoring all the data will likely be more important than quickly restoring partial data.

The full recovery model can use all types of database backups. A typical backup schedule is illustrated in Figure 41-2.

FIGURE 41-2

A typical recovery plan using the full recovery model, using full, differential, and transaction-log backups.

Full Recovery Model Backup Plan

Time	Sun	Mon	Tues	Wed	Thurs	Fri	Sat
1000	Log	Log	Log	Log	Log	Log	Log
1200	Log	Log	Log	Log	Log	Log	Log
1400	Log	Log	Log	Log	Log	Log	Log
1600	Log	Log	Log	Log	Log	Log	Log
2300	Full	Diff	Diff	Full	Diff	Diff	Diff

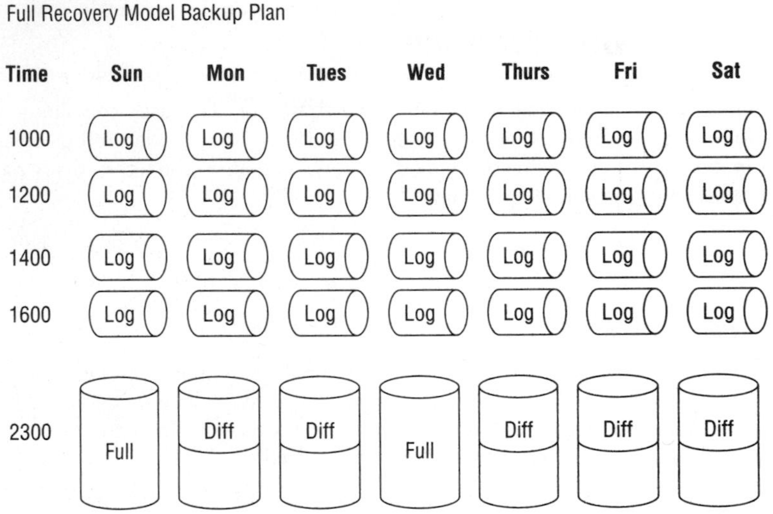

A full recovery backup plan will typically do a full database backup twice a week, and differential backups every other night. The transaction log is backed up throughout the day, from as little as two times to as often as every 15 minutes. The frequency of the transaction log backup is based on the maximum amount of data that will be lost. For example, perform transaction log backup every 15 minutes if you can afford to lose up to 15 minutes of data.

When restoring from the full recovery model, do the following:

1. Back up the current transaction log. This will capture all the log records since the last transaction log backup.

NOTE **If the disk subsystem containing the transaction log is lost, the database is marked suspect by SQL Server and it is not possible to back up the current transaction log. In this case, the best recovery option is to restore to the last transaction-log backup. Other reasons for a database to be marked suspect would be that the database file itself has been removed or renamed.**

2. Restore the most recent full backup.
3. Restore the most recent single differential backup, if one has been made since the last full backup.
4. Restore, in sequence, all the transaction-log backups made since the time of the last full or differential backup. If the last backup was a full backup, then restoring it is sufficient. If the last backup was a differential backup, you need to restore the most recent full backup before restoring the most recent differential.

The Management Studio restore form (discussed in the section "Performing the Restore with Management Studio," later in this chapter) automatically helps you choose the correct set of backups, so it's not as complicated as it sounds.

Bulk-logged recovery model

The bulk-logged recovery model is similar to the full recovery model except that the following operations are minimally logged:

- Bulk import operations (BCP, BULK INSERT, and INSERT ... SELECT * FROM OPENROWSET (BULK...)).
- SELECT INTO operations
- WRITETEXT and UPDATETEXT BLOB operations
- CREATE INDEX (including indexed views)
- ALTER INDEX REBUILD or DBCC DBREINDEX operations
- DROP INDEX

Because this recovery model minimally logs these operations, they run very fast. The transaction log only marks that the operations took place and tracks the *extents* (a group of eight data pages) that are affected by the bulk-logged operation. When the transaction log is backed up, the extents are copied to the transaction log in place of the bulk-logged marker.

The trade-off for bulk-logged operation performance is that the bulk-logged operation is not treated as a transaction. While the transaction log itself stays small, copying all affected extents to the transaction-log backup can make the log-backup file very large.

Because bulk-logged operations are minimally logged, if a failure should occur after the bulk-logged operation but before the transaction log is backed up, the bulk-logged operation is lost and the restore must be made from the last transaction log. Therefore, if the database is using the bulk-logged recovery model, every bulk-logged operation should be immediately followed by a transaction-log backup.

This model is useful only when the database sees a large number of bulk-logged operations, and if it's important to increase their performance. If the database is performing adequately during bulk-logged operations in the full recovery model, bypass the bulk-logged recovery model.

NOTE **The simple recovery model minimally logs bulk-copy operations too.**

Using this setting is essentially the same as setting the SELECT INTO/BULKCOPY database option to true.

Best Practice

It is recommended to minimally use the bulk-logged recovery model because you lose the capability to do point-in-time recovery to any point covered by a transaction log backup that contains even a single minimally logged operation. The best practice for production user databases is to use the full recovery model, take a transaction log backup before performing bulk operations, switch to the bulk-logged model, perform the bulk operations, and then immediately switch back to the full recovery model and take a transaction log backup. This enables point-in-time recovery and fully protects the data.

Setting the recovery model

The model system database's recovery model is applied to any newly created database. The full recovery model is the default for the Standard and Enterprise Editions. The Personal and Desktop editions use the simple recovery model as their default, but you can change the default by setting the recovery model for the model system database.

Using Management Studio, you can easily set the recovery model on the Options tab of the Database Properties dialog. Select the database and right-click to get to the Database Properties dialog.

In code, the recovery model is set with the `ALTER DATABASE` DDL command:

```
ALTER DATABASE DatabaseName SET Recovery Option;
```

The valid options are `FULL`, `BULK_LOGGED`, and `SIMPLE`. The following code sets the `AdventureWorks2008` sample database to the full recovery model:

```
USE AdventureWorks2008;
ALTER DATABASE AdventureWorks2008 SET Recovery FULL;
```

It is recommended to explicitly set the recovery model in the code that creates the database.

The current recovery model for every database can be determined from code using the `sys.databases` catalog view:

```
SELECT name, recovery_model_desc
  FROM sys.databases;
```

Modifying recovery models

While a production user database is typically set to a full recovery model, there's nothing to prevent you from switching between recovery models during operation to optimize performance and suit the specific needs of the moment.

It's perfectly valid to run during the day with the full recovery model for transaction durability, and then to switch to bulk-logged during data imports in the evening.

During recovery it's the full, differential, and transaction-log backups that count. The recovery operation doesn't care how they were made.

Because the simple recovery model does not permanently log the transactions, care must be taken in switching to or from the simple recovery model:

- If you are switching to simple, the transaction log should be backed up prior to the switch.
- If you are switching from simple, a full database backup should be performed immediately following the switch.
- Schedule regular transaction log backups and update your recovery plans.

Backing Up the Database

The actual process of performing a backup presents as many options as the underlying concepts present.

Backup destination

A backup may copy the data to any one of two possible destinations:

- **Disk subsystem:** A backup can be performed either to a local disk (preferably not the same disk subsystem as the database files) or to another server's disk drive by using the Universal Naming Convention (UNC). The SQL Server account must have write privileges to the remote drive in order to save the backup file.

Best Practice

It is recommended to back up the databases to a local disk (not the same disk where databases are stored) and then copy the backup files to tape or DVD (for small databases) using the organization's preferred IT backup method. This method is the fastest for SQL Server, and it enables the IT shop to continue using a familiar single-tape backup-software technique.

- **Tape:** SQL Server can back up directly to most tape-backup devices.

NOTE **Several companies offer a third-party backup for SQL Server. While you may find third-party backup useful, it is a good idea to become familiar with SQL Server's built-in recovery methods before making the decision to use it.**

A disk- or tape-backup file is not limited to a single backup event. The file may contain multiple backups and multiple types of backups.

Backup rotation

If the backup file is being copied to tape, then *media retention* or *rotation*, and the off-site media-storage location, become important.

A common technique is to rotate a set of five tapes for the weekly backups and another set of six tapes for the remaining daily backups. The weekly tapes would be labeled Sunday1, Sunday2, and so on, and the daily tapes would be labeled Monday, Tuesday, Wednesday, Thursday, Friday, and Saturday.

Palindromes also represent a great method for rotating backup tapes. A *palindrome* is a word, phrase, or number that's the same backward or forward, such as "kayak" or "drab as a fool, aloof as a bard." Some numbers when reversed and added to themselves will create a palindrome — for example, 236 + 632 = 868. Palindromes have a rich history: In ancient Greece they inscribed "Nipson anomemata me monan opsin," meaning "wash the sin as well as the face," on fountains.

Using four tapes labeled A through D, a backup rotation might be ABCDCBA ABCDCBA ....

Alternately, the palindrome method can be implemented so that each letter represents a larger interval, such as A for daily, B for weekly, C for monthly, and D for quarterly.

Rotating backup tapes off site is an important aspect of recovery planning. Ideally, a contract should support an off-site recovery location complete with server and workstations.

Performing backup with Management Studio

The first backup must be a full database backup to begin the backup cycles. You can perform a database backup from Management Studio, selecting the database to be backed up. From the database context menu, or from the database Summary Page, select Tasks ➪ Back Up to open the Back Up Database form, shown in Figure 41-3.

The backup source is configured in the General page:

- **Database:** The database to be backed up. By default this is the current database in Management Studio.
- **Backup type:** The type of backup — Full, Differential, or Transaction Log. If the database is set to the simple recovery model, transaction log will not be available. For full or differential backups, the whole database or selected files and filegroups can be backed up.
- **Copy Only Backup:** Allows you to take copy only backup. This will back up all the data without affecting the overall backup and restore procedures for the database. Although this backup type was first introduced in SQL Server 2005, Management Studio in SQL Server 2005 did not support it.
- **Backup Component:** The database component to be backed up: Database or File and Filegroups. If the backup type selected is Transaction Log, the backup component is grayed out. Database indicates that the full database is backed up. File and Filegroups indicates that the specified files and/or filegroups are backed up.

The rest of the Back Up Database form specifies the destination:

- **Name:** The required name of the backup
- **Description:** Optional additional information about the backup
- **Backup set will expire:** SQL Server will prevent another backup from overwriting this backup until the expiration date.
- **Destination:** Sets the destination tape file or disk file. If the current destination is incorrect, delete it and add the correct destination.
- **Contents:** Displays the backups already in the selected destinations

FIGURE 41-3

The General page of the Back Up Database form

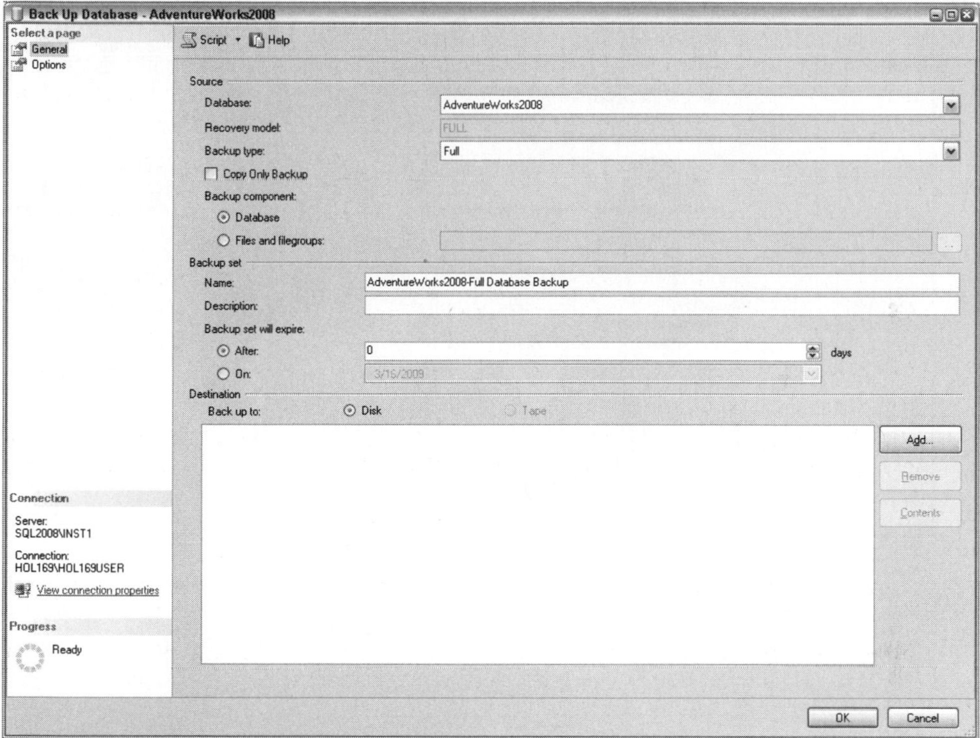

The Options page of the Back Up Database form is shown in Figure 41-4.

The Options page presents the following options:

- **Append to the existing backup set or Overwrite all existing backup sets:** Determines whether the current backup will be added to the backup file or whether the backup media should be initialized and a new series of backups placed in them
- **Check media set name and backup set expiration:** Verifies the name and expiration date for the backup
- **Verify backup when finished:** Verifies that the backup is complete and the file is readable. This option does not compare the data in the backup with the data in the database, nor does it verify the integrity of the backup.
- **Perform checksum before writing to media:** This verifies that the data read from the database is consistent with any checksum or torn-page detection on the database. It also calculates a checksum of the entire backup and saves it in the backup. This can help ensure that the database being backed up does not have any corruption due to the disk subsystem.

FIGURE 41-4

The Options page of the Back Up Database form.

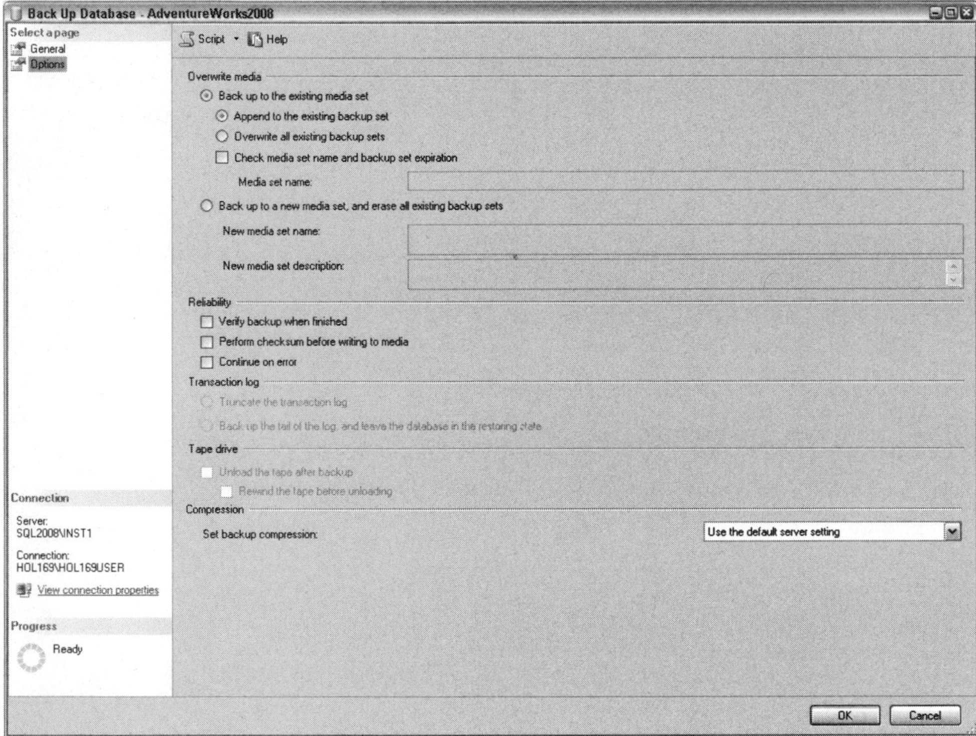

- **Continue on error:** Allows backup to continue even after it encounters one or more errors
- **Unload the tape after backup:** Directs the tape to eject, which helps prevent other backups from overwriting the backup file
- **Rewind the tape before unloading:** This is enabled only if Unload the tape after backup is selected. This rewinds the tape before ejecting it.
- **Truncate the transaction log:** Backs up the transaction log and truncates the inactive transactions to free log space. This is the default option for the Transaction Log backup. This option is available only when Transaction Log is selected for Backup Type on the General page.
- **Back up the tail of the log, and leave the database in the restoring state:** Backs up the transaction log that has not yet been backed up. This option is equivalent to using `NO_TRUNCATE` or `NORECOVERY` in the `BACKUP` statement. This option is available only when Transaction Log is selected for Backup Type on the General page.
- **Set backup compression:** Allows you to choose the default server-level backup compression setting or ignore the server-level default and compress the backup or not compress the backup. At installation the default behavior is no backup compression. You can change this

default by setting the default server-level backup compression setting in Management Studio: Check the Compress Backup check box in the Database Settings tab of Server Properties.

NOTE **Backup compression is a new feature introduced in SQL Server 2008 Enterprise Edition. Compressed backup is smaller than uncompressed backup and therefore requires less I/O and increases backup speed significantly. However, this comes at the price of high CPU usage, which may impact other operations on the server. It is recommended to create low-priority compressed backups in a session whose CPU usage is limited by Resource Governor. For more on Resource Governor, see Chapter 69.**

Backing up the database with code

The BACKUP command offers a few more options than Management Studio, and using the BACKUP command directly is useful for assembling SQL Server Agent jobs by hand, rather than with the Maintenance Plan Back Up Database Task.

Without all the options and frills, the most basic BACKUP command is as follows:

```
BACKUP DATABASE Databasename
  TO DISK = 'file location'
  WITH
    NAME = 'backup name';
```

The following command backs up the AdventureWorks2008 database to a disk file and names the backup AdventureWorks2008Backup:

```
BACKUP DATABASE AdventureWorks2008
  TO DISK = 'e:\AdventureWorks2008Backup.bak'
  WITH
    NAME = 'AdventureWorks2008Backup';
```

Result:

```
Processed 17944 pages for database 'AdventureWorks2008', file
'AdventureWorks2008_Data' on file 1.
Processed 2 pages for database 'AdventureWorks2008', file
'AdventureWorks2008_Log' on file 1.
BACKUP DATABASE successfully processed 17946 pages in 7.954 seconds
(17.625 MB/sec).
```

The backup command has a few important options that deserve to be mentioned first:

- TAPE (Backup To:): To back up to tape instead of disk, use the TO TAPE option and specify the tape-drive location:

  ```
  TO TAPE = '\\.\TAPE0'
  ```

- DIFFERENTIAL: Causes the BACKUP command to perform a differential backup instead of a full database backup. The following command performs a differential backup:

  ```
  BACKUP DATABASE AdventureWorks2008
    TO DISK = 'e:\AdventureWorks2008Backup.bak'
    WITH
      DIFFERENTIAL,
      NAME = 'AdventureWorks2008Backup';
  ```

- To back up a file or filegroup, list it after the database name. This technique can help organize backups.
- PASSWORD: Use this to set the password for the backup. The password will be needed again to restore the backup. The password protection is weak and it is recommended to backup to tapes and store them in a secure location or backup to disks that have an adequate access control list (ACL).

NOTE **Avoid using the password option, as this feature will be removed in a future release of SQL Server.**

- COMPRESSION/NO_COMPRESSION: Overrides the server-level default backup compression. COMPRESSION enables backup compression and performs checksums to detect media corruptions.
- CHECKSUM/NO_CHECKSUM: Identical to the "Perform checksum before writing to media" option within Management Studio.
- STOP_ON_ERROR/CONTINUE_AFTER_ERROR: Identical to the "continue on error" option within Management Studio.

The BACKUP command has numerous additional options:

- DESCRIPTION: Identical to the Description field within Management Studio
- EXPIREDATE: Identical to Management Studio; prevents the backup from being overwritten before the expiration date
- RETAINDAYS: The number of days, as an integer, before SQL Server will overwrite the backup
- STATS = %: Tells SQL Server to report the progress of the backup in the percentage increment specified; the default increment is 10 percent. This option is very useful, particularly while troubleshooting a failed backup, as it gives you an idea of when the backup is failing. Also, for huge databases this indicates what percentage of the backup is completed.
- BLOCKSIZE: Sets the physical block size in bytes. The default is 65,536 bytes for tape devices, and 512 otherwise. This option is usually not required, as backup automatically selects the correct block size of the device. If a backup to disk will later be copied to a CD/RW, try a block size of 2,048.
- MEDIANAME: Specifies the name of the media volume. This option serves as a safety check: If the backup is being added to the media, the name must match.
- MEDIADESCRIPTION: Writes an optional media description
- MEDIAPASSWORD: Creates an optional media password that applies to the entire medium (disk file or tape). The first time the medium is created the password can be set. If the password is specified when the medium is created, then it must be specified every subsequent time the backup medium is accessed to add another backup or to restore.

NOTE **Avoid using the MEDIAPASSWORD option, as this feature will be removed in a future release of SQL Server.**

- INIT/NOINIT: Initializes the tape or disk file, thus overwriting all existing backup sets in the medium. SQL Server will prevent initialization if any of the backups in the medium have not expired or still have the number of retaining days. NOINIT is the default.

- NOSKIP/SKIP: This option "skips" the backup-name and backup-date checking that normally prevents overwriting backups. NOSKIP is the default.
- NOFORMAT/FORMAT: FORMAT writes a new media header on media volumes used for backup and overwrites the existing backup sets; therefore the existing contents of the volume become unusable. NOFORMAT (default behavior) preserves the existing media header and backup sets. FORMAT automatically includes SKIP and INIT.

The last options apply only when backing up to tape:

- REWIND/NOREWIND: REWIND directs SQL Server to rewind the tape. The default is to REWIND.
- UNLOAD/LOAD: UNLOAD automatically rewinds and unloads the tape. This is the default until the user session specifies load.
- RESTART: This option has no effect. It is there for compatibility with previous versions of SQL Server.

Verifying the backup with code

Management Studio's backup includes an option to verify the backup, and the T-SQL BACKUP command does not. Management Studio actually calls the T-SQL RESTORE VERIFYONLY command after the backup to perform the verification:

```
RESTORE VERIFYONLY
  FROM DISK =  'e:\AdventureWorks2008Backup.bak'
```

Result:

```
The backup set is valid.
```

The verification has a few options, such as *Eject tape after backup*. Most of these verification options are for tapes and are self-explanatory.

NOTE **RESTORE VERIFYONLY does not actually restore the database. It only checks whether the backup is complete and readable. By default, it checks the backup checksums if they are present, and proceeds without verification if they are not present.**

Working with the Transaction Log

Sometimes it seems that the transaction log has a life of its own. The space within the file seems to grow and shrink without rhyme or reason. If you've felt this way, you're not alone. This section should shed some light on why the transaction log behaves as it does.

Inside the transaction log

The transaction log contains all the transactions for a database. If the server crashes, the transaction log is used for recovery by rolling back uncommitted partial transactions and by completing any transactions that were committed but not written to the data file.

Virtually, the log can be imagined as a sequential list of transactions sorted by date and time. Physically, however, SQL Server writes to different parts of the physical log file in virtual blocks without a specific order. Some parts might be in use, making other parts available, so the log reuses itself in a loose round-robin fashion.

The active and inactive divide

The transactions in the transaction log can be divided into two groups (see Figure 41-5):

- **Active transactions** are uncommitted and not yet written to the data file.
- **Inactive transactions** are all those transactions before the earliest active transaction.

FIGURE 41-5

The inactive transactions are all those prior to the oldest active transaction.

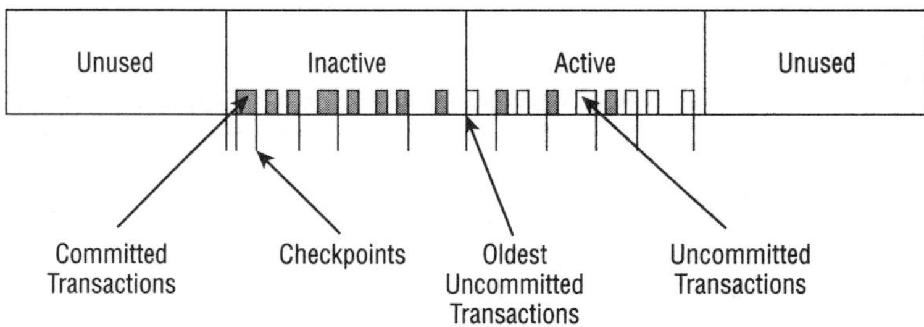

Because transactions are of varying duration, and are committed at different times, it's very likely that committed transactions are in the active portion of the log. The active portion does not merely contain all uncommitted transactions, but all transactions since the start of the oldest uncommitted transaction. One very old uncommitted transaction can make the active portion appear unusually large.

Transaction checkpoints

Understanding how SQL Server uses checkpoints in the transaction log is important to understanding how the transaction log is backed up and emptied. For performance reasons, every time a database page is modified in memory, it is not written to disk immediately. SQL Server generates automatic checkpoints to write the dirty database pages from memory to disk. The time interval between automatic checkpoints is variable and depends on the amount of modifications made to the database and the `recovery interval` SQL Server configuration option. Checkpoints calculate the amount of work that must be done to recover the database during a system restart.

A checkpoint also occurs under any of the following conditions:

- When an `ALTER DATABASE` command is used
- When the SQL Server is shut down

NOTE **If you used the `SHUTDOWN WITH NOWAIT` command to shut down SQL Server, then SQL Server will shut down without performing checkpoints in any database.**

- A minimally logged operation is performed in the database

- Database backup is done
- When an activity requiring database shutdown or database restart is performed
- When the number of log entries exceeds the estimated amount of work required by the SQL Server's `recovery interval` configuration option
- If the database is in simple recovery model and the transaction log becomes 70 percent full

Checkpoints may be manually initiated with a `CHECKPOINT` command. Checkpoints perform the following activities:

- Marks the checkpoint spot in the transaction log
- Writes a checkpoint-log record, including the following:
  - The oldest active transaction
  - The oldest replication transaction that has not been replicated
  - A list of all active transactions
  - Information about the minimum work required to roll back the database
- Marks the space before the oldest uncommitted transaction in a database with simple recovery for reuse
- Writes all dirty data and log pages to disk

Basically, a checkpoint gets everything up to date as best it can and then records the current state of the dividing line between active and inactive in the log.

Backing up the transaction log

Performing a transaction log backup is very similar to performing a full or differential backup, with a few notable differences.

The T-SQL command is as follows:

```
BACKUP LOG AdventureWorks2008
  TO DISK = 'e:\AdventureWorks2008Backup.bak'
  WITH
    NAME = 'AdventureWorks2008Backup';
```

Result:

```
Processed 2 pages for database 'AdventureWorks2008', file
'AdventureWorks2008_Log' on file 2.
BACKUP LOG successfully processed 2 pages in 0.118 seconds
(0.095 MB/sec).
```

The same media options apply to the transaction log backup that apply to the database backup; in addition, two options are transaction-log specific:

- `NO_TRUNCATE\CONTINUE_AFTER_ERROR`: Used for backing up the tail of the log of a damaged database that is offline and does not start. If the data files of a user database are damaged, a tail log backup succeeds only if the transaction log files are not damaged, the state of the database supports tail log backup, and the database does not contain any bulk logged operations.

- `NORECOVERY`: Used to backup the tail of the log of a database that is online and for which you intend to perform `RESTORE` next.

If the data file of the user database and `master` database is damaged, then provided the transaction log is not damaged, to minimize data loss you can still backup the tail of the transaction log as follows:

1. Rename the transaction log files.
2. Rebuild the `master` database with command-line setup.
3. Reapply any SQL Server updates that were previously applied.
4. Create a new user database. The number of data and log files needs to match the number of files of the damaged database. The size of the files can be different.
5. Stop SQL Server.
6. Delete the data files of the new database and replace the log files with the original transaction log files.
7. Start SQL Server.
8. The new database will fail to recover, as we deleted the data file. Run the following command to backup the tail of the log:

```
BACKUP LOG Databasename
  TO DISK = 'file location'
  WITH NO_TRUNCATE;
```

NOTE **If only the data files of the user database are damaged and the master database and transaction log file of the user database are available, the tail of the log can be backed up directly by running the preceding `BACKUP LOG` command with the `NO_TRUNCATE` option.**

The transaction log cannot be backed up if any of the following conditions exist:

- The database is using a simple recovery model.
- The database is using a bulk-logged recovery model, a bulk-logged operation has been executed, and the database files are damaged.
- Database files have been added or removed.

In any of these cases, perform a full database backup instead.

Truncating the log

Updates and deletes might not increase the size of a data file, but to the transaction log every transaction of any type is simply more data. Left to its own devices, the transaction log will continue to grow with every data modification.

The solution is to back up the inactive portion of the transaction log and then remove it. By default, backing up the transaction log will also truncate the log (refer to Figure 41-3).

NOTE **`BACKUP LOG WITH NO_LOG` and `BACKUP LOG WITH TRUNCATE_ONLY` are discontinued in SQL Server 2008. To truncate the log, either take regular transaction log backups or put the database in simple recovery model.**

The transaction log and simple recovery model

When the database is using a simple recovery model, the transaction log ensures that each committed transaction is written to the data file, and that's it. When SQL Server performs a checkpoint and the transaction log is truncated, the free space of the transaction log fluctuates but the minimum is the size of the active portion of the transaction log.

Under the simple recovery model, performing a manual checkpoint will truncate the log and free the log space.

NOTE **Truncating the log marks the inactive portion of the log for reuse and does not reduce the physical size of the transaction log. To reduce the physical size you need to run `DBCC SHRINKFILE` to manually shrink the log file. I have seen many DBAs running the `DBCC SHRINKFILE` command to shrink the log file right after log backup. I highly discourage this because `DBCC SHRINKFILE` can cause severe file-system fragmentation, as the files will likely need to grow again after they have been shrunk, causing performance degradation. Instead, it is important to correctly size the transaction log and perform frequent log backups to keep the size in check.**

To discover the operation that is preventing log truncation, use the `log_reuse_wait_desc` column of the `sys.databases` catalog view.

Recovery Operations

There are any number of reasons to restore a database, including the following:

- A disk subsystem has failed.
- A sleepy programmer forgot a `WHERE` clause in a SQL `UPDATE` statement and updated everyone's salary to minimum wage.
- The server melted into a pool of silicon and disk platters.
- A large import worked, but with yesterday's data.

The best reason to restore a database is to practice the backup/restore cycle, and to prove that the recovery plan works. It is important to perform regular testing of your backup and restore strategy as a fire drill. Without confidence in the recovery, there's little point to doing backups.

Detecting the problem

If a database file is missing, clicking the database in Management Studio pops up a message saying that the database is unavailable. To further investigate a problem, check the SQL Server Errorlog. In Management Studio, the log can be viewed under Management ➪ SQL Server Logs. SQL Server writes errors and events to an error log file in the `\Log` directory under the `MSSQL` directory. SQL Server creates a new file every time the server is started. The six previous versions of the Errorlog file are saved in the same directory. Some errors may also be written to the Windows Application Event Log.

NOTE **To retain more than six Errorlogs, right-click SQL Server Logs in Management Studio and select Configure.**

Recovery sequences

The two most important concepts about recovering a database are as follows:

- A recovery operation always begins by restoring a full backup and then restores any additional differential or transactional backups. The restore never copies only yesterday's work. It restores the entire database up to a certain point.
- There's a difference between restore and recover. A *restore* copies the data back into the database and leaves the transactions open. *Recovery* is the process of handling the transactions left open in the transaction log. If a database-recovery operation requires that four files be restored, only the last file is restored `WITH RECOVERY`.

Only logins who are members of the `sysadmins` fixed server role can restore a database that doesn't currently exist. `sysadmins` and `db_owners` can restore databases that do currently exist.

The actual recovery effort depends on the type of damage and the previous recovery plans. Table 41-2 is a comparative listing of recovery operations.

Performing the restore with Management Studio

As with the `BACKUP` command, there are numerous ways to launch the restore form within Management Studio:

Select the database to be backed up. From the context or Action menu select Tasks ➪ Restore ➪ Database to open the SQL Server Restore Database form.

TABLE 41-2

Recovery Sequences

Recovery Model	Damaged Database File	Damaged Transaction Log
Simple	1) Restore full backup. 2) Restore latest differential backup (if needed).	It is very likely there are unapplied transactions lost with the transaction log and the database is inconsistent. It is recommended to fall back on your backups and use the steps documented for "damaged database file."
Full or Bulk-logged	1) Back up current transaction log with `NO_TRUNCATE` option*. 2) Restore full backup. 3) Restore latest differential backup (if needed). 4) Restore all the transaction-log backups since the last differential or full backup. All committed transactions will be recovered.	1) Restore full backup. 2) Restore latest differential backup (if needed). 3) Restore all the transaction-log backups since the last differential or full backup. Transactions made since the last backup will be lost.

*If the database is using the bulk-logged recovery model and a bulk-insert operation occurred since the last transaction-log backup, the backup will fail. Transactions that occurred after the transaction-log backup will not be recoverable.

The Restore Database form, shown in Figure 41-6, does a great job of intelligently navigating the potential chaos of the backup sequences, and it always offers only legal restore options.

FIGURE 41-6

Only the correct sequence of restoring from multiple backup files is possible from Management Studio's Restore Database form.

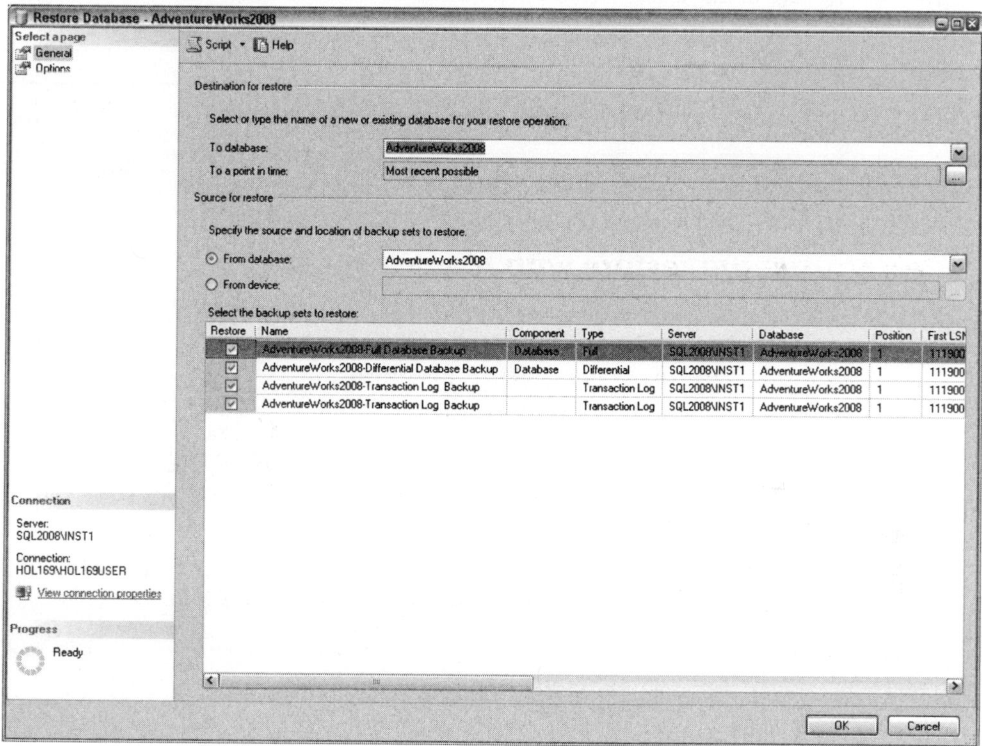

The selection you make at the top of the form is the name of the database after the restore.

The Restore Database form can restore database backups, file backups, or backups from a device (e.g. a tape drive). The Restore Wizard will present a hierarchical tree of backups, while the filegroups or file restore lists the files and must be manually restored in the correct order.

The "Select the backup sets to restore" option displays the available backups. Management Studio uses the backup history in the `msdb` database and creates a restore plan. For example, under the full recovery model, the restore plan selects the full database backup followed by the most recent differential database backup (if available), followed by subsequent log backups.

If the backup history, stored in `msdb`, is not available — because the server is being rebuilt or the database is being restored to a different server — then use the Restore: From Device option to manually select the specific backup disk file and backup instance within the file.

The process of one full backup, the second differential backup, and the following 15 transaction-log backups can be correctly sequenced by selecting the final transaction log to be restored. Restoring the 17 backup files is performed with a single click of the OK button.

If one of the backup files being restored is a transaction log, the Point in Time Restore option becomes available because only a transaction log can restore some of the transactions. The point-in-time restore will restore all transactions committed before the time selected.

The Options page of the Restore Database form is shown in Figure 41-7.

FIGURE 41-7

The Options page of the Restore Database form.

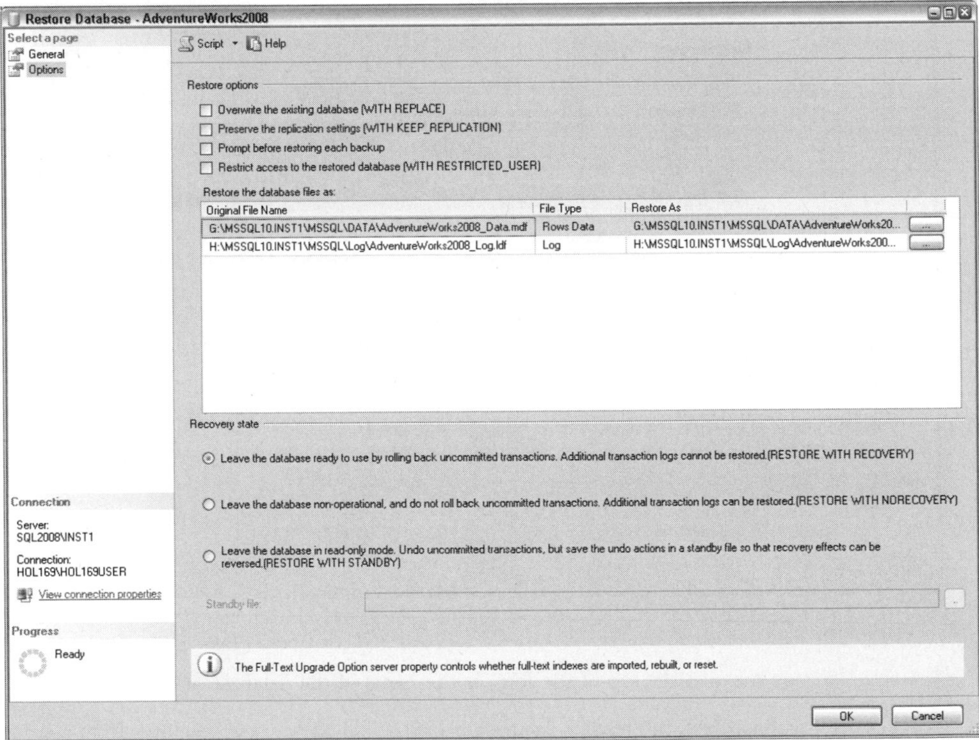

The Options page of the Restore Database dialog offers a few significant options:

- "Overwrite the existing database" disables a safety check that prevents Database A backup from being restored as Database B and accidentally overwriting an existing Database B.
- "Preserve the replication settings" preserves the replication settings when restoring a published database on a different SQL Server (other than the SQL Server where the database was created). This option is available only with the "Leave the database ready for use by rolling back the uncommitted transactions" option.

- "Prompt before restoring each backup" prompts before continuing to restore the next backup in the restore sequence. This option is useful when you are restoring from tape backups and need to swap tapes.
- "Restrict access to the restored database" restricts access to the restored database only to members of db_owner, dbcreator or sysadmin.
- Because it is very possible that the database is being restored to a different file location than the original backup, the "Restore the database files as" section in the Options tab includes a way to assign new file locations.
- "Leave the database ready for use by rolling back the uncommitted transactions" should be used for restoring the final backup. This option recovers the database and does not allow additional transaction logs to be restored.
- "Leave the database non-operational, and do not roll back the uncommitted transactions" enables you to restore additional backups. If you select this option, the "Preserve replication settings" option is unavailable.
- "Leave the database in read-only mode" leaves the database in a standby mode in which the database is available for limited read-only access.

If only certain files or filegroups are being restored, then select Tasks ➪ Restore ➪ File or Filegroups to select the files or filegroups you wish to restore.

Restoring with T-SQL code

Database backup is a regularly scheduled occurrence, so if SQL Server's built-in Maintenance Plan Wizard isn't to your liking, it makes sense to write some repeatable code to perform backups and set up your own SQL Server Agent jobs.

However, unless the backup plan is only a full backup, it's difficult to know how many differential backups or transaction-log backups need to be restored; and because each backup file requires a separate RESTORE command, it's difficult to script the recovery effort beforehand without writing a lot of code to examine the msdb tables and determine the restore sequence properly.

The backupset table in the msdb database contains a row for each backup set. You can query this table to find information on all the successful backups.

The RESTORE command will restore from a full, differential, or transaction-log backup:

```
RESTORE DATABASE (or LOG) DatabaseName
  Optional-File or Filegroup or Page
  FROM BackUpDevice
  WITH
    FILE = FileNumber,
  PARTIAL,

    NORECOVERY or RECOVERY or STANDBY = UnDoFileName,
    REPLACE,
    STOPAT datetime,
    STOPATMARK = 'markname'
    STOPBEFOREMARK = 'markname'
```

To restore a full or differential backup, use the RESTORE DATABASE command; otherwise, use the RESTORE LOG for a transaction log. To restore a specific file or filegroup, add its name after the database name. The PARTIAL option specifies a partial restore that restores the primary filegroup and any specified secondary filegroup(s).

A backup set often contains several backup instances. For example, a backup set might consist of the following:

1: Full backup

2: Differential backup

3, 4, 5, 6: Transaction-log backups

7: Differential backup

8, 9: Transaction-log backups

The WITH FILE option specifies the backup to restore. If it's not included in the command, the first backup instance is restored.

If a password was created with the backup, the password is required to perform a restore from the backup.

NOTE **Avoid using the `password` option, as this feature will be removed in a future release of SQL Server.**

To restore one or more pages, use PAGE = 'file:page[,...n]', where PAGE indicates a list of one or more files and pages, file indicates the file ID containing the page to be restored, page indicates the page ID of the page to be restored in the file, and n indicates multiple pages can be specified.

The RECOVERY/NORECOVERY option is vital to the RESTORE command. Every time a SQL Server starts, it automatically checks the transaction log, rolling back any uncommitted transactions and completing any committed transactions. This process is called *recovery*, and it's a part of the ACID properties of the database.

Therefore, if the restore has the NORECOVERY option, SQL Server restores the log without handling any transactions. Conversely, RECOVERY instructs SQL Server to handle the transactions. In the sequence of the recovery operation, all the restores must have the NORECOVERY option enabled except for the last restore, which must have the RECOVERY option enabled.

Deciding between RECOVERY and NORECOVERY is one of the complications involved in trying to write a script to handle any possible future recovery operation.

The STANDBY option allows the recovery effects to be undone.

If the recovery operation includes a transaction-log restore, the recovery can stop before the end of the transaction log. The options STOPAT and STOPATMARK will leave the end of the transaction log unrestored. The STOPAT accepts a time, and the STOPATMARK restores only to a transaction that was created with a named mark. The STOPBEFOREMARK option restores everything up to the beginning of the marked transaction.

The REPLACE option creates the database and its related files even if another database already exists with the same name.

CROSS-REF **Chapter 26, "Creating DML Triggers," details SQL Server transactions and how to create marked transactions.**

The following script demonstrates an example of a restore sequence that includes a full backup and two transaction-log backups:

```
-- BackUp and recovery example

CREATE DATABASE Plan2Recover;
```

Result:

```
Command(s) completed successfully.
```

Continuing:

```
USE Plan2Recover;

CREATE TABLE T1 (
  PK INT Identity PRIMARY KEY,
  Name VARCHAR(15)
  );
Go
INSERT T1 VALUES ('Full');
go
BACKUP DATABASE Plan2Recover
  TO DISK = 'e:\P2R.bak'
  WITH
    NAME = 'P2R_Full',
    INIT;
```

Result:

```
(1 row(s) affected)
Processed 168 pages for database 'Plan2Recover', file 'Plan2Recover'
on file 1.
Processed 6 pages for database 'Plan2Recover', file 'Plan2Recover_log'
on file 1.
BACKUP DATABASE successfully processed 174 pages in 0.800 seconds
(1.690 MB/sec).
```

Continuing:

```
INSERT T1 VALUES ('Log 1');
go
BACKUP Log Plan2Recover
  TO DISK = 'e:\P2R.bak'
  WITH
    NAME = 'P2R_Log';
```

Result:

```
(1 row(s) affected)
Processed 6 pages for database 'Plan2Recover', file 'Plan2Recover_log'
on file 2.
```

```
BACKUP LOG successfully processed 6 pages in 0.113 seconds
(0.393 MB/sec).
```

Continuing:

```
INSERT T1 VALUES ('Log 2');
go
BACKUP Log Plan2Recover
  TO DISK = 'e:\P2R.bak'
  WITH
    NAME = 'P2R_Log';
```

Result:

```
(1 row(s) affected)
Processed 1 pages for database 'Plan2Recover', file 'Plan2Recover_log'
on file 3.
BACKUP LOG successfully processed 1 pages in 0.082 seconds
(0.005 MB/sec).
```

Continuing:

```
SELECT * FROM T1;
```

Result:

```
PK          Name
----------- ---------------
1           Full
2           Log 1
3           Log 2

(3 row(s) affected)
```

At this point the server is hit with a direct bolt of lightning and all drives are fried, with the exception of the backup files. The following recovery operation goes through the full backup and the two transaction-log backups. Notice the NORECOVERY and RECOVERY options:

```
-- NOW PERFORM THE RESTORE
Use Master;
RESTORE DATABASE Plan2Recover
  FROM DISK = 'e:\P2R.bak'
  With FILE = 1, NORECOVERY;
```

Result:

```
Processed 168 pages for database 'Plan2Recover', file 'Plan2Recover'
on file 1.
Processed 6 pages for database 'Plan2Recover', file 'Plan2Recover_log'
on file 1.
```

```
RESTORE DATABASE successfully processed 174 pages in 0.168 seconds
(8.050 MB/sec).
```

Continuing:

```
RESTORE LOG Plan2Recover
  FROM DISK = 'e:\P2R.bak'
  With FILE = 2, NORECOVERY;
```

Result:

```
Processed 0 pages for database 'Plan2Recover', file 'Plan2Recover'
on file 2.
Processed 6 pages for database 'Plan2Recover', file 'Plan2Recover_log'
on file 2.
RESTORE LOG successfully processed 6 pages in 0.028 seconds
(1.586 MB/sec).
```

Continuing:

```
RESTORE LOG Plan2Recover
  FROM DISK = 'e:\P2R.bak'
  With FILE = 3, RECOVERY;
```

Result:

```
Processed 0 pages for database 'Plan2Recover', file 'Plan2Recover'
on file 3.
Processed 1 pages for database 'Plan2Recover', file 'Plan2Recover_log'
on file 3.
RESTORE LOG successfully processed 1 pages in 0.004 seconds
(0.122 MB/sec).
```

To test the recovery operation:

```
USE Plan2Recover;
Select * from T1;
```

Result:

```
PK          Name
----------- ---------------
1           Full
2           Log 1
3           Log 2
(3 row(s) affected)
```

As this script shows, it is possible to recover using T-SQL, but in this case Management Studio beats code as the best way to accomplish the task.

System Databases Recovery

So far, this chapter has dealt only with user databases, but the system databases are important to the recovery operation as well. The `master` database contains key database and security information, and the `MSDB` database holds the schedules and jobs for SQL Server, as well as the backup history. A complete recovery plan must include the system databases.

Master database

The `master` database, by default, uses the simple recovery model. Using only full backups for the `master` database is OK; it's not a transactional database.

Backing up the master database

The `master` database is backed up in the same manner as user databases. Be sure to back up the `master` database when doing any of the following:

- Creating or deleting databases
- Modifying security by adding logins or changing roles
- Modifying any server or database-configuration options

Because the `MSDB` database holds a record of all backups, back up the `master` database and then the `MSDB`.

Recovering the master database

If the `master` database is corrupted or damaged, SQL Server won't start. Attempting to start SQL Server will have no effect. Attempting to connect to the instance with Management Studio will invoke a warning that the server does not exist or that access is denied. The only solution is to first rebuild the `master` database using the command-line setup (as shown next), reapply any SQL Server updates, start SQL Server in single-user mode, and restore the `master` database.

1. Rebuild the `master` database using the following command-line setup:

   ```
   setup /QUIET /ACTION=REBUILDDATABASE /INSTANCENAME="<instance name>"
   /SQLSYSADMINACCOUNTS="<DomainName\UserName >" /SAPWD="<password>"
   ```

   - `setup.exe` is either from your original installation media or the "local" `setup.exe` as found in the 100\Setup Bootstrap\Release directory.
   - The `/QUIET` switch suppresses all error messages.
   - The `/ACTION=REBUILDDATABASE` switch rebuilds all the system databases.
   - The `/INSTANCENAME` switch specifies the name of your SQL Server named instance. Use `MSSQLServer` for "*<instance_name>*" for the default instance.
   - The `/SQLSYSADMINACCOUNTS` switch corresponds to the currently logged in domain user running this rebuild process. The user must be a member of the SQL Server instance's sysadmin server role.
   - The `/SAPWD` switch is used to indicate a new SA password if you configured SQL Server for mixed authentication.

NOTE **A new feature has been added to rebuilding the system databases. The system databases used for rebuilding the local system databases do not come from the original installation media and are located locally in the \BINN\Templates folder, and setup.exe is located in the 100\Setup Bootstrap\Release folder. Also notice that the switches have changed compared to SQL Server 2005.**

2. Run the following from the command prompt to start a default instance of SQL Server in single-user mode:

```
sqlservr.exe -m
```

To start a named instance of SQL Server in single-user mode, run the following:

```
sqlservr.exe -m -s <instancename>
```

3. Reapply any SQL Server updates, service packs, and hotfixes that were previously applied to the SQL Server.
4. Restore the `master` database as you would a user database. If a `master` backup is not available, then recreate all missing entries for your user databases, logins, endpoints, and so forth.

If the `master` database is accessible, start SQL Server in single-user mode and then restore the `master` database as you would a user database.

NOTE **Rebuilding the master database rebuilds the `msdb` and `model` databases too, so after rebuilding the databases restore the system databases (`master`, `msdb`, `model`) from the most recent good backup.**

Rebuilding the master database installs all system databases to their initial location. If initially one or more system databases were moved to a different location, then a similar move is required again now.

MSDB system database

Like the `master` database, the `msdb` database, by default, uses the simple recovery model.

Because the `msdb` database contains information regarding SQL Server Agent jobs and schedules, as well as the backup history, it should be backed up whenever you do the following:

- Perform backups
- Save SSIS packages
- Create new SQL Server Agent jobs
- Configure SQL Server Agent mail or operators
- Configure replication
- Schedule tasks

The `msdb` database is backed up in the same way that a user database is backed up.

To restore the `msdb` database, you do not need to put the server in single-user mode, as you do with the `master` database. However, it's still not a normal restore, because without a current `msdb`, Management Studio is not aware of the backup history. Therefore, the `msdb` backup can't be chosen as a backup database but must be selected as a backup device.

The Contents button can be used to check the disk device for specific backups. If several backup instances are in the backup device, the Contents dialog can be used to select the correct backup. It then fills in the file number in the restore form.

NOTE **Before restoring the `msdb` database, stop SQL Server Agent. This ensures that the `msdb` database is not being accessed by the SQL Server Agent and allows the restore to complete.**

Performing a Complete Recovery

If the server has completely failed and all the backups must be restored onto a new server, this is the process to follow:

1. Build the Windows server and restore the domain logins to support Windows authentication.
2. Install SQL Server and any service-pack, cumulative updates, security upgrades, or hotfixes.
3. Start SQL Server in single-user mode and restore the `master` database.
4. Verify that SQL Server Agent is stopped. Restore the `msdb` database.
5. If the `model` database was modified, restore it.
6. Restore the user databases.

Best Practice

Performing a flawless recovery is a "bet your career" skill. I recommend taking the time to work through a complete recovery of the production data to a backup server. The confidence it builds will serve you well as a SQL Server DBA.

Summary

The recovery cycle begins with the backup of the databases. The ability to survive hardware failure or human error is crucial to the ACID properties of a database. Without the transaction's durability, the database can't be fully trusted. Because of this, recovery planning and the transaction log provide durability to committed transactions. The recovery cycle transfers data from the past to the present.

They key points from this chapter include the following:

- Invest the time to create a solid backup and recovery plan.
- Just performing regular backups is not enough. Because the only way to know that the backups are good is by restoring them, regularly restore the backups on a test server. This is a boring task but well worth it when a disaster occurs and you need to recover from the backups.

- I recommend that a senior SQL DBA create the backup and recovery plan to ensure that all aspects are taken care of. Once the plan is ready, ascertain that the junior DBA can understand it and perform all the steps in the plan, as it is more than likely that this is the person who will be recovering from the backups in the middle of the night when a disaster occurs.
- Perform a complete recovery to simulate a server and disk subsystem failure at least every six months and update your backup/recovery plan as required.

In the next chapter, you'll learn how to maintain the database.

Chapter 42

Maintaining the Database

The previous chapter covered database recovery planning. This chapter explores various database maintenance tasks that need to be performed regularly, such as database backups, database integrity checks, and index maintenance. It also discusses database maintenance using Transact-SQL Database Console Commands (DBCC) and Maintenance Plans.

IN THIS CHAPTER

Using SQL Server's Database Console Commands (DBCC)

Creating database maintenance plans

DBCC Commands

Microsoft SQL Server Database Console Commands (DBCC) are used for checking database integrity, performing maintenance operations on databases, tables, indexes, and filegroups, and collecting and displaying information during troubleshooting issues.

The first DBCC command to become familiar with is the `DBCC HELP` command, which returns the syntax and all the options for any DBCC command. The following command returns the syntax for `DBCC CHECKDB`:

```
DBCC HELP ('CHECKDB');
```

Result:

```
dbcc CHECKDB
(
    { 'database_name' | database_id | 0 }
    [ , NOINDEX
    | { REPAIR_ALLOW_DATA_LOSS
    | REPAIR_FAST
    | REPAIR_REBUILD
    } ]
)
```

```
        [ WITH
            {
                [ ALL_ERRORMSGS ]
                [ , [ NO_INFOMSGS ] ]
                [ , [ TABLOCK ] ]
                [ , [ ESTIMATEONLY ] ]
                [ , [ PHYSICAL_ONLY ] ]
                [ , [ DATA_PURITY ] ]
                [ , [ EXTENDED_LOGICAL_CHECKS  ] ]
            }
        ]
DBCC execution completed. If DBCC printed error messages, contact your
system administrator.
```

What's New in SQL Server Database Maintenance?

In earlier versions of SQL Server, DBCC stood for ''Database Consistency Checker'' — now it is renamed ''Database Console Commands.'' The following deprecated DBCC commands are still in SQL Server 2008, but they will be removed in the next version. It is recommended to stop using the deprecated DBCC commands for new development work and plan to change existing applications using these commands:

- `DBCC DBREINDEX`
- `DBCC INDEXDEFRAG`
- `DBCC SHOWCONTIG`
- `DBCC PINTABLE`
- `DBCC UNPINTABLE`

While the `DBCC PINTABLE` and `DBCC UNPINTABLE` commands are still in SQL Server 2008, they have no effect on SQL Server. Note also that `DBCC CONCURRENCYVIOLATION` has been discontinued in SQL Server 2008.

You can find a complete list of deprecated (outdated or no longer accessible) DBCC commands in Chapter 1, ''The World of SQL Server,'' in Books Online, and at `http://msdn2.microsoft.com/en-US/library/ms144262.aspx`.

The following command returns all DBCC commands for which help is available:

```
DBCC HELP ('?');
```

Result:

```
checkalloc

checkcatalog
```

```
checkconstraints

checkdb

checkfilegroup

checkident

checktable

cleantable

dbreindex

dropcleanbuffers

free

freeproccache

freesessioncache

freesystemcache

help

indexdefrag

inputbuffer

opentran

outputbuffer

pintable

proccache

show_statistics

showcontig

shrinkdatabase

shrinkfile

sqlperf
```

```
traceoff

traceon

tracestatus

unpintable

updateusage

useroptions
DBCC execution completed. If DBCC printed error messages, contact your
system administrator.
```

All DBCC commands report their activity or errors found, and then conclude with the standard "DBCC execution completed" statement, including any action that might be needed.

Database integrity

`DBCC CHECKDB` performs several operations to check the logical and physical integrity of the database. It's critical for the health of the database that the physical structure is correct. `DBCC CHECKDB` checks things such as index pointers, data-page offsets, the linking between data pages and index pages, and the structural content of the data and index pages. If a hardware hiccup has left a data page half-written, then `DBCC CHECKDB` is the best means of detecting the problem. The following command executes `DBCC CHECKDB` on the `AdventureWorks2008` sample database:

```
DBCC CHECKDB ('AdventureWorks2008');
```

Result (abridged):

```
DBCC results for 'AdventureWorks2008'.
Service Broker Msg 9675, State 1: Message Types analyzed: 14.
Service Broker Msg 9676, State 1: Service Contracts analyzed: 6.
Service Broker Msg 9667, State 1: Services analyzed: 3.
Service Broker Msg 9668, State 1: Service Queues analyzed: 3
.
...
DBCC results for 'sys.sysrscols'.
There are 1406 rows in 14 pages for object "sys.sysrscols".
DBCC results for 'sys.sysrowsets'.
There are 263 rows in 3 pages for object "sys.sysrowsets".
DBCC results for 'sys.sysallocunits'.
...
DBCC results for 'Production.ProductModelProductDescriptionCulture'.
There are 762 rows in 4 pages for object
"Production.ProductModelProductDescriptionCulture".
DBCC results for 'Sales.Store'.
There are 701 rows in 101 pages for object "Sales.Store".
DBCC results for 'Production.ProductPhoto'.
There are 101 rows in 50 pages for object "Production.ProductPhoto".
```

```
CHECKDB found 0 allocation errors and 0 consistency errors in database
'AdventureWorks2008'.
DBCC execution completed. If DBCC printed error messages, contact your
system administrator.
```

NOTE **The results you see could vary from those displayed here depending on your SQL Server configuration and any changes you have made to the database.**

Two options simply determine which messages are reported, without altering the functionality of the integrity check: ALL_ERRORMSGS and NO_INFOMSGS. ALL_ERRORMSGS displays all the error messages; when it is not used, the default displays 200 errors per object. The NO_INFOMSGS option can be used to suppress all informational messages.

The ESTIMATE_ONLY option returns the estimated size of the tempdb required by DBCC CHECKDB without actually running DBCC CHECKDB against the database.

If the database is large, then the NOINDEX option can be used to skip checking the integrity of all user-table non-clustered indexes. For additional time savings, the PHYSICAL_ONLY option performs only the most critical checks on the physical structure of the pages. Use these options only when time prevents a complete DBCC CHECKDB or when the indexes are about to be rebuilt.

If you want to perform logical consistency checks on indexed views, XML indexes, and spatial indexes, then use the new option EXTENDED_LOGICAL_CHECKS. This option increases the performance impact on the SQL Server, and currently its progress cannot be tracked. It is recommended that you first run this on a similar database on a similar test SQL Server to get an estimate of the time it takes to run DBCC CHECKDB with this option and the performance impact on the SQL Server.

For databases upgraded from SQL Server 2000 or earlier, it is recommended to run DBCC CHECKDB with DATA_PURITY as a post-upgrade step to enable the column-value integrity checks, as they are disabled by default on SQL Server 2000 and earlier. After successful completion, column-value integrity checks are enabled for the database, and you do not need to use the DATA_PURITY option for future DBCC CHECKDB executions. Column-value integrity checks are enabled by default beginning with SQL Server 2005.

To reduce blocking and concurrency problems when integrity checks are done, DBCC CHECKDB uses an internal database snapshot to perform the checks. If a snapshot cannot be created or you use the TABLOCK option, then DBCC CHECKDB uses locks, which include a short-term exclusive lock on the database. The TABLOCK option can reduce the time it takes for DBCC CHECKDB to run during peak usage, but it reduces the concurrency on the database. If the TABLOCK option is used, then DBCC CHECKCATALOG is skipped, and Service Broker data is not checked.

TIP **Review the** percent_complete **and** command **columns of the** sys.dm_exec_requests **catalog view to display the progress and current phase of** DBCC CHECKDB**.**

Repairing the database

When an error is found and DBCC CHECKDB can fix it, DBCC CHECKDB indicates the repair level that is needed to repair the error(s). When an error is reported by DBCC CHECKDB, it is recommended to restore the database from a known good backup. Use the repair option with DBCC CHECKDB only when there is no known good backup. Repairing the database is a separate operation from the normal DBCC

CHECKDB command because the database needs to be placed in single-user mode with the ALTER DATABASE command before a DBCC CHECKDB can be executed with the REPAIR option. The following command places the AdventureWorks2008 sample database in single-user mode:

```
ALTER DATABASE AdventureWorks2008 SET SINGLE_USER;
```

More on Single-User Mode

The preceding command will wait indefinitely if there is a lock on the database or users are connected to the database. You can use a termination clause, WITH ROLLBACK AFTER integer [SECONDS] or WITH ROLLBACK IMMEDIATE, to indicate that SQL Server should either roll back incomplete transactions after the specified number of seconds or roll back immediately and close any active connections to the database. The following command places the AdventureWorks2008 sample database in single-user mode and specifies that SQL Server should roll back all incomplete transactions immediately and close any active connections to the database:

```
ALTER DATABASE AdventureWorks2008 SET SINGLE_USER WITH ROLLBACK IMMEDIATE;
```

If the AUTO_UPDATE_STATISTICS_AYSNC option for the database is set to ON, you will be unable to place the database in single-user mode, as the background thread that is used to update the statistics takes a connection against the database. You can query the is_auto_update_stats_async_on column in the sys.databases catalog view to check if the AUTO_UPDATE_STATISTICS_ASYNC option is set to ON. If so, then first set it to OFF using the ALTER DATABASE command.

DBCC offers two repair modes:

- REPAIR_REBUILD: This mode performs a repair that does not lead to any data loss.
- REPAIR_ALLOW_DATA_LOSS: This mode performs the repairs and fixes corrupted database structures. As the name suggests, this mode can result in data loss.

NOTE **Earlier versions of SQL Server included a third repair mode called REPAIR_FAST. This mode still exists in SQL Server 2008 but it does not perform any activity and is kept only for backward compatibility.**

The following example places the AdventureWorks2008 sample database in single-user mode and runs DBCC CHECKDB with the REPAIR_ALLOW_DATA_LOSS option. It then sets the database back to multi-user mode:

```
ALTER DATABASE AdventureWorks2008 SET SINGLE_USER WITH ROLLBACK
IMMEDIATE;
BEGIN TRANSACTION;
DBCC CheckDB ('AdventureWorks2008', REPAIR_ALLOW_DATA_LOSS);
--Check for any data loss
--ROLLBACK TRANSACTION if data loss is not acceptable else COMMIT
TRANSACTION;
ALTER DATABASE AdventureWorks2008 SET MULTI_USER;
```

Result (abridged):

```
DBCC results for 'AdventureWorks2008'.
Service Broker Msg 9675, State 1: Message Types analyzed: 14.
Service Broker Msg 9676, State 1: Service Contracts analyzed: 6.
Service Broker Msg 9667, State 1: Services analyzed: 3.
...
DBCC results for 'sys.sysrowsets'.
There are 291 rows in 3 pages for object "sys.sysrowsets".
...
DBCC results for 'Production.TransactionHistoryArchive'.
There are 89253 rows in 620 pages for object
"Production.TransactionHistoryArchive".
CHECKDB found 0 allocation errors and 0 consistency errors in database
'AdventureWorks2008'.
DBCC execution completed. If DBCC printed error messages, contact your
system administrator.
```

Best Practice

Since SQL Server 7.0, the Storage Engine's quality has significantly improved, reducing the need to run DBCC CHECKDB frequently. However, a foolproof recovery plan will include a full restore and a DBCC CHECKDB to ensure that all portions of the recovery plan are working. The frequency with which you run DBCC CHECKDB depends on your comfort level, your environment, and the importance of your data. I would never say that DBCC CHECKDB is not needed; it is recommended to run it now and then, as well as to restore from backups. It is also recommended to run DBCC CHECKDB after any hardware malfunction. If an error is detected, then restore from a known good database backup. As mentioned, use the repair option only as the last option.

If DBCC CHECKDB asks you to use REPAIR_ALLOW_DATA_LOSS, then take a full database backup first and then run DBCC CHECKDB with the repair option in a user transaction. That way, you can verify the data loss after the command is executed and roll back the transaction if the data loss is not acceptable. After successfully repairing the database, take a full database backup.

Because DBCC CHECKDB is a resource-intensive operation, run it during low peak hours.

Multi-user concerns

DBCC CHECKDB without any repair option can be executed while users are in the database. However, DBCC CHECKDB is very processor- and disk-intensive, so run it when the database has the fewest users. By default, DBCC CHECKDB can check objects in parallel across all CPUs in the box, which can boost the performance of DBCC CHECKDB and reduce the run times. The degree of parallelism is determined by the SQL Server query processor, and the algorithm used is similar to running parallel queries.

Because running DBCC CHECKDB in parallel is processor intensive, you may have environments or situations when you want to disable parallel checking of objects by DBCC CHECKDB. SQL Server enables you to do that using the trace flag 2528.

Object-level validation

DBCC CHECKDB performs a host of database structural-integrity checks. It's possible to run these checks individually. For example, if you have a very large database (VLDB), then it may not be possible to run DBCC CHECKDB on the entire database, but you may be able to run individual checks on key database objects.

If the database requires repair, always use the full DBCC CHECKDB over one of the lesser versions:

- DBCC CHECKALLOC ('database'): A subset of DBCC CHECKDB that checks the allocation of all pages in the database. The report is very detailed, listing the extent count (64KB or eight data pages) and data-page usage of every table and index in the database.
- DBCC CHECKFILEGROUP ('filegroup'): Similar to a DBCC CHECKDB but limited to the specified filegroup only.
- DBCC CHECKTABLE('table'): Performs physical and logical integrity checks on the table and all its non-clustered indexes (unless the NOINDEX option is used).
- DBCC CLEANTABLE ('database', "table"): Reclaims space from a varchar, nvarchar, text, or ntext column that was dropped from the table.

Data integrity

Above the physical-structure layer of the database is the data layer, which can be verified by the following DBCC commands:

- DBCC CHECKCATALOG ('database'): Checks the integrity of the system tables within a database, ensuring referential integrity among tables, views, columns, and data types. While it will report any errors, under normal conditions no detailed report is returned. This is also run as a part of DBCC CHECKDB.
- DBCC CHECKCONSTRAINTS ('table','constraint'): Examines the integrity of a specific constraint, or all the constraints, for a table. It essentially generates and executes a query to verify each constraint, and reports any errors found. As with DBCC CHECKCATALOG, if no issues are detected, then nothing is reported.
- DBCC CHECKIDENT ('table'): Verifies the consistency of the current identity-column value and the identity column for a specific table. If a problem exists, then the next value for the identity column is updated to correct any error. If the identity column is broken, then the new identity value will violate a primary key or unique constraint, and new rows cannot be added to the table. This command can also be used to reseed the current identity value by using the RESEED option and a new_reseed_value.

  The following code demonstrates the use of the DBCC CHECKIDENT command. When needed, this command resets the current identity value of the Employee table in the AdventureWorks2008 sample database:

  ```
  Use AdventureWorks2008;
  DBCC CHECKIDENT ("HumanResources.Employee");
  ```

Result:

```
Checking identity information: current identity value '290', current
column value '290'.
```

```
DBCC execution completed. If DBCC printed error messages, contact your
system administrator.
```

NOTE `DBCC CHECKDB` **also runs** `DBCC CHECKALLOC`, `DBCC CHECKTABLE`, **and** `DBCC CHECKCATALOG`, **so you don't need to run these commands separately if you are executing** `DBCC CHECKDB`. **However,** `DBCC CHECKDB` **does not run** `DBCC CHECKCONSTRAINTS`**; it is recommended to run this separately if your tables have one or more constraints.**

Index maintenance

Indexes provide the performance bridge between the data and SQL queries. Because of data inserts, updates, and deletes, indexes fragment, the data-distribution statistics become out of date, and the fill factor of the pages can be less than optimal. Index maintenance is required to combat these three results of normal wear and tear and prevent reduced performance.

CROSS-REF **Chapter 20, "Creating the Physical Database Schema," and Chapter 64, "Indexing Strategies," both contain more information about index creation.**

Database fragmentation

By default, as data is inserted into the data pages and index pages, the pages fill to 100 percent. At that point, SQL Server performs a page split, creating two new pages with about 50 percent page density each. While this solves the individual page problem, the internal database structure can become fragmented.

To demonstrate the DBCC commands that affect fragmented tables and indexes, a table large enough to become fragmented is required. The following script builds a suitable table and a non-clustered index. The clustered primary key is a GUID, so row insertions will occur throughout the table, generating plenty of fragmentation:

```
USE Tempdb;

CREATE TABLE Frag (
  FragID UNIQUEIDENTIFIER NOT NULL DEFAULT NewID(),
  Col1 INT,
  Col2 CHAR(200),
  Created DATETIME DEFAULT GetDate(),
  Modified DATETIME DEFAULT GetDate()
  );

ALTER TABLE Frag
  ADD CONSTRAINT PK_Frag
  PRIMARY KEY CLUSTERED (FragID);

CREATE NONCLUSTERED INDEX ix_col
  ON Frag (Col1);
```

The following stored procedure will add 100,000 rows each time it is executed:

```
CREATE PROC Add100K
AS
```

```
SET nocount on;
DECLARE @X INT;
SET @X = 0;
  WHILE @X < 100000
    BEGIN
      INSERT Frag (Col1,Col2)
        VALUES (@X, 'sample data');
      SET @X = @X + 1;
    END
GO;
```

The following batch calls Add100K several times and populates the Frag table (be patient, the query can require several minutes to execute):

```
EXEC Add100K;
EXEC Add100K;
EXEC Add100K;
EXEC Add100K;
EXEC Add100K;
```

The dynamic management function sys.dm_db_index_physical_stats reports the fragmentation details and the density for a given table or index. With half a million rows, the Frag table is very fragmented, and most pages are slightly more than half full, as the following command shows:

```
USE tempdb;
SELECT * FROM sys.dm_db_index_physical_stats ( db_id('tempdb'),
object_id('Frag'), NULL, NULL, 'DETAILED');
```

In the following result (abridged), Index ID: 1 is the clustered primary-key index, so it's also reporting the data-page fragmentation. Index ID: 2 is the non-clustered index:

```
index_id: 1
index_type_desc: CLUSTERED INDEX
avg_fragmentation_in_percent: 99.1775717920756
page count: 22008
avg_page_space_used_in_percent: 68.744230294045

index_id: 2
index_type_desc: NONCLUSTERED INDEX
avg_fragmentation_in_percent: 98.1501632208923
page count: 2732
avg_page_space_used_in_percent: 58.2316654311836
```

NOTE **The sys.dm_db_index_physical_stats function requires an Intent-Shared (IS) table lock regardless of the mode it runs in. The DETAILED mode is the most rigorous scan level that can be used with this function. Another mode called LIMITED can provide a rough idea of the fragmentation in less time with less potential impact to the database.**

ALTER INDEX REORGANIZE defragments the leaf level index pages of both clustered and non-clustered indexes. It will reorder the leaf-level index pages and compact the index pages (based on the fill factor value in the sys.indexes catalog view) for faster index scanning performance:

```
ALTER INDEX IndexName ON TableName REORGANIZE;
```

Performing the ALTER INDEX REORGANIZE operation is similar to rebuilding an index (see ALTER INDEX REBUILD, covered in the section "Index density"), with the distinct advantage that defragmenting an index is performed in a series of small transactions that do not block users from performing inserts, updates, and deletes.

NOTE **ALTER INDEX REORGANIZE and ALTER INDEX REBUILD are equivalent to DBCC INDEXDEFRAG and DBCC DBREINDEX, respectively. The sys.dm_db_index_physical_stats dynamic management function replaces DBCC SHOWCONTIG. It is recommended to stop using DBCC INDEXDEFRAG, DBCC DBREINDEX, and DBCC SHOWCONTIG, as they will be removed in the next version of Microsoft SQL Server.**

The following commands defrag both indexes:

```
USE tempdb;
ALTER INDEX PK_Frag ON Frag REORGANIZE;
ALTER INDEX ix_col ON Frag REORGANIZE;
```

A sys.dm_db_index_physical_stats dynamic management function examines the index structure after defragmenting the index. Both the logical-fragmentation and page-density problems created by the insertion of half a million rows are resolved:

```
USE tempdb;
GO
SELECT * FROM sys.dm_db_index_physical_stats ( db_id('tempdb'),
object_id('Frag'), NULL, NULL, 'DETAILED');
GO
```

Result (abridged):

```
index_id: 1
index_type_desc: CLUSTERED INDEX
avg_fragmentation_in_percent: 0.559173738569831
page count: 15201
avg_page_space_used_in_percent: 99.538930071658

index_id: 2
index_type_desc: NONCLUSTERED INDEX
avg_fragmentation_in_percent: 1.23915737298637
page count: 1614
avg_page_space_used_in_percent: 99.487558685446
```

Index statistics

The usefulness of an index is based on the data distribution within that index. For example, if 60 percent of all the customers are in New York City (NYC), then selecting all customers in NYC will likely be faster with a table scan than with an index seek. However, to find the single customer from Delavan, Wisconsin, the query definitely needs the help of an index. The Query Optimizer depends on the index statistics to determine the usefulness of the index for a particular query.

DBCC SHOW_STATISTICS reports the last date the statistics were updated and basic information about the index statistics, including the usefulness of the index. A low density indicates that the index is very selective. A high density indicates that a given index node points to several table rows and may be less useful than a low-density index.

To update the statistics for a specific table, use the UPDATE STATISTICS command. To update the statistics on all the tables in the current database, use the sp_updatestats system stored procedure, which basically runs UPDATE STATISTICS on all the tables in the current database. The sp_updatestats stored procedure does not unnecessarily update every statistic. It updates a specific statistic only if enough data has changed based on rowmodctr information in the sys.sysindexes compatibility view. The following code updates the statistics for all the indexes on the Person.Contact table in the AdventureWorks2008 sample database:

```
USE AdventureWorks2008;
EXEC sp_help 'Person.Contact';
UPDATE STATISTICS Person.Contact;
```

The following code updates the statistics for all the tables in the AdventureWorks2008 sample database:

```
USE AdventureWorks2008;
EXEC sp_updatestats;
```

TIP **To view operational index statistics, query the** sys.dm_db_index_operational_stats **dynamic management view. You can also check usage statistics by querying** sys.dm_db_index_usage_stats, **and check physical statistics by querying** sys.dm_db_index_physical_stats. sys.dm_db_index_operational_stats **and** sys.dm_db_index_physical_stats **require that you provide input arguments or** NULL **values for each of the inputs, such as database ID, object ID, index ID, and partition number.**

To view the T-SQL code that the sp_updatestats **system stored procedure executes, run the** sp_helptext sp_updatestats **command.**

Index density

Index density refers to what percentage of the index pages contains data. If the index density is low, then SQL Server must read more pages from the disk to retrieve the index data. The index's *fill factor* refers to what percentage of the index page contains data when the index is created, but index density will slowly alter during inserts, updates, and deletes.

The ALTER INDEX REBUILD command will completely rebuild the index. Using this command is essentially the equivalent of dropping and creating the index, with the added benefit of enabling users to set the fill factor as the index is recreated. In contrast, the ALTER INDEX REORGANIZE command repairs fragmentation to the index's fill factor but does not adjust the target fill factor.

The following code recreates all the indexes on the Frag table and sets the fill factor to 98 percent:

```
USE tempdb;
ALTER INDEX ALL ON Frag REBUILD WITH (FILLFACTOR = 98);
```

At this point, you have a couple of objects in the tempdb database that you'll want to clean up. Use the following code to perform the task:

```
DROP TABLE Frag;
DROP PROCEDURE Add100K;
```

NOTE **By default, the ALTER INDEX REBUILD operation is an offline operation. In contrast, ALTER INDEX REORGANIZE is always performed online. During the ALTER INDEX REBUILD operation, the underlying tables and indexes are not available for queries and data modification; but if you have SQL Server Enterprise or Developer Editions, then SQL Server allows you to perform online index operations by using the ONLINE=ON option. When you use the ONLINE=ON option, exclusive table locks are held only for a very short amount of time, and then the tables and indexes are available for queries and data modification.**

CROSS-REF **Index density can affect performance. Chapter 64, "Indexing Strategies," also addresses index fill factors.**

Database file size

SQL Server 7.0 moved beyond SQL Server 6.5's method of allocated space with fixed-size files called *devices*. Since SQL Server 7.0, data and transaction logs can automatically grow as required. File size is still an area of database maintenance concern. Without some intervention or monitoring, the data files could grow too large. The following commands and DBCC options deal with monitoring and controlling file sizes.

Monitoring database file sizes

Three factors of file size should be monitored: the size of the database files and their maximum growth size, the amount of free space within the files, and the amount of free space on the disk drives.

The current and maximum file sizes are stored within the sys.database_files database catalog view. The following code displays the name, size, and max size for the AdventureWorks2008 sample database:

```
USE AdventureWorks2008;
SELECT name, size, max_size from sys.database_files;
```

Result:

```
name                                size     max_size
---------                           ------- ---------
AdventureWorks2008_Data                      25080   -1
AdventureWorks2008_Log              256       268435456
```

Here, size is the current size, and max_size is the maximum size of the file, in 8KB pages. A value of -1 for max_size indicates that the file will grow until the disk is full, and 268435456 indicates that the maximum size of the log file will be 2TB.

To check the current and maximum file sizes for all the databases, use the sys.master_files catalog view.

To detect the percentage of the file that is actually being used, use the sp_spaceused system stored procedure. Optionally, you can run the DBCC UPDATEUSAGE command to correct disk space usage inaccuracies or use the @updateusage optional parameter with the sp_spaceused command.

The following command updates the space usage information of the AdventureWorks2008 sample database and then runs the sp_spaceused command:

```
USE AdventureWorks2008;
DBCC UPDATEUSAGE (AdventureWorks2008);
EXEC sp_spaceused;
```

Result:

```
database_name      database_size      unallocated space
-------------------------------------------------------
AdventureWorks2008     197.94 MB           15.62 MB

reserved           data               index_size         unused
------------------ ------------------ ------------------ --------
184648 KB          96672 KB           81440 KB           6536 KB
```

To determine the size and percentage of used space within the transaction log, use the DBCC SQLPERF (LOGSPACE) command:

```
DBCC SQLPERF (LOGSPACE);
```

Result :

```
Database Name          Log Size (MB) Log Space Used (%) Status
-------------------------------------------------------
master                 0.9921875      41.73228         0
tempdb                 0.4921875      76.68651         0
model                  0.4921875      57.14286         0
msdb                   0.4921875      47.61905         0
AdventureWorks2008     1.992188       35.19608         0
DBCC execution completed. If DBCC printed error messages, contact your
system administrator.
```

To monitor the amount of free space on the server's disk drives, you can use the undocumented extended stored procedure xp_fixeddrives:

```
EXEC master..xp_fixeddrives;
```

Result:

```
drive MB Free
----- -------
C     429
F     60358
```

NOTE **Because xp_fixeddrives is an undocumented stored procedure, there is no support for this, and it can be removed from SQL Server at any time.**

CROSS-REF **For more information about configuring the data and transaction log files for autogrowth and setting the maximum file sizes, refer to Chapter 20, "Creating the Physical Database Schema."**

Shrinking the database

Unless the database is configured to automatically shrink in the background, the file space that is freed by deleting unused objects and rows will not be returned to the disk operating system. Instead, the files will remain at the largest size to which the data file may have grown. If data is regularly added and removed, then constantly shrinking and growing the database would be a wasteful exercise. However, if disk space is at a premium, a large amount of data has been removed from the database, and the database is not configured to automatically shrink, then the following commands may be used to manually shrink the database. The database can be shrunk while transactions are working in the database.

Using autoshrink during the day, when users are accessing the database, will definitely affect performance. Normally, you'll want to shrink the database after working hours.

`DBCC SHRINKDATABASE` can shrink the size of the database files by performing two basic steps:

1. Packing data to the front of the file, leaving the empty space at the end of the file
2. Removing the empty space at the end of the file, reducing the size of the file

These two steps can be controlled with the following options:

- The `NOTRUNCATE` option causes `DBCC SHRINKDATABASE` to perform only step 1, packing the database file but leaving the file size the same.
- The `TRUNCATEONLY` option eliminates the empty space at the end of the file, but does not first pack the file.
- The `target_percent` option specifies the desired percentage of free space after the file is shrunk. Because autogrowth can be an expensive operation, leaving some free space is a useful strategy. If the desired free space percentage is larger than the current amount of free space, then this option will not increase the size of the file.

The following command shrinks the `AdventureWorks2008` sample database and leaves 10 percent free space:

```
DBCC SHRINKDATABASE ('AdventureWorks2008', 10);
```

Result:

```
DBCC SHRINKDATABASE: File ID 1 of database ID 9 was skipped
   because the file does not have enough free space to reclaim. Cannot
shrink log file 2 (AdventureWorks2008_Log) because requested size (568KB)
is larger than the start of the last logical log file.
DbId   FileId      CurrentSize MinimumSize UsedPages   EstimatedPages
------ ----------- ----------- ----------- ----------- --------------
9      2           96          63          96          56

(1 row(s) affected)

DBCC execution completed. If DBCC printed error messages,
   contact your system administrator.
```

The results show that not all of the files had space to reclaim. They also indicate which files were changed by displaying the old and new statistics. DBCC SHRINKDATABASE affects all the files for a database, whereas the DBCC SHRINKFILE command shrinks individual files.

Best Practice

DBCC SHRINKDATABASE causes massive index fragmentation and file-system fragmentation of the data files, as they will likely need to grow again after you've shrunk all the space. This will severely affect performance. As a best practice, don't shrink the database, but if you do need to run DBCC SHRINKDATABASE, rebuild all the indexes in your database to remove index fragmentation and boost performance.

Shrinking the transaction log

When the database is shrunk, the transaction log is also shrunk. The NOTRUNCATE and TRUNCATEONLY options have no effect on the transaction log. If multiple log files exist, then SQL Server shrinks them as if they were one large, contiguous file.

A common problem is a transaction log that grows and refuses to shrink. The most likely cause is an old open transaction. The transaction log is constructed of virtual log partitions. The success or failure of shrinking the transaction log depends on the aging of transactions within the virtual logs and log checkpoints. SQL Server can shrink the transaction log only by removing data older than the oldest transaction within the structure of the virtual logs.

To verify that an old transaction has a hold on the transaction log, use the DBCC OPENTRAN command. The following example detects open transaction information for the AdventureWorks2008 sample database:

```
USE AdventureWorks2008;
CREATE TABLE Test(Col1 int);
BEGIN TRAN;
INSERT INTO Test VALUES (1);
DBCC OPENTRAN;
```

Result:

```
Transaction information for database 'AdventureWorks2008'.

Oldest active transaction:
    SPID (server process ID): 51
    UID (user ID) : -1
    Name          : user_transaction
    LSN           : (1246:164:1)
    Start time    : Feb 22 2009  10:56:39:957PM
    SID           : 0x0105000000000005150000000271a6c07352f372aad20fa
5baa200100
DBCC execution completed. If DBCC printed error messages, contact your
system administrator.
```

Based on this information, the errant transaction can be tracked down and the SPID (user connection) can be killed. Management Studio's Current Activity node can provide more information about the SPID's activity. A more drastic option is to stop and restart the server and then shrink the database.

CROSS-REF **The recovery model and transaction log backups both affect how the transaction log grows and automatically shrinks. For more information on these critical issues, refer to Chapter 41, "Recovery Planning."**

Now that you've seen an open transaction, let's close it. The following code rolls back the transaction and verifies that there aren't any other open transactions for the database:

```
ROLLBACK TRAN;
DROP TABLE Test;

DBCC OPENTRAN;
```

Result:

```
No active open transactions.
DBCC execution completed. If DBCC printed error messages,
   contact your system administrator.
```

Miscellaneous DBCC commands

The remaining DBCC commands are used for troubleshooting during testing of stored procedures and triggers. The first five DBCC commands must be used with caution and should not be run against a production SQL Server instance, as it may result in a sudden decrease in query performance:

- `DBCC DROPCLEANBUFFERS`: Cleans the memory of any buffered data so that it doesn't affect query performance during testing. This command is useful for testing queries without recycling SQL Server.
- `DBCC FREEPROCCACHE`: Clears the stored procedure cache for all SQL Server databases
- `DBCC FREEPROCINDB(DBID)`: Clears the stored procedure cache for a specific SQL Server database and not the entire SQL Server
- `DBCC FREESESSIONCACHE`: Clears the cache used by the distributed queries
- `DBCC FREESYSTEMCACHE`: Clears the unused cache entries from all caches. It also clears the plan cache. In addition, it causes an unload of all AppDomains for SQLCLR and frees the CLR memory allocations in the Virtual Address Space/Memory To Leave areas.
- `DBCC INPUTBUFFER SPID)`: Returns the last command executed by a client, as identified by the client's SPID. This command can be executed only by members of the sysadmin server group, for obvious security reasons.
- `DBCC OUTPUTBUFFER SPID)`: Returns the results of the last command executed by a client, in hexadecimal and ASCII format. Like the `DBCC INPUTBUFFER` command, this command can be executed only by members of the sysadmin group.
- `DBCC PROCCACHE`: Reports some basic statistics about the procedure cache as queries and procedures are compiled and stored in memory
- `DBCC PINTABLE`: This command has been deprecated and has no effect on the server.
- `DBCC UNPINTABLE`: This command has been deprecated and has no effect on the server.
- `DBCC CONCURRENCYVIOLATION`: This command has been removed.

- DBCC dllname FREE): Unloads the specified dll from memory
- DBCC MEMORYSTATUS: Provides a snapshot of the current memory status of SQL Server. This command is very useful in troubleshooting issues that relate to SQL Server memory consumption.
- DBCC USEROPTIONS: Returns the active SET options for the current connections

The following three DBCC commands are used with trace flags. Trace flags are used temporarily to set certain specific SQL Server characteristics or turn off some behavior. For example, trace flag 1204 is used to enabled deadlock reporting to SQL Server ErrorLog.

- DBCC TRACEON: Turns on the specified trace flags
- DBCC TRACEOFF: Turns off the specified trace flags
- DBCC TRACESTATUS: Displays the active trace flags

Managing Database Maintenance

SQL Server provides a host of database maintenance commands. Fortunately, it also provides the DBA with ways to schedule maintenance tasks.

Planning database maintenance

Database maintenance plans include the following routine tasks:

- Checking database integrity
- Performing index maintenance
- Updating database statistics
- Performing database backups
- Shrinking the database
- Checking file sizes and free disk space

These maintenance tasks can be automated and scheduled using the SQL Server Agent service. The maintenance tasks are referred to as SQL Server Agent jobs.

Maintenance plan

There are two ways to create a maintenance plan:

- **Maintenance Plan Wizard:** Used to quickly create a basic maintenance plan, this wizard enables you to choose typical predefined maintenance tasks such as performing database backup, rebuilding indexes, updating statistics, checking data integrity, and shrinking the database. It does not allow you to add any custom tasks.
- **Maintenance Plan Design Surface:** Used for designing maintenance plans with more flexibility, this option enables you to create a workflow of typical maintenance tasks and custom maintenance tasks using T-SQL scripts. It also allows extended logging, which can be very useful for troubleshooting purposes.

All of the maintenance plans appear in the Management\Maintenance Plans folder of SQL Server Management Studio. To launch the Maintenance Plan Wizard, right-click the Maintenance Plans folder and choose Maintenance Plan Wizard. Follow the simple step-by-step wizard to create the maintenance plan.

To launch the Maintenance Plan Design Surface, right-click the `Maintenance Plans` folder and choose New Maintenance Plan from the context menu. Type a name for the maintenance plan in the New Maintenance Plan dialog and click OK.

Once you assign a name to your maintenance plan, Management Studio opens a new window that includes the maintenance plan name, a description, the time you want to schedule the maintenance plan, and a list of tasks to perform. Figure 42-1 shows a sample maintenance plan with some tasks already entered.

Adding a task

A maintenance plan must contain at least one task. Fortunately, it isn't difficult to add one. Simply drag and drop the appropriate task from the Toolbox, shown in Figure 42-2, to the design area of the maintenance plan. The resulting task will appear as a square (refer to Figure 42-1).

FIGURE 42-1

Create a maintenance plan by adding some tasks and scheduling a time to perform the tasks.

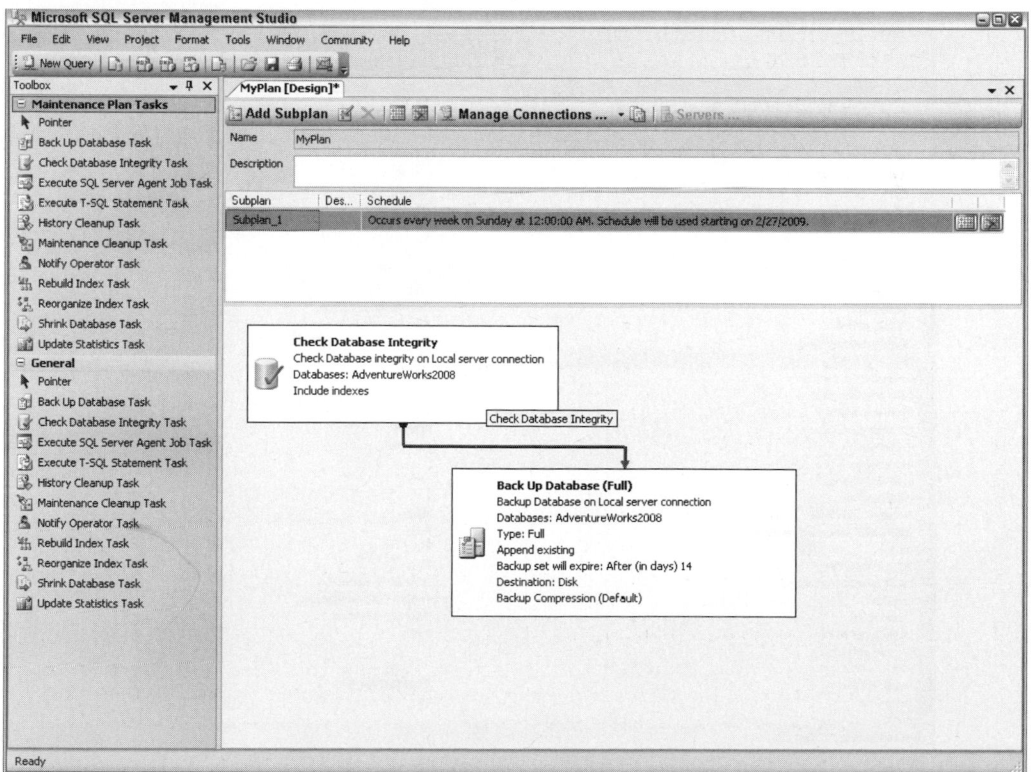

FIGURE 42-2

Use the Toolbox to add new tasks to your maintenance plan.

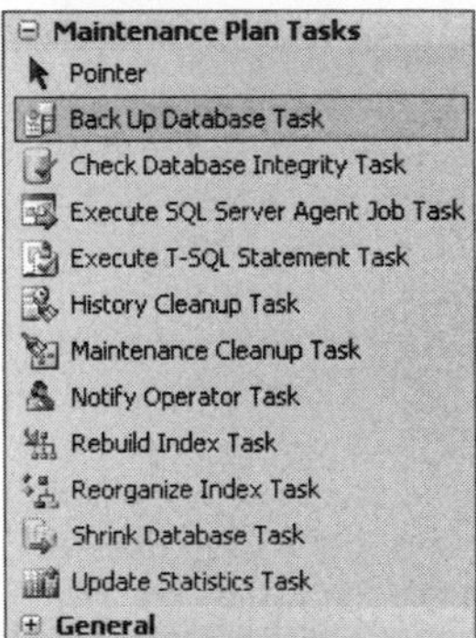

FIGURE 42-3

Define the task specifics using the Properties window.

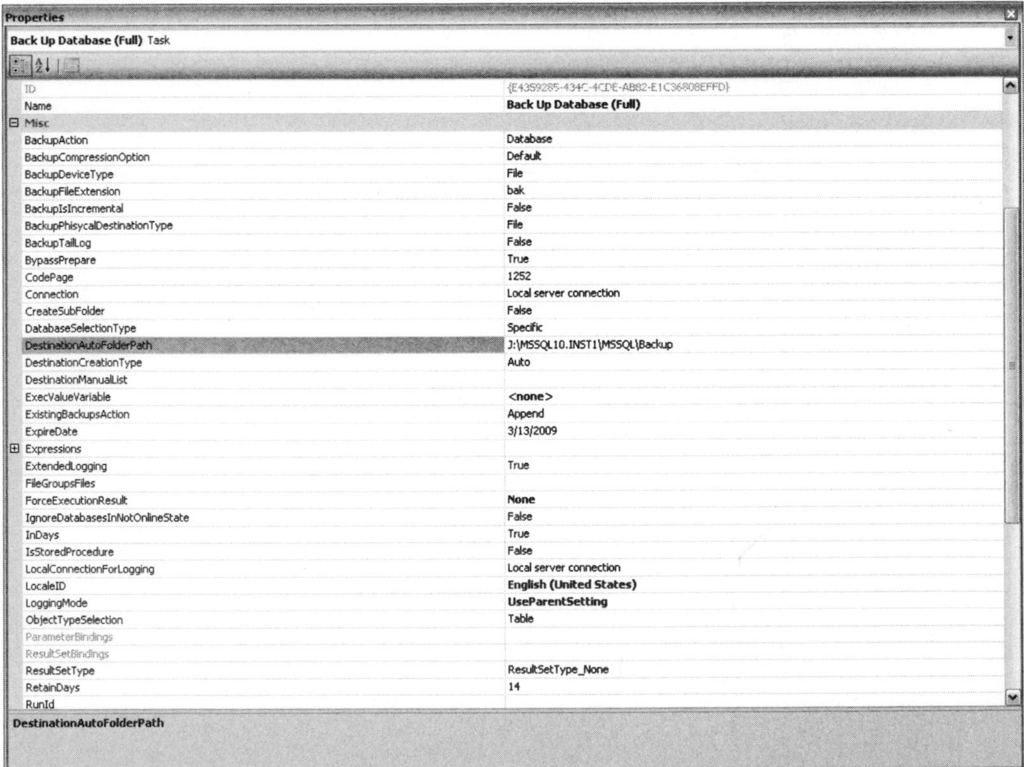

The task isn't configured yet. Use the Properties window, shown in Figure 42-3, to configure the task. The content of the Properties window varies by task. For example, when you select Back Up Database Task, you'll see properties for choosing the kind of database, the backup device type, and other information associated with backing up the database. The upper portion of the Properties window contains the name of the selected task. You can choose other tasks using the drop-down list box. The middle of the Properties window contains a list of properties for the selected task. You can organize the properties by category or in alphabetical order. The lower part of the Properties window contains a description for the selected property. Once you have worked with tasks for a while, the description usually provides enough information to help you remember how to use the selected property.

Sometimes you may not want to use the Properties window. For example, you might be working with a new task. In this case, you can bypass the Properties window by double-clicking the task. A task-specific window like the one shown in Figure 42-4 for a backup task will appear. Unlike the Properties window, this dialog displays the task properties in context. In addition, it grays out task elements until you define the correct functionality. For example, when you choose to back up specific databases, the dialog won't let you perform any other configuration task until you choose one or more databases for the backup.

FIGURE 42-4

In addition to the Properties window, you can use the task-related dialog for configuration.

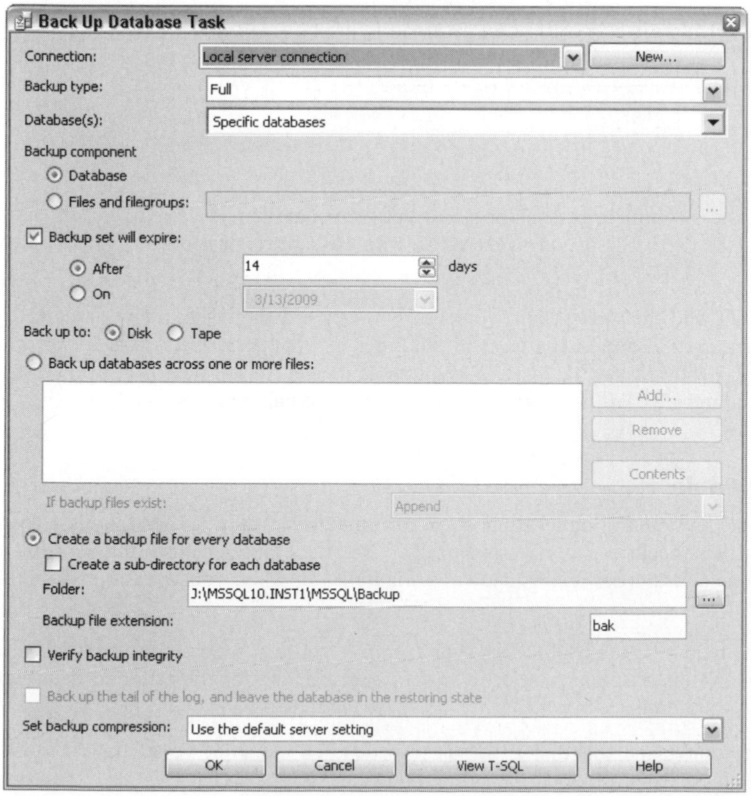

It's interesting to click View T-SQL when you finish configuring the task. The resulting window, like the one shown in Figure 42-5, displays the T-SQL that the task will use. The Transact SQL (Task Generated) window won't let you edit the command, but seeing how the Maintenance Plan Wizard generates the code can prove helpful when you need to create T-SQL commands of your own.

FIGURE 42-5

The View T-SQL button enables you to see the Transact SQL command.

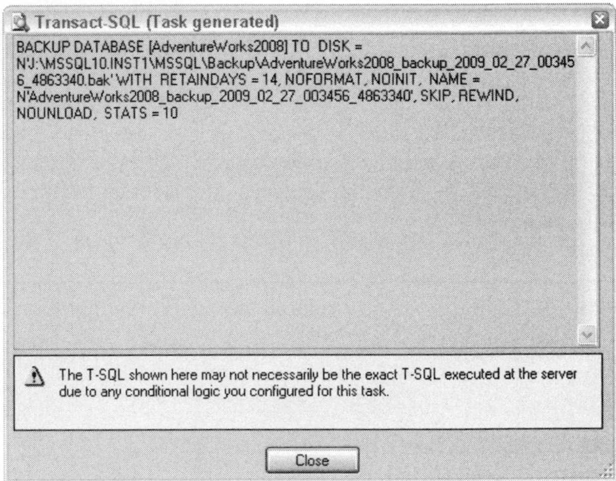

You know when a task is complete by the appearance of the square in the design area. Incomplete tasks, those that won't execute correctly, display a red circle with an X through it on the right side of the window.

After you define a task, add the next task in your list. You can add the tasks in any order and place them in any order onscreen. Connect the tasks in the order in which you want SQL Server to execute them. Figure 42-1 showed two tasks, with one task connected to the next task in the list. In that example, first the integrity of the `AdventureWorks2008` database is checked, and then it is backed up.

Defining the schedule

You can perform tasks on demand or schedule them to run automatically. Generally, it's a good idea to set standard tasks such as backup to run automatically. Click the ellipses next to the Schedule field to display the Job Schedule Properties dialog, shown in Figure 42-6, when you want to change the task schedule.

Select the scheduling requirements for the task. For example, you can set a task to run daily, weekly, or monthly. The dialog also enables you to select a specific starting time for the task and determine when the scheduling begins and ends.

The one form of scheduling that this dialog doesn't provide is on demand. To set the maintenance task to run on demand, simply leave the Job Schedule Properties empty.

FIGURE 42-6

Define a schedule that meets the task requirements; use off-hours scheduling for resource-intensive tasks.

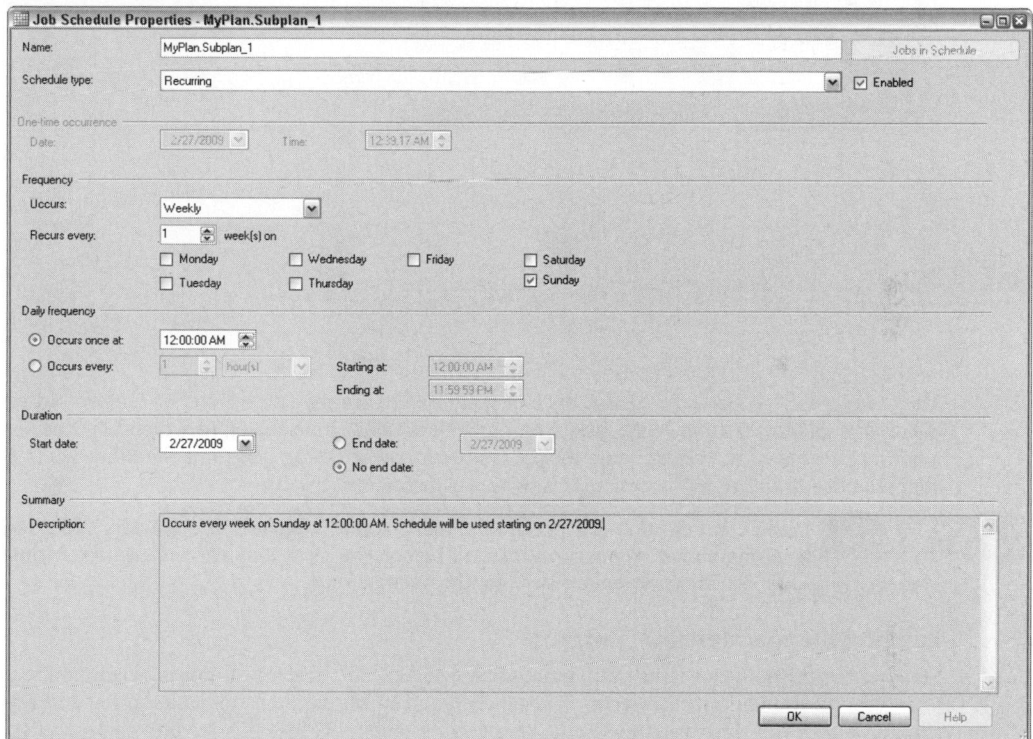

Creating new connections

Depending on your database setup, you might need to create multiple connections to perform a particular task. The maintenance plan always provides a connection to the default instance of the local database. Click Manage Connections to add more connections to the current maintenance plan (any additions won't affect other maintenance plans you create). The Manage Connections dialog shown in Figure 42-7 will appear.

Click Add in the Manage Connections dialog to add a new connection. The New Connection dialog will appear. A connection consists of three elements: connection name, server name, and server security. Choose a connection name that reflects the server and instance. Using a name such as "My Connection" won't be particularly helpful when you need to troubleshoot the maintenance task later. You can either type the server and instance name or select it from a list that the maintenance plan provides when you click the ellipses next to the Select or Enter a Server Name field. Finally, choose between Windows integrated or SQL Server security. Click OK to add the new connection to the list.

FIGURE 42-7

Add new connections as needed to perform maintenance tasks.

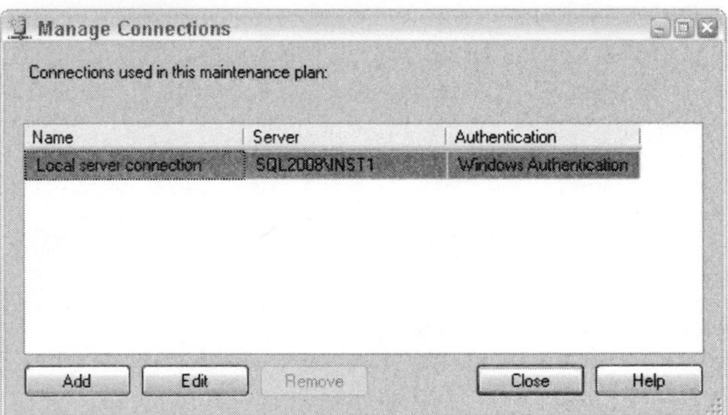

The Manage Connections dialog also enables you to edit existing connections or remove old connections. When you edit an existing connection, you see a New Connection dialog in which you can change the logon arguments or the server name for the connection. The dialog grays out the other fields. Simply click Remove to delete a connection you no longer need from the list.

NOTE **Connection deletion is a one-way process, and it happens quite quickly. Make sure you have the correct connection selected before you click Remove because the maintenance plan won't ask for confirmation before deleting the connection.**

Logging the maintenance progress

Many of the maintenance tasks that you automate will execute during off hours, when you're unlikely to be around to monitor the system. Fortunately, you can set maintenance tasks to log and report their actions so that you don't need to watch them every moment. To use this feature, click the Reporting and Logging icon next to the Manage Connections icon. The Reporting and Logging dialog shown in Figure 42-8 will appear.

The Reporting and Logging dialog includes an option that enables you to send the report to a file or your e-mail. The e-mail feature is quite handy and saves you the time of searching for the file on the hard drive. Conversely, the text file provides an archive that could prove helpful long after you've deleted the e-mail from your inbox. Once you configure the reporting options, click OK, and the maintenance plan will record its actions for you.

Best Practice

You normally want to provide extended information about all maintenance tasks that the system performs without your supervision. Even the smallest piece of information can help you determine where a particular maintenance action went awry.

FIGURE 42-8

Use the Reporting and Logging dialog to monitor your maintenance tasks.

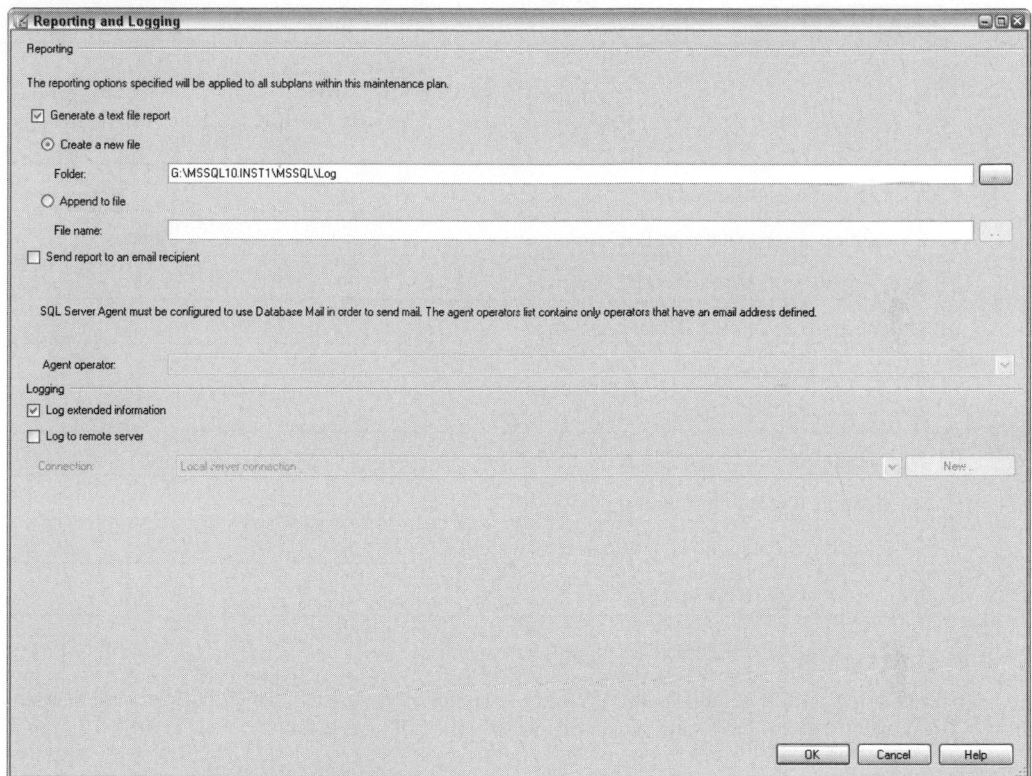

Command-line maintenance

Database maintenance is normally performed within SQL Server Management Studio or automated with SQL Server Agent, but maintenance can be performed from the DOS command prompt by means of the `SQLMaint` utility. This utility has numerous options that can perform backups, update statistics, and run `DBCC`.

NOTE **This feature will be removed in the next version of SQL Server. Do not use this feature in new development work, and plan to change applications that use this feature. To run SQL Server maintenance plans from the command line, use the `dtexec` utility.**

Specific information on `SQLMaint` and `dtexec` can be found in SQL Server 2008 Books Online.

Monitoring database maintenance

It's not enough to simply schedule tasks; they must be monitored as well. In larger installations with dozens of SQL Servers spread around the globe, monitoring the health of SQL Server and the databases is itself a full-time job. Table 42-1 provides a sample DBA daily checklist that can be used as a starting point for developing a database monitoring plan.

TABLE 42-1

DBA Daily Checklist

Item	S	M	T	W	T	F	S
System Databases Backup							
Production User Databases Backup							
SQL Agent, SQL Maint, & DTC Running							
Database Size, Growth, Disk Free Space							
Batch Jobs Execute OK							
DBCC Jobs Execute OK							
SQL Log Errors							
Replication Log Agent Running							
Replication Distribution Cleanup Job Execute OK							
SQL Server Last Reboot							

Depending on the number of servers and the complexity, the DBA daily checklist can be maintained manually with an Excel spreadsheet or tracked in a SQL Server table.

Summary

This chapter covered database maintenance in detail. SQL Server offers a rich set of commands and utilities that can be used to monitor the health of, and perform maintenance on, SQL Server. The Maintenance Plan Wizard is also available to streamline database maintenance. All installations of SQL Server should also include a database maintenance schedule to assist the DBA in keeping track of maintenance performed.

The next chapter explains how to use SQL Server Agent, which may be used to schedule jobs and create custom maintenance jobs, and SQL Server Database Mail, for sending e-mail from SQL Server.

Chapter 43

Automating Database Maintenance with SQL Server Agent

IN THIS CHAPTER

- Setting up SQL Server Agent
- Understanding alerts, operators, and jobs
- Managing alerts
- Managing operators
- Managing jobs
- Setting up Database Mail

The automation of database maintenance is crucial to ensuring that a database is regularly checked, maintained, and optimized. Automated checking consists of monitoring database size to identify issues before they generate mayhem; maintenance includes frequent backups; and optimization involves tweaking the index configuration for optimal performance. Automation ensures that these activities do not consume too much of your time, so you can focus on more pressing issues (such as improving your golf game, perhaps).

Ideally, SQL Server can monitor itself and send alerts when it encounters a critical condition. Luckily Microsoft grants this specific wish, because SQL Server includes a powerful component that can send alerts when specific critical conditions occur. Better still, this same component also enables the scheduling of routine maintenance tasks either on a one-time basis or on a recurring basis — for example, once a month or, say, on the first Saturday of every month. SQL Server Agent is the service responsible for processing alerts and running scheduled jobs.

NOTE **SQL Server Agent service is not available in SQL Server Express Edition, for which scheduling of jobs has to be done using Windows Scheduler. For more information on Windows Scheduler, search the web, using your preferred search engine or consult Microsoft Windows documentation.**

Setting Up SQL Server Agent

Setting up SQL Server Agent is straightforward, as long as you avoid two pitfalls: The first is rather elementary (a startup issue); the second (a security issue) is a bit more subtle. It makes sense to start with the easy one. Because SQL Server Agent is a Windows service, make sure that the service is restarted if anybody reboots the server. (Microsoft sets this service not to start by default when you install SQL Server, so you'll always need to set it to start automatically after an installation.) This is an elementary step, but it is occasionally overlooked (and then, after someone restarts the server, none of the scheduled jobs run and, perhaps even worse, critical alerts go undetected).

Best Practice

The best way to avoid problems with services not restarting is to set them to start automatically. Here's how to do that:

1. Open the Services console found in the Administrative Tools folder of the Control Panel.
2. Right-click the SQL Server Agent (Instance) service and choose Properties from the context menu.
3. Select Automatic in the Startup Type field and click OK.

The SQL Server Agent service is displayed as SQL Server Agent, with the instance name appearing in parentheses. The instance name is MSSQLSERVER for default instance of SQL Server. If more than one SQL Server instance is installed on the server, a SQL Server Agent service will exist for each instance.

As with any service, the SQL Server Agent startup mode can be changed through the Services console in the Control Panel. However, another way to accomplish the same goal is to use the SQL Server Configuration Manager found by selecting Start ➪ Programs ➪ Microsoft SQL Server 2008 ➪ Configuration Tools ➪ SQL Server Configuration Manager.

The SQL Server Configuration Manager appears in Figure 43-1. In this figure, you can see three instances of the SQL Server Agent service. SQL Server Agent (MSSQLSERVER) is the SQL Server Agent for the default SQL Server (MSSQLSERVER) instance. The services named SQL Server Agent (INST1) and SQL Server Agent (INST2) are the SQL Server Agent instances for the SQL Server named instances SQL Server (INST1) and SQL Server (INST2), respectively.

Follow these steps to ensure that the startup mode of the SQL Server Agent service is set to automatic:

1. Open the SQL Server Configuration Manager.
2. Highlight the SQL Server Services folder.
3. Right-click the service you want to change and choose Properties from the context menu. The service's Properties dialog will appear.
4. Select the Service tab.
5. Highlight the Start Mode property and choose the new starting mode from the drop-down list box.
6. Click OK to make the change complete.

FIGURE 43-1

The SQL Server Configuration Manager dialog enables you to change the startup mode of the SQL Server Agent service.

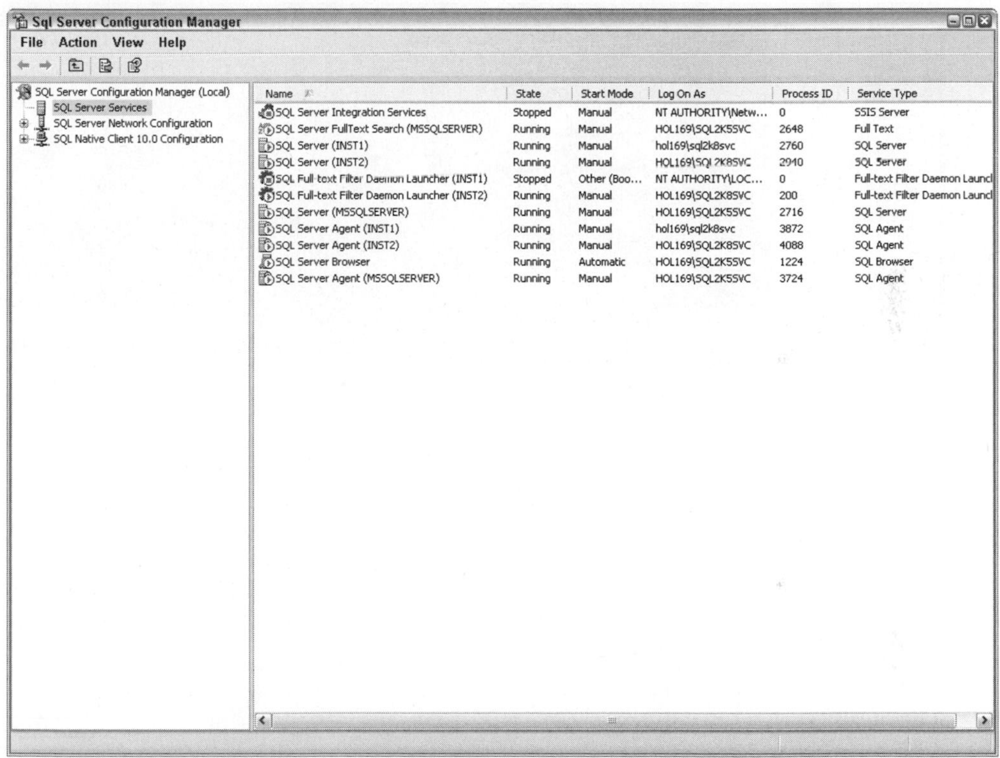

It is a good idea to take one extra step to ensure that SQL Server Agent (and SQL Server, for that matter) restarts if it stops unexpectedly:

1. Start SQL Server Management Studio (its default location is Start ➪ Programs ➪ Microsoft SQL Server 2008 ➪ SQL Server Management Studio).
2. Expand the folders until you find the SQL Server you are configuring. If no SQL Servers are configured, connect to the one you wish to manage.
3. Expand to see the folders below the SQL Server. One of these folders is entitled SQL Server Agent. Right-click the folder and choose Properties from the context menu. Choose the General folder, which offers the options shown in Figure 43-2.
4. Check both of the Auto restart options (refer to Figure 43-2). This ensures that SQL Server and SQL Server Agent restart when they unexpectedly stop.

FIGURE 43-2

The General tab of the SQL Server Agent Properties dialog enables you to configure how the service runs.

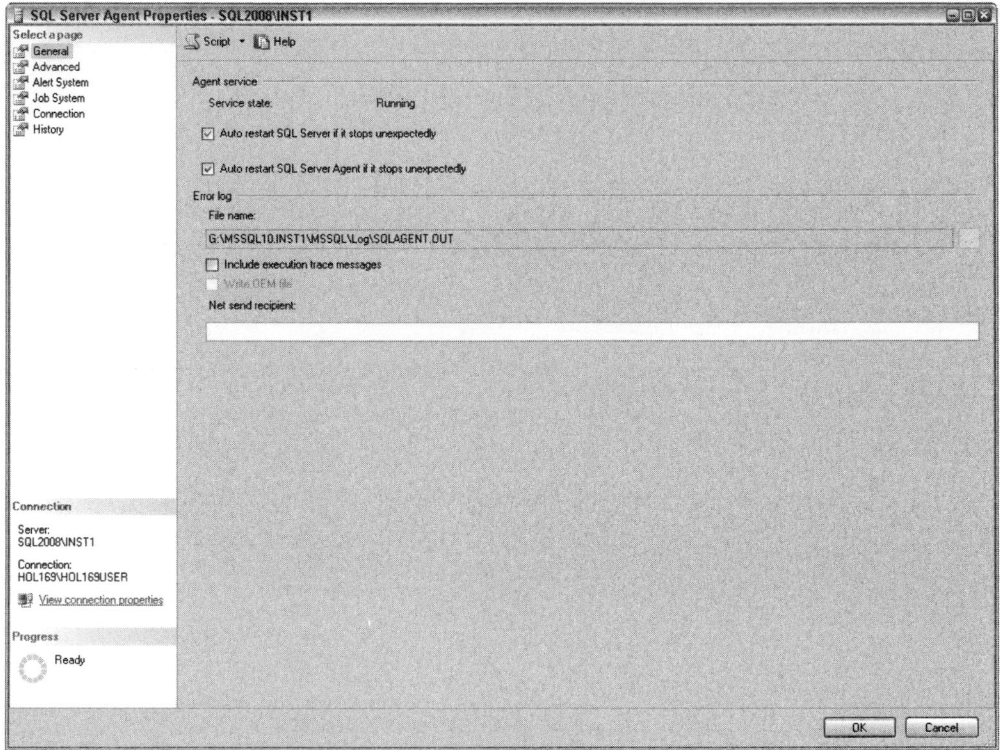

SQL Server Agent Setup Pitfalls

For a SQL Server 2008 Failover Clustering instance, do not set the startup mode of the SQL Server or the SQL Server Agent service to automatic. The startup mode of these services should be left to manual (default), as the cluster service controls the starting and stopping of these services.

The second pitfall to be aware of when setting up SQL Server Agent has to do with security. It's crucial to determine which account will be used to run this service. By default, the system account has access to only local resources. You must use a domain account if you want to access network resources in any of the scheduled jobs (backing up a database to a different server, for example). Typically, a domain account is

continued

continued
also needed to enable SQL Server to send e-mail and pager notifications (the steps to do this are outlined later in this section).

You must also use a domain account in order for replication to work. Typically, SQL Server Agent is configured to use a Windows domain account that is a member of the sysadmin role, so that the necessary permission is in place to run jobs or send notifications.

To change the account used to run the SQL Server Agent service, follow these steps:

1. Open the SQL Server Configuration Manager.
2. Highlight the SQL Server Services folder.
3. Right-click the SQL Server Agent entry and choose Properties from the context menu. The Properties dialog will appear.
4. Select the Log On tab. As shown in Figure 43-3, you can choose between one of the built-in accounts or use a specific account. Choose "This account" and either type in a name or browse a domain account on production SQL Servers where you want to access network resources, and send e-mail and pager notifications.
5. Click OK. A dialog will confirm that the change in account requires a service restart.
6. Click Yes. The account change will appear as soon as the service restarts.

FIGURE 43-3

Choose a built-in or other account to use for log on purposes.

The final step is to set up the SQL Server Agent mail profile so that the service can send e-mail and pager notifications when alerts occur. This requires setting up and configuring a mail service and letting SQL Server Agent know how to access the mail service. SQL Server Agent mail can use either Database Mail or SQL Mail to send e-mails. The section "Database Mail" in this chapter discusses how to configure Database Mail to send e-mails. SQL Mail is not discussed here, as this feature exists only for backward compatibility and will be removed in future versions of SQL Server.

Understanding Alerts, Operators, and Jobs

An alert defines a specific action that is carried out when a certain condition is met. Such a condition can be set up for a variety of performance counters, including number of connections, database file size, and number of deadlocks per second. A condition can also be tied to an error number or degree of error severity. When acting upon an alert condition, SQL Server Agent can notify one or more operators, run a job, or both.

Operators are the people responsible for handling critical conditions on the database server. As pointed out in the previous section, one of the neat things SQL Server Agent does is send messages to operators to report job status or make them aware of server conditions. Operators can be set up to receive messages via e-mail, pager, or Net Send. You can specify at which times an operator is available to receive messages via pager (e.g., 9:00 A.M. to 5:00 P.M., Monday to Friday). You can also suspend notification for a specified operator, such as when the operator is taking time off.

A job is a database task or group of database tasks. Examples of typical jobs are backing up a database, reorganizing the indexes, or executing a SQL Server Integration Services (SSIS) package. SQL Server Agent jobs are also used behind the scenes to implement and schedule a maintenance plan using the Maintenance Plan Wizard in SQL Server Management Studio.

Managing Operators

Just as you need to create logins for the users who will be accessing a SQL Server database, you need to create operators in SQL Server to be able to send alerts to these support people. Creating operators in SQL Server is straightforward. Here's how it works:

1. Start SQL Server Management Studio and find the SQL Server Agent folder below the server you are configuring.
2. Right-click the SQL Server Agent\Operators folder and select New Operator from the context menu. This brings up a dialog similar to the one shown in Figure 43-4. Choose the General folder as shown in the figure.
3. Type in the name of the operator as well as his or her e-mail address, pager e-mail address, and/or Net Send address, depending on how you want the notification to be sent. Filling out a pager address enables you to specify when the operator is available to be paged.
4. Select the Notifications folder and choose the notification method for each alert.
5. Click the Jobs option and set the notification method for each job.

Be sure to revisit the operator configuration every time a new alert or job is created and assign operators to new alerts and jobs as needed.

FIGURE 43-4

The New Operator dialog enables you to specify when an operator is available to receive pager notifications.

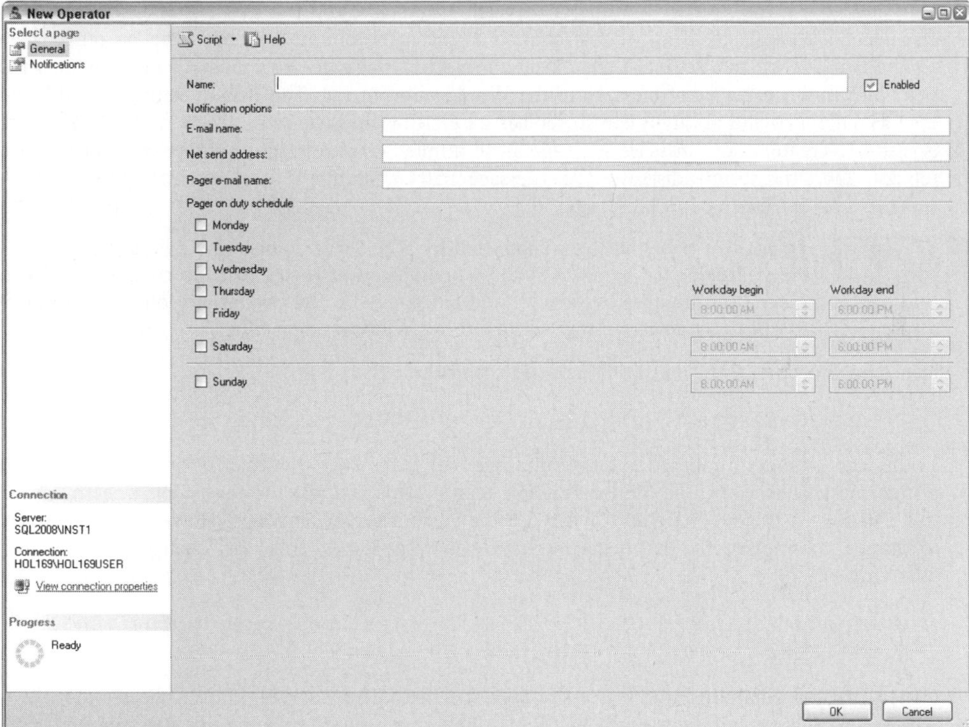

If an operator is unavailable to respond to notification, temporarily disable this operator by clearing the Enabled check box in the General folder. Just remember to ensure that another operator will be notified. Rather than disable an operator, change the e-mail, pager, and Net Send addresses until the operator becomes available again.

Managing Alerts

Depending on how SQL Server is installed, there may be no alerts created by SQL Server. However, SQL Server does create some default alerts when specific product features such as replication are installed. The names of the fourteen replication alerts start with "Replication." By default, SQL Server disables all of the replication alerts except for the warnings, and the alerts have no operators assigned to them. When deciding to use the replication features, be sure to provide operators to receive the alerts so someone is aware if something goes wrong. The "Managing Operators" section of this chapter details one method to add operators to an alert. The following sections describe how to create your own errors and alerts.

Creating user-defined errors

When deploying custom-written applications that use SQL Server as their data store, the application programmers may define their own set of errors. Use the `sp_addmessage` system stored procedure to perform this task. As a minimum, supply the error number (any value between 50,001 and 2,147,483,647), the severity (a number between 1 and 25), and the message text. The stored procedure also accepts a language identifier that consists of the name of any language installed on the server, such as English. The default setting is the currently selected language. You must also determine whether you want to write the error message to the Windows event log. The default setting is `FALSE` in this case. Finally, provide an argument to replace an existing message with a new message. If an attempt is made to create a new message with the same number as an existing number without providing the replace value, the system displays error message `15043`, stating "`You must specify 'REPLACE' to overwrite an existing message`."

TIP **To list the error messages supported by SQL Server, query the `sys.sysmessages` catalog view filtering for `error > 50000` when you want to see just the custom error messages. You can also filter the messages by severity and language ID. The mysterious-looking `dlevel` field has a value of `128` when the error message writes to the Windows event log.**

Here's an example of the `sp_addmessage` command:

```
sp_addmessage 50001, 1, 'This is a test message.';
```

In this case, the command adds a new message with a message identifier of 50001. The severity level of this message is 1 and the human-readable text is "This is a test message." The system won't write this message to the event log and it will use the current server language. However, suppose you decide to change this message so that it does write to the event log. In this case, change the command to the following:

```
sp_addmessage 50001, 1, 'This is a test message.', 'English', TRUE,
REPLACE;
```

Notice that the command now has a language specified. The value of `TRUE` indicates that the system will write the message to the event log. Finally, because you're replacing this message with one that already exists, the command includes the word `REPLACE`.

As far as alerts are concerned, user-defined and native SQL Server messages are handled uniformly. Specify the error number or severity level, and when an error is raised that matches the alert condition, SQL Server Agent will initiate the specified response. The following section covers how to set up these kinds of alerts.

Creating an alert

You can create three kinds of alerts. The first is triggered by an error number or by an error of a specified severity. The second is triggered by a SQL Server performance counter. The third is triggered by a Windows Management Instrumentation (WMI) event. Here is how to set up alerts:

1. Start SQL Server Management Studio.
2. Right-click the SQL Server Agent\Alerts folder and choose New Alert from the context menu. You'll see the New Alert dialog shown in Figure 43-5.
3. Type a name for the alert. Because an alert can affect one or all databases and define any number of events or conditions, name the alert carefully. Use keywords so that the system orders the alert automatically for you — for example, "Event: AdventureWorks: Severity Level 16."

FIGURE 43-5

An error condition is one of the three events that can trigger an alert.

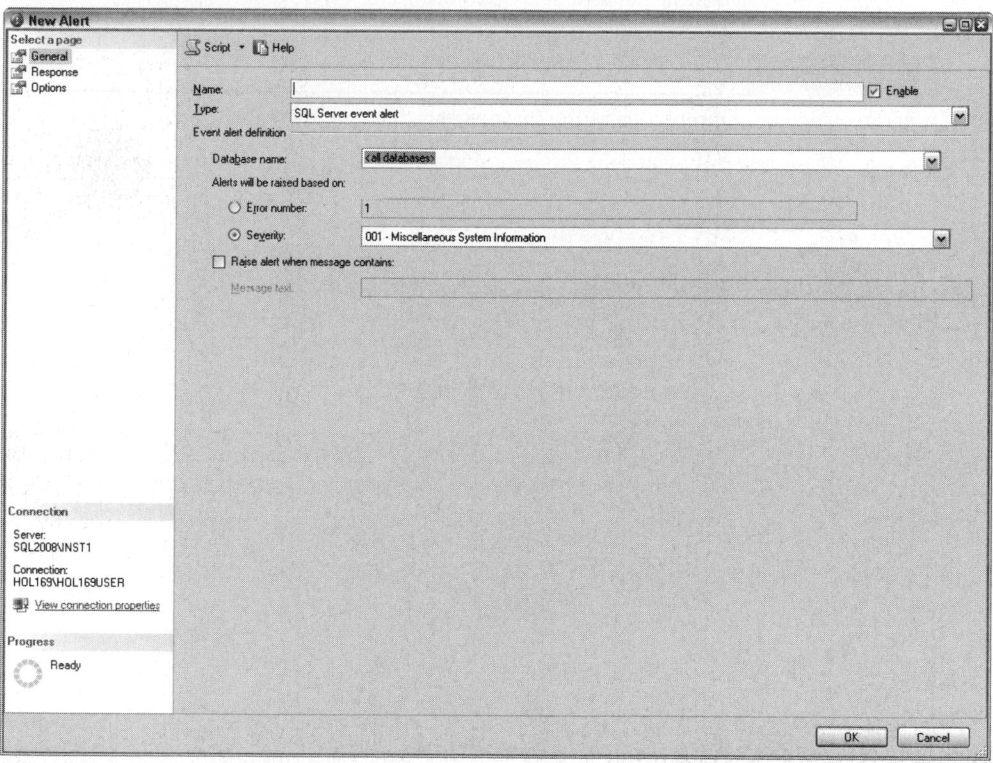

4. Select the type of alert. The Type list box enables you to specify which kind of alert you want to create: a SQL Server event alert (triggered by an error number or level of severity), a SQL Server performance-condition alert, or a WMI event alert. Figure 43-6 shows the changes to make to the New Alert dialog to create a SQL Server performance-condition alert. In this case, the alert will trigger when the size of the `AdventureWorks2008` database log exceeds 4,000 KB (or 4 MB). Use this technique to access any of the SQL Server performance counters.
5. Configure the alert (what to do in this step depends on the choice made in previous step):
   a. When creating a SQL Server event alert, select the severity and enter the error number to monitor. It is possible to monitor either all databases on the server or a specific database. Finally, to restrict alerts to messages containing a specific text string, check the "Raise alert when message contains" check box and enter the text in the "Message text" text box.
   b. When creating a SQL Server performance-condition test alert, select the object and counter to monitor. Then set the threshold for that counter. You can specify that the alert occur when the counter falls below, equals, or exceeds, the specified value. For some counters, you can specify the instance to which the counter is to be applied. For example, you can monitor the data-file size for either all databases on the server or just one specific database.

When creating a WMI event alert, you must provide the namespace for the event, such as `\\.\root\Microsoft\SqlServer\ServerEvents\MSSQLSERVER`. In addition, you must provide a query for that namespace. All WMI queries rely on the Windows Management Instrumentation Query Language (WQL).

FIGURE 43-6

A performance condition is one of the three events that can trigger an alert.

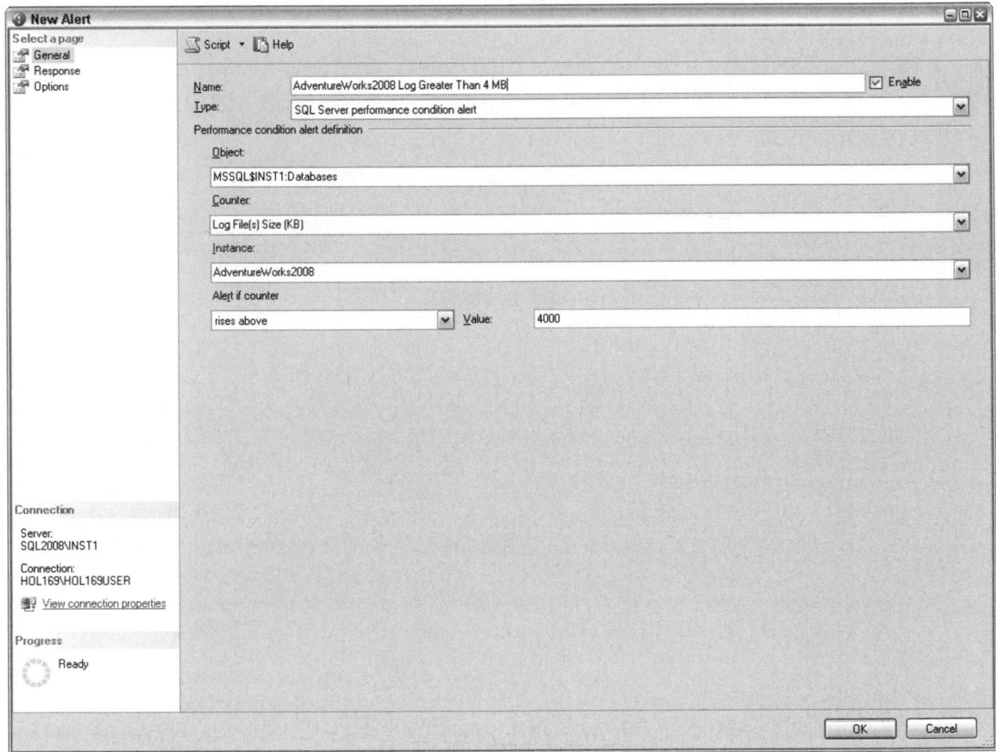

6. Select the Response tab. Determine the kind of response the alert will request. In the Response tab, specify one or more operators to be notified, or which job to run, or both. The next section, "Managing Jobs," covers how to set up jobs. Of course, the New Operator button brings up the New Operator dialog discussed in the previous section, "Managing Operators." Typically, you choose to send the error text in an e-mail or a Net Send, but not when paging an operator. Three check boxes beside the list of operators to be notified control the notification method.

7. Select the Options tab. Choose to send the alert error text in Email, Pager, or Net Send notifications. In addition to the standard error text, it is also possible to provide special text for

this alert. Finally, for recurring alerts, specify the delay between responses in minutes and seconds. This is especially important for SQL Server performance-condition alerts, because these conditions tend to exist for a long time and you don't want to flood the operators with multiple alerts for the same condition.

Managing Jobs

A job is defined as a series of steps with a specific work flow. You can, for example, specify that step 1 will execute step 2 if it succeeds, but will execute step 3 if it fails. Steps come in two basic types. The first type involves replication. The second can execute Transact-SQL script, ActiveX script (Visual Basic script or JScript), or any operating-system command. The latter are the most frequently used. After each step, you can specify the next action depending on whether the step succeeds or fails. There are four options:

- Go to the next step.
- Go to step *x*, where *x* is the number of any step defined in the job.
- Quit the job, reporting success.
- Quit the job, reporting failure.

You can also set the number of times a step will be attempted in case of failure. It is possible to associate one or more schedules with a job. This enables a job to be automatically run at a specified time. A schedule can specify that a job should run once at a specific time or on a recurring basis. You can also schedule a job to run whenever SQL Server Agent starts or whenever the CPU becomes idle.

Specify when you consider the CPU to be idle in the Advanced tab of the SQL Server Agent Properties dialog (see Figure 43-7). This involves selecting the level of average CPU usage that the CPU must fall below for a specified time in seconds. The default idle CPU condition is when average CPU usage falls below 10% and remains below this level for 10 minutes. Finally, you can also set notifications for completion, success, or failure of a job.

Best Practice

It's important to realize that your server is never completely idle. Even a well-tuned setup will usually have 2 percent or 3 percent activity. Consequently, setting the "Average CPU Usage Falls Below" setting to 0 percent means the job will never run. However, nor do you want to set this value so high that it interferes with jobs that must run in the foreground in near real time. Consequently, using a setting between 5 percent and 12 percent normally works best. Likewise, the amount of idle time is important. Using a setting between 360 and 600 seconds works well. However, an administrator for a large system might want to set this value higher to ensure that the server is truly idle, while an administrator for a smaller system might want to use a lower value to maximize use of idle time.

FIGURE 43-7

Set the conditions that you consider equivalent to CPU idle time.

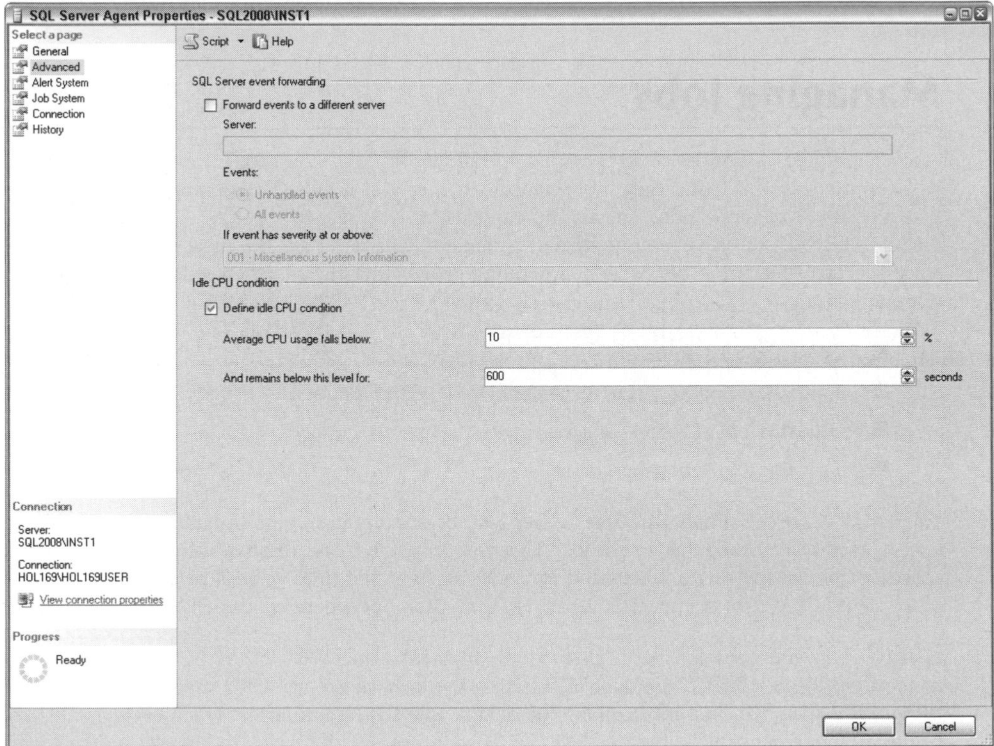

Some wizards such as Maintenance Plan Wizard create jobs behind the scenes when you use them. Any form of replication also creates jobs behind the scenes.

As with alerts, create a new job using the New Job dialog. Creating a job involves five distinct steps:

1. Create a job definition.
2. Set each step to execute.
3. Set the next action for each step.
4. Configure a job schedule.
5. Handle completion-, success-, and failure-notification messages.

The following sections walk through each of these steps. The first section that follows discusses the optional step of creating a job category.

Creating a job category

As you will see in the next section, when defining a job, you can assign a category to it. This enables you to group similar jobs together. Here are the steps you can use to manage job categories:

1. Start SQL Server Management Studio.
2. Right-click the SQL Server Agent\Jobs folder and choose Manage Job Categories from the context menu. This brings up the Manage Job Categories dialog, shown in Figure 43-8.

FIGURE 43-8

The Manage Job Categories dialog enables you to maintain the job categories used when you define a new job.

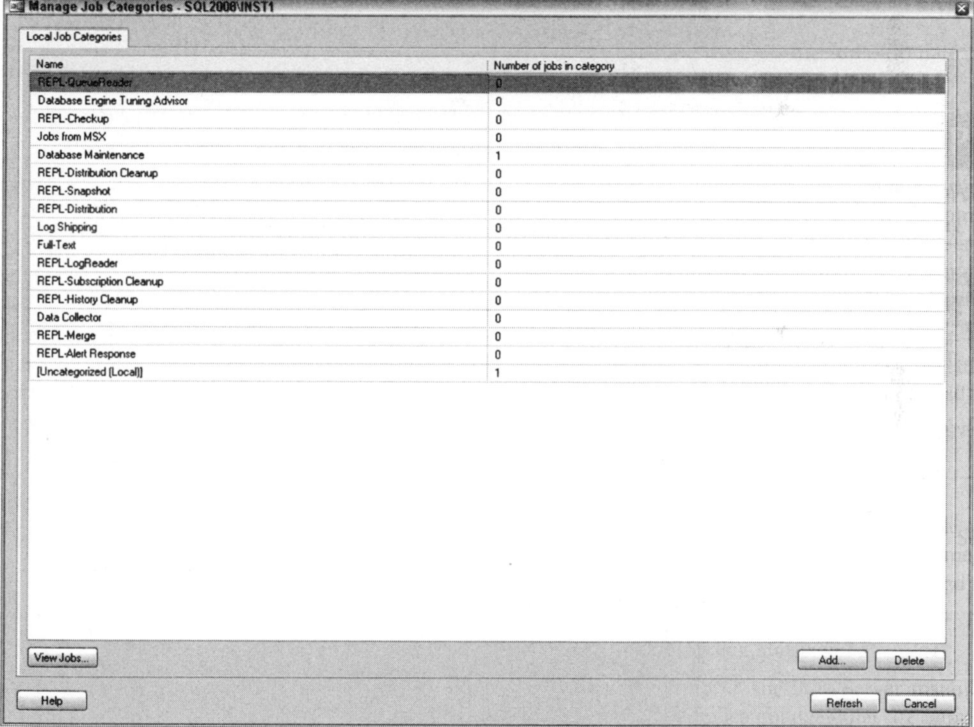

3. Create a new job category by clicking Add. This brings up the New Category properties dialog.
4. Type a descriptive name for the category in the Name field.
5. Add jobs to this category by clicking the Show All Jobs check box and selecting the corresponding check box in the Select column of the job list. Jobs that don't have a category assigned automatically appear in the list. Selecting Show All Jobs will also reveal jobs that already have a category assigned.

6. The Manage Job Categories dialog is also the place to remove existing job categories. Highlight the job category to be deleted and click Delete.
7. In addition, you can see a list of the jobs currently assigned to a particular category. Highlight the job category to view and click View Jobs. Add additional jobs to a category by clicking the Show All Jobs check box and checking the job's entry in the Select column of the New Job Category dialog.

Creating a job definition

The main component of a job definition is the unique name that will be used to refer to the job. Use this unique name, for example, to specify which job to run when an alert is triggered. Here's how to create a job definition:

1. Start SQL Server Management Studio and find the SQL Server Agent folder below the server you are configuring.
2. Expand the SQL Server Agent folder to see the items below it.
3. Right-click the Jobs folder and choose New Job from the context menu. This brings up a New Job dialog similar to the one shown in Figure 43-9.

FIGURE 43-9

You can categorize and assign an owner to a new job in the New Job dialog.

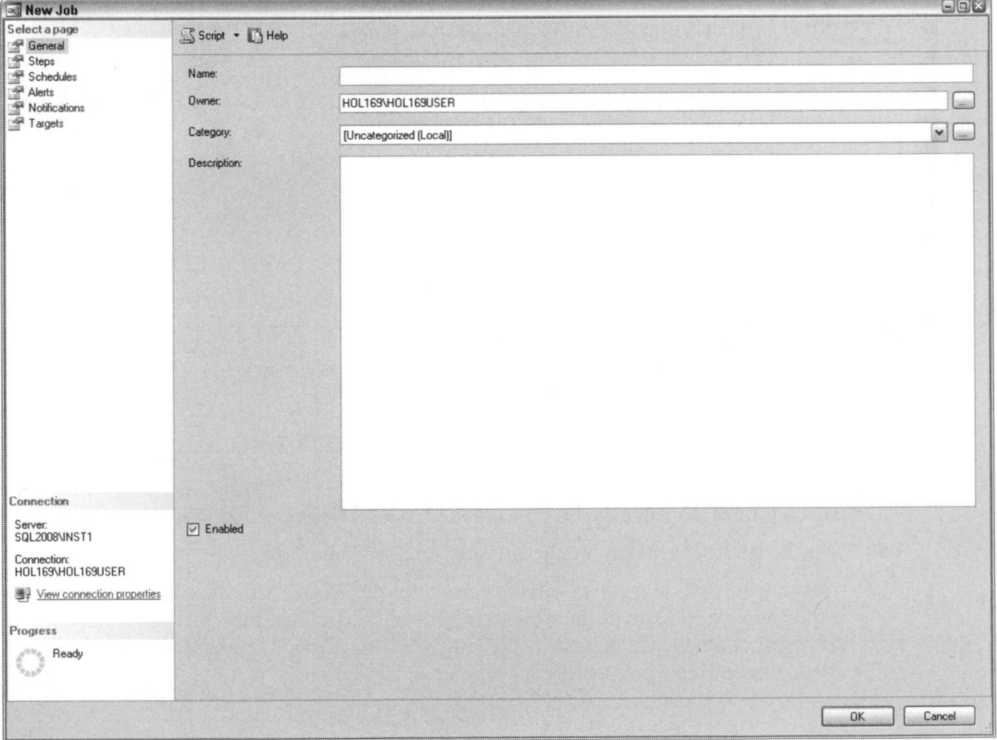

4. In the General tab, give the job a unique name (up to 128 characters), select an appropriate category and owner for the job, and type a description of the job. Only administrators can change the owner of an existing job.

NOTE **Only predefined logins can be used as the owner. If you do not find the login you want to use, exit the job definition by clicking the Cancel button and create a login for the account you want to use. To do this, expand the Security folder in Management Studio, right-click on Logins, and then select New Login.**

5. Select the Targets folder. Select the Target Local Server for jobs that run on a single, local machine. If job scheduling across multiple servers is configured, choose Target Multiple Servers and select which servers acts as the target servers (the servers on which the job runs).
6. Click Apply to create the job definition. You are now ready for the next steps, as explained in the following sections.

Setting up the job steps

After creating a job definition, the next step (if applicable) is to define what steps need to be performed during the job. Do this by clicking the Steps tab (see Figure 43-10) in the Job Properties dialog. The buttons on this screen are as follows:

FIGURE 43-10

A job may consist of one or more steps, which are created in the Steps tab.

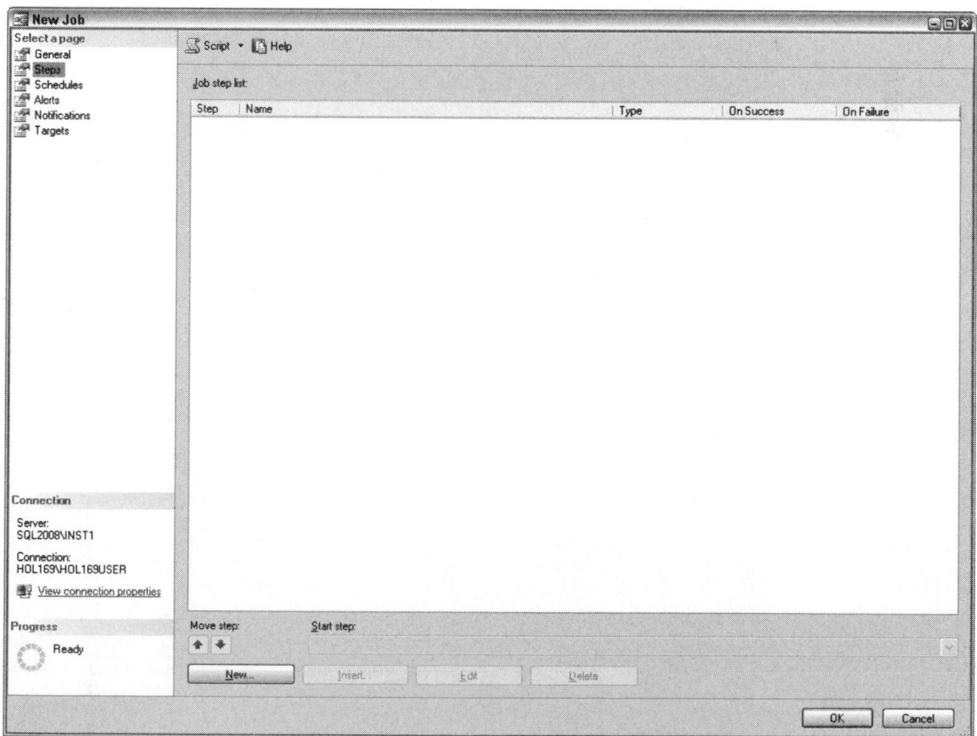

- **New:** Creates a new step
- **Insert:** Inserts a step before the currently highlighted step
- **Edit:** Modifies the currently highlighted step
- **Delete:** Deletes the currently highlighted step
- **Move step up:** Moves the currently highlighted step up one in the list
- **Move step down:** Moves the currently highlighted step down one in the list
- **Start step:** Enables you to choose which step is executed first. This first step is indicated by a green flag.

When creating a new step, you are presented with the New Job Step dialog, shown in Figure 43-11. All steps require a unique name (up to 128 characters). For the three most common types of steps (Transact-SQL Script, ActiveX script, and operating-system commands), simply type in the Command box the code you want executed. You may also click the Open button to load the code from a file. The Parse button enables you to check the syntax of the command.

FIGURE 43-11

A step can execute any Transact-SQL code.

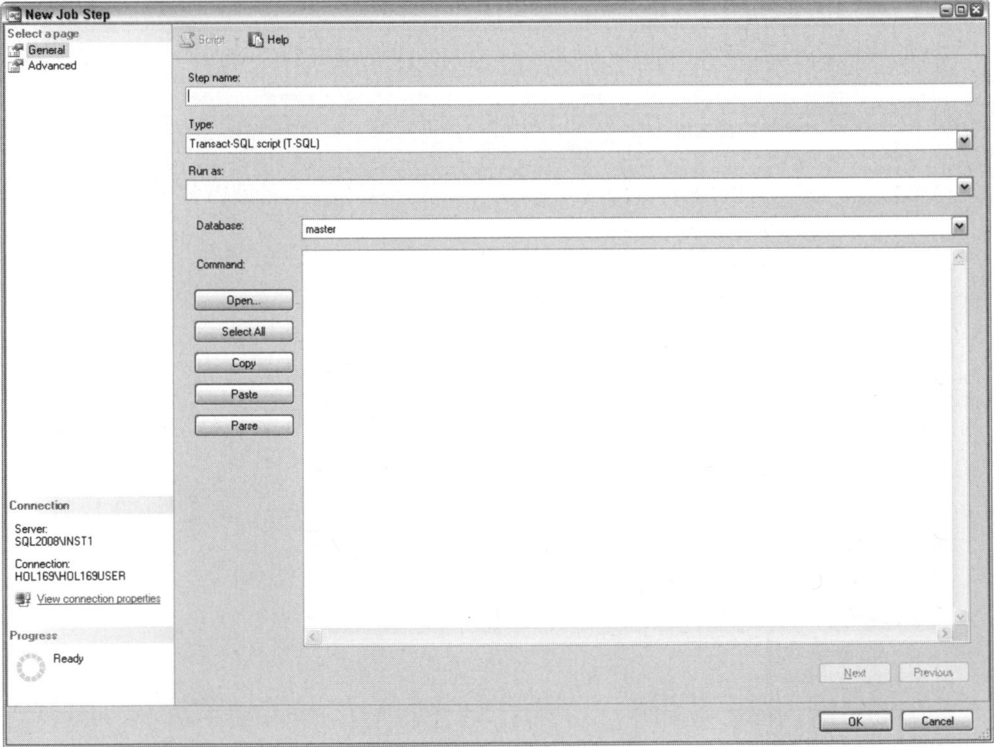

After you have entered the code that should run for the step, you can click the Advanced tab (see Figure 43-12) in the New Job Step dialog to specify what happens after the step executes. You can also specify how many times the step is attempted in case of initial failure, as well as the delay in minutes between the attempts.

FIGURE 43-12

Use the Advanced tab to control what happens after a step executes.

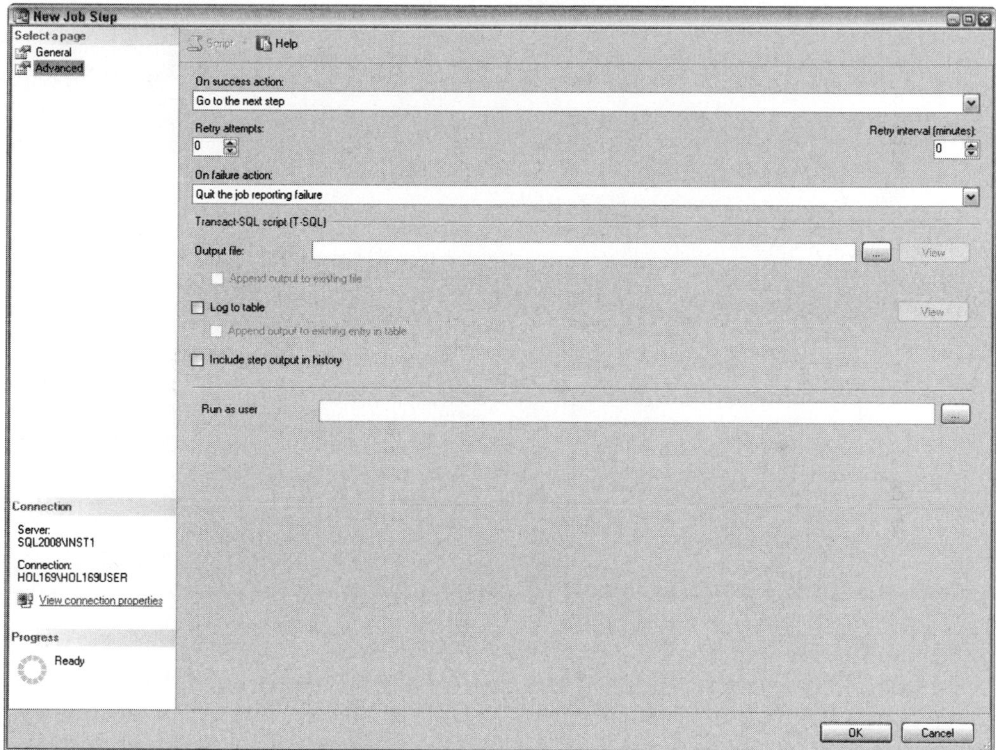

Configuring a job schedule

After entering the steps for a given job, the next step is to specify when the job is to be executed, done in the Schedules tab of the New Job dialog. Clicking the New button on this tab brings up the New Job Schedule dialog, shown in Figure 43-13.

Many maintenance tasks are recurring jobs. If you don't like the default (every week on Sunday at 12:00:00 A.M.), you can define how frequently the task is to be repeated. Figure 43-13 shows there is plenty of flexibility in scheduling a recurring job.

FIGURE 43-13

Jobs can be scheduled on a one-time basis or on a recurring basis.

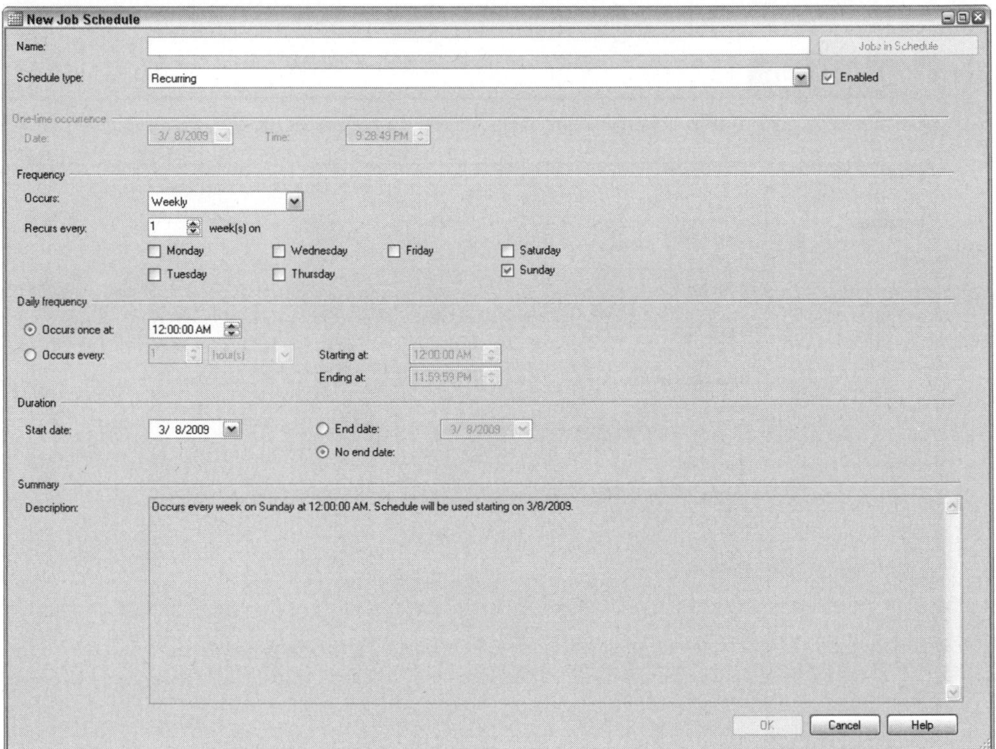

Handling completion-, success-, and failure-notification messages

Finally, click the Notifications tab (see Figure 43-14) of the New Job dialog to specify the type of notification to be used when the job completes, fails, or succeeds. You can send a message to an operator (via e-mail, pager, or Net Send message), log the related event, automatically delete the step, or any combination of these.

Database Mail

Starting with SQL Server 2005, Database Mail was introduced as an enterprise solution to send e-mails from SQL Server. Database Mail features many improvements over SQL Mail, the most important of which is that it is no longer dependent on Messaging Application Program Interface (MAPI). It uses Simple Mail Transfer Protocol (SMTP), and you do not need to install an extended MAPI client (for example, Microsoft Outlook) on your production SQL Server to use Database Mail.

FIGURE 43-14

You can specify the type of notification to be used when the job completes, fails, or succeeds.

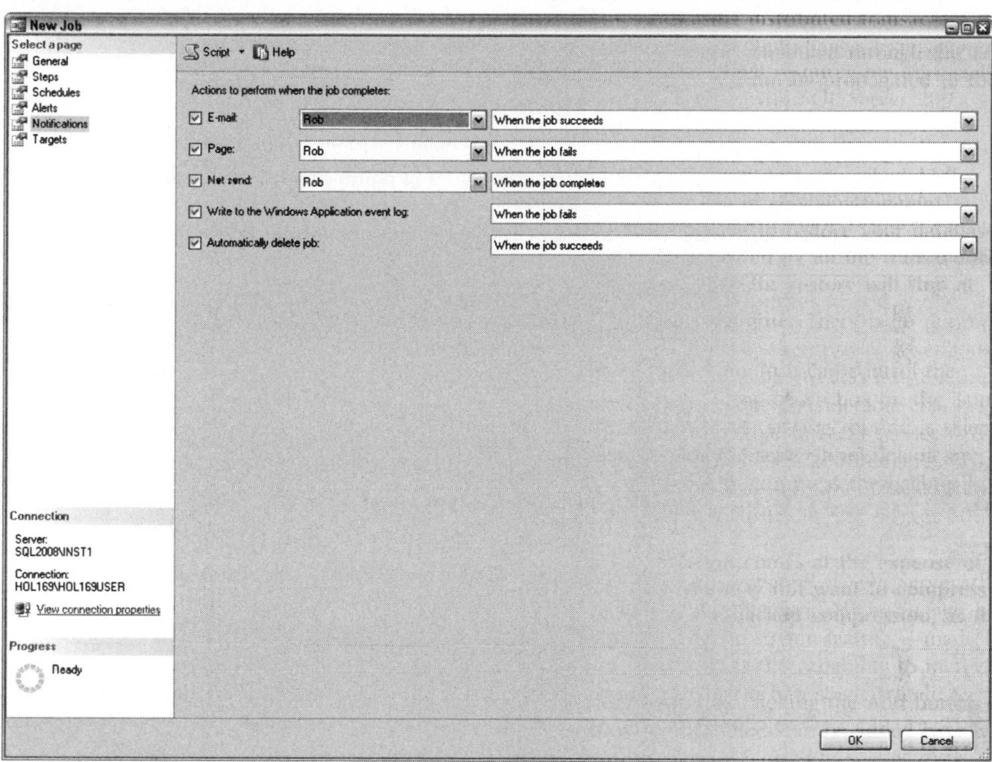

Here are some important advantages of Database Mail:

- Database Mail works in the background. It uses Service Broker queue for the messages, providing asynchronous, out of process delivery.
- It can be configured to use more than one SMTP server, thereby eliminating single point of failure.
- It is cluster aware and fully supported on SQL Server Failover Cluster.
- It is fully supported on 64-bit SQL Server installations.

NOTE **The SQL Mail feature still exists in Microsoft SQL Server 2008 for backward compatibility. It is recommended to stop using SQL Mail and use Database Mail instead, as SQL Mail will be removed in a future version of SQL Server.**

Database Mail is not available in SQL Server Express Edition.

Configuring database mail

Configuring Database Mail is very simple compared to configuring SQL Mail. Microsoft makes it easy by providing a Database Mail Configuration Wizard.

NOTE **By default, Database Mail is not enabled. Enable it one of three ways:**

- **From the Database Mail Configuration Wizard**
- **With the `sp_configure 'Database Mail XPs'` option**
- **Using the Surface Area Configuration Tool of policy-based management.**

Configuring Database Mail involves the following distinct steps:

1. Enable Database Mail.
2. Create a Database Mail profile.
3. Create a Database Mail account.
4. Add the account to the profile.
5. Grant permission for a user or a role to use the Database Mail profile.

Using the Database Mail Configuration Wizard

The following section walks through each of these steps. For configuring database mail for the first time, it is best to use the Database Mail Configuration Wizard. Follow these steps to configure Database Mail:

1. Open SQL Server Management Studio and find the Management folder under the SQL Server you are configuring.
2. Expand the Management folder, right-click the Database Mail folder and select Configure Database Mail from the context menu. This brings up the Database Mail Configuration Wizard. Clicking Next brings up the Select Configuration Task dialog, as shown in Figure 43-15.
3. Because it's the initial Database Mail setup, keep the default selection of Set up Database Mail and click Next to continue. Once you have configured Database Mail, you can select the other options to manage the Database Mail accounts and profiles, manage profile security, and view or change Database Mail system parameters.
4. Because Database Mail is not enabled by default, a dialog similar to the one shown in Figure 43-16 pops up, asking you if you want to enable Database Mail.
5. Click Yes. (Alternately, Database Mail can be enabled by setting the '`Database Mail XPs`' `sp_configure` option to 1). Once Database Mail is enabled, the New Profile dialog will appear, as shown in Figure 43-17.
6. Type a name for the Database Mail profile. Click Add to create a Database Mail Account and add it to the profile. This brings up the New Database Mail Account dialog shown in Figure 43-18. You may have to get the information required for this dialog from your server and/or security team beforehand. Enter the information, select the SMTP authentication, and click OK to continue.

FIGURE 43-15

This handy wizard makes it easy to set up and manage Database Mail.

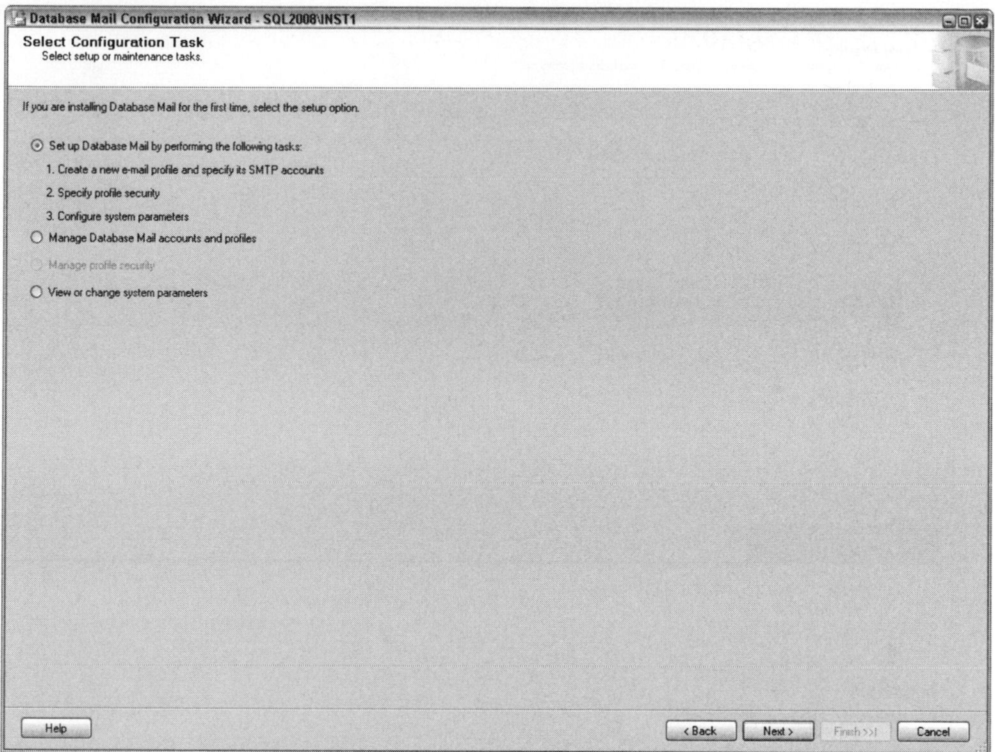

FIGURE 43-16

Enable Database Mail feature.

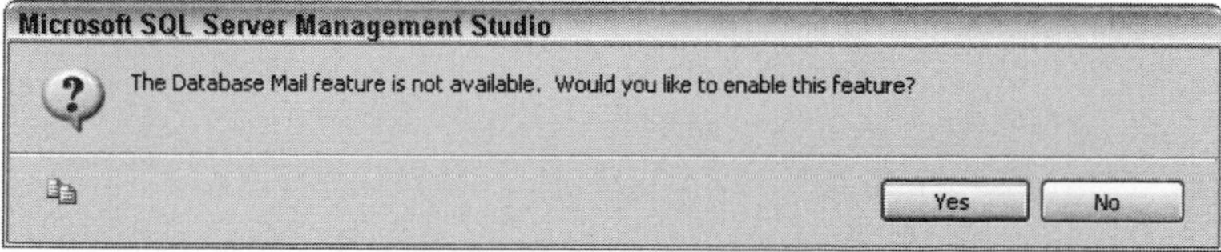

FIGURE 43-17

Create a new profile and add accounts to it.

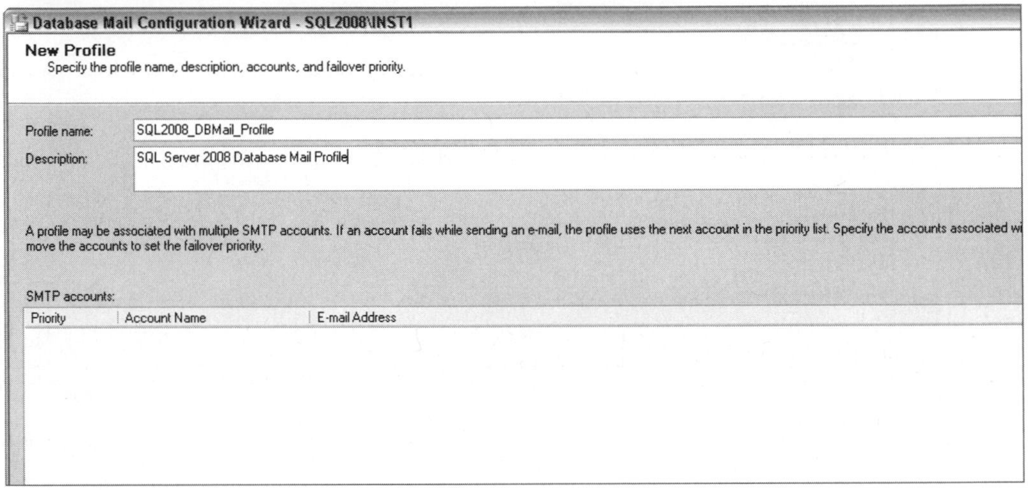

Database Mail Configuration Wizard - SQL2008\INST1

New Profile

Specify the profile name, description, accounts, and failover priority.

Profile name: SQL2008_DBMail_Profile

Description: SQL Server 2008 Database Mail Profile

A profile may be associated with multiple SMTP accounts. If an account fails while sending an e-mail, the profile uses the next account in the priority list. Specify the accounts associated wi
move the accounts to set the failover priority.

SMTP accounts:

Priority	Account Name	E-mail Address

FIGURE 43-18

Create a new account for Database Mail.

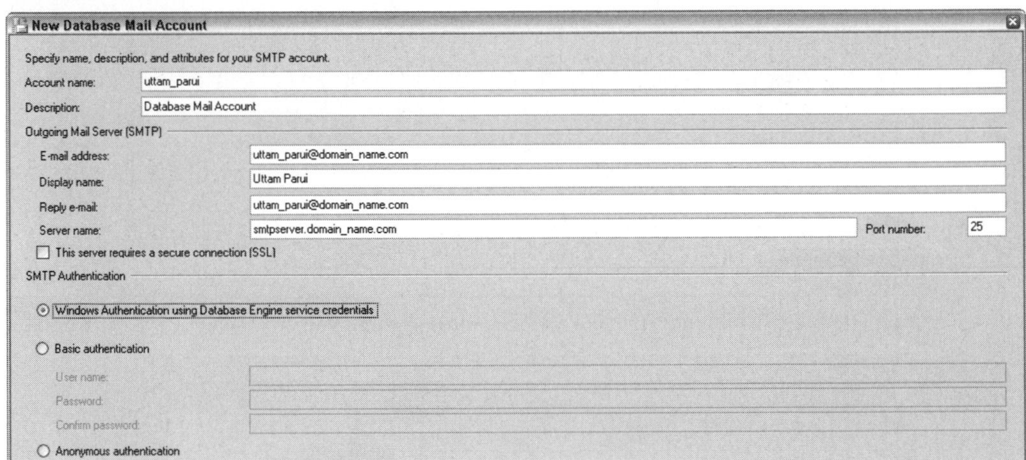

7. Notice that the new account you created in the previous step is added to the profile, as shown in Figure 43-19. Clicking Add sets up multiple accounts for the Database Mail profile to allow for Failover and avoid single points of failure.

FIGURE 43-19

Add an account to the Database Mail profile.

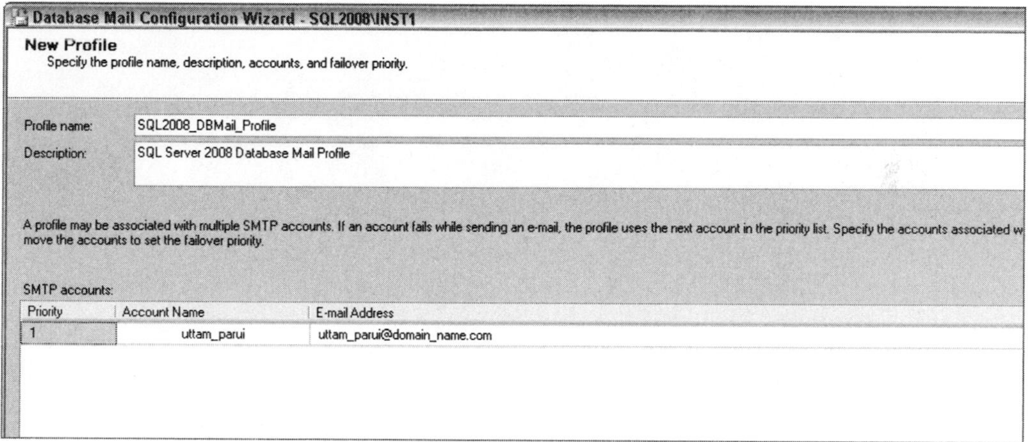

8. Click Next to proceed. This brings up the Manage Profile Security dialog, shown in Figure 43-20. Here you can specify the database users or roles that can access the profiles. The public profile allows all users to access the profile, whereas the private profile allows only specific users to access the profile. This dialog also enables you to specify whether the profile is a default public profile. A default public profile allows you to send e-mail without explicitly specifying the profile.

9. Click Next to bring up the Configure System Parameters dialog, shown in Figure 43-21. Based on your requirements, you can change the Database Mail system parameters in this dialog. You may want to change the retry attempts to 3 instead of the default value of 1.

10. Click Next to review the configuration settings you have made. This brings up the Complete the Wizard dialog, shown in Figure 43-22.

11. Click Finish. This will bring up the Configuring dialog, shown in Figure 43-23.

FIGURE 43-20

You can specify which users have access to the profile and specify the default profile.

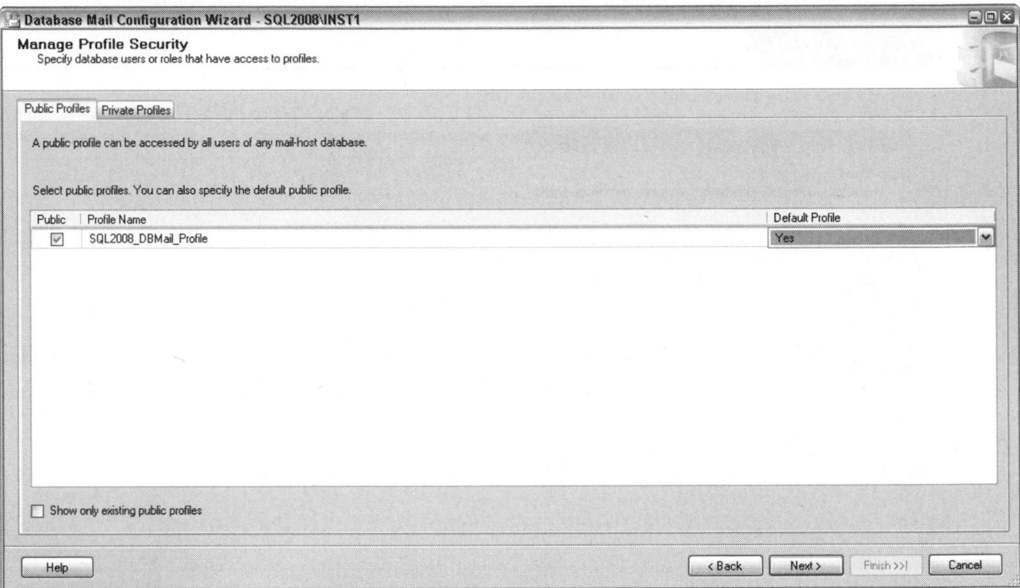

FIGURE 43-21

The Database Mail system parameters can be changed.

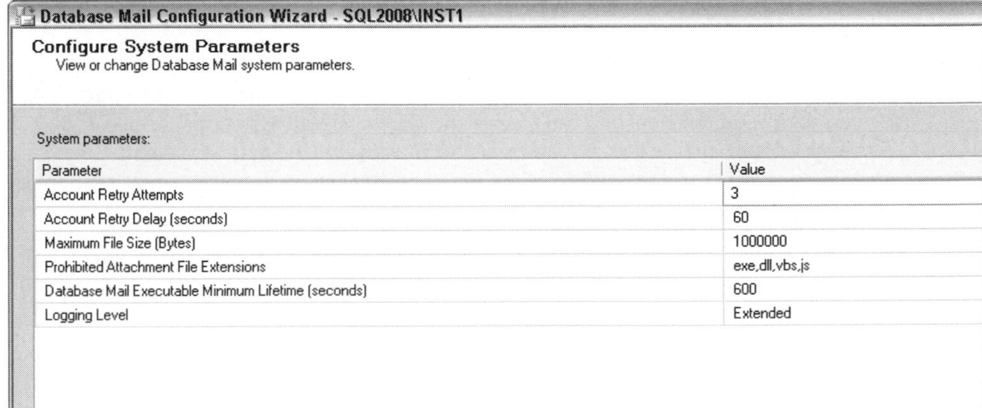

FIGURE 43-22

Review the configuration settings that you have made.

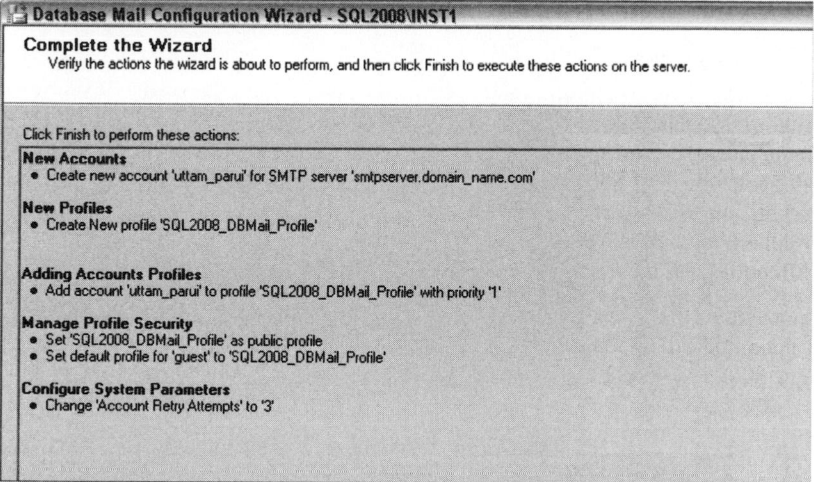

FIGURE 43-23

Underlying stored procedures are being run to configure Database Mail.

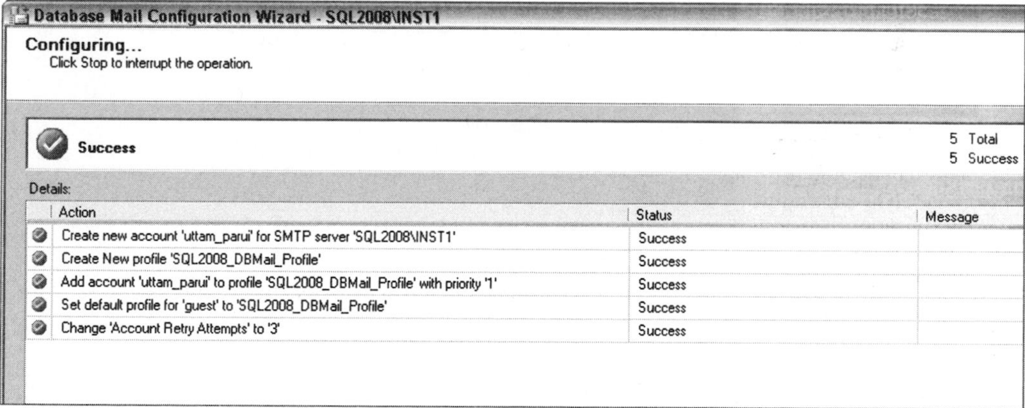

Congratulations. Database Mail is now configured successfully and can be used in a manner similar to SQL Mail. Although the Database Mail Configuration Wizard makes it simple to configure Database Mail, it may not be the fastest way to configure Database Mail on multiple SQL Servers. The following T-SQL script can be used to perform the exact same steps that were achieved with the Database Mail Configuration Wizard:

```
-- Enable Database Mail
sp_configure 'show advanced options', 1;
GO
RECONFIGURE;
GO
sp_configure 'Database Mail XPs', 1;
GO
RECONFIGURE
GO

-- Create a Database Mail profile
EXECUTE msdb.dbo.sysmail_add_profile_sp
@profile_name = 'SQL2008_DBMail_Profile',
@description = 'SQL Server 2008 Database Mail Profile' ;

-- Create a Database Mail account
EXECUTE msdb.dbo.sysmail_add_account_sp
@account_name = 'uttam_parui',
@description = 'Database Mail Account',
@email_address = 'uttam_parui@domain_name.com',
@display_name = 'Uttam Parui',
@replyto_address = 'uttam_parui@domain_name.com',
@mailserver_name = 'smtpserver.domain_name.com' ;

-- Add the account to the profile
EXECUTE msdb.dbo.sysmail_add_profileaccount_sp
@profile_name = 'SQL2008_DBMail_Profile',
@account_name = 'uttam_parui',
@sequence_number =1 ;

-- Grant permission for a user or a role to use the Database Mail
profile
EXECUTE msdb.dbo.sysmail_add_principalprofile_sp
@profile_name = 'SQL2008_DBMail_Profile',
@principal_id = 0,
@is_default = 1 ;
```

Now Database Mail is ready to send e-mails. To do so, use the sp_send_dbmail stored procedure. This stored procedure accepts a lot of parameters, most of which are optional. The following T-SQL code can be used to send a simple text e-mail:

```
EXECUTE msdb.dbo.sp_send_dbmail @profile_name='SQL2008_DBMail_Profile',
@recipients='pauln@sqlserverbible.com',
```

```
@subject='Database Mail Test',
@body='This is a test e-mail sent from Database Mail on SQL2008\INST1'
```

NOTE **To send e-mail using the Database Mail feature, you must be a member of either the** `sysadmin` **fixed server role or the** `DatabaseMailUserRole` **in** `msdb`**.**

To view the status of the e-mails, use the `sysmail_allitems` view as follows:

```
SELECT * FROM msdb.dbo.sysmail_allitems;
```

One of the important columns in this view is `sent_status`. It contains one of the following four values: `sent`, `unsent`, `retrying`, or `failed`. If your e-mails are not going out, check this view to verify that the e-mails are being queued up. If you notice messages with anything other than `sent` status, right-click the Database Mail folder in Management Studio and select View Database Mail Log from the context menu to view detailed error messages.

Best Practice

All the e-mails and attachments are stored in `msdb` internal tables. These tables are not maintained automatically and based on your e-mail activity, they may become very big. It is recommended that you periodically use the system stored procedures `msdb.dbo.sysmail_delete_mailitems_sp` and `msdb.dbo.sysmail_delete_log_sp` to maintain the `msdb` internal tables. You can use the steps learned in this chapter to configure a SQL Server Agent job to run these stored procedures automatically.

Summary

SQL Server Agent is a powerful ally that will ensure you never forget to perform a crucial maintenance task, and that will alert you when something critical requires your attention. The former goal is achieved through recurring jobs, the latter through alerts.

This chapter covered how to set up SQL Server Agent. You learned what alerts, operators, and jobs are, and the steps required to manage them. Finally, you learned how to configure Database Mail so that the SQL Server Agent service can send e-mail and page notifications when alerts occur. In short, you should now be fully equipped to use all features of SQL Server Agent to automate crucial maintenance tasks.

Chapter 44

Transferring Databases

IN THIS CHAPTER

Using the Copy Database Wizard

Generating SQL scripts

Detaching and attaching databases

Using the Import and Export Wizard

Transferring data may be a mundane task, but SQL Server databases are often developed on one server and deployed on other servers. Without a reliable and efficient method of moving database schemas and whole databases, the project won't get very far.

SQL Server enables multiple means of moving databases. As a database developer or database administrator (DBA), you should have basic skills in the following topics, three of which are covered in this chapter:

- Copy Database Wizard
- SQL scripts
- Detach/Attach
- Backup/Restore (covered in Chapter 41, "Recovery Planning")

The keys to determining the best way to move a database are knowing how much of it needs to be moved and whether or not the servers are directly connected by a fast network. Table 44-1 lists the copy requirements and the various methods of moving a database.

Copy Database Wizard

The Copy Database Wizard actually generates a SQL Server Integration Services (SSIS) package that can copy or move one or more databases from one server to another. If the database is being moved to a server on the same network server, this is the premiere method. This method won't work to copy a database from SQL Server 2008 to an older version of SQL Server. In addition, both source and

What's New in SQL Server Configuration?

`sp_attach_db` is a deprecated feature and will be removed in future versions of SQL Server. It is recommended to use `CREATE DATABASE database_name FOR ATTACH` instead.

The SQL Server Import and Export Wizard has additional options for data type conversions that are required by import and export operations. For example, it provides visual cues of the data type mapping for each table or view, which helps to proactively check for errors. Also, the wizard can now be started from Start ➪ Programs ➪ Microsoft SQL Server 2008.

TABLE 44-1

Database Transfer Methods

Requirement	Copy Database Wizard	SQL Scripts	Detaching Attaching	Backup Restore
Exclusive Access to the Database	Yes	No	Yes	No
Copies Between Disconnected Servers	No	Yes	Yes	Yes
Copies Database Schema	Yes	Yes	Yes	Yes
Copies Data	Yes	Depends on the script	Yes	Yes
Copies Security	Server logins, database users, security roles, and permissions	Depends on the script	Database users, security roles, and permissions	Database users, security roles, and permissions
Copies Jobs/ User-Defined Error Messages	Yes	Depends on the script	Yes	Yes

destination servers must have the SQL Server Agent running (it is stopped by default when working with SQL Server 2008). The Copy Database Wizard offers the most flexibility and capability. Its only limitation is that it requires exclusive access to the database. You access the Copy Database Wizard by right-clicking the database you want to copy and choosing Tasks ➪ Copy Database from the context menu. Skip past the Welcome to the Copy Database Wizard page by clicking Next.

CROSS-REF **For more information about starting and stopping SQL Server Agent, refer to Chapter 4, "Installing SQL Server 2008."**

On pages 1 (Select a Source Server) and 2 (Select a Destination Server), as shown in Figure 44-1 and 44-2, respectively, the Copy Database Wizard begins by gathering the name of the source and destination servers and the required security information to log into the server.

FIGURE 44-1

Select the source server

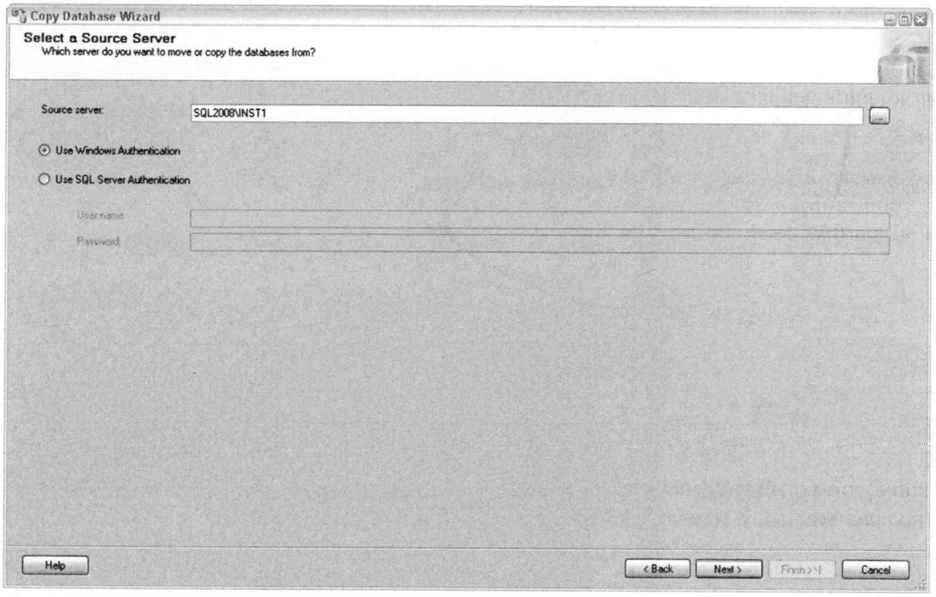

On page 3 (Select the Transfer Method), shown in Figure 44-3, the wizard asks how you want to transfer the database. Using the detach and attach method is faster, but it requires that SQL Server have additional rights to both the source and destination databases, and you must allow exclusive access to both. The detach and attach method works best for large databases. The SQL Management Object (SMO) method doesn't require any special access and users can continue using the source database. However, this method is significantly slower and is not recommended for large databases.

On page 4 (Select Databases), shown in Figure 44-4, the wizard enables you to select the databases you want to move or copy. The status column indicates whether it is OK to move the database; if it isn't, an explanation is provided. For example, system databases (`master`, `msdb`, `model`, and `tempdb`) cannot be moved or copied.

FIGURE 44-2

Select the destination server

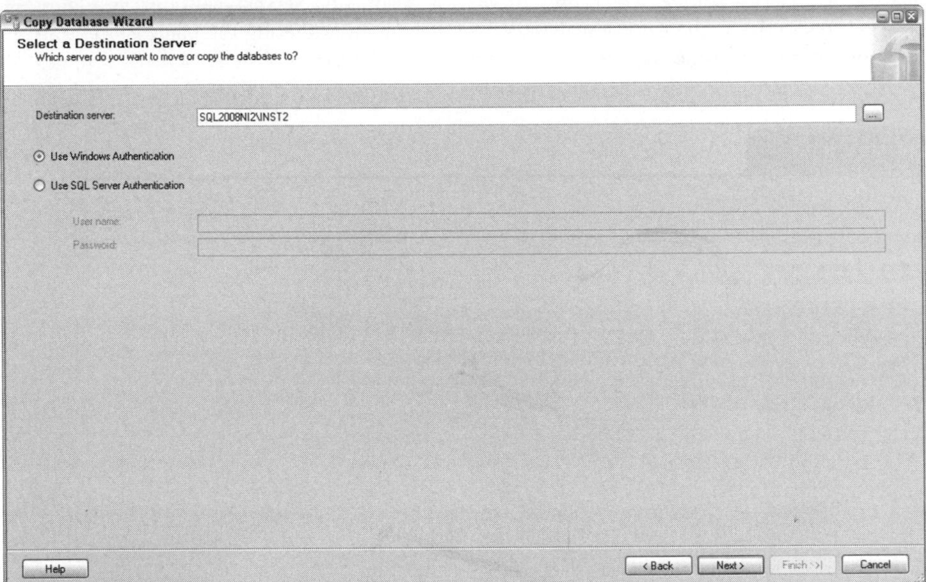

FIGURE 44-3

Select your preferred choice of transfer

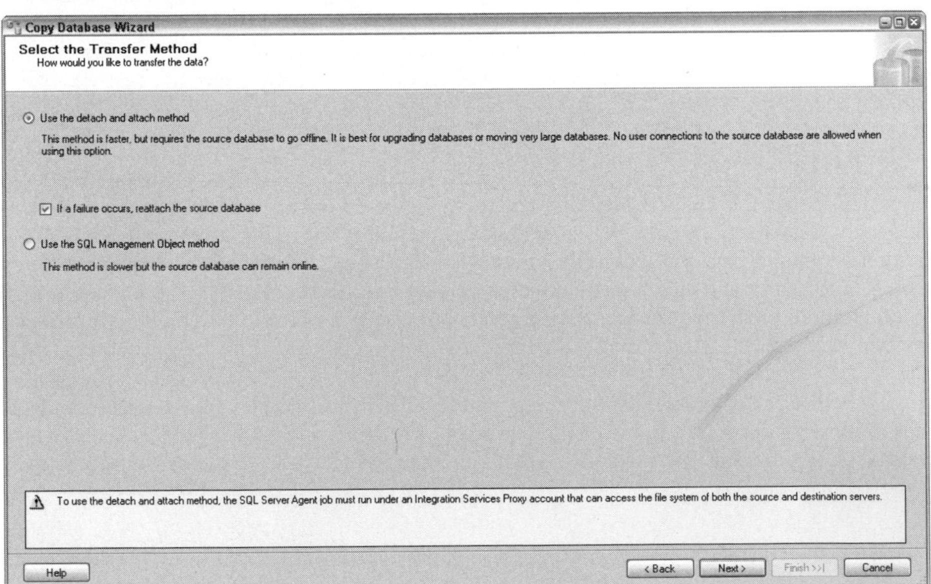

FIGURE 44-4

Select the databases you want to copy or move

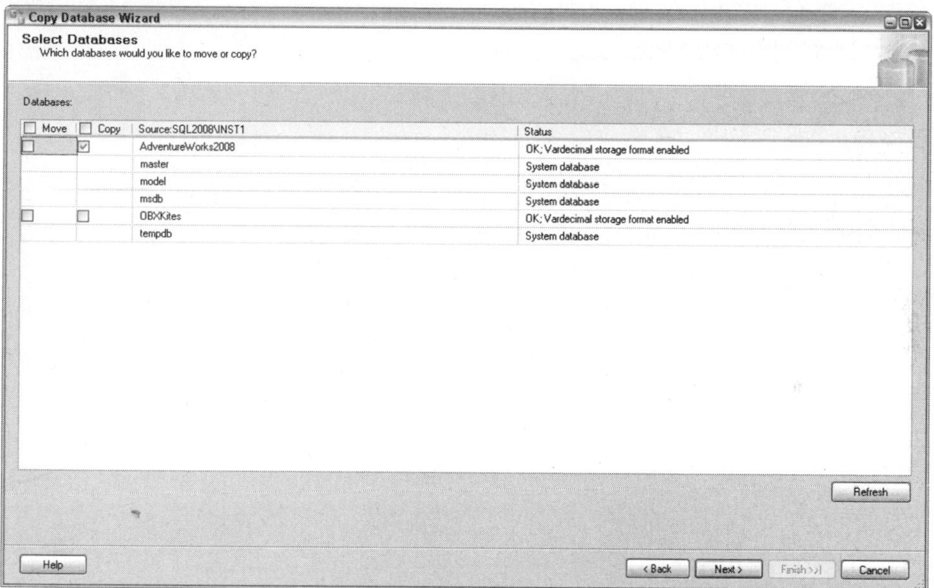

On page 5 (Configure Destination Database), shown in Figure 44-5, the wizard asks you to configure the destination database. You modify the destination database name and the default locations for the database files on the destination server. You also specify how the Copy Database Wizard should react when a database with the requested name already exists on the destination. The options are either stopping the transfer or dropping the existing database and creating a new database with the same name. The wizard will move all the objects and data.

On page 6 (Select Server Objects), shown in Figure 44-6, you can optionally direct the wizard to move the following:

- All logins or only those that have access to the database
- All or selected non-system stored procedures in the `master` database that are used by the database
- All or selected SQL Agent jobs (automated and optionally scheduled tasks)
- All or selected endpoints
- All or selected SSIS packages
- All or selected user-defined error messages (used by the `RAISERROR` T-SQL command)

Click the ellipses button next to each selected option and choose individual objects you want to transfer. If you do not choose individual objects, all the objects of each selection option are transferred by default.

FIGURE 44-5

Configure the destination database

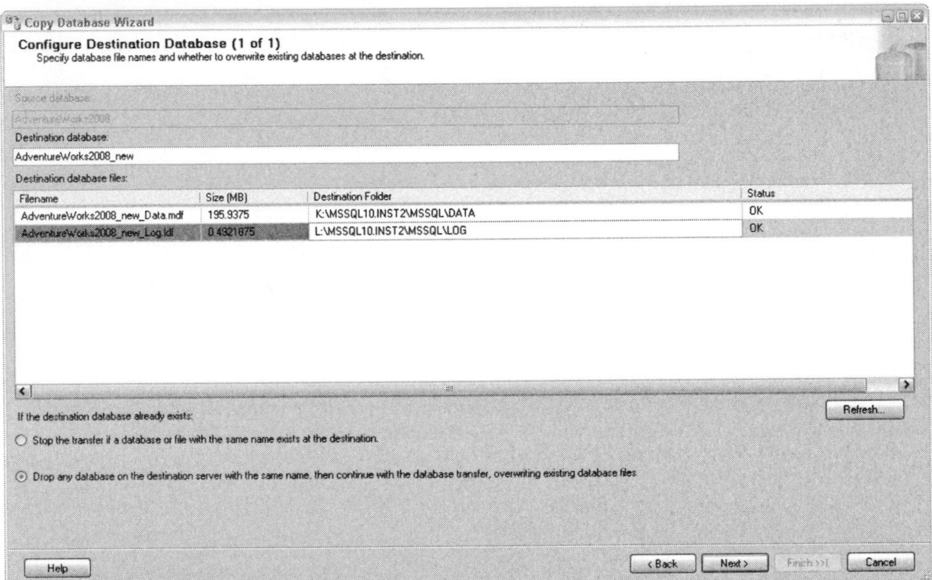

FIGURE 44-6

The Copy Database Wizard can move server-related information as it moves the database

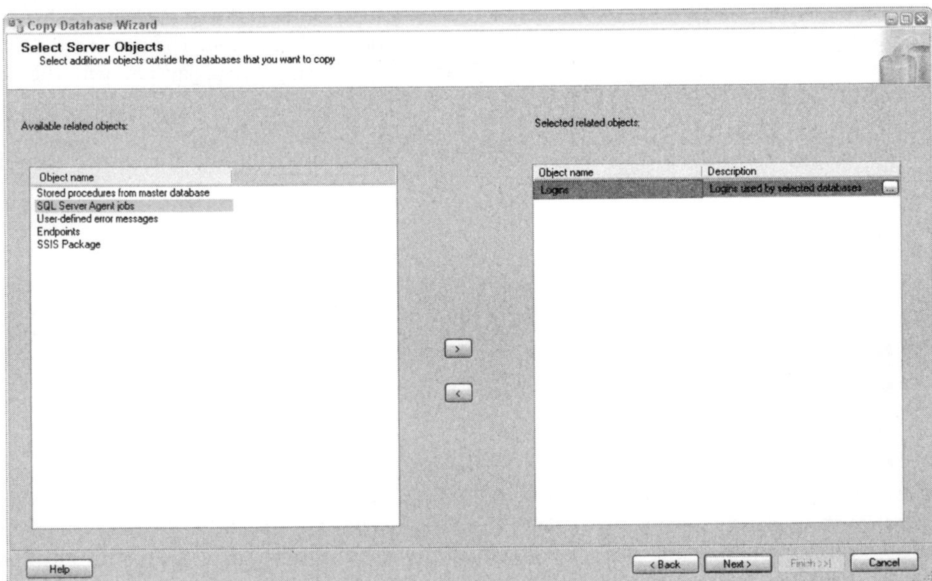

Page 7 (Location of Source Database Files), shown in Figure 44-7, asks you to enter the file share containing the source database files.

FIGURE 44-7

Select the location of the source database files

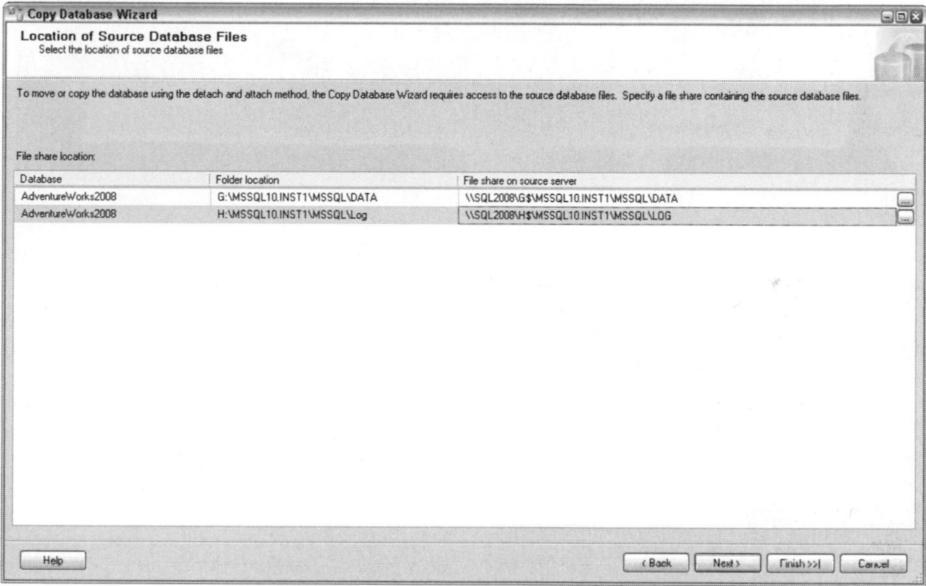

Page 8 (Configure the Package), shown in Figure 44-8, shows the package location. You can also provide a name for the package and choose a method for logging errors. The default method uses the Windows event log. It's also possible to send a list of errors to a text file. The wizard will request a filename when you choose this option.

Page 9 (Schedule the Package), shown in Figure 44-9, directs the wizard to either run the Integration Services package once upon completion of the wizard, run it once later, or set it up on a regular schedule.

Page 10 (Complete the Wizard), shown in Figure 44-10, shows a summary of the choices you made so far. If you want to change something, you can click Back. If you are satisfied with all the choices, click Finish.

When finished, the wizard generates and runs an Integration Services package (see Figure 44-11) and saves it on the destination server.

You can open the generated Integration Services job, as shown in Figure 44-12, by selecting the Jobs node under SQL Server Agent (of the destination SQL Server) in the console tree and then double-clicking on the package. If the name was not edited in the wizard's schedule page, then it should be CDW followed by the two server names and an integer. The creation date is also listed.

FIGURE 44-8

The Copy Database Wizard showing the Integration Services Package location

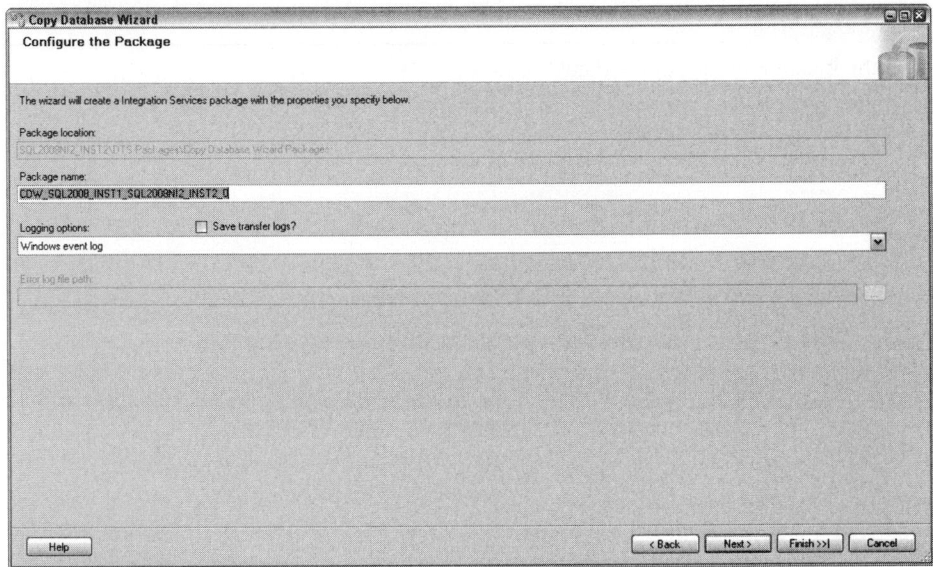

FIGURE 44-9

The Copy Database Wizard can run the Integration Services package once now, once later, or on a schedule

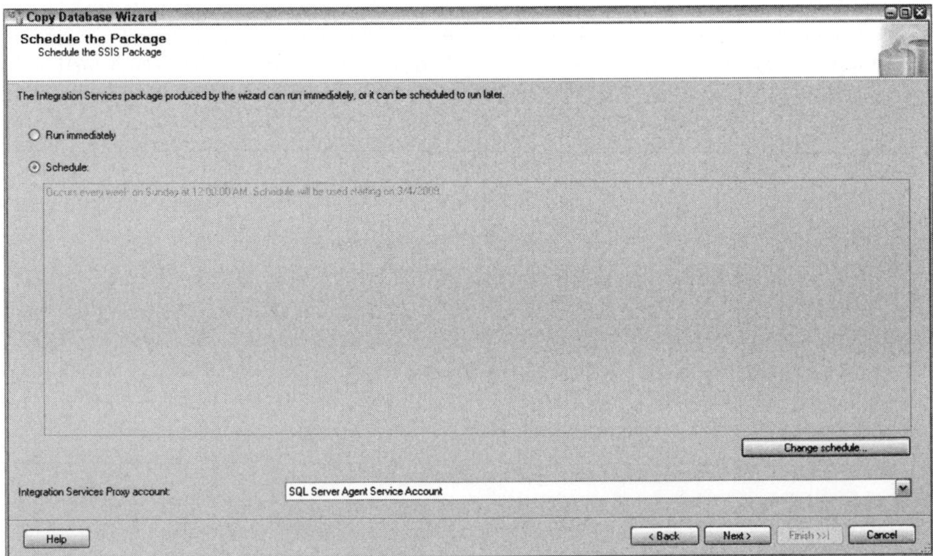

FIGURE 44-10

Copy Database Wizard summary page

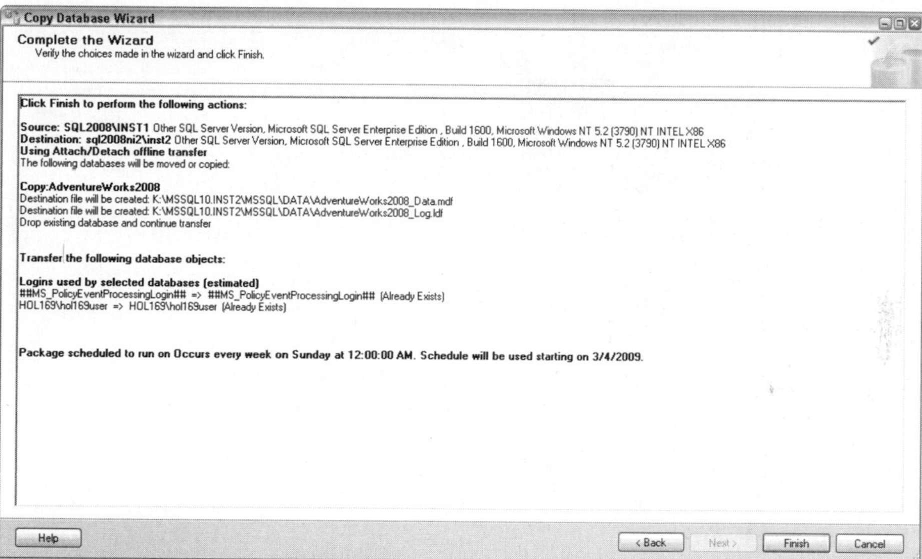

FIGURE 44-11

When the Copy Database Wizard creates the Integration Services package, it displays its progress as it works its way through the steps

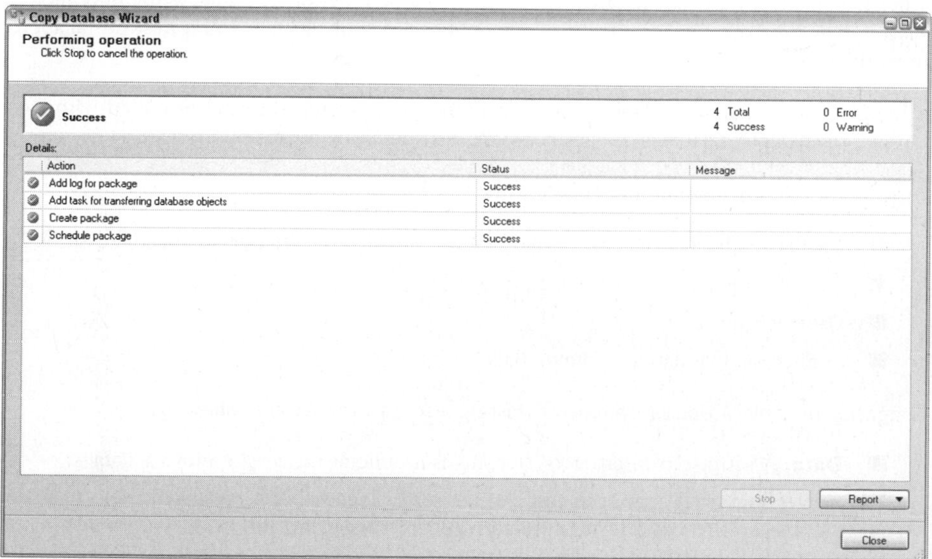

FIGURE 44-12

Job properties for the Integration Services package created by the Copy Database Wizard

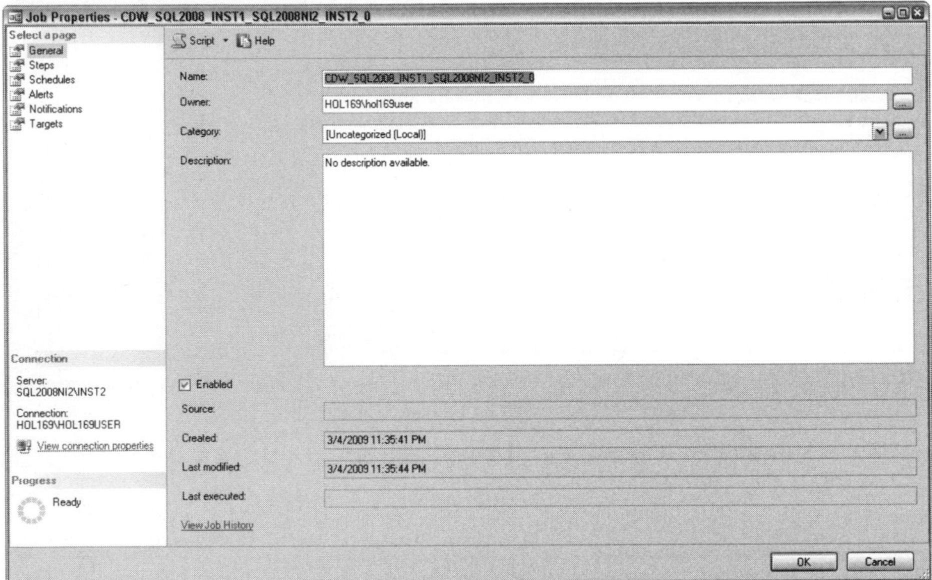

Working with SQL Script

Of the four methods for moving a database, running a SQL Script, or batch, is the only method that creates a new database. Perhaps it's false logic, but the idea of starting with a fresh installation at a client site, without any residue from test data, is a reassuring thought.

Scripts are smaller than databases. They often fit on a floppy, and they can be edited with Notepad. For example, the sample databases for this book are distributed by means of scripts.

Scripts are useful for distributing the following:

- Database schema (databases, tables, views, stored procedures, functions, and so on)
- Security roles
- Database jobs
- Limited sample data or priming data

Though it's possible, I don't recommend creating a script to move the following:

- **Data:** A script can insert rows, but this is a difficult method of moving data.
- **Server logins:** A script can easily create server logins, but server logins tend to be domain specific, so this option is useful only within a single domain.

- **Server jobs:** Server-specific jobs generally require individualized tweaking. While a script may be useful to copy jobs, they will likely require editing prior to execution.

Scripts may also be used to implement a change to a database. The easiest way to modify a client database is to write a script. The change script can be tested on a backup of the database.

Scripts may be generated in several ways:

- The database can be developed initially in Management Studio using a handwritten DDL script. Chapter 20, "Implementing the Physical Database Schema," explains how to create such a script. In addition, the sample databases on the website are all created using a DDL script. This is my preferred method.

CROSS-REF **The code for this chapter may be downloaded from the book's website at** `www.sqlserverbible.com`**.**

- Management Studio can generate a script to create the entire database or a change script for schema changes made with the Table Designer or the Database Designer.
- Most third-party database-design tools generate scripts to create the database or apply changes.

With a focus on generating scripts with Management Studio, open the Management Studio script generator; select the database in the console tree, right-click, and select Tasks ➪ Generate Scripts.

Skip the Welcome to the Generate SQL Server Scripts page. In Management Studio's Script Wizard, use the Select Database page, shown in Figure 44-13, to select the database that you want to script. If you want to script all objects, then check "Script all objects in the selected database."

The Choose Script Options page, shown in Figure 44-14, contains two sets of options. The General options determine script behavior, such as whether Management Studio appends the new script to an existing script file. The Table/View options determine script features, such as whether the script contains code to create foreign keys.

The Choose Object Types page, shown in Figure 44-15, contains a list of objects within the selected databases. At a minimum, you'll see an option to script tables. Note that you will not see this page if you previously checked "Script all objects in the selected database" in the Select Databases page.

The pages that follow vary depending on the objects you select. For example, if you choose to script tables, then you'll see a Choose Tables page in which you select the tables you want to script.

Eventually, you'll reach the Output Option page, shown in Figure 44-16. Use the options on this page to select an output method. If you choose the Script to File option, then you'll also need to choose the output filename and output format.

The next page (Script Wizard Summary) shows a summary of the choices that were made so far. If you want to change something, you can click Back. If you are satisfied with all the choices, click Finish.

FIGURE 44-13

Management Studio can generate scripts for any of the databases within the DBMS

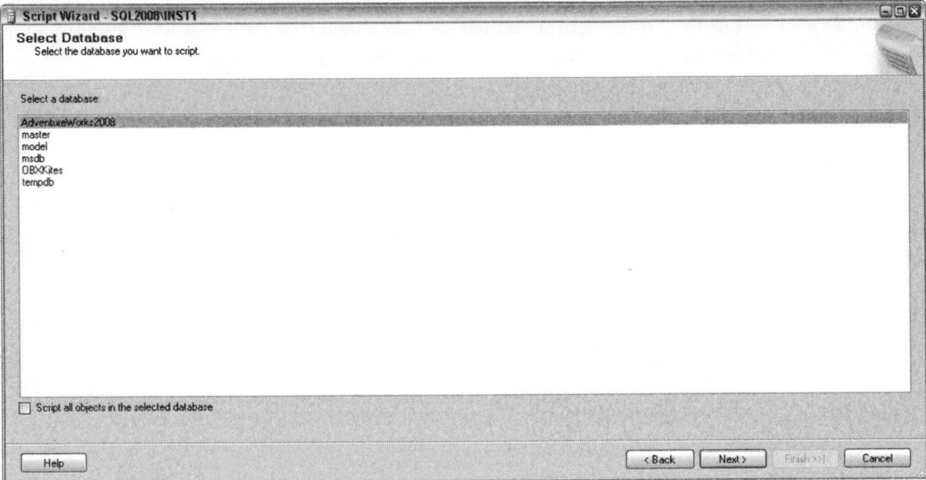

FIGURE 44-14

Set the script options to match the database features you require and to define the behavior you expect from Management Studio

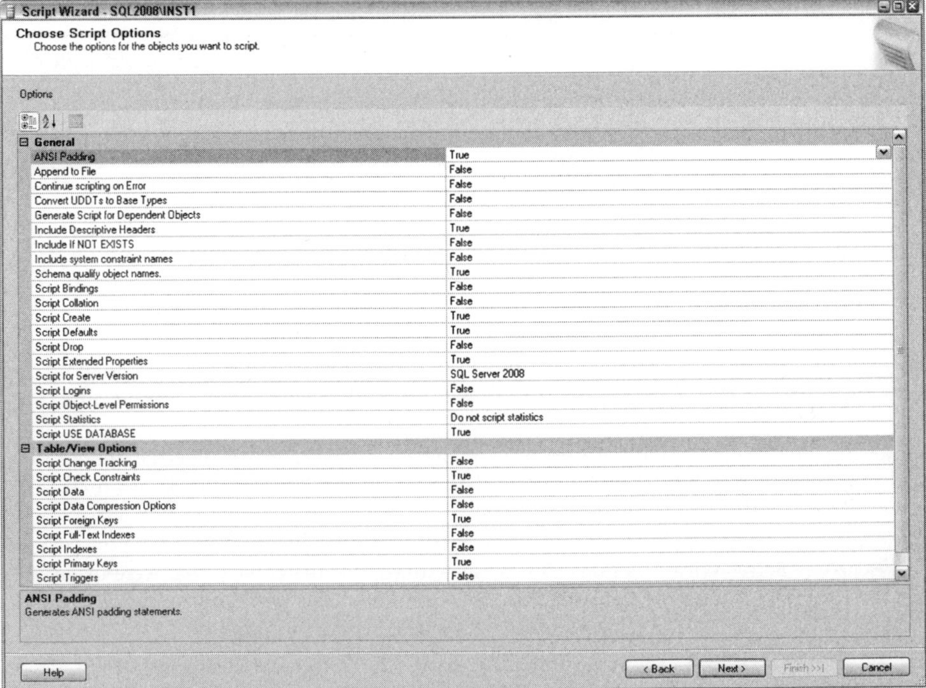

FIGURE 44-15

Select the object types

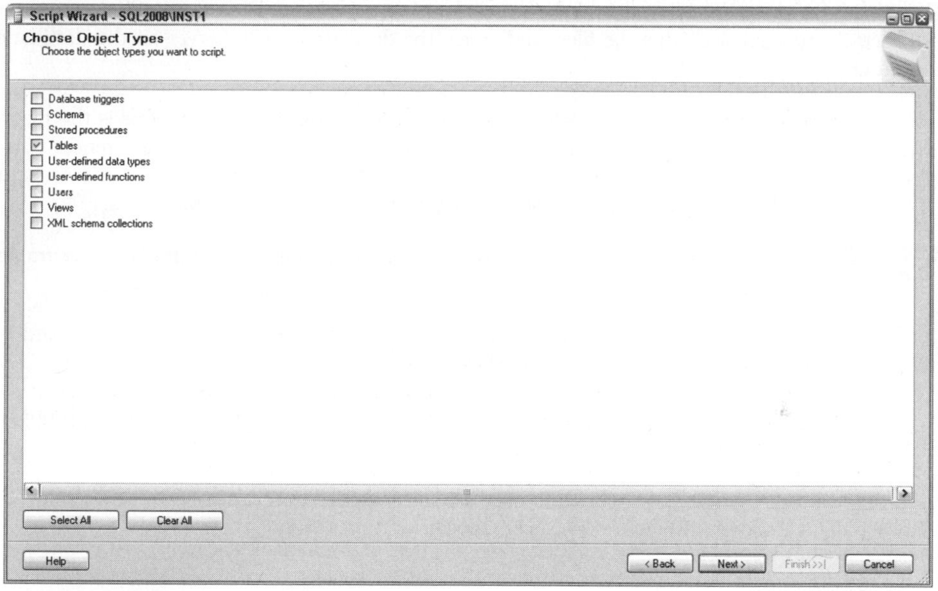

FIGURE 44-16

Choose an output option that matches the kind of database transfer you want to perform

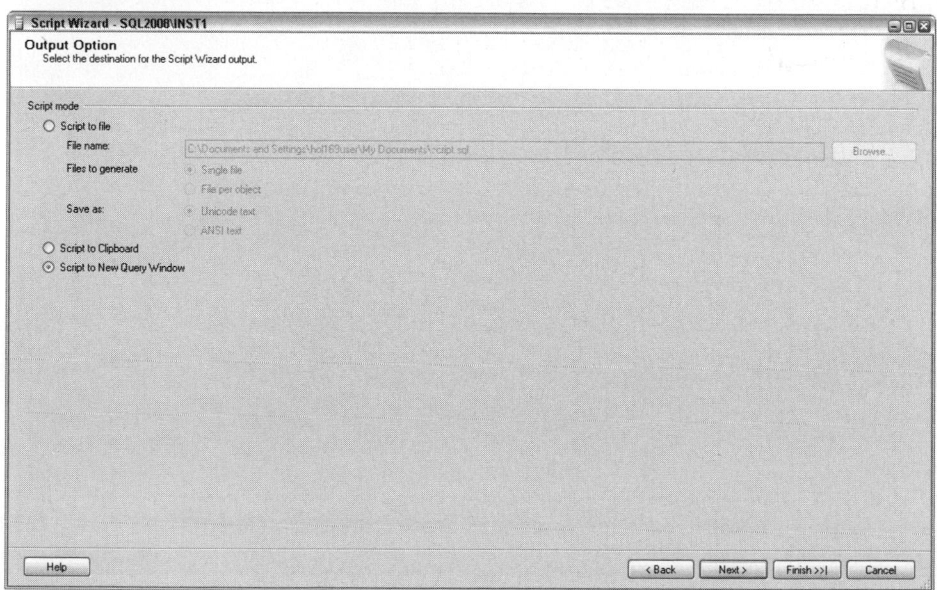

Detaching and Attaching

Though it is often overlooked, one of the easiest ways to move a database from one computer to another is to detach the database, copy the files, and attach the database to SQL Server on the destination computer.

For developers who frequently move databases between notebooks and servers, this is the recommended method. Detaching a database effectively deletes the database from SQL Server's awareness but leaves the files intact. The database must have no current connections and not be replicated if it is to be detached. Only members of the `SysAdmins` fixed server role may detach and attach databases.

CROSS-REF **For more details on the security roles, refer to Chapter 50, "Authorizing Securables."**

Detaching and attaching the database will carry with it any database users, security roles, and permissions, but it will not replicate server logins. These will need to be resolved manually on the destination server. It's best to coordinate security with the network administration folks and leverage their security groups. If the source and destination servers have access to the same network security groups, this will alleviate the security login issues for most installations.

Using Management Studio, right-click the database to be copied and select Tasks ➪ Detach. The Detach Database dialog, shown in Figure 44-17, will appear.

FIGURE 44-17

The Detach Database feature removes the database from SQL Server's list of databases and frees the files for copying

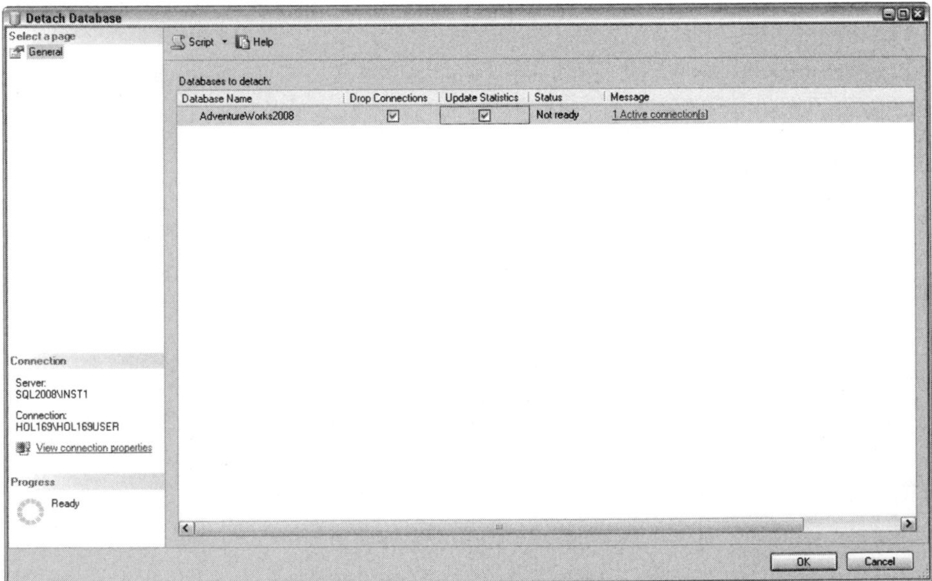

Once the database file is detached, it will disappear from the list of databases in Management Studio. The files may be copied or moved like regular files.

To reattach the database file, select Databases in the Management Studio console tree and Tasks ➪ Attach from the action menu or context menu. The Attach Databases dialog, shown in Figure 44-18, simply offers a place to select the file and verify the file locations and names.

FIGURE 44-18

The database may be reattached by means of Management Studio's Attach Databases tool

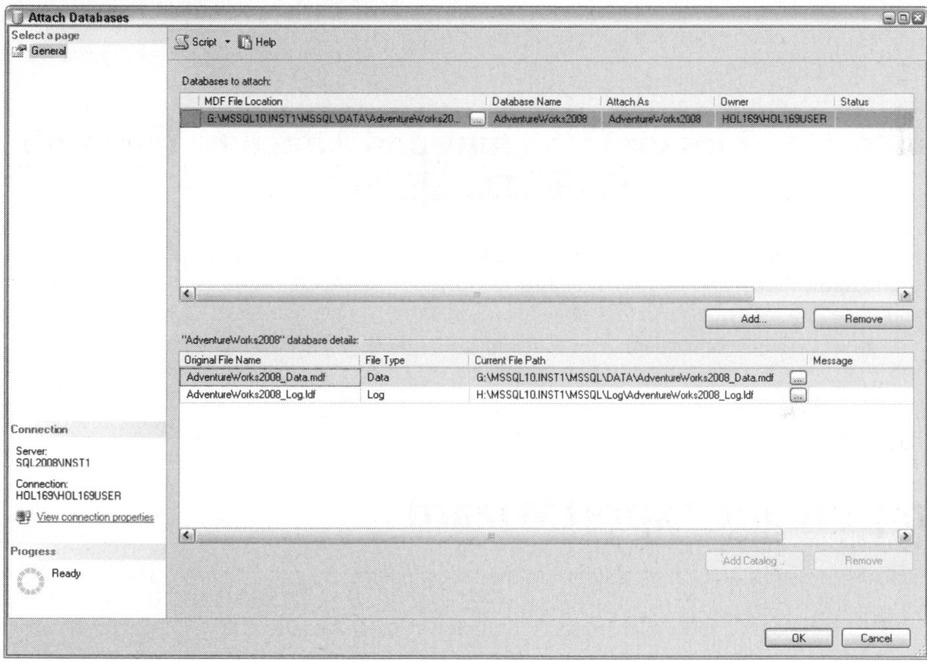

In code, the database is detached by running the `sp_detach_db` system stored procedure. The first parameter is the database to be detached. A second optional parameter simply turns off automatic updating of the index statistics. The following command detaches the `AdventureWorks2008` sample database:

```
sp_detach_db 'AdventureWorks2008'
```

If you wish to reattach a database with code, the counterpart to `sp_detach_db` is the `sp_attach_db` system stored procedure. Attaching a database requires specifying the file locations as well as the database name, as follows:

```
EXEC sp_attach_db @dbname = 'AdventureWorks2008',
   @filename1 = ' G:\MSSQL10.INST1\MSSQL\Data\AdventureWorks2008_
Data.mdf',
   @filename2 = 'H:\MSSQL10.INST1\MSSQL\LOG\AdventureWorks2008_Log.ldf'
```

Best Practice

It is recommended to use `CREATE DATABASE database_name FOR ATTACH` instead of the `sp_attach_db` stored procedure, as it will be removed in a future version of SQL Server. Here is an example:

```
CREATE DATABASE AdventureWorks2008 ON
    (FILENAME = ' G:\MSSQL10.INST1\MSSQL\Data\AdventureWorks2008_Data.mdf'),

    (FILENAME = 'H:\MSSQL10.INST1\MSSQL\LOG\AdventureWorks2008_Log.ldf')
FOR ATTACH;
```

Special Instructions for Detaching and Attaching the msdb and model Databases

Detaching and attaching the `msdb` and `model` databases results in an error by default. In order to detach and attach the `msdb` and `model` databases, you need to start SQL Server with the `-c` option, the `-m` option, and trace flag `3608`. Trace flag `3608` recovers only the `master` database. Once you start SQL Server with these startup parameters, you can detach/attach `msdb` and `model` databases without any error message.

Import and Export Wizard

On many occasions SQL DBAs need to do the following:

- Copy only a few tables from one SQL Server database to another SQL Server database
- Import data from a flat file or Microsoft Office Excel file
- Copy data from one table to another with different collations

To achieve these DBA tasks easily and quickly, Microsoft has provided another powerful wizard called SQL Server Import and Export Wizard. This wizard enables copying data to and from any data source for which a managed .NET Framework data provider or a native OLE DB provider is available.

You can access the Import and Export Wizard from various locations:

- Choose Import and Export Data from Start ➪ Programs ➪ Microsoft SQL Server 2008.
- Open Management Studio, right-click a database and choose Task ➪ Import Data or Export Data from the context menu

- Open SQL Server Business Intelligence Development Studio (BIDS) from Start ➪ Programs ➪ Microsoft SQL Server 2008. Open an SSIS solution, select SSIS Import and Export Wizard from the Project menu or by right-clicking the SSIS Packages folder.
- Run `DTSWizard.exe` (`C:\Program Files\Microsoft SQL Server\100\DTS\Binn`) from the command prompt.

To move data with the Import and Export Wizard, follow these steps:

1. Launch the Import and Export Wizard using one of the preceding methods.
2. Skip past the Welcome to SQL Server Import and Export Wizard by clicking Next.
3. On the Choose a Data Source page, select the source data. If you launched the wizard from Management Studio by right-clicking the database and choosing Task ➪Export Data, the source information is already preconfigured with the server and database name. Depending on the source data, the other options on this page will vary. For example, selecting SQL Server Native Client 10.0 allows you to specify the SQL Server, authentication, and database, as shown in Figure 44-19. Click Next to proceed.

FIGURE 44-19

Selecting SQL Server Native Client 10.0 as the data source and the `AdventureWorks` database

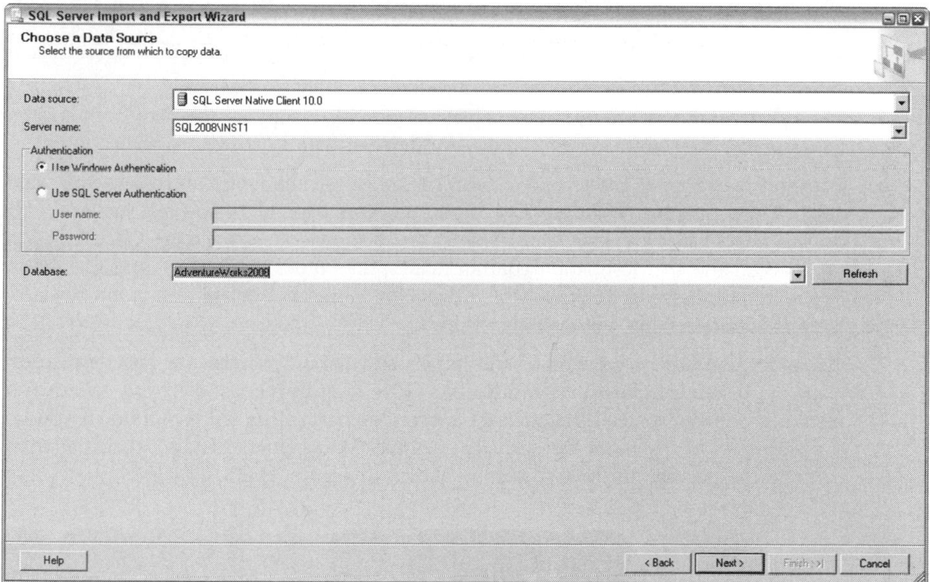

4. On the Choose a Destination page, select the destination target. If you launched the wizard from Management Studio by right-clicking the database and choosing Task ➪Import Data,

the destination information is already preconfigured with the server and database name. This page also allows you to create a new destination database by clicking the New option, which invokes the dialog shown in Figure 44-20.

FIGURE 44-20

Clicking New enables you to create a destination database

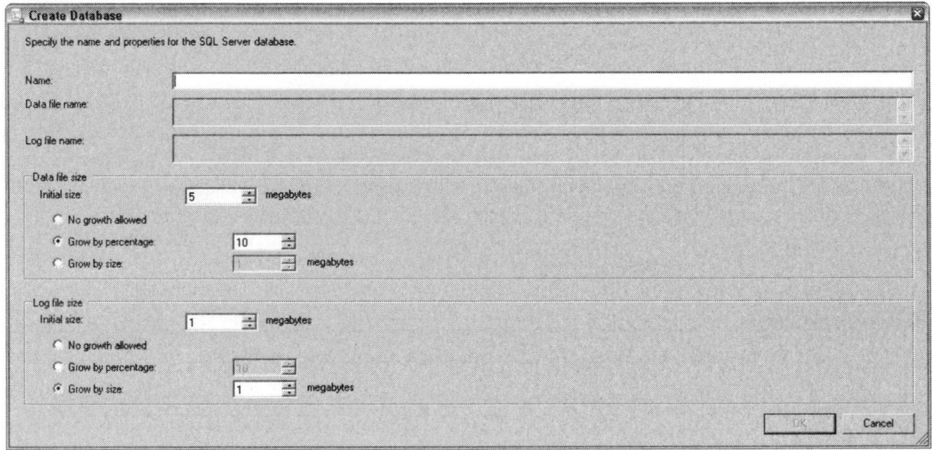

5. The Specify Table or Query page enables you to either copy all the data from existing source tables or views or write a T-SQL query to limit the data to copy.
6. On the Select Source Tables and Views page, select all the tables and views you want to copy. If you opted to write a query on the previous page, then you can just select the query on this page. Click Preview to preview up to 200 rows of source data. Click Edit Mappings to change the destination column names, data types, nullability, and size, as shown in Figure 44-21. If the destination table exists, you can either delete or append rows to it. If there is no destination table, you can create one.
7. Depending on how you launched the Import and Export Wizard, the last step varies. For example, if you launched the wizard from BIDS, then in the last step you cannot run the resulting package; instead the package is saved as part of the SSIS solution. If you launched the wizard from any other method (for example, Management Studio), then the wizard allows running the package in the last step, as shown in Figure 44-22.

Best Practice

To copy the full database or multiple databases, use the Copy Database Wizard instead of the Import and Export Wizard.

FIGURE 44-21

Configuring the destination table and column mappings

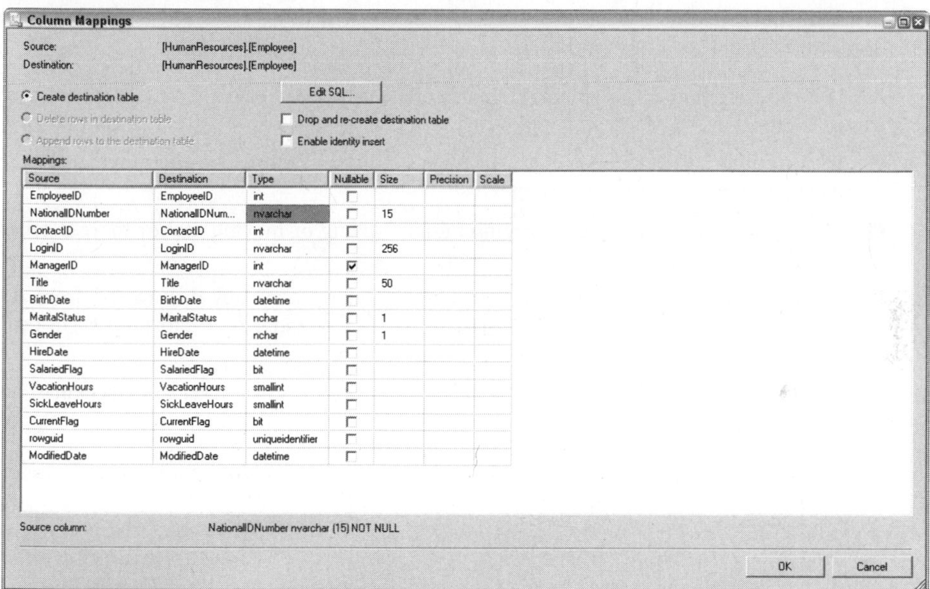

Column Mappings

Source: [HumanResources].[Employee]
Destination: [HumanResources].[Employee]

Create destination table
Delete rows in destination table
Append rows to the destination table
Edit SQL...
Drop and re-create destination table
Enable identity insert

Mappings:

Source	Destination	Type	Nullable	Size	Precision	Scale
EmployeeID	EmployeeID	int	☐			
NationalIDNumber	NationalIDNum...	nvarchar	☐	15		
ContactID	ContactID	int	☐			
LoginID	LoginID	nvarchar	☐	256		
ManagerID	ManagerID	int	☑			
Title	Title	nvarchar	☐	50		
BirthDate	BirthDate	datetime	☐			
MaritalStatus	MaritalStatus	nchar	☐	1		
Gender	Gender	nchar	☐	1		
HireDate	HireDate	datetime	☐			
SalariedFlag	SalariedFlag	bit	☐			
VacationHours	VacationHours	smallint	☐			
SickLeaveHours	SickLeaveHours	smallint	☐			
CurrentFlag	CurrentFlag	bit	☐			
rowguid	rowguid	uniqueidentifier	☐			
ModifiedDate	ModifiedDate	datetime	☐			

Source column: NationalIDNumber nvarchar (15) NOT NULL

OK Cancel

FIGURE 44-22

Running the package immediately and saving the package with encryption

SQL Server Import and Export Wizard

Save and Run Package
Indicate whether to save the SSIS package.

Run immediately
Save SSIS Package
SQL Server
File system

Package protection level:
Encrypt sensitive data with password

Password: ********
Retype password: ********

Help < Back Next > Finish >>| Cancel

Summary

When you need to move a database, don't back it up; there are better ways to move it. Choose the right transfer method based on network proximity of the servers and the objects and/or data to be moved. Some key points to remember are as follows:

- Use the Detach/Attach method to quickly and easily move or copy a database from one server to another.
- If you cannot afford to detach a database, use the good old Backup/Restore method to copy a database from one server to another.
- The Copy Database Wizard is very useful for copying or moving one or more databases from one server to another on the same network.
- To copy only a few tables from one server to another or to copy data to and from any data source for which a managed .NET Framework data provider or a native OLE DB provider is available, use the Import and Export Wizard.
- Use Management Studio to quickly generate scripts to distribute database schemas, security, jobs, and limited data.

Chapter 41, "Recovery Planning," covers not only techniques for performing a backup, but also working with transaction logs and recovering various data objects, up to an entire server.

Chapter 45

Database Snapshots

The Database Snapshot feature, originally introduced in SQL Server 2005, allows for a point-in-time, read-only, consistent view of your user databases to use for reporting, auditing, or recovering purposes. Before database snapshots, this functionality was achieved by running a backup and restoring it to another database. The big advantages provided by database snapshots are the speed at which they can be created, as well as the ability to create multiple database snapshots of the same source database, providing you with snapshots of the database at different times.

IN THIS CHAPTER

- How database snapshots work
- Creating a database snapshot
- Using your database snapshots
- Performance considerations and best practices

NOTE **The Database Snapshot feature is only available in Enterprise and Developer Editions of SQL Server 2008.**

The Database Snapshot feature was primarily designed to do the following:

- Generate reports without blocking the production/source database.
- Perform reporting on a database mirror.
- Recover from user or administrator errors.
- Revert the source database to an earlier time.
- Manage a test database.

Database snapshots are similar to databases in many ways but they do have some limitations of which you should be aware:

- Database snapshots are read-only static copies of the source database.
- Database snapshots cannot be created for system databases (`master`, `model`, and `tempdb`).
- Database snapshots can be created only on an NTFS file system.

- Database snapshots can be created only on the same SQL Server instance where the source database exists.
- Database snapshots depend on the source database, so if the source database is unavailable for any reason, then all its database snapshots will become unavailable too.
- The source database cannot be dropped, detached, or restored as long as it has any database snapshots; but source database backups are not affected by database snapshots.
- You cannot backup or restore a database snapshot. Nor can you attach or detach a database snapshot.
- You cannot revert to the database snapshot if you have multiple database snapshots. You will need to drop all the database snapshots except the one to which you want to revert.
- Database snapshots do not support Filestream.
- Full-text indexing is not supported on database snapshots, and full-text catalogs are not propagated from the source database.
- In a log shipping configuration, database snapshots are allowed only on the primary database, not on the secondary or warm-standby database.
- Database snapshots are I/O intensive and may impact the performance of the system.

If these limitations are acceptable, then Database Snapshots can be an excellent feature that you can use to create point-in-time, read-only copies of your production databases.

How Database Snapshots Work

As discussed earlier, a database snapshot is a point-in-time, read-only, static view of the source database as it existed at the time the database snapshot was created. When a database snapshot is created, SQL Server runs recovery on the database snapshot and rolls back uncommitted transactions to make the database snapshot transactionally consistent. The transactions in the source database are not affected.

A database snapshot is not the same as the source database. It is a different database that has the same number of data files as the source database but it does not have any transaction log file. When it is initially created, the data files in the snapshot database do not contain any user data and are almost empty. That is why creating a database snapshot does not take a long time. Database snapshots use a copy-on-first-write method for each source database page that is updated for the first time after the database snapshot is created.

For every database snapshot, SQL Server creates an in-memory bitmap. It has a bit for each data page indicating if the page is copied to the snapshot. Every time an update is made to the source database, SQL Server checks the bitmap to see if it has been copied to the snapshot. If it is not copied, then SQL Server copies the data page from the source database to the database snapshot and then makes the update. Next time, if the same page is updated, it is not copied, as the database snapshot just contains the data as it existed on the source database when the snapshot was created. This is referred to as copy-on-first-write technology and is shown in Figure 45-1. If a data page on the source database is never updated, it is never copied to the database snapshot.

FIGURE 45-1

Database snapshot using copy-on-first-write technology

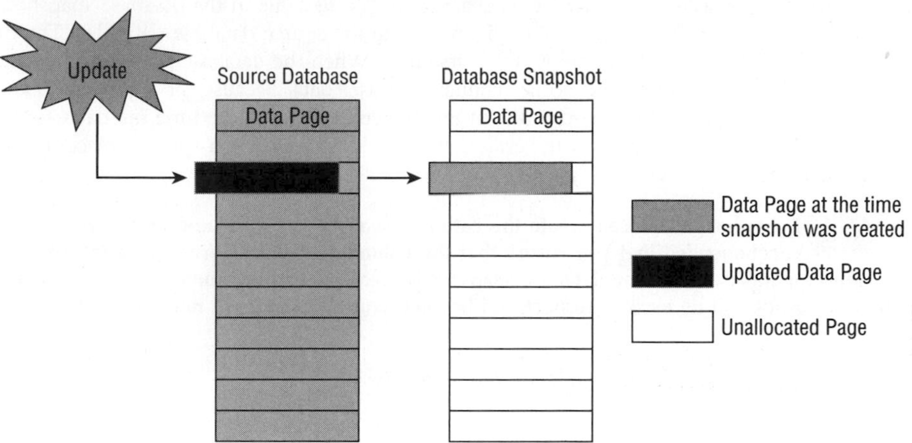

Creating a Database Snapshot

Database snapshots can be only created using the Transact-SQL `CREATE DATABASE...AS SNAPSHOT` command.

SQL Server Management Studio does not have any graphical interface to create database snapshots.

Here are the step-by-step instructions to create a database snapshot of the `AdventureWorks` sample database:

1. The first step is to find out the information about the files in the source database. The following command can be used to retrieve information about the files in the `AdventureWorks` database:

```
USE AdventureWorks;
GO
EXECUTE sp_helpfile;
GO
```

Result (abridged):

```
name                  filename                            size
AdventureWorks_Data   G:\...\AdventureWorks_Data.mdf      200640KB
AdventureWorks_Log    H:\...\AdventureWorks_Log.ldf       504KB
```

2. Note the logical name of the data files listed under the name column and their sizes. In the preceding example, there is only one data file with the logical name AdventureWorks_Data and a size of 200640 KB (or 195 MB).
3. For each data file in the source database there is a data file in the database snapshot. The data files in the database snapshot are different from the source database data files. The data files in the database snapshot are NTFS sparse files. When the database snapshot is created, the sparse files are empty and do not contain any user data. Because the sparse files can potentially grow up to the size of the data file of the source database at the time the database snapshot was created, it is important to verify that the volume where you want to place the database snapshot has enough free space.

NOTE **Even though you can create the database snapshot on a volume with very little space, it is recommended that you ensure that the volume has enough free space (at least the space of the source database when the database snapshot is created). If the volume runs out of space, the database snapshot will be marked suspect and become unusable, and will need to be dropped.**

4. Execute the following Transact-SQL command to create the database snapshot of the AdventureWorks database:

```
CREATE DATABASE AdventureWorks_Snapshot ON
(NAME = AdventureWorks_Data, FILENAME =
'J:\ MSSQL10.INST1\MSSQL\DATABASE SNAPSHOTS\AdventureWorks
_Snapshot.snap' )
AS SNAPSHOT OF AdventureWorks;
GO
```

NOTE **The FILENAME appears to wrap in the preceding code. In actual code, it should not wrap around or you will get the error shown here:**

```
Msg 5133, Level 16, State 1, Line 1
Directory lookup for the file "J:\MSSQL10.INST1\MSSQL\DATABASE
SNAPSHOTS\AdventureWorks_Snapshot.snap" failed with the operating system error
   123(The filename, directory name, or volume label syntax is incorrect.).
```

Best Practice

To make it easier to use the database snapshot, think about how you want to name it before you start. One method is to include the source database name, some indication that it is a snapshot, the time it was created, and a meaningful extension. The preceding example uses the name AdventureWorks_Snapshot and .snap as the extension to differentiate the database snapshot files from regular database files. You might have observed that the preceding example creates the database snapshot on a different volume than the source database. Placing the database snapshot on a physically separate volume is a best practice because it avoids disk contention and provides better performance.

5. Once the database snapshot is created, you can view it using Management Studio. Connect to the SQL Server instance using Object Explorer in Management Studio. Expand Databases and then Database Snapshots to see all the database snapshots, as shown in Figure 45-2.

FIGURE 45-2

Viewing database snapshots in Object Explorer

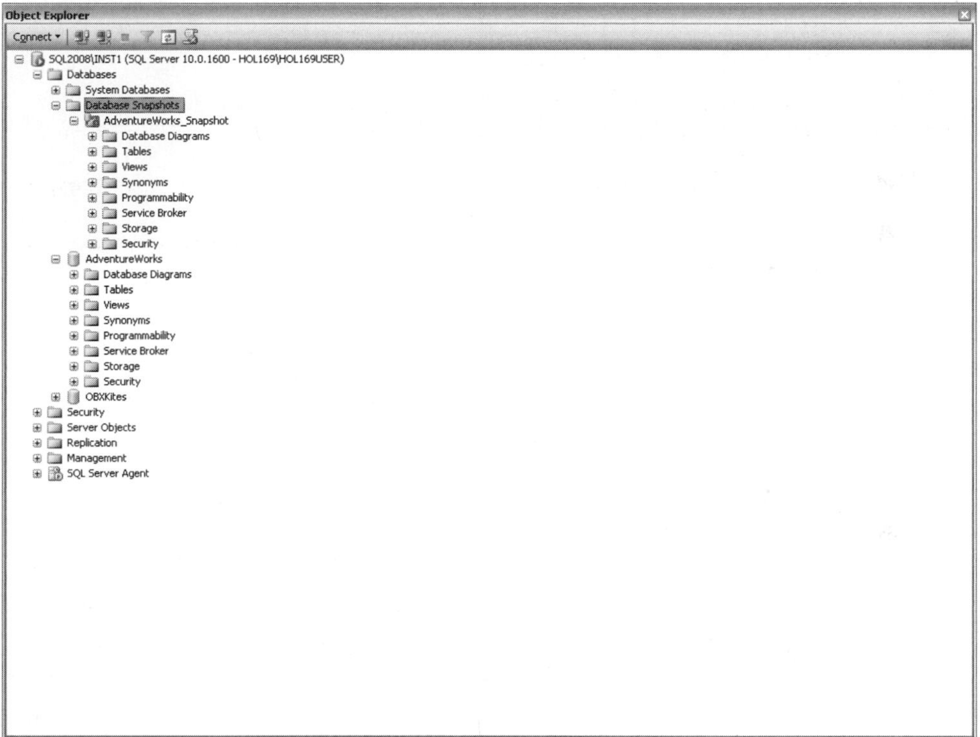

TIP **Query the `sys.databases` catalog view and review the `source_database_id` column. If this column is `NULL`, then it is a regular database; if it is not `NULL`, then it represents the source database ID for the database snapshot.**

6. To find out the space used by the database snapshot, open Windows Explorer, right-click the data file of the database snapshot, and select properties, as shown in Figure 45-3. The Size value (195 MB in Figure 45-3) is not the actual size of the file: It is the maximum size of the file, and it should be about the same size as the source database when the database snapshot was created. The Size on disk value (16,384 bytes in Figure 45-3) is the actual size of the database snapshot data file.

FIGURE 45-3

Viewing the size of the database snapshot data file

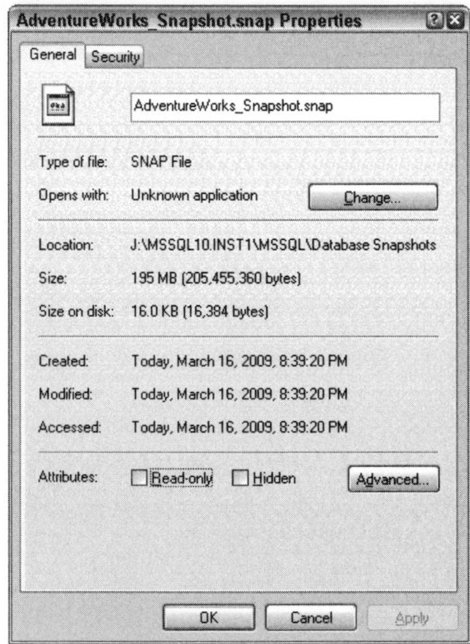

Alternately, you can also find the size using the dynamic management view `sys.dm_io_virtual_file_stats`, as shown here:

```
SELECT size_on_disk_bytes FROM
sys.dm_io_virtual_file_stats(DB_ID(N'AdventureWorks_Snapshot'), 1);
GO

Results
16384
```

Using Your Database Snapshots

Once a database snapshot is created, users can query the database snapshot as if it were a regular database. For example, the following query will retrieve the Name, ProductNumber, and ListPrice from the `Product` table in the `AdventureWorks_Snapshot` database snapshot:

```
USE AdventureWorks_Snapshot;
GO
SELECT Name, ProductNumber, ListPrice
```

```
FROM Production.Product
ORDER BY Name ASC;
GO
```

Users cannot make any updates to the database snapshot, however, as it is read-only. If a user tries to update the database snapshot, he or she will receive `error 3906`, as shown here:

```
Msg 3906, Level 16, State 1, Line 1
Failed to update database "AdventureWorks_Snapshot" because the
database is read-only.
```

When a user reads from the database snapshot, SQL Server accesses the in-memory bitmap and determines whether the data it needs exists on the source database or the database snapshot. If the data page was not updated, it will exist on the source database and SQL Server will read it from the source database. Figure 45-4 shows the read operation accessing the updated page from the database snapshot and the remaining pages from the source database.

FIGURE 45-4

Users querying the database snapshot, accessing the updated pages from the database snapshot and unchanged pages from the source database

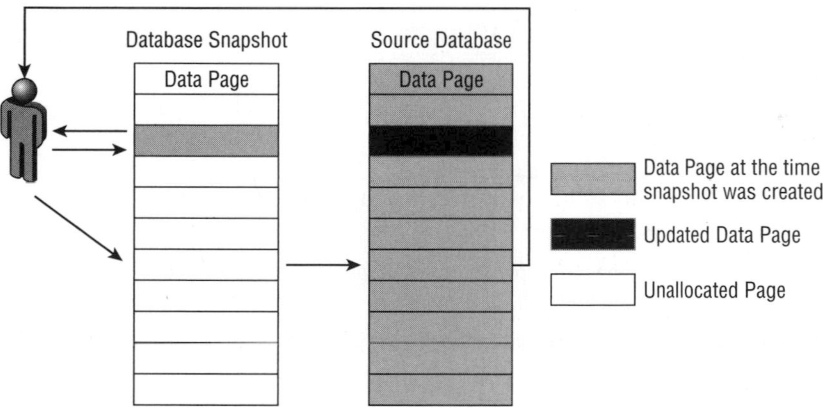

Some common uses of database snapshots include the following:

- **Generate reports without blocking the production/source database:** Database snapshots can be used to run reports based on the data at the time the snapshot was created. When reads are executed on the database snapshot, no locks are held and hence there is no blocking.
- **Maintain historical data:** You can create a database snapshot at a particular time, such as end of the financial year, and run end of financial year reports against the database snapshot.
- **Perform reporting on a mirror database:** The mirror database cannot be queried by default, as it is in `NORECOVERY` mode. If you want to use the mirror database for reporting purposes, you can create a database snapshot on the mirror database and read the database snapshot.

- **Recover from user or administrator errors:** A database snapshot can be recreated periodically and refreshed by a SQL Server Agent job, whereby the previous database snapshot is dropped and recycled. If a user accidentally drops an important table or commits an update wiping out critical data, use the database snapshot to recover that data directly from the snapshot without having to restore the database. For example, if a user accidently drops a table and the table existed when the database snapshot was created, there are several ways to easily recover the data:
  - Use Management Studio and script the table on the database snapshot.
  - Recreate the table by running the preceding script against the source database.
  - Populate the data using the `INSERT INTO...SELECT FROM` statement, whereby you select the data from the table in the database snapshot and insert data into the newly created table in the source database.
- **Revert the source database to an earlier time:** You can use the database snapshot to recover the source database by reverting it to the way it was when you created the snapshot using the Transact-SQL `RESTORE` command.

NOTE **Reverting to a database snapshot rebuilds the transaction log and breaks the log backup chain. This means that you cannot perform point-in-time restores in the period from the last log backup to the time when you reverted to the database snapshot. If you want to perform point-in-time restores in the future, take a full or differential backup and then start taking log backups again.**

The following example reverts the `AdventureWorks` database to the `AdventureWorks_Snapshot` database snapshot:

```
USE master;
GO
RESTORE DATABASE AdventureWorks
FROM DATABASE_SNAPSHOT = 'AdventureWorks_Snapshot';
GO
```

If the source database has multiple database snapshots and you attempt to revert the database to one of the snapshots, you will receive `error 3137`, as shown here:

```
Msg 3137, Level 16, State 4, Line 1
Database cannot be reverted. Either the primary or the snapshot names
are improperly specified, all other snapshots have not been dropped,
or there are missing files.
Msg 3013, Level 16, State 1, Line 1
RESTORE DATABASE is terminating abnormally.
```

As per the error message, you will need to drop all the database snapshots except the one to which you want to revert.

NOTE **Database snapshot is not a replacement for your regular backup and restore strategy. For example, if a disk failure results in the loss of the source database, you cannot use the database snapshot to recover. You will need good backups. You can use database snapshots to supplement your restore strategy only for the purpose of quickly restoring a table that has been accidentally dropped or some rows that have been deleted. I recommend continuing to take regular backups and restoring them to test the backups to protect your data and minimize data loss when a disaster occurs.**

- **Manage a test database:** Database snapshots can be effectively used in a test environment. Before running the tests, you can create a database snapshot of the test database. After the tests are completed, you can quickly return the test database to the original state by reverting to the database snapshot. Before the database snapshot feature was introduced, developers and testers used a backup and restore process to maintain the test database, but the restore process typically takes longer than reverting to a database snapshot.

TIP **Starting with SQL Server 2005, `DBCC CHECKDB` used an internal database snapshot for running online. This database snapshot provides a transactionally consistent view that `DBCC CHECKDB` requires, and prevents blocking and concurrency problems when `DBCC CHECKDB` runs. The internal database snapshot is created in the same location where the database being checked is stored, and you cannot control the location. Depending on the transaction load concurrent with `DBCC CHECKDB`, the internal database snapshot can grow in size. This means it is possible for the disk to run out of space on a SQL Server that has a heavy load. If this happens, the database snapshot files cannot grow, which will stop the progress of your workload and `DBCC CHECKDB`. To proactively avoid this problem, create your own database snapshot and run `DBCC CHECKDB` against it. This is exactly the same as running `DBCC CHECKDB` normally and letting it create its own internal database snapshot.**

As discussed earlier, you cannot back up or restore database snapshots, nor can you attach or detach database snapshots. You can run reports against the database snapshot and drop it when you no longer need it, or it becomes too big, or the disk on which the database snapshot is located runs out of space and the database snapshot becomes suspect.

Dropping a database snapshot is similar to dropping a regular database. The only difference is that users do not have to be terminated before dropping a database snapshot. They will be automatically terminated when the snapshot is dropped. The following example drops the database snapshot named `AdventureWorks_Snapshot`:

```
DROP DATABASE AdventureWorks_Snapshot;
```

The preceding Transact-SQL command drops the database snapshot and deletes the files in it. You can also drop the database snapshot from Management Studio by right-clicking the database snapshot and selecting Delete.

Performance Considerations and Best Practices

Although Database Snapshots is an excellent feature and can be very useful, if there is heavy I/O activity on the source database, database snapshots can negatively affect performance, reducing the throughput and response time of the application running on the source database. This section discusses why database snapshots affect performance and some best practices to minimize the impact.

Creating a database snapshot does not take a long time if there is very little write activity on the source database. Most of the time taken to create database snapshots is spent in the recovery phase that is performed by SQL Server to make the database snapshot transactionally consistent. If the write activity on the source database is high when the database snapshot is being created, recovery will take longer and thereby increase the time taken to create the database snapshot.

After the database snapshot is created, all first-time updates to the source database pages have to be written to the database snapshot. If there are multiple database snapshots, then all first-time updates to the source database pages have to be written to all the database snapshots. This write activity increases the I/O load on the system and affects the throughput and response time of the applications running on the source database.

TIP **To monitor the waits caused by database snapshots, query the** `sys.dm_os_wait_stats` **dynamic management view. The** `REPLICA_WRITES` **wait type occurs when there is a task waiting for the completion of page writes to database snapshots.**

Apart from the increased I/O load on the system, it is important to note that index maintenance operations take longer when there are database snapshots on the source database. Even though data is not updated during index creation or rebuild operations, rows are moved between pages and the original pages need to be written to the database snapshots. The impact is more visible during clustered index creation/rebuild operations.

Best practices to minimize the performance impact of database snapshots include the following:

- To reduce disk contention, isolate the source data files and transaction log file and database snapshot files by placing them on independent disk volumes.
- Use Performance Monitor to see the impact of the database snapshots on the system. If there is a disk bottleneck, then consider reducing the number of database snapshots and/or using more/faster spindles to support your I/O requirements with an acceptable latency.
- Do not create database snapshots during or just before index maintenance operations.
- Ensure that there is enough free disk space for the database snapshot to grow. If the source database is updated frequently, the database snapshot will grow and can become as large as the source database at the time of database snapshot creation.
- Schedule a SQL Server Agent job to drop older versions of database snapshots on the source database.

Summary

Database snapshots bring a new reporting, recovery, and comparison functionality to SQL Server. Some key points from the chapter are as follows:

- Database snapshots enable maintaining previous images of a production database for reporting and recovery purposes.
- Database snapshots enable reporting on the mirror database that is not possible otherwise.
- Although database snapshots are powerful and flexible, they are I/O intensive. If multiple database snapshots are created on a source database that is heavily updated, then the I/O load will increase and may impact the system's performance.

As with any other feature, it is highly recommended that you take a performance baseline of your environment before and after creating database snapshots, and use your performance data to help you determine whether you should use database snapshots or not.

Chapter 46

Log Shipping

IN THIS CHAPTER

Configuring a warm standby server using Management Studio and Transact-SQL

Monitoring log shipping

Modifying or removing log shipping

Switching roles

Returning to the original primary server

The *availability* of a database refers to the overall reliability of the system. The Information Architecture Principle, discussed in Chapter 2, "Data Architecture," lays the foundation for availability in the phrase *readily available*. The definition of readily available varies by the organization and the data. A database that's highly available is one that rarely goes down. For some databases, being down for an hour is not a problem; for others, 30 seconds of downtime is a catastrophe. Organization requirements, budget constraints, and other resources dictate the proper solution.

Of course, availability involves more than just the database, as there are several technologies involved outside of the database: the instance, the server OS, the physical server, the organization's infrastructure, and so on. The quality and redundancy of the hardware, the quality of the electrical power, preventive maintenance of the machines and replacement of the hard drives, the security of the server room — all of these contribute to the availability of the primary database. An IT organization that intends to reach any level of high availability must also have the right people, training, policies, and service-level agreements (SLAs) in place.

NOTE **This chapter is the first of a trilogy of chapters dealing with high-availability technologies: log shipping, database mirroring, and clustering. Backup and recovery, along with replication, and even SQL Data Services (SQL in the cloud) are also part of the availability options. A well-planned availability solution will consider every option and then implement the technologies that best fit the organization's budget and availability requirements.**

A complete plan for high availability will also include a plan to handle true disasters. If the entire data center is suddenly gone, is another off-site disaster recovery site prepared to come online?

Best Practice

Before implementing an advanced availability solution, ensure that the primary server is well thought out and provides sufficient redundancy. The most common issue won't be the data center melting, but hard drive failure or a bad NIC card.

Log shipping is perhaps the most common method of providing high availability. The basic idea is that the transaction log, with its record of the most recent transactions, is regularly backed up and then sent, or shipped, to another server where the log is applied so that server has a pretty fresh copy of all the data from the primary server. Log shipping doesn't require any special hardware or magic, and it's relatively easy to set up and administer.

There are three obstacles to getting log shipping to work smoothly. First, the policies and procedures must be established, implemented, and then regularly tested. The second one is a bit trickier: The client applications need a way to detect that the primary server is down and then switch over to the standby server. The third obstacle is a procedure to switch back to the primary server once it's repaired and ready to step back into the spotlight.

What's New in SQL Server Log Shipping?

SQL Server 2008 log shipping performance can be increased by taking advantage of the new backup compression feature in Enterprise Edition. Backup compression reduces the backup, copy, and restore time. This speeds up log shipping, as now it has to transfer less data. It also reduces the disk space required by the backups, enabling disk cost savings and retaining more backups on the same disks. Although backup compression is supported only in SQL Server 2008 Enterprise Edition, every SQL Server 2008 Edition can restore a compressed backup. This means that you can configure log shipping between a primary SQL Server 2008 Enterprise Edition to a secondary SQL Server 2008 Standard Edition while taking advantage of backup compression.

Starting with SQL Server 2008, log shipping jobs can be scheduled to run as frequently as every 10 seconds or more both through SQL Server Management Studio and stored procedures. SQL Server 2005 allowed the frequency of the log shipping scheduled jobs to be one minute or more.

Availability Testing

A database that's unavailable isn't very useful. The availability test is a simulation of the database restore process assuming the worst. The measurement is the time required to restore the most current production data to a test server and prove that the client applications work.

Warm Standby Availability

Warm standby refers to a database that has a copy set up on separate hardware. A warm standby solution can be achieved with log shipping. Log shipping involves periodically restoring a transaction log backup from the primary server to a warm standby server, making that server ready to recover at a moment's notice. In case of a failure, the warm standby server and the most recent transaction log backups are ready to go. Apart from this, log shipping has the following benefits:

- It can be implemented without exotic hardware and may be significantly cheaper.
- It has been used for many years and is a very robust and reliable technology.
- It can be used for disaster recovery, high availability, and reporting scenarios.
- Implementing log shipping is very simple because Microsoft provides a user-friendly wizard; and once implemented, it is easy to maintain and troubleshoot.
- The primary server and the warm standby server do not have to be in the same domain or subnet. As long as they can talk to each other, log shipping will work.
- There is no real distance limitation between the primary and warm standby servers, and log shipping can be done over the Internet.
- Log shipping allows shipping the transaction log from one primary server to multiple warm standby servers. It also allows having different copy and restore times for each warm standby server. One of my clients is log shipping their production databases to two secondary servers. One of the secondary servers restores the transaction logs immediately as they are ready and is used for disaster recovery. The second secondary server restores the transaction logs nightly and is used for reporting during the day.
- Log shipping can be implemented between different editions of SQL Server (Enterprise Edition to Standard Edition) and between different hardware platforms (x86, x64, or IA64-based SQL Server instance).

However, log shipping has a few drawbacks:

- Only user databases in full or bulk-logged recovery model can be log shipped. A simple recovery model cannot be used because it does not allow transaction log backup. This also means that log shipping will break if the recovery model for a log shipping database is changed from full/bulk-logged to simple recovery model.
- System databases (`master`, `model`, `msdb`, `tempdb`) cannot be log shipped.
- Log shipping provides redundancy at the database level and not at the SQL Server instance level, like SQL Server failover clustering. Log shipping only applies changes that are captured in the transaction log or the initial full backup of the log shipping database. Any database objects such as logins, jobs, maintenance plans, SSIS packages, and linked servers that reside outside the log shipping database need to be manually created on the warm standby server.
- When the primary server fails, any transactions made since the last time the transaction log backup was shipped to the warm standby server may be lost and result in data loss. For this reason, log shipping is usually set to occur every few minutes.

- The switch between primary and warm standby server is not transparent. A series of steps must be manually executed by the DBA on the warm standby server, and front-end application connections must redirect the data source and reconnect to the warm standby server.
- Once the primary server is repaired, returning to the original configuration may require manual DBA intervention.

If these issues are acceptable, log shipping to a warm standby server can be an excellent safeguard against downtime.

Best Practice

Ideally, the primary server and the warm standby server should be in different locations so that a disaster in one location will not affect the other. In addition, log shipping can place a large demand on a network every few minutes while the transaction logs are being moved. If the two servers can be connected with a private high-speed network, log shipping can take place without affecting other network users and the bandwidth they require.

Defining Log Shipping

In SQL Server 2000, log shipping was available only in Developer and Enterprise Editions. Starting with SQL Server 2005, log shipping is available in Workgroup, Standard, Developer, and Enterprise Editions. Developer Edition can be used only for development purposes and not for production.

Microsoft provides a simple-to-use log shipping wizard to create a maintenance plan to back up, copy, and restore the transaction log from the primary server to the warm standby server every few minutes. Log shipping has built-in monitoring that makes it very easy to maintain and troubleshoot.

Log shipping normally involves three SQL Servers: a primary server, a warm standby server, and a monitor server, as shown in Figure 46-1.

- The *primary or source server* is the main production SQL Server to which clients connect. This server contains the log shipping database. The initial full database backup and subsequent transaction log backups are taken on this server. This server should be a high-quality server with redundant disk drives.
- The *warm standby server* is the backup SQL Server, otherwise known as the *secondary server*. If the source server fails, it becomes the primary server. This server should be capable of meeting the minimum performance requirements during a short-term crisis. If your business does not allow any performance degradation, then the warm standby server should be similar to the primary server.

FIGURE 46-1

Typical log shipping configuration

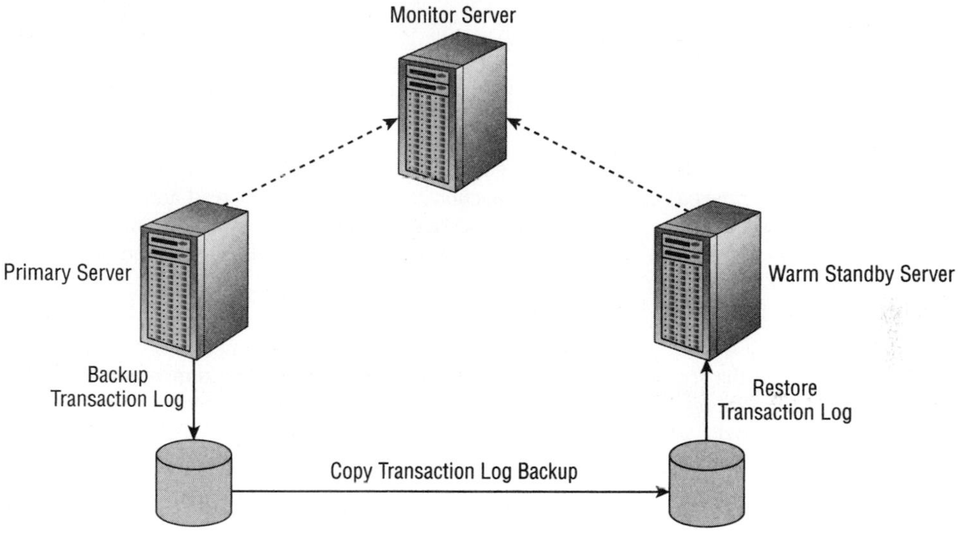

- The *monitor server* polls both the primary server and the warm standby server by keeping track of what files have been sent where, generating an alert when the two are out of sync. A single monitor server can monitor multiple log shipping configurations. The monitor server is optional. If a monitor server is not used, the primary and warm standby servers store the monitoring information.

Best Practice

The monitor server can be an instance on the destination server, but locating the monitor server on the source server would be a self-defeating plan. If the source server physically failed, the monitor server would also fail. The best practice is to assign a monitor server to its own hardware to avoid disrupting monitoring in the event that the primary or warm standby server is lost.

Each primary server database can have only one log shipping plan, and each plan can ship only one database. However, a plan may ship to multiple secondary servers.

Configuring log shipping

Log shipping can be configured using one of two methods: either by using SQL Server Management Studio or by using system stored procedures.

Pre-log shipping configuration

With either method of configuration, the following prerequisites need to be completed before configuring log shipping:

- Disk space needs to be created and shared. This network share is used by the backup job on the primary server to store the transaction log backups. Grant read and write permissions on the network share to the SQL Server service account on the primary server, and read permissions to the proxy account for the copy job (usually the SQL Server Agent service account) on the secondary server.
- The destination folder needs to be created on the secondary servers. The copy job on the secondary server copies the transaction log backups from the network share to the destination folder on the secondary server. The load job then restores these transaction log backups from the destination folder. The SQL Server service accounts on the secondary server need to have read and write permissions on this folder.
- The recovery model of the log shipping database must be set to full or bulk-logged.
- The edition of the SQL Server 2008 participating in log shipping needs to be Enterprise, Standard, or Workgroup Edition.
- If the primary and secondary servers are on different domains, then set up two-way trusts between the domains. If this is not possible, you can also use network pass-through security. With network pass-through security, the SQL Service accounts for all the SQL Servers participating in log shipping use the same network account and the same password, and enough permission to complete the log shipping tasks.
- If you have a very large database, then I recommend taking a full database backup, copying it to the secondary server, and restoring it on the secondary server with `NORECOVERY` or `STANDBY` to put it into a state that will allow restoring the transaction logs. `NORECOVERY` mode will not allow any database access to the secondary database, whereas `STANDBY` mode allows read-only access to the secondary database.

Configuring log shipping using Management Studio

The following steps create a log shipping configuration using SQL Server Management Studio:

1. In the Object Explorer on the primary server in SQL Server Management Studio, right-click on the database that will be log shipped and review the database properties.
2. On the Options page, verify that the recovery model is either Full or Bulk-logged and not Simple.
3. On the Transaction Log Shipping page, shown in Figure 46-2, check the box that enables log shipping configuration.

FIGURE 46-2

Enabling the primary database for log shipping

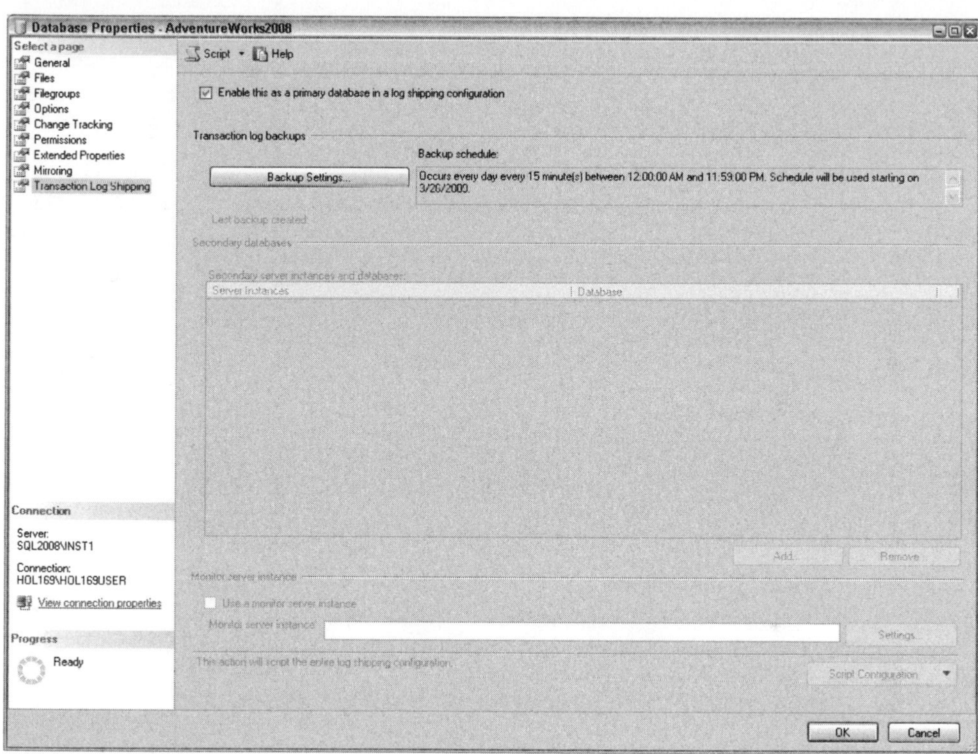

4. Configure the backup settings as shown in Figure 46-3 by clicking the Backup Settings button. Enter the network share where the transaction log backups will be stored before being copied to the secondary server. If the backup folder is local to the primary server, then enter the local folder path too.

A network share that is not located on the primary server will better protect the transaction logs in case of a hardware failure on the primary server.

5. Enter an amount of time after which the transaction log backup files should be deleted. For example, if the files should be deleted after one day, then the "Delete files older than" option should be set to one day.

FIGURE 46-3

Configuring transaction log backup settings for log shipping

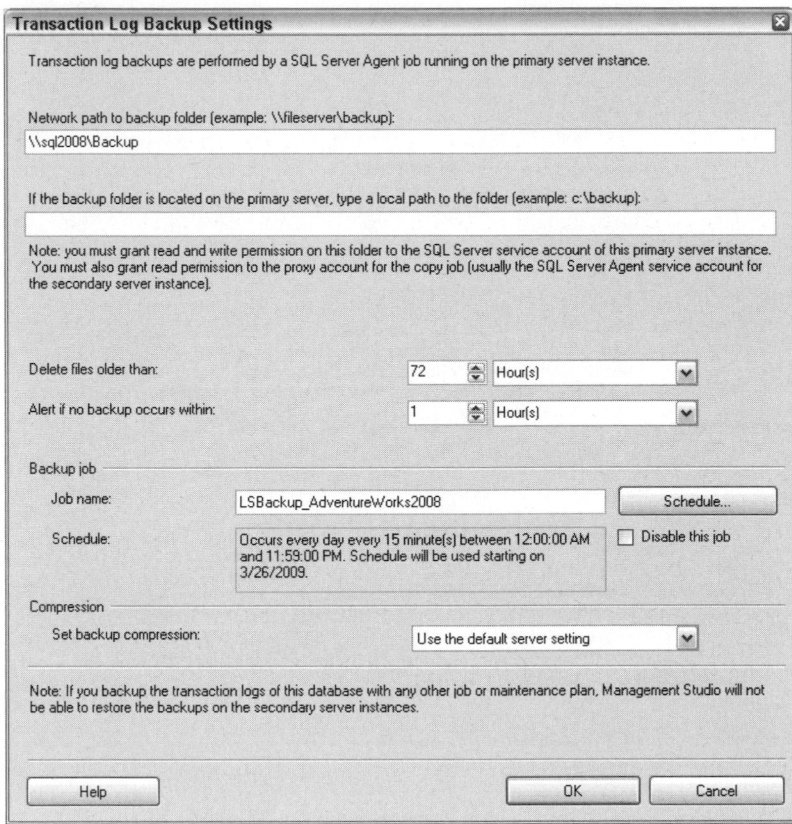

6. Enter an amount of time that the server should wait to send an alert if no new transaction log files are found. For example, if the server has not seen a transaction log backup in the past one hour, then the "Alert if no backup occurs within" option should be set to one hour.

NOTE **The longer the length of the alert time, the higher the risk. With a long alert setting, a transaction log backup failure will result in a larger amount of data loss.**

7. Schedule the job that will back up the transaction log by setting the job's name, time, and frequency by clicking the Schedule button. A shorter duration between transaction log backups will minimize the amount of data that could be lost. By default, the transaction log is backed

up every 15 minutes. The default works for most environments but some of my clients have changed it to 5 minutes to minimize data loss. The frequency of transaction log backups usually is determined by several factors, including service-level agreements, speed of your disk subsystem, and transaction log size.

TIP **Make sure that the only transaction log backup that occurs is scheduled through the Transaction Log Shipping page. Otherwise, all the data changes will not be propagated to the secondary servers and log shipping will break.**

If you have a very powerful server with plenty of resources, you may be tempted to change the transaction log backup frequency to every 1 minute or less. SQL Server 2008 lets you schedule the frequency to every 10 seconds. While it is possible that you may need this in your environment, remember that this creates hundreds of transaction log backups. If you have to restore your database using backups, then you will have to restore the full database backup followed by all the transaction log backups in order; and if one of the transaction log backups is bad, then the restore will stop at that point.

8. SQL Server 2008 Enterprise Edition supports backup compression. You can control the backup compression by clicking the "Set backup compression" drop-down box on the Transaction Log Backup Settings page. By default, "Use the default server setting" option is selected. This uses the default server-level compression. You can bypass the server-level default by selecting the "Compress Backup" option or you can choose not to compress the backup by selecting the "Do not compress backup" option.

NOTE **The performance increase achieved from backup compression comes at the expense of CPU usage. If you have a CPU-bound SQL Server, then you may not want to compress the backup. Thorough testing is recommended to determine the impact of the backup compression, as the CPU increase can impact other operations.**

9. Add the secondary servers to the transaction log configuration by clicking the Add button under the secondary instance's window. Multiple secondary instances can be added here by repeating steps 9 through 16.
10. On the Secondary Database Settings screen, shown in Figure 46-4, connect to the server that will be the secondary server and enter the database name for the secondary database. If the database is not there it will be created.
11. Initialize the secondary database by selecting either the option to have log shipping create a full database backup and restore it on the secondary server or the option to have it use the last known backup. If you select to use the last backup that was created, the name of the directory in which the backup is located needs to be supplied. To create the data and log files on non-default folder locations on the secondary server, click the button "Restore Options" and enter the local folder path on the secondary server where you want the data and log files to exist. The previous two options are best suited for smaller databases. If you have a very large database, it is recommended that you bypass the wizard and manually take a backup of the database, copying it to the secondary database and restoring it. If you take this approach, select the third option, "No, the secondary database is initialized."

FIGURE 46-4

Configuring the secondary server database for log shipping

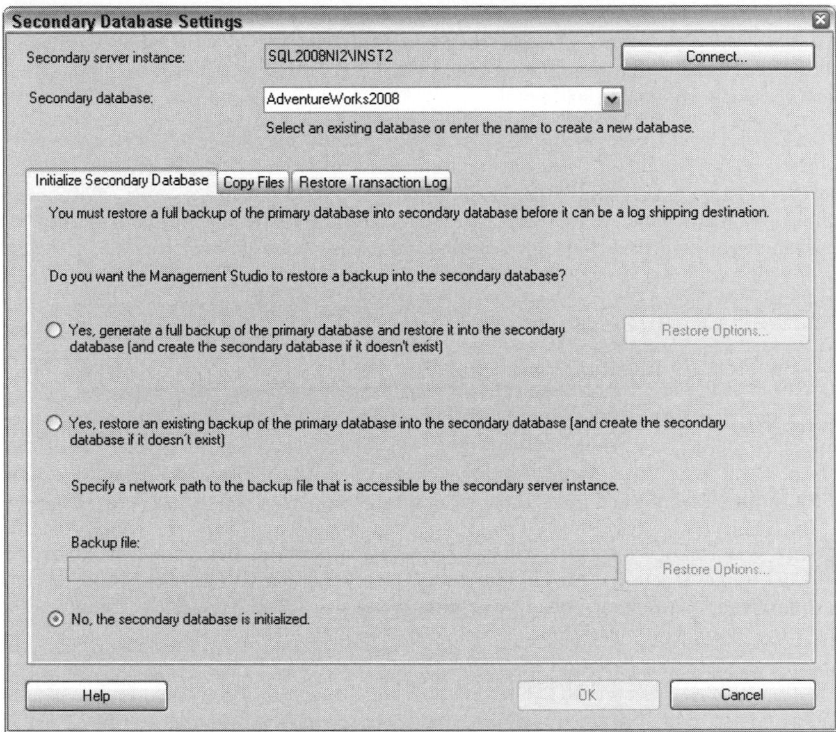

12. The Copy Files tab, shown in Figure 46-5, configures the copy job on the secondary server that copies the transaction log backups from the network share to the destination local folder on the secondary server. This tab also has a setting that enables files to be deleted after a designated amount of time.

13. On the Copy Files tab, enter the local folder on the secondary server to which the transaction log files will be copied. The proxy account for the copy job (usually the SQL Server Agent service) on the secondary server must have read and write permissions on this folder.

14. On the Restore Transaction Log tab, shown in Figure 46-6, choose either No recovery mode or Standby mode. Standby mode allows access to the secondary server for read-only operations. Select this mode if you want to use log shipping for reporting. If the standby mode is selected, the option to have the user connection killed during the transaction log restore is available. If you do not choose to disconnect the users, the transaction log backups will fail and the secondary server will lag behind. The No recovery mode option will not allow any database access to the secondary database. This option is usually selected when log shipping is used for disaster recovery or high-availability scenarios.

FIGURE 46-5

Configuring the copy job on the secondary server

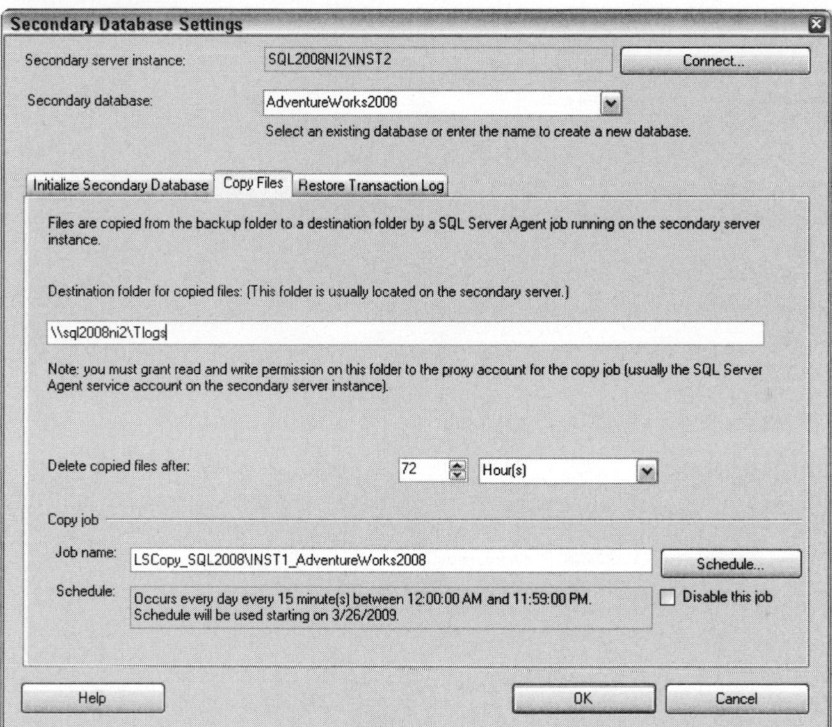

NOTE To use log shipping as a reporting solution you need to select `Standby` mode in the Restore Transaction Log tab. The restore job needs exclusive access to the database and will fail if users are running reports. You may select the option to disconnect the users in the database when restore runs, but this means that longer-running reports may never complete. For example, if you have a restore job that runs every 15 minutes and you have a report that takes 25 minutes to complete, that report will always be killed by log shipping every 15 minutes.

Conversely, you may configure the restore job to occur every few hours, but in that case the secondary server will lag behind the primary server. Because log shipping allows multiple secondary servers, you may have two secondary servers. Set one to no recovery mode and schedule the restore job to run every 15 minutes or earlier, and set the recovery mode to standby mode on the second secondary server. Then, schedule the restore job to run every few hours. This way you will have two copies of your primary database and can use log shipping for a high-availability and reporting solution. If near real-time data is required for reporting, I recommend using transactional replication.

FIGURE 46-6

Configuring the restore transaction log job on the secondary server

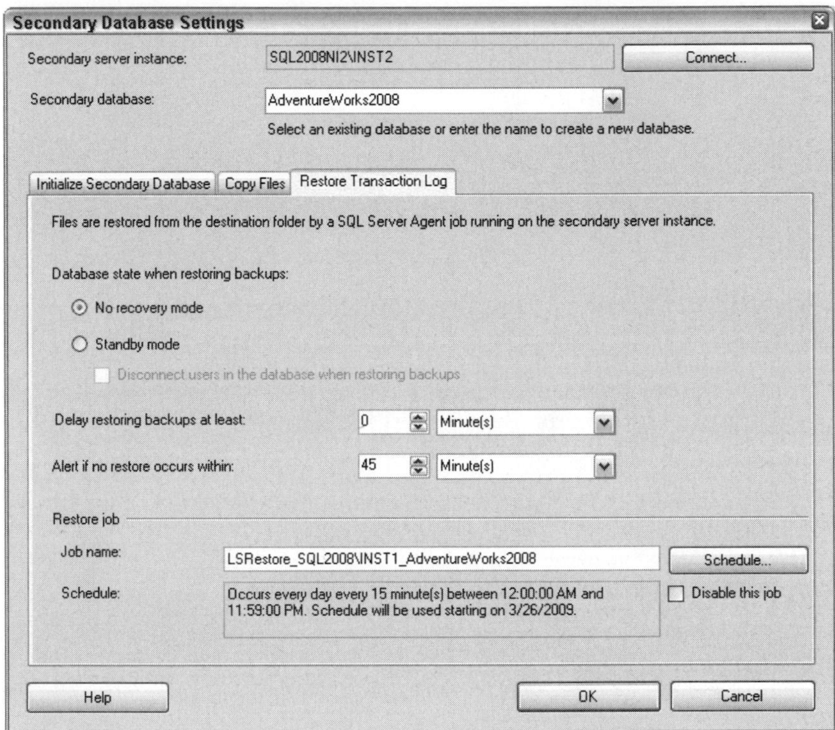

15. On the Restore Transaction Log tab, the option for delaying a restore and alerting is available as well. This configuration option enables all the transaction log backups to be held until the end of the business day or to apply the transaction logs as soon as they are received.

16. The option for more granularities on restores and when they are applied are set in the Restore job by clicking the Schedule button. By default, transaction log backups are restored every 15 minutes on the secondary server.

17. Click OK to complete the secondary database setup, and return to the database's Properties tab.

18. Once the secondary database configuration has been completed, a monitor server can be configured on the primary database's Properties page by checking "Use a monitor server instance" and clicking the Settings button as shown in Figure 46-7.

NOTE **As noted previously, adding a monitor server is optional. But if you do not add a monitor server now you cannot add it later. And if you add a monitor server now, it cannot be changed without removing log shipping first.**

FIGURE 46-7

Configuring the monitor server for log shipping

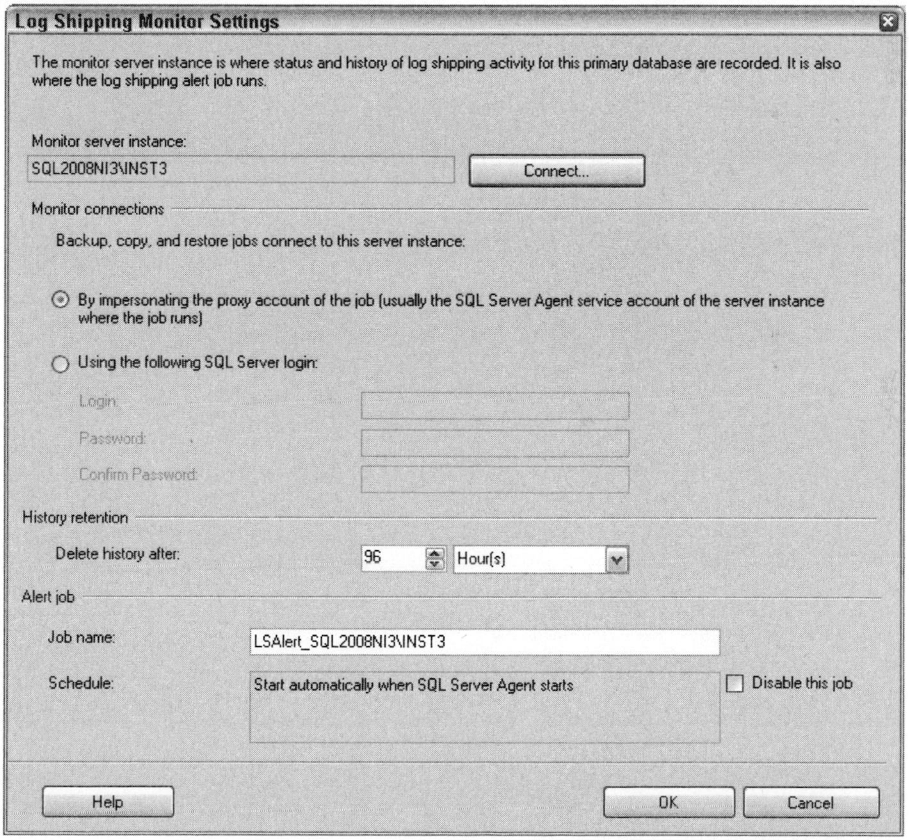

19. Once you have finished configuring log shipping, you will see a page similar to Figure 46-8. Notice that it also has the option of scripting the log shipping configuration.

If your log shipping has a number of non-default options, scripting your changes makes it easier to ensure that each time it is done the configuration stays the same.

FIGURE 46-8

Finished configuring log shipping

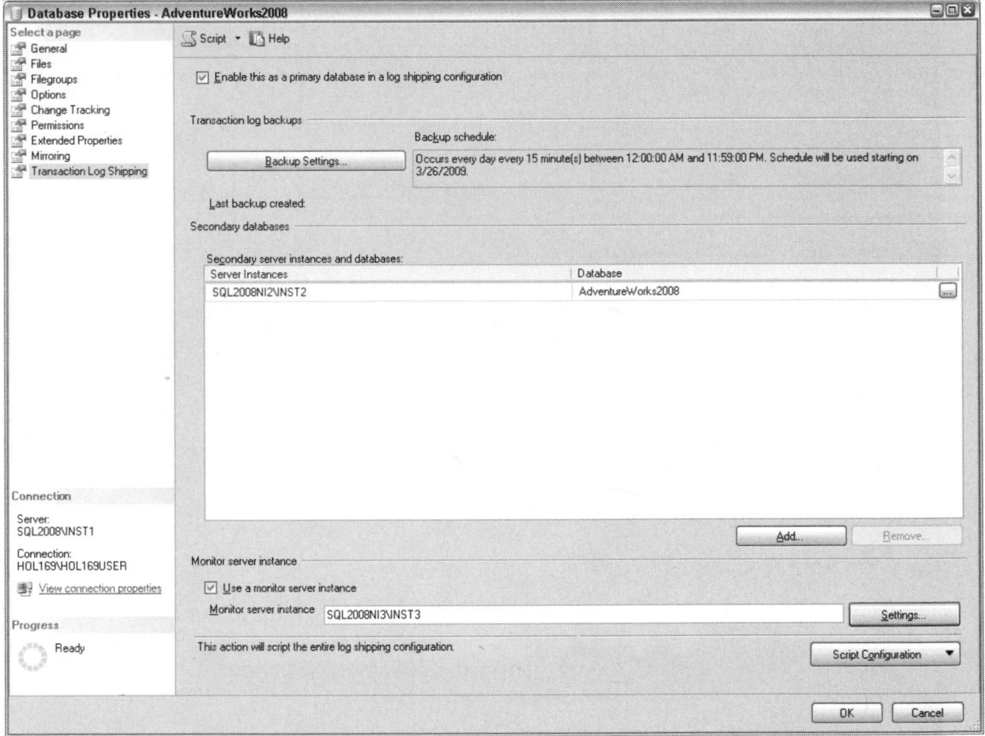

20. Once you click OK, the Save Log Shipping Configuration dialog box sets up the log shipping as shown in Figure 46-9.

FIGURE 46-9

Successful completion of Log Shipping Configuration

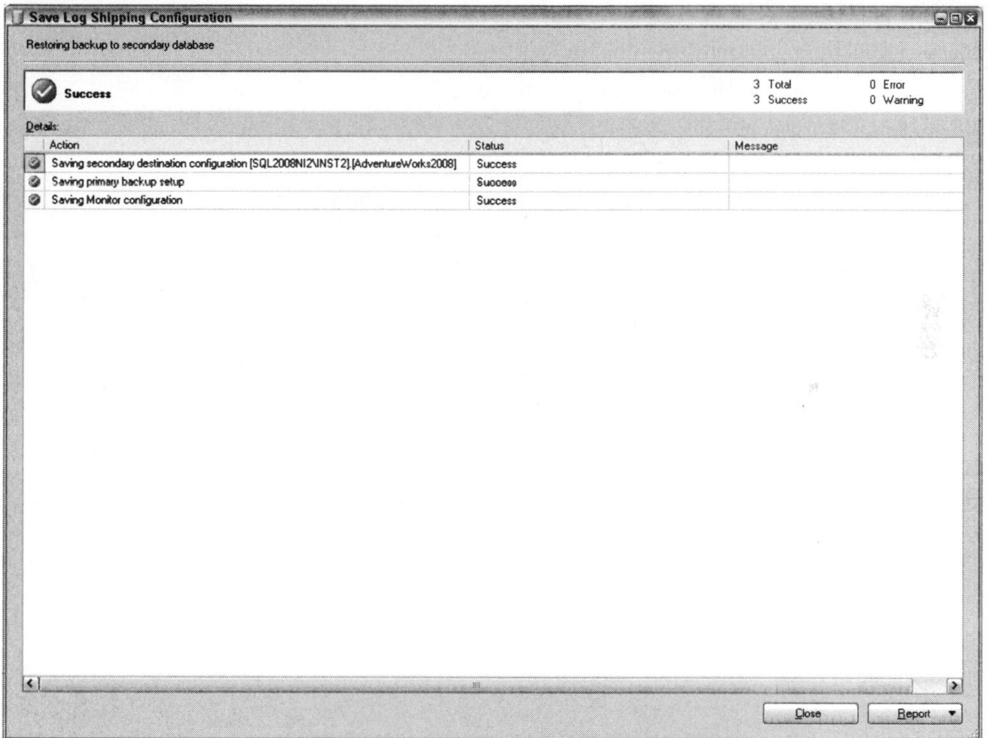

Configuring log shipping using Transact-SQL

Like most other configurations log shipping can also be configured using Transact-SQL. The easiest way to configure log shipping using Transact-SQL is to configure it once using SQL Server Management Studio and click Script Configuration as explained earlier (refer to Figure 46-8). The following system stored procedures need to be executed to configure log shipping:

On the primary server, execute the following system stored procedures:

- `master.dbo.sp_add_log_shipping_primary_database`: Configures the primary database and creates the transaction log backup job

- `msdb.dbo.sp_add_schedule`: Creates the schedule for the backup job
- `msdb.dbo.sp_attach_schedule`: Links the backup job to the schedule
- `msdb.dbo.sp_update_job`: Enables the backup job
- `master.dbo.sp_add_log_shipping_primary_secondary`: Adds an entry for the secondary database on the primary server

On the secondary server, execute the following system stored procedures:

- `master.dbo.sp_add_log_shipping_secondary_primary`: Configures the primary server information and creates the copy and restore jobs
- `msdb.dbo.sp_add_schedule`: Creates the schedule for the copy job
- `msdb.dbo.sp_attach_schedule`: Links the copy job to the schedule
- `msdb.dbo.sp_add_schedule`: Creates the schedule for the restore job
- `msdb.dbo.sp_attach_schedule`: Links the restore job to the schedule
- `master.dbo.sp_add_log_shipping_secondary_database`: Configures the secondary database
- `msdb.dbo.sp_update_job`: Enables the copy job
- `msdb.dbo.sp_update_job`: Enables the restore job

On the monitor server, execute the following system stored procedure:

- `master.dbo.sp_add_log_shipping_alert_job`: Creates the alert job and adds the job ID to the `log_shipping_monitor_alert` table

Post-log shipping configuration

As mentioned earlier, log shipping only applies the changes that are either captured in the transaction log or in the initial full backup of the log shipping database. Any database objects such as logins, jobs, maintenance plans, SSIS packages, and linked servers that reside outside the log shipping database need to be manually created on the warm standby server. After configuring log shipping, it is very important to synchronize the warm standby servers with all objects that live outside the log shipping database. Most of these objects can be easily scripted using Management Studio and can be applied on the warm standby servers. The frequency of applying the changes must meet the rate of changes in your environment.

One of the ways to synchronize the logins is to create an Integration Services (SSIS) job that connects to each server and transfers the logins. The frequency of this job will depend on how often new logins are added to your primary server.

Checking Log Shipping Configuration

Once log shipping is configured, review the following checklist to verify the log shipping setup.

On the primary server:

- Right-click on the log shipping database and look at the database properties. On the Transaction Log Shipping page, note that the database is enabled as the primary database in the log shipping configuration. On this page you can review other log shipping details such as the backup job schedule on the primary server, secondary server details, the copy and restore job schedule on the secondary server, monitor server details, and whether backup compression is being used.
- Expand SQL Server Agent and review the backup transaction log job.

On the secondary server:

- Expand SQL Server Agent and review the copy and restore transaction log backup jobs.

On the monitor server:

- Expand SQL Server Agent and review the Alert job, the log shipping primary server alert, and the log shipping secondary server alert.

Monitoring Log Shipping

To monitor log shipping from SQL Server Management Studio, Microsoft provides a Transaction Log Shipping Status report. This report can be run on any SQL Server participating in the log shipping configuration. To run the Transaction Log Shipping Status report:

1. Connect to the primary, secondary, or monitor server using Object Explorer in SQL Server Management Studio.
2. Right-click the SQL Server instance, and then click Reports.
3. Click Standard Reports.
4. Click Transaction Log Shipping Status.

For a complete picture of the log shipping configuration, run this report on the monitor server, as shown in Figure 46-10.

Another method for monitoring log shipping is to directly review the status of the log shipping jobs. You can review the history of the transaction log backup job on the primary server and the history of the copy and restore jobs on the secondary server.

Log shipping can also be monitored using several monitoring tables and stored procedures. The information that can be retrieved from these sources includes the database name, last backup, last restore, time since the last restore, and whether the alerts are enabled.

FIGURE 46-10

Executing the Transaction Log Shipping Status report on the monitor server

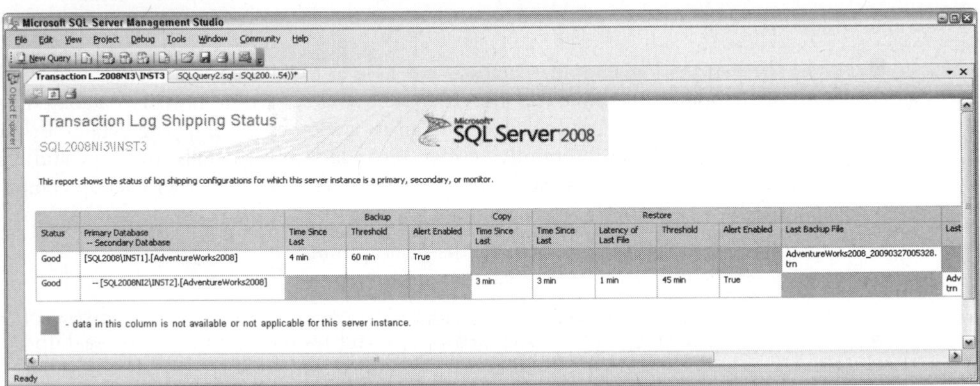

The following is a list of the tables that can be used to monitor log shipping. These tables exist in the MSDB database (because log shipping is mainly executed by a collection of jobs) on all the servers that are involved in the log shipping configuration:

- msdb.dbo.log_shipping_monitor_alert
- msdb.dbo.log_shipping_monitor_error_detail
- msdb.dbo.log_shipping_monitor_history_detail
- msdb.dbo.log_shipping_monitor_primary
- msdb.dbo.log_shipping_monitor_secondary
- msdb.dbo.log_shipping_primary_databases
- msdb.dbo.log_shipping_secondary_databases

The following is a list of stored procedures that can be used to monitor log shipping. They exist on all the servers in the master database that are involved in the log shipping configuration:

- master.sys.sp_help_log_shipping_monitor_primary
- master.sys.sp_help_log_shipping_monitor_secondary
- master.sys.sp_help_log_shipping_alert_job
- master.sys.sp_help_log_shipping_primary_database
- master.sys.sp_help_log_shipping_primary_secondary
- master.sys.sp_help_log_shipping_secondary_database
- master.sys.sp_help_log_shipping_secondary_primary

Modifying or Removing Log Shipping

After configuring log shipping you can edit, add, or remove a log shipping configuration. For example, you can add another secondary server to the log shipping configuration. Or you may want to change the schedule of the backup, copy, or restore jobs. Sometimes you may need to remove a secondary server from the log shipping configuration or remove log shipping completely from all the participating servers.

To modify or remove log shipping:

1. In the Object Explorer on the primary server in SQL Server Management Studio, right-click on the log shipping database and look at the database properties.
2. Under Select a page, click the Transaction Log Shipping page (refer to Figure 46-8).
3. To modify the parameters of the copy or restore jobs on the secondary server, highlight the secondary server under "Secondary Server instances and databases" and click the ellipses (. . .).
4. To add a new secondary server, click Add under "Secondary Server instances and databases." Follow steps 9 through 16 in the section "Configuring Log Shipping using Management Studio."
5. To remove a secondary server, highlight the secondary server under "Secondary Server instances and databases" and click Remove. Log shipping will verify whether you want to remove the secondary server, as shown in Figure 46-11. If you are sure, click Yes.

FIGURE 46-11

Removing a secondary server from the log shipping configuration

When Yes is clicked, log shipping will delete the secondary database on the secondary server as shown in Figure 46-12. Note that the copy and restore jobs on the secondary server are deleted.

6. To completely remove log shipping, clear the "Enable this as a primary database in a log shipping configuration" check box. Log shipping will ask you to confirm that you really want to remove log shipping, as shown in Figure 46-13.

FIGURE 46-12

Deleting the secondary server from the log shipping configuration

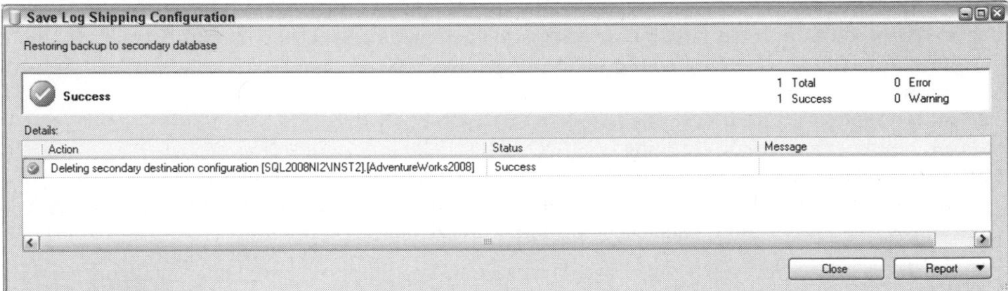

FIGURE 46-13

Checking if you want to completely remove log shipping

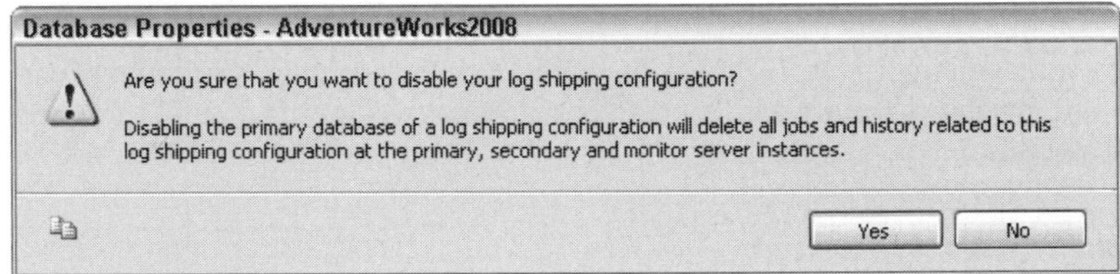

This action will delete all jobs and history related to this log shipping configuration on all the servers involved in this log shipping configuration. If you are sure, then click Yes. Once it completely removes log shipping, the dialog shown in Figure 46-14 will appear.

FIGURE 46-14

Completely removed log shipping configuration

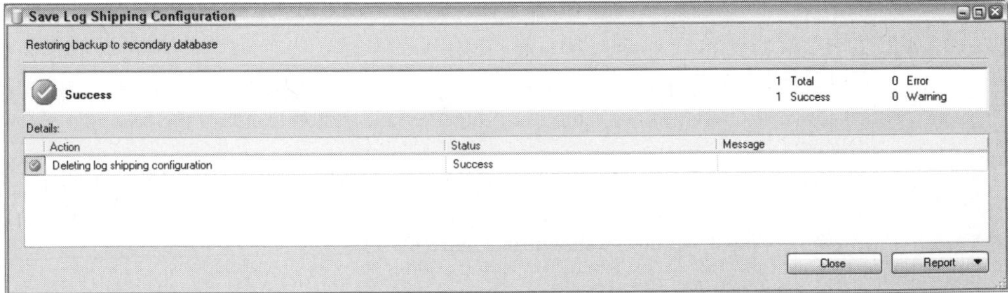

Switching Roles

Log shipping enables the capability to manually switch roles. This action can be performed for maintenance or in the case of a disaster. Depending on the cause of the disaster and its severity, the likely first step is to take a backup of the active transaction log, or tail of the log, on the primary server (if it is still accessible) with the `NORECOVERY` option.

The next step is to transfer all the transaction log backups to the secondary server either using a SQL Server Agent job or copying them manually. Once copied, the transaction log backups need to be restored in sequential order to the secondary server using the `WITH NORECOVERY` or `WITH STANDBY` option for all transaction logs except the last one. The last transaction log is restored using the `WITH RECOVERY` option to close any open transactions and bring the secondary database up to an online state. If all the transaction log backups have been restored using the `WITH NORECOVERY` or `WITH STANDBY` option, then there is no need to panic. You can still recover the database using the `RESTORE DATABASE <database_name> WITH RECOVERY` command. Then disable the log shipping jobs and alerts on the servers participating in the log shipping configuration.

Next, verify that any database objects such as logins, jobs, maintenance plans, SSIS packages, and linked servers that reside outside the log shipping database are created on the warm standby server. For example, if the logins are not created on the warm standby server, then the users will not be able to connect and you will still have a server down situation.

Finally, manually redirect the applications and users to the new primary server.

Best Practice

I highly recommend thoroughly executing the role reversal steps and documenting them prior to needing to failover to the warm standby server. Failure to do this can significantly increase downtime and complexity when you actually need to failover to the warm standby server.

Returning to the original primary server

Once the primary server has been repaired and is ready to return to service, the following steps reinitialize the primary server during a period when users are not connected:

1. Use an Integration Services job to move all the user logins from the warm standby server to the primary server.
2. Transfer the database from the warm standby server to the primary server using either a full database backup and restore method or a detach and attach method. If you had failed over to the warm standby server in a controlled environment, you may be able to avoid taking a complete backup and restore of the database by applying the transaction log backups from the warm standby server to the original primary server.
3. Redirect the applications and users to the original primary server.

Summary

Availability is paramount to the success of most database projects, and it is becoming increasingly important in regard to business requirements. Log shipping, failover clustering, database mirroring, and replication are all high-end features to provide a stable database environment for users.

Log shipping is a robust and reliable high-availability disaster recovery and reporting solution that can be implemented very easily with the hardware you already have; there is no need to purchase any new costly hardware. Log shipping backs up the transaction log on the primary server every few minutes and restores it on the warm standby servers. If the primary server stops working, you can make one of the warm standby servers your new primary server. The main problem with log shipping is that the role change is a manual process and the DBA needs to be present to execute it. It is possible to automate most of the role change process using SQL Server Agent jobs, but some manual intervention is still required and the clients have to be manually redirected to the new primary server.

The next chapter discusses database mirroring, which provides per-database protection like log shipping but also provides an automatic failover option.

Chapter 47

Database Mirroring

IN THIS CHAPTER

Achieving high database availability is one of the most important goals for critical business applications. Database mirroring is a software solution offered by Microsoft SQL Server 2008 to achieve high database availability. Database mirroring enables you to maintain a copy of your production database that could potentially be completely synchronized on a separate server for failover in the event of a failed production server or database. Like log shipping, database mirroring provides high availability at the database level; but unlike log shipping, database mirroring can be configured to provide no data loss and automatic failover.

Database Mirroring Overview

Database mirroring was officially supported with SQL Server 2005 SP1. It is available in Enterprise and Developer Editions, and with some restrictions in Standard Edition. Developer Edition can be used only for development purposes and not for production.

The basic concept of database mirroring is very simple. Database mirroring maintains a hot standby database (mirror database) that is kept in sync with the production database (principal database) by transferring transaction log records from the principal database to a mirror database over the network, either synchronously or asynchronously. In case of a failure, the mirror database can be quickly accessed by the clients. Database mirroring has the following benefits:

- It increases database protection by maintaining a mirror copy of your database.
- It allows you to choose only the databases that you want to mirror from one SQL Server instance to another. There is a 1:1 ratio from the principal server to the mirror server. Multiple databases in a SQL Server instance can be mirrored.

What's New in SQL Server Database Mirroring?

SQL Server 2008 database mirroring has some exciting new features, one of which is called *log compression*. As the name suggests, this feature compresses the transaction log records on the production server before sending them to the mirror server. This feature reduces network bandwidth and increases application performance and throughput at the cost of increased CPU usage.

Another new feature is the capability to automatically repair a page. This means that if the production or mirror server is unable to read a data page due to certain types of errors like 823, 824, or 829, then the server that is unable to read the page requests a copy from the other server participating in database mirroring. Upon successful retrieval of the data page, the server replaces the unreadable page, which resolves the error automatically. This feature is really nice because in order to fix similar errors during a SQL Server 2005 database mirroring session, you may have to manually run the `DBCC REPAIR_ALLOW_DATA_LOSS` option, which, as the name suggests, may result in some data loss.

NOTE **The log compression feature is available in SQL Server 2008 Enterprise, Developer, and Standard Editions. It is on by default and requires no special configuration or switches. However, if the extra CPU usage due to log compression is not desirable in your environment, then you can turn off log compression by turning on the trace flag `1462`.**

The automatic page repair feature is not available in SQL Server 2008 Standard Edition. It is available only in SQL Server 2008 Enterprise and Developer Editions.

- By default, it compresses and encrypts the data between the principal and mirror server.
- It improves the availability of your databases during hardware or software upgrades.
- It can be used for high database availability and disaster recovery purposes. To achieve high database availability, place the principal and mirror SQL Servers in the same data-center. For disaster recovery, place the principal and mirror SQL Servers in different datacenters so that a disaster in one datacenter does not affect the other datacenter.
- By default, it does not support reporting. If you want to use the mirror database for reporting purposes, you can create a database snapshot (refer to Chapter 45 for details on database snapshot) on the mirror database and use the snapshot for reporting purposes.

NOTE **If you are using the mirror database for reporting purposes, then you need to fully license the mirror server. Conversely, if the mirror server is just being used as a hot standby or passive server, then (as per the *Microsoft SQL Server 2008 Pricing and Licensing Guide*) a license is not required, provided that the number of processors in the passive server is equal to or less than those of the active server. The passive server can take the duties of the active server for 30 days. Afterward, it must be licensed accordingly.**

- It provides options for no data loss for committed transactions.
- It can provide an almost instantaneous database failover solution by using an optional server called a *witness*.

- There is no real distance limitation between the principal and mirror servers.
- It can be implemented without exotic hardware and may be significantly cheaper than other high-availability solutions like SQL Server failover clustering. Note that SQL Server failover clustering provides high availability for the entire SQL Server instance, whereas database mirroring provides high availability only at the database level.
- It can complement existing log shipping and failover clustering implementations.
- If your applications use ADO.NET or the SQL Server Native Client to connect to a database, then in case of a failure, the applications can automatically redirect the clients to the mirror database.

However, database mirroring has a few drawbacks:

- Only user databases in `full` recovery model can be used for database mirroring. `Simple` or `bulk-logged` recovery model cannot be used. This also means that database mirroring will break if the recovery model for a mirrored database is changed from `full` to `simple` or `bulk-logged`.
- System databases (`master`, `model`, `msdb`, `tempdb`) cannot be mirrored.
- Database mirroring does not support `FILESTREAM`. This means that databases with a `FILESTREAM` filegroup cannot be mirrored, nor can you create a `FILESTREAM` filegroup on a principal database.
- Database mirroring does not support cross-database transactions or distributed transactions.
- Like log shipping, database mirroring provides redundancy at the database level and not at the entire SQL Server instance level, like SQL Server failover clustering.
- Like log shipping, database mirroring only applies to changes that are captured in the transaction log or the initial full backup of the principal database. Any database objects such as logins, jobs, maintenance plans, SSIS packages, and linked servers that reside outside the mirrored database need to be manually created on the mirror server.
- Unlike log shipping, database mirroring does not support having multiple copies for the same principal database. This means you can only have one mirror database for each principal database.
- The mirror database name needs to be same as the principal database name.
- If the mirror database fails, the transaction log space on the principal database cannot be reused even if you are taking transaction log backup. This means you need to either have enough space for the transaction log to grow, and bring the mirror database online before the log fills up the available disk space and brings the principal database to a halt, or break the database mirroring.
- Depending on the workload, your environment, and the database mirroring configuration, database mirroring may affect application performance. It can also place a large demand on the network while the transaction log records are being sent.

If these drawbacks are acceptable, database mirroring can be an excellent choice for high database availability, disaster recovery, and/or reporting. It is highly recommended that you thoroughly test database mirroring with your application and hardware, and validate your SLAs (service-level agreements), before implementing it in production.

Defining Database Mirroring

Although database mirroring appears to be similar to log shipping, it is not the same. As explained in Chapter 46, log shipping involves periodically restoring a transaction log backup from the primary server to a warm standby server, making that server ready to recover at a moment's notice. Database mirroring continuously transfers the transaction log records (not the transaction log backups) from the principal database and applies them to the mirror database.

Database mirroring normally involves three SQL Servers: a principal server, a mirror server, and an optional witness server, as shown in Figure 47-1.

FIGURE 47-1

Sample database mirroring configuration

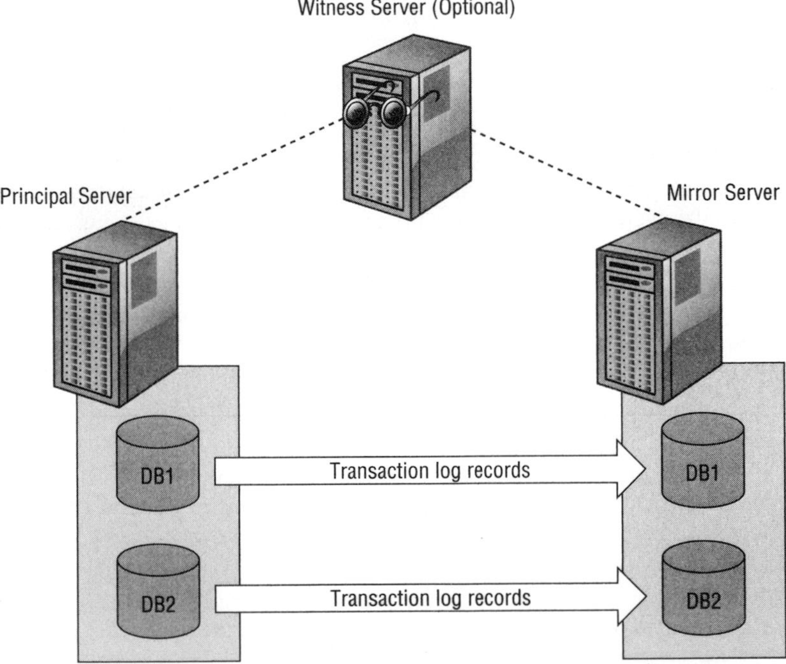

- The *principal server* is the main production SQL Server to which clients connect. This server contains the database for which you want to create a duplicate (also called a hot standby or mirror copy). The initial full database backup is taken on this server, which should be a high-quality server with redundant disk drives.

- The *mirror server* is the hot standby SQL Server. If the principal server fails, the mirror server becomes the new principal server. This server should be capable of meeting the minimum performance requirements during a short-term crisis. If your business does not allow any performance degradation, then the mirror server should be comparable to (same CPU and memory configuration) the principal server.

  The principal server and mirror server are often referred to as *partners* in a database mirroring session.

- The *witness server* is an optional separate SQL Server and is required only when automatic failover is required. The witness server helps create a quorum to ensure that only one SQL Server — either the principal server or the mirror server — owns the database that is accessible by the clients. The witness controls automatic failure to the mirror if the principal becomes unavailable.

NOTE **One witness server can be used for multiple database mirroring sessions, each for different databases and different partners.**

Transaction log records are transferred from the principal server to the mirror server synchronously or asynchronously based on the transaction safety level that you select for the database mirroring session. Database mirroring has two transaction safety levels, `SAFETY FULL` and `SAFETY OFF`, as detailed in Table 47-1. The failover options are described in the section "Role Switching" later in this chapter.

TABLE 47-1

Database Mirroring Safety Levels and Failover Options

Safety Level	Operating Mode	Failover Mode	Witness Server Required
`FULL`	Synchronous Database Mirroring	Automatic and Manual	Yes
`FULL`	Synchronous Database Mirroring	Manual and Forced	No
`OFF`	Asynchronous Database Mirroring	Forced	N/A

`SAFETY FULL` is often referred to as *synchronous database mirroring* or *high-safety mode*. In this mode, the mirror database is in sync with the principal database at all times and provides full data safety. The following steps, shown in Figure 47-2, describe the sequence of events that occurs when you choose `SAFETY FULL`:

1. The client submits a transaction to the principal database. The principal server writes the transaction log records to the transaction log buffer.
2. The transaction log buffer is written to disk (also referred to as *hardening* of the log) and simultaneously transfers the transaction log records from the buffer to the mirror server. The principal server waits for a confirmation from the mirror. Because the principal waits for an acknowledgment from the mirror, application response time increases and transaction throughput is reduced slightly. The actual performance impact depends on various factors, such as your network latency, the disk subsystem, the application, and more.

NOTE There are no specific restrictions on the network for database mirroring, but the network connection between the servers is critical. The process of determining a failover in synchronous database mirroring is based on the network connection. If there is a problem with the network, mirroring will failover or deny access to the database because of the quorum requirement. Although mirroring is working as designed, this behavior may come as a surprise to new database mirroring users, because with a regular standalone server, the database is still available. It is recommended that you have a dedicated network of high quality and high bandwidth. As a rule of thumb, network bandwidth should be three times the maximum log-generation rate.

3. The mirror server writes the transaction log records to the transaction log buffer. The transaction log buffer is then written to disk.
4. The mirror server acknowledges that the transaction has been written.
5. The commit is reported to the client.

FIGURE 47-2

Synchronous database mirroring mode

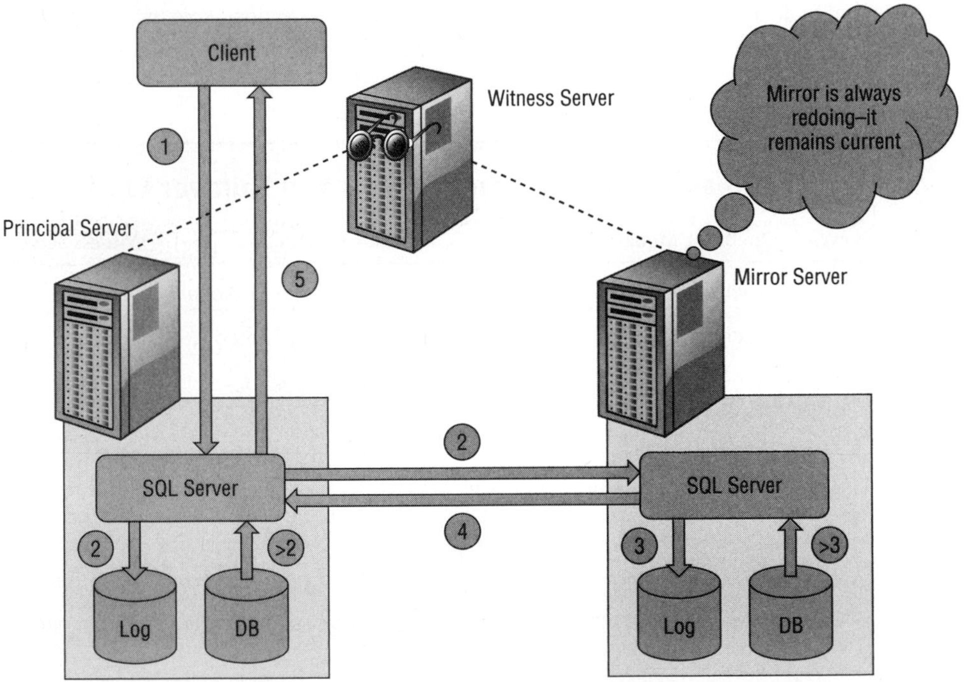

If you choose SAFETY FULL and have a witness server in the database mirroring configuration, then you can achieve automatic failover. This means if the principal database has a failure or is unavailable, the witness server and the mirror server will form a quorum and the mirror server will perform an automatic failover. The mirror server will become the new principal server and will recover the database and start servicing the clients. This operating mode is also referred to as *high-safety mode with automatic failover.*

If you choose SAFETY FULL and you do not have a witness server in the database mirroring configuration, then you cannot achieve automatic failover because if the principal database fails, the mirror server cannot form a quorum, as there is no witness server. In this configuration, you need to perform a manual failover. This operating mode is also referred to as *high-safety mode without automatic failover.*

NOTE **Synchronous database mirroring (high-safety mode) is supported by SQL Server 2008 Enterprise, Developer, and Standard Editions. If you implement synchronous database mirroring using SQL Server 2008 Standard Edition, then you cannot create a database snapshot on the mirror database for reporting purposes, as database snapshots are not supported by SQL Server 2008 Standard Edition.**

SAFETY OFF is often referred to as *asynchronous database mirroring* or *high-performance mode*. This safety level provides high performance with possible data loss. In this mode, the communication between the principal and mirror databases is asynchronous. The sequence of events when you choose SAFETY OFF is shown in Figure 47-3.

FIGURE 47-3

Asynchronous database mirroring mode

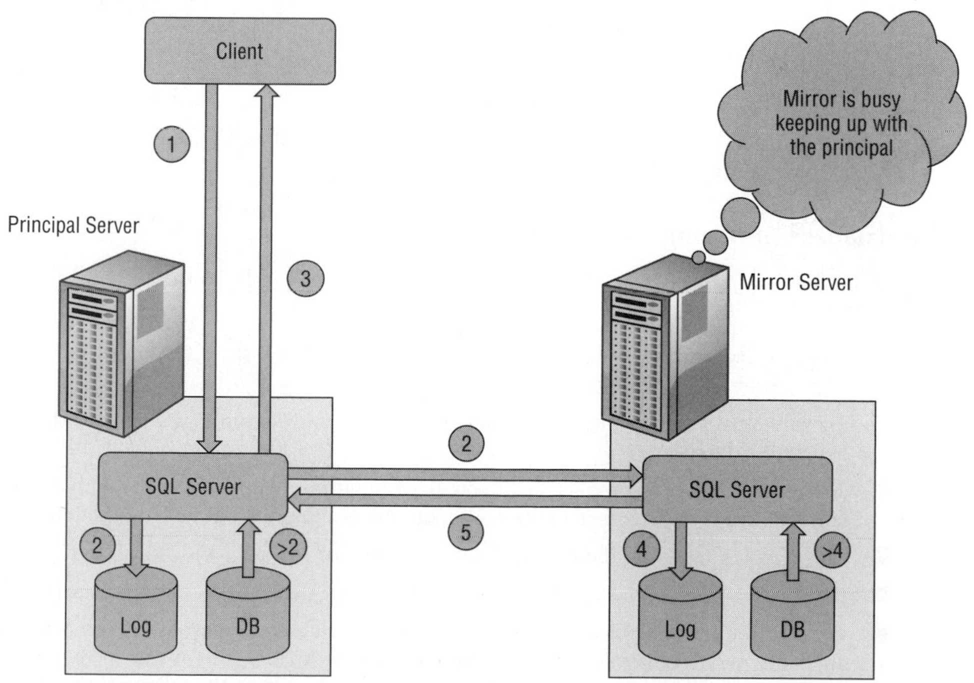

The transaction log records are written to the principal database transaction log and sent to the mirrored database transaction log in the same way as in synchronous mirroring mode. The main difference is that the principal does not wait for the mirror to acknowledge that the transaction has been written to disk. The transactions on the principal database commit as soon as they are written on the principal database transaction log. This increases application performance but creates a heavy load on the principal database, or a network delay could cause the principal database transaction log, which is waiting to be sent to the mirror database, to grow; and in the event of a failure of the principal, the unsent transaction log records may be lost. Automatic and manual failover are not enabled in high performance mode due to possible data loss. Only a forced failover is allowed in this mode.

NOTE **Asynchronous database mirroring (high-performance mode) is only supported by SQL Server 2008 Enterprise or Developer Editions.**

Best Practice

Do not configure a witness server in high-performance operating mode because there is no use of a witness server. In fact, if you use a witness server and for some reason the witness server and mirror server both become unavailable, the principal server will not be able to form a quorum and the principal database will not be accessible to the clients even though the principal server is available and does not have any issues.

Configuring database mirroring

Database mirroring can be configured using one of two methods: either by using SQL Server Management Studio or by using system-stored procedures.

Pre-database mirroring configuration

With either method of configuration, the following prerequisites need to be completed before configuring database mirroring:

- The principal, mirror, and witness servers all must have the same version of SQL Server (SQL Server 2005 or 2008).
- The principal and the mirror server must have the same edition of SQL Server (Enterprise or Standard Edition).
- The edition of the witness server (if you are configuring high-safety mode with automatic failover) can be SQL Server Express, Workgroup, Standard, or Enterprise Edition.
- The recovery model of the principal database must be set to `full`.
- Ensure that there is enough disk space for the mirror database on the mirror server.
- Create the mirror database. To do this, take a full database backup of the principal database and subsequent transaction log backups; copy the backups to the mirror server, and restore it on the mirror server `WITH NORECOVERY` to put it into a state that allows inserting transaction log records. The name of the mirror database should be the same as the principal database.

Before you start mirroring, take a transaction log backup on the principal database and restore it on the mirror database `WITH NORECOVERY`. Do not restore the transaction log backups `WITH STANDBY` — even though it's a loading state, database mirroring will not work.

Best Practice

It is recommended (but not required) that the principal and mirror databases have the same directory structure. If the directory structure is different, adding and removing file operations on the principal database will not be allowed without suspending database mirroring.

CROSS-REF **For more information about backup and restore, refer to Chapter 41, "Recovery Planning."**

- Communication between the SQL Servers in a database mirroring configuration is accomplished over TCP (Transmission Control Protocol) *endpoints*. Each server participating in database mirroring requires its own dedicated database mirroring endpoint. Each endpoint listens on a unique TCP/IP port.
- All the SQL Servers in a database mirroring configuration need to trust one another. If they are on the same domain, you need to ensure that each SQL Server login can connect to the mirroring SQL Server and have `CONNECT` permission on the endpoints. If the SQL Servers do not trust one another, then you need to use certificates for the communication between the servers.

Best Practice

Use a private high-speed network between the principal and mirror servers to reduce the network bandwidth and impact on other users. SQL Server 2008 helps reduce the network bandwidth with the log compression feature.

Configuring database mirroring using Management Studio

The following steps configure database mirroring using SQL Server Management Studio:

1. In the Object Explorer on the principal server in SQL Server Management Studio, right-click on the principal database and select Properties.
2. On the Options page, verify that the recovery model is `full`.
3. On the Mirroring page, shown in Figure 47-4, click Configure Security button to launch the Configure Database Mirroring Security Wizard. Click Next to begin the wizard. This wizard enables you to configure the security of the principal, mirror, and witness (optional) servers.

FIGURE 47-4

Database Properties Mirroring page

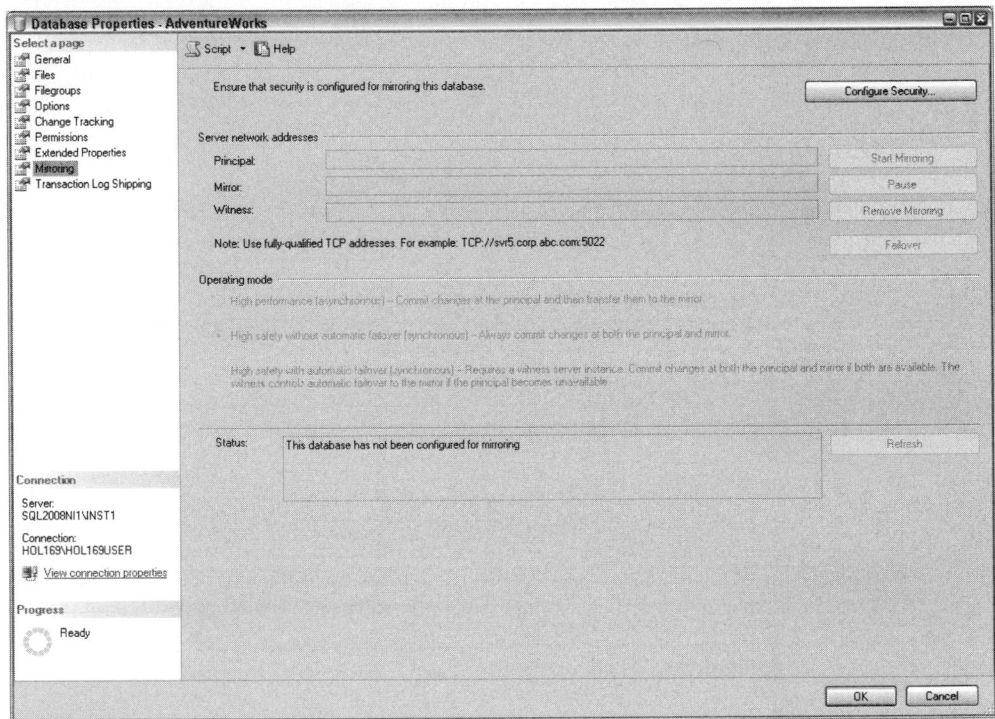

4. On the Include Witness Server page, shown in Figure 47-5, click Yes if you want to operate database mirroring in synchronous (high-safety) mode with automatic failover. For other operating modes (high-safety without automatic failover and high-performance mode), click No.

5. On the Choose Servers to Configure page, shown in Figure 47-6, ensure that the Witness server instance check box is checked. Click Next to continue. If you selected No in the previous step, you will not see this page.

6. The next page is the Principal Server Instance page, shown in Figure 47-7. As discussed earlier, communication between the servers participating in database mirroring is accomplished over TCP endpoints. Each server requires its own, dedicated database mirroring endpoint. Each endpoint listens on a unique TCP/IP port. The default port shown in Figure 47-7 is 5022. For security reasons, it is recommended to use a non-default port. Also, notice that by default the check box for *Encrypt data sent through this endpoint* is selected. It is recommended that you leave this checkbox selected to ensure that the data transferred across the network is encrypted. If for some reason you do not need encryption, uncheck this box. You can also change the endpoint name on this page. Click Next to continue.

FIGURE 47-5

Selecting the witness server

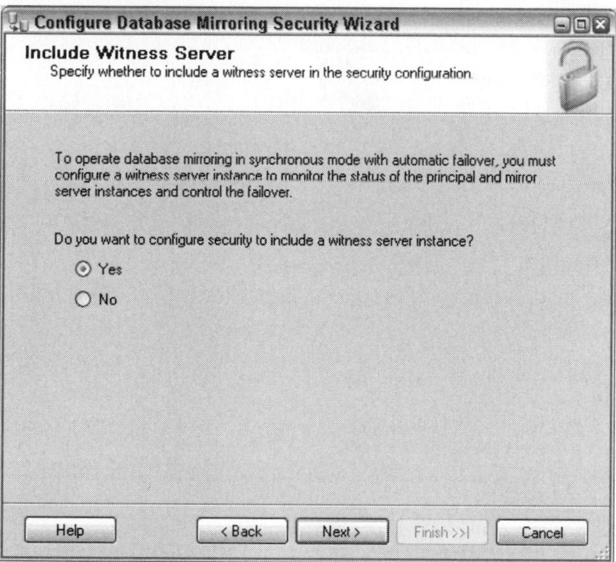

FIGURE 47-6

Selecting the witness server to save the security configuration

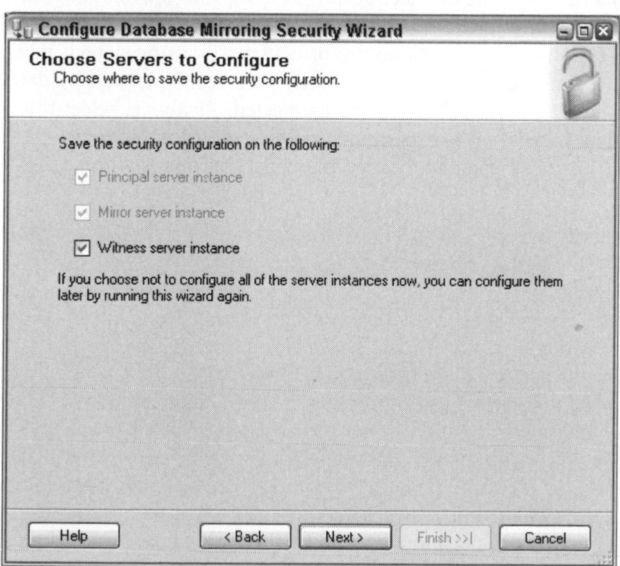

FIGURE 47-7

Configuring the principal server

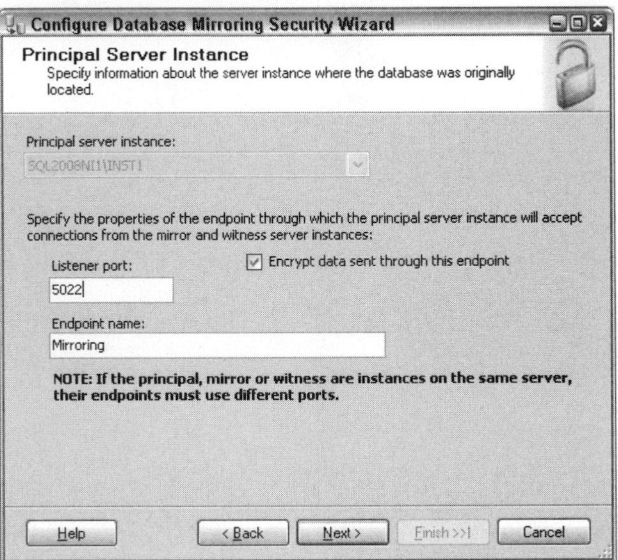

7. On the Mirror Server Instance page, shown in Figure 47-8, click the Connect button to display the Connect to Server dialog. Type the connection properties of the mirror server and click Connect. This will bring you back to the Mirror Server Instance page. Type the TCP/IP port for the endpoint on the mirror server. (Just like the principal server, the default port is 5022; and again, you should use a non-default port for security reasons). Note that by default the check box for *Encrypt data sent through this endpoint* is selected. As above, select this check-box to ensure that the data transferred across the network is encrypted. If you do not need encryption, uncheck this box. You can also change the endpoint name on this page. Click Next to continue.

8. The Witness Server Instance page, shown in Figure 47-9, will be displayed if you selected Witness Server in the Include Witness Server page (refer to Figure 47-5). Click the Connect button to display the Connect to Server dialog. Type the connection properties of the witness server and click Connect. This will bring you back to the Witness Server Instance page. Type the TCP/IP port for the endpoint on the witness server. (You might have already guessed that the default port is 5022 and that you should change it for security.) Also, if your witness server is on the same physical server as the mirror server, use a different port. It is not recommended to have the witness server on the same physical server as the principal server, as loss of the physical server will make both the principal and witness server unavailable and automatic failover cannot be achieved. By default, the check box for *Encrypt data sent through this endpoint* is selected. Leave this check box selected to ensure that data transferred across the network is encrypted. If you do not need encryption, uncheck this box. You can also change the endpoint name on this page. Click Next to continue.

FIGURE 47-8

Configuring the mirror server

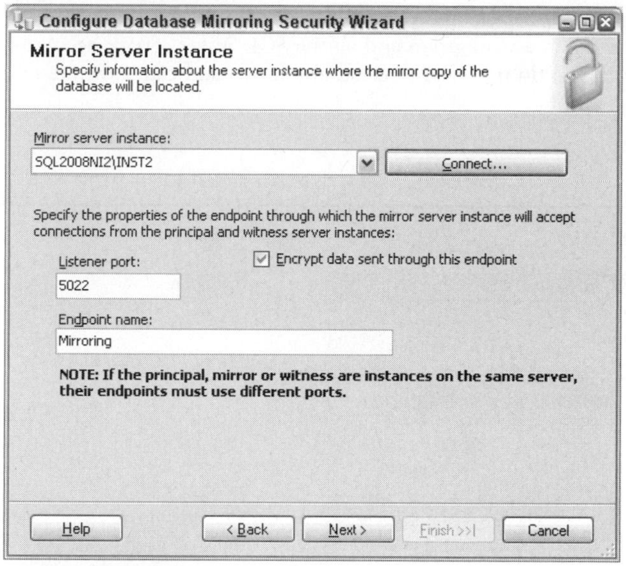

Configure Database Mirroring Security Wizard

Mirror Server Instance

Specify information about the server instance where the mirror copy of the database will be located.

Mirror server instance:

SQL2008NI2\INST2

Connect...

Specify the properties of the endpoint through which the mirror server instance will accept connections from the principal and witness server instances:

Listener port: 5022

Encrypt data sent through this endpoint

Endpoint name: Mirroring

NOTE: If the principal, mirror or witness are instances on the same server, their endpoints must use different ports.

Help | < Back | Next > | Finish >>| | Cancel

FIGURE 47-9

Configuring the witness server

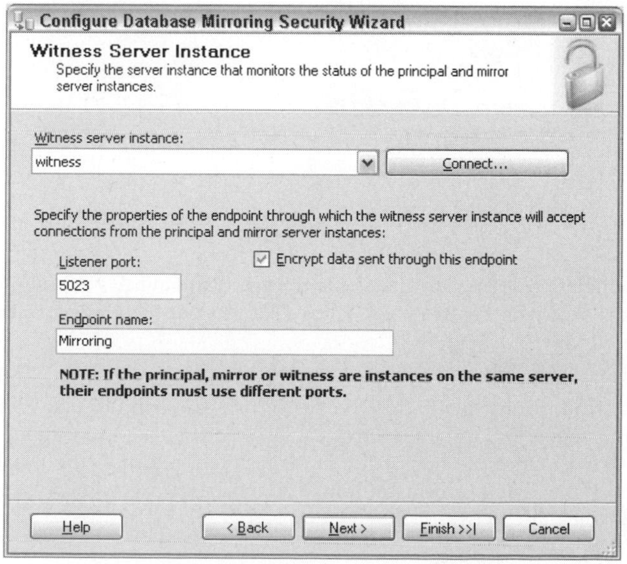

Configure Database Mirroring Security Wizard

Witness Server Instance

Specify the server instance that monitors the status of the principal and mirror server instances.

Witness server instance:

witness

Connect...

Specify the properties of the endpoint through which the witness server instance will accept connections from the principal and mirror server instances:

Listener port: 5023

Encrypt data sent through this endpoint

Endpoint name: Mirroring

NOTE: If the principal, mirror or witness are instances on the same server, their endpoints must use different ports.

Help | < Back | Next > | Finish >>| | Cancel

9. On the Service Accounts page, as shown in Figure 47-10, type the service accounts for all the SQL Server instances (principal, mirror, and witness). After you specify the service accounts, logins are created for each account, if necessary, and will be granted `CONNECT` permission on the endpoints. You do not need to create the logins if all the SQL Server instances use the same domain account or if you are using certificate-based authentication. Similarly, if all the SQL Server instances are in a workgroup and all the SQL Server service accounts use the same login and password, you do not need to create the logins and can leave the fields empty on this page.

FIGURE 47-10

Specifying the service accounts

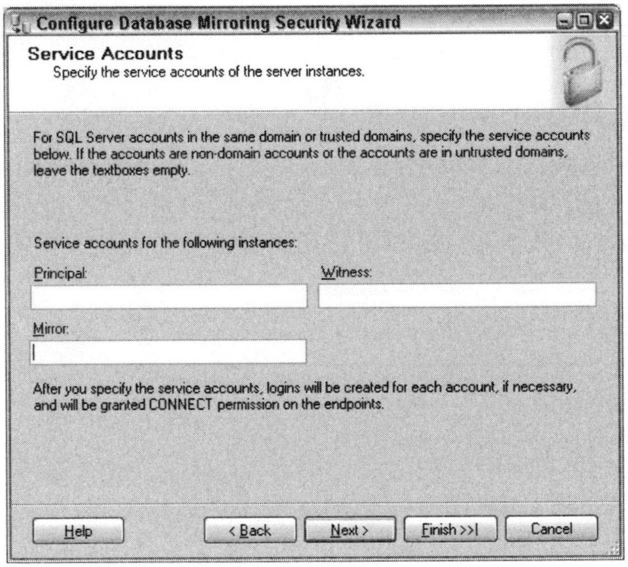

10. On the Complete the Wizard page (not shown), verify the choices made earlier and click Finish.

11. On the Configuring Endpoints page, review the status of each endpoint. A successful configuration of the endpoints is shown in Figure 47-11. Click Close to exit the Configure Database Mirroring Security Wizard.

12. On the Database Properties dialog, shown in Figure 47-12, do not select anything and leave it displayed. Before you start mirroring, verify that the mirror database is up to date. If required, take a backup of the transaction log of the principal database and restore it on the mirror database `WITH NORECOVERY`. Once the transaction log is restored, return to the Database Properties dialog and click the Start Mirroring button. You will see a page similar to what is shown in Figure 47-13. Click OK to exit.

FIGURE 47-11

Configuring endpoints

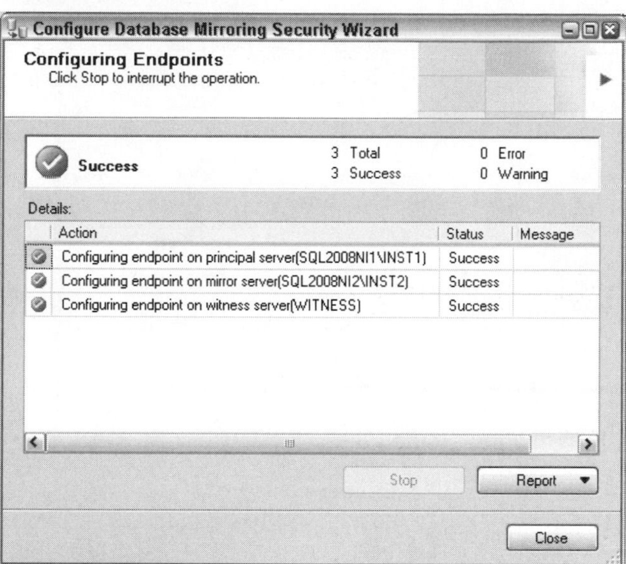

FIGURE 47-12

Starting database mirroring

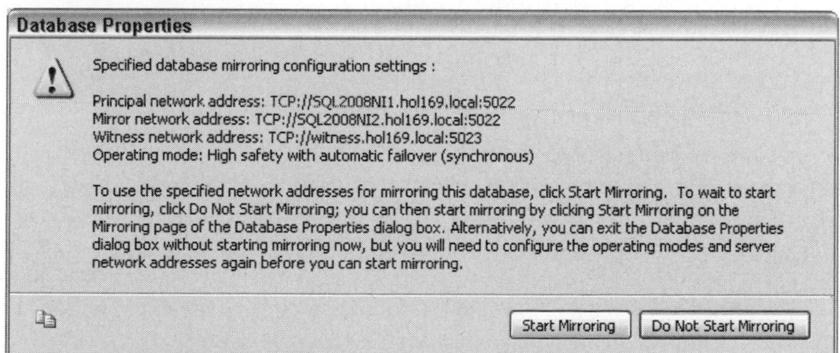

Configuring database mirroring using Transact-SQL

Like most other configurations, database mirroring can also be configured using Transact-SQL. The following example shows the basic steps to configure a database mirroring session for the `AdventureWorks` sample database using Transact-SQL and Windows Authentication. The assumption is that both the partners and the witness run under the same Windows domain service account. This

FIGURE 47-13

Database mirroring in progress

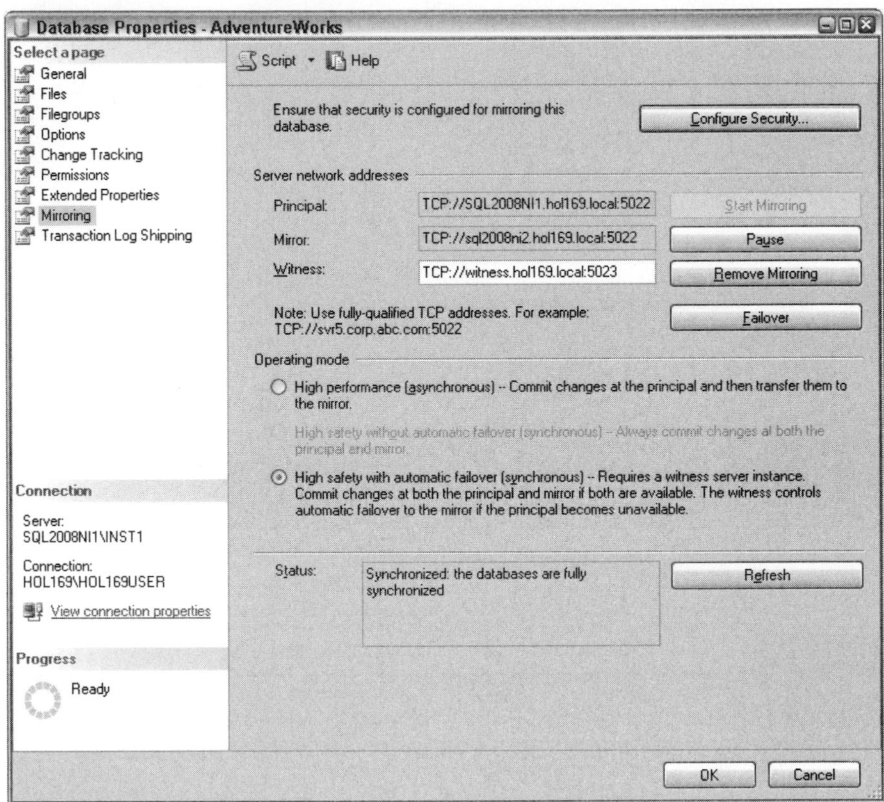

means that we will not need to create a login for each partner, as it already exists. If the partners and witness use different domain user accounts for their service startup accounts, create a login for the account of the server using the `CREATE LOGIN` statement and grant connect permissions on the endpoint to the login using the `GRAND CONNECT on ENDPOINT` command:

1. Connect to the principal server and execute the following code to create an endpoint for the principal. In this example, the principal will use TCP port 5091 for its endpoint:

```
CREATE ENDPOINT Endpoint_Mirroring
    STATE=STARTED
    AS TCP (LISTENER_PORT=5091)
    FOR DATABASE_MIRRORING (ROLE=PARTNER);
```

2. Connect to the mirror server and execute the preceding code.

3. If you are using a witness, connect to the witness server and execute the following code:

```
CREATE ENDPOINT Endpoint_Mirroring
    STATE=STARTED
    AS TCP (LISTENER_PORT=5091)
    FOR DATABASE_MIRRORING (ROLE=WITNESS);
```

4. Execute the following code on the principal server to take a full database backup of the AdventureWorks database:

```
BACKUP DATABASE AdventureWorks
    TO DISK = 'C:\AdventureWorks.bak';
```

5. Copy the AdventureWorks.bak file on the mirror server and execute the following code on the mirror server to restore the AdventureWorks database in restoring mode:

```
RESTORE DATABASE AdventureWorks
    FROM DISK = 'C:\AdventureWorks.bak'
    WITH NORECOVERY;
```

6. Execute the following code on the principal server to take a log backup of the Adventure Works database:

```
BACKUP LOG AdventureWorks
    TO DISK = 'C:\AdventureWorksLog.bak';
```

7. Copy the AdventureWorksLog.bak file on the mirror server and execute the following code on the mirror server to restore the AdventureWorks database in restoring mode:

```
RESTORE LOG AdventureWorks
    FROM DISK = 'C:\AdventureWorksLog.bak'
    WITH NORECOVERY;
```

8. Execute the following code on the mirror server to set the principal server as partner on the mirror database:

```
ALTER DATABASE AdventureWorks
    SET PARTNER =
    'TCP://principal.hol169.local:5091';
```

9. Execute the following code on the principal server to set the mirror server as partner on the principal database. Executing this statement begins the database mirroring session:

```
ALTER DATABASE AdventureWorks
    SET PARTNER =
    'TCP://mirror.hol169.local:5091';
```

10. If you are using a witness, set the witness server as follows:

```
ALTER DATABASE AdventureWorks
    SET WITNESS =
    'TCP://witness.hol169.local:5091';
```

NOTE By default, a database mirroring session is set to run in synchronous mode (SAFETY FULL) without automatic failover. To change the transaction safety level to OFF (asynchronous database mirroring), execute the following command on the principal server:

```
ALTER DATABASE AdventureWorks SET PARTNER SAFETY OFF;
```

CROSS-REF For configuring a database mirroring session using certificates, refer to the SQL Server 2008 Books Online topic "Using Certificates for Database Mirroring."

Post-database mirroring configuration

As mentioned earlier, database mirroring applies either the changes that are captured in the transaction log or the initial full backup of the principal database. Any database objects such as logins, jobs, maintenance plans, SSIS packages, and linked servers that reside outside the principal database need to be manually created on the mirror server. After configuring database mirroring, it is very important to synchronize the mirror server with all objects that live outside the mirrored database. Most of these objects can be easily scripted using Management Studio and can be applied on the mirror server. The frequency of applying the changes must meet the rate of changes in your environment.

One of the ways to synchronize the logins is to create an Integration Services (SSIS) job that connects to each server and transfers the logins. The frequency of this job depends on how often new logins are added to your principal server.

Checking a Database Mirroring Configuration

Once database mirroring is configured, there are several ways to verify the database mirroring setup:

- View the status of the principal and mirror databases.
  - Expand Databases in Management Studio to view the status of the principal and/or mirror databases. An example is shown for the principal database in Figure 47-14.
- Query the `sys.database_mirroring` catalog view to view the database mirroring metadata for each mirrored database. For example, executing the following T-SQL command against the principal and mirror servers displays the results in Table 47-2:

```
SELECT DB_NAME(database_id) AS Database_Name,
mirroring_state_desc,
mirroring_role_desc,
mirroring_safety_level_desc,
mirroring_partner_name,
mirroring_witness_name,
mirroring_witness_state_desc
FROM sys.database_mirroring
WHERE mirroring_state IS NOT NULL;
```

FIGURE 47-14

Status of the principal database

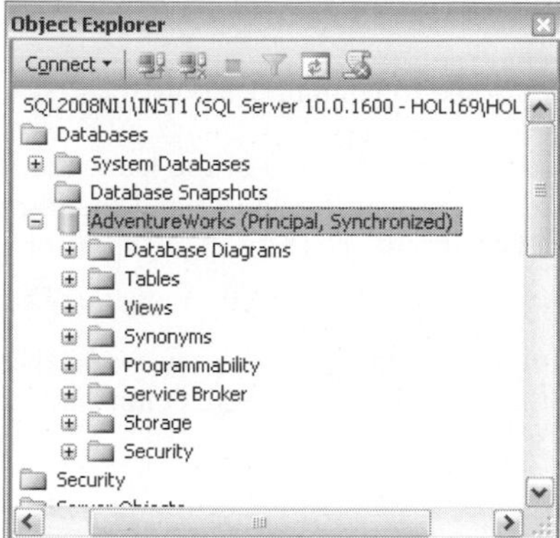

TABLE 47-2

Querying the sys.database_mirroring Catalog View

Column Name	Principal Server Results	Mirror Server Results
Database_Name	AdventureWorks	AdventureWorks
mirroring_state_desc	SYNCHRONIZED	SYNCHRONIZED
mirroring_role_desc	PRINCIPAL	MIRROR
mirroring_safety_level_desc	FULL	FULL
mirroring_partner_name	TCP://sql2008ni2.hol169.local:5022	TCP://sql2008ni1.hol169.local:5022
mirroring_witness_name	TCP://witness.hol169.local:5023	TCP://witness.hol169.local:5023
mirroring_witness_state_desc	CONNECTED	CONNECTED
mirroring_failover_lsn	1120000000012600001	1120000000012600001

Notice that the mirroring state in the table is `SYNCHRONIZED`. This state indicates that the mirror database has sufficiently caught up with the principal database. If you chose `SAFETY FULL`, there will be no data loss. If you chose `SAFETY OFF`, there is a potential for data loss. Other possible mirroring states are as follows:

- `SYNCHRONIZING`: Indicates that the mirror database is trying to catch up with the principal database. This is typically seen when you just start database mirroring or in high-performance mode.

- SUSPENDED: Indicates that the mirror database is not available. During this time the principal is referred to as *running exposed,* as it is processing transactions but not sending any transaction log records to the mirror.
- PENDING_FAILOVER: Indicates the state that the principal goes through before transitioning to the mirror role.
- DISCONNECTED: Indicates that the partners are unable to communicate with each other.

The mirroring_failover_lsn indicates the log sequence number (LSN) of the latest transaction log record that is written to disk. When there is heavy load on the principal database and the mirror is trying to catch up with the principal, you will see that the mirroring_failover_lsn on the principal is ahead of the mirror.

- Query the sys.database_mirroring_witnesses catalog view to review database mirroring session information. For example, executing the following T-SQL command against the witness server displays the results in Table 47-3:

```
SELECT database_name,
principal_server_name,
mirror_server_name,
saftey_level_desc,
partner_sync_state_desc
FROM sys.database_mirroring_witnesses;
```

TABLE 47-3

Querying the sys.database_mirroring_witnesses Catalog View

Column Name	Witness Server Results
database_name	AdventureWorks
principal_server_name	TCP://sql2008ni1.hol169.local:5022
mirror_server_name	TCP://sql2008ni2.hol169.local:5022
saftey_level_desc	FULL
partner_sync_state_desc	IN_SYNC

- Query the sys.database_mirroring_endpoints catalog view to review database mirroring endpoints information. For example, to check that the endpoints are started (STATE=STARTED), execute the following code on each server participating in the database mirroring session:

```
SELECT state_desc FROM sys.database_mirroring_endpoints;
```

Monitoring Database Mirroring

There are many ways to monitor database mirroring. In this section we discuss three methods to monitor database mirroring:

- Using Database Mirroring Monitor
- Using System Monitor
- Using SQL Server Profiler tool.

Monitoring using Database Mirroring Monitor

Microsoft provides a very useful tool called *Database Mirroring Monitor* to monitor database mirroring. You can launch the Database Mirroring Monitor tool from SQL Server Management Studio as follows:

1. Open Management Studio and connect to the principal or mirror server.
2. Expand Databases and right-click the principal database.
3. Select Tasks and then click Launch Database Mirroring Monitor.
4. Click Action menu and select Register Mirrored Database.
5. On the Register Mirrored Database dialog, click the Connect button to display the Connect to Server dialog. Type the connection properties of the principal or the mirror server and click Connect. This will bring you back to the Register Mirrored Database dialog. Click Register. Database Mirroring Monitor will register the database and both partner servers. To modify the credentials used to connect to the partners, click "Show the Manage Server Connections dialog box when I click OK" check box. Click OK to continue.
6. The Database Mirroring Monitor should now show you the principal and mirror server status, the amount of database mirroring traffic and latency, and the operating mode, as shown in Figure 47-15.

NOTE **If no traffic is being produced from the principal to the mirror, then the Database Mirroring Monitor will reflect that as shown in Figure 47-15.**

7. Click the History button to see the database mirroring history. An example is shown in Figure 47-16.
8. Database Mirroring Monitor also allows you to set warning thresholds. Click the Warnings tab. By default thresholds are not enabled. To set the thresholds, click Set Thresholds. On the Set Warning Thresholds dialog, shown in Figure 47-17, check the warning for the principal and/or mirror server and type the value. Click OK to continue. The Warnings tab, shown in Figure 47-18, will now have the thresholds. When a threshold is exceeded, an event will be logged to the Application Event log. To automatically monitor these events, you can configure an alert on the event using either SQL Server Management Studio or Microsoft System Center Operations Manager.

FIGURE 47-15

Monitoring a database mirroring session

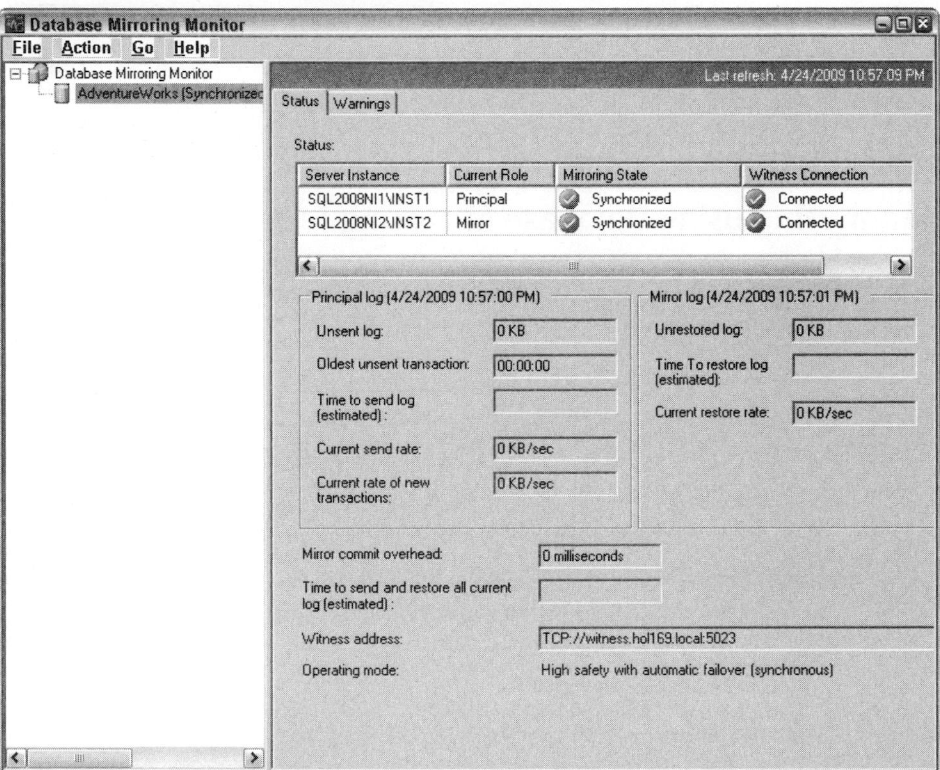

Monitoring using System Monitor

Apart from using the Database Mirroring Monitor, you can also use System Monitor (previously referred to as Performance Monitor) to monitor database mirroring performance. The `SQLServer:Database Mirroring` object contains the database mirroring performance counters. The following list describes some of the key counters.

Key principal server counters:

- **Log Bytes Sent/sec:** Indicates the rate at which the principal is transferring transaction log records to the mirror.
- **Log Send Queue KB:** Indicates the total number of transaction log kilobytes that have not been sent to the mirror yet.
- **Transaction Delay:** Indicates the delay in milliseconds spent waiting for the commit acknowledgment from the mirror. This counter is useful for determining whether database mirroring is impacting performance on the principal server.

FIGURE 47-16

Database mirroring history

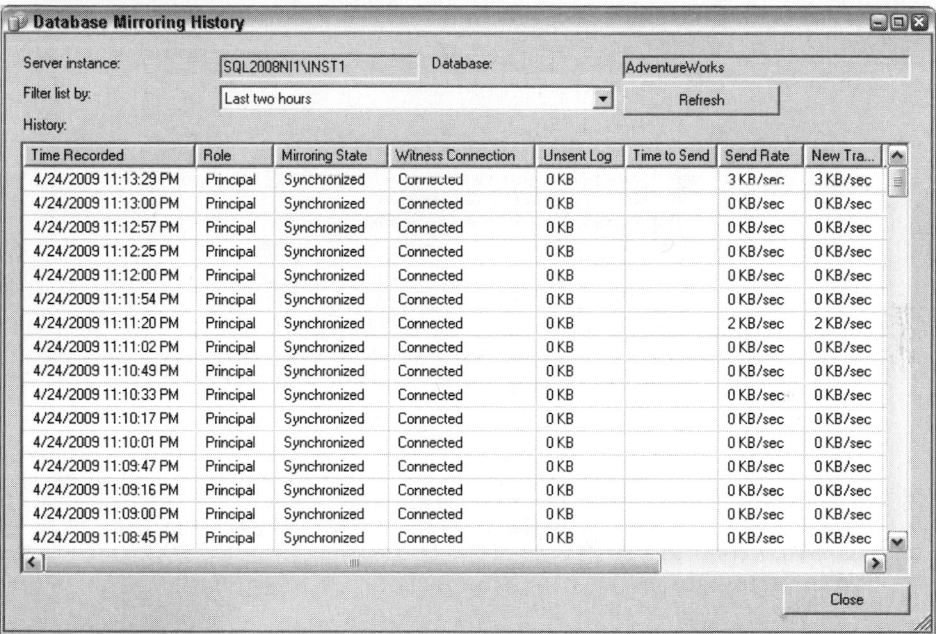

Time Recorded	Role	Mirroring State	Witness Connection	Unsent Log	Time to Send	Send Rate	New Tra...
4/24/2009 11:13:29 PM	Principal	Synchronized	Connected	0 KB		3 KB/sec	3 KB/sec
4/24/2009 11:13:00 PM	Principal	Synchronized	Connected	0 KB		0 KB/sec	0 KB/sec
4/24/2009 11:12:57 PM	Principal	Synchronized	Connected	0 KB		0 KB/sec	0 KB/sec
4/24/2009 11:12:25 PM	Principal	Synchronized	Connected	0 KB		0 KB/sec	0 KB/sec
4/24/2009 11:12:00 PM	Principal	Synchronized	Connected	0 KB		0 KB/sec	0 KB/sec
4/24/2009 11:11:54 PM	Principal	Synchronized	Connected	0 KB		0 KB/sec	0 KB/sec
4/24/2009 11:11:20 PM	Principal	Synchronized	Connected	0 KB		2 KB/sec	2 KB/sec
4/24/2009 11:11:02 PM	Principal	Synchronized	Connected	0 KB		0 KB/sec	0 KB/sec
4/24/2009 11:10:49 PM	Principal	Synchronized	Connected	0 KB		0 KB/sec	0 KB/sec
4/24/2009 11:10:33 PM	Principal	Synchronized	Connected	0 KB		0 KB/sec	0 KB/sec
4/24/2009 11:10:17 PM	Principal	Synchronized	Connected	0 KB		0 KB/sec	0 KB/sec
4/24/2009 11:10:01 PM	Principal	Synchronized	Connected	0 KB		0 KB/sec	0 KB/sec
4/24/2009 11:09:47 PM	Principal	Synchronized	Connected	0 KB		0 KB/sec	0 KB/sec
4/24/2009 11:09:16 PM	Principal	Synchronized	Connected	0 KB		0 KB/sec	0 KB/sec
4/24/2009 11:09:00 PM	Principal	Synchronized	Connected	0 KB		0 KB/sec	0 KB/sec
4/24/2009 11:08:45 PM	Principal	Synchronized	Connected	0 KB		0 KB/sec	0 KB/sec

FIGURE 47-17

Setting warning thresholds

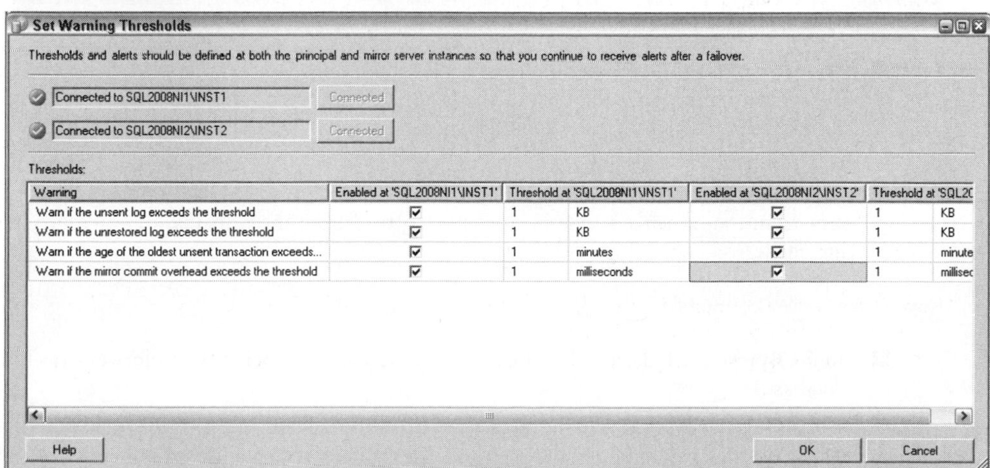

Warning	Enabled at 'SQL2008NI1\INST1'	Threshold at 'SQL2008NI1\INST1'		Enabled at 'SQL2008NI2\INST2'	Threshold at 'SQL2(	
Warn if the unsent log exceeds the threshold	☑	1	KB	☑	1	KB
Warn if the unrestored log exceeds the threshold	☑	1	KB	☑	1	KB
Warn if the age of the oldest unsent transaction exceeds...	☑	1	minutes	☑	1	minute
Warn if the mirror commit overhead exceeds the threshold	☑	1	milliseconds	☑	1	millisec

FIGURE 47-18

Database mirroring warnings

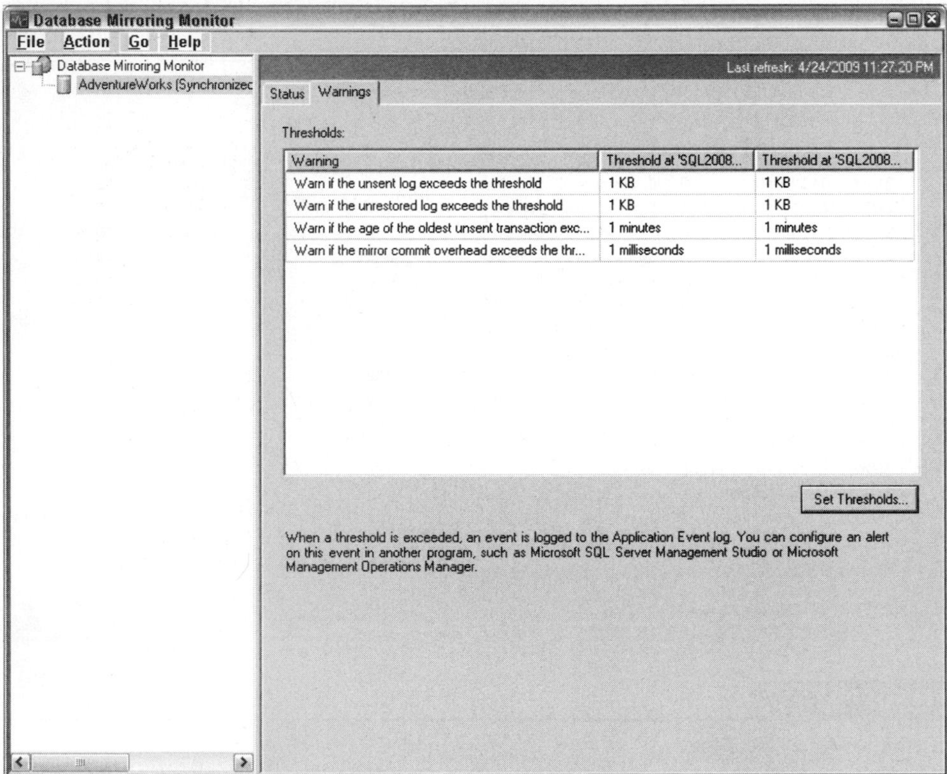

- **Log Compressed Bytes Sent/sec:** Indicates the number of compressed bytes of transaction log sent in the last second. To find the factor by which the transaction log stream has been compressed, also referred to as *log compression ratio*, divide the Log Bytes Sent/sec by Log Compressed Bytes Sent/sec.
- **Log Bytes Sent from Cache/sec:** Indicates how much of the transaction log bytes being sent from the principal to the mirror is being read from the principal's in-memory transaction log cache.

Key mirror server counters:

- **Redo Bytes/sec:** Indicates the rate at which log bytes are being rolled forward on the mirror database.
- **Redo Queue KB:** Indicates the total number of transaction log kilobytes that have not been rolled forward to the mirror database yet. To estimate the time it will take the mirror to redo the log, divide Redo Queue KB by Redo Bytes/sec.

- **Log Bytes Received/sec:** Indicates the rate at which the log bytes are received from the principal. To estimate the time it will take the mirror to catch up with the principal, divide Log Send Queue KB by Log Bytes Received/sec.
- **Log Compressed Bytes Received/sec:** Indicates the number of compressed transaction log bytes received in the last second.
- **Log Bytes Redone from Cache/sec:** Indicates the number of redone transaction log bytes that were read from the mirror's in-memory transaction log cache.

CROSS-REF For more information on all the performance counters available for database mirroring, refer to the SQL Server 2008 Books Online resource "SQL Server, Database Mirroring Object": `http://msdn.microsoft.com/en-us/library/ms189931.aspx`.

Monitoring using SQL Server Profiler

To capture the time taken to switch from the principal to the mirror, launch the SQL Server Profiler tool as follows:

1. From the Start menu, select Programs ➪ Microsoft SQL Server 2008 ➪ Performance Tools ➪ SQL Server Profiler.
2. Select New Trace from the File menu.
3. This is will bring up the Connect to Server dialog. Enter the principal server information and click Connect.
4. On the Trace Properties dialog, enter the trace name in the General tab.
5. On the Trace Properties dialog, click the Events Selection tab. Select the Show all events check box. Expand the Database event and select the Database Mirroring State Change check box. Select the columns *TextData* (gives a description of the database mirroring state change) and *StartTime* (indicates the time at which the event started).
6. Click Run to start the capture.

Pausing or Removing Database Mirroring

After configuring database mirroring you can pause, resume, or remove database mirroring. If database mirroring is affecting your application's performance, you may want to pause a database mirroring session. Pausing a database mirroring session causes the mirroring state to change to `SUSPENDED`. During this time, the principal will not send any transactions to the mirror, and its principal database's transaction log will continue to grow even if you have scheduled transaction log backups. The transaction log will not be truncated because it has to send the transactions to the mirror once the database mirroring session is resumed.

To pause a database mirroring session using SQL Server Management Studio:

1. In the Object Explorer on the principal server in SQL Server Management Studio, right-click on the principal database and select Properties.
2. On the Mirroring page (refer to Figure 47-13), click the Pause button.

3. You will be prompted for confirmation. Click Yes. This will pause the database mirroring session, changing the Pause button to Resume.
4. Click the Resume button to resume the database mirroring session.

To pause the database mirroring session for the `AdventureWorks` database in code, connect to either the principal or mirror server and execute the following:

```
ALTER DATABASE AdventureWorks SET PARTNER SUSPEND;
```

To resume the database mirroring session for the `AdventureWorks` database in code, connect to either the principal or mirror server and execute the following:

```
ALTER DATABASE AdventureWorks SET PARTNER RESUME;
```

To remove a database mirroring session using SQL Server Management Studio:

1. In the Object Explorer on the principal server in SQL Server Management Studio, right-click on the principal database and select Properties.
2. On the Mirroring page (refer to Figure 47-13), click the Remove Mirroring button.
3. You will be prompted for confirmation. Click Yes to confirm, which removes the database mirroring session. This means that the relationship between the partners and witness will be removed and each partner will be left with a separate copy of the database. The mirroring database will be left in the `RESTORING` state, as the database was created using the `RESTORE WITH NORECOVERY` command.
4. To resume a database mirroring session after removing it, you need to configure a new database mirroring session as explained earlier in this chapter.

To remove the database mirroring session for the `AdventureWorks` database in code, connect to either the principal or mirror server and execute the following:

```
ALTER DATABASE AdventureWorks SET PARTNER OFF;
```

Role Switching

Role switching in database mirroring is the process of changing the principal and mirror roles. Three types of role switching exist based on the database mirroring operating mode: automatic failover, manual failover, and forced failover.

Automatic failover is available only in synchronous mode with failover. In this mode, if the principal database becomes unavailable due to any failure and the mirror and witness servers are still connected and the mirroring state is `SYNCHRONIZED`, automatic failover will occur. Here is a high-level sequence of events that occur in an automatic failover scenario:

1. The principal database becomes unavailable due to some failure.
2. If the principal server is still available, the state of the principal database is changed to `DISCONNECTED` and all the clients are disconnected from the principal database.
3. The mirror and the witness server detect the failure.

NOTE **The default timeout for communication between the principal, mirror, and witness servers is 10 seconds. If the principal does not respond within the timeout period, it is considered to be down. If you are using high-safety mode, you can change the timeout period using the `ALTER DATABASE SET PARTNER TIMEOUT` command. The default timeout of 10 seconds works well for most environments. If you do want to change the timeout period, then it is recommended not to set it below 10 seconds, as this may cause false failures.**

4. The mirror server recovers the mirror database.
5. The mirror server forms a quorum with the witness server.
6. The mirror server becomes the new principal server and it brings the mirror database online as the new principal database.
7. The old principal server, when it is back online, takes the mirror role and the old principal database becomes the new mirror database and starts synchronizing with the new principal database.

Manual failover is available only in synchronous mode with and without failover. As the name suggests, you decide whether to switch the roles of the servers and manually failover the database. Manual failover is used for planned downtime (for example, during hardware or software upgrades). Manual failover is allowed only when the partners are connected and the mirroring state is `SYNCHRONIZED`. During a manual failover, the clients are disconnected from the principal database and the roles of the partners are switched.

To perform a manual failover using SQL Server Management Studio:

1. In the Object Explorer on the principal server in SQL Server Management Studio, right-click on the principal database and select Properties.
2. On the Mirroring page (refer to Figure 47-13), click the Failover button.
3. When prompted for confirmation, click Yes to perform a manual failover.

To perform a manual failover for the `AdventureWorks` database in code, connect to the principal server and execute the following:

```
ALTER DATABASE AdventureWorks SET PARTNER FAILOVER;
```

Forced failover, also referred to as *forced service (with possible data loss)* is available only in synchronous mode without failover and asynchronous mode. If the principal server is lost, the principal database will be unavailable to the clients. You can make the database available by manually forcing service on the mirror server by executing the following command on the mirror server:

```
ALTER DATABASE AdventureWorks SET PARTNER FORCE_SERVICE_ALLOW_DATA_LOSS;
```

This will bring the database online on the mirror server, which becomes the new principal server. When the old principal server becomes available, it will automatically assume the mirror role but the database mirroring session will be suspended. To resume the database mirroring session, follow the steps discussed earlier in the chapter.

After any type of failover, clients must reconnect to the new principal database. If your applications use Microsoft ADO.NET or SQL Native Client to connect to a database, then in case of a database mirroring failover, the applications can automatically redirect the clients to the current principal database. You must specify the initial principal server and database and failover partner server in the connection string. The failover partner in the connection string is used as an alternate server name if the connection to the initial principal server fails. If your applications do not use Microsoft ADO.NET or SQL Native Client automatic redirection, you need to use other methods such as network load balancing (NLB), a Domain Name System (DNS) alias, or custom code that will enable your application to failover.

After the role-switching process is completed, verify that any database objects such as logins, jobs, maintenance plans, SSIS packages, and linked servers that reside outside the mirror database are created on the mirror server. For example, if the logins are not created on the mirror server, then users will not be able to connect and you will still have a server down situation.

Best Practice

I highly recommend thoroughly executing the role-switching steps and documenting them prior to needing to failover to the mirror server. Failure to do this can significantly increase downtime and complexity when you actually need to failover to the mirror server.

Summary

Database mirroring is an inexpensive software-based solution to achieve high database availability. Database mirroring works by transferring transaction log records from the production database on one SQL Server to a mirror database on another SQL Server over the network, either synchronously or asynchronously. Asynchronous database mirroring provides the best performance but has the potential for data loss and does not support automatic failover. Synchronous database mirroring provides a higher level of data protection than asynchronous mode and provides automatic and manual failover options at the cost of reduced application performance.

At first glance, database mirroring may appear to be better than log shipping but it is not a replacement for log shipping. Each solution has unique features, and depending on your business requirements you may need to select one or both solutions. For example, log shipping supports multiple copies of the production databases, but database mirroring allows only one copy of the production database. If you need multiple copies of the production database and the features of database mirroring, then you can implement database mirroring and log shipping. Database mirroring also complements existing failover clustering implementations.

As with any other solution, take a performance baseline of your environment before and after configuring database mirroring, and use your performance data to help you determine whether you should use database mirroring or whether you should use synchronous mode or asynchronous mode in your production environment.

The next chapter discusses failover clustering, which is the only Microsoft SQL Server 2008 high-availability solution that provides both high availability for an entire instance of SQL Server and the automatic failover option.

Chapter 48

Clustering

Remember the sitcoms in the 1970s with identical twins? They could switch clothes and fool the teacher, or wear the same clothes and switch boyfriends halfway through a date. I've wondered what life would have been like if I had a twin. I suspect that we would have gotten in more trouble together than I got into alone. Having twins brings a whole new set of "opportunities."

SQL Server failover clustering is like having identical twin SQL Servers. They share the same clothes, and look exactly alike. When one gets into trouble, the other can step right in and continue the job with barely a hiccup. Similarly, like human twins, SQL Server failover clusters bring their own set of challenges. This chapter introduces the SQL Server twins and walks through all their twin tricks so you won't be caught by their jokes.

IN THIS CHAPTER

SQL Server 2008 Failover Clustering Basics

SQL Server 2008 failover clustering is built on top of Windows failover clustering to provide high availability for the entire SQL Server 2008 instance. A high-availability SQL Server solution masks the effects of a hardware or software failure and maintains the availability of SQL Server so that any downtime for users is minimized.

Achieving 100 percent uptime is desirable but virtually impossible, if for no other reason than that at certain times, a security patch or service pack must be applied to the production server to make it secure and stable. This is where the concept of "nines" comes into play. The percentage of uptime all companies should strive for is some variation of 99.*x* percent where *x* is the specified number of nines. Five nines is 99.999 percent uptime for your server, which is considered to be the ultimate in availability, as it means about five minutes of total downtime in a calendar year. Note that not all downtime is planned. We all know that even with the best storage subsystems, disks fail or network interface cards fail or there is a power failure. Also, memory leaks in the application or bugs in the OS or SQL Server can cause a failure. Three nines, which means about nine hours of downtime in a calendar year, is a more practical number to strive for.

What's New in SQL Server 2008 failover clustering?

SQL Server 2008 failover clustering has changed considerably to provide better supportability and reliability and higher availability. The setup architecture has changed completely to enable features that were not possible in earlier versions of SQL Server. There is a completely new setup user interface that supports both SQL Server and Analysis Services failover clustering.

Here are some of the key new features in SQL Server 2008 failover clustering. These features are discussed in detail in the section "Enhancements in SQL Server 2008 failover clustering."

- Reliable setup experience
- Reduced downtime with rolling upgrade and patching
- High availability with Add/Remove node operations
- Integrated with Windows Server 2008 failover cluster features
- Positioned to enable Sysprep and slipstream

SQL Server 2008 failover clustering, shown in Figure 48-1, consists of the following:

- Two or more cluster servers, known as *nodes*
- Shared disk storage
- Two or more networks
- Virtual SQL IP address and SQL Network Name for clients to connect
- Windows Server 2003/2008 Failover Clustering

A SQL Server 2008 failover clustering instance appears on the network as a stand-alone SQL Server 2008 instance, but it has functionality that provides failover from one node to another if the current node becomes unavailable. The failover is handled by the Windows Server failover cluster, which detects that the current node is no longer available and then accordingly handles the failover of the SQL Server to another node. All clients are disconnected during the failover and need to reconnect following it. However, they connect to the same "virtual SQL network name" or "virtual SQL IP address" as before.

Before investing in a SQL Server 2008 failover cluster solution it is very important to know how it works, what it can do, and what it cannot do. Many DBAs are familiar with Oracle clustering and may have different expectations from Microsoft failover clustering. Microsoft failover clustering provides the following benefits:

- **High availability:** Microsoft Windows failover clustering provides protection from machine-level failures such as hardware and software failures, service failures, and site-level failures such as hurricanes, fires, and so on. When a system or application in the cluster fails, the cluster software detects the failure and automatically restarts the failed application on a surviving server. It also allows software/hardware upgrades with minimum downtime.

- **Improved manageability:** It enables managing services within the entire cluster, as if managing a single computer. Applications can be moved to different servers within the cluster. You can manually balance the server workload and free servers for planned maintenance. Using the Cluster Administrator tool in Windows 2003 Failover Cluster or the Failover Cluster Management tool in Windows 2008 Failover Cluster, you can monitor the status of the cluster, all nodes, and resources from anywhere on the network.
- **Increased scalability:** The cluster can grow to meet increased demands. For example, when the load for an application exceeds the resources of the cluster node, it supports the addition of processors, memory, and nodes if required.
- **Instance-level redundancy and automatic failover for SQL Server instances:** When a node or resource (disk, IP address, or network name) fails, Windows failover clustering detects it and automatically restarts the entire SQL server instance on the other node. SQL Server failover clustering is the only high-availability option offered by Microsoft that provides instance-level redundancy. Database mirroring, log shipping, and replication all provide database redundancy, not instance-level redundancy.

FIGURE 48-1

Typical SQL Server 2008 failover cluster

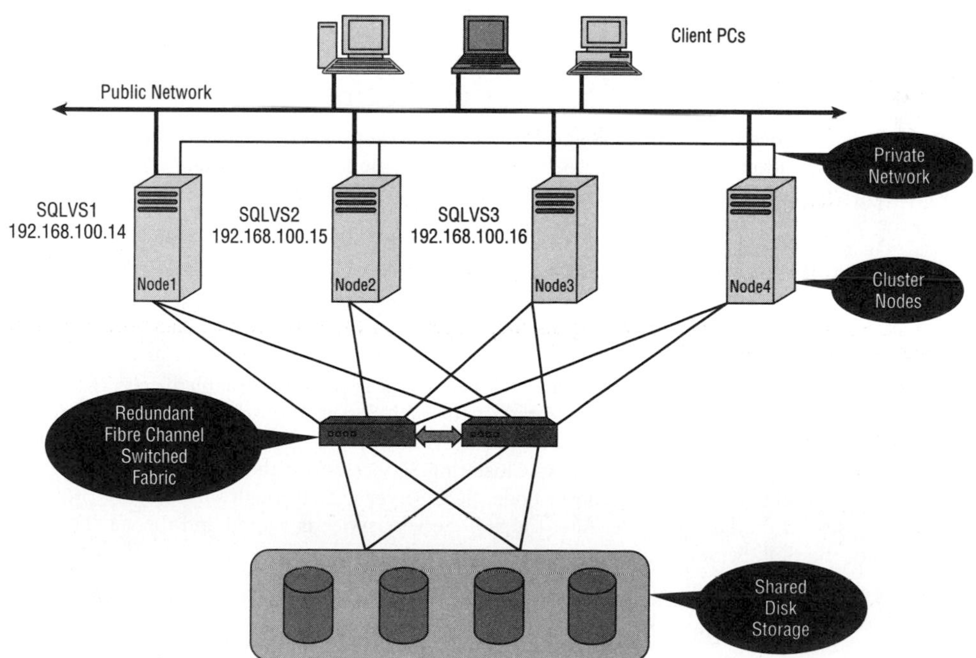

Windows failover clustering is *not* designed to do the following:

- **Provide continuous connectivity:** During the failover process, any active SQL Server client connections are broken. Therefore, all noncommitted transactions need to be performed again unless the transactions are handled within the application. If the application is cluster-aware, the failover is completely transparent.
- **Protect data:** Implementing SQL Server 2008 failure clustering does not obviate the need to take backups or run consistency checks (`DBCC CHECKDB`). Because failover clustering does not protect data, it is still necessary to run backups and restore them on another server, run `DBCC CHECKDB`, etc.
- **Protect a shared disk array from failing:** Failover clustering is not designed to protect against a disk failure. It is recommended to combine failover clustering with hardware redundancy such as SAN to provide data loss protection.
- Prevent hack attacks
- Prevent network failures
- Protect the server from other potential disasters, such as power outages
- **Provide load balancing:** Failover clustering is not like network load balancing. It does not provide any automatic balancing, although DBAs can manually balance the load using Cluster Administrator.

NOTE **Microsoft SQL Server 2008 failover clustering is part of an entire strategy needed to help reduce downtime. Having a failover cluster does not mean that you have a complete high-availability solution.**

How SQL Server 2008 failover clustering works

The clustered nodes use a heartbeat signal to check whether each node is alive, at both the Windows and SQL Server levels. At the Windows level, the cluster nodes are in constant communication, thereby validating the health of all the nodes. After installing SQL Server 2008 failover clustering, the nodes that run the SQL Server resource perform two types of checks:

- `LooksAlive`: Every five seconds, it checks whether the SQL Server service is running.
- `IsAlive`: Every 60 seconds, it runs a simple Transact-SQL command `SELECT @@servername` against the SQL Server to determine whether the server can respond.

If the `LooksAlive` check fails, then the `IsAlive` check is performed immediately. If the `IsAlive` check fails, then, by default, it will try to restart the SQL Server 2008 resource on the same node once. If it fails to restart, then it will failover the SQL Server 2008 group to another node and restart it on the other node. During failover, Windows Clustering Services stops the SQL Server service on the current node and starts it on the failover node. SQL Server goes through the recovery process to start the databases on the failover node. After the SQL Server service is started and the `master` database is recovered, the SQL Server resource is considered to be online.

NOTE **The `LooksAlive` and `IsAlive` setting should not be touched, and the query `select @@servername` that `IsAlive` runs against the SQL Server cannot be changed.**

Even after a SQL Server resource is online, it may not be ready to accept connections yet, as user databases may still be in recovery. Just like in a stand-alone SQL Server recovery, the length of the recovery process depends on how much activity needs to be rolled forward and rolled back on startup. SQL Server 2008 has two important features, *fast recovery* and *instant file initialization*, that can reduce these delays. Fast recovery makes the database available after the REDO phase and during the UNDO phase before it completes. Instant file initialization allows initializing the data files instantly without filling the space with zeros. This feature helps TEMPDB initialization time, as it is recreated every time SQL Server is started.

NOTE **The fast recovery feature is available only in SQL Server 2008 Enterprise Edition. SQL Server 2008 Standard edition does not let users access the database until recovery completes both of the REDO and UNDO phases.**

Instant file initialization is available in all editions of SQL Server 2008. To use this feature, assign the Windows Perform Volume Maintenance Tasks security privilege to the SQL Server 2008 service account.

SQL Server 2008 failover clustering topologies

SQL Server 2008 failover clustering supports many topologies, as shown in Figure 48-2.

FIGURE 48-2

SQL Server 2008 failover cluster topologies

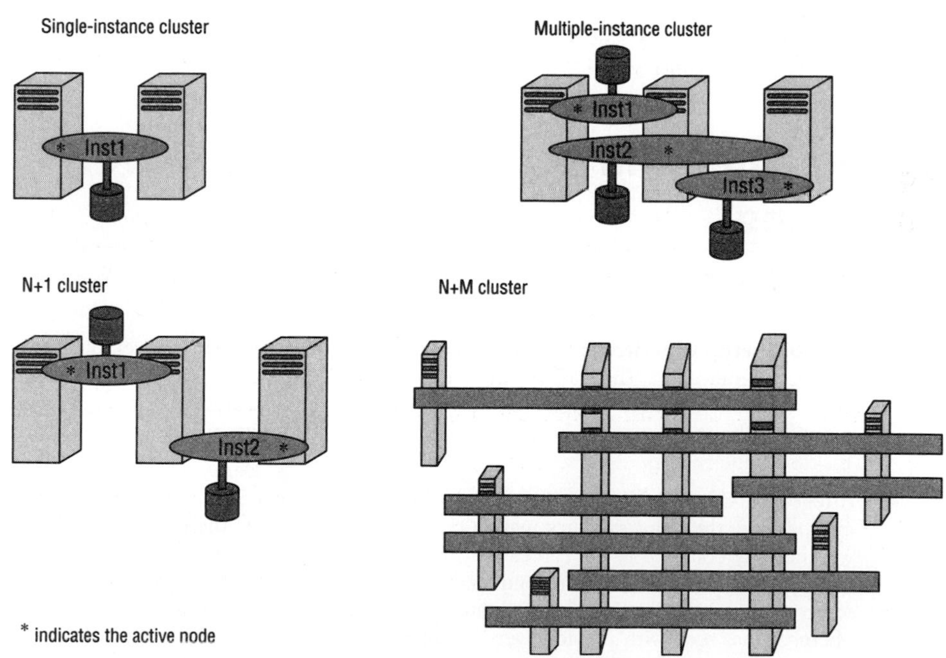

- **Single-instance cluster:** Replaces the Active/Passive terminology. A single-instance cluster has only one active instance of SQL Server owned by a single cluster node, and all other nodes of the cluster are in a wait state. Another node is enabled either in the event of a failure on the active node or during a manual failover for maintenance.

- **Multiple-instance cluster:** Replaces the Active/Active terminology and has more than one SQL Server instance. SQL Server 2008 Enterprise Edition supports up to 25 instances on the same cluster, and SQL Server 2008 Standard Edition is limited to 16 instances on the same cluster. Although 25 instances is the maximum number supported (in the Enterprise Edition), I have not seen any cluster with that many instances. I have seen a two-node cluster with 13 SQL Server instances, and that cluster had many performance issues because it was not properly designed and did not have enough resources for all the instances. The maximum number of instances will be limited to the resources (processor and memory) on the cluster nodes.

NOTE **A multiple-instance cluster is sometimes misunderstood to represent some kind of load-balancing solution for SQL Server 2008. However, this is not true, as the different instances have distinct sets of databases, and there is no shared state between the SQL Server 2008 instances.**

- **N+1 cluster:** Has N active nodes and one passive node. For example, if you need three SQL Server 2008 failover clustering instances, then the best scaling solution would require a four-node cluster. Three of the four nodes would run one SQL Server 2008 failover clustering instance, while the fourth node would provide the failover. This configuration enables each of the SQL Servers to use the maximum resources on each node, still providing failover in case one node goes down. SQL Server 2008 Enterprise Edition supports up to 16 nodes on a Windows Server 2008 failover cluster, and SQL Server 2008 Standard Edition is limited to two nodes.
- **N+M cluster:** A variation of the N+1 cluster that has more than one passive node, which could be used in the event of failover. The N+M cluster has N nodes hosting applications and M passive nodes that are spare.

Enhancements in SQL Server 2008 Failover Clustering

SQL Server 2008 failover clustering has a lot of enhancements compared to previous versions of SQL Server failover clustering:

- **Reliable setup experience:** The setup process in SQL Server 2008 failover clustering has changed significantly. The fragile remote execution has been removed, which means there is no need for Task Scheduler on remote nodes. By removing the remote execution, Microsoft has simplified the installation process and eliminated the possibility of installation failures due to Task Scheduler issues.
- **Integrated OS and SQL checks:** Before actually installing a SQL Server 2008 failover clustering instance, the setup executes many OS and SQL rules on all the cluster nodes to determine whether any common issues can cause the setup to fail. If an issue is found, then it clearly displays the issue along with recommendations. This enables failures to be corrected and the setup to continue. This feature eliminates more than 50 percent of failed installations that Microsoft has seen with previous versions of SQL Server failover clustering.
- **Multiple drive selection:** SQL Server 2000 and 2005 failover clustering allows the selection of only one drive for the databases during setup. After setup, additional drives need to be added, which requires taking the SQL Server resource offline, thereby introducing downtime. With SQL Server 2008 failover clustering, the setup allows selecting multiple drives and specifying different drives for SQL Server data files, log files, tempdb, and backup.

- **Independent of MSDTC:** Unlike SQL Server 2005, a SQL Server 2008 failover clustering installation does not require configuring MSDTC as a clustered resource.

NOTE **SQL Server 2008 setup checks for MSDTC and displays a warning if it does not find it running on the node where setup is running. If you are not using distributed transactions, then you do not need to configure MSDTC and can safely ignore this warning. People have varying opinions about MSDTC. Some believe that MSDTC should be configured as a clustered resource before installing SQL Server 2008 failover clustering — perhaps because of their experience with SQL Server 2005, which required this. Or maybe they saw the warning and interpreted it as a requirement. However, if it were mandatory, then the setup would display a failure and not a warning.**

To configure MSDTC as a clustered resource, a unique IP address resource, a unique Network Name resource, and a unique shared disk (min size 500 MB) are required. Why waste these resources if you know you won't be using distributed transactions? If at a later date you need distributed transactions, then you can configure MSDTC at that time.

- **Full-text and replication installed as part of the database engine:** There is no option to uncheck full-text and replication on a cluster. This is really nice, as in previous versions of SQL Server failover clustering it was very difficult, if not impossible, to add full-text and replication after the installation on a cluster. Full-text has undergone considerable changes and is integrated within the SQL Server service itself. This means that full-text service is no longer installed as a separate service; rather, it is part of the SQL Server 2008 engine itself. Therefore, there is no full-text resource in a SQL Server 2008 cluster group after the setup is completed. Also, when upgrading a SQL Server 2005 failover cluster to SQL Server 2008, full-text resource is removed during the upgrade.
- **Positioned to enable Sysprep and slipstream:** With previous versions of SQL Server, this was not even possible. With the new SQL Server 2008 setup architecture, Microsoft will be able to add this frequently requested feature in the future. The slipstream feature is made available in SQL Server 2008 Service Pack 1. This feature provides the capability to merge RTM and patches (service packs and cumulative updates) and perform a single install. Sysprep is still not supported in RTM or SP1.
- **High availability with Add/Remove node operations:** Starting with SQL Server 2008, adding or removing a node from the SQL Server 2008 failover clustering instance does not affect the node on which SQL Server 2008 is running. This increases the availability of the SQL Server 2008 failover clustering instance.
- **Reduced downtime with rolling upgrade and patching:** For the first time, SQL Server 2008 failover clustering allows rolling upgrade and patching, which significantly increases SQL Server availability. In client tests, in-place SQL Server 2008 failover clustering rolling upgrade processes incurred an average of approximately two to three minutes of downtime. This is a huge improvement compared to previous versions of SQL Server.
- **Integration with Windows Server 2008 failover clustering features:** SQL Server 2008 failover clustering depends on Windows failover clustering, and with the introduction of Windows Server 2008, numerous features have been added. SQL Server 2008 failover clustering is integrated with Windows Server 2008 features, offering the following key benefits:
  - **Certified cluster solution not required:** All the components need to be logoed for Windows Server 2008 and the cluster needs to pass all the Cluster Validation tests included in Windows Server 2008 failover cluster. If any of the cluster validation tests fail, SQL Server 2008 failover clustering will detect it before the actual install, and setup will proceed only after the issue is fixed and all the cluster validation tests have passed.

NOTE **If you are implementing SQL Server 2008 failover clustering on a Windows Server 2003 failover cluster, then you still need a certified cluster solution in the Windows Server Catalog.**

- **Domain groups not required for setup:** To install SQL Server 2005 failover clustering, you first needed to ask your network administrator to create a domain group and place the SQL service accounts in that group. Only then could you proceed with installing SQL Server 2005 failover clustering. Now there is no need for domain groups in order to install SQL Server 2008 failover clustering on Windows Server 2008. You may instead choose to opt for Service Security IDs (SIDs). SIDs is a Windows Server 2008 feature. This means that installing SQL Server 2008 failover clustering on Windows Server 2003 still requires domain groups.
- **DHCP and IPv6 are supported by SQL Server 2008:** The new features of Windows Server 2008 failover clustering, such as DHCP support and IPv6, are supported by SQL Server 2008. Although DHCP is supported in Windows Server 2008 failover clustering, I still recommend using static IP addresses.
- **Node support:** SQL Server 2008 failover clustering supports the maximum number of nodes (16) supported by Windows Server 2008 failover clustering.

NOTE **SQL Server 2008 failover clustering does not support having `OR` dependency between IP addresses (that is, nodes in different subnets) even though Windows Server 2008 failover clustering supports it. This basically leaves the same support for geographically dispersed clusters in SQL Server 2008 failover clustering on Windows Server 2008 as SQL Server 2005 failover clustering on Windows Server 2003.**

SQL Server 2008 Failover Clustering Setup

There are two options for installing a SQL Server 2008 failover clustering instance:

- Integrated installation
- Advanced/Enterprise installation

Integrated installation consists of two steps:

1. Create a single-node SQL Server 2008 failover cluster — During this step, setup is run on the first node of the cluster to create a single-node SQL Server 2008 failover clustering instance. After this step, the SQL Server 2008 service is up and running and is ready to accept client connections. A single-node SQL Server 2008 failover cluster is a fully functional cluster except that it does not provide high availability, as it has only one cluster node.
2. Add the nodes — During this step, setup is run again on each additional cluster node that needs to be added to the single-node failover cluster.

Advanced/Enterprise installation also consists of two steps:

1. Prepare step — During this step, all cluster nodes are defined and prepared. After this step, SQL Server 2008 is not functional and cannot accept client connections.
2. Complete step — After the prepare step is run, the complete step is run on the cluster node that owns the shared disk to complete the SQL Server 2008 failover clustering instance and make it operational. After this step, SQL Server 2008 service is fully functional.

Either option can be used to install a multi-node SQL Server 2008 failover cluster.

Integrated installation is the most popular option for installing SQL Server 2008 failover clustering, especially when an operational SQL Server 2008 failover clustering instance is needed after installing on the node. Additional nodes can be added at any time without causing any downtime.

Planning SQL Server 2008 failover clustering

Before installing a new SQL Server 2008 failover clustering instance, I highly recommend spending a significant amount of time on planning to achieve a high-availability solution. Just installing a SQL Server 2008 failover cluster does not guarantee a high-availability solution. It is just one component of your solution.

Because a SQL Server 2008 failover cluster runs on top of a Windows Server failover cluster, ensure that you have a fully functional Windows Server failover cluster and that there are no errors in the Windows event logs (Application and System logs) on any cluster nodes.

CROSS-REF **Refer to the following Microsoft's whitepapers for creating and configuring the Windows Server failover cluster.**

A step-by-step guide for a Windows Server 2003 failover cluster: `www.microsoft.com/downloads/details.aspx?familyid=96F76ED7-9634-4300-9159-89638F4B4EF7&displaylang=en`

A step-by-step guide for a Windows Server 2008 failover cluster: `www.microsoft.com/windowsserver2008/en/us/clustering-resources.aspx`

NOTE **A SQL Server 2008 failover clustering instance can run on either a Windows Server 2003 SP2 or Windows Server 2008 failover cluster. SQL Server 2008 failover clustering is not supported on Windows Server 2000. If you are installing a new Windows failover cluster, I recommend implementing a Windows Server 2008 failover cluster because it has more enhancements than a Windows Server 2003 failover cluster. For example, with a Windows Server 2008 failover cluster, you no longer need to purchase a certified cluster solution. Now you can build your own cluster with the hardware you might already have purchased. To be supported, all cluster components must be individually certified for Windows Server 2008, and the cluster must pass all tests in the Cluster Validation Wizard.**

Once you have a fully functional Windows Server failover cluster, make sure that you have everything you need to install a SQL Server 2008 failover clustering instance.

A single SQL Server 2008 failover clustering instance requires the following:

- **Unique IP address:** This is the SQL Server IP address that the clients will use to connect to the SQL Server. SQL Server 2008 allows using multiple IP addresses on separate networks, but it does not allow `OR` dependency even though Windows Server 2008 failover clustering supports `OR` dependency. SQL Server 2008 supports `AND` dependency. This means that if multiple IP addresses are used, then all IP addresses must be online in order for SQL Server to be online. If any one of the IP addresses goes offline, then SQL Server will go offline, too. As mentioned earlier, a SQL Server 2008 failover cluster installed on a Windows Server 2008 failover cluster supports DHCP. A dedicated IP is still recommended, though.
- **Unique network name:** This is the SQL network name that the clients will use to connect to the SQL Server. If this is a named instance of SQL Server, then you also need the instance name. For example, consider SQL2008\INST1, where SQL2008 is the SQL network name and INST1 is the instance name. Clients will need to use SQL2008\INST1 to connect to this SQL Server named instance.

- **At least one unique shared disk:** This shared disk will be used for storing the SQL Server databases. Ideally, you should have at least three shared disks: one for data files, one for log files, and a third for `tempdb` files. For important databases, you may want to have separate drives for their log files. I do not recommend using the Quorum drive for storing SQL Server databases. If you are planning to have multiple SQL Server instances, then each instance will need its own dedicated shared disk. SQL Server failover clustering instances cannot use the same shared disk, as it is possible to do with stand-alone SQL Server instances. Also, each shared disk needs a drive letter.
- **Mount points:** With large databases (usually databases that are more than a terabyte in size) and with multiple SQL Server instances, multiple disks are usually needed, and it is very easy to run out of drive letters. In such situations, you can use mount points, as SQL Server 2008 failover cluster supports mount points. A mount point is a drive that is mapped to a folder and is assigned a drive path instead of a drive letter. Therefore, you can surpass the 26 drive-letter limitation by using mount points. When using mount points, note the following:
  - Make sure that each mount point appears as a cluster resource.
  - The root disk must be added as a dependency for the mount points.
  - Each mount point must be added as a SQL Server dependency. Failure to do this may result in data corruption during failover.
  - Do not use the root directory of the mounted drive to store SQL Server databases. Instead, create another folder on the root directory and then place the databases in that directory. Similarly, do not install SQL Server 2008 on the root directory of the mounted drive. Otherwise, SQL Server may not start.
- **SQL Server service accounts:** Each SQL Server clustered service account needs a domain account. For security reasons, it is best to use a separate domain account for each SQL Server service account. Table 48-1 lists the required permissions for SQL Server service accounts.

Best Practice

Do not give domain administrator or local administrator rights to SQL Server service accounts. It is neither necessary nor recommended.

The Lock Pages in Memory policy is disabled by default. This policy determines which accounts can use a process to keep data in physical memory, thereby preventing the system from paging the data to virtual memory on disk. This policy should be enabled on 32-bit SQL Server 2008 only when you need to use AWE memory. On 64-bit SQL Server 2008, only Enterprise Edition can use the Lock Pages in Memory policy. On 64-bit SQL Server 2008, enable Lock Pages in Memory only after thorough testing.

TABLE 48-1

Security Requirements for SQL Server Service Accounts

Local Security Policy	SQL Server	SQL Server Agent	Analysis Services
Adjust memory quotas for a process	Yes	Yes	No
Bypass traverse checking	Yes	Yes	No
Log on as a batch job	Yes	Yes	No
Log on as a service	Yes	Yes	Yes
Replace a process-level token	Yes	Yes	No
Lock Pages in Memory	Yes[1]	No	No
Perform Volume Maintenance Tasks	Yes[2]	No	No

[1]For 32-bit SQL Server, Lock Pages in Memory is required for a SQL Server service account only if you are using Address Windowing Extensions (AWE) memory.
[2]This is required only if you want to use "instant file initialization."

- **Domain groups:** If you are installing a SQL Server 2008 failover cluster on Windows Server 2003, you need domain groups for the SQL Server service accounts. The domain groups control access to registry keys, files, SQL Server objects, and other cluster resources. SQL Server service accounts must be manually added to domain groups before the setup. There is no rule as to how many domain groups need to be created. Some clients choose to use one domain group for all the SQL Server service accounts for simplicity, while others use separate domain groups for each SQL Server service account for security isolation. It is recommended to add the domain groups to the local permissions on the cluster nodes and not give the local permissions directly to the SQL Server service accounts. If you are installing a SQL Server 2008 failover clustering instance on a Windows Server 2008, you can now use Service SIDs instead of domain groups. Service SIDs functionality was introduced in Windows Vista and Windows Server 2008. It allows the provisioning of access control lists (ACLs) to resources and permissions directly to a Windows service.
- **Domain controller:** A SQL Server 2008 failover clustering instance needs a domain controller and is not supported on a cluster node that is a domain controller. It is recommended to have redundant domain controllers, as a single domain controller is a single point of failure; and in a high-availability solution we want to eliminate all single points of failure.
- **Installation media:** The SQL Server 2008 failover clustering feature is available in Enterprise Edition, Developer Edition, Enterprise Evaluation Edition, and Standard Edition. Developer and Enterprise Editions have the same features, but Developer Edition can be used for development purposes only. Enterprise Evaluation Edition is used for short-term testing, as it expires after 180 days. Standard Edition and Enterprise Edition can be used for production purposes.

- Standard Edition is limited to only two nodes, whereas Enterprise Edition supports the maximum of 16 nodes on a Windows Server 2008 failover cluster. Also, Enterprise Edition supports up to 25 instances of SQL Server 2008 on the same cluster, while Standard Edition is limited to 16 instances. Apart from these limitations, SQL Server 2008 Standard Edition does not have a lot of high-availability features such as fast recovery, online indexing, online restore, data compression, backup compression, and many more features that are available only in SQL Server 2008 Enterprise Edition and are very important for highly available clustering solutions.
- SQL Server 2008 failover clustering is supported on x86, x64, and IA64 platforms. The platform for SQL Server 2008 will depend on the Windows Server platform. If you have a Windows Server 2008 x64 failover cluster, then you need SQL Server 2008 x64. SQL Server 2008 x32 failover clustering is not supported on Windows Server 2008 x64. Similarly, if you have a Windows Server 2008 IA64 cluster, then you will need SQL Server 2008 IA64.

SQL Server 2008 prerequisites

Before actually starting the SQL Server 2008 failover cluster setup, the following SQL Server 2008 prerequisites need to be installed on all the cluster nodes:

- Microsoft .NET Framework 3.5 SP1
- Microsoft Windows Installer (MSI) 4.5
- Microsoft Windows hotfix 937444 for FILESTREAM (only for Windows Server 2003 cluster)

The first two prerequisites (.NET Framework and MSI) are located in the installation media under the `redist` folder under the respective platforms. For example, .NET Framework 3.5 SP1 (`dotNetFx35setup.exe`) for the x64 platform is located in the `SQL Server 2008 Developer Binaries\x64\redist\DotNetFrameworks` folder. Microsoft .NET Framework 3.5 SP1 needs to be pre-installed on all platforms except for Windows Server 2003 Itanium (IA64). For Windows Server 2003 IA64, install .NET Framework 2.0 SP2, which is also located in the installation media.

CROSS-REF **If you are installing a SQL Server 2008 failover cluster on a Windows Server 2003, you need to download hotfix 937444 from `http://support.microsoft.com/kb/937444` and install it on all cluster nodes prior to installing SQL Server 2008 failover clustering.**

Best Practice

To minimize downtime, I recommend the following: Install the prerequisites on passive cluster nodes (meaning nodes where no services are running) first, reboot the node, failover the services to a recently updated cluster node, and then install them on the remaining passive cluster node. For example, say you have a three-node Windows Server 2008 failover cluster with SQL1 and SQL2 running on Node1 and Node2, respectively. First install the prerequisites on the passive node (Node3), reboot Node3, and then move either

continued

continued

SQL1 or SQL2 to Node3. Suppose you move SQL2 to Node3, install the prerequisites on Node2, and reboot. Then move SQL1 to Node2, install the prerequisites on Node1, and reboot. This technique will minimize the downtime and give you more control over moving the services from one node to another. Each failover will incur a downtime of approximately 15 seconds, but because you are controlling the failover, you can schedule it properly.

Apart from the prerequisites listed previously, I highly recommend installing the latest SQL Server 2008 Setup Support files. This will enable you to take advantage of known setup fixes that are available and avoid any known issues. To install the latest SQL Server 2008 Setup Support files, download the latest cumulative update for SQL Server 2008 and install it. Note that installing the cumulative update before installing SQL Server 2008 installs only the latest SQL Server 2008 Setup Support files and not the full cumulative update. The next time you are installing SQL Server 2008, setup will see the latest setup support files and use them.

As the slipstream feature is available in SQL Server 2008 Service Pack 1 (SP1), you can slipstream SP1 with SQL Server 2008 RTM and install both of them in a single installation. This approach is even better than installing the latest cumulative update, as with a slipstream install of SQL Server 2008 + SP1 you proactively have the fixes not only to the setup but also in other components of SQL Server 2008.

There is no need to reboot the cluster node after installing each prerequisite. To minimize the number of reboots, apply all the prerequisites on the cluster node and then reboot it once.

Creating a single-node SQL Server 2008 failover cluster

After you have finished planning and have applied the prerequisites, you are ready to install a SQL Server 2008 failover cluster. As discussed earlier, a SQL Server 2008 failover cluster setup performs local installation; it has removed remote execution. So the first step is to create a single-node SQL Server 2008 failover cluster. Here are the step-by-step instructions:

1. Launch the SQL Server Installation Center on the cluster node that owns the shared disk resources that you want to use for SQL Server 2008 databases. To launch the SQL Server Installation Center, double-click `setup.exe` on the root of the SQL Server 2008 installation media.
2. The following message will be displayed if Microsoft .NET Framework 3.5 is not installed:

   ```
   SQL Server 2008 Setup requires Microsoft .NET Framework 3.5 to be
   installed. Download and install .NET Framework from
   http://www.microsoft.com/net/ and then rerun Setup
   OK.
   ```
3. Click OK and install all the prerequisites that were discussed in the previous section.
4. Once all the prerequisites are installed, SQL Server Installation Center, shown in Figure 48-3, will be displayed.

FIGURE 48-3

Select Installation from the left side of the SQL Server Installation Center

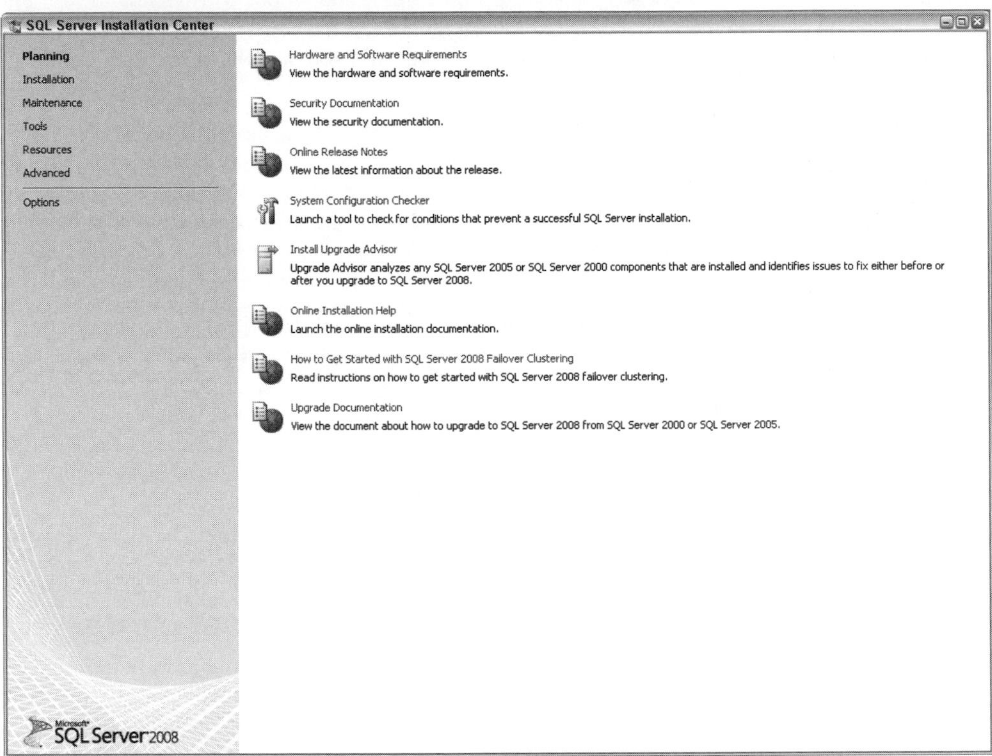

5. Click Installation on the left-hand side of the SQL Server Installation Center. Select "New SQL Server failover cluster installation" to start the single-node SQL Server 2008 failover cluster, as shown in Figure 48-4.

6. Now the wizard runs setup support rules (see Figure 48-5) to identify problems that might occur when setup support files are installed. For example, the wizard checks whether the cluster node has the minimum operating system version, among other checks. The Setup Support Rules page displays all the checks that were performed and gives more information on checking the status. Verify that all the checks pass before proceeding to the next step.

7. On the Setup Support Files page, click Install (see Figure 48-6).

FIGURE 48-4

Launching the wizard to install single-node SQL Server 2008 failover cluster

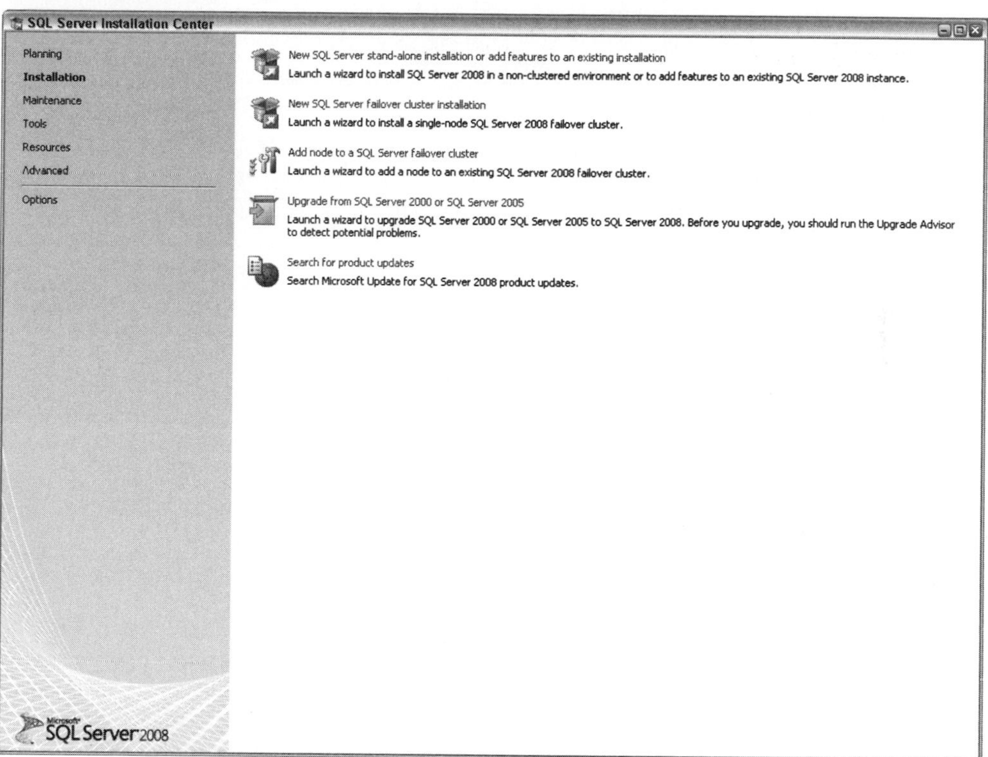

8. On the Setup Support Rules page (see Figure 48-7), the wizard again runs multiple checks to identify problems that might occur when setup support files are installed. Verify that all the checks pass before proceeding to the next step. Click status (Passed, Failed, or Warning) to see more information on the check.

9. On the Product Key page, either select the free edition or enter the product key for production SQL Server 2008.

NOTE **The Product Key page offers Express or Express with Advanced Services editions as selections. Do not select these editions, as they do not support failover clustering and the setup will fail.**

10. On the License Terms page, read the licensing terms and check the box to accept them.

FIGURE 48-5

Wizard running the first set of Setup Support Rules

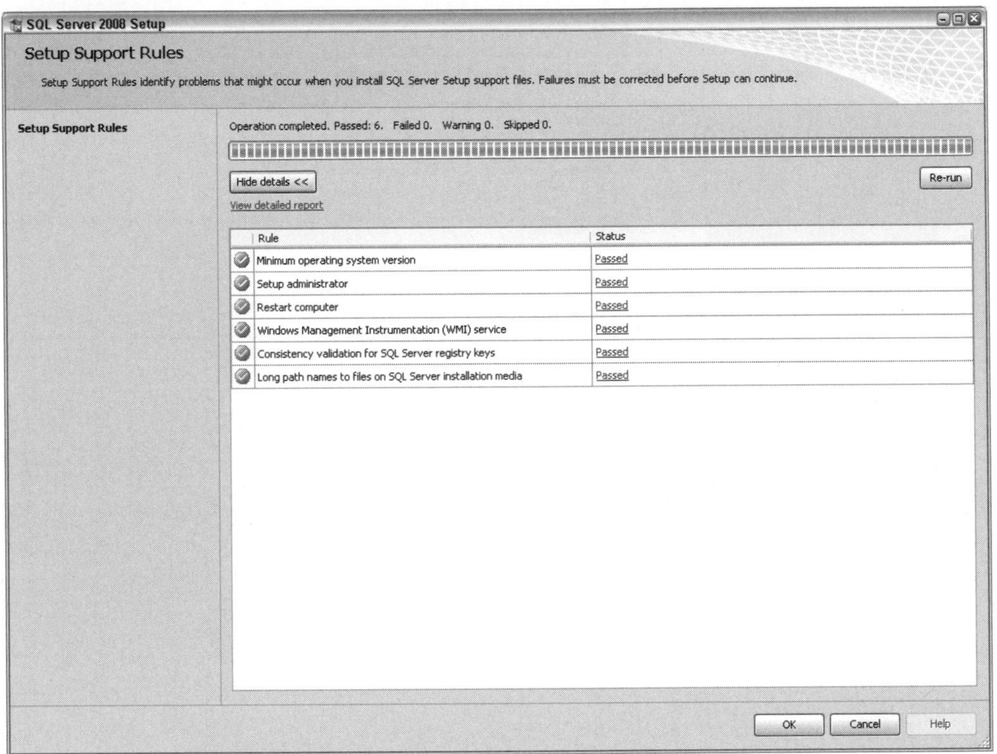

11. The Feature Selection page, shown in Figure 48-8, enables you to select the features you want to install. Only Database Engine Services and Analysis Services features support failover clustering. Other features are stand-alone and will run only on the current cluster node. To install a clustered SQL Server 2008 database engine instance, check Database Engine Services. Note that SQL Server Replication and Full-Text Search are automatically selected when Database Engine Services is checked. There is no option to deselect them in a clustered SQL Server 2008 instance. To install a clustered Analysis Services 2008 instance, check Analysis Services. To install the SQL Server Management tools like SQL Server Management Studio, check Management Tools.

NOTE **If you need any of the shared features on the cluster nodes (e.g., you may need SQL Server Management Studio), then I highly recommend checking it in the Feature Selection page and installing the required shared features along with clustered installation of SQL Server or Analysis**

Server. If you do not install the shared features now, you can still install them later but the installation is not very straightforward.

For one, to install the shared features later, you need to select "New SQL Server stand-alone installation or add features to an existing installation" in the Installation Page. Then when you go through the setup pages, on the Installation Type page, it is important that you select "Perform a new installation of SQL Server 2008." In addition, although it sounds correct because you are adding the shared features for the existing instance of SQL Server 2008, do not select "Add features to an existing instance of SQL Server 2008" because if you do the setup will fail. Continue through the setup and on the Feature Selection page, select only the shared features you want to install and then continue through the setup. Alternatively, you can install only the shared features using command-line setup, as explained in the section "Installing SQL Server 2008 failover cluster using a command prompt" later in this chapter.

FIGURE 48-6

Installing setup support files

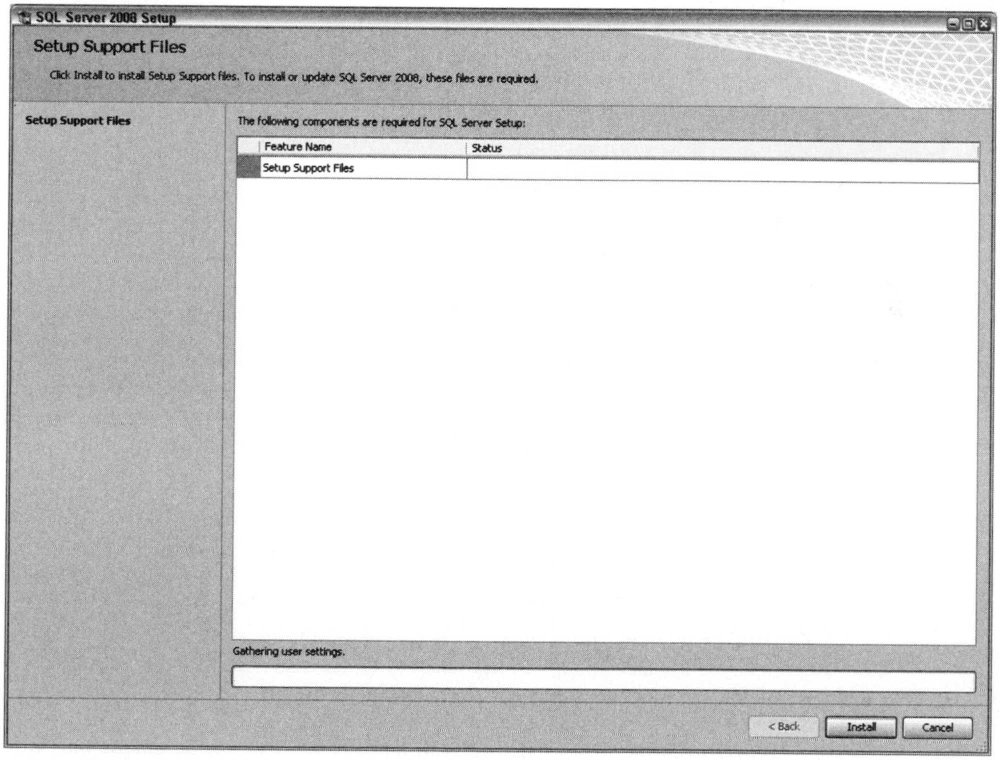

FIGURE 48-7

Wizard running the second set of Setup Support Rules

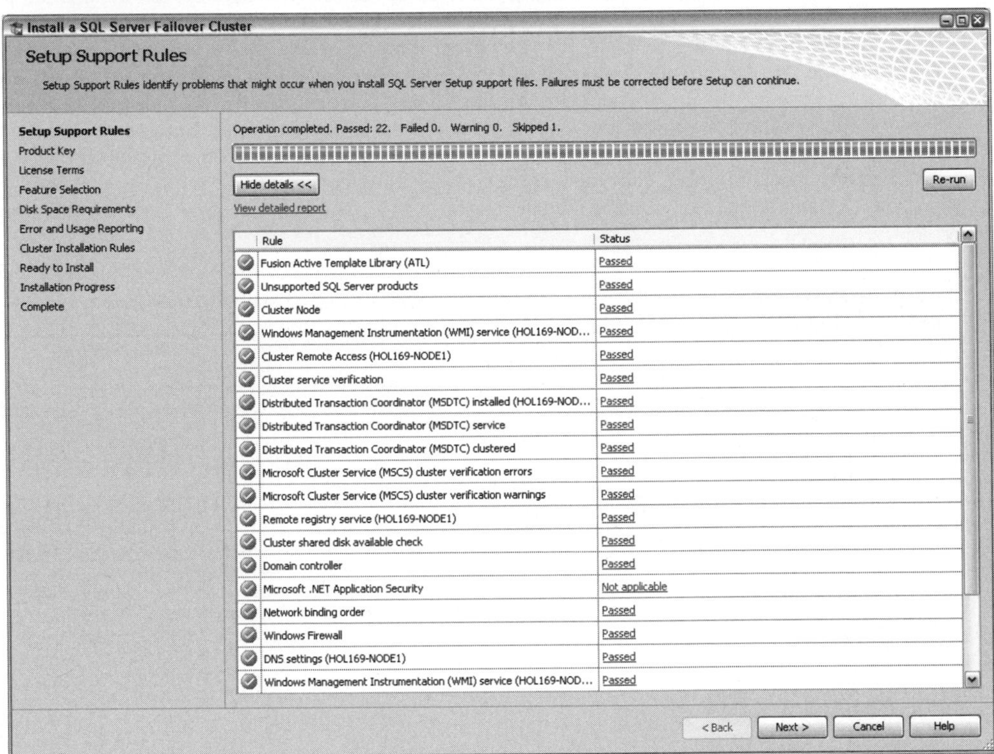

12. The Instance Configuration page, shown in Figure 48-9, displays any SQL Server instances running on the cluster node and allows the following SQL Server instance information to be entered:

- **SQL Server Network Name:** This is the name clients will use to connect to the SQL Server instance. The SQL Server network name cannot be the same as the cluster node name or the Windows failover cluster name, as it needs to be unique in the entire domain.
- **Default or Named instance:** To install a default instance, select Default instance. Only one default instance is allowed in a cluster. Other instances can be named instances. To install a named instance, select Named instance and type the instance name. In order to connect to the named instance, clients will need to use `SQLServerNetworkName\NamedInstanceName`. The named instance name needs to be unique only in this cluster. It can be used again in another cluster.

- **Instance ID:** SQL Server 2008 uses the instance ID to identify the directories and registry entries for the SQL Server instance instead of using MSSQL.*N* (where *N* is an integer 1, 2, 3, . . .). By default, the Instance ID is the same as the named instance name for the SQL Server named instance and MSSQLSERVER for the SQL Server default instance.
- **Instance root directory:** By default, `C:\Program Files\Microsoft SQL Server` is used to install the SQL Server binaries. To use another directory, click the Browse button. This directory needs to be a local disk and not a shared clustered disk.

FIGURE 48-8

Selecting the features to install on a cluster

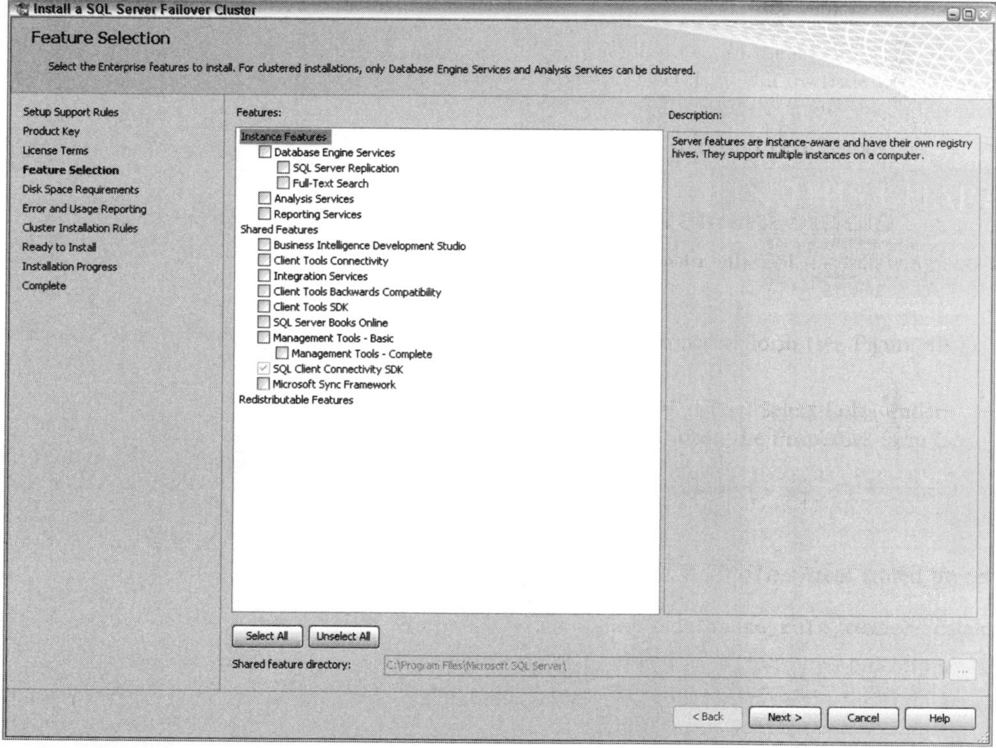

NOTE **SQL Server 2008 setup does not support a drive without a drive letter. Setup fails without a clear message if a drive without a drive letter assigned to it is selected.**

13. The Disk Space Requirements page is informational. It displays the required and available disk space.

FIGURE 48-9

Entering the SQL Server 2008 failover clustering instance information

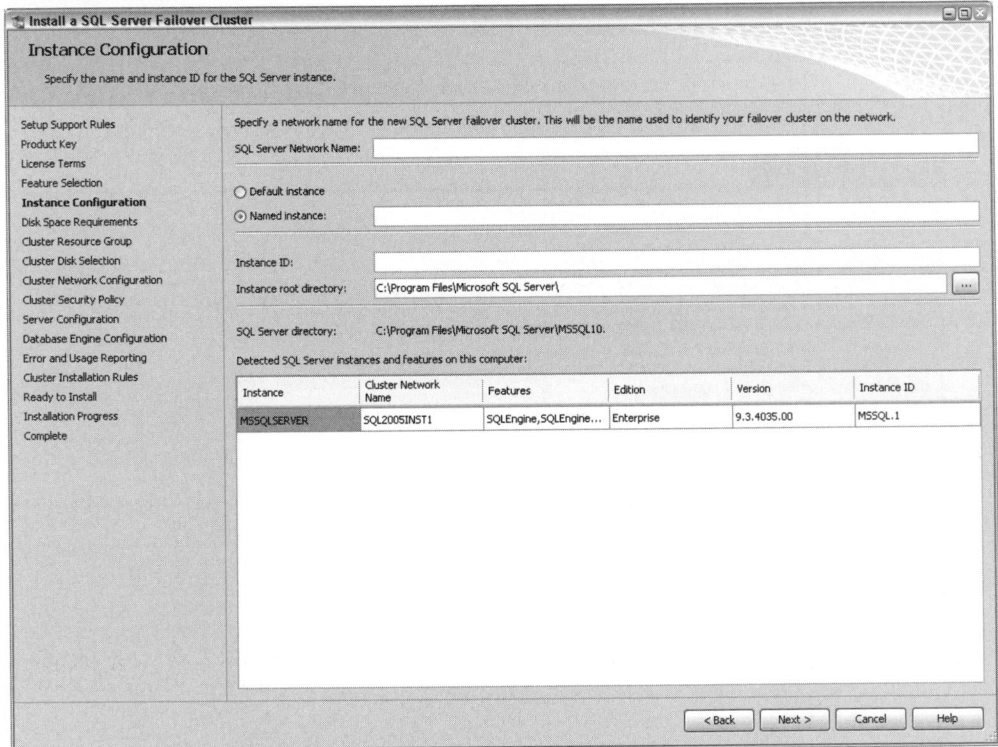

14. The Cluster Resource Group page (see Figure 48-10) enables you to use an existing resource group or enter a new resource group. This is the group where all the SQL Server 2008 resources such as SQL Network Name, IP address, shared disks, SQL Server, and SQL Server Agent will be located.

15. The Cluster Disk Selection page allows you to select the shared disks you want to use for the SQL Server 2008 instance. Figure 48-11 shows the disks that are available for the installation.

NOTE **Starting with SQL Server 2008 failover clustering, setup allows selecting multiple disk drives to use for data, log, tempdb, and backup. This is a very nice feature because now it's not necessary to add additional disks after the setup, which saves the downtime required for that task.**

FIGURE 48-10

Creating a SQL Server cluster resource group

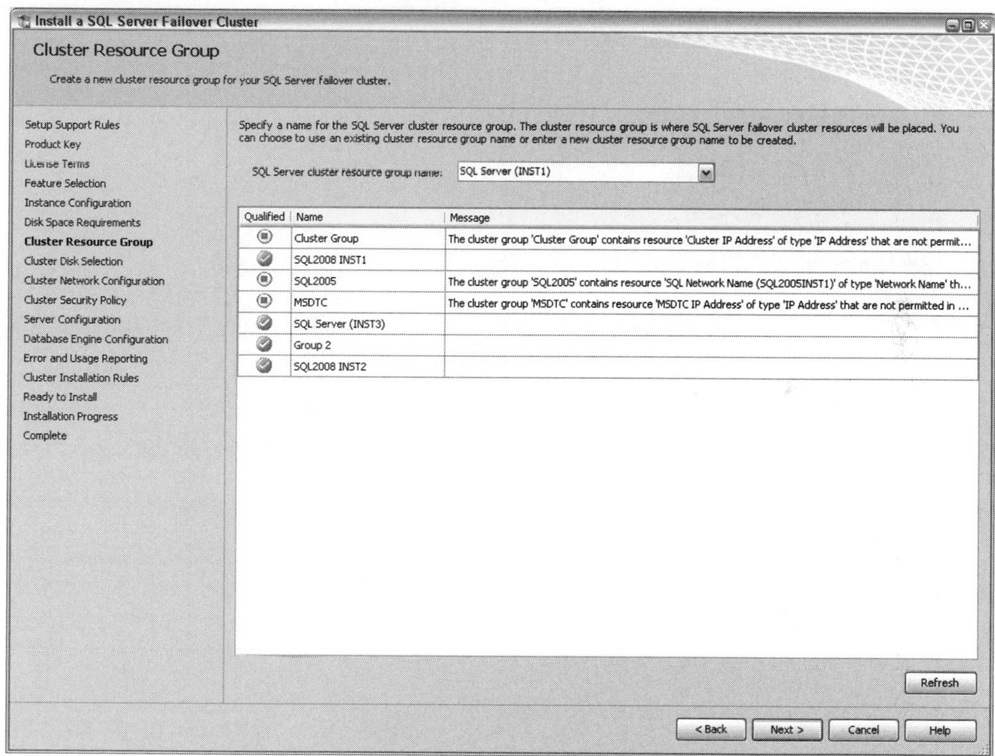

16. The Cluster Network Configuration page allows you to enter the IP address that will be used by the SQL Server 2008 failover clustering instance. An example is shown in Figure 48-12.

17. The Cluster Security Policy page enables you to enter the domain groups for the SQL Server service accounts. On a Windows Server 2008 failover cluster, this page allows you to use Service SIDs instead of the domain groups.

18. The Server Configuration page has two tabs: Service Accounts and Collation. Enter the service accounts for SQL Server and Analysis Services in the Service Accounts tab, as shown in Figure 48-13. This tab also allows you to use the same account for all the SQL Server services.

    The Collation tab enables you to change the SQL Server and Analysis Services collation.

FIGURE 48-11

Selecting multiple shared disks for a SQL Server 2008 failover cluster instance

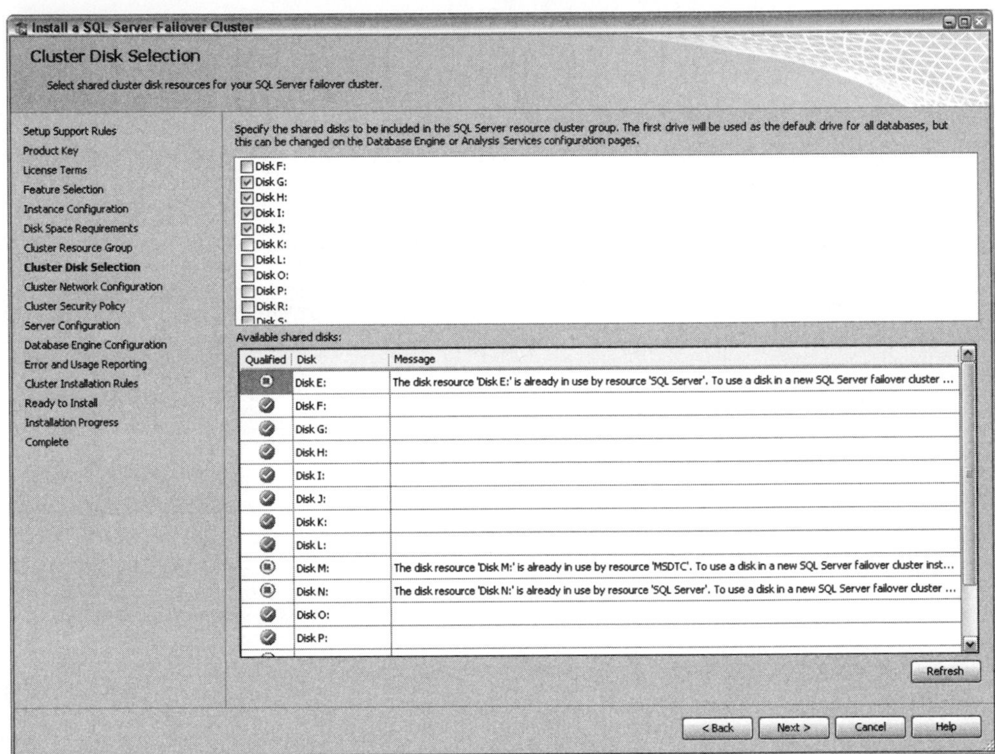

CAUTION When you click "Use the same account for all SQL Server services" it is recommended that you manually enter the correct account name and password. If you instead search the account by clicking Browse and typing a search string, the Account Name text box does not bind the data correctly. When the setup program validates the account, it validates the search string instead of the account you select, and the validation will fail. This issue is fixed in Cumulative Update 1 for SQL Server 2008, so if you proactively installed it before installing SQL Server 2008 or you are using a slip-streamed version of SQL Server 2008 and SP1, then you will not encounter the account validation issue.

Best Practice

In a cluster, the startup type of clustered services should be set to Manual, as the cluster service manages these services. The Server Configuration Service Accounts page allows you to change the startup type of the SQL Server services to a value other than Manual, but the startup of these services will still be Manual after the installation. In a way, this is good and follows best practices.

FIGURE 48-12

Entering an IP address for a SQL Server 2008 failover clustering instance

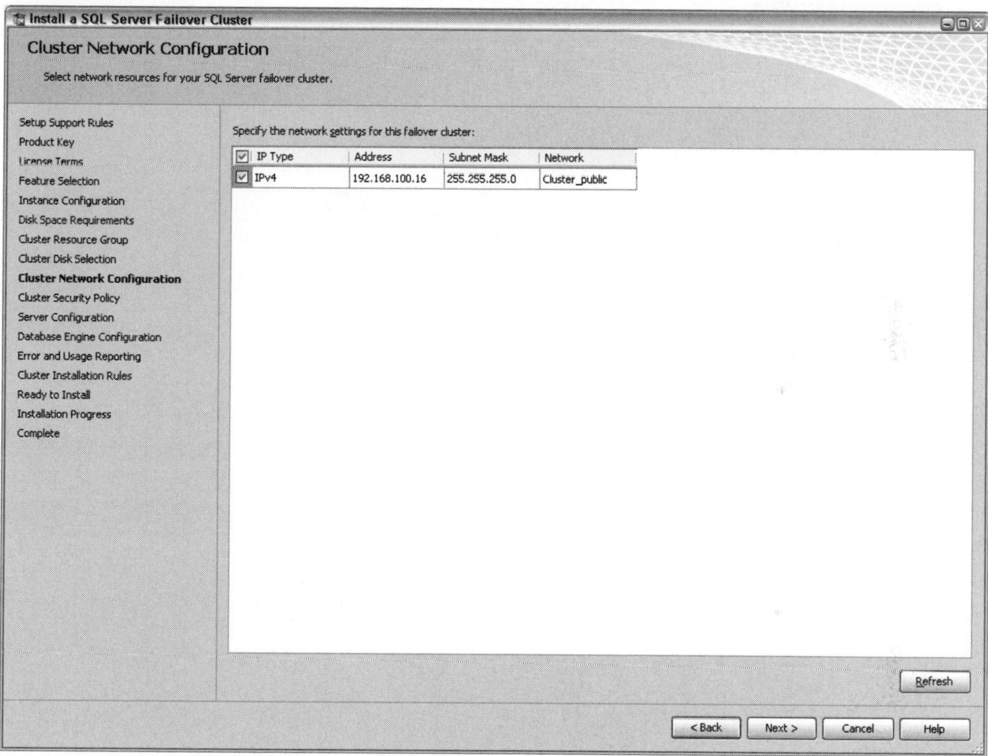

19. The Database Engine Configuration page has three tabs:

- **Account Provisioning:** This tab is used to specify the authentication mode (Windows Authentication mode or mixed mode) and allows specifying SQL Server administrators. Starting from SQL Server 2008, BUILTIN\Administrators are not added to the sysadmin server group by default. Specify at least one SQL Server administrator in this tab by clicking Add. If you want the current logged-in user to be a member of sysadmin, then click "Add current user."
- **Data Directories:** This tab is used to specify the shared disks that you want to use for user database data, log, tempdb, and backup directories. As shown in Figure 48-14, multiple drives can be specified. These drives need to be selected first in the Cluster Disk Selection page.
- FILESTREAM: This tab allows enabling Filestream for Transact-SQL access and filing I/O streaming access.

20. Based on the features that were selected on the Feature Selection page, other configuration pages may be displayed. For example, if Analysis Services was selected in the Feature Selection

page, then the Analysis Services Configuration page will be displayed to configure the Analysis Services.

FIGURE 48-13

Entering the SQL Server service accounts on the Server Configuration page

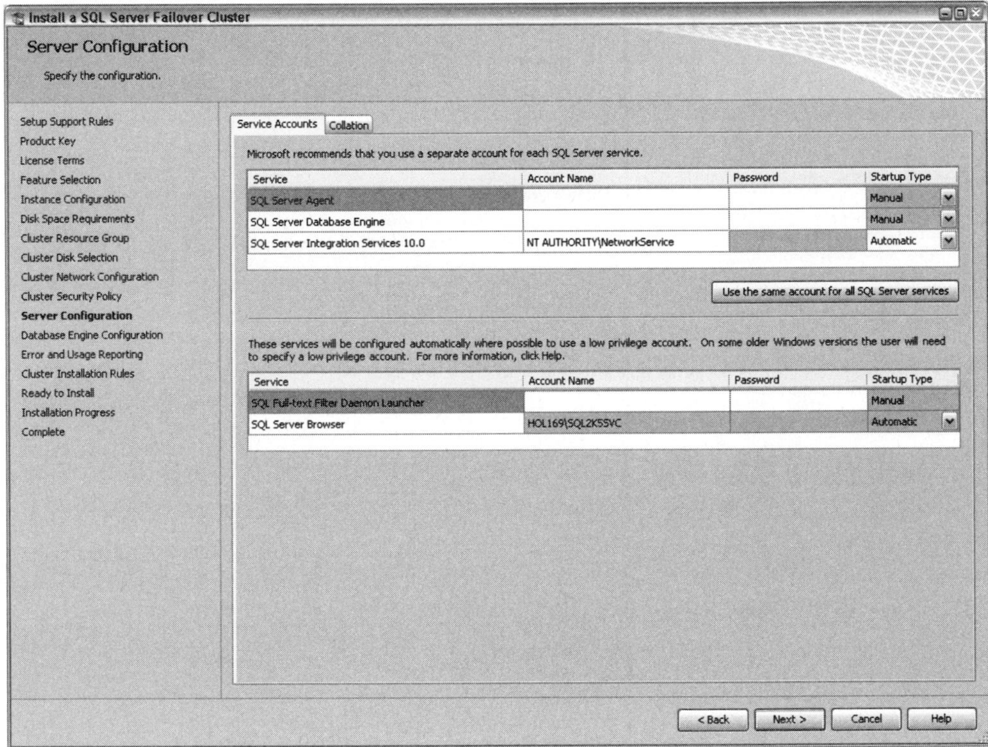

21. On the Error and Usage Reporting page, select the information that you want to automatically send to Microsoft to improve the SQL Server features and services. These settings are optional.

22. The Cluster Installation Rules page runs a set of rules to determine whether the SQL Server 2008 failover cluster installation will be blocked. Verify that all the rules pass before proceeding to the next step.

23. The Ready to Install page, shown in Figure 48-15, displays the features that were selected so far in the setup wizard. Click Install to begin the installation.

NOTE **On the Ready to Install page, notice that the path to the configuration file is specified. SQL Server 2008 setup writes out all the appropriate parameters in the configuration file for the actions that were run, with the exception of sensitive information like passwords. If you want to stop the installation at this time, click Cancel. Later, when you are ready, you can run the installation**

through the command prompt and supply the `ConfigurationFile.ini` using the `ConfigurationFile` parameter. Here is an example of running `setup.exe` using the configuration file:

```
Setup.exe /ConfigurationFile=MyConfigurationFile.ini
```

FIGURE 48-14

Specifying shared disk drives for SQL Server Database engine

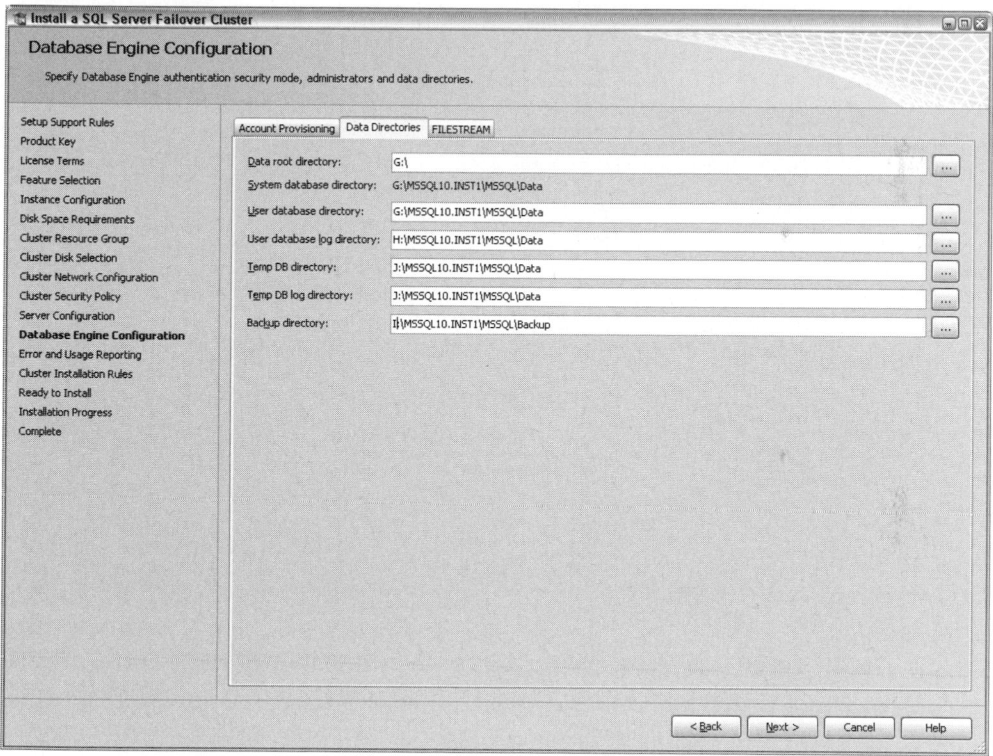

24. During the installation, the Installation Progress page shows the setup progress.
25. On successful completion, the Complete page, shown in Figure 48-16, displays the setup status and a link to the summary log file. Click Close. Reboot the cluster node if the setup wizard instructs you to restart the server.

After the installation of a single-node SQL Server 2008 failover cluster, SQL Server 2008 will be fully functional and ready to accept client connections. All the clustered resources will be created for the SQL Server 2008 instance, except that currently only one node is the possible owner, and the clustered SQL Server 2008 instance cannot failover to another node in the cluster. The next step is to add other cluster nodes to the SQL Server 2008 failover clustering instance to provide high availability.

FIGURE 48-15

Verifying the SQL Server 2008 failover cluster features to be installed

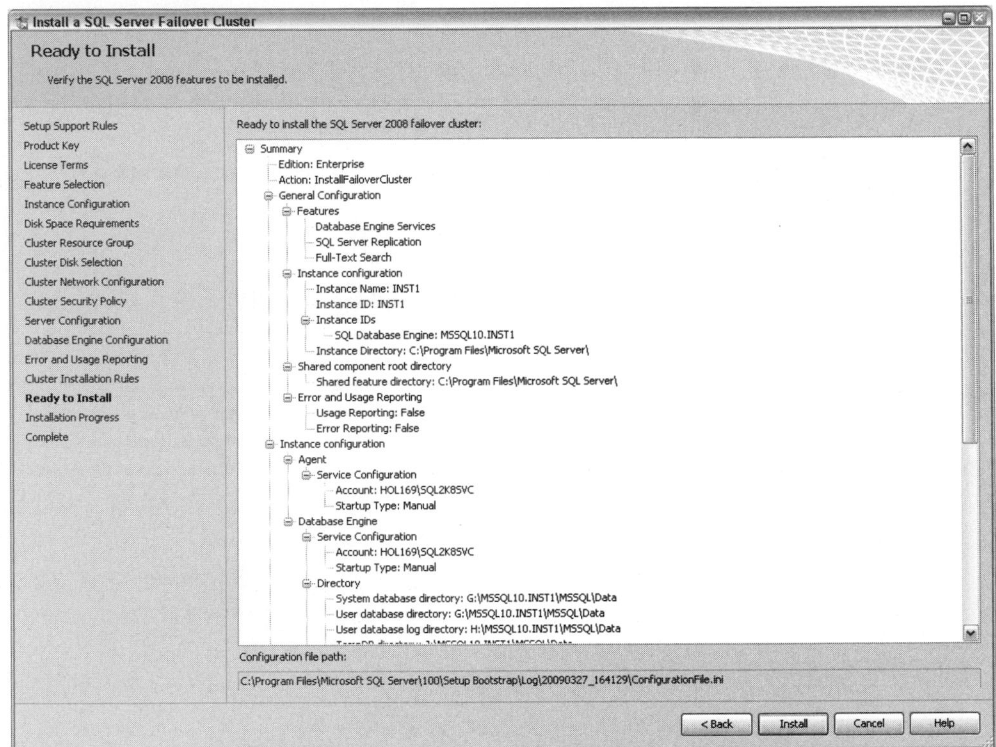

Adding a node to an existing SQL Server 2008 failover cluster

Before adding a cluster node to an existing SQL Server 2008 failover cluster, install all the prerequisites for SQL Server 2008 failover clustering on the node that needs to be added. Once the prerequisites are installed and the node is rebooted, follow these steps to add the node to the SQL Server 2008 failover cluster configuration:

1. Launch the SQL Server Installation Center (by double-clicking `setup.exe` on the root of the SQL Server 2008 installation media) on the node that needs to be added.
2. On the left-hand side of the SQL Server Installation Center, click Installation.
3. Click "Add node to a SQL Server failover cluster."
4. Next, the setup wizard runs setup support rules to identify problems that might occur when setup support files are installed. Verify that all the checks pass before proceeding to the next step.

FIGURE 48-16

Successfully completing the single-node SQL Server 2008 failover cluster installation

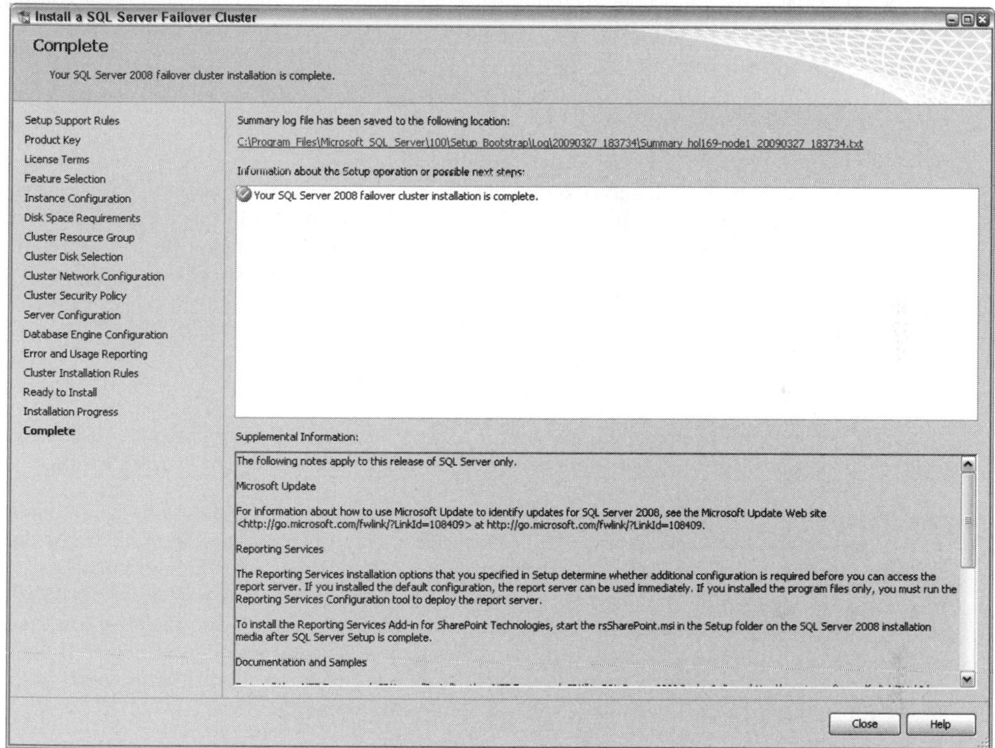

5. On the Product Key page, make the same selection as you did while creating the single-node SQL Server 2008 failover cluster. For example, if you entered a PID key while creating the single-node SQL Server 2008 failover cluster, then enter the same PID key now.

NOTE **When you add a node for a SQL Server 2008 failover cluster from installation media that has a custom `Defaultsetup.ini` file that includes the product key, setup will give you the error message "The current SKU is invalid" even though everything is valid. This issue is fixed in Cumulative Update 1 for SQL Server 2008. Again, if you install Cumulative Update 1 for SQL Server 2008 along with the prerequisites or you are installing a slipstreamed version of SQL Server 2008 and SP1, then you will not encounter this issue.**

6. On the License Terms page, read the licensing terms and check the box to accept them.
7. Use the Cluster Node Configuration page to select the SQL Server 2008 failover clustering instance that you want to add to the current node.

8. On the Service Accounts page, the SQL services are already filled with the ones that were entered while creating the single-node SQL Server 2008 failover cluster. On this page, enter the passwords for the SQL Server services.
9. On the Error and Usage Reporting page, optionally select the information that you want to automatically send to Microsoft to improve the SQL Server features and services.
10. The Add Node Rules page runs a set of rules to determine whether the SQL Server failover cluster installation will be blocked on the new node. Verify that all the rules pass before proceeding to the next step.
11. On the Ready to Add Node page, click Install to begin the installation. Similar to creating the single-node SQL Server 2008 failover cluster, the add node operation also creates a configuration file. The path to the configuration file is displayed in this page. SQL Server 2008 setup writes out all the appropriate parameters in the configuration file for the actions that were run, with the exception of sensitive information like passwords. If you want to stop the installation at this time, click Cancel. Later, when you are ready, you can run the installation through the command prompt and supply the `ConfigurationFile.ini` using the `ConfigurationFile` parameter.
12. The Add Node Progress page shows the progress of the setup.
13. On successful completion, the Complete page displays the setup status and a link to the summary log file. Click Close. Reboot the cluster node if the setup wizard instructs you to restart the server.

At first glance, the new SQL Server 2008 failover cluster setup process may seem like more work for the DBA. Unlike with SQL Server 2005 failover clusters, SQL Server 2008 failover cluster setup is run locally on each node and no remote setup is done. Say we were installing SQL Server 2005 failover cluster on a four-node cluster. To perform this setup, the DBA just needs to run the setup on the node that owns the shared disks and the setup will automatically install on all four cluster nodes. If the installation succeeds on three nodes but fails on the fourth node, then the entire installation is rolled back. Troubleshooting such a failed installation could take hours and sometimes days.

With the new SQL Server 2008 failover cluster setup, installation is performed per node, which is much faster, more reliable, and easier to troubleshoot if the setup fails. More than 50 percent of failed SQL Server 2005 failover cluster installations were related to remote-node operations. Also, once the first node is installed successfully, SQL Server 2008 failover cluster is running and ready to respond to clients. Adding additional nodes to the SQL Server 2008 failover cluster does not incur any downtime, as the add node operation is performed on the node that is being added to the failover cluster and not on the node where SQL Server 2008 is running. Adding additional nodes can be done very easily using command-line setup as explained in the section "Installing SQL Server 2008 failover cluster using a command prompt" later in this chapter.

Post-installation tasks

After successfully installing a SQL Server 2008 failover cluster, perform the following post-installation tasks:

1. Review all the SQL Server resources — Verify that all clustered SQL Server resources and dependencies are created properly and are online. Apart from the shared disk resources that exist before the installation, SQL Server 2008 setup creates the following resources in the SQL Server 2008 group:

- SQL IP Address 1 — Has no dependencies
- SQL Network Name — Dependent on the SQL IP Address 1 resource
- SQL Server — Dependent on the shared drive resources that were selected during setup and SQL Server Network Name resources
- SQL Server Agent — Dependent on SQL Server resources
- SQL Server Filestream share (if Filestream was enabled during installation) — Dependent on disk, SQL Network Name, and SQL Server resources.

NOTE **In SQL Server 2008, there is no separate full-text resource, as it is integrated with the SQL Server Database Engine.**

2. Verify IP and name resolution — Ping the SQL Server and/or Analysis Services IP and network name from all cluster nodes as well as a client machine to test IP address and name resolution, respectively.
3. Verify SQL Server failover — Move SQL Server and/or Analysis Services groups from one cluster node to another. Verify that all the resources failover and become online on all cluster nodes without affecting any other groups, and that users/applications are able to connect to SQL Server.

NOTE **To connect to a SQL Server 2008 failover cluster instance, users/applications need to use the SQL Server network name and/or SQL Server IP address that were entered during the setup. For a named instance, use the SQL Server network name and/or SQL Server IP address followed by a backslash (\) and the instance name.**

4. Set anti-virus exclusions — Verify that the anti-virus software being used is cluster-aware and make sure that the following are excluded:
   - All SQL Server/Analysis Services database and log files (mdf, ldf, ndf)
   - SQL Server/Analysis Services backup directory
   - SQL Server full-text directory
   - Quorum drive
   - `%Systemroot%\Cluster` directory on all cluster nodes
   - `\clusterserviceaccount\Local Settings\Temp` directory on all cluster nodes
   - MSDTC drive (if using MSDTC)

CROSS-REF **Refer to the following Microsoft Knowledge Base articles for configuring anti-virus exclusions:**

Antivirus Software May Cause Problems with Cluster Services **at** `http://support.microsoft.com/kb/250355`**; and** ***Consideration for a Virus Scanner on a Computer That Is Running SQL Server*** **at** `http://support.microsoft.com/kb/309422`**.**

5. Configure new SQL Server installation — After installing a new SQL Server, check the SQL Server configuration to review the features that are enabled and running. For example, dedicated administrator connection (DAC) is off by default on a SQL Server 2008 failover clustering instance. However, enabling DAC will allow you to connect to your SQL Server

using DAC when it is unresponsive to regular connections. The following Transact-SQL code can be used to enable the DAC listener to access a remote connection:

```
EXEC sp_configure 'remote admin connections', 1;

RECONFIGURE;
```

CROSS-REF For more information about configuring SQL Server, refer to Chapter 39, "Configuring SQL Server."

NOTE The SQL Server Surface Area Configuration tool that was a part of SQL Server 2005 has been removed from SQL Server 2008. All the configurations that this tool enabled in SQL Server 2005 can now be done using SQL Server Configuration Manager and SQL Server Management Studio.

To access the Surface Area Configuration features, connect to the SQL Server 2008 failover cluster instance using SQL Server Management Studio. Right-click the server name and select Facets to open the View Facets page. Select Surface Area Configuration from the Facet drop-down list.

6. Test your applications — Test all your applications thoroughly against the new SQL Server 2008 failover clustering instance. Verify that there is retry login to reconnect to the database when the connection is broken during failover. Roll out to production only after successful application testing.
7. Apply the latest SQL Server service packs and security updates — Apply the latest service packs and security updates to help reduce downtime due to known issues that are already fixed in the service packs and security updates. For more information about applying patches, refer to the section "Patching a SQL Server 2008 failover cluster" later in this chapter.

Uninstalling a SQL Server 2008 failover cluster

To uninstall a SQL Server 2008 failover cluster, use the Remove Node operation in SQL Server Installation Center and remove the nodes starting with the passive nodes (nodes on which SQL Server is not currently running). The steps to remove a cluster node are similar to adding a node:

1. On the cluster node that needs to be removed, launch the SQL Server Installation Center by double-clicking `setup.exe` on the root of the SQL Server 2008 installation media. Alternatively, open SQL Server Installation Center from Start ➪ Programs ➪ Microsoft SQL Server 2008 ➪ Configuration Tools ➪ SQL Server Installation Center.
2. On the left-hand side of the SQL Server Installation Center, click Installation.
3. Click Remove Node from a SQL Server failover cluster.
4. The setup wizard will run setup support rules to identify any problems that may block the setup. Verify that all the checks pass before proceeding to the next step.
5. The Cluster Node Configuration page allows selecting the SQL Server 2008 failover clustering instance that needs to be modified. The cluster node that will be removed is displayed in the "Name of this node" field.

NOTE The Remove Node operation needs to be performed on the node that is not running the SQL Server 2008 failover cluster instance. Setup is blocked if the Remove Node operation is run from the active node (the node that is running SQL Server) unless it is the last node that needs to be removed.

6. On the Ready to Remove Node page, click Remove. The Remove Node operation also creates a configuration file, whose path is displayed in this page. SQL Server 2008 setup writes out all the appropriate parameters in the configuration file for the actions that were run, with the exception of sensitive information like passwords. If you want to stop the installation at this time, click Cancel. Later, when you are ready, you can run the installation through the command prompt and supply the `ConfigurationFile.ini` using the `ConfigurationFile` parameter.
7. The Remove Node Progress page shows the progress of the setup.
8. On successful completion, the Complete page displays the setup status and a link to the summary log file. Click close. Follow these steps on other cluster nodes that need to be removed.

NOTE **Similar to the Add Node operation, the Remove Node operation does not incur any downtime, as it is performed on the cluster node that is not running the SQL Server 2008 instance unless it is the last node that needs to be removed.**

Installing a failover cluster using a command prompt

Using the SQL Server Installation Center to install and add/remove SQL Server 2008 may be the easiest way to install a SQL Server 2008 failover cluster. But the SQL Server Installation Center is not the most efficient method for installing a multi-node cluster (e.g., a 4- or 8- or 16-node cluster). Microsoft simplifies the process by offering command line `setup.exe`.

Here is the command-line syntax to install a single-node SQL Server 2008 failover cluster with the Database Engine:

```
setup.exe /q /ACTION=InstallFailoverCluster /FEATURES=SQL
/INSTANCENAME="<Insert SQL Server Instance Name>"
[/INSTANCEIDSUFFIX="<Insert InstanceID Suffix>"]
/INSTANCEDIR="C:\Program Files\Microsoft SQL Server"
/INSTALLSHAREDDIR="C:\Program Files\Microsoft SQL Server"
/SQLSVCACCOUNT="DomainName\UserName" /SQLSVCPASSWORD="XXXXXX"
/AGTSVCACCOUNT="DomainName\UserName" /AGTSVCPASSWORD="XXXXXX"
/SQLDOMAINGROUP="DomainName\DomainGroup"
/INSTALLSQLDATADIR="<Drive>:\<Path>\MSSQLSERVER"
/SQLCOLLATION="CollationName"
/FAILOVERCLUSTERGROUP="<Insert Cluster Group name>"
/FAILOVERCLUSTERDISKS="<Insert Cluster Disk Resource>"
/FAILOVERCLUSTERIPADDRESSES="IPv4;XXX.XXX.XXX.XXX;Cluster
Network;xxx.xxx.xxx.xxx" /FAILOVERCLUSTERNETWORKNAME=
"<Insert SQL Network Name>"
/SQLSYSADMINACCOUNTS=" DomainName\UserName " [/SECURITYMODE=SQL
/SAPWD="StrongPassword"]
```

Here is the command-line syntax to add a node to an existing SQL Server 2008 failover cluster:

```
setup.exe /q /ACTION=AddNode
/INSTANCENAME="<Insert SQL Server Instance Name>"
/SQLSVCACCOUNT="DomainName\UserName" /SQLSVCPASSWORD="XXXXXX"
/AGTSVCACCOUNT="DomainName\UserName" /AGTSVCPASSWORD="XXXXXX"
```

Here is the command-line syntax to remove a node from an existing SQL Server 2008 failover cluster:

```
setup.exe /q /ACTION=RemoveNode /INSTANCENAME="<Insert SQL Server
Instance Name>"
```

The /q parameter implies that setup will run in quiet mode without any user interface. To see the progress of the setup, use the optional /INDICATEPROGRESS parameter. For example, to see the progress of the Remove Node operation, use the following command-line syntax:

```
setup.exe /q /ACTION=RemoveNode /INSTANCENAME="<Insert SQL Server
Instance Name>" /INDICATEPROGRESS
```

Here is the command-line syntax to install only the client tools:

```
setup.exe /q /ACTION=INSTALL /FEATURES=SSMS
```

This installs the SQL Server Management Tools — Basic, which includes the following: SQL Server Management Studio support for the SQL Server Database Engine, SQL Server Express, the sqlcmd utility, and the SQL Server PowerShell provider.

Here is the command-line syntax to install SQL Server Management Tools — Complete:

```
setup.exe /q /ACTION=INSTALL /FEATURES=ADV_SSMS
```

This installs SQL Server Management Tools – Complete, which includes the following components in addition to the components in the Basic version:

- SQL Server Management Studio support for Reporting Services, Analysis Services, and Integration Services
- SQL Server Profiler
- Database Engine Tuning Advisor

Best Practice

Use the /INDICATEPROGRESS parameter to get a better understanding of the setup and see the on-screen progress. This parameter can also be used while installing a single-node SQL Server 2008 failover cluster and adding a node from the command prompt.

CROSS-REF **Most of the options used for the command-line syntax are self-explanatory and are similar to the selection that was entered manually while using the SQL Server Installation Center. For a detailed explanation, refer to the SQL Server Books Online topic "How to: Install SQL Server 2008 from the Command Prompt" at** http://msdn.microsoft.com/en-us/library/ms144259.aspx.

Rolling upgrade and patching

Prior to SQL Server 2008, upgrading and patching a SQL Server failover cluster incurred several minutes downtime as the SQL Server services were shut down and started a few times during the upgrade/patch process. With SQL Server 2008 failover clustering, the downtime is reduced significantly using the rolling upgrade process.

With rolling upgrade you can now upgrade a SQL Server 2000/2005 failover cluster instance one node at a time starting with the passive node without affecting the active node, leaving the SQL Server 2000/2005 failover clustering instance running. A failover only occurs when the active node is upgraded, during which the SQL Server service is stopped on the active node and restarted on the passive node.

Similarly, you can also patch SQL Server 2008 failover clustering instances using rolling upgrade, sometimes referred to as rolling patching, by starting to patch the passive node first, keeping the SQL Server instance up and running on the active node while the passive node is being patched.

NOTE **Recently I worked with a large insurance company to upgrade its production SQL Server 2005 failover cluster to SQL Server 2008 failover cluster using the rolling upgrade process. The SQL Server 2005 failover cluster was used for one of the company's very important 24/7 business applications, which could not afford a long outage. It was a pleasant surprise to see that the in-place SQL Server 2008 cluster rolling upgrade process incurred approximately two minutes downtime (15 seconds failover plus 1.5 minutes database upgrade script execution time upon SQL Server Database Engine start on the upgraded node). The actual upgrade time was approximately 30 minutes per cluster node, but the most important point is that SQL Server was offline for only two minutes during the upgrade process. The rest of the time, it was up and running. You might be wondering if these servers had very tiny databases. Actually, the databases were medium-size, and ranged from 100 GB to 600 GB.**

Consider a two-node failover cluster with one default clustered instance of SQL Server 2005 (SQL2005INST1) running on NODE2. NODE2 is the active node, as SQL2005INST1 is running on this node, and NODE1 is the passive node, as no services are running on it. The following steps walk through the process of upgrading SQL2005INST1 from SQL Server 2005 to SQL Server 2008 using in-place rolling upgrade.

Best Practice

Before proceeding with an upgrade, it's recommended to spend significant time planning it. You may find the following Microsoft upgrade whitepapers helpful:

SQL Server 2000 to 2008 Upgrade Whitepaper at: `http://download.microsoft.com/download/2/0/B/20B90384-F3FE-4331-AA12-FD58E6AB66C2/SQL%20Server%202000%20to%202008%20Upgrade%20White%20Paper.docx`

SQL Server 2005 to 2008 Upgrade Whitepaper at: `http://download.microsoft.com/download/5/3/D/53D72434-7BD5-41C6-A806-8212C1B0DCA1/SQL%20Server%202005%20to%202008%20Upgrade%20White%20Paper.docx`

Also, it's best to run Upgrade Advisor against the SQL Server instances you want to upgrade. Upgrade Advisor will identify issues to fix either before or after you upgrade to SQL Server 2008.

1. Install prerequisites for SQL Server 2008 as discussed earlier on both NODE1 and NODE2. To minimize downtime, install the prerequisites on the passive node (NODE1) first and reboot NODE1. Then, during a scheduled downtime, failover the SQL Server 2005 instance (SQL2005INST1) from NODE2 to NODE1. This incurs a brief downtime of approximately 15 seconds. After the failover, install the prerequisites on NODE2 and reboot NODE2. Now NODE2 is the passive node and NODE1 is the active node.

NOTE **I do not want to paint a rosy picture suggesting that all failovers will take 15 seconds. The actual downtime will depend on your environment. For example, I saw one failover take 10 minutes, as the SQL Server 2005 instance was dependent on 20 drives and it took all the drives approximately 10 minutes to come online and SQL Server can be online only after the drives it is dependent on come online. Also, if there is a long-running transaction running when the failover occurs, SQL Server goes through recovery after failover and will roll back the uncompleted long-running transaction, which again can increase your downtime. This is another reason why you need to have an identical test environment in which to test and observe the actual downtime or at least provide a good estimate of the downtime.**

2. During this step, upgrade the passive node (NODE2). When NODE2 is being upgraded, setup automatically takes NODE2 out of the possible owners for the SQL Network Name resource and then upgrades the binaries on NODE2. Here are the detailed steps:
   - On NODE2, launch the SQL Server Installation Center by double-clicking `setup.exe` on the root of the SQL Server 2008 installation media.
   - On the left-hand side of the SQL Server Installation Center, click Installation.
   - Click Upgrade from SQL Server 2000 or SQL Server 2005 to start the upgrade.
   - On the Setup Support Rules page, verify that there are no errors and click OK.
   - On the Setup Support Files page, click Install.
   - Setup runs another set of setup support rules. On the Setup Support Rules page, verify that there are no errors and click Next.
   - On the Product Key page, enter the product key for your SQL Server 2008 edition.
   - On the License Terms page, read the licensing terms and check the box to accept them.
   - On the Select Instance page, select the instance of SQL Server to upgrade (MSSQLSERVER in this case, as SQL2005INST1 is a default instance), as shown in Figure 48-17. To upgrade only the SQL Server management tools and shared features, select "Upgrade shared features only."
   - The Select Features page will be grayed out, as no changes are allowed during the upgrade.
   - On the Instance Configuration page, review the Instance ID for the SQL Server instance and change it if you do not like the default.
   - The Disk Space Requirements page is informational. It displays the required and available space for the SQL Server features.
   - On the Server Configuration page, enter a low-privilege account for the SQL Full-text Filter Daemon Launcher service. This account should be different from the SQL Server service account. If you are not using full-text, then do not specify a service account. If you are using full-text, then create a local user account to be used specially for this service.
   - On the Full-Text Upgrade page, choose the full-text upgrade option.

FIGURE 48-17

Selecting the instance of SQL Server to upgrade

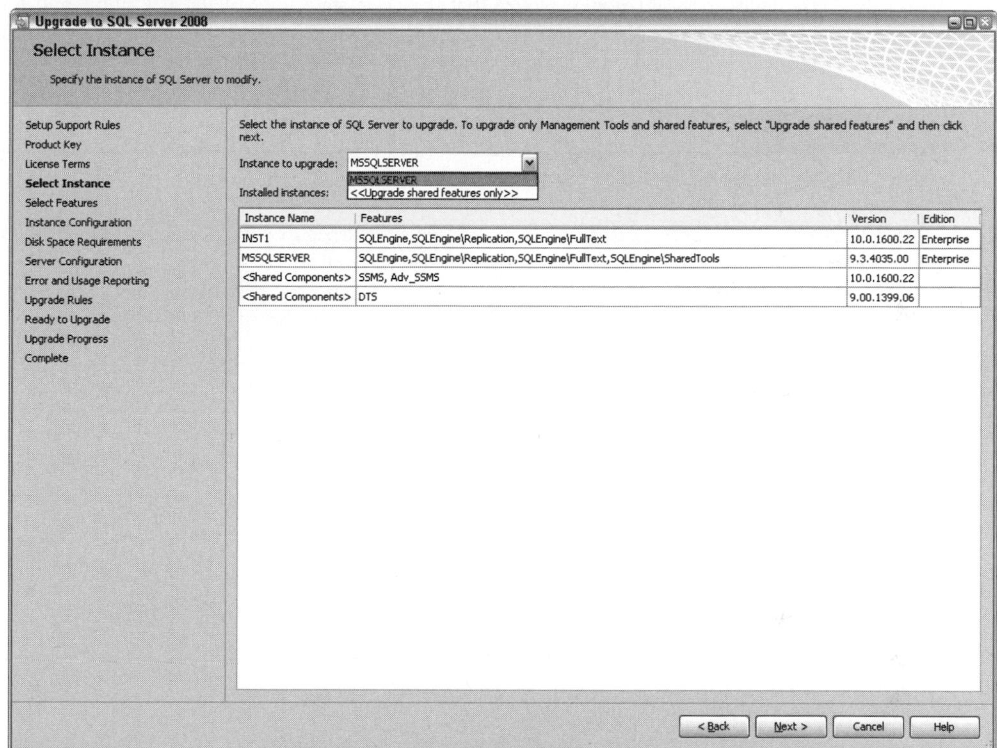

Best Practice

If you are upgrading from SQL Server 2005, all three options in the Full-Text Upgrade page are valid; but if you are upgrading from SQL Server 2000 and you select the Import option in the Full-Text Upgrade page, the Rebuild option is used instead. This means that the catalogs are rebuilt from scratch after the upgrade. Depending on the size of the catalogs and hardware, this may require significant time and resources, which temporarily decreases the server's performance.

To avoid this scenario, it is recommended to select the Reset option on the Full-Text Upgrade page. By selecting this option, the catalogs will remain empty until you manually populate the full-text catalogs after the upgrade is complete.

- On the Error and Usage Reporting page, optionally select the information you want to automatically send to Microsoft to improve the SQL Server features and services.

- The Upgrade Rules page runs a set of rules to determine if the upgrade process will be blocked. Verify that all the rules pass before proceeding to the next step.
- The Cluster Upgrade Report page, shown in Figure 48-18, displays the upgrade status of the failover cluster nodes. Notice that the node state for NODE1 is Online, and for NODE2 it is Passive, as SQL2005INST1 is running on NODE1. The upgrade state for all nodes is Upgrade Pending.

FIGURE 48-18

Cluster Upgrade Report page showing the upgrade status

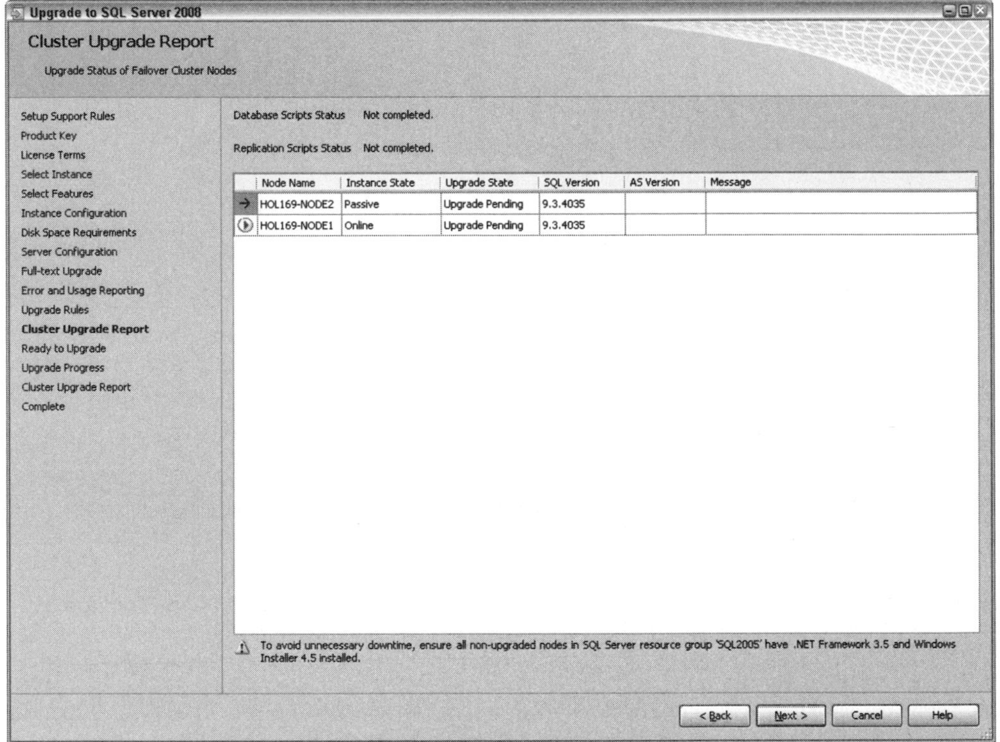

- Verify the SQL Server 2008 features to be upgraded on the Ready to Upgrade page and click Upgrade. An example is shown in Figure 48-19.
- The Upgrade Progress page (see Figure 48-20) shows the upgrade progress. Click Next.
- The Cluster Upgrade Report page, shown in Figure 48-21, displays the upgrade status of the failover cluster nodes. Notice that the state of NODE2 is Offline, and the upgrade state is Upgraded. The state of NODE1 is Online, and the upgrade state is Upgrade Pending. Note also the SQL Version change for NODE2. It has been upgraded to SQL Server 2008 (10.0.1600.22).
- Click Close on the Complete page.

FIGURE 48-19

Ready to Upgrade page showing the features to be upgraded

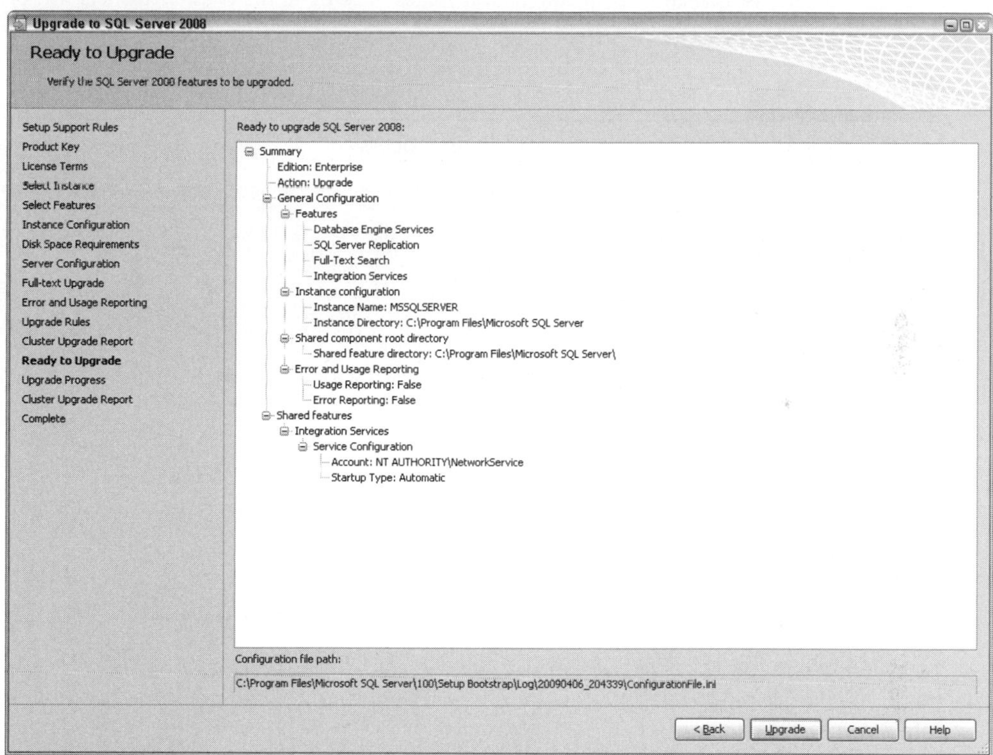

NOTE **At this point, NODE2 is upgraded and NODE1 is the only node in the possible owners for the SQL Network Name resource, as shown in Figure 48-22. Throughout this process, the SQL Server 2005 instance (SQL2005INST1) was online and running as usual on NODE1 while NODE2 was being upgraded. Also, at this point you essentially have a single-node cluster — if something goes wrong on NODE1, no failover is available.**

3. Upgrade NODE1. During this step, upgrade NODE1 by repeating the steps that were used to upgrade NODE2. Before the setup starts upgrading NODE1, it gives a warning: "If you proceed with upgrade, SQL Server Setup will move the SQL Server resource group 'SQLServer-GroupName' to a node that has already been upgraded and complete the database upgrade. Applications will not be able to connect to SQL Server services while the database upgrade is in progress," as shown in Figure 48-23.

   When the upgrade starts on NODE1, setup adds the upgrade node, NODE2, to the possible owners for the SQL Network Name resource and removes NODE1 from the possible owners. This will cause the SQL Server 2005 instance (SQL2005 INST1) to failover to the upgraded node NODE2. This will cause another downtime of approximately 15 seconds. SQL2005INST1 starts on NODE2 and SQL Server 2008 database upgrade scripts are run against it. During my testing, this took approximately 1.5 minutes and then SQL2005INST1 was up and running on NODE2. Therefore, the total downtime was approximately two minutes. In the meantime, the upgrade process will continue on NODE1 and complete the upgrade on NODE1. Once NODE1 is upgraded, setup automatically adds NODE1 in the possible owners list for the SQL Network Name resource.

FIGURE 48-20

Upgrade Progress page showing successful setup process

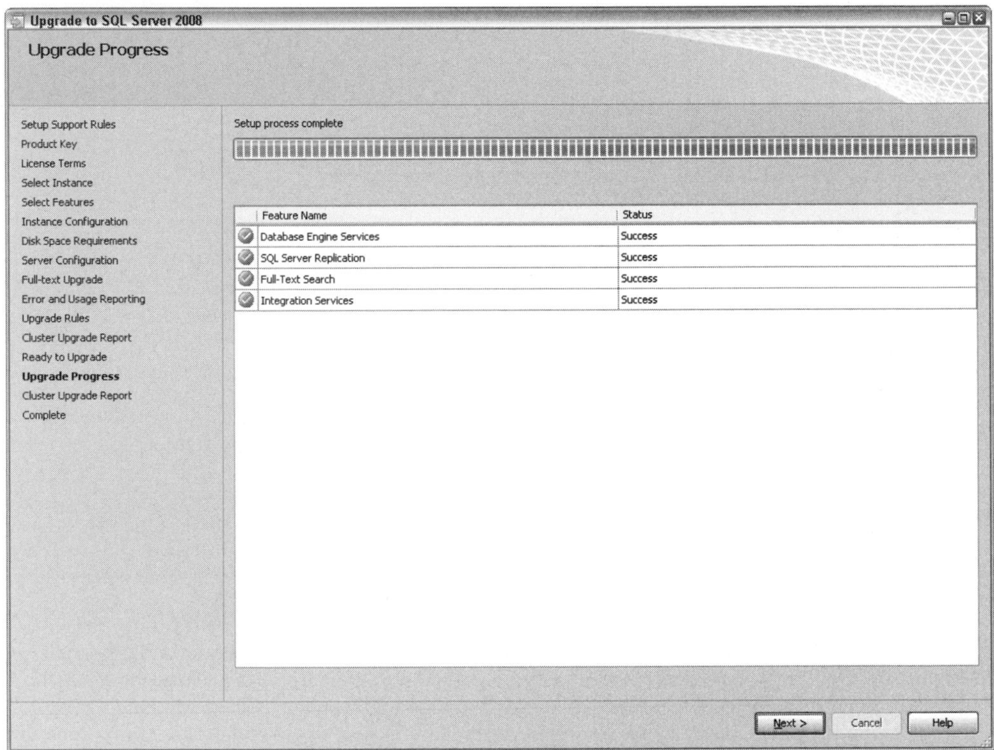

The rolling upgrade process for a cluster with three or more nodes is slightly different. You should still install the prerequisites, starting with the passive nodes first. Then the passive nodes are upgraded to SQL Server 2008. As the upgrade is run on each node, setup automatically removes it from the possible owners for the SQL Network Name resource. When more than 50 percent of the cluster nodes are updated, setup automatically causes a failover of the SQL Server failover clustering instance to any one of the upgraded nodes. Then the setup adds all the upgraded nodes to the possible owners list; and all nodes that are not yet upgraded are removed from the possible owners list. Upon failover, SQL Server starts on an upgraded node and the database upgrade scripts are run against it. Continue upgrading the remaining nodes. As they are upgraded, the setup automatically adds them back to the possible owners list for the SQL Network Name.

FIGURE 48-21

Cluster Upgrade Report page showing the upgrade status

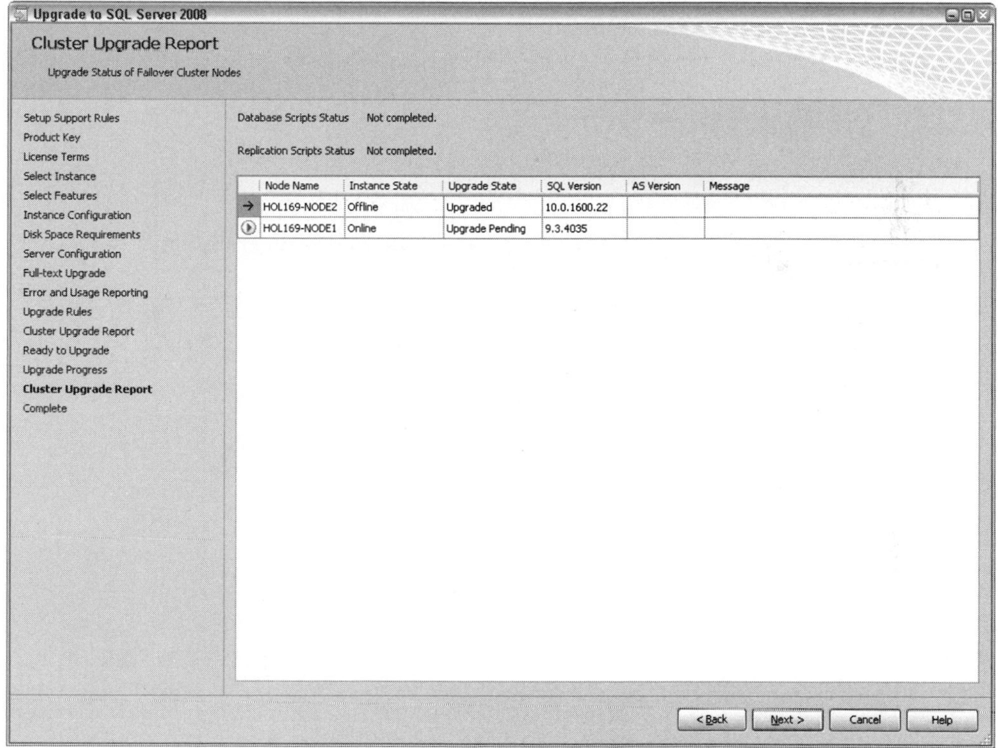

NOTE **During rolling upgrade there is no option to control the failover using the setup user interface. To control the failover, run the setup on the command line by supplying the failover option** `/FAILOVERCLUSTERROLLOWNERSHIP`.

Another important point is that the rolling upgrade can be performed against only one SQL Server 2000/2005 instance at a time. For example, consider a four-node Windows Server 2003 failover cluster with three of them SQL Server 2005 failover clustering instances. It is not possible to upgrade all three SQL Server 2005 failover clustering instances together. You need to repeat the procedure outlined earlier for each instance. Of course, you only need to install the prerequisites once, but the rest of the steps need to be executed once for each instance.

FIGURE 48-22

NODE2 is removed from the possible owners list for SQL Network Name resource.

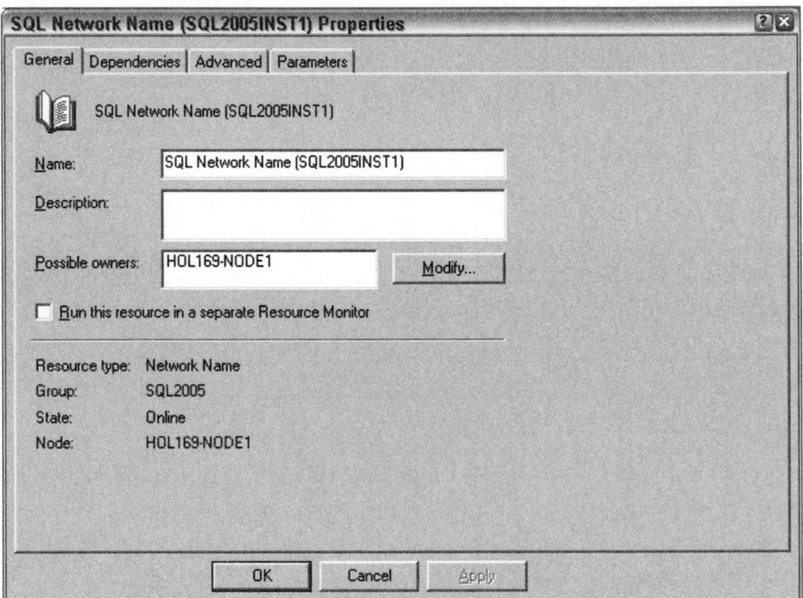

Best Practice

After performing the rolling upgrade, update the statistics on all databases to optimize query performance and run DBCC UPDATEUSAGE on all databases to correct row and page counts. If you upgraded from SQL Server 2000, then run DBCC CHECKDB WITH DATA_PURITY on all databases to enable column-value integrity, as it is not enabled by default on SQL Server 2000.

Patching a SQL Server 2008 failover cluster

Once you have a SQL Server 2008 failover cluster installed, it is recommended that you install the latest service pack for SQL Server 2008 to patch the server with fixes to known issues, which in turn reduces downtime due to known issues. This makes the cluster highly available, stable, and secure, and often increases the server's performance. Of course, before applying the service pack directly on the production cluster, you need to test it thoroughly on a test cluster with all your applications to ensure that everything is working as expected. Microsoft does extensive testing on the service packs but every environment is so different that it is virtually impossible to test each and every scenario.

FIGURE 48-23

Cluster Upgrade Report showing the upgrade status and warning message

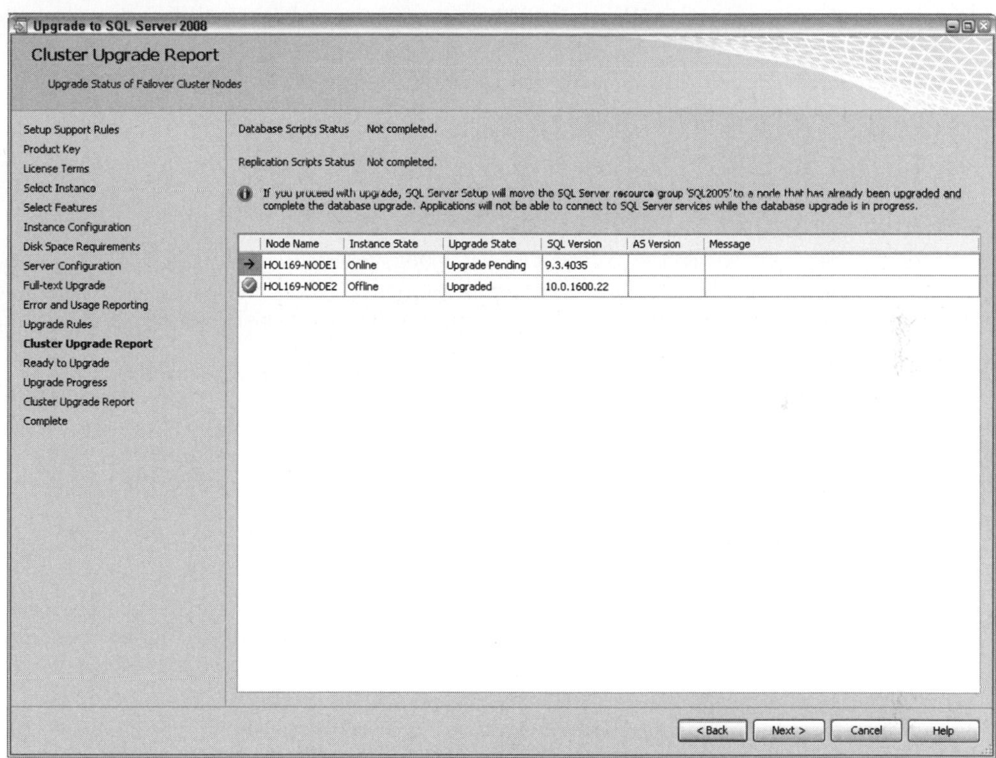

At the time of this writing, there is no service pack released for SQL Server 2008, but Microsoft has released two cumulative updates for SQL Server 2008. Approximately every two months, Microsoft releases a cumulative update. It's not recommended to apply every cumulative update, and frankly it is very difficult if not impossible to thoroughly test every cumulative update every two months against all your applications. Apply a cumulative update only if you need a fix that is included in the cumulative update or if you want to proactively apply the latest cumulative update released by Microsoft. Either way, always test the cumulative update before applying it on your production SQL Server 2008 failover cluster.

NOTE **Starting with SQL Server 2008 SP1, service pack installation is supported. This is great news because now it is not necessary to uninstall/reinstall SQL Server to uninstall a service pack; but this does not mean that you don't have to test your applications thoroughly against the latest service pack. It is still best practice to proactively test the service pack on a test server and verify that all the applications work as expected.**

To minimize downtime and maintain high availability while patching a SQL Server 2008 failover cluster with cumulative updates and/or service packs, use the rolling upgrade process as follows:

1. Open the Cluster Administrator tool in Windows 2003 Failover Cluster or the Failover Cluster Management tool in Windows 2008 Failover Cluster and remove half the passive nodes from the possible owners of the SQL Network Name resource.
2. Apply the update (cumulative update and/or service pack for SQL Server 2008) on the nodes that were removed.

Best Practice

Usually the steps to apply the update for a SQL Server 2008 failover clustering instance are very similar to applying it on a stand-alone SQL Server 2008. Nevertheless, some updates may have special considerations for failover clustering, and it is best to review the documentation that is supplied with the update package.

Before applying the update on a node, verify that no other cluster services are running on the node. For example, you may be applying the cumulative update 2 (CU2) for SQL Server 2008 instance INST1, but another SQL Server 2008 instance INST2 might be currently running on the node on which you are planning to apply CU2. Although the updates do not install the components of other instances, they do update the shared components. To avoid restart that may occur when shared components are updated, move INST2 to another node in the cluster.

3. After applying the updates on the nodes that were removed in step 1, add them back to the possible owners list for the SQL Network Name resource using the Cluster Administrator tool in Windows 2003 Failover Cluster or the Failover Cluster Management tool in Windows 2008 Failover Cluster.
4. At this point, half the cluster nodes have the update installed, but the SQL Server 2008 instance is still running on a node that does not have the update. Move the instance to a node that has the update and verify that all the SQL Server resources come online on the updated node.
5. Repeat steps 1 to 3 except now remove the nodes that were not patched from the possible owners list for the SQL Network Name resource, patch them, and then add them back to the possible owners list.
6. If you still have time and can afford downtime, move the SQL Server on each node to verify that it comes online on each node. Also, connect to the SQL Server instance using SQL Server Management Studio and run `select @@version` against the instance. Verify that the version is the same regardless of the node on which SQL Server is running. If you cannot perform this step now, do it during your next maintenance window. This step is very important to ensure that SQL Server will run on all the cluster nodes after the update is applied.

NOTE **These steps are recommended to attain minimum downtime. Some DBAs install the update directly on the node where the SQL Server 2008 failover clustering instance is running. This was how we installed an update on a SQL Server 2000 and 2005 failover cluster. This method works on SQL Server 2008, but it is not recommend because the number of reboots and down-time is much more compared to the steps just outlined. If one follows the steps, downtime will be**

minimal, and caused only in step 4 when moving the SQL Server 2008 failover clustering instance to an updated node.

It is also important to note that when a SQL Server 2008 patch is installed on a cluster node, it does not automatically install on the remote nodes. It needs to be installed separately on each node just as we installed SQL Server 2008 on each node.

Maintaining a SQL Server 2008 failover cluster

Once a SQL Server 2008 failover clustering instance is installed, you are ready to manage and maintain the instance just as you would on a stand-alone SQL Server 2008 instance. Managing a clustered SQL Server 2008 instance is no different from managing a stand-alone SQL Server 2008 instance.

CROSS-REF **For more information about configuring, recovery planning, and maintaining SQL Server, refer to Chapter 39, "Configuring SQL Server," Chapter 41, "Recovery Planning," and Chapter 42, "Maintaining the Database," respectively.**

Here are some maintenance operations that are slightly different for a SQL Server 2008 failover cluster:

- To start and stop a SQL Server 2008 failover clustering instance, use one of the following tools:
  - SQL Server Management Studio (is cluster-aware)
  - SQL Server Configuration Manager (is cluster-aware)
  - Command-line `cluster.exe` tool
  - Cluster Administrator tool in Windows 2003 Failover Cluster or Failover Cluster Management tool in Windows 2008 Failover Cluster

NOTE **Do not use the Services control panel applet in Windows to stop or start SQL Server 2008 failover clustering instances, as the Services applet is not cluster aware. If SQL Server is stopped from the Services applet, then the Windows cluster service will detect this and try to restart it based on the restart properties of SQL Server.**

- To connect to a SQL Server 2008 failover clustering instance, do not use the actual cluster node name. In fact, it's not necessary to even know the cluster node names; but you need to know the SQL Network Name for the default instance and the instance name for the named instance. For example, to connect to a default SQL Server 2008 failover clustering instance with SQL Network Name as SQL2008VS, use SQL2008VS to connect to the instance. To connect to a named SQL Server 2008 failover clustering instance with SQL Network Name as SQL2008VS1 and named instance name as INST1, use SQL2008VS1\INST1 to connect to the named instance. You can also connect using the SQL IP address instead of the SQL Network Name. Once connected to the SQL Server instance, all other operations are similar to the ones in a stand-alone SQL Server 2008. In fact, for most of the operations you do not even need to know that the SQL Server instance is clustered. Common DBA tasks such as backup, restore, and creating maintenance plans remain the same, without any extra steps.
- Sometimes it may be necessary to determine the actual cluster node name on which the SQL Server 2008 failover clustering instance is currently running. To find the NETBIOS name of the cluster node, execute the following command:

  ```
  SELECT SERVERPROPERTY('ComputerNamePhysicalNetBios');
  ```

Another way to find this information is to open the SQL Server Errorlog and search for the line `"The NETBIOS name of the local node that is running the server is"`. This information becomes especially important during postmortem analysis.

- Sometimes the DBA may not even know if the SQL Server 2008 instance she is administering is a clustered instance or a stand-alone instance. To find out if the current SQL Server instance is clustered, execute the following command:

```
SELECT SERVERPROPERTY('IsClustered');
```

If this is a SQL Server 2008 failover clustering instance, then it will return a value of 1; otherwise, it will return a value of 0.

- To view the cluster nodes on which the SQL Server 2008 failover clustering instance can run, use the `sys.dm_os_cluster_nodes` dynamic management view (DMV) as shown:

```
SELECT * FROM sys.dm_os_cluster_nodes;
```

- To view the shared disks that the SQL Server 2008 failover clustering instance can access, use the `sys.dm_io_cluster_shared_drives` DMV as shown:

```
SELECT * FROM sys.dm_io_cluster_shared_drives;
```

NOTE **A SQL Server 2008 failover clustering instance can only use shared drives for its databases. It cannot use local drives, not even for the `tempdb` database that is created every time SQL Server is started. The `sys.dm_io_cluster_shared_drives` DMV will display all the shared drives SQL Server 2008 can access. These are the drives that were selected during the installation.**

- To add a new shared drive, perform the following steps:
  1. Open the Cluster Administrator tool in Windows 2003 Failover Cluster or the Failover Cluster Management tool in Windows 2008 Failover Cluster.
  2. Move the shared disk to the SQL Server 2008 group.
  3. Right-click the SQL Server resource and select Take Offline. This will disconnect the clients, so it should be planned in advance.
  4. Right-click the SQL Server resource and select Properties. Click the Dependencies tab and select Modify. Add the new shared drive as a dependency to SQL Server.
  5. Bring the SQL Server resource online.
- For security reasons, you may want to change the default TCP/IP port number 1433 for a default SQL Server 2008 failover clustering instance, or you may want to assign a static TCP/IP port for your named SQL Server 2008 failover clustering instance. To assign a static TCP/IP port for a SQL Server 2008 failover clustering instance, follow these steps:
  1. Launch SQL Server Configuration Manager from Start ➪ Programs ➪ Microsoft SQL Server 2008 ➪ Configuration Tools ➪ SQL Server Configuration Manager.
  2. Expand SQL Server Network Configuration in the left pane and select Protocols for `<INSTANCE>`, where `<INSTANCE>` is the SQL Server instance name.
  3. Double-click TCP/IP on the right pane to open the TCP/IP Properties page.

4. Click the IP Addresses tab, scroll to the bottom, and look at the IPALL section. Delete any value that might be there under TCP Dynamic Ports and enter a valid port number for the TCP Port option and click OK.
5. Restart the SQL Server service to enable this change. This will disconnect all client connections, so it must be planned in advance.

- Sometimes it may be necessary to change the SQL IP address or the SQL network name for your SQL Server 2008 failover cluster. Changing the IP address or the network name can be very easily achieved by opening the Cluster Administrator tool in Windows 2003 Failover Cluster or the Failover Cluster Management tool in Windows 2008 Failover Cluster and changing the properties of the resource you want to change.

NOTE **Changing the SQL IP address or the SQL Network Name resource requires taking the SQL Server resource offline, so it needs to be planned in advance. Also, the change takes a few minutes to propagate through a corporate network.**

Although changing the SQL network name is allowed, the named instance name cannot be changed. For example, a SQL Server 2008 failover clustering instance named SQL2008VS1\INST1 can be changed to some other name, such as SQL2008VS2\INST1, but the named instance name INST1 cannot be changed. This is one reason to spend time proactively on the SQL Server 2008 failover cluster naming conventions.

Troubleshooting a SQL Server 2008 failover cluster

Troubleshooting SQL Server 2008 failover clustering is not always the same as diagnosing problems on a stand-alone SQL Server 2008 instance. SQL Server 2008 failover cluster technology is very complex and involves Windows failover clustering, the Windows operating system, the storage subsystem, cluster nodes, the network, hardware drivers, and SQL Server 2008 failover clustering. This makes troubleshooting a SQL Server 2008 failover cluster difficult and time consuming. Due to the dependence on so many components, troubleshooting a SQL Server 2008 failover cluster issue usually involves collaboration with the platforms, networking, storage, and SQL Server teams.

If problems exist on the cluster nodes, then those problems may manifest themselves as issues with your SQL Server 2008 failover clustering instance. Unless it is obvious that the issue is related to SQL Server 2008, troubleshoot a SQL Server 2008 failover clustering issue in the following order:

- Hardware
- Operating system
- Network
- Security
- Windows failover cluster
- SQL Server 2008

Often, a lot of information is required to troubleshoot a SQL Server 2008 failover clustering issue. Here are some of the logs that are useful in getting to the root of the issue:

- Windows application, system, and security event logs on all cluster nodes

- Cluster logs on all cluster nodes: The text file-based `cluster.log` (located in the `%systemroot%\system32\LogFiles\Cluster` folder in Windows Server 2003) is no longer in Windows Server 2008. It has been replaced by a much more sophisticated event-based tracing system. Event trace logging (`.etl`) is now enabled via Event Tracing for Windows (ETW). The `cluster.exe` tool enables you to dump the trace log into a text file. This file looks similar to the cluster log used in previous versions of failover clustering. An example command to generate a cluster log on a Windows failover cluster named `WIN2K8CLUSTER` would be as follows:

  ```
  Cluster.exe /cluster: WIN2K8CLUSTER log /generate /copy "C:\temp"
  ```

  Navigate to the `C:\temp` directory where you will find the `.log` files for each node of your cluster. The cluster log can now be opened in Notepad.
- SQL Server Error logs: Useful for troubleshooting SQL Server errors and SQL Server resource failures
- SQL Server Agent logs: Useful for troubleshooting SQL Server Agent errors and SQL Server Agent resource failures

Troubleshooting SQL Server 2008 setup issues is slightly different. Here are some steps that will assist in troubleshooting the failed installation:

1. Locate the relevant subfolder of the `%ProgramFiles%\Microsoft SQL Server \100\Setup Bootstrap\Log` folder with the latest timestamp to get to the latest installation log files.
2. First, review the `Summary.txt` file.
3. Next, review the `detail.txt` file and look for the keywords `"at Microsoft"` or `"threw an exception during execution"`.
4. Finally, examine the detailed MSI log for the component that failed.
   a. When the installation fails because the MSI failed, find the "`Error:`" string in the `Detail.txt` log.
   b. This error should then indicate which MSI and action failed. The action would be in the format `install_sql_cpu32_action`.
   c. Look into the corresponding MSI log and search for `"Return Value 3"` to determine why the MSI installation failed.

Summary

High availability is paramount to the success of most database projects, and is becoming increasingly important in regard to business requirements.

This chapter explored the key enhancements in SQL Server 2008 failover clustering, installing SQL Server 2008 failover clustering, rolling upgrade and patching, and maintaining and troubleshooting a SQL Server 2008 failover cluster.

SQL Server 2008 failover clustering is one of the high-availability options that Microsoft SQL Server 2008 offers. This is the only option that provides redundancy at the entire SQL Server 2008 instance level. Microsoft SQL Server 2008 offers other high-availability options such as log shipping, database mirroring, and replication. Review these options to determine which high-availability option or options work best for your environment. It is possible that you may need to use more than one option to suit your business requirements.

Part VII

Security

IN THIS PART

The Information Architecture Principle in Chapter 2 states in part:

Information is an organizational asset, and, according to its value and scope, must be organized, inventoried, and secured . . .

In the last edition of this book, security was a single chapter in the Enterprise Database Management part. In this edition, I've given security its own part to give it the space and significance that it deserves.

The basic model of principles and securables has remained constant throughout SQL Server history, but with new features and cryptology, the subject of security is growing more complex. This part also includes my solution for row-based security.

If SQL Server is the box, then this part is about padlocking the box to keep out those who should be out, while extending welcome to those who should be allowed in.

Chapter 49

Authenticating Principals

IN THIS CHAPTER

Understanding SQL Server security

Making sense of the many SQL logins

Server-level security

Server, database, and application roles

When I was a data systems technician in the Navy, I spent almost two years at Combat System Technical School Command (CSTSC) in Mare Island, California. It was good. My class was one of the last groups to be trained on the AN-UYK-7 computer. The CPU was a drawer with about 50 small cards populated with transistors. We learned to troubleshoot the CPU to the logic-gate level. It was very cool. We shared the island with the Crypto-tech school. The sailors in crypto school had it rough; they couldn't carry anything in or out of their school — no notes, no books, nothing. At least we could meet after hours in study groups. I was glad to be on the computer side of the command. Security has never thrilled me, but the Information Architecture Principle clearly states that information must be secured.

It's common practice to develop the database and then worry about security. While there's no point in applying security while the database design is in flux, the project benefits when you develop and implement the security plan sooner rather than later.

Security, like every other aspect of the database project, must be carefully designed, implemented, and tested. Because security may affect the execution of some procedures, it must be taken into account when the project code is being developed.

A simple security plan with a few roles and the IT users as *sysadmins* may suffice for a small organization. Larger organizations — such as the military, banks, or international organizations — require a more complex security plan that's designed as carefully as the logical database schema.

If security is tightly implemented with full security audits performed by server-side traces, the SQL Server installation can be certified at C2-level security. Fortunately, SQL Server's security model is well thought out, and, if fully understood, both logical and flexible. Whereas the tactics of securing a database are creating users and roles and then assigning permissions, the strategy is identifying the rights and responsibilities of data access and then enforcing the plan.

The emphasis on security affects the initial installation. SQL Server installs locked down, and you, as the DBA, must enable features before they can be used. Even remote connections are disabled by default.

The Surface Area Configuration facet of Policy-Based Management is used to enable features and components, thereby controlling the exposed surface area. It's designed to be run after installation. Once configured, the DBA should rarely need to use the tool, which is covered in Chapter 4, "Installing SQL Server 2008."

The SQL Server security model is large and complex. In some ways it's more complex than the Windows security model. Because the security concepts are tightly intertwined, the best way to begin is to walk through an overview of the model.

SQL Server security is based on the concept of securables (see Chapter 50, "Authorizing Securables"), objects that can be secured, and principals, objects that can be granted access to a securable. Principals are logins, users, and roles. Granting `CONTROL SERVER` to a login gives it equivalent rights to being a member of the sysadmin fixed server role. Logins can also be assigned to server roles. Users are assigned to roles, both of which may be granted permission to objects, as illustrated in Figure 49-1. Each object has an owner, and ownership also affects the permissions.

FIGURE 49-1

An overview of the SQL Server security model shows how users are first authenticated to the server, followed by the databases, and finally the objects within the databases. The circles represent how the user is identified.

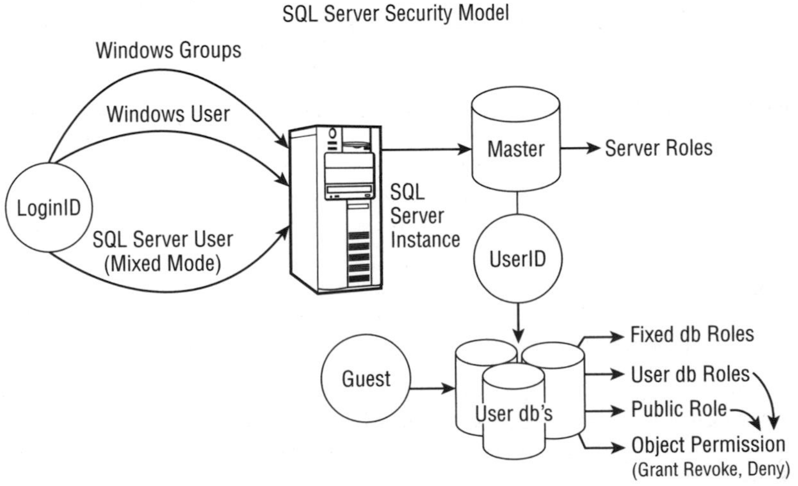

SQL Server Security Model

Server-Level Security

A user may be initially identified to SQL Server via one of three methods:

- Windows user login
- Membership in a Windows user group
- SQL Server-specific login (if the server uses mixed-mode security)

At the server level, users are known by their login name, which is either a SQL Server login, or a Windows domain and username.

Once the user is known to the server and identified, the user has whatever server-level administrative rights have been granted via fixed server roles. If the user belongs to the sysadmin role, he or she has full access to every server function, database, and object in the server. Users also have permissions granted against server securables.

A user can be granted access to a database, and his or her network login ID can be mapped to a database-specific user ID in the process. If the user doesn't have access to a database, he or she can gain access as the guest user with some configuration changes within the database server.

Database-Level Security

At the database level, a user may be granted certain administrative-level permissions by belonging to fixed database roles, but the user still can't access the data. He or she must be granted permission to the database objects (e.g., tables, stored procedures, views, functions). User-defined roles are custom roles that serve as groups. The role may be granted permission to a database object, and users may be assigned to a database user-defined role. All users are automatically members of the public standard database role. Certain database fixed roles also affect object access, such as the right to read from or write to the database.

Object permissions are assigned by means of *grant*, *revoke*, and *deny*. A deny permission trumps a grant permission. Revoke removes the permission assigned, regardless of whether it's deny or grant, which overrides a revoke permission. A user may have multiple permission paths to an object (individually, through a standard database role, and through the public role). If any of these paths are denied, the user is blocked from accessing the object. Otherwise, if any of the paths are granted permission, then the user can access the object.

Object permission is very detailed and a specific permission exists for every action that can be performed (select, insert, update, run, and so on) for every object.

It's entirely possible for a user to be recognized by SQL Server and not have access to any database other than `master`, `msdb`, and `tempdb`. It's also possible for a user to be defined within a database but not recognized by the server. Moving a database and its permissions to another server, but not moving the logins, causes such orphaned users.

Windows Security

Because SQL Server exists within a Windows environment, one aspect of the security strategy must be securing the Windows server.

Using Windows Security

SQL Server databases frequently support websites, so Internet Information Server (IIS) security and firewalls must be considered within the security plan.

Windows security is an entire topic in itself, and therefore outside the scope of this book. If, as a DBA, you are not well supported by qualified network staff, then you should make the effort to become proficient in Windows Server technologies, especially security.

SQL Server login

Don't confuse user access to SQL Server with SQL Server's Windows accounts. The two logins are completely different.

SQL Server users don't need access to the database directories or data files on a Windows level because the SQL Server process, not the user, performs the actual file access. However, the SQL Server process needs permission to access the files, so it needs a Windows account. Three types are available:

- **Local user account:** If network access is not required, this is a viable option. Local user accounts cannot be used outside the server.
- **Local system account:** SQL Server can use the local system account of the operating system for permission to the machine. This option is adequate for single-server installations, but fails to provide the network security required for distributed processing. The local system account has more rights than even a member of the Administrators account because the local system account has implicit privileges in the operating system and Active Directory that go beyond membership in the Administrators group.
- **Domain user account (recommended):** SQL Server can use a Windows user account created specifically for it. The SQL Server domain user account can be granted administrator rights for the server and can access the network through the server to talk to other servers.

CROSS-REF **The SQL Server accounts were initially configured when the server was installed. Installation is discussed in Chapter 4, "Installing SQL Server 2008."**

Server Security

SQL Server uses a two-phase security-authentication scheme. The user is first authenticated to the server. Once the user is "in" the server, access can be granted to the individual databases.

SQL Server stores all login information within the `master` database.

SQL Server authentication mode

When SQL Server was installed, one of the decisions made was which of the following authentication methods to use:

- Windows Authentication mode: Windows authentication only
- Mixed mode: Both Windows authentication and SQL Server user authentication

This option can be changed after installation in Management Studio, in the Security page of the SQL Server Properties dialog, as shown in Figure 49-2.

FIGURE 49-2

Server-level security is managed in the Security tab of the SQL Server Properties dialog.

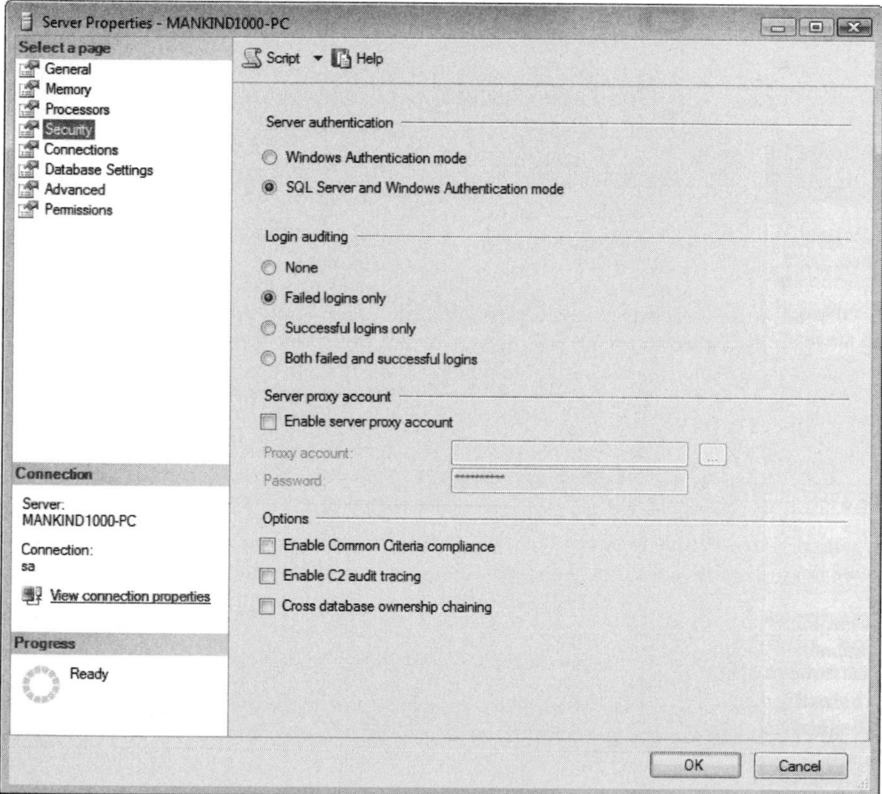

From code, the authentication mode can be checked by means of the `xp_loginconfig` system stored procedure, as follows:

```
EXEC xp_loginconfig 'login mode'
Result:
name            config_value
--------        -----------------------------
login mode      Mixed
```

Notice that the system stored procedure to report the authentication mode is an extended stored procedure. That's because the authentication mode is stored in the registry in the following entry:

```
HKEY_LOCAL_MACHINE\SOFTWARE\Microsoft\
  MicrosoftSQLServer\<instance_name>\MSSQLServer\LoginMode
```

A `LoginMode` value of 1 is for Windows authentication; 0 is for mixed mode. The only ways to set the authentication mode are to use either Management Studio or RegEdit.

Windows Authentication

Windows Authentication mode is superior to mixed mode because users don't need to learn yet another password and because it leverages the security design of the network.

Using Windows Authentication means that users must exist as Windows users in order to be recognized by SQL Server. The Windows SID (security identifier) is passed from Windows to SQL Server.

Windows Authentication is very robust in that it will authenticate not only Windows users, but also users within Windows user groups.

When a Windows user group is accepted as a SQL Server login, any Windows user who is a member of the group can be authenticated by SQL Server. Access, roles, and permissions can be assigned for the Windows user group, and they will apply to any Windows user in the group.

Best Practice

If the Windows users are already organized into groups by function and security level, using those groups as SQL Server users provides consistency and reduces administrative overhead.

SQL Server also knows the actual Windows username, so the application can gather audit information at both the user level and the group level.

Adding a new Windows login

Windows users are created and managed in various places in the different Windows versions. In Windows Vista, local users can be managed by selecting Control Panel ➪ Administrative Tools ➪ Computer Management, as shown in Figure 49-3. Domain users are managed with tools such as the Active Directory Users and Computers snap-in.

Once the users exist in the Windows user list or the Windows domain, SQL Server can recognize them. To add a new login to SQL Server using Object Explorer, follow these steps:

1. Open the Security ➪ Logins node under the server and use the context menu to select New Login.
2. In the General page of the Login-New dialog (see Figure 49-4), use the Search button to locate the Windows user.
3. You may enter a username or group name or use the Advanced button to search for a user.

FIGURE 49-3

Windows users are managed and assigned to Windows groups by means of the Computer Management tool.

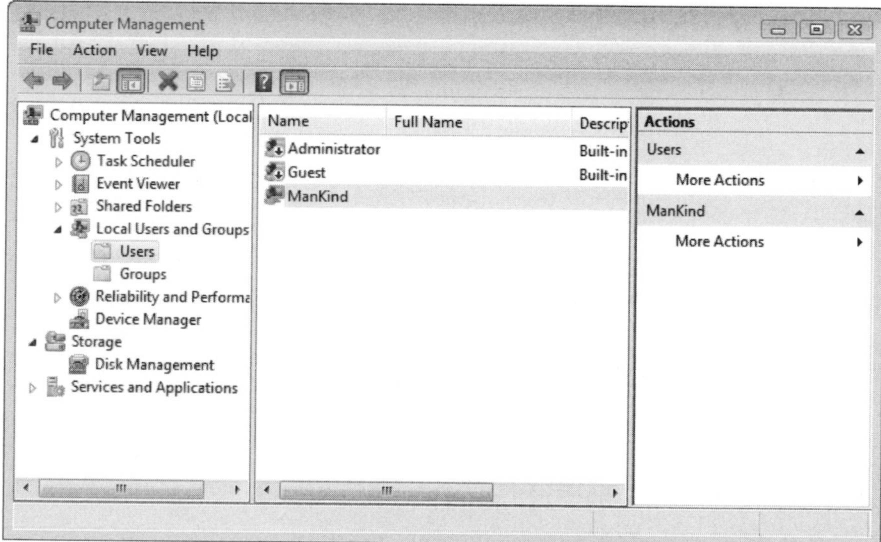

The user may be assigned a default database and language at the bottom of the SQL Server Login Properties dialog. Note that assigning a default database does not automatically grant access to that database. The user may be granted access to databases in the Database Access tab. (Database access is discussed in the next section.)

To use T-SQL code to add a Windows user or group, run the `CREATE LOGIN` command. Be sure to use the full Windows username, including the domain name, as follows:

```
CREATE LOGIN 'XPS\Joe'
```

To view Windows logins using code, query the `sysserver_principals` catalog view.

FIGURE 49-4

Use the General page of the Login-New dialog to create and edit user logins at the server level.

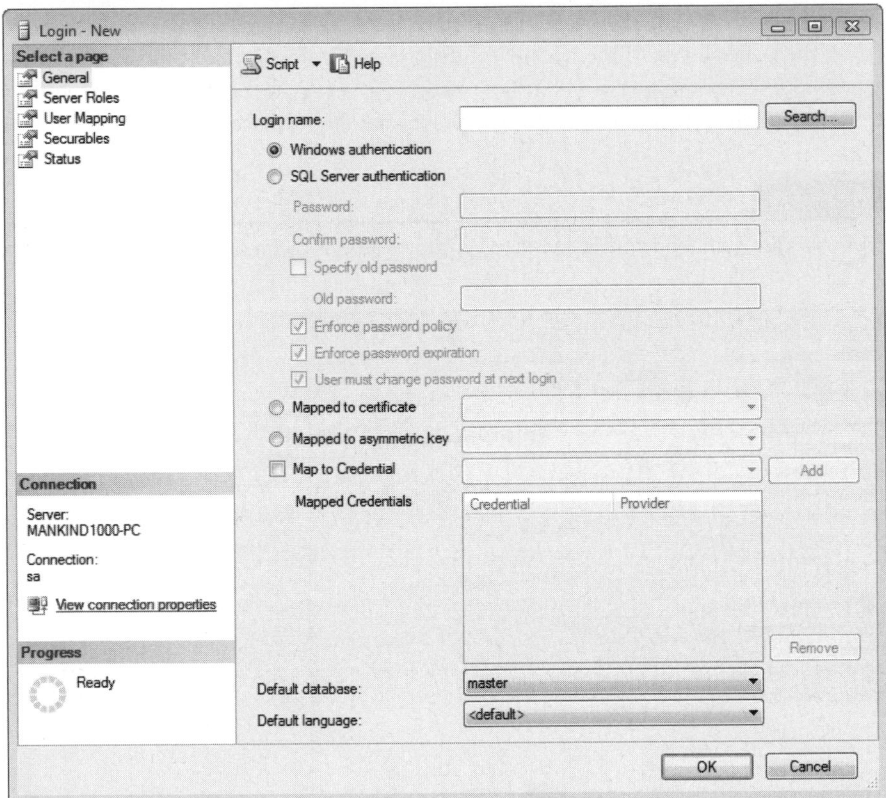

The Login-New dialog is also used to manage existing users. To open the Login Permission version of the dialog for an existing user, select the user under the Security ➪ Logins node and use the context menu's Properties command or double-click the user.

Removing a Windows login

Removing a windows login from SQL Server is simple enough with Management Studio. Select the login in Object Browser and use the context menu to delete the user. Of course, this doesn't delete the user from Windows; it only removes the user from SQL Server.

To remove a Windows user or group from SQL Server, use the `DROP LOGIN` command. The Windows user or group will exist in Windows; it just won't be recognized by SQL Server:

```
DROP LOGIN 'XPS\Joe'
```

Denying a Windows login

Using the paradigm of grant, revoke, and deny, a user may be blocked for access using `ALTER LOGIN` for Windows users and `DENY CONNECT` for Windows groups. This can prevent users or groups from accessing SQL Server even if they could otherwise gain entry from another method.

For example, suppose the Accounting group is granted normal login access, while the Probation group is denied access. Joe is a member of both the Accounting group and the Probation group. The Probation group's denied access blocks Joe from the SQL Server even though he is granted access as a member of the Accounting group, because deny overrides grant.

To deny a Windows user or group, use the `DENY CONNECT` command. If the user or group being denied access doesn't exist in SQL Server, then `DENY CONNECT` adds and then denies him, her, or it:

```
DENY CONNECT 'XPS\Joe'
```

To restore the login after denying access, you must first grant access with the *sp_grantlogin* system stored procedure.

You can deny the ability to log in using T-SQL.

Setting the default database

The default database is set in the Login Properties form in the General page. The default database can be set from code by means of the `ALTER LOGIN` command:

```
ALTER LOGIN 'Sam', 'OBXKites'
```

Orphaned Windows users

When a Windows user is added to SQL Server and then removed from the Windows domain, the user still exists in SQL Server but is considered orphaned. Being an orphaned user means that although SQL Server still has the Windows account listed within SQL Server, it doesn't exist any longer in the domain; therefore, no access is provided as a result. Even if the Windows account is recreated, it will have a new SID and GUID, and therefore won't match up.

The `sp_validatelogins` system stored procedure locates all orphaned users and returns their Windows NT security identifiers and login names. In the following code example, Joe was granted access to SQL Server and then removed from Windows:

```
EXEC sp_validatelogins
Result (formatted):
SID                                                    NT Login
-------------------------------------------            ----------
0x010500000000000515000000FCE31531A931...              XPS\Joe
```

This is not a security hole. Without a Windows login with a matching SID, the user can't log into SQL Server.

To resolve the orphaned user:

1. Remove the user from any database access using *DROP LOGIN*.
2. Revoke the user's server access using *sp_revokelogin*.

Security delegation

In an enterprise network with multiple servers and IIS, logins can become a problem because a user may be logging into one server that is accessing another server. This problem arises because each server must have a trust relationship with the others. For internal company servers, this may not be an issue, but when one of those servers sits in a DMZ on the Internet, you may not want to establish that trust, as it presents a security hole.

Security delegation is a Windows feature that uses Kerberos to pass security information among trusted servers. For example, a user can access IIS, which can access a SQL Server, and the SQL Server will see the user as the username even though the connection came from IIS.

A few conditions must be met in order for Kerberos to work:

- All servers must be running Windows 2000 or later, running Active Directory in the same domain or within the same trust tree.
- The "Account is sensitive and cannot be delegated" option must not be selected for the user account.
- The "Account is trusted for delegation" option must be selected for the SQL Server service account.
- The "Computer is trusted for delegation" option must be selected for the server running SQL Server.
- SQL Server must have a Service Principal Name (SPN), created by `setspn.exe`, available in the Windows 2000 Resource Kit.

Security delegation is difficult to set up and may require the assistance of your network domain administrator. However, the ability to recognize users going through IIS is a powerful security feature. Executing SETSPN to add or delete an SPN does require domain admin rights.

SPN is a powerful security feature, but it does weaken security because the user is being impersonated. Therefore, its use should generally be restricted to those cases where it's absolutely necessary. Unconstrained delegation should be avoided at all costs.

SQL Server logins

The optional SQL Server logins are useful when Windows authentication is inappropriate or unavailable. It's provided for backward compatibility and for legacy applications that are hard-coded to a SQL Server login.

Best Practice

Implementing SQL Server logins (mixed mode) will automatically create an sa user, who will be a member of the sysadmin fixed server role and have all rights to the server. An sa user without a password is very common and the first attack every hacker tries when detecting a SQL Server. Therefore, the best practice is to disable the sa user and assign different users, or roles, to the sysadmin fixed server role instead.

To manage SQL Server users in Management Studio, use the same Login-New dialog used when adding Windows users, but select SQL Server Authentication.

In T-SQL code, use the `CREATE LOGIN` command. Because this requires setting up a user, rather than just selecting one that already exists, it's more complex than adding a `sp_grantlogin`. Only the login name is required:

```
CREATE LOGIN 'login', 'password', 'defaultdatabase',
  'defaultlanguage', 'sid', 'encryption_option'
```

For example, the following code adds Joe as a SQL Server user and sets his default database to the `OBXKites` sample database:

```
EXEC sp_addlogin 'Sam', 'myoldpassword', 'OBXKites'
```

The encryption option (`skip_encryption`) directs SQL Server to store the password without any encryption in the `sysxlgns` system table. This option tells SQL Server that the value being passed is already encrypted, so the password won't work. Avoid this option.

The server user ID, or SID, is an 85-bit binary value that SQL Server uses to identify the user. If the user is being set up on two servers as the same user, then the SIDs need to be specified for the second server. Query the `sys.server_principals` catalog view to find the user's SID:

```
SELECT Name, SID
  FROM sys.server_principals
  WHERE Name = 'Sam'
```

Result:

```
Name            SID
---------       ------------------------------------------
Sam             0x1EFDC478DEB52045B52D241B33B2CD7E
```

Updating a password

The password can be modified by means of the `ALTER LOGIN` command:

```
ALTER LOGIN 'myoldpassword', 'mynewpassword', 'Joe'
```

If the password is empty, use the keyword `NULL` instead of empty quotes (' ').

Removing a login

To remove a SQL Server login, use the `DROP LOGIN` command:

```
DROP LOGIN 'Joe'
```

Removing a login also removes all the login security settings.

Setting the default database

The default database is set in the Login Properties form in the General page, just as it is for Windows users. The default database can be set from code by means of the `ALTER LOGIN` command:

```
ALTER LOGIN 'Sam', 'OBXKites'
```

Server roles

SQL Server includes only fixed, predefined server roles. Primarily, these roles grant permission to perform certain server-related administrative tasks. A user may belong to multiple roles.

The following roles are best used to delegate certain server administrative tasks:

- Bulkadmin: Can perform bulk insert operations
- Dbcreator: Can create, alter, drop, and restore databases
- Diskadmin: Can create, alter, and drop disk files
- Processadmin: Can kill a running SQL Server process
- Securityadmin: Can manage the logins for the server
- Serveradmin: Can configure the serverwide settings, including setting up full-text searches and shutting down the server
- Setupadmin: Can configure linked servers, extended stored procedures, and the startup stored procedure
- Sysadmin: Can perform any activity in the SQL Server installation, regardless of any other permission setting. The sysadmin role even overrides denied permissions on an object.

SQL Server automatically creates a user, BUILTINS/Administrators, that includes all Windows users in the Windows Admins group and allows a choice of what groups or users are added during setup. The BUILTINS/Administrators user can be deleted or modified if desired.

If the SQL Server is configured for mixed-mode security, it also configures the sa account to be disabled. The sa user is there for backward compatibility.

Best Practice

Disable or rename the sa user, or at least assign it a password, but don't use it as a developer and DBA sign-on. In addition, delete the BUILTINS/Administrators user. Instead, use Windows authentication and assign the DBAs and database developers to the sysadmin role.

A user must reconnect for the full capabilities of the sysadmin role to take effect.

The server roles are set in Management Studio in the Server Roles page of the Login Properties dialog (see Figure 49-5).

FIGURE 49-5

The Server Roles page is used to assign server administrative rights to users. Here, the Windows Admin group is granted the sysadmin role.

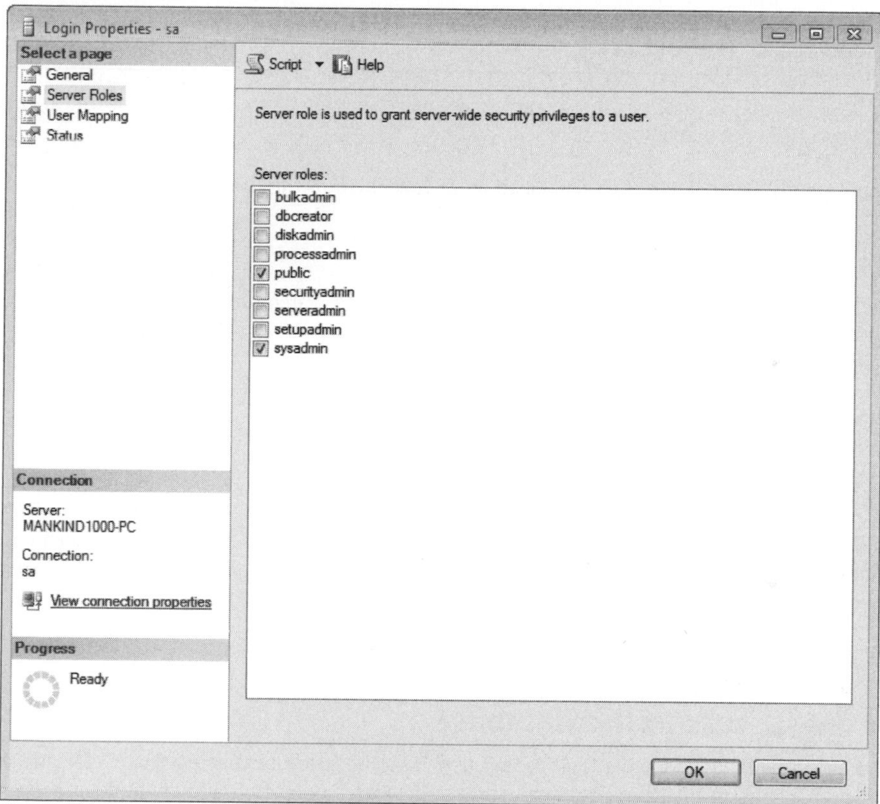

In code, a user is assigned to a server role by means of a system stored procedure:

```
sp_addsrvrolemember
  [ @loginname = ] 'login',
  [ @rolename = ] 'role'
```

For example, the following code adds the login "XPS\Lauren" to the sysadmin role:

```
EXEC sp_addsrvrolemember  'XPS\Lauren', 'sysadmin'
```

The counterpart of sp_addsrvrolemember, sp_dropsrvrolemember, removes a login from a server fixed role:

```
EXEC sp_dropsrvrolemember  'XPS\Lauren', 'sysadmin'
```

TIP **To view the assigned roles using code, query the `sysserver_principals` catalog view to select the members, joined with the `sysserver_role_members`, and joined again to the `sysserver_principals` to select the roles.**

Database Security

Once a user has gained access to the server, access may be granted to the individual user databases. Database security is potentially complex.

Users are initially granted access to databases by adding them to the database.

Guest logins

Any user who wishes to access a database but has not been declared a user within the database will automatically be granted the user privileges of the guest database user if the guest user account exists (refer to Figure 49-1).

The guest user is not automatically created when a database is created. It must be specifically added in code or as a database user. The guest login does not need to be predefined as a server login:

```
EXEC sp_adduser 'Guest'
```

CAUTION **Be very careful with the guest user. While it may be useful to enable a user to access the database without setting him or her up, the permissions granted to the guest user apply to everyone without access to the database.**

The guest user must be removed from a database when guests are no longer welcome.

Granting access to the database

Users must be explicitly granted access to any user database. Because this is a many-to-many relationship between logins and database, you can manage database access from either the login side or the database side.

When a login is granted access to the database, the login is also assigned a database username, which may be the same as the login name or some other name by which the login will be known within the database.

To grant access to a database from the login side using Object Explorer, use the User Mapping page of the Login Properties form (shown in Figure 49-6).

NOTE **Many security settings involve multiple objects such as users and databases or roles and object permissions. These settings can be made from either the Login Permissions form or the role's or object's Properties page.**

To grant access from the database point of view, use the New User Context Menu command under the Database ➪ Security ➪ Users node to open the Database User-New form, shown in Figure 49-7. Enter the login to be added in the Login Name field. To search for a login, use the ellipses (...) button. You must enter a name by which the user will be known within the database in the User Name field.

FIGURE 49-6

You can use the Login Properties form to grant a login access to any database and to assign database roles.

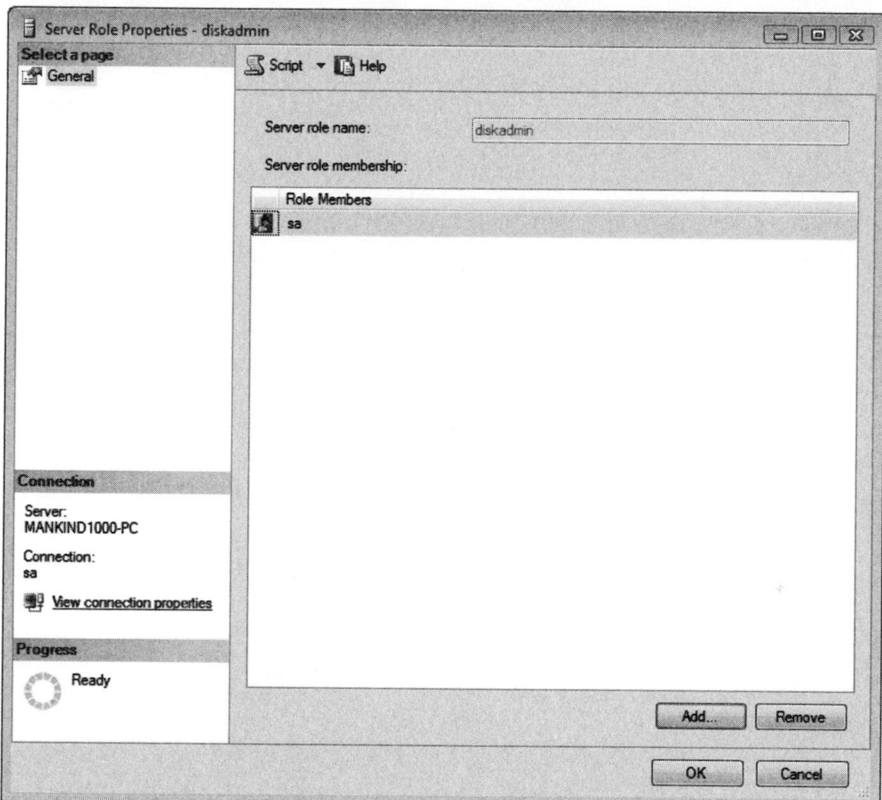

Granting access using T-SQL code

Of course, a stored procedure is available to grant database access to a user: *CREATE USER*. The stored procedure must be issued from within the database to which the user is to be granted access. The first parameter is the server login, and the second is the optional database username:

```
USE Family
CREATE USER 'XPS\Lauren', 'LRN'
```

Lauren now appears in the list of database users as "LRN."

To remove Lauren's database access, the system stored procedure *DROP USER* requires her database username, not her server login name:

```
USE Family
DROP USER 'LRN'
```

FIGURE 49-7

The Login dialog box can be used to add a new user to the database or to manage the current user.

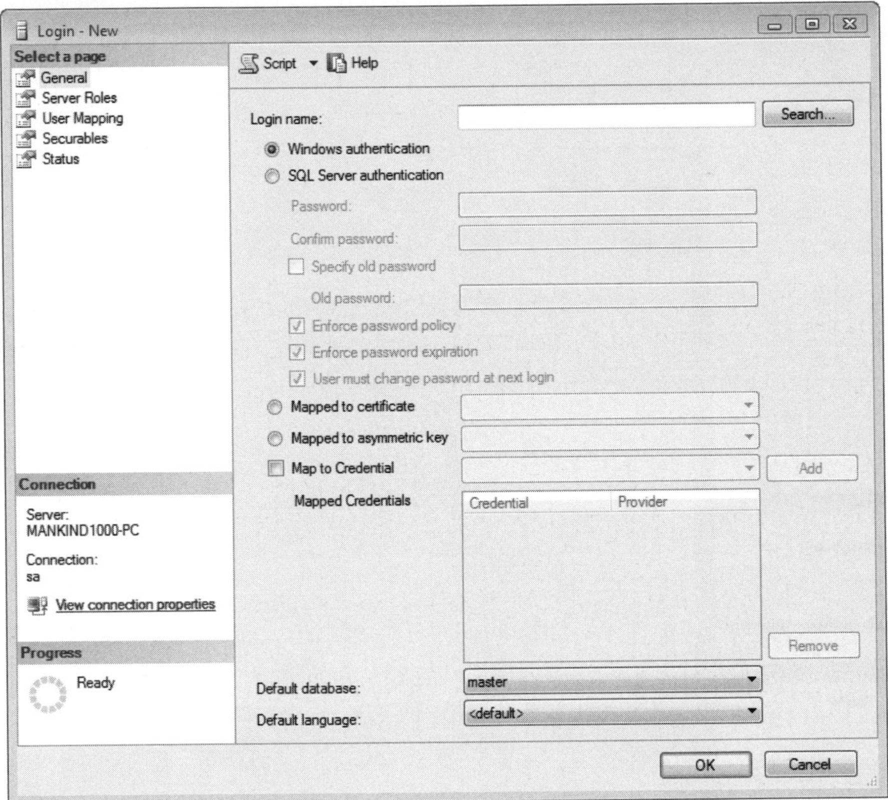

TIP **To query a database user using T-SQL, select from the** `sys.database_principals` **catalog view.**

Fixed database roles

SQL Server includes a few standard, or fixed, database roles. Like the server fixed roles, these primarily organize administrative tasks. A user may belong to multiple roles. The fixed database roles include the following:

- db_accessadmin: Can authorize a user to access the database, but not manage database-level security

- db_backupoperator: Can perform backups, checkpoints, and DBCC commands, but not restores (only server sysadmins can perform restores)
- db_datareader: Can read all the data in the database. This role is the equivalent of a grant on all objects, and it can be overridden by a deny permission.
- db_datawriter: Can write to all the data in the database. This role is the equivalent of a grant on all objects, and it can be overridden by a deny permission.
- db_ddladmin: Can issue DDL commands (create, alter, drop)
- db_denydatareader: Can read from any table in the database. This deny will override any object-level grant.
- db_denydatawriter: Blocks modifying data in any table in the database. This deny will override any object-level grant.
- db_owner: A special role that has all permissions in the database. This role includes all the capabilities of the other roles. It is different from the dbo user role. This is not the database-level equivalent of the server sysadmin role; an object-level deny will override membership in this role.
- db_securityadmin: Can manage database-level security — roles and permissions

Assigning fixed database roles with Management Studio

The fixed database roles can be assigned with Management Studio with either of the following two procedures:

- Adding the role to the user in the user's Database User Properties form (see Figure 49-7), either as the user is being created or after the user exists.
- Adding the user to the role in the Database Role Properties dialog. Select Roles under the database's Security node, and use the context menu to open the Properties form (see Figure 49-8).

Assigning fixed database roles with T-SQL

From code, you can add a user to a fixed database role with the `sp_addrole` system stored procedure.

To examine the assigned roles in T-SQL, query the `sysdatabase_role_members` catalog view joined with `sysdatabase_principal`.

Application roles

An application role is a database-specific role intended to allow an application to gain access regardless of the user. For example, if a specific Visual Basic program is used to search the *Customer* table and it doesn't handle user identification, the VB program can access SQL Server using a hard-coded application role. Anyone using the application gains access to the database.

Because using an application role forfeits the identity of the user, I strongly advise against using application roles. The user can regain identity context using `sp_unsetapprole`.

FIGURE 49-8

The Database Role Properties dialog lists all users assigned to the current role. To add or remove users from the role, use the Add and Remove buttons, respectively.

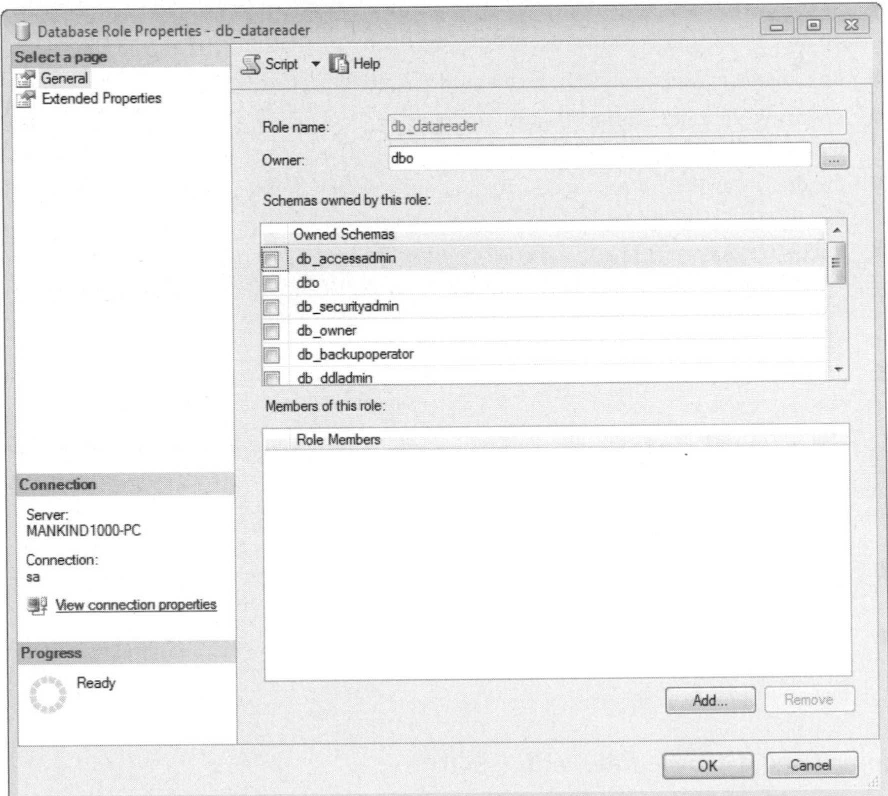

Summary

In this era of cybercrime, data security is more important than ever. Security is integral to the Information Architecture Principle. While it's possible to set all the users to sysadmin and ignore security, with a little effort SQL Server security is functional and flexible enough to meet the needs presented by a variety of situations.

Chapter 50

Authorizing Securables

This chapter adds another important piece to the SQL Server security puzzle — securables. These are objects (for example, tables, views, stored procedures, columns) that can be secured in order to prevent unauthorized access.

IN THIS CHAPTER

Object ownership

Securables permissions

Object security

Views and security

Object Ownership

A very important aspect of SQL Server's security model involves object ownership. Every object is contained by a schema. The default schema is dbo — not to be confused with the dbo role.

Ownership becomes critical when permission is being granted to a user to run a stored procedure when the user doesn't have permission to the underlying tables. If the ownership chain from the tables to the stored procedure is consistent, then the user can access the stored procedure, and the stored procedure can access the tables as its owner. However, if the ownership chain is broken, meaning there's a different owner somewhere between the stored procedure and the table, then the user must have rights to the stored procedure, the underlying tables, and every other object in between.

There is a fine point in the details. A schema is owned; and because a schema is owned, anything that is contained by it has the same owner.

Most security management can be performed in Management Studio. With code, security is managed by means of the `GRANT`, `REVOKE`, and `DENY` Data Control Language (DCL) commands and several system stored procedures.

Object Security

If a user has access to the database, then permission to the individual database objects may be granted. Permission may be granted either directly to the user or to a standard role and the user assigned to the role. Users may be assigned to multiple roles, so multiple security paths from a user to an object may exist.

Standard database roles

Standard database roles, sometimes called user-defined roles, can be created by any user in the server sysadmin, database `db_owner`, or database security admin role. These roles are similar to those in user groups in Windows. Permissions, and other role memberships, can be assigned to a standard database role, and users can then be assigned to the role.

Best Practice

The cleanest SQL Server security plan is to assign object permissions and fixed roles to standard database roles, and then to assign users to the roles.

Object permissions

Several specific types of permissions exist:

- **Select:** The right to select data. Select permission can be applied to specific columns.
- **Insert:** The right to insert data
- **Update:** The right to modify existing data. Update rights for which a `WHERE` clause is used require select rights as well. Update permission can be set on specific columns.
- **Delete:** The right to delete existing data
- **DRI (References):** The right to create foreign keys with DRI
- **Execute:** The right to execute stored procedures or user-defined functions

Object permissions are assigned with the SQL DCL commands, `GRANT`, `REVOKE`, and `DENY`. The permissions in SQL Server work like they do in the operating system. SQL Server aggregates all the permissions a given user might have, whether directly assigned against the user or through the roles. Then SQL Server gives the `MAXIMUM` of what has been granted. `DENY` is an exception. `DENY` functions as a trump. If anywhere a `DENY` has been issued, then just like in Windows, the user is blocked. For instance, if a user can `SELECT` against a table directly assigned, but a role the user is a member of has a `DENY` for `SELECT`, then the user is blocked from issuing a `SELECT` against the table. Whether security is being managed from Management Studio or from code, it's important to understand these three commands.

Granting object permission interacts with the server and database roles. Here's the overall hierarchy of roles and grants, with 1 overriding 2, and so on:

1. The sysadmin server role. A Windows login that owns a database will be mapped to dbo, and because it maps to dbo, it ignores all security on the database.
2. Deny object permission or the db_denydatareader database role or the db_denydatawriter database role.
3. Grant object permission or object ownership or the db_datareader database role or the db_datawriter database role.

Best Practice

An easy way to test security is to configure the server for mixed mode and create a SQL Server Login test user. Using Management Studio, it's easy to create additional connections as different users — much easier than it is to change the server registration and log into Management Studio as someone else.

Since SQL Server 2005 it has been possible to create a database principal that does not map to a server principal using the `CREATE USER` command and specifying `WITHOUT LOGIN`. Then, using `EXECUTE AS USER = '<username>'` to switch security contexts, the security can be tested. `REVERT`, of course, switches the context back.

If your environment prohibits mixed-mode security, then the easiest way to check security is to right-click Management Studio or Query Analyzer and use the `RUN AS` command to run as a different user, but this entails creating dummy users in the Windows domain. Generally speaking, in a "production" Windows domain, most auditors would flag dummy users as an audit point. Since workstations belonging to DBAs tend to belong in production domains, this recommendation wouldn't work where the auditors are being diligent.

Granting object permissions with code

Setting an object's permission is the only security command that can be executed without a system stored procedure being called:

```
GRANT Permission, Permission
  ON Object
  TO User/role, User/role
  WITH GRANT OPTION
```

The permissions may be `ALL`, `SELECT`, `INSERT`, `DELETE`, `REFERENCES`, `UPDATE`, or `EXECUTE`. The role or username refers to the database username, any user-defined public role, or the public role. For example, the following code grants select permission to Joe for the `Person` table:

```
GRANT Select ON Person TO Joe
```

The next example grants all permissions to the public role for the `Marriage` table:

```
GRANT All ON Marriage TO dbcreator
```

Multiple users or roles, and multiple permissions, may be listed in the command. The following code grants select and update permission to the guest user and to LRN:

```
GRANT Select, Update ON Person to Developer, LRN
```

The `WITH GRANT` option provides the ability to grant permission for the object. For example, the following command grants Joe the permission to select from the `Person` table and grant select permission to others:

```
GRANT Select ON Person TO Joe WITH GRANT OPTION
```

Revoking and denying object permission with code

Revoking and denying object permissions uses essentially the same syntax as granting permission. The following statement revokes select permissions from Joe on the `Marriage` table:

```
REVOKE All ON Marriage TO Joe
```

If the permission included the `WITH GRANT OPTION`, then the permission must be revoked or denied with the `CASCADE` option so that the `WITH GRANT OPTION` will be removed. The following command denies select permissions to Joe on the `Person` table:

```
DENY Select ON Person TO Joe CASCADE
```

Because using `CASCADE` will revoke not only the `WITH GRANT OPTION` permission, the DBA can get rid of the ability to `GRANT` but must first get rid of the permission, including `WITH GRANT OPTION`, and then re-`GRANT` the original permission, but this time without specifying `WITH GRANT OPTION`.

The public role

The public role is a fixed role, but it can have object permissions like a standard role. Every user is automatically a member of the public role and cannot be removed, so the public role serves as a baseline or minimum permission level.

CAUTION **Be careful when applying permissions to the public role because it will affect everyone except members of the sysadmin role. Granting access will affect everyone; more important, denying access will block all users except members of the sysadmin role, even object owners, from accessing data.**

Managing roles with code

Creating standard roles with code involves using the `sp_addrole` system stored procedure. The name can be up to 128 characters and cannot include a backslash, be null, or be an empty string. By default, the roles will be owned by the dbo user. However, you can assign the role an owner by adding a second parameter. The following code creates the manager role:

```
CREATE ROLE 'Manager'
```

Result:

```
New role added.
```

The counterpart of creating a role is removing it. A role may not be dropped if any users are currently assigned to it. The `sp_droprole` system stored procedure will remove the role from the database:

```
DROP ROLE 'Manager'
```

Result:

```
Role dropped.
```

Once a role has been created, users may be assigned to the role by means of the `sp_addrolemember` system stored procedure. The following code sample assigns Joe to the manager role:

```
EXEC sp_addrolemember 'Manager', Joe
```

Result:

```
'Joe' added to role 'Manager'.
```

Not surprisingly, the system stored procedure `sp_droprolemember` removes a user from an assigned role. This code frees Joe from the drudgery of management:

```
EXEC sp_dropRoleMember 'Manager', Joe
```

Result:

```
'Joe' dropped from role 'Manager'.
```

Hierarchical role structures

If the security structure is complex, then a powerful permission-organization technique is to design a hierarchical structure of standard database roles. In other words, you can nest user-defined database roles.

- The worker role may have limited access.
- The manager role may have all worker rights plus additional rights to look up tables.
- The administrator role may have all manager rights plus the right to perform other database administration tasks.

To accomplish this type of design, follow these steps:

1. Create the worker role and set its permissions.
2. Create the manager role and set its permissions. Add the manager role as a user to the worker role.
3. Create the admin role. Add the admin role as a user to the manager role.

The advantage of this type of security organization is that a change in the lower level affects all upper levels. As a result, administration is required in only one location, rather than dozens of locations.

Object security and Management Studio

Object permissions, because they involve users, roles, and objects, can be set from numerous places within Management Studio. It's almost a maze.

From the object list

Follow these steps to modify an object's permissions:

1. From an object node (tables, views, stored procedures, or user-defined functions) in the Object Browser, select Properties from the context menu to open the Properties dialog for that object type.
2. Click the Permissions page to open the Object Properties dialog.

The top portion of the form is for selecting a user or role to assign or check permissions. The user must have access to the database to be selected.

As with setting statement permissions in the Database Properties Security tab, you can select grant, with grant, or deny. The object list at the top of the dialog lists all the objects in the database. This list can be used to quickly switch to other objects without backing out of the form to the console and selecting a different object.

If the user or role has permission to the table, the Columns button opens the Column Permissions dialog. Select the user and then click the button to set the columns permission for that user. Only select and update permissions can be set at the column level, because inserts and deletes affect the entire row.

From the user list

From the list of database users in Management Studio, select a user and double-click, or select Properties from the right-click context menu. The Database User Properties dialog is used to assign users to roles.

Clicking the Properties button will open the properties of the selected role.

In the Database User Properties dialog, the Securables page is used to assign or check object permissions. This dialog is similar to the Permissions tab of the Database Object Properties dialog.

From the role list

The third way to control object permissions is from the database role. To open the Database Role Properties dialog, double-click a role in the list of roles, or select Properties from the right-click context menu. The Database Role Properties dialog can be used to assign users or other roles to the role, and to remove them from the role.

The Permissions button opens the permissions dialog for the role. This form operates like the other permission forms except that it is organized from the role's perspective.

Ownership chains

In SQL Server databases, users often access data by going through one or several objects. Ownership chains apply to views, stored procedures, and user-defined functions. For example:

- A program might call a stored procedure that then selects data from a table.
- A report might select from a view, which then selects from a table.
- A complex stored procedure might call several other stored procedures.

In these cases, the user must have permission to execute the stored procedure or select from the view. Whether the user also needs permission to select from the underlying tables depends on the ownership chain from the object the user called to the underlying tables.

If the ownership chain is unbroken from the stored procedure to the underlying tables, the stored procedure can execute using the permission of its owner. The user only needs permission to execute the stored procedure. The stored procedure can use its owner's permission to access the underlying tables. The user doesn't require permission to the underlying tables.

Ownership chains are great for developing tight security where users execute stored procedures but aren't granted direct permission to any tables.

If the ownership chain is broken, meaning there's a different owner between an object and the next lower object, then SQL Server checks the user's permission for every object accessed.

It's important to note that if dynamic SQL is used, then the `EXECUTE AS` clause for `CREATE PROCEDURE` was added to SQL Server 2005. Since it executes as a separate batch, it breaks ownership chaining.

When the chain is broken:

- The ownership chain from dbo.A to dbo.B to dbo.Person is unbroken, so dbo.A can call dbo.B and access dbo.Person as dbo.
- The ownership chain from dbo.A to Sue.C to Joe.Purchase is broken because different owners are present. Therefore, dbo.A calls Sue.C using Joe's permissions, and Sue.C accesses Joe.Purchase using Joe's permissions.
- The ownership chain from dbo.A through dbo.B to Joe.Person is also broken, so dbo.A calls dbo.B using dbo's permissions, but dbo.B must access Joe.Purchase using Joe's permissions.
- It is possible for dbo, Sue, and Joe to all have the same owner. In that case, the ownership chain will work.

Stored procedure execute as

When developing stored procedures, the effective security access of the code within the stored procedures can be explicitly determined. This is far better than just guessing that the security, or the ownership chain, will be correct.

The `execute as` stored procedure option defines how the ownership is determined.

Although `execute as` is typically associated with stored procedures, it also applies to scalar user-defined functions, multi-line table-valued user-defined functions, and DML and DDL triggers.

The following example creates a stored procedure that will execute with the permissions of the user with created the stored procedures:

```
CREATE PROCEDURE AddNewCustomer (
  LastName VARCHAR(50),
  FirstName VARCHAR(50)
  )
WITH EXECUTE AS SELF
AS
SET NO COUNT ON
```

The options for execute as are:

- `Caller` — execute with the owner permissions of the user executing the stored procedure.
- `Self` — execute with the permission of the user who created or altered the stored procedure.
- `Owner` — execute with the permissions of the owner of the stored procedure.
- `'hard-coded user name'` — execute with the permission of the specific named user.

A Sample Security Model Example

For a few examples of permissions using the `OBXKites` database, Table 50-1 lists the permission settings of the standard database roles. Table 50-2 lists a few of the users and their roles.

TABLE 50-1

OBXKites Fixed Roles

Standard Role	Hierarchical Role Structures	Primary Filegroup Tables	Static Filegroup Tables	Other Permissions
IT	sysadmin server role	–	–	–
Clerk	–	–	–	Execute permissions for several stored procedures that read from and update required day-to-day tables
Admin	db_owner database fixed role	–	–	–
Customer	–	Select permissions	–	–

TABLE 50-2

OBXKites Users

User	Database Standard Roles
Sammy	Admin
Joe	Public
LRN	IT DBA
Clerk Windows group (Betty, Tom, Martha, and Mary)	Clerk

Using this security model, the following users can perform the following tasks:

- Betty, as a member of the Clerk role, can execute the application that executes stored procedures to retrieve and update data. Betty can run select queries as a member of the Public role.
- LRN, as the IT DBA, can perform any task in the database as a member of the sysadmin server role.
- Joe can run select queries as a member of the public role.
- As a member of the admin role, Sammy can execute all stored procedures. He can also manually modify any table using queries. As a member of the admin role that includes the db_owner role, Joe can perform any database administrative task and select or modify data in any table.
- Only LRN can restore from the backups.

Views and Security

A popular, but controversial, method of designing security is to create a view that projects only certain columns, or that restricts the rows with a `WHERE` clause and a `WITH CHECK` option, and then grants permission to the view to allow users limited access to data. Some IT shops require that all access go through such a view. This technique is even assumed in the Microsoft certification tests.

CROSS-REF **Chapter 14, "Projecting Data Through Views," explains how to create a view and use the `WITH CHECK` option.**

Those opposed to using views for a point of security have several good reasons:

- Views are not compiled or optimized.
- Column-level security can be applied with standard SQL Server security.
- Using views for row-level security means that the `WITH CHECK` option must be manually created with each view. As the number of row-level categories grows, the system requires manual maintenance.

Summary

It's essential to secure the database objects. This is an integral part of the SQL Server security model. This chapter covered such securables, and you should now be able to handle the design and maintenance of this part of the database.

The next chapter continues with another security-related topic, data encryption, which keeps data confidential.

Chapter 51

Data Cryptography

When I was a kid, I remember playing with the secret decoder ring from a cereal box. How cool was that?! Now I'm all grown up and still playing with secret decoder rings. Hmmm.

Usually, securing access to the table is sufficient; if not, securing the column will suffice. However, for some information, such as credit card numbers or secret government data, the information's sensitivity warrants further security by encrypting the data stored in the database.

SQL Server 2008 can encrypt data inside SQL Server with passwords, keys, or certificates. All editions of SQL Server support data encryption.

IN THIS CHAPTER

Introduction to cryptography

Using the SQL Server data encryption tools

Introduction to Cryptography

Data encryption is basically a scrambling of the data with a secret key to produce an encoded copy of the data called the *cipher data*. Without the key, the data is impossible to unscramble.

Types of encryption

Symmetric encryption uses the same key to both encrypt and decrypt the data. While this method is simpler to administer and faster than asymmetric encryption, it's considered riskier because the encryption algorithm is weaker, and more tasks (people) need copies of the key. This may not be a problem when encrypting and decrypting data inside SQL Server.

What's new with data cryptography?

SQL Server 2005 introduced data encryption with master keys and certificates. Although it's complex, it was well received.

Not to rest on their laurels, for SQL Server 2008 Microsoft adds transparent data encryption that encrypts the whole database file for theft protection. Also new is extensible key management, which lets SQL Server use third-party enterprise key management software and hardware-based encryption key.

Asymmetric encryption is considered stronger than symmetric encryption because one key, a private key, is paired with a second public key. If the data is encrypted with one of those two keys, then it can be decrypted with the other. In other words, if I encrypt some data using my private key and you already have my public key, then you can decrypt the data. If I've had to share my public key with several partners and I want to ensure that only you can decrypt the data, then we can double the encryption using both our private and public keys. I encrypt using my private key and encrypt it again using your public key. You reverse the order, decrypting with your private key and then my public key.

NOTE **Data can also be encrypted and decrypted using .NET at the middle tier or at the front end. This offers the advantage that the database server never sees readable data. A number of years ago, I used this method for a SQL Server 2000 project storing credit card data. It required that I write a C# .NET class that employed the** `System.Security.Cryptography` **class to use a Rinjdael (explained later in this chapter) encryption algorithm. It worked well, and the data was encrypted from the time it was initially received until the authorized user viewed the report.**

Certificates are similar to keys but are generally issued by an organization, such as VeriSign, to certify that the organization associated with the certificate is legitimate. It's possible, and recommended, to generate local certificates within SQL.

The hierarchy of keys

SQL Server encryption is based on a hierarchy of keys. At the top of the hierarchy is a unique *service master key* generated by SQL Server for encryption the first time it's needed.

At the next level is the *database master key*, which is a symmetric key SQL Server uses to encrypt private certificates and asymmetric keys. You create a database master key using the `CREATE MASTER KEY` DDL command. SQL Server then encrypts the database master using the service master key and stores it in both the user database and the master database:

```
CREATE MASTER KEY
  ENCRYPTION BY PASSWORD = 'P@$rw0rD';
```

The password must meet Windows' strong password requirements.

TIP **To view information about the master keys, use the** `syssymmetric_keys` **and the** `sysdatabases.is_master_key_encrypted_by_server` **catalog views.**

Within the database, and below the database master key in SQL Server's cryptographic hierarchy, are certificates and private keys.

Encrypting Data

When it comes to actually encrypting data, SQL Server provides four methods:

- Passphrase
- Symmetric key
- Asymmetric key
- Certificate

Encrypting with a passphrase

The first method of encrypting data is to use a passphrase, similar to a password but without the strong password requirements, to encrypt the data. The encrypted data will be binary, so the example code uses a `varbinary` data type for the `creditcardnumber` column. You should test your situation to determine the required binary length.

The actual encryption is accomplished using the `EncryptbyPassPhrase()` function. The first parameter is the passphrase, followed by the data to be encrypted.

This example demonstrates encrypting data using the `INSERT` DML command:

```
CREATE TABLE CCard (
  CCardID INT IDENTITY PRIMARY KEY NOT NULL,
  CustomerID INT NOT NULL,
  CreditCardNumber VARBINARY(128),
  Expires CHAR(4)
  );
INSERT CCard(CustomerID, CreditCardNumber, Expires)
  VALUES(1,EncryptByPassPhrase('Passphrase', '12345678901234567890'),
      '0808');
```

A normal select query views the encrypted value actually stored in the database:

```
SELECT *
  FROM CCard
  WHERE CustomerID = 1;
```

Result (binary value abridged):

```
CCardID       CustomerID   CreditCardNumber          Expires
-----------   -----------  --------------------      -------
1             1            0x01000000C8CF68C         0808
```

To decrypt the credit card data into readable text, use the `DecryptByPassPhrase()` function and convert the binary result back to a readable format:

```
SELECT CCardID, CustomerID,
  CONVERT(VARCHAR(20), DecryptByPassPhrase('Passphrase',
```

```
        CreditCardNumber)), Expires
    FROM CCard
    WHERE CustomerID = 1;
```

Result:

```
CCardID        CustomerID   CardNo                 Expires
-----------    -----------  --------------------   -------
1              1            12345678901234567890   0808
```

Sure enough, the data decrypted to the same value previously inserted. If the passphrase were incorrect, then the result would have been null.

There is one other option to the passphrase encryption method. An authenticator may be added to the encryption to further enhance it. Typically, some internal hard-coded value unknown by the user is used as the authenticator to make it more difficult to decrypt the data if it's removed from the database.

The following code sample adds the authenticator to the passphrase encryption. The code, 1, enables the authenticator, and the last parameter is the authenticator phrase:

```
INSERT CCard(CustomerID, CreditCardNumber, Expires)
  VALUES(3,EncryptbyPassPhrase('Passphrase','12123434565678788989',
      1, 'hardCoded Authenticator'), '0808');

SELECT CCardID, CustomerID,
  CONVERT(VARCHAR(20),DecryptByPassPhrase('Passphrase',
      CreditCardNumber, 1, 'hardCoded Authenticator')), Expires
  FROM CCard
  WHERE CustomerID = 3;
```

Result:

```
CCardID        CustomerID   CardNo                 Expires
-----------    -----------  --------------------   -------
2              3            12123434565678788989   0808
```

Encrypting with a symmetric key

Using a symmetric key provides an actual object for the encryption, rather than just a human-readable passphrase. Symmetric keys can be created within SQL Server using the CREATE DDL command:

```
CREATE SYMMETRIC KEY CCardKey
WITH ALGORITHM = TRIPLE_DES
ENCRYPTION BY PASSWORD = 'P@s$wOrD';
```

Once the keys are created, they are listed in Management Studio's Object Explorer under the database's Security ⇨ Symmetric Keys node.

TIP **To view information about the symmetric keys using T-SQL, query the** `syssymmetric_keys` **catalog view.**

Keys are objects and can be altered or dropped like any other SQL Server object.

Encryption algorithms

The algorithm defines how the data will be encrypted using this key. There are nine possible algorithms: DES, TRIPLE_DES, RC2, RC4, RC4_128, DESX, AES_128, AES_192, and AES_256. They differ in speed and strength.

The Data Encryption Standard (DES) algorithm was selected as the official data encryption method for the U.S. government in 1976, but it can be broken by brute force using today's computers in as little as 24 hours. The triple DES (TRIPLE_DES) algorithm uses a longer key and is considerably stronger.

The RC algorithms (such as RC2 and RC4) were invented by Ron Rivest in the mid-eighties. Like the DES algorithm, they too are fairly easy to crack.

The Advanced Encryption Standard (AES), also known as Rijndael (pronounced "Rhine-dahl"), was approved by the National Institute of Standards and Technology (NIST) in November 2001. The 128, 192, or 256 in the algorithm name identifies the bit size of the key. The strongest algorithm in SQL Server's toolbox is the AES_256.

NOTE **SQL Server leverages Windows' encryption algorithms, so if an algorithm isn't installed on Windows, then SQL Server can't use it. AES is not supported on Windows XP or Windows 2000.**

Because the symmetric key might be transported in the open to the client, the key itself can also be encrypted. SQL Server can encrypt the key using one, or multiple, passwords, other keys, or certificates. A `key_phrase` can be used to seed the generation of the key.

A temporary key is valid only for the current session and should be identified with a pound sign (#), similar to temporary tables. Temporary keys can use a GUID to help identify the encrypted data using the `indentity_value = 'passphrase'` option.

Using the symmetric key

To use the symmetric key, the first step is to `open` the key. This decrypts the key and makes it available for use by SQL Server:

```
OPEN SYMMETRIC KEY CCardKey
  DECRYPTION BY PASSWORD = 'P@s$wOrD';
```

Using the same `CCard` table created previously, the next code snippet encrypts the data using the CCardKey key. The `EncryptByKey()` function accepts the GUID identifier of the key, which can be found using the `key_guid()` function, and the actual data to be encrypted:

```
INSERT CCard(CustomerID, CreditCardNumber, Expires)
  VALUES(7,EncryptByKey(Key_GUID('CCardKey'),'11112222333344445555'),
     '0808');
```

To decrypt the data, the key must be open. The `decryptbykey()` function will identify the correct key from the data and perform the decryption:

```
SELECT CCardID, CustomerID,
  CONVERT(varchar(20), DecryptByKey(CreditCardNumber)) as
```

```
    CreditCardNumber, Expires
  FROM CCard
  WHERE CustomerID = 7;
```

Result:

```
CCardID         CustomerID   CreditCardNumber        Expires
-----------     ----------   ---------------------- -------
3               7            1111222233334444555 5   0808
```

It's a good practice to close the key after the transaction:

```
CLOSE SYMMETRIC KEY CCardKey
```

For most applications, you'll want to encrypt the data as it goes into the database and decrypt it as it is selected. If you want to move the data to another server and decrypt it there, then both servers must have identical keys. To generate the same key on two servers, the key must be created with the same algorithm, `identity_value`, and `key_phrase`.

Using asymmetric keys

Using asymmetric keys involves encrypting and decrypting with matching private and public keys. Generating an asymmetric key is similar to generating a symmetric key:

```
CREATE ASYMMETRIC KEY AsyKey
  WITH ALGORITHM = RSA_512
  ENCRYPTION BY PASSWORD = 'P@s$w0rD';
```

SQL Server supports RSA_512, RSA_1024, and RSA_2048 (algorithms for public-key cryptography) as possible asymmetric algorithms. The difference is the bit length of the private key.

Asymmetric keys can also be generated from existing key files:

```
CREATE ASYMMETRIC KEY AsyKey
  FROM FILE  = ' C:\SQLServerBible\AsyKey.key'
  ENCRYPTION BY PASSWORD = 'P@s$w0rD';
```

Encrypting and decrypting data with an asymmetric key is very similar to using symmetric keys except that the key doesn't need to be open in order to be used.

Using certificates

Certificates are typically used to encrypt data over the web for HTTPS endpoints. SQL Server includes certificates, as they fit into some companies' security standards. Certificates are typically obtained from a certificate authority such as VeriSign or Thawte.

Transparent Data Encryption

Data encryption is great, but what if the thief simply steals the whole server? Few shops encrypt every column. With enough time and hacker's utilities, eventually they will gain access to the disk. Using a hex editor, the data in the SQL Server data file is right there for anyone to read. So while they might not be able to run SQL queries, they can still read the raw data.

If the data is encrypted using the methods discussed previously in the chapter, the data is still safe. Transparent data encryption is for the rest of the data in case of theft of the data file or backup file.

On nice aspect of transparent data encryption (TDE) is that it's completely transparent. The Storage Engine encrypts or decrypts the data as it's being written to or read from the disk. There's no code change required at any layer of code.

Using transparent data encryption requires a master key:

```
USE master;
go --
CREATE MASTER KEY ENCRYPTION BY PASSWORD = 'Pa@sWOrD';
go --
CREATE CERTIFICATE SQLBibleCert WITH SUBJECT = 'SQLBibleCert'
```

To encrypt a user database a database key is required:

```
USE AdventureWorks2008
go --
CREATE DATABASE ENCRYPTION KEY
WITH ALGORITHM = AES_128
ENCRYPTION BY SERVER CERTIFICATE SQLBibleCert
```

With the database key created, the database can be encrypted or decrypted using either an `alter` command or Management Studio's Database Properties ➪ Options page:

```
ALTER DATABASE AdventureWorks2008
SET ENCRYPTION ON
```

If you have the time, download a freeware hex editor, take a look at your database file, then encrypt the database and take a second look – it's a cool experiment.

CAUTION **If you use TDE, be absolutely certain to back up the encryption keys. If you need to restore a database that's been encrypted using TDE, and you don't have the encryption key, your backups are worthless.**

Summary

Cryptography can provide another level of security beyond authentication. It converts normal readable data that can be understood to data that cannot be understood. In this way, the data cannot be used by the wrong parties. SQL Server gives you many options for cryptography and makes it easy to use.

The next chapter continues the discussion of security by covering row-level security, which is another necessary tool for keeping data safe.

Chapter 52

Row-Level Security

IN THIS CHAPTER

Extending the abstraction layer for custom row-level security

Components of row-level security

Assigning and checking permissions

SQL Server is excellent at vertical security (tables and columns), but it lacks the ability to dynamically enforce row-level security. Views, using `with check option`, can provide a hard-coded form of row-level security, but developing a row-based security schema for an entire database using dozens or hundreds of views would create a maintenance headache.

Enterprise databases often include data that is sensitive on a row level. Consider these four real-life business-security rules:

- Material data, inventory-cost data, and production scheduling are owned by a department and should not be available to those outside that department. However, the MRP system contains materials and inventory tracking for all locations and all departments in the entire company.
- HR data for each employee must be available to only the HR department and an employee's direct supervisors.
- A companywide purchasing system permits only lumber buyers to purchase lumber, and only hardware buyers to purchase hardware.
- Each bank branch should be able to read any customer's data, but only edit those customers who frequent that branch.

I believe the best possible solution for these requirements is to build the security into the abstraction layer.

In Chapter 2, "Data Architecture," I tried to make the case for database encapsulation and a strong abstraction layer as a means toward database extensibility; but a strong abstraction layer also enables the security objective:

> "The sixth database objective based on the Information Architecture Principle is security. For any organizational asset, the data must be secured depending on its value and sensitivity.

> Security is enforced by ... enforcing a strong database abstraction layer for all data access ... and permitting no direct ad-hoc SQL access to the raw tables."

Implementing a server-side code version of row-level security requires four components:

- **Security table:** Can contain the list of users and their departments, or branches, with their appropriate read and write rights
- **Security procedure:** Checks the user's rights against the data being requested and returns a status of approved or denied
- **Fetch procedure:** Checks the security procedure for permission to return the data
- **Triggers:** Call the security procedure to check the user's right to perform the DML statement on the requested rows

To demonstrate this design, the following topics implement row-level security to the `OBXKites` database. Each employee in the `Contact` table can be granted read, write, or administrator privileges for each location's inventory and sales data. With this row-based security scheme, security can be checked by means of a stored procedure, function, NT login, and trigger.

Although this is only an example of how to construct row-level security, the concepts here should help you as you design and develop your own custom row-level security solution.

This code is a work in progress. To download the latest version, please check `www.sqlserverbible.com`**.**

The Security Table

The `security` table serves as a many-to-many associative table (junction table) between the `contact` and `location` tables. The security level determines the level of access:

0 (or no rows): 0 access

1: Read access

2: Write access

3: Admin access

Alternately, three-bit columns could be used for read, write, and administrator rights, but the privileges are cumulative, so an integer column seems appropriate.

The `security` table has two logical foreign keys. The foreign key to the `location` table is handled by a standard foreign key constraint; however, the reference to the `contact` table should allow only contacts who are flagged as employees, so a trigger is used to enforce that complex referential-integrity requirement. The security assignment is meaningless without its contact or location, so both foreign keys are cascading deletes. A constraint is applied to the security-level column to restrict entry to the valid security codes (0–3), and a unique constraint ensures that a contact may have only one security code per location:

```
USE OBXKites;

CREATE TABLE dbo.Security (
  SecurityID UniqueIdentifier NOT NULL
    PRIMARY KEY NONCLUSTERED,
```

```
ContactID UniqueIdentifier NOT NULL
  REFERENCES dbo.Contact(ContactID) ON DELETE CASCADE,
LocationID UniqueIdentifier NOT NULL
  REFERENCES dbo.Location(LocationID) ON DELETE CASCADE,
SecurityLevel INT NOT NULL DEFAULT 0
);
```

The following three commands add the constraints to the Security table:

```
CREATE TRIGGER ContactID_RI
ON dbo.Security
AFTER INSERT, UPDATE
AS
SET NOCOUNT ON;
IF EXISTS(SELECT *
            FROM Inserted
              INNER JOIN dbo.Contact
                ON Inserted.ContactID = Contact.ContactID
            WHERE Contact.ContactID IS NULL
              OR IsEmployee = CAST(0 AS bit))
  BEGIN;
    RAISERROR
      ('Foreign Key Constraint: Security.ContactID', 16, 1);
    ROLLBACK TRANSACTION;
    RETURN;
  END;
GO
ALTER TABLE dbo.Security
  ADD CONSTRAINT ValidSecurityCode CHECK
    (SecurityLevel IN (0,1,2,3));

ALTER TABLE dbo.Security
  ADD CONSTRAINT ContactLocation UNIQUE
    (ContactID, LocationID);
```

Assigning Permissions

Implementing row-level security requires a set of basic admin procedures to set up and maintain the security settings. These procedures handle assigning security levels to users.

Assigning security

In order for the Security table to be viewed, the first procedure created is pSecurity_Fetch. This procedure returns all the row-based security permissions, or it can be restricted to return permissions for a single user or a single location:

```
CREATE PROCEDURE pSecurity_Fetch
  @LocationCode VARCHAR(15) = NULL,
  @ContactCode VARCHAR(15) = NULL
AS
```

```
SET NOCOUNT ON;
SELECT c.ContactCode,
       l.LocationCode,
       s.SecurityLevel
    FROM dbo.Security AS s
      INNER JOIN dbo.Contact AS c
        ON s.ContactID = c.ContactID
      INNER JOIN dbo.Location AS l
        ON s.LocationID = l.LocationID
          WHERE (l.LocationCode = @LocationCode
                        OR @LocationCode IS NULL)
            AND (c.ContactCode = @ContactCode
                        OR @ContactCode IS NULL);
```

Row-level security permissions are set by adding or altering rows in the `Security` table, which serves as a junction between contact and location. In keeping with the theme of server-side code, the `pSecurity_Assign` stored procedure assigns a security level to the contact/location combination. There's nothing new about this procedure. It accepts a contact code and location code, converts the codes into GUID IDs, and then performs the `INSERT`:

```
CREATE PROCEDURE pSecurity_Assign
  @ContactCode VARCHAR(15),
  @LocationCode VARCHAR(15),
  @SecurityLevel INT
AS
  SET NOCOUNT ON;
  DECLARE
    @ContactID UNIQUEIDENTIFIER,
    @LocationID UNIQUEIDENTIFIER;

  -- Get ContactID
  SELECT @ContactID = ContactID
    FROM dbo.Contact
    WHERE ContactCode = @ContactCode;
  IF @@ERROR <> 0 RETURN -100
  IF @ContactID IS NULL
    BEGIN;
      RAISERROR
        ('Contact: "%s" not found', 15,1,@ContactCode);
      RETURN -100;
    END;

  -- Get LocationID
  SELECT @LocationID = LocationID
    FROM dbo.Location
    WHERE LocationCode = @LocationCode;
  IF @@ERROR <> 0 RETURN -100;
  IF @LocationID IS NULL
    BEGIN;
```

```
      RAISERROR
        ('Location: "%s" not found', 15,1,@LocationCode);
      RETURN -100;
    END;

  -- Insert
  INSERT dbo.Security (ContactID,LocationID, SecurityLevel)
    VALUES (@ContactID, @LocationID, @SecurityLevel);
  IF @@ERROR <> 0 RETURN -100;
  RETURN;
```

With the pSecurity_Fetch and pSecurity_Assign stored procedures created, the following batch adds some test data. The first two queries return some valid data for the test:

```
SELECT ContactCode
  FROM dbo.Contact
  WHERE IsEmployee = CAST(1 AS bit);
```

Result:

```
ContactCode
---------------
118
120
119
```

The next query returns valid locations:

```
SELECT LocationCode FROM dbo.Location;
```

Result:

```
LocationCode
---------------
CH
Clt
ElC
JR
KH
W
```

Based on this data, the next four procedure calls assign security:

```
EXEC pSecurity_Assign
  @ContactCode = '118',
  @LocationCode = 'CH',
  @SecurityLevel = 3;

EXEC pSecurity_Assign
  @ContactCode = '118',
```

```
    @LocationCode = 'Clt',
    @SecurityLevel = 2;

  EXEC pSecurity_Assign
    @ContactCode = '118',
    @LocationCode = 'Elc',
    @SecurityLevel = 1;

  EXEC pSecurity_Assign
    @ContactCode = '120',
    @LocationCode = 'W',
    @SecurityLevel = 2;
```

The following two commands test the data inserts using the `pSecurity_Fetch` procedure. The first test examines the security settings for the `'W'` location:

```
EXEC pSecurity_Fetch @LocationCode = 'W';
```

Result:

```
ContactCode     LocationCode    SecurityLevel
--------------- --------------- -------------
120             W               3
```

The next batch examines the security setting for “Dave Boston” (contact code 118):

```
EXEC pSecurity_Fetch @ContactCode = '118';
```

Result:

```
ContactCode     LocationCode    SecurityLevel
--------------- --------------- -------------
118             Clt             2
118             CH              3
118             ElC             1
```

The row-based security schema includes several constraints. The following commands test those constraints using the stored procedures.

Testing the unique constraint:

```
EXEC pSecurity_Assign
  @ContactCode = '120',
  @LocationCode = 'W',
  @SecurityLevel = 2;
```

Result:

```
Server: Msg 2627, Level 14, State 2,
  Procedure pSecurity_Assign, Line 35
```

```
Violation of UNIQUE KEY constraint 'ContactLocation'.
Cannot insert duplicate key in object 'Security'.
The statement has been terminated.
```

Testing the valid security-code check constraint:

```
EXEC pSecurity_Assign
  @ContactCode = '118',
  @LocationCode = 'W',
  @SecurityLevel = 5;
```

Result:

```
Server: Msg 547, Level 16, State 1,
  Procedure pSecurity_Assign, Line 35
INSERT statement conflicted with COLUMN CHECK constraint
  'ValidSecurityCode'. The conflict occurred in database
  'OBXKites', table 'Security', column 'SecurityLevel'.
The statement has been terminated.
```

Testing the employees-only complex-business-rule trigger:

```
Select ContactCode FROM dbo.Contact WHERE IsEmployee = CAST(0 AS bit);
EXEC pSecurity_Assign
  @ContactCode = '102',
  @LocationCode = 'W',
  @SecurityLevel = 3;
```

Result:

```
Foreign Key Constraint: Security.ContactID
```

The next execution of the stored procedure tests the contact foreign key constraint and generates an error because 999 is an invalid contact:

```
EXEC pSecurity_Assign
  @ContactCode = '999',
  @LocationCode = 'W',
  @SecurityLevel = 3;
```

Result:

```
Server: Msg 50000, Level 15, State 1, Procedure pSecurity_Assign,
  Line 19
Contact: '999' not found
```

Test the location-code foreign key constraint. It's also checked within the stored procedure:

```
EXEC pSecurity_Assign
  @ContactCode = '118',
```

```
    @LocationCode = 'RDBMS',
    @SecurityLevel = 3;
```

Result:

```
Server: Msg 50000, Level 15, State 1, Procedure pSecurity_Assign,
  Line 30
Location: 'RDBMS' not found
```

Handling security-level updates

The pSecurity_Assign procedure used in the previous examples handles new security assignments but fails to accept adjustments to an existing security setting.

The following alteration to the procedure checks whether the security combination of contact and location is already in the Security table, and then performs the appropriate INSERT or UPDATE. Security permissions may be created or adjusted with the new version of the procedure and the same parameters. Here's the improved procedure:

```
ALTER PROCEDURE pSecurity_Assign(
  @ContactCode VARCHAR(15),
  @LocationCode VARCHAR(15),
  @SecurityLevel INT
  )
AS
  SET NOCOUNT ON;
  DECLARE
    @ContactID UNIQUEIDENTIFIER,
    @LocationID UNIQUEIDENTIFIER;
  -- Get ContactID
  SELECT @ContactID = ContactID
    FROM dbo.Contact
    WHERE ContactCode = @ContactCode;
  IF @ContactID IS NULL
    BEGIN;
      RAISERROR
        ('Contact: "%s" not found', 15,1,@ContactCode);
      RETURN -100;
    END;
  -- Get LocationID
  SELECT @LocationID = LocationID
    FROM dbo.Location
    WHERE LocationCode = @LocationCode;
  IF @LocationID IS NULL
    BEGIN;
      RAISERROR
       ('Location: "%s" not found', 15,1,@LocationCode);
      RETURN -100;
    END;
```

```
-- IS Update or Insert?
IF EXISTS(SELECT *
           FROM dbo.Security
           WHERE ContactID = @ContactID
             AND LocationID = @LocationID)
-- Update
  BEGIN;
    UPDATE dbo.Security
      SET SecurityLevel = @SecurityLevel
      WHERE ContactID = @ContactID
        AND LocationID = @LocationID;
    IF @@ERROR <> 0 RETURN -100;
  END;

-- Insert
ELSE
  BEGIN;
    INSERT dbo.Security
        (ContactID,LocationID, SecurityLevel)
      VALUES (@ContactID, @LocationID, @SecurityLevel);
    IF @@ERROR <> 0 RETURN -100;
  END;
RETURN;
```

The following script tests the new procedure's ability to modify a security permission for a contact/location combination. The first command modifies contact 120's security for location W:

```
EXEC pSecurity_Assign
  @ContactCode = '120',
  @LocationCode = 'W',
  @SecurityLevel = 2;

EXEC pSecurity_Fetch
  @ContactCode = '120';
```

Result:

```
ContactCode     LocationCode    SecurityLevel
--------------- --------------- -------------
120             W               2
```

The following two commands issue a new security permission and edit an existing security permission. The third command fetches the security permissions for contact code 120:

```
EXEC pSecurity_Assign
  @ContactCode = '120',
  @LocationCode = 'CH',
  @SecurityLevel = 1;
```

```
EXEC pSecurity_Assign
  @ContactCode = '120',
  @LocationCode = 'W',
  @SecurityLevel = 3;

EXEC pSecurity_Fetch
  @ContactCode = '120';
```

Result:

```
ContactCode     LocationCode    SecurityLevel
--------------- --------------- -------------
120             W               3
120             CH              1
```

Checking Permissions

The value of row-level security is in actually allowing or blocking reads and writes. The following procedures, functions, and triggers are examples demonstrating how to build row-level read/write validation.

The security-check stored procedure

The security-check stored procedure, p_SecurityCheck, is central to the row-based security system. It's designed to return a true or false value for a security request for a user, a location, and a requested security level.

The procedure selects the security level of the user for the given location and then compares that value with the value of the requested security level. If the user's permission level is sufficient, then a 1 (indicating true) is returned; otherwise, a 0 (for false) is returned:

```
CREATE PROCEDURE p_SecurityCheck
  @ContactCode VARCHAR(15),
  @LocationCode VARCHAR(15),
  @SecurityLevel INT,
  @Approved BIT OUTPUT
AS
SET NOCOUNT ON;
DECLARE @ActualLevel INT = 0;
SELECT @ActualLevel = s.SecurityLevel
  FROM dbo.Security AS s
    INNER JOIN dbo.Contact AS c
      ON s.ContactID = c.ContactID
    INNER JOIN dbo.Location AS l
      ON s.LocationID = l.LocationID
  WHERE c.ContactCode = @ContactCode
    AND l.LocationCode = @LocationCode;
```

```
IF    @ActualLevel < @SecurityLevel
  SET @Approved = CAST(0 AS bit);
ELSE
  SET @Approved = CAST(1 AS bit);

RETURN 0;
```

The following batch calls the p_SecurityCheck procedure and uses the @OK local variable to capture the output parameter. When testing this from the script on the web, try several different values. Use the pSecurity_Fetch procedure to determine possible parameters. The following code checks whether contact code 118 has administrative privileges at the Charlotte warehouse:

```
DECLARE @OK BIT;
EXEC p_SecurityCheck
  @ContactCode = '118',
  @LocationCode = 'Clt',
  @SecurityLevel = 3,
  @Approved = @OK OUTPUT;
SELECT @OK;
```

Result:

```
0
```

The security-check function

The security-check function, fSecurityCheck, includes the same logic as the pSecurity_Check stored procedure. The advantage of a function is that it can be used directly within an IF command without a local variable being used to store the output parameter. The function uses the same three input parameters as the stored-procedure version and the same internal logic, but it returns the approved bit as the return of the function, rather than as an output parameter. Here's the function's code:

```
CREATE FUNCTION dbo.fSecurityCheck (
  @ContactCode VACHAR(15),
  @LocationCode VARCHAR(15),
  @SecurityLevel INT)
RETURNS BIT
AS
BEGIN;
DECLARE @Approved BIT = CAST(0 AS bit);

IF (SELECT s.SecurityLevel
  FROM dbo.Security AS s
    INNER JOIN dbo.Contact AS c
      ON s.ContactID = c.ContactID
    INNER JOIN dbo.Location AS l
      ON s.LocationID = l.LocationID
  WHERE c.ContactCode = @ContactCode
```

```
    AND l.LocationCode = @LocationCode) >= @SecurityLevel
  BEGIN;
  SET @Approved = CAST(1 AS bit);
  END;

RETURN @Approved;
END;
```

The next code fragment demonstrates how to call the function to test security within a stored procedure. If the function returns a 0, then the user does not have sufficient security, and the procedure terminates:

```
-- Check within a Procedure
IF dbo.fSecurityCheck( '118', 'Clt', 3) = CAST(0 AS bit)
  BEGIN;
    RAISERROR('Security Violation', 16,1);
    ROLLBACK TRANSACTION;
    RETURN -100;
  END;
```

Using the NT login

Some applications are designed so that the user logs in with the application, and, so far, the row-based security code has assumed that the username is supplied to the procedures. However, if the SQL Server instance is using NT authentication, then the security routines can use that identification.

Rather than request the contact code as a parameter, the security procedure or function can automatically use `suser_sname()`, the NT login, to identify the current user. The login name (domain and username) must be added to the `Contact` table. Alternately, a secondary table could be created to hold multiple logins per user. Some wide-area networks require users to log in with different domain names according to location, so a `ContactLogin` table is a good idea.

The following function is modified to check the user's security based on his or her NT login and a `ContactLogin` table. The first query demonstrates retrieving the login within T-SQL code:

```
SELECT SUSER_SNAME();
```

Result:

```
--------------
NOLI\Paul
```

The following code creates the secondary table to store the logins:

```
CREATE TABLE dbo.ContactLogin(
  ContactLogin UNIQUEIDENTIFIER
    PRIMARY KEY NONCLUSTERED DEFAULT NEWID(),
  ContactID UNIQUEIDENTIFIER NOT NULL
    REFERENCES dbo.Contact(ContactID) ON DELETE CASCADE,
  NTLogin NVARCHAR(128) UNIQUE CLUSTERED);
```

With the table in place, a simple INSERT will populate a single row using my login so the code can be tested:

```
INSERT dbo.ContactLogin (ContactID, NTLogin)
  SELECT ContactID, 'NOLI\Paul'
    FROM dbo.Contact
    WHERE ContactCode = 118;
```

Check the data:

```
SELECT c.ContactCode, cl.NTLogin
  FROM dbo.Contact AS c
    INNER JOIN ContactLogin AS cl
      ON c.ContactID = cl.ContactID;
```

Result:

```
ContactCode     NTLogin
--------------- --------------
118             Paul/NOLI
```

The security-check function is modified to join the ContactLogin table and to restrict the rows returned to those that match the NT login name. Because the contact code is no longer required, this SELECT can skip the contact table and join the Security table directly with the ContactLogin table:

```
CREATE FUNCTION dbo.fSecurityCheckNT (
  @LocationCode VARCHAR(15),
  @SecurityLevel INT)
RETURNS BIT
AS
BEGIN;
DECLARE @Approved BIT = CAST(0 AS bit);

IF (SELECT s.SecurityLevel
  FROM dbo.Security AS s
    INNER JOIN dbo.Location AS l
      ON s.LocationID = l.LocationID
    INNER JOIN dbo.ContactLogin AS cl
      ON s.ContactID = cl.ContactID
  WHERE cl.NTLogin = suser_sname()
    AND l.LocationCode = @LocationCode) >= @SecurityLevel
  BEGIN;
  SET @Approved = CAST(1 AS bit);
  END;

RETURN @Approved;
END;
```

To test the new function, the following code fragment repeats the security check performed in the last section, but this time the user will be captured from the NT login instead of being passed to the function:

```
IF dbo.fSecurityCheckNT('Clt', 3) = 0
  BEGIN;
    RAISERROR('Security Violation', 16,1);
    ROLLBACK TRANSACTION;
    RETURN;
  END;
```

The function did not return an error, so I'm allowed to complete the procedure.

The security-check trigger

The security-check stored procedure and function both work well when included within a stored procedure, such as the FETCH, ADDNEW, UPDATE, or DELETE procedures mentioned in the beginning of this chapter; but to implement row-based security in a database that allows access from views, ad-hoc queries, or direct table DML statements, you must handle the row-based security with a trigger. The trigger can prevent updates, but it will not be able to check data reads. If row-based security is a requirement for reads, then all reads must go through a stored procedure.

The following trigger is similar to the security-check function. It differs in that the trigger must allow for multiple orders with potentially multiple locations. The joins must match up [Order] rows and their locations with the user's security level for each location. The join can go directly from the ContactLogin table to the Security table. Because this is an INSERT and UPDATE trigger, any security level below 2 for any order being written will be rejected and a security-violation error will be raised. The ROLLBACK TRANSACTION command will undo the original DML command that fired the trigger and all other modifications made as part of the same transaction:

```
CREATE TRIGGER OrderSecurity ON dbo.[Order]
AFTER INSERT, UPDATE
AS
IF @@ROWCOUNT = 0 RETURN;
IF EXISTS (
SELECT *
  FROM dbo.Security AS s
    INNER JOIN dbo.ContactLogin  AS cl
      ON s.ContactID = cl.ContactID
    INNER JOIN Inserted AS i
      ON i.LocationID = s.LocationID
  WHERE cl.NTLogin = suser_sname()
    AND s.SecurityLevel < 2 )
  BEGIN;
    RAISERROR('Security Violation', 16,1);
    ROLLBACK TRANSACTION;
  END;
```

Summary

SQL Server has a solid reputation for security, but it lacks row-based security. If the database is well architected with a carefully implemented abstraction layer, then adding a custom row-based security schema is not difficult.

This concludes Part VII, "Security," which is so critical for production databases. SQL Server security is based on matching privileges between principals and securables, and a chapter was devoted to each side of the equation.

The third security chapter covered data cryptography — introduced in SQL Server 2005 and extended with SQL Server 2008.

From here, the book moves into Part VIII, "Monitoring and Auditing." The sheer number of technologies and options available for monitoring and auditing has grown such that what was a single chapter in *SQL Server 2005 Bible* grew into a 10-chapter part in this edition.

Part VIII

Monitoring and Auditing

Wow! SQL Server has seen an explosion of monitoring and auditing technologies. SQL Server 2000 and before offered these traditional monitoring technologies:

- Trace and Profiler
- System Monitor and Performance Monitor
- DML triggers and custom audit trails
- Wait states

SQL Server 2005 added:

- Dynamic management views
- DDL triggers (Logon triggers with SP2)
- Event notification
- SSMS reports
- Performance Dashboard (downloadable add-on)

SQL Server 2008 doubles the core monitoring technologies with the following:

- Extended events
- SQL Server auditing
- Change tracking
- Change Data Capture
- Management Data Warehouse
- Policy-Based Management (covered in Chapter 43)

If SQL Server is the box, then this part is about the many ways to be a SQL whisperer and listen to the box. The table on the following page clearly delineates the monitoring and auditing functions available in SQL Server.

IN THIS PART

Technology	Introduced	Events Tracked	Data Available	Performance
DML Triggers — fires T-SQL code on table events	Beginning of time	Instead Of or After Insert, Update, Delete, Merge	Inserted and deleted tables, all columns, all changes with user context	Synchronous within transaction; depending on width of table and amount of code, may have a significant impact
PerfMon/SysMon — Windows utilities	Beginning of time	Listens for hundreds of Windows/SQL Server events	Counters for nearly any event, no actual data	Virtually no impact
SQL Trace and Profiler — SQL Server internal monitoring and UI	6.5	Monitors 179 SQL Server internal events	Event data, no actual data	Profiler may have an impact, trace alone has little impact
Wait States — tracks system waits	7	Every time a process waits for a resource	Aggregate count of waits by wait type	No impact
C2 Auditing — combines SQL Trace and security settings for compliance	2000	All security events	All security-related data	Minor impact
Common Criteria Compliance — combines SQL Trace and security settings for compliance	2005	All security events	All security-related data	Minor impact
DMVs — dynamic management views, catalog views	2005	–	Massive details for all metadata and current status	No impact
Management Studio Reports — easy way to view DMV data	2005	–	Builds on many of the DMVs	Some impact depending on report
Performance Dashboard — downloadable add-on with extra reports	2005	–	Builds on many of the DMVs	Some impact depending on report
DDL Triggers — responds to server and database DDL events	2005	All server and database DDL events and logins	`EventDate()` provides all info in XML format	Rarely called, so no real impact
Change Tracking — synchronously records which rows have been updated	2008	Row inserts, updates, and deletes	PK with net change, columns changed, very limited user context	Little impact
Change Data Capture — asynchronously reads T-Log and records data changes	2008	Insert, Update, Delete, Merge	All or net data changed, all column values, no user context	Reads from the log, so no impact during the transaction, but impact of the overall work
Extended Events — lightweight windows monitoring technology	2008	Nearly any server or database event, similar to SQL Trace	Event detail – similar to SQL Trace/Profiler	Very lightweight
SQL Auditing — SQL Server interface for extended events	2008	Any extended event	Detail dependent on extended events	Very lightweight
Management Data Warehouse — collects performance data	2008	Nearly continuous recording of performance data	Aggregate historical performance data	Lightweight, but requires server to collect data
Policy-Based Management — enforces and reports on configuration policies	2008	Any defined configuration policy	Can view health level of any object	No impact

Chapter 53

Data Audit Triggers

IN THIS CHAPTER

Creating a robust data-audit trail

Rolling back changes

Undeleting rows

Thinking through auditing complications

My consulting firm once developed a legal compliance/best-practices document-management system for a Fortune 100 company whose law firm was populating the database with regulatory laws. The law firm fell behind on its schedule and claimed that it was unable to enter data for two weeks because of software problems. When a list of the more than 70,000 column-level data changes made during those two weeks was provided from the data-audit trail, the claim vanished.

Data auditing is just a plain good idea.

The section "Data Architecture" in Chapter 2 lists data auditing as a key contributor toward the security and integrity database objectives.

Although Microsoft has added several auditing technologies, there's still a place for the old trigger/audit table solution. It's still the best way to build a complete audit trail of every value change ever made to a row since the inception of the database.

A trigger based data-audit trail can provide very detailed history of the data, including the following:

- All data changes to a row since it was inserted
- All data changes made by a specific user last week
- All data changes from a certain workstation during lunch
- All data changes made from an application other than the standard front-end application

I've seen published methods of auditing data that add a few columns to the table, or duplicate the table, to store the last change. Neither of these methods is worthwhile. A partial audit, or a last-value audit, is of no real value. A robust audit trail should track every change, from every table, in a generic audit table.

Audit triggers that write every DML change to a generic audit table come in two basic flavors — fixed and dynamic:

- **Fixed audit triggers:** These are custom written for each table and include hard-coded code for each column. There are two problems inherent with fixed audit triggers. First, they are a pain to write: tedious, back-breaking, repetitive, time intensive, and error prone code.

  Second, the only task worse than coding a fixed audit trigger is maintaining it. The audit triggers must be kept in perfect sync with every `ALTER TABLE`; otherwise, either the trigger generates an error, or the data audit trail is incomplete.
- **Dynamic audit triggers:** These investigate the metadata and either pass the data to the CLR or use dynamic SQL to insert into the audit table. There are a couple dynamic audit trigger solutions on the Internet, and I published a dynamic SQL audit trigger in the *SQL Server 2000 Bible*. These solutions are easy to implement but perform as well as a slug on a lazy day. Plus, the use of dynamic SQL requires the end-users to have more privileges in the database than is typically desired in most database applications.

AutoAudit

The hybrid solution I'm proposing in this chapter is to dynamically code-gen perfect fixed audit trail triggers using the techniques covered in Chapter 29, "Dynamic SQL and Code Generation."

The result is the best performance possible from a trigger, but no manual coding. When the schema changes, just rerun the code-gen procedure to recreate the audit trigger.

CROSS-REF **As I'm writing, version 1.09a of AutoAudit is available on www.codeplex.com/AutoAudit. It's a work in progress, so check for updates.**

Besides recording every column value change to an audit table, I like to record some generic audit data right in the row:

- `Created` column to record the date the row was inserted
- `Modified` column to timestamp the last update
- `Version` column to count the number of times the row has been updated

AutoAudit adds these three columns to any table, and code-gens the trigger code to keep the `modified` and `version` columns up-to-date.

This version is limited to tables with single-column primary keys. (That's not likely to change anytime soon, because modifying the audit table on the fly to handle composite primary keys adds too much complexity and only a few have requested the feature.) It's written to be compatible with SQL Server 2005 and SQL Server 2008.

Installing AutoAudit

The first time the AutoAudit script is run in a database it creates the `dbo.Audit` table and four stored procedures:

- `dbo.pAutoAudit`: Code-gens the changes required for a single table
- `dbo.pAutoAuditAll`: Executes AutoAudit on every table in the database
- `dbo.pAutoAuditDrop`: Backs out the changes made by AutoAudit for a single table
- `dbo.pAutoAuditDropAll`: Backs out the changes made by AutoAudit for every table in the database

The audit table

The `Audit` table's purpose is to provide a single location in which to record data changes for the database. The following audit-trail table can store all non-BLOB changes to any table. The `Operation` column stores an `I`, `U`, or `D`, depending on the DML statement. This is the table created by executing the AutoAudit script:

```
CREATE TABLE dbo.Audit (
  AuditID BIGINT NOT NULL IDENTITY PRIMARY KEY CLUSTERED,
  AuditDate DATETIME NOT NULL,
  HostName sysname NOT NULL,
  SysUser VARCHAR(50) NOT NULL,
  Application VARCHAR(50) NOT NULL,
  TableName SYSNAME NOT NULL,
  Operation CHAR(1) NOT NULL, -- i,u,d
  PrimaryKey INT NOT NULL, -- edit to suite
  RowDescription VARCHAR(50) NULL,-- Optional
  SecondaryRow VARCHAR(50) NULL, -- Optional
  ColumnName SYSNAME NULL, -- required for i,u not for D
  OldValue VARCHAR(50) NULL, -- edit to suite - varchar(MAX)?
  NewValue VARCHAR(50) NULL
  Version INT NULL
  );
```

The `PrimaryKey` column stores the pointer to the row that was modified, and the `RowDescription` column records a readable description of the row. These two columns enable the audit trail to be joined with the original table or viewed directly. The `PrimaryKey` column is important because it can quickly find all changes to a single row regardless of how the description has changed over time.

Running AutoAudit

Once the AutoAudit script is run in the current database, `pAutoAudit` may be executed for any table. The parameters are self-explanatory:

```
EXEC pAutoAudit @Schema, @Table;
```

The stored procedure makes several changes to the table:

1. Adds the `created`, `modified`, and `version` columns to the table
2. Code-gens and creates the _`modified` update trigger, which updates the `modified` and `rowversion` columns

3. Code-gens and creates the _update trigger, which writes any updated column values to the audit table
4. Code-gens and creates the _delete trigger, which writes any deleted column values to the audit table

   The stored procedure then creates two new objects in the database:

5. Code-gens and creates the _deleted view, which reassembles the deleted rows from the audit table
6. Code-gens and creates the _RowHistory user-defined function, which presents a historical view of the data for any row

The following code executes pAutoAudit in the AdventureWorks2008 database on the Department table:

```
EXEC pAutoAudit 'HumanResources', 'Department'
```

Executing pAutoAuditAll will run pAutoAudit against every table in the current database.

_Modified trigger

The generated Product_ Modified trigger isn't very complicated. The trigger simply updates the modified column to the current date time and increments the rowversion column. As with any trigger, joining the inserted table with the base table limits the rows affected to those rows being updated:

```
CREATE TRIGGER [HumanResources].[Department_Modified] ON
  [HumanResources].[Department]
 AFTER Update
 NOT FOR REPLICATION AS
 SET NoCount On
 -- generated by AutoAudit on Apr 28 2009  3:38PM
 -- created by Paul Nielsen
 -- www.SQLServerBible.com

 Begin Try
 If Trigger_NestLevel
     (object_ID(N'[HumanResources].[Department_Modified]')) > 1
     Return;
 If (Update(Created) or Update(Modified)) AND Trigger_NestLevel() = 1
     Begin; Raiserror('Update failed.', 16, 1); Rollback;  Return; End;
 -- Update the Modified date
 UPDATE [HumanResources].[Department]
 SET Modified = getdate(),
     [Version] = [Department].[Version] + 1
   FROM [HumanResources].[Department]
     JOIN Inserted
       ON [Department].[DepartmentID] = Inserted.[DepartmentID] End Try
 Begin Catch
   Raiserror('error in [HumanResources].[Department_modified] trigger',
```

```
      16, 1 ) with log
   End Catch
  GO
```

Auditing changes

The real workhorse of AutoAudit is the `_Update` trigger, which writes every update, column by column, to the `audit` table. The trigger is a bit repetitive, but here's a sample of the code it creates for each column (slightly formatted for readability):

```
IF UPDATE([Name])
   INSERT dbo.Audit
     (AuditDate, SysUser, Application, HostName, TableName,
      Operation, PrimaryKey, RowDescription, SecondaryRow,
      ColumnName, OldValue, NewValue, RowVersion)
   SELECT @AuditTime, suser_sname(), APP_NAME(), Host_Name(),
        'HumanResources.Department', 'u', Convert(VARCHAR(50),
        Inserted.[DepartmentID]),
        NULL, -- Row Description (e.g. Order Number)
        NULL, -- Secondary Row Value
                     (e.g. Order Number for an Order Detail Line)
        '[Name]',
        Convert(VARCHAR(50), Deleted.[Name]),
        Convert(VARCHAR(50), Inserted.[Name]),
        DELETED.Rowversion + 1
     FROM Inserted
       JOIN Deleted
         ON Inserted.[DepartmentID] = Deleted.[DepartmentID]
            AND isnull(Inserted.[Name],'') <> isnull(Deleted.[Name],'')
```

Here's how this works. The `INSERT` statement joins the `Inserted` and `Deleted` tables on the primary key to correctly handle multiple-row inserts and updates. The join is also restricted with a `not-equals` <> join condition so that when a multiple-row update only affects some of the rows for a given column, only those rows that are actually changed are recorded to the audit trail.

The `_Insert` trigger audits all inserts. In AutoAudit version 1.09b, inserts are minimally logged to save space. The only row written to the `Audit` table is the insert event with the primary key value. The idea is that between the base table, the insert event, and the fully audited updates, the complete history can be reconstructed. A popular request is the verbose insert, which would audit every value on insert — I'll probably add that to the next version.

With AutoAudit's code-generated "fixed audit trigger" installed, the following batch exercises it by inserting and updating work order data:

```
INSERT Production.WorkOrder
       (ProductID, OrderQty, ScrappedQty,
        StartDate, EndDate, DueDate, ScrapReasonID)
  VALUES (757, 25, 3,
        '2008-9-20', '2008-9-23', '2008-9-24', 2)
```

```
UPDATE Production.WorkOrder
  SET DueDate = '2008-10-12'
  WHERE WorkOrderID = 72592
```

With these two changes made, AutoAudit recorded these audits:

```
SELECT AuditDate, SysUser, Operation, PrimaryKey as Key, ColumnName,
    OldValue as Old, NewValue as New, Version
  FROM dbo.Audit
```

Result:

```
AuditDate               SysUser Op Key   ColumnName    Old   New   Version
----------------------- ------- -- ----- ------------- ----- ----- --------
2009-04-28 20:10:50.567 Maui\Pn i  72592 [WorkOrderID] NULL  72592 1
2009-04-28 20:10:53.137 Maui\Pn u  72592 [ScrappedQty] 3     5     2
```

The trigger is the right place to implement an audit trail because it will catch all the changes, even those made directly to the table with DML commands.

Viewing and undeleting deleted rows

The `_Delete` trigger writes all the final values for every column to the `audit` table. From this information, the final state of the row can be easily recreated using a case expression-style crosstab query like this one for the `AdventureWorks2008` products table (abbreviated for space):

```
SELECT
    Max(Case ColumnName
       WHEN '[ProductID]' THEN OldValue
       ELSE '' END) AS [ProductID],
    Max(Case ColumnName
       WHEN '[Name]' THEN OldValue
       ELSE '' END) AS [Name],
    Max(Case ColumnName
       WHEN '[ProductNumber]' THEN OldValue
       ELSE '' END) AS [ProductNumber],
    . . .
    Max(Case ColumnName
      WHEN '[ModifiedDate]' THEN OldValue
      ELSE '' END) AS [ModifiedDate],
    Max(Case ColumnName
      WHEN '[Created]' THEN OldValue
      ELSE '' END) AS [Created],
    Max(Case ColumnName
      WHEN '[Modified]' THEN OldValue
      ELSE '' END) AS [Modified],
    Max(Case ColumnName
      WHEN '[RowVersion]' THEN OldValue
      ELSE '' END) AS [RowVersion],
```

```
  MAX(AuditDate) AS 'Deleted'
FROM Audit
Where TableName = 'SalesLT.Product' AND Operation = 'd'
GROUP BY PrimaryKey;
```

For every table audited by AutoAudit, it creates a view, named `v`*`tablename`*`_Deleted`, that contains the code-genned crosstab query. Selecting from this view displays all the rows deleted from the table.

To undelete rows, it's trivial to `insert...select` from the `_deleted` view.

Viewing row history

A feature I've recently added and am still enhancing is the row history user-defined function. Its purpose is to provide a visual history. The function is code-genned when AutoAudit is applied to a table. After four updates to the `DB Audit` row in the `HumanResources.Department` table, the `_RowHistory()` function returns the following story:

```
SELECT AuditDate, Version AS Ver, Name, GroupName
  FROM HumanResources.Department_RowHistory(22)
```

Result:

```
AuditDate            Ver  Name              GroupName
-------------------- ---- ----------------- ----------------------------
2009-04-29 10:46:23  1    DB Audit          Compliance Dept
2009-04-29 10:46:52  2    Data Audit        Compliance Dept
2009-04-29 10:47:13  3    Data Auditing     Compliance Dept
2009-04-29 10:47:26  4    Data Auditing     Compliance and Audit Dept
2009-04-29 10:48:04  5    Data Forensics    Data Audit
```

Note that the `_RowHistory()` function requires the primary key as a parameter. To return multiple histories, use the `CROSS APPLY` command.

Backing out AutoAudit

AutoAudit makes several changes to the database schema, modifying tables and creating objects. It would be irresponsible to not provide an automated way to roll back these changes. The following command removes all changes made by `pAutoAudit`, with one key exception: It does not drop the `audit` table, so any saved audit values are retained:

```
dbo.pAutoAuditDrop @Schema, @Table
```

Auditing Complications

While AutoAudit provides a rather complete audit trail solution, there are other factors that you should consider when implementing it, modifying it, or creating your own custom solution.

Best Practice

Develop the entire database and prove that the data schema is correct prior to implementing a data-audit trail. Changes to the data schema are more complex once audit-trail triggers are in place.

Auditing related data

The most significant complication involves auditing related data such as secondary rows. For example, a change to an `OrderDetail` row is actually a change to the order. A user will want to see the data history of the order and all changes to any of the data related to the order. Therefore, a change to the `OrderDetail` table should be recorded as a change to the `[Order]` table, and the line number of the order detail item that was changed is recorded in the `SecondaryRow` column.

Recording foreign key changes is another difficult aspect of a full audit trail. A user does not want to see the new GUID or identity value for a foreign-key update. If the order-ship-method foreign key is changed from "Slow Boat" to "Speedy Express," the audit-trail viewing procedure might want to look up the meaningful value and display that instead of the surrogate key value.

Auditing select statements

Data-audit triggers are limited to auditing `INSERT`, `UPDATE`, and `DELETE` DML statements. To audit data reads, implement the read audit in the `FETCH` stored procedure. Use SQL Server security to limit access to the table so that all reads must go through a stored procedure or a function.

In my software product I record every `objectfetch` operation with the `objectID`, `username`, and `datetime` in a separate table. This table serves as a select audit and feeds the user's recently viewed objects feature.

Data auditing and security

Another concern for those creating a full data-audit history is the security of the data-audit trail. Anyone who has read rights to the audit table will be able to effectively see all the data from every audited table. If users will be able to see the data history for a given row, use a stored procedure to fetch the audit data so that security can be preserved.

Data auditing and performance

A full data-audit trail will add some level of overhead to the system. A single row insert to a 20-column-wide table will add 20 inserts to the audit table. To reduce the performance impact of the audit trail, do the following:

- Limit the indexes on the audit table.
- Locate the audit table on its own filegroup and disk subsystem. A separate filegroup will make backups easier as well.

- Consider archiving older audits and then using distributed partitioned views to see all the audit data.
- Edit the fixed audit trigger to limit the auditing to those columns that require such a high level of data integrity.

One question when creating an audit trail is whether or not to write the insert DML values to the audit trail. Including the inserts completes the audit trail, and the rows may theoretically be completely recreated from the audit trail alone. The problem, of course, with writing inserts is that the audit trail grows larger than the original base tables.

Most OLTP databases see significantly more inserts than updates. Most rows are inserted and never updated. Therefore, if the original tables are used to store the original data, and the audit trail records only insert events and changes, then the `audit` table is significantly smaller than if every insert were fully audited. This improves performance by eliminating the audit during inserts and reduces the size of the audit table.

AutoAudit only records update values, but the commented out code to code-gen an insert audit trigger is in the AutoAudit stored procedure.

Summary

With all the new compliance regulations and requirements, auditing is more important than ever. But auditing is a pain. I've wasted way too many hours keeping a fixed audit trail in sync with schema changes, and the best dynamic audit triggers are slow.

I've created AutoAudit to help you solve some of your auditing problems. If after using it you have any suggestions, e-mail them to me, or add a request in CodePlex and vote for your idea.

Key points from this chapter include the following:

- A single audit table is easier to query for changes across the whole database than an individual audit-table-per-base-table approach.
- AutoAudit will code-gen triggers, views, and user-defined functions for your auditing solution.
- Deleted rows can be viewed or undeleted using the `v`*`table`*`_deleted` view.
- Row history can be viewed using the well-named `_RowHistory` user-defined function.
- AutoAudit requires a single-column primary key.
- Suggest improvements and vote for enhancements on `www.CodePlex.com/AutoAudit`.

The next chapter continues the thread of auditing with triggers, but it moves from auditing data to auditing the schema.

Chapter 54

Schema Audit Triggers

IN THIS CHAPTER

Tracking schema changes

In some shops, the path to production can be complicated. For a recent contract, the client had 20 servers dedicated to the project, which included a dev environment, a QA testing environment, an integration testing environment, a performance testing environment, and a production environment. Because the project scaled out using four servers, each environment had four identical servers. Adding my development notebook to the mix pushed us to 21 machines.

At least once, as I was deploying change scripts, I missed a server — and of course I wouldn't catch it in my testing. If I was lucky, another DBA would catch it before it broke something for one of the app programmers.

No doubt you've been there too.

While the schema audit trigger presented in this chapter couldn't have prevented my error, it would have made it much easier to diagnose and correct.

CROSS-REF **This chapter builds on its sister chapter, Chapter 27, "Creating DDL Triggers." That chapter demonstrates how to create a DDL trigger, while this chapter applies the technology for a specific purpose.**

DDL triggers are easy enough to code, but it's not a common task, so I've tried to automate the process for you with `SchemaAudit`, an open-source schema auditing script available for download from my website, `www.sqlserverbible.com`, or from `CodePlex.com`. The `SchemaAudit` script creates a `SchemaAudit` table and installs the DDL trigger to track all schema changes.

CROSS-REF **You can (and should) download the most recent version of the `SchemaAudit` script from `www.sqlserverbible.com`. It's quite likely this script will be updated over time.**

SchemaAudit Table

Just as with the Audit table in the previous chapter, any audit system needs a repository. The following table is designed to track schema changes:

```
CREATE TABLE dbo.SchemaAudit (
 AuditDate DATETIME NOT NULL,
 UserName sysname NOT NULL,
 [Event] sysname NOT NULL,
 [Schema] sysname NULL,
 [Object] VARCHAR(50) NULL,
 [TSQL] NVARCHAR(MAX) NOT NULL,
 [XMLEventData] XML NOT NULL);
```

The SchemaAudit script creates this table.

SchemaAudit Trigger

The following DDL trigger captures information about any database changes in the user database and records the changes to an audit table. The key is the EventData() XML function, which contains information generic to any DDL command. The SchemaAudit script creates this trigger:

```
CREATE TRIGGER [SchemaAuditDDLTrigger] ON DATABASE
  FOR DDL_DATABASE_LEVEL_EVENTS
AS
  BEGIN
  -- www.SQLServerBible.com
  -- Paul Nielsen
    SET NoCount ON
    DECLARE @EventData XML,
      @Schema SYSNAME,
      @Object SYSNAME,
      @EventType SYSNAME,
      @SQL VARCHAR(MAX)

    SET @EventData = EventData()

    SET @Schema = @EventData.value
                    ('data(/EVENT_INSTANCE/SchemaName)[1]', 'VARCHAR(50)')
    SET @Object = @EventData.value
                    ('data(/EVENT_INSTANCE/ObjectName)[1]', 'VARCHAR(50)')
    SET @EventType = @EventData.value
                    ('data(/EVENT_INSTANCE/EventType)[1]', 'VARCHAR(50)')


    INSERT SchemaAudit (AuditDate, UserName, [Event], [Schema],
```

```
                         Object, TSQL, [XMLEventData])
        SELECT
          GETDATE(),
          @EventData.value('data(/EVENT_INSTANCE/UserName)[1]', 'SYSNAME'),
          @EventType, @Schema, @Object,
          @EventData.value('data(/EVENT_INSTANCE/TSQLCommand/CommandText)[1]',
                              'VARCHAR(max)'),
          @EventData

    END
```

With the trigger in place, it's time to make several schema changes:

```
CREATE TABLE Test (
  PK INT NOT NULL Primary Key,
  Col1 VARCHAR(1)
   );

GO
ALTER TABLE Test
  DROP Column Col1

ALTER TABLE Test
  ADD Col1 CHAR(1)

DROP TABLE Test
```

Use the following to view the Schema Audit log and see the full history of the database schema changes:

```
SELECT AuditDate, User, [Event], [Schema] + '.' + [Object] as Object,
  TSQL FROM SchemaAudit;
```

Result:

```
AuditDate           User Event          Object      TSQL
------------------- ---- -------------- ----------- --------------------
2009-03-29 18:36:00 dbo  CREATE_TABLE   dbo.Test    CREATE TABLE Test
                                                    (PK INT NOT NULL
                                                     Primary Key,
                                                     Col1 VARCHAR(1);
2009-03-29 18:36:00 dbo ALTER_TABLE     dbo.Test    ALTER TABLE Test
                                                     DROP Column Col1
2009-03-29 18:36:00 dbo ALTER_TABLE     dbo.Test    ALTER TABLE Test
                                                     DROP Column Col1
2009-03-29 18:36:00 dbo ALTER_TABLE     dbo.Test    ALTER TABLE Test
                                                     ADD Col1 CHAR(1)
2009-03-29 18:37:00 dbo DROP_TABLE      dbo.Test    DROP TABLE Test
```

Summary

Although this chapter is short, auditing schema changes is a critical task for any database, whether it's a dev database, test environment, or production. I strongly recommend adding schema auditing to every database, and the `SchemaAudit` script automates the process.

The next chapter in this part covering monitoring and auditing discusses tracing and profiling, the ability to see into SQL Server and its traffic.

Chapter 55

Performance Monitor

IN THIS CHAPTER

Observing server performance

Saving counter logs

When I tuned the search feature in Nordic (my T-SQL based O/R DBMS) I pushed the database up to five million objects by running several instances of Query Editor, each running a loop to generate random names using the distribution of names from the 1990 U.S. Census. To be as efficient as possible, I played with the number of Query Editor instances and found that, on my machine, about ten instances with a .025-second pause produced the highest number of transactions per second.

The tool I used to watch the transactions per second, and the number of objects in the database, was PerfMon.

Performance Monitor, or "PerfMon," has been around for quite a while. Anyone working with Windows as an IT platform is familiar with PerfMon. These are the first tools used for high-level diagnostics and health of any server.

SQL Server extends PerfMon by adding dozens of SQL Server–specific counters. While PerfMon alone doesn't provide enough detail to fully diagnose SQL Server, it does a great job of illustrating the overall server performance issues and highlighting SQL Server themes.

PerfMon is more than just a pretty face. PerfMon's counter logs can write data to a binary perflog (`*.blg`) file or to a comma-delimited file (universal across Windows versions). Either type of file can be integrated into SQL Server Profiler.

All in all, anyone working with SQL Server needs to be proficient with PerfMon.

Using Performance Monitor

Performance Monitor (PerfMon) includes two snap-ins: *System Monitor* and *Performance Logs and Alerts*. Some servers have it installed in the Administrative Tools menu. It's also found at Control Panel ➪ Administrative Tools ➪ Performance, and it can be launched from SQL Server Profiler's Tools ➪ Performance Monitor menu command.

System monitor

System Monitor, or "sysmon," is familiar to anyone with experience with Windows server administration. System Monitor graphically displays multiple counters, aggregate but detailed data from the server internals. It looks a bit like a heart EKG monitor for Windows and SQL Server, as shown in Figure 55-1.

FIGURE 55-1

System Monitor is useful for watching the overall activity within SQL Server.

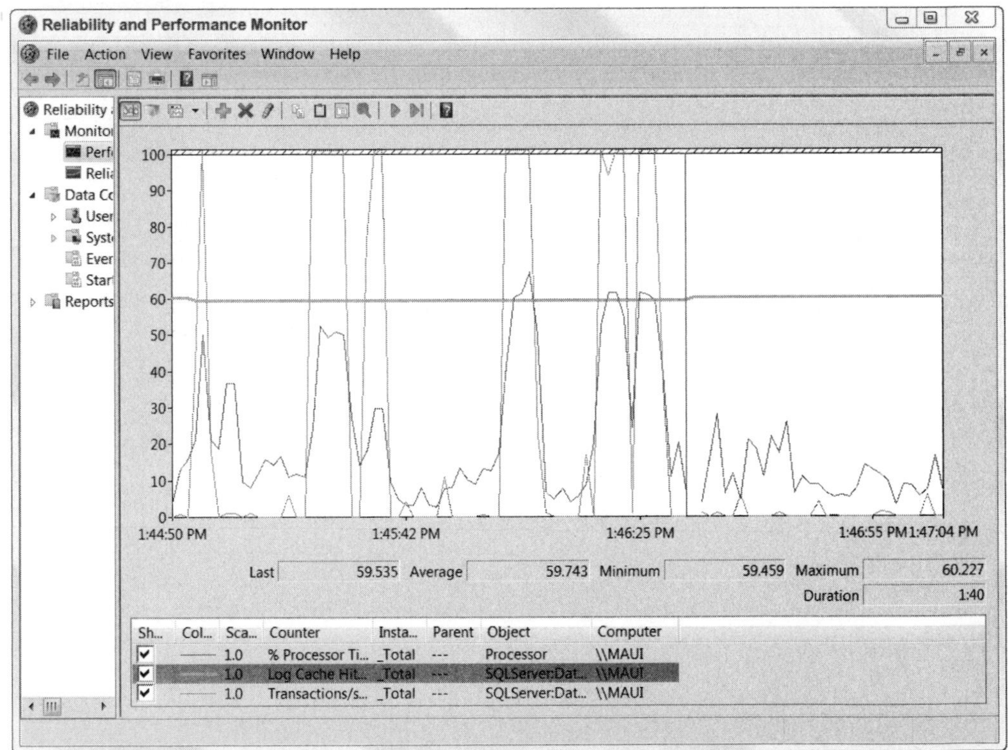

The performance counters are added to System Monitor one counter at a time using the plus-symbol button in the toolbar. A performance counter can watch the local server or a remote server, so it isn't necessary to run System Monitor at the SQL Server machine. The counters can be watched as a timed line graph, a histogram bar graph, or a real-time report.

Counters are organized by object and, sometimes, instance. For example, in Figure 55-1, the `SQL Server: Databases` object exposes many counters, including the Transactions/sec counter. This counter can be watched for All Instances (all databases), or as selected instances (the PerfTest database).

NOTE **The SQL Server Database Engine isn't the only server to expose counters to System Monitor. Analysis Services, Reporting Services, .NET, ASP, BizTalk, and other servers all add counters to System Monitor.**

Typically, a new counter will display as a line at the top or bottom of the graph because the scale needs adjustment. Using the System Monitor Properties dialog, available from the context menu, you can adjust the scale of the graph, the scale of each counter, and the presentation of each counter.

Although there are hundreds of possible System Monitor counters, Table 55-1 describes the counters commonly used when investigating a SQL Server installation.

The "best counter" list seems to change with every performance conference presentation. These are the counters I had success with, but by no means am I saying there aren't other counters worth watching. So, read the blogs, experiment, and keep track of the ones you find meaningful.

Additionally, the SQL Server: Wait Statistics counters are useful windows into potential SQL Server bottlenecks; and there are a number of interesting memory counters in SQL Server: Resource Pool Stats.

TIP **A complete list of SQL Server counters and their current values can be queried from the `sys.dm_os_performance_counters` dynamic management view. This is cool, because you can get the counter data from within Transact-SQL code.**

You can create custom counters using T-SQL to pass data from your database code to System Monitor. This can be useful to show the number of transactions processed by a performance test or the number of rows inserted by a data generator. There are ten possible user counters. The following trivial example increments one of the counters:

```
DECLARE @Counter Int
SET @Counter = 0
While @Counter < 100
  BEGIN
    SET @Counter = @Counter + 1
    EXEC sp_user_counter1 @Counter
    WAITFOR Delay '00:00:02'
  END
```

TABLE 55-1

Key Performance-Monitor Counters

Object	Counter	Description	Usefulness
SQLServer: Buffer Manager	Buffer-cache hit ratio	Percentage of reads found already cached in memory	SQL Server typically does an excellent job of pre-fetching the data into memory. If the ratio is below 95 percent, more memory will likely improve performance.
Processor	Percentage of processor time	Total percentage of processor activity	If CPUs are regularly more than 60 percent active, additional CPU cores or a faster server will increase performance.
SQLServer: SQL Statistics	Batch requests per second	SQL batch activity	A good indicator of user activity
Physical Disk	Average disk-queue length	Number of both reads and writes waiting on the disk; an indication of disk throughput; affected by the number of disk spindles on multi-disk RAID configurations. According to Microsoft, the disk-queue length should be less than the number of disk spindles plus two. (Check the scale when applying.)	Disk throughput is a key hardware performance factor. Carefully splitting the database across multiple disk subsystems will probably improve performance.
SQLServer: SQL Statistics	Failed auto-params per second	Number of queries for which SQL Server could not cache the query execution plan in memory; an indication of poorly written queries. (Check the scale when applying.)	Locating and correcting the queries will improve performance.
SQLServer: Locks	Average wait time (in milliseconds), lock waits, and lock timeouts per second	A cause of serious performance problems; lock waits, the length of the wait, and the number of lock timeouts are all good indicators of the level of locking contention within a database.	If locking issues are detected, the indexing structure and transaction code should be examined.
SQLServer: User Connections	User connections	Number of current connections	Indicates potential database activity
SQLServer: Databases	Transactions per second	Number of current transactions within a database	A good indicator of database activity

Best Practice

Use System Monitor to get an overall picture of the health of the server and to get an idea of the types of issues that might be occurring within SQL Server. Then, armed with this information, move to SQL Server Profiler to target the specific problem.

The configuration of System Monitor, including every counter, can be saved to a configuration file using File ➪ Save As, and later restored using File ➪ Open. Using this technique, you can export a System Monitor configuration to other servers.

There is one catch: the counter must be monitoring the local server to move from server to server. However, if the counters monitor a remote server, then the configuration will monitor that remote server regardless of where the System Monitor configuration file is opened. Because DBAs are seldom physically at the SQL Server being monitored, this is a problem. If this bothers you as much as it bothers me, e-mail me; one of these days I'm going to write a custom system monitor to fix this and other problems.

Counter Logs

Performance Monitor also includes the Performance Logs and Alerts plug-in, which includes counter logs, Trace Alerts, and Alerts. This section focuses on counter logs. Counter logs use the same server counters as System Monitor, but instead of graphically displaying the data in real time, the counter logs write the counter data to a log file. This means the data can be analyzed after the fact or even replayed within SQL Server Profiler (more on this cool feature in the next chapter).

Counter log configurations are listed under the counter logs node in Performance Monitor. To see the resulting log files you have to look in the output directory.

To create a new counter log, use the counter log's context menu and choose New Log Settings. After naming the log, the SQL Server Trace Property dialog (shown in Figure 55-2) is used to define the log. Adding an object adds every counter for the object, while adding counters provides a more granular capability to select counters similarly to System Monitor.

Counter Logs can be scheduled to run in the Counter Log Property dialog, or manually started and stopped using the log's context menu or the start and stop toolbar buttons.

If the Counter Log file was defined as a text file (comma-delimited or tab-delimited), you can open it using Excel. Each column is a counter value, and each row is a sample interval.

FIGURE 55-2

The SQLServerTrace Counter Log is configured to write server performance counter data to the C:\PerfLogs directory.

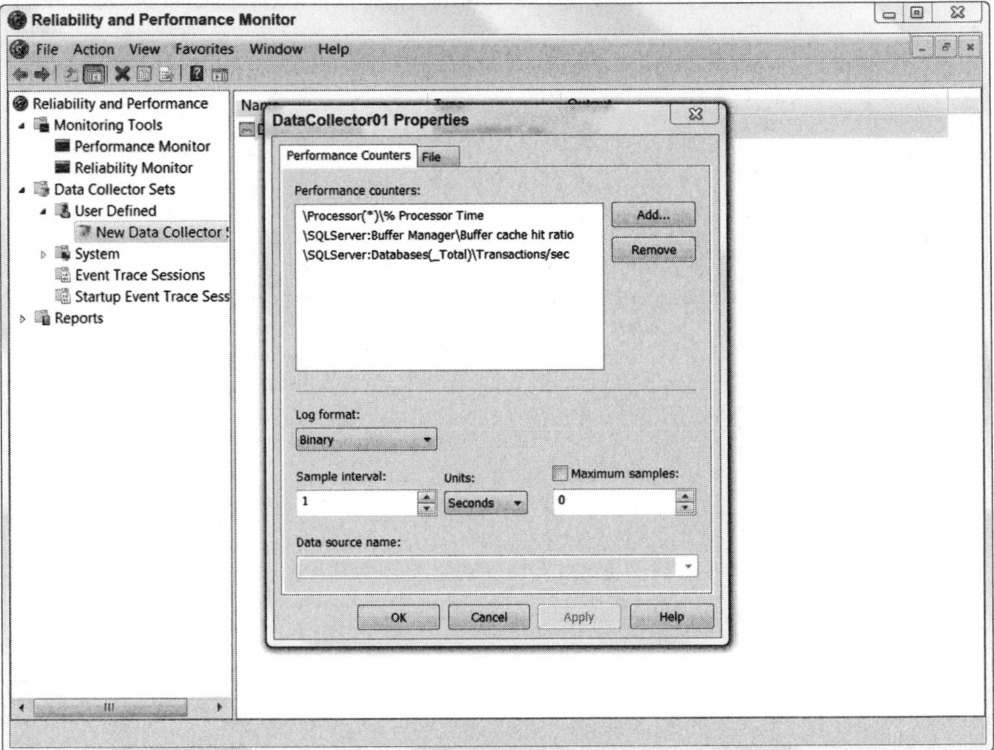

Summary

PerfMon is a small but powerful tool in any DBA's toolbox. Used alone, it provides a comprehensive overview of the server's status — both Windows and SQL Server. Used in conjunction with Profiler (covered in the next chapter), it opens up a visual microscope into performance.

The key to PerfMon is understanding the overwhelming number of counters. If you know which counters to focus on, you'll find that PerfMon can be efficient. If not, you'll waste time and fail to come to any useful conclusion.

The next chapter looks at Profiler, by far the most popular SQL Server monitoring tool, and for good reason. Profiler is indeed an excellent tool. With PerfMon, it's even better.

Chapter 56

Tracing and Profiling

I love SQL Server Profiler.

IN THIS CHAPTER

Viewing SQL Server events

Establishing traces

Merging Profiler data with SysMon

When tuning my own application, or as a consultant when I arrive at a job site, one of the first things I do is to fire up Profiler to capture a full trace of every ad hoc SQL query and stored procedure call. (You can read more about my performance trace in Chapter 64, "Indexing Strategies.")

I use a Dell Latitude E6400 notebook, which is great for traveling, but in the SQL Dungeon (my basement), I attach the notebook to a normal keyboard, a mouse, and a large monitor. The notebook screen becomes a second monitor off to the left. When I code, the second monitor runs Profiler and displays performance stats as I code.

Of all the SQL Server programs and icons, I have only three pinned to my main Start menu: Management Studio, Books Online, and Profiler.

Profiler is to the DBA what a camera is to a photographer. Any photographer who doesn't have an affection for his favorite camera must not be much of a photographer. (I just got a Nikon D60 for my fiftieth birthday!) Likewise, any SQL Server professional needs to be intimately familiar with Profiler. When I help clients by doing tech interviews, I always ask the candidate if he or she loves Profiler. It's one of the mandatory minimum skills.

If you're new to SQL Server, let me introduce you to SQL Server Profiler:

- SQL Trace is a lightweight, but powerful, technology that can run on SQL Server; it collects performance data selected from hundreds of possible performance data points ranging from locks, to connections, to SQL DML statements, to recompiles, to you name it.

- SQL Server Profiler is a separate application that can configure, start, and stop SQL Trace as well as capture and display data from SQL Trace. You can think of SQL Server Profiler as the optional UI for SQL Trace.
- Profiler data can scroll on the screen or be saved to a file or table for further analysis.
- Data can be filtered in numerous ways, including viewing only events related to a specific database, excluding events from a specific application, or capturing only the queries that exceed a specified duration.
- Profile configurations can be saved and reused later.
- Profile event data can be merged with server counter data collected by Perfmon/SysMon for a great visual representation of what's happening on the server.

To be accurate, Profiler is actually just the front-end UI for SQL Trace. The two are different components and technologies. SQL Trace runs on the server, is lightweight, and collects data points to be passed to Profiler or written to a file.

What's New with SQL Server Profiler and Trace?

To be honest, there's not a lot new with Profiler for SQL Server 2008. Management Studio adds the capability to open Profiler preset to filter for the current connection.

To fill in the history of SQL Server Profiler, SQL Trace was first introduced with SQL Server version 6.5. The interface was enhanced with SQL Server 2005, merging the events and data points. SQL Server 2005 also introduced the Default Trace, a high-performance specific trace configuration.

Running Profiler

SQL Server Profiler can be opened from several locations:

- From the Start menu, Profiler is under SQL Server 2008 ➪ Performance menu.
- In Management Studio, Profiler is in the Tools menu.
- Within Management Studio's Query Editor, the context menu includes the option to Trace Query in SQL Server Profiler. This option opens Profiler filtered to the current connection.

Defining a new trace

When a new trace is created (with the New Trace toolbar button or File ➪ New Trace), a connection is created to a SQL Server, and the Trace Properties dialog (see Figure 56-1) is presented. The Trace Properties General tab sets up the trace (name, file destination, etc.), and the Events Selection tab defines the events and data columns to be recorded, as well as the filter. If the trace is running, the properties may be viewed but not changed. A trace configuration can be saved as a template to make creating new traces easier.

FIGURE 56-1

This SQL Server Profiler is using the T-SQL Duration template and will write information to a file.

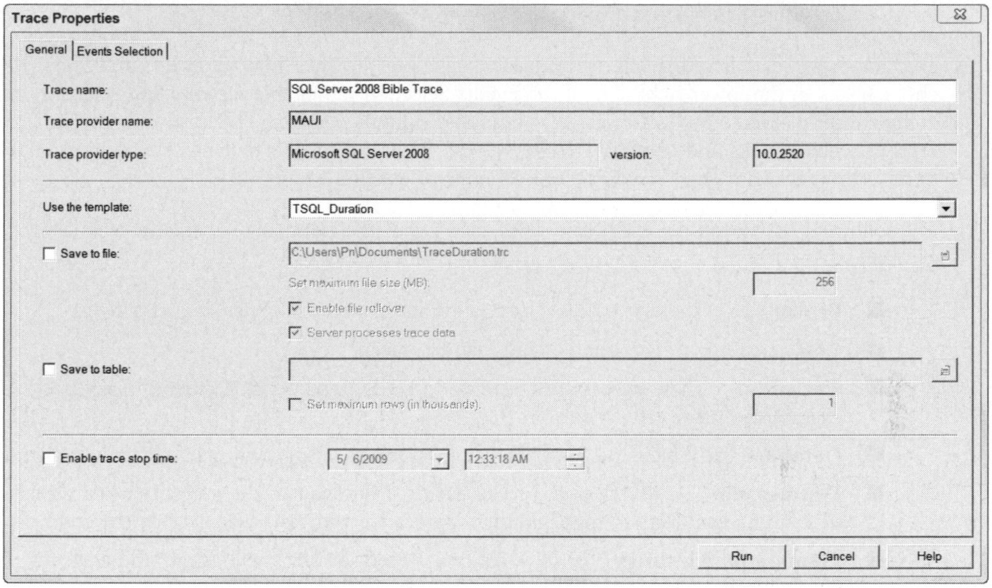

A Profiler trace is primarily viewed interactively, but the data can also be written to a file or a SQL Server table. This is useful for further manual analysis, viewing alongside System Monitor counter data, or importing into the Database Engine Tuning Advisor.

When Profiler data is written to a file, SQL Server writes 128-KB chunks of data at a time for performance. Conversely, writing data to a table involves a series of row inserts that doubles the transaction log workload and seriously hinders SQL Server's performance. Never trace directly to a table on the server being traced, although writing to a different server is OK.

Best Practice

To save Profiler data for further analysis, use the high-performance file method and a server-side trace (discussed later). If you want to analyze the data using T-SQL (and analyzing trace data with SQL aggregate queries and `WHERE...LIKE` clauses is way cool), save the trace to a file; and after the trace is complete, open the trace file using Profiler and select File ⇨ Save As ⇨ Table.

Selecting events and data columns

The Events Selection tab (see Figure 56-2) determines the data points that SQL Trace will capture. SQL Trace can monitor 179 key SQL Server events. The default templates configure a trace with a few preselected events, but there's so much more.

Two important details of the interface are easily overlooked: The Show all events and Show all columns check boxes in the lower-right side of the Events Selection tab enable viewing and selecting from the complete set of events and columns. Without those options checked, the form only displays the currently selected events and columns. While this can be useful to filter out noise, you must enable these options to select additional events or add columns to existing events.

The following list shows the event categories, along with the number of events in each category and a comment:

- **Broker** (13): The first category covers events related to Service Broker activity.
- **CLR** (1): Only CLR assembly loads can be traced.
- **Cursors** (7): These events are not related to T-SQL server-side cursors. They track ADO client-side cursor activity.
- **Database** (6): Tracks database file activity such as autogrowth and mirror connections.
- **Deprecation** (2): A very useful set of events. I always run these events when exercising code or running unit tests to highlight any deprecated features being used in the code.
- **Errors and Warnings** (16): Any abnormal event or error will trigger these events; useful when watching for errors in an active system.
- **Full text** (3): The Full text events only track Full-Text Search crawl activity. There are no events for Full-Text Search configuration changes. More information about Full-Text Search queries is hidden in the Performance: FullTextQuery events.
- **Locks** (9): While enabling lock events can be great for learning about locks in a controlled setting, using these events in a production environment can instantly fill Profiler with thousands of events, so be careful with this category. A noteworthy exception is the Deadlock Graph event, which captures a full set of data about the deadlock and even displays a graph.
- **OLEDB** (5): These events track OLE-DB distributed query calls made by SQL Server to other providers.
- **Objects** (3): DDL events (`CREATE`, `ALTER`, `DROP`) can be tracked with these events.
- **Performance** (14): These events track data about query plans and plan guides. A notable event is the ShowPlan XML event, which can display the query execution plan.
- **Progress Report** (1): This event category tracks the progress of online reindexing.
- **Query Notifications** (4): These show information about query notification activity, including subscriptions activity.
- **Scans** (2): When watching for performance issues, this category can trace index scans and table scans.
- **Security Audit** (42): With a nod to the *Hitchhiker's Guide to the Galaxy*, the Security Audit category includes numerous events to support C2 and Common Criteria compliance.
- **Server** (3): This odd category includes mount tape, memory change, and trace stop events.

- **Sessions** (1): This event fires when a trace is started and returns an event for every existing connection, including its properties.
- **Stored Procedures** (15): This rich category includes a number of events related to stored procedure execution, compilation, and cache hits.
- **TSQL** (9): These events fire for individual T-SQL statements.
- **Transactions** (13): SQL transactions events at the level of begin transaction, commit transaction, and rollback transaction are traced with this category. Playing with this event will reveal how much activity actually happens with SQL Server. Unfortunately, there's no event to capture changing the transaction isolation level.
- **User Configurable** (10): To gather custom data about the environment or application's activity, the application can call the `sp_trace_generateevent` system stored procedure to fire an event and pass custom data to SQL Trace.

FIGURE 56-2

The Trace Properties Events Selection page enables you to select the events tracked by Profiler.

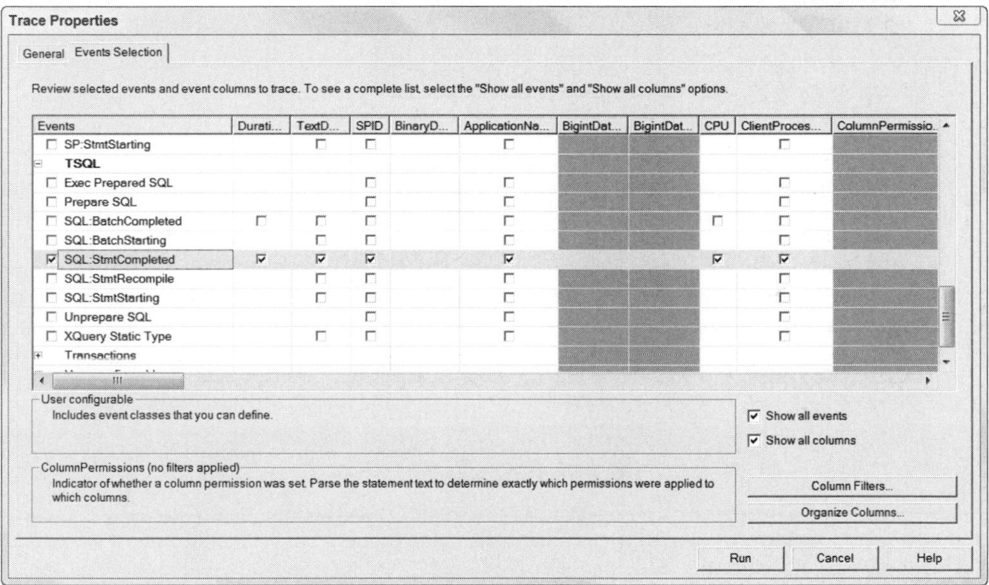

Depending on the events, different data becomes relevant to the trace. The data columns automatically offer the appropriate data. Although the SPID data column appears optional, it's only fooling you — it's mandatory. A useful data column to capture is StartDate, which is required if the trace will be correlated with Perfmon data later.

Filtering events

Profiler can capture so much information that it can fill a drive with data. Fortunately, the Profiler Trace Filter (see Figure 56-3) can narrow the scope of your search to the data of interest.

FIGURE 56-3

The Edit Filter dialog serves as a where clause for the trace, restricting it to certain events only. Here, only events for the OBXKites database will be captured.

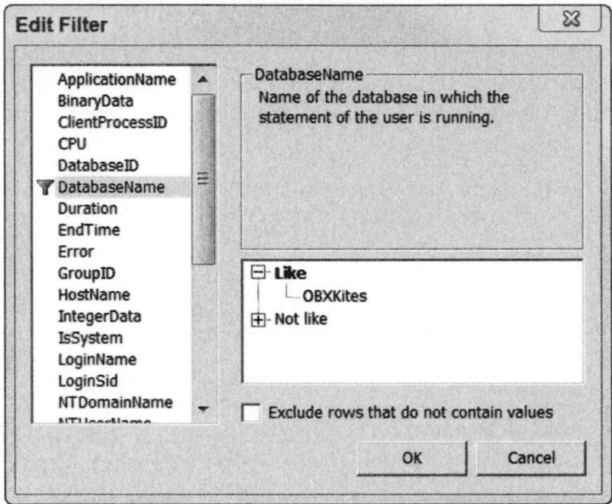

The filter uses a combination of `equal` and `like` operators, depending on the data types captured. A frustrating aspect of the filter is that it only works against collected data, and the data collected for some columns may not be what was expected. For example, if you want to filter the trace to only those batches that reference a specific table or column, filtering by object name won't work. Defining a `like` filter using wildcards on the `text data` column, however, will cause Profiler to select only those batches that include that column name.

The Exclude system IDs check box sets the filter to select only user objects.

Best Practice

By default, SQL Server Profiler filters out the calls made by SQL Server Profiler, but it's a good idea to regularly also filter out the Reporting Services and SQL Agent applications to avoid any unnecessary event clutter.

Organizing columns

To add a column to the `GROUP BY` (not shown in a figure), select `GROUP BY` in the right-hand column before clicking the Add button. Columns can also be escalated to group status by means of the Up button. Any `GROUP BY` columns become the first columns in the trace window; and as new events are added to the trace window, those events are automatically added within their group.

Running the trace

Although Profiler is just a UI that consumes data generated by SQL Trace, it's pretty good at controlling live traces. Profiler can start, pause, and stop the trace using the typical icons in the toolbar.

A few details worth pointing out are as follows:

- The eraser toolbar button will clear the results in Profiler.
- If the trace is flying by too fast to view but you don't want to pause or stop the trace, the Auto Scroll Window toolbar button enables Profiler to continue to add new events at the bottom of the list without scrolling the window.
- While a trace is stopped, its events and data columns may be changed using the Properties button.

Using the trace file

Once the trace is captured it can be browsed through using the Profiler trace window, and a Find toolbar button can help navigate the data. However, the trace is likely to be so large that it will be difficult to manually use the data.

The solution is to save the trace file to a SQL table using File ⇨ Save As; the data can then be analyzed and manipulated as in any other SQL table.

SQL Server Profiler has the ability to replay traces. However, the restrictions on the replay option are such that it's unlikely to be useful for most databases. If the trace is to be replayed, certain events must be captured. For example, the SQL Batch Start event can be replayed, but SQL Batch Complete cannot. Also, if data inserts are replayed, you'll want to reset the database to the same state as the beginning of the trace; otherwise, you'll likely have unique data conflicts, and issues with identity column values.

Additionally, the entire trace file can be submitted as a workload to the Database Engine Tuning Advisor so that it can tune for multiple queries. However, I'm not a big fan of the Database Engine Tuning Advisor, as I explain in Chapter 64, "Indexing Strategies."

Integrating Performance Monitor data

Both System Monitor and Profiler present their own unique perspective on the state of the server. The two sets of information can be merged to produce a synchronized walk-through scenario viewing both perspectives using SQL Server Profiler.

To set up the dual-perspective experience, simultaneously capture server performance logs using both Performance Monitor's Counter Logs and SQL Server Profiler. These steps are specific:

1. Configure System Monitor with the exact counters you want to view later. Be sure to get the scale and everything just right. Set up the Counter Log to the exact same configuration.
2. Configure Profiler with the right set of trace events. They must include the start and end time data columns so Profiler can integrate the two logs later. Script the trace to T-SQL code. Close Profiler.
3. Manually start the Counter Log. Execute the T-SQL trace code to start the server-side trace.

4. Exercise the server with the code and load you want to analyze.
5. When the test is complete, stop both the Counter Log and the server-side trace.
6. Open Profiler and then open the saved trace file.
7. Use the File ➪ Import Performance Data menu command to import the Counter Log.

Profiler responds to the import by adding a pane that displays the System Monitor graph, as shown in Figure 56-4. Select a Profiler event or a time in the System Monitor graph; the two stay in sync. Cool, eh?

FIGURE 56-4

SQL Server Profiler can integrate Performance Monitor data and move through the events in sync.

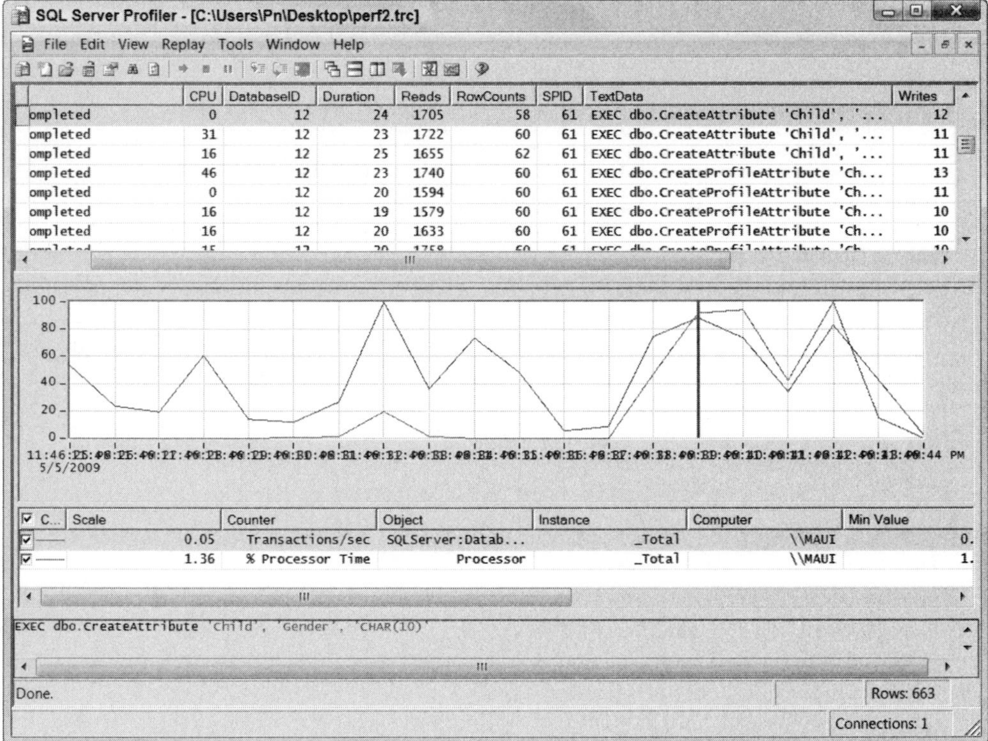

Using SQL Trace

SQL Server Profiler is usually used interactively, and for ad hoc data gathering this is probably sufficient. However, running Profiler on a heavy transaction server can lead to problems:

- If Profiler can't keep up, some events will be dropped. I've seen this happen frequently on heavy transaction servers with Profiler.
- There's a measurable performance impact on the server when running Profiler. The heavier the transaction traffic on the server, the greater the percentage of performance impact from Profiler.
- The workstation gathering the events may run out of memory.

The solution is to run the SQL Trace directly on the server without collecting the data using the Profiler UI.

SQL Traces are started by the `sp_trace_create` system stored procedure. Once the trace exists, events are added to it using `sp_tracesetevent`.

While it's possible to code stored procedures to configure SQL Traces, the most common method is to define the trace in Profiler and then script the trace to run on the server. Once the trace is set up and tested in SQL Server Profiler, select File ➪ Export ➪ Script Trace Definition ➪ For SQL Server 2005 - 2008 to generate a T-SQL script that will launch the server-side trace.

Best Practice

For production systems running server-side traces, writing to a file is the best way to collect performance data with the least overhead to the server.

To view all the traces currently running in the server, query `sys.traces`:

```
SELECT id, path, start_time, last_event_time,
  event_count, dropped_event_count
  FROM sys.traces t
```

Result (abbreviated to fit):

```
id start_time          last_event_time     event_count dropped_event_count
-- ------------------- ------------------- ----------- -------------
1  2009-04-27 03:07:49 2009-04-27 22:49:22 2770        NULL
2  2009-04-27 22:27:20 NULL                0           0
```

To programmatically view the events and data columns being collected by a trace, use the following query (you'll need to modify the parameter for `fn_trace_geteventinfo`):

```
SELECT tcat.name +':' + te.name AS 'Event', tcol.NAME AS 'Column'
  FROM fn_trace_geteventinfo (2) tinfo
    JOIN sys.trace_events te
      ON tinfo.eventid = te.trace_event_id
    JOIN sys.trace_categories tcat
      ON te.category_id = tcat.category_id
```

```
    JOIN sys.trace_columns tcol
      ON tinfo.columnid = tcol.trace_column_id
```

Result:

```
Event                      Column
-------------------------- -----------------------
TSQL:SQL:StmtCompleted     TextData
TSQL:SQL:StmtCompleted     DatabaseID
TSQL:SQL:StmtCompleted     ApplicationName
TSQL:SQL:StmtCompleted     SPID
TSQL:SQL:StmtCompleted     Duration
TSQL:SQL:StmtCompleted     StartTime
TSQL:SQL:StmtCompleted     RowCounts
TSQL:SQL:StmtCompleted     IsSystem
TSQL:SQL:StmtCompleted     EndTime
TSQL:SQL:StmtCompleted     Reads
TSQL:SQL:StmtCompleted     Writes
TSQL:SQL:StmtCompleted     CPU
TSQL:SQL:StmtCompleted     DatabaseName
```

To stop a server-side trace use the `sp_trace_setstatus` system stored procedure. The first parameter is the `traceid`, and the second parameter specifies the action: 0 = stop the trace, 1 = start the trace, and 2 = close and delete the trace. The sample code uses trace as 2:

```
EXEC sp_trace_setstatus 2, 0
```

Another useful trace system stored procedure is `fn_trace_gettable`, which reads a trace file and returns the data in table form:

```
SELECT *
  FROM fn_trace_gettable
   ('C:\Program Files\Microsoft SQL Server
         \MSSQL10.MSSQLSERVER\MSSQL\Log\log_195.trc', 1)
```

Preconfigured traces

SQL Server automatically runs a trace called the Default Trace that gathers basic events like server start and stop, file growth, and creating or dropping objects. As the default trace, its trace ID is 1. Theoretically, it could be stopped without any ill effects, but there's no reason to do so.

Another preconfigured trace is the *blackbox* trace, which is used to diagnose server crashes. Starting a trace with `option = 8` starts this trace. Typically this trace is not run unless there's a specific problem and Microsoft PSS has asked for data from the trace.

Common Criteria and the older C2 Audit security levels also involve running a specific trace that gathers login and other security data. Executing `sp_trace_create` with `option = 4` configures these traces.

Summary

SQL Server Profiler and SQL Trace are two technologies you need if you're interested in what's really happening with your server. Profiler and SQL Trace may be venerable technologies compared to Change Tracking or Extended Events, but they're still two of the more useful tools in the DBA toolbox. Whereas some SQL Server technologies are optional — you can survive as a DBA without learning much about XML or SMO — Profiler and SQL Trace are mandatory.

Key points about SQL Trace and Profiler:

- Trace is a server-side technology that collects data that may be consumed by Profiler or written to a file.
- Profiler is a slick UI for Trace, but it may impact performance, so for heavy traces on a production server, it's best to use Profiler to configure the trace, generate a script, and then run the trace on the server.
- Because there are 179 SQL Trace events, it's worth it to become familiar with them.
- Events can be filtered; typically, Reporting Services and SQL Agent are filtered out.
- SQL Trace can be completely configured and controlled by T-SQL code alone, but this is an advanced skill.
- SQL Trace events and Performance Monitor data can be integrated after the fact to produce a complete picture of what was happening on the server.

The next chapter stays in the mode of monitoring and auditing SQL Server. Similar to SQL Trace, but at a finer granularity, wait states track every process and every time it pauses for any reason.

Chapter 57

Wait States

IN THIS CHAPTER

Querying for wait states

Detecting CPU pressure

Analyzing hardware performance

I wonder how much of the gross national product is wasted annually waiting at traffic lights. I've thought about using the chronometer feature on my Timex Ironman watch to time my monthly aggregate red light wait time. (It would be a good reason to actually use my watch for more than telling time, as there's little chance I'm going to do a triathlon anytime soon.) There's no doubt that our fast-food culture obsesses about avoiding waiting at any cost.

SQL Server has to wait too. Sometimes it's waiting for I/O, sometimes for the CLR, sometimes for CPU. These waits are system bottlenecks. Fortunately, you don't need a stopwatch to measure how SQL Server waits. The data is all there in a dynamic management view (DMV), just waiting for you.

Most of my optimization strategies involve reducing the aggregate workload of the database by improving the schema, queries, and indexes.

Wait states are about tuning the environment — the hardware and server operating system. By analyzing what SQL Server is waiting for, you can identify the bottlenecks in the system.

The SQL Server Operating System (SQLOS) uses one scheduler per logical CPU core. Each scheduler manages a set of sessions that rotate through three states. A session that's *running* eventually has to wait for something, so it becomes *suspended* while waiting. When the wait is over, the session is *runnable* and waiting for the CPU to pick it up again:

- **Running:** Only one session per scheduler can be running at any given time. The session runs until it reaches a point when it's waiting for something, and then it yields control cooperatively back to the scheduler. The scheduler does not preempt sessions.
- **Suspended:** A session that's waiting is said to be suspended, and it stays suspended until the wait is satisfied.

- **Runnable:** A session that's no longer waiting and is ready to run again is put into the Runnable list, from which the scheduler can pick to run sessions.

To examine this round-robin from a practical point of view:

- If the session is spending time as runnable, then it's waiting on the CPU. This CPU pressure is referred to as *signal wait time*. It means the server needs more CPU cycles.
- The amount of time that the session is suspended is the time it spends waiting for some resource — disk I/O, for example. There no clearer way to see the hardware deficiencies than analyzing wait states.

Of course, these three states assume that the session has work to do. Sessions that are just waiting will show up as background or sleeping.

What's New with Wait States?

Looking at wait states was a bit of an undocumented mystery when they were first exposed in SQL Server 7, but Microsoft has steadily increased the number of wait states and their reliability.

With SQL Server 2005, new dynamic management views were introduced, making it easier to view wait states. SQL Server 2008 brings wait states into the limelight by including wait states in Activity Monitor.

Observing Wait State Statistics

Wait states are easier to observe with SQL Server 2008 than ever before. SQL Server automatically collects statistics on wait states as the server runs. There's nothing to enable or start as with SQL Trace/Profiler. For each type of wait state, SQL Server simply keeps a count of the instances and durations.

The normal behavior is to see the wait state statistics since the start of the server. It's probably more beneficial to see the wait states for a period of time (e.g., during a specific test). To reset all the wait states back to zero, run the following `dbcc` command:

```
dbcc sqlperf ('sys.dm_os_waiting_tasks', clear)
```

There are several ways to view wait states in SQL Server 2008.

Querying wait states

The most common method of viewing wait states is to query the DMVs.

The first wait state DMV lists every wait state type and its related statistics. This is also where the aggregate signal wait time (waiting on the CPU) is found:

```
SELECT *
  FROM sys.dm_os_wait_stats;
```

Result (abbreviated):

```
wait_type     waiting_tasks_count wait_time_ms  max_wait_time_ms signal_wait_time_ms
------------- ------------------- ------------- ---------------- -------------------
MISCELLANEOUS 0                   0             0                0
LCK_M_SCH_S   1                   29            29               0
LCK_M_SCH_M   12                  160           40               5
LCK_M_S       21                  12718         2029             35
LCK_M_U       7                   4             1                4
LCK_M_X       35                  611           76               126
LCK_M_IS      7                   2             1                0
...
```

The versatile `sys.dm_exec_requests` DMV has a wealth of information about the current sessions, including their current wait status:

```
SELECT session_id, status, command, wait_type, wait_time, last_wait_type
  FROM sys.dm_exec_requests
  WHERE Status NOT IN ('background', 'sleeping');
```

Result:

```
session_id status    command         wait_type      wait_time  last_wait_type
---------- --------- --------------- -------------- ---------  --------------
65         running   SELECT          NULL           0          MISCELLANEOUS
66         suspended CREATE DATABASE PAGEIOLATCH_SH 6          PAGEIOLATCH_SH
```

The third DMV with wait state information is a subset of the previous DMV:

```
SELECT *
  FROM sys.dm_os_waiting_tasks
```

Activity Monitor

Activity Monitor has been around for nearly a decade, but it's completely redesigned for SQL Server 2008. (Personally, I prefer the old Activity Monitor — it showed more detail about locks and wasn't as buggy a UI. The new Activity Monitor refuses to size the columns correctly for widths less than 1,180 pixels.)

The new Activity Monitor has a section for waits that basically presents the key information from the `sys.dm_os_wait_stats` DMV, as shown in Figure 57-1.

CROSS-REF **If you're running Enterprise Edition and exploring the new Management Data Warehouse (MDW), you'll find that the MDW also collects wait state information. You can read more about it in Chapter 62, "Management Data Warehouse."**

FIGURE 57-1

The new Activity Monitor displays basic wait state activity.

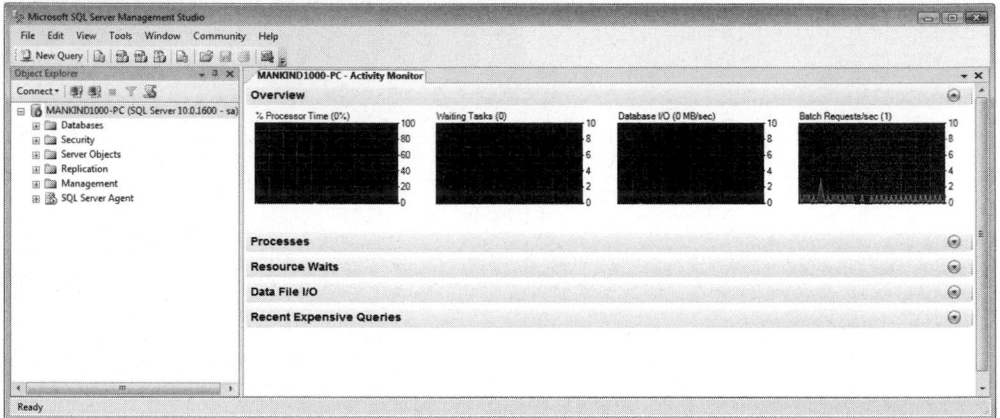

Analyzing Wait States

Since wait state is available, the key question is, what does it mean? There are over 400 wait types, but many are normal, similar, or rarely seen. Some common wait types to look for include the following:

- **Locks:** Sessions are waiting on other sessions to release locks. Consider improving the indexing to reduce query duration.
- **Latches** and **page latches:** Sessions are waiting on memory or I/O.
- **I/O Completion**, **Write Completion, Asynch I/O Completion:** Sessions are waiting on writes to the data file.
- **Asynch Network I/O:** Sessions are waiting on a network resource.
- **CXPacket:** Parallel query synchronization
- **LogMgr, Write Log I/O:** Sessions are waiting on the transaction log.

Summary

Understanding wait states is vital to diagnosing server performance. After all, what's more important to analyzing hardware performance than analyzing why it's waiting? Key points from this chapter include the following:

- Every session (with work to do) rotates through three states: running, suspended, and runnable.

- A high volume of runnable sessions, tracked as signal wait time, means there's not enough CPU cycles to meet the demand.
- While a resource is waiting for another resource (typically I/O or a lock), it's considered suspended.
- Wait states can be seen in Activity Monitor or DMVs.

The next chapter propels the topic of monitoring and auditing into the newest capabilities of SQL Server 2008 with Change Tracking, a new way to track which rows have been altered in a certain time frame.

Chapter 58

Extended Events

IN THIS CHAPTER

Extended Events packages and objects

Starting XE sessions

Querying XE data with XPath

If it ain't broke don't fix it.

In my humble opinion, there's nothing broken with SQL Trace and SQL Profiler, wait states, and DMVs. I've found these tools satisfactory for monitoring and diagnostics.

Nulltheless, the shiny new Extended Events (XE) feature, new in SQL Server 2008, is faster and more extensible than SQL Trace. SQL Trace has an easy UI: SQL Profiler. Extended Events has no (Microsoft provided) UI, and it has a steep learning curve. XE is also compatible with Event Tracing for Windows (ETW). You don't need to learn Extended Events to be successful with SQL Server 2008 today.

So why learn Extended Events? Two reasons. First, Extended Events is powerful and more granular than SQL Trace. Second, Extended Events is strategic to Microsoft. It's the foundation for event analysis going forward.

XE Components

The core of Extended Events is the Extended Events engine, which can handle any event, and because the payload (the data about the event) is XML based, the engine can include different data for different events as appropriate.

The engine can see events synchronously, but can process events and send event data to the target (the consumer of the event data) synchronously or asynchronously, which is an improvement over SQL Trace and enables Extended Events to handle a greater load than SQL Trace.

NOTE **SQL Server MVP and all-around smart guy, Jonathan Kehayias, has developed "Extended Events Manager," a UI for Extended Events that you can download from** `www.codeplex.com/ExtendedEventManager`**.**

Jonathan is also writing a white paper on Extended Events for Microsoft. Having read a draft, if you're interested in implementing an Extended Events solution, I highly recommend it. See `www.sqlserverbible.com` **for a link.**

Packages

At the top level, Extended Events organizes its components into three Microsoft-developed packages (it's really four, but the fourth package, `SecAudit`, is a private package dedicated to SQL Audit):

- `Package0`: Provides base functionality used by the other packages
- `sqlos`: Works with the SQL/OS events
- `sqlserver`: Works with the rest of SQL Server

Each of these packages contains several objects. To see the full list of objects within packages, query the following DMVs:

```
SELECT p.NAME AS Package, o.object_type,
       o.NAME AS Object,  o.description
  FROM sys.dm_xe_objects o
    JOIN sys.dm_xe_packages p
      ON o.type_package_guid = p.guid
  ORDER BY p.NAME, o.object_type
```

Result (abbreviated):

```
Package     object_type  Object                     description
----------- ------------ -------------------------- ---------------------------
package0    action       tsql_stack                 Collect Transact-SQL stack
package0    action       sql_text                   Collect SQL text
package0    action       plan_handle                Collect plan handle
package0    action       create_dump_single_thread  Create mini dump for the
                                                    current thread
package0    action       create_dump_all_threads    Create mini dump including
                                                    all threads
...
```

The `object_type` column reveals seven types of objects: actions, events, maps, pred_compares, pred_sources, targets, and types.

Building a crosstab query from the previous query analyzes the distribution of object types within the packages:

```
SELECT Package, action, event, map, pred_compare, pred_source, target, type
  FROM (SELECT o.Name AS Object, p.Name AS Package, o.object_type
          FROM sys.dm_xe_objects o
            JOIN sys.dm_xe_packages p
```

```
            ON o.type_package_guid = p.guid) sq
    PIVOT (COUNT(Object)
      FOR object_type IN
        (action, event, map, pred_compare, pred_source, target, type)
      ) AS pt;
```

Result:

```
Package    action  event   map    pred_compare pred_source target  type
---------- ------- ------- ------ ------------ ----------- ------- -----
package0   35      254     61     111          29          13      27
sqlos      1       0       0      0            0           0       1
sqlserver  1       0       0      0            0           0       1
```

Objects

Within each package is a host of objects. Creating an Extended Event is basically a process of evoking the right objects. To dig into these object types:

- **Events:** Similar to SQL Trace events, XE has more events and their columns are listed in `sys.dm_xe_object_columns`.

  Extended Events borrows the concept of event channels from Event Tracing for Windows (ETW). In the `Channel` read-only column, every event is in one of four predetermined channels: admin, analytic, debug, or operational.
- **Actions:** XE actions fire as the result of an event and can gather additional data about the context of the event.
- **Types and Maps:** A high-performance optimization, types and maps both serve as pointers to data. Instead of having to gather every data point synchronously, a type or map can point to the data in memory.
- **Pred_Compares** and **Pred_Sources:** Predicates are essentially filters, similar to SQL Trace filters.
- **Targets:** The target object defines the destination for the event data and the synchronous or asynchronous nature of the target.

XE Sessions

The Extended Events equivalent of starting a SQL Trace is a session. Sessions can be launched, queried, and stopped using T-SQL code.

The following example launches a simple event that tracks when SQL Server performs checkpoints. Using the `ring_buffer` as the target captures the data in memory:

```
CREATE EVENT SESSION [CheckPoint]
  ON SERVER
  ADD EVENT sqlserver.checkpoint_end
  ADD TARGET package0.ring_buffer;
```

The session is now created, but it's not running until an ALTER command actually starts the session:

```
ALTER EVENT SESSION [CheckPoint]
  ON SERVER
  State = START;
```

The session can now be seen in the session DMV:

```
SELECT address, name
  FROM sys.dm_xe_sessions
```

Result:

```
address            name
------------------ ---------------------------
0x0000000080576081 system_health
0x0000000080360D61 CheckPoint
```

Sure enough, there's the CheckPoint session. SQL Server automatically started a default system_health session as well, which is worth exploring.

Joining the session DMV with sys.dm_xe_session_targets will retrieve the event data from the ring_buffer target and expose the data for every captured event within a single XML value:

```
SELECT CONVERT(XML, st.target_data) AS ring_buffer
          FROM sys.dm_xe_sessions s
            JOIN sys.dm_xe_session_targets st
              ON  s.address = st.event_session_address
          WHERE NAME = 'CheckPoint'
```

Result (abbreviated and opened in the browser window):

```
<RingBufferTarget eventsPerSec="0" processingTime="0"
      totalEventsProcessed="13"
  eventCount="13" droppedCount="0" memoryUsed="546">
  <event name="checkpoint_end" package="sqlserver" id="86" version="1"
      timestamp="2009-05-11T07:12:00.220Z">
    <data name="database_id">
      <type name="uint16" package="package0" />
      <value>3</value>
      <text />
    </data>
  </event>
  <event name="checkpoint_end" package="sqlserver" id="86" version="1"
      timestamp="2009-05-11T07:12:00.719Z">
    <data name="database_id">
      <type name="uint16" package="package0" />
      <value>12</value>
      <text />
```

```
      </data>
    </event>
  ...
```

Other types of events and actions will return other elements within the XML data. You can find additional examples on the chapter's downloadable SQL script.

Extracting the data from the XML into relational data requires a little XPath:

```
SELECT
    node.event_data.value('(data/value)[1]', 'BIGINT') AS
      source_database_id,
    node.event_data.value('(timestamp)[1]', 'Datetime') AS test
  FROM (SELECT CONVERT(XML, st.target_data) AS ring_buffer
          FROM sys.dm_xe_sessions s
            JOIN sys.dm_xe_session_targets st
              ON  s.address = st.event_session_address
          WHERE NAME = 'CheckPoint' ) AS sq
    CROSS APPLY sq.ring_buffer.nodes('//RingBufferTarget/event') node
         (event_data)
```

Result:

```
source_database_id   test
-------------------- -----------------------
3                    2009-05-11T07:12:00.220Z
12                   2009-05-11T07:12:00.719Z
```

To stop the session, use another ALTER command. Removing the session configuration requires a DROP command:

```
ALTER EVENT SESSION [CheckPoint]
  ON SERVER
  State = STOP;

DROP EVENT SESSION [CheckPoint]
  ON SERVER
```

Summary

Extended Events may seem cryptic at first, but with a few attempts, I think you'll find they're not that complicated. They offer better performance and granularity than SQL Trace, but at the cost of raw T-SQL and XPath.

The key to working with Extended Events is exploring the objects so you know which events and actions to monitor.

The next chapter also deals with a new monitoring technology in SQL Server 2008, Change Tracking.

Chapter 59

Change Tracking

Change Tracking is one of the best-named software features I've come across. All Change Tracking does is track changes; it says to the world: "This row was changed, here's the PK." Clean and simple, no fuss, no muss. It's a piece of cake to configure and easy to query.

IN THIS CHAPTER

Lightweight synchronization for data warehouse ETL and mobile applications

Net changes

Auto cleanup

While Change Data Capture (another of the new auditing technologies in SQL Server 2008, covered in the next chapter) is limited to only the Enterprise Edition, Change Tracking is available in all the SQL Server editions, even SQL Server Express.

Change Tracking occurs synchronously within the transaction. It simply records in an internal table the primary key values of the rows that are modified. Although there's a cost to recording the changes within the transaction, it means that SQL Agent is not required.

Optionally, Change Tracking can store which columns were changed, using a bit-mapped method similar to how triggers know which column was included in the DML code.

The real purpose of Change Tracking is to support synchronization. By easily and reliably recording the primary keys of which rows were inserted, updated, or deleted since the last synchronization, it becomes much simpler to perform the synchronization.

Change Tracking returns the net changes. If a row is inserted and updated since the last synchronization, then Change Tracking will list it as an insert. If the row is inserted and deleted, then it won't even show in the Change Tracking results — which is perfect for applications that need synchronization.

Several applications can benefit from using Change Tracking:

- The Microsoft Synch Framework
- ETL processes that keep a data warehouse in synch with the OLTP database
- Caching data in middle tiers for performance
- Synchronizing occasionally connected mobile applications

There is a performance hit for using Change Tracking, but it's a lightweight feature with about the same performance hit as adding an index. The performance cost depends on the size of the primary key and the number of rows affected by the transaction. A single column integer primary will have less performance cost than a wide composite primary key. Adding column tracking also adds to the performance overhead.

As cool as Change Tracking is for applications that need synchronization, it isn't adequate for OLTP auditing (who changed what rows to what new values when and from where?) for two reasons. First, Change Tracking does have a context option, but it's not very pretty. Second, Change Tracking returns the net changes, so intermediate changes wouldn't be audited.

Configuring Change Tracking

Compared to other optional SQL Server technologies, Change Tracking is relatively easy to turn on and configure. It's simply turned on for the database, and then for each table.

Enabling the database

Change Tracking may be enabled for the database in Object Explorer's Database Properties dialog, available from each database's context menu (as shown in Figure 59-1). Changing the values in the drop-down boxes immediately changes the database settings when you close the properties dialog.

Change Tracking may also be configured with T-SQL. I like that it uses normal SQL `ALTER SET` commands and not system stored procedures:

```
ALTER DATABASE  AdventureWorks2008
SET Change_tracking = on
(change_retention = 24 hours,
auto_cleanup = on);
```

The current Change Tracking database configuration can be viewed in the Object Explorer Database Properties dialog, or by querying the `sys.change_tracking_databases` DMV:

```
SELECT d.name, ct.is_auto_cleanup_on, ct.retention_period,
   ct.retention_period_units, ct.retention_period_units_desc
  FROM sys.change_tracking_databases ct
    JOIN sys.databases d
      ON ct.database_id = d.database_id;
```

The database must be in 9.0 compatibility mode, and at least db_owner role permission is required, to enable the database for Change Tracking.

FIGURE 59-1

The Database Properties' Change Tracking page displays the current settings and may be used to enable or disable Change Tracking.

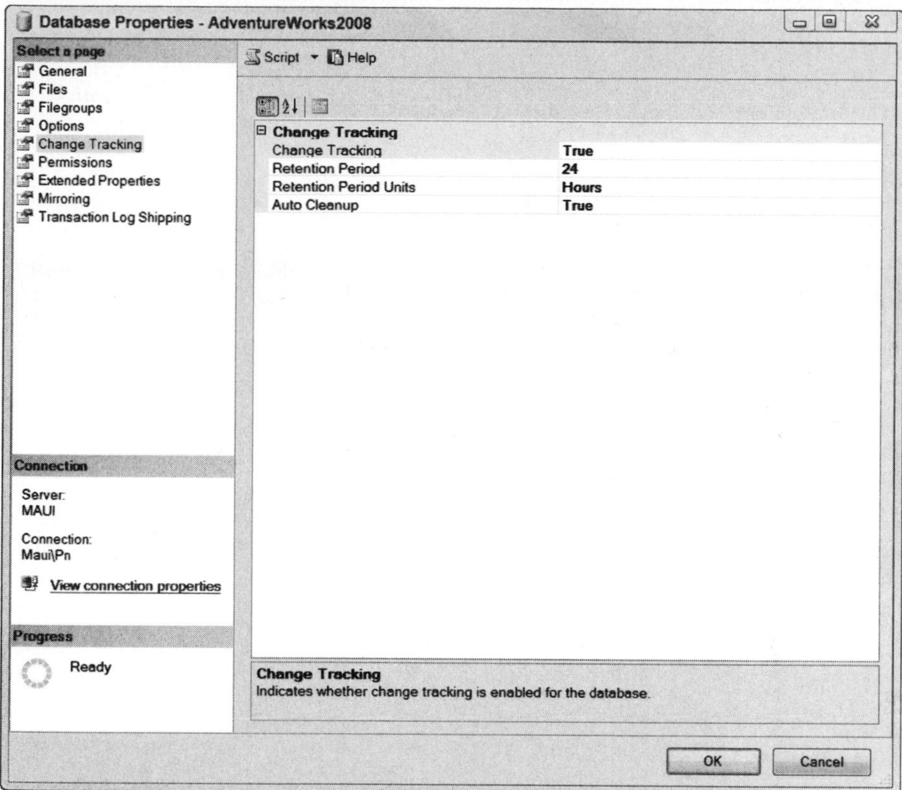

Auto cleanup

Change Tracking can create a lengthy audit trail, but it can also optionally automatically clean up old Change Tracking data. The retention period can be set to any number of `Days`, `Hours`, or `Minutes`. The default is to retain the data for two days (which is probably too short for most applications).

`Auto_cleanup` and the retention period can be set when Change Tracking is initially enabled, or it can be modified later by reissuing the set `Change_Tracking` option with the new retention settings. In this situation, because Change Tracking is already enabled, re-enabling Change Tracking would generate an error. It's only necessary to change the option setting:

```
ALTER DATABASE [AdventureWorks2008]
SET change_tracking (change_retention = 7 days)
```

Be careful with the auto cleanup retention period. Change Tracking doesn't know when synchronizations occur. If the synchronization application doesn't run before the retention period expires, then the changes will not be seen by the synchronization.

If there's a problem and the synchronization won't occur, then use the ALTER DATABASE command to toggle auto cleanup:

```
ALTER DATABASE [AdventureWorks2008]
  SET change_tracking (auto_cleanup = off)
```

Best Practice

Estimate the longest possible period between synchronizations and then triple that time. Other than the disk space usage, there's no risk in a longer retention period, but there's considerable risk in a retention period that's too short.

Enabling tables

The ease of configuring Change Tracking continues with enabling Change Tracking of each table. Using Management Studio, table Change Tracking is viewed or enabled/disabled in the Table Properties dialog, on the Change Tracking page, as shown in Figure 59-2.

Like the database, Change Tracking is enabled using T-SQL for tables with an ALTER command:

```
ALTER TABLE HumanResources.Department
  Enable Change_tracking
  With (track_columns_updated = on);
```

The only option is to enable or disable whether Change Tracking tracks which columns were changed. By default, column tracking is disabled. There's a section later in this chapter that explains how to use column tracking.

The ALTER TABLE permission is required to enable the table for Change Tracking.

Enabling Change Tracking for a table can affect other tasks:

- The primary key constraint/index cannot be dropped while Change Tracking is enabled.
- If the table is dropped, then Change Tracking is first removed from the table.
- The table can't use a partitioned table's ALTER TABLE...SWITCH PARTITION command.
- Change Tracking does not track changes made by the TRUNCATE TABLE command. In this case, the synch target table should also be truncated.

FIGURE 59-2

The Table Properties dialog may be used to view the table's Change Tracking settings.

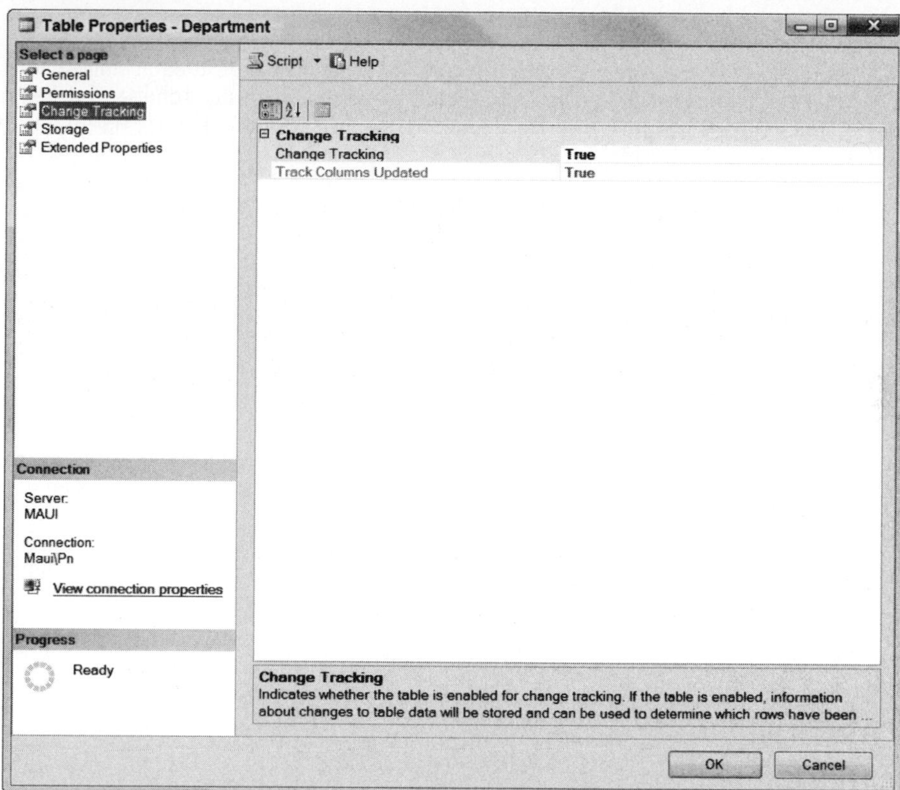

To view the current tables with Change Tracking enabled, query the sys.change_tracking_tables DMV:

```
SELECT s.name + '.' + t.name as [table],
    ct.is_track_columns_updated_on,ct.min_valid_version,
    ct.begin_version, ct.cleanup_version
  FROM sys.change_tracking_tables ct
    JOIN sys.tables t
      ON ct.object_id = t.object_id
    JOIN sys.schemas s
      ON t.schema_id = s.schema_id
  ORDER BY [table];
```

Enabling all tables

Enabling every table in a large database for Change Tracking can be cumbersome — scripting the ALTER command for every table. Fortunately, sp_MSforeachtable, an undocumented Microsoft stored procedure, is the salve that binds the wound.

sp_MSforeachtable executes like a cursor, executing a command, enclosed in single quotes, for every table in the current database. The ? placeholder is replaced with the schema.tablename for every table. If an error occurs, then it's reported in the message pane, but sp_MSforeachtable trudges along with the next table.

This script enables Change Tracking for every table in the current database:

```
EXEC sp_MSforeachtable
  'ALTER TABLE ?
    Enable Change_tracking
    With (track_columns_updated = on);';
```

Internal tables

Change Tracking stores its data in internal tables. There's no reason to directly query these tables to use Change Tracking. However, it is useful to look at the space used by these tables when considering the cost of using Change Tracking and to estimate disk usage.

Query sys.internal_tables to find the internal tables. Of course, your Change Tracking table(s) will have a different name:

```
SELECT s.name + '.' + o.name as [table],
    i.name as [ChangeTracking],
    ct.is_track_columns_updated_on,
    ct.min_valid_version,
    ct.begin_version, ct.cleanup_version
  FROM sys.internal_tables i
    JOIN sys.objects o
      ON i.parent_id = o.object_id
    JOIN sys.schemas s
      ON o.schema_id = s.schema_id
    JOIN sys.change_tracking_tables ct
      ON o.object_id = ct.object_id
  WHERE i.name LIKE 'change_tracking%'
  ORDER BY [table]
```

Result (abbreviated):

```
table                           ChangeTracking
------------------------------- ---------------------------------
HumanResources.Department       sys.change_tracking_757577737
```

Armed with the name, it's easy to find the disk space used. Because Change Tracking was just enabled in this database, the internal table is still empty:

```
EXEC sp_spaceused 'sys.change_tracking_757577737'
```

Result:

```
name                          rows reserved data index_size unused
----------------------------- ---- -------- ---- ---------- -------
change_tracking_757577737     0    0 KB     0 KB 0 KB       0 KB
```

This query combines the Change Tracking configuration with the internal name:

```
SELECT s.name + '.' + o.name as [table],
    i.name as [ChangeTracking],
    ct.is_track_columns_updated_on,
    ct.min_valid_version,
    ct.begin_version, ct.cleanup_version
  FROM sys.internal_tables i
    JOIN sys.objects o
      ON i.parent_id = o.object_id
    JOIN sys.schemas s
      ON o.schema_id = s.schema_id
    JOIN sys.change_tracking_tables ct
      ON o.object_id = ct.object_id
  WHERE i.name LIKE 'change_tracking%'
  ORDER BY [table]
```

Querying Change Tracking

Once Change Tracking is enabled for a table, SQL Server begins to store information about which rows have changed. This data may be queried to select only the changed data from the source table — perfect for synchronization.

Version numbers

Key to understanding Change Tracking is that Change Tracking numbers every transaction with a database-wide version number, which becomes important when working with the changed data. This version number may be viewed using a function:

```
SELECT Change_tracking_current_version();
```

Result:

```
0
```

The current version number is the number of the latest Change Tracking version stored by Change Tracking, so if the current version is 5, then there is a version 5 in the database, and the next transaction will be version 6.

The following code makes inserts and updates to the HumanResources.Department table while watching the Change Tracking version number:

```
INSERT HumanResources.Department (Name, GroupName)
  VALUES ('CT New Row', 'SQL Rocks'),
         ('Test Two'  , 'SQL Rocks');

SELECT Change_tracking_current_version();
```

Result:

```
1
```

The inserts added two new rows, with primary key values of DepartmentID 17 and 18.

And now an update:

```
UPDATE HumanResources.Department
  SET Name = 'Changed Name'
  WHERE Name = 'CT New Row';
```

The update affected row DepartmentID = 17.

Testing the Change Tracking version shows that it has been incremented to 2:

```
SELECT Change_tracking_current_version();
```

Result:

```
2
```

The version number is critical to querying ChangeTable (explained in the next section), and it must be within the range of the oldest possible version number for a given table and the current database version number. The old data is probably being cleaned up automatically, so the oldest possible version number will likely vary for each table.

The following query can report the valid version number range for any table. In this case, it returns the current valid queryable range for HumanResources.Department:

```
SELECT
  Change_tracking_min_valid_version
    (Object_id(N'HumanResources.Department')) as 'oldest',
  Change_tracking_current_version() as 'current';
```

Result:

```
oldest               current
-------------------- --------------------
0                    2
```

Changes by the row

Here's where Change Tracking shows results. The primary keys of the rows that have been modified since (or after) a given version number can be found by querying the `ChangeTable` table-valued function, passing to it the Change Tracking table and a beginning version number. For example, passing table `XYZ` and version number `10` to `ChangeTable` will return the changes for version 11 and following that were made to table `XYZ`. Think of the version number as the number of the last synchronization, so this synchronization needs all the changes after the last synchronization.

In this case, the Change Tracking table is `HumanResources.Department` and the beginning version is `0`:

```
SELECT *
  FROM ChangeTable
    (Changes HumanResources.Department, 0) as CT;
```

Result:

```
           SYS
SYS        CHANGE     SYS         SYS       SYS
CHANGE     CREATION   CHANGE      CHANGE    CHANGE
VERSION    VERSION    OPERATION   COLUMNS   CONTEXT  DepartmentID
--------   ---------  ----------  --------  -------- --------------
2          1          I           NULL      NULL     17
1          1          I           NULL      NULL     18
```

Since version number 0, two rows have been inserted. The update to row 17 is still reported as an insert because, for the purposes of synchronization, row 17 must be inserted.

If version number 1 is passed to `ChangeTable`, then the result should show only change version 2:

```
SELECT *
  FROM ChangeTable
    (Changes HumanResources.Department, 1) as CT;
```

Result (formatted to include the `syschangecolumns` data):

```
           SYS
SYS        CHANGE     SYS         SYS       SYS
CHANGE     CREATION   CHANGE      CHANGE    CHANGE
VERSION    VERSION    OPERATION   COLUMNS   CONTEXT     DepartmentID
--------   ---------  ----------  --------  ----------  --------------
2          1          U           0x0000000002000000    17
                                             NULL
```

This time row 17 shows up as an update, because when version 2 occurred, row 17 already existed, and version 2 updated the row. A synchronization based on changes made since version 1 would need to update row 17.

Note that as a table-valued function, `ChangeTable` must have an alias.

Synchronizing requires joining with the source table. The following query reports the changed rows from HumanResources.Department since version 1. The left outer join is necessary to pick up any deleted rows which, by definition, no longer exist in the source table and would therefore be missed by an inner join:

```
SELECT CT.SYS_CHANGE_VERSION as Version,
    CT.DepartmentID, CT.SYS_CHANGE_OPERATION as Op,
    d.Name, d.GroupName
  FROM ChangeTable (Changes HumanResources.Department, 1) as CT
    LEFT OUTER JOIN HumanResources.Department d
      ON d.DepartmentID = CT.DepartmentID
  ORDER BY CT.SYS_CHANGE_VERSION;
```

Result:

```
Version  DepartmentID Op  Name           GroupName
-------- ------------ --- -------------  -------------
2        17           U   Changed Name    SQL Rocks
```

As expected, the result shows row 17 being updated, so there's no data other than the primary key returned by the ChangeTable data source. The join pulls in the data from HumanResources .Department.

Coding a synchronization

Knowing which rows have been changed means that it should be easy to merge those changes into a synchronization table. The trick is synchronizing a set of data while changes are still being made at the source, without locking the source.

Assuming the previous synchronization was at version 20, and the current version is 60, then 20 is passed to ChangeTable. But what becomes the new current version? The current version just before the ChangeTable is queried and the data is merged? What if more changes occur during the synchronization?

The new SQL Server 2008 MERGE command would seem to be the perfect solution. It does support the output clause. If the version is stored in the synchronization target table, then the output clause's inserted table can return the insert and update operation new versions, and the max() versions can be determined. But deletion operations return only the deleted virtual table, which would return the version number of the last change made to the deleted row, and not the version number of the deletion event.

The solution is to capture all the ChangeTable data to a temp table, determine the max version number for that synchronization set, store that version number, and then perform the synchronization merge. As much as I hate temp tables, it's the only clean solution.

The following script sets up a synchronization from HumanResources.Department to HRDeptSynch. Synchronization typically occurs from one device to another, or one database to another. Here, AdventureWorks2008 is the source database, and tempdb will serve as the target database. Assume the tempdb.dbo.HRDeptSynch table was last synchronized before any changes were made to AdventureWorks2008.HumanResources.Department in this chapter. By including the database name in the code, there's no need to issue a USE DATABASE command:

```
-- create synch master version table
CREATE TABLE Tempdb.dbo.SynchMaster (
    TableName SYSNAME,
    LastSynchVersion INT,
    SynchDateTime DATETIME
    )

-- initialize for HRDeptSynch
INSERT Tempdb.dbo.SynchMaster (TableName, LastSynchVersion)
  VALUES ('HRDeptSynch', 0)

-- create target table
CREATE TABLE Tempdb.dbo.HRDeptSynch (
    DepartmentID SmallINT,
    Name NVARCHAR(50),
    GroupName NVARCHAR(50),
    Version INT
    )

-- Populate Synch table with baseline original data
INSERT Tempdb.dbo.HRDeptSynch (DepartmentID, Name, GroupName)
  SELECT DepartmentID, Name, GroupName FROM HumanResources.Department;
```

Another good idea in this process is to check

```
Check Change_tracking_min_valid_version
    (Object_id(N'HumanResources.Department')) as 'oldest'
```

to verify that the synchronization won't miss cleaned-up data.

The following stored procedure uses Change Tracking, a synch master table, a temp table, and the new SQL Server `MERGE` command to synchronize any changes in the source table (`HumanResources.Department`) into the target table (`Tempdb.dbo.HRDeptSynch`):

```
USE AdventureWorks2008;

CREATE PROC pHRDeptSynch
AS
SET NoCount ON;

  DECLARE
    @LastSynchMaster INT,
    @ThisSynchMaster INT;

  CREATE TABLE #HRDeptSynch (
    Version INT,
    Op CHAR(1),
    DepartmentID SmallINT,
    Name NVARCHAR(50),
```

```
    GroupName NVARCHAR(50)
    );

  SELECT @LastSynchMaster = LastSynchVersion
    FROM Tempdb.dbo.SynchMaster
    WHERE TableName = 'HRDeptSynch';

  INSERT #HRDeptSynch
      (Version, Op, DepartmentID, Name, GroupName)
    SELECT CT.SYS_CHANGE_VERSION as Version,
        CT.SYS_CHANGE_OPERATION as Op,
        CT.DepartmentID, d.Name, d.GroupName
      FROM ChangeTable
         (Changes HumanResources.Department, @LastSynchMaster)
         as CT
        LEFT OUTER JOIN HumanResources.Department d
          ON d.DepartmentID = CT.DepartmentID
      ORDER BY CT.SYS_CHANGE_OPERATION;

  MERGE INTO Tempdb.dbo.HRDeptSynch as Target
    USING
      (SELECT
        Version, Op, DepartmentID, Name, GroupName
        FROM #HRDeptSynch)
          AS Source (Version, Op, DepartmentID, Name, GroupName)
    ON Target.DepartmentID = Source.DepartmentID
    WHEN NOT MATCHED AND Source.Op = 'I'
      THEN INSERT (DepartmentID, Name, GroupName) VALUES (DepartmentID,
        Name, GroupName)
    WHEN MATCHED AND Source.Op = 'U'
      THEN UPDATE
             SET Name = Source.Name,
                 GroupName = Source.GroupName
    WHEN MATCHED AND Source.Op = 'D'
      THEN DELETE;

  UPDATE Tempdb.dbo.SynchMaster
    SET LastSynchVersion = (SELECT Max(Version) FROM #HRDeptSynch),
        SynchDateTime = GETDATE()
    WHERE TableName = 'HRDeptSynch';
Go --
```

To put the stored procedure through its paces, the following script makes several modifications to the source table and calls pHRDeptSynch:

```
INSERT HumanResources.Department (Name, GroupName)
  VALUES ('Row Three', 'Data Rocks!'),
         ('Row Four'  , 'SQL Rocks!');
```

```
UPDATE HumanResources.Department
  SET GroupName = 'SQL Server 2008 Bible'
  WHERE Name = 'Test Two';

EXEC pHRDeptSynch;

DELETE FROM HumanResources.Department
  WHERE Name = 'Row Four';

EXEC pHRDeptSynch;

EXEC pHRDeptSynch;

DELETE FROM HumanResources.Department
  WHERE Name = 'Test Two';

EXEC pHRDeptSynch;
```

To test the results, the next two queries search for out of synch conditions. The first query uses a set-difference query with a FULL OUTER JOIN and two IS NULLs to find any mismatched rows on either side of the join:

```
-- check for out-of-synch rows:
SELECT *
  FROM HumanResources.Department Source
    FULL OUTER JOIN tempdb.dbo.HRDeptSynch Target
      ON Source.DepartmentID = Target.DepartmentID
  WHERE Source.DepartmentID IS NULL
    OR Target.DepartmentID IS NULL
```

There is no result set.

The second verification query simply joins the tables and compares the data columns in the WHERE clause to return any rows with mismatched data:

```
-- Check for out-of-synch data
SELECT *
  FROM HumanResources.Department Source
    LEFT OUTER JOIN tempdb.dbo.HRDeptSynch Target
      ON Source.DepartmentID = Target.DepartmentID
  WHERE Source.Name != Target.Name
    OR Source.GroupName != Target.GroupName
```

There is no result set.

Good. The Change Tracking and the synchronization stored procedure worked — and the stored version number is absolutely the correct version number for the next synchronization.

To check the versions, the next two queries look at Change Tracking's current version and the version stored in SynchMaster:

```
SELECT Change_tracking_current_version();
```

Result:

```
6

SELECT * FROM tempdb.dbo.SynchMaster;
```

Result:

```
TableName    LastSynchMaster SynchDateTime
------------ --------------- ---------------------------
HRDeptSynch  6               2009-01-16 18:00:42.643
```

Although lengthy, this exercise showed how to leverage Change Tracking and the new MERGE command to build a complete synchronization system.

Change Tracking Options

It's completely reasonable to use only the ChangeTable function to design a Change Tracking system, but three advanced options are worth exploring.

Column tracking

If Change Tracking was enabled for the table with the track_columns_updated option on (it's off by default), then SQL Server stores which columns are updated in a bitmap that costs four bytes per changed column (to store the column's column_id). The CHANGE_TRACKING_IS_COLUMN_IN_MASK function returns a Boolean true if the column was updated. It requires two parameters: the column's column_id and the bit-mapped column. The bit-mapped column that actually stored the data is the SYS_CHANGED_COLUMNS column in the ChangeTable row. The following query demonstrates the function, and the easiest way to pass in the column_id:

```
SELECT CT.SYS_CHANGE_VERSION, CT.DepartmentID, CT.SYS_CHANGE_OPERATION,
    d.Name, d.GroupName, d.ModifiedDate,
    CHANGE_TRACKING_IS_COLUMN_IN_MASK(
        ColumnProperty(
          Object_ID('HumanResources.Department'),
            'Name', 'ColumnID'),
        SYS_CHANGE_COLUMNS) as IsChanged_Name,
    CHANGE_TRACKING_IS_COLUMN_IN_MASK(
            ColumnProperty(
          Object_ID('HumanResources.Department'),
            'GroupName', 'ColumnID'),
      SYS_CHANGE_COLUMNS) as IsChanged_GroupName
  FROM ChangeTable (Changes HumanResources.Department, 1) as CT
    LEFT OUTER JOIN HumanResources.Department d
      ON d.DepartmentID = CT.DepartmentID;
```

Determining latest version per row

The Change Tracking version is a database-wide version number, but it is possible to determine the latest version for every row in a table, regardless of the last synchronization, using the ChangeTable's version option. The CROSS APPLY calls the table-valued function for every row in the outer query:

```
SELECT d.DepartmentID, CT.SYS_CHANGE_VERSION
  FROM HumanResources.Department d
    CROSS APPLY ChangeTable
       (Version HumanResources.Department, (DepartmentID),
         (d.DepartmentID)) as CT
  ORDER BY d.DepartmentID;
```

Result (abbreviated):

```
DepartmentID Sys_Change_Version
------------ ----------------
15           NULL
16           NULL
17           2
19           3
```

To find the last synchronized version per row since a specific version, use ChangeTable with the Changes option. In this example, row 17 was last updated with version 2, so requesting the most recent versions since version 2 returns a NULL for row 17:

```
SELECT d.DepartmentID, CT.SYS_CHANGE_VERSION
  FROM HumanResources.Department d
    LEFT OUTER JOIN
     ChangeTable (Changes HumanResources.Department, 2) as CT
     ON d.DepartmentID = CT.DepartmentID
  ORDER BY d.DepartmentID;
```

Result (abbreviated):

```
DepartmentID Sys_Change_Version
------------ ----------------
15           NULL
16           NULL
17           NULL
19           3
```

Capturing application context

It's possible to pass information about the DML's context to Change Tracking. Typically the context could be the username, application, or workstation name. The context is passed as a varbinary data type. Adding context to Change Tracking opens the door for Change Tracking to be used to gather OLTP audit trail data.

Here's the catch: The context isn't automatic — it must be added to each and every DML command. In addition, it uses a WITH clause, just like a common table expression, so the syntax is confusing. While I'm glad it's possible to capture the context, I'm not a huge fan of the implementation.

The following code creates the varbinary variable and passes it to Change Tracking as part of an UPDATE command.

```
DECLARE @AppContext VARBINARY(128)
  = CAST('Maui/Pn' as VARBINARY(128));

WITH Change_Tracking_Context (@AppContext)
UPDATE HumanResources.Department
  SET GroupName = 'Certified Master w/Context'
  WHERE Name = 'Row Three';
```

When querying ChangeTable, the sys_Change_Context column returns the context data. The CAST() function converts it to readable text:

```
SELECT CT.SYS_CHANGE_VERSION, CT.DepartmentID, CT.SYS_CHANGE_OPERATION,
    d.Name, d.GroupName, D.ModifiedDate,
    CAST(SYS_CHANGE_CONTEXT as VARCHAR) as ApplicationContext
  FROM ChangeTable (Changes HumanResources.Department, 5) as CT
    LEFT OUTER JOIN HumanResources.Department d
      ON d.DepartmentID = CT.DepartmentID
  ORDER BY CT.SYS_CHANGE_VERSION;
```

Removing Change Tracking

It's as easy to remove Change Tracking as it is to enable it: Disable it from every table, and then remove it from the database.

If the goal is to reduce Change Tracking by a single table, then the same ALTER command that enabled Change Tracking can disable it:

```
ALTER TABLE HumanResources.Department
  Disable Change_tracking;
```

When Change Tracking is disabled from a table, all stored ChangeTable data — the PKs and columns updated — are lost.

If the goal is to remove Change Tracking from the database, then Change Tracking must first be removed from every table in the database. One way to accomplish this is to leverage the sp_MSforeachtable stored procedure:

```
EXEC sp_MSforeachtable
  'ALTER TABLE ?
    Disable Change_tracking;';
```

However, after much testing, I can only warn that in many cases sp_msforeachtable often fails to remove Change Tracking from every table.

A less elegant, but more reliable, method of ensuring that Change Tracking is completely removed from every table in the database is to actually cursor through the sys.change_tracking_tables table:

```
DECLARE @SQL NVARCHAR(MAX)='';
SELECT @SQL = @SQL + 'ALTER TABLE ' + s.name + '.' + t.name +
  ' Disable Change_tracking;'
FROM sys.change_tracking_tables ct
JOIN sys.tables t
  ON ct.object_id = t.object_id
JOIN sys.schemas s
  ON t.schema_id = s.schema_id;
PRINT @SQL;
EXEC sp_executesql @SQL;
```

Only after Change Tracking is disabled from every table can Change Tracking be removed from the database:

```
ALTER DATABASE AdventureWorks2008
  SET Change_tracking = off;
```

Even though Change Tracking is removed from the database, it doesn't reset the Change Tracking version number, so if Change Tracking is restarted it won't cause a synchronization nightmare.

Summary

Designing a DIY synchronization system involves triggers that either update row timestamps or write keys to a table. Change Tracking does all the hard work, adds auto cleanup, is relatively easy to set up and use, and reliably returns the net changes. Without question, using Change Tracking sets you up for success with ETL processes and mobile device synchronization.

Microsoft introduces several new auditing and monitoring technologies with SQL Server 2008. The next chapter continues exploring these new technologies with Change Tracking's big brother, Change Data Capture.

Chapter 60

Change Data Capture

IN THIS CHAPTER

High-end BI ETL

Leveraging the T-Log

I know almost nothing about the CDC in Atlanta. The little I do know about the Centers for Disease Control comes from watching Dustin Hoffman in the movie *Outbreak*. Fortunately for me and you, this chapter is about the other CDC — Change Data Capture.

There's power hidden in the transaction log (T-Log), and Change Data Capture (CDC) harnesses the transaction log to capture data changes with the least possible impact on performance.

Any data written to the transaction log can be asynchronously captured using CDC from the transaction log after the transaction is complete, so it doesn't affect the original transaction's performance. CDC can track any data from the T-Log, including any DML `INSERT`, `UPDATE`, `DELETE`, and `MERGE` command, and DDL `CREATE`, `ALTER`, and `DROP`.

Changes are stored in change tables — tables created by CDC with the same columns as the tracked tables plus a few extra CDC-specific columns. All the changes are captured, so CDC can return all the intermediate values or just the net changes.

Because CDC gathers its data by reading the log, the data in the change tables is organized the same way the transaction log is organized — by T-log log sequence numbers, known as LSNs. (Kalen Delaney told a joke about Oracle's founder Larry Ellison being inside SQL Server — just look at the transaction log and there's LSN! Ha!)

There are only a few drawbacks to CDC:

- **Cost:** It requires Enterprise Edition.
- **Code:** Personally, this really irks me. CDC uses system stored procedures instead of standardized `ALTER` statements.

- **Code:** There's no UI for configuring change data capture in Management Studio.
- **T-Log I/O:** The transaction log will experience about twice as much I/O because CDC reads from the log.
- **Performance hit:** Although it can vary greatly, expect an approximate 10% performance hit on the OLTP server running CDC.
- **Disk space:** Because CDC essentially stores copies of every transaction data, there's the potential that it can grow like a transaction log gone wild.

Where change data capture shines is in gathering data for ETL from a high-traffic OLTP database to a data warehouse. Of the possible options, change data capture has the least performance hit, and it does a great job of providing the right set of data for the Business Intelligence ETL (extract-transform-load). When you think big-dollar BI, think change data capture.

Enabling CDC

Change Data Capture is enabled at the database level first, and then for every table that needs to be tracked. Because change data capture reads from the transaction log, one might think that CDC requires the database to be set to full recovery model so that the transaction log is kept. However, SQL Server doesn't flush the log until after the transactions have been read by CDC, so CDC will work with any recovery model, even simple.

Also, and this is very important, change data capture uses SQL Agent jobs to capture and clean up the data, so SQL Agent must be running or data will not be captured.

Enabling the database

To enable the database, execute the `sys.sp_cdc_enable_db` system stored procedure in the current database. It has no parameters:

```
EXEC sys.sp_cdc_enable_db
```

The `is_cdc_enabled` column in `sys.databases` can be used to determine which databases have CDC enabled on them:

```
SELECT *
FROM sys.databases
WHERE is_cdc_enabled = 1
```

This procedure creates six system tables in the current database:

- `cdc.captured_columns`: Stores metadata for tracked table's columns
- `cdc.change_tables`: Stores metadata for tracked tables
- `cdc.ddl_history`: Tracks DDL activity
- `cdc.index_columns`: Tracks table indexes
- `cdc.lsn_time_mapping`: Used for calculating clean-up time

- dbo.systranschemas: Tracks schema changes

These are listed in Object Explorer under the Database ➪ Tables ➪ System tables node.

Enabling tables

Once the database has been prepared for CDC, tables may be set up for CDC using the sys.sp_cdc_enable_table stored procedure, which has several options:

- @source_schema: The name of the table to be tracked
- @source_name: The tracked table's schema
- @role_name: The role with permission to view CDC data

The last six parameters are optional:

- @capture_instance: May be used to create multiple capture instances for the table. This is useful if the schema is changed.
- @supports_net_changes: Allows seeing just the net changes, and requires the primary key. The default is true.
- @index_name: The name of the unique index, if there's no primary key for the table (but you'd never do that, right?)
- @captured_column_list: Determines which columns are tracked. The default is to track all columns.
- @filegroup_name: The filegroup the CDC will be stored on. If not specified, then the change table is created on the default filegroup.
- @allow_partition_switch: Allows ALTER TABLE... SWITCH PARTITION on CDC table

Note that the last parameter, @allow_partition_switch, was changed late in development of SQL Server 2008, and some sources incorrectly list it as @partition_switch.

The following batch configures CDC to track changes made to the HumanResources.Department table:

```
EXEC sys.sp_cdc_enable_table
  @source_schema = 'HumanResources',
  @source_name = 'Department',
  @role_name = null;
```

With the first table that's enabled, SQL Server generates two SQL Agent jobs:

- cdc.dbname_capture
- cdc.dbname_cleanup

With every table that's enabled for CDC, SQL Server creates a change table:

- cdc.change_tables

- cdc.index_columns
- cdc.captured_columns

NOTE For an excellent article on tuning the performance of change data capture under various loads, see http://msdn.microsoft.com/en-us/library/dd266396.aspx.

Working with Change Data Capture

It isn't difficult to work with change data capture. The trick is to understand the transaction log's log sequence numbers.

Assuming AdventureWorks2008 has been freshly installed, the following scripts make some data changes so there will be some activity in the log for change data capture to gather:

```
INSERT HumanResources.Department (Name, GroupName)
  VALUES ('CDC New Row', 'SQL Rocks'),
         ('Test Two'   , 'CDC Rocks ');

UPDATE HumanResources.Department
  SET Name = 'Changed Name'
  WHERE Name = 'CDC New Row';


INSERT HumanResources.Department (Name, GroupName)
  VALUES ('Row Three', 'PBM Rocks'),
         ('Row Four'   , 'TVP Rocks');

UPDATE HumanResources.Department
  SET GroupName = 'T-SQL Rocks'
  WHERE Name = 'Test Two';

DELETE FROM HumanResources.Department
  WHERE Name = 'Row Four';
```

With five transactions complete, there should be some activity in the log. The following DMVs can reveal information about the log:

```
SELECT *
  FROM sys.dm_cdc_log_scan_sessions

SELECT *
  FROM sys.dm_repl_traninfo

SELECT *
  FROM sys.dm_cdc_errors
```

Examining the log sequence numbers

The data changes are organized in the change tables by log sequence number (LSN). Converting a given date time to LSN is essential to working with change data capture. The `sys.fn_cdc_map_time_to_lsn` function is designed to do just that. The first parameter defines the LSN search (called *LSN boundary options*), and the second parameter is the point in time. Possible searches are as follows:

- smallest greater than
- smallest greater than or equal
- largest less than
- largest less than or equal

Each of the search options defines how the function will locate the nearest LSN in the change tables.

The following sample query defines a range beginning with Jan 20 and ending with Jan 24, and returns the LSNs that bound that range:

```
select
  sys.fn_cdc_map_time_to_lsn
    ('smallest greater than or equal', '20090101')
    as BeginLSN,
  sys.fn_cdc_map_time_to_lsn
    ('largest less than or equal', '20091231')
    as EndLSN;
```

Result:

```
BeginLSN               EndLSN
---------------------- ----------------------
0x0000002F000001330040 0x0000003B000002290001
```

The `sys.fn_cdc_get_min_lsn()` and `sys.fn_cdc_get_max_lsn()` functions serve as anchor points to begin the walk through the log. The `min` function requires a table and returns the oldest log entry. The `max` function has no parameters and returns the most recent LSN in the change tables:

```
DECLARE
  @BeginLSN VARBINARY(10) =
    sys.fn_cdc_get_min_lsn('HumanResources_Department');
SELECT @BeginLSN;

DECLARE
  @EndLSN VARBINARY(10) =
    sys.fn_cdc_get_max_lsn();
SELECT @EndLSN;
```

There's not much benefit to knowing the hexadecimal LSN values by themselves, but the LSNs can be passed to other functions to select data from the change tables.

Querying the change tables

Change tracking creates a function for each table being tracked using the name cdc.fn_cdc_get_all_changes concatenated with the schema and name of the table. The following script uses the sys.fn_cdc_map_time_to_lsn function to determine the LSN range values, store them in variables, and then pass the variables to the department tables' custom change data capture function:

```
-- with variables
DECLARE
  @BeginLSN VARBINARY(10) =
    sys.fn_cdc_map_time_to_lsn
      ('smallest greater than or equal', '20090101'),
  @EndLSN VARBINARY(10) =
    sys.fn_cdc_map_time_to_lsn
      ('largest less than or equal', '20091231');
SELECT __$start_lsn, __$seqval, __$operation,
    __$update_mask, DepartmentID Name, GroupName, ModifiedDate
  FROM cdc.fn_cdc_get_all_changes_HumanResources_Department
    (@BeginLSN, @EndLSN, 'all')
  ORDER BY __$start_lsn
```

Result:

```
__$start_lsn           __$seqval              __$operation
---------------------- ---------------------- ------------
0x0000005400001D6E0008 0x0000005400001D6E0003 2
0x0000005400001D6E0008 0x0000005400001D6E0006 2
0x0000005400001D700007 0x0000005400001D700002 4
0x0000005400001D7D0008 0x0000005400001D7D0003 2
0x0000005400001D7D0008 0x0000005400001D7D0006 2
0x0000005400001D7F0004 0x0000005400001D7F0002 4
0x0000005400001D810005 0x0000005400001D810003 1

__$update_mask Name    GroupName     ModifiedDate
-------------- ------------------- -----------------------
0x0F           17      SQL Rocks     2009-03-07 11:21:48.720
0x0F           18      CDC Rocks     2009-03-07 11:21:48.720
0x02           17      SQL Rocks     2009-03-07 11:21:48.720
0x0F           19      PBM Rocks     2009-03-07 11:21:55.387
0x0F           20      TVP Rocks     2009-03-07 11:21:55.387
0x04           18      T-SQL Rocks   2009-03-07 11:21:48.720
0x0F           20      TVP Rocks     2009-03-07 11:21:55.387
```

It's also possible to pass the functions directly to the table's change data capture function. This is essentially the same code as the previous query, but slightly simpler, which is usually a good thing:

```
SELECT *
  FROM cdc.fn_cdc_get_all_changes_HumanResources_Department
    (sys.fn_cdc_map_time_to_lsn
```

```
            ('smallest greater than or equal', '20090101'),
        sys.fn_cdc_map_time_to_lsn
            ('largest less than or equal', '20091231'),
        'all') as CDC
    ORDER BY __$start_lsn
```

You can also convert an LSN directly to a time using the `fn_cdc_map_lsn_to_time()` function. The next query extends the previous query by returning the time of the transaction:

```
-- with lsn converted to time
SELECT
  sys.fn_cdc_map_lsn_to_time(__$start_lsn) as StartLSN, *
  FROM cdc.fn_cdc_get_all_changes_HumanResources_Department
    (sys.fn_cdc_map_time_to_lsn
        ('smallest greater than or equal', '20090101'),
     sys.fn_cdc_map_time_to_lsn
        ('largest less than or equal', '20091231'),
     'all') as CDC
  ORDER BY __$start_lsn
```

The `__$Operation` column returned by the change data capture custom table functions identifies the type of DML that caused the data change. Similar to a DML trigger, the data can be the before (deleted table) or after (inserted table) image of an update.

The default `'all'` parameter directs CDC to only return the after, or new, image from an update operation. The `'all update old'` option, shown in the following example, tells CDC to return a row for both the before update image and the after update image.

This query uses a row constructor subquery to spell out the meaning of the operation:

```
SELECT
    sys.fn_cdc_map_lsn_to_time(__$start_lsn) as StartLSN,
    Operation.Description as 'Operation',
    DepartmentID, Name, GroupName
  FROM cdc.fn_cdc_get_all_changes_HumanResources_Department
   (sys.fn_cdc_map_time_to_lsn('smallest greater than or equal',
       '20090101'),
    sys.fn_cdc_map_time_to_lsn('largest less than or equal',
       '20091231'),
    'all update old') as CDC
  JOIN
    (VALUES
      (1, 'delete'),
      (2, 'insert'),
      (3, 'update/deleted'), -- 'all update old' option to view
      (4, 'update/inserted')
    ) as Operation(OperationID, Description)
    ON CDC.__$operation = Operation.OperationID
  ORDER BY __$start_lsn
```

Result:

```
StartLSN                Operation        DepartmentID Name         GroupName
----------------------- ---------------- ------------ ------------ ---------
2009-03-07 19:49:26.383 insert           21           CDC New Row  SQL Rocks
2009-03-07 19:49:26.383 insert           22           Test Two     CDC Rocks
2009-03-07 19:49:26.390 update/deleted   21           CDC New Row  SQL Rocks
2009-03-07 19:49:26.390 update/inserted  21           Changed Name SQL Rocks
2009-03-07 19:49:26.393 insert           23           Row Three    PBM Rocks
2009-03-07 19:49:26.393 insert           24           Row Four     TVP Rock
2009-03-07 19:49:26.400 update/deleted   22           Test Two     CDC Rocks
2009-03-07 19:49:26.400 update/inserted  22           Test Two     T-SQL Rocks
2009-03-07 19:49:26.403 delete           24           Row Four     TVP Rock
```

Querying net changes

All the previous queries returned all the changes within the requested time frame. But for many ETL operations or synchronizations, only the final net values are needed. Change data capture can automatically determine the net, or final, values. Use the `cdc.fn_cdc_get_net_changes_schema_table` function to return the net changes:

```
-- Querying Net Changes - 'all' option
SELECT
    sys.fn_cdc_map_lsn_to_time(__$start_lsn) as StartLSN,
    Operation.Description as 'Operation',
    DepartmentID, Name, GroupName
  FROM cdc.fn_cdc_get_net_changes_HumanResources_Department -- net
    changes
    (sys.fn_cdc_map_time_to_lsn('smallest greater than or equal',
        '20090101'),
     sys.fn_cdc_map_time_to_lsn('largest less than or equal',
        '20091231'),
     'all') as CDC
  JOIN
    (VALUES
      (1, 'delete'),
      (2, 'insert'),
      (3, 'update/deleted'), -- 'all update old' option to view
      (4, 'update/inserted')
    ) as Operation(OperationID, Description)
    ON CDC.__$operation = Operation.OperationID
  ORDER BY __$start_lsn
```

Result:

```
StartLSN                Operation  DepartmentID Name           GroupName
----------------------- ---------- ------------ --------------------------
2009-03-07 19:49:26.390 insert     21           Changed Name   SQL Rocks
2009-03-07 19:49:26.393 insert     23           Row Three      PBM Rocks
2009-03-07 19:49:26.400 insert     22           Test Two       T-SQL Rocks
```

When querying net changes using Change Data Capture, it's also possible to work with a column mask to determine whether a given column has changed. In the following query, the `all with mask` option and `sys.fn_cdc_has_column_changed` function are used together to test for changes in the `GroupName` column:

```
-- update the GroupName column
UPDATE HumanResources.Department
  SET GroupName = 'Updated 2'
  WHERE Name = 'Test Two';

-- Querying Net Changes - 'all with mask' option
SELECT
    Operation.Description as 'Operation',
    DepartmentID AS DeptID, GroupName,
    sys.fn_cdc_is_bit_set
          (sys.fn_cdc_get_column_ordinal
          ('HumanResources_Department',
          'GroupName') ,
          __$update_mask
          )
          as GroupNameUpdated,
     sys.fn_cdc_has_column_changed
          ('HumanResources_Department', -- wrong in BOL
            'GroupName',
          __$update_mask)
          as GroupNameHasChanged
  FROM cdc.fn_cdc_get_net_changes_HumanResources_Department -- net
    changes
    (sys.fn_cdc_map_time_to_lsn('smallest greater than or equal',
      '20090307 8:40pm'), -- change datetime to pick up update as
      net change
     sys.fn_cdc_map_time_to_lsn('largest less than or equal',
      '20091231'),
     'all with mask') as CDC
  JOIN
    (VALUES
      (1, 'delete'),
      (2, 'insert'),
      (3, 'update/deleted'), -- 'all update old' option to view
      (4, 'update/inserted')
    ) as Operation(OperationID, Description)
    ON CDC.__$operation = Operation.OperationID
  ORDER BY __$start_lsn
```

Result:

```
Operation        DeptID  GroupName  GroupNameUpdated  GroupNameHasChanged
---------------- ------- ---------- ----------------- ---------------------
update/inserted  22      Updated 2  1                 1
```

Walking through the change tables

For most ETL and synchronization operations, selecting the data as a set is the best practice, but change data capture also supports walking through the change table data iteratively. Think of these functions as CDC cursors.

The following script uses the `sys.fn_cdc_get_min_lsn()` function to identify a starting point in the change table and then iterates through the entries sequentially using the `sys.fn_cdc_increment_lsn()` function, which finds the next entry following the one passed in as a parameter:

```
DECLARE
 @BeginLSN VARBINARY(10) =
   sys.fn_cdc_get_min_lsn('HumanResources_Department');
SELECT @BeginLSN;

SET @BeginLSN = sys.fn_cdc_increment_lsn(@BeginLSN);
SELECT @BeginLSN;

SET @BeginLSN = sys.fn_cdc_increment_lsn(@BeginLSN);
SELECT @BeginLSN;
```

Result (obviously, your result will be different):

```
----------------------
0x000000420000136A003D
----------------------
0x000000420000136A003E
----------------------
0x000000420000136A003F
```

Likewise, CDC can move backward through the entries:

```
SET @BeginLSN = sys.fn_cdc_decrement_lsn(@BeginLSN);
SELECT @BeginLSN;
```

Result:

```
----------------------
0x000000420000136A003E
```

Removing Change Data Capture

Removing change data capture is a flexible and simple process. CDC can be disabled table by table, or for the whole database. When CDC is disabled for the database, it automatically disables all tables, removing the SQL Agent jobs, and dropping the custom tracked table functions. There's no need to remove CDC from each table individually before disabling CDC from the database:

```
EXEC sys.sp_cdc_disable_db;
```

To remove CDC from a specific table, use the following system stored procedure:

```
EXEC sys.sp_cdc_disable_table
  @source_schema = 'HumanResources',
  @source_name = 'Department',
  @capture_instance = 'all';
```

Summary

Change Data Capture, Change Tracking's big brother, is Microsoft's high-end feature intended for heavy transaction OLTP systems to capture changes for ETL to the data warehouse.

- CDC uses the transaction log asynchronously to reduce the impact on OLTP transactions, but there will be some impact.
- Working with CDC means working with transaction log sequence numbers, or LSNs.
- Using CDC, you can query for all changes or net changes.

The next chapter continues the trend of examining new auditing technologies in SQL Server 2008 with a look at yet another all-new technology: SQL Audit. Based on eExtended Events, SQL Audit can audit any action in SQL Server.

Chapter 61

SQL Audit

IN THIS CHAPTER

Configuring SQL Audit

Tracking server events

At one of the pre-Katmai (the code name for SQL Server 2008 while it was being developed) NDA (non-disclosure agreement — that is, secret) sessions for MVPs, the SQL Server team asked how many of us would like an easy way to audit selects. Nearly every MVP's hand went up. The SQL Server community has wanted a more powerful auditing mechanism for a long time.

SQL Audit is the answer.

Based on the new Extended Events technology, SQL Audit is both lightweight and powerful. While it's possible to "roll your own" auditing solution from Extended Events, SQL Audit is an out-of-the-box solution to leverage Extended Events and collect server and database events. It's blazingly fast, easy to configure, and cool.

While Extended Events is available for all editions of SQL Server, SQL Audit is available only for Enterprise (and Developer) Edition.

SQL Audit Technology Overview

It takes several SQL Audit components working together to create a functioning Audit. A *SQL Server Audit* object is a bucket that collects the audit events defined by a *Server Audit Specification* and the *Database Audit Specification*, and sends the audited events to a target. Here are the facts:

- A SQL Server Audit object can be written to by one Server Audit Specification and one Database Audit Specification per database.
- A SQL Server Audit can belong to only one SQL Server instance, but there may be several SQL Server Audits within an instance.

- A Server Audit Specification defines which server-level events will be captured and passed to the SQL Audit.
- A Database Audit Specification defines which database-level events are captured and passed to the SQL Audit.
- Both Server Audit Specifications and Database Audit Specifications can define sets of events or groups to be captured. Event groups encapsulate a number of related events. Database actions include select, insert, update, and delete, and they capture the user context and the entire DML query.
- The audited data includes user context information.
- The SQL Server Audit sends all the captured events to a single target: a file, the Windows Security event log (not in Windows XP), or the Windows Application event log. The Management Studio SQL Audit UI includes a tool for browsing the audit logs.
- SQL Server Audits, Server Audit Specifications, and Database Audit Specifications can all be created and managed either with Object Explorer or by using T-SQL.
- SQL Server Audits, Server Audit Specifications, and Database Audit Specifications can all be enabled or disabled. They may be modified only while disabled. All are disabled by default when they are first created, because that's how Extended Events works.
- SQL Server Audits, Server Audit Specifications, and Database Audit Specifications can all be managed by Policy-Based Management.
- SQL Audits are serious. The SQL Server Audit object can be configured to shut down the server if the audit doesn't function properly.

Creating an Audit

The first step to working with SQL Audit is to create a SQL Server Audit object.

In Object Explorer, SQL Server Audit objects are listed under the server ⇨ Security ⇨ Audits node. The New Audit command in the Audits node context menu opens the Create Audit dialog shown in Figure 61-1.

The queue delay, which determines how long SQL Server can wait before processing the Extended Event, ranges from 1 second (1,000 milliseconds) to almost 25 days (2,147,483,647 milliseconds). The default (1 second) is reasonable for most situations. If the server is hit with very heavy traffic, increasing the queue delay gives SQL Audit more flexibility.

Selecting true for "Shut down server on auditing failure" ensures that the target file or log receiving the events can be written to. If SQL Audit can't write to the target, then it will write a `MSG_AUDIT_FORCED_SHUTDOWN` event to the error log and shut down the server.

Fortunately, except for the name, all of the SQL Server Audit attributes may be changed after the object is created.

FIGURE 61-1

The Create Audit dialog is used to define SLQ Server Audit objects, which collect events defined by the Server Audit Specification or the Database Audit Specification.

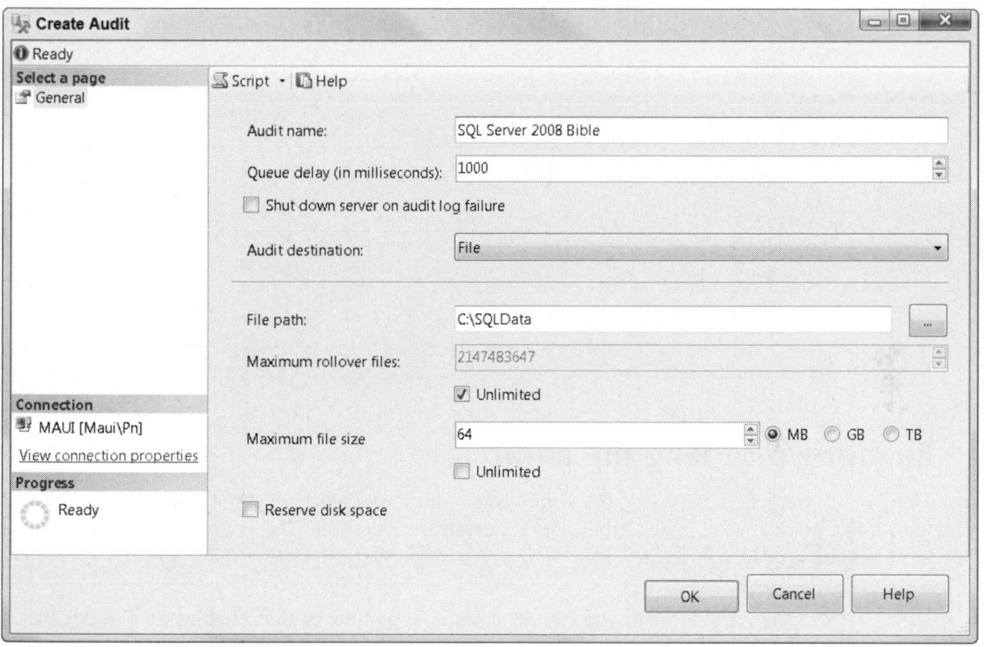

NOTE **If "Shut down on auditing failure" is set to true, and SQL Audit does indeed shut down the server, here's what to do: Start SQL Server with the minimal configuration option using the** `-f` **flag. This will start SQL Server in single-user mode, and put SQL Audit into** `Auditing failure=continue` **mode.**

Defining the target

The events can be sent to either a file, the Windows Security event log (not available in Windows XP), or the Windows Application event log. If the target is the log, then there are no other options.

If the target is a file, then the receiving directory, the size of the file, and the number of rollover files may be defined. The minimum file size is 1024 KB. SQL Server will automatically name the files and place them in the specified directory. I recommend using a dedicated local directory and limiting the file size to a few MB.

If the target is the Windows Security Log, then there are special security permissions and configurations required. See `http://msdn.microsoft.com/en-us/library/cc645889.aspx` for detailed information.

Using T-SQL

Of course, the SQL Server Audit object can be created using the CREATE SERVER AUDIT command. The following example creates the same SQL Server Audit object shown in Figure 61-1:

```
CREATE SERVER AUDIT [SQL Server 2008 Bible Audit]
  TO FILE (
    FILEPATH = N'C:\SQLData',
  MAXSIZE = 64 MB,
  MAX_ROLLOVER_FILES = 2147483647,
  RESERVE_DISK_SPACE = OFF
    )
  WITH (
    QUEUE_DELAY = 1000,
    ON_FAILURE = CONTINUE
    )
```

The SQL Server Audit object can also be modified using an ALTER command.

Enabling/disabling the audit

Object Explorer's SQL Server Audit node visually indicates whether the Audit is enabled or disabled with a red mark on the node if the item is currently turned off. The context menu includes commands to enable or disable the Audit.

Using T-SQL, the ALTER command has an additional parameter that enables or disables the SQL Server Audit. The following command enables the SQL Server 2008 Bible Audit:

```
ALTER SERVER AUDIT [SQL Server 2008 Bible]
  WITH (State = ON)
```

Server Audit Specifications

A new Server Audit Specification may be created from Object Explorer using the Security ➪ Server Audit Specifications' context menu ➪ New Server Audit Specification command, which opens the Create Server Audit Specification dialog, shown in Figure 61-2.

Each SQL Server Audit object may have only one Server Audit Specification, but there may be multiple Server Audits running, and each may have a Server Audit Specification.

The new Server Audit Specification can't be created unless it points to an existing SQL Server Audit object and that SQL Server Audit object currently does not have a Server Audit Specification connected to it.

FIGURE 61-2

Creating a new Server Audit Specification using Management Studio

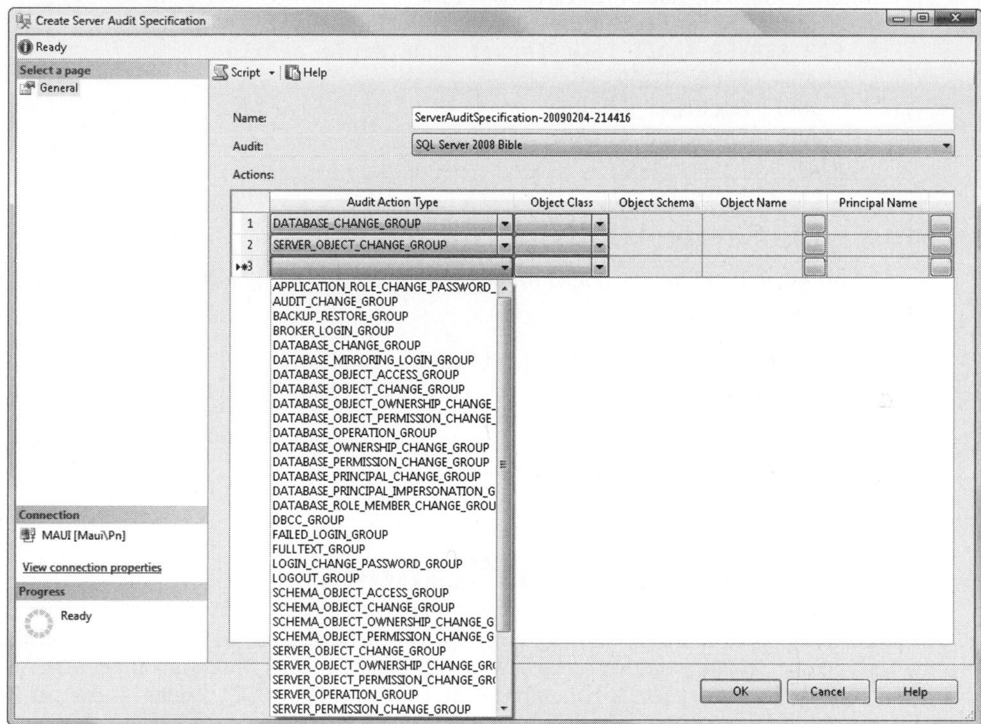

Adding actions

Without a doubt, the most important part of defining the Server Audit Specification is adding actions to the specification. Unfortunately, these actions aren't in a hierarchy like the DDL Triggers events and groups; each action group must be added individually.

The server-related events that can be audited are organized into 35 action groups (most are shown in the drop-down list in Figure 61-2). Potentially, a Server Audit Specification could have all 35 action groups.

The Server Audit State Change Audit group, which audits whether SQL Audit is enabled or disabled, is automatically audited.

Creating with T-SQL

Using T-SQL's `CREATE` command, it's easy to create a new Server Audit Specification. The principal parameter is the `ADD(`*`ACTION GROUP`*`)` option, which configures the Server Audit Specification with action groups. The following command creates a Server Audit Specification and assigns it to the SQL Server 2008 Bible Audit:

```
CREATE SERVER AUDIT SPECIFICATION
        [ServerAuditSpecification-20090204-212943]
  FOR SERVER AUDIT [SQL Server 2008 Bible Audit]
    ADD (DBCC_GROUP),
    ADD (FULLTEXT_GROUP),
    ADD (DATABASE_CHANGE_GROUP)
  WITH (STATE = ON)
```

Modifying Server Audit Specifications

New Action Audit Types may be added to the Server Audit Specification if the Server Audit Specification is disabled:

```
Alter Server Audit Specification name
  Add (Action Group)
```

To redirect a Server Audit Specification to a new SQL Server Audit, both the Server Audit Specification and the new SQL Server Audit must be disabled.

Database Audit Specifications

Database Audit Specifications are created using the same UI dialog as the Server Audit Specification. Like the Server Audit Specification there may only be one Database Audit Specification per SQL Audit. To create multiple Database Audit Specifications there must be multiple SQL Audits — one per Database Audit Specification.

The critical point is that Database Audit Specifications can audit DML events such as select, insert, update, and delete, as shown in Figure 61-3. You can also see the list of possible Database Audit Action Types in the drop-down list.

Viewing the Audit Trail

The easiest way to view the audit trail is to select the SQL Server Audit in Object Explorer and select View Logs in the context menu. This opens the Log File Viewer to the Audit Collection, as shown in Figure 61-4. The filter is useful to narrow the event viewed.

Using T-SQL, the logs can be read with the `fn_get_audit_file` function.

FIGURE 61-3

This Database Audit Specification will record every select statement executed by the dbo user in the AdventureWorks2008 database, and pass the audit data to the SQL Server 2008 Bible SQL Audit bucket.

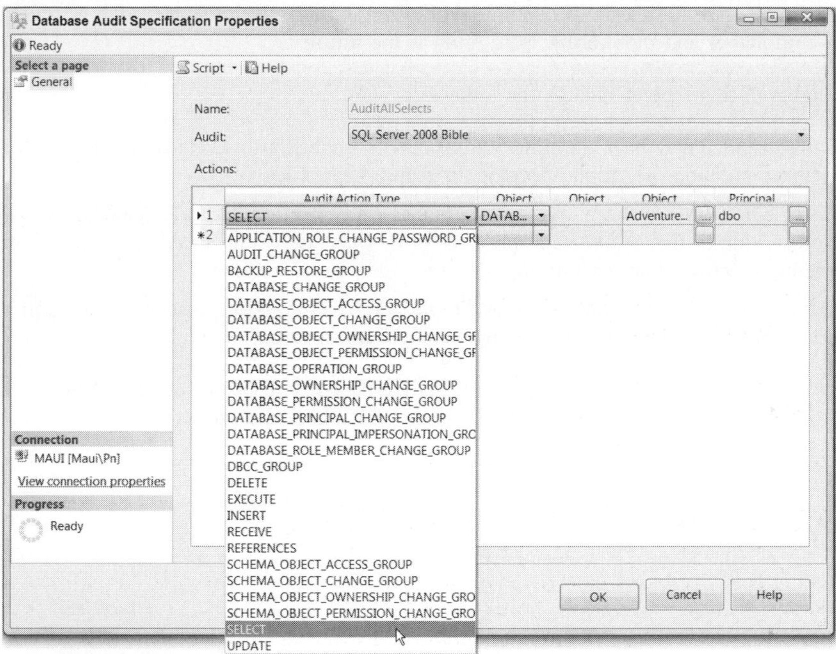

FIGURE 61-4

Viewing the audit history using Management Studio's Log File Viewer. Here, select statements issued in AdventureWorks2008 are being audited on a per-table basis.

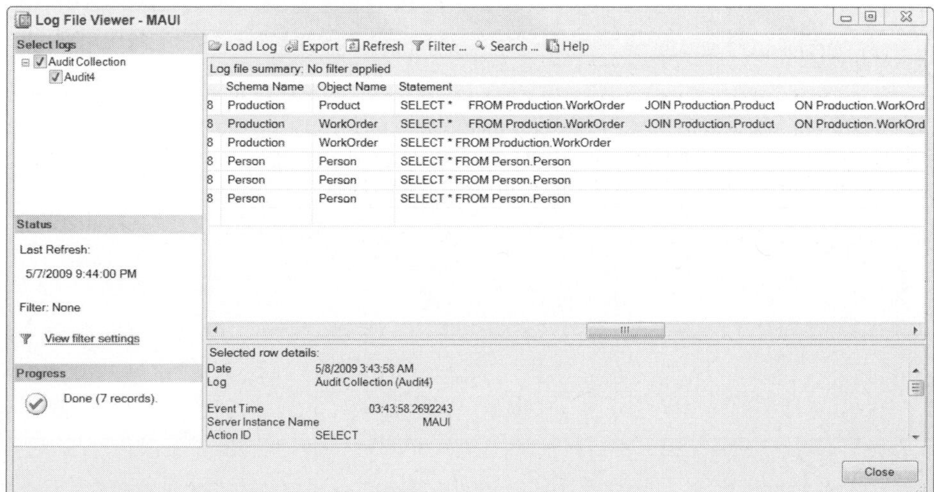

Summary

Extended Events is a powerful new auditing technology for Windows and SQL Server. But by itself, it takes a lot of work to use Extended Events. SQL Audit is a powerful collection of objects, easily configured, that extend and leverage Extended Events and makes it useful today. If your shop is running Enterprise Edition, I see no reason to continue with other auditing technologies such as tracing or triggers for compliance and monitoring. SQL Audit is the future.

Major highlights of this chapter include the following:

- Each instance may have multiple SQL Audits — collection buckets for audit data that can write to an audit file, application log, or security event log.
- Each SQL Audit can have one Server Database Specification and one Database Audit Specification writing to that SQL Audit. Each Server or Database Audit Specification may have multiple events or actions that it's auditing.
- Database Audit Specifications can audit DML statements: select, insert, update, and delete. In addition, the audit details include user context information.

This part covers another new monitoring technology targeted at enterprise servers. Management Data Warehouse is a strategic tool, both for Microsoft and the IT shops that adopt it.

Chapter 62

Management Data Warehouse

IN THIS CHAPTER

Collecting management data

Configuring MDW

The default collection set

Denmark is primarily an Oracle country. SQL Server accounts for perhaps 10% of the database servers, but that number is growing. So at the SQL Open World 2007 (hosted by Miracleas.dk)at Lalandia in Rødby, Denmark, most of the attendees were Oracle DBAs and developers wanting to learn more about SQL Server. For me, as a presenter, it was a great time to learn more about the gap between SQL Server and Oracle. At Lalandia, the guests stay in cottages near the conference center (and indoor beach, but that's another story). While walking to the cottages I asked the Oracle DBAs, "What could SQL Server do better? What do you as Oracle DBAs take for granted with Oracle that you don't see in SQL Server?" The singular answer was that Oracle DBAs build a data warehouse to gather performance stats, and then they use this data warehouse to analyze the baselines and performance trends. And they were right, that's a wonderful practice missing from the SQL Server community.

Allow me to introduce the Management Data Warehouse.

New to SQL Server 2008 Enterprise Edition, the Management Data Warehouse (MDW) is a significant strategic development in the progress of SQL Server.

The collection of management data is what has been missing in Microsoft's plans to take SQL Server to the next level. Even if you don't see much benefit to the MDW now, believe me, it's one of the most strategic SQL Server new features in this decade.

Of course, there are other third party systems that collect management data for later analysis, and it's not hard to develop one yourself. But, with a well-designed management data warehouse solution built into SQL Server 2008 Enterprise Edition, it's worth trying it before going down an alternative route.

Configuring MDW

As with any data warehouse, there are basically three key elements:

- The collection of source data.
- The extract-transform-load (ETL), process that populates the data warehouse.
- The schema of the data warehouse itself.

MDW is designed for large enterprises, so the assumption is that there's a dedicated server for the MDW database, but it's possible to collect data from any server and post it to any server.

MDW has a default collection set, default data warehouse schema, default programmability objects, and default reports, but it's possible to create and configure custom collection sets. While the default collection set has a lame name, it's actually a rather powerful and complete collection set. Don't consider designing your own, or extending the default set until you've mastered the details of the default collection set.

MDW can be configured and operate using only context menus, wizards, and property pages, but it's possible to create and control collection sets with T-SQL code.

Configuring a data warehouse

It's easy to configure and start a default configuration.

The data warehouse that will receive the data must be created prior to configuring a collection that will collect and send that data to the warehouse.

To create a MDW data warehouse, connect Object Explorer to the server that will house the data warehouse, open the server's Management ➪ Data Collection context menu and select Configure Management Data Warehouse, which launches the wizard.

The Configure Management Data Warehouse Wizard can perform one of two tasks. In this case, select the first task: Create or upgrade a management data warehouse. This lets you select an existing database or create a new database which will serve as the MDW data warehouse. The wizard will create all the required objects (tables, views, stored procedures, etc) in the new data warehouse.

Configuring a data collection

The data collection is created on the server that will have its management data gathered by MDW. So, on the server that will be tracked, in Management Studio's Object Explorer, open the server's Management ➪ Data Collection context menu and select Configure Management Data Warehouse.

Choosing the wizard's second task option will set-up all the objects in the source server for collecting the management data. The only significant option is choosing the MDW database that will be the destination of the collected data.

Once data collection has been install, it can be enabled or disable on the source server using Management ➪ Data Collection context menu.

The default collection actually includes three separate collection sets: Disk Usage, Query Statistics, and Server Activity (shown in Figure 62-1). Each collection set can be started, stopped, and manually uploaded using their respective context menus.

FIGURE 62-1

In this view of MDW, the three collection sets are open in Object Explorer and the central portion of the default MDW data warehouse schema is open in the database diagramming tool.

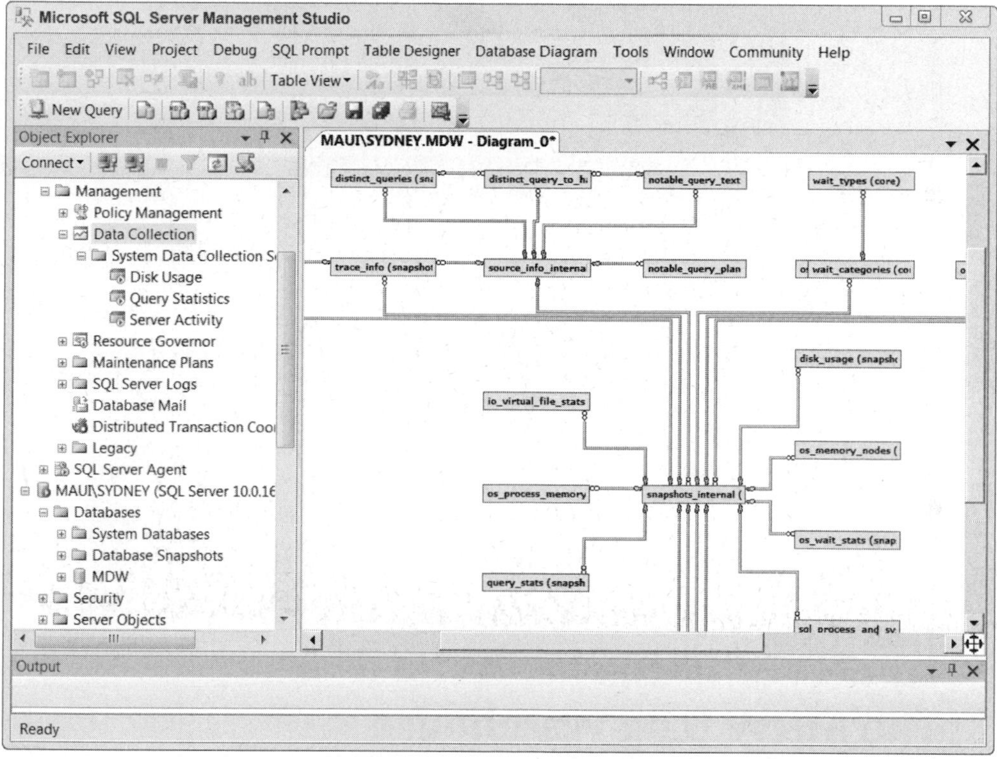

The collection set can be further configured in the Collection Set Properties page, illustrated in Figure 62-2. It's opened from the collection set's context menu.

Each collection set may actually include multiple collection items, each defining a script or query that will typically select management of performance data from SQL Server's system stored procedures or Dynamic Management Views (DMVs). The properties page is also used to set the ETL schedule and retention duration.

FIGURE 62-2

The Collection Set Properties page is used to fine tune each collection set. A key point on this page is the duration retention.

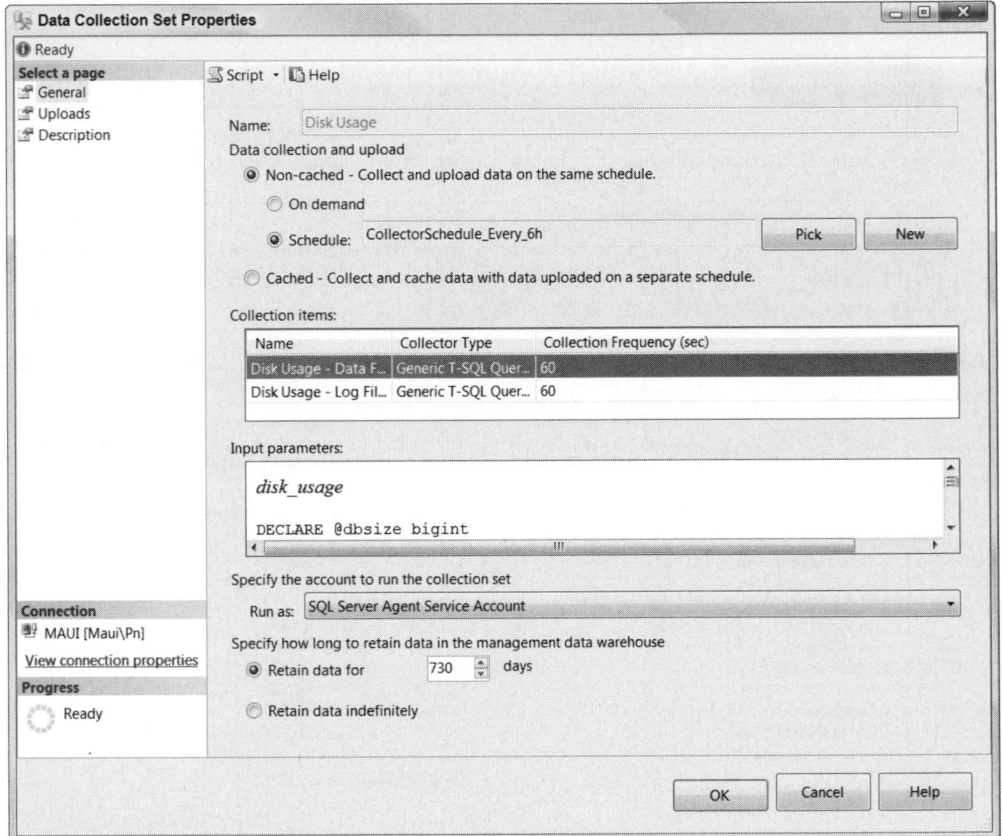

The MDW Data Warehouse

When initialized, MDW includes a default collection set which gathers a rather extensive set of performance and operational data about SQL Server. The default MDW data warehouse actually consists of:

- 30 tables in the data warehouse database (some of which are shown in Figure 62-1)
- 5 views, 64 stored procedures, and 9 user-defined functions all designed to extract information from the data warehouse

The data warehouse is designed in a star schema design around a central snapshot table. Each snapshot is one point in time, or one ETL upload of the management data.

The default MDW data warehouse supports three preconfigured reports. To find the three reports, look under the Management ➪ Data Collection context menu in the source server.

Summary

Management Data Warehouse is a great way to collect data for baselining performance, finding trends, or diagnosing issues, which begs the question: what will you do with all that information? I believe that MDW is the strategic foundation for lots of good things to come.

As a side note, third-party vendors who create add-on software for Microsoft applications who survive by dancing with an elephant — they had better be nimble and quick. They need to exploit a feature gap for a version of two and move on. The feature gap in SQL Server 2008 is right here at the end of MDW. The third party vendors who are smart will write reports and create tools that analyze MDW data and offer tuning advice.

This chapter completes Part VIII — a survey of monitoring and auditing technologies in SQL Server 2008. No one can ever accuse SQL Server of not being transparent.

The next part logically builds on this part and moves into the realm of the performance tuning and optimization skill set.

Part IX

Performance Tuning and Optimization

It seems everyone wants a quick fix.

On one optimization job, I identified and prioritized numerous issues with the schema, queries, and indexes that together would have reduced the aggregate workload by 60–80 percent. I thought I'd done a great job. The client didn't think so. They actually said they were hoping that as an MVP I'd know of an undocumented "go fast" switch.

The switch is in the design!

But once the schema and queries are right and the workload is known, it's time to tune the indexes and optimize the server. From reading query execution plans, to query paths and indexing, to data compression, this part is filled with some of my favorite SQL Server topics. If you thought left outer joins were fun, well, you're in for a real treat.

If SQL Server is the box, this part is about making the box scream.

IN THIS PART

Chapter 63

Interpreting Query Execution Plans

IN THIS CHAPTER

The language of performance tuning and optimization

Viewing, saving, and working with query execution plans

Reading query execution operators

I believe that intelligence is the ability to abstract — to create something new at a higher lever based on more primitive constructs. The ability to express thoughts using words composed of letters and simple sounds is abstraction; to turn beats and notes into a melody is abstraction; and to turn 1s a 0s in CPU registers into a programming language and then use that language to develop an application represents multiple layers of abstraction.

Interpreting SQL Server query execution plans is abstraction inside-out.

SQL, as a declarative language, is an interesting study of abstraction because the underlying primitive operations that execute the query are dynamically determined based on more than just the SQL query.

The art of SQL Server performance tuning and optimization (PTO) is essentially the skill of reading the query execution plans and understanding how to manipulate the factors that determine the physical operations in an effort to improve performance. The operations inside a query execution plan are the language of SQL Server PTO, which is why this part of the book begins with reading and interpreting the query execution plan.

Viewing Query Execution Plans

The SQL Server development team has exposed the query execution plan in several places and in several formats, making it easy to find, view, and work with query execution plans:

- Management Studio's Query Editor can display the estimated or actual query execution plan as a graphic or as XML.
- Showplans return the query plan as a message or a result set.

- SQL Profiler can capture the query execution plan as plain text or as XML that can be viewed in graphic form.
- Query plans in cache may be viewed using dynamic management views.

Additionally, the query execution plan can be saved as an XML file and opened later using Management Studio's Query Editor.

What's New with Query Execution Plans?

There's very little that's new regarding viewing query execution plans, but there are a few new tricks to working with query execution plans in SQL Server 2008:

- Management Studio's Query Editor can switch the graphical query execution plan into XML from the context menu.
- A saved query execution plan now includes the full query, so when it's re-opened, the original source query can be viewed in the Query Editor.
- The XML query execution plan is formatted better.
- The Query Editor can now open the XML query execution plan that's returned from the `sys.dm_exec_query_plan()`dynamic management function as a graphical plan with a single click.

Estimated query execution plans

SQL Server can return just the estimated query execution plan before the query is executed, or it can return the actual query execution plan with the results of the query.

The difference between the estimated and the actual isn't the plan — the sequence of logical and physical operations is identical; the only difference is the estimated vs. actual number of rows returned by each operation. Before the query is executed, the Query Optimizer will estimate the number of rows based on statistics and use that estimate in determining the plan. After the query is executed, the query processor can add to the plan the actual number of rows processed by each operation.

The estimated query execution plan may be viewed by selecting the query in the Query Editor and either clicking the Display Estimated Execution Plan button in the toolbar, selecting Query ➪ Display Estimated Execution Plan, or by pressing Ctrl+L.

Because the query isn't actually executed, the estimated query execution plan should display in the Execution Plan tab rather quickly.

The Query Editor's execution plan

The data flow in a query plan is from right to left, bottom to top, as shown in Figure 63-1. Each operation is presented as an icon. The Query Editor isn't just a static display:

- Mousing over the logical operation causes a dialog to appear containing detailed information about the logical operation, including the logical cost and the portion of the query handled by the operation.
- Mousing over a connector line presents detailed information about how much data is being moved by that connector.
- The Property window also presents detailed information about any operation or connector.

The display may be zoomed or sized to fit using the right-click context menu.

FIGURE 63-1

Query execution plans show the operations SQL Server uses to solve the query.

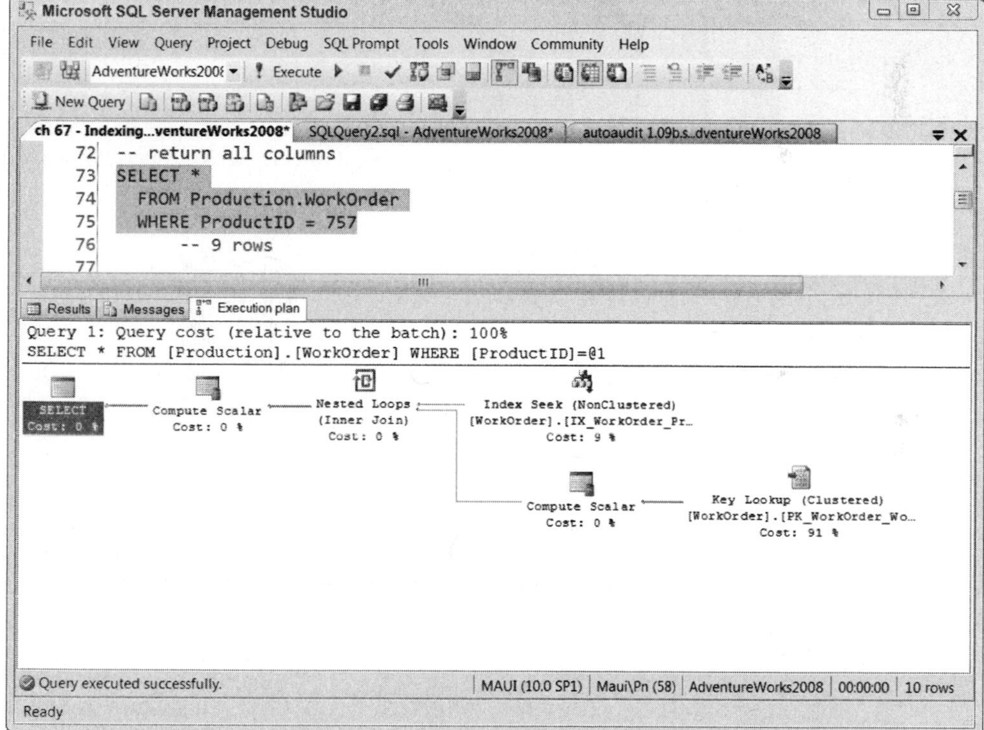

To walk through the query execution plan shown in Figure 63-1:

1. In the upper-right corner of the plan, the index seek operation is finding every row with `ProductID = 757` using an index seek operation against the `[WorkOrder.IX_WorkOrder_ProductID]` non-clustered index.

2. The nested loop operation receives every row from the index seek, and asks for those same rows from the clustered index, calling the key lookup operation. Just ignore the compute scalar operation, as it's only handling a type conversion.
3. The nested loop assembles, or joins, the data from the index seek and key lookup and passes the data to the select operation, which returns the correct columns to the client.

Note the following key pieces of information on the query plan:

- The type of operation. Key operations are listed later in Table 63-1.
- The object, listed below the operator and in the pop-up info box, is the actual index hit by the operation.
- The estimated number of rows, as the Query Optimizer uses the estimated number of rows to choose the best query execution plan.
- The estimated operator cost and the estimated subtree cost are relative values used by the Query Optimizer. When tuning a query, these are critical values to watch. I typically read the cost as cost times 1,000. For example, I'll read .0051234 as 5, or .3255786 as 325, to make it easier to think through the plans.

Plans can also be saved to a plan file (`.sqlplan`) to be reexamined later. Re-opening a plan opens the graphical execution plan. The context menu has a new option to edit the SQL query, which opens the original SQL statement in a new Query Editor tab.

Returning the plan with showplans

In addition to the graphical execution plan, the `Showplan` options reveal the execution plan with some additional detail.

Just as the display-estimated-execution-plan Query Editor option, when showplan is on, SQL Server will return the query execution plan but won't execute the statement. `SET SHOWPLAN` must be the only statement in the batch.

`SET SHOWPLAN` comes is three flavors: `ALL`, `TEXT`, and `XML`:

- `SHOWPLAN_ALL` displays the operators as a result set. It exposes the same information as the graphical execution plan. The executing statement is returned in the first row and every operator is returned as subsequent rows. (This is a deprecated feature and will be eliminated in a future version.)
- `SHOWPLAN_TEXT` is very similar to `SHOWPLAN_ALL` except that the executing statement and the operations are in separate result sets and only the `stmt text` (first column) is displayed. The `SHOWPLAN_TEXT` option, along with the `SET STATISTICS` options, may also be toggled graphically within Query Editor. Use the context menu's Query Options command to open the Query Properties and you can find the showplan options by selecting Execution ➪ Advanced. (This is also a deprecated feature that will be eliminated in a future version.)
- `SHOWPLAN_XML` displays more detail than any other method of viewing the execution plan, and it offers the benefit of storing and displaying unstructured data, so it can display additional information that may not pertain to all execution plans. For example, in the `<Statement>` element, `SHOWPLAN_XML` displays the Query Optimizer optimization level, or the reason why the Query Optimizer returned this execution plan. For the XML version of

SHOWPLAN, the "Include actual execution" Query Editor option must be off. In addition, if the query results are set to grid, then the grid will offer a link to open the XML using the browser.

Another way to gather the execution plan is the SET STATISTICS PROFILE ON command, which executes the query and then supplies the same detail as SHOWPLAN_ALL with the addition of actual row counts and execution counts. This is the result set equivalent of the SHOW ACTUAL execution plan. This is a deprecated feature, to be eliminated in a future version.

SQL Profiler's execution plans

Within the Performance event category, SQL Server Profiler includes several showplan events. The Showplan XML event includes the XML for the query execution plan, which SQL Profiler displays in a graphical form. It includes the same features as the Query Editor to mouse over the operation to see more properties and zoom the display.

Saving the plan is possible with SQL Profiler, but it's well hidden: If you right-click anywhere in the upper pane on the line of a Showplan XML or Showplan XML Statistics Profile event, you can choose to "Extract Event Data." This enables you to save the plan as a .sqlplan file. Cool add!

Examining plans using dynamic management views

Dynamic management views, or DMVs, previously introduced with SQL Server 2005, provide an excellent window into SQL Server's internals. Three of the DMVs expose the query execution plans currently in the cache:

- sys.dm_exec_cached_plans: Returns the plan type, memory size, and usecounts
- sys.dm_exec_query_stats: Returns several aggregate execution statistics (e.g., last_execution_time, max_elapsed_time)
- sys.dm_exec_requests: Returns plans that are currently executing

Each of these DMVs returns a plan handle (a binary identifier of the query execution plan in memory) that can be passed to one of the following dynamic management functions with a CROSS APPLY to extract the query text or the query execution plan:

- sys.dm_exec_query_plan(plan_handle): Returns the query execution plan in XML. Note that for some very complex queries, if the XML nesting level is greater than 128, this method of extracting the query plan will fail. Use the next method instead.
- sys.dm_exec_text_query_plan(plan_handle): Returns the query execution plan as a text showplan
- sys.dm_exec_sql_text(plan_handle): Returns the query SQL statement

The code example in Figure 63-2 pulls together data from the DMVs to view the original SQL statements and query execution plans from the cache.

FIGURE 63-2

Using DMVs, it's possible to view the SQL code and the query execution plan in the procedure cache. Clicking the XML in the right-most column opens another tab with a graphical view of the selected query execution plan.

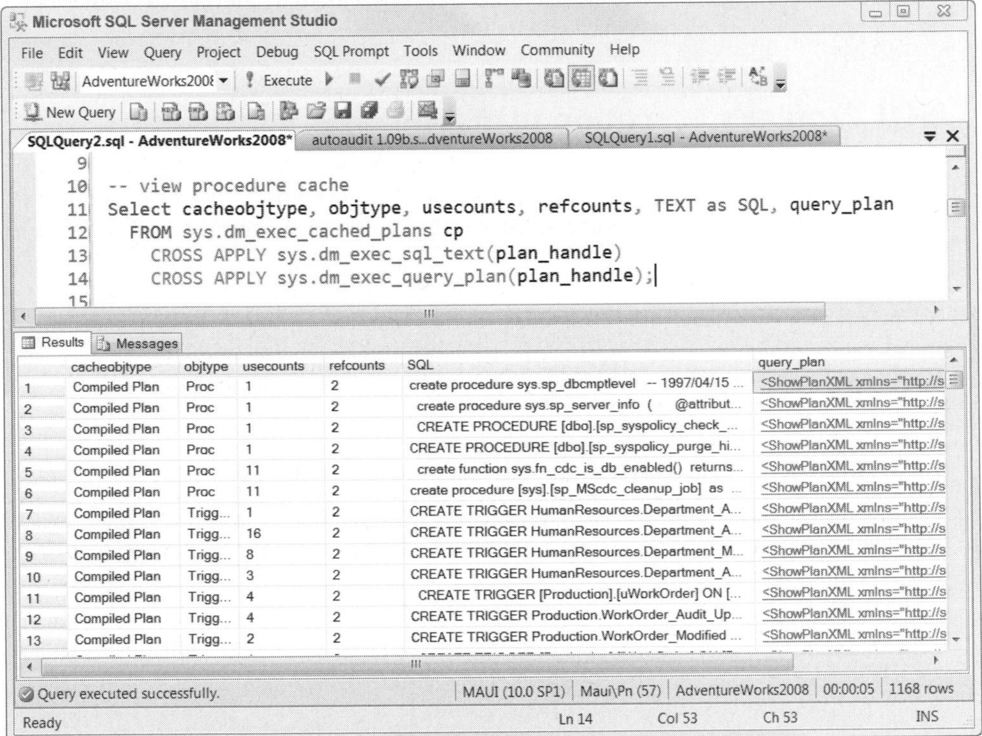

Interpreting the Query Execution Plan

Reading query execution plans may seem difficult at first; there are several types of complex icons, a ton of detail, and the sheer scope of some query plans can be overwhelming.

SQL server uses about 60 operators. Some represent specific physical tasks, while most logically represent a collection of hidden tasks. Table 63-1 lists the key operators regarding select queries and indexing.

TABLE 63-1

Query Execution Plan Operators

Icon	Definition	Description
	Clustered index scan	In a clustered index scan, SQL Server reads the entire clustered index, typically sequentially, but it can be otherwise depending on the isolation level and the fragmentation. SQL Server chooses this operation when the set of rows requested by the WHERE clause or join condition is a large percentage of rows needed from the table or no index is available to select the range.
	Table scan	A table scan is similar to a clustered index scan but it scans a heap.
	Clustered index seek	In a clustered index seek, SQL Server rapidly navigates the clustered index b-tree to retrieve specific rows. The benefit of the clustered index seek is that when the row(s) are determined, all the columns are immediately available.
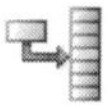	Hash match	A hash match is an unordered join method that builds a temp table and iteratively matches with data from another table. A hash match is more efficient if one table is significantly larger than the other table. This is the worst-case join method and is used when no suitable index is available.
	Merge join	The merge join is the fastest method of joining two tables if both tables are pre-sorted.
	Nested loop	A nested loop iterates through the first table (or intermediate result set if in the middle of the query plan), finding matching row(s) in the second table for each row from the first. Typically, nested-loop joins are best when a large index is joined with a small table.
	Index scan (non-clustered)	In a non-clustered index scan, SQL Server reads through the entire index sequentially looking for the data.
	Index seek (non-clustered)	A non-clustered index seek navigates the b-tree index from the root node, through the intermediate node(s), to the leaf node, and finally to the row. The benefit of a nonclustered index seek is that it tends to be narrow (have few columns), so more rows can fit on a page. Once the correct row is identified, if all the required columns are found in the index, then the seek is complete because the index covers the needs of the query. If a range is required, an index seek operation can seek to the start of the range and then sequentially read to the end of the range.
	RID lookup	The RID lookup locates rows in the data pages of a heap (a table without a clustered index). Typically, a RID lookup works with a nested loop to locate the data pages following a non-clustered index seek or scan.
	Filter	In some situations, SQL Server retrieves all the data from a table and then uses filter operations to select the correct rows. Sometimes the Query Optimizer uses a Filter for performance reasons, but it's more often due to the lack of a useful index.
	Sort	In some situations SQL Server retrieves all the data from a table and then sorts the data to prepare it for operations to perform the ORDER BY. While the filters and sorts are themselves fast operations, they need to examine all the data, which means a slower scan is required. These typically indicate a lack of useful indexes.
	Spool	In a spool operation, SQL Server has to save a temporary set of data.

Summary

If you're new to SQL Server performance tuning and optimization, the mechanics of reading a query execution plan can't be underestimated. Fortunately, SQL Server exposes the internals of query execution in several ways: graphically, with text showplans, and with XML, and makes them relatively easy to read once they make sense.

This chapter covered the how-to of reading and working with query execution plans. The key point to remember is that both estimated and actual query execution plans show the actual plan. The difference is that the estimated plan doesn't perform the query, so it can't show the actual row count in the connector's properties.

The next chapter transitions into the whys and wherefores of query execution plans and how to manipulate them with indexes — an execution plan one-two punch.

Chapter 64

Indexing Strategies

IN THIS CHAPTER

- Indexing for improving performance
- Interpreting query execution plans
- A database strategy for improving performance

My son Dave and I love to watch "MythBusters." Even if we know Adam and Jamie aren't going to get the pig's head to blow up, it's a blast to see them try.

If there's any aspect of SQL Server populated with misconceptions (or shall I say, "*mythconceptions*"), it's indexing — and that's unfortunate, because sound indexing isn't all that complicated.

My Smart Database Design Seminar is based on the notion (described in Chapter 2) that an elegant physical schema lends itself to writing great set-based queries that respond well to indexing. It's the theory I use when I design a database and when I go on a performance-tuning and optimization consulting job. One aspect of Smart Database Design is that no layer can overcome deficiencies in lower layers, i.e., no index will solve an inappropriate cursor and a sorry database schema.

Nulltheless, indexes are at the heart of SQL Server performance; they are the bridge from the question to the data — from the query to the schema.

Indexes are so critical to SQL Server performance that I've spent two months longer than my writing schedule allowed to explain how to think about indexes, work through the twelve query paths, and present a solid indexing strategy.

Zen and the Art of Indexing

Right up front, here's my secret to designing effective indexes: When I'm indexing, in my mind's eye I don't see tables and indexes, I see only indexes. Some indexes have more data attached to the leaf level than other indexes, but there are only indexes. When indexing, there's no such thing as a table in SQL Server.

Indexes only become useful as they serve the needs of a query, so designing indexes means thinking about how the query will navigate the indexes to reach the data. "Zen and the Art of Indexing" means that you see the query path in your mind's eye and design the shortest path from the query to the data.

What's New With Indexes?

Indexing is critical to SQL Server performance, and Microsoft has steadily invested in SQL Server's indexing capabilities. Back in SQL Server 2005, my favorite new feature was included columns for non-clustered indexes, which made non-clustered indexes more efficient as covering indexes.

With SQL Server 2008, Microsoft has again added several significant new indexing features.

Filtered indexes means that a non-clustered index can be created that indexes only a subset of the data. This is perfect for situations like a manufacturing orders table with 2% active orders.

The new star-join optimization uses bitmap filters for up to seven times performance gains when joining a single table (fact table) with several lookup (dimension) tables.

The new `Forceseek` table hint, as the name implies, forces the Query Optimizer to choose a seek operation instead of a scan.

Indexing Basics

You can't master indexing without a solid understanding of how indexes work. Please don't skip this section. To apply the strategies described later in this chapter, you must grok the b-tree.

The b-tree index

Conventional wisdom says that SQL Server has two types of indexes: clustered and non-clustered; but a closer look reveals that SQL Server has in fact only one type of index: the *b-tree*, or balanced tree, index, because internally both clustered and non-clustered indexes are b-tree indexes.

B-tree indexes exist on index pages and have a root level, one or more intermediate levels, and a leaf or node level. The columns actually sorted by the b-tree index are called the index's *key columns*, as shown in Figure 64-1. The difference between clustered and non-clustered indexes is the amount and type of data stored at the leaf level.

CROSS-REF **While this chapter discusses the strategies of designing and optimizing indexes and does include some code examples that demonstrate creating indexes, the sister Chapter 20, "Creating the Physical Database Schema," details the actual syntax and Management Studio methods of creating indexes.**

Over time, indexes typically become fragmented, which significantly hurts performance. For more information on index maintenance, turn to Chapter 42, "Maintaining the Database."

After you've read this chapter, I highly recommend digging deeper into the internals of SQL Server's indexes with my favorite SQL Server book, Kalen Delaney's *SQL Server 2008 Internals* (Microsoft Press, 2009).

FIGURE 64-1

The b-tree index is the most basic element of SQL Server. This figure illustrates a simplified view of a clustered index with an identity column as the clustered index key. The first name is the data column.

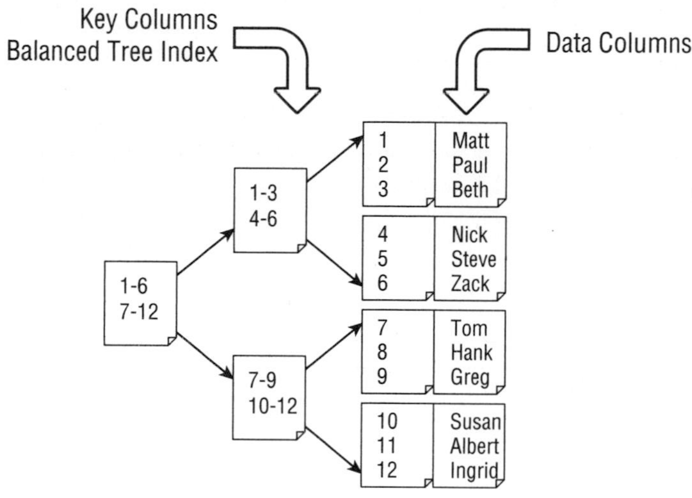

Clustered indexes

In SQL Server, when all the data columns are attached to the b-tree index's leaf level, it's called a *clustered index,* and some might call it a table or base table (refer to Figure 64-1). A clustered index is often called the physical sort order of the table, which is mostly, or at least logically, true.

Logically, the clustered index pages will have the data in the clustered index sort order; but physically, on the disk, those pages are a linked list — each page links to the next page and the previous page in the list. In a perfect world the pages would be in the same order as the list, but in reality they are often moved around due to page splits and fragmentation (more on page splits later in this chapter). In this case, the links probably jump around a bit.

A table may only have one physical sort order, and therefore, only one clustered index. The quintessential example of a clustered index is a telephone book (the old-fashioned printed kind, not the Internet search type). The telephone book itself is a clustered index. The last name and first name columns are the index keys, and the rest of the data (address, phone number) is attached to the index.

A telephone book even simulates a b-tree index. Open a telephone book to the middle. Choose the side with the name you want to find, and then split that side in half. In a few halves and splits, you'll be at the page with the name you're looking for. Your eye can now quickly scan that page and find the last name and first name you want. Because the address and phone number are printed right next to the names, no more searching is needed.

Non-clustered indexes

SQL Server can also create *non-clustered indexes*, which are similar to the indexes in the back of a book. This type of index is keyed, or sorted, by the keywords, and the page numbers are pointers to the book's content.

Internally, SQL Server non-clustered indexes are b-tree indexes and point to the base table, which is either a clustered index or a heap. If the base table is a clustered index, then the clustered index keys (every sort-by column) are included at every level of the non-clustered index b-tree and leaf level. If the base table is a heap, then the heap RID (row ID) is used.

For example, the non-clustered index illustrated in Figure 64-2 uses the first name column as its key column, so that's the data sorted by the b-tree. The non-clustered index points to the base table by including the clustered index key column. In Figure 64-2, the clustered index key column is the identity column used in Figure 64-1.

Since SQL Server 2005, additional unsorted columns can be *included* in the leaf level. The employee's title and department columns could be added to the previous index, which is extremely useful in designing covering indexes (described in the next section).

A SQL Server table may have up to 999 non-clustered indexes, but I've never seen a well-normalized table that required more than a dozen well-designed indexes.

FIGURE 64-2

This simplified illustration of a non-clustered index has a b-tree index with first name as the key column. The non-clustered index includes pointers to the clustered index key column.

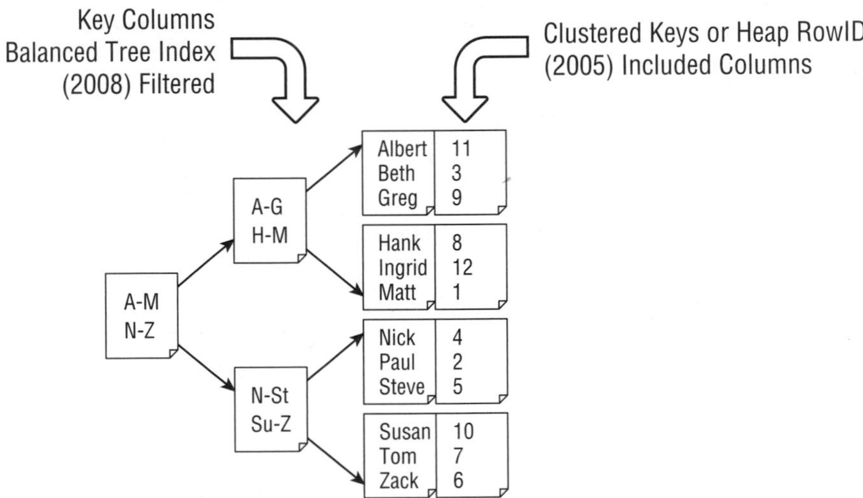

Composite indexes

A *composite index* is a clustered or non-clustered index that is keyed, or sorted, on multiple columns. Composite indexes are common in production.

The order of the columns in a composite index is important. In order for a search to take advantage of a composite index it must include the index columns from left to right. If the composite index is `lastname, firstname`, a search for `firstname` can't seek quickly through the b-tree index, but a search for `lastname`, or `lastname` and `firstname`, will use the b-tree.

CROSS-REF **Various methods of indexing for multiple columns are examined in Query Paths 9 through 11 later in this chapter.**

A similar problem is searching for words within a column but not at the beginning of the text string stored in the column. For these word searches, SQL Server can use Integrated Full-Text Search (iFTS), covered in Chapter 19, "Using Integrated Full-Text Search."

Unique indexes and constraints

Because primary keys are the unique method of identifying any row, indexes and primary keys are intertwined — in fact, a primary key must be indexed. By default, creating a primary key automatically creates a unique clustered index, but it can optionally create a unique non-clustered index instead.

A unique index limits data to being unique so it's like a constraint; and a unique constraint builds a unique index to quickly check the data. In fact, a unique constraint and a unique index are the exact same thing — creating either one builds a unique constraint/index.

The only difference between a unique constraint/index and a primary key is that a primary key cannot allow nulls, whereas a unique constraint/index can permit a single null value.

The page split problem

Every b-tree index must maintain the key column data in the correct sort order. Inserts, updates, and deletes will affect that data. As the data is inserted or modified, if the index page to which a value needs to be added is full, then SQL Server must split the page into two less-than-full pages so it can insert the value in the correct position. Turning again to the telephone book example, if several new Nielsens moved into the area and the Nie page 515 had to now accommodate 20 additions, a simulated page split would take several steps:

1. Cut page 515 in half making two pages; call them 515a and 515b.
2. Print out and tape the new Nielsens to page 515a.
3. Tape page 515b inside the back cover of the telephone book.
4. Make a note on page 515a that the Nie listing continues on page 515b located at the end of the book, and a note on page 515b indicating that the listing continues on page 515a.

Pages splits cause several performance-related problems:

- The page split operation is expensive because it involves several steps and moving data. I've personally seen page splits reduce an intensive insert process' performance by 90 percent.
- If, after the page split, there still isn't enough room, then the page will be split again. This can occur repeatedly depending on certain circumstances.
- The data structure is left fragmented and can no longer be read in a single contiguous pass.

The data structure has more empty space, which means less data is read with every page read and less data is stored in the buffer per page.

Index selectivity

Another aspect of index tuning is the selectivity of the index. An index that is very selective has more distinct index values and selects fewer data rows per index value. A primary key or unique index has the highest possible selectivity; each index key only relates to one row.

An index with only a few distinct values spread across a large table is less selective. Indexes that are less selective may not even be useful as indexes. A column with three values spread throughout the table is a poor candidate for an index. A bit column has low selectivity and cannot be indexed directly.

SQL Server uses its internal index statistics to track the selectivity of an index. `DBCC Show_Statistic` reports the last date on which the statistics were updated, and basic information about the index statistics, including the usefulness of the index. A low density indicates that the index is very selective. A high density indicates that a given index node points to several table rows and that the index may be less useful, as shown in this code sample:

```
Use CHA2;
DBCC Show_Statistics (Customer, IxCustomerName);
```

Result (formatted and abridged; the full listing includes details for every value in the index):

```
Statistics for INDEX 'IxCustomerName'.
                  Rows                      Average
Updated    Rows   Sampled   Steps  Density  key length
---------  -----  --------  ------ -------- -----------
May 1,02   42     42        33     0.0      11.547619

All density     Average Length  Columns
--------------  --------------  ---------------------------
3.0303031E-2    6.6904764       LastName
2.3809524E-2    11.547619       LastName, FirstName

DBCC execution completed. If DBCC printed error messages,
contact your system administrator.
```

Sometimes changing the order of the key columns can improve the selectivity of an index and its performance. Be careful, however, because other queries may depend on the order for their performance.

Unordered heaps

It's also possible to create a table without a clustered index, in which case the data is stored in an *unordered heap*. Instead of being identified by the clustered index key columns, the rows are identified internally using the heap's RowID. The RowID is an actual physical location composed of three values, `FileID:PageNum:SlotNum`, and cannot be directly queried. Any non-clustered indexes store the heap's RowID in all levels of the index to point to the heap instead of using the clustered index key columns to point to the clustered index.

Because a heap does not include a clustered index, a heap's primary key must be a non-clustered index.

Why Use Heaps?

I believe heaps add no value and nearly always require a bookmark lookup (explained in Query Path 5), so I avoid creating heaps.

Developers who like heaps tend to be the same developers who prefer natural primary keys (as opposed to surrogate primary keys). Natural primary keys are nearly always unordered. When natural primary keys are used for clustered indexes they generate a lot of page splits, which kills performance. Heaps simply add new rows at the end of the heap and they avoid the natural primary key page split problem.

Some developers claim that heaps are faster than clustered indexes for inserts. This is true only when the clustered index is designed in a way that generates page splits. Comparing insert performance between heaps and clustered surrogate primary keys, there is little measurable difference, or the clustered index is slightly faster.

Heaps are organized by RIDs—row IDs (includes file, page, and row). Any seek operation (detailed soon) into a heap must use a non-clustered index and a bookmark lookup (detailed in Query Path 5 later in this chapter).

Query operations

Although there are dozens of logical and physical query execution operations, SQL Server uses three primary operations to actually fetch the data:

- **Table scan:** Reads the entire heap and, most likely, passes all the data to a secondary filter operation
- **Index scan:** Reads the entire leaf level (every row) of the clustered index or non-clustered index. The index scan operation might filter the rows and return only those rows that meet the criteria, or it might pass all the rows to another filter operation depending on the complexity of the criteria. The data may or may not be ordered.
- **Index seek:** Locates specific row(s) data using the b-tree and returns only the selected rows in an ordered list, as illustrated in Figure 64-3

The Query Optimizer chooses the fetch operation with the least cost. Sequentially reading the data is a very efficient task, so an index scan and filter operation may actually be cheaper than an index seek with a bookmark lookup (see Query Path 5 below) involving hundreds of random I/O index seeks. It's all about correctly guessing the number of rows touched and returned by each operation in the query execution plan.

Path of the Query

Indexes exist to serve queries — an index by itself serves no purpose. The best way to understand how to design efficient indexes is to observe and learn from the various possible paths queries take through the indexes to locate data.

FIGURE 64-3

An index-seek operation navigates the b-tree index, selects a beginning row, and then scans all the required rows.

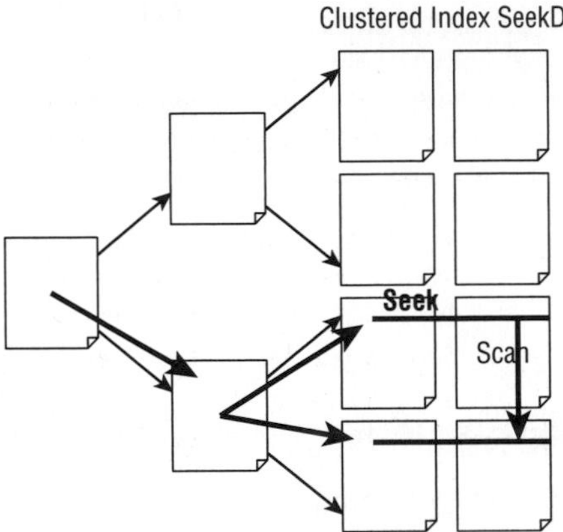

There are ten *kata* (a Japanese word for martial arts choreographed patterns or movements), or query paths, with different combinations of indexes combined with index seeks and scans. These kata begin with a simple index scan and progress toward more complex query paths.

Not every query path is an efficient query path. There are nine good paths, and three paths that should be avoided.

A good test table for observing the twelve query paths in the `AdventureWorks2008` database is the `Production.WorkOrder` table. It has 72,591 rows, only 10 columns, and a single-column clustered primary key. Here's the table definition:

```
CREATE TABLE [Production].[WorkOrder](
[WorkOrderID] [int] IDENTITY(1,1) NOT NULL,
[ProductID] [int] NOT NULL,
[OrderQty] [int] NOT NULL,
[StockedQty]  AS (isnull([OrderQty]-[ScrappedQty],(0))),
[ScrappedQty] [smallint] NOT NULL,
[StartDate] [datetime] NOT NULL,
[EndDate] [datetime] NULL,
[DueDate] [datetime] NOT NULL,
[ScrapReasonID] [smallint] NULL,
[ModifiedDate] [datetime] NOT NULL,
 CONSTRAINT [PK_WorkOrder_WorkOrderID] PRIMARY KEY CLUSTERED
  ([WorkOrderID] ASC)
    WITH (PAD_INDEX  = OFF, STATISTICS_NORECOMPUTE  = OFF,
    IGNORE_DUP_KEY = OFF, ALLOW_ROW_LOCKS  = ON,
    ALLOW_PAGE_LOCKS  = ON) ON [PRIMARY]
) ON [PRIMARY];
```

As installed, the WorkOrder table has the three indexes, each with one column as identified in the index name:

- PK_WorkOrder_WorkOrderID (clustered)
- IX_WorkORder_ProductID (non-unique, non-clustered)
- IX_WorkOrder_ScrapReasonID (non-unique, non-clustered)

Performance data for each kata, listed in Table 64-1, was captured by watching the T-SQL ➪ SQL:StmtComplete and Performance ➪ Showplan XML Statistics Profile events in Profiler, and examining the query execution plan.

The key performance indicators are the query execution plan optimizer costs (Cost), and the number of logical reads (Reads).

For the duration column, I ran each query multiple times and averaged the results. Of course, your SQL Server machine is probably beefier than my notebook. I urge you to run the script on your own SQL Server instance, take your own performance measurements, and study the query execution plans.

The Rows per ms column is calculated from the number of rows returned and the average duration.

Before executing each query path, the following code clears the buffers:

```
DBCC FREEPROCCACHE;
DBCC DROPCLEANBUFFERS;
```

Query Path 1: Fetch All

The first query path sets a baseline for performance by simply requesting all the data from the base table:

```
SELECT *
  FROM Production.WorkOrder;
```

Without a WHERE clause and every column selected, the query must read every row from the clustered index. A clustered index scan (illustrated in Figure 64-4) sequentially reads every row.

This query is the longest query of all the query paths, so it might seem to be a slow query, but when comparing the number of rows returned per millisecond, the index scan returns the highest number of rows per millisecond of any query path.

Query Path 2: Clustered Index Seek

The second query path adds a WHERE clause to the first query and filters the result to a single row using a clustered key value:

```
SELECT *
  FROM Production.WorkOrder
  WHERE WorkOrderID = 1234;
```

TABLE 64-1

Query Path Performance

Path	Kata	Execution Plan	Rows	Cost	Reads	Missing Index	Duration (ms)	Rows per ms
1	Fetch All	C Ix Scan	72,591	.485	526		1,196	60.71
2	Clustered Index Seek	C Ix Seek	1	.003	2		7	.14
3	Range Seek Query (narrow)	C Ix Seek (Seek keys start-end)	11	.003	3		13	.85
	Range Seek Query (wide)	C Ix Seek (Seek keys start-end)	72,591	.485	526		1,257	57.73
4	Filter by non-Key Column	C Ix Scan → filter (predicate)	55	.519	526	NC (include all columns)	170	.32
5	Bookmark Lookup (Select *)	NC Ix Seek → BML	9	.037	29		226	.04
	Bookmark Lookup (Select clustered key, non-key col)	NC Ix Seek → BML	9	.037	29		128	.07
6	Covering Index (narrow)	NC Ix Seek (Seek Predicate)	9	.003	2		30	.30
	Covering Index (wide)	NC Ix Seek (Seek Predicate)	1,105	.005	6		106	10.46
	NC Seek Selecting Clustered Key (narrow)	NC Ix Seek (Seek Predicate)	9	.003	2		46	.20
	NC Seek Selecting Clustered Key (wide)	NC Ix Seek (Seek Predicate)	1,105	.004	4		46	24.02
	Filter by Include Column	NC Ix Seek (Seek Predicate + Predicate)	1	.003	2		51	.02
7	Filter by 2 x NC Indexes	2 x NC Ix Seek (Predicate → Merge Join	1	.012	4		63	.02
8	Filter by Ordered NC Composite Index	NC Ix Seek (Seek Predicate w/ 2 prefixes)	1	.003	2		56	.02
9	Filter by Unordered NC Composite Index	NC Ix Scan	118	.209	173	NC by missing key, include C Key	72	1.64
10	Filter by Expression	NC Ix Scan	9	.209	173		111	.08

FIGURE 64-4

The clustered index scan sequentially reads all the rows from the clustered index.

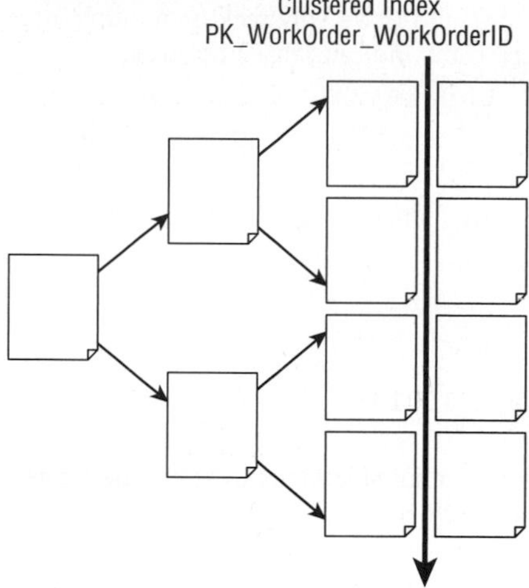

The Query Optimizer offers two clues that there's only one row that meets the `WHERE` clause criteria: statistics and the fact that `WorkOrderID` is the primary key constraint so it must be unique. `WorkOrderID` is also the clustered index key, so the Query Optimizer knows there's a great index available to locate a single row. The clustered index seek operation navigates the clustered index b-tree and quickly locates the desired row, as illustrated in Figure 64-5.

FIGURE 64-5

A clustered index seek navigates the b-tree index and locates the row in a snap.

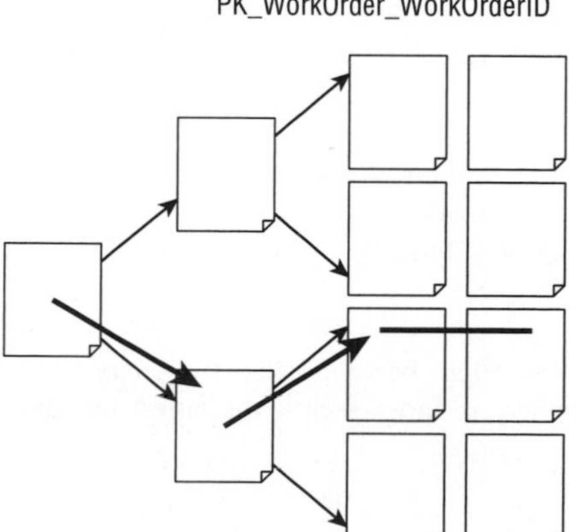

Conventional wisdom holds that this is the fastest possible query path, and it is snappy when returning a single row; however, from a rows-returned-per-millisecond perspective, it's one of the slowest query paths.

A common myth is that seeks can only return single rows and that's why seeking multiple rows would be very slow compared to scans. As the next two query paths indicate, that's not true.

Query Path 3: Range Seek Query

The third query path selects a narrow range of consecutive values using a `between` operator in the `WHERE` clause:

```
SELECT *
  FROM Production.WorkOrder
  WHERE WorkOrderID between 10000 and 10010;
```

The Query Optimizer must first determine whether there's a suitable index to select the range. In this case it's the same key column in the clustered index as in Query path 2.

A range seek query has an interesting query execution plan. The seek predicate (listed in the index seek properties), which defines how the query is navigating the b-tree, has both a start and an end, as shown in Figure 64-6. This means the operation is seeking the first row and then quickly scanning and returning every row to the end of the range, as illustrated in Figure 64-7.

To further investigate the range seek query path, this next query pushes the range to the limit by selecting every row in the table. Both queries are tested just to prove that `between` is logically the same as >= with <=:

```
SELECT *
  FROM Production.WorkOrder
  WHERE WorkOrderID >= 1 and WorkOrderID <= 72591;

SELECT *
  FROM Production.WorkOrder
  WHERE WorkOrderID between 1 and 72591;
```

At first blush it would seem that this query should generate the same query execution plan as the first query path (`select * from table`), but, just like the narrow range query, the `between` operator needs a consecutive range of rows, which causes the Query Optimizer to select index seek to return ordered rows.

Keep in mind that there's no guarantee that another row might be added after the query plan is generated and before it's executed. Therefore, for range queries, an index seek is the fastest possible way to ensure that only the correct rows are selected.

FIGURE 64-6

The clustered index seek's seek predicate has a start and an end indicating the range of rows searched for using the b-tree index.

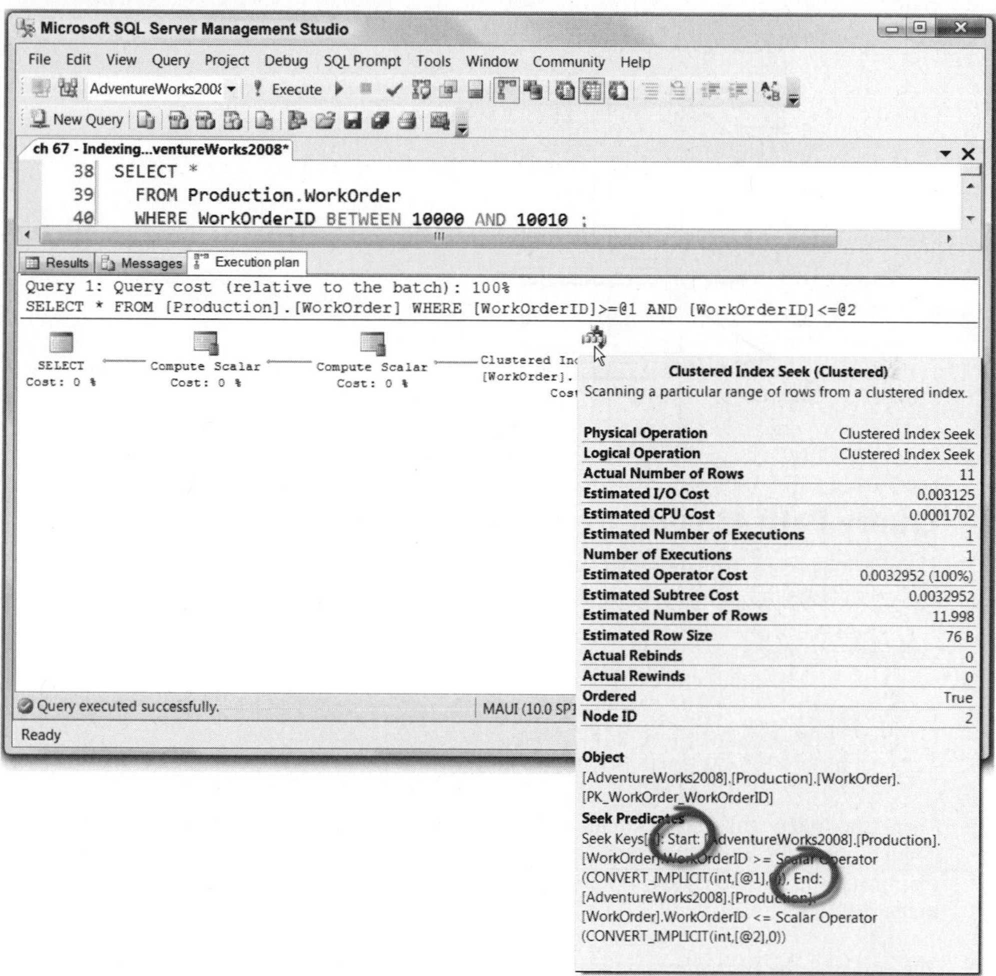

Index seeks and index scans both perform well when returning large sets of data. The minor difference between the two query's durations listed in the performance chart (refer to Table 64-1) is more likely due to variance in my computer's performance. There were some iterations of the index seek that performed faster than some iterations of the index scan.

FIGURE 64-7

An index seek operation has the option of seeking to find the first row, and then sequentially scanning on a block of data.

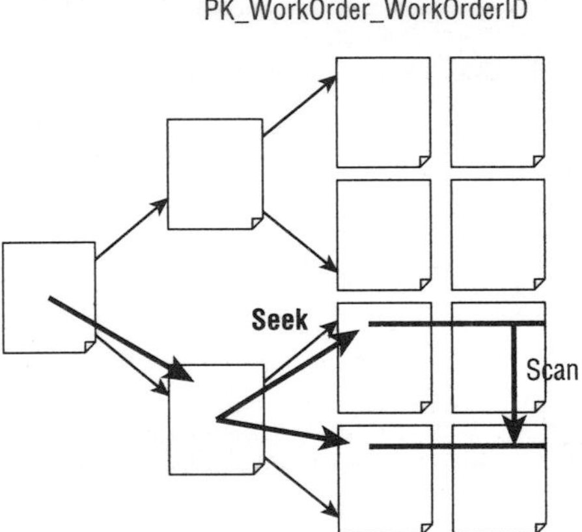

Query Path 4: Filter by non-key column

The previous query paths were simple to solve because the filter column matched the clustered index key column and all the data was available from one index; but what if that isn't the case?

Consider this query:

```
SELECT *
  FROM Production.WorkOrder
  WHERE StartDate = '2003-06-25';
```

There's no index with a key column of `StartDate`. This means that the Query Optimizer can't choose a fast b-tree index and must resort to scanning the entire table and then manually searching for rows that match the `WHERE` clause. Without an index, this query path is 23 times slower than the clustered index seek query path.

The cost isn't the filter operation alone (which is only 7 percent of the total query cost). The real cost is having to scan in every row and pass 72,592 rows to the filter operation, as shown in the query execution plan in Figure 64-8.

Note that this query execution plan suggests a missing index. Management Studio will even generate the code to create the missing index using the context menu, not that I'd suggest using that as an indexing strategy. (Too often the missing index is not the best index, and it often wants to build a non-clustered index that includes every column.)

FIGURE 64-8

Query path 4 (filter by non-key column) passes every row from an index scan to a filter operation to manually select the rows.

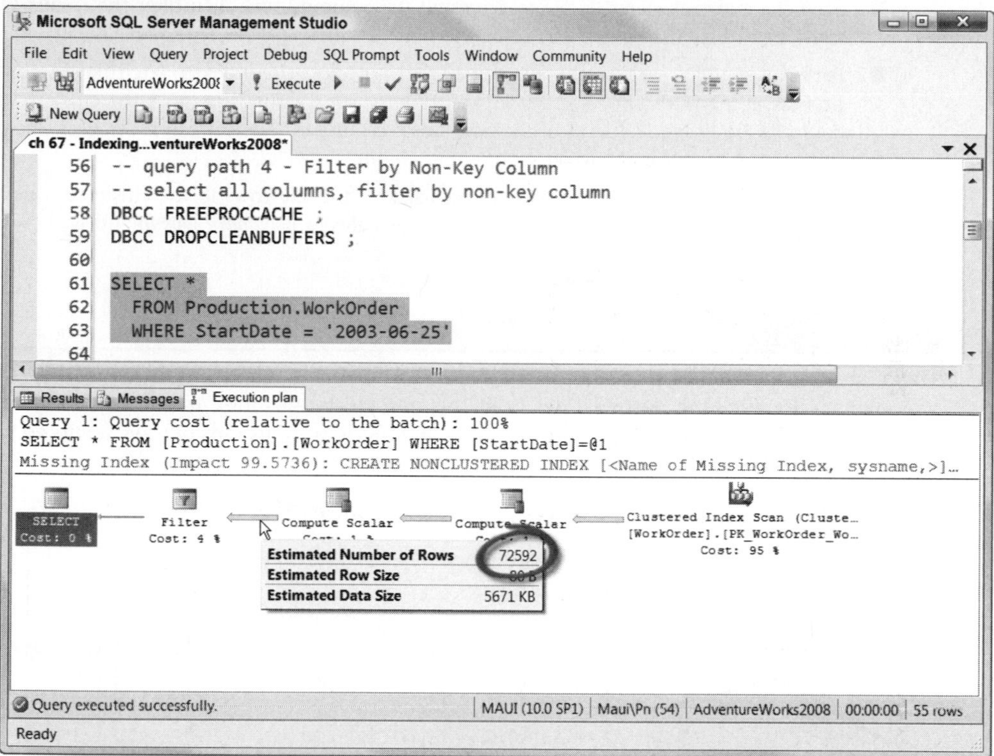

Query Path 5: Bookmark Lookup

This bookmark lookup query path is a two-edged sword. For infrequent queries, it's the perfect query path, but for the handful of queries that consume the majority of the server's CPU, this query path will kill performance.

To demonstrate a bookmark lookup query path, the following query filters by ProductID while returning all the base table's columns:

```
SELECT *
  FROM Production.WorkOrder
  WHERE ProductID = 757;
```

To rephrase the query in pseudo-code, *find the rows for Product 757 and give me all the columns for those rows.*

There is an index on the `ProductID` column, so the Query Optimizer has two possible options:

- Scan the entire clustered index to access all the columns, and then filter the results to find the right rows. Essentially, this would be the same as query path 4.
- Perform an index seek on the `IX_Workload_ProductID` index to fetch the 11 rows. In the process, it learns the `WorkOrderID` values for those 11 rows (because the clustered index key columns are in the leaf level of the non-clustered index). Then it can index seek those 11 rows from the clustered index to fetch the other columns.

  This jump, from the non-clustered index used to find the rows to the clustered index to complete the columns needed for the query, is called a *bookmark lookup* and is shown in Figure 64-9.

FIGURE 64-9

The non-clustered index is missing a column. To solve the query, SQL Server has to perform a bookmark lookup (the dashed line) from the non-clustered index to the clustered index. This illustration shows a single row. In reality it's often hundreds or thousands of rows scattered throughout the clustered index.

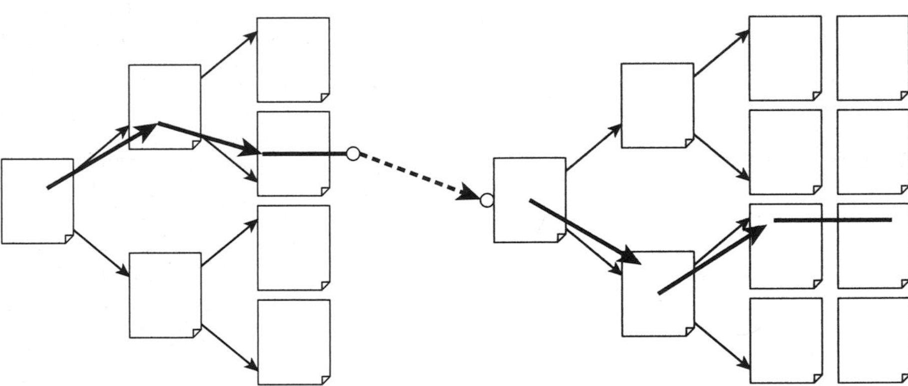

The real cost of the bookmark lookup is that the rows are typically scattered throughout the clustered index. Locating the 11 rows in the non-clustered index was a single page hit, but those 11 rows might be on 11 different pages in the clustered index. With a larger number of selected rows the problem intensifies. Selecting 1,000 rows with a bookmark lookup might mean reading 3–4 pages from the non-clustered index and then reading more than a thousand pages from the clustered index b-tree and leaf level. Eventually, SQL Server will decide that the bookmark lookup is more expensive than just scanning the clustered index.

In the Zen mindset of indexing, the best query path is one that can return all the data by navigating a single index. The bookmark lookup has to navigate two indexes, which is wasteful.

The query execution plan for a bookmark lookup shows the two indexes as data sources for a nested loop join (as shown in Figure 64-10). For each row returned by the seek of the non-clustered index, the nested loop join is requesting the matching rows from the clustered index by calling the key lookup.

If you think of SQL Server as having tables with indexes, this query execution plan appears confusing; but if you think of SQL Server as a collection of indexes with varying amounts of data, then fetching data from two indexes and joining the results makes sense.

FIGURE 64-10

The query execution plan shows the bookmark lookup as an index seek being joined with a key lookup.

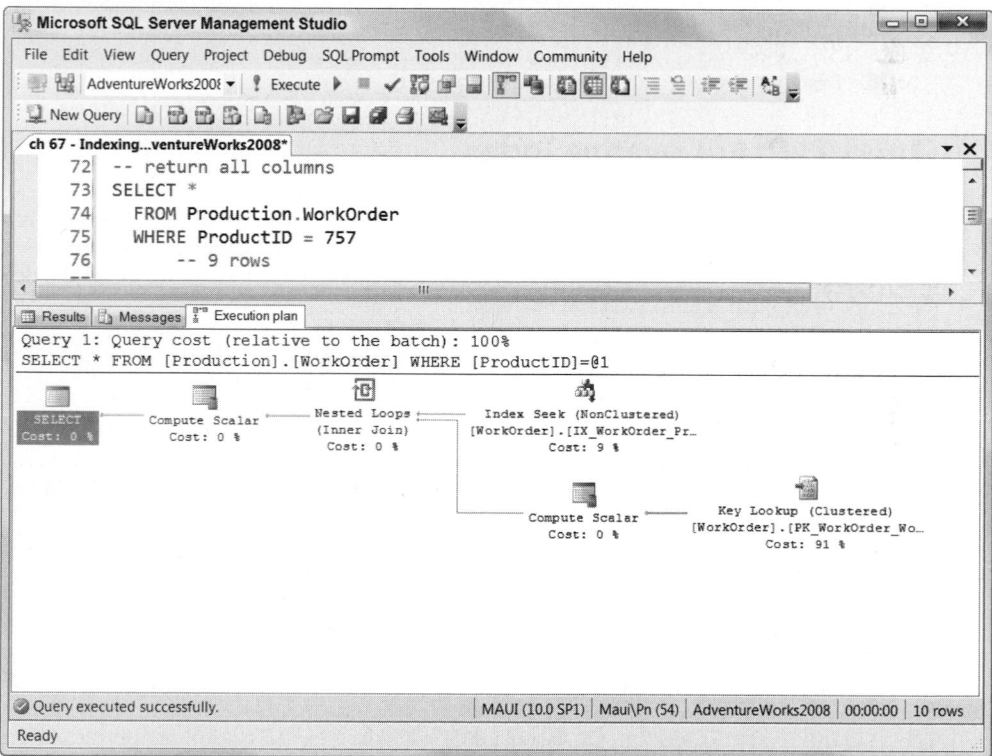

It's frequently said that `Select *` is wrong because it returns too many columns — the extra data is considered wasteful. I agree that `Select *` is wrong, but the real reason isn't the extra network traffic, it's the bookmark lookup that is almost always generated by a `Select *`.

The following query builds on the last bookmark lookup query and demonstrates more about the bookmark lookup problem; the difference is that this query requests only one column that's not available from the non-clustered index:

```
SELECT WorkOrderID, StartDate
  FROM Production.WorkOrder
  WHERE ProductID = 757;
```

Consider the performance difference (again, refer to Table 64-1) between this query path and the `select *` bookmark lookup query path. Their performance is nearly identical.

It doesn't take many columns to force a bookmark lookup; a single column missing from the non-clustered index means SQL Server must also look to the clustered index to solve the query.

There are only two ways to avoid the bookmark lookup problem:

- Filter by the clustered index key columns so the query can be satisfied using the clustered index (Query path 2 or 3).
- Design a covering index (the next query path).

Query Path 6: Covering Index

If a non-clustered index includes every column required by the query (and that means every column referenced by the query: `SELECT` columns, `JOIN ON` condition columns, `GROUP BY` columns, `WHERE` clause columns, and windowing columns), then SQL Server's Query Optimizer can choose to solve the query using only that non-clustered index. When this occurs the index is said to cover the needs of the query — in other words, it's a *covering index*.

An index by itself isn't a covering index, rather it becomes a covering index for a specific query when the Query Optimizer can solve the query using only the non-clustered index.

Query Path 5's second query selected the `StartDate` column. Because `StartDate` isn't part of the `IX_WorkOrder_ProductID` index, SQL Server was forced to use an evil bookmark lookup. To solve the problem, the following code adds `StartDate` to the `IX_WorkOrder_ProductID` index so the index can cover the query:

```
DROP INDEX Production.WorkOrder.IX_WorkOrder_ProductID

CREATE INDEX IX_WorkOrder_ProductID
  ON Production.WorkOrder (ProductID)
  INCLUDE (StartDate);
```

The `INCLUDE` option (added in SQL Server 2005) adds the `StartDate` column to the leaf level of the `IX_WorkOrder_ProductID` index. The Query Optimizer can now solve the queries with an index seek (as show in Figure 64-11):

```
SELECT WorkOrderID, StartDate
  FROM Production.WorkOrder
  WHERE ProductID = 757;  -- 9 rows
```

```
SELECT WorkOrderID, StartDate
  FROM Production.WorkOrder
  WHERE ProductID = 945; -- 1,105 rows
```

FIGURE 64-11

With the StartDate column included in the index, the queries are solved with an index seek — a perfect covering index.

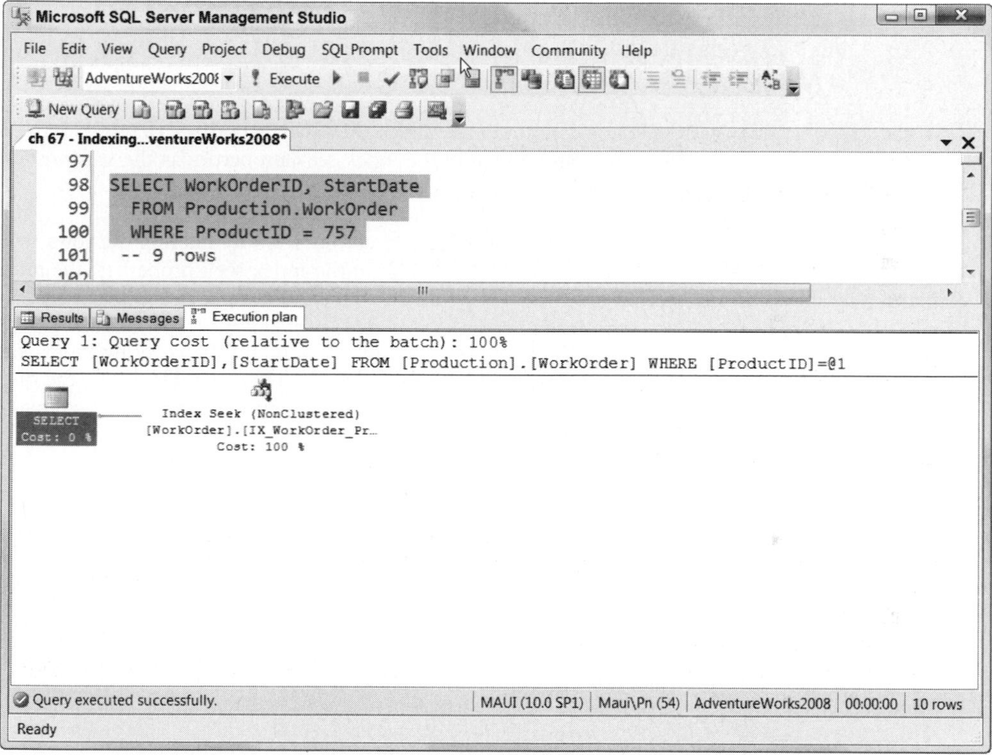

A nuance of the non-clustered index structure proves to be useful when designing covering indexes. This next query filters by the non-clustered index key and returns the clustered index key value:

```
SELECT WorkOrderID
  FROM Production.WorkOrder
  WHERE ProductID = 757;
```

The `Ix_WorkOrder_ProductID` non-clustered index has the `ProductID` column as the key column, so that data is available in the b-tree.

Even though the clustered index key, `WorkOrderID`, doesn't show up anywhere in the `Ix_WorkOrder_ProductID` dialogs in Management Studio, it's there. `WorkOrderID` is the clustered index key column, so every work order table's non-clustered index includes ProductID in the index.

The next query is a rare example of a covering index. Compared to the previous query path, this query adds the StartDate column in the WHERE clause. Conventional wisdom would say that this query requires an index scan because it filters by a non-key column (StartDate is an included column in the index and not a key column):

```
SELECT WorkOrderID
  FROM Production.WorkOrder
  WHERE ProductID = 945
    AND StartDate = '2002-01-04';
```

In this case the index seek operator uses the b-tree index (keyed by ProductID) to seek the rows matching ProductID = 945. This can be seen in the index seek properties as the *seek predicate* (as illustrated in Figure 64-12).

But then, the index seek operator continues to select the correct rows by filtering the rows by the included column (AND StartDate = '2002-01-04'). In the index seek properties, the *predicate* is filtering by the StartDate column.

The performance difference between the bookmark lookup solution and the covering index is dramatic. When comparing the Query Optimizer cost and the logical reads (refer to Table 64-1), the query paths that use a covering index are about 12 times more efficient. The duration appears less so due to my limited hardware.

Query Path 7: Filter by 2 x NC Indexes

A common indexing dilemma is how to index for multiple WHERE clause criteria. Is it better to create one composite index that includes both key columns? Or do two single-key column indexes perform better? Query Paths 7 through 9 evaluate the options.

The following code reconfigures the indexes: one index keyed on ProductID, and one with StartDate:

```
DROP INDEX Production.WorkOrder.IX_WorkOrder_ProductID;

CREATE INDEX IX_WorkOrder_ProductID
  ON Production.WorkOrder (ProductID);

CREATE INDEX IX_WorkOrder_StartDate
  ON Production.WorkOrder (StartDate);
```

With these indexes in place, this query filters by both key columns:

```
SELECT WorkOrderID, StartDate
  FROM Production.WorkOrder
  WHERE ProductID = 757
    AND StartDate = '2002-01-04';
```

FIGURE 64-12

The index seek operator can have a seek predicate, which uses the b-tree; and a predicate, which functions as a non-indexed filter.

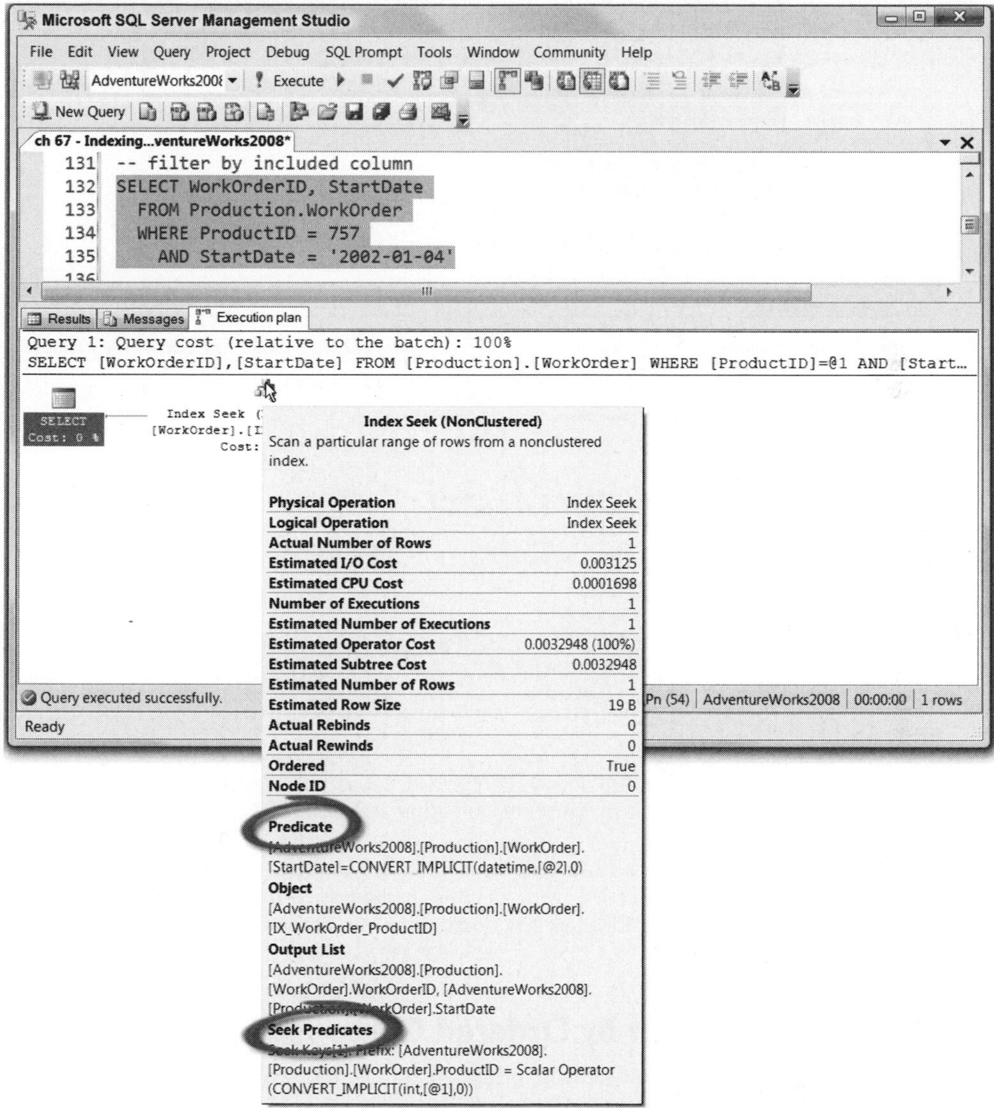

To use both indexes, SQL Server uses a merge join to request rows from each index seek and then correlate the data to return the rows that meet both criteria, as shown in Figure 64-13.

FIGURE 64-13

Filtering by two indexes adds a merge join into the mix.

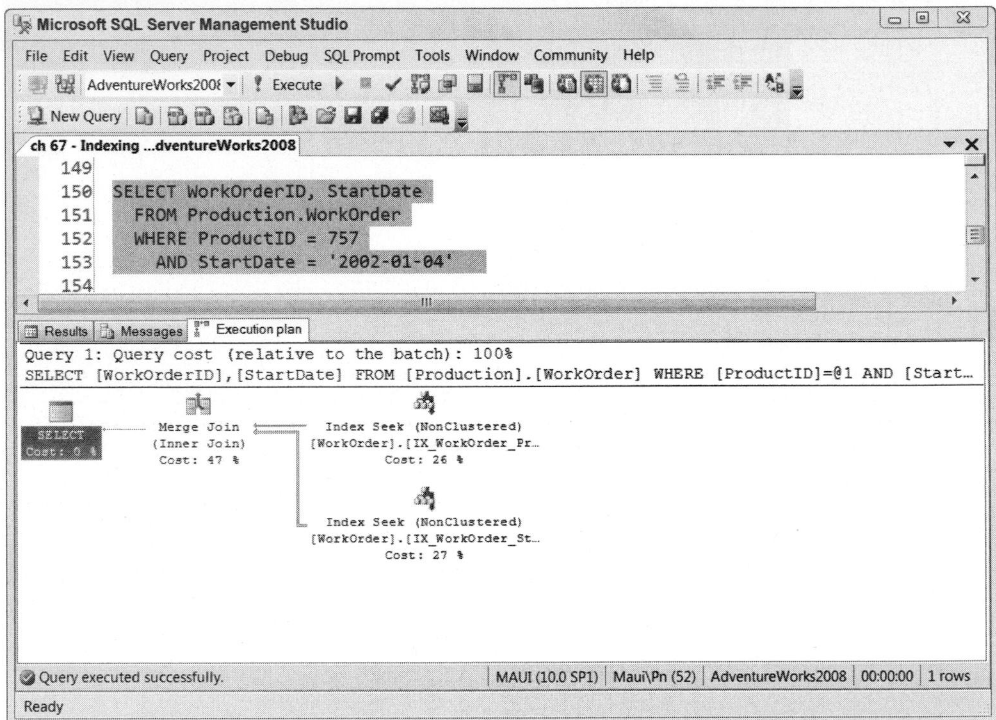

Examining the performance stat in Table 64-1, multiple indexes has a Query Optimizer cost of .12 and uses four logical reads.

For infrequent queries, Query Path 7, with its multiple indexes, is more than adequate, and much better than no index at all. However, for those few queries that run constantly, the next query path is a better solution for multiple criteria.

Query Path 8: Filter by Ordered Composite Index

For raw performance, the fastest solution to the "multiple `WHERE` clause criteria" problem is a single composite index, as demonstrated in Query Path 8.

Creating a composite index with `ProductID` and `StartDate` as key columns sets up the test:

```
DROP INDEX Production.WorkOrder.IX_WorkOrder_ProductID
DROP INDEX Production.WorkOrder.IX_WorkOrder_StartDate

CREATE INDEX IX_WorkOrder_ProductID
  ON Production.WorkOrder (ProductID, StartDate);
```

Rerunning the same query:

```
SELECT WorkOrderID, StartDate
  FROM Production.WorkOrder
  WHERE ProductID = 757
    AND StartDate = '2002-01-04';
```

The query execution plan, show in Figure 64-14, is a simple single-index seek operation and it performs wonderfully.

FIGURE 64-14

Filtering two criteria using a composite index performs like greased lighting.

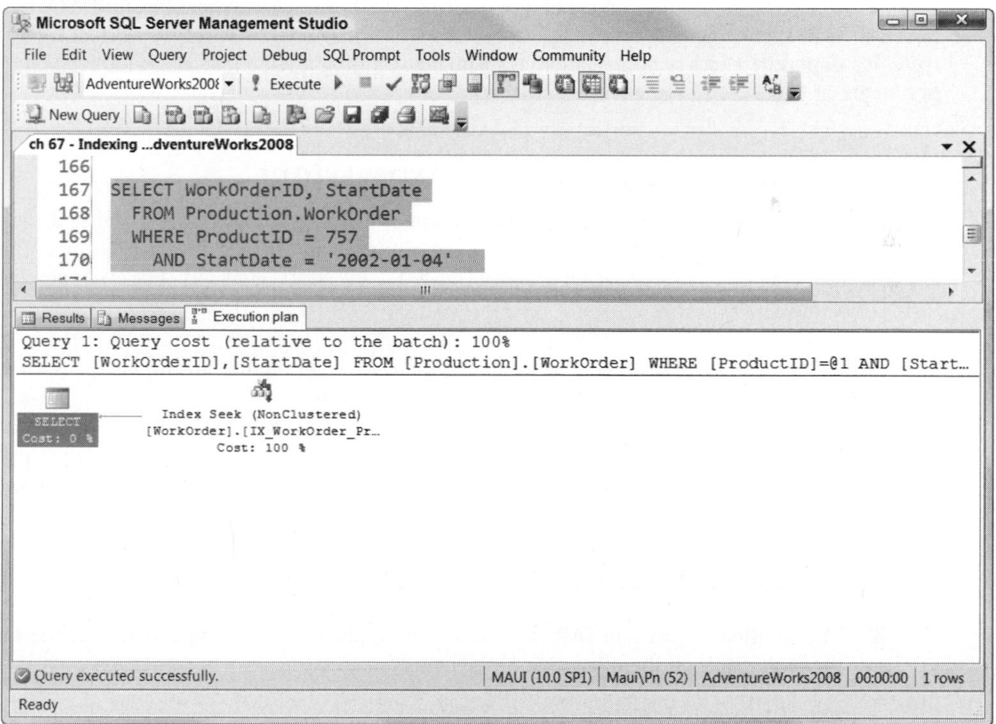

Query Path 9: Filter by Unordered Composite Index

One common indexing myth is that the order of the index key columns doesn't matter — that is, SQL Server can use an index so long as the column is anywhere in the index. Like most myths, it's a half truth.

Searching b-tree indexes requires the data for the leading columns in the order of the columns. Searching for col1, col2, and so on works great, but searching for the columns out of order — e.g., col2 without col1 — requires scanning all the leaf-level data.

Query Path 9 demonstrates the inefficiency of filtering by an unordered composite index. In the following example, `StartDate` is the second key in the composite index, so the data is there. Will the query use the index?

```
SELECT WorkOrderID
  FROM Production.WorkOrder
  WHERE StartDate = '2002-01-04';
```

The Query Optimizer uses the `IX_WorkOrder_ProductID` composite non-clustered index, as shown in Figure 64-15, because it's narrower than the clustered index, enabling more rows to fit on a page. But because the filter is by the second column, it can't use the b-tree of the index; instead, SQL Server is forced to scan every row and manually filter (in the scan operation) to select the correct rows. Essentially, it's doing the exact same operation as manually scanning a telephone book for everyone with a first name of Paul.

Query Path 10: Non-SARGable Expressions

SQL Server's Query Optimizer examines the conditions within the query's `WHERE` clause to determine which indexes are actually useful. If SQL Server can optimize the `WHERE` condition using an index, the condition is referred to as a *search argument,* or *SARG* for short. However, not every condition is a "SARGable" search argument.

The final query path walks through a series of anti-patterns — designing `WHERE` clauses with conditions that can't use b-tree indexes and that fall back to an index scan.

- Wrapping the column in an expression forces SQL Server to evaluate the data using the expression for every row before it can determine if the row passes the `WHERE` clause criteria:

  ```
  SELECT WorkOrderID
    FROM Production.WorkOrder
    WHERE ProductID + 2 = 759;
  ```

- The solution to this non-SARGable issue is to apply a little algebra and rewrite the query with the expression on the other side of the equals:

  ```
  SELECT WorkOrderID
    FROM Production.WorkOrder
    WHERE ProductID = 759 - 2;
  ```

FIGURE 64-15

Filtering by the second key column of an index forces an index scan.

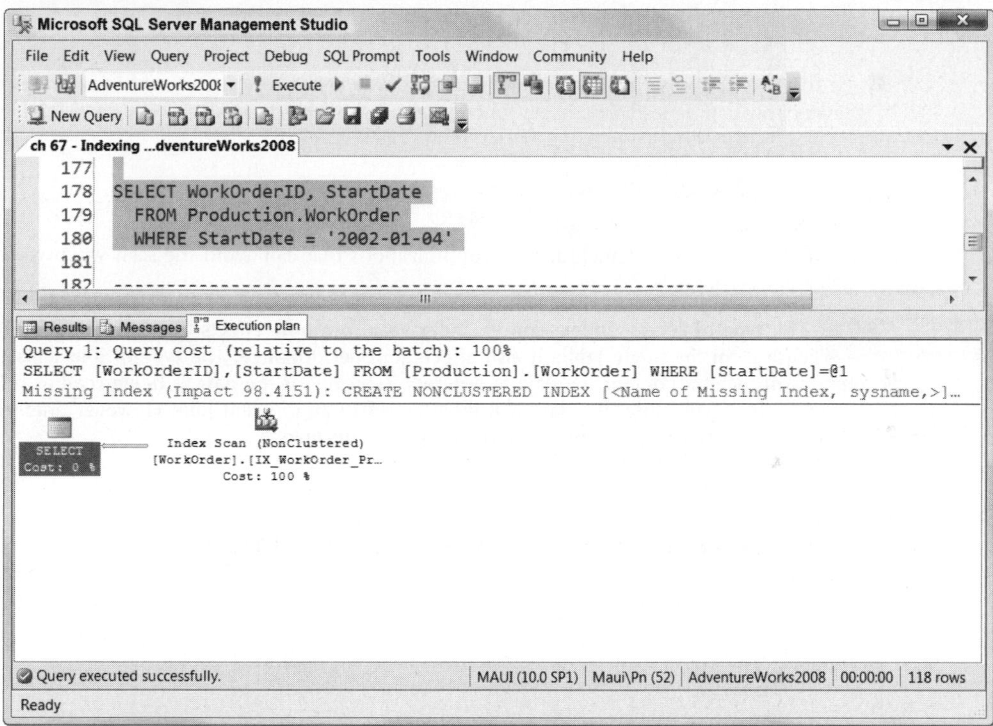

- Multiple conditions that are ANDed together are SARGs, but ORed conditions might not be useful for the b-tree:

```
SELECT WorkOrderID, StartDate
  FROM Production.WorkOrder
  WHERE ProductID = 757
    OR  StartDate = '2002-01-04';
```

- Negative search conditions (<>, !>, !<, Not Exists, Not In, Not Like) are not easily optimizable. It's easy to prove that a row exists, but to prove it doesn't exist requires examining every row:

```
SELECT WorkOrderID, StartDate
  FROM Production.WorkOrder
  WHERE ProductID NOT IN (400,800, 950);
```

However, sometimes, a few negative values can be SARGable, so it's worth testing. Often, it's the number of rows returned that forces a scan, not the negative condition.

- Conditions that begin with wildcards aren't SARGable. An index can quickly locate `WorkOrderID = 757`, but must scan every row to find any `WorkOrderID`'s ending in 7:

  ```
  SELECT WorkOrderID, StartDate
    FROM Production.WorkOrder
    WHERE WorkOrderID like '%7';
  ```

- If the `WHERE` clause includes a function, such as a string function, a table scan is required so every row can be tested with the function applied to the data:

  ```
  SELECT WorkOrderID, StartDate
    FROM Production.WorkOrder
    WHERE DateName(dw, StartDate) = 'Monday';
  ```

  SQL Server 2008 does include some optimizations that can avoid the scan when working with date conversions.

NOTE **The type of access (index scan vs. index seek) not only affects the performance of reading data from the single table, it also affects join performance. The type of join chosen by SQL Server depends on whether or not the data is ordered. Typically, if the data is being read as efficiently as possible from the single table, the data will then passed to an efficient join. However, inefficient table access is compounded by the subsequent inefficient join performance.**

A Comprehensive Indexing Strategy

An index strategy deals with the overall application, rather than fixing isolated problems to the detriment of the whole. In my consulting practice, I've found that the key to indexing is knowing when you need a bookmark lookup vs. when to design indexes to avoid bookmark lookups.

Identifying key queries

Analyzing a full query workload, which includes a couple days of operations (and nightly or weekend workloads) will likely reveal that although there may be a few hundred distinct queries, the majority of the CPU time is spent on the top handful of queries. I've tuned systems on which 95 percent of the CPU time was spent on only five queries. Those top queries demand flat-out performance, while the other queries might be able to afford a bookmark lookup.

To identify those top queries:

1. Create a Profiler trace to capture all queries or stored procedures:
   - Profiler event: `T-SQL SQL:Completed` and `Remote Procedure Call:Completed`
   - Profiler columns: `TextData`, `ApplicationName`, `CPU`, `Reads`, `Writes`, `Duration`, `SPID`, `EndTime`, `DatabaseName`, and `RowCounts`.

   It's terribly important to *not* filter the trace to capture only long-running queries (a common suggestion is to set the filter to capture only queries with a duration > 1 sec). Every query must be captured.
2. Test the trace definition using Profiler for a few moments, and then stop the trace. Be sure to filter out applications or databases not being analyzed.

3. In the trace properties, add a stop time to the trace definition (so it will capture a full day's and night's workload), and set up the trace to write to a file.
4. Generate a trace script using the File ➪ Export ➪ Script Trace Definition ➪ for SQL Server 2005–2008 menu command.
5. Check the script. You may need to edit it to supply a filename and path, and double-check the start and stop times. Execute the trace script on the production server.
6. Pull the trace file into Profiler and then save it to a table using the File ➪ Save As ➪ Trace Table menu command.
7. Profiler exports the `TextData` column as an `nText` data type, and that just won't do. The following code creates an `nVarChar(max)` column, which is much friendlier, with string functions:

```
alter table trace
  alter column textdata nvarchar(max);
```

8. Run the following aggregate query to summarize the query load. This query assumes that the trace data was saved to a table creatively named `trace`:

```
select substring(querytext, 1, CHARINDEX(' ',querytext, 6)),
    count(*) as 'count',
    sum(duration) as 'SumDuration',
    avg(duration) as 'AvgDuration',
    max(duration) as 'MaxDuration',
    cast(SUM(duration) as numeric(20,2))
      / (select sum(Duration) from trace) as 'Percentage',
    sum(rowcounts) as 'SumRows'
  from trace
  group by substring(querytext, 1, charindex(' ',querytext, 6))
  order by sum(Duration) desc;
```

The top queries will become obvious.

Table CRUD analysis

For each table involved with one of the top queries, it's important to collect together in one presentation these top queries and stored procedures that hit that table. Plot the access using a CRUD (create, retrieve, update, delete) matrix, as shown in Table 64-2. This example analyzes a fictitious `OrderDetail` table and examines only three fictitious procedures for simplicity.

The abbreviations are as follows: S for selected column, O for order by column, W for a column referenced in the `WHERE` clause, and G for the group by function.

The next step is to design the fewest number of indexes that satisfies the table's needs. This process first determines the clustered index and then creates indexes for every procedure and query that accesses the table, as shown in the following list and Table 64-3. The numbers in the chart indicate the ordinal position of the column in the index. An included column is listed as `I`.

TABLE 64-2

Table CRUD Usage Analysis

Column	pGetOrder	pCheckQuantity	pShipOrder
OrderDetailID	S		W
OrderID	W	W	
ProductID	S	S	
NonStockProduct	S		
Quantity	S	S	
UnitPrice	S		
ExtendedPrice	S		
ShipRequestDate	S	W	
ShipDate	S		U
ShipComment	S		U

TABLE 64-3

Table Strategic Index Plan

Column	CI	Ix2	Ix1
OrderDetailID			1
OrderID	1	(cl)	(cl)
ProductID		I	
NonStockProduct			
Quantity		I	
UnitPrice			
ExtendedPrice			
ShipRequestDate		1	
ShipDate			
ShipComment			

Because the `OrderDetail` table is often selected using the `OrderID` column, and this column can also be used to gather multiple rows into a single data page, `OrderID` is the best candidate for the clustered index (`CI`). The clustered index will consist of one column — the `OrderID` — so a `1` goes in the ordered row for the clustered index, indicating that it's the first column of the clustered index.

The clustered index satisfies the `pGetOrder` procedure.

The `pCheckQuantity` procedure verifies the quantity on hand prior to shipping. It filters the rows by `ShipRequestDate` and `OrderID`. Creating a non-clustered index with `ShipRequestDate` will index both the `ShipRequestDate` column and the `OrderID` column, as the clustered index is present in the leaf node of the non-clustered index. Because the procedure needs only four columns, adding `ProductID` and `Quantity` as included columns will enable `Ix1` to completely cover the needs of the query and significantly improve performance.

The third procedure can be satisfied by adding a non-clustered index, Ix2, with the `OrderDetailID` column.

Although this example had only three procedures, and may seem simplistic, if the plan focuses on the top queries, most production tables will, in fact, have only a handful of queries or stored procedures.

NOTE **The Database Engine Tuning Advisor is a SQL Server 2008 utility that can analyze a single query or a set of queries and recommend indexes and partitions to improve performance.**

My indexing strategy is based on knowing when to use a bookmark lookup vs. when to avoid a bookmark lookup. The Database Engine Tuning Advisor doesn't know whether a given query should or should not have a bookmark lookup so it can't follow the strategy. Therefore, I recommend that you avoid the Database Engine Tuning Advisor. If you understand how queries work, you don't need the Advisor anyway.

Selecting the clustered index

Selecting the clustered index is a critical piece of the performance puzzle, perhaps the most important piece of the physical schema. A clustered index can affect performance in several ways:

- When an index seek operation finds a row using a clustered index, the data is right there — no bookmark lookup. This makes the column used to select the row, probably the primary key, an ideal candidate for a clustered index.
- Clustered indexes gather rows with the same or similar values to the smallest possible number of data pages, thus reducing the number of data pages required to retrieve a set a rows. Clustered indexes are therefore excellent for columns that are often used to select a range of rows, such as secondary table foreign keys like `OrderDetail.OrderID`.
- Inserting data in the middle of a clustered index is always a bad idea. The page splits can cripple performance, so carefully consider the actual data usage for every clustered index.

NOTE **The MOC (Microsoft Official Curriculum) used to teach that the primary purpose of the clustered index was gathering together similar rows (the second bullet above). When I wrote the *SQL Server 2000 Bible*, I also believed that was the primary reason for a clustered index. I now believe that avoiding a bookmark lookup is a stronger case for designing a clustered index, and the second bullet only sometimes applies.**

Creating base indexes

Even before tuning, the locations of a few indexes are easy to determine. These base indexes are the first step in building a solid set of indexes. Here are a few steps to keep in mind when building these base indexes:

1. Create a clustered index for every table. For primary tables, cluster on the column most likely used to select the row — probably the primary key.

   For secondary tables that are most commonly retrieved by a set of related rows, create a clustered index for the most important foreign key to group those related rows together.
2. Create non-clustered indexes for the columns of every foreign key, except for the foreign key that was indexed in step 1. Use only the foreign key values as index keys. I've developed a script that will create a non-clustered index for every foreign key (download from `www.sqlserverbible.com`).
3. Create a single-column index for every column expected to be referenced in a `WHERE` clause, an `ORDER BY`, or a `GROUP BY`.

While this indexing plan is far from perfect, and it's definitely *not* a final indexing plan, it provides an initial compromise between no indexes and tuned indexes, and can serve as a baseline performance measurement to compare against future index tuning.

Additional tuning will likely involve creating composite indexes and removing unnecessary indexes.

Best Practice

When planning indexes, there's a subtle tension between serving the needs of select queries vs. update queries. While an index may improve query performance, there's a performance cost because when a row is inserted, updated, or deleted, the indexes must be updated as well. Nonetheless, some indexing is necessary for write operations. The update or delete operation must locate the row prior to performing the write operation, and useful indexes facilitate locating that row, thereby speeding up write operations.

Therefore, when planning indexes, be careful to include the fewest number of indexes to accomplish the job.

TIP **SQL Server exposes index usage statistics via dynamic management views. Specifically,** `sys.dm_db_index_operational_stats` **and** `sys.dm_index_usage_stats` **uncover information about how indexes are being used. In addition, there are four dynamic management views that reveal indexes that the Query Optimizer looked for but didn't find:** `sys.dm_missing_index_groups`, `sys.dm_missing_index_group_stats`, `sys.dm_missing_index_columns`, **and** `sys.dm_missing_index_details`.

Specialty Indexes

Beyond the standard clustered and non-clustered indexes, SQL Server offers two type of indexes I refer to as specialty indexes. *Filtered indexes*, new in SQL Server 2008, include less data, and *indexed views*, available since SQL Server 2000, build out custom sets of data. Both are considered high-end performance-tuning indexes.

Filtered indexes

Until SQL Server 2008, every non-clustered index indexed every key value and every row. Filtered indexes allow adding a WHERE clause to the CREATE INDEX statement. This option is only available for non-clustered indexes (how could a clustered index not include some rows?) A filtered index not only includes fewer rows at the leaf level, but also includes fewer values in the intermediate levels. It's this reduction in intermediate levels that causes the reads to be fewer for any index seek.

An example of employing a filtered index in AdventureWorks2008 is the ScrappedReasonID column in the Production.WorkOrder table. Fortunately for Adventure Works, they scrapped only 612 (.8%) parts over the life of the database. The existing IX_WorkOrder_ScrapReasonID includes every row. The ScrapReasonID foreign key in the Production.WorkOrder table allows nulls for work orders that were not scrapped. The index includes all the null values with pointers to the WorkOrder rows with NULL ScrapReasonIDs. The current index uses 109 pages.

The following script recreates the index with a WHERE clause that excludes all the NULL values:

```
DROP INDEX Production.WorkOrder.IX_WorkOrder_ScrapReasonID

CREATE INDEX IX_WorkOrder_ScrapReasonID
  ON Production.WorkOrder(ScrapReasonID)
  WHERE ScrapReasonID IS NOT NULL
```

The new index uses only two pages. Interestingly, the difference isn't noticeable between using the filtered or a non-filtered index when selecting all the work orders with a scrap reason that's not null. That's because there aren't enough intermediate levels to make a significant difference. For a much larger table, the difference would be worth testing, and most likely the filtered index would provide a benefit.

Filtered indexes, because of their compact size, not only reduce the disk usage but are easier to maintain.

Best Practice

When designing a covering index (see index kata #6) to solve a specific query — probably one that represents the top handful of CPU duration according to the indexing strategy — if the covering index works with a relatively small subset of data, and the overall table is a large table, consider filtering the covering index.

Another situation that might benefit from filtered indexes is building a unique index that includes multiple rows with null values. A normal unique index allows only a single row to include a null value in the key columns. However, building a unique index that excludes null in the WHERE clause creates a unique index that permits an unlimited number of null values.

In a sense, SQL Server has had filtered indexes since SQL Server 2000 with indexed view. There no reason why an indexed view couldn't have included a `WHERE` clause and included data from a filtered set of rows; but filtered indexes are certainly easier to create than indexed views, and they function as normal non-clustered indexes, which is an excellent segue into the next topic, indexed views.

Indexed views

For strictly OLTP operations (insert, update, delete, small selects), I firmly believe that a purely normalized design performs best. However, for reporting, analysis, and selecting large complex queries, a solution that denormalizes and pre-aggregates data is the answer.

When the denormalized and pre-aggregated data needs to be real-time, an excellent alternative to base tables includes indexed views — a custom designed clustered index that is updated when the base tables are modified and can serve as a materialized view to denormalize and pre-aggregate data.

Instead of building tables to duplicate data and denormalize a join, a view can be created that can join the two original tables and include the two source primary keys and all the columns required to select the data. Building a clustered index on the view then physically materializes every column in the select column list of the view. The resulting indexed view is in effect a custom multiple-table covering index.

CROSS-REF **Although indexed views build on normal views, they should not be confused. A normal view is nothing more than a saved `SELECT` statement — no data is physically stored, as explained in Chapter 14, "Projecting Data Through Views." Indexed views actually store the data on disk. An indexed view is Microsoft's terminology for a materialized view.**

Numerous restrictions exist on indexed views, including the following:

- The ANSI null and quoted identifier must be enabled when the view is created, and when any connection attempts to modify any data in the base tables.
- The index must be a unique clustered index; therefore, the view must produce a unique set of rows without using `DISTINCT`.
- The tables in the view must be tables (not nested views) in the local database and must be referenced by means of the two-part name (`schema.table`).
- The view must be created with the option `WITH SCHEMABINDING`.

NOTE **Because indexed views require schema binding, they can't be mixed with table partition switching or rolling partitions. To switch a table partition, you must drop the indexed view, perform the switch, and then rebuild the indexed view.**

As an example of an indexed view being used to denormalize a large query, the following view selects data from the `Product`, `WorkOrder`, and `ScrapReason` tables to produce a view of scrapped products:

```
USE OBXKites;

SET ANSI_Nulls ON;
SET ANSI_Padding ON;
SET ANSI_Warnings ON;
```

```
SET ArithAbort ON;
SET Concat_Null_Yields_Null ON;
SET Quoted_Identifier ON;
SET Numeric_RoundAbort OFF;

GO

CREATE VIEW vScrap
WITH SCHEMABINDING
AS
  SELECT WorkOrderID, P.NAME AS Product,
    P.ProductNumber,
     S.NAME AS ScrappedReason, ScrappedQty
    FROM Production.WorkOrder W
      JOIN Production.Product P
        ON P.ProductID = W.ProductID
      JOIN Production.ScrapReason S
        ON W.ScrapReasonID = S.ScrapReasonID
```

With the view in place, the index can now be created on the view, resulting in an indexed view:

```
CREATE UNIQUE CLUSTERED INDEX ivScrap
  ON vScrap
   (WorkOrderID, Product, ProductNumber,
      ScrappedReason, ScrappedQty) ;
```

Indexed views can also be listed and created in Management Studio under the Views ➪ Indexes node.

To drop an indexed view, the DROP statement must refer to the view instead a table:

```
DROP INDEX ivscrap ON dbo.vScrap
```

Dropping the view will automatically drop the indexed view created from the view.

An advanced application of indexed views leverages the fact that an indexed view is a clustered index. It's possible to build non-clustered indexes on the indexed view's clustered index to create some pretty wild covering indexes.

Indexed Views and Queries

When SQL Server's Query Optimizer develops the execution plan for a query, it includes the indexed view's clustered index as one of the indexes it can use for the query, even if the query doesn't explicitly reference the view. This only happens with Enterprise Edition, which is only a very last resort if a suitable plan is not found. Often a suitable plan is found and the indexed view is never considered. More often than not you have to force the indexed view using the WITH (NOEXPAND) option.

This means that the indexed view's clustered index can serve as a covering index to speed queries. When the Query Optimizer selects the indexed view's clustered index, the query execution plan indicates it with an index scan. Both of the following queries use the indexed view:

```
SELECT WorkOrderID, P.NAME AS Product,
```

```
    P.ProductNumber,
     S.NAME AS ScrappedReason, ScrappedQty
    FROM Production.WorkOrder W
      JOIN Production.Product P
        ON P.ProductID = W.ProductID
      JOIN Production.ScrapReason S
        ON W.ScrapReasonID = S.ScrapReasonID

SELECT * FROM vScrap
```

While indexed views are essentially the same as they were in SQL Server 2000, the Query Optimizer can now use indexed views with more types of queries.

Best Practice

Just adding indexed views without fully analyzing how the queries use them may hurt performance more than it helps. As with any index, SQL Server must work to keep them correct with inserts, updates, or deletes. All index updates must take place within the transaction. If updating a single row in a base table must update hundreds of rows in the indexed view, or updating a row in the base table must force SQL Server to recalculate an aggregate query in an indexed view that draws from thousands of rows, there will be a performance cost. However, if real-time data is required, this still may be the best solution.

Updating indexed views

As with any denormalized copy of the data, the difficulty is keeping the data current. Indexed views have the same issue. As data in the underlying base tables is updated, the indexed view must be kept in sync. This process is completely transparent to the user and is more of a performance consideration than a programmatic issue.

Summary

The third layer of Smart Database Design, (in Chapter 2, "Data Architecture"), is indexing. To intelligently create indexes you need to understand not only the technologies — the Query Optimizer, index pages, and indexing options — but also both your schema and your queries inside out. Indexing is essentially a bridge from the query to the data. While indexes can't fully overcome a poor schema or poorly written queries, a database without good indexing is sure to perform poorly.

To highlight the key ideas about indexing:

- There's no such thing as a table in SQL Server, only indexes — some with more data than others at the leaf level.
- Clustered indexes store all the data of the base table, logically organized by the index keys.

- Non-clustered indexes are subsets of data with their own keys and optionally included columns.
- A non-clustered index that completely solves the query without having to jump over to the clustered index (using a bookmark lookup) is referred to as a covering index.
- Bookmark lookups are the crux of indexing. For the queries that consume the most CPU duration, avoid them with clustered indexes or covering indexes. For the other queries, bookmark lookups are the preferable method to reduce the number of indexes.
- Filtered non-clustered indexes include only a small subset of rows, are faster to maintain, and can make perfect covering indexes.
- Indexed views are custom indexes that actually materialize data and can pull from multiple base tables or pre-aggregate data.

The next chapter continues the theme of understanding SQL Server internals and pragmatically using that knowledge to leverage performance from the system.

Chapter 65

Query Plan Reuse

IN THIS CHAPTER

Compiling SQL

Working with the query Plan Cache

CSC 101 taught that programming languages are either compiled or interpreted. SQL is neither.

A SQL query is declarative, meaning that the SQL statement describes the question but does not specifically code how to best solve the problem.

The best solution has to consider the available indexes and the mix of the data compared to the query parameters, and the hardware constraints. The indexes, data mix, and parameters are bound to fluctuate, so generating a query execution plan (also called compiling the SQL query) when the query is created would be foolish.

On the other hand, the process of generating a query execution plan can be expensive, sometimes more expensive than performing the query, so it doesn't make sense to generate the query execution plan every time the query is executed.

As a compromise, SQL Server generates a query execution plan the first time the query is executed and then stores that query execution plan in memory. The next time the same query is executed, SQL Server uses the stored query execution plan instead of generating a new plan.

Query Compiling

When SQL Server compiles a query, it's stored in the Plan Cache, a portion of memory reserved for query plans, where it stays for a while, ready to be used again. SQL Server compiles both SQL queries and stored procedures into query execution plans.

The Query Optimizer

The technology that compiles a SQL query is commonly called the *Query Optimizer* — the magic that makes SQL Server scream. But in fact, there are several components and stages to compiling a query.

First, the *parser* dissects the T-SQL code, ensures that it is valid, and generates a parse tree, a logical representation of the query broken down into a sequence.

Second, the *Algebrizer* attempts to simplify any arguments, and resolves any object names and aliases, identifies any data type conversions required, and binds any aggregate functions (e.g., `group by`, `count(*)`). The result is a *query processor tree* — a corrected version of the parse tree ready for the Query Optimizer.

Delayed name resolution means that SQL Server will allow a stored procedure to be created even if the objects it references don't yet exist. The idea is that the object might be created by the time the code is executed. Objects aren't physically checked until the Algebrizer checks for them.

Best Practice

Delayed name resolution is one more reason why a simple parse check is insufficient when developing SQL code. Unit testing against sample data that exercises every use case, including dynamically created objects, is the only way to fully test any SQL code.

The Query Optimizer will generate several possible query execution plans to solve the query and evaluate them according to the estimated cost. The estimated cost isn't a concrete figure that correlates to actual execution time but a relative cost in order to choose the best operation. The cost per operation also considers the amount of data, available indexes, and the data statistics to determine the best operation to read the data. The Query Optimizer must also determine the best order in which to read the data sources and the best join operators to combine the data.

The job of the Query Optimizer is to guess the amount of data that will be required by and produced by each operation and then plan the best operations for that amount of data.

Once the query execution plan is generated, SQL Server will store it in the Plan Cache and inform the query processor that the plan is ready to be executed.

CROSS-REF **Chapter 63, "Interpreting Query Execution Plans," has more details on reading and viewing the plans and interpreting the query operations within the plans.**

Viewing the Plan Cache

There are dynamic management views (DMVs) that expose the Plan Cache. You can look at the query Plan Cache to verify that the query is in fact cached. The procedure cache can be large. While it's not recommended in a production environment, clearing the cache will make checking for a specific query easier:

```
DBCC FREEPROCCACHE
```

To examine the procedure cache, use the `sys.dm_exec_cached_plans` DMV, which returns the plan handle, which can be passed to `sys.dm_exec_sql_text(plan_handle)` and `sys.dm_exec_query_plan(plan_handle)` to view the original SQL code and the query execution plan, as shown in Figure 65-1.

FIGURE 65-1

Viewing the Plan Cache is easy with a few DMVs. The SQL source is right there, and the query execution plan can be viewed by clicking on the XML in the `query_plan` column.

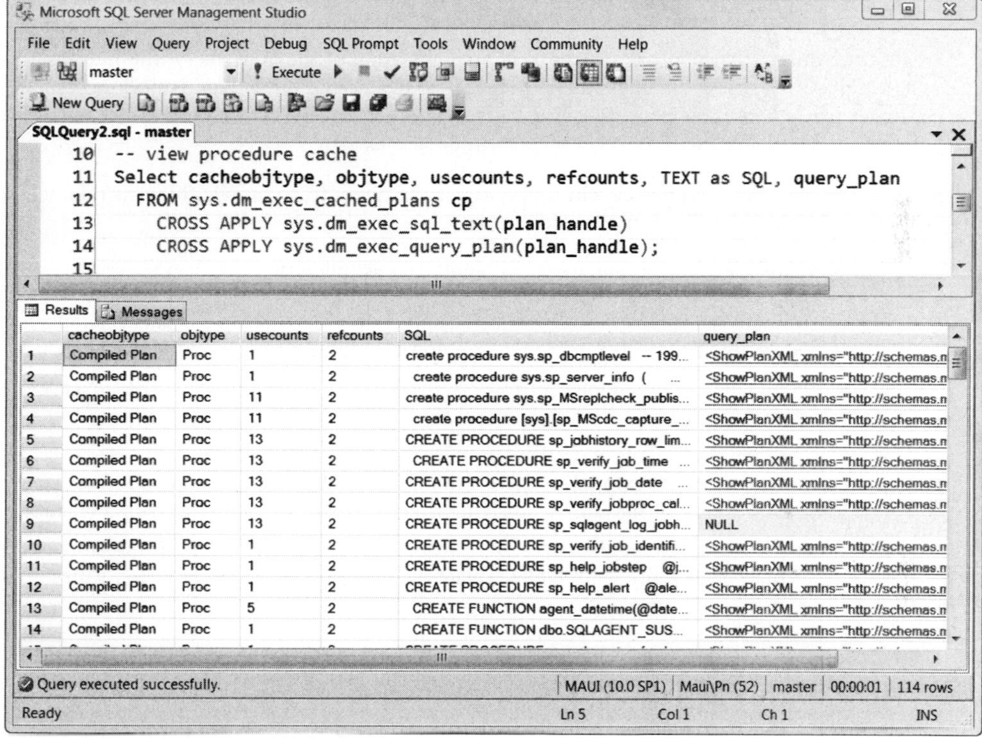

Plan lifetime

All the query plans in memory stay in the Plan Cache until SQL Server experiences "memory pressure" — softie speak for when the Plan Cache becomes about 75% full. Then SQL Server begins to age-out query plans based on how much time has elapsed since they were last executed and how complex they are. A complex query plan with a high query cost will stay in memory much longer than a simple query that was easy to compile.

Query plan execution

When the query processor needs to execute a query, it first checks to see whether the query can reuse a query execution plan already in the Plan Cache. It's much faster to find and reuse a query execution plan than to generate a new plan. In order to use a plan from the Plan Cache, the query must use qualified object names (`schema.object`).

If the query qualifies, then the query processor will search the Plan Cache for an identical SQL statement (minus parameters). If a match is found, then an *execution context* is used to hold the data and variables for that instance of the query execution plan. This enables multiple users to execute the same query execution plan simultaneously.

Query Recompiles

Because the query execution plan is based on a combination of the SQL query, the indexes, and the data, a number of changes might cause SQL Server to decide the query plan is no longer valid, or no longer the best possible plan. SQL Server then marks the query execution plan as unusable and generates a new query execution plan the next time it is executed.

Single-statement query recompiles will simply cause the query to recompile the next time it is executed, but stored procedures will recompile mid-stream.

The most common causes of an automatic recompile are as follows:

- Out of date statistics can cause poor plans; therefore, if statistics for data referenced by the query are updated, SQL Server will stop and recompile based on the newer statistics.
- A large change in the number of rows in the base table referenced by the query, even rows inserted by a trigger
- Mixing DML statements and DDL statements in a stored procedure will cause a recompile. For example, creating a temp table, then running an update, then creating another temp table will force a recompile of the stored procedure following the second temp table's creation.
- A table, view, or index referenced by the query is altered. Therefore, if the stored procedure batch creates any temp tables, create them all at the beginning of the stored procedure or batch.

Query recompilation was a greater problem with SQL Server 2000 and earlier, which would recompile the entire batch or stored procedure. Fortunately, beginning with SQL Server 2005, individual statements can be recompiled, rather than whole batches. This means that recompiles are less costly, even if they occur more frequently.

The `Sp_recompile object` system stored procedure will force a recompile of any query plan stored that references that object (be it a stored procedure, a table, or a view) the next time the query is executed.

Recompiles may be monitored using SQL Profiler using the `SQL:StmtRecompile` event. Ignore the `SP:Recompile` event — it offers incomplete information.

A stored procedure can be created with the recompile options, which forces SQL Server to recompile it every time it's executed.

`DBCC FreeProcCache` clears out the procedure cache, so any queries that are reissued must be compiled again.

NOTE **This chapter has presented the query execution plan default behavior, which is perfect for nearly all situations. I plan on updating this chapter with additional information on controlling the query execution plan for those rare exceptions when the Query Optimizer needs help. Watch** `www.sqlserverbible.com` **or subscribe to the SQL Server Bible eNewsletter to download the updated chapter.**

Summary

The heart of SQL Server is the Query Optimizer, the technology that analyzes the query, the indexes, and the data to compile the best query execution plan for that query for that moment. The best way to optimize queries is to provide the Query Optimizer with the best indexing. From there, SQL Server will handle the rest.

The next chapter moves from single-user queries to multi-user contention and scalability and deals with transactions, isolation, and the ACID test. For some, the next topic is considered one of the harder topics in the database world, but I think it's foundational to developing SQL Server databases. My goal is to carefully walk you through the different scenarios, so that you too will fully grok transactions.

Chapter 66

Managing Transactions, Locking, and Blocking

IN THIS CHAPTER

- Transactional integrity theory
- The transaction log and why it's important
- SQL Server locks and performance
- Handling and preventing deadlocks
- Implementing optimistic and pessimistic locking

Any route is fast at 4:00 A.M. with no traffic and all green lights. The trick is designing a route that works during rush hour. Concurrency is about contention. Contention is "a struggling together in opposition" in which two users are trying to get hold of the same thing, and it can apply to system resources or data. Managing resource contention is about writing code that uses as few resources as possible to enable as many users as possible to execute code at the same time.

With database contention, more than one user is trying to access the same resource within the database. For any complex system, as the number of users increases, performance decreases as each user competes for the same resources and the contention increases. This chapter focuses on the contention for data. Most people focus on system resource contention, not on contention for database resources. Chapter 2 defined six database architecture design goals: usability, integrity, scalability, extensibility, availability, and security. Scalability is all about concurrency — multiple users simultaneously attempting to retrieve and modify data.

Here's why: To ensure transactional integrity, SQL Server (by default) uses locks to protect transactions from affecting other transactions. Specifically, transactions that are reading data will lock that data, which prevents, or blocks, other transactions from writing the same data. Similarly, a transaction that's writing will prevent other transactions from writing or reading the same data.

SQL Server maintains locks for the duration of a transaction, so as more transactions occur simultaneously, especially long transactions, more resources are locked, which results in more transactions being blocked. This can create a locking and blocking domino effect that bogs down the whole system.

To reduce contention you need to reduce the amount of resources being locked and reduce the length of time those are locks are held. Relational database design (as described in Chapter 3) states that a well-defined schema, set-based queries, and a sound indexing strategy all work together to reduce the aggregate workload of the database and thus reduce transaction duration. Reducing the aggregate workload of the database addresses both of the requirements listed previously and thus increases concurrency (the number of users who can share a resource) and sets up the database for the more advanced high-scalability features such as table partitioning.

That's why concurrency is relational database design's fourth level, following schema, set-based queries, and indexing. I can't stress enough that if you have a transaction locking and blocking problem, the solution isn't found at the concurrency level, but in the deeper layer of Smart Database Design — that is, in modifying either the schema, query, or indexing.

This chapter has four goals:

- Detail how transactions affect other transactions
- Explain the database theory behind transactions
- Illustrate how SQL Server maintains transactional integrity
- Explain how to get the best performance from a high-concurrency system

What's New with Transactions?

SQL Server has always had transactional integrity, but Microsoft has improved it over the versions. SQL Server 7 saw row locking, which eliminated the "insert last page hot spot" issue and dramatically improved scalability. SQL Server 2000 improved how deadlocks are detected and rolled back. SQL Server 2005 introduced an entirely rewritten lock manager, which simplified lock escalation and improved performance. Beyond the ANSI standard isolation levels, SQL Server 2005 added *snapshot isolation,* which makes a copy of the data being updated in its own physical space, completely isolated from any other transactions, which enables readers to not block writers. Try-catch error handling, introduced in SQL Server 2005, can catch a 1205 deadlock error.

SQL Server 2008 continues the performance advances with the new capability to restrict lock escalation on a table, which forces row locks and can improve scalability.

Transactions and locking in SQL Server can be complicated, so this chapter explains the foundation of ACID transactions (described in the next section) and SQL Server's default behavior first, followed by potential problems and variations.

If you want the very short version of a long story, I believe that the `READ COMMITTED` transaction isolation level (SQL Server's default) is the best practice for *most* OLTP databases. The exceptions are explained in the section "Transaction Isolation Levels."

The ACID Properties

Transactions are defined by the ACID properties. ACID is an acronym for four interdependent properties: *atomicity*, *consistency*, *isolation*, and *durability*. Much of the architecture of any modern relational database is founded on these properties. Understanding the ACID properties of a transaction is a prerequisite for understanding SQL Server.

Atomicity

A transaction must be *atomic*, meaning all or nothing. At the end of the transaction, either all of the transaction is successful, or all of the transaction fails. If a partial transaction is written to disk, the atomic property is violated. The ability to commit or roll back transactions is required for atomicity.

Consistency

A transaction must preserve database *consistency*, which means that the database must begin the transaction in a state of consistency and return to a state of consistency once the transaction is complete. For the purposes of ACID, consistency means that every row and value must agree with the reality being modeling, and every constraint must be enforced. For example, if the order rows were written to disk but the order detail rows are not written, the consistency between the `Order` and `OrderDetail` tables, or more specifically, the `OrderDetail` table's `OrderID` foreign key constraint, would have been violated, and the database would be in an inconsistent state. This is not allowed.

Consistency allows the database to be in an inconsistent state during the transaction. The key is that the database is consistent at the completion of the transaction. Like atomicity, the database must be able to commit the whole transaction or roll back the whole transaction if modifications resulted in the database being inconsistent.

Isolation

Each transaction must be *isolated,* or separated, from the effects of other transactions. Regardless of what any other transaction is doing, a transaction must be able to continue with the exact same data sets it started with. Isolation is the fence between two transactions. A proof of isolation is the ability to replay a serialized set of transactions on the original set of data and always receive the same result.

For example, assume Joe is updating 100 rows. While Joe's transaction is under way, Sue tries to read one of the rows Joe is working on. If Sue's read takes place, then Joe's transaction is affecting Sue's transaction, and their two transactions are not fully isolated from each another. This property is less critical in a read-only database or a database with only a few users.

SQL Server enforces isolation with locks and row versioning.

Durability

The *durability* of a transaction refers to its permanence regardless of system failure. Once a transaction is committed, it stays committed in the state it was committed. Another transaction that does not modify the data from the first transaction should not affect the data from the first transaction. In addition, the Database Engine must be designed so that even if the data drive melts, the database can be restored up to the last transaction that was committed a split second before the hard drive died.

SQL Server ensures durability with the write-ahead transaction log.

Programming Transactions

A *transaction* is a sequence of tasks that together constitute a logical unit of work. All the tasks must complete or fail as a single unit. For example, in the case of an inventory movement transaction that reduces the inventory count from one bin and increases the inventory count in another bin, both updates to the bins must be written to the disk, or neither should be written to the disk. If this didn't happen, then your total inventory count would be wrong.

In SQL Server, every DML operation (`SELECT`, `INSERT`, `UPDATE`, `DELETE`, `MERGE`) is a transaction, whether or not it has been executed within a `BEGIN TRANSACTION`. For example, an `INSERT` command that inserts 25 rows is a logical unit of work. Each and every one of the 25 rows must be inserted. An `UPDATE` to even a single row operates within a transaction so that the row in the clustered index (or heap) and the row's data in every non-clustered index are all updated. Even `SELECT` commands are transactions; a `SELECT` that should return 1,000 rows must return all 1,000 rows. Any partially completed transaction would violate transactional integrity.

In ancient Hebrew poetry (a passion of mine), an *inclusio* is a line or phrase that begins a poem and is repeated at the close of the poem, providing a theme or wrapper for the poem. In the same way, you can think of a transaction as a wrapper around a unit of work.

Logical transactions

If the logical unit of work involves multiple operations, some code is needed to define the perimeter of a transaction: two markers — one at the *beginning* of the transaction, and the other at its completion, at which time the transaction is *committed* to disk. If the code detects an error, then the entire transaction can be *rolled back*, or undone. The following three commands appear simple, but a volume of sophistication lies behind them:

- **BEGIN** TRANSACTION
- **COMMIT** TRANSACTION
- **ROLLBACK** TRANSACTION

(The text in bold is the required portion of the command.)

A transaction, once begun, should be either committed to disk or rolled back. A transaction left hanging will eventually cause an error — either a real error or a logical data error, as data is never committed.

Putting T-SQL code to the inventory movement example, if Michael Ray, Production Supervisor at Adventure Works, moves 100 bicycle wheel spokes from miscellaneous storage to the subassembly area, the next code example records the move in the database.

The two updates that constitute the logical unit of work (the update to `LocationID = 6` and the update to `LocationID = 50`) are wrapped inside a `BEGIN TRANSACTION` and a `COMMIT TRANSACTION`. The transaction is then wrapped in a `TRY` block for error handling:

```
BEGIN TRY;
  BEGIN TRANSACTION;
    UPDATE Production.ProductInventory
      SET Quantity -= 100
```

```
      WHERE ProductID = 527
        AND LocationID = 6  -- misc storage
        AND Shelf = 'B'
        AND Bin = 4;
    UPDATE Production.ProductInventory
      SET Quantity += 100
      WHERE ProductID = 527
        AND LocationID = 50 -- subassembly area
        AND Shelf = 'F'
        AND Bin = 11;
  COMMIT TRANSACTION;
END TRY
BEGIN CATCH;
  ROLLBACK TRANSACTION;
  RAISERROR('Inventory Transaction Error', 16, 1);
  RETURN;
END CATCH;
```

CROSS-REF **If you're not familiar with** `Try-Catch`**, the improved error-handling code introduced in SQL Server 2005, it's covered in Chapter 23, "T-SQL Error Handling."**

If all goes as expected, both updates are executed, the transaction is committed, and the `TRY` block completes execution. However, if either `UPDATE` operation fails, execution immediately transfers down to the `CATCH` block, the `COMMIT` is never executed, and the `CATCH` block's `ROLLBACK TRANSACTION` will undo any work that was done within the transaction.

NOTE **SQL Server 2008 Books Online and some other sources refer to transactions using** `BEGIN TRANSACTION` **as *explicit transactions*. I prefer to call these *logical transactions* instead because the name makes more sense to me and helps avoid any confusion with *implicit transactions* (covered soon).**

When coding transactions, the minimum required syntax is only `BEGIN TRAN`, `COMMIT`, `ROLLBACK`, so you'll often see these commands abbreviated as such in production code.

Xact_State()

Every user connection is in one of three possible transaction states, which may be queried using the `Xact_State()` function, introduced in SQL Server 2005:

- 1: Active, healthy transaction
- 0: No transaction
- -1: Uncommittable transaction. It's possible to begin a transaction, experience an error, and not be able to commit that transaction (consider the consistency part of ACID). In prior versions of SQL server these were called *doomed transactions*.

Typically, the error-handling catch block will test the `Xact_State()` function to determine whether the transaction can be committed or must be rolled back. The next `CATCH` block checks `Xact_State()` and determines whether it can `COMMIT` or `ROLLBACK` the transaction:

```
BEGIN CATCH
  IF Xact_State() = 1 -- there's an active committable transaction
    COMMIT TRAN;
  IF Xact_State() = -1 -- there's an uncommittable transaction
    BEGIN
      ROLLBACK TRANSACTION;
      RAISERROR('Inventory Transaction Error', 16, 1);
    END
END CATCH;
```

CAUTION **Use `Xact_State()` for single DML transactions, but avoid it if the transaction includes multiple DML commands that must be committed or rolled back as an atomic unit. If one of the DML commands failed and the transaction were still committable, committing the logical transaction would write a partial transaction. Horrors!**

Although the `XactState()` function is normally used within the error-handling catch block, it's not restricted to the catch block and may be called at any time to determine whether the code is in a transaction.

Xact_Abort

A common SQL Server myth is that an error condition will roll back the transaction. In fact, unless there's try-catch error handling in place, many error conditions only abort the statement. The batch continues, and the transaction is completed even though an error occurred.

Turning on `Xact_Abort` solves some of these problems by doing two things to the error. First, it promotes statement-level errors into batch-level errors, solving the single-statement error issue. Second, `Xact_Abort` automatically rolls back any pending transaction. Therefore, `Xact_Abort` is a very good thing and should often be set in code. `Xact_Abort` also triggers the try-catch code and sends execution into the catch block.

CROSS-REF **Heads up: There's significant overlap between transaction error handling in this chapter and T-SQL error handling in general in Chapter 23, "T-SQL Error Handling."**

Nested transactions

Multiple transactions can be nested, although they are rarely nested within a single stored procedure. Typically, nested transactions occur because a stored procedure with a logical transaction calls another stored procedure that also has a logical transaction. These nested transactions behave as one large transaction: Changes made in one transaction can be read in a nested transaction — they do not behave as isolated transactions, where actions of the nested transaction can be committed independently of a parent transaction.

When transactions are nested, a `COMMIT` only marks the current nested transaction level as complete. It does not commit anything to disk, but a rollback undoes all pending transactions. At first this sounds inconsistent, but it actually makes sense, because an error within a nested transaction is also an error in the outer transaction. The `@@TranCount` indicates the current nesting level. A commit when the trancount > 1 has no effect except to reduce trancount by 1. Only when trancount is 1 are the actions within all levels of the nested transaction committed to disk. To prove this behavior, the next code sample examines the @@TranCount global variable, which returns the current transaction nesting level:

```
SELECT @@TRANCOUNT; -- 0
BEGIN TRAN;
  SELECT @@TRANCOUNT; -- 1
  BEGIN TRAN;
    SELECT @@TRANCOUNT; -- 2
    BEGIN TRAN;
      SELECT @@TRANCOUNT; -- 3
      ROLLBACK; - undoes all nested transactions
 SELECT @@TRANCOUNT; -- 0
```

Results:

```
0
1
2
3
0
```

If the code might have nested transactions, then it's a good idea to examine @@TranCount (or XactState()) because attempting to COMMIT or ROLLBACK a transaction if no pending transactions exist will raise a 3902 or 3903 error with a 16 severity code to the client.

Implicit transactions

While SQL Server requires an explicit BEGIN TRANSACTION to initiate a logical transaction, this behavior can be modified so that every DML statement starts a logical transaction if one is not already started (so you don't end up with numerous nested transactions). It's as if there were a hidden BEGIN TRANSACTION before every DML statement. This means that once a SQL DML command is issued, a COMMIT or ROLLBACK is required.

To demonstrate implicit transactions, the following code alone will not commit the UPDATE:

```
USE AdventureWorks2008;
SET Implicit_Transactions ON;

UPDATE HumanResources.Department
  SET Name = 'Department of Redundant Departments'
  WHERE DepartmentID = 2;
```

Viewing the @@TranCount global variable does indeed show that there's one pending transaction level awaiting a COMMIT or rollback:

```
SELECT @@TRANCOUNT;
```

Result:

```
1
```

Adding a COMMIT TRANSACTION to the end of the batch commits the transaction, and the update is finalized:

```
COMMIT TRANSACTION;
```

Multiple DML commands or batches will occur within a single logical transaction, so it doesn't create a bunch of nested transactions — what a mess that would be.

NOTE **Turning off implicit transactions, as shown here, only affects future batches. It does not commit any pending transactions:**

```
SET Implicit_Transactions OFF;
```

NOTE Implicit_transactions ON **is the default behavior for Oracle, and adjusting to explicit transactions takes getting used to for Oracle developers moving up to SQL Server. On the other hand, setting your buddy's connection (to the development server) to** Implicit_transactions ON **might make for a good April Fool's Day joke!**

Save points

It is also possible to declare a *save point* within the sequence of tasks and then roll back to that save point only. However, I believe that this mixes programmatic flow of control (IF, ELSE, WHILE) with transaction handling. If an error makes it necessary to redo a task within the transaction, it's cleaner to handle the error with standard error handling than to jury-rig the transaction handling.

Default Locking and Blocking Behavior

When two transactions both need the same resource, SQL Server uses locks to provide transactional integrity between the two transactions. Locking and blocking isn't necessarily a bad thing — in fact, I think it's a good thing. It ensures transactional integrity.

There are different types of locks, including *shared* (reading), *update* (getting ready to write), *exclusive* (writing) and more. Some of these locks work well together (e.g., two people can have shared locks on a resource); however, once someone has an exclusive lock on a resource, no one can get a shared lock on that resource — this is blocking. The different types of locks, and how compatible they are with each other, are documented in BOL.

SQL Server's default transaction isolation is *read committed*, meaning that SQL Server ensures that only committed data is read. While a writer is updating a row, and the data is still yet uncommitted, SQL Server makes other transactions that want to read that data wait until the data is committed.

To demonstrate SQL Server's default locking and blocking behavior, the following code walks through two transactions accessing the same row. Transaction 1 will update the row, while transaction 2 will attempt to select the row. The best way to see these two transactions is with two Query Editor windows, as shown in Figure 66-1.

FIGURE 66-1

Opening multiple Query Editor windows and sending the second tab into a New Vertical Tab Group (using the tab's context menu) is the best way to experiment with transactions.

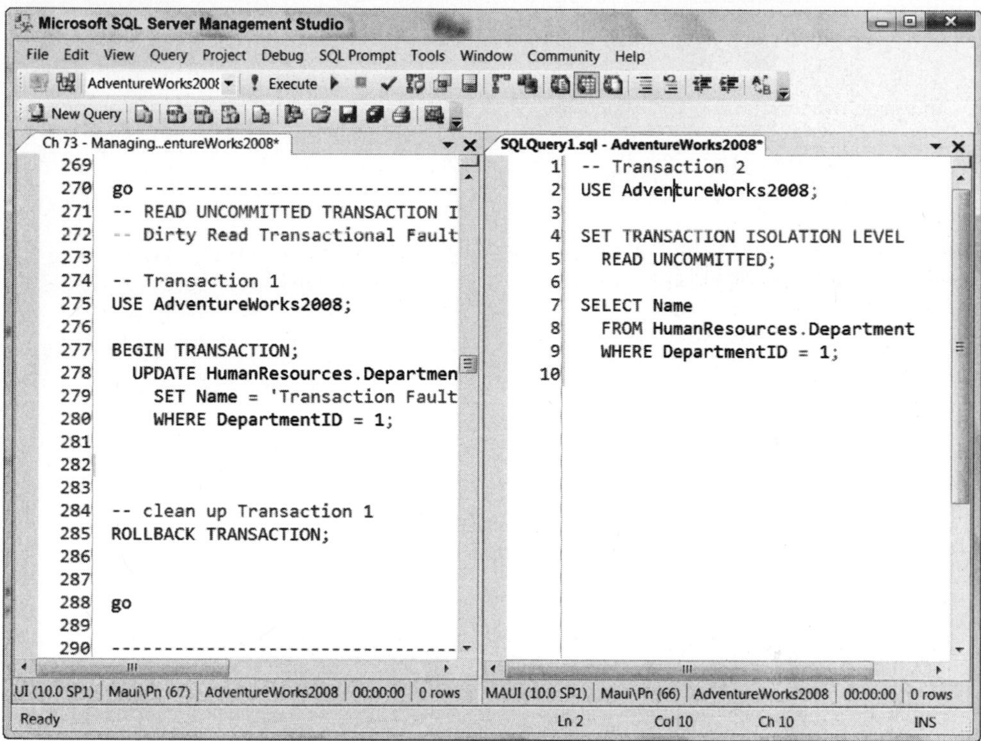

Transaction 1 opens a logical transaction and updates the `Department` table:

```
-- Transaction 1
USE AdventureWorks2008;

BEGIN TRANSACTION;
  UPDATE HumanResources.Department
    SET Name = 'New Name'
    WHERE DepartmentID = 1;
```

Transaction 1 (on my machine it's on connection, or SPID, 54) now has an exclusive (X) write lock on the row being updated by locking the key of the record I'm updating. The locks can be viewed using the DMV `sys.dm_tran_locks` (the full query and more details about locks appear later in this chapter).

Result:

```
Spid Object                     Type  Mode  Status
---- -------------------------- ----- ----- ----------
54   HumanResources.Department  PAGE  IX    GRANT
54   HumanResources.Department  KEY    X    GRANT
```

Transaction 2 ensures that the transaction isolation level is set to the default and then attempts to read the same row transaction 1 is updating:

```
-- Transaction 2
USE AdventureWorks2008;

SET TRANSACTION ISOLATION LEVEL
  READ COMMITTED;

SELECT Name
  FROM HumanResources.Department
  WHERE DepartmentID = 1;
```

There is no result yet for transaction 2. It's waiting for transaction 1 to complete — blocked by transaction 1's exclusive lock.

Requerying `sys.dm_tran_locks` reveals that the second transaction (SPID 51) has an *intent to share (IS)* read lock and is waiting for a *share (S)* read lock.

Result:

```
Spid Object                     Type  Mode  Status
---- -------------------------- ----- ----- ----------
51   HumanResources.Department  PAGE  IS    GRANT
51   HumanResources.Department  PAGE  S     WAIT
54   HumanResources.Department  KEY   X     GRANT
54   HumanResources.Department  PAGE  IX    GRANT
54   HumanResources.Department  PAGE  IX    GRANT
54   HumanResources.Department  KEY   X     GRANT
54   HumanResources.Department  KEY   X     GRANT
```

While transaction 1 is holding its exclusive lock, transaction 2 has to wait. In other words, transaction 1 is blocking transaction 2.

Now, transaction 1 commits the transaction and releases the exclusive lock:

```
-- Transaction 1
COMMIT TRANSACTION
```

Immediately, transaction 1 completes and releases its locks. Transaction 2 springs to life and performs the select, reading the committed change.

Result:

```
Name
----------------------
New Name
```

The point of transaction isolation level read committed is to avoid reading uncommitted data. What if the update doesn't change the data? If transaction 1 updates the data from "John" to "John," what's the harm of reading "John"?

SQL Server handles this situation by not respecting an exclusive lock if the page hasn't been changed, i.e., if the page isn't flagged as dirty. This means that sometimes (because there's probably more data on the page than just the data in question) SQL Server can avoid locking and blocking if the data isn't actually being changed. Cool, no?

You can prove this behavior by reexecuting the previous locking and blocking sample code with the same update value.

Monitoring Locking and Blocking

Without the ability to see the lock, the various types of locks and their durations may seem like pure theory. Fortunately, SQL Server is a relatively open environment, and it's easy to inspect the current locks from several possible points of view.

Viewing blocking with Management Studio reports

With Management Studio, transaction information for a server or database may be seen using the Standard Reports, available from the server or database context menus, which pull data from the dynamic management views. The transaction-related reports include All Transactions, All Blocking Transactions (shown in Figure 66-2), Top Transactions by Age, Top Transactions by Blocked Transaction Count, Top Transactions by Lock Count, Resource Locking by Object, and User Statistics.

Viewing blocking with Activity Monitor

The Activity Monitor (see Figure 66-3) is completely rewritten for SQL Server 2008 and includes process information. It's available both on the toolbar and in the Object Explorer's server context menu.

For more information on the Activity Monitor, refer to Chapter 6, "Using Management Studio."

Using Profiler

You can also use SQL Server Profiler to watch blocked processes using the Error and Warnings: Blocked Process Report event.

FIGURE 66-2

Management Studio's All Blocking Transactions Report is a quick way to view key transaction locking and blocking information.

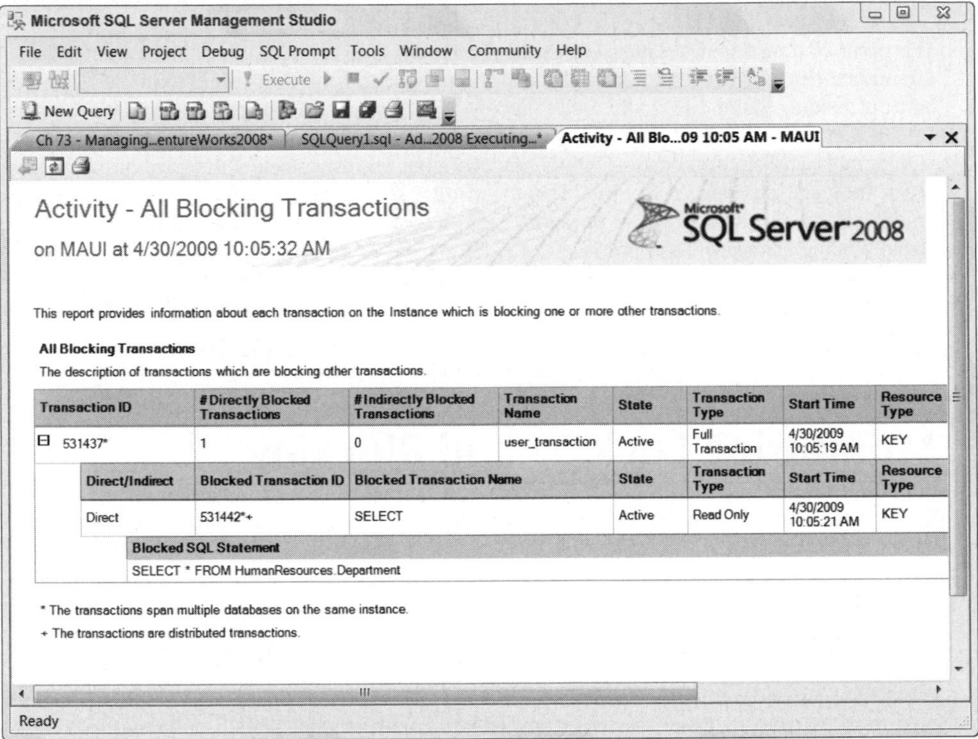

Best Practice

Of the many possible methods to monitor locking and blocking, Activity Monitor and Management Studio's Summary page provide the best overall view to determine whether locking and blocking is a problem. To home in on the specific locking and blocking issues, Profiler provides the actual code for the transactions involved.

The catch to using Profiler is that by default the server is not configured to fire the blocked process event. To enable it, you have to configure the `blocked process threshold` setting. Because that's an advanced option, you must enable "Show advanced options" first. The following snippet sets the blocking duration to one second:

```
sp_configure 'show advanced options', 1;
```

FIGURE 66-3

Activity Monitor displays information about the current locks and any blocking going on. In this instance, SPID 53 is blocking SPID 54.

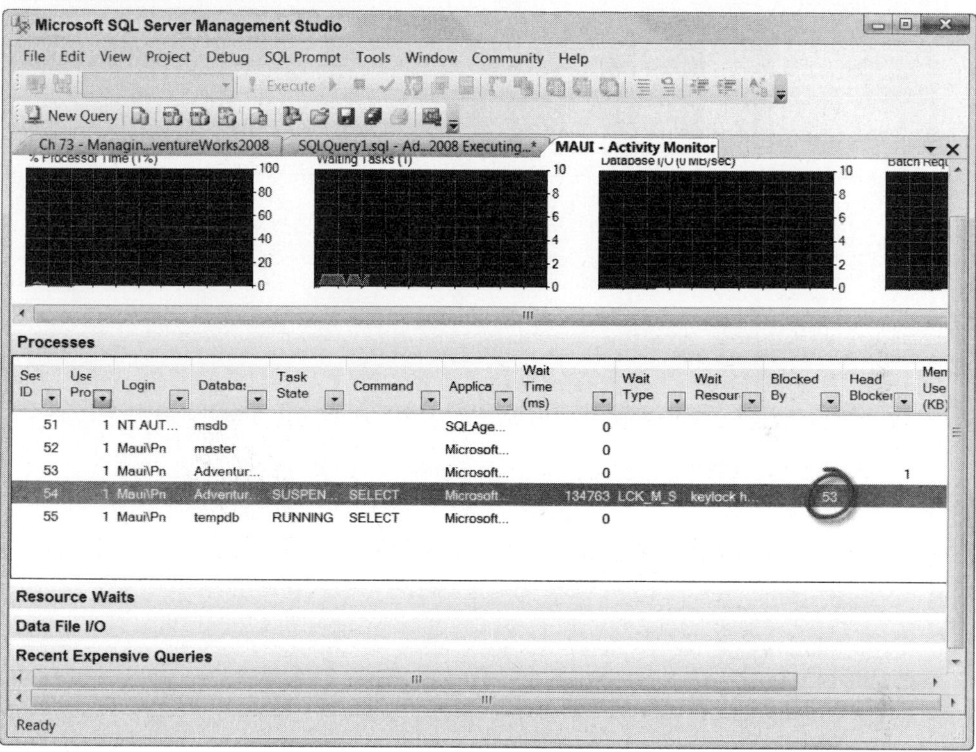

```
GO
RECONFIGURE;
GO
sp_configure 'blocked process threshold', 1;
GO
RECONFIGURE;
```

This means that the server will check every second for blocked statements, and for any statement that has been blocked for longer than one second, the blocked process report event will fire. Depending on when the last check was done, a statement may be blocked for more than the threshold value before it is reported. This can be seen by setting the threshold to a large value, say 10 seconds.

The result is a complete XML-formatted disclosure of the blocked and blocking process (see Figure 66-4). Saving this trace to a file and analyzing it in total is an excellent locking and blocking debugging technique.

FIGURE 66-4

SQL Server Profiler can monitor and display the blocked and blocking code in XML.

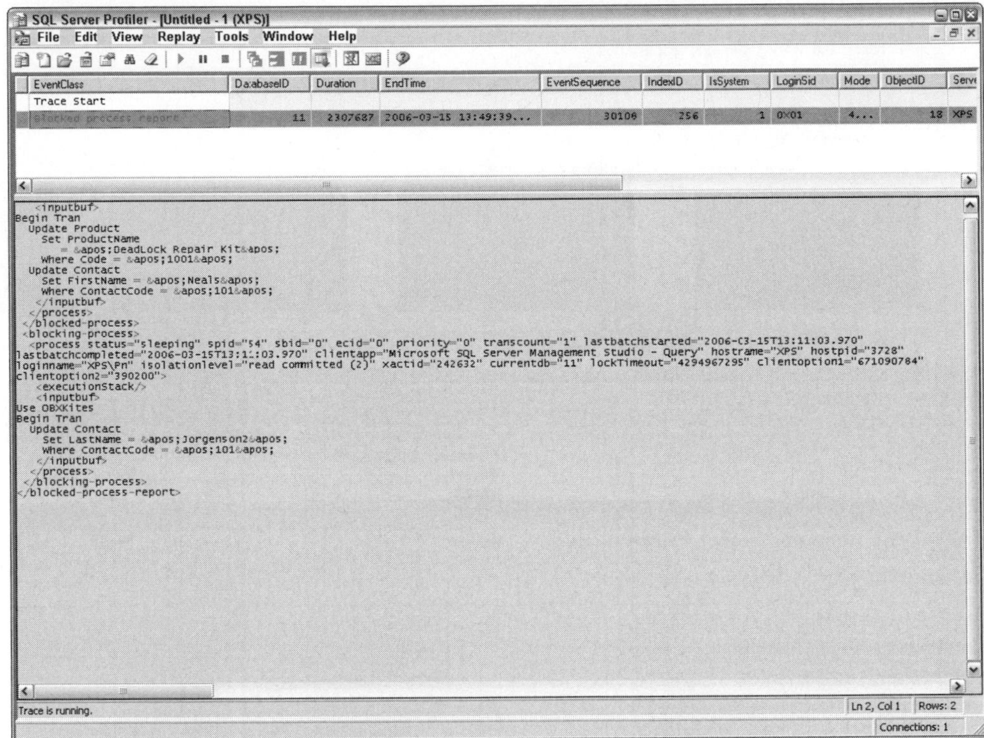

Querying locks with DMVs

Personally, I'm a big fan of SQL Server dynamic management views, but then I like to write queries. The `sys.dm_exec_requests` DMV reports several interesting facts about current sessions, including the blocking session ID:

```
SELECT session_id, blocking_session_id
  FROM sys.dm_exec_requests
  WHERE blocking_session_id > 0
```

NOTE **My friend and SQL Server MVP Adam Machanic has developed an extensive script based on this DMV that reports all active sessions, their statements, and their blocking status. It's available at:** `http://sqlblog.com/blogs/adam_machanic/archive/2008/12/31/a-gift-of-script-for-2009-who-is-active-redux.aspx`.

Viewing all the locks is possible with the `sys.dn_tran_locks` DMV. The following query joins with other DMVs to provide a complete picture of the locks in a database:

```
SELECT
    request_session_id as Spid,
    Coalesce(s.name + '.' +  o.name + isnull('.' + i.name,''),
    s2.name + '.' +  o2.name,
    db.name) AS Object,
    l.resource_type as Type,
    request_mode as Mode,
    request_status as Status
  FROM sys.dm_tran_locks l
    LEFT JOIN sys.partitions p
      ON l.resource_associated_entity_id = p.hobt_id
    LEFT JOIN sys.indexes i
      ON p.object_id = i.object_id
     AND p.index_id  = i.index_id
    LEFT JOIN sys.objects o
      ON p.object_id = o.object_id
    LEFT JOIN sys.schemas s
      ON o.schema_id = s.schema_id
    LEFT JOIN sys.objects o2
      ON l.resource_associated_entity_id = o2.object_id
    LEFT JOIN sys.schemas s2
      ON o2.schema_id = s2.schema_id
    LEFT JOIN sys.databases db
      ON l.resource_database_id = db.database_id
  WHERE resource_database_id = DB_ID()
  ORDER BY Spid, Object, CASE l.resource_type
                               When 'database' Then 1
                               when 'object' then 2
                               when 'page' then 3
                               when 'key' then 4
                               Else 5  end
```

Deadlocks

A deadlock is a special situation that occurs only when transactions with multiple tasks compete for the same data resource out of order. For example:

- Transaction 1 has a lock on data A and needs to lock data B to complete its transaction.

and

- Transaction 2 has a lock on data B and needs to lock data A to complete its transaction.

Each transaction is stuck waiting for the other to release its lock, and neither can complete until the other does. Unless an outside force intercedes, or one of the transactions gives up and quits, this situation could last until the end of time.

While a deadlock typically involves two transactions, it can be a cyclic locking and blocking problem involving several transactions — for example, A is waiting on B, which is waiting on C, which is waiting on A.

Deadlocks used to be a serious problem. Fortunately, SQL Server handles deadlocks refreshingly well.

CAUTION **I've seen deadlocks result from a single parallelized `UPDATE` query. The parallel threads of the query deadlocked on index updates. This is why I strongly recommend that OLTP servers run with maximum degree of parallelism (maxdop) set to 1.**

Creating a deadlock

It's easy to create a deadlock situation in SQL Server using two connections in Management Studio's Query Editor, as illustrated in Figure 66-5. Transaction 1 and transaction 2 will simply try to update the same rows but in the opposite order. Use a third window to watch the locks using Activity Monitor or one of the DMV queries.

FIGURE 66-5

Creating a deadlock situation in Management Studio using two connections tiled vertically

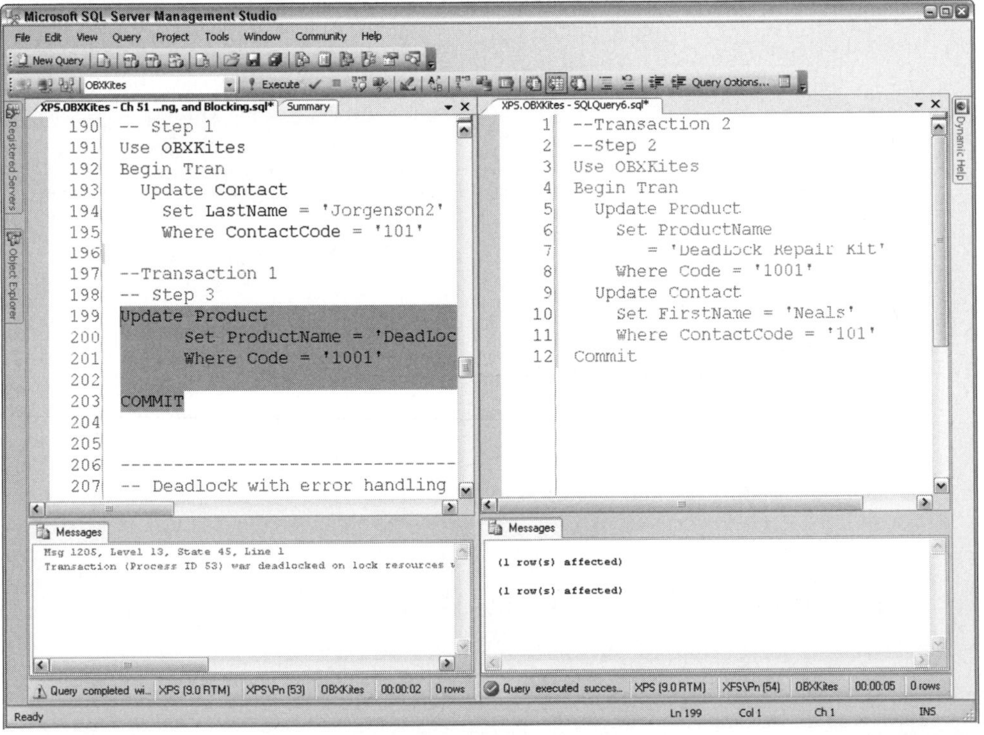

To execute the code, you'll need to do the following:

1. Create two query windows. In one paste the following:

```
-- Transaction 1
-- Step 1
USE OBXKites
BEGIN TRANSACTION
Update Contact
  SET LastName = 'Jorgenson'
  WHERE ContactCode = '101'

-- Transaction 1
-- Step 3
Update Product
  SET ProductName
     = 'DeadLock Identification Tester'
  Where ProductCode = '1001'
COMMIT TRANSACTION
```

2. Paste the following in the second window:

```
-- Transaction 2
-- Step 2
USE OBXKites
BEGIN TRANSACTION
  Update Product
    SET ProductName
      = 'DeadLock Repair Kit'
    Where ProductCode = '1001'
  Update Contact
    SET FirstName = 'Neals'
    Where ContactCode = '101'
COMMIT TRANSACTION
```

Execute in the code in the first query window:

```
-- Transaction 1
-- Step 1
USE OBXKites
BEGIN TRANSACTION
Update Contact
  SET LastName = 'Jorgenson'
  WHERE ContactCode = '101'
```

Transaction 1 now has an exclusive lock on `ContactCode` 101.

Execute step 2 in the second window:

```
-- Transaction 2
-- Step 2
USE OBXKites
BEGIN TRANSACTION
  Update Product
    SET ProductName
      = 'DeadLock Repair Kit'
    Where ProductCode = '1001'

  Update Contact
    SET FirstName = 'Neals'
    Where ContactCode = '101'
COMMIT TRANSACTION
```

Transaction 2 will gain an exclusive lock on `ProductCode 1001` and then try to grab an exclusive lock on `ContactCode 101`, but transaction 1 already has it locked.

It's not a deadlock yet because although transaction 2 is waiting for transaction 1, transaction 1 is not waiting for transaction 2. At this point, if transaction 1 finished its work and issued a `COMMIT TRANSACTION`, the data resource would be freed; transaction 2 could get its lock on the contact row and be on its way as well.

The trouble begins when transaction 1 tries to update `ProductCode 1001`. It can't get an exclusive lock because transaction 2 already has an exclusive lock. So when the following code is executed:

```
-- Transaction 1
-- Step 3
Update Product
  SET ProductName
    = 'DeadLock Identification Tester'
  Where ProductCode = '1001'
COMMIT TRANSACTION
```

transaction one returns the following friendly error message in about two seconds. The deadlock can also be viewed using SQL Server Profiler (as shown in Figure 66-6).

```
Server: Msg 1205, Level 13,
 State 50, Line 1
Transaction (Process ID 5173) was
 deadlocked on lock resources with
 another process and has been chosen
 as the deadlock victim. Rerun the
 transaction.
```

Transaction 2 completes as if there's no problem. Result:

```
(1 row(s) affected)
(1 row(s) affected)
```

FIGURE 66-6

SQL Server Profiler can monitor deadlocks using the Locks: Deadlock Graph event and can display the resource conflict that caused the deadlock.

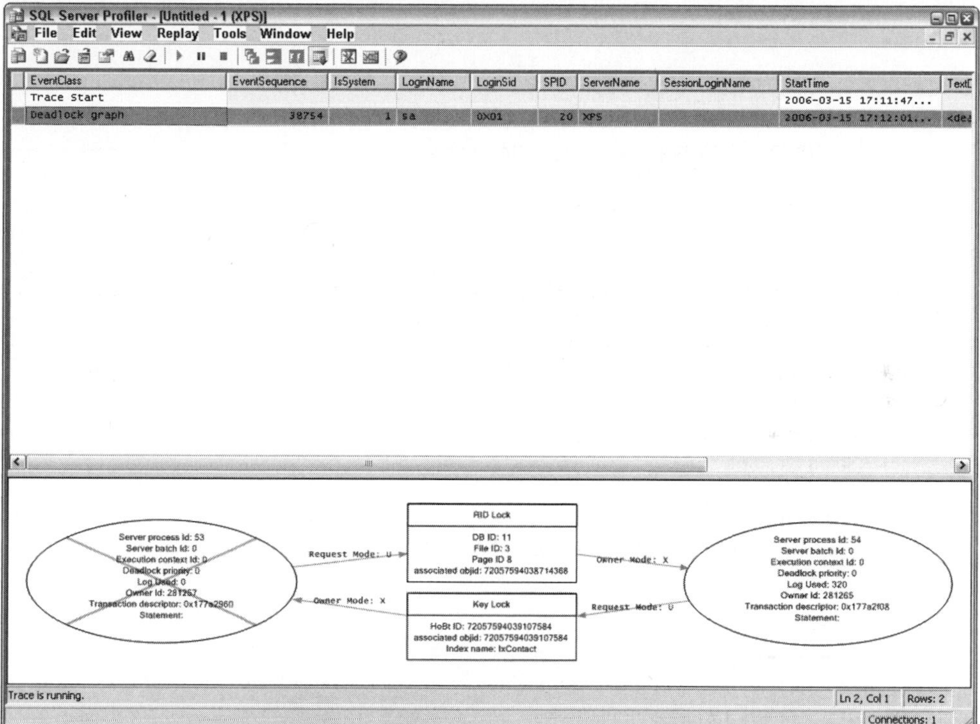

Automatic deadlock detection

As the previous deadlock code demonstrated, SQL Server automatically detects a deadlock situation by examining the blocking processes and rolling back the transaction that has performed the least amount of work. A process within SQL Server is constantly checking for cross-blocking locks and even detects deadlocks that span multiple servers using distributed queries. The deadlock-detection delay is typically instantaneous.

Handling deadlocks

Once a deadlock occurs, SQL Server will determine the transaction to roll back based on an estimate of the amount of work it requires. The transaction selected as the deadlock victim will need to be performed again.

Before SQL Server 2005, trapping a deadlock could only occur at the client, but fortunately try-catch error-handling code can trap a 1205 error, and deadlocks can now be handled in the catch block. If you catch the deadlock within the transaction, your only option is to roll back the transaction. However, you can then rerun your transaction using T-SQL logic, as shown in the following example:

```
declare @retry int
set @retry = 1
while @retry = 1
begin
  begin try
  set  @retry  = 0

    begin transaction

    UPDATE HumanResources.Department
      SET Name = 'qq'
      WHERE DepartmentID = 2;


    UPDATE HumanResources.Department
      SET Name = 'x'
      WHERE DepartmentID = 1;
     commit transaction

  end try
  begin catch
  if error_number() = 1205
  begin
    print error_message()
    set  @retry  = 1
    end
  rollback transaction
  end catch
end
```

Instead of letting SQL Server decide which transaction will be the "deadlock victim," a transaction can "volunteer" to serve as the deadlock victim. That is, the transaction with the lowest deadlock priority will be rolled back first. Assuming the deadlock priorities are the same, SQL will fallback to the rollback cost to determine which to rollback. The following code inside a transaction will inform SQL Server that the transaction should be rolled back in case of a deadlock:

```
SET DEADLOCK_PRIORITY LOW
```

The setting actually allows for a range of values from -10 to 10, or normal (0), low (-5), and high (5).

Minimizing deadlocks

Even though deadlocks can be detected and handled, it's better to avoid them altogether. The following practices will help prevent deadlocks:

- Set the server setting for maximum degree of parallelism (maxdop) to 1.
- Keep a transaction short and to the point. Any code that doesn't have to be in the transaction should be left out of it.

- Never code a transaction to depend on user input.
- Try to write batches and procedures so that they obtain locks in the same order — for example, `TableA`, then `TableB`, then `TableC`. This way, one procedure will wait for the next, avoiding a deadlock.
- Plan the physical schema to keep data that might be selected simultaneously close on the data page by normalizing the schema and carefully selecting the clustered indexes. Reducing the spread of the locks will help prevent lock escalation. Smaller locks help prevent lock contention.
- Ensure that locking is done at the lowest level. This includes locks held at the following: database, object, page, and key. The lower the lock level, the more can be held without contention.
- Don't increase the isolation level unless it's necessary. A stricter isolation level increases the duration of the locks and what types of locks are held during the transaction.

Understanding SQL Server Locking

SQL Server implements the ACID isolation property with locks that protect a transaction's rows from being affected by another transaction. SQL Server locks are not just a "page lock on" and "page lock off" scheme, but rather a series of lock levels. Before they can be controlled, they must be understood.

If you've written manual locking schemes for other database engines to overcome their locking deficiencies (as I have), you may feel as though you still need to control the locks. Let me assure you that the SQL Server lock manager can be trusted. Nevertheless, SQL Server exposes several methods for controlling locks.

Within SQL Server, you can informally picture two processes: a query processor and a lock manager. The goal of the lock manager is to maintain transactional integrity as efficiently as possible by creating and dropping locks.

Every lock has the following three properties:

- **Granularity:** The size of the lock
- **Mode:** The type of lock
- **Duration:** The isolation mode of the lock

Locks are not impossible to view, but some tricks make viewing the current set of locks easier. In addition, lock contention, or the compatibility of various locks to exist or block other locks, can adversely affect performance if it's not understood and controlled.

Lock granularity

The portion of the data controlled by a lock can vary from only one row to the entire database, as shown in Table 66-1. Several combinations of locks, depending on the lock granularity, could satisfy a locking requirement.

TABLE 66-1

Lock Granularity

Lock Size	Description
Row Lock	Locks a single row. This is the smallest lock available. SQL Server does not lock columns.
Page Lock	Locks a page, or 8 KB. One or more rows may exist on a single page.
Extent Lock	Locks eight pages, or 64 KB
Table Lock	Locks the entire table
Database Lock	Locks the entire database. This lock is used primarily during schema changes.
Key Lock	Locks nodes on an index

For best performance, the SQL Server lock manager tries to balance the size of the lock against the number of locks. The struggle is between concurrency (smaller locks allow more transactions to access the data) and performance (fewer locks are faster, as each lock requires memory in the system to hold the information about the lock).

SQL Server automatically manages the granularity of locks by trying to keep the lock size small and only escalating to a higher level when it detects memory pressure.

Lock mode

Locks not only have granularity, or size, but also a mode that determines their purpose. SQL Server has a rich set of lock modes (such as shared, update, exclusive). Failing to understand lock modes will almost guarantee that you develop a poorly performing database.

Lock contention

The interaction and compatibility of the locks plays a vital role in SQL Server's transactional integrity and performance. Certain lock modes block other lock modes, as detailed in Table 66-2. For example, if transaction 1 has a shared lock (S) and transaction 2 requests an exclusive lock (X), then the request is denied, because a shared lock blocks an exclusive lock.

Keep in mind that exclusive locks are ignored unless the page in memory has been updated, i.e., is dirty.

Shared lock (S)

By far the most common and most abused lock, a *shared lock* (listed as an "S" in SQL Server) is a simple "read lock." If a transaction has a shared lock, it's saying, "I'm looking at this data." Multiple transactions are allowed to view the same data, as long as no one else already has an incompatible lock.

TABLE 66-2

Lock Compatibility

T1 has:	T2 Requests: IS	S	U	IX	SIX	X
Intent shared (IS)	Yes	Yes	Yes	Yes	Yes	Yes
Shared (S)	Yes	Yes	Yes	No	No	No
Update (U)	Yes	Yes	No	No	No	No
Intent exclusive (IX)	Yes	No	No	Yes	No	No
Shared with intent exclusive (SIX)	Yes	No	No	No	No	No
Exclusive (X)	No	No	No	No	No	No

Exclusive lock (X)

An exclusive lock means that the transaction is performing a write to the data. As the name implies, an exclusive lock means that only one transaction may hold an exclusive lock at one time, and that no transactions may view the data during the exclusive lock.

Update lock (U)

An update lock can be confusing. It's not applied while a transaction is performing an update — that's an exclusive lock. Instead, the update lock means that the transaction is getting ready to perform an exclusive lock and is currently scanning the data to determine the row(s) it wants for that lock. Think of the update lock as a shared lock that's about to morph into an exclusive lock.

To help prevent deadlocks, only one transaction may hold an update lock at any given time.

Intent locks (various)

An intent lock is a yellow flag or a warning lock that alerts other transactions to the fact that something more is going on. The primary purpose of an intent lock is to improve performance. Because an intent lock is used for all types of locks and for all lock granularities, SQL Server has many types of intent locks. The following is a sampling of the intent locks:

- Intent Shared Lock (IS)
- Shared with Intent Exclusive Lock (SIX)
- Intent Exclusive Lock (IX)

Intent locks serve to stake a claim for a shared or exclusive lock without actually being a shared or exclusive lock. In doing so they solve two performance problems: hierarchical locking and permanent lock block.

Without intent locks, if transaction 1 holds a shared lock on a row and transaction 2 wants to grab an exclusive lock on the table, then transaction 2 needs to check for table locks, extent locks, page locks, row locks, and key locks.

Instead, SQL Server uses intent locks to propagate a lock to higher levels of the data's hierarchical levels. When transaction 1 gains a row lock, it also places an intent lock on the row's page and table.

The intent locks move the overhead of locking from the transaction needing to check for a lock to the transaction placing the lock. The transaction placing the lock needs to place three or four locks, i.e., key, page, object, or database. The transaction checking only needs to check for locks that contend with the three or four locks it needs to place. That one-time write of three locks potentially saves hundreds of searches later as other transactions check for locks.

Jim Gray (memorialized in Chapter 1) was the brains behind this optimization.

The intent locks also prevent a serious shared-lock contention problem — what I call "permanent lock block." As long as a transaction has a shared lock, another transaction can't gain an exclusive lock. What would happen if someone grabbed a shared lock every five seconds and held it for 10 seconds while a transaction was waiting for an exclusive lock? The `UPDATE` transaction could theoretically wait forever. However, once the transaction has an intent exclusive lock (IX), no other transaction can grab a shared lock. The intent exclusive lock isn't a full exclusive lock, but it lays claim to gaining an exclusive lock in the future.

Schema lock (Sch-M, Sch-S)

Schema locks protect the database schema. SQL Server will apply a schema stability (Sch-S) lock during any query to prevent data definition language (DDL) commands.

A schema modification lock (Sch-M) is applied only when SQL Server is adjusting the physical schema. If SQL Server is in the middle of adding a column to a table, then the schema lock will prevent any other transactions from viewing or modifying the data during the schema-modification operation.

Controlling lock timeouts

If a transaction is waiting for a lock, it will continue to wait until the lock is available. By default, no timeout exists — it can theoretically wait forever.

Fortunately, you can set the lock time using the `set lock_timeout` connection option. Set the option to a number of milliseconds or set it to infinity (the default) by setting it to `-1`. Setting the `lock_timeout` to `0` means that the transaction will instantly give up if any lock contention occurs at all. The application will be very fast, and very ineffective.

The following query sets the lock timeout to two seconds (2,000 milliseconds):

```
SET Lock_Timeout 2000
```

When a transaction does time out while waiting to gain a lock, a 1222 error is raised.

Best Practice

I recommend setting a lock timeout in the connection. The length of the wait you should specify depends on the typical performance of the database. I usually set a five-second timeout.

Lock duration

The third lock property, lock duration, is determined by the transaction isolation level of the transactions involved — the more stringent the isolation, the longer the locks will be held. SQL Server implements four transaction isolation levels (transaction isolation levels are detailed in the next section.)

Index-level locking restrictions

Isolation levels and locking hints are applied from the connection and query perspective. The only way to control locks from the table perspective is to restrict the granularity of locks on a per-index basis. Using the `ALTER INDEX` command, rowlocks and/or pagelocks may be disabled for a particular index, as follows:

```
ALTER INDEX AK_Department_Name
  ON HumanResources.Department
  SET (ALLOW_PAGE_LOCKS = OFF)
```

This is useful for a couple of specific purposes. If a table frequently causes waiting because of page locks, setting `ALLOW_PAGE_LOCKS` to `OFF` will force rowlocks. The decreased scope of the lock will improve concurrency. In addition, if a table is seldom updated but frequently read, then row-level and page-level locks are inappropriate. Allowing only table locks is suitable during the majority of table accesses. For the infrequent update, a table-exclusive lock is not a big issue.

`Sp_indexoption` is for fine-tuning the data schema; that's why it's on an index level. To restrict the locks on a table's primary key, use `sp_help` *`tablename`* to find the specific name for the primary key index.

The following commands configure the `ProductCategory` table as an infrequently updated lookup table. First, `sp_help` reports the name of the primary key index:

```
sp_help ProductCategory
```

Result (abridged):

```
index                        index         index
name                         description   keys
---------------------------- ------------ ----------------
PK__ProductCategory__79A81403 nonclustered, ProductCategoryID
                             unique,
                             primary key
                             located
                             on PRIMARY
```

Having identified the actual name of the primary key, the ALTER INDEX command can be set as shown previously.

Transaction Isolation Levels

Any study of how transactions affect performance must include *transactional integrity*, which refers to the quality, or fidelity, of the transaction. Three types of problems violate transactional integrity: dirty reads, nonrepeatable reads, and phantom rows.

The level of isolation, or the height of the fence between transactions, can be adjusted to control which transactional faults are permitted. The ANSI SQL-92 committee specifies four isolation levels: read uncommitted, read committed, repeatable read, and serializable.

SQL Server 2005 introduced two additional row-versioning levels, which enables two levels of optimistic transaction isolation: *snapshot* and *read committed snapshot*. All six transaction isolation levels are listed in Table 66-3 and detailed in this section.

TABLE 66-3

ANSI-92 Isolation Levels

Isolation Level (Transaction isolation level is set for the connection)	Table Hint (override the connection's transaction isolation level)	Dirty Read (Seeing another transaction's noncommitted changes)	Non-Repeatable Read (Seeing another transaction's committed changes)	Phantom Row (Seeing additional rows selected by where clause as a result of another transaction)	Reader/Writer Blocking (A write transaction blocks a read transaction)
Read Uncommitted (least restrictive)	NoLock, Read-Uncommitted	Possible	Possible	Possible	Yes
Read Committed (Sql Server default; moderately restrictive)	ReadCommitted	Prevented	Possible	Possible	Yes
Repeatable Read	RepeatableRead	Prevented	Prevented	Possible	Yes
Serializable (most restrictive)	Serializable	Prevented	Prevented	Prevented	Yes
Snapshot		Prevented	Prevented	Possible	No
Read Committed Snapshot		Prevented	Possible	Possible	No

Internally, SQL Server uses locks for isolation (except for the snapshot isolations), and the transaction isolation level determines the duration of the share lock or exclusive lock for the transaction, as listed in Table 66-4.

TABLE 66-4

Isolation Levels and Lock Duration

Isolation Level	Share-Lock Duration	Exclusive-Lock Duration
Read Uncommitted	None	Held only long enough to prevent physical corruption; otherwise, exclusive locks are neither applied nor honored
Read Committed	Held while the transaction is reading the data	Held until `TRANSACTION COMMIT`
Repeatable Read	Held until `TRANSACTION COMMIT`	Held until `TRANSACTION COMMIT`
Serializable	Held until `TRANSACTION COMMIT`	Held until `TRANSACTION COMMIT`. The exclusive lock also uses a keylock (also called a *range lock*) to prevent inserts.
Snapshot Isolation	n/a	n/a

Setting the transaction isolation level

The transaction isolation level can be set at the connection level using the `SET` command. Setting the transaction isolation level affects all statements for the duration of the connection, or until the transaction isolation level is changed again (you can't change the isolation level once in a transaction):

```
SET TRANSACTION ISOLATION LEVEL
  READ COMMITTED;
```

To view the current connection transaction isolation level, use `DBCC UserOptions`, or query `sys.dm_exec_sessions`:

```
SELECT TIL.Description
  FROM sys.dm_exec_sessions dmv
    JOIN (VALUES(1, 'Read Uncommitted'),
                (2, 'Read Committed'),
                (3, 'Repeatable Read'),
                (4, 'Serializable'))
                AS TIL(ID, Description)
      ON dmv.transaction_isolation_level = TIL.ID
  WHERE session_id = @@spid;
```

Result:

```
READ COMMITTED
```

Alternately, the transaction isolation level for a single DML statement can be set by using table-lock hints in the FROM clause (WITH is optional). These will override the current connection transaction isolation level and apply the hint on a per-table basis. For example, in the next code sample, the Department table is actually accessed using a read uncommitted transaction isolation level, not the connection's read committed transaction isolation level:

```
SET TRANSACTION ISOLATION LEVEL
  REPEATABLE READ;

SELECT Name
  FROM HumanResources.Department WITH (NOLOCK)
  WHERE DepartmentID = 1;
```

Level 1 – Read uncommitted and the dirty read

The lowest level of isolation, read uncommitted, is nothing more than a line drawn in the sand. It doesn't really provide any isolation between transactions, and it allows all three transactional faults.

A dirty read, when one transaction can read uncommitted changes made by another transaction, is possibly the most egregious transaction isolation fault. It is illustrated in Figure 66-7.

FIGURE 66-7

A dirty read occurs when transaction 2 can see transaction 1's uncommitted changes.

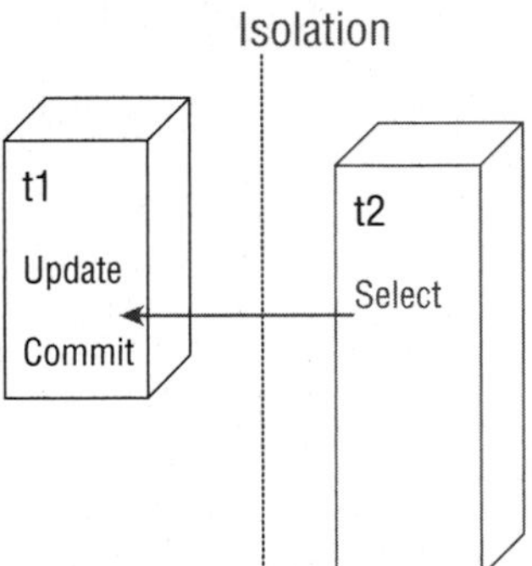

To demonstrate the read uncommitted transaction isolation level and the dirty read it allows, the following code uses two connections — creating two transactions: transaction 1 is on the left, and transaction 2 is on the right. The second transaction will see the first transaction's update before that update is committed:

```
USE AdventureWorks2008;
```

```
BEGIN TRANSACTION;
  UPDATE HumanResources.Department
    SET Name = 'Transaction Fault'
    WHERE DepartmentID = 1;
```

In a separate Query Editor window (refer to Figure 66-1), execute another transaction in its own connection window. (Use the Query tab context menu and New Vertical Tab Group to split the windows.) This transaction will set its transaction isolation level to permit dirty reads. Only the second transaction needs to be set to read uncommitted for transaction 2 to experience a dirty read:

```
-- Transaction 2
USE AdventureWorks2008;

SET TRANSACTION ISOLATION LEVEL
  READ UNCOMMITTED;

SELECT Name
  FROM HumanResources.Department
  WHERE DepartmentID = 1;
```

Result:

```
Name
----------------------
Transaction Fault
```

Transaction 1 hasn't yet committed the transaction, but transaction 2 was able to read "Transaction Fault." That's a dirty read violation of transactional integrity.

To finish the task, the first transaction will roll back that transaction:

```
-- Transaction 1
ROLLBACK TRANSACTION
```

Best Practice

Never use read uncommitted or the With (NOLOCK) table hint. It's often argued that read uncommitted is OK for a reporting database, the rationale being that dirty reads won't matter because there's little updating and/or the data is not changing. If that's the case, then the reporting locks are only share locks, which won't block anyway. Another argument is that users don't mind seeing inconsistent data. However, it's often the case that users don't understand what "seeing inconsistent data" means.

There are other issues about reading uncommitted data related to how the SQL engine optimizes such a read that can result in your query reading the same data more than once.

Level 2 – Read committed

SQL Server's default transaction isolation level, read committed, (described previously) is like a nice, polite white-picket fence between two good neighbors. It prevents dirty reads, but doesn't bog the system down with excessive lock contention. For this reason, it's SQL Server's default isolation level and an ideal choice for most OTLP projects.

Best Practice

Unless there's a specific reason to escalate the transaction isolation level, I strongly recommend that you keep your transactions at read committed.

Level 3 – Repeatable read

The third level of isolation, repeatable read, is like a 10-foot chain-link fence with barbed wire on top. There's a significant difference between read committed's white-picket fence and repeatable read. Read committed only has to lock the transaction that's doing the writing. To ensure that reads are consistent, share locks on the reading transaction have to be extended as well.

First, here's a walk-through of a nonrepeatable read fault.

Nonrepeatable read fault

A *nonrepeatable read* is similar to a dirty read, but a nonrepeatable read occurs when a transaction can see the committed updates from another transaction (see Figure 66-8). True isolation means that one transaction never affects another transaction. If the isolation is complete, then no data changes from outside the transaction should be seen by the transaction. Reading a row inside a transaction should produce the same results every time. If reading a row twice results in different values, that's a nonrepeatable read type of transaction fault.

FIGURE 66-8

A nonrepeatable read transaction fault is when transaction 2 selects the same data twice and sees different values.

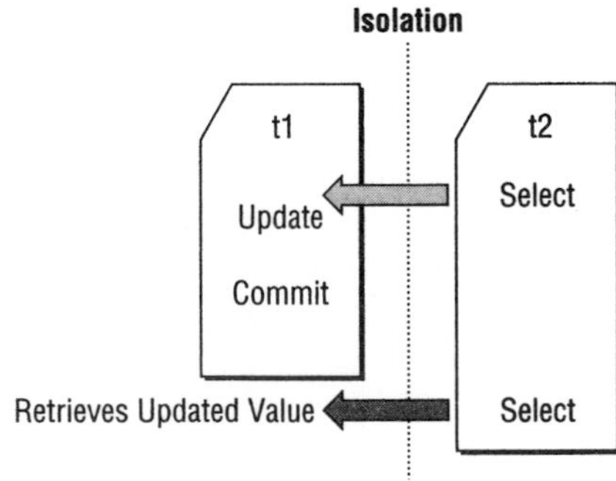

To demonstrate a nonrepeatable read, the following sequence sets up two concurrent transactions. Transaction 2, on the right side, is in the default read committed transaction isolation level, which allows the nonrepeatable read fault.

Assuming an unaltered copy of `AdventureWorks2008`, transaction 2 begins a logical transaction and then reads the department name as "Engineering":

```
-- Transaction 2
USE AdventureWorks2008;

SET TRANSACTION ISOLATION LEVEL
  READ COMMITTED;

BEGIN TRANSACTION;
  SELECT Name
    FROM HumanResources.Department
    WHERE DepartmentID = 1;
```

Result:

```
Name
------------------------
Engineering
```

Transaction 1 on the left side now updates the department name to "Non-Repeatable Read":

```
-- Transaction 1
USE AdventureWorks2008;

UPDATE HumanResources.Department
  SET Name = 'Non-Repeatable Read'
  WHERE DepartmentID = 1;
```

Transaction 2, back on the right side, reads the row again. If it sees the value updated by transaction 1, that will be a nonrepeatable read transaction fault:

```
  SELECT Name
    FROM HumanResources.Department
    WHERE DepartmentID = 1;
COMMIT TRANSACTION;
```

Result:

```
Name
------------------------
Non-Repeatable Read
```

Sure enough, transaction 2's read was not repeatable.

Preventing the fault

Rerunning the same scripts with transaction 2's transaction isolation level to Repeatable Read will result in a very different behavior (assuming an unaltered copy of AdventureWorks2008):

```
-- Transaction 2
USE AdventureWorks2008;

SET TRANSACTION ISOLATION LEVEL
  REPEATABLE READ;

BEGIN TRANSACTION;
  SELECT Name
    FROM HumanResources.Department
    WHERE DepartmentID = 1;
```

Result:

```
Name
------------------------
Engineering
```

Transaction 1 on the left side now updates the department name to "Non-Repeatable Read":

```
-- Transaction 1
USE AdventureWorks2008;

UPDATE HumanResources.Department
  SET Name = 'Non-Repeatable Read'
  WHERE DepartmentID = 1;
```

Here's the first major difference: There's no "1 row(s) affected" message indicating that the update is paused, waiting for transaction 2's share lock.

Transaction 2, back on the right side, reads the row again. If it sees the value updated by transaction 1, then that's a nonrepeatable read transaction fault:

```
SELECT Name
  FROM HumanResources.Department
  WHERE DepartmentID = 1;
```

Result:

```
Name
------------------------
Engineering
```

But the result is not the updated value from transaction 1. Instead, the original value is still in place. The read was repeatable and the nonrepeatable read fault has been prevented.

When transaction 2 completes the transaction, it releases the share lock:

```
COMMIT TRANSACTION;
```

Immediately, transaction 1, on the left side, is now free to complete its update and the "1 `row(s)affected`" message appears in the Messages pane.

Repeatable read protects against the selected rows being updated, but it doesn't protect against new rows being added to or deleted from the selected range. Therefore, you could get a different value/set of results, if new rows are added or deleted. To avoid this, use the serializable transaction isolation level of protection.

Best Practice

Repeatable read has significant overhead, but it's perfect for situations when a transaction must be able to read the data multiple times, perhaps performing calculations, and guarantee that no other transaction updates the data during these calculations.

The key to using repeatable read is applying it conservatively — if an application requires repeatable read in some cases, be careful to only set repeatable read for those transactions that require it. Leave all the other transactions at the default read committed transaction isolation level.

Level 4 – Serializable

This most restrictive isolation level prevents all transactional faults and is like a high-security prison wall. Serializable protects against all three transactional faults: dirty reads, nonrepeatable reads, and phantom rows.

Just as serialized inventory means that each item is uniquely identified and accounted for, the serialized transaction isolation level means that each row in every select's result set is accounted for; and if that select is reissued, then the result will not include any row additions or deletions made by any other transaction.

This mode is useful for databases for which absolute transactional integrity is more important than performance. Banking, accounting, and high-contention sales databases, such as the stock market, typically use serialized isolation.

Best Practice

Use the serialized transaction level when performing multiple aggregations on a ranged set of rows and there's a risk that another connection might add or remove rows from that range during the transaction. An example might be when a transaction is reconciling multiple accounts and must ensure that no other transaction inserts within the same range as the adjustments during the reconciliation.

Phantom rows

The least severe transactional-integrity fault is a *phantom row*, which means that one transaction's insert, update, or delete causes different rows to be returned in another transaction, as shown in Figure 66-9.

FIGURE 66-9

When the rows returned by a select are altered by another transaction, the phenomenon is called a *phantom row*.

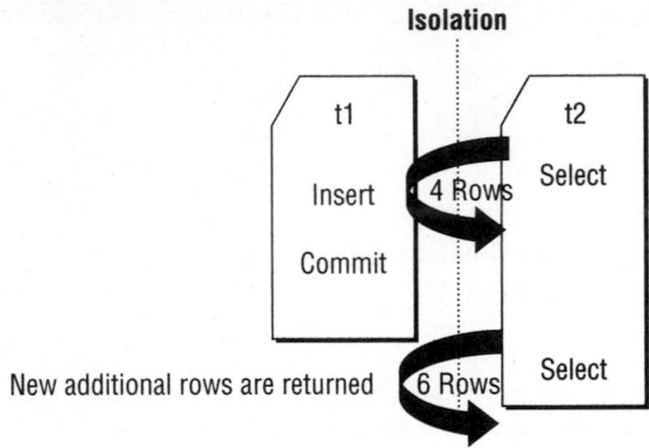

Beginning with a clean copy of AdventureWorks2008, transaction 2 selects all the rows in a specific range (Name BETWEEN 'A' AND 'G'):

```
-- Transaction 2
USE AdventureWorks2008

SET TRANSACTION ISOLATION LEVEL
  REPEATABLEREAD

BEGIN TRANSACTION
  SELECT DepartmentID as DeptID, Name
    FROM HumanResources.Department
    WHERE Name BETWEEN 'A' AND 'G'
```

Result:

```
DeptID     Name
---------- ---------------------
12         Document Control
1          Engineering
16         Executive
14         Facilities and Maintenance
10         Finance
```

Transaction 1 now inserts a new row into the range selected by transaction 2:

```
-- Transaction 1
-- Insert a row in the range
INSERT HumanResources.Department (Name, GroupName)
  VALUES ('ABC Dept', 'Test Dept')
```

When transaction 2 selects the same range again, if 'ABC Dept' is in the result list, then a phantom row transaction fault occurred:

```
-- Transaction 2
-- re-selecting the same range
  SELECT DepartmentID as DeptID, Name
    FROM HumanResources.Department
    WHERE Name BETWEEN 'A' AND 'G'
COMMIT TRANSACTION
```

Result:

```
DeptID     Name
---------- ---------------------
17         ABC Dept
12         Document Control
1          Engineering
16         Executive
14         Facilities and Maintenance
10         Finance
```

Sure enough, 'ABC Dept' is in the result list, and that's the phantom row.

Serialized transaction isolation level

The highest transaction isolation level can defend the transaction against the phantom row.

Transaction 2 will first insert a sample row, 'Amazing FX Dept,' so transaction 1 will have a row that can be deleted without worrying about referential integrity issues. It then sets the transaction isolation level, begins a transaction, and reads a range of data:

```
-- Transaction 2
USE AdventureWorks2008

-- insert test row for deletion
INSERT HumanResources.Department
  (Name, GroupName)
  VALUES
    ('Amazing FX Dept', 'Test Dept')

SET TRANSACTION ISOLATION LEVEL
  SERIALIZABLE

BEGIN TRANSACTION

  SELECT DepartmentID as DeptID, Name
    FROM HumanResources.Department
    WHERE Name BETWEEN 'A' AND 'G'
```

Result:

```
DeptID     Name
---------- ---------------------
17         Amazing FX Dept
12         Document Control
1          Engineering
16         Executive
14         Facilities and Maintenance
10         Finance
```

Transaction 2's SELECT returned six rows.

With transaction 2 in a transaction and serialized transaction isolation level protecting the range of names from 'A' to 'G', transaction 1 will attempt to insert, update, and delete into and from that range:

```
-- Transaction 1
-- Insert a row in the range
INSERT HumanResources.Department (Name, GroupName)
  VALUES ('ABC Dept', 'Test Dept')

-- Update Dept into the range
UPDATE HumanResources.Department
  SET Name = 'ABC Test'
  WHERE DepartmentID = 1 -- Engineering

-- Delete Dept from range
DELETE HumanResources.Department
  WHERE DepartmentID = 17 -- Amazing FX Dept
```

The significant point here is that none of transaction 1's DML commands produced a "1 row(s)affected" message.

Transaction 2 now reselects the same range:

```
-- Transaction 2
  SELECT DepartmentID as DeptID, Name
    FROM HumanResources.Department
    WHERE Name BETWEEN 'A' AND 'G'
```

Result:

```
DeptID     Name
---------- ---------------------
17         Amazing FX Dept
12         Document Control
1          Engineering
16         Executive
14         Facilities and Maintenance
10         Finance
```

The SELECT returns the same six rows with the same values. Transactional integrity is intact, and the phantom row fault has been thwarted.

Transaction 1 is still on hold, waiting for transaction 2 to complete its transaction:

```
COMMIT TRANSACTION
```

As soon as transaction 2 issues a commit transaction and releases its locks, transaction 1 is free to make its changes, and three "1 row(s)affected" messages appear in transaction 1's Messages pane:

```
SELECT *
  FROM HumanResources.Department
```

Result:

```
DeptID     Name
---------- ---------------------
18         ABC Dept
1          ABC Test
12         Document Control
1          Engineering
16         Executive
14         Facilities and Maintenance
10         Finance
```

Selecting the range after transaction 2 is committed and transaction 1 has made its updates reveals the inserted and updated rows added to the range. In addition, the Amazing FX department has disappeared.

Concurrency and the serialized isolation level are not friends because in order to get the protection needed for the serialized isolation level, more locks are required; worse, those locks have to be on key ranges to prevent someone else from inserting rows. In the event that you don't have the correct indexes, the only way SQL can prevent phantoms is to lock the table. Locking the table is obviously not good for concurrency. For this reason, if you need to use serialized transactions, you must ensure that you have the correct indexes in order to avoid table locks.

Snapshot isolations

Traditionally, writers block readers, and readers block writers, but version-based isolations are a completely different twist. When version-based isolations are enabled, if a transaction modifies (irrespective of the isolation level) data, a pre-modification version of the data is stored. This allows other transactions to read the original version of the data even while the original transaction is in an uncommitted state.

Therefore, snapshot isolation eliminates writer versus reader contention. Nevertheless, contention isn't completely gone — you still have writers conflicting with writers. If a second writer attempts to update a resource that's already being updated, the second resource is blocked.

There are two version-based isolations — *snapshot isolation* and *read committed snapshot isolation*:

- **Snapshot isolation:** Operates like serializable isolation without the locking and blocking issues. The same select within a transaction will see before image of the data.
- **Read committed snapshot isolation:** Sees any committed data, similar to SQL Server's default isolation level of read committed. However, importantly, it doesn't place any shared locks on the data being read.

Best Practice

Oracle's default transaction behavior is just like snapshot isolation, which is why some DBAs moving up to SQL Server love snapshot isolation, and why some assume snapshot isolation must be better somehow than traditional transaction isolation levels.

It's true that snapshot isolation can eliminate some locking and blocking issues and therefore improves performance given the right hardware.

However, the best practice is as follows: If you choose snapshot isolation, it should be an architecture issue, not a performance issue. If another transaction is updating the data, should the user wait for the new data, or should the user see the before image of the data? For many applications, returning the before image would paint a false picture.

Enabling row versioning

Snapshot actually leverages SQL Server's row-versioning technology, which copies any row being updated into TempDB. Configuring snapshot isolation, therefore, requires first enabling row versioning for the database. Besides the TempDB load, row versioning also adds a 14-byte row identifier to each row. This extra data is added to the row when the row is modified if it hasn't been done previously. It is used to store the pointer to the versioned row.

CAUTION **Because snapshot isolation uses row versioning, which writes copies of the rows to TempDB, this can put an incredible load on TempDB. If you enable the row-version-based isolations, be prepared to watch TempDB and perhaps locate TempDB's data and transaction logs on their own disk subsystems.**

Row versioning alters the row structure so that a copy of the row can be sent to TempDB.

The following code enables snapshot isolation. To alter the database and turn on snapshot isolation, there can no other connections to the database:

```
USE Aesop;

ALTER DATABASE Aesop
SET ALLOW_SNAPSHOT_ISOLATION ON
-- check snapshot isolation
select name,
  snapshot_isolation_state,
  snapshot_isolation_state_desc,
```

```
  is_read_committed_snapshot_on
from sys.databases
where database_id = DB_ID()
```

Transaction 1 now begins a reading transaction, leaving the transaction open (uncommitted):

```
USE Aesop
SET TRANSACTION ISOLATION LEVEL Snapshot;

BEGIN TRAN
SELECT Title
  FROM FABLE
  WHERE FableID = 2
```

Result:

```
Title
--------
The Bald Knight
```

A second transaction begins an update to the *same* row that the first transaction has open:

```
USE Aesop;
SET TRANSACTION ISOLATION LEVEL Snapshot;

BEGIN TRAN

UPDATE Fable
  SET Title = 'Rocking with Snapshots'
  WHERE FableID = 2;

SELECT * FROM FABLE WHERE FableID = 2
```

Result:

```
Title
--------------------------
Rocking with Snapshots
```

This is pretty amazing. The second transaction is able to update the row even though the first transaction is still open. Going back to the first transaction, it will still see the original data:

```
SELECT Title
  FROM FABLE
  WHERE FableID = 2
```

Result:

```
Title
--------
The Bald Knight
```

If you were to open a third or fourth transaction, they would all still see the original value, The Bald Knight.

Even after the second transaction committed the change, the first transaction would still see the original value, The Bald Knight. This is the same behavior as the serializable isolation but without the blocking that occurs with serializable isolation. Any new transactions would see updated value, Rocking with Snapshots.

Using read committed snapshot isolation

Read committed snapshot isolation is enabled using a similar syntax:

```
ALTER DATABASE Aesop
  SET READ_COMMITTED_SNAPSHOT ON
```

Like snapshot isolation, read committed snapshot isolation uses row versioning to stave off locking and blocking issues. In the previous example, transaction 1 would see transaction 2's update once it was committed.

The difference with snapshot isolation is that you don't specify a new isolation level. This just changes the behavior of the standard read committed isolation level, which means you shouldn't have to change your application to benefit from it.

Handling write conficts

Transactions that write to the data within a snapshot isolation can be blocked by a previous uncommitted write transaction. This blocking won't cause the new transaction to wait; instead, it generates an error. Be sure to use try-catch to handle these errors, wait a split second, and try again.

Using locking hints

Locking hints enable you to make minute adjustments to the locking strategy. Whereas the isolation level affects the entire connection, locking hints are specific to one table within one query (see Table 66-5). The WITH (locking hint) option is placed after the table in the FROM clause of the query. You can specify multiple locking hints by separating them with commas.

The following query uses a locking hint in the FROM clause of an UPDATE query to prevent the lock manager from escalating the granularity of the locks:

```
USE OBXKites
UPDATE Product
  FROM Product WITH (RowLock)
  SET ProductName = ProductName + ' Updated'
```

If a query includes subqueries, don't forget that each query's table references will generate locks and can be controlled by a locking hint.

TABLE 66-5

Locking Hints

Locking Hint	Description
ReadUnCommitted	Isolation level. Doesn't apply or honor locks. Same as no lock.
ReadCommitted	Isolation level. Uses the default transaction-isolation level.
RepeatableRead	Isolation level. Holds share and exclusive locks until `COMMIT TRANSACTION`.
Serializable	Isolation level. Applies the serializable transaction isolation level durations to the table, which holds the shared lock until the transaction is complete.
ReadPast	Skips locked rows instead of waiting
RowLock	Forces row-level locks instead of page, extent, or table locks
PagLock	Forces the use of page locks instead of a table lock
TabLock	Automatically escalates row, page, or extent locks to the table-lock granularity
NoLock	Doesn't apply or honor locks. Same as ReadUnCommitted.
TablockX	Forces an exclusive lock on the table. This prevents any other transaction from working with the table.
HoldLock	Holds the share lock until `COMMIT TRANSACTION`. (Same as serializable.)
Updlock	Uses an update lock instead of a shared lock and holds the lock. This blocks any other reads or writes of the data between the initial read and a write operation. This can be used to escalate locks used by a `SELECT` statement within a serializable isolation transaction from causing deadlocks.
XLock	Holds an exclusive lock on the data until the transaction is committed

Application Locks

SQL Server uses a very sophisticated locking scheme. Sometimes a process or a resource other than data requires locking. For example, a procedure might need to run that would be ill affected if another user started another instance of the same procedure.

Several years ago, I wrote a program that routed cables for nuclear power plant designs. After the geometry of the plant (what's where) was entered and tested, the design engineers entered the cable-source equipment, destination equipment, and type of cable to be used. Once several cables were entered, a procedure wormed each cable through the cable trays so that cables were as short as possible. The procedure also considered cable fail-safe routes and separated incompatible cables. While I enjoyed writing that database, if multiple instances of the worm procedure ran simultaneously, each instance attempted to route the cables, and the data became fouled. An application lock is the perfect solution to that type of problem.

Application locks open up the whole world of SQL Server locks for custom uses within applications. Instead of using data as a locked resource, application locks use any named user resource declared in the `sp_GetAppLock` stored procedure.

Application locks must be obtained within a transaction. As with the locks the engine puts on the database resources, you can specify the lock mode (`Shared`, `Update`, `Exclusive`, `IntentExclusive`, or `IntentShared`) . The return code indicates whether or not the procedure was successful in obtaining the lock, as follows:

- 0: Lock was obtained normally
- 1: Lock was obtained after another procedure released it
- -1: Lock request failed (timeout)
- -2: Lock request failed (canceled)
- -3: Lock request failed (deadlock)
- -999: Lock request failed (other error)

The `sp_ReleaseAppLock` stored procedure releases the lock. The following code shows how the application lock can be used in a batch or procedure:

```
DECLARE @ShareOK INT
EXEC @ShareOK = sp_GetAppLock
                 @Resource = 'CableWorm',
                 @LockMode = 'Exclusive'
IF @ShareOK < 0
   ...Error handling code

 ... code ...

EXEC sp_ReleaseAppLock @Resource = 'CableWorm'
Go
```

When the application locks are viewed using Enterprise Manager or `sp_Lock`, the lock appears as an "APP"-type lock. The following is an abbreviated listing of `sp_lock` executed at the same time as the previous code:

```
Sp_Lock
```

Result:

```
spid  dbid  ObjId  IndId  Type Resource       Mode  Status
----- ----- ------ ------ ---- -------------- ----- ------
57    8     0      0      APP  Cabllf94c136   X     GRANT
```

Note two minor differences from the way application locks are handled by SQL Server:

- Deadlocks are not automatically detected.
- If a transaction gets a lock several times, it has to release that lock the same number of times.

Application Locking Design

Aside from SQL Server locks, another locking issue deserves to be addressed. How the client application deals with multi-user contention is important to both the user's experience and the integrity of the data.

Implementing optimistic locking

The two basic means of dealing with multi-user access are *optimistic locking* and *pessimistic locking*. The one you use determines the coding methods of the application.

Optimistic locking assumes that no one else will attempt to change the data while a user is working on the data in a form. Therefore, you can read the data and then later go back and update the data based on what you originally read. Optimistic locking does not apply locks while a user is working with data in the front-end application. The disadvantage of optimistic locking is that multiple users can read and write the data because they aren't blocked from doing so by locks, which can result in lost updates.

The pessimistic (or "Murphy") method takes a different approach: If anything can go wrong it will. When a user is working on some data, a pessimistic locking scheme locks that data until the user is finished with it.

While pessimistic locking may work in small workgroup applications on desktop databases, large client/server applications require higher levels of concurrency. If SQL Server locks are held while a user is viewing the data in an application, performance will be unreasonably slow.

The accepted best practice is to implement an optimistic locking scheme using minimal SQL Server locks, as well as a method for preventing lost updates.

Lost updates

A lost update occurs when two users edit the same row, complete their edits, and save the data, and the second user's update overwrites the first user's update. For example:

1. Joe opens Product 1001, a 21-inch box kite, in the front-end application. SQL Server applies a shared lock for a split second while retrieving the data
2. Sue also opens Product 1001 using the front-end application.
3. Joe and Sue both make edits to the box-kite data. Joe rephrases the product description, and Sue fixes the product category.
4. Joe saves the data in the application, which sends an update to SQL Server. The `UPDATE` command replaces the old product description with Joe's new description.
5. Sue presses the "save and close" button, and her data is sent to SQL Server in another `UPDATE` statement. The product category is now fixed, but the old description was in Sue's form, so Joe's new description was overwritten with the old description.
6. Joe discovers the error and complains to the IT vice president during the next round of golf about the unreliability of that new SQL Server–based database.

Because lost updates only occur when two users edit the same row at the same time, the problem might not occur for months. Nonetheless, it's a flaw in the transactional integrity of the database and should be prevented.

Minimizing lost updates

If the application is going to use an optimistic locking scheme, you can minimize the chance that a lost update can occur, as well as minimize the effects of a lost update, using the following methods:

- Normalize the database so that it has many long, narrow tables. With fewer columns in a row, the chance of a lost update is reduced. For example, the OBXKites database has a separate table for prices. A user can work on product pricing and not interfere with another user working on other product data.
- If the UPDATE statement is being constructed by the front-end application, have it check the controls and send an update for only those columns that are actually changed by the user. This technique alone would prevent the lost update described in the previous example of Joe's and Sue's updates and most lost updates in the real world. As an added benefit, it reduces client/server traffic and the workload on SQL Server.
- If an optimistic locking scheme is not preventing lost updates, the application is using a "he who writes last, writes best" scheme. Although lost updates may occur, a data-audit trail can minimize the effect by exposing updates to the same row within minutes and tracking the data changes.

Preventing lost updates

A stronger solution to the lost update problem than just minimizing the effect is to block lost updates where the data has changed since it was read. This can be done in two ways. The more complicated version checks the current value of each column against the value that was originally read. Although it can be very complicated, it offers you very fine-grain control over doing partial updates.

The second way is to use the RowVersion method. The rowversion data type, previously known as a timestamp in earlier versions of SQL Server, automatically provides a new value every time the row is updated. By comparing the RowVersion value retrieved during the row select and the RowVersion value at the time of update, it's trivial for code to detect whether the row has been changed and a lost update would occur.

The RowVersion method can be used in SELECT and UPDATE statements by adding the RowVersion value in the WHERE clause of the UPDATE statement.

The following sequence demonstrates the RowVersion technique using two user updates. Both users begin by opening the 21-inch box kite in the front-end application. Both SELECT statements retrieve the RowVersion column and ProductName:

```
SELECT RowVersion, ProductName
  FROM Product
  WHERE ProductCode = '1001'
```

Result:

```
RowVersion         ProductName
------------------ -------------------------
0x0000000000000077 Basic Box Kite 21 inch
```

Both front-end applications can grab the data and populate the form. Joe edits the ProductName to "Joe's Update." When Joe is ready to update the database, the "save and close" button executes the following SQL statement:

```
UPDATE Product
  SET ProductName = 'Joe's Update'
  WHERE ProductCode = '1001'
    AND RowVersion = 0x0000000000000077
```

Once SQL Server has processed Joe's update, it automatically updates the RowVersion value as well. Checking the row again, Joe sees that his edit took effect:

```
SELECT RowVersion, ProductName
  FROM Product
  WHERE ProductCode = '1001'
```

Result:

```
RowVersion         ProductName
------------------ -------------------------
0x00000000000000B9 Joe's Update
```

If the update procedure checks to see whether any rows were affected, it can detect that Joe's edit was accepted:

```
SELECT @@ROWCOUNT
```

Result:

```
1
```

Although the RowVersion column's value was changed, Sue's front-end application isn't aware of the new value. When Sue attempts to save her edit, the UPDATE statement won't find any rows meeting that criterion:

```
UPDATE Product
  SET ProductName = 'Sue's Update'
  WHERE ProductCode = '1001'
    AND RowVersion = 0x0000000000000077
```

If the update procedure checks to see whether any rows were affected, it can detect that Sue's edit was ignored:

```
SELECT @@ROWCOUNT
```

Result:

```
0
```

This method can also be incorporated into applications driven by stored procedures. The FETCH or GET stored procedure returns the RowVersion along with the rest of the data for the row. When the application is ready to update and calls the UPDATE stored procedure, it includes the RowVersion as one of the required parameters. The UPDATE stored procedure can then check the RowVersion and raise an error if the two don't match. If the method is sophisticated, the stored procedure or the front-end application can check the audit trail to see whether or not the columns updated would cause a lost update and report the changes to the last user in the error dialog.

Transaction-Log Architecture

SQL Server's design meets the transactional-integrity ACID properties, largely because of its write-ahead transaction log. The write-ahead transaction log ensures the durability of every transaction.

Transaction log sequence

Every data-modification operation goes through the same sequence in which it writes first to the transaction log and then to the data file. The following sections describe the 12 steps in a transaction.

Database beginning state

Before the transaction begins, the database is in a consistent state. All indexes are complete and point to the correct row. The data meets all the enforced rules for data integrity. Every foreign key points to a valid primary key.

Some data pages are likely already cached in memory. Additional data pages or index pages are copied into memory as needed. Here are the steps of a transaction:

1. The database is in a consistent state.

Data-modification command

The transaction is initiated by a submitted query, batch, or stored procedure, as shown in Figure 66-10.

2. The code issues a BEGIN TRANSACTION command. Even when the DML command is a stand-alone command without a BEGIN TRANSACTION and a COMMIT TRANSACTION, it is still handled as a transaction.
3. The code issues a single DML INSERT, UPDATE, or DELETE command, or a series of them.

   To give you an example of the transaction log in action, the following code initiates a transaction and then submits two UPDATE commands:

```
USE OBXKites;
BEGIN TRANSACTION;

UPDATE Product
  SET ProductDescription = 'Transaction Log Test A',
      DiscontinueDate = '12/31/2003'
  WHERE Code = '1001';

UPDATE Product
```

```
SET ProductDescription = 'Transaction Log Test B',
    DiscontinueDate = '4/1/2003'
WHERE Code = '1002';
```

Notice that the transaction has not yet been committed.

FIGURE 66-10

The SQL DML commands are performed in memory as part of a transaction.

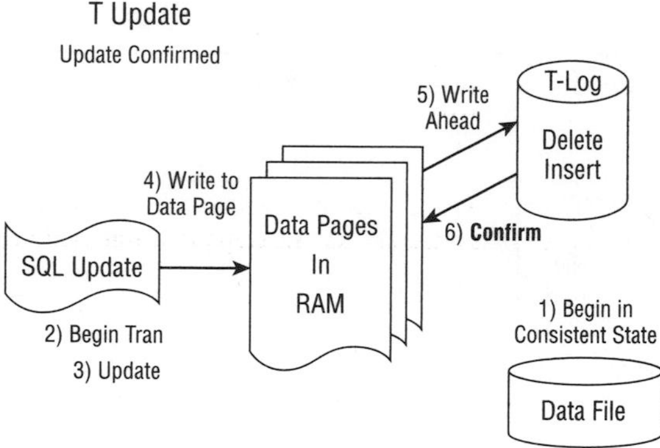

4. The query optimization plan is either generated or pulled from memory. Any required locks are applied, and the data modifications, including index updates, page splits, and any other required system operations, are performed in memory. At this point the data pages in memory are different from those that are stored in the data file.

The following section continues the chronological walk through the process.

Transaction log recorded

The most important aspect of the transaction log is that all data modifications are written to it and confirmed prior to being written to the data file (refer to Figure 66-10).

Best Practice

The write-ahead nature of the transaction log is what makes it critical that the transaction log be stored on a different disk subsystem from the data file. If they are stored separately and either disk subsystem fails, then the database will still be intact, and you will be able to recover it to the split second before the failure.

Conversely, if they are on the same drive, a drive failure will require you to restore from the last backup. If the transaction log fails, it can't be recovered from the data file, so it's a best practice to invest in redundancy for the T-Log files along with regular T-Log backups.

5. The data modifications are written to the transaction log.
6. The transaction log DML entries are confirmed. This ensures that the log entries are in fact written to the transaction log.

Transaction commit

When the sequence of tasks is complete, the `COMMIT TRANSACTION` closes the transaction. Even this task is written to the transaction log, as shown in Figure 66-11.

FIGURE 66-11

The commit transaction command launches another insert into the transaction log.

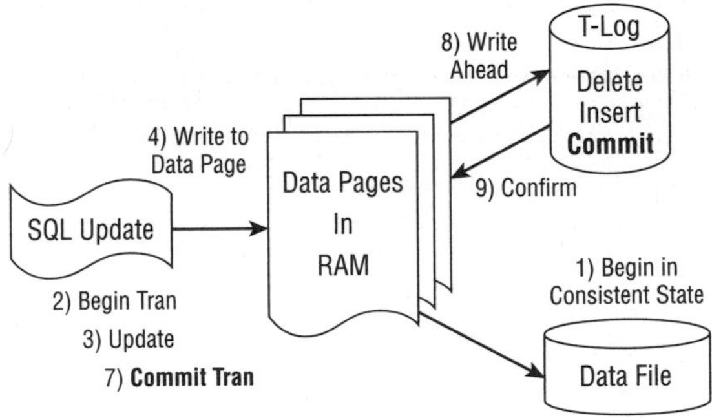

7. The following code closes the transaction:

```
COMMIT TRANSACTION
```

CROSS-REF **To watch transactions post to the transaction log, watch the Transaction screencast on `www.sqlserverbible.com`.**

8. The `COMMIT` entry is written to the transaction log.
9. The transaction-log `COMMIT` entry is confirmed (see Figure 66-12).

NOTE **If you're interested in digging deeper into the transaction log, You might want to research `::fn_dblog(startlsn, endlsn)`, an undocumented system function that reads the log. Also, Change Data Capture leverages the transaction log, so there are some new functions to work with the transaction log and LSNs, as described in Chapter 60, "Change Data Capture."**

Data-file update

With the transaction safely stored in the transaction log, the last operation is to write the data modification to the data file, as shown in Figure 66-13.

FIGURE 66-12

Viewing committed transactions in the transaction log using ApexSQL Log, a third-party product

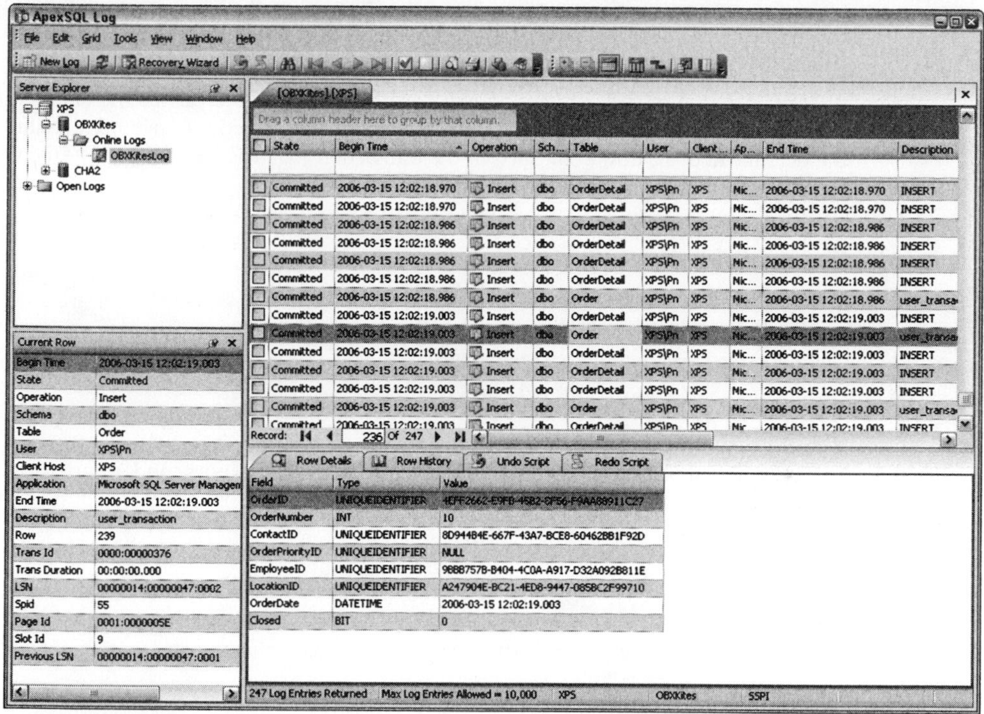

FIGURE 66-13

As one of the last steps, the data modification is written to the data file.

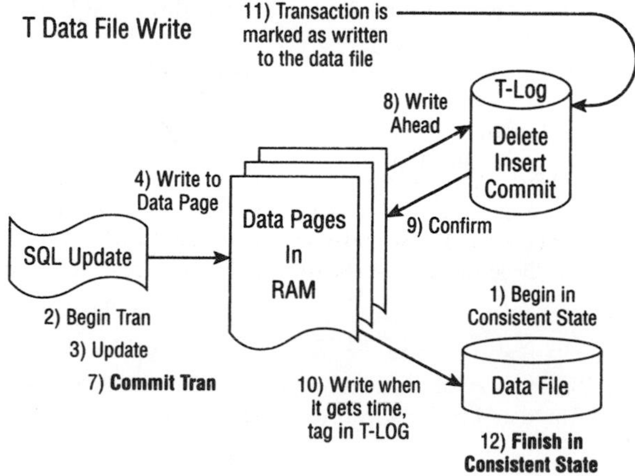

10. In the background, when a checkpoint occurs (a SQL Server internal event) or the lazy writer runs, SQL Server writes any dirty (modified) data pages to the data file. It tries to find sequential pages to improve the performance of the write. Even though I've listed it here as step 10, this can happen at nearly any point during the transaction or after it depending on the amount of data being changed and the memory pressure on the system. SQL Server receives a "write complete" message from Windows.
11. At the conclusion of the background write operation, SQL Server marks the oldest open transaction in the transaction log. All older, committed transactions have been confirmed in the data file and are now confirmed in the transaction log. The `DBCC OpenTran` command reports the oldest open transaction.

Transaction complete

The sequence comes full circle and returns the database to a consistent state.

12. The database finishes in a consistent state.

Transaction-log rollback

If the transaction is rolled back, the DML operations are reversed in memory, and a transaction-abort entry is made in the log. More often than not, the time taken to perform a rollback will be greater than the time taken to make the changes in the first place.

Transaction log recovery

The primary benefit of a write-ahead transaction log is that it maintains the atomic transactional property in the case of system failure.

If SQL Server should cease functioning (perhaps due to a power failure or physical disaster), the transaction log is automatically examined once it recovers, as follows:

- If any entries are in the log as DML operations but are not committed, they are rolled back.
- To test this feature you must be brave. Begin a transaction and shut down the SQL server before issuing a `COMMIT transaction (using the Services applet). This does a shutdown with nowait`. Simply closing Query Analyzer won't do it; Query Analyzer will request permission to commit the pending transactions and will roll back the transactions if permission isn't given. If SQL Server is shut down normally (this varies greatly, as there are many ways to stop, some of which gracefully shut down, others which don't), it will wait for any pending tasks to complete before stopping.
- If you have followed the steps outlined previously and you disable the system just before step 7, the transaction log entries will be identical to those shown later (refer to Figure 66-10).
- Start SQL Server, and it will recover from the crash very nicely and roll back the unfinished transaction. This can be seen in the SQL Server ErrorLog.
- If any entries are in the log as DML operations and committed but not marked as written to the data file, they are written to the data file. This feature is nearly impossible to demonstrate.

Transaction Performance Strategies

Transaction integrity theory can seem daunting at first, and SQL Server has numerous tools to control transaction isolation. If the database is low usage or primarily read-only, transaction locking and blocking won't be a problem. However, for heavy-usage OLTP databases, you'll want to apply the theory and working knowledge from this chapter using these strategies. Also if you are mixing reporting and OLTP systems, you are facing large blocking issues, as reporting systems generally place locks at the page or table level, which isn't good for your OLTP system that wants row-level locks. Because locking and blocking comprise the fourth optimization strategy, ensure that steps one through three are covered before tackling locking and blocking:

1. Begin with Smart Database Design: Start with a clean simplified schema to reduce the number of unnecessary joins and reduce the amount of code used to shuttle data from bucket to bucket.
2. Use efficient set-based code, rather than painfully slow iterative cursors or loops. Large set-based operations can cause locking and blocking. Chapter 22, "Kill the Cursor!," explains how to break up large set-based operations into smaller batches to alleviate this problem.
3. Use a solid indexing strategy to eliminate unnecessary table scans and increase the speed of transactions.

To identify locking problems, use the Activity Monitor or SQL Profiler.

To reduce the severity of a locking problem, do the following:

- Evaluate and test using the read committed snapshot isolation level. Depending on your error handling and hardware capabilities, snapshot isolation can significantly reduce concurrency contention.
- Check the transaction isolation level and ensure that it's not any higher than required.
- Make sure transactions begin and commit quickly. Redesign any transaction that includes a cursor that doesn't have to use a cursor. Move any code that isn't necessary to the transaction out of the transaction unless it is needed to ensure transactional consistency.
- If two procedures are deadlocking, make sure they lock the resource in the same order.
- Make sure client applications access the database through the data abstraction layer.
- Consider forcing rowlocks locks with the `(rowlock)` hint to prevent the locks from escalating.

Evaluating database concurrency performance

It's easy to build a database that doesn't exhibit lock contention and concurrency issues when tested with a handful of users. The real test occurs when several hundred users are all updating orders.

Concurrency testing requires a concerted effort. At one level, it can involve everyone available running the same front-end form concurrently. A .NET program that constantly simulates a user viewing data and updating data is also useful. A good test is to run 20 instances of a script that constantly pounds the database and then let the test crew use the application. Performance Monitor (covered in Chapter 55, "Performance Monitor") can watch the number of locks.

Best Practice

Multi-user concurrency should be tested during the development process several times. To quote the MCSE exam guide, "... don't let the real test be your first test."

Summary

A transaction is a logical unit of work. Although the default SQL Server transaction isolation level works well for most applications, there are several means of manipulating and controlling the locks. To develop a serious SQL Server application, your understanding of the ACID database principles, SQL Server's transaction log, and locking will contribute to the quality, performance, and reliability of the database.

Major points from this chapter include the following:

- Transactions must be ACID: atomic (all or nothing), consistent (before and after the transaction), isolated (not affected by another transaction), and durable (once committed always committed).
- SQL Server transactions are durable because of the write-ahead transaction log.
- SQL Server transactions are isolated because of locks or snapshot isolation.
- Using traditional transaction isolation, readers block writers, and writers block readers and other writers.
- SQL Server offers four traditional transaction isolation levels: read uncommitted, read committed, repeatable read, and serializable. Read committed, the default transaction isolation level, is the right isolation for most OLTP databases.
- Never ever use read uncommitted (or the `NOLOCK` hint).
- Snapshot isolation means reading the before image of the transaction instead of waiting for the transaction to commit. Using snapshot isolation, readers don't block writers, and writers don't block readers; only writers block other writers.

The next chapter continues the optimization theme with one of my favorite new features — data compression. High-transaction databases always struggle with I/O performance, and data compression is the perfect solution for reducing I/O.

Chapter 67

Data Compression

Pushing a database into the tens of thousands of transactions per second requires massive amounts of raw I/O performance. At those rates, today's servers can supply the CPU and memory, but I/O struggles. By reducing the raw size of the data, data compression trades I/O for CPU, improving performance.

Data compression is easy — easy to enable, and easy to benefit from, so why a full chapter on data compression?

Data compression is the sleeper of the SQL Server 2008 new feature list. Like online indexing in SQL Server 2005, I believe that data compression will become the compelling reason to upgrade for many large SQL Server IT shops.

In other words, data compression doesn't warrant an entire chapter because of its complexity or length, but because of its value. Its impact is such that it deserves center stage, at least for this chapter.

IN THIS CHAPTER

Understanding Data Compression

Every IT professional is familiar with data compression, such as zip files and .jpg compression, to name a couple of popular compression technologies.

But SQL Server data compression is specific to the SQL Server storage engine and has a few database-specific requirements. First, there has to be zero risk of loss of data fidelity. Second, it has to be completely transparent — enabled without any application code changes.

SQL Server data compression isn't like .jpg compression, where you can choose the level of compression and more compression means more data loss. With SQL Server data compression, the data is transparently compressed by the storage engine and every compressed data page retains every data value when decompressed.

NOTE **Don't confuse data compression with backup compression — the two technologies are completely independent.**

The following data objects may be compressed:

- Entire heap
- Entire clustered index
- Entire non-clustered index
- Entire indexed view (specifically, the materialized clustered index of an indexed view)
- Single partition of partitioned table or index

NOTE **While indexes can be compressed, they are not automatically compressed with the table's compression type. All objects, including indexes, must be individually, manually enabled for compression.**

Data compression limitations:

- Heaps or clustered indexes with sparse data may not be compressed.
- File stream data or LOB data is not compressed.
- Tables with rows that potentially exceed 8,060 bytes and use row overflow cannot be compressed.
- Data compression does not overcome the row limit. The data must always be able to be stored uncompressed.

Data compression pros and cons

Data compression offers several benefits and a few trade-offs, so while using data compression is probably a good thing, it's worth understanding the pros and cons.

The most obvious con is the financial cost. Data compression is only available with the Enterprise Edition. If you already are using Enterprise Edition, great; if not, then moving from Standard to Enterprise is a significant budget request.

Data compression uses CPU. If your server is CPU pressured, then turning on data compression will probably hurt performance. Depending on the data mix and the transaction rate, enabling data compression might slow down the application.

Not all tables and indexes compress well. In my testing, some objects will compress up to 70%, but many tables will see little compression, or even grow in size when compressed. Therefore, you shouldn't simply enable compression for every object; it takes some study and analysis to choose compression wisely.

With these three possible drawbacks understood, there are plenty of reasons to enable data compression (assuming the data compresses well):

- Data compression significantly reduces the I/O bottleneck for a high-transaction database.
- Data compression significantly reduces the memory footprint of data, thus caching more data in memory and probably improving overall performance.
- More rows on a page mean that scans and `count(*)` type operations are faster.
- Compressed data means SAN shadow copies are smaller.
- Database snapshots are smaller and more efficient with data compression.
- SANS and high-performance disks are expensive. Compressed data means less disk space is required, which means more money is left in the budget to attend a SQL Server conference in Maui.
- Compressed data means backup duration and restore duration is reduced, and less storage space is used for backups.

NOTE **There are hardware-based data compression solutions that compress data as it's written to disk. While these can reduce disk space and off-load the CPU overhead of compression, they fail to reduce the I/O load on SQL Server, or reduce the data's memory footprint within SQL Server.**

There are two types, or levels, of data compression in SQL Server 2008: *row level* and *page level*. Each has a specific capability and purpose. So you can best understand how and when to employ data compression, the following sections describe how they work.

Row compression

Row compression converts the storage of every fixed-length data type column (both character and numeric data types) to a variable-length data type column. Row compression grew out of the vardecimal compression added with SQL Server 2005 SP2. Depending on the number of fixed-length columns and the actual length of the data, this level may, or may not, provide significant gain.

While you'll still see the columns as fixed length when viewing the database, under the covers the storage engine is actually writing the values as if the columns were variable length. A `char(50)` column is treated as if it's a `varchar(50)` column.

When row compression is enabled, SQL Server also uses a new variable-length row format that reduces the per-column metadata overhead from 2 bytes to 4 bits.

Row-level data compression is designed specifically for third-party databases that have several fixed-length columns but don't allow schema changes.

Page compression

SQL Server page compression automatically includes row compression and takes compression two steps further, adding prefix compression and then dictionary compression. Page compression applies only to leaflevel pages (clustered or heaps) and not to the b-tree root or intermediate pages.

Prefix compression may appear complex at first, but it's actually very simple and efficient. For prefix compression the storage engine follows these steps for each column:

1. The storage engine examines all the values and selects the most common prefix value for the data in the column.
2. The longest actual value beginning with the prefix is then stored in the compression information (CI) structure.
3. If the prefix is present at the beginning of the data values, a number is inserted at the beginning of the value to indicate *n* number of prefix characters of the prefix. The non-prefix portion of the value (the part to the right of the prefix) is left in place.

Prefix compression actually examines bytes, so it applies to both character and numeric data.

For example, assume the storage engine were applying prefix compression to the following data, which includes two columns, shown in Figure 67-1.

FIGURE 67-1

The sample data before page compression is enabled.

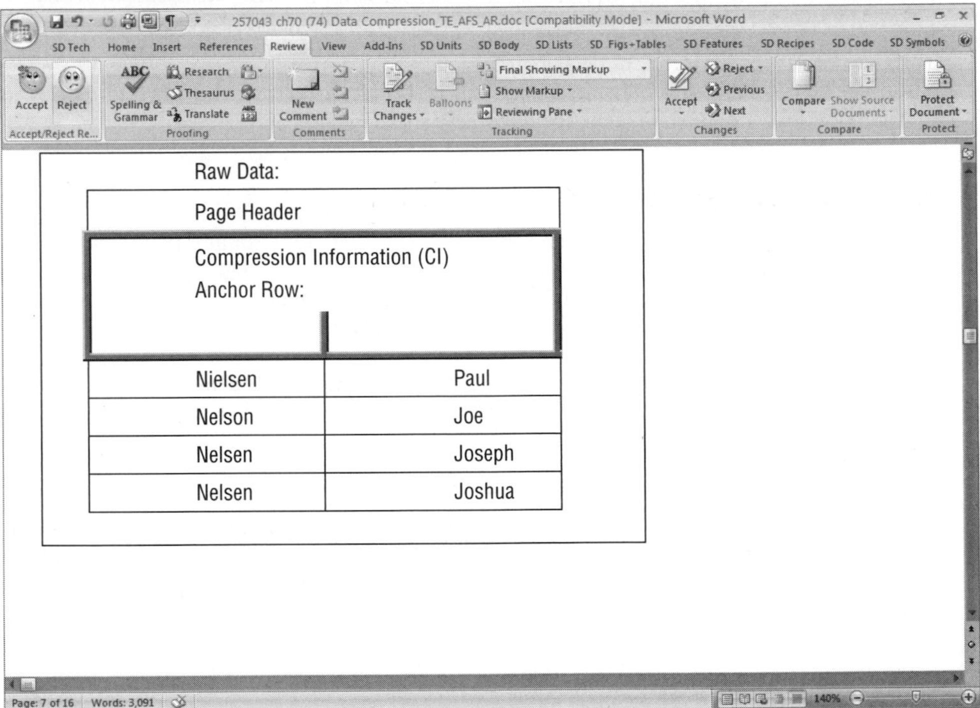

For the first column, the best prefix is `Nels`. The longest value beginning with the prefix is `Nelson`, so that's written to the CI structure, as shown in Figure 67-2. For the second column, the best prefix is `Jos` and the longest value is `Joseph`. The prefixes are written to an anchor row at the beginning of each page.

The values are then updated with the prefix (see Figure 67-2). The first value, `Nielsen`, begins with one letter of the prefix, so `1ielsen` is written, which doesn't save any space. But the compression ratio is much better for values that include more of the prefix — for instance, `Nelson` is compressed into just the number 6 because it contains six characters of the prefix with nothing remaining. `Nelsen` is compressed into `4en`, meaning that it begins with four letters of the compression followed by `en`.

FIGURE 67-2

Prefix compression identifies the best prefix for each column and then stores the prefix character count in each row instead of the prefix characters.

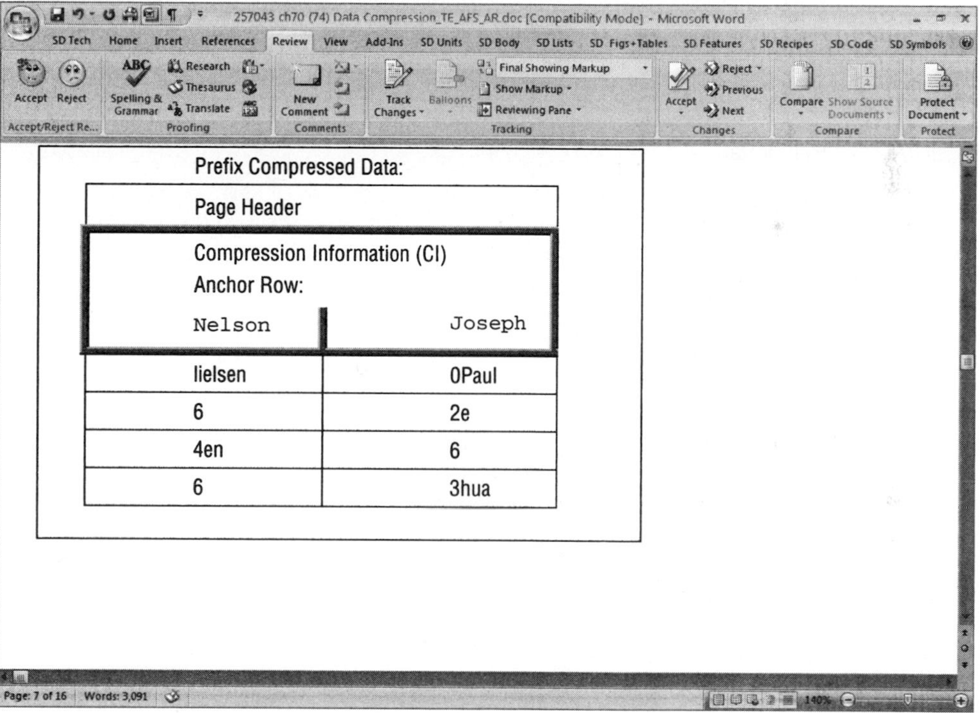

As demonstrated, depending on the commonality of the data set, prefix compression can significantly compress the data without any loss of data fidelity. In this simple example, prefix compression alone reduced the data from 42 bytes to 29 bytes, saving 30%.

Notice that in this example, one value, `Paul`, doesn't match the prefix at all. It's stored as `0Paul`, which increases the length. If this is the case for most of the rows, and prefix compression offers no benefit for a given column, the storage engine will leave the anchor row null and not use prefix compression for that column. This is one reason why sometimes tables will actually grow when compressed.

Once the data is prefix compressed, the storage engine applies *dictionary compression*. Every value is scanned and any common values are replaced with a token that is stored in the compression information area of the page. Prefix compression occurs on the column level, while dictionary compression occurs across all columns on the page level.

Compression sequence

The cool thing about data compression is that it's completely handled by the storage engine and transparent to every process outside of the storage engine. This means that the data is compressed on the disk and is still compressed when it's read into memory. The storage engine decompresses the data as it's being passed from the storage engine to the query processor, as illustrated in Figure 67-3.

FIGURE 67-3

The storage engine compresses and decompresses data as it's written to and read from the buffer.

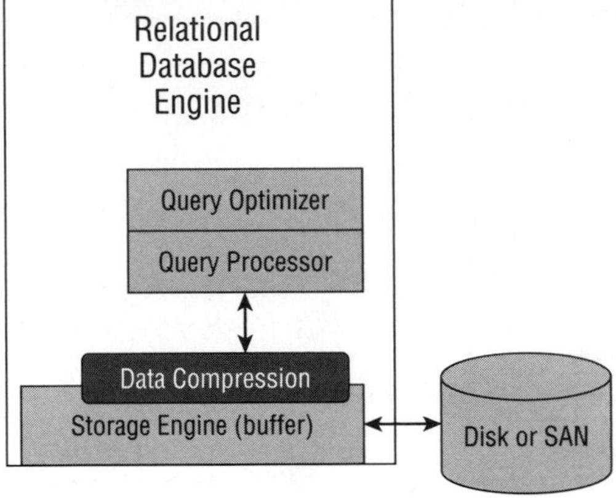

If the object is row compressed, or page compressed (which automatically includes row compression), then row compression is always enabled for every page of the object. Page compression, however, is a different story:

- The storage engine enables page compression on a page-by-page basis when there's a benefit for that page. When the storage engine creates a new page, it's initially uncompressed and remains uncompressed as rows are added to the page. Why compress a page that's only half full anyway?
- When the page is full but SQL Server wants to add another row to it, the storage engine tests the page for compression. If the page compresses enough to add the new rows, then the page is compressed.
- Once the page is a compressed page, any new rows will be inserted compressed (but they won't trigger recalculation of the compression information, the prefix anchor row, or the dictionary tokens).

- Pages might be recompressed (and the prefixes and dictionary tokens recalculated) when the row is updated, based on an algorithm that factors in the number of updates to a page, the number of rows on the page, the average row length, and the amount of space that can be saved by page compression for each page, or when the row would again need to be split.
- Heaps are recompressed only by an index rebuild or bulk load.
- In the case of a page split, both pages inherit the page compression information (compression status, prefixes, and dictionary tokens) of the old page.
- During an index rebuild of an object with page compression, the point at which the page is considered full still considers the fill factor setting, so the free space is still guaranteed.
- Row inserts, updates, and deletes are normally written to the transaction log in row compression, but not in page compression format. An exception is when page splits are logged. Because they are a physical operation, only the page compression values are logged.

Applying Data Compression

Although data compression is complicated, actually enabling data compression is a straightforward task using either the Data Compression Wizard or an ALTER command.

Determining the current compression setting

When working with compression, the first task is to confirm the current compression setting. Using the Management Studio UI, there are two ways to view the compression type for any single object:

- The Table Properties or Index Properties Storage page displays the compression settings as a read-only value.
- The Data Compression Wizard, found in Object Explorer (context menu ➪ Storage ➪ Manage Compression), opens with the current compression selected.

To see the current compression setting for every object in the database, run this query:

```
SELECT O.object_id, S.name AS [schema], O.name AS [Object],
    I.index_id AS Ix_id, I.name AS IxName, I.type_desc AS IxType,
    P.partition_number AS P_No, P.data_compression_desc AS Compression
  FROM sys.schemas AS S
    JOIN sys.objects AS O
      ON S.schema_id = O.schema_id
    JOIN sys.indexes AS I
      ON O.object_id = I.object_id
    JOIN sys.partitions AS P
      ON I.object_id = P.object_id
         AND I.index_id = P.index_id
  WHERE O.TYPE = 'U'
  ORDER BY S.name, O.name, I.index_id ;
```

Abbreviated result when executed in the AdventureWorks database:

```
object_id  schema Object ix_id ixName              ixType       P_No Comp
---------- ------ ------ ----- ------------------- ------------ ---- ----
1509580416 Person Person 1     PK_Person_Busines... CLUSTERED    1    NONE
1509580416 Person Person 2     IX_Person_LastName... NONCLUSTERED 1    NONE
1509580416 Person Person 3     AK_Person_rowguid    NONCLUSTERED 1    NONE
...
```

Estimating data compression

Because every object can yield a different compression ratio, it's useful to have some idea of how much compression is possible before actually performing the compression. Toward this end, SQL Server 2008 includes the ability to pre-estimate the potential data reduction of data compression using the sp_estimate_data_compression_savings system stored procedure.

Specifically, this system stored procedure will copy 5% of the data to be compressed into tempdb and compress it. The 5% is not a random sample but every twentieth page, so it should give consistent results:

```
EXEC sp_estimate_data_compression_savings
  @schema_name = 'Production',
  @object_name = 'BillOfMaterials',
  @index_id = NULL,
  @partition_number = NULL,
  @data_compression = 'page';
```

The result displays the following columns for each object (base table and index):

```
object_name
schema_name
index_id
partition_number
size_with_current_compression_setting(KB)
size_with_requested_compression_setting(KB)
sample_size_with_current_compression_setting(KB)
sample_size_with_requested_compression_setting(KB)
```

The Data Compression Wizard, shown in Figure 67-4, uses this same system stored procedure to estimate the compression. Select the type of compression to estimate and press the Calculate button.

Enabling data compression

Data compression alters the structure of the data on the disk, so it makes sense that data compression is enabled using a CREATE or ALTER statement.

Using the UI, the only way to adjust an object's data compression is by using the same Data Compression Wizard used previously to estimate the compression gain.

FIGURE 67-4

The Data Compression Wizard will estimate the compression ratio and apply the selected type of data compression.

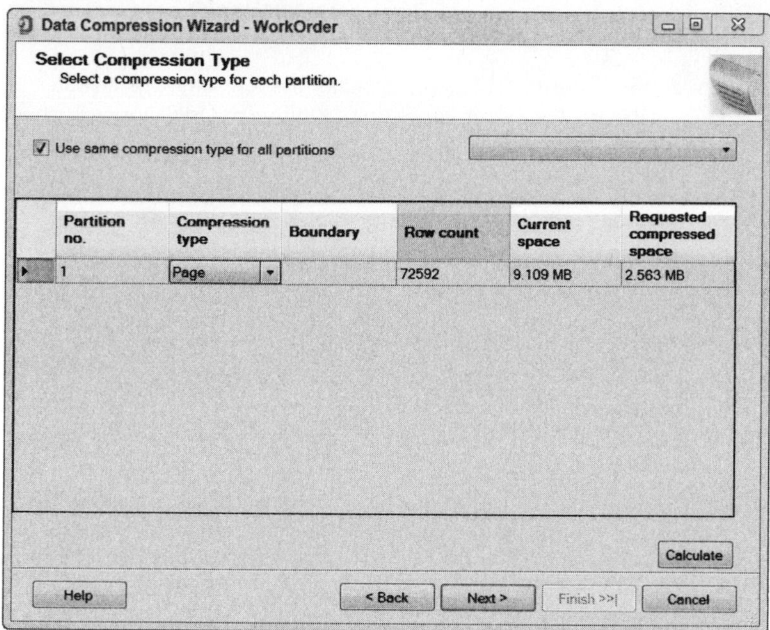

With T-SQL, compression may be initially set when the object is created by adding the data compression setting to the CREATE statement with the following option:

```
WITH (DATA_COMPRESSION = [none, row, or page])
```

Use the following to create a new table with row compression:

```
CREATE TABLE CTest (col1 INT, Col2 CHAR(100))
WITH (Data_Compression = Row);
```

To change the compression setting for an existing object, use the ALTER statement:

```
ALTER object REBUILD
WITH (DATA_COMPRESSION = [none, row, or page])
```

For instance, the following code changes the BillOfMaterials table to page compression:

```
ALTER TABLE 'Production'. 'BillOfMaterials'
Rebuild with (data_compression = Page);
```

Whole Database Compression

I'm a big fan of data compression, so I've expended some effort in trying to make compression more accessible to the busy DBA by creating two stored procedures that automate estimating and applying data compression for the whole database.

The first stored procedure, `db_compression_estimate`, estimates the row and page compression gain for every object and index in the database. For `AdventureWorks2008` on my VPC it runs in about 2:35, producing the following results:

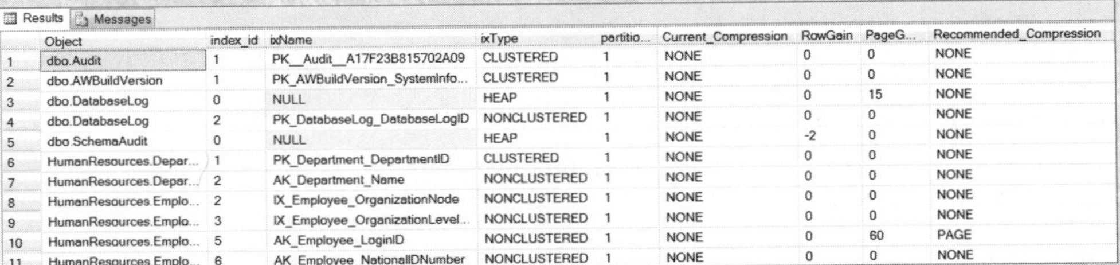

Results | Messages

	Object	index_id	ixName	ixType	partitio...	Current_Compression	RowGain	PageG...	Recommended_Compression
1	dbo.Audit	1	PK__Audit__A17F23B815702A09	CLUSTERED	1	NONE	0	0	NONE
2	dbo.AWBuildVersion	1	PK_AWBuildVersion_SystemInfo...	CLUSTERED	1	NONE	0	0	NONE
3	dbo.DatabaseLog	0	NULL	HEAP	1	NONE	0	15	NONE
4	dbo.DatabaseLog	2	PK_DatabaseLog_DatabaseLogID	NONCLUSTERED	1	NONE	0	0	NONE
5	dbo.SchemaAudit	0	NULL	HEAP	1	NONE	-2	0	NONE
6	HumanResources.Depar...	1	PK_Department_DepartmentID	CLUSTERED	1	NONE	0	0	NONE
7	HumanResources.Depar...	2	AK_Department_Name	NONCLUSTERED	1	NONE	0	0	NONE
8	HumanResources.Emplo...	2	IX_Employee_OrganizationNode	NONCLUSTERED	1	NONE	0	0	NONE
9	HumanResources.Emplo...	3	IX_Employee_OrganizationLevel...	NONCLUSTERED	1	NONE	0	0	NONE
10	HumanResources.Emplo...	5	AK_Employee_LoginID	NONCLUSTERED	1	NONE	0	60	PAGE
11	HumanResources.Emplo...	6	AK_Employee_NationalIDNumber	NONCLUSTERED	1	NONE	0	0	NONE

The `db_compression (@minCompression)` stored procedure automatically compresses using a few intelligent choices: It checks the size of the object and the current compression setting, and compares it to potential row and page compression gains. If the object is eight pages or less, no compression is applied. For larger objects, the stored procedure calls `sp_estimate_data_compression_savings` to estimate the savings with row and page compression. If the estimated gain is equal to or greater than the `@minCompression` parameter (default 25%), it enables row or page compression, whichever offers greater gain. If row and page have the same gain, then it enables row compression.

If the estimated gain is less than the `@mincompression` parameter, then its alters the object to set compression to none.

If the stored procedure is rerun and the gains have changed, it will change the object to the compression method (or no compression) that is now the recommended option.

The `db_compression_estimate` and `db_compression` stored procedures may be downloaded from `www.sqlserverbible.com` or `codeplex.com`. This is the first version of these stored procedures; check back or watch my blog for any updates.

Data compression strategies

Data compression is new to SQL Server and at this early stage, applying compression is more an art than science. With this in mind, here are my recommendations on how to best use data compression:

1. Establish a performance baseline.
2. Run the `db_compress` stored procedure.

3. If specific procedures or queries run noticeably slower, decide, on a case-by-case basis, if the space savings and I/O reduction is worth the performance hit, and adjust compression as needed.
4. Carefully monitor the use of data compression on high-transaction tables, in case the CPU overhead exceeds the I/O performance gains.

In practice I've seen row compression alone offer disk space gains up to 50%, but sometimes it actually increases the size of the data. Seldom does row compression alone beat page compression, but they often provide the same result. When row compression and page compression offer the same compression ratio, it's better to apply only row compression and save the CPU from having to perform the additional page compression.

For small lookup tables that are frequently accessed by queries, use row compression but avoid page compression — the CPU overhead versus compression benefit isn't worth it in this case.

If the object is partitioned using partition tables (covered in the next chapter), carefully consider data compression on a per-partition basis — especially for sliding window–style partitioning.

Summary

Data compression is the sleeper feature of SQL Server 2008. With both row compression and page compression, including both prefix and dictionary compression, SQL Server offers the granularity to tune data compression. Using data compression carefully, you'll be able to push the envelope for an I/O bound, high-transaction database.

The next chapter continues the thread of technologies used for highly scalable database design with a look at several types of partitioning.

Chapter 68

Partitioning

IN THIS CHAPTER

Scaling out with multiple tables and multiple servers.

Distributed partition views

Table partitioning

Custom partitioning design

Divide and conquer.

Dividing a terabyte table can be as effective as dividing an enemy tank division or dividing the opposing political party.

Dividing data brings several benefits:

- It's significantly easier to maintain, back up, and defragment a divided data set.
- The divided data sets mean smaller indexes, fewer intermediate pages, and faster performance.
- The divided data sets can reside on separate physical servers, thus scaling out and lowering costs and improving performance.

However, dividing, or partitioning, data has its own set of problems to conquer. E. F. Codd recognized the potential issues with physical partitioning of data in October 1985 in his famous "Is Your DBMS Really Relational?" article, which outlined 12 rules, or criteria, for a relational database. Rule 11 specifically deals with partitioned data:

Rule 11: Distribution independence

The distribution of portions of the database to various locations should be invisible to users of the database. Existing applications should continue to operate successfully:

1. when a distributed version of the DBMS is first introduced; and

2. when existing distributed data are redistributed around the system.

In layperson's terms, rule 11 says that if the complete set of data is spread over multiple tables or multiple servers, then the software must be able to search for any piece of that data regardless of its physical location.

There are several ways to try to solve this problem. SQL Server offers a couple of technologies that handle partitioning: *partitioned views* and *partitioned tables*. And later in this chapter, I offer a design pattern that I've had some success with.

Partitioning Strategies

The partitions are most effective when the partition key is a column often used to select a range of data, so that a query has a good chance of addressing only one of the segments. For example:

- A company manages sales from five distinct sales offices; splitting the order table by sales region will likely enable each sales region's queries to access only that region's partition.
- A manufacturing company partitions a large activity-tracking table into several smaller tables, one for each department, knowing that each of the production applications tends to query a single department's data.
- A financial company has several terabytes of historical data and must be able to easily query across current and old data. However, the majority of current activity deals with only the current data. Segmenting the data by era enables the current-activity queries to access a much smaller table.

Best Practice

Very large, frequently accessed tables, with data that can logically be divided horizontally for the most common queries, are the best candidates for partitioning. If the table doesn't meet this criteria, don't partition the table.

In the access of data, the greatest bottleneck is reading the data from the drive. The primary benefit of partitioning tables is that a smaller partitioned table will have a greater percentage of the table cached in memory.

Partitioning can be considered from two perspectives:

- *Horizontal partitioning* means splitting the table by rows. For example, if you have a large 5,000-row spreadsheet and split it so that rows 1 through 2,500 remain in the original spreadsheet and move rows 2,501 to 5,000 to a new additional spreadsheet, that move would illustrate horizontal partitioning.
- *Vertical partitioning* splits the table by columns, segmenting some columns into a different table. Sometimes this makes sense from a logical modeling point of view, if the vertical partitioning segments columns that belong only to certain subtypes. But strictly speaking, vertical partitioning is less common and not considered a best practice.

All the partitioning methods discussed in this chapter involve horizontal partitioning.

A Brief History of SQL Server Partitioning

Microsoft introduced partitioned views and distributed partitioned views with SQL Server 2000 and improved their performance with SQL Server 2005, but the big news regarding partitioning in SQL Server 2005 was the new partitioned tables.

SQL Server 2008 doesn't change the feature set or syntax for partitioned views or partitioned tables, but the new version significantly improves how the Query Processor uses parallelism with partitioned tables.

Considerable research is still ongoing regarding SQL Server scale-out and partitioning. Microsoft has already publicly demonstrated Synchronicity — an incredible scale-out middle layer technology for SQL Server.

Partitioned Views

Of the possible ways to partition data using SQL Server, the most straightforward solution is partitioned views.

To *partition* a view is to split the table into two or more smaller separate tables based on a partition key and then make the data accessible, meeting Codd's eleventh rule, using a view. The individual tables can all exist on the same server, making them local partitioned views.

With the data split into several partition tables, of course, each individual table may be directly queried. A more sophisticated and flexible approach is to access the whole set of data by querying a view that unites all the partition tables — this type of view is called a *partitioned view*.

The SQL Server query processor is designed specifically to handle such a partitioned view. If a query accesses the union of all the partition tables, the query processor will retrieve data only from the required partition tables.

A partitioned view not only handles selects; data can be inserted, updated, and deleted through the partitioned view. The query processor will engage only the individual table(s) necessary.

SQL Server supports two types of partition views: local and distributed.

- A *local-partition view* unites data from multiple local partition tables on a single server.
- A *distributed-partition view*, also known as a *federated database*, spreads the partition tables across multiple servers and connects them using linked servers, and views that include distributed queries.

NOTE **The individual tables underneath the partitioned view are called partition tables, not to be confused with partitioned tables, a completely different technology, covered in the next major section in this chapter.**

Local-partition views

Local-partition views access only local tables. For a local-partition view to be configured, the following elements must be in place:

- The data must be segmented into multiple tables according to a single column, known as the *partition key*.
- Each partition table must have a check constraint restricting the partition-key data to a single value. SQL Server uses the check constraint to determine which tables are required by a query.
- The partition key must be part of the primary key.
- The partition view must include a union statement that pulls together data from all the partition tables.

Segmenting the data

To implement a partitioned-view design for a database and segment the data in a logical fashion, the first step is to move the data into the partitioned tables.

As an example, the `Order` and `OrderDetail` tables in the `OBXKites` sample database can be partitioned by sales location. In the sample database, the data breaks down as follows:

```
SELECT LocationCode, Count(OrderNumber) AS Count
  FROM Location
    JOIN [Order]
      ON [Order].LocationID = Location.LocationID
   GROUP BY LocationCode
```

Result:

```
LocationCode      Count
----------------- ---------
CH                6
JR                2
KH                2
```

To partition the sales data, the `Order` and `OrderDetail` tables will be split into a table for each location. The first portion of the script creates the partition tables. They differ from the original tables only in the primary-key definition, which becomes a composite primary key consisting of the original primary key and the `LocationCode`. In the `OrderDetail` table the `LocationCode` column is added so it can serve as the partition key, and the `OrderID` column foreign-key constraint points to the partition table.

The script then progresses to populating the tables from the non-partitioned tables. To select the correct `OrderDetail` rows, the table needs to be joined with the `OrderCH` table.

For brevity's sake, only the Cape Hatteras (CH) location is shown here. The chapter's sample code script includes similar code for the Jockey Ridge and Kill Devil Hills locations. The differences between the partition table and the original tables, and the code that differs among the various partitions, are shown in bold:

```
--Order Table
CREATE TABLE dbo.OrderCH (
```

```
  LocationCode CHAR(5) NOT NULL,
  OrderID UNIQUEIDENTIFIER NOT NULL  -- Not PK
    ROWGUIDCOL DEFAULT (NEWID()),
  OrderNumber INT NOT NULL,
  ContactID UNIQUEIDENTIFIER NULL
    FOREIGN KEY REFERENCES dbo.Contact,
  OrderPriorityID UNIQUEIDENTIFIER NULL
    FOREIGN KEY REFERENCES dbo.OrderPriority,
  EmployeeID UNIQUEIDENTIFIER NULL
    FOREIGN KEY REFERENCES dbo.Contact,
  LocationID UNIQUEIDENTIFIER NOT NULL
    FOREIGN KEY REFERENCES dbo.Location,
  OrderDate DATETIME NOT NULL DEFAULT (GETDATE()),
  Closed BIT NOT NULL DEFAULT (0) -- set to true when Closed
   )
  ON [Primary]
go

-- PK
ALTER TABLE dbo.OrderCH
  ADD CONSTRAINT
    PK_OrderCH PRIMARY KEY NONCLUSTERED
      (LocationCode, OrderID)

-- Check Constraint
ALTER TABLE dbo.OrderCH
  ADD CONSTRAINT
    OrderCH_PartitionCheck CHECK (LocationCode = 'CH')

go
-- Order Detail Table
CREATE TABLE dbo.OrderDetailCH (
  LocationCode CHAR(5) NOT NULL,
  OrderDetailID UNIQUEIDENTIFIER NOT NULL -- Not PK
    ROWGUIDCOL DEFAULT (NEWID()),
  OrderID UNIQUEIDENTIFIER NOT NULL, -- Not FK
  ProductID UNIQUEIDENTIFIER NULL
    FOREIGN KEY REFERENCES dbo.Product,
  NonStockProduct NVARCHAR(256),
  Quantity NUMERIC(7,2) NOT NULL,
  UnitPrice MONEY NOT NULL,
  ExtendedPrice AS Quantity * UnitPrice,
  ShipRequestDate DATETIME,
  ShipDate DATETIME,
  ShipComment NVARCHAR(256)
  )
  ON [Primary]
go
```

```
ALTER TABLE dbo.OrderDetailCH
  ADD CONSTRAINT
    FK_OrderDetailCH_Order
      FOREIGN KEY (LocationCode,OrderID)
      REFERENCES dbo.OrderCH(LocationCode,OrderID)

ALTER TABLE dbo.OrderDetailCH
  ADD CONSTRAINT
    PK_OrderDetailCH PRIMARY KEY NONCLUSTERED
      (LocationCode, OrderDetailID)

ALTER TABLE dbo.OrderDetailCH
  ADD CONSTRAINT
    OrderDetailCH_PartitionCheck CHECK (LocationCode = 'CH')

go

-- move the data
INSERT dbo.OrderCH (LocationCode,
    OrderID, OrderNumber, ContactID, OrderPriorityID,
    EmployeeID, LocationID, OrderDate, Closed)
  SELECT
      'CH',
      OrderID, OrderNumber, ContactID, OrderPriorityID,
      EmployeeID, [Order].LocationID, OrderDate, Closed
    FROM [Order]
      JOIN Location
        ON [Order].LocationID = Location.LocationID
    WHERE LocationCode = 'CH'

INSERT dbo.OrderDetailCH (
    LocationCode, OrderDetailID, OrderID, ProductID,
    NonStockProduct, Quantity, UnitPrice, ShipRequestDate,
    ShipDate, ShipComment)
  SELECT 'CH',
      OrderDetailID, OrderDetail.OrderID,
      ProductID, NonStockProduct, Quantity, UnitPrice,
      ShipRequestDate, ShipDate, ShipComment
    FROM OrderDetail
      JOIN OrderCH
      ON OrderDetail.OrderID = OrderCH.OrderID
```

Creating the partition view

With the data split into valid partition tables that include the correct primary keys and constraints, SQL Server can access the correct partition table through a partition view. The `OrderAll` view uses a `UNION ALL` to vertically merge data from all three partition tables:

```
CREATE VIEW OrderAll
AS
```

```
  SELECT
      LocationCode,
      OrderID, OrderNumber, ContactID, OrderPriorityID,
      EmployeeID, LocationID, OrderDate, Closed
    FROM OrderCH
UNION ALL
  SELECT
      LocationCode,
      OrderID, OrderNumber, ContactID, OrderPriorityID,
      EmployeeID, LocationID, OrderDate, Closed
    FROM OrderJR
UNION ALL
  SELECT
      LocationCode,
      OrderID, OrderNumber, ContactID, OrderPriorityID,
      EmployeeID, LocationID, OrderDate, Closed
    FROM OrderKDH
```

Selecting through the partition view

When all the data is selected from the `OrderAll` partition view, the query plan, shown in Figure 68-1, includes all three partition tables as expected:

```
SELECT LocationCode, OrderNumber
  FROM OrderAll
```

Result (abridged):

```
LocationCode OrderNumber
------------ -----------
CH           1
...
JR           4
JR           7
KDH          9
KDH          10
```

What makes partition views useful for advanced scalability is that the SQL Server query processor will use the partition tables' check constraints to access only the required tables if the partition key is included in the `WHERE` clause of the query calling the partition view.

The following query selects on the Kill Devil Hills orders from the partition view. The `LocationCode` column is the partition key, so this query will be optimized for scalability. Even though the view's union includes all three partition tables, the query execution plan, shown in Figure 68-2, reveals that the query processor accesses only the `OrderCH` partition table:

```
SELECT OrderNumber
  FROM OrderAll
  WHERE LocationCode = 'KDH'
```

Result:

```
OrderNumber
-----------
9
10
```

FIGURE 68-1

The partition table's query plan, when run without a where clause restriction, includes all the partition tables as a standard union query.

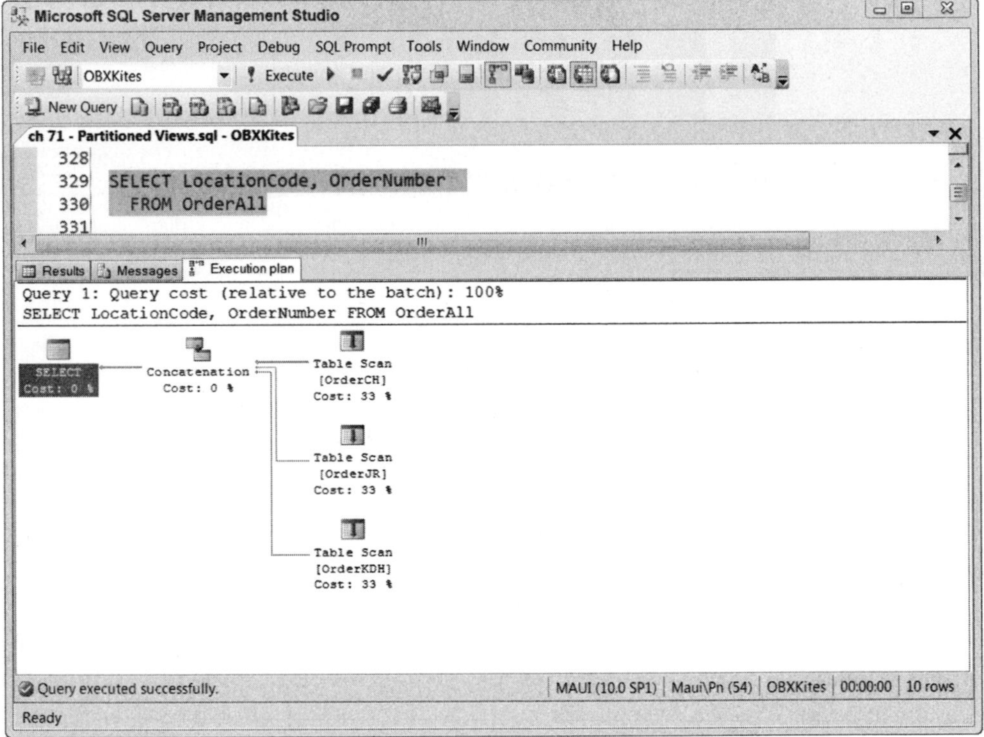

Updating through the partition view

Union queries are typically not updateable. Yet, the partition tables' check constraints enable a partition view based on a union query to be updated, as long as a few conditions are met:

- The partition view must include all the columns from the partition tables.
- The primary key must include the partition key.

- Partition table columns, including the primary key, must be identical.
- Columns and tables must not be duplicated within the partition view.

FIGURE 68-2

When a query with a where clause restriction that includes the partition key retrieves data through the partition view, SQL Server's query processor accesses only the required tables.

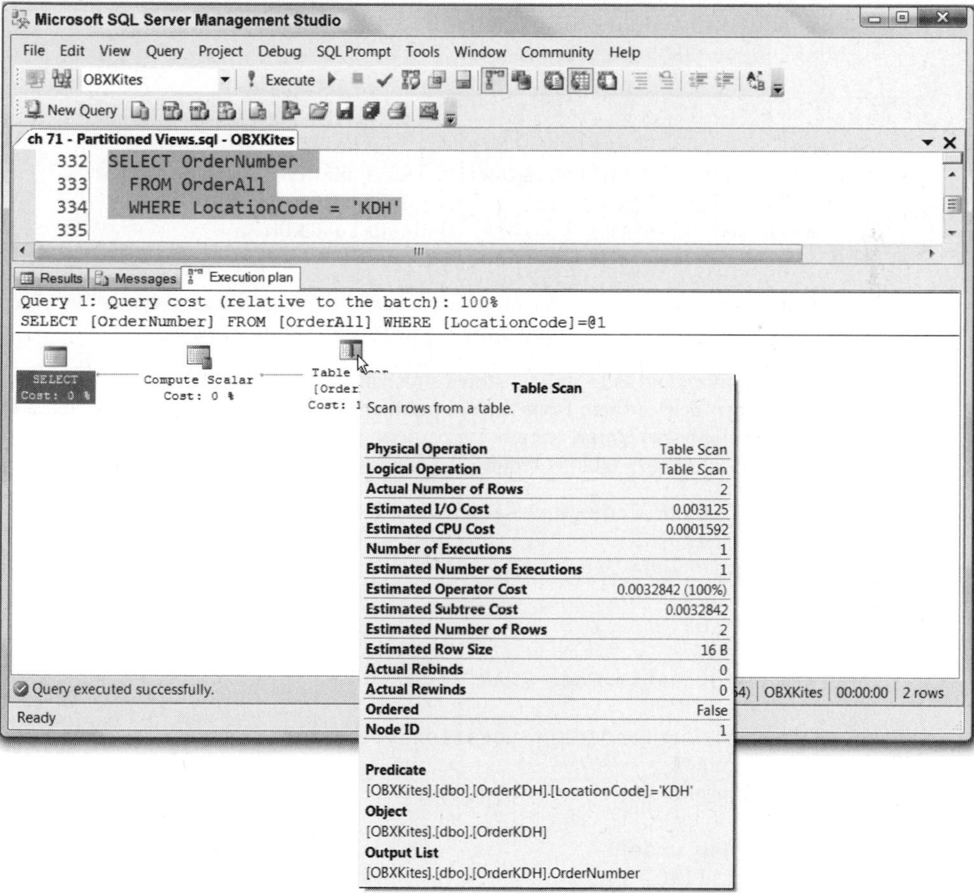

The following UPDATE query demonstrates updating through the OrderAll view:

```
UPDATE OrderAll
  SET Closed = 0
  WHERE LocationCode = 'KDH'
```

Unfortunately, an UPDATE does not benefit from query optimization to the extent that a SELECT does. For heavy transactional processing at the stored-procedure level, the code should access the correct partition table.

Moving data

An issue with local-partition views is that data is not easily moved from one partition table to another partition table. An UPDATE query that attempts to update the partition key violates the check constraint:

```
UPDATE OrderAll
  SET Locationcode = 'JR'
  WHERE OrderNumber = 9
```

Result:

```
Server: Msg 547, Level 16, State 1, Line 1
UPDATE statement conflicted with TABLE REFERENCE constraint
  'FK_OrderDetailKDH_Order'. The conflict occurred in
   database 'OBXKites', table 'OrderDetailKDH'.
The statement has been terminated.
```

For implementations that partition by region or department, moving data may not be an issue, but for partition schemes that divide the data into current and archive partitions, it is.

The only possible workaround is to write a stored procedure that inserts the rows to be moved into the new partition and then deletes them from the old partition. To complicate matters further, a query that inserts into the partition view cannot reference a partition table in the query, so an INSERT...SELECT query won't work. A temporary table is required to facilitate the move:

```
CREATE PROCEDURE OrderMovePartition (
  @OrderNumber INT,
  @NewLocationCode CHAR(5) )
AS
SET NoCount ON

DECLARE @OldLocationCode CHAR(5)

SELECT @OldLocationCode = LocationCode
  FROM OrderAll
  WHERE OrderNumber = @OrderNumber

-- Insert New Order
  SELECT DISTINCT
      OrderID, OrderNumber, ContactID, OrderPriorityID,
      EmployeeID, LocationID, OrderDate, Closed
    INTO #OrderTemp
    FROM OrderAll
    WHERE OrderNumber = @OrderNumber
      AND LocationCode = @OldLocationCode

INSERT dbo.OrderAll (LocationCode,
    OrderID, OrderNumber, ContactID, OrderPriorityID,
```

```
    EmployeeID, LocationID, OrderDate, Closed)
  SELECT
      @NewLocationCode,
      OrderID, OrderNumber, ContactID, OrderPriorityID,
      EmployeeID, LocationID, OrderDate, Closed
    FROM #OrderTemp

-- Insert the New OrderDetail
  SELECT DISTINCT
      OrderDetailID, OrderDetailAll.OrderID,
      ProductID, NonStockProduct, Quantity, UnitPrice,
      ShipRequestDate, ShipDate, ShipComment
    INTO #TempOrderDetail
    FROM OrderDetailALL
      JOIN OrderALL
      ON OrderDetailALL.OrderID = OrderALL.OrderID
    WHERE OrderNumber = @OrderNumber

Select * from #TempOrderDetail

INSERT dbo.OrderDetailAll (
    LocationCode, OrderDetailID, OrderID, ProductID,
    NonStockProduct, Quantity, UnitPrice, ShipRequestDate,
    ShipDate, ShipComment)
  SELECT @NewLocationCode,
      OrderDetailID, OrderID,
      ProductID, NonStockProduct, Quantity, UnitPrice,
      ShipRequestDate, ShipDate, ShipComment
    FROM #TempOrderDetail

-- Delete the Old OrderDetail
DELETE FROM OrderDetailAll
  FROM OrderDetailAll
    JOIN OrderALL
      ON OrderAll.OrderID = OrderDetailAll.OrderID
  WHERE OrderNumber = @OrderNumber
    AND OrderDetailAll.LocationCode = @OldLocationCode

-- Delete the Old Order
DELETE FROM OrderALL
  WHERE OrderNumber = @OrderNumber
    AND LocationCode = @OldLocationCode
```

To test the stored procedure, the following batch moves order number 9 from the Kill Devils Hill store to the Jockey's Ridge location:

```
EXEC OrderMovePartition 9, 'JR'
```

To see the move, the following query reports the LocationCode from both the OrderAll and the OrderDetailAll tables:

```
Select
    OrderAll.OrderNumber,
    OrderALL.LocationCode as OrderL,
    OrderDetailALL.LocationCode AS DetailL
  FROM OrderDetailAll
    JOIN OrderAll
      ON OrderAll.OrderID = OrderDetailAll.OrderID
  WHERE OrderNumber = 9
```

Result:

```
OrderNumber OrderL DetailL
----------- ------ -------
9           JR     JR
9           JR     JR
9           JR     JR
```

Distributed-partition views

Because partition views often segment data along natural geographic lines, it logically follows that a partition view that spans multiple servers is very useful. Distributed-partition views build upon local-partition views to unite data from segmented tables located on different servers. This technique is also referred to as a *federated-database configuration* because multiple individual components cooperate to complete the whole. This is how Microsoft gains those incredible performance benchmarks.

The basic concept is the same as that of a local-partition view, with a few differences:

- The participating servers must be configured as linked servers with each other.
- The distributed-partition view on each server is a little different from those of the other servers, because it must use distributed queries to access the other servers.
- Each server must be configured for lazy schema validation to prevent repeated requests for metadata information about the databases.

NOTE **Turning on lazy schema validation means that SQL Server will not check remote tables for the proper schema until it has executed a script. This means that if a remote table has changed, then scripts that depend on that table will error out. Turning this feature on can result in certain bad effects on scripts but does help increase performance.**

The following script configures a quick distributed-partition view between `Maui` and `Maui\Copenhagen` (my two development instances). To save space, I list only the `Maui` half of the script. Similar code is also run on the second server to establish the distributed view. The script creates a database with a single table and inserts a single row. Once a link is established, and lazy schema validation is enabled, the distributed-partition view is created. This partition view is created with a four-part name to access the remote server. Selecting through the distributed-partition view retrieves data from both servers:

```
CREATE DATABASE DistView
go
USE DistView
```

```
CREATE TABLE dbo.Inventory(
  LocationCode CHAR(10) NOT NULL,
  ItemCode INT NOT NULL,
  Quantity INT )
ALTER TABLE dbo.Inventory
  ADD CONSTRAINT PK_Inventory
        PRIMARY KEY NONCLUSTERED(LocationCode, ItemCode)
ALTER TABLE dbo.Inventory
  ADD CONSTRAINT Inventory_PartitionCheck
      CHECK (LocationCode = 'MAUI')

INSERT dbo.Inventory
  (LocationCode, ItemCode, Quantity)
  VALUES ('MAUI', 12, 1)

-- Link to the Second Server
EXEC sp_addlinkedserver
  @server = 'MAUI\COPENHAGEN',
  @srvproduct = 'SQL Server'

EXEC sp_addlinkedsrvlogin
  @rmtsrvname = 'MAUI\COPENHAGEN'

-- Lazy Schema Validation
EXEC sp_serveroption 'MAUI\COPENHAGEN',
  'lazy schema validation', true

-- Create the Distributed Partition View
CREATE VIEW InventoryAll
AS
  SELECT *
    FROM dbo.Inventory
UNION ALL
  SELECT *
    FROM [MAUI\COPENHAGEN].DistView.dbo.Inventory

SELECT *
  FROM InventoryAll
Result:
LocationCode     ItemCode    Quantity
---------------- ----------- -----------
MAUI             12          1
MAUI\COPENHAGEN  14          2
```

Updating and moving data with distributed-partition views

One fact that makes distributed-partition views an improvement over local-partition views is that a distributed-partition view can move data without complication. MS Distributed Transaction Coordinator must be running and `xact_abort` enabled because the transaction is a distributed transaction. The following update query changes the `LocationCode` of the first server's row to `Maui\Copenhagen`, and effectively moves the row from `Maui` to `Maui\Copenhagen`:

```
SET XACT_ABORT ON
UPDATE InventoryAll
  SET LocationCode = 'MAUI\COPENHAGEN'
    WHERE Item = 12
```

To show you the effect of the update query, the next query selects from the distributed-partition view and demonstrates that item 14 is now located on `Maui`:

```
SELECT *
  FROM InventoryAll
```

Result:

```
LocationCode ItemCode    Quantity
------------ ----------- -----------
MAUI         12          1
MAUI         14          2
```

Highly scalable distributed-partition views

SQL Server's query processor handles distributed-partition views much like it handles local-partition views. Where the local-partition view accesses only the required tables, a distributed-partition view performs distributed queries and requests the required data from the remote servers. Each server executes a portion of the query.

In the following example, the query is being executed on `Maui`. A remote query request is sent to `Maui\Copenhagen`, and the results are passed back to `Maui`. The query processor knows not to bother looking at the table on `Maui`. Even better, the query passes the row restriction to the remote server as well. `Maui\Copenhagen` has two rows, but only one is returned:

```
SELECT *
  FROM InventoryAll
    WHERE LocationCode = 'MAUI\COPENHAGEN'
      AND Item = 14
```

Result:

```
LocationCode       ItemCode    Quantity
------------------ ----------- -----------
MAUI\COPENHAGEN    14          2
```

Partitioned Tables and Indexes

Partitioned tables are similar to partitioned views — both involve segmenting the data. However, whereas partitioned views store the data in separate tables and use a view to access the tables, partitioned tables store the data in a segmented clustered index and use the table to access the data.

Partitioning tables reduces the sheer size of the clustered and non-clustered b-tree indexes, which provides these scalability benefits:

- Inserts and update operations must also insert and update index pages. When a table is partitioned, only the affected partition's indexes are updated.
- Index maintenance can be a costly operation. A partition's index is significantly smaller and reduces the performance cost of reindexing or defragmenting the index. However, the partitions can't be indexed off-line, which is still a major drawback.
- Backing up part of a table using Backup Filegroups eases backups.
- The index b-tree is slightly smaller — perhaps an intermediate level or two smaller — but the performance gain is probably not going to be noticeable.
- A partitioned table can segment the data by one `WHERE` clause filter and perhaps improve the selectiveness of another filtering predicate so that the index is used when perhaps it wasn't without partitioning.
- With partitioned data, a scan might only need to retrieve a partition, rather than the entire table, which can result in a huge performance difference and avoid memory bloat.

Best Practice

The performance benefit of partitioned tables doesn't kick in until the table is extremely large — billion-row tables in terabyte-size databases. In fact, in some testing, partitioned tables actually hurt performance on smaller tables with less than a million rows, so reserve this technology for the big problems. Maybe that's why table partitioning isn't included in Standard Edition.

On the other hand, even for tables with fewer than one million rows, partitioning can be an effective part of archiving old data into one partition while keeping current data in another partition.

Creating SQL Server 2008 table partitions is a straightforward four-step process:

1. Create the partition function that will determine how the data is partitioned.
2. Create the partition scheme that assigns partitions to filegroups.
3. Create the table with a non-clustered primary key.
4. Create a clustered index for the table using the partition scheme and partition function.

Partition functions and partition schemes work together to segment the data as illustrated in Figure 68-3.

Creating the partition function

A partition function is simply a means to define the range of values that each partition will contain. A table partition can segment the data based on a single column. Even though the table isn't yet defined, the function must know the segmenting column's data type, so the partition function's parameter is the data type that will be used to segment the data.

In the following example, the function `fnYears` takes a datetime value. The function defines the boundary values for the ranges of each partition. An important aspect of boundary values is that you

FIGURE 68-3

The partition function is used by the partition scheme to place the data in separate filegroups.

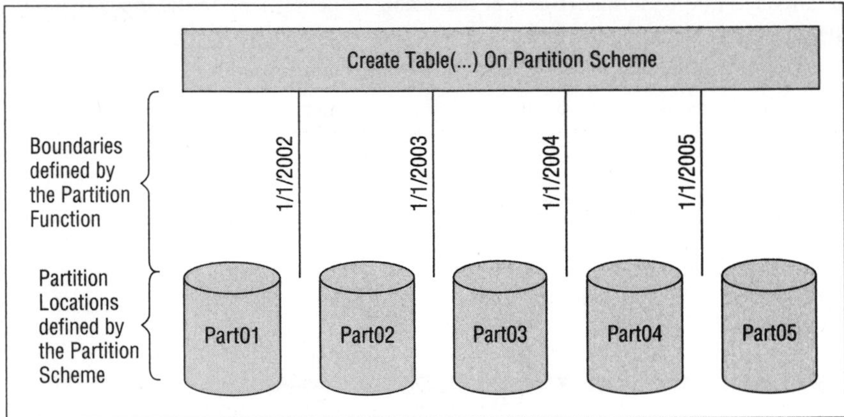

only specify the boundary values between ranges; they don't define the upper or lower values for the whole table.

A boundary value can only exist in one partition. The ranges are defined as left or right. If a row has a partition column value that is the same as a boundary value, then SQL Server needs to know in which partition to put the row.

Left ranges mean that data equal to the boundary is included in the partition to the left of the boundary. A boundary of `'12/31/2004'` would create two partitions. The lower partition would include all data up to and including `'12/31/2004'`, and the right partition would include any data greater than `'12/31/2004'`.

Right ranges mean that data equal to the boundary goes into the partition on the right of the boundary value. To separate at the new year starting 2008, a right range would set the boundary at `'1/1/2008'`. Any values less than the boundary go into the left, or lower, boundary. Any data with a date equal to or later than the boundary goes into the next partition. These two functions use left and right ranges to create the same result:

```
CREATE PARTITION FUNCTION pfyears(DateTime)
AS RANGE LEFT FOR VALUES
('12/31/2001', '12/31/2002', '12/31/2003', '12/31/2004');
```

or

```
CREATE PARTITION FUNCTION pfYearsRT(DateTime)
AS RANGE RIGHT FOR VALUES
('1/1/2002', '1/1/2003', '1/1/2004', '1/1/2008');
```

These functions both create four defined boundaries, and thus five partitions.

NOTE **SQL Server 2008's table partitions are declarative, meaning the table is segmented by data values. A hash partition segments the data randomly. SQL Server does not have hash partitioning. You can create a hash function on a computed column but your client application needs to understand this computation to allow for partition elimination. Another option to randomly spread the data across multiple disk subsystems is to define the table using a filegroup and then add multiple files to the filegroup. See Figure 68-4.**

FIGURE 68-4

The partition configuration can be viewed in Object Explorer.

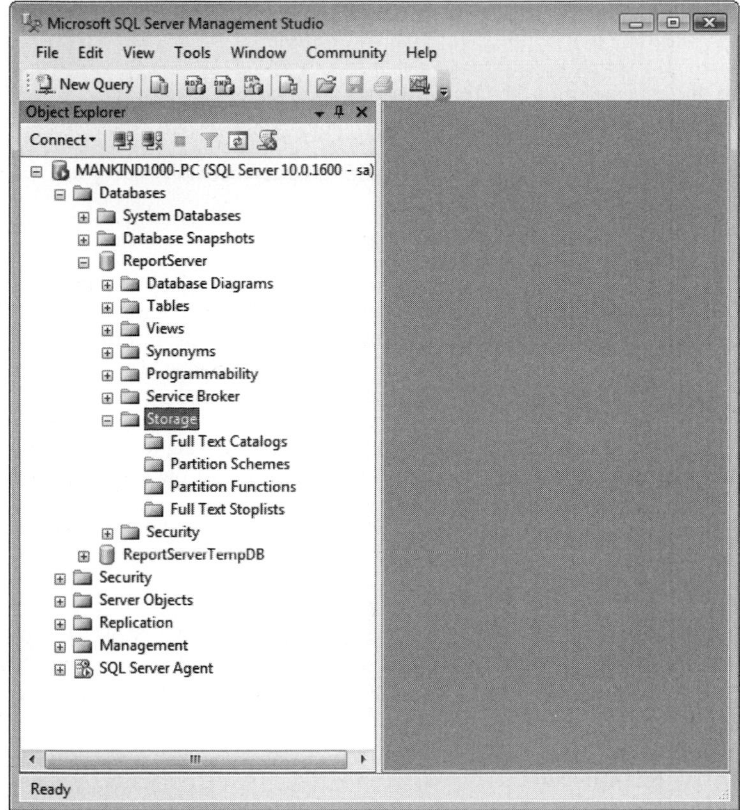

TIP **Three catalog views expose information about partition function:** `syspartition_functions`, `syspartition_function_range_values`, **and** `syspartition_parameters`.

Creating partition schemes

The partition schema builds on the partition function to specify the physical locations for the partitions. The physical partition tables may all be located in the same filegroup or spread over several filegroups.

The first example partition scheme, named psYearsAll, uses the pfYearsRT partition function and places all the partitions in the Primary filegroup:

```
CREATE PARTITION SCHEME psYearsAll
AS PARTITION pfYearsRT
  ALL TO ([Primary]);
```

To place the table partitions in their own filegroup, omit the ALL keyword and list the filegroups individually. This creates five partitions to match the four boundary values specific in the function:

```
CREATE PARTITION SCHEME psYearsFiles
AS PARTITION pfYearsRT
  TO (Part01, Part02, Part03, Part04, Part05);
```

The partition functions and schemes must be created using T-SQL code, but once they've been created you can view them in Management Studio's Object Explorer under the database Storage node.

TIP **To examine information about partition schemes programmatically, query** sys.partition_schemes.

Creating the partition table

Once the partition function and partition schemes are in place, actually creating the table is a piece of cake (pun intended). I recommend creating a partition table with a non-clustered primary key. Adding a clustered index to a table will partition the table based on the partition scheme. The WorkOrder Table Properties page also displays the partition scheme being used by the table.

Partition functions and partition schemes don't have owners, so when referring to partition schemes or partition functions, you don't need to use the four-part name or the schema owner in the name.

The following table is similar to the AdventureWorks WorkOrder table in the production scheme:

```
CREATE TABLE dbo.WorkOrder (
  WorkOrderID INT NOT NULL PRIMARY KEY NONCLUSTERED,
  ProductID INT NOT NULL,
  OrderQty INT NOT NULL,
  StockedQty INT NOT NULL,
  ScrappedQty INT NOT NULL,
  StartDate DATETIME NOT NULL,
  EndDate DATETIME NOT NULL,
  DueDate DATETIME NOT NULL,
  ScrapReasonID INT NULL,
  ModifiedDate DATETIME NOT NULL
  );
CREATE CLUSTERED INDEX ix_WorkORder_DueDate
  ON dbo.WorkOrder (DueDate)
    ON psYearsAll(DueDate);
```

The next script inserts 7,259,100 rows into the WorkOrder table in 2 minutes and 42 seconds, as confirmed by the database Summary page:

```
DECLARE @Counter INT;
SET @Counter = 0;

WHILE @Counter < 100
BEGIN
  SET @Counter = @Counter + 1;
  INSERT dbo.WorkOrder (ProductID, OrderQty, StockedQty, ScrappedQty,
     StartDate, EndDate, DueDate, ScrapReasonID, ModifiedDate)
    SELECT WorkOrderID, ProductID, OrderQty, StockedQty, ScrappedQty,
      StartDate, EndDate, DueDate, ScrapReasonID, ModifiedDate
    FROM AdventureWorks.Production.WorkOrder;
END;
```

It's possible for multiple partition schemas to share a single partition function. Architecturally, this might make sense if several tables should be partitioned using the same boundaries, because this improves the consistency of the partitions. To verify which tables use which partition schemes, based on which partition functions, use the Object Dependencies dialog for the partition function or partition scheme. You can find it using the partition function's context menu.

To see information about how the partitions are being used, look at `sys.partitions` **and** `sys.partition_counts`.

Querying partition tables

The nice thing about partition tables is that no special code is required to query either across multiple underlying partition tables or from only one partition table. The Query Optimizer automatically uses the right tables to retrieve the data.

The `$partition` operator can return the partition table's integer identifier when used with the partition function. The next code snippet counts the number of rows in each partition:

```
SELECT $PARTITION.pfYearsRT(DueDate) AS Partition,
    COUNT(*) AS Count
  FROM WorkOrder
  GROUP BY $PARTITION.pfYearsRT(DueDate)
  ORDER BY Partition;
```

Result:

```
Partition        Count
-----------      --------
1                703900
2                1821200
3                2697100
4                2036900
```

The next query selects data for one year, so the data should be located in only one partition. Examining the query execution plan (not shown here) reveals that the Query Optimizer used a high-speed clustered index scan on partition ID `PtnIds1005`:

```
SELECT WorkOrderID,ProductID, OrderQty, StockedQty, ScrappedQty
  FROM dbo.WorkOrder
  WHERE DueDate between '1/1/2002' and '12/31/2002'
```

Altering partition tables

In order for partition tables to be updated to keep up with changing data, and to enable the performance testing of various partition schemes, they are easily modified. Even though the commands are simple, modifying the design of partition tables never executes very quickly, as you can imagine.

Merging partitions

Merge and split surgically modify the table partition design. The `ALTER PARTITION...MERGE RANGE` command effectively removes one of the boundaries from the partition function and merges two partitions. For example, to remove the boundary between 2003 and 2004 in the `pfYearsRT` partition function, and combine the data from 2003 and 2004 into a single partition, use the following `ALTER` command:

```
ALTER PARTITION FUNCTION pfYearsRT()
  MERGE RANGE ('1/1/2004');
```

Sure enough, following the merge operation, the previous count-rows-per-partition query now returns three partitions, and scripting the partition function from Object Explorer creates a script with three boundaries in the partition function code.

If multiple tables share the same partition scheme and partition function being modified, then multiple tables will be affected by these changes.

Splitting partitions

To split an existing single partition, the first step is to designate the next filegroup to be used by the partition scheme. This is done using the `ALTER PARTITION...NEXT USED` command. If you specify too many filegroups when creating a scheme, you will get a message that the next filegroup used is the extra file group you specified. Then the partition function can be modified to specify the new boundary using the `ALTER PARTITION...SPLIT RANGE` command to insert a new boundary into the partition function. It's the `ALTER FUNCTION` command that actually performs the work.

This example segments the 2003–2004 work order data into two partitions. The new partition will include only data for July 2004, the last month with data in the `AdventureWorks` table:

```
ALTER PARTITION SCHEME psYearsFiles
  NEXT USED [Primary];
```

```
ALTER PARTITION FUNCTION pfYearsRT()
  SPLIT RANGE ('7/1/2004');
```

Switching tables

Switching tables is the cool capability to move an entire table into a partition within a partitioned table, or to remove a single partition so that it becomes a stand-alone table. This is very useful when importing new data, but note a few restrictions:

- Every index for the partition table must be a partitioned index.
- The new table must have the same columns (excluding identity columns), indexes, and constraints (including foreign keys) as the partition table, except that the new table cannot be partitioned.
- The source partition table cannot be the target of a foreign key.
- Neither table can be published using replication, or have schema-bound views.
- The new table must have check constraint restricting the data range to the new partition, so SQL Server doesn't have to re-verify the data range (and it needs to be validated; no point loading and then creating the constraint with nocheck).
- Both the stand-alone table and the partition that will receive the stand-alone table must be on the same filegroup.
- The receiving partition or table must be empty.

In essence, switching a partition is rearranging the database metadata to reassign the existing table as a partition. No data is actually moved, which makes table switching nearly instantaneous regardless of the table's size.

Prepping the new table

The `WorkOrderNEW` table will be created to demonstrate switching. It will hold August 2004 data from `AdventureWorks`:

```
CREATE TABLE dbo.WorkOrderNEW (
  WorkOrderID INT IDENTITY NOT NULL,
  ProductID INT NOT NULL,
  OrderQty INT NOT NULL,
  StockedQty INT NOT NULL,
  ScrappedQty INT NOT NULL,
  StartDate DATETIME NOT NULL,
  EndDate DATETIME NOT NULL,
  DueDate DATETIME NOT NULL,
  ScrapReasonID INT NULL,
  ModifiedDate DATETIME NOT NULL
  )
  ON Part05;
```

Indexes identical to those on the preceding table will be created on the partitioned table:

```
ALTER TABLE dbo.WorkOrderNEW
  ADD CONSTRAINT WorkOrderNEWPK
  PRIMARY KEY NONCLUSTERED (WorkOrderID, DueDate) go
CREATE CLUSTERED INDEX ix_WorkOrderNEW_DueDate
  ON dbo.WorkOrderNEW (DueDate)
```

The following adds the mandatory constraint:

```
ALTER TABLE dbo.WorkOrderNEW
  ADD CONSTRAINT WONewPT
    CHECK (DueDate BETWEEN '8/1/2004' AND '8/31/2004');
```

Now import the new data from AdventureWorks, reusing the January 2004 data:

```
INSERT dbo.WorkOrderNEW (ProductID, OrderQty, StockedQty, ScrappedQty,
    StartDate, EndDate, DueDate, ScrapReasonID, ModifiedDate)
  SELECT
      ProductID, OrderQty, StockedQty, ScrappedQty,
      DATEADD(mm,7,StartDate), DATEADD(mm,7,EndDate),
      DATEADD(mm,7,DueDate), ScrapReasonID, DATEADD(mm,7,ModifiedDate)
    FROM AdventureWorks.Production.WorkOrder
    WHERE DueDate BETWEEN '1/1/2004' and '1/31/2004';
```

The new table now has 3,158 rows.

Prepping the partition table

The original partition table, built earlier in this section, has a non-partitioned, non-clustered primary key. Because one of the rules of switching into a partitioned table is that every index must be partitioned, the first task for this example is to drop and rebuild the WorkOrder table's primary key so it will be partitioned:

```
ALTER TABLE dbo.WorkOrder
  DROP CONSTRAINT WorkOrderPK

ALTER TABLE dbo.WorkOrder
  ADD CONSTRAINT WorkOrderPK
  PRIMARY KEY NONCLUSTERED (WorkORderID,DueDate)
    ON psYearsAll(DueDate);
Next, the partition table needs an empty partition:
ALTER PARTITION SCHEME psYearsFiles
  NEXT USED [Primary]

ALTER PARTITION FUNCTION pfYearsRT()
  SPLIT RANGE ('8/1/2004')
```

Performing the switch

The ALTER TABLE...SWITCH TO command will move the new table into a specific partition. To determine the empty target partition, select the database Summary page ➪ Disk Usage report:

```
ALTER TABLE WorkOrderNEW
  SWITCH TO WorkOrder PARTITION 5
```

Switching out

The same technology can be used to switch a partition out of the partition table so that it becomes a stand-alone table. Because no merger is taking place, this is much easier than switching in. The following code takes the first partition out of the WorkOrder partition table and reconfigures the database metadata so it becomes its own table:

```
ALTER TABLE WorkOrder
  SWITCH PARITION 1 to WorkOrderArchive
```

Rolling partitions

With a little imagination, the technology to create and merge existing partitions can be used to create rolling partition designs.

Rolling partitions are useful for time-based partition functions such as partitioning a year of data into months. Each month, the rolling partition expands for a new month. To build a 13-month rolling partition, perform these steps each month:

1. Add a new boundary.
2. Point the boundary to the next used filegroup.
3. Merge the oldest two partitions to keep all the data.

Switching tables into and out of partitions can enhance the rolling partition designs by switching in fully populated staging tables and switching out the tables into an archive location.

Indexing partitioned tables

Large tables mean large indexes, so non-clustered indexes can be optionally partitioned.

Creating partitioned indexes

Partitioned non-clustered indexes must include the column used by the partition function in the index, and must be created using the same ON clause as the partitioned clustered index:

```
CREATE INDEX WorkOrder_ProductID
  ON WorkOrder (ProductID, DueDate)
    ON psYearsFiles(DueDate);
```

Maintaining partitioned indexes

One of the advantages of partitioned indexes is that they can be individually maintained. The following example rebuilds the newly added fifth partition:

```
ALTER INDEX WorkOrder_ProductID
  ON dbo.WorkOrder
  REBUILD
  PARTITION = 5
```

Removing partitioning

To remove the partitioning of any table, drop the clustered index and add a new clustered index without the partitioning ON clause. When dropping the clustered index, you must add the MOVE TO option to actually consolidate the data onto the specified filegroup, thus removing the partitioning from the table:

```
DROP INDEX ix_WorkOrder_DueDate
  ON dbo.Workorder
  WITH (MOVE TO [Primary]);
```

Data-Driven Partitioning

The third method doesn't involve any Microsoft partitioning technology. Instead, it's an architectural pattern that I've used in large, heavy transaction databases. It's rather simple, but very fast.

A data-driven partitioning scheme segments the data into different servers based on a partition key. Each server has the same database schema, but the data stored is only the required data partition key or ranges. For example, server A could hold accounts 1–999. Server B could hold accounts 1,000–1,999. Server C could hold all accounts greater than or equal to 2,000.

A partition mapping table stores the server name for each partition key value or range of values. In the previous example, the partition key table would hold the from and to account numbers and the server name.

The middle tier reads and caches the partition mapping table, and for every database access it checks the partition mapping table to determine which server holds the needed data.

This method works best when the data is self-contained and the complete query can be solved using only the subset of data. If the servers need to do much cross-server querying to solve the queries, then the benefits are likely lost.

What's nice about data-driven partitioning is that it's very easy to scale out. Adding another server only requires moving some data and updating the partition-mapping table.

Summary

Not every database will have to scale to higher magnitudes of capacity, but when a project does grow into the terabytes, SQL Server 2008 provides some advanced technologies to tackle the growth. However, even these advanced technologies are no substitute for Smart Database Design.

Key points on partitioning include the following:

- Partitioned views use a union all to merge data from several user-created base tables. Each partition table must include the partition key and a constraint.
- The Query Processor can carefully choose the minimum number of underlying tables when selecting through a partitioned view, but not when updating.
- Distributed partitioned views add distributed queries to combine data from multiple servers.
- Partitioned tables are a completely different technology than partitioned views and use a partition function, schema, and clustered index to partition a single table.
- Data-driven partitioning is an architectural pattern that involves custom coding, but it delivers the best possible scale-out performance and flexibility.

The next chapter wraps up this part covering optimization with a new feature for SQL Server 2008 Enterprise Edition that's getting quite a bit of buzz.

Chapter 69

Resource Governor

Whenever I think of the Resource Governor, I get a picture of an old southern gentleman in a white suit with a white bow tie.

"Excuse me, Gov'nor, but I'd be much obliged but you could please restrict the CPU traffic so my job could run smooth. . . . Many thanks to you, sir. Why sure, I'd love a cold lemonade. Thank you kindly."

Fitting right in with Microsoft's theme of SQL Server for the large enterprise, Resource Governor is designed to limit CPU and proc cache memory for specific queries, which improves SQL Server's ability to handle conflicting loads. For example, a few reports pulling data from a parallelized query can tie up a normally fast order processing database. But limit those reports to 10% of the CPU, the reports will take longer to run but the call center doesn't swamp the help desk with complaints.

Although Resource Governor sounds like a panacea for all sorts of server performance ills, it does have its limitations:

- Sessions must be assigned to the workload group at the beginning of the session. As the DBA, you can't alter the workload group of a runaway query to corral it into submission. If it's an assigned runaway session, it stays a runaway session.
- Resource Governor requires Enterprise Edition, so it can't help the organization with a single dual-core server running Standard Edition that desperately needs to control reporting queries.
- A poorly indexed query that is scanning a few million rows will still scan a few million rows even after its CPU has been limited by the Resource Governor. The poorly indexed query will take even longer to run — its poor performance has simply been spread around so that others don't feel its pain quite so badly. The root source of the poor performance still needs to be addressed.

IN THIS CHAPTER

Determining whether Resource Governor is the right tool for the job

Configuring Resource Governor

Resource Governor performance monitoring

- It's been criticized for not including the ability to limit I/O; however, I prefer limiting I/O by limiting the CPU that makes the I/O requests. I'd rather not have to balance CPU limits and I/O limits, or have the two limits waiting for one another, so I don't agree with this perceived limitation.

On the bright side, assuming the queries are well written and supported by the right indexes, Resource Governor is the right tool to smooth the conflicts between competing tasks.

Configuring Resource Governor

The Resource Governor is designed around the concepts of *resource pools* (named units that allocate CPU and memory) and *workload groups* (named units that include user sessions). As a user session is initiated it is assigned to a workload group. Workload groups are connected to a resource pool.

Resource Governor is not on by default. It can be enabled in Object Explorer using the [*server name*] ➪ Management ➪ Resource Governor enable or disable command context menu.

Using T-SQL, the Resource Governor can be enabled or disabled using `ALTER` commands:

```
ALTER RESOURCE GOVERNOR Reconfigure;
GO
ALTER RESOURCE GOVERNOR Enable;
```

Resource pools

A resource pool is a defined limit of CPU and memory resources. There are two predefined resource pools (internal and default):

- **Internal pool:** The resources used by SQL Server to run SQL Server. This pool is never restricted in any way. Any dedicated administrator connection (DAC) sessions run in the internal pool.
- **Default pool:** This is a mandatory pool (can't be dropped) for any session that falls into the default workload group. The default pool is unrestricted.
- **User-defined resource pools:** Additional resource pools can be created for more granular configuration of resources.

For each resource pool, the `min%` and `max%` CPU and memory can be configured. The total of all the resource pools' `min%` settings must be equal to or less than 100%.

The granularity of the `min%` and `max%` setting is 5%, which fits perfectly with 20 as the maximum number of resource pools (including the internal and default pool, leaving 18 possible user-defined resource pools).

NOTE **The memory pool controlled by the Resource Governor is the procedure cache used to compile and store query execution plans, not the memory used to buffer data. Any data page might be accessed by any session, so there's no good reason or method to limit the data buffer by resource pool. SQL Server normally does a good job of managing the procedure cache, but if you**

do decide to limit it, be sure to use the CPU to limit the data workload, and use memory to limit the number of cached query execution plans.

Best Practice

Be careful when setting `min%` above 0 because it can lead to some strange results. To simplify the formula: The total `min%` setting of the other pools reduces any user-defined pool's effective `max%` settings. For example, if pool A has a `min%` of 20 and pool B has a `min%` of 30, then pool C's effective `max%` is reduced to only 50%. I recommend leaving the `min%` setting to 0 and only restricting the `max%`.

To create a resource pool using Object Explorer, use the Management ➪ Resource Governor ➪ Resource Pools context menu and select the New Resource Pool menu item. The Resource Governor Properties page, shown in Figure 69-1, is used to create, alter, and drop resource pools and workload groups.

FIGURE 69-1

A user-defined resource pool, Reporting, is limited to 20% of CPU and is connected to the Reports workload group.

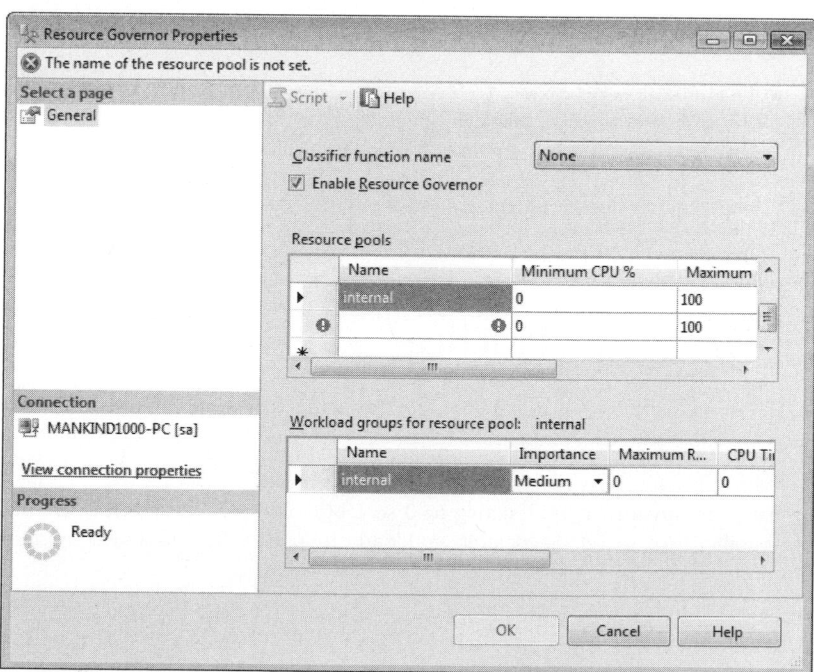

Resource pools can also be scripted using standard CREATE, ALTER, and DROP DDL commands.

NOTE **The Resource Governor Properties page is pretty buggy (using SP1). If you prefer it to T-SQL, here's how I got it to work: It only enables the OK button, which allows you to save changes if you've added a new resource pool. Therefore, no matter what you need to change, be sure to add a new resource pool so you can save changes. It is hoped that this will be fixed in a subsequent service pack.**

Workload groups

Workload groups are the named item that ties a session to resource pools. Multiple workgroups can be connected to a single resource group.

Workload groups can optionally provide additional resource limits. The critical ones are as follows:

- **Importance (low|medium|high):** The relative importance within the resource pool (this is relevant only when multiple workload groups are assigned to the resource pool).
- **Max_Dop:** The maximum degree of parallelism setting for any session assigned to this workload group.
- **Group_Max_Request:** This limits the number of sessions for a workload group.

Workload groups can be created, altered, and dropped in the same Management Studio property page as resource pools. They can also be managed using the CREATE, ALTER, and DROP DDL commands. The following DDL query creates the SSMS workload group, sets MAX_DOP to 1, and assigns the workload group to the default resource pool:

```
CREATE WORKLOAD GROUP SSMS
  WITH (MAX_DOP = 1)
  USING "default"
```

That's right, the syntax requires double quotes around the resource group name in the USING clause. Weird.

Best Practice

Controlling MAX_DOP using query hints is a real pain, but this actually becomes another great reason to use the Resource Governor. Use workload groups to control MAX_DOP. MAX_DOP query hints override workload group settings, which override the server configuration.

This enables you to leave the server MAX_DOP setting to 0 so DBCC can parallelize. OLTP transactional queries should avoid parallelizing, so set the default workload group MAX_DOP to 1. Reporting queries benefit from parallelism, so set MAX_DOP to 0.

Classifier functions

The whole point of the Resource Governor is to control individual queries. The classifier function includes specific sessions into workload groups so they can be limited by the resource pool.

The classifier function is executed with every new session, assigning the session to a workload group. Below is a sample classifier function:

```
CREATE
-- alter
FUNCTION ResourceGovClassifer()
RETURNS SYSNAME
WITH SCHEMABINDING
BEGIN
 DECLARE @WorkLoad sysname

 --workload based on login names
 IF SUSER_SNAME()= 'Maui\Pn'
   SET @WorkLoad='PowerUsers';

 --workload based on application
 IF APP_NAME() = 'Microsoft SQL Server Management Studio'
   SET @WorkLoad= 'SSMS';

 IF APP_NAME() LIKE '%REPORT SERVER%'
   SET @WorkLoad= 'Reports';

RETURN @WorkLoad;
END
```

Once the function has been created it must be selected in the Resource Governor Properties page to be the current classifier function. To change the current classifier function using T-SQL, use the `ALTER` command:

```
ALTER RESOURCE GOVERNOR WITH (CLASSIFIER_FUNCTION=dbo. ResourceGovClassifer);
GO
ALTER RESOURCE GOVERNOR RECONFIGURE;
```

To view information about the classifier function and logons, check the `sys.dm_exec_sessions` and `sys.dm_exec_requests` DMVs.

Monitoring Resource Governor

Of course, with Resource Governor enabled, you'll want to watch the CPU usage by watching `SQL Server: Resource Pool Stats` and `SQL Server: Workload Stats` in Performance Monitor.

Best Practice

Various loads can be first collected into workload groups and attached to the default resource pool to track them for CPU usage before assigning them to other resource pools.

I strongly recommend keeping the resource pools simple. Keep the primary workload using the default resource pool and group the workloads that you want to restrict into one or more user-defined resource pools.

To check on the Resource Governor configuration, there are four catalog views/DVMs:

- `sys.resource_governor_configuration`
- `sys.resource_governor_resource_pools`
- `sys.resource_governor_workload_groups`
- `sys.dm_resource_governor_workload_groups`

To monitor usage and limits, use these DMVs:

- `sys.dm_resource_governor_configuration`
- `sys.dm_resource_governor_resource_pools`

Summary

Resource Governor won't be used by most DBAs, and without careful planning the Resource Governor could royally mess up a heavy transaction system. But if you're one of the few for whom the Resource Governor is the solution, in the hands of a skilled DBA, it's the perfect tool to fine-tune a conflicting workload.

A few highlights about the Resource Governor:

- Resource pools define a set of `min%` and `max%` restrictions for CPU and memory.
- Workload groups are used to assign sessions to resource pools.
- Besides CPU and memory, the workload groups can control `MAXDOP`.
- The classifier function runs as part of the logon sequence to assign incoming session to a workload group.
- Performance Monitor can be used to watch stats about the individual resource pools and workload groups.

This concludes part IX, "Performance Tuning and Optimization," as well as the majority of this book that deals with SQL Server's Relational Database Engine. The next part moves into the BI world and explains topics such as star schemas, cubes, and data warehouse designs.

Part X

Business Intelligence

If the Information Architecture Principle stated in Chapter 2 is true, then information is useful not only for daily operations, but also for current and future analysis. Hence, extract, transform, and load (ETL) processes collect data from the daily operations and store it in data warehouses using patterns organized for analysis, rather than daily operations. Cubes, MDX queries, and Reporting Services pull from the data warehouse and present the data for analysis.

This whole process of analyzing historical and current data, both today and in the future, is the proactive side of IT and is collectively called *business intelligence* (BI).

In the past four releases of SQL Server, Microsoft has been steadily growing SQL Server's BI services, and SQL Server 2008 brings to fruition years of planning and development. From the enterprise-grade ETL tool and the rich and easy-to-build cubes to the slick reporting interface, SQL Server 2008 is more than ready to help you conquer your BI requirements.

BI, by definition, does not exist in a vacuum. Not only is the data warehouse dependent on numerous operational databases, but the BI toolset frequently includes multiple tools from multiple vendors. While non-SQL Server tools are beyond the scope of this book, this part covers using Excel, the most popular data analysis tool on the planet, as a front end for SQL Server's BI suite.

If you're an old hand at BI, then welcome to SQL Server 2008's sweet BI suite. If you've been around operational data for a while but never had the chance to work on the analysis side, welcome.

If SQL Server is the box, Part X is about getting the box to talk.

IN THIS PART

Chapter 70

BI Design

IN THIS CHAPTER

- Differences between OLTP and OLAP
- Data warehousing concepts
- Warehouse structures and relationships
- Loading dimensions and fact tables
- Managing changing dimension data

Having worked with various organizations and data systems, over time I've noticed a progression of reporting and analysis solutions. First queries are run directly against the online transactional processing (OLTP) database, but this approach conflicts with production use of the database and generally limits access to a very few staff due to security concerns.

Often the next step is to make a copy of the OLTP database for the express purpose of running analytical or reporting queries. These attempts at using an OLTP database for online analytical processing (OLAP) are problematic on a number of fronts:

- OLTP data structures are optimized for single, atomic transactions, whereas OLAP queries summarize large volumes of data. Thus, queries are painfully slow.
- OLTP data may reflect limited history, whereas OLAP tends to be interested in historical trends.
- OLTP data structures are understood by a relatively small population of experts in the organization, whereas OLAP is most effective when exposed to the widest possible audience.

A common refinement on querying the OLTP database is to create a new database that contains tables of summary data. When done carefully, this approach can address some speed and history issues, but it is still understood by a relatively small population. Consistent interpretation tends to be a problem as well, because summary tables are often created at different times for different purposes.

These two concepts of consistent interpretation and availability to a wide audience are key strategies for successful OLAP in particular and for business intelligence (BI) in general. An organization needs to have widely understood data on which to base its business decisions — the only alternatives are rumor and intuition.

These concepts are also in direct support of the Information Architecture Principle described in Chapter 2, making data "readily available in a usable format for daily operations and analysis. . ."

This chapter describes key concepts and practices behind the BI, enabling the availability and usability that maximizes your data's value.

Data Warehousing

Data warehousing is a key concept behind both the structure and the discipline of a BI solution. While increasingly powerful tools provided in the latest release of SQL Server ease some of the requirements around warehousing, it is still helpful to understand these concepts in considering your design.

Star schema

The data warehouse is the industry-standard approach to structuring a relational OLAP data store. It begins with the idea of dimensions and measures, whereby a dimension is a categorization or "group by" in the data, and the measure is the value being summarized. For example, in "net sales by quarter and division," the measure is "net sales," and the dimensions are "quarter" (time) and "division" (organization).

Deciding which dimensions and measures to include in the warehouse should be based on the needs of the business, bringing together an understanding of the types of questions that will be asked and the semantics of the data being warehoused. Interviews and details about existing reports and metrics can help gain a first approximation, but for most organizations a pilot project is needed to fully define requirements.

Best Practice

Organizations that are not familiar with what BI solutions can deliver have a difficult time understanding the power they represent. Kick-start your effort by developing a simple prototype that demonstrates some of what is possible using data that everyone understands. Choose a small but relevant subset of data and implement a few dimensions and one or two measures to keep implementation time to a minimum.

Business needs can then provide a basis for building the star schema that is the building block of the warehouse (see Figure 70-1).

The star schema derives its name from its structure: a central fact table and a number of dimension tables clustered around it like the points of a star. Each dimension is connected back to the fact table by a foreign key relationship.

FIGURE 70-1

Simple star schema

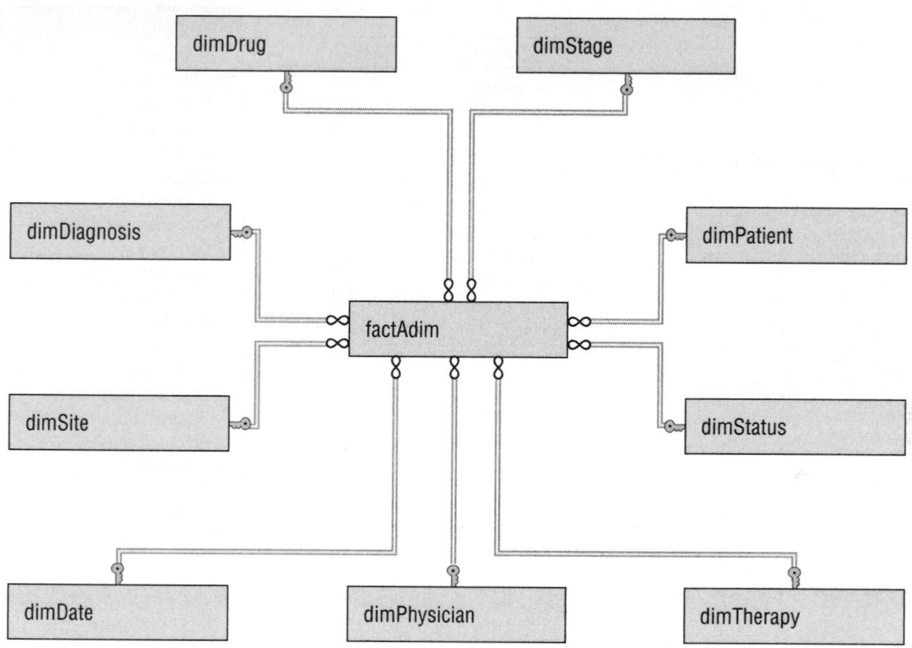

The fact table consists of two types of columns: the keys that relate to each dimension in the star and the facts (or measures) of interest.

Each dimension table consists of a primary key by which it relates back to the fact table, and one or more attributes that categorize data for that dimension. For example, a customer dimension may include attributes for name, e-mail address, and zip code. In general, the dimension represents a denormalization of the data in the OLTP system. For example, the AdventureWorksDW customer dimension is derived from the `AdventureWorks` tables `Sales.Individual` and `Person.Contact`, and fields parsed from the XML column describing demographics, among others.

Snowflake schema

Occasionally, it makes sense to limit denormalization by making one dimension table refer to another, thus changing the star schema into a snowflake schema. For example, Figure 70-2 shows how the product dimension has been snowflaked in `AdventureWorks`' Internet Sales schema. Product category and subcategory information could have been included directly in the product `DimProduct` table, but instead separate tables have been included to describe the categorizations. Snowflakes are useful for complex dimensions for which consistency issues might otherwise arise, such as the assignment of subcategories to categories in Figure 70-2, or for large dimensions where storage size is a concern.

FIGURE 70-2

Snowflake dimension

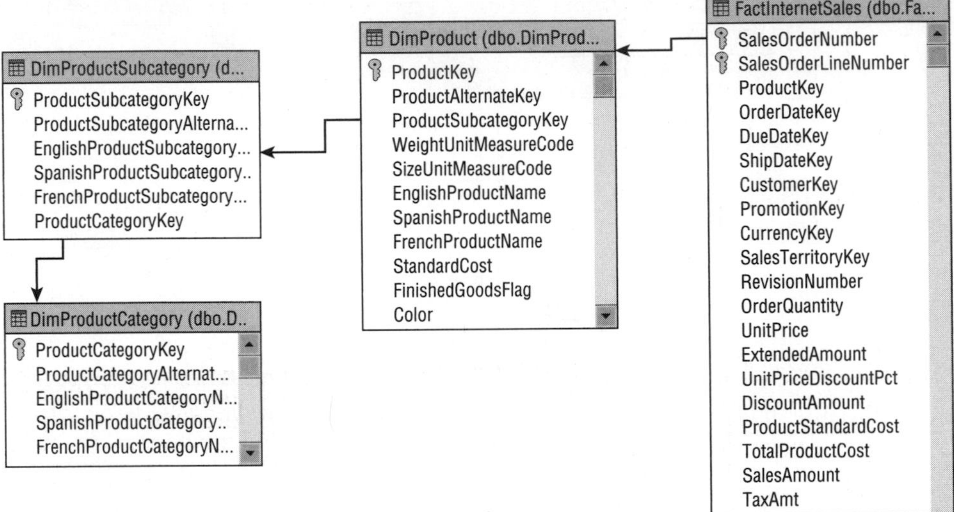

NOTE **Traditionally, snowflake schema have been discouraged because they add complexity and can slow SQL operations, but recent versions of SQL Server eliminate the majority of these issues. If a dimension can be made more consistent using a snowflake structure, then do so unless: (1) the procedure required to publish data into the snowflake is too complex or slow to be sustainable or (2) the schema being designed will be used for extensive SQL queries that will be slowed and complicated by the snowflake design.**

Surrogate keys

Foreign key relationships are the glue that holds the star schema together, but avoid using OLTP keys to relate fact and dimension tables, even though it is often very convenient to do so. Consider a star schema containing financial data when the accounting package is upgraded, changing all the customer IDs in the process. If the warehouse relation is based on an identity column, changes in the OLTP data can be accomplished by changes to the relatively small amount of data in the customer dimension. If the OLTP key were used, then the entire fact table would need to be converted.

Instead, create local *surrogate keys*, usually an identity column on dimension tables, to relate to the fact table. This helps avoid ID conflicts and adds robustness and flexibility in a number of scenarios.

Consistency

Defining the star schema enables fast OLAP queries against the warehouse, but gaining needed consistency requires following some warehousing rules:

- When loading data into the warehouse, null and invalid values should be replaced with their reportable equivalents. This enables the data's semantics to be researched carefully once and then used by a wide audience, leading to a consistent interpretation throughout the organization. Often, this involves manually adding rows to dimension tables to allow for all the cases that can arise in the data (e.g., Unknown, Internal, N/A, etc.).

- Rows in the fact table should never be deleted, and no other operations should be performed that will lead to inconsistent query results from one day to the next. Often this leads to delaying import of in-progress transactions. If a summary of in-progress transactions is required, keep them in a separate fact table of "provisional" data and ensure that the business user is presented with distinct summaries of data that will change. Nothing erodes confidence in a system like inconsistent results.

A key design consideration is the eventual size of the fact table. Fact tables often grow such that the only practical operation is the insertion of new rows — large-scale delete and update operations become impractical. In fact, database size estimates can ignore the size of dimension tables and use just the size of the fact tables.

Best Practice

Keeping large amounts of history in the warehouse doesn't imply keeping data forever. Plan to archive from the beginning by using partitioned fact tables that complement the partitioning strategy used in Analysis Services. For example, a large fact table might be broken into monthly partitions, maintaining two years of history.

Loading data

Given the architecture of the star/snowflake schema, adding new data begins at the points and moves inward, adding rows to the fact table last in order to satisfy the foreign key constraints. Usually, warehouse tables are loaded using Integration Services, but examples are shown here as SQL inserts for illustration.

Loading dimensions

The approach to loading varies with the nature of the source data. In the fortunate case where the source fact data is related by foreign key to the table containing dimension data, only the dimension data needs to be scanned. This example uses the natural primary key in the source data, product code, to identify rows in the `Products` staging table that have not yet been added to the dimension table:

```
INSERT INTO Warehouse.dbo.dimProduct (ProductCode, ProductName)
SELECT stage.Code, stage.Name FROM Staging.dbo.Products stage
  LEFT OUTER JOIN Warehouse.dbo.dimProduct dim
    ON stage.Code=dim.ProductCode
WHERE dim.ProductCode is NULL;
```

Often, the source dimension data will not be related by foreign key to the source fact data, so loading the dimension table requires a full scan of the fact data in order to ensure consistency.

This next example scans the fact data, picks up a corresponding description from the dimension data when available, or uses "Unknown" as the description when none is found:

```
INSERT INTO Warehouse.dbo.dimOrderStatus (OrderStatusID,
  OrderStatusDesc)
SELECT DISTINCT o.status, ISNULL(mos.Description,'Unknown')
FROM Staging.dbo.Orders o
  LEFT OUTER JOIN Warehouse.dbo.dimOrderStatus os
    ON o.status=os.OrderStatusID
  LEFT OUTER JOIN Staging.dbo.map_order_status mos
    ON o.status = mos.Number
WHERE os.OrderStatusID is NULL;
```

Finally, a source table may contain both fact and dimension data, which opens the door to inconsistent relationships between dimension attributes. The following example adds new codes that appear in the source data, but guards against multiple product name spellings by choosing one with an aggregate function. Without using `MAX` here, the query may return multiple rows for the same product code:

```
INSERT INTO Warehouse.dbo.dimProduct (ProductCode, ProductName)
SELECT stage.Code, MAX(stage.Name)
FROM Staging.dbo.Orders stage
  LEFT OUTER JOIN Warehouse.dbo.dimProduct dim ON
    stage.Code=dim.ProductCode
WHERE dim.ProductCode is NULL;
```

Loading fact tables

Once all the dimensions have been populated, the fact table can be loaded. Dimension primary keys generally take one of two forms: the key is either a natural key based on dimension data (e.g., `ProductCode`) or it is a surrogate key without any relationship to the data (e.g., the `identity` column). Surrogate keys are more general and adapt well to data from multiple sources, but each surrogate key requires a join while loading. For example, suppose our simple fact table is related to `dimTime`, `dimCustomer`, and `dimProduct`. If `dimCustomer` and `dimProduct` use surrogate keys, the load might look like the following:

```
INSERT INTO Warehouse.dbo.factOrder
  (OrderDate, CustomerID, ProductID, OrderAmount)
SELECT o.Date, c.CustomerID, p.ProductID, ISNULL(Amount,0)
FROM Staging.dbo.Orders o
  INNER JOIN Warehouse.dbo.dimCustomer c
    ON o.CustCode = c.CustomerCode
  INNER JOIN Warehouse.dbo.dimProduct p
    ON o.Code = p.ProductCode;
```

Because `dimTime` is related to the fact table on the date value itself, no join is required to determine the dimension relationship. Measures should be converted into reportable form, eliminating nulls whenever possible. In this case, a null amount, should it ever occur, is best converted to 0.

Best Practice

The extract-transform-load (ETL) process consists of a large number of relatively simple steps that evolve over time as source data changes. Centralize ETL logic in a single location as much as possible, document non-obvious aspects, and place it under source control. When some aspect of the process requires maintenance, this will simplify rediscovering all the components and their revision history. Integration Services and SourceSafe are excellent tools in this regard.

Changing data in dimensions

Proper handling of changes to dimension data can be a complex topic, but it boils down to how the organization would like to track history. If an employee changes her last name, is it important to know both the current and previous values? How about address history for a customer? Or changes in credit rating?

Following are the four common scenarios for tracking history in dimension tables:

- **Slowly Changing Dimension Type 1:** History is not tracked, so any change to dimension data applies across all time. For example, when the customer's credit rating changes from excellent to poor, there will be no way to know when the change occurred or that the rating was ever anything but poor. Such tracking makes it difficult to explain why the customer's purchase order was accepted last quarter without prepayment. Conversely, this simple approach will suffice for many dimensions. When implementing an Analysis Services database on OLTP data instead of a data warehouse, this is usually the only option available, as the OLTP database rarely tracks history.
- **Slowly Changing Dimension Type 2:** Every change in the source data is tracked as history by multiple rows in the dimension table. For example, the first time a customer appears in OLTP data, a row is entered into the dimension table for that customer and corresponding fact rows are related to that dimension row. Later, when that customer's information changes in the OLTP data, the existing row for that customer is expired, and a new row is entered into the dimension table with the new attribute data. Future fact rows are then associated with this new dimension table row. Because multiple surrogate keys are created for the same customer, aggregations and distinct counts must use an alternate key. Generally, this alternate key will be the same one used to match rows when loading the dimension (see "Loading dimensions" earlier in this chapter).
- **Slowly Changing Dimension Type 3:** Combines both type 1 and 2 concepts, whereby history on some but not all changes is tracked based on business rules. Perhaps employee transfers within a division are treated as type 1 changes (just updated), while transfers between divisions are treated as type 2 (a new dimension row is inserted).
- **Rapidly Changing Dimension:** Occasionally an attribute (or a few attributes) in a dimension will change rapidly enough to cause a type 2 approach to generate too many records in the dimension table. Such attributes are often related to status or rankings. This approach resolves the combinatorial explosion by breaking the rapidly changing attributes out into a separate dimension tied directly to the fact table. Thus, instead of tracking changes as separate rows in the dimension table, the fact table contains the current ranking or status for each fact row.

Accommodating possible changes to dimensions complicates our "loading dimensions" example from the previous section. For example, a Type 1 dimension requires that each dimension value encountered must first be checked to see if it exists. If it does not, then it can be inserted as described. If it does exist, then a check is performed to determine whether attributes have changed (e.g., whether the employee name changed), and an update is performed if required.

This type of conditional logic is another reason to use Integration Services to load data, as it simplifies the task and performs most operations quickly in memory. A common practice for detecting changes is to create and store a checksum of the current data values in the dimension, and then calculate the checksum on each dimension row read, comparing the two checksums to determine whether a change has occurred. This practice minimizes the amount of data read from the database when performing comparisons, which can be substantial when a large number of attributes are involved. While there is a small chance that different rows will return the same checksum, the risk/reward of this approach is frequently judged acceptable.

Type 2 dimensions extend the idea of Type 1's insert-or-update regimen. If a dimension row does not exist, it is still inserted, but if it exists two things need to happen. First, the existing row of data is expired — it continues to be used by all previously loaded fact data, but new fact data will be associated with the new dimension row. Second, the new dimension row is inserted and marked as active.

There are a number of ways to accomplish this expire/insert behavior, but a common approach adds three columns to the dimension table: effective start and end dates, plus an active flag. When a row is initially inserted, the effective start is the date when the row is first seen, the end date is set far in the future, and the active flag is on. Later, when a new version of the row appears, the effective end date is set and the active flag is cleared. It is certainly possible to use only the active flag or date range alone, but including both provides both easy identification of the current rows and change history for debugging.

Summary

All organizations use BI whether they realize it or not, because every organization needs to measure what is happening in its business. The only alternative is to make every decision based on intuition, rather than data. The quest for BI solutions usually begins with simple queries run against OLTP data and evolves into an inconsistent jumble of numbers. The concepts of BI and data warehousing help organize that chaos.

Storing data in a separate warehouse database avoids the contention, security, history, and consistency pitfalls associated with directly using OLTP data. The discipline of organizing dimensions and facts into a star schema using report-ready data delivers both the quality and the performance needed to effectively manage your data.

The concepts introduced in this chapter should help prepare and motivate you to read the Analysis Services and Integration Services chapters in this section.

Chapter 71

Building Multidimensional Cubes with Analysis Services

A naïve view of Analysis Services would be that it is the same data used in relational databases with a slightly different format. Why bother? One could get by with data relational format only, without needing new technology. One can build a house with only a handsaw as well — it is all about the right tool for the job.

Analysis Services is fast. It serves up summaries of billions of rows in a second — a task that would take relational queries several minutes or longer. And unlike creating summary tables in a relational database, you don't need to create a different data structure for each type of summary.

Analysis Services is all about simple access to clean, consistent data. Building a database in Analysis Services eliminates the need for joins and other query-time constructs requiring intimate knowledge of the underlying data structures. The data modeling tools provide methods to handle null and inconsistent data. Complex calculations, even those involving period over period comparisons, can be easily constructed and made to look like just another item available for query to the user.

Analysis Services also provides simple ways to relate data from disparate systems. The facilities provided in the server combined with the rich design environment provide a compelling toolkit for data analysis and reporting.

IN THIS CHAPTER

Analysis Services Quick Start

One quick way to get started with both data warehousing and Analysis Services is to let the Business Intelligence Development Studio build the Analysis Services database and associated warehouse tables for you, based on templates shipped with SQL Server. Begin by identifying or creating a SQL Server warehouse (relational) database. Then open Business Intelligence Development Studio and create a new Analysis Services project.

Right-click on the Cubes node in the Solution Explorer and choose New Cube to begin the Cube Wizard. On the Select Creation Method page of the wizard, choose "Generate tables in the data source" and choose the template from the list that corresponds to your edition of SQL Server. Work through the rest of the wizard choosing measures and dimensions that make sense in your business. Be sure to pause at the Define Time Periods page long enough to define an appropriate time range and periods to make the time dimension interesting for your application.

At the Completing the Wizard page, select the Generate Schema Now option to automatically start the Schema Generation Wizard. Work through the remaining wizard pages, specifying the warehouse location and accepting the defaults otherwise. At the end of the Schema Generation Wizard, all the Analysis Services and relational objects are created. Even if the generated system does not exactly meet a current need, it provides an interesting example. The resulting design can be modified and the schema regenerated by right-clicking the project within the Solution Explorer and choosing Generate Relational Schema at any time.

Analysis Services Architecture

Analysis Services builds on the concepts of the data warehouse to present data in a multidimensional format instead of the two-dimensional paradigm of the relational database. How is Analysis Services multidimensional? When selecting a set of relational data, the query identifies a value via row and column coordinates, while the multidimensional store relies on selecting one or more items from each dimension to identify the value to be returned. Likewise, a result set returned from a relational database is a series of rows and columns, whereas a result set returned by the multidimensional database can be organized along many axes depending on what the query specifies.

CROSS-REF **Background on Business Intelligence and Data Warehousing is presented in Chapter 70, "BI Design." Readers unfamiliar with these areas will find this background helpful for understanding Analysis Services.**

Instead of the two-dimensional table, Analysis Services uses the multidimensional cube to hold data in the database. The cube thus presents an entity that can be queried *via multidimensional expressions (MDX)*, the Analysis Services equivalent of SQL.

Analysis Services also provides a convenient facility for defining calculations in MDX, which in turn provides another level of consistency to the Business Intelligence information stream.

CROSS-REF **See Chapter 72, "Programming MDX Queries," for details on creating queries and calculations in MDX.**

Analysis Services uses a combination of caching and pre-calculation strategies to deliver query performance that is dramatically better than queries against a data warehouse. For example, an existing query to summarize the last six months of transaction history over some 130 million rows per month takes a few seconds in Analysis Services, whereas the equivalent data warehouse query requires slightly more than seven minutes.

Unified Dimensional Model

The Unified Dimensional Model (UDM) defines the structure of the multidimensional database, including attributes presented to the client for query and how data is related, stored, partitioned, calculated, and extracted from the source databases.

At the foundation of the UDM is a data source view that identifies which relational tables provide data to Analysis Services and the relations between those tables. In addition, the data source view supports giving friendly names to included tables and columns. Based on the data source view, measure groups and dimensions are defined according to data warehouse facts and dimensions. Cubes then define the relations between dimensions and measure groups, forming the basis for multidimensional queries.

Server

The UDM, or database definition, is hosted by the Analysis Services server, as shown in Figure 71-1.

FIGURE 71-1

Analysis Services server

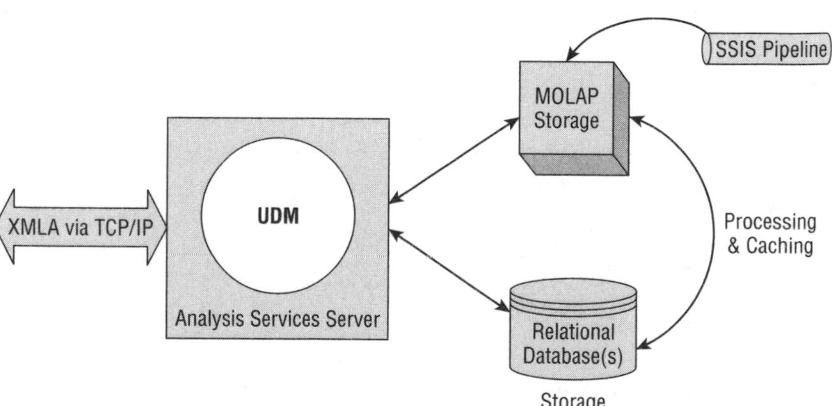

Data can be kept in a Multidimensional OLAP (MOLAP) store, which generally results in the fastest query times, but it requires pre-processing of source data. Processing normally takes the form of SQL queries derived from the UDM and sent to the relational database to retrieve underlying data. Alternately, data can be sent directly from the Integration Services pipeline to the MOLAP store.

In addition to storing measures at the detail level, Analysis Services can store pre-calculated summary data called *aggregations*. For example, if aggregations by month and product line are created as part of the processing cycle, queries that require that combination of values do not have to read and summarize the detailed data, but can use the aggregations instead.

Data can also be left in the relational database, or ROLAP store, which generally results in the fastest processing times at the expense of query times. Without aggregations, queries against a ROLAP store cause the equivalent SQL to be executed as needed. Aggregations can be pre-calculated for ROLAP, but doing so requires processing all the detailed data, so MOLAP is the preferred option. A relational database in this context is not limited to SQL Server, but may be any data source for which an OLE DB provider exists.

A compromise between the speed of MOLAP storage and the need for preprocessing, called *proactive caching*, serves queries out of MOLAP storage when possible, but queries the relational database to retrieve the latest data not yet processed into the MOLAP store.

Finally, the Analysis Services server uses XML for Analysis (XMLA) as its sole protocol, which is why you see XMLA inside the arrow in Figure 71-1.

Client

Clients communicate with Analysis Services, like any other Web Service, via the Simple Object Access Protocol (SOAP). Client applications can hide XMLA and SOAP details by using the provided data access interfaces to access Analysis Services:

- All .NET languages can use ADOMD.NET.
- Win32 applications (such as C++) can use the OLE DB for OLAP driver.
- Other COM-based applications (such as VB6, VBA, scripting) can use ADOMD.

While the server will only speak XMLA via TCP/IP, clients have the option of using the HTTP protocol for their communications, if an appropriately configured IIS server is available to translate.

In addition to custom applications, Analysis Services can be accessed by several provided tools, including the following:

- Business Intelligence Development Studio, for defining database structure
- SQL Server Management Studio, for managing and querying the server
- Reporting Services, which can base report definitions on Analysis Services data
- Excel features and add-ins, for querying and analyzing data

A wide variety of third-party tools are also available to exploit the features of Analysis Services.

Building a Database

An Analysis Services database is built by identifying the data to include in the database, specifying the relationships between that data, defining dimension structures on that data, and finally building one or more cubes to combine the dimensions and measures. This section describes the overall process with an emphasis on gathering the data needed to define the database. Subsequent sections describe the many facets of dimensions and cubes.

Business Intelligence Development Studio

The process of building an Analysis Services database begins by opening a new Analysis Services project in the Business Intelligence Development Studio. Each project corresponds to a database that will be created on the target server when the project is deployed.

Best Practice

Along with opening an Analysis Services project, it is also possible to directly open an existing database in Business Intelligence Development Studio. While this is a useful feature for examining the configuration of a running server, changes should be made in a project, deployed first to a development server, and deployed to production only after testing. Keep the project and related files in source control.

Be sure to set the target server before attempting to deploy your new database. Right-click on the project in the Solution Explorer and choose Properties. Set the target server in the deployment property page for the configuration(s) of interest (for example, development vs. production). Taking care with this setup when you create a project will prevent inadvertently creating a database on the wrong server.

Data sources

Define a data source for each distinct database or other source of data needed for the Analysis Services database. Each data source encapsulates the connection string, authentication, and properties for reading a particular set of data. A data source can be defined on any data for which an OLE DB provider exists, enabling Analysis Services to use many types of data beyond the traditional relational sources.

Start the New Data Source Wizard by right-clicking the Data Sources folder in the Solutions Explorer and selecting the New option. After you view the optional welcome screen, the "Select how to define a connection" screen appears and presents a list of connections. Select the appropriate connection if it exists.

If the appropriate connection does not exist, bring up the connection manager by clicking the New button and add it. Within the connection manager, choose an appropriate provider, giving preference to native OLE DB providers for best performance. Then enter the server name, authentication information, database name, and any other properties required by the chosen provider. Review entries on the All tab and test the connection before clicking OK to complete the connection creation.

Work through the remaining wizard screens, choosing the appropriate login (impersonation) information for the target environment and finally the name of the data source. The choice of impersonation method depends on how access is granted in your environment. Any method that provides access to the necessary tables is sufficient for development.

- **Use a specific Windows user name and password** allows the entry of the credential to be used when connecting to the relational database. This option is best when the developer and target server would not otherwise have access to the necessary data.

- **Use the service account** will use the account that the Analysis Server service is logged in under to connect to the relational database. This is the simplest option provided that the login specified for the service has been granted access to the relational database.
- **Use the credentials of the current user** uses the current developer's login to read the relational database. This can be a good choice for development, but it won't work when the database is deployed to a server because there is no "current user."
- **Inherit** uses the Analysis Services database impersonation method, which defaults to using the service account, but it can be changed in database properties.

When managing multiple projects in a single solution, basing a data source in one project on information in another project can be useful. For those cases, instead of choosing a connection at the "Select how to define a connection" window, select the option to "Create a data source based on another object." This leads the wizard through the "Data sources from existing objects" page. This page offers two alternatives:

- "Create a data source based on an existing data source in your solution" minimizes the number of places in which connection information must be edited when it changes.
- "Create a data source based on an Analysis Services project" enables two projects to share data. This functionality is similar to using the Analysis Services OLE DB provider to access an existing database, but in this case the databases can be developed simultaneously without deployment complications.

Data source view

Whereas a data source describes where to look for tables of data, the data source view specifies which available tables to use and how they relate to each other. The data source view also associates metadata, such as friendly names and calculations, with those tables and columns.

Creating the data source view

The following steps create a data source view:

1. Add needed tables and named queries to a data source view.
2. Establish logical primary keys for tables without a primary key.
3. Establish relationships between related tables.
4. Annotate tables/columns with friendly names and calculations.

Begin by creating the data source view via the wizard: Right-click on the Data Source Views folder and select the New option. There are several pages in the wizard:

- **Select a Data Source:** Choose one of the data sources to be included in this data source view. If more than one data source is to be included in the data source view, then the first data source must be a SQL Server data source. Pressing the Advanced button to limit the schemas retrieved can be helpful if there are many tables in the source database.
- **Name Matching:** This page appears only when no foreign keys exist in the source database, providing the option of defining relationships based on a selection of common naming conventions. Matching can also be enabled via the `NameMatchingCriteria` property once the data source view has been created, identifying matches as additional tables added to an existing view.

- **Select Tables and Views:** Move tables to be included from the left pane (available objects) to the right (included objects) pane. To narrow the list of available objects, enter any part of a table name in the Filter box and press the Filter button. To add objects related to included objects, select one or more included objects and press the Add Related Tables button. This same dialog is available as the Add/Remove Tables dialog after the data source view has been created.
- **Completing the Wizard:** Specify a name for the data source view.

Once the data source view has been created, more tables can be added by right-clicking in the diagram and choosing Add/Remove Tables. Use this method to include tables from other data sources as well.

Similar to a SQL view, named queries can be defined, which behave as if they were tables. Either right-click on the diagram and choose New Named Query or right-click on a table and choose Replace Table/with New Named Query to bring up a Query Designer to define the contents of the named query. If the resulting named query will be similar to an existing table, then it is preferable to replace that table because the Query Designer will default to a query that is equivalent to the replaced table. Using named queries avoids the need to define views in the underlying data sources and allows all metadata to be centralized in a single model.

As tables are added to the data source view, primary keys and unique indexes in the underlying data source are imported as primary keys in the model. Foreign keys and selected name matches (see Name Matching presented earlier in the section "Creating the data source view") are automatically imported as relationships between tables. For cases in which primary keys or relationships are not imported, they must be defined manually.

For tables without primary keys, select one or more columns that define the primary key in a given table, right-click and select Set Logical Primary Key. Once primary keys are in place, any tables without appropriate relationships can be related by dragging and dropping the related columns between tables. If the new relationship is valid, the model will show the new relationship without additional prompting. If errors occur, the Edit Relationship dialog will appear. Resolving the error may be as simple as pressing Reverse to correct the direction of the relationship, as shown in Figure 71-2, or it may take additional effort depending on the type of error.

A common issue when working with multiple data sources is different data types. For example, a key in one database may be a 16-bit integer, while another database may store the same information in a 32-bit integer. This situation can be addressed by using a named query to cast the 16-bit integer as its 32-bit equivalent.

The Edit Relationship dialog can also be accessed by double-clicking an existing relationship, by right-clicking the diagram, and from toolbar and menu selections. Be sure to define all relationships, including relationships between different columns of the fact table and the same dimension table (for example, OrderDate and ShipDate both relate to the Time dimension table), as this enables role-playing dimension functionality when a cube is created.

Managing the data source view

As the number of tables participating in the data source view grows, it can become difficult to view all the tables and relationships at once. An excellent way to manage the complexity is to divide the tables into a number of diagrams. The Diagram Organizer pane in the upper-left corner of the Data Source View page is initially populated with a single <All Tables> diagram. Right-click in the Diagram

Organizer pane and choose the New Diagram option to define a new diagram, and then drag and drop tables from the lower-left corner Tables pane to add tables to the new diagram. Alternately, right-click the diagram and use the Show Tables dialog to include tables currently in the <All Tables> diagram. However, don't confuse the Show Tables dialog, which determines the data source view in which tables appear in a given diagram, with the Add/Remove Tables dialog, which determines which tables are in the data source view as a whole.

FIGURE 71-2

The Edit Relationship dialog

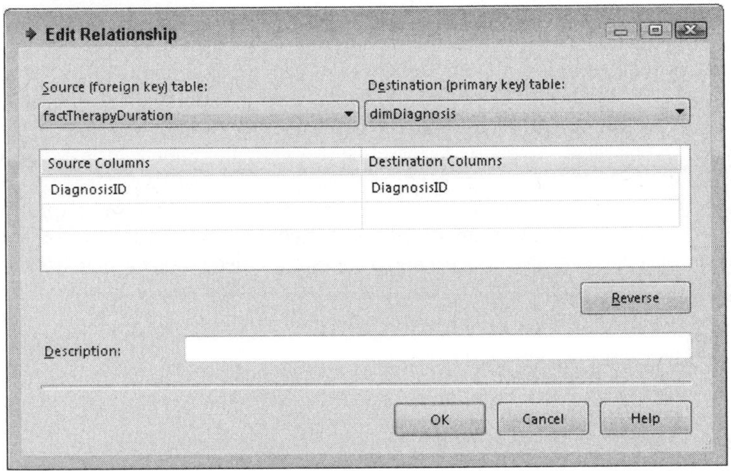

Other tools for managing data source views include the following:

- **Tables pane:** All the tables in a data source view are listed in the Tables pane. Click on any table, and it will be shown and highlighted in the current diagram (provided the table exists in the current diagram). You can also drag tables from the Tables pane onto diagrams as an alternative to the Show Tables dialog.
- **Find Table:** Invoked from toolbar or menu, this dialog lists only tables in the current diagram and allows filtering to speed the search process. Once chosen, the diagram shows and highlights the selected table.
- **Locator:** The locator tool enables quick scrolling over the current diagram. Find it at the lower-right corner at the intersection of the scroll bars. Click and drag the locator to move around quickly within the diagram.
- **Switch layout:** Right-click the diagram to toggle between rectangular and diagonal layout. The rectangular layout is table oriented and good for understanding many relationships at once. The diagonal layout is column oriented and thus good for inspecting relationship details.

- **Explore data:** Looking at a sample of the data in a table can be very useful when building a data source view. Right-click any table to open the Explore page, which presents four tabbed views: The table view provides a direct examination of the sample data, while the pivot table and pivot chart views enable exploration of patterns in the data. The chart view shows a series of charts, breaking down the sample data by category based on columns in the sample data. The columns selected for analysis are adjustable using the drop-down at the top of the page, as are the basic charting options. The size and type of sample is adjustable from the Sampling Options button on the page's toolbar. After adjusting sampling characteristics, press the Resample button to refresh the currently displayed sample.

The data source view can be thought of as a cache of underlying schemas that enables a responsive modeling environment, and like all cache it can become outdated. When the underlying schema changes, right-click on the diagram and choose Refresh to reflect the latest version of the schema in the data source view. The refresh function, also available from the toolbar and menu, opens the Refresh Data Source View dialog, which lists all the changes affecting the data source view. Before accepting the changes, scan the list for deleted tables, canceling changes if any deleted tables are found. Inspect the underlying schema for renamed and restructured tables to determine how equivalent data can be retrieved, and resolve any conflicts before attempting the refresh again. For example, right-click on a renamed table and choose Replace Table/with Other Table to select the new table. This approach prevents losing relationship and other context information during the refresh.

Refining the data source view

One of the strengths of the UDM is that queries against that model do not require an understanding of the underlying table structures and relationships. However, even the table name itself often conveys important semantics to the user. For example, referencing a column as `accounting.hr.staff.employee.hourly_rate` indicates that this hourly rate is on the accounting server, `hr` database, staff schema, and `employee` table, which suggests this hourly rate column contains an employee pay rate and not the hourly charge for equipment rental. Because the source of this data is hidden by the unified dimensional model, these semantics will be lost.

The data source view enables the definition of friendly names for every table and column. It also includes a description property for every table, column, and relationship. Friendly names and descriptions enable the preservation of existing semantics and the addition of others as appropriate.

Best Practice

Make the data source view the place where metadata lives. If a column needs to be renamed to give it context at query time, give it a friendly name in the data source view, rather than rename a measure or dimension attribute — the two names are displayed side by side in the data source view and help future modelers understand how data is used. Use description properties for non-obvious notes, capturing the results of research required in building and modifying the model.

Add a friendly name or description to any table or column by selecting the item and updating the corresponding properties in the Properties pane. Similarly, add a description to any relationship by selecting the relationship and updating the Properties pane, or by entering the description from the Edit Relationship dialog. The display of friendly names can be toggled by right-clicking the diagram.

Best Practice

Applications and reports based on Analysis Services data are likely a large change for the target organization. Assign friendly names that correspond to the names commonly used throughout the organization to help speed adoption and understanding.

Many simple calculations are readily included in the data source view as well. As a rule of thumb, place calculations that depend on a single row of a single table or named query in the data source view, but implement multi-row or multi-table calculations in MDX. Add calculations to named queries by coding them as part of the query. Add calculations to tables by right-clicking the table and choosing New Named Calculation. Enter a name and any expression the underlying data provider can interpret. For example, if SQL Server's relational database is your data source, basic math, null replacement, and data conversion are all available for creating named calculations (think of any expression that can be written in T-SQL).

Creating a cube

The data source view forms the basis for creating the cubes, which in turn present data to database users. Running the Cube Wizard generally provides a good first draft of a cube. Begin by right-clicking the Cubes folder and selecting New, and then work through these pages:

- **Select Build Method:** Choose "Use existing tables." The "generate tables in the data source" option is outlined previously in the "Analysis Services Quick Start" section. The option "Create an empty cube" does exactly that, essentially bypassing the wizard.
- **Select Measure Group Tables:** Choose the appropriate data source view from the drop-down, and then indicate which tables are to be used as fact tables — meaning they will contain measures. Pressing the Suggest button will make an educated guess about which tables to check, but the guesses are not accurate in all cases.
- **Select Measures:** The wizard presents a list of numeric columns that may be measures from the measure group tables. Check/uncheck columns as appropriate; measures can also be added/removed/adjusted at the conclusion of the wizard. Both Measure Groups and Measures can be renamed from this page.
- **Select Existing Dimensions:** If the current project already has dimensions defined, then this page will be displayed to enable those dimensions to be included in the new cube. Check/uncheck dimensions as appropriate for the created cube.
- **Select New Dimensions:** The wizard presents a list of dimensions and the tables that will be used to construct those dimensions. Deselect any dimensions that are not desired or any tables that should not be included in that dimension. Dimensions, but not tables, can be renamed from this page.

- **Completing the Wizard:** Enter a name for the new cube and optionally review the measures and dimensions that will be created.

Upon completion of the wizard, a new cube and associated dimensions will be created.

Dimensions

Recall from the discussion of star schema that dimensions are useful categorizations used to summarize the data of interest, the "group by" attributes that would be used in a SQL query. Dimensions created by a wizard generally prove to be good first drafts, but they need refinement before deploying a database to production.

CROSS-REF **Background on Business Intelligence and Data Warehousing concepts is presented in Chapter 70, "BI Design."**

Careful study of the capabilities of a dimension reveal a complex topic, but fortunately the bulk of the work involves relatively simple setup. This section deals first with that core functionality and then expands into more complex topics in "Beyond Basic Dimensions."

Dimension Designer

Open any dimension from the Solution Explorer to use the Dimension Designer, shown in Figure 71-3. This designer presents information in four tabbed views:

- **Dimension Structure:** Presents the primary design surface for defining the dimension. Along with the ever-present Solution Explorer and Properties panes, three panes present the dimension's structure:
  - **Data Source View (right):** Shows the portion of the data source view on which the dimension is built
  - **Attributes (left):** Lists each attribute included in the dimension
  - **Hierarchies (center):** Provides a space to organize attributes into common drill-down paths
- **Attribute Relationships:** Displays a visual designer to detail how dimension attributes relate
- **Translations:** Provides a place to define alternative language versions of both object captions and the data itself
- **Browser:** Displays the dimension's data as last deployed to the target analysis server

Unlike data sources and data source views, cubes and dimensions must be deployed before their behavior (e.g., browsing data) can be observed. The process of deploying a dimension consists of two parts. First, during the build phase, the dimension definition (or changes to the definition as appropriate) is sent to the target analysis server. Examine the progress of the build process in the Output pane. Second, during the process phase, the Analysis Services server queries underlying data and populates dimension data. Progress of this phase is displayed in the Deployment Progress pane, usually positioned as a tab of the Properties pane. The Business Intelligence Development Studio attempts to build or process only the changed portions of the project to minimize the time required for deployment.

FIGURE 71-3

Dimension Designer with AdventureWorks Customer dimension

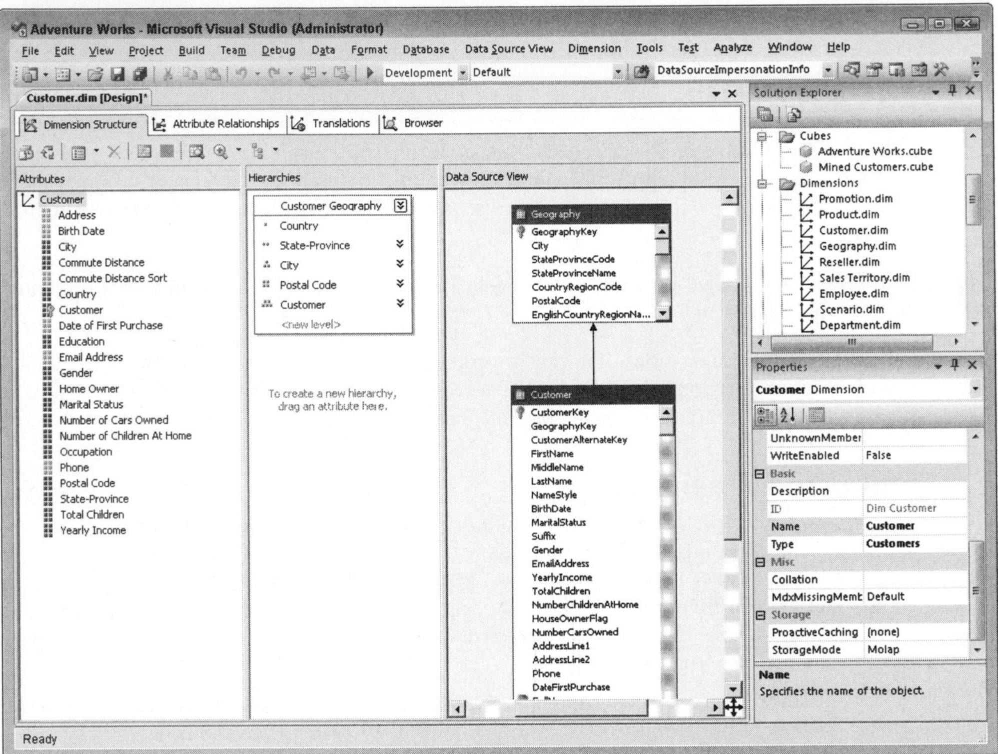

New in 2008

Best Practice warnings are now displayed in the Dimension Designer, appearing as either caution icons or blue underlines. These warnings are informational and are not applicable to every situation. Following the procedures outlined below, such as establishing hierarchies and attribute relationships, will eliminate many of these warnings. See the "Best Practice Warnings" topic later in this chapter for additional details.

Attributes

Attributes are the items that are available for viewing within the dimension. For example, a time dimension might expose year, quarter, month, and day attributes. Dimensions built by the Cube Wizard only have the key attribute defined. Other attributes must be manually added by dragging columns from the Data Source View pane to the Attributes pane. Within the attribute list, the key icon denotes the key attribute (Usage property = Key), which corresponds to the primary key in the source data used to relate to the fact table. There must be exactly one key attribute for each dimension.

Attribute source columns and ordering

Columns from the data source view are assigned to an attribute's KeyColumns and NameColumn properties to drive which data is retrieved in populating the attribute. During processing, Analysis Services will include both key and name columns in the SELECT DISTINCT it performs against the underlying data to populate the attribute. The KeyColumns assignment determines which items will be included as members in the attribute. The optional NameColumn assignment can give a display value to the key(s) when the key itself is not adequately descriptive.

For example, a product dimension might assign a ProductID to the KeyColumn and the ProductName to the NameColumn. For the majority of attributes, the single key column assigned when the attribute is initially created will suffice. For example, an Address attribute in a customer dimension is likely to be a simple string in the source table with no associated IDs or codes; the default of assigning that single Address column as the KeyColumns value with no NameColumn will suffice.

Some scenarios beyond the simple case include the following:

- **Attributes with both an ID/code and a name:** The approach for this case, which is very common for dimension table primary keys (key attributes), depends on whether the ID or code is commonly understood by those who will query the dimension. If the code is common, then leave its NameColumn blank to avoid hiding the code. Instead, model the ID/Code and Name columns as separate attributes. If the ID or code is an internal application or warehouse value, then hide the ID by assigning both the KeyColumns and NameColumn properties on a single attribute.
- **ID/Code exists without a corresponding name:** If the ID or code can take on only a few values (such as Yes or No), then derive a column to assign as the NameColumn by adding a named calculation in the data source view. If the ID or code has many or unpredictable values, then consider adding a new snowflaked dimension table to provide a name.
- **Non-Unique keys:** It is important that the KeyColumns assigned uniquely identify the members of a dimension. For example, a time dimension table might identify months with numbers 1 through 12, which are not unique keys from one year to the next. In this case, it makes sense to include both year and month columns to provide a good key value. Once multiple keys are used, a NameColumn assignment is required, so add a named calculation to the data source view to synthesize a readable name (e.g., Nov 2008) from existing month and year columns.

In the preceding non-unique keys scenario, it might be tempting to use the named calculation results (e.g., Jan 2009, Feb 2009) as the attribute's key column were it not for ordering issues. Numeric year and month data is required to keep the attribute's members in calendar, rather than alphabetic, order. The attribute's OrderBy property enables members to be sorted by either key or name. Alternately, the OrderBy options AttributeKey and AttributeName enable sorting of the current attribute's members based on the key or name of another attribute, providing that the other attribute has been defined as a member property of the current attribute. Member properties are described in detail in the next section.

Change the KeyColumns property for the currently selected attribute by clicking on the current value and then clicking the ellipses to launch the Key Columns dialog. The left pane of the Key Columns dialog shows each of the current key members. Use the left and right arrows to build a key in the right pane as shown in Figure 71-4.

FIGURE 71-4

The Key Columns dialog

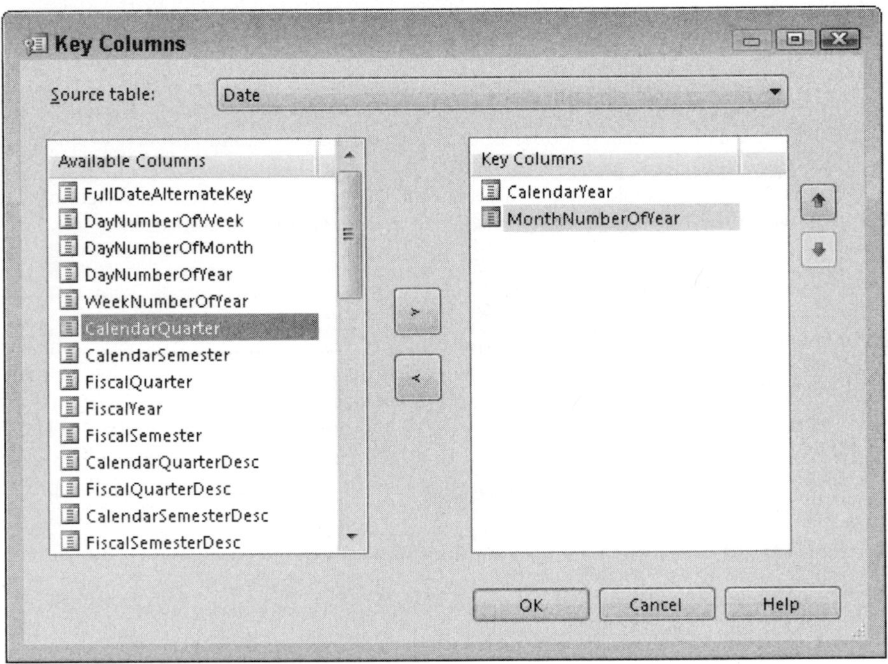

Likewise, add or change an attribute's NameColumn binding by clicking the ellipses to invoke the Name Column dialog. Highlight the column that contains the desired value.

Hierarchies and attribute relationships

Once deployed, each attribute not specifically disabled becomes an *attribute hierarchy* for browsing and querying. The attribute hierarchy generally consists of two levels: the All level, which represents all possible values of the attribute, and a level named after the attribute itself that lists each value individually.

The Hierarchies and Levels pane of the Dimension Designer enables the creation of *user hierarchies*, which define drill-down paths by organizing attributes into multiple levels. For example,

Figure 71-3 shows a user hierarchy that first presents the browser with a list of countries, which can be expanded into a list of states, then cities, and so on. Ultimately, the user will experience the dimension as some combination of attribute and user hierarchies.

One of the most important practices to optimize cube performance is the careful construction of user hierarchies in conjunction with attribute relationships. This follows from how Analysis Services pre-calculates data summaries, called aggregations, to speed query performance. For example, totals by year or month might be pre-calculated along the time dimension.

To understand attribute relationships, consider a simple time dimension with attributes for year, quarter, month, and day, with day relating to the fact table (key attribute). By default, every attribute in a dimension is related directly to the key attribute, resulting in the default relationships shown in Figure 71-5(a) and (b). The value for each non-key level summarizes all the day values. Contrast this to the properly assigned relationships in Figure 71-5(c), in which values for the month level must reference all the day values, but the quarters level need only reference the months, and the years need only reference the quarters.

FIGURE 71-5

Attribute relationships

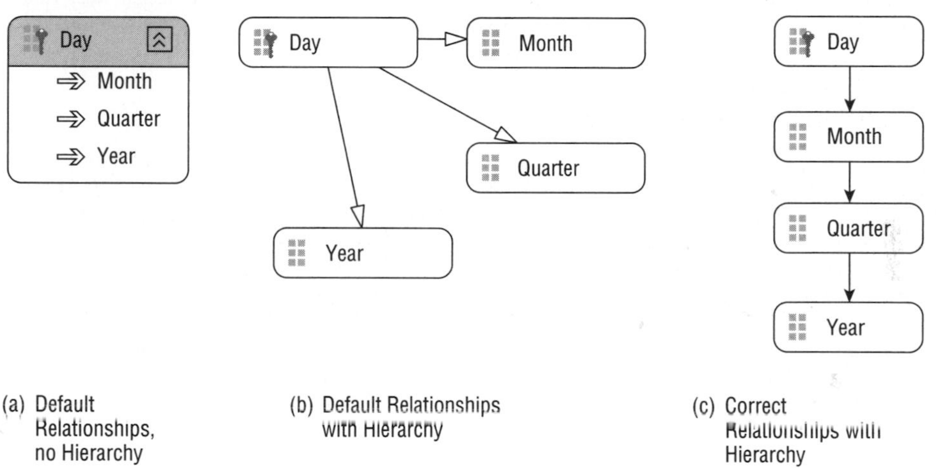

When relationships are established in a dimension and a user hierarchy is created that mirrors those relationships, it is considered a *natural hierarchy*. The combination of creating the natural hierarchy and associated relationships is what enables effective aggregations to be created and used to speed query processing. Relationships describe how aggregations can be built, and only members of a natural hierarchy are considered in the aggregation creation process.

Best Practice

While natural hierarchies are important for cube performance, user hierarchies provide drill-down paths for users who will interactively browse the contents of a cube, so it is important to define paths that make sense to the user of the cube as well. Spend time exploring how various users think about the data being presented and adapt the design to their perspective.

Creating user hierarchies

Drag an attribute to an empty spot of the Hierarchies and Levels pane to start a new hierarchy. Likewise, new attributes can be added by dragging attributes onto an existing hierarchy. Remember to rename each hierarchy with a user-friendly title, as the default names are "Hierarchy," "Hierarchy 1," and so on.

The browser view is a good place to get a feel for how the user will experience the hierarchies as created. Right-click on the dimension name in the Solution Explorer and choose Process to update the server with the latest dimension definition. Then switch to the Browser tab of the Dimension Designer, choose the hierarchy to view in the toolbar, and explore the hierarchy in the pane. If the latest changes do not appear in the Browser tab, press the refresh button in the toolbar. Notice names, values, and ordering associated with each hierarchy, and adjust as needed. Note the differing icons to distinguish between user and attribute hierarchies while browsing.

Establishing attribute relationships

Switch to the Attribute Relationships tab of the Dimension Designer, which contains three panes. The diagram pane provides a graphical representation of the relationships like those shown in Figure 71-5. This mirrors the information presented in the Attribute Relationships pane, which shows a pair-wise list of relationships. Finally, the Attributes pane is a simple list of attributes — identical to the list shown on the Dimension Structure tab.

The relationships diagram will look like that in Figure 71-5(a) after the attributes have been defined but no user hierarchy has been defined. This diagram shows how month, quarter, and year are all directly related to the day. Once the user hierarchy has been defined as described earlier, the relationships look like Figure 71-5(b), breaking each level of the hierarchy out into a separate box. One trick for interpreting the diagram is to read each arrow as "determines." For example, knowing the day determines the corresponding month, knowing the month determines the quarter, and so on.

Right-click on the design surface to add a new relationship, or right-click on an existing relationship to edit it; both operations launch the Edit Attribute Relationship dialog shown in Figure 71-6. Set the source/related attributes for each relationship until you have all the attributes correctly related, such as shown in Figure 71-5(c). Two important properties are associated with each relationship: Type and Cardinality. The Relationship Type appears in the dialog as well as in the Properties pane, and can take on two values:

- **Rigid:** Denotes that the values of these two attributes will have static relationships over time. If those relationships change, then a processing error will result. This is more efficient than the flexible alternative, however, because Analysis Services can retain aggregations when the dimension is processed. Examples include quarter's relationship to month, and state's relationship to city.

- **Flexible:** Used for attribute values and member property values that change in relationship over time. Aggregations are updated when the dimension is processed to allow for changes. For example, the relationship between employee and department would be flexible to reflect the movement of employees between departments.

FIGURE 71-6

Relationship Editor

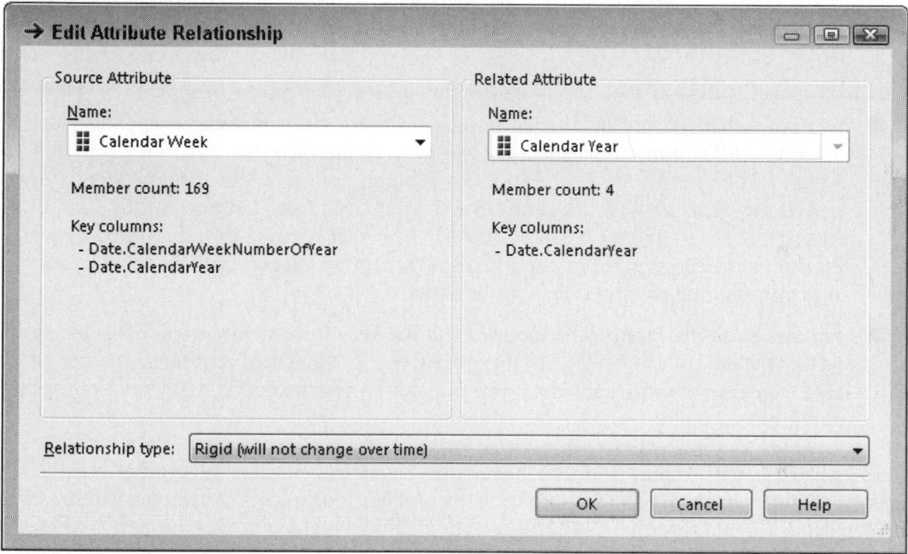

Note that flexible relationships appear as hollow arrows, and rigid relationships as solid arrows, in the designer.

The other important relationship property is Cardinality, which appears only in the Properties pane. Choose "Many" when there is a one-to-many relationship, such as the day to month relationship. Choose "One" when there is a one-to-one relationship, such as that between a customer ID and social security number. When all user hierarchies have been defined, one-to-many relationships will tend to be represented as separate boxes, whereas one-to-one relationships will tend to appear in the same box. Boxes with more than one attribute represented can be toggled to show or hide attribute details — choose Expand All from the toolbar to see all attributes across the diagram.

You can set the Attribute Relationships diagram to auto-arrange boxes or you can manually position boxes. To manually position boxes, turn off auto-arrange using the toolbar, then select the box and move it using the top border (dragging other portions of the shape will not move it).

Visibility and organization

Most cubes will have a large number of dimension attributes, which can overwhelm the user. Using familiar names will help, but the simplest way to combat attribute overload is to not expose attributes that won't be useful to the user. Specific strategies include the following:

- Delete attributes that are not useful to users. This includes items not well understood and any alternative language information that can be specified in the translation view.
- Some attributes can be presented to users only within a user hierarchy. For example, when interpreting a list of cities without knowing their corresponding country and state information, it may be challenging to tell the difference between Paris, Texas, and Paris, France. For these cases, build the appropriate user hierarchy and set the `AttributeHierarchyVisible` property to `False` for the corresponding attributes. For example, setting the `City` attribute's `AttributeHierarchyVisible` to `False` will hide the city hierarchy itself while allowing the city to appear in any user hierarchies.
- Attributes that will not be queried but are still needed for member properties, such as columns used only for sorting or calculations, can be fully disabled. Set `AttributeHierarchyEnabled` to `False` and note how the attribute icon is now grayed out. Also set `AttributeHierarchyOptimizedState` to `NotOptimized`, and `AttributeHierarchyOrdered` to `False` so that Analysis Services doesn't spend unnecessary time processing. Most client tools now support displaying properties in query results, although filtering on properties can be slow.
- For attributes that need to be modeled but are very infrequently used, consider setting their `AttributeHierarchyVisible` property to `False`. These attributes will not be available to users browsing cube data, but can still be referenced via MDX queries for custom applications.

Once the list of visible attribute and user hierarchies has been determined, consider organizing dimensions with more than a handful of visible hierarchies into folders. Attributes will organize under the folder name entered into the `AttributeHierarchyDisplayFolder` property, whereas user hierarchies have an equivalent property named `DisplayFolder`. In general, these properties should be left blank for the most frequently used hierarchies in a dimension so that those items will display at the root level.

Best Practice

Well-organized dimensions using well-understood names are essential to gaining acceptance for interactive applications — most users will be overwhelmed by the amount of available attributes. Excluding unused attributes not only helps simplify the user's view of the data, it can greatly speed performance — especially for cubes with substantial calculations because the more attributes, the larger the number of cells each calculation must consider.

Basic setup checklist

After creating a basic dimension via either the Dimension or the Cube wizards, review the following checklist, which outlines a first-order refinement. This level of attention is adequate for the majority of circumstances:

- Ensure that attribute names are clear and unambiguous in the context of all dimensions in the model. If changes are required, consider modifying names in the data source view and regenerating the dimension to keep all names consistent within the model.
- Review each attribute's source (`KeyColumns` and `NameColumn` properties) and ordering. Make frequent use of the browser view to check the results.
- Create natural hierarchies and attribute relationships for every dimension to optimize aggregations and query speed.
- Review stakeholder needs for any additional user hierarchies and add them.
- Remove unneeded attributes and adjust visibility as outlined above.
- Organize dimensions with many hierarchies into folders.

Best Practice Warnings

SQL Server 2008 implements best practice warnings throughout the Analysis Services design environment, but dimension design is the first place they are normally encountered. The warnings appear as blue underlines on the object in question, such as the dimension name as viewed in the Dimension Designer. Don't confuse these advisories with actual errors, which appear as red underlines and which will prevent a design from operating. Best practice warnings flag designs that are valid but may not be optimal, depending on the application being built. For example, when a new dimension is created, a warning is generated that relationships have not yet been defined.

A full list of best practice warnings for the project is also generated in the Error List window whenever the cube is deployed. Read the advice associated with each of these, and if it does not apply to a given item, dismiss that particular warning by right-clicking in the Error List window and choosing Dismiss. Comments can be entered to document why a warning was dismissed.

Warnings that don't apply to a given project can be disabled globally by right-clicking on the project within the Solution Explorer and choosing Edit Database. Select the Warnings tab to see a list of all warning rules. Disabling a rule prevents a warning from being checked anywhere in the project. This same page provides both a list of individual warnings that have been dismissed and any comments provided.

Beyond regular dimensions

Dimension concepts described so far in this chapter have focused on the basic functionality common to most types of dimensions. It is somewhat challenging, however, to understand what exactly is meant by the "type" of a dimension. Some sources refer to dimensions as being of only two types: data mining and standard, which encompasses everything else. Each dimension has a type property that assigns values such as Time, Geography, Customer, Accounts, and Regular, which corresponds to everything else not on the list. Furthermore, other characteristics of a dimension, such as parent-child organization, write-enabled dimensions, or linking a dimension from another database, can be thought of as different dimension types.

For clarity, this chapter limits the discussion to standard dimensions and uses "type" only in the context of the dimension property, but it is important to understand how "type" is overloaded when reading other documents.

Time dimension

Nearly every cube needs a time dimension, and a great many production cubes exist with poorly implemented time dimensions. Fortunately, the Dimension Wizard will automatically create a time dimension and a corresponding dimension table, and populate the table with data. Right-click on the dimension folder in the Solution Explorer pane and choose New Dimension to start the wizard.

- **Select Creation Method:** Select "Generate a time table" in the data source.
- **Define Time Periods:** Choose the date range and periods that should appear in the dimension.
- **Select Calendars:** In addition to the standard calendar, choose and configure any other calendars that should appear in the dimension.
- **Completing the Wizard:** Modify the name if desired; leave the "Generate schema now" check box unchecked.

Review the structure of the dimension created by the wizard. Note that the dimension's `type` property is set to `Time`, and that each attribute has an appropriate type set as well: days, months, quarters, and so on. Perform the basic checklist on the dimension design and adjust as necessary. `KeyColumns` and `NameColumn` properties do not require attention, but names assigned to attributes and hierarchies can be adjusted to work for the target audience. Attribute relationships will require refinements. Once the dimension has been adjusted, click the link in the Data Source View pane to create the time dimension table using appropriate naming and location choices.

Assigning an attribute's proper `type` property provides documentation, and may enable features in applications that use a cube. Attribute types are also used for some features within Analysis Services, including Business Intelligence calculations.

Time dimensions can be developed from existing dimension tables as well, using the Dimension Wizard. The challenge with this approach is specifying the attribute type for each of the columns in the time dimension. Using the wizard to generate a similar dimension table can also act as a guide when integrating a custom time table.

A *server time dimension* is an alternative to a traditional time dimension that relies on an underlying relational table. The server time dimension is created internally to Analysis Services, and while not as flexible as the traditional approach, it can be a great shortcut for building a simple cube or quick prototype. Create a server time dimension by starting the Dimension Wizard as described earlier, but choose "Generate a time table on the server" as the creation method.

Because server time dimensions do not have an underlying dimension table, they will not appear in the data source view, so the relationship to the fact table(s) cannot be described there. Instead, use the Cube Designer's dimension usage view to establish relationships to selected fact tables (also known as *measure groups*).

Other dimension types

In addition to the time dimension, Analysis Services recognizes more than a dozen other dimension types, including Customers, Accounts, and Products. Included templates can define a table similar to the process described for generating time dimensions. Start the Dimension Wizard and choose "Generate a non-time table in the data source" and then select a template. Existing tables can be cast as a special type as well by assigning the `Type` property for the dimension (such as `Account`) and the `Type` property for the dimension's attributes (such as `AccountNumber`).

Parent-child dimensions

Most dimensions are organized into hierarchies that have a fixed number of levels, but certain business problems do not lend themselves to a fixed number of levels. For example, a minor organizational change may add a new level to the organizational chart. Relational databases solve this problem with self-referential tables. Analysis Services solves this problem using parent-child dimensions.

A self-referential table involves two key columns — for example, an employee ID and a manager ID. To build the organizational chart, start with the president and look for employees that she manages; then look for the employees they manage, and so on. Often this relationship is expressed as a foreign key between the employee ID (the primary key) and the manager ID. When such a relationship exists on the source table, the Dimension Wizard will suggest the appropriate parent-child relationship. In the employee table example, the `employee ID` attribute will be configured with the `Usage` property set to `Key`, while the `manager ID` attribute will be configured with a `Usage` of `Parent`. Other important properties for configuring a parent-child dimension include the following:

- **`RootMemberIf`:** As set on the parent attribute, this property tells Analysis Services how to identify the top level of the hierarchy. Values include `ParentIsBlank` (null or zero), `ParentIsSelf` (parent and key values are the same), `ParentIsMissing` (parent row not found). The default value is all three, `ParentIsBlankSelfOrMissing`.
- **`OrderBy`:** The `OrderBy` of the `Parent` attribute will organize the hierarchy's display.
- **`NamingTemplate`:** By default, each level in the hierarchy is named simply Level 01, Level 02, etc. Change this naming by clicking the ellipses on the parent attribute's `NamingTemplate` property and specifying a naming pattern in the Level Naming Template dialog. Levels can be given specific names, or a numbered scheme can be specified using an asterisk to denote the level number's location.
- **`MembersWithData`:** As set on the parent attribute, this property controls how non-leaf members with data are displayed. Under the default setting, `NonLeafDataVisible`, Analysis Services will repeat parent members at the leaf level to display their corresponding data. For example, if you browse a cube using a parent-child employee dimension to display sales volume by salesperson, then the sales manager's name will show first at the manager level and then again at the employee level so that it can be associated with the sales the manager made. The alternative setting, `NonLeafDataHidden`, will not repeat the parent name or show data associated with it. This can be disconcerting in some displays because, as the totals do not

change, the sum of the detail rows will not match the total: In the sales manager example, the totals will differ by the sales manager's contribution.

- **MembersWithDataCaption:** When MembersWithData is set to NonLeafDataVisible, this parent attribute property instructs Analysis Services how to name the generated leaf members. Left at the default, blank, generated leaf members will have the same names as their corresponding parents. Enter any string using an asterisk to represent the parent name to change the default name generation. For example, "* (mgr)" will cause the string "(mgr)" to be suffixed to each sales manager's name.
- **UnaryOperatorColumn:** This is a custom rollup function often used with account dimensions, enabling the values associated with different types of accounts to be added or subtracted from the parent totals as needed. Set on the parent attribute, this property identifies a column in the source data table that contains operators to direct how totals are constructed. The column is expected to contain "+" for items that should be added to the total, "−" for subtracted, and "~" for ignore. The column can also contain "*" to multiply a value and the current partial total, or "/" to divide a value by the partial total, but these operators produce different results depending on which values are accumulated first. To control the order of operation, a second column can be added as an attribute in the parent-child dimension, given the type of sequence. For example, "+" and "−" operators could be used to calculate a net from a series of debit and credit accounts. Blank operators are treated as "+".

Once the parent-child relationship is configured, the parent attribute presents a multi-level view of the dimension's data. In addition, all the other attributes of the dimension are available and behave normally. The basic setup checklist applies to a parent-child dimension, although the name of the parent attribute will likely need to be adjusted within the dimension instead of in the data source view, given the unique usage.

Dimension refinements

Once a dimension has been built, a large number of properties are available to refine its behavior and that of its attributes. This section details some of the more common and less obvious refinements possible.

Hierarchy (All) level and default member

The (All) level is added to the top of each hierarchy by default, and represents every member in that hierarchy. At query time, the (All) level allows everything in a hierarchy to be included, without listing each member out separately. In fact, any hierarchy not explicitly included in a query is implicitly included using its (All) level. For example, a query that returns products sold by state explicitly is implicitly products sold by state for all years, all months, all customers, etc.

By default, the name of the (All) level will be All, which is quite practical and sufficient for most applications, but it is possible to give the (All) level a different name by setting the dimension property AttributeAllMemberName or the user hierarchy property AllMemberName. For example, the top level of the employee dimension could be changed to "Everyone."

Regardless of name, the (All) member is also the default member, implicitly included in any query for which that dimension is not explicitly specified. The default member can be changed by setting the dimension's DefaultMember property. This property should be set with care. For example, setting the DefaultMember for the year attribute to 2009 will cause every query that does not explicitly specify the year to return data for only 2009. Default members can also be set to conflict: Setting the `DefaultMember` for the year to 2009 and the month to August 2008 will cause any query that does not explicitly specify year and month to return no data.

Default members are often set when data included in a cube is not commonly queried. Consider a cube populated with sales transactions that are mostly successful but sometimes fail due to customer credit or other problems. Nearly everyone that queries the cube will be interested in the volume and amount of successful transactions. Only someone doing failure analysis will want to view other than successful transactions. Thus, setting the status dimension's default member to success would simplify queries for the majority of users.

Another option is to eliminate the (All) level entirely by setting an attribute's `IsAggregatable` property to `false`. When the (All) level is eliminated, either a `DefaultMember` must be specified or one will be chosen at random at query time. In addition, the attribute can participate in user hierarchies only at the top level, because appearing in a lower level would require the attribute to be aggregated.

Grouping dimension members

The creation of member groups, or discretization, is the process of grouping the values of a many-valued attribute into discrete "buckets" of data. This is a very useful approach for representing a large number of continuous values, such as annual income or commute distance. Enable the feature on an attribute by setting the `DiscretizationBucketCount` property to the number of groups to be created and by choosing a `DiscretizationMethod` from the list.

A `DiscretizationMethod` setting of Automatic will result in reasonable groupings for most applications. Automatic allows Analysis Services to choose an algorithm to match the data being grouped. Should the Automatic setting not yield acceptable groupings, try other methods. Once the groupings have been created they are not necessarily static — changes to the underlying data may cause new groupings to be calculated during cube processing.

An attribute that is being grouped must not have any member properties — that is, other attributes cannot rely on a discretized attribute as the source of their aggregations. If the attribute to be discretized must participate in the natural hierarchy (for example, if it is the key or greatly affects performance), consider adding a second dimension attribute based on the same column to provide the grouped view.

Take care to configure the attribute's source columns and ordering because the `OrderBy` property will determine both how the data is examined in creating member groups and the order in which those groups are displayed.

Cubes

A cube brings the elements of the design process together and exposes them to the user, combining data sources, data source views, dimensions, measures, and calculations in a single container.

A cube can contain data (measures) from many fact tables organized into measure groups. The data to be presented in Analysis Services is generally modeled with as few cubes and databases as is reasonable, with advantages to both the designer and the end user. Users that need only a narrow slice of what is presented in the resulting cube can be accommodated by defining a perspective, rather like an Analysis

Service view, exposing only what makes sense to them. From the designer's perspective, limiting the number of cubes and databases keeps the number of linked dimensions and measures to a minimum.

Using the Cube Wizard has been covered in earlier sections, both from the top-down approach (see "Analysis Services Quick Start") using the cube design to generate corresponding relational and Integration Services packages, and from the bottom-up approach (see "Creating a Cube"). Once the cube structure has been created, it is refined using the Cube Designer.

Open any cube from the Solution Explorer to use the Cube Designer, shown in Figure 71-7. The Cube Designer presents information in several tabbed views described in the remainder of this section.

FIGURE 71-7

Cube Designer

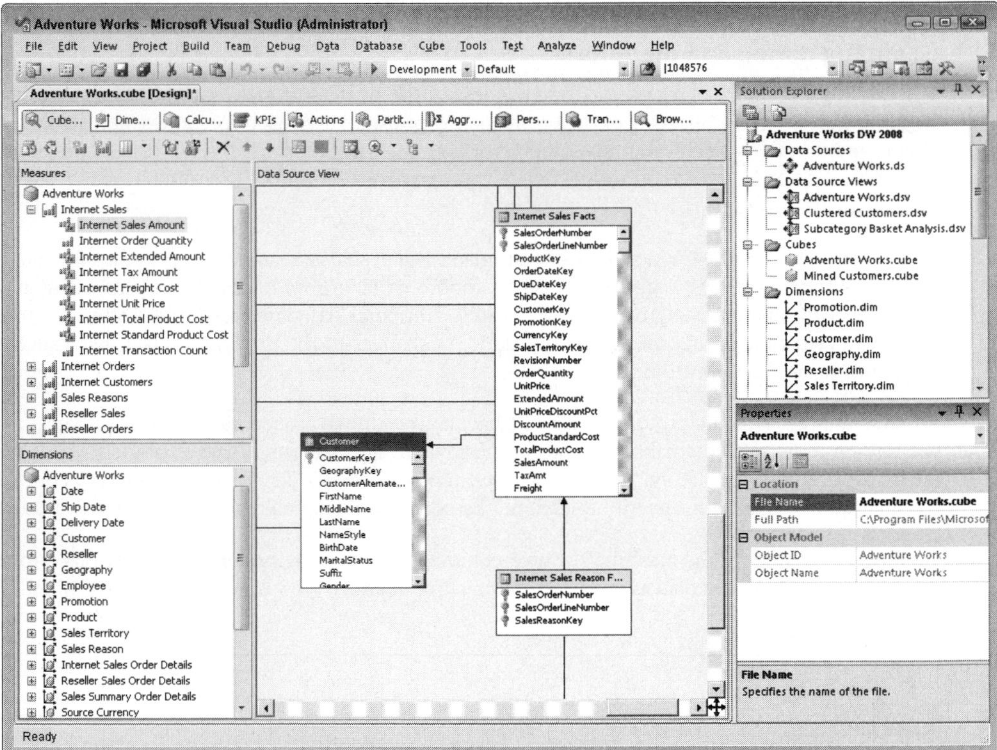

Cube structure

The cube structure view is the primary design surface for defining a cube. Along with the ever-present Solution Explorer and Properties panes, three panes present the cube's structure:

- **Data Source View:** This pane, located in the center of the view, shows a chosen portion of the data source view on which the cube is built. Each table is color-coded: yellow for fact tables, blue for dimensions, and white for neither. The tables available can be changed by right-clicking on the design surface and choosing an option from the context menu. Right-clicking a table presents options to hide that table or to show related tables. Diagrams defined within the data source view can be used as well by selecting the Copy Diagram From option on the context menu. Additionally, the toolbar can be used to toggle between diagram and tree views of the table and relationship data; the tree view can be very useful for answering questions about complex diagrams.

- **Measures:** This pane, located in the upper-left section of the view, lists all of the cube's measures organized by measure group. Both the toolbar and the context menu toggle between the tree and grid view of measures.
- **Dimensions:** This pane, located in the lower-left section of the view, lists all dimensions associated with the cube. This list may be a subset of the defined dimensions from the Solution Explorer if not every dimension is in the current cube. Each dimension in the Dimensions pane shows the user hierarchies and attributes, and has a link to edit that dimension in the Dimension Designer.

Because the order in which measures and dimensions appear in their respective lists determines the order in which users see them presented, the lists can be reordered using either the right-click Move Up/Move Down options or drag-and-drop while in tree view. Like the Dimension Designer, changes to a cube must be deployed before they can be browsed.

Measures

Each measure is based on a column from the data source view and an aggregate function. The aggregate function determines how data is processed from the fact table and how it is summarized. For example, consider a simple fact table with columns of day, store, and sales amount being read into a cube with a sales amount measure, a stores dimension, and a time dimension with year, month, and day attributes. If the aggregate function for the sales amount measure is `Sum`, then rows are read into the cube's leaf level by summing the sales amount for any rows with the same store/day combinations. Higher levels, such as the store/month level, are determined by adding up individual days in that month. However, if the aggregate function is `Min`, then the smallest value is saved from all the sales on a given day, and the store/month level would be determined as the smallest of all the days in that month.

Available aggregate functions include the following:

- **Sum:** Adds the values of all children
- **Min:** Minimum value of children
- **Max:** Maximum value of children
- **Count:** Count of the corresponding rows in the fact table
- **Distinct Count:** Counts unique occurrences of the column value (e.g., Unique Customer Count)
- **None:** No aggregation performed. Any value not read directly from the fact table will be null.
- **AverageOfChildren:** Averages non-empty children
- **FirstChild:** Value of the first child member as evaluated along the time dimension.
- **FirstNonEmpty:** Value of the first non-empty child member as evaluated along the time dimension.

- **LastChild:** Value of the last child member as evaluated along the time dimension.
- **LastNonEmpty:** Value of the last non-empty child member as evaluated along the time dimension.
- **ByAccount:** Aggregation varies based on the values in the Account Dimension. The dimension's `Type` property must be `Accounts`, and one of the dimension's attributes must have the `Type` property set to `AccountType`. The column corresponding to `AccountType` contains defined strings that identify the type of account, and thus the aggregation method, to Analysis Services.

The best way to add a new measure is to right-click in the Measures pane and choose New Measure. Specify the aggregation function and table/column combination in the New Measure dialog. The new measure will automatically be added to the appropriate measure group. Measure groups are created for each fact table plus any distinct count measure defined. These groups correspond to different SQL queries that are run to retrieve the cube's data.

Beyond measures derived directly from fact tables, calculated measures can be added by the Business Intelligence Wizard and directly via the calculations view.

CROSS-REF **For more information about calculated measures, see Chapter 72, "Programming MDX Queries."**

Measures can be presented to the user grouped in folders by setting the `DisplayFolder` property to the name of the folder in which the measure should appear. It is also good practice to assign each measure a default format by setting the `FormatString` property, either by choosing one of the common formats from the list or by directly entering a custom format.

Each cube can have a default measure specified if desired, which provides a measure for queries when no measure is explicitly requested. To set the default measure, select the cube name at the top of the Measures pane tree view, and set the `DefaultMeasure` property by selecting a measure from the list.

Cube dimensions

The hierarchies and attributes for each dimension can be either disabled (`Enabled` and `AttributeHierarchyEnabled` properties, respectively) or made invisible (`Visible` and `AttributeHierarchyVisible` properties, respectively) if appropriate for a particular cube context (see "Visibility and Organization" earlier in the chapter, for example scenarios). Access these settings in the Dimensions pane and then adjust the associated properties. These properties are specific to a dimension's role in the cube and do not change the underlying dimension design.

Dimensions can be added to the cube by right-clicking the Dimensions pane and choosing New Dimension. Once the dimension has been added to the cube, review the dimension usage view to ensure that the dimension is appropriately related to all measure groups.

Dimension usage

The dimension usage view displays a table showing how each dimension is related to each measure group. With dimensions and measure groups as row and column headers, respectively, each cell of the table defines the relationship between the corresponding dimension/measure group pair. Drop-down lists in the upper-left corner enable rows and columns to be hidden to simplify large views.

The Cube Designer creates default relationships based on the data source view relationships, which are accurate in most cases, although any linked objects require special review because they are not derived from the data source view. Click on the ellipses in any table cell to launch the Define Relationship dialog and choose the relationship type. Different relationship types require different mapping information, as described in the following sections.

No relationship

For a database with more than one fact table, there will likely be dimensions that don't relate to some measure groups. Signified by gray table cells with no annotation, this setting is expected for measure group/dimension pairs that don't share a meaningful relationship. When a query is run that specifies dimension information unrelated to a given measure, it is ignored by default.

Regular

The regular relationship is a fact table relating directly to a dimension table, as in a star schema. Within the Define Relationship dialog, choose the Granularity attribute as the dimension attribute that relates directly to the measure group, usually the dimension's key attribute. Once the granularity attribute has been chosen, specify the fact table column names that match the granularity attribute's key columns in the relationships grid at the bottom of the dialog.

Choosing to relate a dimension to a measure group via a non-key attribute does work, but it must be considered in the context of the dimension's natural hierarchy (see "Attribute Relationships," earlier in the chapter). Think of the natural hierarchy as a tree with the key attribute at the bottom. Any attribute at or above the related attribute will be related to the measure group and behave as expected. Any attribute below or on a different branch from the related attribute will have "no relationship," as described in the preceding section.

Fact

Fact dimensions are those derived directly from the fact table when a fact table contains both fact and dimension data. No settings are required beyond the relationship type. Only one dimension can have a fact relationship with a given measure group, effectively requiring a single fact dimension per fact table containing all dimension data in that fact table.

Referenced

When dimension tables are connected to a fact table in a snowflake schema, the dimension could be implemented as a single dimension that has a regular relationship with the measure group, or the dimension could be implemented as a regular dimension plus one or more referenced dimensions. A referenced dimension is indirectly related to the measure group through another dimension. The single dimension with a regular relationship is certainly simpler, but if a referenced dimension can be created and used with multiple chains of different regular dimensions (e.g., a Geography dimension used with both Store and Customer dimensions), then the referenced option will be more storage and process efficient. Referenced relationships can chain together dimensions to any depth.

Create the referenced relationship in the Define Relationship dialog by selecting an intermediate dimension by which the referenced dimension relates to the measure group. Then choose the attributes by which the referenced and intermediate dimensions relate. Normally, the Materialize option should be selected for best performance.

Many-to-Many

Relationships discussed so far have all been one-to-many: One store has many sales transactions, one country has many customers. For an example of a many-to-many relationship, consider tracking book sales by book and author, whereby each book can have many authors and each author can create many books. The many-to-many relationship can be modeled in Analysis Services, but it requires a specific configuration beginning with the data source view (see Figure 71-8). The many-to-many relationship is implemented via an intermediate fact table that lists each pairing of the regular and many-to-many dimensions. For other slightly simpler applications, the regular dimension can be omitted and the intermediate fact table related directly to the fact table.

FIGURE 71-8

Example of a many-to-many relationship

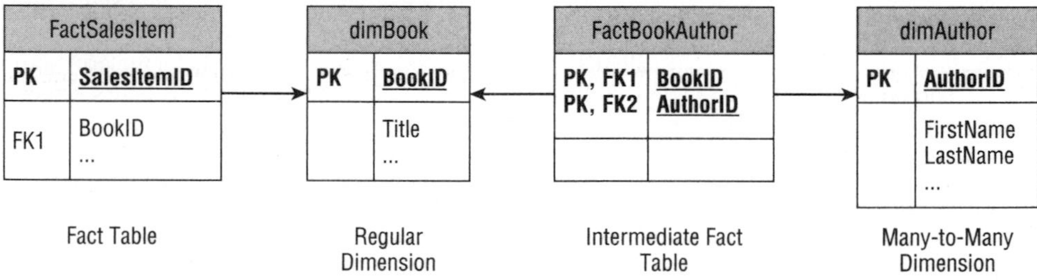

The Define Relationship dialog only requires the name of a measure group created on the intermediate fact table to configure the many-to-many relationship. Other configuration is derived from the data source view.

Many-to-many relationships have the query side effect of generating result sets that don't total in an intuitive way. Using the book sales example, assume that many of the books sold have multiple authors. A query showing books by author will display a list of numbers whose arithmetic total is greater than the total number of books sold. Often, this will be expected and understood behavior, although some applications will require MDX scripting to gain the desired behavior in all views of the cube.

Calculations

The Calculations tab enables the definition of calculated measures, sets of dimension members, and dynamic control over cube properties. While the Calculations tab offers forms to view many of the objects defined here, the underlying language is MDX (Multidimensional Expressions), so details on how to manipulate calculations are covered in the next chapter.

CROSS-REF **For more information about defining scripting, see Chapter 72, "Programming MDX Queries."**

KPIs

A *Key Performance Indicator (KPI)* is a server-side calculation meant to define an organization's most important metrics. These metrics, such as net profit, client utilization, or funnel conversion rate, are frequently used in dashboards or other reporting tools for distribution at all levels throughout the organization. Using a KPI to host such a metric helps ensure consistent calculation and presentation.

Within the KPI's view, an individual KPI consists of several components:

- The actual value of the metric, entered as an MDX expression that calculates the metric
- The goal for the metric — for example, what the budget says net profit should be. The goal is entered as an MDX expression that calculates the metric's goal value.
- The status for the metric, comparing the actual and goal values. This is entered as an MDX expression that returns values between -1 (very bad) to +1 (very good). A graphic can also be chosen as a suggestion to applications that present KPI data, helping to keep the presentation consistent across applications.
- The trend for the metric, showing which direction the metric is headed. Like status, trend is entered as an MDX expression that returns values between -1 and +1, with a suggested graphic.

As KPI definitions are entered, use the toolbar to switch between form (definition) and browser mode to view results. The Calculations Tools pane (lower left) provides cube metadata and the MDX functions list for drag-and drop-creation of MDX expressions. The Templates tab provides templates for some common KPIs.

Actions

The Actions tab of the Cube Designer provides a way to define actions that a client can perform for a given context. For example, a drillthrough action can show detailed rows behind a total, or a reporting action can launch a report based on a dimension attribute's value. Actions can be specific to any displayed data, including individual cells and dimension members, resulting in more detailed analysis or even integration of the analysis application into a larger data management framework.

New in 2008

Drillthrough actions now use cube data to display their results. Prior versions required access to the underlying relational data to provide the display of detail data.

Partitions

Partitions are the unit of storage in Analysis Services, storing the data of a measure group. Initially, the Cube Designer creates a single MOLAP partition for each measure group. MOLAP is the preferred storage mode for most scenarios, but setting partition sizes and aggregations is key to both effective processing and efficient query execution.

Partition sizing

Cube development normally begins by using a small but representative slice of the data, yet production volumes are frequently quite large, with cubes summarizing a billion rows per quarter and more. A partitioning strategy is needed to manage data through both the relational and Analysis Services databases, beginning with the amount of data to be kept online and the size of the partitions that will hold that data.

The amount of data to be kept online is a trade-off between the desire for access to historical data and the cost of storing that data. Once the retention policy has been determined, there are many possible ways to partition that data into manageable chunks, but a time-based approach is widely used, usually keeping either a year's or a month's worth of data in a single partition. For partitions being populated on the front end, the size of the partition is important for the time it takes to process — processing time should be kept to a few hours at most. For partitions being deleted at the back end, the size of the partition is important for the amount of data it removes at one time.

Matching the partition size and retention between the relational database and Analysis Services is a simple and effective approach. As the number of rows imported each day grows, smaller partition sizes (such as week or day) may be required to expedite initial processing. As long as the aggregation design is consistent across partitions, Analysis Services will allow smaller partitions to be merged, keeping the overall count at a manageable level.

Best Practice

Take time to consider retention, processing, and partitioning strategies before an application goes into production. Once in place, changes may be very expensive given the large quantities of data involved.

Creating partitions

The key to accurate partitions is including every data row exactly once. Because it is the combination of all partitions that is reported by the cube, including rows multiple times will inflate the results. A common mistake is to add new partitions while forgetting to delete the default partition created by the Designer; because the new partitions contain one copy of all the source data, and the default partition contains another, cube results are exactly double the true values.

The partition view consists of one collapsible pane for each measure group, each pane containing a grid listing the currently defined partitions for that measure group. Highlighting a grid row will select that partition and display its associated properties in the Properties pane.

Start the process of adding a partition by clicking the New Partition link, which launches a series of Partition Wizard dialogs:

- **Specify Source Information:** Choose the appropriate Measure group (the default is the measure group selected when the wizard is launched). If the source table is included as part of the data source view, then it will appear in the Available tables list and can be selected there. If the source table is not part of the data source view, then choose the appropriate data source from the Look in list and press the Find Tables button to list other tables with the same structure. Optionally, enter a portion of the source table's name in the Filter Tables text box to limit the list of tables returned.

- **Restrict Rows:** If the source table contains exactly the rows to be included in the partition, then skip this page. If the source table contains more rows than should be included in the partition, then select the "Specify query to restrict rows" option, and the Query box will be populated with a fully populated `SELECT` query missing only the `WHERE` clause. Supply the missing constraint(s) in the Query window and press the Check button to validate syntax.
- **Processing and Storage Locations:** The defaults will suffice for most situations. If necessary, choose options to balance load across disks and servers.
- **Completing the Wizard:** Supply a name for the partition — generally the same name as the measure group suffixed with the partition slice (e.g., `Internet_Orders_2004`). If aggregations have not been defined, define them now. If aggregations have already been defined for another partition, then copy these existing aggregations from that partition to ensure consistency across partitions.

Once a partition has been added, the name and source can be edited by clicking in the appropriate cell in the partition grid.

Aggregation design

The best trade-off between processing time, partition storage, and query performance is defining only aggregations that help answer queries commonly run against a cube. Analysis Services' usage-based optimization tracks queries run against the cube and then designs aggregations to meet that query load. However, representative query history usually requires a period of production use, so the aggregations can also be based on intelligent guesses.

New in 2008

The Cube Designer now includes an Aggregations tab that allows summary and detailed views of aggregations for each partition. It introduces the concept of named aggregation designs, which are groups of aggregations specific to a measure group that can be assigned to its associated partitions.

A good approach is to first create a modest number of aggregations using the Aggregation Design Wizard and assign that design to all active partitions. Then deploy the cube for use to collect a realistic query history by enabling query logging (see Analysis Server "Log" properties by right clicking on the server in SQL Server Management Studio). Finally, use the query log to generate a more efficient aggregation design based on usage-based optimization.

Aggregation Design Wizard

The Aggregation Design Wizard will create aggregations based on intelligent guesses. Invoke the wizard from the toolbar on the Aggregations tab of the Cube Designer. The wizard steps through several pages:

- **Select Partitions to Modify:** Each run of the wizard is specific to the measure group selected when the wizard is invoked. Check all the partitions to be updated with the new aggregation design. At least one partition must be selected, and designs can also be moved to other partitions later.

- **Review Aggregation Usage:** All the attributes for every dimension related to the measure group are presented with their usage settings. The default generally suffices, but options include the following:
  - **Full:** Include this attribute in every aggregation.
  - **None:** Don't include this attribute in any aggregation.
  - **Unrestricted:** Considers this attribute for inclusion in the design without restrictions.
- **Specify Object Counts:** Accurate row counts for each partition and dimension table drive how aggregations are calculated. Pressing the Count button will provide current row counts, with the Estimated Count reflecting the total number of rows currently in the database, and the Partition Count reflecting the number of rows that will be included in the first partition. Numbers can be manually entered if the current data source is different from the target design (e.g., a small development data set).
- **Set Aggregation Options:** This page actually designs the aggregations. Options on the left tell the designer when to stop creating new aggregations, while the graph on the right provides estimated storage versus performance gain. Press the Continue button to create an aggregation design before pressing the Next button.

  There are no strict rules, but some general guidelines may help:
  - Unless storage is the primary constraint, target an initial performance gain of 10–20 percent. On the most complex cubes this will be difficult to obtain with a reasonable number of aggregations (and associated processing time). On simpler cubes more aggregations can be afforded, but they are already so fast that the additional aggregations don't buy much.
  - Keep the total number of aggregations under 200 (aggregation count is shown at the bottom, just above the progress bar).
  - Look for an obvious knee (flattening of the curve) in the storage/performance graph and stop there.
- **Completing the Wizard:** Give the new aggregation design a name. Choose either to save the design or to save and process it.

Best Practice

The best aggregations are usage-based: Collect usage history in the query log and use it to optimize each partition's aggregation design periodically. Query logging must be enabled in Analysis Server's Server properties, in the Log\QueryLog section: Set `CreateQueryLogTable` to `true`, define a `QueryLogConnectionString`, and specify a `QueryLogTableName`.

Aggregations tab

The toolbar of this tab can launch the wizard as described earlier and the usage-based optimization wizard as well. The pane itself toggles between standard and advanced views. Standard view lists all the measure groups and summarizes which aggregation designs are assigned to which partitions. Right-click a design's name to assign partitions to it.

The advanced view allows detailed exploration and manual modification of an aggregation design. Choose the measure group and design name in the header, and a table of dimensions vs. individual aggregations appears. Any check that appears in the table indicates that the aggregation (such as A5) includes summaries by the indicated dimension attributes (such as Product Line and Quarter). Manual updates to a design are generally not effective because usage-based optimization tends to be more accurate than individual judgment, but cases do arise in which problem queries can be addressed by a well-placed aggregation. Use the toolbar to copy an existing design to a new name, and then modify as needed. New columns (aggregations) can be copied/added to the table using the toolbar as well.

Perspectives

A perspective is a view of a cube that hides items and functionality not relevant to a specific purpose. Perspectives appear as additional cubes to the end user, so each group within the company can have its own "cube," each just a targeted view of the same data.

Add a perspective by either right-clicking or using the toolbar, and a new column will appear. Overwrite the default name at the top of the column with a meaningful handle, and then uncheck the items not relevant to the perspective. A default measure can be chosen for the perspective as well — look for the `DefaultMeasure` object type in the second row of the grid.

Data Storage

The data storage strategy chosen for a cube and its components determines not only how the cube will be stored, but also how it can be processed. Storage settings can be set at three different levels, with parent settings determining defaults for the children:

- **Cube:** Begin by establishing storage settings at the cube level to set defaults for the entire cube (dimensions, measure groups, and partitions). Access the Cube Storage Settings dialog by choosing a cube in the Cube Designer and then clicking the ellipses on the Proactive Caching property of the cube.
- **Measure Group:** Used in the unlikely case that storage settings for a particular measure group differ from cube defaults. Access the Measure Group Storage Settings dialog by either clicking the ellipses on the measure group's Proactive Caching property in the Cube Designer or by choosing the Storage Settings link in partition view without highlighting a specific partition.
- **Object level (specific partition or dimension):** Sets the storage options for a single object. Access the Dimension Storage Settings dialog by clicking the ellipses on the dimension's Proactive Caching property in the Dimension Designer. Access the Partition Storage Settings dialog by selecting a partition in the partition view and clicking the Storage Settings link.

Each of the storage settings dialogs are essentially the same, differing only in the scope of the setting's effect. The main page of the dialog contains a slider that selects preconfigured option settings — from the most real-time (far left) to the least real-time (far right). Each "stop" on the slider displays a summary of the options available. Alternately, position the slider and click the Options button to examine the options associated with a particular position. Beyond these few presets, the Storage Options dialog enables a wide range of behaviors.

By default, the pure MOLAP setting is chosen. This setting works well for traditional data warehousing applications because the partitions can be processed by the same procedure that loads large batches of data into the warehouse. Pure MOLAP is also an excellent choice for historical partitions for which data additions and updates are not expected. However, if a partition is built based on frequently changing source data (e.g., directly on OLTP tables), then proactive caching can manage partition updates automatically.

Proactive caching

Proactive caching is used to describe the many ways in which Analysis Services can automatically update the contents of a cube based on a relational data source. It is controlled by the many options on the Storage Options dialog, but these options are all controls on the same basic procedure: Analysis Services is notified each time underlying data is updated; it waits for a pause in the updates, and then begins rebuilding the cache (partition). If an update notification is received before the rebuild completes, then the rebuild will be restarted. If the rebuild process takes longer than allowed, then the cache reverts to ROLAP (SQL Queries) until the rebuild is complete.

The options that control the rebuild process are located on the Storage Options' General tab (select the Enable Proactive Caching check box to enable updates):

- **Silence Interval:** Amount of quiet time since the last update notification before beginning the rebuild process. An appropriate setting depends on the table usage profile, and should be long enough to identify when a batch of updates has completed.
- **Silence Override Interval:** After this amount of time, begin the rebuild even if no silence interval has been detected.
- **Latency:** The amount of time from receipt of the first notification until queries revert to ROLAP. Essentially, this guarantees that data returned by Analysis Services will never be more outdated than the specified amount of time. Of course, this may represent a significant extra load against the SQL database(s) and server(s) that must service the queries in the interim, depending on the number and complexity of the queries.
- **Rebuild Interval:** Causes a cache rebuild even when no update notifications are received. The value specifies the time since the last rebuild that a new rebuild will be triggered. This option can be used independently of data changes (e.g., don't listen for notifications, just rebuild this partition every four hours) or as a backup to update notifications, as update notification may not be guaranteed.
- **Bring online immediately:** Causes a newly created cube to come online immediately in ROLAP mode without waiting for the MOLAP build process to complete. Improves availability at the possible expense of extra load on the relational database(s) and server(s) that will process the ROLAP queries.
- **Enable ROLAP aggregations:** Creates views to support ROLAP aggregations.
- **Apply storage settings to dimension:** Only available at the cube or measure group levels, this option applies the same storage settings to all dimensions related to the cube or measure group.

The Notifications tab specifies how Analysis Services will be notified of underlying relational data changes. Notifications options must be set for each object (partition and dimension) individually. These options are relevant only when rebuilds on data change are enabled (for example, Silence Interval and Silence Override Interval are set).

SQL Server notifications

SQL Server notifications use trace events to tell Analysis Services when either an insert or an update has occurred in the underlying table. Because event delivery is not guaranteed, this approach is often coupled with periodic rebuilds to ensure that missed events are included on a regular schedule. Enabling trace events requires that Analysis Services connects to SQL Server with an appropriately privileged account.

A partition that relies directly on an underlying table, without the use of query binding or a named query in the data source view, does not require tracking tables to be specified. Other partitions will need to have tracking tables specified, listing the underlying tables that when changed indicate the partition is out of date. Dimensions must always list tracking tables. These tracking tables are simply the tables on which the intermediate named query or view are based.

Client-initiated notifications

Client-initiated notification enables a custom application that changes data tables to notify Analysis Services when a table has been changed. The application sends a `NotifyTableChange` command to the server to specify which table has been changed. Otherwise, processing behaves much like SQL Server notification.

Scheduled polling notifications

Scheduled polling notification is simple to configure and works for non-SQL Server data sources, but only recognizes when new rows have been added to the table. If update-only transactions are common against a table, then combine polling with the periodic rebuild option to incorporate missed updates.

Polling works by running a query that returns a high-water mark from the source table and notices when the mark changes. For example, a partition built on the `factSales` table with an always increasing primary key `SalesID` can poll using the following query:

```
SELECT MAX(SalesID) FROM factSales;
```

Enable polling by selecting the polling interval and entering the corresponding polling query. Multiple polling queries can be used if the object (such as a multi-table dimension) relies on multiple tables for data.

Notification based on polling can help implement incremental updates. Incremental updates become important as partition sizes grow, increasing processing time and resource requirements beyond convenient levels. Incremental processing is based on a query that returns only data added since the partition was last processed. Continuing the preceding example, Analysis Services replaces the first parameter (?) with the last value previously processed, and the second parameter with the current polled value:

```
SELECT * FROM factSales WHERE SalesID > COALESCE(?,-1) AND SalesID <= ?;
```

The `COALESCE` function handles the empty table case where no data had been previously processed. Enable incremental updates by selecting the Enable Incremental Updates check box and entering a processing query and tracking table for each polling query.

Data Integrity

Data integrity functionality in Analysis Services addresses inconsistencies that would otherwise cause improper data presentation. Analysis Services views these inconsistencies in two categories:

- **Null Processing:** When nulls are encountered in source data. For example, if a measure contains a null, should it be reported as zero or remain a null value?
- **Key Errors:** When keys are missing, duplicated, or otherwise don't map between tables. For example, how should a CustomerID in the fact table without a corresponding entry in the customer dimension be handled?

Basing a cube on a traditional data warehouse helps minimize data integrity issues by addressing these problems during the warehouse load.

Best Practice

A key strength of OLAP in general and the UDM in particular is consistent interpretation of data. Data integrity settings and centralized calculations are examples of the many ways that UDM centralizes data interpretation for downstream data consumers. Address these issues in the design of the warehouse and UDM to deliver the most useful product. Think of it as building a "data object" complete with information hiding and opportunities for reuse.

Null processing

How nulls are treated depends on the `NullProcessing` property of the object in question. For measures, the `NullProcessing` property appears as part of the source definition with four possible values:

- **ZeroOrBlank:** The server converts nulls to zero for numeric data items, and to blank for string data items.
- **Automatic:** Same as ZeroOrBlank
- **Error:** The server will trigger an error and discard the record.
- **Preserve:** Stores the null value without change

A good way to choose among these settings is to consider how an average value should be calculated on the data for a given measure. If the best interpretation is averaging only the non-null values, then `Preserve` will yield that behavior. Otherwise, `ZeroOrBlank` will yield an average that considers null measures as zero.

For dimensions, the `NullProcessing` property can take on an additional value:

- **UnknownMember:** Interprets the null value as the unknown member

The NullProcessing property appears in several contexts for dimensions:

- Each dimension attribute's NameColumn, if defined, contains NullProcessing as part of the source definition. This setting is used when a null name is encountered when building the dimension.
- Each dimension attribute's KeyColumns collection contains a NullProcessing property for every column in the collection. This setting is used when null key column(s) are encountered when building the dimension.
- Each cell on the Dimension Usage tab that relates a measure group and dimension via a regular relationship contains a NullProcessing property. The NullProcessing property is located on the Advanced (Measure Group Bindings) dialog, and is used when the related column in the fact table is null.

For dimension relationships, the default setting of Automatic NullProcessing is actually quite dangerous. As the key column is read as null, it will be converted to 0 (or blank), which may be a valid key into some dimensions, causing null entries to be assigned to that member. Usually a better setting is UnknownMember if nulls are expected, or Error if nulls are not expected. Alternately, a dimension member could be created for a 0 (or blank) key value and assigned a name such as "Invalid" to match the automatic processing behavior.

Unknown member

Choosing an unknown member option, either as part of null processing or in response to an error, requires the unknown member to be configured for the affected dimension. Once the unknown member is enabled for a dimension, the member will be added to every attribute in the dimension. The UnknownMember dimension property can take on three possible settings:

- **None:** The unknown member is not enabled for this dimension and any attempt to assign data to the unknown member will result in an error. This is the default setting.
- **Visible:** The unknown member is enabled and is visible to queries.
- **Hidden:** The unknown member is enabled, but not directly visible in queries. However, the (All) level of the dimension will contain the unknown member's contribution and the MDX UnknownMember function can access the unknown member's contribution directly.

The default name of the unknown member is simply "Unknown," which can be changed by entering a value for the dimension's UnknownMemberName property.

Error Configuration

For data integrity errors as described and several others, the ErrorConfiguration property specifies how errors will be handled. Initially, the setting for this property will be (default), but choose the (custom) setting from the list and eight properties will appear. The ErrorConfiguration properties are available on several objects, but are primarily set for dimensions and measure groups.

The error configuration properties are as follows:

- **KeyDuplicate:** Triggered when a duplicate key is seen while building the dimension. The default is `IgnoreError`; other settings are `ReportAndContinue` and `ReportAndStop`. `IgnoreError` will cause all the attribute values to be incorporated into the dimension, but Analysis Services randomly chooses which values to associate with the key. For example, if a product dimension table has two rows for productID 73, one with the name "Orange" and the other with the name "Apple," then both Orange and Apple will appear as members of the product name attribute, but only one of those names will have transactions associated with it. Conversely, if both product names are Apple, then there will be only one Apple in the product name dimensions, and users of the cube will be unable to tell that there were any duplicate records.
- **KeyErrorAction:** Triggered when a `KeyNotFound` error is encountered. This occurs when a key value cannot be located in its associated table. For measure groups, this happens when the fact table contains a dimension key not found in the dimension table. For snowflaked dimension tables, it similarly implies one dimension table referencing a non-existent key in another dimension table. Settings are either `ConvertToUnknown` (the default) or `DiscardRecord`.
- **KeyErrorLimit:** The number of key errors allowed before taking the `KeyErrorLimitAction`. The default value of `0` causes the first error to trigger the `KeyErrorLimitAction`. Set to `-1` for no limit.
- **KeyErrorLimitAction:** The action triggered by exceeding the `KeyErrorLimit`. Settings are either `StopProcessing` (default) or `StopLogging`. `StopLogging` will continue processing and allow any number of key errors, but will log only the first `KeyErrorLimit` errors.
- **KeyErrorLogFile:** File to log all key errors.
- **KeyNotFound:** Determines how `KeyNotFound` errors interact with the `KeyErrorLimit`. The default setting of `ReportAndContinue` counts the error against `KeyErrorLimit`, whereas a setting of `IgnoreError` does not count the error against `KeyErrorLimit`. The setting of `ReportAndStop` will log the error and stop processing immediately without regard for any `KeyErrorLimit` or `KeyErrorAction` settings. The `IgnoreError` setting is useful when multiple `KeyNotFound` errors are expected, allowing the expected mapping to an unknown member to occur while counting other types of key errors against the `KeyErrorLimit`.
- **NullKeyConvertedToUnknown:** Identical in concept to the `KeyNotFound` property, but for null keys converted to an unknown member (`NullProcessing=UnknownMember`) instead of `KeyNotFound` errors. The default setting is `IgnoreError`.
- **NullKeyNotAllowed:** Identical in concept to the `KeyNotFound` property, but for disallowed null keys (`NullProcessing=Error`) instead of `KeyNotFound` errors. The default setting is `ReportAndContinue`.

These same properties can be set as server properties to establish different defaults. They can also be set for a particular processing run to provide special handling for certain data.

Summary

Analysis Services provides the capability to build fast, consistent, and relevant repositories of data suitable for both end-user and application use. The details are extensive, but generally simple problems can be resolved easily by using default behaviors, and more complex problems need the flexibility provided by the breadth of this server and its design environment.

Other chapters in this section detail the design, loading, analyzing, querying, and reporting of BI data.

Chapter 72

Programming MDX Queries

IN THIS CHAPTER

Cube addressing basics

MDX `SELECT` statements

Commonly used MDX functions

MDX named sets and calculated members

Adding named sets, calculated members, and business intelligence to cube definitions

Multidimensional Expressions (MDX) is to Analysis Services what SQL is to the relational database, providing both definition (DDL) and query (DML) capabilities. MDX queries even look somewhat like SQL, but the ideas behind them are dramatically different. Certainly, MDX returns multidimensional cell sets instead of two-dimensional result sets, but more important, MDX does not contain a `JOIN` statement, as the cube contains explicit relationships between all the data it summarizes. Instead, hierarchically organized dimension data is manipulated in sets to determine both the content and structure of the result.

Learning to write basic MDX queries goes quickly for most people, especially those with other database experience. However, many beginners have a tendency to stall at the basic query level. This learning plateau seems to stem from a lack of understanding of only a dozen or so terms and concepts. These are the same concepts presented at the beginning of this chapter: tuples, sets, the parts of a dimension, and so on.

To avoid being stalled, attack MDX in manageable bites:

1. Read the "Basic Select Query" section following this list, and then practice basic queries until you become comfortable with them.
2. Return to and reread "Basic Select Query" carefully until you master the concepts and terminology. These basics will enable you to read the documentation of advanced features in "Advanced Select Query" later in this chapter with confidence. Practice advanced queries.
3. Get started defining sets and calculations within the cube structure by reading the "MDX Scripting" section toward the end of this chapter.

CROSS-REF **For background in creating the cubes that MDX queries, see Chapter 71, "Building Multidimensional Cubes with Analysis Services."**

Basic Select Query

Like SQL, the SELECT statement in MDX is the means by which data is retrieved from the database. A common MDX form is as follows:

```
SELECT { Set1 } ON COLUMNS, { Set2 } ON ROWS
FROM  Cube
WHERE ( Set3 )
```

This query will return a simple table, with Set1 and Set2 defining the column and row headers, Cube providing the data, and Set3 limiting which parts of the cube are summarized in the table.

Cube addressing

A set is a list of one or more tuples. A *tuple* is an address that references some portion of the cube. Consider the example cube in Figure 72-1, which has been limited to three dimension hierarchies (Product, Year, Measure) so that it can be represented graphically. An MDX query summarizes the individual blocks of the cube, called *cells,* into the geometry specified by the query.

FIGURE 72-1

A simple cube with three dimension hierarchies

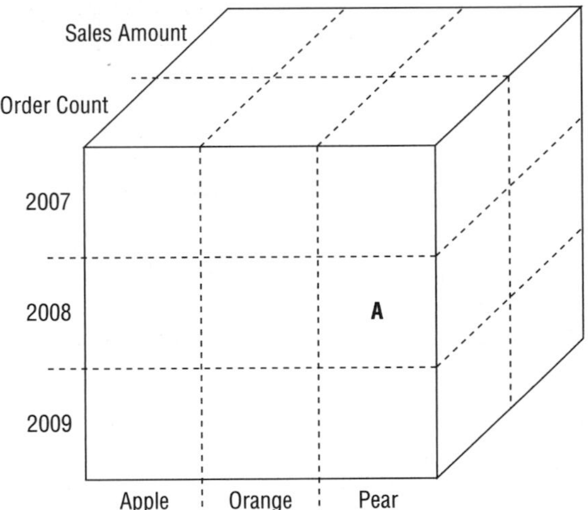

Tuples are specified by listing entries from every hierarchy providing coordinates in the cube, selecting all the cells where those coordinates intersect. For example, (Pear, 2008, Order Count) addresses the cell marked as "A" in Figure 72-1. Tuples can also address groups of cells using a dimension's All level — for example, (Pear, All Years, Order Count) refers to three cells: the cell marked as "A" and the cells immediately above (Pear, 2007, Order Count) and below (Pear, 2009, Order Count) it. In fact, even when a tuple does not explicitly list a dimension, MDX uses the dimension's default member (usually the All level) to fill in the missing information. Thus, (Sales Amount) is the same as (All Products, All Years, Sales Amount).

Sets are built from tuples, so {(Pear, 2008, Order Count)} is a set of one cell, while {(Apple), (Orange)} consists of 12 cells — all the cells that don't have Pear as the product. Of course, the MDX syntax is a bit more formal than these examples show, and practical cubes are more complex, but the addressing concepts remain the same.

Dimension structure

Each dimension is a subject area that can be used to organize the results of an MDX query. Within a dimension are hierarchies, essentially topics within that subject area. For example, a customer dimension might have hierarchies for city, country, and postal code, describing where a customer lives. Each hierarchy in turn has one or more levels that actually contain the members or dimension data. Members are used to build the sets that form the basis of MDX queries.

Dimension references

Referring to one of the components of a dimension is as simple as stringing together its lineage separated by periods. Here are some examples:

```
[Customer]                                   -- Customer dimension
[Customer].[Country]                         -- Country hierarchy
[Customer].[Country].[Country]               -- Country level
[Customer].[Country].[Country].&[Germany]    -- Germany member
```

While it is technically acceptable to omit the square brackets around each identifier, many cube names have embedded spaces and special characters, so it is customary to include them consistently. The ampersand (&) before the member denotes a *reference by* key — every member can be referenced by either its key or its name, although keys are recommended. In this case, the key and the name are the same thing, so`[Customer].[Country].[Country].[Germany]`refers to the same member as the sample does. Members from other hierarchies may have more cryptic keys — for example, `[Customer].[Customer].[Customer].&[20755]`may be equivalent to`[Customer].[Customer].[Customer].[Mike White]`.

In addition to referring to individual members in a dimension, most dimensions also have an [All] level that refers to all the members in that dimension. The default name for this level is [All], but it can be changed by the cube developer. For example, the [All] level for the AdventureWorks Customer dimension is named [All Customers]. The [All] level can be referenced from either the dimension or the hierarchy with equivalent results:

```
[Customer].[All Customers]             -- Customer [All] level from
                                          dimension
[Customer].[Country].[All Customers]-- Customer [All] level from
                                          hierarchy
```

Tuples and simple sets

As outlined earlier in the section "Cube Addressing," tuples are constructed by listing one member from each hierarchy; or, if no member is explicitly specified for a particular hierarchy, the default member (usually the [All] level) for that hierarchy is implicitly included in the tuple. Parentheses are used to group the tuple's member list. For example, the following tuple references all the cells that contain Internet sales volume for German customers over all time, all territories, all products, and so on:

```
([Customer].[Country].[Country].&[Germany],
 [Measures].[Internet Sales Amount])
```

This example includes a *measure*, which is part of every tuple. Unlike a dimension, it is not possible to have an [All] level when it is omitted, but the cube can be configured with a default measure, which will be used if no measure is specified. Also notice the simplified syntax to refer to a measure:

```
[Measures].[Measure Name].
```

When a simple tuple is specified with only one hierarchy member, the parentheses can be omitted, so all German customers becomes the following:

```
Customer].[Country].[Country].&[Germany].
```

The simplest way to build a set is by listing one or more tuples inside of braces. For example, using simple tuples without parentheses, the following is a set of French and German customers:

```
{[Customer].[Country].[Country].&[France],
 [Customer].[Country].[Country].&[Germany]}
```

Basic SELECT statement

Simple sets enable the construction of a basic SELECT statement. The following example query returns Internet sales to French and German customers for the calendar years 2003 and 2004:

```
SELECT
{[Customer].[Country].[Country].&[France],
 [Customer].[Country].[Country].&[Germany]} ON COLUMNS,
{[Date].[Calendar Year].[Calendar Year].&[2003],
 [Date].[Calendar Year].[Calendar Year].&[2004]} ON ROWS
FROM [Adventure Works]
WHERE ([Measures].[Internet Sales Amount])
```

CROSS-REF **All queries in this chapter are constructed to run against the AdventureWorks Cube samples for SQL Server 2008. See** `www.codeplex.com/SqlServerSamples` **to download the sample Analysis Services and Relational databases.**

Result:

	France	Germany
CY 2003	$1,026,324.97	$1,058,405.73
CY 2004	$ 922,179.04	$1,076,890.77

This example places sets on two axes, rows and columns, which become the row and column headers. The WHERE clause in this example limits the query to only cells containing Internet sales amount. The WHERE clause is often called the *slicer*, as it limits the scope of the query to a particular slice of the cube. Think of the slicer as determining how each hierarchy that isn't part of some axis definition will contribute to the query.

Any number of headers can be specified for an axis by including more than one non-default hierarchy in each tuple that builds the axis set. The following example creates two row headers by listing both the Product Line and Sales Reason Type hierarchies in each row tuple:

```
SELECT
{[Customer].[Country].[Country].&[France],
 [Customer].[Country].[Country].&[Germany]} ON COLUMNS,
{([Product].[Product Line].[Product Line].&[S],
    [Sales Reason].[Sales Reason Type].[Sales Reason Type].
       &[Marketing]),
 ([Product].[Product Line].[Product Line].&[S],
    [Sales Reason].[Sales Reason Type].[Sales Reason Type].
       &[Promotion]),
 ([Product].[Product Line].[Product Line].&[M],
    [Sales Reason].[Sales Reason Type].[Sales Reason Type].
       &[Marketing]),
 ([Product].[Product Line].[Product Line].&[M],
    [Sales Reason].[Sales Reason Type].[Sales Reason Type].
       &[Promotion])
 } ON ROWS
FROM [Adventure Works]
WHERE ([Measures].[Internet Sales Amount],
       [Date].[Calendar Year].[Calendar Year].&[2004])
```

Result:

		France	Germany
Accessory	Marketing	$ 962.79	$ 349.90
Accessory	Promotion	$ 2,241.84	$ 2,959.86
Mountain	Marketing	$ 189.96	$ 194.97
Mountain	Promotion	$100,209.88	$126,368.03

This hierarchy-to-header mapping provides a way to control the geometry of the result set, but it also places a restriction on creating sets for an axis: The hierarchies specified for tuples in the set must remain consistent for every item in the set. For example, having some of the tuples in the preceding example use the Product Category hierarchy instead of the Product Line hierarchy would not be allowed. Think of inconsistencies between the tuples as causing blank header cells, which MDX doesn't know how to handle.

Another restriction on creating sets for an MDX query is that each hierarchy can appear on only one axis or slicer definition. If the Calendar Year hierarchy is explicitly named in the row definition, then it cannot appear again in the slicer. This restriction applies purely to the hierarchy — another hierarchy that contains the calendar year data (for example, the Calendar hierarchy in AdventureWorks) can appear on one axis while the Calendar Year hierarchy appears elsewhere.

Measures

Measures are the values that the cube is created to present. They are available in MDX as members of the always present Measures dimension. The Measures dimension has no hierarchies or levels, so each measure is referenced directly from the dimension level as `[Measures].[measure name]`. If no measure is specified for a query, then the cube's default measure is used.

Generating sets from functions

Developing MDX code would quickly become very tedious if every set had to be built by hand. Several functions can be used to generate sets using data within the cube; some of the most popular are listed below. To save space, each example has been constructed such that it provides the missing row set for this example query:

```
SELECT
{[Measures].[Internet Sales Amount],
 [Measures].[Internet Total Product Cost]} ON COLUMNS,
{ } ON ROWS
FROM [Adventure Works]
```

- `.Members`: Lists all of the individual members of either a hierarchy or a level. Used with a level, all the members of that level are listed (e.g., `[Date].[Calendar].[Month].Members` returns all calendar months). When used with a hierarchy, all members from every level are listed (e.g., `[Date].[Calendar].Members` returns every year, semester, quarter, month, and day).
- `.Children`: Lists all the children of a given member (e.g., `[Date].[Calendar].[Calendar Quarter].&[2002]&[1].Children` returns all the months in the first quarter of 2002).
- `Descendants(start [,depth [,show]])`: Lists the children, grandchildren, and so on, of a member or set of members. Specify `start` as the member or set of members, `depth` as either a specific level name or the number of levels below `start`. By default, if `depth` is specified, only descendants at that depth are listed; the `show` flag can alter that behavior by allowing levels above, at, or below to be shown as well — values include `SELF`, `AFTER`, `BEFORE`, `BEFORE_AND_AFTER`, `SELF_AND_AFTER`, `SELF_AND_BEFORE`, `SELF_BEFORE_AFTER`. Some examples are as follows:
  - `Descendants([Date].[Calendar].[Calendar Year].&[2003])` lists the year, semesters, quarters, months, and days in 2003.
  - `Descendants([Date].[Calendar].[Calendar Year].&[2003],[Date].[Calendar].[Month])` lists the months in 2003.
  - `Descendants([Date].[Calendar].[Calendar Year].&[2003],3,SELF_AND_AFTER)` lists the months and days in 2003.

- LastPeriods(n, member): Returns the last n periods ending with member (e.g., LastPeriods(12,[Date].[Calendar].[Month].&[2004]&[6])lists July 2003 through June 2004). If n is negative, then future periods are returned beginning with member.
- TopCount(set, count [,numeric_expression]): Returns the top n (count) of a set sorted by the numeric_expression (e.g., TopCount([Date].[Calendar].[Month].Members, 5, [Measures].[Internet Sales Amount]) returns the top five months for Internet sales). Omitting the numeric_expression argument just returns the first count entries of the set. Very similar to functions BottomCount, TopPercent, and BottomPercent.

Unlike TopCount and its cousins, most set functions do not involve sorting as part of their function, and instead return a set with members in their default cube order. The Order function can be used to sort a set:

```
Order(set, sort_by [ , { ASC | DESC | BASC | BDESC } ]).
```

Specify the set to be sorted, the expression to sort by, and optionally the order in which to sort (defaults to ASC). The ASCending and DESCending options sort within the confines of the hierarchy. For example, sorting months within the AdventureWorks Calendar hierarchy using one of these options, months will move around within a quarter, but will not cross quarter (hierarchy) boundaries. The "break hierarchy" options, BASC and BDESC, will sort without regard to the parent under which a member normally falls.

Generated sets frequently have members for which no measure data are available. These members can be suppressed by prefixing the axis definition with NON EMPTY. The following example shows sales by salesperson for months in 2004; NON EMPTY is used for the column headers because the cube does not contain data for all months in 2004, and NON EMPTY is useful in the row definition because not every employee is a salesperson. In addition, the Order function is used to rank the salespeople by total sales in 2004. Note that the sort_by is a tuple specifying sales for the year of 2004. Had the [Date].[Calendar].[Calendar Year].&[2004]been omitted, the ranking would have instead been sales over all time.

```
SELECT
NON EMPTY {Descendants([Date].[Calendar].[Calendar Year].&[2004], 3)}
ON COLUMNS,
NON EMPTY {
  Order(
    [Employee].[Employee].Members,
    ([Date].[Calendar].[Calendar Year].&[2004],
     [Measures].[Reseller Sales Amount]),
    BDESC
  )
} ON ROWS
FROM [Adventure Works]
WHERE ([Measures].[Reseller Sales Amount])
```

The preceding query yields the following:

	January 2004	February 2004	...	June 2004
All Employees	$1,662,547.32	$2,700,766.80		$3,415,479.07
Linda C. Mitchell	$ 117,697.41	$ 497,155.98		$ 282,711.04
Jae B. Pak	$ 219,443.93	$ 205,602.75		$ 439,784.05
...	...			
Stephen Y. Jiang	$ 70,815.36	(null)		$ 37,652.92
Amy E. Alberts	$ 323.99	$ 42,041.96		(null)
Syed E. Abbas	$ 3,936.02	$ 1,376.99		$ 4,197.11

These generated sets all contain a single hierarchy, so how are multiple headers generated? The `Crossjoin` function will generate the cross-product of any number of sets, resulting in a single, large set with tuples made in every combination of the source sets. For example, the following query provides two levels of headers listing Product Line and Sales Territory Country. Alternately, the cross-join operator "*" can be placed between sets to generate the cross-product:

```
SELECT
NON EMPTY {Descendants([Date].[Calendar].[Calendar Year].&[2004], 3)}
ON COLUMNS,
NON EMPTY {
  Crossjoin([Product].[Product Line].[Product Line].Members,
    [Sales Territory].[Sales Territory Country].[Sales Territory
Country].Members)
} ON ROWS
FROM [Adventure Works]
WHERE ([Measures].[Reseller Sales Amount])
```

Using SQL Server Management Studio

The names of objects within a cube can be very long and difficult to type correctly. Fortunately, SQL Server Management Studio provides a convenient drag-and-drop interface for specifying both object names and MDX functions. Begin by opening a new Analysis Services MDX query, and choose the appropriate Analysis Services database in the toolbar, and the target cube in the upper left-hand corner of the query window. The Metadata tab (see Figure 72-2) is automatically populated with all the measures, dimensions, and so on, for that cube. MDX queries can then be built up by dragging objects onto the script pane or by switching to the Functions tab and similarly dragging function definitions.

CROSS-REF **For more details about working in SQL Server Management Studio, see Chapter 6, "Using Management Studio."**

The cube developer may choose to group dimension hierarchies into folders, also shown in Figure 72-2. Folders provide a handy way to organize long lists of hierarchies and have no effect on the structure of the cube or how MDX is written.

FIGURE 72-2

SQL Server Management Studio Metadata tab

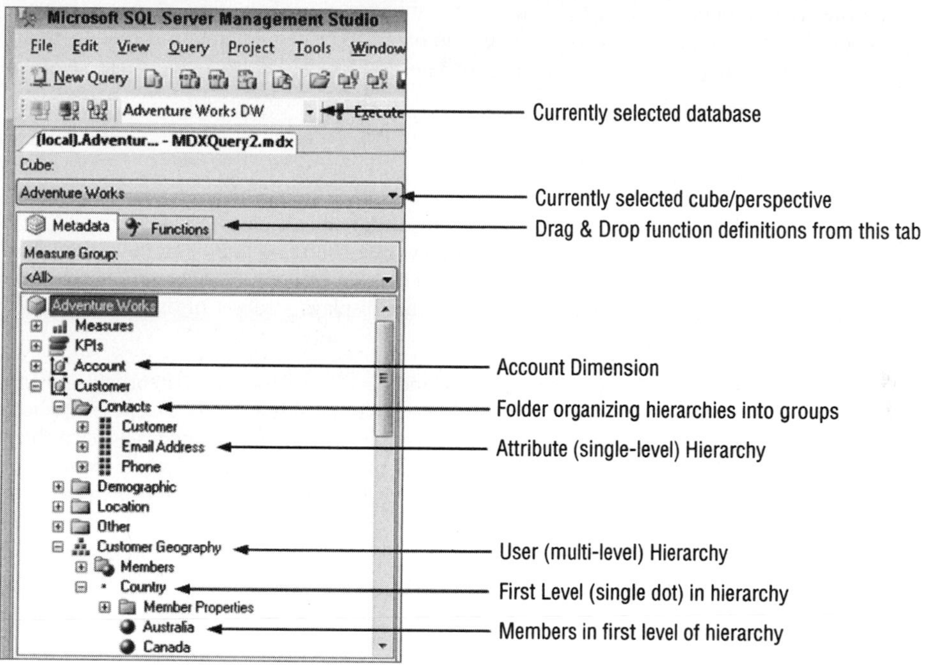

Advanced Select Query

Beyond the basic table generation described so far in this chapter, the syntax described here includes the most commonly used features:

```
[ WITH <calc | set> [ , <calc | set> ... ] ]
SELECT [ <set> on 0
    [ , <set> on 1 ... ] ]
FROM <cube> | <subcube>
[ WHERE ( <set> ) ]
```

The `SELECT` statement can return from 0 to 128 axes, with the first five having aliases of `ROWS`, `COLUMNS`, `PAGES`, `SECTIONS`, and `CHAPTERS`. Alternately, axis numbers can be specified as AXIS(0), AXIS(1), etc.

Best Practice

As the complexity of a query increases, the need for clarity and documentation increases as well. Break long queries onto several lines and use indentation to organize nested arguments. Add comments about the intent and meaning using "--" or "//" for end of line comments, or /*comment*/ for embedded or multi-line comments.

Subcubes

Subcubes are helpful for breaking complex logic into manageable segments. They can also be helpful for building applications when either a consistent view of a changing population (e.g., top five salespeople) or a fixed population with alternate views (e.g., only displaying sales figures to employees of that department) is desired. For example, an application that displays a subset of data based on which user is logged in could build all its queries based on a user-specific subcube.

Specify a subcube in the `FROM` clause by enclosing another `SELECT` within parentheses where a cube name would normally appear. This works much like a derived table in SQL, except that whereas a derived table includes only the columns explicitly identified, a subcube includes all hierarchies in the result, though some of the hierarchies will have limited membership. The following example creates a subcube of the top five products and top five months for U.S. Internet sales, and then summarizes order counts by day of the week and subcategory:

```
SELECT
    {[Date].[Day Name].Members} on Columns,
    {[Product].[Subcategory].[Subcategory].Members} ON ROWS
FROM (SELECT
            {TOPCOUNT([Product].[Model Name].[Model Name].Members, 10,
                  [Measures].[Internet Sales Amount])} ON COLUMNS,
            {TOPCOUNT([Date].[Calendar].[Month], 5,
                  [Measures].[Internet Sales Amount])} ON ROWS
        FROM [Adventure Works]
        WHERE ([Customer].[Country].&[United States]))
WHERE ([Measures].[Internet Order Count])
```

WITH clause

The `WITH` clause enables the creation of sets and calculated members. While some of the functionality provided can be performed directly within axis definitions, it is good practice to use sets and members to break logic apart into units that can be more easily constructed and understood. Don't confuse these constructs with similar syntax in T-SQL, as they behave quite differently.

Best Practice

Sets and calculations can also be defined as part of the cube (see the "MDX Scripting" section that follows). If any item is to be used in more than a handful of queries, create it as part of the cube, making it globally available and adjustable by changes in a single location.

Sets

Add a named set to the WITH clause using the syntax SET set_name AS definition, where set_name is any legal identifier, and definition specifies a set appropriate for use in an axis or WHERE clause. The following example builds three sets to explore the nine-month trends on products with ratios over 5% in 2004:

```
WITH
  SET [ProductList] AS
    Filter( [Product].[Product].[Product].Members,
      ([Date].[Calendar Year].&[2004],
         [Measures].[Internet Ratio to All Products])>0.05
      )
  SET [TimeFrame] AS
   LastPeriods(9,[Date].[Calendar].[Month].&[2004]&[6])
  SET [MeasureList] AS {
   [Measures].[Internet Order Count],
   [Measures].[Internet Sales Amount]
    }
SELECT
    {[MeasureList]*[ProductList]} ON COLUMNS,
    {[TimeFrame]} ON ROWS
FROM [Adventure Works]
```

The preceding query yields the following:

	Internet Order Count Mountain-200 Silver, 38	. . .	**Internet Order Count Mountain-200 Black, 46**	**Internet Sales Amount Mountain-200 Silver, 38**	. . .	**Internet Sales Amount Mountain-200 Black, 46**
October 2003	29	. . .	29	$ 67,279.71	. . .	$ 66,554.71
November 2003	28		31	$ 64,959.72		$ 71,144.69
December 2003	32		42	$ 74,239.68		$ 96,389.58
January 2004	28		36	$ 64,959.72		$ 82,619.64
February 2004	36		34	$ 83,519.64		$ 78,029.66
March 2004	35		33	$ 81,199.65		$ 75,734.67
April 2004	45		34	$104,399.55		$ 78,029.66
May 2004	48		50	$111,359.52		$114,749.50
June 2004	62		44	$143,839.38		$100,979.56

This example uses the Filter function to limit the set of products to those with ratios over 5%. The Filter function has the following general form:

```
Filter(set, condition).
```

Best Practice

Perhaps the most important query optimization available is limiting the size of sets as early as possible in the query, before cross joins or calculations are performed. Many optimizations a developer can expect when writing T-SQL queries are not available in MDX.

Calculated Members

Although the syntax of a calculated member is similar to that of a set, `MEMBER member_name as definition`, the member name must fit in to an existing hierarchy, as shown in the following example:

```
WITH
   MEMBER [Measures].[GPM After 5% Increase] AS
    ( [Measures].[Internet Sales Amount]*1.05 -
      [Measures].[Internet Total Product Cost] ) /
      [Measures].[Internet Sales Amount], FORMAT_STRING = 'Percent'
  MEMBER [Product].[Subcategory].[Total] AS
      [Product].[Subcategory].[All Products]
SELECT
  {[Measures].[Internet Gross Profit Margin],
   [Measures].[GPM After 5% Increase]} ON 0,
  NON EMPTY{[Product].[Subcategory].[Subcategory].Members,
   [Product].[Subcategory].[Total]} ON 1
FROM [Adventure Works]
WHERE ([Date].[Calendar].[Calendar Year].&[2004])
```

This query yields the following:

	Internet Gross Profit Margin	GPM after 5% Increase
Bike Racks	62.60%	67.60%
Bike Stands	62.60%	67.60%
Bottles and Cages	62.60%	67.60%
...	...	
Touring Bikes	37.84%	42.84%
Vests	62.60%	67.60%
Total	41.45%	46.45%

This query examines the current and what-if gross profit margin by product subcategory, including a subcategory "total" across all products. Note how the names are designed to match the other hierarchies used on their query axis. `FORMAT_STRING` is an optional modifier to set the display format for a calculated member. The source cube contains default formats for each measure, but new measures created by calculation will likely require formatting. [Product].[Subcategory].[Total], like most totals and subtotals, can rely on a parent member (in this case, the [All] level) to provide the appropriate value:

```
WITH
  SET [Top20ProductList] AS
    TOPCOUNT([Product].[Product].[Product].Members,
    20,
    ([Date].[Calendar].[Calendar Year].&[2004],
    [Measures].[Internet Order Count]))
  SET [NotTop20ProductList] AS
     Order(
    Filter(
     {[Product].[Product].[Product].Members - [Top20ProductList] },
      NOT IsEmpty([Measures].[Internet Order Count])),
     [Measures].[Internet Order Count],BDESC)
  MEMBER [Measures].[Average Top20ProductList Order Count] AS
    AVG([Top20ProductList],[Measures].[Internet Order Count])
  MEMBER [Measures].[Difference from Top20 Products] AS
    [Measures].[Internet Order Count] -
    [Measures].[Average Top20ProductList Order Count]
  MEMBER [Product].[Product].[Top 20 Products] AS
    AVG([Top20ProductList])
SELECT
    {[Measures].[Internet Order Count],
     [Measures].[Difference from Top20 Products] } ON COLUMNS,
    {[Product].[Product].[Top 20 Products],
     [NotTop20ProductList]} ON ROWS
  FROM [Adventure Works]
  WHERE ([Date].[Calendar].[Month].&[2004]&[6])
```

Result:

	Internet Order Count	Difference from Top 20 Products
Top 20 Products	176	0
Hydration Pack - 70 oz.	76	−100
Mountain-200 Silver, 38	62	−114
...	...	
Touring-3000 Yellow, 54	4	−172
Touring-3000 Yellow, 58	4	−172
Mountain-500 Black, 40	2	−174

This example compares the average June 2004 order count of the top 20 products to the other products ordered that month. A contrived example to be sure, but it demonstrates a number of concepts:

- Top20ProductList: Builds a set of the top 20 products based on orders for the entire year of 2004.

- `NotTop20ProductList`: Builds the list of everything not in the top 20. The "except" set operator (`-`) is used to remove the top 20 products from the list of all products. That list is filtered to exclude empty members and is in turn ordered by order count descending.
- `Average Top20ProductList Order Count`: Calculates the average order count across the set of top 20 products. Similar aggregate functions, including `SUM`, `MIN`, `MAX`, and `MEDIAN`, share this syntax: `AVG(set [, numeric_expression])`. In practice, this calculation would likely be implemented as part of the next calculation, but it's included here to show one calculation depending on another.
- `Difference from Top20 Products`: Difference between a given product's order count and the top 20 average.
- `Top 20 Products`: Created as part of the product hierarchy to get a row to display showing the top 20 average. Because this row will display for a couple of measures, the `numeric_expression` is omitted so that it is calculated in the context of the cell being displayed.

Dimension considerations

There are several things to understand about dimensions and the properties of the cube being queried, as they affect query execution, including the following:

- `MdxMissingMemberMode`: This dimension property, when set to `true`, causes invalid members specified as part of a query to be ignored without generating an error. For example, if an axis is defined as `{[Product].[Product].[Mountain-100 Silver, 38], [Product].[Product].[Banana]}`and Banana is not a valid product name, then no error will be generated. Instead, the result will list the mountain bike and not the fruit. When `MdxMissingMemberMode` is set to `false`, an error is generated for invalid member names. MDX scripts (calculations described within the cube definition) always throw an error for missing members, regardless of this property setting.
- `IgnoreUnrelatedDimensions`: When `true`, this measure group property tells MDX to ignore dimensions unrelated to a measure being queried. For example, the employee dimension of Adventure Works is not related to the Internet measures because no salesperson is involved with an Internet sale. Thus, the query

  ```
  SELECT {[Measures].[Internet Sales Amount]} ON COLUMNS,
         {[Employee].[Employee].[Employee].Members} ON ROWS
    FROM [Adventure Works]
  ```

  will list every employee with the total Internet sales amount, satisfying both the requirement to list all employees and the requirement to ignore the unrelated employee dimension when evaluating Internet sales. The alternative setting would result in null values being returned for every employee. An `IgnoreUnrelatedDimensions` setting of `true` is both the default and the more flexible option, but it requires some care by MDX query writers.
- If a default member has been specified for a hierarchy, then results will be limited to that default unless another value for that hierarchy is explicitly listed in the query. For example, if `[Date].[Calendar].[Calendar Year].&[2003]` is the default member for year, then referencing `[Date].[Calendar].[Month].&[2004]&[6]`in a query without referencing the calendar year hierarchy will result in no data being returned. To retrieve the June 2004 data,

either reference the [All] level of calendar year, or, if the cube developer has suppressed the [All] level, reference the 2004 member of the year hierarchy. Default members are generally avoided, but they can be useful in some situations, and a query writer should be aware of any hierarchy that has a default member.

- Autoexists vs. Non Empty: Placing the set `{[Date].[Calendar Year].[Calendar Year].Members * [Date].[Calendar].[Month].Members}` on a query axis will result in listing the year 2001 with the months from 2001, the year 2002 with the months from 2002, etc. Why doesn't the cross-join result in a true cross-product (e.g., 2001 appears with months from 2002) between the years and months? Analysis Services automatically detects which members of the hierarchies exist with each other, and returns only the valid combinations. This behavior is referred to as *autoexists,* and it only functions for hierarchies within a single dimension. `Non Empty` is used to further restrict sets to only those that have corresponding measure values.

MDX Scripting

Sets and calculations like those described in this chapter can be created directly within the cube. Using the Business Intelligence Development Studio, open the Cube Designer for the cube of interest and switch to the Calculations tab.

CROSS-REF **For more information on designing cubes specifically, see Chapter 71, "Building Multidimensional Cubes with Analysis Services."**

The cube contains a single declarative script that describes all the calculations and sets, although, by default, the designer presents this script as a series of forms (see Figure 72-3). Even if no calculated members or sets exist in the cube, a single `CALCULATE` statement should exist, instructing the cube to populate non-leaf cells within the cube.

New in 2008

SQL Server 2008 exposes the "Associated Measure Group" and "Display Folder" properties of calculated members directly in the calculation definition (refer to Figure 72-3). These items can still be set by choosing Calculation Properties from the Cube menu, but their new location simplifies design. Likewise, Display folders can also be specified for named sets in this manner. Specifying these groupings organizes the client's browsing experience. For example, placing calculated measures into measure groups displays calculated and physical measures in the same groupings.

Calculated members and named sets

Click on an existing calculated member (refer to Figure 72-3) or select New Calculated Member from the toolbar. A form appears with several options:

- **Name:** Name of the calculated member, without its parent hierarchy.

FIGURE 72-3

Calculations tab of the Business Intelligence Development Studio Cube Designer

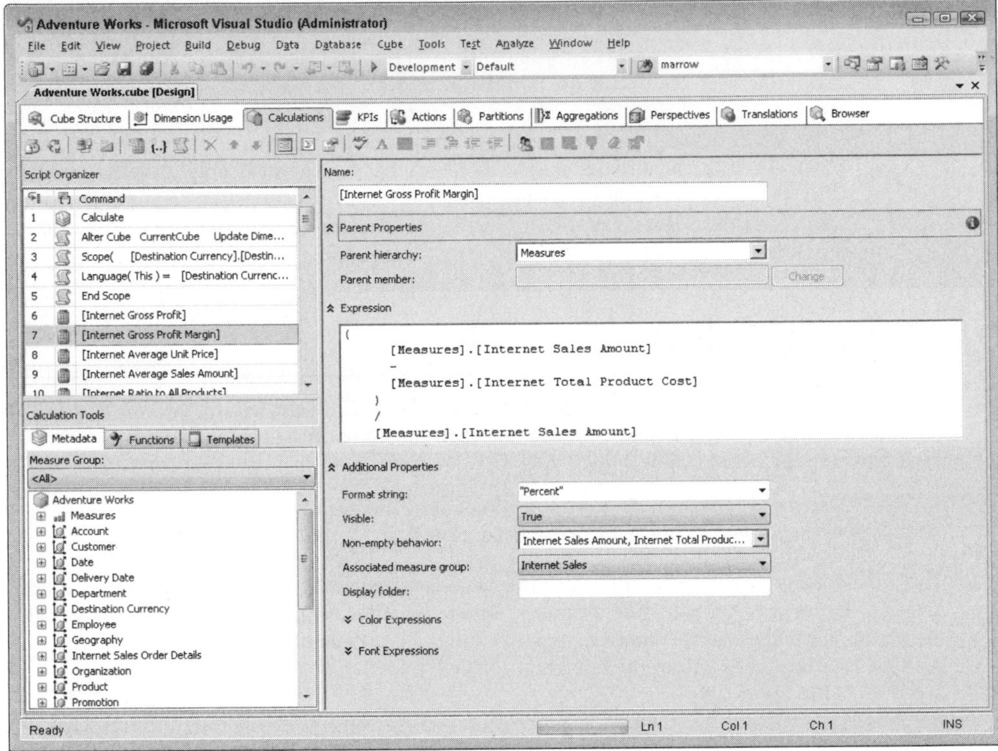

- **Parent Hierarchy:** Hierarchy to which this member should be added. For measures, this will be simply Measures; for other hierarchies, use the built-in navigation to locate the appropriate dimension.hierarchy combination.
- **Parent Member:** Only applies to multi-level hierarchies; specify the parent member of the calculated member. Essentially, this specifies the drill-down path in the multi-level hierarchy to reach the calculated member.
- **Expression:** The formula that calculates the appropriate member value; equivalent to the expression used for a `WITH MEMBER` definition.
- **Format String:** Optional format string; generally specified for measures.
- **Visible:** Calculations are sometimes made not visible when they form the basis for other calculations but are not themselves valuable to the end-user.
- **Non-Empty Behavior:** Select one or more measures to specify how to determine whether a specific cell will be empty. If not specified, the calculated member must be evaluated at every possible cell to determine whether it is empty. If specified, the listed physical measure(s) are used to determine whether a cell will be empty, dramatically speeding the calculation.

- **Color and Font Expressions:** Display attributes can be changed, as long as the client is using software that supports the appropriate display, based on any MDX expression. For example, values within budget could appear in green, and those outside of budget could be displayed in red.

Sets are defined in a similar fashion to calculated members, but only the set name and defining expression need to be specified.

New in 2008

Sets created in SQL Server 2008 can be specified as either *static* or *dynamic*. Static sets are evaluated only once when the CREATE SET statement is evaluated. Dynamic sets are evaluated each time they are used in a query. Therefore, in addition to the low-overhead static sets available in SQL Server 2005, dynamic sets handle definitions that change depending on context, such as the 10 top-selling products, which may change depending upon the month being queried.

Adding Business Intelligence

The Cube Designer's Business Intelligence Wizard can add calculations to a cube from standard templates. Templates include currency conversion, combining values based on a chart of accounts, and time-based calculations such as moving averages and period to date. Each template has individual requirements and purposes documented in Books Online, but time calculations are described here because they are most widely applicable.

Using time intelligence requires a properly configured time dimension, with attribute types assigned, based on a dimension table (not a server dimension). Time intelligence is generally added late in the cube development cycle so that all the manually built calculated members are available for creating time-based calculations. Start the wizard by opening the cube of interest in the Cube Designer and selecting Add Business Intelligence from the toolbar. The wizard presents a series of pages:

- **Choose Enhancement:** Select Define time intelligence.
- **Choose Target Hierarchy and Calculations:** Calculations defined by the wizard will apply to a single time hierarchy. If the cube has multiple roles (e.g., Order vs. Ship date) or calendar types (e.g., Calendar vs. Fiscal), multiple runs of the wizard will be required to create calculations for different target hierarchies. Generally, a multi-level hierarchy is chosen as the target hierarchy.

  Choose the target hierarchy at the top of the page, and then choose the calculations to be created for this hierarchy (e.g., Twelve Month Moving Average).
- **Define Scope of Calculations:** Choose the measures that will be averaged, summarized, and so on, by the time calculations.
- **Completing the Wizard:** Review the changes the wizard will make to the cube.

The wizard adds the following: a named calculation to the data source view in the time table, a new hierarchy in the time dimension to contain the calculated members, and the MDX script that defines the calculated members. Calculation results are accessed by queries that combine the target hierarchy and the hierarchy containing the calculated members. Results will be one of the following: a value when one can be calculated, null when not enough data is available, or "NA" if the calculation does not apply to the cell (e.g., a 12-month average calculation in a cell corresponding to one year).

Summary

MDX provides a way to define and query constructs within Analysis Services databases much the way SQL provides those capabilities for relational databases. Unlike SQL, MDX accommodates the multi-dimensional data by specifying sets along multiple axes that identify the geometry of the resulting cell set. Functions are available to generate, order, and filter sets. The `WITH` keyword can be used to create building blocks for larger and more complex queries.

MDX can also be used as the basis for calculations and sets defined within a cube definition. These MDX scripts are an excellent place to include commonly used calculations and groupings that are then available to any query.

These features combine to create an extraordinarily rich and efficient data query and analysis environment.

Chapter 73

Authoring Reports with Reporting Services

Reporting Services delivers a powerful toolset for report authoring. The Report Designer in Visual Studio provides robust capabilities for developers, while nontechnical users can build and update reports using the Report Builder. This chapter demonstrates how to build reports using Visual Studio.

Building good reports requires an odd and often conflicting set of skills. Reports bridge the gap between nontechnical decision-makers and the database you've worked so hard to make understandable, robust, complete, consistent, and stable. Given this, it is worth stating the result that report developers strive to achieve:

- Speed and availability
- Accuracy and timeliness
- The right amount of detail — not too much, not too little
- Consistent, organized, and easily interpreted formatting and presentation

This chapter explores the anatomy of a report, demonstrates the steps required to create a report, and covers several additional features of Reporting Services to satisfy nearly any reporting need.

IN THIS CHAPTER

Anatomy of a Report

A Reporting Services report consists of data sources, datasets, parameters, and the report layout or design all wrapped up in an XML file that describes the report. This section explains each of these report components.

Report Definition Language (RDL)

The Report Definition Language (RDL) is an open XML schema used to represent data retrieval and layout information for a report. This includes elements to define datasets, parameters, charts, tables, and so on — everything needed to retrieve the report data and format it for display.

This report definition in Reporting Services is nothing more than an XML file that conforms to the RDL specification. Microsoft provides two tools for creating RDL report definitions so that you don't have to handwrite the XML: Visual Studio and Report Builder. This chapter focuses on building reports using Visual Studio. The Report Builder tool is part of the Report Manager deployment and provides end-users (nontechnical) with the ability to author and update reports.

CROSS-REF **See Chapter 74, "Administering Reporting Services," for more information on how to configure and deploy reports.**

One powerful facet of Reporting Services is the capability to extend the RDL schema. Because the RDL schema is an open schema, it is possible to accommodate advanced or custom scenarios by adding elements and attributes to it. This can be accomplished by hand or programmatically using the classes in the `System.XML` namespace.

It is also possible to programmatically build, deploy, and execute reports, which means the possibilities are endless when it comes to creating custom report authoring tools, authoring reports on-the-fly, and integrating reports into applications. For example, a developer could use the `XmlTextWriter` .NET class to programmatically create an RDL report definition, and then use the Report Server Web Service to deploy and render the report from within an application. The Report Server Web Service also contains methods to manage nearly all aspects of the report server.

Data Sources

A data source contains the connection information for a database or data file and includes the data source type, connection string, and credentials. A data source is required to retrieve data for a report. It can be defined and stored within a single report, or it can be shared by multiple reports within the project. Like a report, shared data sources can be deployed to the report server. Both shared data sources and report-specific data sources can be modified using the Report Manager once they are deployed to the report server.

Data Source types

While it is possible to extend Reporting Services by creating a custom data extension, several data source types are available out of the box:

- Microsoft SQL Server
- Microsoft SQL Server Analysis Services
- OLE DB (Object Linking and Embedding for Databases)
- XML (Extensible Markup Language)
- ODBC (Open Database Connectivity)
- Report Server Model
- Oracle
- SAP NetWeaver BI

- Hyperion Essbase
- DB2
- Teradata

Data source connection strings

Adding a new data source as either a shared or a report-specific source will invoke the Data Source Properties dialog. Give the source a meaningful name, choose the data source type, and enter the connection string. For most connection types, pressing the Edit button will assist in building the connection string.

The XML data source type does not provide an editor. To connect to an XML data source, select the XML data type and provide a URL as the connection string. The following example shows a connection string to connect to the Report Server Web Service on the local machine.

```
http://localhost/reportserver/reportservice2006.asmx
```

The following connection string shows how to connect to an XML file named `StateList.xml` located on the local web server:

```
http://localhost/StateList.xml
```

Using expressions in a connection string

Connection strings can contain expressions, allowing the connection string to be determined at runtime. For example, the following connection string will connect to the server and database specified by the parameter:

```
="data source=" & Parameters!ServerName.Value & ";initial catalog=" &
Parameters!Database.Value
```

Adding parameters to the report for the server and database enables the user to specify the data source of the report. Because reports often execute under the credentials of someone other than the end-user, care must be taken to avoid inappropriate data access.

Setting data source credentials

The data source credentials can be set to use Windows Authentication database authentication (such as SQL Server Authentication) or none. The credentials can be stored in the Report Server database, or users can be prompted for the credentials upon report execution. The best configuration option depends on your network and security environment.

CROSS-REF **For more information about configuring report and data access, see the "Managing Roles" and "Managing Security" sections in Chapter 74, "Administering Reporting Services."**

Reporting Services datasets

Once a data source is defined, it can be used as the basis for queries that result in Reporting Services datasets. Datasets provide the data that can appear on a report. Because a single report can use several data sources and datasets, a report can integrate data from multiple databases, XML sources, or ODBC sources, and so on.

New in 2008

The report design environment has been dramatically changed and enhanced in SQL Server 2008 compared to the 2005 version. The Report Data pane provides easy access to Data Sources, Datasets, Fields, and Parameters. The Grouping pane likewise shows all the row and column groups defined in the reports. Enhanced object display and positioning, right-click menus, and pop-up properties dialogs streamline the design experience.

Defining a new report using the wizard prompts for a query to define the new report's initial dataset, which is handy for simple reports. Otherwise data sources and their corresponding datasets can be added in the Report Data pane in the design environment. Defining or changing a dataset will launch the Dataset Properties dialog, which includes several tabs:

- **Query:** Can consist of most any string that is appropriate to the data source, including SQL statements, stored procedure calls, or XML queries
- **Parameters:** Displays the parameters used in the query and the mapping to the report's parameters
- **Fields:** Lists all fields returned by the query and the corresponding names used in the dataset. When the names of the fields can't be determined at design time, these names must be manually entered. Calculated fields may also be added here, which helps centralize expressions that are referred to frequently in the report (e.g., defining profit as [revenue]-[expenses] enables profit to be referred to throughout the report as if it came from the source data).
- **Options:** Provides source-specific options such as collation
- **Filters:** Allows the definition of filters on the data returned from the source. Filters are run in-memory after the entire dataset has been returned, and are often used in conjunction with report parameters to enable users to display a subset of the data without querying the source a second time.

The resulting dataset is available for use in report layout. The challenge of properly defining a dataset frequently involves properly setting up the associated parameters.

Query parameters and report parameters

Parameters can be used to empower the user to specify the report criteria and control report formatting. Query parameters are included in the dataset definition and are used to select or filter data. For example, the parameter `@CategoryID` can be used to return the subcategories for a selected category, as demonstrated in the following example:

```
Select * From Subcategory Where CategoryID = @CategoryID
```

Query parameters can also be used to specify the values passed to a stored procedure. The following example calls a stored procedure named `uspSubcategories` that contains a parameter for the `CategoryID`:

```
EXEC uspSubcategories @CategoryID
```

Report parameters can also be used to control report formatting and behavior. For example, adding a Boolean parameter can control the visibility of report items used to display additional details in the report (see "Working with Expressions" later in this chapter).

Many options are available to control the way parameters are presented in the report header. For example, setting the parameter data type to `Boolean` will render the parameter as radio buttons, enabling the user to select True or False. Setting the data type to `Integer` and adding a list of available values will render the parameter as a drop-down list. Selecting a parameter's Multi-Value option and entering available values will render as a multi-value drop-down list (see Figure 73-1).

FIGURE 73-1

Multi-value drop-down list for colors to be included in a report

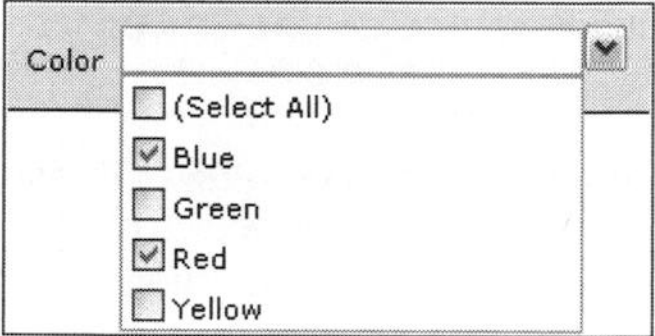

Three options are available for specifying parameter values and parameter defaults: `None`, `Specify values`, and `Get values from a query`. Selecting None adds a textbox to the report, enabling the user to enter any value. Providing values using the `Specify values` and `Get values from a query` options adds a drop-down list to the report, enabling the user to select from the available values. The `Specify values` option enables the report author to manually enter the parameter values as part of the parameter definition, while the `Get values from a query` option retrieves the parameter values from a dataset.

Report content and layout

Report content and layout is defined using the Design tab in the Report Designer. Reports contain header, body, and footer sections (header and footer are not displayed by default in 2008). Many report items are available to accommodate virtually any report formatting requirement.

New in 2008

The Table and Matrix items have been combined into a single, more flexible Tablix item in the report definition. Anytime a Table, Matrix, or List item is placed on the report surface, it is rendered in the .RDL code as a Tablix element. This enables the report author to use any feature from the three items regardless of which control is used in the report design. By default, the Table and Matrix cells each contain a textbox, making it easy to display data in each cell, while the List item contains a rectangle by default, making it easy to nest other items within the List.

Table 73-1 contains the report items included with Visual Studio 2008.

TABLE 73-1

Visual Studio 2008 Report Items

Report Item	Description
Textbox	Adds report content that is not located within a table or matrix. The textbox can contain static text or an expression or can be bound to a data field.
Line, Rectangle	Adds visual separation and formatting to a report. Rectangles can also be used to group other items, enabling them to be treated as a group for placement and/or visibility. They also enable multiple controls to be placed where, by default, you can only place a textbox.
Image	Places an image in the report. The image source can be Embedded, Project, Database, or the Web.
Table	Renders the dataset in a Tablix with a fixed set of columns. The item contains many options to control how the data is grouped, sorted, exported, and presented. A report can contain multiple tables, providing the capability to include data from multiple datasets and data sources in a single report. Begin with a Table instead of a Matrix if the data will be presented primarily as fixed columns.
Matrix	Renders a dataset as a crosstab. For example, the Matrix report item could show total sales by region as row headers, and periods as column headers, enabling the column headers to change over time based on the underlying dataset. Multiple column, row, and detail criteria can be added to the Matrix report item. Begin with a Matrix instead of a Table when the data will be presented primarily with variable column headers.
List	The list is bound to a dataset. The content of a list is repeated for each row in the dataset or for each grouped row if group criteria are specified. The body of the list represents the template for the report items to be displayed. The report author places items within the template, free-form, without the spatial constraints of a table.
Chart	This item includes a wide variety of charts and provides extensive control over the chart type and formatting.
Gauge	Similar to charts, gauges come in a wide variety of shapes and sizes. But unlike charts, which show many data points, gauges display a single data point. For example, a gauge might be used to display actual sales vs. a planned sales goal.
Subreport	Use this item to render another report within the current report, usually displaying some details not available from the dataset driving the current report.

The Report Authoring Process

The report authoring process includes creating a new Reporting Services project using SQL Server Business Intelligence Development Studio, defining a data source for the report, adding a report to the project, creating a dataset to retrieve the report data, and formatting the report content. This section describes the primary tasks required to create a report and provides an example to illustrate the process.

Creating a Reporting Services project

Business Intelligence Development Studio, a version of Visual Studio 2008 shipped with SQL Server, contains the tools required to author and deploy Reporting Services reports. Alternately, developers with a license for Visual Studio can open a reporting project within that environment. Follow these steps to create a new Reporting Services project:

1. Run the Business Intelligence Development Studio (BIDS).
2. Select File ➪ New ➪ Project to open the New Project dialog. Alternately, you can click the Create Project link in the Recent Projects section of the Start Page tab to open the New Project dialog. By default, the Start Page tab is displayed when opening BIDS.
3. Select the Business Intelligence Projects project type in the Project Types pane on the left side.
4. Select the Report Server Project template in the Templates pane on the right side.
5. Name the project.
6. Specify the location of the project. To create a folder to contain the Solution file with a subfolder containing the report project, check the option to Create Directory for Solution. The value provided for the Solution Name field specifies the name of the solution folder, while the value provided for the Name field specifies the name of the report project. To create the solution and project under a single folder, uncheck the option Create Directory for Solution.
7. Select OK to create the new Reporting Services project.

An alternative to the Report Server Project is the Report Server Project Wizard, which invokes the Report Wizard to guide the creation of an initial report in addition to creating a project.

Creating a report

Two methods are available to create a report: using the report wizard and adding a blank report. The following steps describe the tasks required to create a report, regardless of the method:

1. Add a report to the report project by selecting Project ➪ Add New Item. Select the Report Wizard template to have the wizard help you create a report, or select the Report template to create a blank report.
2. Create a (or select an existing) data source.
3. Create one or more report datasets.
4. Design the report layout.
5. Add and configure Report Parameters.
6. Use the Preview tab on the Report Designer to preview the report.

Using the Report Wizard to create reports

The Report Wizard is a good way to build a simple report quickly. The Report Wizard will walk you through selecting (or creating) the data source, designing the report query, choosing the report type, adding data fields to the report, choosing the report style, and naming the report. This takes as little as 60 seconds, and when completed you have a report that's ready to run.

If you could satisfy all of your report requirements using the wizard, that would be wonderful. However, this is typically just a starting point. After creating a report using the wizard, the Report Designer can be used to customize the report.

Authoring a report from scratch

Starting with a blank report requires manual completion of all six steps outlined above, but it allows for more flexibility. The following example demonstrates how to build a simple product list report using the `AdventureWorks2008` sample database.

Creating a shared data source

Figure 73-2 shows the Shared Data Source Properties dialog configured for the `AdventureWorks2008` database.

FIGURE 73-2

Creating a shared data source

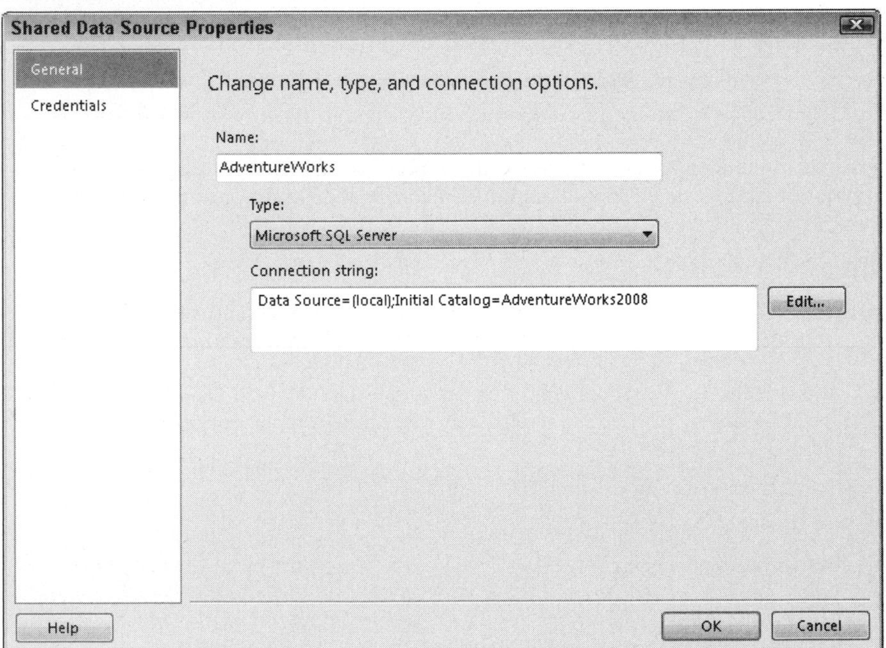

Best Practice

While it is possible to create report data sources without referring to a shared data source, it is generally best to avoid this practice. When reports are deployed to different environments, or systems undergo a configuration change, it is much easier to adjust a handful of shared data sources than every deployed report. A report-specific data source can be converted to a shared data source by right-clicking it in the Report Data pane and choosing "Convert to Shared Data Source."

Follow these steps to create a new shared data source:

1. With the Solution Explorer displaying the reporting project, right-click on the Shared Data Sources folder and choose Add New Data Source. The Shared Data Source Properties dialog will appear.
2. Name the Data Source "AdventureWorks".
3. Select Microsoft SQL Server from the Type drop-down list.
4. Enter the connection string to the `AdventureWorks2008` database. You can click the Edit button to build the connection string.
5. Switch to the Credentials tab and choose an appropriate login method for the data source.
6. Click OK to add the new data source to the project.

Adding a blank report

Follow these steps to create a blank report:

1. With the Solution Explorer displaying a reporting project, right-click on the Reports folder and choose Add ⇨ New Item.
2. From the Add New Item dialog, select the Report template.
3. Name the report "Project List".
4. Click Add.

The new empty report is added to your project and opened in the Report Designer. The Report Designer window contains two tabs: Design and Preview. Supporting panes (usually located to the left of the design surface) are the Toolbox that contains items to be placed on the design surface and the Report Data pane, which shows the sources of data available to build up the report, as well as parameters and images.

Creating a dataset

Follow these steps to create a dataset to return product information:

1. Define a data source that refers to the shared data source created earlier. In the Report Data pane, choose New ⇨ Data Source. In the Data Source Properties dialog, name the Data Source "AdventureWorks", select the "Use shared Data Source reference" option, and choose the AdventureWorks shared data source from the drop-down.

2. Right-click on the AdventureWorks data source in the Report Data pane and choose Add Dataset. The Dataset Properties dialog will appear (see Figure 73-3).

FIGURE 73-3

Use the Data Properties dialog to define the query that will populate the dataset.

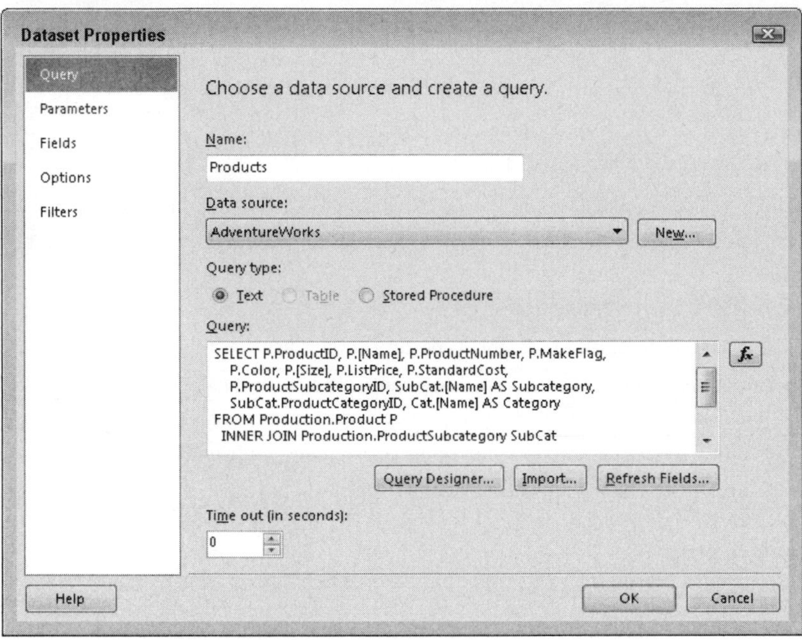

3. Name the dataset "Products".
4. Select the AdventureWorks data source.
5. Enter the following SQL (this SQL statement returns the product information, including the Category and Subcategory names and IDs from the `AdventureWorks2008` database):

```
SELECT P.ProductID, P.[Name], P.ProductNumber, P.MakeFlag,
    P.Color, P.[Size], P.ListPrice, P.StandardCost,
    P.ProductSubcategoryID, SubCat.[Name] AS Subcategory,
    SubCat.ProductCategoryID, Cat.[Name] AS Category
FROM Production.Product P
  INNER JOIN Production.ProductSubcategory SubCat
    ON P.ProductSubcategoryID = SubCat.ProductSubcategoryID
  INNER JOIN Production.ProductCategory Cat
    ON SubCat.ProductCategoryID = Cat.ProductCategoryID
```

6. Press the Refresh Fields button to verify the SQL, or press the Query Designer button to preview the data. Once the Dataset Properties dialog has been dismissed using the OK button, the new dataset and associated fields will appear under the data source in the Report Data pane.

Displaying data in the report

The results can be displayed in the report using either the list, table, or matrix report items. Working with these items is covered in more depth later in this chapter. To display the results of the dataset, follow these steps to add a table to the body of the report, bind it to the dataset, and add data fields to the table:

1. Select the Design tab on the Report Designer.
2. Add a table to the body of the report by dragging a table report item from the Toolbox and dropping it on the report body.
3. Add fields from the dataset by dragging fields from the Report Data pane and dropping them in the details row of the table.

Previewing the report

Select the Preview tab to review the report. The report currently consists of a single table that displays data from the Products dataset, which in turn queries data from the AdventureWorks data source. Details on how to refine both the data and display of the report follow in the next sections.

Working with Data

Once the basics of building up a report are understood, the next step is to dive into the details of structuring data to meet reporting needs. The Query Designer provides assistance in constructing queries for different data sources, while parameters provide a way to limit and filter result sets returned by those queries. Expressions provide a way to combine results and parameters to synthesize data and behaviors.

Best Practice

Offloading as much work to the source database as possible will increase the speed of report execution. Use query parameters to return only the data actually required for display. When a report represents a summary of source data, let the source database aggregate to the granularity of the report. Reporting Services can filter and summarize data as well, but it will never match a database engine's speed.

Working with SQL in the Query Designer

The Query Designer can be invoked from the Dataset Properties dialog by clicking the Query Designer button, or by right-clicking on a dataset in the Report Data pane and choosing Query. The default view, Edit as Text, displays the query as text in the upper pane, and the query results in the lower pane. Click the exclamation point in the toolbar to execute the query.

Many programmers find that developing queries in their favorite SQL tool and pasting the query text into the Query Designer or Dataset Properties dialogs provides the most efficient workflow, but the Query Designer also offers a graphical mode. Click the Edit as Text button to toggle to the graphical designer, which contains the Diagram, Grid, SQL, and Results panes. Figure 73-4 shows the graphical designer view containing the Products query used earlier in this chapter.

FIGURE 73-4

The Advanced Query Designer simplifies writing SQL command text.

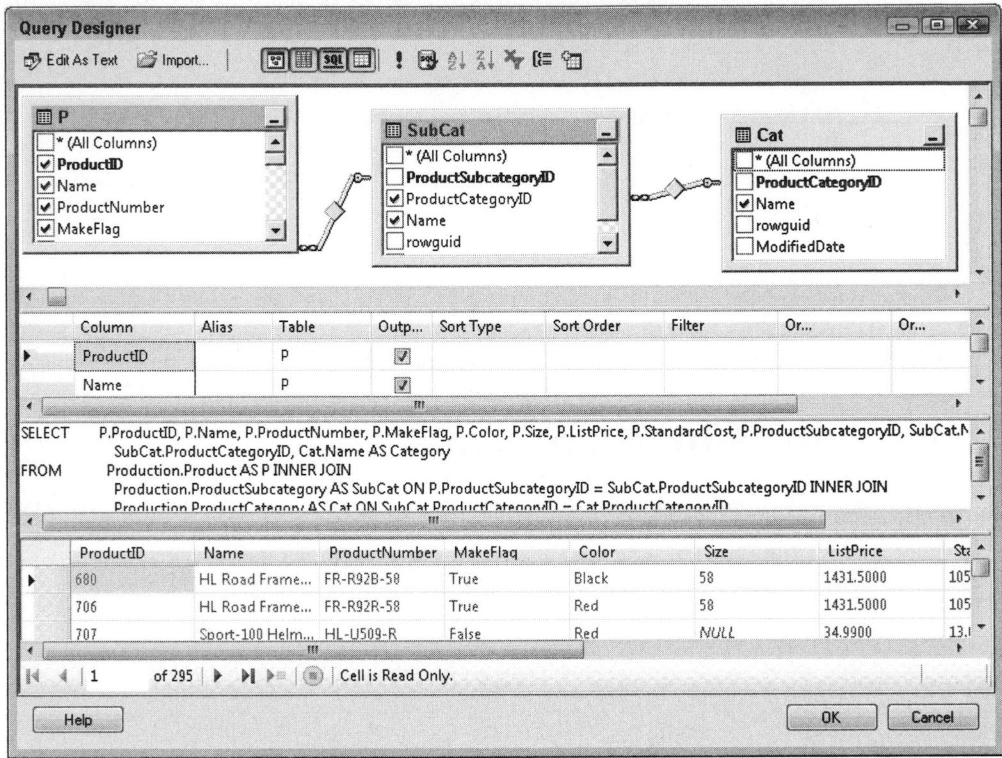

Using query parameters to select and filter data

Query parameters appear in a query much like a T-SQL variable would for SQL Server data sources. For example, the following query limits the rows returned to only those with a specific subcategory:

```
SELECT * FROM Production.Product
WHERE ProductSubcategoryID = @ProductSubcategoryID
```

This example refers to a query parameter named `@ProductSubcategoryID`, which in turn is mapped to either a report parameter or an expression. The mapping is specified on the Parameters tab of the Dataset Properties dialog. However, if a query parameter is to be mapped to a report parameter of the same name, simply refer to the query parameter, as shown, and the corresponding report parameter will be created and mapped when the dataset is saved.

Query parameters are specific to a particular dataset and are visible only in the Dataset Properties dialog. Report parameters are global to the report, can be set to prompt the user when the report runs, and appear in the Report Data pane under the Parameters folder.

Nested report parameters

This section offers an interesting example of how to prompt the user for report parameters and how those parameters can interact. The goal is to generate a report that lists products within a given product category and subcategory. For usability, the report user will be prompted for both the category and the subcategory. Of course, the subcategories change with each selection of a category — these are referred to as *nested parameters*.

To create this nested parameter example, you'll add two datasets to the Product List report created earlier. Both new datasets use the AdventureWorks data source. The first dataset, named `CategoryList`, returns the list of categories using the following SQL:

```
SELECT ProductCategoryID, Name
FROM Production.ProductCategory
ORDER BY Name
```

The second dataset, named `SubcategoryList`, returns the list of subcategories and includes a parameter to select only the subcategories for the selected category:

```
SELECT ProductSubcategoryID, ProductCategoryID, Name
FROM Production.ProductSubcategory
WHERE (ProductCategoryID = @ProductCategoryID)
ORDER BY Name
```

Update the `Products` dataset with the following SQL to include the new parameters:

```
SELECT P.ProductID, P.[Name], P.ProductNumber, P.MakeFlag,
   P.Color, P.[Size], P.ListPrice, P.StandardCost,
   P.ProductSubcategoryID, SubCat.[Name] AS Subcategory,
   SubCat.ProductCategoryID, Cat.[Name] AS Category
FROM Production.Product P
   INNER JOIN Production.ProductSubcategory SubCat
    ON P.ProductSubcategoryID = SubCat.ProductSubcategoryID
   INNER JOIN Production.ProductCategory Cat
    ON SubCat.ProductCategoryID = Cat.ProductCategoryID
WHERE P.ProductSubcategoryID = @ProductSubcategoryID
    AND SubCat.ProductCategoryID = @ProductCategoryID
```

When a dataset that refers to a new query parameter is saved, such as in these examples, a new report parameter with the same name is automatically created. A mapping between the corresponding query parameter and report parameter is also established on the Dataset Parameters tab.

Configure a report parameter by right-clicking on the parameter in the Report Data pane and choosing Parameter Properties. Figure 73-5 shows the Report Parameter Properties dialog with the `ProductSubcategoryID` parameter selected.

Follow these steps to configure the parameters:

1. Select the `ProductCategoryID` parameter.
2. Change the prompt to something user-friendly, such as "Category".

3. Change the data type to `Integer`. Select the Allow null value option.
4. Switch to the Available Values tab, and select "Get values from a query," which will populate the available categories from the dataset you defined earlier.
5. Select the `CategoryList` dataset.
6. From the Value Field drop-down list, select `ProductCategoryID`.
7. From the Label Field drop-down list, select `Name`.
8. Repeat this process for the `ProductSubcategoryID` report parameter, using the Prompt "SubCategory", `SubcategoryList` as the dataset, `ProductSubcategoryID` as the value field, and `Name` as the label field.
9. Make sure that the `ProductCategoryID` parameter is listed before `ProductSubcategoryID` in the Report Data pane. Because the subcategory depends on the category, it must be defined first. If the order is not correct, then highlight one of the entries and use the up and down arrows in the Report Data pane's toolbar to adjust the order.

FIGURE 73-5

The Report Parameter Properties dialog controls report parameters.

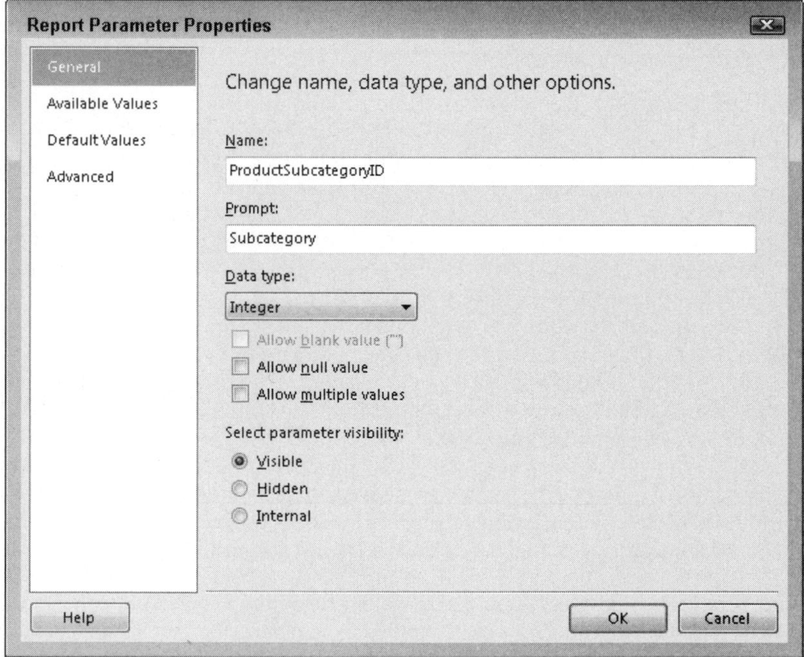

Preview the report. Note that the `SubCategory` parameter is disabled until you select a value from the `Category` parameter. Once you select a category, the `SubCategory` parameter is enabled and contains the list of subcategories for the selected category. Click the View Report button to return only the products within the selected subcategory.

Multi-value report parameters

The previous example demonstrated how to build a report with nested parameters. Let's enhance the report now to enable the user to select multiple values from each parameter and include all products matching the criteria.

Changing the parameters to multi-value parameters requires some minor modifications to the SQL for the `SubcategoryList` and `Products` datasets. Specifically, the `WHERE` clause must change to use the `IN` statement instead of `"="`. Update the SQL for the `SubcategoryList` dataset as follows:

```
SELECT ProductSubcategoryID, ProductCategoryID, Name
FROM Production.ProductSubcategory
WHERE ProductCategoryID IN (@ProductCategoryID)
ORDER BY Name
```

Update the `Products` dataset:

```
SELECT P.ProductID, P.[Name], P.ProductNumber, P.MakeFlag,
  P.Color, P.[Size], P.ListPrice, P.StandardCost,
  P.ProductSubcategoryID, SubCat.[Name] AS Subcategory,
  SubCat.ProductCategoryID, Cat.[Name] AS Category
FROM Production.Product P
  INNER JOIN Production.ProductSubcategory SubCat
         ON P.ProductSubcategoryID = SubCat.ProductSubcategoryID
  INNER JOIN Production.ProductCategory Cat
         ON SubCat.ProductCategoryID = Cat.ProductCategoryID
WHERE P.ProductSubcategoryID IN (@ProductSubcategoryID)
  AND SubCat.ProductCategoryID  IN (@ProductCategoryID)
```

At execution time, Reporting Services will replace the multi-value parameter with a list of values selected by the user. For example, `IN (@ProductSubcategoryID)` might become `IN (1,3,7)` when the SQL is executed.

Follow these steps to configure the parameters as multi-value parameters:

1. Right-click on the `ProductCategoryID` parameter in the Report Data pane, select the "Allow multiple values" check box, and click OK to save the changes.
2. Right-click on the `ProductSubcategoryID` parameter in the Report Data pane, select the "Allow multiple values" check box, and click OK to save the changes.

Now run the report and select Accessories and Clothing from the `Category` parameter. The `Subcategory` parameter now contains all subcategories for Accessories and Clothing, as shown in Figure 73-6. Select several subcategories and run the report. It should now contain all products for the selected subcategories. The report is no longer limited to the selection of a single parameter value.

Some caution should be used when designing reports that use multi-value parameters, because every value selected is passed in as part of the SQL Query. In this example, selecting all values will only grow the size of the query by about 100 characters (a short list of integer IDs is passed in); but other reports could have many more values and/or longer text strings, which could lead to extremely large queries and poor performance.

FIGURE 73-6

Example of multi-value nested parameters

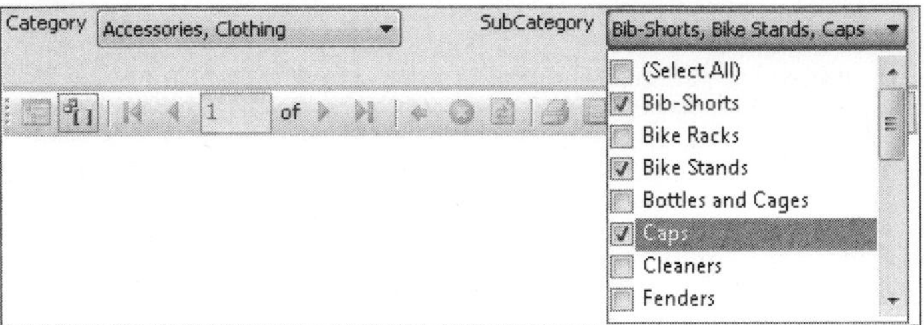

Adding calculated fields to a dataset

Once the dataset is defined, it is possible to add fields to it and specify an expression for the field value. For example, you could add a field to the `Products` dataset named "Margin", and set the expression to calculate it as `ListPrice - StandardCost`. To add a field, follow these steps:

1. Right-click on the `Products` dataset and choose Add Calculated Field. The Dataset Properties dialog displays, showing a blank row on the Fields tag.
2. Enter "Margin" for the new Field Name.
3. Enter the following expression as the Field Source. Alternately, click the fx button to launch the expression editor and build the expression using the fields listed there.

```
=Fields!ListPrice.Value - Fields!StandardCost.Value
```

4. Select OK and the new field is added to the dataset.

Best Practice

While it is possible to achieve the same result by including the calculation in the SQL statement, this approach is very convenient when calling a stored procedure that you don't want to include the calculation in, or that you don't have permission to update. However, the report expression language requires careful coding to handle any `NULL` values or data type conversions.

It is also possible to include expressions in the report layout, but this may require writing and maintaining the expression multiple times within the report. Adding the calculated field to the dataset ensures that the expression is defined in one place and simplifies report construction and maintenance.

Working with XML data sources

XML can be a very useful data source for reports. Individual files can provide easy-to-deploy datasets that are not otherwise available. Web Service access allows reports to be enhanced by services available inside and outside the organization. The example in this section demonstrates both types of data sources, using an XML file to populate a report parameter and a Web Service to provide the dataset for reporting. The ultimate goal is to choose a company from the parameter and view its stock quote in the report.

The following XML file contains the stock symbols and their associated companies:

```
<?xml version="1.0" encoding="utf-8" ?>
<StockSymbols>
  <Symbol Value="AAPL" Name="Apple Computer, Inc. (AAPL)" />
  <Symbol Value="CSCO" Name="Cisco Systems (CSCO)" />
  <Symbol Value="MSFT" Name="Microsoft Corporation (MSFT)" />
  <Symbol Value="ORCL" Name="Oracle Corporation (ORCL)" />
  <Symbol Value="JAVA" Name="Sun Microsystems, Inc (JAVA)" />
</StockSymbols>
```

Follow these steps to create a new dataset for the `StockSymbols.xml` file:

1. Create a file named `StockSymbols.xml` containing the stock symbols XML code above.
2. Place the file on a handy web server.
3. Create a new data source with the name "Stocks", the type XML, and a connection string that points to the newly created file — for example, `http://localhost/StockSymbols.xml` for a file saved on the root of the local web server.
4. Add a dataset under the Stocks data source, name it "StockSymbols", and use the following query:

```
<Query>
  <ElementPath IgnoreNamespaces="true">
    StockSymbols/Symbol{@Value, @Name}
  </ElementPath>
</Query>
```

5. Use the Query Designer to execute the query to ensure successful connection and configuration.

Now create a report parameter named `Symbols` and use the `StockSymbols` dataset to populate the values. Follow these steps:

1. Right-click the Parameters folder in the Report Data pane and choose Add Parameter.
2. Name the parameter `Symbols`, set the prompt to something user-friendly such as "Stock Symbol", and set the data type to `Text`.
3. Under the Available Values tag, select "Get values from query." Set the dataset to `Stock Symbols`, the Value to `Value`, and the Label to `Name`.
4. Click OK to save the new parameter.

When the report is executed, the user will be prompted to select a stock symbol from the parameter to obtain a quote. Now create a dataset to retrieve stock quote information from a Web Service. CDYNE Corporation provides a Web Service to return delayed stock quotes. The `GetQuote` method of the Web Service retrieves a current stock quote and requires two parameters: `StockSymbol` and `LicenseKey`.

You will associate the StockSymbol query parameter to the Symbols Report parameter just created and hard-code the LicenseKey query parameter with a value of 0; the key is provided for testing purposes. Follow these steps to create the Stock Quote dataset:

1. Create a new data source named StockQuote as an XML data source and use the following URL for the connection string:

   ```
   http://ws.cdyne.com/delayedstockquote/delayedstockquote.asmx
   ```

2. Create a dataset named Quote under the new data source, using the following code:

   ```
   <Query>
   <Method Namespace="http://ws.cdyne.com/" Name="GetQuote">
      <Parameters>
          <Parameter Name="StockSymbol">
              <DefaultValue>MSFT</DefaultValue>
          </Parameter>
          <Parameter Name="LicenseKey">
              <DefaultValue>0</DefaultValue>
          </Parameter>
      </Parameters>
   </Method>
   <SoapAction>http://ws.cdyne.com/GetQuote</SoapAction>
   <ElementPath IgnoreNamespaces="true">*</ElementPath>
   </Query>
   ```

3. On the Parameters tab, add a new Parameter named StockSymbol mapped to the [@Symbols] report parameter (available in the drop-down). Add a second parameter named LicenseKey and set the value to 0. Be aware that the parameter names are case sensitive. These parameters correspond to the parameter placeholders in the XML and override the default values specified there.

4. Use the Query Designer to execute the query to ensure successful connection and configuration.

Now place fields from the Quote dataset in the report — a List item works well here because it is difficult to fit all the fields across the page. Then run the report, choose a company, and view the Web Service results in the output.

For a detailed description of query syntax, see the "XML Query Syntax for Specifying XML Report Data" topic in Books Online.

Working with expressions

Expressions are a powerful resource for report authors. They can be used as data for any item that appears on the report design surface, which enables calculations on source data and a variety of summarizations. Expressions can also be included in most object properties, enabling items to be selectively hidden, formatted, and change most any other behavior controlled by properties.

Figure 73-7 shows the Expression Editor used to build expressions.

To open the Expression Editor, select <Expression...> from a property value list, right-click on an object, and select Expression from the context menu, or select the function button labeled "fx" next to a property in a property page. The Expression Editor contains the expression code window, a category tree, category items, and a description pane. Double-clicking a value in the Item pane or Description pane inserts code into the code window.

FIGURE 73-7

The Expression Editor now contains advanced features such as IntelliSense and a list of available functions.

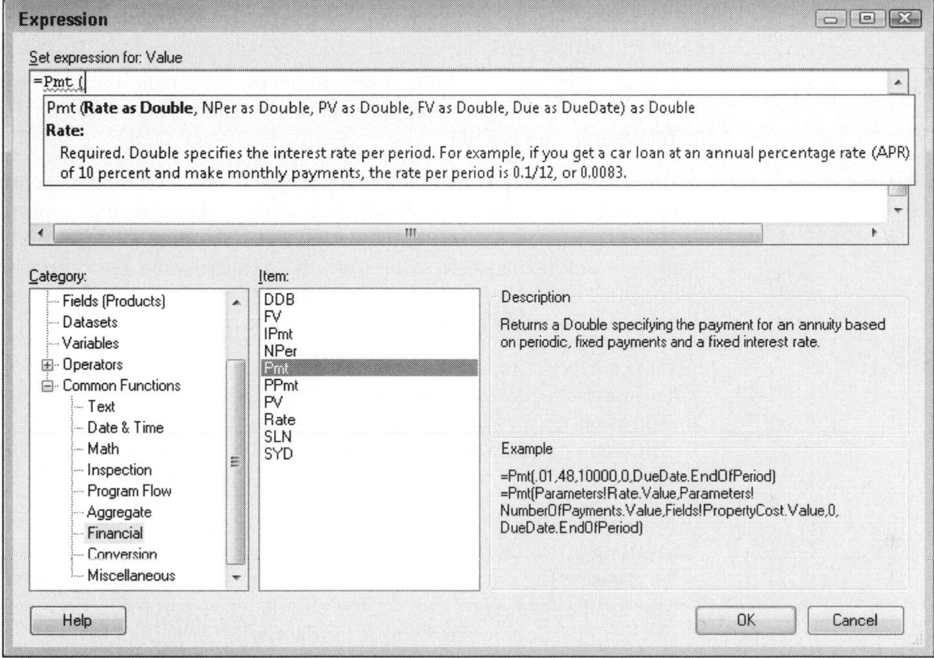

Table 73-2 describes the categories available in the Expression Editor.

Expression scope

Aggregate functions enable you to specify the scope for performing a calculation. Scope refers to either the name of a dataset or the name of a grouping or data region that contains the report item in which the aggregate function is used.

For example, consider a Sales by Product report containing a table with a group named `grpProduct`. To add a Running Total column to the report that resets the running total on each product, use the following expression:

```
=RunningValue(Fields!LineTotal.Value, Sum, "grpProduct")
```

TABLE 73-2

Expression Editor Categories

Category	Description
Constants	Constants are not available for all report items and properties. This category will contain the constant values available for the property for which the expression is being written. For example, when editing an expression to set the background color for a row in a table, the Constants category contains the list of colors available and exposes controls enabling the addition of a custom color.
Built-in Fields	This category contains built-in tags to access information about the report and the execution of the report, such as ExecutionTime, PageNumber, TotalPages, and UserID.
Parameters	This category contains the list of report parameters. Note that special handling is required for multi-value parameters because they represent a list of values instead of a single value. For example, the `Join` function can be used to produce a single string from the multiple values; an expression like `Join(Parameters!ProductCategoryID.Value,",")` will produce a comma-separated list of category IDs.
Fields	This category contains the list of fields for the dataset within the scope of the selected report item or property. For example, when editing the expression for a cell in a table bound to the `Products` dataset, the Fields expression category will list all of the fields available in the `Products` dataset.
Datasets	This expression category contains each dataset defined in the report. Selecting a dataset displays the default aggregation function for each field in the dataset. The default aggregation function varies according to the data type for the field. For example, the default aggregation function of the `ListPrice` field in the `Products` dataset is `Sum(ListPrice)`. Double-clicking this field adds the following code to the code window: `Sum(Fields!ListPrice.Value, "Products")`
Operators	This expression category contains Arithmetic, Comparison, Concatenation, Logical/Bitwise, and Bit Shift operators to assist with expression syntax and construction.
Common Functions	This expression category contains functions for working with Text, Date and Time, Math, Inspection, Program Flow, Aggregate, Financial, Conversion, and Miscellaneous.

To add a Running Total column to the report that does not reset by product, use this expression:

```
=RunningValue(Fields!LineTotal.Value, Sum)
```

Expression scope can also be important when adding an expression to a textbox. Because the textbox report item cannot be bound directly to a dataset, the expression must include the dataset's scope. The following expression calculates the sum of the `LineTotal` field in the `Sales` dataset:

```
=Sum(Fields!LineTotal.Value, "Sales")
```

Expressing yourself with common expressions

The following examples demonstrate several common expressions used in reports. Using the following expression as the `BackgroundColor` property for the detail row in a table will set the background color for the even rows to `AliceBlue`:

```
=IIf(RowNumber(nothing) mod 2 = 1, "AliceBlue", "White")
```

It's a good idea to include the date and time a report was executed. The following expression produces output like "Report Executed on Monday, August 15, 2005 at 2:24:33 P.M.":

```
="Report Executed On " & Globals!ExecutionTime.ToLongDateString &
" at " & Globals!ExecutionTime.ToLongTimeString
```

Expressions can be used to format text. The following expression calculates the sum of the `LineTotal` field in the `Sales` dataset and formats the result as a currency string such as $4,231,205.23:

```
=FormatCurrency(Sum(Fields!LineTotal.Value, "Sales"),
2, true, true, true)
```

Sometimes it doesn't make sense to show certain report items based on the parameters selected. To toggle the visibility of a report item or even just a cell in a table, use an expression similar to the following in the `Visibility.Hidden` property:

```
=IIf(Parameters!CategoryID.Value = 10, true, false)
```

Designing the Report Layout

The Report Designer contains a rich feature set for designing reports. This section discusses the basics of report design and demonstrates creating a report design, grouping and sorting data, and adding charts to a report.

Design basics

The Design tab in the Report Designer contains rich features to make formatting even the most complicated reports possible. The page layout contains three sections: header, body, and footer. Table 73-3 summarizes the behavior and purpose of each section. Designing the report layout is similar to working with Windows Forms. Report items are added by dragging them from the Toolbox onto the report.

Best Practice

Because a report represents the state of a dataset at a particular moment in time, it is important to include enough information in the report to answer the "5 Ws" of the report: who, what, when, where, and why? Who ran the report? Where did they run it? What criteria were provided to execute the report? When was the report generated? Why does the report exist? Communicating these facts on the report in a consistent manner avoids confusion and debate over the report's content.

TABLE 73-3

Report Sections

Section	Description
Header	By default, content in the header will appear on every page. This is a good place to include the report title to indicate why the report exists. The `PrintOnFirstPage` and `PrintOnLastPage` properties can be used to prevent the header from appearing on the first and last pages.
Body	If the report contains parameters, it's a good idea to add a section to the top or bottom of the body to show the value of the parameters used to execute the report, and perhaps a short description of what the report represents. Adding this detail at the top or bottom of the body ensures that the information is printed only once, rather than on every page.
Footer	Like the header, the footer also appears on every page by default and can be turned off for the first and last pages. This is a good place to include information specifying who ran the report, when they ran it, the report version, and page numbering.

Designing the report header

To add a report title, follow these steps:

1. Right-click the left margin of the report and select Page Header to show the page header section. Be aware that once you have added content to a report section, the content is lost if you toggle that section off.
2. Add a textbox to the header from the Toolbox.
3. Type the report title and format the textbox. You may want the title to be dynamic based on the report content or parameters selected. This can be achieved by using an expression. Nearly all visual aspects of the textbox permit expressions too.

Designing the report footer

The footer should include information such as who ran the report, when the report was executed, and page numbering. This type of information can be added using expressions. Follow these steps to build the footer:

1. Right-click the left margin of the report and select Page Footer to show the page footer section.
2. Add three textboxes using these expressions:

```
=User!UserID
=Globals!PageNumber & " of " & Globals!TotalPages
=Globals!ExecutionTime
```

3. Add a line above the textboxes to provide visual separation.

Adding and formatting a Table report item

Use the Table report item to render the data from a row-oriented dataset — the type of data that might present well in a simple Excel spreadsheet. Follow these steps to add a table showing the data from a dataset named `Products`:

1. Add a table to the body of the report from the Toolbox.
2. Drag fields from the dataset to the detail section of the table. Notice how the indicator highlights where the field will be placed — either in an empty column or between columns. If necessary, highlight and right-click column headers and delete columns as necessary. Column headers are automatically set based on the field name. Note that dropping fields into the header and footer sections of the table will create an expression to either return the value for that field from the first row in the dataset or to calculate the sum of a numeric dataset field.
3. Format the report by using the numerous formatting options available in the toolbar and properties pane to control data presentation. Table formatting can be set at the table, row, column, and cell level — each parent's formatting can be overridden at the child level. Property values can be specified as expressions to dynamically change the formatting based on data values (e.g., exceptions could be highlighted by changing the font color or weight).

Figure 73-8 shows the layout of the report, including the header, table, and footer. Figure 73-9 shows the rendered report.

Adding and formatting a List report item

Adding a List item to a report places both a Tablix and a Rectangle item on the design surface. Because it includes a Tablix, it can present anything that a Table or Matrix can present, but the List item is in a convenient form to contain other items, suggesting a number of uses:

- Place other items within the List item, such as textboxes, images, charts, etc. All these nested items will be repeated for each row of the dataset associated with the list. This is an excellent approach for data that does not fit cleanly into a grid because the arrangement of items within the List is free-form.

FIGURE 73-8

Report layout with formatted header, body, and footer

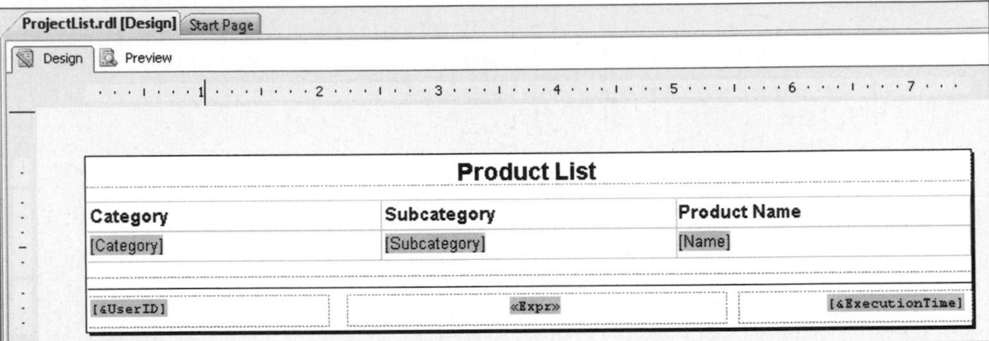

FIGURE 73-9

Rendered report with formatted header, body, and footer

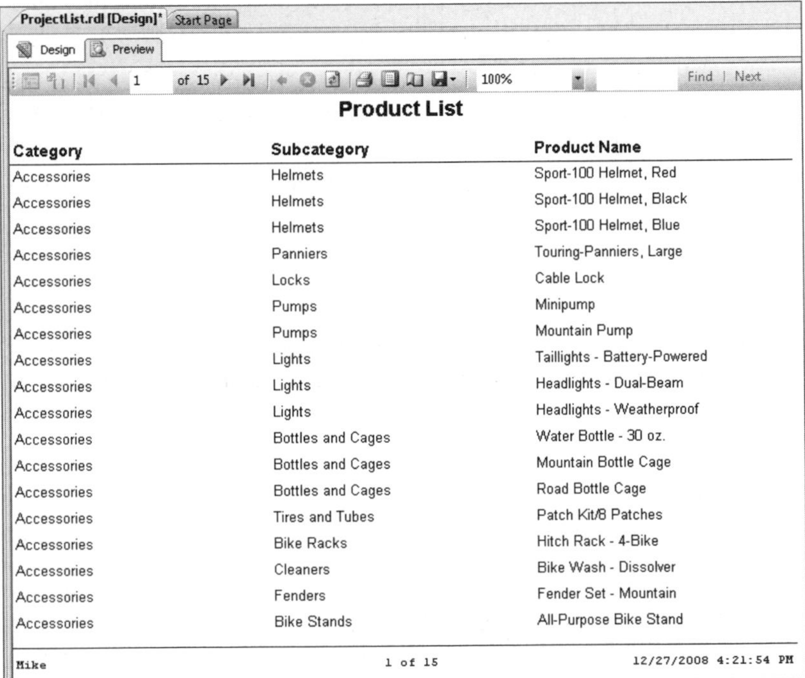

Category	Subcategory	Product Name
Accessories	Helmets	Sport-100 Helmet, Red
Accessories	Helmets	Sport-100 Helmet, Black
Accessories	Helmets	Sport-100 Helmet, Blue
Accessories	Panniers	Touring-Panniers, Large
Accessories	Locks	Cable Lock
Accessories	Pumps	Minipump
Accessories	Pumps	Mountain Pump
Accessories	Lights	Taillights - Battery-Powered
Accessories	Lights	Headlights - Dual-Beam
Accessories	Lights	Headlights - Weatherproof
Accessories	Bottles and Cages	Water Bottle - 30 oz.
Accessories	Bottles and Cages	Mountain Bottle Cage
Accessories	Bottles and Cages	Road Bottle Cage
Accessories	Tires and Tubes	Patch Kit/8 Patches
Accessories	Bike Racks	Hitch Rack - 4-Bike
Accessories	Cleaners	Bike Wash - Dissolver
Accessories	Fenders	Fender Set - Mountain
Accessories	Bike Stands	All-Purpose Bike Stand

Mike | 1 of 15 | 12/27/2008 4:21:54 PM

- By adding group(s) to the List (see "Grouping and Sorting Data in a Tablix" later in this chapter), it is simple to show both master and detail data in flexible layouts. For example, textboxes in a group header can show customer information, while a table in the group footer can list all of the customer's associated order detail.
- Adding a group to a List item (and eliminating the detail section) can summarize a dataset that is reported in detail elsewhere.

Using the Tablix property pages

Use the Tablix property pages to define key behaviors as described in Table 73-4. Invoke the property pages by clicking somewhere within the Tablix to expose the row and column handles, then right-click one of the handles and choose Tablix Properties. While the options vary slightly among the Table, Matrix, and List report items, the process to work with them is very similar.

TABLE 73-4

Table and Matrix Property Pages

Property Page	Description
General	Name the table/matrix/list, bind a dataset, set the tooltip text, control page breaks, and control where row/column headers appear. Note that row/column headers are not simply the first row or column displayed, but group or other headers as designated by dotted lines around the cells in design mode.
Visibility	Control the initial visibility of the item upon report execution. Allow the item visibility to be toggled by another report item.
Filters	Supply filter criteria. Use expressions to apply values from report parameters or other data for filtering.
Sorting	Set the sort order of the details section of the Tablix.

Many of the same properties are available in the Properties pane of the design environment. For example, the dataset can be set directly in the Properties pane. The property pages can also be launched from the icon in the Properties pane, or by choosing the ellipses of some property values (e.g., `SortExpressions`).

Grouping and sorting data in a Tablix

Grouping within a Tablix provides the power to organize data in many ways. Figure 73-10 shows a matrix item with groups. The row and column groups displayed at the bottom show the name and order of the groups of the currently selected report item. This grouping display is enabled by checking the Grouping option of the Report menu of the design environment. The scope of the grouping in the Tablix is indicated by the brace markings within the row and column handles, indicating which portions will be repeated for each group.

Groups can be created by dragging fields into the Row Groups or Column Groups areas, or by clicking the drop-down on each group. The drop-down also allows a group to be removed, or totals, such as the Sub Total and Grand Total rows in Figure 73-10, to be added.

FIGURE 73-10

Matrix item configured to group by Category and Subcategory on rows, plus Year and Quarter on columns.

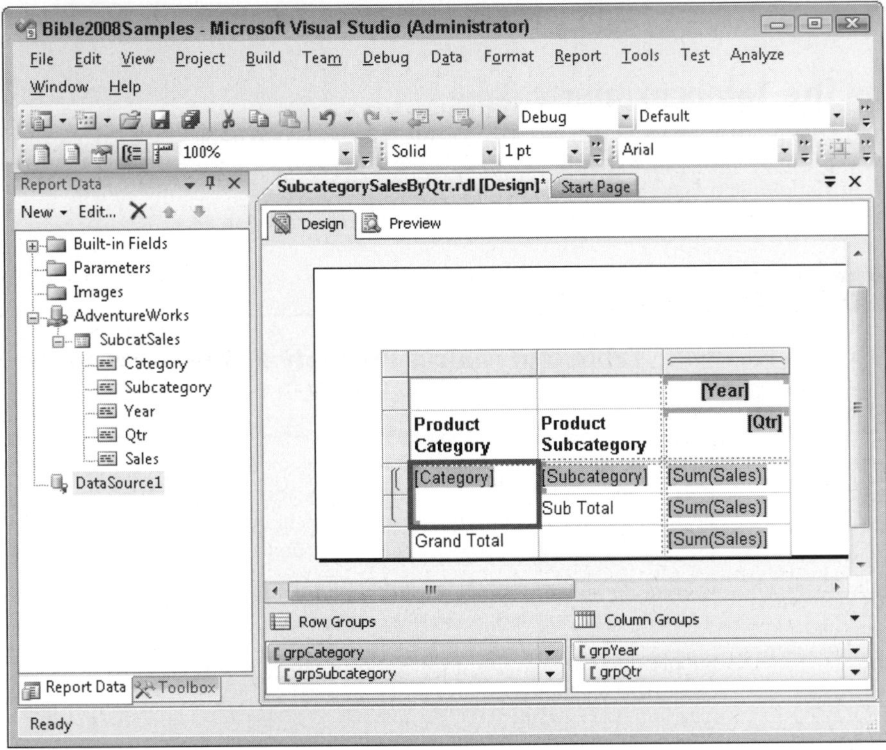

The drop-down is also a convenient way to access the Group Properties dialog, shown in Figure 73-11, to control the details of a grouping. While the ability to group data seems simple, the effect on report presentation can be stunning.

Each of the tabs in the Group Properties dialog provides control over a different aspect of the group:

- **General:** Allows the entry of a meaningful group name, and the definition of a group based on one or more fields or expressions. Each group exists in the context of its parent, so only specify what should define a "section" at the current level.

Best Practice

To simplify writing expressions in a table or matrix, it is important to provide a name for each group.

- **Page Breaks:** Specify whether page breaks should appear between, before, or after the group.
- **Sorting:** The order in which unique group values appear can be adjusted based on the group values themselves, other fields, or even an expression.
- **Visibility:** When the report executes, a group can be set to show itself, to be hidden (e.g., detail remains hidden until toggled on by users), or to be visible based on an expression (e.g., users select show/hide detail via a report parameter). Specify the report item that toggles visibility here when user control over specific sections is desired.
- **Filters:** Define expressions to limit the values available in the group.
- **Variables:** Group variables are evaluated when each new group value is encountered, and not evaluated again until the group value changes. The variable can be referenced in the current or child group expressions via the syntax `Variables!MyVar.Value` (for the group variable `MyVar`).
- **Advanced:** Specify the field or expression that will appear in the document map for this group. A document map will appear as different types of table-of-contents features depending on the output format of the rendered report (PDF, Excel, or Word). Recursive parent provides a way to display self-referential datasets, such as an employee list that refers to other rows as the manager.

FIGURE 73-11

The Group Properties dialog manages the behavior of Tablix groups.

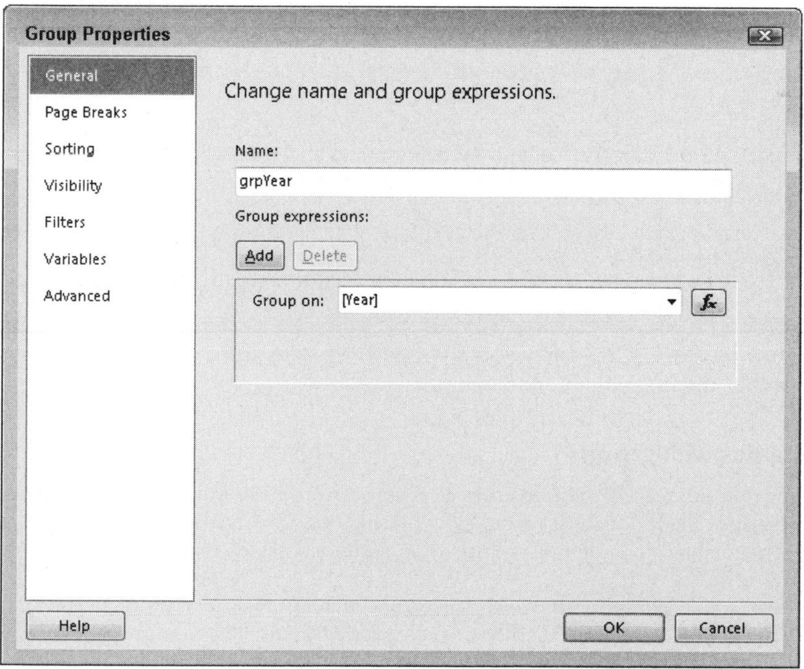

A Matrix report item, such as the one shown in Figure 73-10, contains only groups and does not display detailed data. This is why all values are reported using aggregate functions, such as the `Sum(Sales)` shown in the figure. Table and List items do display detailed data (one row on the report for each row in the dataset), which they accomplish by including a special group named Details by default, with no group expression. Implementing the detail level in this way enables details to be included or excluded from any Tablix by simply adding or removing the Details group.

The most intuitive way to use groups together is in a hierarchy. For example, countries are the parent group of regions, regions are the parent group of cities, and so on. Reporting Services also uses the concept of Adjacent groups, which are presented one after the other. Adjacent groups are often used in conjunction with filters at the group level. For example, filters could be defined to show products grossing in the top 10% for the current quarter in one group and the bottom 10% for another group. If these two were arranged as Adjacent groups as children of the Product category, then the report would list only the outliers in each category.

Setting the sort order for a Tablix

Because sort order can be specified at both the Tablix and group level, it is important to understand that group sort definitions override Tablix definitions. This is in keeping with the Reporting Services theme of child property settings overriding the parent settings.

Interactive sorting can also be enabled in a variety of ways. Traditionally, this has been implemented by adding sort arrows to the column header of a table. Pressing the arrows on the rendered report causes the report to re-sort as desired. While column headers are the normal place to enable sorting, there are no real restrictions regarding how interactive sorting is enabled, and it can be used for detail rows, groups, or various combinations. For example, follow these steps to enable interactive sorting of the Category column on the ProductList report described earlier in this chapter:

1. Right-click on the Category column header textbox, and choose Text Box Properties.
2. Select the Interactive Sort tab.
3. Check "Enable interactive sort on this text box" and "Detail rows." Choose`[Category]` for the "Sort by" option.
4. Select OK to apply the changes.

When the report is rendered, users can now re-sort categories using the sort arrows. This process can easily be repeated for the Subcategory and Product columns.

Formatting tables with groups

The ways in which groups can be used to enhance reports are endless, but this example demonstrates a simple way to enhance the ProductList report shown in Figures 73-8 and 73-9. At this point, the earlier example has been enhanced by adding List Price as an additional table column.

Begin by deleting the two left columns, which currently contain Category and Subcategory. Then drag Category and Subcategory fields from the Report Data pane onto the Row Groups pane to achieve the order shown in Figure 73-12.

FIGURE 73-12

The ProductList report design with groups defined for category and subcategory

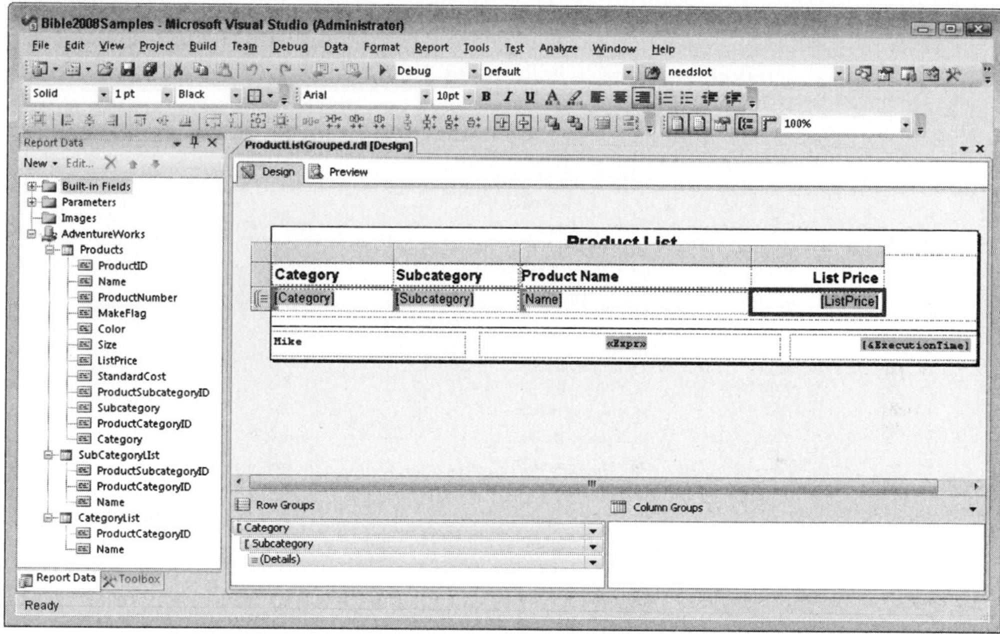

Switch to the preview tab and note that with groups defined, the category and subcategory render only when necessary, instead of being repeated for every row as they were when part of the Details group. This cleans up the presentation substantially; however, also note that the second and subsequent pages do not display column headers — this will definitely hurt the report's readability.

Repeating headers on each page requires that a true header row be added to the report. The procedure to do this is a bit clunky, but very fast once practiced:

1. Drag the Size field (it could be any field) from the Report Data pane to the Column Groups pane. This causes a true header row to be added above the table.
2. Use the drop-down to immediately delete the new group. When prompted by the pop-up, choose the "Delete group only" option, which removes the group but leaves the new header row.
3. The new row will have several columns merged together at the right side of the table. Right-click in the large cell and choose Split Cells.
4. Copy the text labels from the old header row to the new one.
5. Delete the old header row by right-clicking on the row handle and choosing Delete Rows.
6. Right-click on a row or column header and choose Tablix Properties. Check the "Repeat header rows on each page" option.

The preview tab now shows both suppressed duplicates from the row groupings and column headers that repeat on each page (see Figure 73-13).

FIGURE 73-13

The ProductList report preview with both groups defined and repeating column headers

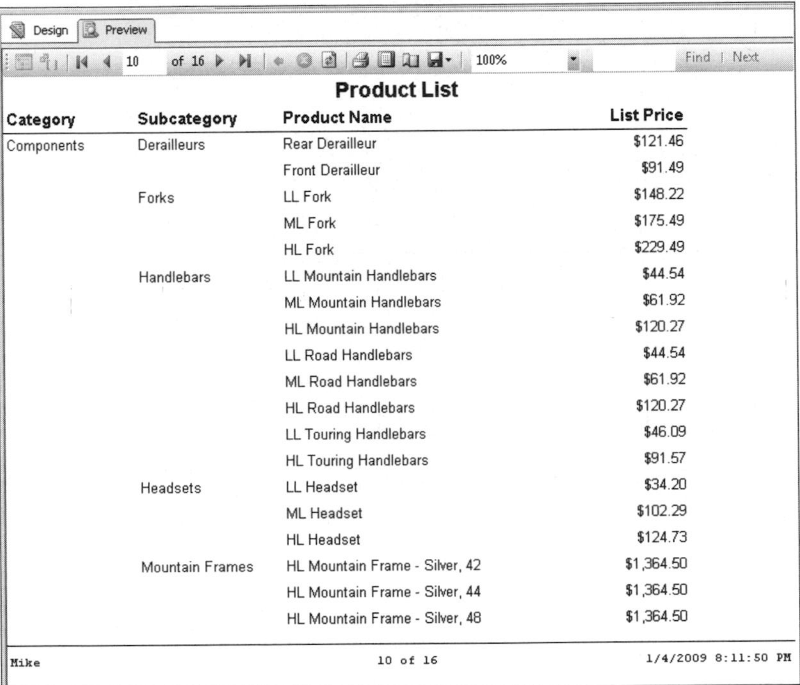

Product List

Category	Subcategory	Product Name	List Price
Components	Derailleurs	Rear Derailleur	$121.46
		Front Derailleur	$91.49
	Forks	LL Fork	$148.22
		ML Fork	$175.49
		HL Fork	$229.49
	Handlebars	LL Mountain Handlebars	$44.54
		ML Mountain Handlebars	$61.92
		HL Mountain Handlebars	$120.27
		LL Road Handlebars	$44.54
		ML Road Handlebars	$61.92
		HL Road Handlebars	$120.27
		LL Touring Handlebars	$46.09
		HL Touring Handlebars	$91.57
	Headsets	LL Headset	$34.20
		ML Headset	$102.29
		HL Headset	$124.73
	Mountain Frames	HL Mountain Frame - Silver, 42	$1,364.50
		HL Mountain Frame - Silver, 44	$1,364.50
		HL Mountain Frame - Silver, 48	$1,364.50

Mike 10 of 16 1/4/2009 8:11:50 PM

Illustrating data with charts and gauges

Reporting Services 2008 has greatly enhanced graphics to present report data. Charts show proportion, trends, and comparisons of series of data. Drag a chart onto the design surface and click to select the item. Three areas appear ready for data fields to be dragged onto them:

- **Series:** This is the field that separates the data into groups that appear in the legend. For example, Year is the Series field in Figure 73-14.
- **Category:** This is the field that subdivides a series into distinct bars or points on a line. For example, Product Category is the Category field in Figure 73-14.
- **Data:** These are the actual values to be charted.

FIGURE 73-14

Sample chart of sales comparisons with scale breaks enabled on the vertical axis

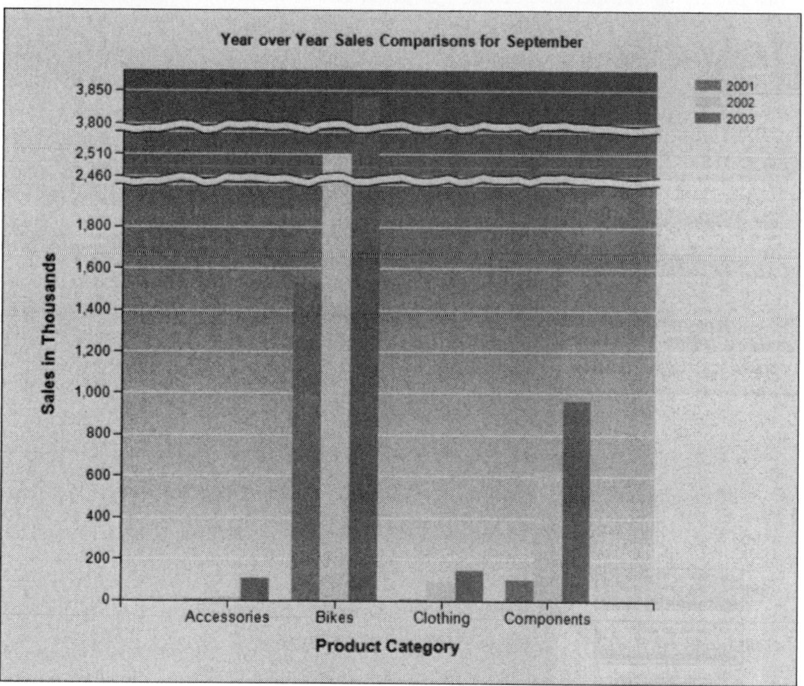

Fields can be dragged directly from the Report Data pane where the dataset is defined to a chart. Titles, placement, and many formatting details can now be set by directly typing on or moving items within the chart. An exhaustive set of additional properties is available via the right-click menu to control nearly every detail of the chart.

New in 2008

Gauges are new in Reporting Services 2008. They provide an eye-catching way to call out key metrics in a report, such as plan vs. budget.

A gauge is conceptually a much simpler control. It displays how far a value falls on a scale, like a gas gauge or thermometer. The dataset that drives the gauge need only provide a single value (or for some gauges a few), and, optionally, the minimum and maximum values for the scale. For example, a gauge could display how all salespeople are performing against their sales quota.

Drag a gauge onto the design surface and select it to see the data handle. Drop the field from the dataset to be displayed into this handle. Then right-click to access the scale properties to enter the minimum and maximum scale values, or choose the dataset fields to associate them with.

Summary

Reporting Services delivers abundant features that enable report authors and developers to empower business decision-makers by providing access to interactive reports. The Reporting Services Project in the Business Intelligence Development Studio contains a rich set of tools to make report authoring possible. The 2008 release removes many of the barriers that developers have encountered in previous versions.

For authors who have previously used other reporting products, the switch from writing code to accomplish advanced tasks to the expressions in properties paradigm of Reporting Services can be challenging at times, but well worth the investment. Development is faster, the paradigm is more flexible, and changing an existing report is much easier.

Even the best development environment does not guarantee good reports. Like any development effort, creating useful reports requires talking to prospective users to understand the questions they are trying to answer, and prototyping different reports to get feedback on the effectiveness of different presentations. Push the boundaries in prototypes because most users will be unfamiliar with the power available in Reporting Services.

Chapter 74

Administering Reporting Services

Once reports have been developed in Reporting Services, they must be delivered to be of value. Certainly most users won't be interested in loading up the development environment to view the latest sales report!

The Reporting Services server addresses this need. The server can run on the same hardware as the relational database but need not if system load requires scale-out. Installing the server creates one windows service and installs two relational databases: one that contains deployed report definitions and other metadata, and a second for temporary objects used in processing. After installation, be sure to visit the Reporting Services Configuration Manager to adjust settings and back up the encryption keys and save them in a safe place. Keeping all the metadata in the `ReportServer` database makes it simple to back up, but without the encryption key a restore will be difficult.

All access to the Reporting Services service happens via a Web Service, which enables reports to be uploaded and managed, security settings modified, and so on. The Web Service can be accessed in several ways:

- Business Intelligence Development Studio will deploy reports to the Web Service.
- Applications and browsers can explore and render reports by referencing a URL.
- Programmatically, custom applications can access all of the server's features. SharePoint has made good use of these capabilities by adding Reporting Services web parts and integration.
- The Report Manager, an ASP.NET application installed with Reporting Services, provides interactive access to the server.
- SQL Server Management Studio can connect to Reporting Services for managing server properties and roles.

IN THIS CHAPTER

Structure of the report server

Report deployment options

Security model and guidelines

General server configuration

Leveraging existing development with linked reports

User and data-driven subscriptions

New in 2008

Reporting Services no longer requires IIS to be installed. It now uses the HTTP listener (HTTP.SYS) to process requests to the Web Service. This implementation enables IIS to be omitted from Reporting Services servers entirely, but does not interfere with IIS implementations when run on the same server.

The role of tools in managing Reporting Services has changed in 2008 to support the enhanced architecture and SharePoint integration. SQL Server Management Studio no longer manages report server content or subscriptions.

The Report Manager application provides the tools required to administer the report server and deploy items, including reports, shared data sources, and data models. The Report Manager also provides the interface for users to access, manage, and execute reports. The default URL for the Report Manager is `http://localhost/reports`. Figure 74-1 shows the Report Manager application on its default page.

FIGURE 74-1

The Report Manager comes with Reporting Services. It provides an interactive interface for both users and administrators.

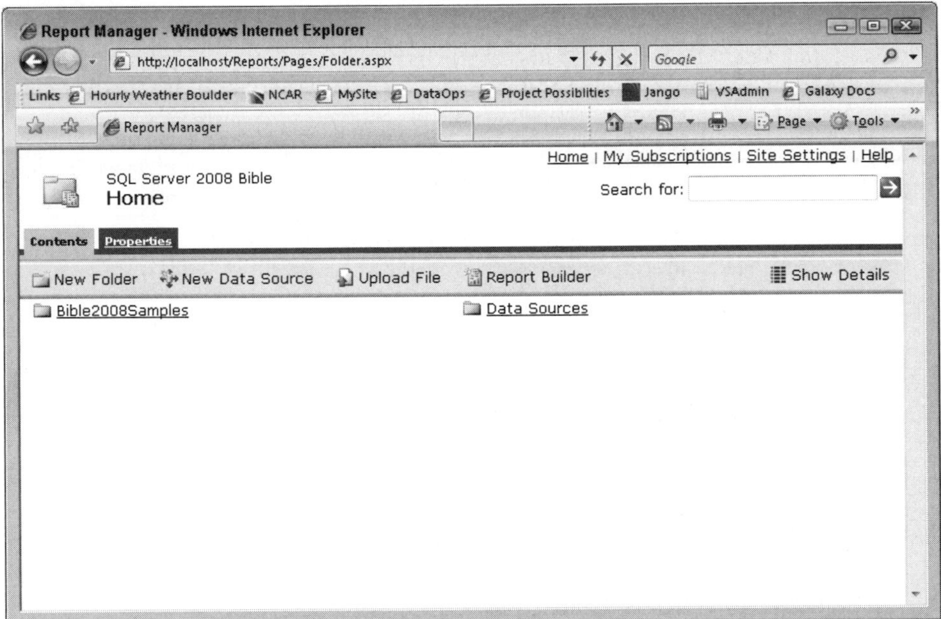

This chapter describes the tools and methods to administer the report server, beginning with deploying reports onto the server.

Deploying Reporting Services Reports

This section explores the options and strategies to deploy the reports to the report server. Deploying directly from the development environment, Business Intelligence Development Studio (BIDS) is the simplest method for the developer, but it may not always be possible or desirable depending upon configuration and security constraints.

Deploying reports using BIDS

Deploying reports using BIDS requires some basic configuration of the Reporting Services project. Once configured, reports (and other resources such as data sources and images) can be deployed individually or the entire project can be deployed.

To configure the deployment properties for a Reporting Services project, open the project's property page by right-clicking on the Reporting Services project and selecting Properties. Figure 74-2 shows the property page for a Reporting Services project, and Table 74-1 summarizes the deployment properties available for a Reporting Services project.

FIGURE 74-2

Use the settings on the property page of a Reporting Services project to configure the deployment options.

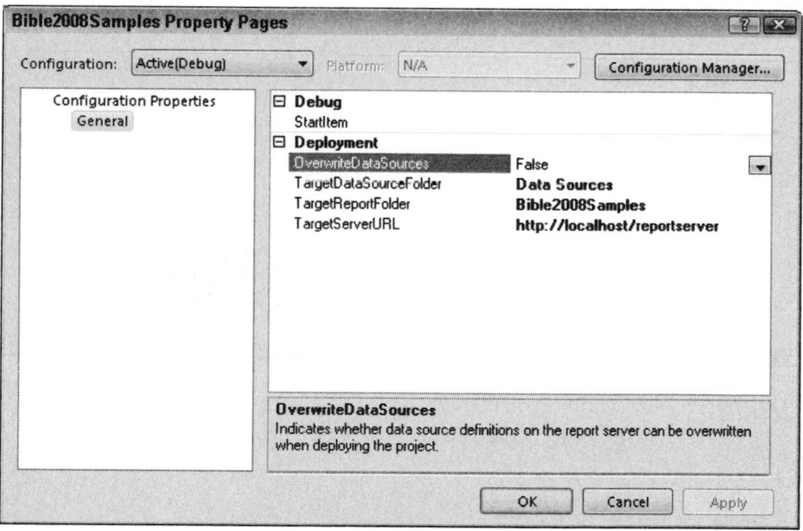

Deploying a single report or data source

Once the deployment properties are configured for a Reporting Services project, a report or data source can be deployed by simply right-clicking on the item and selecting Deploy in Solution Explorer. The status bar at the bottom of Visual Studio indicates the deployment's progress. During deployment, progress and any errors appear in the output window.

TABLE 74-1

Reporting Services Project Deployment Properties

Property	Description
`OverwriteDataSources`	Set this to `True` if you want to overwrite data sources on the report server with data sources in the report project. The default value is `False`, which prevents data sources from being overwritten. This is helpful if the data source used for development is different from the data source used on the report server. Note this does not prevent the initial deployment of a data source, only the subsequent overwriting.
`TargetDataSourceFolder`	This is the path of the folder to which you wish to deploy shared data sources. Using this parameter enables the definition of a common data source that can be deployed to a common location and used by reports across multiple folders (or projects in development). Using a common shared connection minimizes administration efforts for the data source object. Leave this property blank to deploy the shared data source(s) to the folder specified in the `TargetReportFolder` property (not recommended).
`TargetReportFolder`	This is the path of the folder to which you wish to deploy reports. In BIDS, you must create a project for each folder (or subfolder) to which you wish to deploy reports. For example, to simplify deploying reports to two folders named `Sales` and `Customers`, set up two Reporting Services projects in Visual Studio and specify the respective folder name in the `TargetReportFolder` property. Then move the reports between the projects to control their deployment destination. It is also possible to use the `TargetReportFolder` variable to deploy to subfolders on the report server. For example, setting this value to `Sales/Regional` would create a nice home for your regional sales reports.
`TargetServerURL`	This is the URL of the report server you wish to deploy to. The default location of your local report server is `http://localhost/ReportServer`. If you named the instance SQL08, the local report server would be `http://localhost/ReportServer$SQL08`.

This method of deploying objects to the report server is convenient when you want to update only selected objects on the report server, rather than all objects in the project.

Deploying a Reporting Services project

To deploy all objects in the Reporting Services project, ensure that the project deployment properties are correctly configured, and then right-click on the project and select Deploy. Note that the `OverwriteDataSources` project property can be used to prevent overwriting data source objects.

This is an important feature because the data source for your reports on the report server will often require different configuration than the data source used for report development.

Deploying reports using the Report Manager

While BIDS provides an easy way to deploy reports to the report server, it is not required for report deployment. It is possible to deploy and configure individual Reporting Services objects using the Report Manager. The Report Manager includes features that enable the creation of new folders and data sources, and it provides the capability to upload and update report definitions (.rdl files), report data sources (.rds files), and any other file type you wish to make available on the report server (such as a PDF, Word document, Power Point presentation, Excel file, etc.).

To deploy a report using the Report Manager, follow these steps:

1. Open the Report Manager application in a web browser. The default location for the Report Manager is `http://localhost/reports`.
2. Navigate to the folder to which you want to deploy the report.
3. Click the Upload File button.
4. Enter the path to the file or use the Browse button to find the file.
5. Enter the report name.
6. If you want to overwrite an existing report with the same name, check the option to "Overwrite item" if it exists.
7. Click the OK button to upload the file and return to the contents of the folder. The new report now appears in the list and is marked as New to grab the user's attention.

It's a good idea to execute the report and verify that the data source is valid. You may need to use the Data Sources link on the Properties tab of the report to either select a shared data source or specify a custom data source for the report. You should also review the other links available on the Properties tab to set parameter defaults and configure report execution, history, and security settings.

Deploying reports programmatically using the Reporting Services Web Service

The Reporting Services Web Service exposes methods to deploy reports and enables custom applications to be written to perform such tasks. Remember that the Report Manager is an ASP.NET user interface that leverages the Reporting Services Web Service to manage the report server. All functionality available in the Report Manager is available for your application development pleasure using the Reporting Services Web Service.

To begin developing an application that will use the Reporting Services Web Service, create a project in Visual Studio and add a web reference to the Reporting Services Web Service. The default location of the Web Service on the local machine is `http://localhost/reportserver/reportservice2006.asmx`. After adding this web reference, you will have access to classes that enable your custom application to perform any task on the report server, including deploying and executing reports. The `ReportingService` class on the Web Service contains methods that enable the creation (and deletion) of folders, reports, data sources, schedules, and subscriptions, along with many other operations on the report server. It also contains methods to render reports in any of the formats summarized in Table 74-6, later in the chapter.

An alternative to a full-blown custom application is using the `rs.exe` utility. This utility provides methods for scripting report deployment tasks; and while it lacks some of the flexibility of the custom application option, it can be very effective for specific deployments.

Configuring Reporting Services Using Management Studio

SQL Server Management Studio (SSMS) has limited functionality in Reporting Services 2008, but it excels at configuring the basic server options and managing role definitions. While many of the operations described in this section are also possible from within the Report Manager application, SSMS has more options, and interactions are simpler within that familiar interface.

CROSS-REF **For background on working in SQL Server Management Studio, see Chapter 6, "Using Management Studio."**

Configuring Reporting Services server properties

Access server properties by connecting a Reporting Services server via the Object Explorer in SSMS. Once connected, right-click on the server and choose Properties. The resulting Server Properties dialog is shown in Figure 74-3.

NOTE **Use Report Manager for all content-related management and permission assignments, and use SQL Server Management Studio for server properties, role definitions, and shared schedules. The Reporting Services Configuration Manager is similar in function to its 2005 counterpart, setting service properties such as execution account, URL, and database connections, but its function has been streamlined and adapted to the 2008 architecture.**

The following sections describe the more commonly adjusted server properties.

General

By default, the option to enable My Reports is turned off. Turning this feature on enables users to manage a personal folder named My Reports, where they can publish their own reports, create linked reports, and manage their own content. Each user has his or her own My Reports folder, similar to the My Documents folder in Windows. Reporting Services contains a default role named My Reports to provide appropriate security access for this folder. Later in the chapter you'll see how to customize roles and create new roles, but note that you can specify the role applied to the My Reports folder.

Enabling the My Reports option provides a location where users can save the reports they build using the Report Builder. This tool enables users to create their own reports based on predefined data models.

Configuring report execution settings

The Execution tab (refer to Figure 74-3) enables you to set the default report execution timeout for Reporting Services. The default server limit is set to 1,800 seconds (30 minutes). Alternately, choose the

"Do not timeout report execution" option on the same page to remove an execution timeout limit. Any policy established at the server level can be overridden for individual reports using Report Manager.

FIGURE 74-3

Use the Server Properties dialog in Management Studio to administer server options.

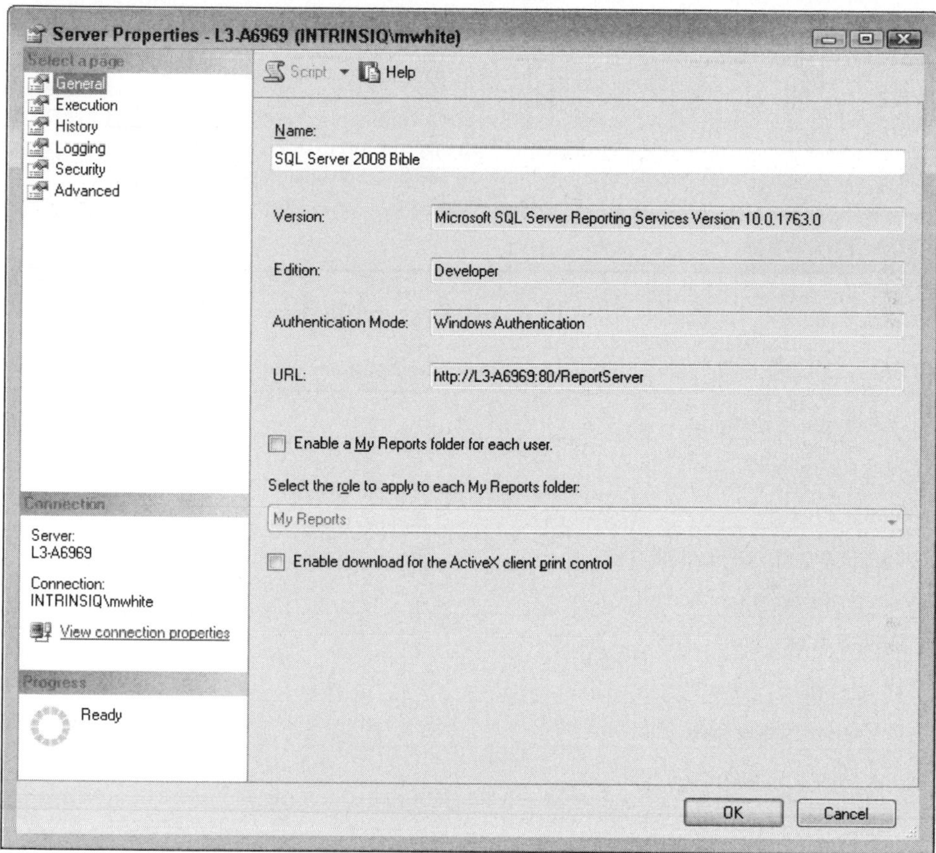

Configuring report history settings

Reporting Services can retain snapshots of reports to allow rendering of those older versions. The default behavior for keeping report history can be set to either an unlimited number of snapshots or a number that you specify (the former being the default setting, which can be overridden for specific reports if necessary). To override this for a specific report, select the Properties tab on the report in Report Manager, and then select the History link. The settings here plus those on the Execution tab enable control over how snapshots are generated, stored, and used in report rendering. Limiting the number of snapshots at the site level can help ensure that the `ReportServer` database does not grow beyond available storage.

Security: managing roles

The security model in Reporting Services leverages Active Directory to grant access to the Report Manager and to items (folders, reports, shared data sources, etc.) within the report server. Security is administered by assigning users or groups to roles. Roles contain selected tasks that enable specific actions within the Report Manager application. Two types of predefined roles and tasks exist: system-level and item-level. Most Reporting Services installations do not actually require changes to the default roles, but rather focus on managing membership in those roles via Report Manager.

System-level roles

System-level roles grant access to server functions that are not item-specific. Two system-level roles are created when the report server is installed: System Administrator and System User. Table 74-2 shows the tasks granted to these roles by default. To change the predefined roles or create new roles, select the "Configure System-level Role Definitions" link on the Site Settings page.

TABLE 74-2

Default System Roles

Task	System Administrator	System User
Execute report definitions	X	X
Generate events		
Manage jobs	X	
Manage report server properties	X	
Manage report server security	X	
Manage roles	X	
Manage shared schedules	X	
View report server properties		X
View shared schedules		X

The default role definitions can be changed by expanding the System Roles folder in Object Explorer, right-clicking on the role to be changed, and selecting Properties. If necessary, additional roles can be created by right-clicking the System Roles folder and choosing New System Role. Once defined in SSMS, managing the membership of these roles is handled by the Report Manager application as described in the following section.

Item-level roles

Item-level roles manage permissions associated with the reports, folders, and so on stored in the report server. SSMS presents them in the Roles folder of the Object Explorer, with the same functionality (right-click the role to edit, and then right-click the folder to add) as used with system folders. Of course, the capabilities being granted differ as described in the next section.

Configuring Reporting Services Using Report Manager

Report Manager is a web application included with Reporting Services. It provides features required to administer the report server, and features for end-users to access and execute reports. Report Manager is an ASP.NET user interface built upon the Reporting Services Web Service. The default URL for Report Manager is `http://localhost/reports`.

Managing security

Whether you are using the default role definitions or custom definitions, as described earlier, the majority of security management generally falls to assigning membership in those roles.

Granting system access to users and groups

By default, the BUILTIN\Administrators group is assigned the System Administrator role. Follow these steps to grant system access to additional users or Active Directory groups:

1. Start the Report Manager application by entering the appropriate URL into a browser.
2. Click the Site Settings link in the upper-right corner and then choose the Security tab. A list of current users assigned to system roles is displayed.
3. Click the New Role Assignment button on the System Role Assignments page.
4. Enter the Group or User name — for example, *myDomain*\jdoe or *myDomain* \SRSAdminstrators.
5. Select one or more system roles to assign to the group or user.
6. Click the OK button to save.

Best Practice

It is important to be consistent regarding your approach to granting access to the Report Manager and to items within the Report Manager. Consider your environment when choosing how to manage and assign access and whether you grant access to Active Directory groups or to individual users. If you have already taken the time to create Active Directory groups in your organization, you can most likely leverage your existing groups to administer access to your report server.

For example, if you have an Active Directory group for accounting, you can simply create a new system role assignment for that group to grant all of the accounting members access to the report server. Perhaps you will have an Accounting folder with accounting reports to which only accounting employees should have access. When creating this folder, simply adjust the inherited role assignments to ensure that only the accounting group has access.

Regardless of which strategy you choose (user vs. groups), maintain a consistent approach in order to minimize maintenance, research, and troubleshooting efforts in the future.

Item-level permissions

Item-level roles are used to control the tasks available for managing folders, reports, shared data sources, models, and other resources in the Report Manager application. Table 74-3 describes the default item-level roles created when the report server is installed. SQL Server Management Studio can be used to modify or add to these roles as described in the preceding section.

To access item-level roles, select the Security link on the Property tab of any item beneath the root directory in the Report Manager. Next, click either the Edit link for an existing assignment or the New Role Assignment button. Notice how this model differs from the relational permissioning model: These roles are bundles of rights that are applied to users or groups for each object, whereas the relational database role is a bundle of users which are in turn granted permissions.

TABLE 74-3

Default Item-Level Roles

Task	Browser	Content Manager	My Reports	Publisher	Report Builder
Consume reports		X			X
Create linked reports		X	X	X	
Manage all subscriptions		X			
Manage data sources		X	X	X	
Manage folders		X	X	X	
Manage individual subscriptions	X	X	X		X
Manage models		X		X	
Manage report history		X	X		
Manage reports		X	X	X	
Manage resources		X	X	X	
Set security for individual items		X			
View data sources		X	X		
View folders	X	X	X		X
View models	X	X			X
View reports	X	X	X		X
View resources	X	X	X		X

Controlling item-level security

By default, every item-level resource inherits the security settings of its parent. If the security settings for an item have not been modified (they still inherit from their parent item), then the Security page for that item contains an Edit Item Security button. After modifying the security settings (and breaking the inheritance from the parent item), the Security page for the item contains item-level access to a user or group.

Best Practice

Once inheritance has been broken, it can be very complex to make broad changes to sitewide permissions. Because of this, planning ahead for the folder hierarchy can be a big win. Keep the structure simple so that permissions can be granted on a few parent folders. For complex cases, it is sometimes easier to use linked reports to provide appropriate access, rather than break inheritance.

You must belong to a system role with the Set Security for Individual Items task to complete these tasks. Follow these steps:

1. Select the Security link on the Properties tab for the item for which you wish to modify security settings.
2. If the item still inherits its security settings from its parent, click the Edit Item Security button. An alert will be displayed indicating that the security is inherited, and that if you continue to edit the item's security, you will break the inheritance. Select OK to continue. Note that you can also delete roles that were assigned to the parent.
3. Click the New Role Assignment button.
4. Enter the group or username, e.g., *myDomain*\accounting.
5. Select one or more roles to assign to the group or user.
6. Click the OK button to save the new role assignment.

Remember that in order for users to access an item-level resource, they must also be granted system-level access (See the earlier topic "Granting System Access to Users and Groups").

In addition, modifying an item's security will automatically apply the security to all child items that inherit that security. To restore the inherited security for an item that has been customized, click the Revert to Parent Security button. An alert will be displayed prompting for confirmation before the security settings defined for that item are replaced by the security settings of its parent.

Working with linked reports

A linked report is a shortcut to an actual report. It enables configuration of the report parameters, execution, history, and security — independent of the actual report. If the report server is configured to allow user-owned folders for publishing and running personalized reports, users can create a linked report and configure the parameter defaults to suit their specific needs.

Linked reports also provide a powerful way to administer report security and limit the available parameters by user, group, or role. For example, consider a regional sales report with an optional parameter used to execute the report for a selected region. Certain users should be able to execute the report for all regions, while other users should only be able to execute the report for their own region. You can limit access to the actual report to the users (or an Active Directory group) who should be able to view all regions, and then create a linked report for each region and limit access to the linked reports according to the user's privileges. For each linked report, hide the region parameter and set the default value to the desired region.

You could also create a folder for each region and save the linked reports in these folders. That way, security can be controlled for the folder and multiple linked reports can be saved to the folder, thereby eliminating the need to administer security on each linked report.

Creating linked reports

To create a linked report, select the Properties tab on the report to which you wish to create a link and select the Create Linked Report button. Name the new linked report and enter a description and location for it. Click OK to create the report. Once created, select the Properties tab on the new linked report to administer parameters, execution, history, and security. It is also possible to create subscriptions and set up history snapshots for the linked report.

To simplify analysis of dependencies and management of linked reports, it's a good idea to include the actual report name either in the name of the linked report or in the description of the linked report. This way, you can enter the actual report name in the Search criteria (see the Search feature in the header of Report Manager) to retrieve a list of all linked reports and the actual report.

Leveraging the power of subscriptions

The capability to subscribe to reports represents an extremely valuable feature in Reporting Services to automate report delivery. Reporting Services supports both push-and-pull paradigms for report delivery. For example, upon scheduled report execution, a subscription can send an e-mail with an attachment containing the report content (push), with the report content in the body of the e-mail (push), or with a link to the report stored on the report server (pull). Alternatively, reports can be written to a file share where users or other systems can access the report or exported data.

Report subscriptions require that the SQL Server Agent service is running on the relational database hosting the `ReportServer` database. This service executes jobs, monitors SQL Server, fires alerts, and allows automation of some administrative tasks for the report server. Before creating a subscription, ensure that this service is started. In addition, to successfully create a report subscription, the connection credentials for the report data source must be stored. For example, setting a data source to connect using user credentials will not work for reports running as subscriptions, as there is no interactive user at the time the subscription runs.

To begin creating a subscription, select the report you wish to subscribe to and click the New Subscription button in the report control header. Figure 74-4 shows the options available for an e-mail subscription. You can configure options for report delivery, subscription processing and scheduling, and the report parameter values. More information about each of these options is detailed in the next section, which describes how to create data-driven subscriptions, which enables these options to be set using the results from a query.

FIGURE 74-4

Create a report subscription to be delivered by e-mail by configuring these options.

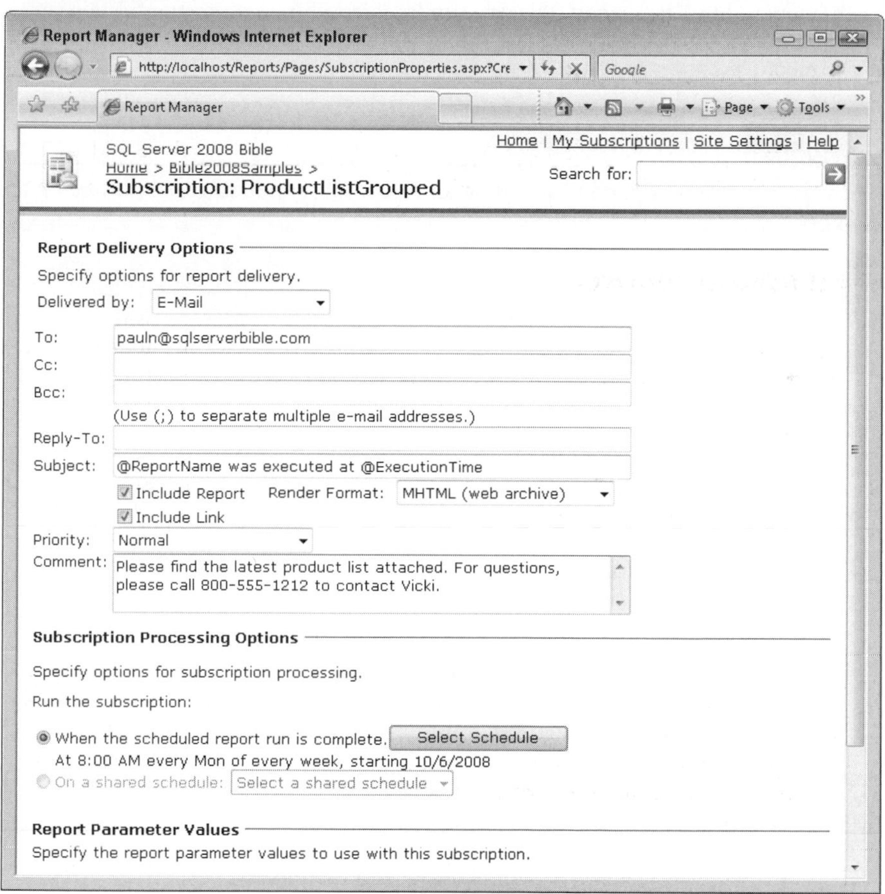

Creating a data-driven subscription

A data-driven subscription enables delivery settings and report parameters to be set dynamically using the results of a query. This is an excellent way to deliver reports and to customize the content of the reports being delivered. (Note that this feature is available only in the Enterprise Edition of SQL Server.) For example, instead of creating linked reports for each region as described earlier, a data-driven subscription could obtain the list of recipients and their corresponding region from a data source and automatically generate and deliver the reports with the content appropriate to each recipient.

To create a data-driven subscription, select the Subscriptions tab on the report you wish to deliver and click the New Data-driven Subscription button. This will guide you through the process of creating a data-driven subscription. Data-driven subscriptions can be delivered by e-mail or written to a file share. In either case, you can specify a data source containing the dynamic data for the report and write a query to return the appropriate data.

Figure 74-5 shows the options available to specify the command or query that returns data for the data-driven subscription. Just like a report, this data can be accessed from a variety of data sources, including Microsoft SQL Server, Oracle, and XML. The values returned in the command or query can be used to execute the report, as shown in Figure 74-6.

FIGURE 74-5

Use the Data-Driven Subscription feature to tailor report subscriptions to users based on another data source.

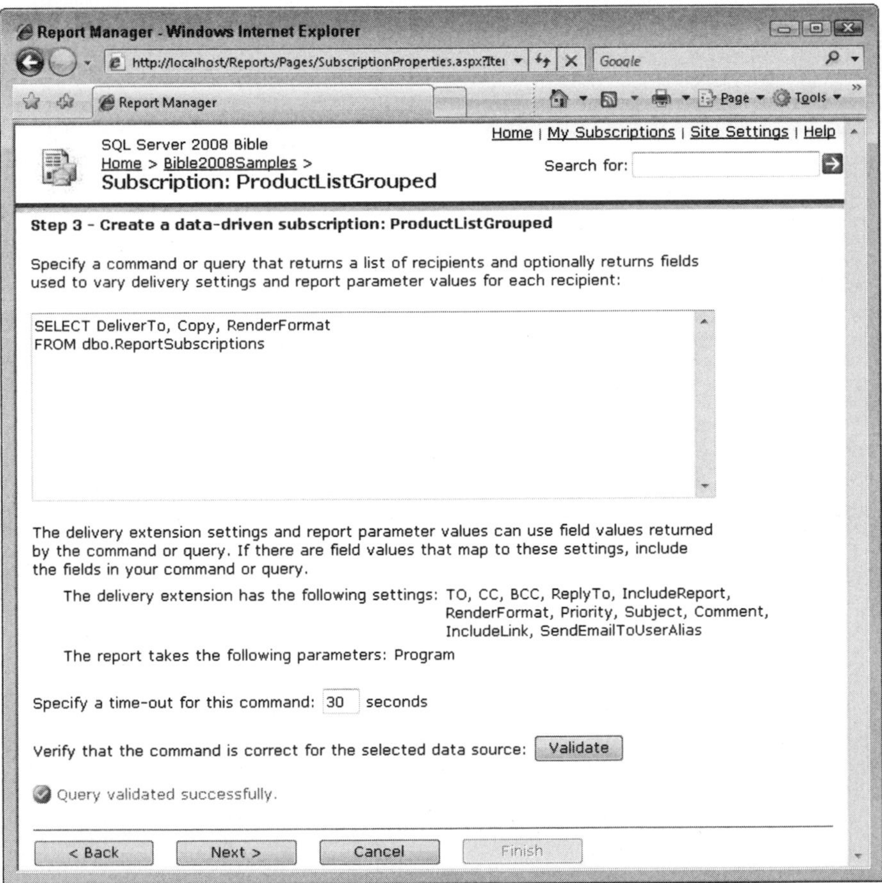

FIGURE 74-6

To control report execution, provide static values or use values from the database.

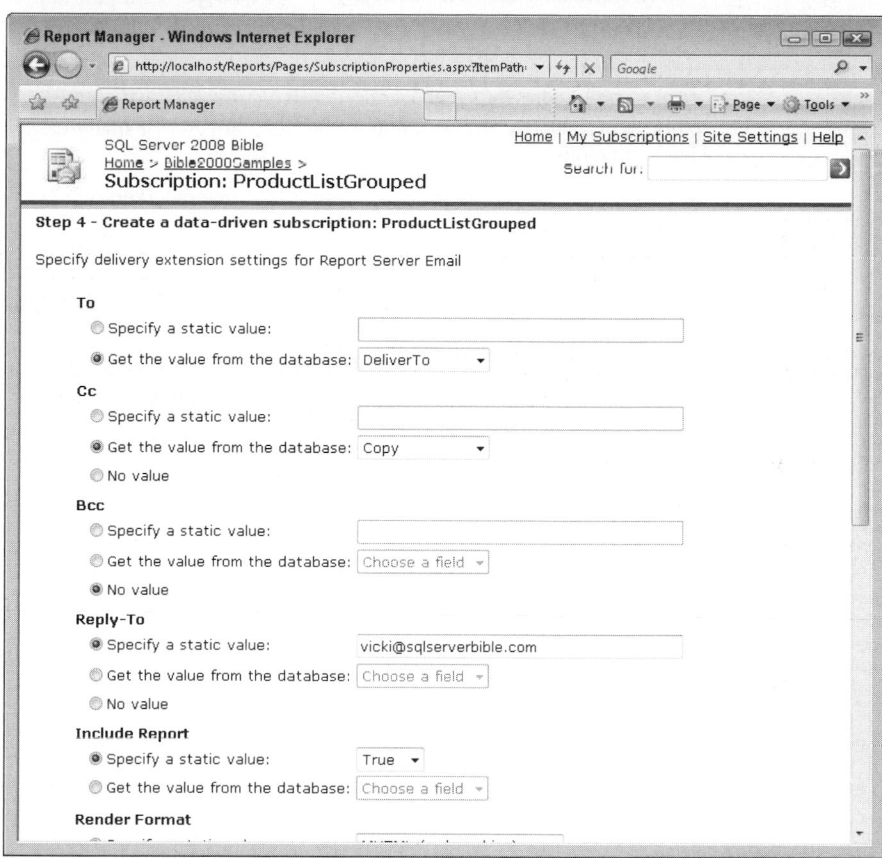

In addition to dynamically setting the delivery settings for the report, the query fields can also set values for the report parameters. This powerful feature enables you to dynamically deliver the right report with the right content to the right user. Table 74-4 contains the delivery settings available for an e-mail subscription, and Table 74-5 contains the delivery settings available for a file share subscription.

Subscriptions can generate a variety of output formats, as detailed in Table 74-6. This provides great flexibility to accommodate different usage of the output. For example, one user might prefer to receive the report as a PDF because all of the formatting of the report remains intact and the file may be easily distributed, while another user might prefer to receive the report as a comma-delimited file (CSV) so the data can be imported into another system. Both CSV and Excel formats are a good choice if the user wants the data in Excel, although Excel will attempt to retain the formatting of the report within Excel, while the CSV will simply export the raw data used in the report.

TABLE 74-4

Available E-Mail Delivery Settings

Field Name	Description	Sample Value
`TO`	List of e-mail addresses to which the report will be sent. Separate multiple addresses with semicolons. Required.	myself@xyz.com; myboss@xyz.com
`CC`	List of e-mail addresses to which the report should be copied. Separate multiple addresses with semicolons. Optional.	mycoworker@xyz.com
`BCC`	List of e-mail addresses to which the report should be blind copied. Separate multiple addresses with semicolons. Optional.	mysecretinformer@xyz.com
`ReplyTo`	The e-mail address to which replies should be sent. Optional.	reportReplies@xyz.com
`IncludeReport`	True or False value. Set to True to include the report in the e-mail message. Use `RenderFormat` to control the format.	True
`RenderFormat`	The format of the report. See Table 74-6 for the list of valid values. Required when `IncludeReport` is True.	PDF
`Priority`	Use High, Normal, or Low to set the priority of the e-mail message.	High
`Subject`	The subject of the e-mail message	Daily sales summary
`Comment`	Text to be included in the body of the e-mail message	This is the daily sales summary. Please review.
`IncludeLink`	True or False value. Set to True to include a link in the e-mail body to the report on the report server. Note that this is a link to the actual report with the parameters used to execute the report for this subscription; it is not a link to a snapshot of the report.	True

Data-driven subscriptions allow the same scheduling or trigger options as normal subscriptions. Once you create a data-driven subscription, it will appear in the list of subscriptions on the My Subscriptions page. Use this page to view information about the subscription, including trigger type, last run date and time, and the subscription's status. You can also edit the subscription from this page.

TABLE 74-5

Available File Share Delivery Settings

Field Name	Description	Sample Value
FILENAME	The name of the file to be written to the shared folder	MyReport_1
FILEEXTN	True or False value. When this is True, the file extension will be appended to the filename based on the specified render format.	True
PATH	The UNC path for the shared folder to which the file will be written	\\computer\sharedFolder
RENDER_FORMAT	The format of the report. See Table 74-6 for the list of valid values.	PDF
USERNAME	The username credential required to access the file share	myDomain\bobUser
PASSWORD	The password credential required to access the file share	Bobpasswd
WRITEMODE	Valid values include None, AutoIncrement, and OverWrite	AutoIncrement

TABLE 74-6

Available Report Formats

Value	Description
MHTML	Web archive
WORD	Microsoft Word
HTML4.0	Web page for IE 5.0 or later (.htm)
CSV	CSV (comma delimited)
EXCEL	Microsoft Excel
PDF	Acrobat (PDF) file
XML	XML file with report data
RPL	Report Page Layout — Reporting Services internal binary format
IMAGE	TIFF file

Summary

Reporting Services provides a robust set of facilities to enable administration of the report server. SQL Server Management Studio configures the basic server features and defines roles, while Report Manager configures the application of those roles to individual objects. Up-front planning of report server permissioning, including both the granularity with which permissions will be managed and the reports both shared and not shared between various users, can drive deployment strategies, especially the folder hierarchy.

Deploying reports and related objects via BIDS, Report Manager, or custom applications provide many options to meet the needs of individual environments. Consider deploying documentation and related information directly to the report server as well — users welcome such supporting information and the report server is happy to provide ad-hoc access to nearly any file type.

Linked reports provide a way to customize report execution in many ways, enabling a "develop once, deploy many times" strategy. They also can be used to simplify permission schemes. Standard subscriptions provide users with a way to be notified of reports containing the latest information or periodic updates. Data-driven subscriptions provide enterprise installations with a convenient way to manage centralized report generation and distribution.

Given a reasonably well-thought-out configuration, these features combine to provide a platform that can be an effective tool for users, developers, and administrators alike.

Chapter 75

Analyzing Data with Excel

Reporting Services provides a method to create reports that expose trends, exceptions, and other important aspects of data stored in SQL Server. Reports can be created with a level of interactivity, but even the most interactive reports limit how the end-user interacts with the data.

Using Microsoft Excel to analyze data gives users much greater flexibility and interactivity. Because Excel is in common use and most staff already know how to use at least the basic features, it also lowers the training hurdles that prospective users face. This enables a much larger audience to undertake data analysis, so they won't have to make do with canned reports.

The advantage of data analysis is the ability to discover trends and relationships that are not obvious, and to look at data in ways and combinations not normally performed. Ad-hoc analysis is also a good way to quickly prototype reports, enabling report development to happen once requirements are well understood. With the addition of data mining features to Excel 2007, options for including mining models in routine analysis can be explored as well.

This chapter focuses on the features of Microsoft Excel 2007 that use SQL Server data or features — how to retrieve data from relational and multidimensional databases, common ways of analyzing such data, and how data mining features can help you understand the data.

Organizational interest in data analysis tends to be focused among a small population, with the majority of staff satisfied with reports created by others. Interested staff tend to share the following characteristics:

- They perceive the value of data to their professional success (or feel hindered by a lack of data).
- They have mastered basic office automation skills (e.g., spreadsheet construction).
- They have a basic understanding of the data being analyzed (e.g., know the difference between a product category and a product line).

IN THIS CHAPTER

Understanding the benefits of ad-hoc data analysis

Building connections to both relational and multidimensional data

Sorting, filtering, and reviewing relational data in Excel tables

Discovering data relationships and trends using PivotTables and PivotCharts

Taking analysis to the next level using data mining add-ins

Using data mining to detect erroneous data based only on data set patterns

Forecasting time series data based on historical trends

Championing data analysis among staff likely to have these characteristics can have a positive impact on the organization, increasing the availability of data to staff while decreasing the number of reports needed.

Data Connections

A *data connection* describes how to connect to a server or other source of data, and optionally the query or table from which to retrieve data. This may seem like a mundane topic, but how a workbook's connections are defined has important implications for validity, reuse, and sharing of analyses. The Data tab of Excel's Ribbon provides several functions to create and manage connections:

- **Get External Data:** Invokes wizards and dialogs to create a new connection. Once the connection has been defined for the workbook, a connection file containing a description of the connection is created to enable that connection to be reused. While connections can be defined to a variety of data sources, this chapter focuses on getting data from SQL Server. The primary ways to define these connections are located on the From Other Sources menu, and include From SQL Server, From Analysis Services, and From Microsoft Query.
- **Existing Connections:** Lists all the connections that Excel can find, including those in the current workbook, any connection files found on the network (in a SharePoint Data Connection Library), or any connection files in the user's local My Data Sources folder. Selecting a connection file makes that connection part of the workbook and invokes dialogs to import its data.

  While the Existing Connections dialog often contains all the connections of interest, connection files located in other folders can be retrieved by pressing the Browse for More button. If the desired file is not found, it can be created by pressing the New Source button on the Browse dialog, which invokes the Data Connection Wizard, similar to choosing Get External Data, described above.
- **Connections:** Choosing Connections from the Data tab of Excel's Ribbon will display the connections currently in use by the workbook. The workbook's copy of a connection can be viewed and modified via the properties dialog, removed from the workbook with the Remove button, or new connections can be added by clicking the Add button, which invokes the Existing Connections dialog described above. In addition, the properties of all existing connections can be examined and modified.

By default, a connection is cached by each workbook in which it is used, and that cached copy is used to retrieve data until that data source becomes unavailable, at which point the corresponding data connection file is read to see if anything has changed. Alternately, setting the connection property "Always use connection file" (on the Definition tab) will reverse Excel's search order (file first, cached connection last). This alternate setting would be useful when data sources could change without the old one being eliminated — then only the connection file would require update instead of every workbook that references a connection.

Other important connection properties to consider include the following:

- **Save password:** Found on the Definition tab, this determines whether a password is saved in the connection and thus visible to others, or not saved, whereby each user is prompted for the password. This issue can be avoided by using integrated security connections.

- **Refresh options:** Found on the Usage tab, this enables external data to be refreshed either when the workbook is opened and/or on a regular interval.
- **OLAP options:** Found on the Usage tab, this determines which server formatting will appear for query results and how many rows will be displayed on drill-through operations.

Managing Connections in Microsoft Office SharePoint Server

It is generally desirable to deploy task or subject-specific data connections, rather than train staff about servers, databases, tables, and so on; but deploying data connections in an organization can be challenging as well, especially when database locations or structural changes require updates to an unknown number of workbooks stored in an unknown number of locations.

SharePoint offers a good solution for centrally storing and managing connection information via a Data Connection Library. Connections stored in such a library appear as "Connection files on the Network" for Excel users. Setting up the connection library takes a few steps:

1. Choose the site on which the connection library will be hosted, select Create from the Site Actions menu, and then choose Data Connection Library. Give it a name and click the Create button. Save the URL of the new library.
2. The new library must then be marked as trusted to work as expected. Run SharePoint Central Administration, choose the Application Management tab, and then select "Create or configure this farm's shared services" link to display a list of shared service providers. Choose the provider that hosts the services of interest (e.g., SharedServices1) to view available operations. Select "Trusted data connection libraries" to view the list of trusted libraries and add the URL of the library created above. When copying URLs from the address bar of a browser, eliminate the `/Forms/AllItems.aspx` suffix. For example, `http://home.mysite.com/Sitename/Libraryname/Forms/AllItems.aspx` becomes `http://home.mysite.com/Sitename/Libraryname` when specifying the library location.
3. Upload connection files to your new Data Connection Library either by using the library's Upload function or by exporting connections from Excel. Find the Export Connection File button on the Connection Properties dialog in Excel.

Sharing connections requires a bit of planning. Server names must make sense for the audience that is sharing the connection (e.g., referring to the "localhost" server implies a different server for each user of the connection). In addition, choose authentication methods that enable the intended audience to read the target data.

Data Connection Libraries are a good approach to sharing connection information in an organization, and a requirement if Excel Services is used.

Data Connection Wizard

Choosing to create a new connection to either SQL Server or Analysis Services will invoke the Data Connection Wizard to define the server, credentials, database, and optionally the table/cube to be queried. Specifying only a database results in a very generic connection that can be widely used by an audience that understands which database object they desire access to, but a generic connection to a relational database also prompts the Excel user to choose the appropriate database object every time the data is refreshed.

Because the Data Connection Wizard does not offer the opportunity to enter a query, it is best suited to relational scenarios in which views have been built to present large, flattened data sets appropriate for performing analyses without requiring joins to other tables or views. For other scenarios, modify the connection to include a query:

1. Create a connection that defines the appropriate server and database using the wizard.
2. Construct the T-SQL required to return the data of interest in another environment, such as SQL Server Management Studio.
3. Launch the Connections dialog from the Data tab, locate the new connection and examine its properties. On the Definition tab of the dialog, change the command type to SQL, and then paste the T-SQL into the connection.

NOTE **When the wizard creates the connection, it automatically creates an `.odc` file containing the connection details in the user's My Data Sources folder. This enables future references to the same data to be chosen from the Existing Connections list, a handy reuse that is improved by carefully naming connections.**

Anytime the properties of a connection are altered, such as described above, Excel warns that the cached and file copies of the connection will be different. They can be made identical again by using the Export Connection File function in the Connection Properties dialog.

Several types of connection files are discussed in the following sections. The wizards described previously will generate Office Data Connection (`.odc`) files, whereas the From Microsoft Query wizards will generate an Excel ODBC Query. Excel OLEDB Query (`.rqy`) and Excel OLAP Query (`.oqy`) files provide an alternative that enables the placement of queries in easily edited connection files without the baggage associated with ODBC.

Microsoft Query

Microsoft Query provides a graphical design environment for relational queries. While this is somewhat complex and relies on the deprecated ODBC technology, it can be effective for some users that have difficulty with other methods of query construction.

Create a new Microsoft Query connection by choosing From Microsoft Query on the Data tab's From Other Sources menu. The wizard walks through choosing or defining a data source, and launches the Microsoft Query applet to define the query that will return data to Excel. Once the query has been defined, simply exit the applet to return the selected data to Excel for analysis. Note the "Use the Query Wizard to create/edit queries" check box at the bottom of the first wizard dialog. Checking this box will insert into the dialog additional steps that attempt to simplify the query definition process, but many users will find these additional steps confusing.

Unlike the Data Connection Wizard, the Microsoft Query process saves only a Data Source Name (.dsn) file, which omits the query definition. Fortunately, the full connection information, including the query, can be saved to an .odc file by using the Export Connection File function in the Connection Properties dialog.

Connection file types

Excel 2007 emphasizes the use of Office Data Connection (.odc) files, which are XML documents that define the connection details. These files are easily created using Excel's wizards and tools as described above, but not easy to create or edit outside of Excel.

The Excel OLE DB Query (.rqy) file is useful to define extensions outside of Excel. Consider the following example that defines a relational query against AdventureWorksDW:

NOTE **The connection files in this section contain long lines that may not be broken onto multiple lines. Unfortunately, they appear that way in print due to space limitations. In the samples below, make sure to continue indented text on the previous line.**

```
QueryType=OLEDB
Version=1
Connection=Provider=SQLOLEDB;Server=(local);Database=AdventureWorksDW;
  Trusted_Connection=yes
CommandText=SELECT LastName, Gender, EmailAddress FROM dbo.DimCustomer
```

The connection string uses the standard format and the command text can be any valid query, although it must be listed on a single line. For queries against Analysis Services, the similar Excel OLAP Query (.oqy) file, shown next, provides a simple format to define a cube connection:

```
QueryType=OLEDB
Version=1
CommandType=Cube
Connection=Provider=MSOLAP.3;Initial Catalog=Adventure Works DW;
  Data Source=(local);Location=(local)
CommandText=Adventure Works
```

Alternately, connections using MDX queries can be defined using the format shown here:

```
QueryType=OLEDB
Version=1
CommandType=MDX
Connection=Provider=MSOLAP.3;Initial Catalog=Adventure Works DW;
  Data Source=(local);Location=(local)
CommandText=select [Measures].[Internet Order Count] on 0,
  [Date].[Calendar Year].members on 1 from [Adventure Works]
```

Basic Data Analysis

Data can be retrieved using connections into three forms within Excel. A data table provides a simple list of data, with one row in Excel for each row returned from the relational query it is based on. PivotTables and PivotCharts provide an aggregate view of the underlying data set, providing a richer environment for analysis, and may use both relational and cube queries as source data.

Data tables

Data retrieved into a table takes on all the capabilities of an Excel table:

- **Table formatting and totals:** Click inside the table, then choose a style from the Design tab, and the entire table's formatting will change to that style. The Total Row check box here enables a row at the bottom of the table for summary functions (e.g., `SUM`, `AVERAGE`, `COUNT`) that will apply to all extracted data, regardless of how many rows are returned at the next refresh.
- **Conditional formatting:** Select a column in the table, choose a format from the Conditional Formatting menu on the Home tab, and the color, data bars, or icons will overlay the table data to highlight variations in values.
- **Filter and sort:** Clicking on the column header menu enables visible rows to be filtered by picking individual values in that column, by defining conditions (e.g., greater or less than value or average, top 10, etc.), or based on conditional formatting applied to that column. Similarly the column can be sorted by either value or conditional formatting.
- **Add/Remove columns:** Insert a new column into the table and enter an Excel formula into any cell within that column to create a calculated column. Additionally, entire columns can be eliminated from the table by deleting that column without the need to change the connection definition. Similarly, you can also remove rows from the table. However, these rows will reappear the next time the table is refreshed.

The latest data from the database can be retrieved at any time by right-clicking on the table and choosing the Refresh item, or by choosing one of the Refresh options from the Data tab. None of the changes made to the Excel table will change data in the source database.

PivotTables

PivotTables and PivotCharts are powerful analysis tools that work for both relational and Analysis Services data. The way Excel interacts with the source data is fundamentally different between these two types of data, however. For relational data sources, Excel reads the entire data set from the database as soon as the PivotTable is created, storing it invisibly within the workbook in a `PivotCache` object. This enables the PivotTable to respond to changes without querying the underlying data each time, but it can make for a very large workbook when the data set is large.

By contrast, Analysis Services data sources are queried for each update to the PivotTable, keeping the workbook size down and relying on the responsiveness of Analysis Services. PivotTables created on Analysis Services data sources reflect the latest data with every change to the PivotTable, whereas relationally based PivotTables only reflect new data when explicitly refreshed (or refreshed by the connection definition).

Start a PivotTable by either choosing a connection from the Data tab or choosing PivotTable from the Insert tab. The idea of *pivoting* data is to display summaries based on categories that are placed as row and column headers. As categories are dropped onto the header areas, the table quickly reformats itself to display values grouped by all the currently selected category values, as shown in Figure 75-1.

FIGURE 75-1

Excel PivotTable based on Analysis Services cube

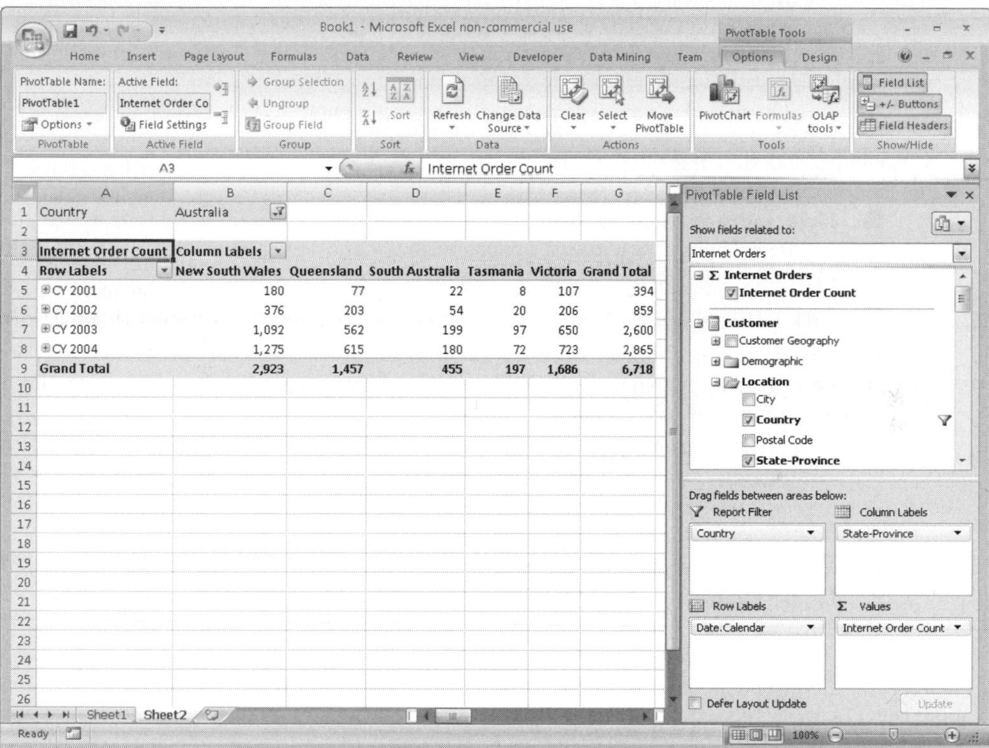

Once the PivotTable is added to a worksheet, available data fields are displayed in the PivotTable Field List, ready for dragging onto one of the four table areas:

- **Values:** The center of the table that displays data aggregates, such as the Internet Order Count shown in Figure 75-1
- **Row Labels:** Category data that provides row headers on the left side of the table (e.g., Calendar Year in Figure 75-1)
- **Column Labels:** Category data that provides column headers along the top of the table (e.g., Stage-Province in Figure 75-1)
- **Report Filter:** Provides an overall filter for the PivotTable that does not change the layout of the table (e.g., Country in Figure 75-1)

While the Field List panel is basically the same for both relational and Analysis Services data sources, the Analysis Services version includes additional information. Values (called measures in Analysis Services) are differentiated from category items by the $\sum$ symbol. In addition, the "Show fields related to" filter at the top of the panel restricts the Field List to only those items in the selected group of values (called measure groups in Analysis Services). Category items within Field List can be organized into folders by setting an item's AttributeHierarchyDisplayFolder property in Analysis Services, which cause the folders to appear next to Contacts and other category groups in Figure 75-1. Finally, Analysis Services defines hierarchies that allow drill-down paths, such as Calendar and Customer Geography in Figure 75-1, which enable details to be toggled in outline form.

Once fields have been placed in the PivotTable, field-specific settings are available. Right-click on a field in the PivotTable to access the following:

- **Field settings:** These provide control over subtotals, layout, number format, and how values are calculated. Calculation options include basic aggregation functions (`SUM`, `COUNT`, `AVERAGE`, etc.), as well as "% of," "Running total," and several other options.
- **Sort settings:** Choose to sort rows or columns based on either headers or values.
- **Filter:** Individual header values can be selected, Label filters can be defined (e.g., State-Province does not contain "Wales"), or Value filters can be defined (e.g., show only periods with more than 100 orders).
- **Properties:** Analysis Services data sources associate properties with many of the values listed in the header. Some of these values may not be available directly in the Field List. Properties may be exposed either directly as columns in the spreadsheet or as a tooltip when the cursor hovers over a header.
- **Additional Actions:** Analysis Services can associate actions, such as running reports, with header values.

Because PivotTables display summary data, it is often useful to drill into the details behind a sum or count. Double-clicking on any value will create a new worksheet with the associated detail rows. By default, Analysis Services data sources limit the rows returned by a drill-through to 1,000, but this maximum is configurable via the Connection Properties dialog.

After a bit of practice, generating a desired view in this environment is extremely time efficient, limited mostly by the speed of the underlying data source. Insights into data can be gained at a surprising rate.

PivotCharts

PivotCharts (see Figure 75-2 for an example) are bound to a PivotTable, displaying the contents of the table as it changes. The PivotTable's row headers appear as axis labels in the chart, and its column headers appear as entries in the legend. You can create a PivotChart either by choosing the PivotChart option when the PivotTable is created or by clicking inside of an existing PivotTable and inserting an Excel chart.

You can control the content of the PivotChart with either the full-featured PivotTable Field List or the simplified PivotChart Filter pane. The majority of Excel chart functions are available for a PivotChart, including creating a full-page chart by right-clicking and choosing the Move option.

FIGURE 75-2

Excel PivotChart based on Analysis Services cube

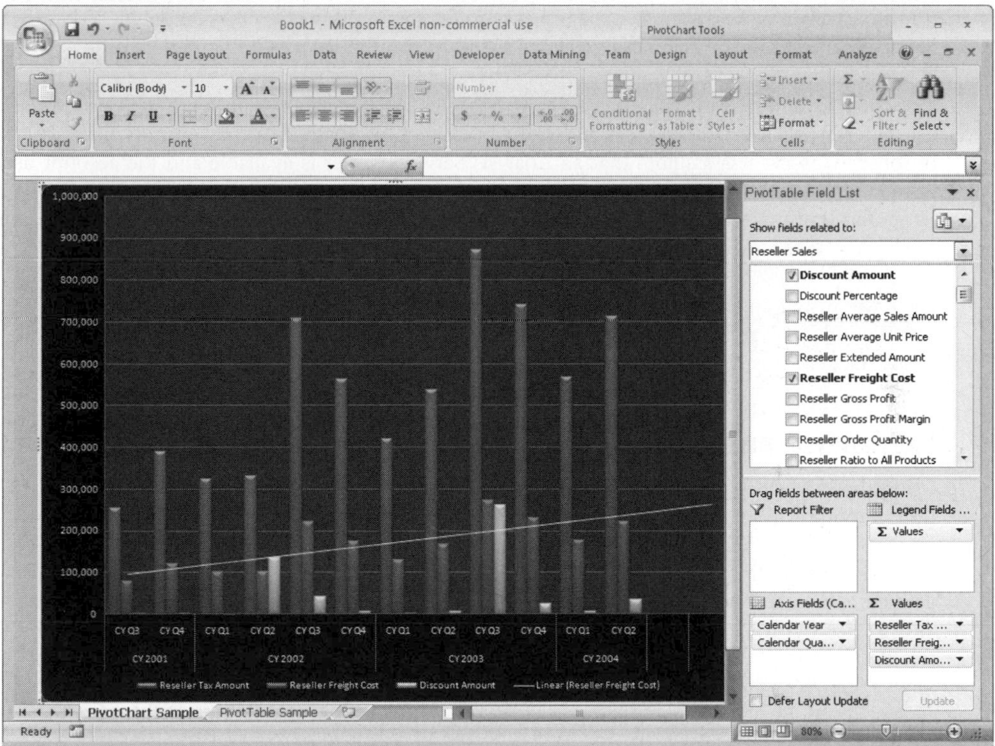

Advanced Data Analysis

The SQL Server Data Mining Add-ins for Office 2007 make a number of additional features available in Excel for analyzing data. This free download enhances Excel with features that make it easier to explore and prepare data sets, perform common analyses using data mining, and allow Excel to act as a full data mining client.

This approach of encapsulating common data mining analyses in Excel is extremely powerful, allowing a much wider audience to use data mining than would otherwise access them. Note that most of these features require an Analysis Services server to execute the associated data mining processing.

CROSS-REF **See Chapter 76, "Data Mining with Analysis Services" for more detail on how to approach data mining projects and available algorithms.**

Installing the data mining add-ins

Start by downloading and installing the add-ins. The product page for the add-ins, www.microsoft.com/sqlserver/2008/en/us/data-mining-addins.aspx, includes pointers to the download, tutorials, webcasts, and labs. Because executing the data mining algorithms requires access to an Analysis Services server, setup installs and provides a link to run the Server Configuration Utility.

The configuration wizard will set up a new Analysis Services database in which Excel mining models can be created, or it enables you to identify an existing database if one has already been created for that purpose. This process assumes that an Analysis Services server is available and the account used for installation has adequate permissions. The configuration utility will also suggest enabling the creation of temporary mining models, which is important to prevent the database becoming filled with junk objects as a result of the models Excel will create.

Once the install and configuration steps are complete, Excel's Ribbon will have two new tabs: Data Mining and Analyze (select some portion of a table to see the Analyze tab, described in "Table Analysis Tools" later in this chapter).

Exploring and preparing data

Using these advanced functions is easiest when the data set being analyzed is defined as an Excel table. Data imported from external sources is automatically defined as a table, but other data, such as that entered into Excel via a copy/paste operation, will not automatically be defined as a table. A simple way to check whether a data set has been defined as a table is to select a cell in the table, and if it has been defined as a table, the Table Tools group of tabs will appear in Excel's Ribbon. Convert a range of cells into a table by first ensuring that the top row of cells contains column headers for the table, selecting a cell in the range to be converted, and then choosing Table from the Insert tab. Excel assigns table names that may be less than intuitive. Table names can be adjusted by selecting a cell in a table, choosing the "Table Tools" Design tab, and typing over the name that appears on the left-hand side of the Ribbon.

Once the data has been organized as desired, there are three actions in the Data Preparation group of the Data Mining tab described in this section. While these functions are intended to prepare data for use by the data mining client, they can be useful for a wide variety of situations. None of these explore and prepare data functions rely on data mining algorithms, nor do they communicate with the Analysis Services server.

Explore Data

Choose Explore Data and the wizard will prompt for a table and column name, and then display a histogram of rows for each value in that column. For example, Figure 75-3(a) shows the count of rows for each value in the NumberChildrenAtHome column. For numeric data, an alternate display can be toggled via the icons at the lower left, allowing the data to be grouped into equally sized buckets of values, as shown in Figure 75-3(b). This is very useful for columns that contain a large number of values, such as dates, salaries, and so on.

Displays in numeric mode can also add a new column to the source table to denote into which bucket each row falls. The copy button will snapshot the histogram chart for pasting in any application that accepts bitmap graphics.

FIGURE 75-3

Explore Data histograms in (a) Discrete and (b) Numeric displays

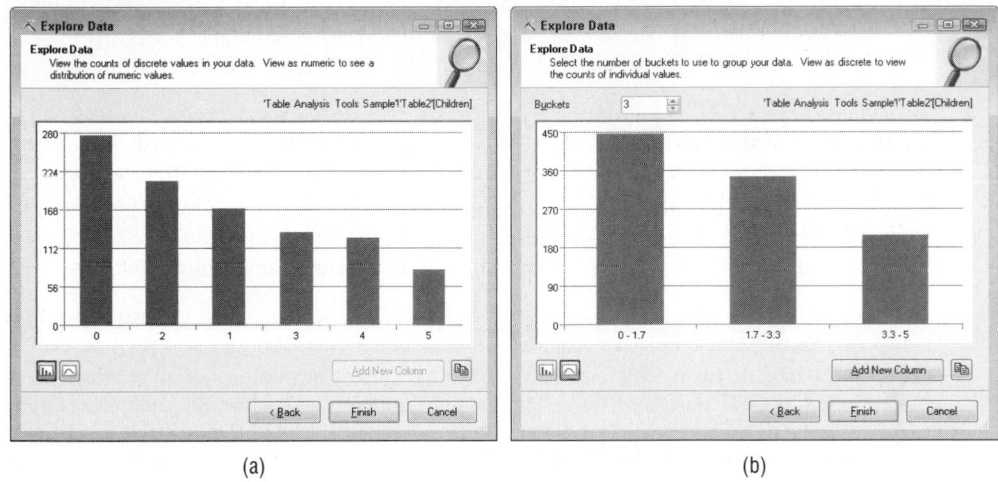

Clean Data

Choose Clean Data and two options will appear: Outliers and Re-label. Outliers is very similar to Explore Data as described above, except that when the histogram displays, sliders appear that allow the elimination of extreme data values in the table. For numeric values, this includes identifying minimum and maximum allowable values, with several handling options: replacing an outlier with limit values, replacing an outlier with a mean value, simply clearing the outlier, or totally removing the offending row. For text values, infrequently used values can be defined as outliers. This enables, for example, the top 10 occurring cities to be surfaced in an analysis, with less frequently occurring cities to be grouped under an Other category. In addition to replacing values, text values can be cleared or the associated rows removed from the table.

The Re-label variant can be thought of as a structured search and replace. After identifying the table and column of interest, the wizard presents a list of current values in that column, prompting for the new values with which they should be replaced. This function is useful for fixing data entry problems, mapping abbreviations to reporting descriptions, or even grouping data into categories.

Partition Data

Choose this function to copy rows from a source table to new tables in useful ways:

- **Split data into training and testing sets:** When building data mining models, it is necessary not only to train a model using part of the available data, but also to reserve a part of that data for testing the trained model to assess how well it will perform on data it has not yet seen. This option will split the source table into two separate tables for this purpose based on a chosen ratio, randomly selecting which rows fall into each set.
- **Random sampling:** This option extracts a random sample of the rows based on a supplied ratio or row count. While very similar in function to the Split option, it more directly

addresses the need to select a small sample from a large one, or generate multiple training sets to assess differences that training a model on different data slices present.

- **Oversampling to balance data distribution:** Data sets sometimes do not accurately represent the populations they are meant to model. Oversampling is a method to compensate for sampling bias in a data set. Indicate to the wizard the column and associated value to sample, and the resulting new data set will guarantee a representation of rows with a specified ratio.

Table analysis tools

Select a cell inside of a table and the Table Tools tabs will become available, including the Analyze tab. The functions on this tab are common data mining operations that have been made nearly single-click operations. All of these operations use Analysis Services to run the associated data mining algorithms. The server and database used can be changed by choosing Connection from the Ribbon.

Analyze Key Influencers

Data sets that include predictable outcome(s) often have many attributes, not all of which are important in determining the outcome. Select a cell in the table, choose the Analyze Key Influencers option, tell the wizard which column contains the outcome, and Excel will build a Naïve Bayes model to determine which attributes (columns) are most influential in determining the outcome. Excel will automatically add a worksheet and report on key influencers. Additional report sections can be generated to contrast influencers for selected outcomes.

The resulting report provides some initial insight into the data set being analyzed, and suggests attributes that should definitely be included when developing a predictive analysis. However, it is important to understand that these are often not the only attributes that influence the outcome. Naïve Bayes is the simplest of algorithms and will only detect very direct relationships.

Detect Categories

It is often useful to group cases (rows) in a data set into groups to better understand the population. For example, grouping customers by common traits could yield insights that lead to more targeted marketing campaigns. Tell the wizard which columns to consider in determining the categories, limit the number of categories that will be created if desired, and click Run. Excel will build a clustering model to put similar cases into distinct buckets, add the category names as a new column to the source table, and then add a worksheet that enables the exploration and naming of the associated categories.

The Categories Report page contains three sections, including notes about how to use each. The top-level summary shows how many cases fall into each category and allows the categories to be renamed. The second section shows the characteristics of the selected category — change the filter on the category column to display other categories. The third section shows how a selected column varies across all categories — change the column displayed by right-clicking on the x-axis and choosing the "Sort and Filter" menu item.

Highlight Exceptions

The wizard and algorithm for this analysis is identical to Detect Categories described above, but instead of presenting a report that enables exploration of the categories, cases that don't fall inside the categories are identified. This extends the idea of outlier detection to the next level, looking not just at the range of a single column, but at how that column's value fits with other attributes in that row. The result finds combinations that while not impossible are unlikely, such as managers with entry-level salaries. Basic outlier detection would not recognize this problem because the salary is in a valid range for the data set as a whole.

Excel builds the categories and then looks at every table row in turn, using the model to predict the likelihood of that row given the category definition. When the likelihood falls below the user-defined threshold, that row in the table is highlighted. In addition, the value in each column is evaluated for its likelihood as well, and the least likely value is highlighted. Excel automatically adds a report worksheet that summarizes the exceptions found by the least-likely column. The report also contains the threshold that determines which likelihoods are considered exceptions — adjust this value to see fewer or more exceptions.

TIP **When reviewing exceptions in a large table, it is helpful to sort by color to put all the exceptions in one place: Right-click on an exception, and select Sort ➪ Put selected cell color on top.**

Fill from Example

Excel will build a logistic regression model to detect patterns and estimate data for a column with missing data. Tell the wizard the column to be filled in and the columns to be used to detect patterns, and Excel will add a new column to the table with all the values filled. In addition, a report is added summarizing the patterns used to determine the missing values. This feature is meant to handle a variety of missing data cases, such as surveys that are missing some responses, assuming that patterns in the known attributes will be a good predictor of the missing attribute.

The model that Excel builds will always supply a value for the missing attribute even when it is not correct, so before accepting the values provided, find some way to validate the model before blindly accepting its results. For example, add some test rows (cases with known values for the attribute in question) to the table without values for the attribute in question and compare the value generated by the model to their actual values.

Forecasting

Forecasting estimates the next steps of a series given its history. For example, what will next quarter's sales be? Set up a table with all the related series in columns, with one time column. It is best to include related series, as the Time Series algorithm finds relationships between series that can help build better forecasts. For example, last year's software sales numbers may help predict this year's maintenance sales.

Indicate in the wizard the series to be predicted, which column contains time, and the number of periods to be predicted. If the data has an inherent periodicity, such as a quarterly sales cycle, supplying that information in the wizard as a hint to the algorithm may improve the forecast. Excel will extend the source table with new rows at the bottom containing predicted values. In addition, a forecasting report worksheet is added showing a graph with the existing and predicted values.

A good test for the reliability of the forecast is to copy the source worksheet, remove the last few periods, and run the forecast to predict known values. Comparing the actual and predicted values will give you an indication of the reliability of the forecast going forward.

Scenario Analysis

Scenario Analysis investigates how changes to the source data set affect the outcome. The "What-if" option enables the user to form an exact question — for example, "How many more customers would purchase a bike if their income went up 20%?" The "Goal Seek" option asks Excel to find the value at which the desired outcome occurs — for example, "How much more income would our customers need before purchasing a bike?" Excel builds a logistic regression model to estimate the impact of changes.

Upon completion of a "What-if" scenario for the entire table, new columns are added to the source table showing the new value of the outcome column and the confidence in the result. "Goal Seek" for the entire table adds columns for the new value of the outcome column and the new value for the column being adjusted.

Prediction Calculator

The Prediction Calculator functions by first using the data in an Excel table to train a *logistic regression* model to predict an outcome, and then makes the resulting model available as a calculator in Excel to evaluate individual cases without being connected to the Analysis Services server. For example, a model could be trained to predict component failure based on measurable attributes, and then made available to technicians performing preventive maintenance. Inform the wizard of what attribute and attribute value is to be predicted, and it will create up to three new sheets in the workbook:

- **Prediction Report:** Lists all the significant attribute/value combinations found in building the model and their impact on the result. In addition, if the user enters costs associated with correct and incorrect guesses into the interactive profit calculator (e.g., cost of a component failure vs. cost of replacing a component that would not have failed), a threshold will be calculated for how likely an outcome must be before it is predicted. This threshold is then used in the calculator pages.
- **Prediction Calculator (optional):** Enter the values for a case and see the predicted outcome.
- **Printable Calculator (optional):** This contains a printable form that can be used for data collection and later entry into Excel, or even manual calculation without entry into Excel.

Shopping Basket Analysis

The Shopping Basket Analysis is a quick way to build an *association rules* model based on the data in an Excel table. This model will identify groups of items that normally appear together in a transaction, allowing better product organization and/or suggestions to customers — for example, the famous "Customers who bought this book also bought . . ."

The Excel table must contain certain columns that are indicated in the wizard:

- **Transaction ID:** The Order Number, Session ID, or some other identifier that ties multiple rows together into a single transaction
- **Item:** The name or other identifier of the item purchased
- **Item Value (optional):** The price or value of the item included in that transaction. This enables the results to be sorted on the total value that a "basket" represents (average price of the basket * number of sales). As a result, a priority can be placed on suggestions that will likely yield greater revenue.

After the model has been built, two sheets are added to the workbook. The Bundled Items report details all the bundles (item combinations) found and their associated sales and price information. The Recommendations report lists recommendation rules by item, the proposed recommendation, and supporting statistics.

Data mining client

The Data Mining tab added by installing the SQL Server Data Mining Add-ins for Office 2007 provides a full data mining environment, equivalent to the data mining environment provided by Visual Studio (also known as Business Intelligence Development Studio). Unlike the table analysis tools described earlier, whereby tables and reports are created directly in Excel, the primary focus here is on creating, training, browsing, and querying data mining models in an Analysis Services database.

Working from within Excel to develop models can have advantages over the Visual Studio environment, especially when working with small amounts of data early in the process, when cleaning and exploring the data set, as the data set can be quickly changed in Excel and used to train and test models in Analysis Services. However, there are limitations to the Excel environment, such as the inability to show the accuracy of competing models in the same accuracy chart.

CROSS-REF **See Chapter 76, "Data Mining with Analysis Services," to learn more about the data mining features of Analysis Services and the functions detailed here.**

Functions exposed on the Data Mining tab include the following:

- **Data Preparation:** This is described in the section "Exploring and Preparing Data" earlier in the chapter.
- **Data Modeling:** Allows the creation of mining structures and models. Several of the most popular models are listed as separate functions, while the Advanced option provides access to all available algorithms.
- **Accuracy and Validation:** Provides different views of model performance on test data
- **Browse:** Enables the examination of model details for any model in the current database
- **Document Model:** Adds a new sheet to the current workbook listing model details
- **Query:** Provides a friendly environment for constructing and executing DMX queries against mining models
- **Manage Models:** Enables structures and models in the current database to be deleted, renamed, processed, and so on
- **Connection:** Manages connections to the Analysis Services database
- **Trace:** Provides a history of every command sent to the Analysis Services server. Use of session models for table analysis functions can also be enabled or disabled here.

Summary

Microsoft Excel has long been the most frequently used tool for analyzing data, and with the advent of the 2007 version, it is easier than ever to include relational and Analysis Services data in those analyses. Relational data can be included in data tables that remain linked to the underlying table or query for easy refresh as data changes. PivotTables and PivotCharts provide a flexible analysis environment for both relational and Analysis Services data that queries the current database contents for every update.

SQL Server Data Mining Add-ins for Office 2007 make a host of sophisticated data mining capabilities available within the familiar Excel environment. Use the Data Preparation features to explore and clean data, and the Table Analysis Tools to perform a number of common analyses with minimal effort. Excel even offers an alternative to Visual Studio as a client for data mining in Analysis Services.

Most every organization can benefit from better data availability and analysis and Excel is a great place to start.

Chapter 76

Data Mining with Analysis Services

Many business questions can be answered directly by querying a database — for example, "What is the most popular page on our website?" or "Who are our top customers?" Other, often more important, questions require deeper exploration — for example, the most popular paths through the website or common characteristics of top customers. Data mining provides the tools to answer such non-obvious questions.

The term *data mining* has suffered from a great deal of misuse. One favorite anecdote is the marketing person who intended to "mine" data in a spreadsheet by staring at it until inspiration struck. In this book, data mining is not something performed by intuition, direct query, or simple statistics. Instead, it is the algorithmic discovery of non-obvious information from large quantities of data.

Analysis Services implements algorithms to extract information addressing several categories of questions:

- **Segmentation:** Groups items with similar characteristics. For example, develop profiles of top customers or spot suspect values on a data entry page.
- **Classification:** Places items into categories. For example, determine which customers are likely to respond to a marketing campaign or which e-mails are likely to be spam.
- **Association:** Sometimes called *market basket analysis*, this determines which items tend to occur together. For example, which web pages are normally viewed together on the site, or "Customers who bought this book also bought . . ."
- **Estimation:** Estimates a value. For example, estimating revenue from a customer or the life span of a piece of equipment.
- **Forecasting:** Predicts what a time series will look like in the future. For example, when will we run out of disk space, or what revenue do we expect in the upcoming quarter?

IN THIS CHAPTER

- **Sequence analysis:** Determines what items tend to occur together in a specific order. For example, what are the most common paths through our website? Or, in what order are products normally purchased?

These categories are helpful for thinking about how data mining can be used, but with increased comfort level and experience, many other applications are possible.

The Data Mining Process

A traditional use of data mining is to train a data mining model using data for which an outcome is already known and then use that model to predict the outcome of new data as it becomes available. This use of data mining requires several steps, only some of which happen within Analysis Services:

- **Business and data understanding:** Understand the questions that are important and the data available to answer those questions. Insights gained must be relevant to business goals to be of use. Data must be of acceptable quality and relevance to obtain reliable answers.
- **Prepare data:** The effort to get data ready for mining can range from simple to painstaking depending on the situation. Some of the tasks to consider include the following:
  - Eliminate rows of low data quality. Here, the measure of quality is domain specific, but it may include too small an underlying sample size, values outside of expected norms, or failing any test that proves the row describes an impossible or highly improbable case.
  - General cleaning by scaling, formatting, and so on; and by eliminating duplicates, invalid values, or inconsistent values.
  - Analysis Services accepts a single primary *case* table, and optionally one or more child *nested* tables. If the source data is spread among several tables, then denormalization by creating views or preprocessing will be required.
  - Erratic time series data may benefit from smoothing. Smoothing algorithms remove the dramatic variations from noisy data at the cost of accuracy, so experimentation may be necessary to choose an algorithm that does not adversely impact the data mining outcome.
  - Derived attributes can be useful in the modeling process, typically either calculating a value from other attributes (e.g., Profit = Income − Cost) or simplifying the range of a complex domain (e.g., mapping numeric survey responses to High, Medium, or Low).

    Some types of preparation can be accomplished within the Analysis Services data source view using named queries and named calculations. When possible, this is highly recommended, as it avoids reprocessing data sets if changes become necessary.
  - Finally, it is necessary to split the prepared data into two data sets: A training data set that is used to set up the model, and a testing data set that is used to evaluate the model's accuracy. Testing data can be held out either in the mining structure itself or during the data preparation process. The Integration Services Row Sampling and Percentage Sampling transforms are useful to randomly split data, typically saving 20 to 30 percent of rows for testing.
- **Model:** Analysis Services models are built by first defining a data mining structure that specifies the tables to be used as input. Then, data mining models (different algorithms) are added to the structure. Finally, all the models within the structure are trained simultaneously using the training data.

- **Evaluate:** Evaluating the accuracy and usefulness of the candidate mining models is simplified by Analysis Services' Mining Accuracy Chart. Use the testing data set to understand the expected accuracy of each model and compare it to business needs.
- **Deploy:** Integrate prediction queries into applications to predict the outcomes of interest.

CROSS-REF **For a more detailed description of the data mining process, see** www.crisp-dm.org.

While this process is typical of data mining tasks, it does not cover every situation. Occasionally, exploring a data set is an end in itself, providing a better understanding of the data and its relationships. The process in this case may just iterate between prepare/model/evaluate cycles. At the other end of the spectrum, an application may build, train, and query a model to accomplish a task, such as identifying outlier rows in a data set. Regardless of the situation, understanding this typical process will aid in building appropriate adaptations.

Modeling with Analysis Services

Open an Analysis Services project within Business Intelligence Development Studio to create a data mining structure. When deployed, the Analysis Services project will create an Analysis Services database on the target server. Often, data mining structures are deployed in conjunction with related cubes in the same database.

Begin the modeling process by telling Analysis Services where the training and testing data reside:

- Define data source(s) that reference the location of data to be used in modeling.
- Create data source views that include all training tables. When nested tables are used, the data source view must show the relationship between the case and nested tables.

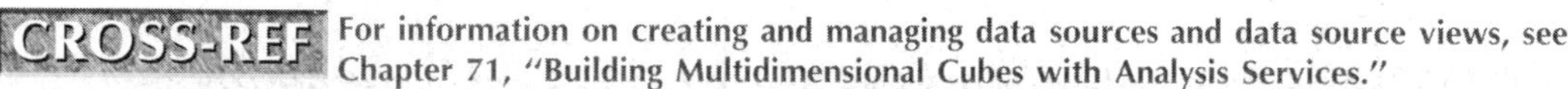

CROSS-REF **For information on creating and managing data sources and data source views, see Chapter 71, "Building Multidimensional Cubes with Analysis Services."**

Data Mining Wizard

The Data Mining Wizard steps through the process of defining a new data mining structure and optionally the first model within that structure. Right-click on the Mining Structures node within the Solution Explorer and choose New Mining Model to start the wizard. The wizard consists of several pages:

- **Select the Definition Method:** Options include relational (from existing relational database or data warehouse) or cube (from existing cube) source data. For this example, choose relational. (See the section "OLAP Integration" later in this chapter for differences between relational-based and cube-based mining structures.)
- **Create the Data Mining Structure:** Choose the algorithm to use in the structure's first mining model. (See the "Algorithms" section in this chapter for common algorithm usage). Alternately, a mining structure can be created with no models, and one or more models can be added to the structure later.
- **Select Data Source View:** Choose the data source view containing the source data table(s).
- **Specify Table Types:** Choose the case table containing the source data and any associated nested tables. Nested tables always have one-to-many relationships with the case table, such as a list of orders as the case table, and associated order line items in the nested table.

- **Specify the Training Data:** Categorize columns by their use in the mining structure. When a column is not included in any category, it is omitted from the structure. Categories are as follows:
  - **Key:** Choose the columns that uniquely identify a row in the training data. By default, the primary key shown in the data source view will be marked as the key.
  - **Input:** Mark each column that may be used in prediction — generally this includes the predictable columns as well. The Suggest button may aid in selection once the predictable columns have been identified by scoring columns by relevance based on a sample of the training data, but take care to avoid inputs with values that are unlikely to occur again as input to a trained model. For example, a customer ID, name, or address might be very effective at training a model, but once the model is built to look for a specific ID or address, it is very unlikely new customers will ever match those values. Conversely, gender and occupation values are very likely to reappear in new customer records.
  - **Predictable:** Identify all columns the model should be able to predict.
- **Specify Columns' Content and Data Type:** Review and adjust the data type (Boolean, Date, Double, Long, Text) as needed. Review and adjust the content type as well; pressing the Detect button to calculate continuous versus discrete for numeric data types may help. Available content types include the following:
  - **Key:** Contains a value that, either alone or with other keys, uniquely identifies a row in the training table.
  - **Key Sequence:** Acts as a key and provides order to the rows in a table. It is used to order rows for the sequence-clustering algorithm.
  - **Key Time:** Acts as a key and provides order to the rows in a table based on a time scale. It is used to order rows for the time series algorithm.
  - **Continuous:** Continuous numeric data — often the result of some calculation or measurement, such as age, height, or price.
  - **Discrete:** Data that can be thought of as a choice from a list, such as occupation, model, or shipping method.
  - **Discretized:** Analysis Services will transform a continuous column into a set of discrete buckets, such as ages 0–10, 11–20, and so on. In addition to choosing this option, other column properties must be set once the wizard is complete. Open the mining structure, select the column, and then set the `DiscretizationBucketCount` and `DiscretizationMethod` properties to direct how the "bucketization" will be performed.
  - **Ordered:** Defines an ordering on the training data but without assigning significance to the values used to order. For example, if values of 5 and 10 are used to order two rows, then 10 simply comes after 5; it is not "twice as good" as 5.
  - **Cyclical:** Similar to ordered data but repeats values, thus defining a cycle in the data, such as day of month or month of quarter. This enables the mining model to account for cycles in the data such as sales peaks at the end of a quarter or annually during the holidays.
- **Create Testing Set:** In SQL Server 2008, the mining structure can hold both the training and the testing data directly, instead of manually splitting the data into separate tables. Specify the percentage or number of rows to be held out for testing models in this structure if testing data is included in the source table(s).

- **Completing the Wizard:** Provide names for the overall mining structure and the first mining model within that structure. Select Allow Drill Thru to enable the direct examination of training cases from within the data mining viewers.

Once the wizard finishes, the new mining structure with a single mining model is created, and the new structure is opened in the Data Mining Designer. The initial Designer view, Mining Structure, enables columns to be added or removed from the structure, and column properties, such as `Content` (type) or `DiscretizationMethod`, to be modified.

Mining Models view

The Mining Models view of the Data Mining Designer enables different data mining algorithms to be configured on the data defined by the mining structure. Add new models as follows (see Figure 76-1):

FIGURE 76-1

Adding a new model to an existing structure

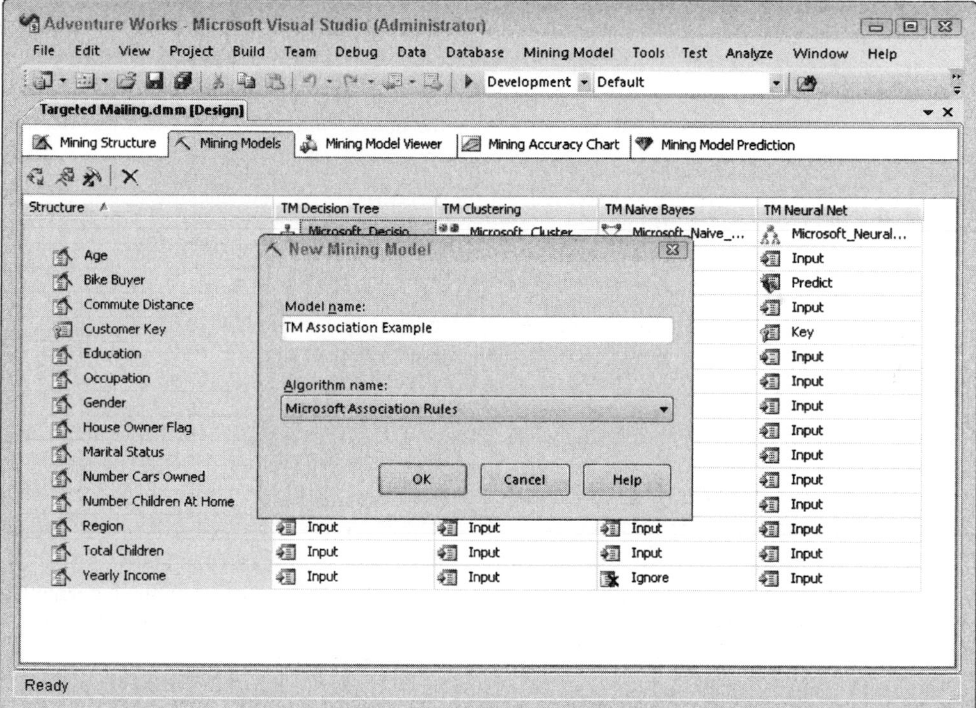

1. Right-click the structure/model matrix pane and choose New Mining Model.
2. Supply a name for the model.
3. Select the desired algorithm and click OK.

Depending on the structure definition, not all algorithms will be available — for example, the Sequence Clustering algorithm requires that a Key Sequence column be defined, while the Time Series algorithm requires a Key Time column to be defined. In addition, not every algorithm will use each column in the same way — for example, some algorithms ignore continuous input columns (consider using discretization on these columns).

SQL Server 2008 allows filters to be placed on models, which can be useful when training models specific to a subset of the source data. For example, targeting different customer groups can be performed by training filtered models in a single mining structure. Right-click on a model and choose Set Model Filter to apply a filter to a model. Once set, the current filter is viewable in the model's properties.

In addition to the optional model filter, each mining model has both properties and algorithm parameters. Select a model (column) to view and change the properties common to all algorithms in the Properties pane, including Name, Description, and AllowDrillThrough. Right-click on a model and choose Set Algorithm Parameters to change an algorithm's default settings.

Once both the structure and model definitions are in place, the structure must be deployed to the target server to process and train the models. The process of deploying a model consists of two parts:

1. During the build phase, the structure definition (or changes to the definition as appropriate) is sent to the target Analysis Services Server. Examine the progress of the build in the output pane.
2. During the process phase, the Analysis Services server queries the source data, caches that data in the mining structure, and trains the models with all the data that has not been either filtered out or held out for testing.

Before the first time a project is deployed, set the target server by right-clicking on the project in the Solution Explorer pane containing the mining structure and choose Properties. Then, select the Deployment topic and enter the appropriate server name, adjusting the target database name at the same time (deploying creates an Analysis Services database named, by default, after the project).

Deploy the structure by choosing either Process Model or Process Mining Structure and All Models from the context menu. The same options are available from the Mining Model menu as well. After processing, the Mining Model Viewer tab contains processing results; here, one or more viewers are available depending on which models are included in the structure. The algorithm-specific viewers assist in understanding the rules and relationships discovered by the models (see the "Algorithms" section later in this chapter).

Model evaluation

Evaluate the trained models to determine which model predicts the outcome most reliably, and to decide whether the accuracy will be adequate to meet business goals. The Mining Accuracy Chart view provides tools for performing the evaluation.

The charts visible within this view are enabled by supplying data for testing under the Input Selection tab. Choose one of three sources:

- **Use mining model test cases:** Uses test data held out in the mining structure but applies any model filters in selecting data for each model
- **Use mining structure test cases:** Uses test data held out in the mining structure, ignoring any model filters

- **Specify a different data set:** Allows the selection and mapping of an external table to supply test data. After selecting this option, press the ellipses to display the Specify Column Mapping dialog. Then, press the Select Case Table button on the right-hand table and choose the table containing the test data. The joins between the selected table and the mining structure will map automatically for matching column names, or they can be manually mapped by drag-and-drop when a match is not found. Verify that each non-key column in the mining structure participates in a join.

If the value being predicted is discrete, then the Input Selection tab also allows choosing a particular outcome for evaluation. If a Predict Value is not selected, then accuracy for all outcomes is evaluated.

Lift charts and scatter plots

Once the source data and any Predict Value have been specified, switch to the Lift Chart tab, and verify that Lift Chart (Scatter Plot for continuous outcomes) is selected from the Chart Type list box (see Figure 76-2). Because the source data contains the predicted column(s), the lift chart can compare each model's prediction against the actual outcome. The lift chart plots this information on the Target Population % (percent of cases correct) versus Overall Population % (percent of cases tested) axes, so when 50 percent of the population has been checked, the perfect model will have predicted 50 percent correctly. In fact, the chart automatically includes two useful reference lines: the Ideal Model, which indicates the best possible performance, and the Random Guess, which indicates how often randomly assigned outcomes happen to be correct.

The profit chart extends the lift chart and aids in calculating the maximum return from marketing campaigns and similar efforts. Press the Settings button to specify the number of prospects, the fixed and per-case cost, and the expected return from a successfully identified case; then choose Profit Chart from the Chart Type list box. The resulting chart indicates profit versus population percent included, offering a guide as to how much of the population should be included in the effort either by maximizing profit or by locating a point of diminishing returns.

Classification matrix

The simplest view of model accuracy is offered by the Classification Matrix tab, which creates one table for each model, with predicted outcomes listed down the left side of the table and actual values across the top, similar to the example shown in Table 76-1. This example shows that for red cases, this model correctly predicted red for 95 and incorrectly predicted blue for 37. Likewise, for cases that were actually blue, the model correctly predicted blue 104 times while incorrectly predicting red 21 times.

TABLE 76-1

Example Classification Matrix

Predicted	Red (Actual)	Blue (Actual)
Red	95	21
Blue	37	104

The classification matrix is not available for predicting continuous outcomes.

FIGURE 76-2

Lift Chart tab

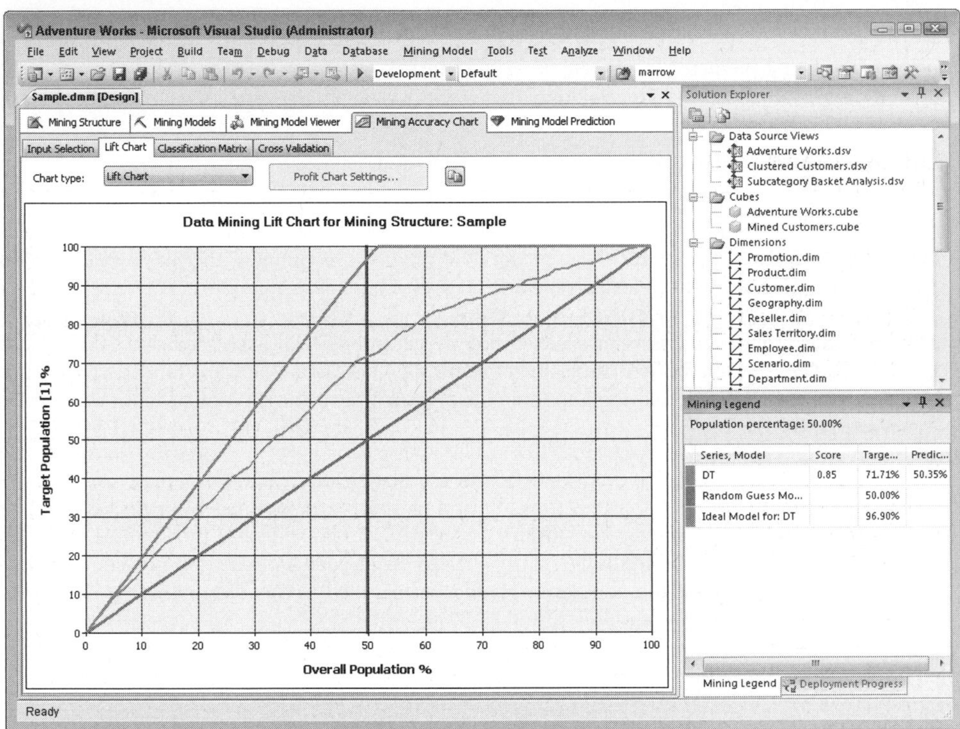

Cross validation

Cross validation is a very effective technique for evaluating a model for stability and how well it will generalize for unseen cases. The concept is to partition available data into some number of equal sized buckets called *folds*, and then train the model on all but one of those folds and test with the remaining fold, repeating until each of the folds has been used for testing. For example, if three folds were selected, the model would be trained on 2 and 3 and tested with 1, then trained on 1 and 3 and tested on 2, and finally trained on 1 and 2 and tested on 3.

Switch to the Cross Validation tab and specify the parameters for the evaluation:

- **Fold Count:** The number of partitions into which the data will be placed.
- **Max Cases:** The number of cases from which the folds will be constructed. For example, 1,000 cases and 10 folds will result in approximately 100 cases per fold. Because of the large amount of processing required to perform cross validation, it is often useful to limit the number of cases. Setting this value to 0 results in all cases being used.

- **Target Attribute and State:** The prediction to validate.
- **Target Threshold:** Sets the minimum probability required before assuming a positive result. For example, if you were identifying customers for an expensive marketing promotion, a minimum threshold of 80 percent likely to purchase could be set to target only the best prospects. Knowing that this threshold will be used enables a more realistic evaluation of the model.

Once the cross-validation has run, a report like the one shown in Figure 76-3 displays the outcome for each fold across a number of different measures. In addition to how well a model performs in each line item, the standard deviation of the results of each measure should be relatively small. If the variation is large between folds, then it is an indication that the model will not generalize well in practical use.

FIGURE 76-3

Cross Validation tab

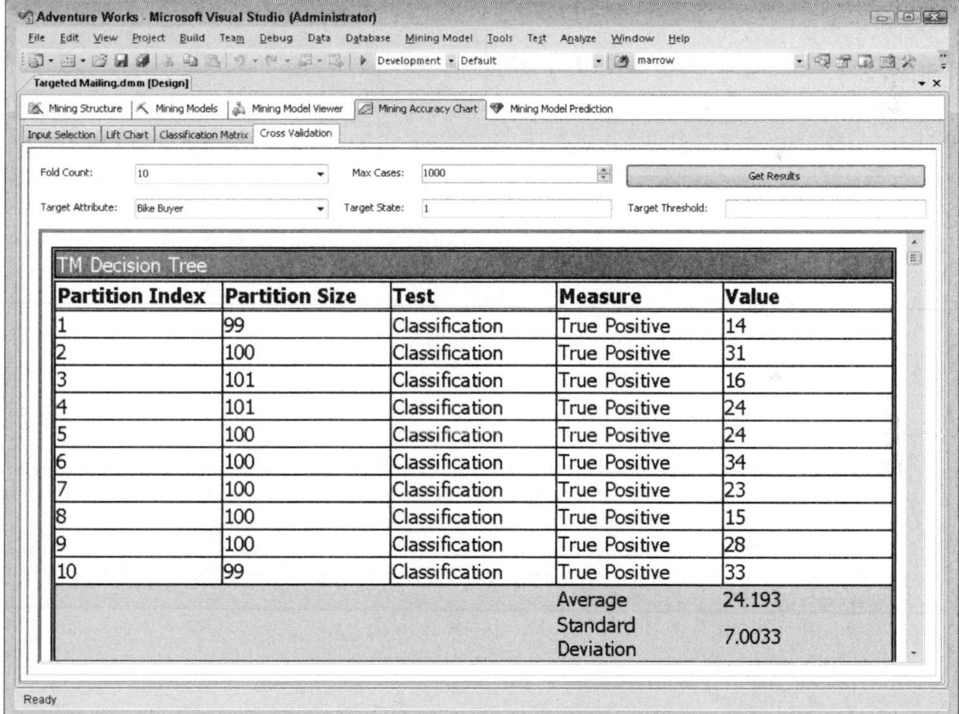

Partition Index	Partition Size	Test	Measure	Value
1	99	Classification	True Positive	14
2	100	Classification	True Positive	31
3	101	Classification	True Positive	16
4	101	Classification	True Positive	24
5	100	Classification	True Positive	24
6	100	Classification	True Positive	34
7	100	Classification	True Positive	23
8	100	Classification	True Positive	15
9	100	Classification	True Positive	28
10	99	Classification	True Positive	33
			Average	24.193
			Standard Deviation	7.0033

Troubleshooting models

Models seldom approach perfection in the real world. If these evaluation techniques show a model falling short of your needs, then consider these common problems:

- A non-random split of data into training and test data sets. If the split method used was based on a random algorithm, rerun the random algorithm to obtain a more random result.

- Input columns are too case specific (e.g., IDs, names, etc.). Adjust the mining structure to ignore data items containing values that occur in the training data but then never reappear for test or production data.
- Too few rows (cases) in the training data set to accurately characterize the population of cases. Look for additional sources of data for best results. If additional data is not available, then better results may be obtained by limiting the special cases considered by an algorithm (e.g., increasing the `MINIMUM_SUPPORT` parameter).
- If all models are closer to the Random Guess line than the Ideal Model line, then the input data does not correlate with the outcome being predicted.

Note that some algorithms, such as `Time_Series`, do not support the Mining Accuracy Chart view at all. Regardless of the tools available within the development environment, it is important to perform an evaluation of the trained model using test data held in reserve for that purpose. Then, modify the data and model definitions until the results meet the business goals at hand.

Deploying

Several methods are available for interfacing applications with data mining functionality:

- Directly constructing XMLA, communicating with Analysis Services via SOAP. This exposes all functionality at the price of in-depth programming.
- Analysis Management Objects (AMO) provides an environment for creating and managing mining structures and other meta-data, but not for prediction queries.
- The Data Mining Extensions (DMX) language supports most model creation and training tasks and has a robust prediction query capability. DMX can be sent to Analysis Services via the following:
  - ADOMD.NET for managed (.NET) languages
  - OLE DB for C++ code
  - ADO for other languages

DMX is a SQL-like language modified to accommodate mining structures and tasks. For purposes of performing prediction queries against a trained model, the primary language feature is the prediction join. As the following code example shows, the prediction join relates a mining model and a set of data to be predicted (cases). Because the DMX query is issued against the Analysis Services database, the model `[TM Decision Tree]` can be directly referenced, while the cases must be gathered via an `OPENQUERY` call against the relational database. The corresponding columns are matched in the `ON` clause like a standard relational join, and the `WHERE` and `ORDER BY` clauses function as expected.

DMX also adds a number of mining-specific functions such as the `Predict` and `PredictProbability` functions shown here, which return the most likely outcome and the probability of that outcome, respectively. Overall, this example returns a list of IDs, names, and probabilities for prospects who are more than 60 percent likely to purchase a bike, sorted by descending probability:

```
SELECT t.ProspectAlternateKey,t.FirstName, t.LastName,
  PredictProbability([TM Decision Tree].[Bike Buyer]) as Prob
FROM [TM Decision Tree]
PREDICTION JOIN
  OPENQUERY([Adventure Works DW],
```

```
    'SELECT
      ProspectAlternateKey, FirstName, LastName, MaritalStatus,
      Gender, YearlyIncome, TotalChildren, NumberChildrenAtHome,
      Education, Occupation, HouseOwnerFlag, NumberCarsOwned, StateProvince-
Code
    FROM dbo.ProspectiveBuyer;') AS t
ON
  [TM Decision Tree].[Marital Status] = t.MaritalStatus AND
  [TM Decision Tree].Gender = t.Gender AND
  [TM Decision Tree].[Yearly Income] = t.YearlyIncome AND
  [TM Decision Tree].[Total Children] = t.TotalChildren AND
  [TM Decision Tree].[Number Children At Home] = t.NumberChildrenAtHome AND
  [TM Decision Tree].Education = t.Education AND
  [TM Decision Tree].Occupation = t.Occupation AND
  [TM Decision Tree].[House Owner Flag] = t.HouseOwnerFlag AND
  [TM Decision Tree].[Number Cars Owned] = t.NumberCarsOwned AND
  [TM Decision Tree].Region = t.StateProvinceCode
WHERE PredictProbability([TM Decision Tree].[Bike Buyer]) > 0.60
AND   Predict([TM Decision Tree].[Bike Buyer])=1
ORDER BY PredictProbability([TM Decision Tree].[Bike Buyer]) DESC
```

Another useful form of the prediction join is a singleton query, whereby data is provided directly by the application instead of read from a relational table, as shown in the next example. Because the names exactly match those of the mining model, a `NATURAL PREDICTION JOIN` is used, not requiring an `ON` clause. This example returns the probability that the listed case will purchase a bike (i.e., `[Bike Buyer]=1`):

```
SELECT
  PredictProbability([TM Decision Tree].[Bike Buyer],1)
FROM [TM Decision Tree]
NATURAL PREDICTION JOIN
(SELECT 47 AS [Age], '2-5 Miles' AS [Commute Distance],
  'Graduate Degree' AS [Education], 'M' AS [Gender],
  '1' AS [House Owner Flag], 'M' AS [Marital Status],
  2 AS [Number Cars Owned], 0 AS [Number Children At Home],
  'Professional' AS [Occupation], 'North America' AS [Region],
  0 AS [Total Children], 80000 AS [Yearly Income]) AS t
```

Business Intelligence Development Studio aids in the construction of DMX queries via the Query Builder within the mining model prediction view. Just like the Mining Accuracy Chart, select the model and case table to be queried, or alternately press the singleton button in the toolbar to specify values. Specify `SELECT` columns and prediction functions in the grid at the bottom. SQL Server Management Studio also offers a DMX query type with meta-data panes for drag-and-drop access to mining structure column names and prediction functions.

Numerous prediction functions are available, including the following:

- **Predict:** Returns the expected outcome for a predictable column
- **PredictProbability:** Returns the probability (between 0 and 1) of the expected outcome, or for a specific case if specified

- **PredictSupport:** Returns the number of training cases on which the expected outcome is based, or on which a specific case is based if specified
- **PredictHistogram:** Returns a nested table with all possible outcomes for a given case, listing probability, support, and other information for each outcome
- **Cluster:** Returns the cluster to which a case is assigned (clustering algorithm specific)
- **ClusterProbability:** Returns the probability the case belongs to a given cluster (clustering algorithm specific).
- **PredictSequence:** Predicts the next values in a sequence (sequence clustering algorithm specific)
- **PredictAssociation:** Predicts associative membership (association algorithm specific)
- **PredictTimeSeries:** Predicts future values in a time series (time series algorithm specific). Like PredictHistogram, this function returns a nested table.

Algorithms

When working with data mining, it is useful to understand mining algorithm basics and when to apply each algorithm. Table 76-2 summarizes common algorithm usage for the problem categories presented at the beginning of this chapter.

TABLE 76-2

Common Mining Algorithm Usage

Problem Type	Primary Algorithms
Segmentation	Clustering, Sequence Clustering
Classification	Decision Trees, Naive Bayes, Neural Network, Logistic Regression
Association	Association Rules, Decision Trees
Estimation	Decision Trees, Linear Regression, Logistic Regression, Neural Network
Forecasting	Time Series
Sequence Analysis	Sequence Clustering

These usage guidelines are useful as an orientation, but not every data mining problem falls neatly into one of these types, and other algorithms will work for several of these problem types. Fortunately, with evaluation tools such as the lift chart, it's usually simple to identify which algorithm provides the best results for a given problem.

Decision tree

This algorithm is the most accurate for many problems. It operates by building a decision tree beginning with the All node, corresponding to all the training cases (see Figure 76-4). Then, an attribute is chosen that best splits those cases into groups, and each of those groups is examined for an attribute that best splits those cases, and so on. The goal is to generate leaf nodes with a single predictable outcome. For example, if the goal is to identify who will purchase a bike, then leaf nodes should contain cases that are either bike buyers or not bike buyers, but no combinations (or as close to that goal as possible).

FIGURE 76-4

Decision Tree Viewer

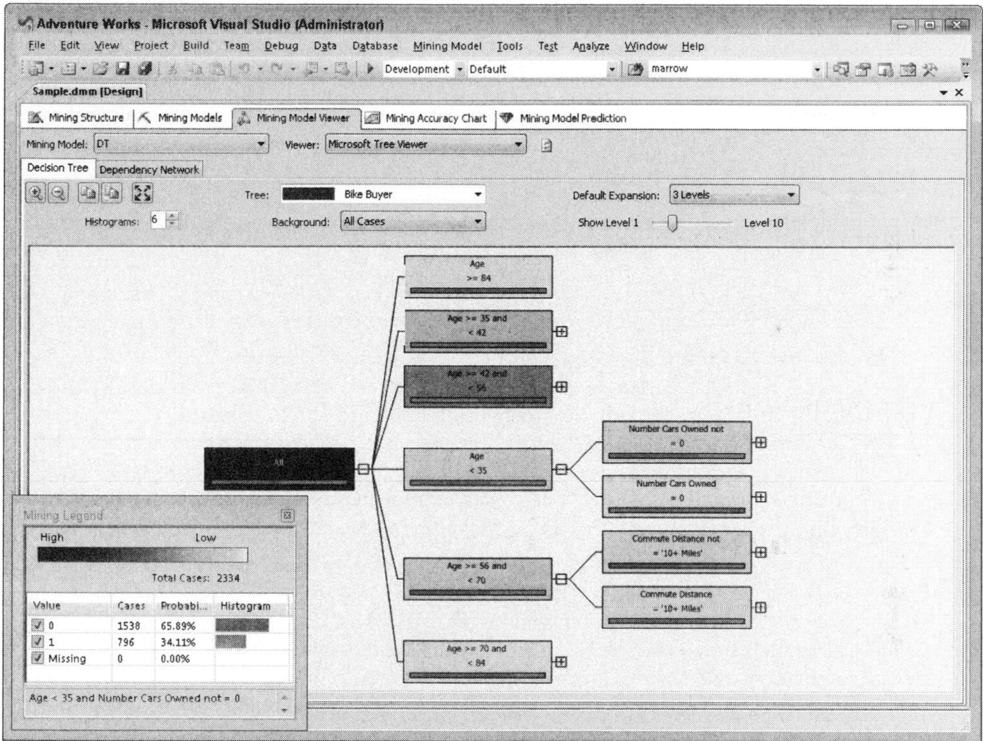

The Decision Tree Viewer shown in Figure 76-4 graphically displays the resulting tree. Age is the first attribute chosen in this example, splitting cases into groups such as under 35, 35 to 42, and so on. For the under-35 crowd, Number Cars Owned was chosen to further split the cases, while Commute Distance was chosen for the 56 to 70 cases. The Mining Legend pane displays the details of any selected node, including how the cases break out by the predictable variable (in this case, 796 buyers and 1,538 non-buyers) both in count and probability. Many more node levels can be expanded using the Show Level control in the toolbar or the expansion controls (+/-) on each node. Note that much of the tree is not expanded in this figure due to space restrictions.

The Dependency Network Viewer is also available for decision trees, displaying both input and predictable columns as nodes, with arrows indicating what predicts what. Move the slider to the bottom to see only the most significant predictions. Click on a node to highlight its relationships.

Linear regression

The *linear regression algorithm* is implemented as a variant of decision trees and is a good choice for continuous data that relates more or less linearly. The result of the regression is an equation in the form

$$Y = B_0 + A_1{}^*(X_1 + B_1) + A_2{}^*(X_2 + B_2) + \ldots$$

where Y is the column being predicted, X_i is the input columns, and A_i/B_i are constants determined by the regression. Because this algorithm is a special case of decision trees, it shares the same mining viewers. While, by definition, the Tree Viewer will show a single All node, the Mining Legend pane displays the prediction equation. The equation can be either used directly or queried in the mining model via the Predict function. The Dependency Network Viewer provides a graphical interpretation of the weights used in the equation.

Clustering

The *clustering algorithm* functions by gathering similar cases together into groups called *clusters* and then iteratively refining the cluster definition until no further improvement can be gained. This approach makes clustering uniquely suited for segmentation/profiling of populations. Several viewers display data from the finished model:

- **Cluster Diagram:** This viewer displays each cluster as a shaded node with connecting lines between similar clusters — the darker the line, the more similar the cluster. Move the slider to the bottom to see only lines connecting the most similar clusters. Nodes are shaded darker to represent more cases. By default, the cases are counted from the entire population, but changing the Shading Variable and State pull-downs specifies shading to be based on particular variable values (e.g., which clusters contain homeowners).
- **Cluster Profiles:** Unlike node shading in the Cluster Diagram Viewer, where one variable value can be examined at a time, the Cluster Profiles Viewer shows all variables and clusters in a single matrix. Each cell of the matrix is a graphical representation of that variable's distribution in the given cluster (see Figure 76-5). Discrete variables are shown as stacked bars describing how many cases contain each of the possible variable values. Continuous variables are shown as diamond charts, with each diamond centered on the mean (average) value for cases in that cluster, while the top and bottom of the diamond are the mean +/− the standard deviation, respectively. Thus, the taller the diamond, the less uniform the variable values in that cluster. Click on a cell (chart) to see the full distribution for a cluster/variable combination in the Mining Legend, or hover over a cell for the same information in a tooltip. In Figure 76-5, the tooltip displayed shows the full population's occupation distribution, while the Mining Legend shows Cluster 3's total children distribution.
- **Cluster Characteristics:** This view displays the list of characteristics that make up a cluster and the probability that each characteristic will appear.
- **Cluster Discrimination:** Similar to the Characteristics Viewer, this shows which characteristics favor one cluster versus another. It also enables the comparison of a cluster to its own complement, clearly showing what is and is not in a given cluster.

Once you gain a better understanding of the clusters for a given model, it is often useful to rename each cluster to something more descriptive than the default "Cluster *n*." From within either the Diagram or Profiles Viewer, right-click on a cluster and choose Rename Cluster to give it a new name.

FIGURE 76-5

Cluster Profiles Viewer

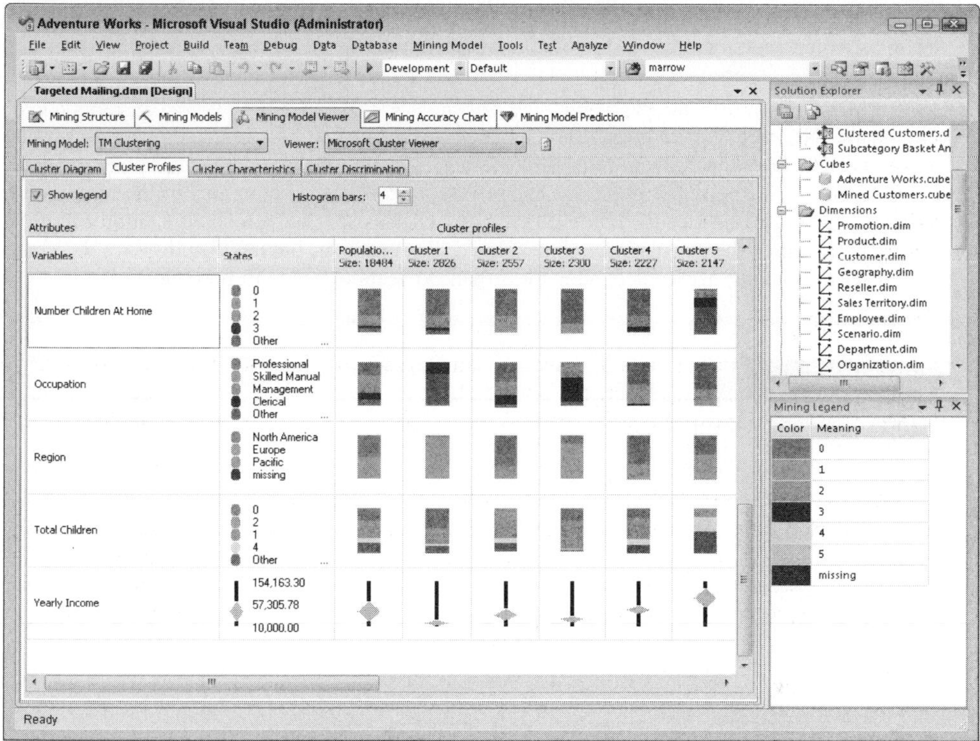

Sequence clustering

As the name implies, this algorithm still gathers cases together into clusters, but based on a sequence of events or items, rather than on case attributes. For example, the sequence of web pages visited during user sessions can be used to define the most common paths through that website.

The nature of this algorithm requires input data with a nested table, whereby the parent row is the session or order (e.g., shopping cart ID) and the nested table contains the sequence of events during that session (e.g., order line items). In addition, the nested table's key column must be marked as a Key Sequence content type in the mining structure.

Once the model is trained, the same four cluster viewers described above are available to describe the characteristics of each. In addition, the State Transition Viewer displays transitions between two items (e.g., a pair of web pages), with its associated probability of that transition happening. Move the slider to the bottom to see only the most likely transitions. Select a node to highlight the possible transitions from that item to its possible successors. The short arrows that don't connect to a second node denote a state that can be its own successor.

Neural Network

This famous algorithm is generally slower than other alternatives, but often handles more complex situations. The network is built using input, hidden (middle), and output layers of neurons whereby the output of each layer becomes the input of the next layer. Each neuron accepts inputs that are combined using weighted functions that determine the output. Training the network consists of determining the weights for each neuron.

The Neural Network Viewer presents a list of characteristics (variable/value combinations) and how those characteristics favor given outputs (outcomes). Choose the two outcomes being compared in the Output area at the upper right (see Figure 76-6). Leaving the Input area in the upper left blank compares characteristics for the entire population, whereas specifying a combination of input values allows a portion of the population to be explored. For example, Figure 76-6 displays the characteristics that affect the buying decisions of adults less than 36 years of age with no children.

FIGURE 76-6

Neural Network Viewer

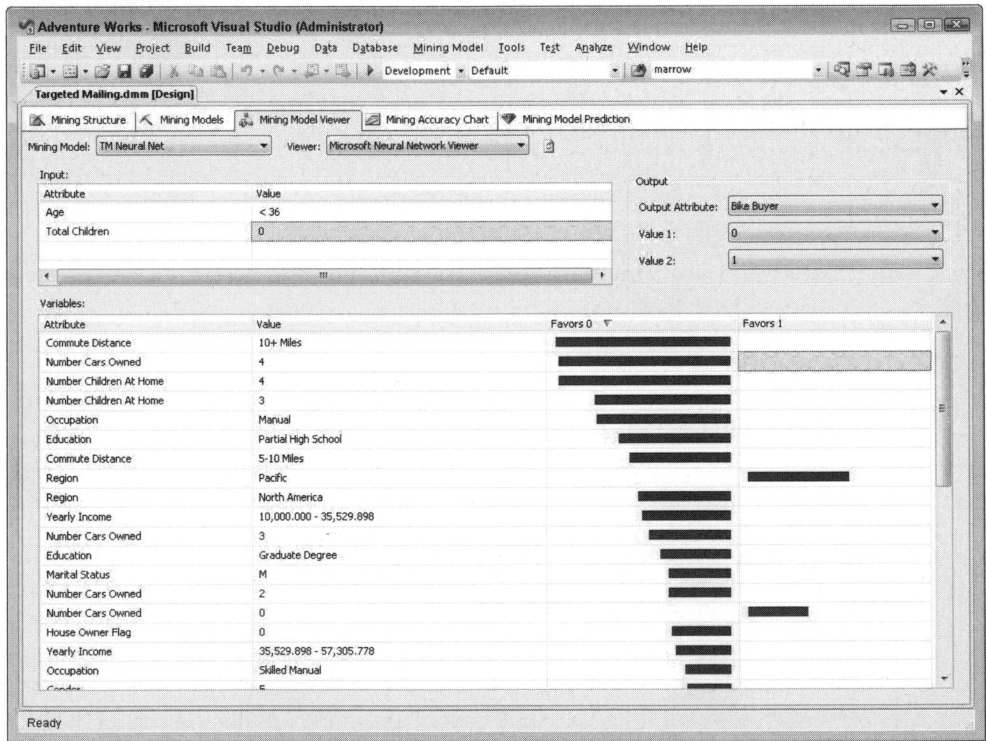

Logistic regression

Logistic regression is a special case of the neural network algorithm whereby no hidden layer of neurons is built. While logistic regression can be used for many tasks, it is specially suited for estimation problems for which linear regression would be a good fit. However, because the predicted value is discrete, the linear approach tends to predict values outside the allowed range — for example, predicting probabilities over 100 percent for a certain combination of inputs.

Because it is derived from the neural network algorithm, logistic regression shares the same viewer.

Naive Bayes

Naive Bayes is a very fast algorithm with accuracy that is adequate for many applications. It does not, however, operate on continuous variables. The Naive portion of its name derives from this algorithm's assumption that every input is independent. For example, the probability of a married person purchasing a bike is computed from how often married and bike buyer appear together in the training data without considering any other columns. The probability of a new case is just the normalized product of the individual probabilities.

Several viewers display data from the finished model:

- **Dependency Network:** Displays both input and predictable columns as nodes with arrows indicating what predicts what; a simple example is shown in Figure 76-7. Move the slider to the bottom to see only the most significant predictions. Click on a node to highlight its relationships.
- **Attribute Profiles:** Similar in function to the Cluster Profiles Viewer, this shows all variables and predictable outcomes in a single matrix. Each cell of the matrix is a graphical representation of that variable's distribution for a given outcome. Click on a cell (chart) to see the full distribution for that outcome/variable combination in the Mining Legend, or hover over a cell for the same information in a tooltip.
- **Attribute Characteristics:** This viewer displays the list of characteristics associated with the selected outcome.
- **Attribute Discrimination:** This viewer is similar to the Characteristics Viewer, but it shows which characteristics favor one outcome versus another.

Association rules

This algorithm operates by finding attributes that appear together in cases with sufficient frequency to be significant. These attribute groupings are called *itemsets*, which are in turn used to build the rules used to generate predictions. While Association Rules can be used for many tasks, it is specially suited to market basket analysis. Generally, data will be prepared for market basket analysis using a nested table, whereby the parent row is a transaction (e.g., Order) and the nested table contains the individual items. Three viewers provide insight into a trained model:

- **Rules:** Similar in layout and controls to itemsets, but lists rules instead of itemsets. Each rule has the form A, B ≥ C, meaning that cases that contain A and B are likely to contain C (e.g., people who bought pasta and sauce also bought cheese). Each rule is listed with its probability (likelihood of occurrence) and importance (usefulness in performing predictions).

- **Itemsets:** Displays the list of itemsets discovered in the training data, each with its associated size (number of items in the set) and support (number of training cases in which this set appears). Several controls for filtering the list are provided, including the Filter Itemset text box, which searches for any string entered (e.g., "Region = Europe" will display only itemsets that include that string).
- **Dependency Network:** Similar to the Dependency Network used for other algorithms, with nodes representing items in the market basket analysis. Note that nodes have a tendency to predict each other (dual-headed arrows). The slider will hide the less probable (not the less important) associations. Select a node to highlight its related nodes.

FIGURE 76-7

Naive Bayes Dependency Network Viewer

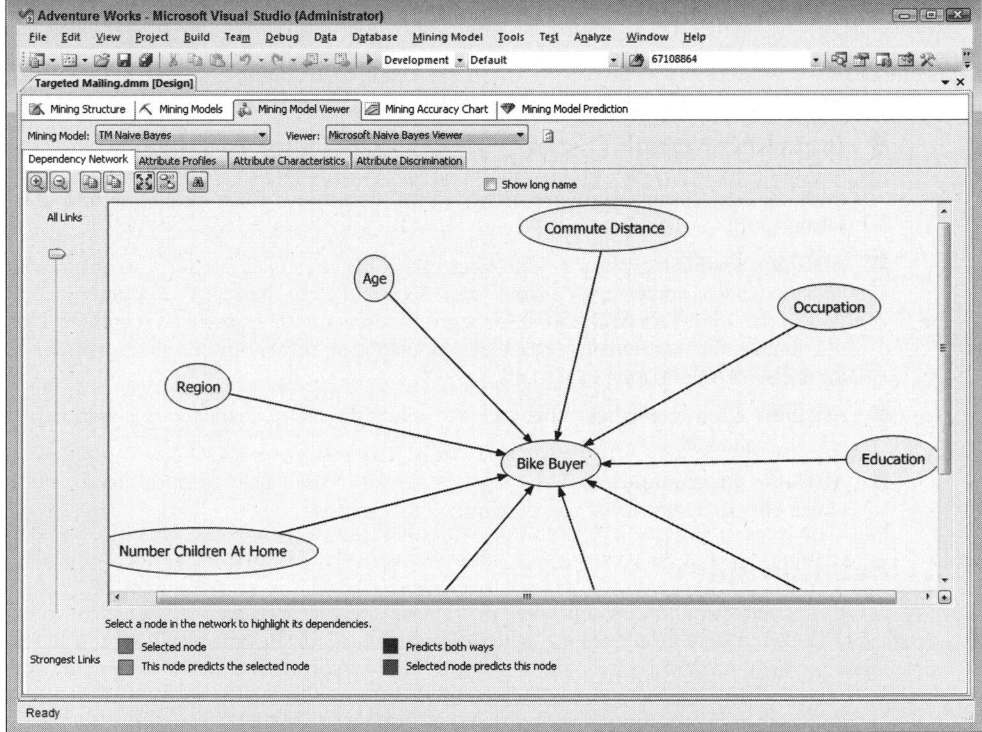

Time series

The time series algorithm predicts the future values for a series of continuous data points (e.g., web traffic for the next six months given traffic history). Unlike the algorithms already presented, prediction does not require new cases on which to base the prediction, just the number of steps to extend the series into the future. Input data must contain a *time key* to provide the algorithm's time attribute. Time keys can be defined using date, double, or long columns.

Once the algorithm has run, it generates a decision tree for each series being forecast. The decision tree defines one or more regions in the forecast and an equation for each region, which can be reviewed using the Decision Tree Viewer. For example, a node may be labeled `Widget.Sales-4 < 10,000`, which is interpreted as "use the equation in this node when widget sales from four time-steps back is less than 10,000." Selecting a node will display two associated equations in the Mining Legend, and hovering over the node will display the equation as a tooltip — SQL Server 2008 added the second equation, providing better long-term forecasts by blending these different estimation techniques.

Note the Tree pull-down at the top of the viewer that enables the models for different series to be examined. Each node also displays a diamond chart whose width denotes the variance of the predicted attribute at that node. In other words, the narrower the diamond chart, the more accurate the prediction.

The second Time Series Viewer, labeled simply Charts, plots the actual and predicted values of the selected series over time. Choose the series to be plotted from the drop-down list in the upper-right corner of the chart. Use the Abs button to toggle between absolute (series) units and relative (percent change) values. The Show Deviations check box will add error bars to display expected variations on the predicted values, and the Prediction Steps control enables the number of predictions displayed. Drag the mouse to highlight the horizontal portion of interest and then click within the highlighted area to zoom into that region. Undo a zoom with the zoom controls on the toolbar.

Because prediction is not case based, the Mining Accuracy Chart does not function for this algorithm. Instead, keep later periods out of the training data and compare predicted values against the test data's actuals.

Cube Integration

Data mining can use Analysis Services cube data as input instead of using a relational table (see the first page of the Data Mining Wizard section earlier in this chapter); cube data behaves much the same as relational tables, with some important differences:

- Whereas a relational table can be included from most any data source, the cube and the mining structure that references it must be defined within the same project.
- The case "table" is defined by a single dimension and its related measure groups. When additional data mining attributes are needed, add them via a nested table.
- When selecting mining structure keys for a relational table, the usual choice is the primary key of the table. Choose mining structure keys from dimension data at the highest (least granular) level possible. For example, generating a quarterly forecast requires that quarter to be chosen as the key time attribute, not the time dimension's key (which is likely day or hour).
- Data and content type defaults tend to be less reliable for cube data, so review and adjust type properties as needed.
- Some dimension attributes based on numeric or date data may appear to the data mining interface with a text data type. A little background is required to understand why this happens: When a dimension is built, it is required to have the Key column property specified.

Optionally, a Name column property can also be specified, giving the key values friendly names for the end user (e.g., June 2008 instead of 2008-06-01T00:00:00). However, data mining uses the Name column's data type instead of the Key column's data type, often resulting in unexpected text data types showing up in a mining structure. Sometimes the text data type works fine, but for other cases, especially Key Time or Key Sequence attributes, it can cause the mining structure not to build or to behave incorrectly once built.

- Resolving this issue requires either removing the Name column property from the dimension attribute or adding the same column to the dimension a second time without using the Name column property. If a second copy of the attribute is required, then it can be marked as not visible to avoid confusing end users.
- The portion of cube data to be used for training is defined via the mining structure's cube slice. Adjust this slice to exclude cases that should not be used in training (e.g., discontinued products and future time periods). Consider reserving a portion of the cube data for model evaluation (e.g., train a forecast on 18 of the last 24 months of data and compare actual and forecast values for the final six months).
- A lift chart cannot be run against cube test data, so model evaluation requires either test data in a relational table or some strategy that does not rely on the tools of the Mining Accuracy Chart.

Using a cube as a mining data source can be very effective, providing access to what is often large quantities of data for training and testing, and providing the ability to create a dimension or even an entire cube based on the trained model.

Summary

Data mining provides insights into data well beyond those provided by reporting, and Analysis Services streamlines the mining process. While the data must still be prepared, mining models hide the statistical and algorithmic details of data mining, enabling the modeler to focus on analysis and interpretation.

Beyond one-time insights, trained models can be used in applications to allocate scarce resources, forecast trends, identify suspect data, and a variety of other uses.

This book has been quite the journey — from a foundation of Smart Database Design and normalization, through selects, aggregating data, joins, and merge. Microsoft has steadily extended SQL Server's capability to handle data beyond the traditional relational data type, but SQL queries and T-SQL programming are still the power of SQL Server. Several chapters detailed setting up, configuring, maintaining, and securing SQL Server. Part IX looked into the black art of indexing and tuning. At the close, SQL Server's BI features, with Analysis Services at the core, showed how to build cubes and data mine for insights.

The analogy of SQL Server as a box has been woven throughout the part introductions, so it makes sense to close with that analogy. The informal motto for database design and normalization is "the key, the whole key, and nothing but the key." If SQL Server is the box, then think "the box, the whole box, and nothing but the box."

Appendix A

SQL Server 2008 Specifications

Table A-1 provides a thorough and complete listing of all the different versions of SQL Server specifications.

IN THIS APPENDIX

Comparison of SQL Server specifications for versions 6.5 through 2008

TABLE A-1

SQL Server Specifications

Feature	6.5	7.0	2000	2005	2008
Server Features					
Automatic Configuration	No	Yes	Yes	Yes	Yes
Page Size	2 KB	8 KB	8 KB	8 KB + extendable	8 KB + extendable
Max Row Size	1,962 bytes	8,060 bytes	8,060 bytes	8,060 bytes extendable based on data types	8,060 bytes extendable based on data types
Page-Level Locking	Yes	Yes	Yes	Yes	Yes
Row-Level Locking	Insert only	Yes	Yes	Yes	Yes
Files Located	Devices	Files and filegroups	Files and filegroups	Files and filegroups	Files and filegroups

TABLE A-1 *(continued)*

Feature	6.5	7.0	2000	2005	2008
Kerberos and Security Delegation	No	No	Yes	Yes	Yes
C2 Security Certification	No	No	Yes	Yes	Yes
Common Criteria Certification	No	No	No	Yes	Yes
Bytes per Character Column	255	8,000	8,000	8,000	8,000
Automatic Log Shipping	No	No	Yes	Yes	Yes
Persisted Computed Column	No	No	No	Yes	Yes
Max Batch Size	128 KB	65,536 * network packet–size bytes	65,536 * network packet–size bytes	65,536 * network packet–size bytes	65,536 * network packet–size bytes
Bytes per Text/Image	2 GB	2 GB	2 GB	2 GB	2 f
Bytes per VarChar(max)	–	–	–	2 GB	2 GB
Objects in Database	2 billion	2,147,483,647	2,147,483,647	2,147,483,647	2,147,483,647
Parameters per Stored Procedure	255	1,024	1,024	1,024	2,100
References per Table	31	253	253	253	253
Rows per Table	Limited by available storage	Limited by available storage	Limited by available storage	Limited by available storage	Limited by available storage
Tables per Database	2 billion	Limited by number of objects in database	Limited by number of objects in database	Limited by number of objects in database	Limited by number of objects in database

TABLE A-1 *(continued)*

Feature	6.5	7.0	2000	2005	2008
Tables per SELECT Statement	16	256	256	256	256
Triggers per Table	3	Limited by number of objects in database	Limited by number of objects in database	Limited by number of objects in database	Limited by number of objects in database
Bytes per GROUP BY or ORDER BY	900	8,060	8,060	8,060	8,060
Bytes of Source Text per Stored Procedure	65,025	Batch size or 250 MB, whichever is less	Batch size or 250 MB, whichever is less	Batch size or 250 MB, whichever is less	Batch size or 250 MB, whichever is less
Columns per Key (Index, Foreign, or Primary)	16	16	16	16	19
Bytes per Key (Index, Foreign, or Primary)	900	900	900	900	900
Columns in GROUP BY or ORDER BY	16	Limited by bytes	Unspecified	Unspecified	Unspecified
Columns per Table	255	1,024	1,024	1,024	1,024 (w/Sparse Columns 30,000)
Columns per SELECT Statement	4,096	4,096	4,096	4,096	4,096
Columns per INSERT Statement	250	1,024	1,024	1,024	4,096
Database Size	1 TB	1,048,516 TB	1,048,516 TB	524,272 TB	524,272 TB
Databases per Server	32,767	32,767	32,767 (per instance)	32,767 (per instance)	32,767 (per instance)
File Groups per Database	–	256	256	256	32,767

TABLE A-1 *(continued)*

Feature	6.5	7.0	2000	2005	2008
Files per Database	32	32,767	32,767	32,767	32,767
Data-File Size	32 GB	32 TB	32 TB	16 TB	16 TB
Log-File Size	32 GB	4 TB	32 TB	2 TB	2 TB
Foreign-Key References per Table	16	253	253	253	253
Identifier Length (Table, Column Names, etc.)	30	128	128	128	128
XML Indexes	–	–	–	249	249
Instances per Server	1	1	16	16 (Standard) 50 (Enterprise)	50 (32 bit Workgroup limited to 16 instances)
Locks per Instance	2,147,483,647	2,147,483,647 or 40 percent of SQL Server memory	2,147,483,647 or 40 percent of SQL Server memory	32 bit: 2,147,483,647 or 40 percent of SQL Server memory 64 bit: limited only by memory	32 bit: 2,147,483,647 or 40 percent of SQL Server memory 64 bit: limited only by memory
Parallel Query Execution	No	Yes	Yes	Yes	Yes
Federated Databases	No	No	Yes	Yes	Yes
Indexes per Table Used in Query Execution	1	Multiple	Multiple	Multiple	Multiple
Administration Features					
Automatic-Data and Log-File Growth	No	Yes	Yes	Yes	Yes
Automatic Index Statistics	No	Yes	Yes	Yes	Yes

TABLE A-1 *(continued)*

Feature	6.5	7.0	2000	2005	2008
Profiler Tied to Optimizer Events	No	Yes	Yes	Yes	Yes
Alert on Performance Conditions	No	Yes	Yes	Yes	Yes
Conditional Multistep Agent Jobs	No	Yes	Yes	Yes	Yes
Programming Features					
Recursive Triggers	No	Yes	Yes	Yes	Yes
Multiple Triggers per Table Event	No	Yes	Yes	Yes	Yes
`INSTEAD OF` Triggers	No	No	Yes	Yes	Yes
Unicode Character Support	No	Yes	Yes	Yes	Yes
User-Defined Functions	No	No	Yes	Yes	Yes
Indexed Views	No	No	Yes	Yes	Yes
Cascading DRI Deletes and Updates	No	No	Yes	Yes	Yes
Collation Level	Server	Server	Server, database, table, query	Server, database, table, query	Server, database, table, query
Nested Stored-Procedure Levels	16	32	32	32	32
Nested Subqueries	16	32	32	32	32
Nested Trigger Levels	16	32	32	32	32

TABLE A-1 *(continued)*

Feature	6.5	7.0	2000	2005	2008
XML Support	No	No	Yes	Yes	Yes
Replication Features					
Snapshot Replication	Yes	Yes	Yes	Yes	Yes
Transactional Replication	Yes	Yes	Yes	Yes	Yes
Merge Replication with Conflict Resolution	No	Yes	Yes	Yes	Yes
Enterprise Manager/Management Studio Features					
Database Diagram	No	Yes	Yes	Yes	Yes
Graphical Table Creation	Yes	Yes	Yes	Yes	Yes
Database Designer	No	Yes	Yes	Yes	Yes
Query Designer	No	Yes	Yes	Yes	Yes
T-SQL Debugger	No	Yes	Yes	No	Yes
IntelliSense	No	No	No	No	Yes
Multi-Server Queries	No	No	No	No	Yes

SQL Server 2008 Edition Features Table

The best thing for you to do if you're looking for a list of features is to go to: `www.microsoft.com/sqlserver/2008/en/us/editions-compare.aspx` or `http://msdn.microsoft.com/en-us/library/cc645993.aspx`. The table is already organized and set up in the best possible fashion; if I reorganized it for the sake of reprinting it, it would lose its usability.

Appendix B

Using the Sample Databases

IN THIS CHAPTER

The file list, background, requirements, diagrams, and descriptions for the five sample databases

In addition to Microsoft's AdventureWorks sample database, this book draws examples from the following five sample databases, each designed to illustrate a particular design concept or development style:

- *Cape Hatteras Adventures* is actually two sample databases that together demonstrate upsizing to a relational SQL Server database. Version 1 consists of a simple Access database and an Excel spreadsheet — neither of which is very sophisticated. Version 2 is a typical small- to mid-size SQL Server database employing identity columns and views. It uses an Access project as a front end and publishes data to the Web using the SQL Server Web Publishing Wizard and stored procedures.
- The *OBXKites* database tracks inventory, customers, and sales for a fictitious kite retailer with four stores in North Carolina's Outer Banks. This database is designed for robust scalability. It employs GUIDs for replication and Unicode for international sales. In various chapters in the book, partitioned views, full auditing features, and Analysis Services cubes are added to the OBXKites database.
- The *Family* database stores family tree history. While the database has only two tables, `person` and `marriage`, it sports the complexities of a many-to-many self-join and extraction of hierarchical data.
- Twenty-five of *Aesop's Fables* provide the text for Chapter 19, "Using Integrated Full-Text Search."

This appendix documents the required files (Table B-1) and the database schemas for the sample databases.

CROSS-REF All the files to create these sample databases, and chapter code files, can be downloaded from www.sqlserverbible.com.

The Sample Database Files

The sample files should be installed into the C:\SQLServerBible directory. The SQL Server sample web applications are coded to look for template files in a certain directory structure. The DTS packages and distributed queries also assume that the Access and Excel files are in that directory.

TABLE B-1

Sample Database Files

Cape Hatteras Adventures Version 2	
C:\SQLServerBible\Sample Databases\CapeHatterasAdventures	
CHA2_Create.sql	Script that generates the database for Cape Hatteras Adventures Version 2, including tables, constraints, indexes, views, stored procedures, and user security
CHA_Convert.sql	Distributed queries that convert data from Access and Excel into the Cape Hatteras Adventures Version 2 database. This script mirrors the DTS package and assumes that the Access and Excel source files are in the C:\SQLServerBible directory.
CHA1_Customers.mdb	Access database of the customer list, used prior to SQL Server conversion. Data is imported from this file into the CHA1 SQL Server database.
CHA1_Schdule.xls	Excel spreadsheet of events, tours, and guides, used prior to SQL Server conversion. Data is imported from this file into the CHA1 SQL Server database.
CHA2_Events.xml	Sample XML file
CHA2_Events.dtd	Sample XML Data Type Definition file
CHA2.adp	Sample Access front end to the CHA2 database
OBXKites	
C:\SQLServerBible\Sample Databases\OBXKites	
OBXKites_Create.sql	Script that generates the database for the OBXKites database, including tables, views, stored procedures, and functions

TABLE B-1 *(continued)*

OBXKites_Populate.sql	Script that populates the database for the OBXKites database with sample data by calling the stored procedures
OBXKites_Query.sql	A series of sample test queries with which to test the population of the OBXKites database
The Family	
C:\SQLServerBible\Sample Databases\Family	
Family_Queries.sql	Script that creates the Family database tables and stored procedures and populates the database with sample data
Family_Create.sql	A set of sample queries against the Family database
AESOP'S FABLES	
C:\SQLServerBible\Sample Databases\Aesop	
`Aesop_Create.sql`	Script that creates the Aesop database and `Fable` table and populates the database with 25 of Aesop's fables. This sample database is used with full-text search
`Aesop.adp`	Access front end for browsing the fables
MATERIAL SPECIFICATIONS	
C:\SQLServerBible\Sample Databases\MaterialSpec	
`MS_Create.sql`	Script to create the Material Specification database
`MS_Populate.sql`	Script to populate the Material Specification to database with sample data from a computer-clone store

To create one of the sample databases, run the `create` script within Query Analyzer. The script will drop the database if it exists. These scripts make it easy to rebuild the database, so if you want to experiment, go ahead. Because the script drops the database, no connections to the database can exist when the script is run. Enterprise Manager will often keep the connection even if another database is selected. If you encounter an error, chances are good that Enterprise Manager, or a second connection in Query Analyzer, is holding an open connection.

Cape Hatteras Adventures Version 2

The fictitious Cape Hatteras Adventures (CHA) is named for the Cape Hatteras lighthouse in North Carolina, one of the most famous lighthouses and life-saving companies in America. Cape Hatteras is the easternmost point of North Carolina's Outer Banks, known for incredible empty beaches and the graveyard of the Atlantic.

Cape Hatteras Adventures leads wild and sometimes exotic adventures for the rich and famous. From excursions down the gnarly Gauley River in West Virginia to diving for sunken treasure off the Outer Banks to chopping through the Amazon jungle, Cape Hatteras Adventures gets its guests there and brings them back, often alive and well.

The staff and management of CHA are outdoors folks, and their inclination to avoid the indoors shows in the effort that's been put into IT. The customer/prospect list is maintained in Access 2000 in a single-table database. It's used primarily for mailings. The real workhorse is an Excel spreadsheet that tracks events, tours, and tour guides in a single flat-file format. In the same page, a second list tracks customers for each event. Although the spreadsheet is not a proper normalized database, it does contain the necessary information to run the business.

QuickBooks handles all financial and billing activities, and both the company president and the bookkeeper are very satisfied with that setup. They foresee no need to improve the financial or billing software.

Application requirements

CHA has grown to the point that it realizes the need for a better scheduling application; however, it desires to "keep the tough work in the rapids and not in the computer." CHA has contracted for the development and maintenance of the database.

All scheduling and booking of tours takes place at the main office in Cape Hatteras, North Carolina. CHA launches tours from multiple sites, or base camps, throughout the world. The base camps generally have no computer access and sometimes no electricity. Guides are dispatched to the base camp with a printed guest list. If it's determined in the future that a base camp may need to be staffed and have access to the schedule online, a web page will be developed at that time.

Each base camp may be responsible for multiple tours. A tour is a prearranged, repeatable experience. Each time the tour is offered, it's referred to as an *event*. An event will have one lead guide, who is responsible for the safety and enjoyment of the guests. Other guides may also come along as needed.

As CHA brings on more guides with broader skills, the database must track the guides and which tours each one is qualified to lead.

Database design

The database design uses typical one-to-many relationships between customer type and customer, and from guide to base camp to tour to event. Many-to-many relationships exist between customer and event, guide and tour, and guide and event.

Concerning the development style, there is currently no need for multiple database sites, so identity columns will be used for simplicity of design. The primary means of access to the data is through views and direct `SELECT` statements.

Data conversion

The `CHA2_Create.sql` script creates an empty database. The data resides in the Access and Excel spreadsheets. Both the `CHA_Conversion` DTS package and the `CHA_Convert.sql` script can extract the data from Access and Excel and load it into SQL Server.

CHA2.adp front end

Because the Cape Hatteras Adventures staff is comfortable with Access forms and does not require the robustness of a full Visual Basic or .NET application, a simple front end has been developed using Access.adp project technology.

OBX Kites

OBX Kites is a high-quality kite retailer serving kite enthusiasts and vacationers around the Outer Banks, where the winds are so steady the Wright brothers chose the area (Kill Devil Hills) for their historic glider flights and their first powered flights. OBX Kites operates a main store/warehouse and four remote retail locations and is planning to launch an e-commerce website.

Application requirements

OBX Kites needs a solid and useful order/inventory/purchase order system with a middle-of-the-road set of features. For simplicity, all contacts are merged into a single table, and the contact type is signified by flags. A contact can be a customer, employee, or vendor. Customers have a lookup for customer type, which is referenced in determining the discount. Full details are maintained on customers, including both a summer location and the home location. The product/inventory system must handle multiple suppliers per product, price history, multiple inventory items per product, multiple locations, and inventory transactions to track inventory movement.

Database design

The database design uses standard one-to-many relationships throughout.

The database construction must support replication and Unicode for international customers. For performance and flexibility, the database implements two filegroups — one for heavy transactions and the other for static read-mostly data.

The database design is a standard inventory, order-processing database.

The Family

This small database demonstrates multiple hierarchical reflexive relationships for interesting queries and both cursors and queries to navigate the genealogical hierarchy.

Application requirements

The Family database must store every person in the family, along with genealogical information, including both biological and marital relationships. The database is populated with five generations of a fictitious family for query purposes.

Database design

The Family database consists of two tables and three relationships, as configured in the Database Designer. Each person has an optional reflexive `MotherID` and `FatherID` foreign key back to the `PersonID`. The `marriage` table has a foreign key to the `PersonID` for the husband and the wife. The primary keys are integer columns for simplicity.

Aesop's Fables

Aesop's collection of fables is an excellent test bed for string searches and full-text search. The fables are relatively short and familiar, and they're in the public domain.

Application requirements

The primary purpose of this database is to enable you to experience SQL Server's full-text search. Therefore, the database must include a few character columns, a BLOB or image column, and a BLOC-type column.

Database design

The database design is very simple — a single table with one fable per row.

Index

Symbols and Numbers

A

B

C

D

E

F

G

N

O

P

Q

R

S

T

U